THE GOOD
RESTAURANT GUIDE
1996

In association with
RENAULT

Produced by:
AA Publishing

Atlas prepared by:
The Cartographic Department of
The Automobile Association
Maps © The Automobile Association 1995

Restaurant assessments and rosette awards
are based on reports of visits carried out
anonymously by the AA's Hotel and
Restaurant Inspectors.

Restaurant descriptions have been
contributed by the following team of
writers:
Liz Carter (Co-Editor),
Jackie Bates, William Boden,
Beth Dobson, Russell Cronin,
Clarissa Hyman, Julia Hynard,
Philip Bryant, Denise Laing,
Daphne Jolley, Joy Nelson,
James Wydenbach.

Typeset by:
Anton Graphics, Andover, England

Printed and bound in Italy by
Amilcare Pizzi S.p.A., Milan

The contents of this book are believed
correct at the time of going to printing.
Nevertheless, the Publisher cannot be held
responsible for any errors or omissions or
for changes in the details given in this
guide or for the consequences of any
reliance on the information provided in
the same. Assessments of AA inspected
establishments are based on the experience
of the Hotel and Restaurant Inspectors on
the occasion of their visit(s) and therefore
descriptions given in this guide necessarily
contain an element of subjective opinion
which may not reflect or dictate a reader's
own opinion on another occasion. We
have tried to ensure accuracy in this guide
but things do change and we would be
grateful if readers would advise us of any
inaccuracies they may encounter.

A CIP catalogue record for this book is
available from the British Library

Published by:
AA Publishing, which is a trading
name of Automobile Association
Developments Limited whose
registered office is Norfolk House,
Priestley Road, Basingstoke,
Hampshire RG24 9NY
Registered number 1878835.

ISBN 0 7495 1114 1

Contents

Abbey Well
Natural Mineral Water

RESTAURANTS

How to Use this guide

How restaurants have been selected

Every restaurant in this guide, and a great many more, has had a meal visit from at least one anonymous inspector. Many, especially at the higher award levels, have been visited more than once by different inspectors at different times.

Every item of the meal has been assessed – from the quality of the bread and butter and wine list to the strength and freshness of the coffee – not forgetting the service, the surroundings and the overall atmosphere. AA visits are anonymous; no favours are accepted; no charge is made for entries in this guide.

All assessment is subjective

Although our inspectors are a highly-trained and very experienced professional men and women, it must be stressed that the opinions expressed are only opinions, based on the experience of one or more particular occasions. Assessments are therefore to some extent necessarily subjective. AA inspectors are experienced enough to make a balanced judgement, but they are not omniscient. We do ask our readers to bear this in mind.

Omissions

If a restaurant is not featured in this edition it does not necessarily mean that the AA has decided against a rosette award. It may be that there was no time to make a visit before the editorial deadline, or that our information network had failed us, and in that case we should be extremely grateful to our readers for their views.

Rosette Awards

Every restaurant included has been awarded one or more rosettes for the quality of the food, up to a maximum of five. The rosette symbol or symbols are printed immediately after the restaurant name. See page 8 for a clear explanation of how they are graded.

Locations

London has so many good restaurants that we feel it qualifies for a section on its own. Restaurants in London are listed alphabetically by name. Throughout the book those with Le, La or Les as part of their name have been listed alphabetically under L. In the rest of Britain, establishments are listed alphabetically under county, then town or village location, and within that town or village alphabetically by name.

In the London section, each restaurant has a map reference number to help locate its approximate position on the Central or Greater London maps on pages 747. In the remainder of the guide, the map references refer to the 16 pages of maps of Britain from page 750.

Summary line

Every restaurant description begins with a short summary of its style of cuisine and atmosphere to help readers to see at a glance if it might suit their needs.

☺ At the beginning of each entry where we are confident you can obtain a good meal for under £25 a head (excluding wine) we have inserted a smiley face.

Information column

Most of the statistical information about each restaurant is supplied in the narrow column. For the one-rosette entries, a slightly different format has been used and some information is located under their brief description. Although we try to keep our database as up-to-date and full as possible, occasionally restaurants do not supply us with new information and up-to-date costs or are awarded a rosette just before going to press. Where information is omitted or appears in italics, it is because we have been unable to confirm our data.

Telephone numbers

During the currency of this guide it is possible that a telephone number may change, but the numbers in the guide were current at the time of going to press.

Cost

Where applicable, we have calculated the average cost of an *à la carte (alc)* meal, for one person, of three courses including coffee and service but not wine. Fixed-price lunch and/or dinner menus come next. If these meals have more or less than three courses we have indicated this. Food prices are followed by the cost of the house wine or one of the cheaper wines on the list. Prices quoted are a guide only, and are subject to change without notice.

For restaurants where a good choice of wines can be purchased by the glass we have inserted a wine glass symbol.

Credit cards

Credit cards are shown by the following symbol.

Access/Eurocard/ Mastercard

American Express

Visa/Barclaycard

Diners Club

OTHER - indicates a cash card such as Switch or Delta or lesser known brands of credit card.

If no credit card details are given, please check with the restaurant whether or not they take credit cards before booking.

Times

Where possible we have given the latest time at which a meal may be ordered. Not all restaurants are open for both lunch and dinner all week. Remember that opening times are liable to change without notice.

Chefs and Proprietors

These names are as accurate and as up-to-date as we could make them at the time of going to press, but changes in personnel often occur, and may affect both the style and the quality of the restaurant.

Seats and Additional Information

Information about smoking regulations and special needs have been carefully checked, but if these are important to you, please telephone for confirmation before booking.

Where a vegetarian choice is always offered on a menu we have used the standard V symbol. Almost all the restaurants featured in the guide will prepare a vegetarian dish or accommodate a special diet if given prior notice.

Villeroy & Boch

and

AA ROSETTE AWARDS

Villeroy & Boch and AA Hotel Services are delighted to celebrate their long-standing partnership in the recognition of the very Best Restaurants in Britain

For the past 5 years Villeroy & Boch have sponsored the superb plates which are presented annually to winners of Three, Four and Five AA Rosettes for exceptionally high standards of cuisine

Rosette Awards

A brief guide to the Rosette Award scheme and how
AA inspectors assess the level of the award

One rosette denotes simple, carefully prepared food, based on good quality, fresh ingredients, cooked in such a way as to emphasise honest flavours. Sauces and desserts will be home-made and the cooking will equate to first-class home cooking.

Two rosettes denote cooking that displays a high degree of competence on the part of the chef. The menus should include some imaginative dishes, making use of very good raw ingredients, as well as some tried and tested favourites. Flavours should be well balanced and complement or contrast with one another, not over-dominate.

Only ten percent of the restaurants receiving rosette awards will achieve high enough standards of cooking, presentation of dishes and service to merit the AA's top awards of three, four and five rosettes.

Only cooking of the highest national standard receives three or more rosettes. Menus will be imaginative; dishes should be accurately cooked, demonstrate well-developed technical skills and a high degree of flair in their composition. Ingredients will be first-class, usually from a range of specialist suppliers, including local produce only if its quality is excellent. Most items – breads, pastries, pasta, petits fours – will be made in the kitchens, but if any are bought in, for example, breads, the quality will be excellent.

At this level, cuisine should be innovative, daring, highly accomplished and achieve a noteworthy standard of consistency, accuracy and flair throughout all the elements of the meal. Excitement, vibrancy and superb technical skill will be the keynotes.

Five rosettes is the supreme accolade, made to chefs at the very top of their profession. This award recognises superlative standards of cuisine at an international level, evident at every visit in every element of the meal. Creativity, skill and attention to detail will produce dishes cooked to perfection, with intense, exciting flavours in harmonious combinations and faultless presentation. Menus may be innovative or classical, and may use luxury ingredients like lobster, truffles, foie gras, etc. often in unexpected combinations and with secret ingredients that add an extra dimension of taste and interest.

Above: The first presentation – Peter Lewis, Director, Villeroy & Boch Hotelware, with Raymond Blanc of Le Manoir aux Quat' Saisons and Albert Hampson, Business Manager, AA Hotel Services.

The Top Ten Per Cent

LONDON

Four Seasons Hotel, *Hamilton Place,*
Park Lane W1, ☎ *0171 499 0888*
La Tante Claire Restaurant,
68 Royal Hospital Rd SW3,
☎ *0171 352 6045*
Le Gavroche Restaurant,
43 Upper Brook St W1, ☎ *0171 408 0881*
Les Saveurs, *37a Curzon St W1,*
☎ *0171 491 8919*
Nico at Ninety, *90 Park Lane W1,*
☎ *0171 409 1290*
The Restaurant, *The Hyde Park Hotel,*
66 Knightsbridge SW1, ☎ *0171 259 5380*

BERKSHIRE

Waterside Inn, *Ferry Road, BRAY,*
Maidenhead, ☎ *01628 20691*
L'Ortolan Restaurant, *Church Lane,*
SHINFIELD, Reading, ☎ *01734 883783*

OXFORDSHIRE

Le Manoir Aux Quat' Saisons,
GREAT MILTON, nr Oxford,
☎ *01844 278881*

ENGLAND-LONDON

Aubergine, *11 Park Walk SW10,*
☎ *0171 352 3449*
Bibendum, *Michelin House, 81 Fulham Rd*
SW3, ☎ *0171 581 5817*
The Capital, *Basil Street, Knightsbridge*
SW3, ☎ *0171 589 5171*
L'Escargot, *Greek St W1,*
☎ *0171 437 2679*
Pied a Terre, *34 Charlotte St W1,*
☎ *0171 636 1178*

AVON

Restaurant Lettonie, *9 Druid Hill,*
Stoke Bishop, BRISTOL, ☎ *0117 968 6456*

DEVON

Gidleigh Park, *CHAGFORD, Newton*
Abbot, ☎ *01647 432367*

LANCASHIRE

Paul Heathcotes Restaurant,
104-106 Higher Rd, LONGRIDGE,
Preston, ☎ *01772 784969*

LEICESTERSHIRE

Hambleton Hall, *Hambleton,*
OAKHAM, ☎ *01572 756991*

SOMERSET

Castle Hotel, *Castle Green,*
TAUNTON, ☎ *01823 272671*

WEST SUSSEX

Manleys Restaurant, *Manleys Hill,*
STORRINGTON, Pulborough,
☎ *01903 742331*

SCOTLAND-HIGHLAND

Altnaharrie Inn, *ULLAPOOL,*
Ross-shire, ☎ *01854 633230*

ENGLAND-LONDON

NW1

Odettes, *130 Regents Park Rd,*
☎ *0171 586 5486*

SW1

Auberge de Provence,
St James Court Hotel, 41 Buckingham
Gate, ☎ *0171 821 1899*
Le Caprice, *Arlington House, Arlington St,*
☎ *0171 629 2239*
The Halkin Hotel, *Halkin St,*
Belgravia, ☎ *0171 333 1000*
The Lanesborough, *Hyde Park Corner,*
☎ *0171 259 5599*
Simply Nico, *48a Rochester Row,*
☎ *0171 630 8061*
The Square, *32 King St, St James's,*
☎ *0171 839 8787*

SW10

The Canteen, *Harbour Yard, Chelsea*
Harbour, ☎ *0171 351 7330*

SW17

Chez Bruce, *2 Bellevue Rd, Wandsworth*
Common, ☎ *0181 672 0114*

SW3

Daphne's, *110-112 Draycott Av, Chelsea*
☎ *0171 584 6883*
Turners, *87-89 Walton St,*
☎ *0171 584 6711*
Fulham Road Restaurant,
257-259 Fulham Rd, ☎ *0171 351 7823*

SW7

Downstairs at 190 Queensgate,
190 Queensgate, ☎ *0171 581 5666*
Hilaire, *68 Old Brompton Rd,*
☎ *0171 584 8993*

W1

Alastair Little, *49 Frith St,*
☎ *0171 734 5183*
Atelier, *41 Beak St, West Soho,*
☎ *0171 2872057*
Bistrot Bruno, *63 Frith St,*
☎ *0171 734 4545*

Bon at The Mirabelle,
56 Curzon St, ☎ *0171 499 4636*
Café Royal Grill Room,
68 Regent St, ☎ *0171 437 9090*
Connaught Hotel, *Carlos Place,*
☎ *0171 499 7070*
The Dorchester, *Park Lane,*
☎ *0171 629 8888*
The Greenhouse, *27A Hay's Mews,*
☎ *0171 499 3331*
Hotel Inter-Continental,
1 Hamilton Pl, Hyde Park Corner,
☎ *0171 409 3131*
Interlude, *5 Charlotte St,*
☎ *0171 637 0222*
Le Meridien Piccadilly,
21 Piccadilly, ☎ *0171 734 8000*
The London Hilton on Park Lane,
22 Park Lane, ☎ *80171 493 8000*
Nico Central, *35 Great Portland St,*
☎ *0171 436 8846*
Ritz Hotel, *Piccadilly,*
☎ *0171 493 8181*
Stephen Bull, *5-7 Blandford St,*
☎ *0171 486 9696*

W11

Halcyon Hotel, *81 Holland Park,*
☎ *0171 727 7288*
Leith's Restaurant, *92 Kensington Park Rd,*
☎ *0171 229 4481*

W14

Chinon Restaurant, *23 Richmond Way,*
☎ *0171 602 5968*

W6

River Café, *Thames Wharf Studio's,*
Rainville Rd, Hammersmith,
☎ *0171 381 8824*

W8

Clarke's, *124 Kensington Church St,*
☎ *0171 221 9225*

WC2

Neal St Restaurant, *26 Neal St,*
☎ *0171 836 8368*
The Ivy, *1 West St, Covent Garden,*
☎ *0171 836 4751*
The Savoy, *Strand,* ☎ *0171 836 4343*
Savoy Grill, *Strand,* ☎ *0171 836 4343*

AVON

Royal Crescent, *16 Royal Crescent,*
BATH, ☎ *01225 739955*
Harveys, *12 Denmark St, BRISTOL,*
☎ *0117 927 5034*
Hunstrete House Hotel,
CHELWOOD, Bristol, ☎ *0176 490490*
Homewood Park Hotel,
HINTON CHARTERHOUSE, Bath,
☎ *01225 723731*

BEDFORD
Flitwick Manor Hotel, *Church Rd,*
FLITWICK, ☎ *01525 712242*

BERKSHIRE
Fredrick's Hotel, *Shoppenhangers Rd,*
MAIDENHEAD, ☎ *01628 35934*
Royal Oak Hotel, *The Square,*
YATTENDON, Newbury, ☎ *01635 201325*

BUCKINGHAMSHIRE
Cliveden Hotel, *TAPLOW, Maidenhead,*
☎ *01628 668561*

CHESHIRE
Crabwall Manor Hotel, *Parkgate Rd,*
Mollington,CHESTER, ☎ *01244 851666*
The Chester Grosvenor Hotel,
Eastgate, CHESTER, ☎ *01244 324024*
Rookery Hall, *Worleston, NANTWICH,*
☎ *01270 610016*
Nunsmere Hall Hotel, *Tarporley Rd,*
Oakmere, SANDIWAY, Northwich,
☎ *01606 889100*

CORNWALL
Well House Hotel, *St Keyne,*
LISKEARD, ☎ *01579 342001*
The Seafood Restaurant,
Riverside, PADSTOW, ☎ *0184 532485*

CUMBRIA
Uplands Hotel, *Haggs Lane,*
CARTMEL, Grange-Over-Sands,
☎ *01539 536248*
Michael's Nook Hotel, *GRASMERE,*
Ambleside, ☎ *015394 35496*
Sharrow Bay Hotel, *Sharrow Bay,*
HOWTOWN, Penrith, ☎ *017684 86301*
Rampsbeck Hotel, *WATERMILLOCK,*
Penrith, ☎ *017684 86442*

DERBYSHIRE
Fischer's, Baslow Hall, *Calver Rd,*
BASLOW, ☎ *01246 583259*
The Old Vicarage, *Ridgeway Moor,*
RIDGEWAY, ☎ *01742 475814*

DEVON
Carved Angel, *2 South Embankment,*
DARTMOUTH, ☎ *01803 832465*
The Horn of Plenty, *GULWORTHY,*
Tavistock, ☎ *01822 832528*
Arundell Arms, *LIFTON,*
☎ *01566 784666*
Chez Nous, *13 Frankfort Gate,*
PLYMOUTH, ☎ *01752 266793*
Whitechapel Manor,
SOUTH MOLTON, ☎ *01769 573377*
The Table Restaurant,
135 Babbacombe Rd, TORQUAY,
☎ *01803 324292*

DORSET
Summer Lodge, *EVERSHOT, Dorchester,*
☎ *01935 83424*

Stock Hill Hotel, *Stock Hill,*
GILLINGHAM, ☎ *01747 823626*

EAST SUSSEX
Roser's Restaurant, *64 Eversfield Place,*
ST LEONARDS-ON-SEA, Hastings,
☎ *01424 712218*
Horsted Place, *Little Horsted,*
UCKFIELD, ☎ *01825 750581*

GLOUCESTERSHIRE
Greenway Hotel, *Shurdington,*
CHELTENHAM, ☎ *01242 862352*

Le Champignon Sauvage,
24 Suffolk Rd, CHELTENHAM,
☎ *01242 573449*
Lower Slaughter Manor,
LOWER SLAUGHTER,
☎ *0145 820456*
Washbourne Court Hotel,
LOWER SLAUGHTER, ☎ *0145 822143*
Wyck Hill House Hotel,
Burford Rd, STOW-ON-THE-WOLD,
☎ *0145 831936*
Lords of the Manor,
UPPER SLAUGHTER, Cheltenham,
☎ *0145 820243*

GREATER MANCHESTER
Normandie Hotel, *Elbut Lane, Birtle,*
BURY, Lancs, ☎ *016 764 3869*

HAMPSHIRE
Le Poussin, *The Courtyard, Brookley Rd,*
BROCKENHURST, ☎ *01590 23063*
Hollington House, *Woolton Hill,*
HIGHCLERE, nr Newbury, Berks,
☎ *01635 255100*
Gordleton Mill Hotel, *Silver St, Hordle,*
LYMINGTON, ☎ *01590 682219*
Chewton Glen Hotel, *Christchurch Rd,*
NEW MILTON, ☎ *01425 275341*

The Dew Pond, *OLD BURGHCLERE,*
nr Newbury, Berks, ☎ *01635 278408*
Old Manor House, *21 Palmerston St,*
ROMSEY, ☎ *01794 517353*

HEREFORD & WORCESTERSHIRE
Buckland Manor, *BUCKLAND,*
Broadway, ☎ *01386 852626*
Poppies, Roebuck Inn, *BRIMFIELD,*
nr Ludlow, Shrops, ☎ *01584 711230*

HERTFORDSHIRE
Hanbury Manor, *WARE,* ☎ *01920 487722*

HUMBERSIDE
Winteringham Fields,
WINTERINGHAM, ☎ *01724 733096*

KENT
Eastwell Manor, *Eastwell Park, Boughton*
Lees, ASHFORD, ☎ *01233 219955*
Wallet's Court Hotel, *West Cliffe,*
St Margarets-at-Cliffe, DOVER,
☎ *01304 852424*
Read's Restaurant, *Painters Forstal,*
FAVERSHAM, Kent, ☎ *01795 535344*
Thackeray's House, *85 London Rd,*
ROYAL TUNBRIDGE WELLS,
☎ *01892 511921*

LINCOLNSHIRE
Harry's Place, *17 High St,*
Great Gonerby, GRANTHAM,
☎ *01476 61780*

NORFOLK
Adlard's Restaurant, *79 Upper St Giles St,*
NORWICH, ☎ *01603 633522*

NORTH YORKSHIRE
Millers, The Bistro, *1 Montpellier*
Mews, HARROGATE, ☎ *01423 530708*

OXFORDSHIRE
Beetle & Wedge Hotel, *Ferry Lane,*
MOULSFORD, Wallingford,
☎ *0149 651381*
Stonor Arms, *STONOR,*
Henley-on-Thames, ☎ *0149 638345*

SHROPSHIRE
Merchant House, *62 Lower Corve St,*
LUDLOW, ☎ *01584 875438*
Old Vicarage Hotel, *WORFIELD,*
Bridgnorth, ☎ *01746 716497*

SOMERSET
Ston Easton Park, *STON EASTON,*
Bath, ☎ *0176 241631*
White House Hotel, *Long St,*
WILLITON, Taunton,
☎ *01984 632306*

STAFFORDSHIRE
Old Beams Restaurant, *Leek Rd,*
WATERHOUSES, ☎ *01538, 308254*

Above: Design – Beaulieu

SUFFOLK
Mr Underhills Restaurant,
Norwich Rd, EARL STONHAM,
Stowmarket, ☎ *01449 711206*
Fox & Goose Inn, *FRESSINGFIELD,*
Nr Diss, ☎ *01379 586247*
Hintlesham Hall Hotel,
HINTLESHAM, Ipswich,
☎ *01473 652334*

SURREY
Pennyhill Park Hotel, *London Rd,*
BAGSHOT, ☎ *01276 471774*
Fleur de Sel, *23/27 Lower St,*
HASLEMERE, ☎ *01428 651462*
Michels Restaurant, *13 High St,*
RIPLEY, ☎ *01483 224777*

TYNE & WEAR
21 Queen St, *Quayside, NEWCASTLE*
UPON TYNE, ☎ *0191 222 0755*

WARWICKSHIRE
Mallory Court Hotel, *Harbury Lane,*
Bishop's Tachbrook, LEAMINGTON SPA,
☎ *01926 330214*
Billesley Manor Hotel,
Billesley, Alcester, STRATFORD-UPON
AVON, ☎ *01789 279955*

WEST MIDLANDS
Swallow Hotel,
12 Hagley Rd, Five Ways,
BIRMINGHAM, ☎ *0121 452 1144*
Nuthurst Grange Hotel, *Nuthurst*
Grange Lane, HOCKLEY HEATH,
Solihull, ☎ *01564 783972*

WEST SUSSEX
Bailiffscourt Hotel, *CLIMPING,*
Littlehampton, ☎ *01903 723511*
Angel Hotel, *North St, MIDHURST,*
☎ *01730 812421*

WEST YORKSHIRE
Restaurant Nineteen, *19 North Park Rd,*
Heaton, BRADFORD, ☎ *01274 492559*
Box Tree Restaurant, *35-37 Church St,*
ILKLEY, ☎ *01943 608484*

WILTSHIRE
Woolley Grange, *Woolley Green,*
BRADFORD ON AVON,
☎ *01225 864705*
Lucknam Park, *COLERNE,*
Chippenham, ☎ *01225 742777*
Howard's House Hotel,
Teffont Evias, SALISBURY,
☎ *01722 716392*

THE CHANNEL ISLANDS
Broome's, *The Bulwarks, ST AUBIN,*
Jersey, ☎ *01534 42760*
Longueville Manor Hotel,
ST SAVIOUR, Jersey, ☎ *01534 25501*

SCOTLAND-CENTRAL
Braeval, *Braeval, ABERFOYLE,*
Stirlingshire, ☎ *01877 382711*

DUMFRIES & GALLOWAY
Collin House, *AUCHENCAIRN, Castle*
Douglas, Kircudbrightshire,
☎ *01556 640292*
Knockinaam Lodge, *PORTPATRICK,*
Stranraer, Wigtownshire, ☎ *01776 810471*

FIFE
Cellar Restaurant, *24 East Green,*
ANSTRUTHER, ☎ *01333 310378*
Ostlers Close Restaurant,
Bonnygate, CUPAR, ☎ *01334 655574*
Peat Inn, *PEAT INN, Cupar,*
☎ *01334 840206*

HIGHLAND
Inverlochy Castle Hotel, *Torlundy,*
FORT WILLIAM, Inverness-shire,
☎ *01397 702177*
The Cross, *Tweed Mill Brae, Ardbroilach*
Rd, KINGUSSIE, Inverness-shire,
☎ *01540 661166*

LOTHIAN
Atrium, *Cambridge St, Edinburgh,*
☎ *0131 228 8882*
La Potinière, *Main St, GULLANE,*
East Lothian, ☎ *01620 843214*
Champany Inn, *LINLITHGOW,*
West Lothian, ☎ *0150683 4532*

STYRATHCLYDE
Cameron House Hotel, *BALLOCH,*
Alexandria, Dubartonshire,
☎ *01389 755565*
Airds Hotel, *PORT APPIN, Appin,*
Argyll, ☎ *0163173 236*

TAYSIDE
Kinloch House Hotel,
BLAIRGOWRIE, Perthshire,
☎ *01250 884237*
Kinnaird, *Kinnaird Estate, DUNKELD,*
Perthshire, ☎ *01796 482440*

WALES - CLWYD
Bryn Howel Hotel,
LLANGOLLEN, ☎ *01978 860331*

GWENT
Walnut Tree Inn, *LLANDDEWI*
SKYRRID, ☎ *01873 852797*

GWYNEDD
The Old Rectory Country House,
Llanrwst Rd, Llansanffraid Glan Conwy,
☎ *01492 580611*
St Tudno Hotel, *Promenade,*
LLANDUDNO, ☎ *01492 874411*
Tre-Ysgawen Hall, *Capel Coch,*
LLANGEFNI, Isle of Anglesey,
☎ *01248 750750*
Maes y Neuadd Hotel,
TALSARNAU, Harlech, ☎ *01766 780200*

NORTHERN IRELAND

CO ANTRIM
Roscoff, *7 Lesley House, Shaftesbury*
Square, BELFAST, ☎ *01232 331532*

CO DOWN
Shanks, *The Blackwood, Crawfordsburn Rd,*
BANGOR, ☎ *01247 853313*

The following do not appear in AA Best
Restaurants in Britain sponsored by Abbey
Well Mineral Water
*   The telephone numbers are local - please*
use international dialling code from Britain

REPUBLIC OF IRELAND

CO CORK
Sea View Hotel, *BALLYLICKEY,*
☎ *027 50073*
Longueville House Hotel, *MALLOW,*
☎ *022 47156*

CO DONEGAL
Harvey's Point Hotel, *Lough Eske,*
DONEGAL, ☎ *073 22208*

CO KERRY
Park Hotel Kenmore, *KENMARE,*
☎ *064 41200*
Aghadoe Heights Hotel, *KILLARNEY,*
☎ *064 31766*

CO KILDARE
The Kildare Hotel, *STRAFFAN,*
☎ *01 6273333*

CO LIMERICK
Dunraven Arms Hotel, *ADARE,*
☎ *061 396633*

WEXFORD
Marlfield House Hotel, *GOREY,*
☎ *055 21124*

Above: Design – Jardins français, La Jarre

Enhancing your Lifestyle

Villeroy & Boch, the renowned tableware company, is delighted to be once again working in close association with the AA's Rosette Awards to the Best Restaurants throughout Britain.

Villeroy & Boch offers an incredibly wide selection of tableware, crystal, cutlery, cookware, gifts and decorative accessories that fit very comfortably into any lifestyle. Fashion and style led, yet with timeless, classic, subtle and refined designs, the company represents excellent quality and expert crafts-manship. Working with major international designer names such as Paloma Picasso, their designs have always captured attention, creating fashion for the table, but fashion that beckons everyday use.

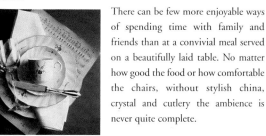

Villeroy & Boch was founded in 1748 and from its inception has been known equally for its manufacturing innovations as well as the aesthetic quality of its china. Today, Villeroy & Boch is one of the world's largest tableware manufacturers, with factories in Germany, Luxembourg and France. Its fine products can be found in leading shops and stores the world over, bringing colour, elegance and style to the homes of millions.

Lifestyle – in our rapidly changing world – is something of which Villeroy & Boch is particularly aware. With people increasingly moving away from the idea of using one formal or 'best' dinner service and another for more informal entertaining, Villeroy & Boch has recently launched SWITCH 1, 2 and 3. These three 'Mix and Match' designs can stand alone or be happily co-ordinated, representing the trend towards a more casual approach to entertaining, but still maintaining the excellence and quality associated with this famous name. With its contemporary colours, and exciting designs, the SWITCH range is an excellent example of Villeroy & Boch's diversity.

There can be few more enjoyable ways of spending time with family and friends than at a convivial meal served on a beautifully laid table. No matter how good the food or how comfortable the chairs, without stylish china, crystal and cutlery the ambience is never quite complete.

The Hotel and Restaurant industry is focused not only on excellence in food, but on interior design and equally on tabletop presentation. Villeroy & Boch's use of colour, innovative design and superb quality has been a major influence in setting the high standards with the industry. **It is hardly surprising, therefore, that out of the establishments who have qualified for the prestigious Five, Four and Three Rosette Award categories, well over half have already chosen Villeroy & Boch china and accessories to reflect their high standard of culinary skills.**

When only the best is good enough, the obvious choice is always Villeroy & Boch.

For brochure and stockist list, write to Villeroy & Boch Limited, 267 Merton Road, London SW18 5JS or Telephone: 0181 871 0011 or Fax: 0181 871 1062

Left: Design: 'Switch 3'
Above: Design: 'Old Luxembourg' – one of the patterns used by Raymond Blanc at Le Manoir aux Quat' Saisons

NEW FOR 1996

Hundreds of colour photographs

AA

The
Hotel Guide
1996

WIN A LUXURY WEEKEND FOR TWO

In association with Royal Mail   **Royal Mail**

- Over 4000 inspected hotels with AA Star Rating

- Many Special Award winners

- Up-to-date details and colour location maps

- Free Prize Draw to Win a Luxury Weekend for Two

- Published November 1995

- Price £13.99 from all good bookshops

THE EUROPEAN PREFERENCE for bottled drinking water is gradually being adopted by Britain. Over the course of the past decade our consumption has increased more than tenfold to its current level of almost ten litres per person, per year. Compare this to the European average consumption of 75 litres per person, per year, however, and it is clear that we have a lot of drinking to do to catch up.

The Germans currently drink an annual 95 litres per head and the French and Belgians 111 litres, while the Italians top the table with an annual per capita consumption of 135 litres - that's over fourteen times more than we drink in Britain.

TAKING THE WATERS

AS BRITAIN GRADUALLY ADOPTS THE EUROPEAN BOTTLED WATER HABIT, WE TAKE A LOOK AT WHAT EXACTLY IT IS THAT WE ARE DRINKING

But what exactly is it that we are drinking? The term bottled water refers to the vast range of different carbonated or still varieties of water described variously as 'spring', 'natural', 'purified', 'table water', and 'natural mineral water', all very different in source and composition. Of all these, the most coveted designation is natural mineral water.

Here is the reason why. The term 'natural mineral water' may only be used in connection with waters that comply with the enormously stringent procedures and rules laid down by the European and British Natural Mineral Waters Regulations, which have been developed to ensure that a natural mineral water is just that and nothing more.

To this end, the regulations require natural mineral waters to conform to a whole range of compositional, bottling and labelling conditions, for example:

- *The only treatment permitted is filtration to remove unstable constituents*
- *The water must contain naturally occurring minerals*
- *The water must contain no pathogenic bacteria*
- *The typical mineral analysis and source must be officially recognised*
- *In addition to the standard legislation, labels must state that it is a natural mineral water and where the water comes from*
- *The mineral analysis must be shown on the label or be available to the public on request*
- *Bottles must have tamper-proof seals which must be intact upon purchase*
- *The water must be bottled at source*

ABBEY WELL®
NATURAL MINERAL WATER

The different characteristics of natural mineral waters depend upon the type of rock strata they travel through, with different journeys yielding different minerals. Abbey Well Natural Mineral Water for instance comes from deep in the Northumberland hillside where, far away from the atmosphere and pollution, it percolates slowly through 315 million year old water-bearing white sandstone.

It is a very different story for many other bottled waters such as spring, natural, purified or table waters. These may be drawn from any source including underground or surface water and the source does not have to be recognised or protected. The water may be artificially purified and chemically treated to destroy both pathogenic and benign bacteria. Other processing may include blending, UV treatment, filtration and pasteurisation or ozonization. Such waters are regulated by the Water in Container Regulations 1992 and are bottled in accordance with EC Directive 778 which governs the quality of tap water.

Abbey Well Natural Mineral Water was discovered by Thomas Robson in 1910 and is named after his favourite Northumbrian landmark, a 12th century Cistercian Abbey.

Abbey Well is still taken from the original underground source and is recognised as a natural mineral water under the Natural Mineral Waters Regulations (1985). The company remains a British-owned family concern and today is run by Tony Robson, Thomas Robson's grandson.

Both still and sparkling natural mineral waters are available from Abbey Well, in returnable or recyclable glass and recyclable plastic bottles in a range of sizes to suit most occasions.

"The term 'natural mineral water' may only be used in connection with waters that comply with enormously stringent procedures and rules."

A SPLASH OF COLOUR

ART CRITIC NICHOLAS USHERWOOD
EXAMINES THE ENDURING
FRIENDSHIP BETWEEN BRITISH POP
ARTISTS PETER BLAKE AND
DAVID HOCKNEY

IF, AS THE SAYING GOES, 'every picture tells a story', the Peter Blake painting 'Portrait Of David Hockney In A Hollywood Spanish Interior' that appears on the labels of Abbey Well bottles tells a tale of warmth and friendship and high artistic achievement that is longer and much more interesting than most.

The painting, which exemplifies the contemporary, refreshing and individual taste of Abbey Well Natural Mineral Water, was begun in 1964 but not 'completed' until a year or two ago. However, the origins of the picture go back almost as far as the friendship between Hockney and Blake itself. Both artists were products of the Royal College of Art in its glory days, the late 50s and early 60s, when the place became virtually synonymous with Swinging London, though Blake had, in fact, already left the Royal College three years before Hockney arrived there from Bradford in 1959.

However, under the benevolent dictatorship of the then Rector, Sir Robin Darwin, old students were encouraged to come back and visit the studios, and it was in the course of one of these visits that Blake and Hockney met for the first time. Blake recognised him even then as a 'star', both as a painter and as a vivid personality; and it was the wish to celebrate this admiration and the feelings of immediate friendship that formed between the two men that accounts for the unlikely choice of party balloons and confetti which forms such a distinctive part of the image here.

Indeed Blake says that he originally intended there to be a great deal more confetti, so much so that it would virtually cover up the whole of Hockney's body. In the end though, that never materialised, the very delicate sprinkling of confetti we now see conveying an altogether gentler, more reflective approach to a friendship that has, particularly over the last fifteen years or so, become closer than ever.

During that time there have been numerous visits between London and Los Angeles, the most notable occurring in 1979 when Peter Blake and Sir Howard Hodgkin paid Hockney a lengthy visit in his Hollywood Hills home. To commemorate it, both men decided to produce a series of paintings on a Californian theme, one of which, Peter Blake's 'The Meeting' or 'Have a Nice Day Mr Hockney', now hangs in The Tate Gallery.

A witty update of Gustave Courbert's 19th century masterpiece 'Bonjour Monsieur Courbet' but with a Venice Beach/Los Angeles setting, the work pays affectionate tribute to Hockney's full-blown adoption of Californian lifestyle.

'Portrait Of David Hockney In A Hollywood Spanish Interior', on the other hand, was started in 1964, shortly after Hockney first decided to settle there.

This accounts for the curious background setting of the painting,

the boy with blond, hairy legs, lolling against a wall. This striking image was chosen by Hockney himself from a Hollywood pin-up magazine, the photograph then being blown up by Blake to the full six foot life size of the painting itself. He then painted Hockney sitting in front of it, so that he, in effect, became part of the photograph. Or vice versa!

Worked on, exhibited spasmodically over the years - a 'work in progress' as Blake himself liked to describe it - the painting then became part of an artistic swap between them, Hockney giving Blake a set of his famous 'Rake's Progress' etchings in return.

The portrait, however, remained in Blake's studio (a bad swap for Hockney, some might say!) until a year or two ago when, for various reasons, Blake decided to return it to him whatever state of completion it was in. Blake has come to feel that, in the very act of doing this, the painting became 'finished' emotionally - always, perhaps, the crucial moment for an artist in deciding when to stop working on a painting.

In reality too, what you see on the label and the painting as it is now is very much the same - the story of 'Portrait Of David Hockney In A Hollywood Spanish Interior' has now come full circle, a celebration of an artistic friendship between two of the elder statesmen of British contemporary art. There are not many bottle labels that can say that!

Peter Blake

David Hockney

STILL SPARKLING

FOOD WRITER AND
RESTAURANT CRITIC
LINDSEY BAREHAM
MEETS RICK STEIN,
CHEF PROPRIETOR
OF THE SEAFOOD
RESTAURANT, PADSTOW

IN PRIME POSITION on the seafront at Padstow stands a typically Cornish four-square granite building fronted by a distinctive conservatory and a modest sign that advertises The Seafood Restaurant.

The first thing you notice about the large white-washed dining room is the profusion of rattan armchairs. Conveying a mood of relaxed conviviality in total contrast to the formality of the starched white linen tablecloths and well-schooled waiting staff. Large mirrors and an eclectic mix of paintings, most of which involve seafood, give the room a contemporary, almost funky, ambience. By day the restaurant has a constant stream of visitors, holiday-makers popping in on the off-chance of a table, and by night, when it glows like a beacon, it attracts people from all over Cornwall. Some, like Hugh Grant and Liz Hurley, hole up in one of its upstairs rooms and work their way through Rick Stein's idiosyncratic menu which features dishes such as the Mediterranean fish soup he cooked on his BBC TV series Taste of the Sea, and his famous grilled Padstow lobster with fines herbes.

Everything about this very special restaurant revolves around Rick Stein's unconventional style. He shares with Raymond Blanc and Alastair Little the advantage of being entirely self-taught. That might sound a contradiction in terms but it means he's learnt to cook the kind of food he likes to eat. And in Rick's case, the food he loves most is fish and shellfish, particularly when it comes from the waters of his beloved Cornwall.

Rick Stein was born in 1947 and brought up in Oxfordshire on the family farm. One of five children, he was youngest son in a family of high achievers and, inevitably, the young Rick rebelled.

At Uppingham his studies took second place to his rock band and his happiest times were the summer when the family repaired to a magnificent white, bow-fronted villa overlooking the sea at Padstow's Trevose Head. Although he took no particular interest in food and cooking, those summers spent fishing for mackerel and bass, eating crabs and lobsters with a dollop of homemade mayonnaise made an impression. Years later, they were to form the linchpin of his menu at The Seafood Restaurant and the crux of his philosophy. "To me," says Rick, "that's what English food is. Good materials, simply turned out."

Rick failed to get into university and left school with no idea what to do and found himself in the midst of an acute identity crisis. Out of desperation he turned to catering and a traineeship with British Transport Hotels, but quit within months. Depressed, he decided to go away and spent the next two years on a 'voyage of discovery' working his way round Australia, New Zealand, America and Mexico, returning home via Canada with his sights set on Oxford. This time he made it. At Oxford he edited Cherwell by day and earnt a fortune running a mobile disco by night. In 1975, with a degree in English under his belt, he headed for Padstow and within months had his eye on that square granite building, but only as a home for the mobile disco. The thought of running a restaurant couldn't have been further from his mind. Fate, however, had a joker up its sleeve.

The small fishing port wasn't used to late night clubbing and a series of brawls lost the disco all its licenses. All, that is, except for one: the restaurant license for the steak bistro at the top of the building. It took two years for The Seafood Restaurant to evolve into its current state.

An early influence was a small seafood bistro in Falmouth where Rick and Jill were regulars. The heady smell of shellfish, garlic and mussels planted the idea of capitalising on the vast wealth of seafood on their doorstep. Combine this with Rick's determination not to create yet another twee faux bistro (and there were plenty of those in Cornwall in the seventies) and the result is a restaurant that broke new ground. Rick is still stressing, even after years of critical acclaim, that he's more concerned with people enjoying themselves than impressing them with his skills as a cook.

It took seven hard years - "I was cooking to save my life," recalls Rick - before the restaurant moved up a notch from being a seasonal place for holiday-makers to somewhere that attracted visitors all the year round. The break came in 1984 when the restaurant won an award in the Sunday Times. From that moment the pressure was on and Rick has built on a success that's inextricably linked with his passion for fresh fish and his love of Cornwall.

Rick's interests in Padstow now extend to a hotel, café and food shop. Then there's his TV career. The next project is to go to the Eastern Sea Board of the USA and make what he describes as "the first road movie about fish". No matter how good a time he has, no matter how sweet the Maine lobsters are, he'll hurry back to Padstow. Lucky Cornwall.

"Rick is still stressing that he's more concerned with people enjoying themselves than impressing them with his skills as a cook."

SUPER MARKET WATER

SUPER WATER

ABBEY WELL®
NATURAL MINERAL WATER

NOT SOLD IN SUPERMARKETS

Phone the Abbey Well Supplyline today 01670 513113

LONDON

Each entry has a map number referring to the London maps at the back of the book. Those with GtL refer to Greater London Map.

The Academy

Operating as a private dining club in the evening, a hotel restaurant offering a good choice of brasserie-style dishes

Service at this elegant Georgian townhouse hotel is mainly provided by friendly young Danish staff, under the supervision of general manager Mette Doessing. Public areas are limited to a small foyer lounge and a cosy library, with a pleasant walled garden and summer terrace leading off. Downstairs is the bar, and the GHQ Restaurant, which runs as a private dining club in the evening, though hotel guests are automatically given temporary membership. Chef John O'Riordan offers a short *carte* with a varied choice of freshly prepared and uncomplicated dishes, including a vegetarian option. Successful dishes at a spring meal included duck confit with garlic mash, red cabbage and cassis sauce, and roast rump of lamb served with some creamy gratin dauphinoise and crunchy french beans. Another main course of roast cod with beurre blanc and meaux mustard was less pleasing, with its thin sauce and powerful mustard flavour. A short list of reasonably priced wines is also available.

Directions: Five mins walk from Oxford Street, Tottenham Court Road Tube, Goodge Street

WC1 17-21 Gower Street
WC1E 6HG
Map no: D4
Tel: 0171 636 7612
Chef: John O'Riordan
Proprietor: Consort Hotels.
Manager: Mette Doessing
Cost: Fixed-price L £14.95/D £16.95. H/wine £9.95 Service exc
Credit cards: 🔲 🔲 🔲 🔲 OTHER
Times: 7am-last L 3pm, last D 11pm
Menus: Fixed-price, pre-theatre, bar menu
Seats: 45. Smoking permitted, air-conditioning
Additional: Children welcome, children's portions and menu; ❶ dishes, vegan/other diets on request

Ajimura Japanese Restaurant

The longest established Japanese restaurant in London featuring authentic dishes served in two small dining-rooms. Look out for good hamachi and brill sushi, served with the usual strong green mustard and shredded horseradish, or skewered conger eel and pot-steamed soup

Menus: A la carte, fixed-price L & D **Seats:** 58. No-smoking area, air-conditioning **Additional:** Children welcome; ❶ dishes, vegan/other diets on request
Directions: Halfway up Frith Street from Shaftesbury Ave on the left. Nearest Tubes – Tottenham Court Rd and Leicester Square

WC2 51-53 Shelton Street
WC2H 9HE
Map no: D4
Tel: 0171 240 0178
Chef: Tatsuo Tanizawa
Proprietor: Tatsuo Tanizawa
Cost: Alc £22 (sashimi large), fixed-price L £8.90/D £35 ❢ Service exc
Credit cards: 🔲 🔲 🔲 🔲
Times: Noon-last L 3pm, 6pm-last D 11pm. Closed Sat L, Sun & Bhs

Alastair Little Restaurant

Influential, much imitated restaurant that still draws the Soho crowds

The small, blue, shop-fronted restaurant, in the busy Soho street, does not immediately catch the eye. The place has the sort of casual air only achieved by studied determination, with casually attired staff providing casual service with a rather casual air. The cooking, however, is far from casual – and neither is the bill – and Alastair Little continues to lead the pack with his characteristic, vibrant European dishes based on a foundation of impeccable, fresh, seasonal produce.

W1 49 Frith Street W1V 5TE
Map no: D4
Tel: 0171 734 5183
Chefs: Alastair Little and Andy Parle
Proprietor: Mercedes Andre-Vega, Alastair Little and Kirsten Tormod Pedersen
Cost: Alc £35, fixed-price L £25 (3 courses). H/wine £12 ❢ Service exc
Credit cards: 🔲 🔲 🔲 OTHER

That said, occasional inconsistencies have been reported this year. Tender asparagus spears wrapped in a mature Parma ham and crisp filo pastry, set on a bed of mustard leaf salad, was unquestionably excellent, a good combination of clean, individual flavours. The same went for another starter of fine, homemade tagliatelle combined with wild mushrooms and asparagus. The success of main course dishes, however, was rather more mixed. Baked turbot was perfectly cooked, served with a wild mushroom sauce, but calves' kidneys proved unacceptably tough and chewy. Desserts feature many favourites, such as creamy, vanilla crème brûlée and apple, almond and pecan tart. Prices are high. The no choice, set lunch menu is £25, for which one might get celeriac rémoulade with crispy Parma ham, new season salmon with spinach, sorrel and herb dressing, and either pudding or cheese.

There is a cheaper £12.50 lunchtime alternative downstairs, less the place to see and be seen, but still somewhere to enjoy items such as pasta ceci, crostini Toscana, bourride of Dover sole and prawns, and spicy sausages with beans.

Directions: Nearest Tube stations: Tottenham Court Road, Piccadilly Circus, Leicester Square

Times: Noon-last L 3pm, 6pm-last D 11.30pm. Closed Sat L, Sun & Bhs
Menus: *A la carte*, fixed-price, pre-theatre, bar menu
Seats: 59. Smoking permitted, air-conditioning
Additional: Children welcome, children's portion's on request; ❤ dishes, vegan/other diets on request

Alba Restaurant ❀❀

Seasonally based northern Italian food in a simple modern setting

Freshly arranged foxgloves and bowls of fruit, attractively displayed near the entrance, created a favourable impression at one inspection visit. With its black metal-framed chairs and efficient, well-timed service, Alba provides a simple modern setting with that kind of authentic feel of a restaurant in any northern Italian city. The predominant influence in the kitchen is the Piedmont region, with the chef content to concentrate on seasonal produce, eschewing trendy flourishes. For example, among the antipasti there might be a salad of artichoke hearts, Parma ham with mango, or a vegetarian asparagus cake. Pasta is represented by a few choice dishes, such as 'tagliolini al ragu Piedmontese' – fresh pasta with rich pork and beef sauce. Main courses comprise fish or meat with simple accompaniments, perhaps fresh swordfish steak with sun-dried tomatoes and capers, or calves' liver with butter and sage served with spinach. The dessert trolley is laden with several chocolate confections, and coffee is served with nutty Cantucci biscuits. The wine list is all Italian, and for diners in a hurry there is an informal wine bar.

Directions: 100 yards from entrance to Barbican Arts Centre; three mins walk from Barbican Station

EC1 107 Whitecross Street EC1Y 8JH
Map no: F4
Tel: 0171 588 1798
Chef: Armando Liboi
Proprietor: Rudi Venerandi
Cost: *Alc* £25, fixed-price D £16.90. H/wine £10.50 ❢
Service inc
Credit cards: 🔳 💳 💳 💳 OTHER
Times: Noon-last L 3pm, last D 11pm. Closed Sat, Sun & Bhs
Menus: *A la carte*, fixed-price D, pre-theatre
Seats: 60. No-smoking area, air-conditioning
Additional: Children welcome, children's portions; ❤ dishes, vegan/other diets on request

'Pithiviers' is a large round puff-pastry tart filled with an almond cream. It is a speciality of Pithiviers, in the Orleans region, and is traditionally served on Twelfth Night, when it contains a dried broad bean. The town is famous for another tart, also made of puff pastry, but this time filled with crystallised fruit and covered with white fondant icing. Nowadays, modern chefs interpret pithiviers in various ways, in both savoury and sweet dishes.

Al Bustan ❀

Brightly decorated with flowers and plants, there is a friendly, informal atmosphere to this stylish Lebanese restaurant. The meze is good. 'Lahem bil agine' – a Lebanese pizza with minced meat, tomatoes, onions and pine kernals on a pastry base – and baby chicken oven cooked with onions and somak are recommended

Menus: A la carte, fixed-price L & D
Seats: 65. No-smoking area, air-conditioning
Additional: Children welcome, children's portions; ❖ dishes, vegan/other diets on request
Directions: Off Sloane Street, turn left by Carlton Tower Hotel, straight at T junction with Motcombe Street. Off Lowndes Street

SW1 Motcomb Street SW1X 8JU
Map no: B2
Tel: 0171 235 8277
Chef: Inam Atalla
Proprietor: Riyad Atalla
Cost: Alc £22, fixed-price L £18/D £20. H/wine £11 Service exc
Credit cards: 🎴 📰 📰 📳
Times: Noon-last D 11pm. Closed Xmas/Boxing Day, New Year's Day

Al San Vincenzo ❀❀

Skilfully prepared, imaginative Italian food from a talented, self-taught chef

The imaginative menu and the style of the cooking might indicate the skills of somebody who had spent many youthful years in the kitchens of Naples. But chef/owner Vincenzo Borgonzola began to cook late in life and is entirely self taught. A native of Naples, he has lived for many years in this country. At our last visit, the two daily specials were fish based, though other dishes could feature calves' sweetbreads with Savoy cabbage, smoked duck with mustard and mint chutney, and snails with cannellini beans, for example, with main courses including pheasant with apples and chestnuts, pig's trotter, or octopus stewed with potato. Raw materials are brought together in wonderful combinations, as demonstrated at a recent meal by soft melting gnocchi with caviar and chives, followed by red mullet with lentils and spinach, then bread and butter pudding made with panattone, an Italian fruit bread. Caring service is overseen by Elaine Borgonzolo. There is a short but interesting all-Italian wine list.

Directions: 2nd left in Edgeware Road, from Marble Arch

W2 30 Connaught Street W2 2AF
Map no: B3
Tel: 0171 262 9623
Chef: Vincenzo Borgonzolo
Proprietor: Elaine & Vincenzo Borgonzolo
Cost: Alc £35. H/wine £11 Service exc
Credit cards: 🎴 📰
Times: 12.30-last L 2pm, 7pm-last D 10pm. Closed Sat L, Sun & 2 wks at Xmas
Menus: A la carte
Seats: 22
Additional: Children over 12 permitted

Alfred ❀❀

☺ *An informal cafe-style restaurant serving simple British dishes*

There is a relaxed and casual atmosphere at this cafe-style restaurant, which offers an extensive *carte* and a short daily set-price menu of British dishes. Chef Robert Gutteridge's cooking is perfectly straightforward and honest. Typical starters might be Glamorgan patties, salad of wood pigeon, and nettle soup, with main courses including the likes of aubergine, artichoke and goats' cheese crumble tart, and some comforting dishes such as toad in the hole (also available as a starter), rabbit in beer and sage sauce, and faggots with minted peas and champ potatoes. All the bread is baked on the premises, and at a test meal a rosemary-flavoured loaf was served with crab soup. This was followed by saddle of lamb with sweetbreads, liver and kidneys, mashed vegetables and potato pancake. Desserts are also along traditional lines, with treacle tart and custard, gingerbread and lavender ice-cream, and a heavily

W2 245 Shaftesbury Avenue WC2 8EH
Map no: D3
Tel: 0171 240 2566
Chef: Robert Gutteridge
Proprietors: Fred Taylor and Robert Gutteridge
Cost: Alc £20, fixed-price L £15.90. H/wine £11 ♥ Service exc
Credit cards: 🎴 📰 📰 📳 OTHER
Times: noon-last L 3.30pm, 6pm-last D 11.30pm. Closed Sun, Bhs, Christmas, N/Year
Menus: A la carte, fixed-price L, pre-theatre, bar menu
Seats: 60 + 30 outside Summer

endorsed sticky toffee pudding. The wine list presents a nicely balanced list of inexpensive wines.

Directions: near British Museum, junction New Oxford Street

The Angel ❀

The Angel boasts one of London's best views – overlooking the Thames and London Bridge with St Paul's in the distance. The pub restaurant offers traditional English dishes, braised lamb shank, or ale sausages with potato and spring onion mash, for example. Best of British puddings too: spotted dick perhaps, or apricot crumble

Additional: children welcome; children's menu, ❶ dishes, vegan/other diets on request

SE16 101 Bermondsey Wall East SE16 4NB
Map no: GtL D3
Tel: 0171 237 3608 / 252 0327
Chef: Andrew Harland
Proprietors: Forte.
Manager: Joanne Grimwood
Cost: *Alc* £23.50, fixed price D £15.50, Sun L £15.50. H/wine £8.25 Service exc
Credit cards: ▨ ▩ ▨ ▨ OTHER
Times: noon-last L 1.45pm, 7pm-last D 9.45pm. Closed Sat lunch, Sun eve and Bhs
Seats: 50
Additional: Children permitted; ❶ dishes

Directions: From south of Tower Bridge follow Jamaica Road towards Rotherhithe Tunnel. Cathay Street is the last turning before the tunnel, the Angel is straight ahead on the river

Annas Place Restaurant ❀❀

A small, friendly restaurant offering a short menu of honestly presented, freshly made Swedish dishes

The welcome is warm and service both friendly and informal at this pleasant little Swedish restaurant, situated just off Newington Green. The blue of the national flag is taken up in the decor, set off by the wooden floor and small vinyl-clothed tables; in summer a vine-covered rear courtyard provides an inviting extension. What is offered here is honest, accurately cooked food, from the short menu. There are several daily dishes and these are verbally announced. 'Sill tallrik' – two types of marinated herring – and gravad lax are regular starters. Then there is 'tre kroner', a selection of Swedish delicacies. To follow there might be 'biff strindberg' – diced fillet of beef marinated in mustard and pan sautéed – or spiced crabcakes. Favourite puddings include a rich chocolate cake, and waffles with blueberry compote and whipped cream. There is also a wine list, supplemented by ice-cold schnapps and Swedish beer. In the evening it is essential to book, and diners should bear in mind that no credit cards are accepted.

N1 90 Mildmay Park N1 4PR
Map no: GtL D3
Tel: 0171 249 9379
Chef: Beth Daidon
Proprietor: Anna Hegarty
Cost: *Alc* £25. H/wine £8.50 ❢ Service exc
Credit cards: None taken
Times: Noon-last L 2.15pm, 7pm-last D 10.45pm. Closed Sun, Mon & 2 wks at Xmas & Easter, 4 wks in August
Menus: *A la carte*
Seats: 42 & 20 in garden. Cigars allowed in dining room
Additional: Children welcome, children's portions; ❶ dishes, vegan/other diets on request

Directions: Left off Balls Pond Road into Mildmay Park. On the corner of Newington Green. Bus 73, 171, 141 to Newington Green

Arcadia ❀❀

☺ *A new chef at this attractive restaurant offering modern cooking*

A change of chef at this colourful Kensington restaurant, with Steve Taylor (ex Leith's) taking over the running of the kitchen. The menu style has hardly changed and still features modern British cooking. Meals begin with warm home-baked bread, and at lunchtime the set-price selection offers simple dishes, such as cured salmon salad with dill dressing, or grilled veal chops with braised red cabbage and roast potatoes. In the evening the *carte* is more adventurous, but dishes remain uncomplicated. Marinated squid with Thai vegetables, coriander and gaufrettes, or pressed sardine and tomato terrine with olive and parsley dressing, followed perhaps by braised oxtail off the bone, with butter beans, port wine and roast vegetables, or grilled baby chicken in sweet spice marinade, lemon cous cous and rocket salad, are typical of the style. The dessert choice is not large, but there could be plum and almond tart with vanilla ice-cream or a delicious cherry and chocolate trifle. There is nothing outstanding in the wine list, but the wines complement the menu and are reasonably priced.

Directions: From High Street Kensington Tube turn right and take 3rd turning on right. Signed footpath leads to Kensington Court

W8 Kensington Court
35 Kensington Street W8 5EB
Map no: GtL C3
Tel: 0171 937 4294
Chef: Steve Taylor
Proprietor: A V Garcia-Quires
Cost: *Alc £19, fixed-price lunch £13.50 (2 courses), £16. H/wine £9.75* ❢ *Service exc*
Credit cards: 🔳 💳 💳 💳 OTHER
Times: *Last L 2.30pm, Last D 11.15pm. Lunch not served Sat, Sun. Closed 3 days Xmas*
Menus: *A la carte, fixed-price lunch*
Seats: *78. No-smoking area. No pipes or cigars*
Additional: *Children welcome; children's portions.* ❷ *dishes; Vegan/other diets on request*

Atelier ❀❀❀

Exciting modern British cooking in minimalist Soho setting

Stephen Bulmer takes an intelligent approach to his work. His dishes show excitingly original combinations of textures, colours and flavours, with harmonious and well-balanced sauces. Five starters and main courses might prove a restricted choice for some, but they are well thought out, with descriptions that come straight to the point. Dishes such as warm spinach mousse with white anchovies, garnished with tomato and parsley, roasted lamb chump with basil potato, tomato fondue and rosemary, and pan-fried tuna with vegetable pistou, saffron mash, red pepper and sauce leave the diner in no doubt as to what they are about to receive. Quail boudin on spinach and pea purée exemplified the style, blending light and rich flavours in a pan-fried sausage, the jus additionally textured with whole girolles and morels. Pan-fried monkfish with mussels, on our inspection, were all perfectly fresh, but even so the mussels took some chewing. These central ingredients were backed up with a turban of perfectly cooked, home-made linguine and a butter mustard seed sauce, constructed from fish and vegetable stock and flavoured with tarragon. Vegetables included haricots verts and spot-on mashed potatoes. Only a chocolate tart, a sort of reconstructed Black Forest job, with fresh black cherries flavoured with cinnamon and Kirsch plus crème Chantilly, lacked zip – but, to be fair, a new pâtissier was in the process of being recruited at the time. The largely French wine list is as focused as the food, and there are a fair number of wines by the glass and half bottle.

Directions: From Piccadilly Tube go north up Regent Street. Beak Street is on the right

W1 41 Beak Street W1R 3LE
Map no: C3
Tel: 0171 287 2057
Chef: Stephen Bulmer
Proprietor: J S B Restaurants Ltd

Athenaeum Hotel ❀❀

Modern British cooking with a strong Mediterranean influence, aimed at a cosmopolitan clientele

A multi-million pound refit has revitalised one of London's most popular and friendly hotels. In Bullochs Restaurant, named after their own executive manager, the names of the famous can be seen on some of the chair-backs. It is a rare day indeed when a statesman, actor or sportsman cannot be seen. Chef David Marshall's realistically priced *carte* is founded on fixed prices for each course, plus a few supplements. An inspection dinner began with freshly made ricotta and tarragon ravioli, served with a light, creamy sauce, followed by a generous portion of rack of pink lamb with a provençale herb crust. A dish of fresh leaf spinach, with garlic added on our inspector's request, caused the restaurant manager to say how good it smelt. Other starters might include chilled crayfish, and lobster and coriander ravioli, which is also available as a main course. There are plenty of meat dishes, including duck, steak and calves' liver, while the fish section includes turbot, swordfish and grilled carp. Restaurant staff are friendly but seemed inclined to prefer to chat with the pianist on the night we were there.

Directions: Hyde Park Corner/Green Park on Piccadilly

W1 116 Piccadilly W1V 0BJ
Map no: C3
Tel: 0171 499 3464
Chef: David Marshall
Proprietor: The Athenaeum Hotel & Apartments.
Manager: David Plant
Cost: *Alc* £23.45. H/wine £12.95 ♥ Service exc
Credit cards: ▨ ▧ ▧ ▨ OTHER
Times: Mon-Fri Noon-last L 2.30pm, Mon-Sat 6pm-last D 11.30pm, Sun 7pm-last D 10pm
Menus: A la carte
Seats: 65. No-smoking area, air-conditioning
Additional: Children's portions; ♥ dishes, vegan/other diets on request

The Atlantic ❀❀

Vast Art Deco basement where the decibel levels are high and the clientele know that cuttlefish isn't just for budgerigars

A former marbled function room of the Regent Palace Hotel, with Odeon cinema-style lighting, makes a perfect setting for one of the most sought after places in Town. In fact, it is so sought after that queuing may be necessary. The modern international menu reflects the customers, or maybe it's the other way round. Chef Richard Sawyer pulls together ideas from southern California and the Mediterranean to create an intriguing list of dishes. Ceviche of Azura tomatoes, blue fin tuna and salmon with lemon juice and avocado, or warm truffled potato layers with shiitake and girolle mushrooms, foie gras and a sweet and sour dressing, for example. Or perhaps lobster ravioli, filled with pink fish mousse with collops of crunchy fresh lobster, set in a golden chicken consommé, and textured with chopped spring onion, carrot, and deep-fried leeks, suprême of Bresse chicken with snap peas, shredded bacon and lemon thyme, or new season lamb rosette with roasted garlic fritters and red shallots. Such an unusual array of dishes requires a wide choice of wines; Atlantic offers just that.

Directions: Just off Piccadilly Circus

W1 20 Glasshouse Street W1 5RQ
Map no: D3
Tel: 0171 734 4888
Chef: Richard Sawyer
Proprietor: Oliver Peyton
Cost: *Alc* £25, fixed-price L £11.90. H/wine £11.50 ♥ Service exc
Credit cards: ▨ ▧ ▧ OTHER
Times: Noon-last L 2.30pm, last D 11.30pm. Closed 24-26 Dec
Menus: A la carte, fixed-price, bar menu
Seats: 160. Cigars allowed in restaurant & bars, air-conditioning
Additional: ♥ dishes, vegan/other diets on request in advance

Auberge de Provence ❀❀❀

French Provençal cuisine in the grand style

After a bumpy patch last year, the cooking is once more broadly 'comme il faut'. Renowned for its ongoing links with the village of Les Baux and L'Oustau de Baumanière (founded by Raymond

SW1 41 Buckingham Gate SW1E 6AF
Map no: D2
Tel: 0171 821 1899
Chef: Bernard Brique
Proprietor: St James Court Hotel.

Thuilier), the restaurant, which forms part of the St James Court Hotel, offers both a seasonal *carte* and a three course Provençal menu priced at £32. After enjoying a warm appetiser of glazed monkfish with cabbage, and a choice of breads such as onion, walnut and olive, our inspection meal continued with a banon cheese soufflé, somewhat marred by a loose texture bordering on the scrambled. An additional course of 'ravioli pétoncles à la crème thym' was perfectly cooked, with a light and delicious coral-thickened sauce and pasta filled with fresh salmon mousse, but the queen scallops were gritty and lacked delicacy. The highlight of this year's inspection meal were the noisettes of lamb, served with a barquette of sliced salsify in basil cream, set alight by a wonderful marjoram jus. Whilst most desserts are still offered from the trolley, worth ordering in advance is the apple tart, constructed from French Golden Delicious apples and puff pastry with frangipan; try it with the wonderful, home-made vanilla ice-cream. There is a choice of coffee, and the espresso comes rich and full-bodied, with excellent petits fours and chocolate truffles. Service is very correct, with flashing silver cloches, and is well supervised by the affable restaurant manager Christian Berger. The wine list, as one might expect, is totally French, with all the principal growers represented. Prices are good value for money, and there are some interesting house wines. The Chateau Monjouan 1ère Côte de Bordeaux 1990, is worth seeking out for its well developed bouquet and round flavour.

Directions: Off Victoria Street, five mins walk from Buckingham Palace

Manager: Christian Berger
Cost: *Alc* £43, fixed-price L £24.50/D £32. H/wine £12.50
❗ Service exc
Credit cards: 🅴 ▦ ▧ 🅿 OTHER
Times: Last L 2.30pm, last D 11pm. Closed Sat L, Sun & one wk Jan, 2 wks Aug
Menus: *A la carte*, fixed-price L & D
Seats: 70. No-smoking area, air-conditioning
Additional: Children welcome, children's portions; ❷ dishes, other diets on request

Aubergine ❀❀❀❀

Bright, fashionable modern restaurant serving innovative modern cooking

The restaurant bustles with activity, yet remains airy, sunny and calm. Everyone goes there. The staff are mainly French and seem devoted to their mission of making sure that the right dishes and wines are chosen, sometimes with over zealous dedication. You have to admire Gordon Ramsay. Last year he was fêted as the new kid on the block. This year has been one of consolidation, an amalgamation of technique acquired in London where he trained with Albert Roux and Marco Pierre White, and in Paris, with Joel Robuchon and Guy Savoy. While his cooking pays tribute, Ramsay has his own direct approach. It is sheer joy, innovativeness combined with a purity and accuracy of flavour and texture, yet with simplicity as the keyword.

A meal taken in winter could be an exemplar. A ballotine of foie gras was followed by an appetiser of quite delicate chilled gazpacho. The ballotine was layered livers coated in aspic with port jelly around the edges, the texture smooth, the flavour spot on. Pot au feu of pigeon 'heralded a gasp of delight' for its pungent aroma generated by truffle and two small breasts, succulent, pink and tender, swimming in pure bouillon with cabbage stuffed with foie gras; only a pot of spiced tomato chutney seemed superfluous. Tarte tatin was equally well executed, served with a creamy black pepper ice. The cooking consistently retains an edge. At a meal in May rabbit terrine – pieces of potato, rabbit, foie gras, mushroom, green cabbage and truffle, all perfectly judged to give bite and set in a jelly – was light in effect but bursting with flavour. A curl of

SW10 11 Park Walk SW10
Map no: A1
Tel: 0171 352 3449
Chef: Gordon Ramsay
Proprietor: Gordon Ramsay
Cost: Fixed-price L £19.50/D £44 (six courses). H/wine £15 ❗ Service exc
Credit cards: 🅴 ▦ ▧ 🅿 OTHER
Times: 12.15-last L 2.30pm, 7pm-last D 11pm. Closed Sat L, Sun & 1 wk at Easter, 2 wks in August, 2 wks at Xmas
Menus: Fixed-price
Seats: 50
Additional: ❷ /other diets on request

acidulated, creamy vinaigrette added zest. Its neighbour, lobster ravioli, came with a frothy ginger sauce. Sea bass was crisped on top, set on spinach, batons of salsify and baby fennel with a vanilla sauce. This was full flavoured and slightly sweet, pushing the boundaries, but it worked. Crème brûlée was creamy and smooth, not heavy within, crisp thin top, set on rhubarb with a strawberry coulis. A raspberry soufflé with an eau de vie sauce poured in was perfect. The meal was typical of the style and worked well because every part of it was on form. Bread is excellent: sun-dried tomato, walnut, plain white and brown. Petits fours are 'delightful'.

The wine list is sound; outside Bordeaux and Burgundy bottles under £20 are to be found. The selection of half bottles is excellent.

Directions: Fulham Road, 2nd road left after the MGM cinema

Au Jardin des Gourmets ☻☻

A much loved Soho restaurant with dependable standards of traditional French cooking and courteous, formal service

Now 65 years old, this well established restaurant maintains its popularity with a showbiz clientele. Consistency is the key to its success, and there are high hopes of new chef Vincent Hiss. The cooking is a mixture of classical and provincial French, offered from a choice of fixed-price menus and a *carte*, along with a superb wine list featuring many classic wines of good vintage. From a selection that could include smoked wild boar salad, or a fricassée of snails and pig's trotter, our inspector opted for a first course of lightly grilled fresh scallops on a potato tartlet with corn lettuce and a lemon and herb vinaigrette. This was followed by fillet of lamb topped with foie gras and served with an excellent truffle and Madeira sauce. Dessert was a winter pudding of light sponge filled with fresh fruit and almonds and served with caramel sauce. There are also some five fish dishes, such as braised sea bass with broad beans in a tomato and tarragon sauce. Main courses are served with a substantial garnish; vegetables and salads are charged separately.

Directions: Near Soho Square and Oxford Street; nearest Tube – Tottenham Court Road

W1 5 Greek Street
Soho Square W1V 5LA
Map no: D4
Tel: 0171 437 1816
Chef: Vincent Hiss
Proprietor: Novoport Group.
Manager: Franco Zoia
Cost: *Alc* £28.50, fixed price
L & D £17.50. H/wine £9.50 ⬤
Service exc. Cover charge £1.50
for *Alc*
Credit cards: ▨ ▤ ▨ ▨ OTHER
Times: Last L 2.30pm /
D 11.15pm. Closed Sat lunch,
Sun, Christmas, Good Fri
Menus: *A la carte*, fixed-price
L & D, brasserie menu, pre-
theatre
Seats: 95. Air conditioned,
smoking areas
Additional: Children welcome;
childrens portions, ⬤ dishes,
vegan/other diets on request

Ayudhya Thai Restaurant 🏵🏵

☺ *Hard to beat as an introduction to Thai cooking; a wide choice with excellent explanatory notes and helpful staff*

The colourful modern interior, with Thai murals and ornaments, creates a striking first impression. The huge choice of dishes gives a real test of Thai cooking. Dishes sampled have included 'hoy jaw', a mixture of minced prawn, crab and pork with spring onion and coriander leaves, steamed with beancurd, deep fried, and served with a sweet and sour sauce, 'popia pad', tender pieces of duck with spring onions and cucumber, wrapped in a thin rice pancake, and served with a yellow bean sauce, 'kai yang', pieces of barbecued chicken marinated in herbs and spices and served with a sweet, hot chilli sauce, and 'neua paht bai kaprow', thin strips of tender beef stir-fried with chilli and fresh sweet basil leaves. Salads, such as green mango, or roasted aubergine, are worth exploring, as are some of the Thai curries, especially 'gaeng Mussaman', a rich beef curry based on coconut milk, lemon grass and galanga. Some typical Thai desserts are offered featuring coconut milk, bananas and pumpkin. To drink there is a short, inexpensive wine list, plus Singha Thai beer.

Directions: 0.5 mile from Kingston town centre on A308, and 2.5 miles from Robin Hood Roundabout at the junction of A3M

14 Kingston Hill
Kingston upon Thames
KT2 7NH
Map no: GtL B2
Tel: 0181 549 5984/546 5878
Chef: Somjai Thanpho
Proprietor: Somjai Thanpho
Cost: Alc £20. H/wine £6.95 ⸙
Service inc
Credit cards: 🄰 ▦ ▧ 🄳 OTHER
Times: Noon-last L 2.30pm, last D 11pm. Closed Mon L & Easter Sun, 25/6 Dec & New Year's Day
Menus: A la carte
Seats: 82. Cigars allowed
Additional: Children welcome, children's portions; ❶ dishes, vegan/other diets on request

Baboon 🏵🏵

☺ *A popular basement restaurant and piano bar offering modern British cooking from a talented chef*

Baboon is located below the New Mandeville Hotel in Jason Court. A comfortable bar lounge and two dining rooms are the setting for chef Redmond Hayward's honest, full flavoured dishes from a short *carte* and fixed-price market menu. A recent inspection meal began with chicken liver parfait set on crunchy green beans with a shallot salad and strongly flavoured balsamic vinegar dressing. Roast brill followed, accompanied by a well seasoned saffron mash and grain mustard dressing which acted as a perfect foil to the richness of the fish. A feuilleté of apples was outstanding, especially the contrast of the crisp puff pastry and excellent, intensely flavoured cider and Calvados butter sauce. Attention to small detail is excellent. Bread is made on the premises and rich, strong espresso comes with hand-made chocolate truffles. A few fine wines can be found on the all-French list, and there is a short selection of half bottles. Baboon is a restaurant and piano bar, so entertainment is provided, and being a popular establishment booking is recommended, particularly at lunchtime.

Directions: Off Wigmore Street, opposite Christophers Place, near Bond Street Tube

W1 76 Wigmore Street
W1M 6BE
Map no: C4
Tel: 0171 224 2992
Chef: Redmond Hayward
Proprietor: Tony Kitons.
Manager: Norman Barke
Cost: Alc £20, fixed-price L £12.50/D £17. H/wine £9 ⸙
Service exc
Credit cards: 🄰 ▦ ▧ 🄳 OTHER
Times: Noon-last L 3pm, 6pm-last D 11pm. Closed Sat L, Sun & Bhs, Easter, Xmas
Menus: A la carte, fixed-price, bar menu
Seats: 65. No-smoking area, no pipes allowed, cigars in lounge
Additional: Children welcome; ❶ dishes, other diets on request

Babur Brasserie ❀❀

☺ *Smart, modern Indian restaurant, some radically different dishes, and above average cooking*

SE23 119 Brockley Rise
Forest Hill SE23 1JP
Map no: GtL D2
Tel: 0181 291 2400/4881
Chef: Enam Rahman
Proprietor: Babur Ltd.
Manager: Emdad Rahman
Cost: *Alc* £14.50. H/wine £6.95
Service exc
Credit cards: ▨ ▨ ▨ ▨ OTHER
Times: Last L 2.15pm, last D
11.15pm. Closed 25/26 Dec
Menus: *A la carte*, Sunday
lunch, once a year festival
Seats: 54. No-smoking area,
air-conditioning
Additional: Children welcome;
❶/vegan dishes

Although an Indian restaurant, Babur does things differently. Even the names of some of the dishes are unfamiliar, especially those from Goa: 'beef xacuti', with roasted star anise, nutmeg, javantri, fenugreek, red chillies, coconut and cinnamon and 'baingan badam', baby aubergines cooked with roasted mustard and onion seed, ginger and garlic purée, finished in a delicious peanut sauce. 'Murgh tikka lasania' is a departure from the usual tikka. Chicken is marinated in a special strained yoghurt and garlic purée, then cooked in the tandoor. An inspector tried 'pathia purée', an appetiser of spiced prawns with vegetables on a light, crispy Moghlai pancake, 'shugati masala' (large pieces of tender chicken cooked in spices and a masala sauce, with coconut and white poppy seed), 'poodina gosht' (minted lamb cooked with honey, lemon juice and special spices), and 'shah jahani', chunks of river fish, marinated then cooked over the tandoor with onions, capsicums and tomatoes and served with tomato and coconut sauce. Indian lagers and a range of wines, virtually all under £10, are available.

Directions: Off S Circular – Stansted RD1. Nearest BR Honor Oak Park

Bahn Thai Restaurant ❀❀

Thai restaurant with an unwieldy menu but delicious, if pricey, food

You should not say 'That's my dish' at a Thai table; everything belongs to everyone. If a 'green torpedo' blows the roof off your mouth, eat lots of plain rice. Water is of very little help in dealing with chillies. These and other hints are offered to those who are unfamiliar with Thai food. Despite its well-meant attempts to help, the menu is rather daunting, with symbols denoting the spiciness and temperature of each dish, a dish number, its name in Thai characters, in phonetic English and in English translation. A recent meal began with a peanut-laden satay, and excellent minced pork dumplings with garlic and soya sauce. This was followed by wok-fried pork with garlic, pepper and coriander paste, as enjoyable for its subtle flavours as was a green chicken curry for its fiery heat. Some curries can be 'stronger than paint stripper', while others are

W1 21a Frith Street W1V 5TS
Map no: D4
Tel: 0171 437 8504
Chef: Mrs Penn
Proprietor: Philip Harris.
Manager: Valentino Henkel
Cost: *Alc* £25, fixed-price from
£37.10 for two. H/wine £7.95
Service inc
Credit cards: ▨ ▨ ▨ ▨ OTHER
Times: Noon-last L 2.45pm,
6.30pm-last D 11.15pm. Closed
Bhs, Xmas & Easter
Menus: *A la carte*, fixed-price D,
pre-theatre
Seats: 93. Smoking permitted

very delicate. According to the tasting notes, all the wines go with the food, and the house wines are 'eminently drinkable with all the kitchen can produce'. Chilled Thai beer is a good alternative. Beware the steep compulsory service charge.

Directions: On the right hand side of Frith Street when approaching from Shaftesbury Avenue. Nearest Tube – Tottenham Court Road

Additional: Children welcome; ❶ /vegan dishes

Basil Street Hotel ❁

☺ *A fine Edwardian hotel which has not changed ownership since 1910. The elegant, candlelit dining-room is the setting for the likes of a salad of fresh spinach, mushrooms, avacado, and bacon, with a hazelnut oil dressing, followed by deep fried goujons of sole, squid and scampi, tossed in a lime and olive oil dressing*

Menus: Fixed-price **Seats:** 70
Additional: Children welcome, children's portions; ❶ dishes, vegan/other diets on request
Directions: Off Sloane Street, behind Harrods

SW3 3 Basil Street
Knightsbridge SW3 1AH
Map no: B2
Tel: 0171 581 3311
Chef: James Peake
Cost: Fixed-price L £16.50
(3 course)/D £22 (3 course).
H/wine £10.95 Service inc
Credit cards: ▨ ▨ ▨ ▨
Times: Noon-last L 2.30pm,
6.30pm-last D 10.15pm. Closed
Sat L

The Bedlington Café ❁

Simple Thai restaurant made popular by its unpretentious atmosphere, tightly packed tables, mixed crockery and large mugs of jasmine tea. A meal here might feature steamed dumplings filled with pork and prawn, hot and sour chicken soup, and rice sticks fried with egg, peanuts, shrimps and spring onions

Additional: Children welcome; ❶ dishes, vegan/other diets on request
Directions: From Chiswick High Road take Sutton Court Road and cross motorway, at next junction turn right into Fauconberg Road

W4 24 Fauconberg Road
Chiswick W4
Map no: GtL E3
Tel: 0181 994 1965
Chef: S Srisawad
Proprietor: P Priyanu
Credit cards: None taken
Times: 8am-2pm, 6.30pm-10pm
Menus: A la carte
Seats: 30

Belgo ❁❁

☺ *Be transported to a place of mussels, frites, and beer so successful that a sister restaurant, Belgo Central, has opened*

The atmosphere at this unusual place has obviously been a reason for its great success; waiters dressed as Trappist monks and bawdy comments are scrawled on the walls. A new head chef has brought added authenticity to the cooking in the form of more classic Belgian dishes, and some remarkable bargains, such as 'lunch for a fiver' – large pot of moules marinière or wild boar sausages, plus a beer – and 'beat the clock' pricing (weekdays, six until eight). Mussels and frites are available, obviously, coming by the kilo in various ways: with green peppercorns, au provençal, with coconut and lemongrass, or with beer and lardons. The beef braised in Trappist beer with plums and apples was an instant hit with our inspector, who also recommended the 'waterzooi de la Mer du Nord', a light, creamy stew of brill and grey and red mullet, served with a julienne of fresh vegetables and new potatoes. More than 50 national beers of all types and a large selection of gins are there to be tried.

Directions: Nearest Tube – Chalk Farm

NW1 72 Chalk Farm Road NW1
Map no: GtL C3
Tel: 0171 267 0718
Chef: Poul Jensen
Proprietor: Denis Blais & Andre
Plisnier
Cost: Alc £20, fixed-price
L £5/D £10. H/wine £8.95 ❶
Service inc
Credit cards: ▨ ▨ ▨ ▨ OTHER
Times: Weekdays Noon-last
L 3pm, 6pm-last D 11.30pm;
weekends Noon-11.30pm.
Closed Xmas day
Menus: A la carte, fixed-price
L & D
Seats: 120. Smoking permitted,
air conditioning
Additional: Children welcome,
children's portions; ❶ dishes

Belvedere ❀❀

A restaurant in the middle of a park, isolated from the noise and dust of the crowded streets, serving mainly British food

Jacobean Holland House was once known as Hope Castle, after the man who had it built. It stands, not only in the middle of one of London's most fashionable parks, but in one of the capital's most fashionable areas. The bar and reception area are on the ground floor, the first-floor dining-room, bedecked with colourful cartoons and photographs of celebrity visitors, commands leafy views of the park. The *carte* features a range of dishes, some available as either starters or main courses, such as tagliatelle with artichoke pesto, and saffron risotto with wild mushroom sauce, which were both well reported. So too was a main course typical of Duncan Wallace's modern style, namely pan-fried calves' liver on a bed of bubble and squeak with an onion gravy and crispy bacon. Beefsteak sausages with cheesy mash and vegetable crisps is popular, or there is grilled fillets of red and grey mullet on a bed of crunchy vegetables with fennel oil and minted potatoes. The selection of puddings always features a hot soufflé and a daily special. A dozen or so well chosen reds outnumber a smaller selection of whites.

Directions: Nearest Tubes – Holland Park, High Street Kensington. Restaurant behind Holland Park car park

W8 Abbotsbury Road
Holland Park W8 6LU
Map no: GtL C3
Tel: 0171 602 1238
Chef: Duncan Wallace
Proprietor: J Gold and W Zofner.
Manager: Ian MacRae
Cost: *Alc* £25. H/wine £10.50
Service exc
Credit cards: ▨ ▨ ▨ ▨ OTHER
Times: Noon-last L 3pm,
7pm-last D 11pm (open at 6pm in summer). Closed Sun D & Xmas, New Year's Day
Menus: *A la carte*, set-menus for parties 20+, Summer pre/post-theatre
Seats: 120 plus some seating outside, air-conditioning
Additional: Children welcome, children's portions; ✆ dishes, vegan/other diets on request

The Bengal Clipper ❀❀

☺ *Strongly spiced Bengali food contrasts with more delicate dishes in the historic setting of Butler's Wharf*

Bringing the spice trade full circle, this Indian restaurant is appropriately located on London's historic spice wharf, close to Tower Bridge on the south side of the Thames. A twice-yearly *carte* and daily changing set-price menu offer an interesting and varied selection of Bengali dishes. Delicately balanced sauces accompany dishes such as 'murgh tikka masala', tender pieces of chicken in a house-speciality sauce made with fenugreek and cream, lamb 'pasanda', marinated lamb in a sauce of cream and almonds, and 'golda chingri masala', large prawns from the Bay of Bengal, baked in a clay oven and simmered in a spicy red masala sauce. Among the hotter dishes is 'kadi ghost', a hot lamb stew originating from central India, made with coriander seed and bulb chilli sauce. Breads include nan, and a very good, lightly spiced papadom; pilaf rice with cinnamon, cloves, cassia leaf, aniseed and rosewater was also highly recommended.

Directions: By Tower Bridge. Nearest Tube – Tower Hill

SE1 Butler's Wharf SE1
Map no: GtL D3
Tel: 0171 357 9001
Chef: Ruf Uddin
Proprietor: Mukit Choudhury
Cost: *Alc* £18.95, fixed-price L £12.95. H/wine £8.95 ❢
Service exc
Credit cards: ▨ ▨ ▨ ▨ OTHER
Times: Noon-last L 3pm. Closed 25/26 Dec
Menus: *A la carte*, fixed-price L
Seats: 175. Air-conditioning
Additional: Children welcome, children's portions; ✆ dishes, vegan/other diets on request

Bentley's ❀❀

New owners are transforming one of London's most famous fish restaurants

The tradition of serving fish began in 1916. Under new owners Oscar Owide and his son Daniel, Bentley's Seafood Restaurant and Oyster Bar, to give it its full title, feels more like a gentlemen's club. Keith Stanley (ex Ritz) has moved the goalposts a little so that

W1 11/15 Swallow Street
W1R 7HD
Map no: C3
Tel: 0171 734 4756/439 6903
Chef: Keith Stanley
Proprietor: Oscar Owide

alongside classic starters like rock oysters, dressed crab and lobster and avocado salad, the Orient is now represented by grilled giant Thailand prawns with chilli salsa, and tempura crab claws with black bean sauce. The sheer variety of fish and seafood on the *carte* and set-price menu makes choice difficult. Other starters include gazpacho of crab and fennel at the inexpensive end, and work their way up through skate and artichoke terrine, and lobster and avocado salad, to seafood platter at £42.00 (for two) or Beluga caviar. Main courses are of seared salmon on wilted greens, bouillabaisse with rouille, charred tuna with lemon couscous, or maybe a non-fish dish like fillet of lamb with tomato and spinach cake. A separate desserts menu includes a hot pudding of the day. On the ground floor is the less formal Oyster Bar.

Directions: Nearest Tube – Piccadilly Circus. Swallow Street links Regent Street & Piccadilly and is opposite St James's Church on Piccadilly

Cost: *Alc* £35, fixed-price L/D £19.50 (3 course). H/wine £11.50 ❗ Service exc
Credit cards: ▨ ▤ ▤ ▣ OTHER
Times: Noon-last L 2.30pm, 6pm-last D 11.30pm. Closed Sun & Bhs
Menus: A la carte, fixed-price, oyster bar menu
Seats: 80. Cigars permitted, air-conditioning
Additional: Children welcome; ❷ dishes, other diets on request in advance

The Berkeley ❀❀

Sound, quality cooking in one of the smartest parts of London

Wilton Place
Knightsbridge SW1
Map no: B2
Tel: 0171 235 6000
Chef: John Williams
Proprietor: Savoy Group.
Manager: Stefphen Boxall
Cost: *Alc* from £35, fixed price L £21.50/ D £24. H/wine £15 Service inc
Credit cards: ▨ ▤ ▤ ▣
Times: 12.30-last L 2.45pm, 6.30pm-last D 10.45pm. Closed Sat
Menus: A la carte, fixed-price L & D
Seats: 65. Air conditioned
Additional: children permitted; children's menu, ❷ dishes, vegan/other on request

The atmosphere is serene and comforting, the furnishings discreet; they whisper quality. Of the two dining-rooms, the Berkeley Restaurant offers a range of dishes which, while following a strong classical inclination, keep up with current tastes. Few will dispute the standard of the food, or the service; the waiters have a style which reflects their surroundings perfectly. A typical meal will kick off with 'terrine de foie gras d'oie', or ravioli of Dublin Bay prawns doused in a rich and pungent cream sauce. Then there may be delice of turbot with rosemary and thyme crust, fillet of zander with a purée of potatoes, artichokes and sage, magret of duck with spiced apples and pepper sauce, or noisettes of lamb with baked tomato and basil fondue. Puddings are mostly from the trolley, 'a great range', with a 'lovely' bread and butter pudding, and 'full of flavour' lemon tart. The second restaurant, the Perroquet, serves contemporary Italian food. The extensive wine list is comprehensive and has some very strong candidates from Bordeaux and Burgundy.

Directions: The Berkeley is 200yds from Hyde Park Corner, on the corner of Knightsbridge and Wilton Place; nearest Tube – Hyde Park Corner

The Berkshire ❀

A popular place with both business clients and shoppers for its prized location on Oxford Street, almost opposite New Bond Street. Ascot's panelled restaurant offers a short daily menu and a seasonal carte. Typical dishes include duck and pigeon terrine with kumquats, or hot oak-smoked salmon with watercress sauce

Seats: 50. Air conditioned
Additional: Children welcome; children's portions; ❂ menu; Vegan/other diets on request
Directions: From Bond Street Tube cross Oxford Street. The hotel is next to Debenhams, entrance in Marylebone Lane

W1 Oxford Street W1
Map no: C4
Tel: 0171 629 7474
Chef: James Chapman
Proprietor: Radisson Edwardian.
Manager: Steven Hobden
Cost: Alc £33, fixed-price L £17.50 (2 courses), £23.40/D £17.50 (2 courses) £23.40. Wine £13.75. Service inc
Credit cards: ▨ ▆ ▆ ▨ OTHER
Times: Last L 2.30pm/D 10.30pm. Closed L Sat, Sun and BH

Bibendum Restaurant ❀❀❀❀

Still one of the most fashionable places to eat in London, Matthew Harris continues the successful promotion of modern bistro-style cooking

You can hardly see the join. Simon Hopkinson has been replaced by his former number two, Matthew Harris with apparently no loss of standard, or commitment to the simple cooking of dishes using the best raw materials. The flagship of Sir Terence Conran's restaurant empire, Bibendum is set on the first floor of the Michelin building; it is a bright, airy and very popular place – booking is essential. The kitchen style remains the one pioneered by Hopkinson who has been influenced by the recipes of Elizabeth David, the cuisine of the Mediterranean and the Far East, and the reworking of British traditional dishes. Thus, deep-fried goujons of sole with Thai dipping sauce, roast pigeon with braised lettuce, bacon and truffles, and steamed maple syrup and walnut sponge with custard, could happily form the components of a meal.

Recent inspections have sung the praises of Matthew Harris's cooking. One meal began with herbed olives and freshly baked baguette, then a bright dish of confit of fresh tasting tuna with a crunchy green bean salad set off with a first-class garlic cream dressing. Its companion, stewed squid, was remarkable for a lightness of texture, and for the well judged, robust tomato sauce and braised fennel. A poached fillet of cod came with a heavily perfumed Thai broth. Adorned with Chinese spinach this dish was quite outstanding in concept and depth of individual flavours; simply cooked, but faultless vegetable accompanied. Another main course of intensely flavoured roast saddle of rabbit was set off with butter beans and a rich basil infused sauce. To finish, featherlight chocolate cake, richly flavoured with smooth orange sauce, and an Amaretto parfait with a reduced orange sauce. First-class espresso coffee and excellent chocolate truffles.

The wine list is encyclopaedic, concentrating on France region by region, but there are choice bottles from around the world. The Italian section in particular, is outstanding.

Directions: Michelin Building at crossroads of Fulham Road & Sloane Avenue

SW3 81 Fulham Road SW3 6RD
Map no: A1
Tel: 0171 581 5817
Chef: Matthew Harris and James Kirby
Manager: Graham Williams
Cost: Fixed-price L £27. H/wine £9.50 ▮ Service inc
Credit cards: ▨ ▆ ▆ OTHER
Times: Last L 2.30pm, last D 11pm. Closed 24-28 Dec
Menus: A la carte, fixed-price L
Seats: 72. Cigars allowed – no pipes, air-conditioning
Additional: Children welcome, children's portions; ❂ dishes

Bice ❀❀

Mayfair haunt – Louis Vuitton bags are almost de rigueur – serving food from the Italian regions

Bice is a chain with a difference – the dozen or so branches are countries, even continents, apart. The style here is definitely upmarket Italian, with not a pizza in sight, but plenty of northern regional dishes. Prices reflect the salubrious Mayfair setting. On offer might be a mixed salad with artichokes and Parmesan flakes, or Tuscan-style beans and vegetable soup, followed by pasta with taleggio cheese and rocket salad, or pan-fried fillets of trout with herb butter sauce. Selected from the main menu, an inspection starter of soft, home-made tagliatelle was served with a restrained bolognese sauce. Slightly tough calamari rings filled with a mixture of peas, garlic and breadcrumbs, were given some much-needed pzazz by a rich tomato and black olive sauce. Traditional Italian desserts include coffee panna cotta and tiramisu, as well as mousses, tarts and sorbets.

Directions: Off Piccadilly/near Old Bond St; nearest tube Green Park

W1 13 Albermarle Street
W1X 3HA
Map no: C3
Tel: 0171 409 1011
Chef: Antonello Tagliabue
Proprietor: S Frittella and
Roberto Rugeri.
Managers: Umberto Tosi and
Yolanda Ruggeri
Cost: Alc £32.50, fixed-price
L £20. H/wine £15 Service exc
Credit cards: 🜲 🜲 🜲 🜲 OTHER
Times: Noon-last L 2.45pm, last
D 11pm. Closed Sat L, Sun &
Bhs, Xmas & Easter
Menus: A la carte, fixed-price L
Seats: 105. Smoking permitted,
air-conditioning
Additional: Children welcome;
♥ dishes, vegan/other diets on
request in advance

Big Night Out ❀❀

Stunning food of memorable taste and texture, cooked to order and served in simple surroundings

There is no doubting that the Big Night Out is big on flavour, with well-executed sauces and original ideas from talented young chef and co-owner Richard Coates. He and partner Hugh O'Doyle (both ex-Ritz) work together on the three-monthly menu to provide the kind of dishes the more regular local diners have come to expect. Hugh looks after service, supported by a friendly and industrious team of staff. Ingredients are carefully sourced and results are fresh and robust. Commitment to quality is evident in the memorable flavours and textures, though kitchen delays are inevitable. Bread is made on the premises and for early diners it comes straight from the oven. Dishes sampled this year include rabbit sausages with braised lentils and button mushrooms accompanied by a good beef stock reduction, and roast guinea fowl with wild mushrooms and a shallot confit served with an excellent truffle and mushroom fumet sauce. For dessert raspberry soufflé tartlet with strawberry sauce.

Directions: near to Primrose Hill, 750yds from Chalk Farm tube, on left going N

148 Regents Park NW1
Map no: Q29
Tel: 0171 586 5768
Chef: Richard Coates
Proprietor: Hugh O'Boyle and
Richard Coates
Cost: Alc £29.50, fixed-price
L £18.50 / D £18.50 H/wine
£9.50 ❗ Service exc
Credit cards: 🜲 🜲 🜲 🜲 OTHER
Times: Midday-last L 3pm,
7.30pm-midnight. D not served
Sun, L not served Mon
Menus: A la carte, fixed-price
L & D, Sun brunch
Seats: 65. Air conditioned
Additional: Children welcome;
♥ dishes

Bistro Bistret ❀

☺ *A busy, bustling restaurant which serves well prepared, wholesome dishes. A spring meal here featured mussels in a white wine, cream, and onion stock, lamb with rosemary and garlic, and a fresh fruit tart with crisp shortcrust pastry*

Menus: A la carte, fixed-price, pre-theatre, bar menu
Additional: Children welcome, children's portions; ♥ dishes, vegan/other diets on request
Directions: Opposite Gloucester Road Tube station

SW7 140 Gloucester Road
SW7 4QH
Map no: A2
Tel: 0171 373 6000/5044
Chef: Ray Morgan
Proprietor: Ray Morgan
Cost: Alc £15, fixed-price
L £7.50/D 9.50. H/wine £9.90 ❗
Service exc
Credit cards: 🜲 🜲 🜲 🜲 OTHER
Times: 7am-10am, noon-last
L 2.30pm, 5.30pm-last D 11pm

Bistro 190 ❀❀

A popular, vibrant South Ken bistro with an original approach to modern Mediterranean food

The high-ceilinged front room of the delightful Gore Hotel works well for Anthony Worrall-Thompson's modern bistro. Walls are heavily hung with pictures and wooden tables stand on bare floorboards. It is noisy, but even so the atmosphere remains relaxing. The menu is keenly priced, offering a range of simple dishes ranging from soups and salads, pasta with thick tomato sauce and chorizo, and moules marinière, to pappardelle with chicken livers, porcini and red wine, herbed salmon with garlic cream and new potatoes, Italian sausages with black pudding and lentil, char-grilled rump steak, Gorgonzola butter and peperonata, or seared tuna with artichoke salad, aubergine and wild onions. The Worrall-Thompson formula of good country bread and olives, and simple desserts complete the picture. Wines are served by small pitcher as well as by bottle. Reveille is sounded at 7am with a huge breakfast selection.

Directions: Hyde Park end of Queen's Gate

SW7 190 Queen's Gate
SW7 5EU
Map no: A1
Tel: 0171 581 5666
Chef: Adrian McCormack
Proprietor: Simpsons of Cornhill.
Gen. Manager: Graham Wells
Credit cards: 🔳 🔳 🔳 🔳 OTHER
Times: 7am-12.30am. Closed 25/6 Dec
Menus: *A la carte*, pre-theatre
Seats: 60
Additional: Children welcome, ❂ dishes, vegan/other diets on request

Bistrot Bruno ❀❀❀

Lively Soho restaurant with bold, at times brilliant, French cooking

This is not food for the faint-hearted. Chef/co-owner Bruno Loubet has an open fondness for the earthy, rustic cooking of his native hearth. This refined country food is the main attraction here, with starters such as black pudding and potato pancake with French bean and leaf salad, evidence of his love of the 'cuisine de terroir' he grew up with. A starter of snails with garlic cream, balanced on a rich shallot tarte tatin, was perfectly executed, the crisp pastry a counterpoint to the caramelised shallots and tender snails.
A celeriac and morel ravioli was served in a sparkling but intensely flavoured game bouillon, yet another example of the fusion of fine technical skills and robust approach that typifies the kitchen. A signature main dish of braised oxtail stuffed with kidney mince on parsley-flavoured mash showed the love of offal one would expect from such a traditionalist. There is a nod to fashion on the *carte* offered at both lunch and dinner, and a red mullet dish served with an intense saffron risotto showed an awareness of current trends. Desserts include the novel roast pineapple with star anise on rice pudding, and the classic hot chocolate tartlette. Brioche and butter pudding is a witty mixed marriage. Details are all well up to the mark; a ramequin of olives sits on the table, and crusty, brown pain de campagne arrives with good, unsalted butter. Petits fours are fabulous fruit sorbets dipped in chocolate, and espresso coffee is good and strong.
The recently opened Café Bruno next door shares the philosophy, offering equally hearty dishes, but in a simpler style, and at a lower price. One can expect to enjoy pork liver pâté with home-made pickles or, perhaps, a roast poussin with gratin dauphinoise and a herb jus. The wine list in the café is fairly short but features a carefully selected range of fine suppliers.

Directions: Tottenham Court Road Tube station

W1 63 Frith Street W1V 5TA
Map no: D4
Tel: 0171 734 4545
Chef: Bruno Loubet
Proprietor: Pierre & Kathleen Condou
Cost: *Alc* £30. H/wine £8.75 ❢ Service exc
Credit cards: 🔳 🔳 🔳 🔳 OTHER
Times: 12.30pm-last L 2.30pm, last D 11.30pm. Closed Sat L, Sun & Xmas
Menus: *A la carte*, pre-theatre
Seats: 40. No cigars or pipes
Additional: ❂ dishes

Blue Print Café ❀❀

Business customers, locals and tourists alike love the buzz and the food here – a typical Conran venture

One of a growing number of Sir Terence Conran's successes, the Blue Print Café is in the stylishly refurbished Butlers Wharf, within the building housing the Design Museum. There are glorious views of the River Thames and Tower Bridge, and in fine weather it is possible to eat al fresco on the balcony; duels are fought over these tables, booking is essential. A talented team regard freshness, quality and the importance of balancing flavours as a triumvirate of equals, which the menu projects through its reasonably wide selection. Starters like buffalo mozzarella with roast tomatoes and pesto, or sherry herrings with potato and pancetta salad provide an insight to the style. From the list of main courses, there could be steamed halibut with stir-fried noodles and Oriental dressing, rib-eye steak with Jerusalem artichoke mash, or even simple deep-fried plaice with chips and tartare sauce. Service is well paced, efficient and polite – staff have a very pleasant attitude to customers. And 'le patron mange ici' at least once a week.

Directions: SE of Tower Bridge, on mezzanine of the Design Museum

SE1 The Design Museum Shad Thames SE1 2YD
Map no: G3
Tel: 0171 378 7031
Chefs: Lucy Crab and Jeremy Lee
Proprietor: Sir Terence Conran and Joel Kissin.
Manager: Kieran de Lange
Cost: *Alc* £28.30. H/wine £10.50 ❢ Service inc
Credit cards: ▨ ▧ ▨ ▨
Times: Noon-last L 3pm, 6pm-last D 11pm. Closed Sun D & 4 days at Xmas
Menus: *A la carte*
Seats: 86 + 40 outside. No pipes allowed

Bombay Brasserie ❀❀

A colonial-style Indian restaurant that's a cut above the average

The wide range of dishes on offer from around the Indian Sub-continent cannot be disputed: Goan fish curries, Moghlai specialities, and Parsi dishes such as 'papri ma gosht', a mild casserole of lamb with flat beans, herbs and garlic. There is a hint of the British Raj with mulligatawny soup, and familiar curry house staples such as chicken tikka and vegetable samosas. Of the more interesting dishes, 'patrani macchi', a Parsi speciality, features pomfret (fish) left on the bone, wrapped in banana leaves, and served with a striking, aromatic mint and coconut paste, or crab 'bhujanee', a simple but effective combination of flaked crab meat, spices, coconut, mustard and tamarind. Indian beers and lassis, or fruit juices, are often the most sensible thing to drink. Service is agreeable but, in a restaurant of this size, it can be patchy. The same might be said for the food, but generally it is a cut above the average Indian restaurant in the capital.

Directions: Opposite Gloucester Road Tube adjacent to Bailey's Hotel

Courtfield Close
Courtfield Road SW7
Map no: A1
Tel: 0171 370 4040
Chef: Udit Sarkhel
Proprietor: Taj International.
General Manager: Adi Modi
Cost: *Alc* £25, buffet lunch £14.95. H/wine £10.50
Service exc
Credit cards: ▨ ▧ ▨ ▨
Times: noon-last L 3pm, 7pm-last D midnight
Menus: *A la carte* D, fixed price buffet L, bar menu
Seats: 180. No-smoking area. Air conditioned
Additional: Children welcome for lunch; ❤ dishes, vegan/other diets on request

Bon, Japanese Cuisine at the Mirabelle ❀❀❀

Classical Japanese cooking in two Teppanyaki counter rooms

Times change. Once the Mirabelle was at the hub of London café society, now the original dining rooms are reserved for private corporate and party use. The name lives on, however. The cuisine has moved from classic French to classic Japanese. Bon means supreme in Chinese character writing, but the word originates from

W1 56 Curzon Street W1Y 8DL
Map no: C3
Tel: 0171 499 4636
Manager: Graziano Zoina
Cost: H/wine £16 Service inc
Credit cards: ▨ ▧ ▨ ▨ OTHER
Times: Noon-last L 2pm, 6pm-last D 10.30pm. Closed Sun, Sat L & 2 wks Aug, Xmas & Bhs
Menus: *A la carte*, fixed-price, pre-theatre

ancient Sanskrit. Of the two Teppanyaki rooms, one is traditional – diners are required to remove their shoes and sit on the floor – the other is plainer in style, with normal counter seating, and is mostly used by Europeans. Chef Kunio Sekine San sets a high standard with excellent dashi and some well-developed, fermented sake soy sauces, fresh ingredients and top quality seafood from exclusive London suppliers. The Bon Kaiseki Menu has come in for much praise, with eleven easy-to-understand courses at an excellent value for money price of £38 per person. A range of other interesting Teppanyaki menus are also featured. Our inspection meal started with an enjoyable crunchy seaweed appetiser, followed by top-class sashimi of fresh, white eel and raw tuna, served with shredded white radish, green mustard, soy sauce and green nettle leaf. Teppanyaki grilled vegetables included asparagus, onion, courgettes, mushrooms and red and green peppers, served with a soy sauce blended with radish, sake vinegar, chives, garlic and chilli pepper. Seafood teppanyaki comprised langoustines, scallops, salmon and sea bass served with slices of lemon and a mixed lettuce leaf salad dressed with soy vinegar and oil. Miso soup was crystal clear dashi stock with fermented soybean paste, blended with tofu and mushrooms.

Seats: 70. Air-conditioning
Additional: Children welcome, children's portions; vegan dishes

Directions: At Berkeley Square end of Curzon Street. NCP car parks close by. Nearest Tube – Green Park

Boyd's Restaurant ❀❀

Uncomplicated modern British cooking and an adventurous wine list served in a relaxed environment by helpful staff

Simple and honest cooking is offered at this bright split-level restaurant at the northern end of Kensington Church Street. Chef/ patron Boyd Gilmour presents a short fixed-price lunch menu, which changes daily, and a *carte* of modern British dishes which includes all the current fashionable influences. Starters include seared scallops with chargrilled provençale vegetables; salads, such as avocado pear with crab mayonnaise and pink grapefruit; and a soup – a well flavoured chilled leek and potato at the time of one inspector's visit. Main courses, such as a skilfully prepared roast breast of pigeon on a potato rösti with sweet and sour red cabbage and black truffle sauce, or roast lambs' sweetbreads in a puff pastry case with spring vegetables, show the range. To finish, there are English and Irish cheeses and a selection of desserts; perhaps French apple tart with vanilla ice-cream, or prune and Armagnac terrine with Armagnac caramel. The wine list includes some fine French bottles – 1976 Chateau d'Yquem at £300 and a 1981 Chateau Latour at £86.50 – though there are, of course, quite a number of rather less expensive wines.

35 Kensington Church Street W8
Map no: P34
Tel: 0171 727 5452
Chef: Boyd Gilmour
Proprietor: Boyd Gilmour
Cost: *Alc* £35, fixed-price L £14. H/wine £10 ! Service exc
Credit cards: 🂠 🂡 🂢 🂣
Times: 12.30pm-last L 2.30pm, 7pm-last D 11pm. Closed Sun, Bhs
Menus: *A la carte* L & D, fixed-price lunch
Seats: 40. Air conditioned
Additional: children permitted (no infants), ❶ dishes, other diets on request

Directions: Nearest Tube Notting Hill Gate, 2 blocks South

The Brackenbury ❀❀

Good modern food at neighbourhood restaurant that should be the norm not the exception

The Brackenbury is situated at the heart of Shepherd's Bush, and is the sort of easy-going, quality local restaurant every neighbourhood should have. The exceptionally good value-for-money *carte* attracts

W6 129 Brackenbury Road W6
Map no: GtL C3
Tel: 0181 748 0107
Chef: Adam Robinson and Patricia Hilferty
Proprietor: Adam & Kate Robinson.
Manager: Jane Blum

customers as much as the honest, robust cooking. Sometimes, however, the restaurant can be a victim of its own popularity, and the demands placed upon kitchen and staff can result in lack of attention to detail and clumsy presentation. Nonetheless, the modern British *carte* is varied and imaginative, and, admirably, changes daily at both lunch and dinner. Dishes available on a July day included lobster soup with coriander, broccoli and purple chicory with warm anchovy dressing, roast hake with chickpeas, tomato and chorizo, and chump of lamb with courgette and tomato gratin. Offal makes a regular appearance. Lambs' tongues may be cooked with broad beans and capers, sweetbreads with peas, lettuce and sorrel, and brains served on a crostini with salsa verde. The wine list offers the majority of wines by the glass, and non-wine drinkers will enjoy the James White Special Edition Cider.

Directions: Nearest Tubes – Hammersmith Broadway, Goldhawk Road. Off Goldhawk Road

Cost: Alc £16.75. H/wine £8.50
! Service exc
Credit cards: ◪ ▦ ▨ ▨ OTHER
Times: 12.30pm-last L 2.45pm, 7pm-last D 10.45pm. Closed Sat & Mon L, Sun D & Bhs, 10 days at Xmas
Menus: A la carte
Seats: 60
Additional: Children's portions; ❻ dishes, other diets on request

Britannia Inter-Continental ❀

Situated in the heart of Mayfair, this smart hotel offers contemporary cooking in Adam's Restaurant. A meal here might feature quenelles of pike with lobster sauce, followed by pot roasted duck with pancetta and lentils, or beef with Madeira sauce, mushrooms and artichokes

W1 Grosvenor Square W1A 3AN
Map no: C3
Tel: 0171 629 9400
Chef: Neil Gray
Proprietor: Inter-Continental Hotels.
Manager: Mohamed Sayed
Cost: Alc £28, fixed-price L £17.50/D £24. H/wine £12.95
! Service exc
Credit cards: ◪ ▦ ▨ ▨ OTHER
Times: 12.30pm-last L 2.30pm, 6.30pm-last D 10pm. Closed Sat/Sun & August

Menus: A la carte, fixed-price L & D, pre-theatre, bar menu
Seats: 60. Air-conditioning **Additional:** Children welcome, children's portions & menu; ❻ dishes, vegan/other diets on request
Directions: 5 mins walk from Oxford Street, access from Adams Row or Grosvenor Square

Brown's ❀❀

Traditional and modern influences combine in the cooking at this famous Mayfair hotel

Traditional dishes are given a modern interpretation in the comfortable, well-appointed restaurant of Brown's. Situated in the heart of Mayfair, the famous hotel, with its country house atmosphere, was opened in 1837 and is now one of Forte's 'exclusive hotels of the world'. Diners can choose from a short but

W1 Dover Street W1A 4SW
Map no: C3
Tel: 0171 493 6020
Chef: John King
Proprietor: Forte.
Manager: R Davis
Cost: A la carte £40, fixed-price L 24.50 (3 courses)/D £29 (3 courses). ! Service exc
Credit cards: ◪ ▦ ▨ ▨ OTHER

interesting *carte* or from a fixed-price menu, where typical dishes might be traditional favourites such as neck of mutton with green peas, or calves' liver with bubble and squeak. An inspection meal produced rilletes of rabbit which lacked the promised roasted langoustines, but had good flavour, and a chump of lamb, served with pearl barley and carrots, turnips and swedes. The dessert trolley offered four or five choices; the tiramisu chosen was rather average. However, coffee was excellent, served with decent petits fours. Service is old-fashioned and wonderfully correct. Canapés are served with drinks in the atmospheric panelled bar.

Directions: Main entrance in Albermarle Street, off Piccadilly. Nearest Tubes – Piccadilly Circus, Green Park

Times: 7am-10.30am, 12.30pm-last L 2.15pm, 6pm-last D 10pm. Closed Sat L
Menus: *A la carte*, fixed-price L & D, pre-theatre, bar menu, afternoon tea
Seats: 60. No pipes allowed, air-conditioning
Additional: ✪ dishes, other diets on request

Buchan's ✿✿

Wide choice of popular, keenly priced dishes with more than a hint of Scottish influence

A popular restaurant noted for an informal atmosphere and friendly, helpful service, Buchan's benefits from the close involvement of owners Jeremy and Denise Bolam. Chef Alain Jeannon produces some interesting dishes, some with a strong Scottish influence, such as Cullen skink, haggis and whisky soufflé, Scottish sirloin steak flambéed in whisky, Scottish cheese and Gaelic coffee. The choice is varied. A café/bar menu offers soups, sandwiches, salads and snacks plus the likes of Buchan's beef burger, deep fried Brie with chilli jelly and green salad, and tagliatelle squid provençale. From the reasonably priced *carte* a fresh tasting smoked salmon with lime was chosen, followed by roast lambs' kidneys in filo pastry with basil sauce. The kidneys were good, balancing the disappointment of rather heavy pastry. Dessert was a high point, a dark and white chocolate terrine with firm texture and good flavour, served with a fruit coulis. The wine list offers some 39 wines, mostly French, with a few New World and one Scottish wine.

Directions: 200 yards S of Battersea Bridge

SW11 62-64 Battersea Bridge Road SW11 3AG
Map no: GtL C2
Tel: 0171 228 0888
Chef: Alain Jeannon
Proprietor: Jeremy Bolam
Cost: *Alc* £17.50, fixed-price L £7.50/D £5.95. H/wine £8.95 ⚑ Service exc
Credit cards: 🟦 💳 💳 💳 OTHER
Times: Noon-last L 3pm, 6pm-last D 10.45pm. Closed Boxing Day
Menus: *A la carte*, fixed-price L & D, bar menu
Seats: 70. Smoking permitted, air-conditioning
Additional: Children welcome, children's portions on request; ✪ dishes, vegan/other diets on request

Bu San ✿

One of the few Korean restaurants in London, Bu-San is a well-established neighbourhood haunt. The menu seems endless, but staff will happily offer advice to the uninitiated; it is best to avoid the set meals which offer the blandest examples of the national cuisine – the reliance on sesame and garlic means that many dishes taste similar

N7 43 Holloway Road N7
Map no: D4
Tel: 0171 607 8264
Chef: Young Hyung Lee
Proprietor: Kim Lee

Butlers Wharf Chop House ✿✿

A haven for the lovers of traditional British cooking at the fashionable riverside Butlers Wharf Building

Part of Sir Terence Conran's burgeoning restaurant empire, this old-fashioned British chop house offers solid, comfortable-sounding food for traditionalists fed up with olive oil and roasted vegetables. The only thing roasted here is meat, and some may take pleasure in a menu that ignores vegetarian, vegan or any other alternative diet.

SE1 36e Shad Thames SE1 2YE
Map no: D3
Tel: 0171 403 3403
Chef: Rod Eggleston
Proprietors: Sir Terence Conran and Joel Kissin.
Managers: Finlay Macleod and Delfo Melli

The restaurant offers a fixed-price three-course lunch – a busy time – and a comprehensive *carte* ; the bar has its own separate menu of sandwiches, pies, fish and grills. Starters from the *carte* might include Lincolnshire chine with mustard leeks, and Chop-House terrine with pickles. A separate fish section offers plaice and chips with tartare sauce and Brixham fish stew, while under 'main courses' the nostalgic litany continues with steak and kidney pudding (available with oysters), chicken and ham pie, and roast veal kidney with bubble and squeak, black pudding and mustard sauce. Grills and chops include lamb, veal, beef and venison, plus sirloin steak. To finish there is cherry trifle, fruit crumble and similar delights, or a plate of British cheeses.

Cost: *Alc* £40.45, fixed-price L £22.75. H/wine £11.35 ❢
Service inc
Credit cards: 💳 💳 💳 💳
Times: Noon-last L 3pm, 6pm-last D 11pm. Closed Sat L, Sun D & New Year's Day
Menus: *A la carte*, fixed-price L, bar menu
Seats: 115 + 45 outside

Directions: On riverfront, on SE side of Tower Bridge

Café des Arts 🏵

A Hampstead restaurant with a decidedly relaxed and informal atmosphere. Expect a short but well-balanced menu supplemented by specials of the day, plus a selection of inexpensive wines. Dishes might include smoked haddock rillettes, seared lambs' liver, and Cafe des Arts fish stew

NW37 82 Hampstead High Street NW3
Map no: GtL C4
Tel: 0171 435 3608
Chef: *Sally James*
Proprietor: *Brian Stein*
Seats: *65*

Directions: Middle of Hampstead High Street, next door to the Post Office. Nearest Tube – Hampstead

Café Fish 🏵

Busy, bustling fish restaurant which is consistent in maintaining good standards. The menu offers thoughtfully prepared dishes and a selection of daily specials. Good examples are 'soupe de poisson', which has plenty of flavour, and a main course of excellent fillet of sea bass with ragout of scallops

Menus: *A la carte*, bar menu **Seats:** 94. No-smoking area
Additional: Children welcome; ♥ dishes
Directions: Nearest Tube Piccadilly Circus. Panton Street is off the Haymarket

SW1 39 Panton Street Haymarket SW1
Map no: D3
Tel: 0171 930 3999
Chef: Andrew Magson
Proprietor: Groupe Chez Gerard. Manager: Marie Jeanne Collins
Cost: *Alc* £25. H/wine £8.50 ❢
Service exc
Credit cards: 💳 💳 💳 💳 OTHER
Times: Last L 3pm, last D 11.30pm. Closed Sat L, Sun & 25-26 Dec

Café Nico

As we went to press distinctive green awnings appeared on Park Lane bearing, in gold, the legend Café Nico. Grosvenor House's old Pavilion restaurant has been refurbished with an understated good taste that is Nico Ladenis's trademark. Gone are the blinds from the huge windows, allowing not only light to pour into the lovely, spacious room but also giving uninterrupted views of Park Lane. Andrew Barber, from Simply Nico, heads the kitchen and the menu is in classic French brasserie style. The room has a raised internal dais where full meals are served at formal times. Otherwise, a simpler, all day menu, which includes light meals and salads, is available in the café/bar area.

W1 Grosvenor House Hotel Park Lane W1A 3AA
Map no: B3
Tel: 0171 499 6363
Chef: Andrew Barber

Directions: Ground floor of Grosvenor House Hotel

Café Royal Grill Room ❀❀❀

Modern variations on a classic theme given a suitable sense of occasion by baroque decor

W1 68 Regent Street W1R 5PJ
Map no: C3
Tel: 0171 437 9090
Chef: Herbert Berger
Proprietor: Forte.
Manager: David Arcusi
Cost: *Alc* £50, fixed-price L
£24/D £39. H/wine £14.95
Service exc
Credit cards: ▩ ▩ ▩ ▩
Times: Noon-last L 2.30pm,
6pm-last D 10.45pm. Closed Sat
L, Sun & Bhs
Menus: *A la carte*, fixed-price L
& D, pre-theatre
Seats: 45. No pipes allowed, air-conditioning
Additional: Children 12+
welcome, ❷ /vegan dishes

Situated within this great banqueting institution, the Grill Room has changed little since opening in 1865. The Rococo style may be heavy but no one can deny the splendour of the gilded, mirrored walls, frescoed ceiling and burgundy banquettes. Staff are old school and, for the most part, utterly professional without being ingratiating. Under the enthusiastic leadership of executive chef Herbert Berger, a menu has been devised which mixes the classic with the contemporary. Chateaubriand and crèpes Suzette are theatrically prepared at the the table, but more modern dishes may be along the lines of open ravioli of langoustines with tarragon butter sauce, or roasted monkfish with rosemary jus.

A special promotional meal sampled by one of our inspectors offered a variation on a mille-feuille by using crispy Savoy cabbage layered between slices of slightly dry Scottish salmon,with a sharp beurre blanc sauce. The main course of Welsh lamb with leeks and foie gras in a truffle sauce balanced its components well, though the young lamb understandably lacked depth of flavour and the sauce could have been hotter. Luxurious ingredients, however, do not come cheap, and best value is the set price dinner. It was here that lambs' kidneys were enjoyed, succulent and pink, stuffed with shallot, wrapped in crépinette and served with wild mushrooms. Combinations were also well judged in a melt-in-the-mouth caramel mousseline, the sweetness cut by a mango and lime compote. A well-prepared Cox's apple pithivier with blackberry coulis and vanilla ice-cream has also impressed. The attentive sommelier offers willing guidance through the comprehensive wine list.

Directions: End of Regent Street, near Piccadilly Circus

'Brandade' is a speciality of Languedoc and Provence. In its basic form it is a purée of salt cod, olive oil and milk, but in the Toulon and Marseilles areas crushed garlic was added and this has become the standard recipe. Nowadays potato purée is also included. The word is derived from the Provençal verb 'brandar' meaning to stir.

Café St Pierre ✿

Popular establishment which features a brasserie on the ground floor and a more formal restaurant on the first. A recent inspection meal began with a flan of salmon mousse topped with scallops and parsley sauce, followed by steak with Madeira and truffle sauce. Desserts include home-made sorbets and ice-cream

EC1 29 Clerkenwell Green
EC1R 0DU
Map no: GtL D3
Tel: 0171 253 0994

Canal Brasserie ✿✿

Good value one-plate meals from an imaginative and eclectic menu

A former chocolate factory, beside the Regent Canal, converted into a complex of media offices as well as the Canal Brasserie. Sometimes the brasserie is franchised out to other operators in the evening, so it is best to check beforehand. When the chef is in residence, the kitchen is noted for its one-plate meals, all freshly cooked, full of flavour and representing good value for money. The daily *carte* offers a modern eclectic approach, with starters such as sweet pepper, potato and ginger soup, gumbo mussels with Cajun spices, chillies and tomatoes, and kedgeree with smoked cod, saffron rice and mustard sauce. Main courses might be Atlantic shark pan-fried in butter with tomato cous cous and roast red onions, shredded Chinese 'sticky duck' on sesame salad with cucumber and noodles, and 'yellow Thai chicken' cooked in fresh spices and coconut milk. Puddings range from Cointreau and blood orange parfait to chocolate brownies with chocolate sauce.

Directions: Turn right at top of Ladroke Grove, just before crossing canal

W10 222 Kensal Road
W10 5BN
Map no: GtL C3
Tel: 0181 960 2732
Chef: John Goodall
Proprietor: Antony Harris
Cost: *Alc* £16, fixed-price £7.50.
H/wine £9.25 ❢ Service inc
Credit cards: 🂠 💳 💳 OTHER
Times: 9am-7pm, last L 3pm.
Closed Sat/Sun, Bhs & Xmas
Menus: *A la carte*, fixed-price L
Seats: 60
Additional: Children welcome,
❶ dishes, vegan/other diets on request

Cannizaro House ✿✿

Gracious country house surroundings for sound modern cooking

This restored and sympathetically extended handsome Georgian mansion, on the western edge of Wimbledon Common, has a graceful atmosphere. Public rooms feature fine paintings, antique furniture, painted ceilings, original fireplaces and huge flower arrangements. The fine dining room boasts crystal chandeliers, gilt mirrors and well spaced tables and is a suitably impressive setting for Stephen Wilson's modern cooking. The seasonally changing *carte* offers a wide range of dishes which include a number of enterprising vegetarian dishes, and some unusual flavour combinations such as cod with foie gras and wild mushrooms. The highlight of one meal was an excellent sea bass served with deep-fried squid, a fresh tomato and basil compote and a sweet pepper butter sauce. Desserts are largely fruit based and for the indecisive, a selection of five of the ten desserts make up the Cannizaro 'Grand Dessert'. A large staff provide formal but friendly and attentive service. There is a suitably extensive wine list, strongest in the French department.

Directions: From A3 (London Road) Tibbets Corner, take A219 (Parkside), right into Cannizaro Road, the right into West Side

SW19 West Side
Wimbledon Common
SW19 4UE
Map no: GtL C2
Tel: 0181 879 1464
Chef: Stephen Wilson
Proprietor: Thistle.
General Manager: Ray Slade
Cost: *Alc* £30, fixed-price L
£21.55/D £25.75. H/wine
£16.50 Service exc
Credit cards: 🂠 💳 💳 💳
Times: Noon-last L 2.30pm,
3pm-last tea 5pm, 7pm-last D
10.30pm
Menus: *A la carte*, fixed-price L
& D, pre-theatre, afternoon tea
Seats: 45. No-smoking area
Additional: Over eight children's portions on request; ❶ dishes, vegan/other diets on request

The Canteen 🏵🏵🏵

Standards remain high at this perennially fashionable and consistently praiseworthy establishment

Marco Pierre White can justifiably lay claim to running the country's premier finishing school for top chefs. Graduates include Gordon Ramsay at Aubergine, Phillip Howard at The Square, Richard Neat at Pied à Terre, and Tim Powell, who is now in command of The Canteen's kitchen. Universally acclaimed from the moment it opened, the buzz about this stylish, split-level restaurant shows no sign of abating and it's easy to see why. The decor is bright and fun and so, too, are the staff. The food is consistently good and it doesn't cost a fortune. Small wonder, then, that the place is so popular that they run two sittings for dinner and while service at the earlier one tends to be brisk, it is not brusque. The menu offers around a dozen imaginative choices at each course, all at the same price and described in a clipped style. Hence: 'grilled tuna, piperade and salad frisée, langoustine oil and balsamic.' On the plate, this translates as a juicy tuna steak accompanied by a sort of super-charged scrambled egg with tomatoes and peppers, accompanied by some crisp and bitter salad leaves with an interesting dressing. It's good! Indeed, most things here are good, our inspector's one cavil being calves' liver that sadly showed little pinkness, but was redeemed by paper fine Alsace ham, crisp cos lettuce and a piquant sauce. The unmissable dessert is a dark chocolate marquise, which our inspector thought 'pure heaven', its rich flavour set off by a well-judged caramel sauce with just the right amount of sweetness. The wine list is well-paced, includes an interesting selection from the New World, and majors in the grand cru of Bordeaux which may well be a concession to the preferences of co-proprietor, Michael Caine.

Directions: Off Kings Road, Chelsea

SW10 Harbour Yard
Chelsea Harbour SW10
Map no: GtL C2
Tel: 0171 351 7330
Chef: Tim Powell
Proprietors: Michael Caine and Claudio Pulze
Cost: *Alc* £23.85, fixed-price D £23.85. H/wine £12 ❢ Service exc
Credit cards: 🆑 🆑
Times: Last L 3pm, last D midnight
Menus: *A la carte*, fixed-price D
Seats: 150. Air-conditioning
Additional: Children welcome, children's portions on request; ❷ dishes, vegan/other diets on request

Cantina del Ponte 🏵

Both deliberately simple furnishing and cooking prove popular at this Mediterranean-style restaurant. The frequently-changing menu might feature such dishes as Parmesan and semolina gnocchi on tomato sauce, followed by squid with red onions, coriander and orange confit

Menus: *A la carte*
Seats: 90 + 40 outside
Additional: ❷ dishes
Directions: SE side of Tower Bridge, by riverfront

SE1 The Butlers Wharf Building
36c Shad Thames SE1 2YE
Map no: GtL G3
Tel: 0171 403 5403
Chef: Mark O'Brien
Proprietors: Sir Terrence Conran, Joel Kissin and David Burke
Cost: *Alc* £30. ❢ Service exc
Credit cards: 🆑 🆑 🆑 🆑
Times: Noon-last L 3pm, 6pm-last D 11pm. Closed Sun D & Good Friday, 4 days at Xmas

Ravigote sauce can be served either hot or cold but it is always highly seasoned. Cold ravigote is a vinaigrette mixed with capers, chopped herbs and finely chopped onion. A hot ravigote sauce is made by adding veal velouté sauce (a basic, flour-based white sauce) to equal quantities of white wine and wine vinegar reduced with chopped shallots, and finished with chopped herbs. Savoury butter and mayonnaise à la ravigote have chopped herbs and shallots and occasionally mustard added.

Capital Hotel ❀❀❀❀

Polished and precise cooking with vibrant flavours and a renewed sense of confidence

SW3 Basil Street
Knightsbridge SW3
Map no: B2
Tel: 0171 589 5171
Chef: Philip Britten
Proprietor: David Levin
Cost: Alc £35, fixed-price
L £25/D £40 (6 courses). H/wine
£12.50 ♥ Service inc
Credit cards: 🔲 💳 💳 💳 OTHER
Times: 12.30pm-last L 2.30pm
/last D 11.15pm
Menus: A la carte, fixed-price L
& D, bar menu
Seats: 35. Air conditioned
Additional: children over 8
welcome ; ♥ dishes,
vegan/other diets by
arrangement

One of the great strengths of The Capital Hotel is the fact it is small and exclusive, as well as being a mere credit card's throw from both Harrods and Harvey Nichols. Since last year, the hotel has had a major facelift, and the restaurant given a complete new look. David Linley designed the wonderful etched glass and burr walnut inlaid shutters, and there is now a sense of greater light and space. Philip Britten is back on top form. The effort that goes into the cooking really shows, and the result is grand, luxurious and rarely off-key. The set lunch is still the best value, since the cost at dinner doubles with items priced individually. There is a £30 minimum evening charge, but on the whole the price is reasonable, given the quality and location. The menu is written in lucid and concise English, despite the pronounced French influence in the food. Great canapés lift the mood instantly: onion tart, delicate smoked fish mousse, fish goujon or stunning seared tuna and yellow pepper kebab with orange zest. There is a stroke of genius in a starter/main course of nage of lobster with ginger, peas and caviar, the meat perfectly cooked, a julienne of vegetables and whole sugarsnaps providing textural contrast, and all the flavours singing sweetly together. Boudin of foie gras, too, marinated in Sauternes with toasted brioche and artichoke, was skilfully made, the artichoke adding a subtle smoky dimension. A main course of grilled veal sweetbreads came correctly cooked, set on a crisp potato galette and served with a buttery tomato sauce, infused with non-evident rosemary. A turbot gratin was less memorable, perhaps best described as a modern day sole véronique; this version included foamy Muscadet sabayon and savoury cabbage along with the peeled grapes, but the combination failed to gel. The hallmark, five course fish menu still works well, with exquisitely tempting dishes such as lobster salad with orange and ginger. Assiette of vanilla is a virtuoso display – light, moist vanilla soufflé with Armagnac and vanilla sauce, delicious vanilla parfait topped with a caramel sauce. In contrast, a high-rise pear tart tatin is served with a no-nonsense cinnamon ice-cream. The wine list is a canter through the French classics, but there are also a few inexpensive parvenus such as owner David Levin's own Vins de Levin.

Directions: Between Harrods and Sloane Street, nearest Tube –
Knightsbridge

Cecconi's ❀❀

*Probably the most exclusive Italian restaurant in London,
notwithstanding Harry's Bar*

Attentive, smartly dressed Italian waiters help to create a lively
atmosphere in which to enjoy the cooking of the eponymous owner.
This is Italian food at its best, and high prices do not seem to deter
customers; tables are keenly sought after. Saucing is a strength,
noted not for delicacy or finesse as in French cooking, but for gutsy
flavour. Cannelloni Cecconi comes with a full-flavoured cheese,
cream and tomato sauce, scallopine of veal capricciosa is served
with a rich, pungent sauce of cream, tomatoes, mushrooms and red
peppers. The modern Italian dessert, tiramisu, is very popular,
Cecconi's version being light and moist. The wine list is
predominantly Italian, some of them a little overpriced.

Directions: Visible at end of Burlington Arcade. Nearest Tubes –
Green Park, Piccadilly Circus

W1 5a Burlington Gardens W1
Map no: C3
Tel: 0171 434 1509
Chef: E Cecconi
Proprietor: E Cecconi
Cost: Alc £40. Service charge
15%. Cover charge £2.50
Credit cards: ▨ ▨ ▨ ▨ OTHER
Times: 12.30pm-last L 2.30pm,
7.30pm-last D 11.30pm. Closed
Sat lunch, all day Sun, Bhs
Menus: A la carte
Seats: 120. No-smoking area.
No pipes. Air conditioned
Additional: Children welcome;
❷ dishes; other diets by prior
arrangement

Charco's ❀❀

An established wine bar with an imaginative and offbeat menu

The arrival of chef Jon Bentham at this established Sloaney wine
bar has put Charco's firmly on the culinary map. The upstairs is still
predominantly a watering hole but the basement is for diners only.
It's an unfussy room with bottle green decor, crisp linen and plenty
of fresh flowers. Similarly, the service is amiable and focused, with
no frills. The menu on the other hand is offbeat, imaginative and
eclectic, with Chinese braised duck with bok choy and egg noodles
sitting alongside Mexican fish stew. There are some daring
combinations, too, such as grilled rabbit, snails, chorizo and rocket,
and the more understandable addition of crispy fried sweet onions
to a wonderful oak smoked Cheddar soufflé. A main course of
grilled breast of veal with butterbeans was enlivened by a perky
salsa verde, and a perfectly cooked noisette of lamb was topped
with a peppery mousse and accompanied by a feuilletté of
sweetbreads. The wine list is reasonably priced and offers wine by
the glass, but there is little of interest outside France, though there
is an Indian sparkling wine, Omar Khayam 1987.

Directions: From Kings Rd turn into Anderson Street, first right,
entrance in Coulson Street

SW3 1 Bray Place SW3
Map no: B1
Tel: 0171 584 0765
Chef: Jon Bentham
Proprietor: Sylvie Poster
Cost: Alc £21, fixed-price D
£21.50. H/wine £8 ! Service exc
Credit cards: ▨ ▨ ▨ ▨
Times: Noon-last L 2.30pm, last
D 10.30pm. Closed Sun & 2 wks
Aug, Bhs
Menus: A la carte, fixed-price D
Seats: 60. Air-conditioning
Additional: Children welcome;
❷ dishes

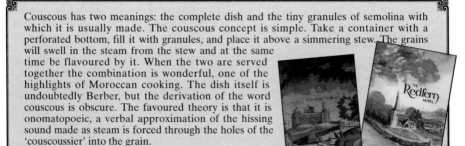

Couscous has two meanings: the complete dish and the tiny granules of semolina with
which it is usually made. The couscous concept is simple. Take a container with a
perforated bottom, fill it with granules, and place it above a simmering stew. The grains
will swell in the steam from the stew and at the same
time be flavoured by it. When the two are served
together the combination is wonderful, one of the
highlights of Moroccan cooking. The dish itself is
undoubtedly Berber, but the derivation of the word
couscous is obscure. The favoured theory is that it is
onomatopoeic, a verbal approximation of the hissing
sound made as steam is forced through the holes of the
'couscoussier' into the grain.

Chelsea Hotel ❀

Sandwiched between Christian Dior and Gucci, this design-led hotel offers a fashion conscious carte to its international clientele. Lobster and tomato ravioli, John Dory with a compote of cherry tomatoes, lightly steamed vegetables, or pan-fried corn-fed chicken with scallops and creamed lentils, are typical offerings

SW1 17-25 Sloane Street
Knightsbridge SW1
Map no: B2
Tel: 0171 235 4377
Chef: Darren Roberts
Manager: CDL Hotels. Food &
Beverage.
Manager: M Regenhardt
Cost: *Alc* £25, fixed-price L
£11.95 (2 course). H/wine £12 ❢
Service inc
Credit cards: 🔳 🔳 🔳 🔳
Times: noon-last L 2pm / D
10pm
Menus: *A la carte,* fixed-price L,
Sun brunch
Seats: 90. Air conditioned
Additional: Children welcome;
children' portions, ❤ dishes,
vegan/other diets on request

Directions: Two minutes from Knightsbridge Tube

Chesterfield Hotel ❀❀

A hotel restaurant in the heart of Mayfair offering imaginative modern English cooking

Modern British cooking with Mediterranean and Californian influences, is on offer at this West London hotel, just off Berkeley Square. Blackened cod with beer hushpuppies and remoulade butter sauce, and sticky toffee pudding is a good example of the eclectic style. The seasonal *carte* provides a comprehensive selection, with starters of carpaccio of beef with 'tête de moine', and seared five-pepper tuna with smoked tomato marmalade and buttered spinach leaves. These might be followed by calves' liver 'saltimbocca' with basil gravy, polenta and honey-roast onions, and the vegetarian main course, filo parcel of wild mushroom dijonaise served with artichoke risotto. The Conservatory 'Let's Do Lunch' *carte* ranges from Caesar salad to chargrilled Scotch sirloin steak with tobacco onions, wild mushrooms and frites. The wine list offers 60 wines from around the world, including half bottles and wines by the glass.

W1 35 Charles Street W1X 8LX
Map no: C3
Tel: 0171 491 2622
Chef: David Needed
Proprietor: Peter Wood
Cost: *Alc* £25, fixed-price L
£10/D £20.50. H/wine £12.95 ❢
Service exc
Credit cards: 🔳 🔳 🔳 🔳 OTHER
Times: Noon-2pm last L, last D
10pm. Closed Sat L
Menus: *A la carte,* fixed-price L
& D, bar menu
Seats: 60. No-smoking area, air-
conditioning
Additional: Children welcome,
children's portions; ❤ dishes,
vegan/other diets on request

Directions: Nearest Tube Green Park. Bottom of Berkley Square, on corner of Charles Street & Queen Street

Chez Bruce ❀❀❀

Vivid French food in new solo chef/patron venture

Chez Bruce is located on the very same site that launched Marco Pierre White to greater glory. No doubt, Bruce Poole is hoping a bit of the magic will rub off and, to date, this does not seem such a far-

SW17 2 Bellevue Road
Wandsworth Common
SW17 7EG
Map no: GtL C2
Tel: 0181 672 0114
Chef: Bruce Poole
Proprietor: Bruce Poole.

fetched possibility. Classically trained, with a pedigree acquired at
Bibendum, The Square and Chez Max, he cooks in a lucid,
gimmick-free, traditional French style. The food shouts confidence,
and bursts with flavour and unerring accuracy of execution.
Overlooking an expanse of green and a busy main road, the place
is justifiably packed nightly, and only a little quieter during the day.
A short, fixed-price menu is decided upon each morning, with an
abbreviated but keenly-priced version on offer at lunchtime.
The dinner menu might have a choice of eight dishes or so at each
course, and there is the additional, indulgent bonus of a succinctly
chosen wine list offering each bottle by the glass. A rustic white
loaf, baked with olive oil and rock salt, showed the form straight
away. 'Imam Bayildi' (or 'the priest who fainted') was a Turkish
departure from the Gallic norm, but shone with the captivating
flavours of aubergine, tomato, onion and olive oil laced with a good
dose of pungent seasoning. A main course of 'navarin d'agneau
printanier' (spring lamb stew) was a perfectly judged dish of braised
Welsh lamb fillet with a light wine and rosemary sauce.
It was served in a pot with individually cooked and seasoned
vegetables – baby broad beans and carrots, young asparagus,
shallots and new potatoes – finished off in the cooking liquid.
A tarte tatin showed technical precision and exact flavours
producing a spot on combination of dark and light caramel, apple
and buttery pastry, with the sweetness balanced by a generous
dollop of crème fraîche.

Directions: 2 mins walk from Wandsworth Common (BR), 5 mins
from Balham Tube

Manager: Maurice Bernard
Cost: Fixed-price L £15/D £22.
H/wine £8.50 ●
Credit cards: ▨ ▨ ▨ ▨ OTHER
Times: Last L 2pm, last D
10.30pm. Closed Sun D,
Sat/Mon am
Menus: Fixed-price L & D
Seats: 75. No-smoking area, air-
conditioning
Additional: ✿/vegan/other diets
on request in advance

Chez Max ❀❀

*Classic French cookery of dependable quality served with great good
humour in an atmospheric Earls Court basement*

An atmospheric – some might say claustrophobic – basement in a
residential backwater that pretends to be a bistro in an obscure
arrondisment of Paris and pulls off the illusion with panache.
The secret is the rampant Francophilia of the Renzland twins, who
won recognition at Le Petit Max in Hampton Wick before making
their triumphant London debut in 1994. These days, Max runs this
place and Marc shuttles between the two, concocting sauces here
in the afternoons and leaving the service of dinner in the capable
hands of Christopher Eve. The result is hearty portions of food
that is unequivocally French, à la façon Max, with the odd pasta or
risotto and occasional English dish. Expect well made terrines,
braised meats, daubs and stews with great depth of flavour and
confidently handled meat dishes from a series of set-price menus,
with the odd supplement for foie gras and sea bass. The wine list
has been expanded to include some German dessert wines, but
remains essentially French. Now open for every meal save Saturday
lunch, Max also offers a bargain plat du jour at weekday lunch
times.

Directions: Turn off the Fulham Road into Ifield Road, restaurant is
500yds on the left

SW10 168 Ifield Road SW10
Map no: C2
Tel: 0171 835 0874
*Proprietors: Marc & Max
Renzland and Graham Thomson
Cost: Fixed-price dinner £23.50.
H/wine £11.50. Corkage £3.50
min. Service exc*
Credit cards: *None taken*
Times: *12.30-last L 2.30pm,
7pm-last D 11pm. Lunch not
served Sat and Mon. Closed Sun,
Easter, Xmas, Bhs*
Menu: *Fixed-price dinner*
Additional: *Children over 12
permitted.* ✿ *dishes on request*

Chez Max Restaurant ❀❀

☺ *Sound French cooking in a leafy suburban setting*

Surbiton is a London suburb trying hard to retain its Surrey leafiness, is well worth exploring and the restaurant Chez Max is worth seeking out. It is unrelated to Chez Max in Chelsea or le Petit Max in Hampton Wick but is a sister establishment to C'est La Vie in Ewell in Surrey which serves French-style cooking. Clive Lane has bought the place from the Makarian family who ran the place with proprietal charm for 13 years. A typical meal could be salad of goats' cheese or fricasée of snails, followed perhaps by lamb in a creamy garlic sauce or beef in red wine sauce. Fish is well represented on the *carte*, and desserts include crème brûlée, strawberry gâteaux and chocolate charlotte.

Directions: From Surbiton Station walk down St James Road, turn right at end, Chez Max in to the left

85 Maple Road, Surbiton, Surrey
Map no: GtL B1
Tel: 0181 394 2933
Chef: Frederic Dervin
Proprietor: Clive Lane
Cost: Alc £20, fixed-price L £14.75/D £14.75. H/wine £8.50 Service inc
Credit cards: 🔲 🔲 🔲 🔲 OTHER
Times: Noon-last L 2.30pm, 7pm-last D 10pm. Closed Sun D
Menus: A la carte, fixed-price L & D
Seats: 42. No-smoking area, air-conditioning
Additional: Not suitable for young children; ❂ dishes, vegan/other diets on request

Chez Moi ❀❀

The long established partnership of proprietors Richard Walton and Colin Smith has turned this well-loved restaurant into an institution

With a devoted following from globe-trotting corporate Americans to neighbourhood socialites, this restaurant continues to improve and achieve greater levels of comfort. The food is French, offered from the *carte* or set-price lunch menu, written in French, with English sub-titles, but there are some alternative influences – borsch, the classic Polish beetroot soup, garnished with sour cream and dill and served with spicy turnovers, and seared scallops served with a Japanese inspired futo-maki roll (nori, wasabi, sticky rice, smoked salmon, avocado, spring onion and cucumber), for example. Main courses include fillet of sole sautéed in butter, lemon juice and parsley, and served with diced tomato, potatoes and artichokes, or rack of lamb with a herb crust served with boulangère potatoes and vegetables. Desserts range from crêpes to Moroccan pastries. The wine list is mostly French with some New World wines, and has a section of 19 half bottles.

Directions: N side of Holland Park Avenue, opp Kensington Hilton. Nearest Tube Holland Park

W11 1 Addison Avenue
W11 4QS
Map no: GtL C3
Tel: 0171 603 8267
Chef: Richard Walton
Proprietors: Richard Walton, Colin Smith and Philippe Bruyer
Cost: Alc £25, fixed-price L £14. H/wine £8.75 ❗ Service exc
Credit cards: 🔲 🔲 🔲 🔲
Times: 12.30pm-last L 2pm, 7pm-last D 11pm. Closed Sat L, Sun & Bhs
Menus: A la carte, fixed-price L
Seats: 45. No pipes allowed, air-conditioning
Additional: Children welcome, children's portions; ❂ dishes, other diets on request

In the Middle Ages, the word 'plum' meant virtually any dried fruit, hence names such as plum pudding and plum cake. The earliest cultivation of plums took place in Syria, and the fruit was first recorded by Roman authors in the 1st century AD. The Crusaders introduced the plum to western Europe. In 14th century England, Chaucer commented on a garden where plums grew and they were certainly a feature in the gardens of medieval monasteries. Greengages are considered the finest dessert plums. Thought to have originated in Armenia, they reached France in the 16th century during the reign of François I (the greengage is still known there as 'Reine Claude' after his wife). Sir Thomas Gage gave his name to the fruit when he introduced it to Britain in the 18th century.

Chiaroscuro ✸

Modern, fashionable restaurant decorated with works of art. A typical meal might include chicken liver parfait with apple and grape chutney, followed by blackened mackerel fillets with a celery and fennel confit, and poached pear on brioche with caramel sauce and vanilla ice

Directions: Nearest Tubes – Holborn (Kingsway), Tottenham Court Road

WC1 Townhouse
24 Coptic Street WC1
Map no: D4
Tel: 0171 636 2731
Chef: Sally James
Proprietors: Carl & Sally James

Chinon ✸✸✸

Relaxed surroundings for reasonably priced modern British cooking

Jonathan Hayes has a real understanding of the raw materials featured in his repertoire, and treats them with proper respect. His short, handwritten *carte*, available at both lunch and dinner, offers an imaginative choice of some eight starters and main courses. At a meal in early spring a simple starter of crab ravioli was well received, as was its neighbour, a warm smoked eel with potato galette and crispy bacon. Breast of duck was full of natural flavours, though presentation was rather clumsy. Vegetables were an integral part and again the freshness and flavours were superb. Pan-fried scallops were beautifully cooked, subtly flavoured with ginger and presented with crispy greens.

There are half a dozen desserts, or a selection of French cheeses with fresh fruits. Chocolate tart was a definite highlight, a delicious chocolate filling on buttery sweet pastry, home-made vanilla ice-cream providing the perfect foil to the richness of the tart. Vanilla bavarois was slightly marred by strands of undissolved gelatine, but the accompanying passion fruit sorbet was a delight. Friendly and relaxed service is provided by partner Barbara Deane, with the assistance of a young waiter. The loyal clientele are clearly at ease in this relaxed, informal atmosphere, taking their food seriously and openly trying forkfuls of each others' dishes. The wine list is predominantly French with a selection of half bottles and a short section of wines from around the world.

Directions: Behind Olympia Exhibition Hall, round the corner to Sinclair Road, close to Kensington & Olympia Hiltons

W14 23 Richmond Way
W14 0AS
Map no: GtL C3
Tel: 0171 602 5968/4082
Chefs: Jonathan Hayes
Proprietors: Barbara Deane and Jonathan Hayes
Cost: *Alc* £25. H/wine £9.50
Credit cards: 🔳 💳 💳 OTHER
Times: Last L 2pm, last D 10.45pm. Closed Xmas
Menus: *A la carte*, pre-theatre
Seats: 60. Air-conditioning
Additional: Children over 10 welcome; ♥ dishes

The Chiswick ✸✸

☺ *Good food at reasonable prices*

The style is uncomplicated, the sky-blue decor minimalist, and the range evolving modern British. Such is the formula for this good neighbourhood restaurant where chef Ian Bates uses his skill well. Recent recommendations have included ragout of snails, chorizo and chickpeas, lightly flavoured with fresh coriander and served with a rich tomato and garlic herb sauce, and a garlicky sauté of cuttlefish, pasta and tomato. The escalope of wild salmon with fennel purée and a black olive dressing also impressed with its rich and lasting flavour. Less successful has been rather hard calves' kidneys with lentils, bacon and mustard. Professionally constructed and well thought out desserts may include apricot and almond tart, chocolate bavarois, and panna cotta with poached plums. Excellent value set menus are available both lunch and dinner, and a good list

W4 131/133 Chiswick High Road W4
Map no: B3
Tel no: 0181 994 6887
Chef: Ian Bates
Proprietor: Clive Greenhalgh
Cost: *Alc* £20, fixed-price L & D £8.50 fixed-price D 7-8pm only. H/wine £9.50. Service exc
Credit cards: 🔳 💳 💳 OTHER
Times: 12.30pm-last L 2.45pm, 7pm-last D 11.30pm. Closed Sat lunch, Sun evening, 1 week Xmas
Menus: *A la carte*, fixed-price L & D

of wines from around the world has a welcome number of 50 cl bottles. Sunday lunches are pepped up with jugs of Bloody Mary.

Directions: On Chiswick High Road close to junction with Turnham Green Terrace. 3 mins walk from Tube station

Christopher's ❀❀

US-style burgers, steaks, fish and fries in grand English surroundings

Since it opened in an old Victorian casino, this American-style restaurant in Covent Garden has grown in popularity. It apes the brash steak houses of New York and Chicago and is popular with the financial crowd. Indeed, it is so popular booking is essential. New York chef Andrew Searing can take a fair share of the credit. The menus – Sunday brunch, lunch, theatre and dinner – are governed by market availability, but generally, apart from the steaks, shellfish come from New England, and Florida supplies the fish. Fries and char-grilling (including the daily specials) predominate. Inspection produced a crab flan, made mostly with brown meat, served with a coriander sabayon, grilled leg of lamb steak with parsley caper salsa with superb mashed potato, light and delicious. The date and pine nut pudding could have been more datey, but the accompanying pistachio sauce provided some additional flavour. The wine list has Californian and southern hemisphere wines and includes a few fine Burgundies. Sandwiches and other simpler items are available in the downstairs café bar. Attentive, friendly staff give an efficient and helpful service.

Directions: 100 yards from the Royal Opera House; nearest Tube – Covent Garden

WC2 18 Wellington Street WC2
Map no: E3
Tel: 0171 240 4222
Chef: Adrian Searing
Proprietor: Christopher Gilmour
Cost: Alc £25, fixed-price pre-theatre £15 (3 course), Sun brunch £12 (2 courses). H/wine £12. Service exc
Credit cards: 🔳 💳 💳 🔳 OTHER
Times: noon-last L 2.30pm, 6pm-last D 11.30pm. Closed Sun eve, Bhs
Menus: A la carte, fixed-price pre-theatre & Sun brunch,
Seats: 120. Air conditioned
Additional: Children permitted; ❶ dishes; other diets on request

Churchill Inter-Continental ❀❀

Much improved carte with skilful dishes cooked consistently well

The menu at Clementine's Restaurant is heavily international. Chef Idris Caldora has put together an inventive and enjoyable range of dishes, such as a crisp fritto misto of seafood and balsamic dressed salad, baby chicken stuffed with couscous, and beef with wild mushrooms. On our inspection, slices of tender duck breast, layered with rösti, were topped with a slice of pink foie gras. Dessert pleasingly played on the theme name of the restaurant – clementine mousse with clementine sorbet in a crisp gingersnap basket, topped with delicate swirls of spun sugar. A daily market menu might include cream of courgette soup, loin of lamb served on a bed of red onion confit with grilled vegetables, and dark chocolate terrine with a Cointreau syrup. The club-like Churchill Bar, however, serves up more aptly traditional British food, such as Lincolnshire sausages 'n mash, Cornish crabcakes, homemade steak and kidney pie, and East Coast cod 'n' chips fried in beer batter. A splendid selection of cocktails includes daiquiris, Manhattans and Cuba Libras made with fresh lime juice.

Directions: Close to Marble Arch, just off Oxford Street

W1 30 Portman Square W1A 4ZX
Map no: B4
Tel: 0171 486 5800
Chef: Idris Caldora
Proprietor: Inter-Continental.
Manager: Luciano Daris
Cost: Alc £27.50, fixed-price L £19.50/D £19.50. H/wine £10.50 ❗ Service exc
Credit cards: 🔳 💳 💳 🔳 OTHER
Times: Noon-last L 3pm, last D 11pm. Closed Sat L
Menus: A la carte, fixed-price L & D, pre-theatre, bar menu
Seats: 100. No-smoking area, air-conditioning
Additional: Children welcome; ❶ dishes, vegan/other diets on request

Chutney Mary Restaurant ❀❀

Indian cooking from the days of the Raj, served in a smart basement restaurant on the King's Road

Anglo-Indian cuisine from the days of the Raj includes dishes not to be found elsewhere on Indian menus. The smart, colonial style restaurant – paddle fans, potted palms and conservatory extension – marks the place out as not your usual curry house, with prices to match. The menu has much to interest. A test meal in May began with freshly cooked nan, 'Memsahib's lamb cutless' – so called because Indian cooks could not pronounce cutlets – which were in fact small patties of minced lamb, pistachio chicken korma, made with tender pieces of chicken breast in a rich, delicately-spiced cream sauce, and a good 'makhmi dahl' flavoured with dried mango powder and black pepper. Basmati rice was freshly cooked. A coffee cream caramel for dessert was more Anglo than Indian. It was a light mousse with good coffee flavour, but the accompanying caramel sauce was thin and bland. The wine list is well chosen, and covers a number of countries including New World wines.

Directions: On corner of Kings Road and Lots Road; 2 mins from Chelsea Harbour, nearest Tube – Fulham Broadway

535 King's Road
Chelsea SW10
Map no: L59
Tel: 0171 351 3113
Chef: Hardev Singh Bhatty
Proprietor: Chelsea Plaza Restaurants.
Manager: Joe Mirrelson
Cost: *Alc* £30, fixed-price L/D (Mon-Sat) £10 (2 course) H/wine £9.25 ❢ Service inc 12.5%. Cover charge £1.50
Credit cards: 🆔 🆔 🆔 🆔 OTHER
Times: 12.30-last L 2.30pm (3pm Sun), 7pm-last D 11.30pm (10.30pm Sun)
Seats: 110. No-smoking area. Air conditioned
Menus: *A la carte* and fixed-price L & D, bar menu
Additional: Children welcome; ❤ dishes, vegan/other diets on request

Cibo ❀❀

A convivial restaurant-bar providing pleasant surroundings for fashionable Italian dishes

Cibo is a friendly neighbourhood place with a lively atmosphere. The cheerful service is overseen by proprietor Gino Taddei. A moderately sized *carte* of regional Italian dishes offers the likes of 'baccala mantecato', cream of salt cod mousse on bread with olive oil, 'calamari di granchio in salsa', baby squid filled with crab with a light tomato sauce, or raw beef marinated with lemon and olive oil with wild rocket and shavings of Parmesan or pasta of ravioli with duck in mushroom sauce, and home-made gnocchi with tomato and melted mozzarella. Fish and seafood figure prominently among the main courses with dishes such as whole sea bass baked or grilled with fresh herbs, and a mixed grill of lobster, prawns and langoustines with fish, mussels and clams. Alternatively there may be grilled new season lamb with broad beans and Parma ham, or roast quails with saffron risotto; and to finish, perhaps the ever popular tiramisu.

Directions: Russell Gardens is a resisdential area off Holland Road. Nearest Tubes – Kensington (Olympia); Shepherds Bush

W14 3 Russell Gardens W14 8EZ
Map no: GtL C3
Tel: 0171 371 2685/6271
Chef: Robert Frederic
Proprietor: Gino Taddei
Cost: *Alc* £25, fixed-price L £12.50. H/wine £8.90 ❢
Credit cards: 🆔 🆔 🆔 🆔
Times: Opens noon
Menus: *A la carte*, fixed-price L
Seats: 50. Air-conditioning
Additional: Children welcome, children's portions; ❤ dishes, vegan/other diets on request

> Wild rice is not a rice at all. It is the seed of an aquatic grass which comes from the northern United States. It was originally harvested by native American tribes. The seeds grow one by one up the stalk and resemble little black sticks. It is extremely expensive and is not uncommon to buy it mixed with brown rice.
> Perfumed rice is a long grain rice from Vietnam and Thailand which has a distinctive taste.

City Miyama Restaurant ❀

Popular and stylish Japanese restaurant with a ground floor sushi bar and teppanyaki counter, and main dining area downstairs. Try egg-battered and deep-fried soya bean curd, and prawn and chicken poached with vegetables in a 'dashi' consommé

Times: Noon-last L 2.30pm, 6pm-last D 10pm
Menus: A la carte, Teppan-Yaki
Seats: 75. Air-conditioning
Additional: Children welcome; ❶ /vegan dishes
Directions: S side of St Paul's behind city info centre

EC4 17 Godliman Street
EC4V 5BD
Map no: F3
Tel: 0171 489 1937/329 4225
Chef: I Ebina
Proprietor: K Furuya (Managing Director)
Cost: Alc £20, fixed-price L £15/D £30. H/wine £15 ❢
Service exc
Credit cards: 🔳 🔳 🔳 🔳 OTHER

Claridge's ❀❀

Elegant surroundings in a choice of two restaurants at this notable Mayfair establishment

Renowned as a home-from-home for visiting royalty, heads of state and the British aristocracy, there is an inevitable cachet to a meal at Claridge's. Rapidly approaching its centenary, the hotel retains many original features, the most striking of which is the stunning black and white marbled hall and foyer lounge. The atmosphere in the restaurant is generally dignified (less formal dining is offered in the Causerie). The cooking is classically based but the food has an agreeable lightness, although some flavours could be better balanced – shellfish made little impact in a moist risotto sampled at a test meal, for example, and the flavour of morels was not really incorporated with partridge. Still, this is grand cooking for a grand hotel restaurant where luxury items such as terrine of goose liver with truffles and Sauternes wine jelly, steamed turbot with spinach, roasted scallops and langoustines, and tournedos of beef with truffles, are menu staples. Prices are not cheap, with main courses from the *carte* ranging from around £19.50 to £26, and vegetables charged at an additional £6, but the experience is certainly memorable.

Directions: Two minutes from Bond Street Tube, take Davies Street exit

Brook Street W1
Map no: C3
Tel: 0171 629 8860
Chef: Marjan Lesnik
Proprietor: Savoy Hotels PLC
Manager: Mr F Touzin
Cost: Alc £50, fixed-price L £29 / D £40. H/wine £15 ❢ Service inc
Credit cards: 🔳 🔳 🔳 🔳 OTHER
Times: 12.30pm-last L 3.15pm, 7pm-last D 11.15pm.
Menus: A la carte; fixed-price L & D,
Seats: 100. Air conditioned
Additional: Children welcome; children's portions, ❶ menu, vegan/other diets on request

Clarke's ❀❀❀

Limited choice formula does not detract from the popularity of this individual and excellent Kensington restaurant

For many people, the agonising act of menu perusal is an essential part of the whole dining experience. A no-choice menu sometimes lead to frustration but it's not a worry which seems to concern Sally Clarke's regular following. As the four-course dinner menu is available for the whole week, it may be worth checking for likes and dislikes before booking.

At lunchtime, however, when Sally Clarke herself is cooking, the menu offers three choices and is priced for two or three courses. Located next to her retail shop at the Notting Hill end of Kensington Church Street, the busy, stylish restaurant takes up two floors. Upstairs, the high ceilings, together with the wooden flooring and bright lighting, create a clever sense of space. Downstairs, try and request a table away from the draughts

W8 124 Kensington Church Street W8 4BH
Map no: GtL C3
Tel: 0171 221 9225
Chefs: Sally Clarke and Elizabeth Payne
Proprietor: Sally Clarke.
Manager: Sarah Dickinson
Cost: Fixed-price L £26 (3 courses)/ D £37. H/wine £8.50
❢ Service inc
Credit cards: 🔳 🔳 OTHER
Times: 12.30pm-last L 2pm, 7pm-last D 10pm. Closed Sat, Sun & Bhs, 10 days at Xmas, 2wks in Aug
Menus: Fixed-price

caused by constant use of the front door. Typical dishes from the ever-changing repertoire may include chargrilled Scottish scallops with spring vegetables and ribbons of deep-fried leek, and breast of Hereford duck grilled with crackling, potato pancake and blood orange glaze. The duck leg frequently comes slow-baked with crisp polenta, as was the case at our inspection meal. Succulent and tender, with a powerful flavour and dry, crispy skin, it arrived with a reduction of the cooking juices delicately scented with roasted apple, leek and red onion. A starter of freshly picked crab was served simply flaked with diced cucumber, roughly chopped herbs and herb mayonnaise. Dessert kept up the pace with a memorable, light and crisp puff pastry tartlette filled with poached pears and pecan nuts, and served with creamy maple syrup ice-cream. The wine list is reasonably priced, and Californian bins feature strongly. A good selection of wines is also available by the glass.

Directions: Near Notting Hill Gate

Seats: 90. No-smoking area, air-conditioning
Additional: Children welcome; ❶ dishes, vegan/other diets on request

Clifton-Ford Hotel ❀

A purpose-built hotel handy for the Oxford Street shops. Doyle's Restaurant provides a relaxed atmosphere in which to enjoy some modern British cooking. Look out for duck in a green chilli sauce, pan-fried scallops with spinach and bacon, and rabbit stuffed with herb mousse. Summer fruit mille-feuille for dessert

Menus: *A la carte,* bar menu, ❶
Seats: 96. No-smoking area, air-conditioning
Additional: Children's portions; ❶ /vegan dishes
Directions: By car: Welbeck St is last turning left off New Cavendish St, both one way. Nearest Tube: Bond Street

W1 47 Welbeck Street
W1M 8DN
Map no: C4
Tel: 0171 486 6600
Chef: Mark Dancer
Proprietor: Doyle Hotels.
Manager: Stephen French
Cost: *Alc* £23. H/wine £11
❢ Service inc
Credit cards: ▨ ▧ ▨ ▨
Times: Last L 2.30pm, last D 10pm. Closed 3 days at Xmas

Coast ❀❀

Modish Med, Pacific rim and West Coast cooking all combine at the latest hot spot

A former car showroom has been so transformed that it manages to combine both futuristic and retro looks with bulbous light fittings, utilitarian yellow chairs and lacquered tables with pedestal bases. Stephen Terry's recent tour of the USA has probably had the greatest influence on the menu. There are some daring ideas, some of which miss the mark. A sauté of perfectly cooked scallops came with lettuce hearts and a creamed vanilla and lemon dressing that lacked the promised balance of sweet and sour. Similarly, a fine salad of lobster and Chinese radish was overpowered by a thick vinaigrette. Main courses fared better with a stunning adaptation of Chinese noodle soup – fine egg noodles and choi sum, topped with honey roasted Gressingham duck and surrounded by duck stock infused with lemongrass and lime leaves. Salmon came on noodles too, a first-class tagliatelle of pasta and cucumber served with a frothy cucumber and mint fondue, finished with lightly poached oyster and caviar. For dessert, an old favourite of rhubarb and custard was reworked as a firm vanilla custard with a soup of the fruit. Wines are well chosen.

Directions: Nearest Tube – Green Park

W1 Albermerle Street W1
Map no: C3
Tel: 0171 495 5999
Chef: Steven Terry
Proprietor: Oliver Peyton
Cost: *Alc* £25, H/wine £12.50
Credit cards: ▨ ▧ ▨ OTHER
Times: noon-last L 3pm, 6pm-last D midnight
Menus: *A la carte*
Seats: 153. Air conditioned
Additional: ❶ dishes, other diets on prior request

FLETCHER RESTAURANT

The Connaught ❀❀❀

A relic of a more refined age where standards of service are irreproachable and the classic cuisine highly accomplished

Change is unthinkable at this bastion of traditional values and, if it were ever contemplated, would provoke consternation in Mayfair and cause an outcry throughout the civilised world. Michel Bourdin, chef de cuisine, has notched up a decade of service and, with his dedicated team, continues to produce daily lunch and dinner menus as well as the lengthy *carte*, which mixes grand cuisine in the style of Escoffier with robust yet refined English classics.

Our inspector's lunch commenced with a kipper pâté that resembled a rillete in texture and taste, its fishy flavour softened with the addition of onions, potato and bacon, and the terrine topped with a layer of rendered fat; after a couple of mouthfuls it all began to taste a bit boring. Crab bisque was enlivened at the table with a splash of flaming brandy, a spectacular way of thinning a soup which was heavy on the beurre manie. Poultry provided by the famous butcher, Allen's, across the road, is always of excellent quality and well-handled. Guinea fowl was taken off the bone and served with a duo of sauces which had run into each other before our man got to eat it, giving a powerful flavour of wild mushrooms heightened by shaved truffles. It was accompanied by mixed white and wild rice which added nothing to the dish, especially as it was served in a crescent dish on the side. But the bird itself had great flavour and was perfectly cooked. Grand Marnier soufflé came with a vanilla anglaise of wonderful sheen and consistency, but the soufflé itself was rather heavy, though still moist and intensely flavoured. Not, then, the most exciting food ever eaten, but well-prepared with top quality ingredients, served with great aplomb.

Directions: On corner of Mount Street and Carlos Place, between Oxford Street and Hyde Park Lane. Nearest Tubes – Bond Street, Hyde Park Corner

W1 Carlos Place W1
Map no: C3
Tel: 0171 499 7070
Chef: Michel Bourdin
Proprietor: The Savoy Group plc
Cost: Alc £80, fixed-price £25
Credit cards: ▩ ▦ ▦ ▣ OTHER
Menus: A la carte, fixed-price
Seats: 75 (Restaurant), 35 (Grill Room). No smoking. Air conditioned
Additional: Some vegetarian dishes

The Copthorne Tara ❀

A large, modern hotel, set in a quiet cul-de-sac, convenient for Kensington High Street. Despite its size the staff maintain a personal approach. The restaurant menu emphasis is on international dishes with a pronounced English streak; there is a separate grill menu with a good choice of steaks and mixed grills

Seats: 40. No-smoking area. Air conditioned
Additional: Children welcome; children's menu, ✿ dishes, vegan/other diets on request
Directions: Two minutes from High St Kensington underground

W8 Scarsdale Place (off Wrights Lane) W8
Map no: GtL C3
Tel: 0171 937 7211
Chef: Klaus Hohenauer
Proprietor: Copthorne.
Cost: Alc from £20, fixed-price L & D £17. H/wine £11.50 Service inc
Credit cards: ▩ ▦ ▦ ▣ OTHER
Times: last L 3pm/D 11pm

Coulsdon Manor ❀❀

Careful, assured Anglo-French cooking at a stately Surrey hotel

A popular hotel set in 140 acres of landscaped parkland with wide leisure and corporate facilities. Attentive service and hospitality are hallmarks. Chef Michael Neal's careful style reflects his serious and dedicated approach to his craft. An inspection meal yielded a

Coulsdon Road
Croydon CR5 2LL
Map no: GtL D1
Tel: 0181 668 0414
Chef: Michael Neal
Proprietor: Marstons Hotel.
General Manager: John Harrison

terrine of leek and duck: a creamy parfait wrapped in wilted leaves of leek and served with an excellent orange marmalade. Then mignons of beef, pan fried, tender, and set on a well-made buttery galette topped with slices of black truffle and a cheese sabayon. It was served with a rich glace de viande port sauce and garnished with mange tout, cauliflower, haricot vert, broccoli and turned swedes and carrots. Dessert, queen of hearts, was a disappointment. An individually made hot egg custard topped with an uncooked piped meringue, and served with raspberry coulis and crème anglaise was very sweet with 'lots of overkill'. A vegetarian menu featuring dishes such as spiced black bean soup and tagliatelle with beetroot is also available. The wine list features a particularly good New World selection and each bottle is well described.

Directions: From M23/M25 Jnc 7 follow M23 N until road becomes A23. Follow A23 2.5mile, take right after Coulsdon S Railway Station onto B2030. Follow uphill 1mile, turn left past pond, follow B2030 (Purley) 0.5mile and turn right into Coulsdon Court Rd. Manor at end of road

Cost: *Alc* from £23.45, fixed-price L £14.95/D £18.50. H/wine £10.95 ! Service exc
Credit cards: ▨ ▧ ▧ ▨ OTHER
Times: Noon-last L 2.30pm, 7pm-last D 9.30pm. Closed Sat L
Menus: *A la carte*, fixed-price, carvery, bar menu, ♥
Seats: 120. No smoking in dining room, air-conditioning
Additional: Children welcome, children's portions & menu; ♥ dishes, vegan/other diets on request

Crowthers ❀❀

Moderately priced modern Anglo-French cooking at this small family-run restaurant

The Crowthers' popular little restaurant is noted for attentive service. Philip Crowther cooks a manageable and moderately priced menu of two or three courses. Described as 'essentially French/British', the style admits to a wider European influence in such starters as tortellini of seafood with cream and basil sauce, and grilled aubergine with tomato, feta cheese and pesto. To follow, favourite main courses are rib-eye beef steak with rösti potato and shallot sauce, or boned and stuffed quails served with a casserole of flageolet beans, smoked bacon and garlic. Puddings have classic appeal with choices such as tarte au citron, three chocolate parfaits with raspberry coulis, or sticky toffee pudding with butterscotch sauce. There is a short, reasonably priced wine list which complements the style of cooking.

Directions: Bus 33 or 337. BR to Mortlake. Between Jct of Sheen Lane & Clifford Avenue

SW14 481 Upper Richmond Road West SW14 7PU
Map no: GtL B2
Tel: 0181 876 6372
Chef: Philip Crowther
Proprietor: Philip & Shirley Crowther
Cost: Fixed-price L £18 (3 courses)/D £22 (3 courses). H/wine £8.50 ! Service exc
Credit cards: ▨ ▧
Times: Noon-last L 2pm, 7pm-last D 10pm. Closed Sat L, Sun, Mon & 1 wk Xmas, 2 wks Aug
Menus: Fixed-price L & D
Seats: 35. Air-conditioning
Additional: Children welcome, children's portions; ♥ dishes, vegan/other diets on request

Dan's Restaurant ❀

A warm, friendly atmosphere and honest cooking combine to make this a popular place. Modern ideas feature in poached haddock with coriander, charred marinated chicken with lime, or grilled calves' liver with sweet and sour onions. Walnut tart is recommended

Seats: *50*
Directions: At the Kings Road end of Sydney Street. Nearest Tube – South Kensington

SW3 119 Sydney Street SW3
Map no: B1
Tel: *0171 352 2718*
Chef: *Thierry Rousseau*
Proprietor: *Dan Whitehead*
Cost: *Alc £24.50, fixed-price L/D £14 (2 courses), £16.50. H/wine £9.50* ! *Service inc*
Credit cards: ▨ ▧ ▧
Times: *Last L 2.30pm/D 10.30pm. Closed Sat L, Sun D, Xmas week, Bhs*

Daphne's Restaurant ❀❀❀

Fashionable rendezvous for Hello! readers, with exemplary Tuscan cooking

Well-heeled ladies-who-lunch flock to Daphne's for the excellent food and, perhaps, also for the charms of the handsome young Danish owner, Morgens Tholstrup. He is proud of his Italian restaurant where the *carte*, at both lunch and dinner, offers a wide range of interesting dishes. Kamel Benamar is now in control of the kitchen, and previous high cooking standards have been retained. Cooking style can best be described as simple with clean textures and flavours, and no superflous distractions. Around ten starters, such as beef carpaccio with rucola and Parmesan or forest mushrooms with grilled polenta, sharpen the taste buds adroitly. Our inspector raved about the sweet and fresh pan-fried scallops with pancetta and salsa, although felt slightly cheated when three of the six scallops turned out to be potatoes shaped to look like scallops. A rack of lamb, cooked pink to order, could not have been bettered in either Wales or Yorkshire. It is worth noting that vegetables are charged separately and are quite expensive. There is an interesting pasta and risotto section, where vegetarians will find something to their tastes, if they're not heretically tempted by the lobster ravioli or tortelloni with crab and aubergine. Puddings are not to be missed; tiramisu, almond and prune tart or a well-made crème brûlée with a vanilla-speckled creamy texture, are amongst the difficult choices. Espresso is rich, strong and superbly flavoured. The wine list presents bottles from around the world, but does have a Pisa-like leaning towards Italy. The service is slick, friendly and knowlegable, and the atmosphere bustles with catchy European style. Advance booking is essential.

Directions: Jnc of Draycott Avenue & Walton Street, Brompton Cross

SW3 110-112 Draycott Avenue
SW3 3AE
Map no: B1
Tel: 0171 589 4257
Chef: Karmel Benamar
Proprietor: Mogens Tholstrup.
Manager: Annie Foster Firth
Cost: *Alc* L £23.50/D £40.
H/wine £9.50 ▮ Serice inc
Credit cards: 🗗 💳 💳 💷
Times: Noon-last L 3pm, 7pm-last D 11pm. Closed 25/26 Dec
Menus: *A la carte*, Sunday brunch
Seats: 110. No pipes allowed, air-conditioning
Additional: Children welcome at Sunday L only; ♥ dishes, vegan/other diets on request

dell'Ugo ❀❀

Bastion of the new Soho establishment in danger of losing its cutting edge through complaisant cooking

dell'Ugo can be like the curate's egg – fine in parts, disappointing in others. The place still buzzes, particularly at ground floor level. Things quieten down as you pass through the first floor café to the wood-panelled restaurant above. The menu remains mostly Tuscan-led Mediterranean, and includes a number of popular dishes regulars have come to expect. For our inspector, after a poor start with sub-standard country bread and tapenade, things picked up with a well-made white bean and fresh pesto soup. Main course calves' liver was tender and of good quality, with a refined shallot jus; the smoked bacon, however, was so fatty as to be quite inedible. A colcannon cake was heavy and dull, made with potato and little else. Classic lemon tart arrived drenched in icing sugar and without its advertised orange confit, but was otherwise perfectly fine. It is a worrying sign when the high point of an inspection meal is felt to be a cup of espresso coffee, however excellent. Service is laid-back, but dishes arrive without delay. Wines of the month are a regular feature, and list some of the more interesting young bottles from around the world.

Directions Soho Square end of Frith Street

W1 56 Frith Street W1V 5TA
Map no: D4
Tel: 0171 734 8300
Chef: Mark Emberton
Proprietor: Simpsons of Cornhill.
Gen Manager: Max Alderman
Cost: *Alc* £21.95. H/wine £8.75
▮ Service exc
Credit cards: 🗗 💳 💳 💷 OTHER
Times: Closed Sun & Bhs
Menus: *A la carte*, pre-theatre, bar menu
Seats: 180. Air-conditioning
Additional: Children welcome; ♥ dishes, vegan/other diets on request

The Dorchester, Grill Room ❀❀❀

Traditional British dishes, formally served in sumptuously decorated surroundings

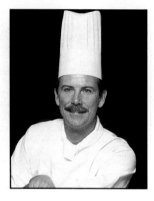

The Grill Room at the Dorchester has remained virtually unchanged since it opened in 1931, with its opulent Spanish decor, formal atmosphere and correct service. Michael DiFiore, the Grill Room manager supervises the professional, white aproned staff with quiet authority, while executive chef Willi Elsener offers traditional British dishes from the *carte* and the fixed-price menu of the day. Luncheon specialities are printed on the *carte* with steak and kidney pie on Wednesdays, for example, and Cornish fisherman's pie on Friday. On a recent inspection visit, our inspector was impressed with the range of breads available from the trolley, including one with a delicious Stilton flavour, a nut and sultana bread and a moist wholemeal loaf.

Chicken liver and bacon salad, a successful combination of textures and flavours with a generous amount of the carefully cooked, pink liver, opened the meal. This was followed by salmon pancakes with a sorrel sauce, the dish delivering all its promised flavours, accompanied by a colourful combination of fine French beans and Vichy carrots. Hard to resist is the sweet trolley with its array of artistically presented desserts – crème caramel, trifle, and syllabub with raspberry coulis among them. Alternatively, there is a selection of well kept English cheeses. Full-flavoured espresso coffee completed an enjoyable meal, served with a plate of petits fours.

The Dorchester's wine list, available in each of the hotel's restaurants, offers an extensive choice of superb wines with excellent vintages.

Menus: *A la carte*, fixed-price L & D
Seats: 81. Air conditioning
Additional: Children welcome, children's portions; ❂ dishes, vegan/other diets on prior request
Directions: Two-thirds of the way down Park Lane, fronting a small island garden. Nearest Tube – Hyde Park

W1 The Dorchester Hotel
Park Lane W1A 2HJ
Map no: C3
Tel: 0171 629 8888
Chef: Willi Elsener
Proprietors: The Dorchester Hotel Ltd
Cost: *Alc* £35, fixed-price L 24.50, fixed-price D £32. H/wine £17.50 Service inc
Credit cards: 🟥 ▦ ▦ 🔳 OTHER
Times: 12.30pm-2.30pm-last L 2.30pm, 6pm-11pm-last D 11pm (10.30pm Sun & Bhs)

The Dorchester, The Oriental ❀❀❀

Refined Chinese cooking as befits the most elegant surroundings

The Oriental is expensive, but the surroundings are suitably extravagant. Best quality ingredients, well judged flavour combinations and accurate cooking characterise the exemplary Chinese food, and presentation is exquisite. Service has all the focus and flourish one would expect from an exclusive hotel. It is worth the expense.

A meal taken in summer started with an appetiser spring roll filled with chicken and vegetables and served with fried seaweed and Worcestershire sauce. Julienne of moist chicken and roast duck served with matchsticks of cucumber and Charentais melon, tossed at the table with chilli-flavoured rice vinegar, proved an excellent combination of flavours, textures and colours. Fish mousse stuffed with spring onions and bacon and fried in crisp batter came attractively sliced in the diagonal, with a good sweet and sour sauce. Pan-fried rice noodles with vegetables and strips of barbecue pork made for a fresh and simple dish, and hot pot of crisp vegetables with cellophane noodles, tender squid and dried shrimps had a

W1 The Dorchester Hotel
Park Lane W1A 2HJ
Map no: C3
Tel: 0171 317 6328
Chef: Simon Yung
Proprietors: The Dorchester Hotel Ltd
Cost: *Alc* £50, fixed-price L £24.50 (3 courses), fixed-price D £32 (5 courses). H/wine £17.50 Service inc
Credit cards: 🟥 ▦ ▦ 🔳 OTHER
Times: Noon-2.30pm-last L 2.30pm, 7pm-11pm, last D 11pm. Closed Sun & month of Aug

The Dorchester, The Oriental

good seafood flavour. Steamed chicken, abalone and Chinese mushrooms with mustard greens and light soya sauce provided an effective contrast between the perfectly cooked chicken and the chewy abalone, which had an 'earthy fishiness'. Moist, fragrant duck came on a bed on thinly sliced cucumber and pickled ginger with steamed rice. Oriental Delight, an expensive selection of desserts, didn't quite live up to its name, but was the only disappointment.

The extensive wine list is common to all the Dorchester's restaurants, and is outstanding in its quality and choice.

Menus: *A la carte*, fixed-price L & D
Seats: 81. Air conditioning
Additional: Children welcome, children's portions; ❶ dishes, vegan other diets on prior request
Directions: See The Dorchester Grill

Downstairs at 190 Queensgate ❀❀❀

Consistently good fish cookery at this ever-popular Kensington watering-hole

Ever since traditional English fish and chips was reclaimed by the chattering classes, it has been a daily favourite at this informal basement restaurant, cooked in a beer batter. Fresh fish and seafood dominate the menu, which changes according to the market. There may be at least half a dozen varieties to choose from on any one day – salmon, sea bream, Dover sole, parrot fish, cod and turbot were all available on our visit. Steamed or chargrilled mussels and clams come by the half and full kilo, and there are five different ways with lobster. Carnivores don't miss out, however, with dishes along the lines of marinated duck breast with stir-fried vegetables, soy and sesame dressing, and peppered rump steak, Taleggio mushrooms and frites.

Marinated olives whet the appetite, and tapenade is served with home-made bread and slices of fresh, crispy baguette. A starter of deep-fried salmon fishcakes was well seasoned, set on wilted leaves of fresh spinach cooked in oil, and served with a sorrel sauce. More wilted spinach leaves arrived under a succulent, steamed fillet of sea bream, accompanied by a light fish jus textured with chopped

SW7 190 Queensgate SW7 5EU
Map no: A1
Tel: 0171 581 5666
Chefs: Antony Worral Thompson and Adrian McCormack
Proprietors: Simpsons of Cornhill.
Manager: Julian Peters
Cost: *Alc* £23.50. H/wine £10.50 Service exc
Credit cards: 🔲 💳 💳 💳 OTHER
Times: 7pm-last D midnight. Closed L, Sun & Bhs, 1 wk at Xmas
Menus: *A la carte*
Seats: 70. Air-conditioning
Additional: Children welcome, children's portions on request; ❶ dishes, vegan/other diets on request

Downstairs at 190 Queensgate

parsley. Yet more wilted spinach leaves were included in the vegetables served with the dish. (Happily, there was no sign of any in a generously filled portion of cherry and cinammon tart.) The wine list comes in for special praise, with a fine selection from most of the principal wine growing areas of the world, and we can recommend the Poggio alle Gazze 1992 from Tuscany. However, there are also good value selected wines of the month and many half bottles, as well as some expensive vintage wines from Bordeaux and Burgundy. Despite a change of ownership, Antony Worrall-Thompson remains consultant chef, assisted by head chef Adrian MacCormack.

Directions: From Kensington High St, go down Queen's gate. Left hand side next to Gore Hotel. Nearest Tubes: High Street Kensington, Gloucester Road & South Kensington

Drury Lane Moat House ❀

☺ *Modern, purpose-built hotel in a convenient Covent Garden location. Interesting cooking ensures the popularity of Maudie's Restaurant where straightforward menus feature dishes such as seafood quenelles*

Menus: *A la carte*, fixed-price L & D, pre-theatre, bar menu
Seats: No-smoking area
Additional: Children welcome, children's portions & menu;
❤ dishes, other diets on request
Directions: Nearest Tubes: Tottenham Court Road, Covent Garden, Holborn

WC2 10 Drury Lane WC2B 5RE
Map no: E4
Tel: 0171 208 9988
Chef: Charles Cooper
Proprietors: Moat House.
Manager: S van Herwijnen
Cost: *Alc* £15.85, fixed-price
L £10 (1 course)/D £13.85
(2 courses). H/wine £11.40
Service exc
Credit cards: 🂠 🂡 🂢 🂣 OTHER
Times: L from noon, last D
10.30pm

'En papillote' describes a manner of cooking and serving. It is quite simply a way of wrapping food so that it is tightly enclosed in buttered or oiled greaseproof paper or aluminium foil and then cooked in the oven. The wrapping swells during cooking and the dish is served piping hot before the wrapping collapses. This preserves the flavour and is a method often employed with fish which requires a short cooking time.
A 'papillote' on the other hand, is a small decorative paper frill used to decorate the bone end of a lamb or veal chop, rack of lamb or chicken drumstick.

The Eagle ❀

☺ *Bustling, popular converted pub, strong on basic decor and modern Brit meets Med food. Cooking is open plan, there's no booking, tables (cramped) are shared, and it is all great fun. Expect Italian sausages with rocket and red onions, and barracuda with garlic, lemon and spinach. Finish with Portuguese custard tart*

Menus: *A la carte*
Seats: 55
Additional: Children welcome, children's portions; ❷ dishes
Directions: North end of Farringdon Rd opp National Car Park

EC1 159 Farringdon Road
EC1R 3AL
Map no: E5
Tel: 0171 837 1353
Chef: David Eyre
Proprietors: Michael Belben and David Eyre
Cost: *Alc* £3.50-£10 (1 course) ❢
Credit cards: None taken
Times: Noon-last L 2.30pm, last D 10.30pm

Elena's L'Etoile ❀❀

Veritable cuisine grandmére served by an inimitable hostess

Elena Salvoni has been cosseting the great and good of Soho for more years than many of her customers probably prefer to remember. It's entirely appropriate, then, that she should have crossed Oxford Street to preside over the grand old institution that is L'Etoile. The food, prepared by a Roux-trained chef, has been pepped up and is less resolutely old fashioned than during former incarnations of this rather lovely old place, but still firmly in the mould of a traditional brasserie – which is no bad thing. An inspection meal began with garlicky tomato soup enhanced with herbs, blended with cream and garnished with chopped parsley. Expertly seared calves' liver was very pink, garnished with rashers of smoked streaky bacon and sauced with a well made veal reduction. Lemon tart to finish had all the zest one might expect from an apprentice of the brothers Roux. Cuisine grandmére, indeed. The well-balanced wine list is divided into Elena's house selection, featuring 30 bottles at decent prices, plus a 'French Connoisseurs List' which is just that.

Direction: Southside of Goodge Street, between Goodge Street and Oxford Street. Nearest Tube – Tottenham Court Road

W1 30 Charlotte Street W1
Map no: C4
Tel: 0171 636 1496
Chef: Kevin Hopgood
Manager: John Robel
Cost: *Alc* £25. H/wine £10.50
Credit cards: ▨ ▨ ▨ ▨ OTHER
Times: 12.30pm-4.30pm, 6.30pm-11.30. Closed Sat L, Sun, Bhs
Menus: *A la carte*
Seats: 75
Additional: ❷ dishes, other diets on prior request

Ellington's ❀

☺ *Simple, well-prepared dishes are served at this café-style restaurant with a jazz theme. Potato parcels are filled with chicken livers, leeks and sage, and a tender, lightly cooked sirloin steak is served with red wine sauce. Desserts include a lemon and orange cheesecake with custard sauce*

Menus: fixed-price L & D
Seats: 67 Air conditioned
Additional: children welcome; children's portions, ❷ dishes, vegan/other diets on request
Directions: opposite Chingford Station

E4 140 Station Road
Chingford E4
Map no: GtL E5
Tel: 0181 524 5544
Chefs: David Simpson, Karen Neish and Carl Fordham
Proprietor: Brian Hutchinson.
Manager: Greg Simpson
Cost: fixed-price L £4.95 (1 course)/D £17.95. H/wine £9.50 Service exc
Credit cards: ▨ ▨ ▨ ▨ OTHER
Times: 10am-last L 3pm, 7pm-last D 10pm. Closed Mon, Dec 25-Jan 2

English Garden Restaurant ❀❀

Assured cooking in an attractive and friendly environment

SW3 10 Lincoln Street SW3 2TS
Map no: B1
Tel: 0171 584 7272
Chef: Brian Turner
Proprietor: Roger Wren.
Manager: Colin Livingstone
Cost: *A/c* £28, fixed-price L
£14.75. H/wine £9.50 Service
exc
Credit cards: 🖾 📰 📧 📳
Times: 12.30pm-last L 2.30pm,
7.30pm-last D 11.30pm. Closed
25/26 Dec
Menus: *A la carte*, fixed-price L
Seats: 55. No pipes allowed, air-
conditioning
Additional: Children welcome,
children's portions; ❂ dishes,
vegan/other diets on request

A bright conservatory extension is almost de rigour for a restaurant with a name like English Garden. It certainly enhances this well-appointed, popular Chelsea restaurant which offers sound, uncomplicated cooking based on traditional English dishes with a modern slant. The set lunch is good value, and there is a *carte*; both feature carefully-prepared dishes based on quality ingredients. An inspector was impressed by a first course of leek and goats' cheese tart, the pastry light, the filling fluffy, and a main course of gamey grilled duck breast garnished with caramelised oranges. Only pudding – brown sugar meringue with coffee cream – was slightly disappointing, the texture too loose, the chewy centre lacking. Other dishes typical of the style include grilled lobster with scallop, saddle of hare, Lancashire hot pot, and chicken curry. Service is formal but attentive. The wine list offers a good selection of reasonably-priced clarets and Burgundies.

Directions: Nearest Tube: Sloane Square

The English House Restaurant ❀❀

Modern English cooking in a small, friendly Chelsea restaurant

SW3 3 Milner Street SW3
Map no: B1
Tel: 0171 584 3002
Chef: Danny Leahy
Proprietor: Roger Wren.
Manager: Dieter Durgensen
Cost: *A/c* £28, fixed-price L
£14.75, H/wine £9.50. Service
exc
Credit cards: 🖾 📰 📧 📳
Times: 12.30-last L 2.30pm
(2pm Sun & Bhs), 7.30pm-last D
11.30pm (10pm Sun & Bhs).
Closed 26 Dec
Menus: *A la carte*, fixed-price L
Seats: 58. No-smoking area
Additional: children welcome;
children's portions, ❂ dishes,
vegan/other diets on request

A smart, intimate English restaurant that is slap-bang in the heart of Chelsea. Danny Leahy (ex-Dukes) has taken over the kitchen although the Englishness of the menu remains the same. Plain, no-frills cooking tends to be the style. Soused mackerel with apple and potato, chicken liver pâté with sweet onion marmalade, grilled fillet of beef with celeriac pancake, grilled calves' liver with bacon and bubble and squeak, are all typical offerings. One inspector enjoyed a meal that began with celery and Stilton soup, followed by a main course of tender, moist, boned guinea fowl, its skin light and crisp, served on a bed of shredded Savoy cabbage with caraway cream sauce and a dessert of excellent orange cheesecake with a light fluffy filling, but a slightly heavy, bitter chocolate sauce. Bread is good, as is the coffee and chocolate fudge. The wine list is all French. Service is young, helpful and willing.

Directions: between South Kensington & Sloane Square tubes

Enoteca ❀

☺ *Popular neighbourhood restaurant, close to Putney Bridge, offering regional Italian cooking. Look out for rabbit marinated in olive oil with garlic and sage, roast salmon with artichokes, pesto and oyster muchrooms, and ginger baskets with mascarpone and strawberries to finish*

SW15 28 Putney High Street SW15 1SQ
Map no: GtL C2
Tel: 0181 785 4449
Chef: G Turi
Proprietor: G & T Turi
Cost: *Alc* £18.20, fixed-price L £9.50. H/wine £9 Service exc
Credit cards: ⬛ ▦ ▦ ▣ OTHER
Times: 12.30-last L 2.30pm, 7pm-last D 11pm. Closed Sun & 25-30 Dec
Menus: *A la carte,* fixed-price L
Seats: 75
Additional: Children welcome, children's portions; ❶ dishes, vegan/other diets on request

Directions: Opposite MGM cinema. Nearest Tube: Putney Bridge. Buses 14, 220, 22, 9, 74

Fifth Floor Restaurant ❀❀

An appropriately stylish restaurant on the fifth floor of Harvey Nichols, offering modern British cooking

SW1 Knightsbridge SW1
Map no: B2
Tel: 0171 235 5250
Chef: Henry Harris
Proprietors: Harvey Nichols. Manager: Edward Hyde
Cost: *Alc* £26, fixed-price L & D £21.50. H/wine £9.75 ❗ Service charge inc 12.5%
Credit cards: ⬛ ▦ ▦ ▣ OTHER

The fifth floor of this stylish store is a haven for gourmets. The food market purveys all manner of delights; the café is popular for coffee and light snacks, and the restaurant provides a relaxed setting for some delicious food. The latter is a huge, hangar-like room, decorated in blue and white and hung with rather garish paintings. It could easily lack atmosphere, but actually buzzes with happy chatter. The lunch menu is a short, two or three-course affair while dinner is both more elaborate and extensive. An inspection meal

Fifth Floor Restaurant

Times: noon-last L 3pm (Sat 3.30pm), 6.30pm-last D 11.30pm. Closed Sun, B/hol eves, Dec 25/6
Menus: *A la carte*, fixed-price L & D, bar menu
Seats: 110. Air conditioned
Additional: children welcome; children's portions, ❂ menu, vegan/other diets on reqest

began with good home-made bread and succulent grilled duck breast, cooked rosy pink and set on lentils and peas with an aromatic salsa verde. Calves' kidneys followed, served with a creamy Meaux mustard sauce. The lemon tart to finish was delightfully zesty, though the pastry was a little soft. A separate menu is presented for vegetarians with dishes such as leek and truffle tart with Gruyère cheese, and asparagus and pea risotto. The wine list offers everything listed in the store's wine shop, plus a good selection of half bottles and wines by the glass. Mobile phones are banned and smoking discouraged.

Directions: on the Knightsbridge corner of Sloane Street, nearest Tube Knightsbridge

Forte Crest – The Cavendish ❀

A large, purpose-built hotel with a wide range of amenities. Dishes served in the restaurant have a strong Mediterranean bias and may include a rich, home-cured salmon and prawns with a sweet pepper and pesto salsa, or boldly flavoured but delicately textured sea bass

SW1 81 Jermyn Street SW1Y 6JF
Map no: C3
Tel: 0171 839 6379
Chef: Jack Rivas
Proprietor: Forte.
Manager: Julian Groom
Cost: Alc £23.30, fixed-price L £15.50/D £15.50. H/wine £11.95 ❢ Service exc
Credit cards: 🔳 💳 💳 💳
Times: 12.30pm-last L 2.30pm, 6pm-last D 11pm
Menus: *A la carte*, fixed-price L & D, bar menu
Seats: 82. No-smoking area, no pipes or cigars, air-conditioning
Additional: Children welcome, children's portions & menu; ❂ dishes, vegan/other diets on request

Directions: 5 mins walk from Green Park or Piccadilly Tube stations. Behind Fortnum & Masons, near Royal Academy

Forum Hotel ✱

☺ *The Ashburn Restaurant is on the first floor of this, the tallest hotel in London. France and the Mediterranean are the predominant influences in the kitchen. Look out for porchini and ricotta ravioli, supreme of parrot fish with a creamy seafood and white wine ragout, and chocolate truffle cake*

Menus: a la carte, fixed-price buffet L & D,bar menu **Seats:** 246 No-smoking area. Air conditioned **Additional:** children welcomed; children's menu, ❶ dishes, vegan/other diets on request
Directions: 3 mins from Gloucester Road tube

SW7 97 Cromwell Road SW7
Map no: A2
Tel: 0171 370 5757
Chef: Roy Thompson
Proprietor: Inter-Continental Hotels.
Manager: Stephen Mulligan
Cost: Alc from £19, fixed-price buffet L £12.50/D £15.50.
H/wine £12.50 ❗ Service inc
Credit cards: 🖃 🖃 🖃 🖃 OTHER
Times: 12.30pm-last L 2.30pm / D 10.30pm

Four Seasons Hotel ✱✱✱✱✱✱

Smart hotel restaurant where a talented chef is producing some stunning food

Jean Christophe Novelli is a chef whose style is still developing; it makes him rather exciting to watch. The Four Seasons has given him the stable base he so needed, allowing him to consolidate his bold technique. And indeed, recent meals have shown him to be more in control of his ideas, producing dishes of stunning visual impact, with tastes managing to be all at once full, complex, imaginative and well integrated.

Superlatives were strewn across one inspector's report for modern cooking fizzing with ideas and combinations that can, at times, be startling: a stick of lemon grass skewered with scallops and mackerel, gently spiced with a hint of orange and cardamom, accompanied by slivers of beetroot and orange rind and a well balanced beetroot oil; sea bream on a marvellous purée of potato and leek, with a dark, sun-dried tomato sauce; saddle of rabbit, sautéed liver and braised leg on a rich creamy risotto, topped with finely shredded salsify. Desserts were visually breath-taking. A glazed banana tatin, with banana crisp sails looked like a vessel, rum and raisin ice-cream was on deck. A hot chocolate sponge was rich but not heavy with its bitter chocolate centre and white chocolate ice-cream. Crème brûlée catalane had a delicate mandarin flavour and a perfect crisp top.

Offal is a feature here. Braised ox tongue, cheek, lamb's trotter, ox tail and lamb's brain are served with a purée of white beans and honey sauce. Braised pig's trotter is lightly smoked and stuffed with offal and flavoured with black pudding. Or there is roast fillet of beef on a marrow bone topped with a thin, crispy potato crown with baby turnips and red wine sauce. Fish is also well represented. Fillet of turbot poached in coconut milk is served on a bed of almonds and cauliflower purée, on top of bazelle and spinach leaves, lightly sweetened with honey. Or there is marinated pan-fried tuna fillet and star anise set between layers of pasta with baby spinach and fennel. This is lively, adventurous, modern, and it works.

Find time to consult the finely moustachioed sommelier who knows his stuff. His enthusiasm for his subject, plus his knowledge of the detail of the dishes (which rather puts to shame one or two of the waiting staff) make his recommendation worth seeking out. The wine list itself is extensive, pricey, but covers just about every wine growing region in the world. On the other hand there is an excellent list of half bottles and house wines starting at £15.

Directions: Off Park Lane. Nearest Tubes: Hyde Park & Green Park

W1 Park Lane W1A 1AZ
Map no: C3
Tel: 0171 499 0888
Chef: Jean-Christophe Novelli
Proprietor: Four Seasons/Regent Hotels & Resorts.
Rest Manager: Vinicio Paolin
Cost: Alc from £39.50, fixed-price L £25 (3 courses); D £45 (5 courses). H/wine £15 ❗ Service inc
Credit cards: 🖃 🖃 🖃 🖃 OTHER
Times: 12.30pm-last L 3pm, 7pm-last D 10.30pm
Menus: A la carte L & D, fixed-price L & D
Seats: 55. No pipes allowed, air-conditioning
Additional: Children welcome, children's portions & menu; ❶ dishes, vegan/other diets on request

The Fox Reformed ❀

A popular restaurant offering good value for money. The daily-changing blackboard menu features cooking that is bang up-to-date. Expect sliced sweet peppers in olive oil, glazed smoked haddock pot cooked with English mustard, cream and tarragon, or smoked breast of duck with honey vinaigrette

Seats: *40*
Additional: *Children welcome; childen's portions;* ❂ *dishes*
Directions: Opposite the junction with Woodlea Road

N16 176 Stoke Newington Church Street N16
Map no: GtL D4
Tel: 0171 254 5975
Chef: Paul Harper
Proprietors: *Robbie & Carol Richards*
Costs: *Alc £14.50. H/wine £7.35. No service charge*
Credit cards: ▨ ▨
Times: *Last L 2pm/D 10.30pm. Closed Xmas*

French House Dining Room ❀

Set in the heart of Soho, the French House is a lively restaurant with a modern approach. Fashionable up-to-the-minute dishes include grilled ox-tongue, and hake, squid and mussel stew. Highlights of an inspection meal were venison sausages with shallots and apple, and orange and almond cake

Times: 12.30-last L 3pm / D 11.15pm Closed Sun, B/hols, Christmas, Easter
Directions: above the French House pub; nearest Tube Leicester Square

W1 49 Dean Street W1
Map no: D4
Tel: 0171 437 2477
Chef: Margot Clayton
Proprietors: M Clayton, F Henderson and J Spiteri.
Manager: Catherine Bolton
Cost: *Alc* £20. H/wine £8.95
Credit cards: ▨ ▨ ▨ ▨ OTHER

Friends Restaurant ❀

A charming 400 year old timbered restaurant where diners are well looked after. The sound cooking includes such dishes as chicken terrine with roasted tomatoes, bream with angel hair pasta and tartare butter, with lemon cheesecake to finish

Directions: Nearest Tube – Pinner

11 High Street
Pinner
Map no: GtL A4
Tel: 0181 866 0286
Proprietor: Mr Farr

Fulham Road ❀❀❀

As we went to press we were informed that Richard Corrigan had left Fulham Road and was to be replaced by Adam Newell, formerly of St George's, The Heights. This is what we had to say about Newell's cooking at The Heights.

Adam Newell's distinctive cooking style succeeded in marrying flavours in startling ways; indeed, if he keeps on current form, his talent promises great things for the future. However, outré ingredients make one reach for the diners' dictionary: breast of cannette, roasted mahi mahi and cups of ristretto and macchiato and the like frankly need elucidation. Tarts in various guises, fresh anchovy or red mullet with tapenade and rouille, have been high-powered starters. Main courses may include a fair number of game and poultry dishes; pot roasted pigeon comes with shallot tarte tatin, medallion of rabbit with herb risotto and baby beetroot, and chicken two ways – fricassée of corn-fed chicken with peas and broad beans, and breast of black-legged chicken with pearl barley and truffle oil. Puddings can be stunning, as in a chocolate and pear brûlée with raisin madeleines.

At Fulham Road surroundings are elegant but unostentatious, with parquet flooring, walls chequered in shades of honey and

SW3 257-259 Fulham Road SW3
Map no: A1
Tel: 0171 351 7823
Chef: Adam Newell
Proprietor: Stephen Bull
Cost: *Alc* £35, fixed-price L £22 (3 courses). H/wine £13 ▮
Service exc
Credit cards: ▨ ▨ ▨
Times: 12.15pm-last L 2.30pm, last D 11pm. Closed Sat L & Bhs, 1 wk at Xmas
Menus: *A la carte*, fixed-price L
Seats: 80. Air-conditioning
Additional: Children welcome, children's portions; ❂ dishes, vegan/other diets on request

Fulham Road Restaurant

yellow, monochrome prints and an animal frieze banquette; seating is comfortable and tables sufficiently far apart to ensure privacy (the latter a prerequisite, in view of some guests' status). Competent young servers evince an attentive interest in keeping with the lively "buzz" of the atmosphere. In the stylish setting of this Chelsea restaurant, proprietor Stephen Bull presents innovative and assured cooking in the tradition of haute cuisine. His recipe for success – and overriding philosophy – is based on bringing minimal interference to bear on the finest of fresh raw ingredients, which are interpreted by his head chef.

Directions: Close to junction of Fulham Rd & Old Church St

Fung Shing Restaurant ❀❀

☺ *Popular Chinese in the heart of Chinatown serving food that stands head and shoulders above many others*

London's Chinatown is choc-a-bloc with restaurants, especially in flamboyant Gerrard Street. Lisle Street's less brash, more down-at-heel appearance, and Fung Shing's understated exterior, however, does not prevent it from being one of the better Cantonese restaurants. Chef Kwan Fu has been here since opening about 11 years ago, plenty of time in which to build up a regular following for his extensive *carte*. It specialises in seafood and includes a section devoted to bean curd. The most interesting meals are likely to be chosen from the weekly and chef's specials. Succulent, plump lobster, steamed to perfection and served with garlic and mandarin peel, boned eel with the lightest, crispest of batters, fried chilli and seasoned salt, or hearty hotpot of braised duck with cubes of yam and fermented bean curd, its richness cut by fresh leaves and stalks of coriander, for example. Cooking is balanced and carefully judged. Seasonal greens, enlivened with ginger and garlic make the ideal accompaniment, whatever your choice. The wine list is better chosen than many in this area, and there is Chinese beer.

Directions: Nearest Tube: Leicester Square. Behind Empire Cinema

WC2 15 Lisle Street WC2
Map no: D3
Tel: 0171 437 1539
Chef: Kwun Fu
Proprietor: Jimmy Jim
Cost: Alc £20, fixed-price L/D from £12.50. H/wine £9 ❢
Service exc
Credit cards: 🟦 📰 🈺 💳 OTHER
Times: Noon-last D 11.15pm.
Closed 24-26 Dec
Menus: A la carte, fixed-price L & D
Seats: 85. Air-conditioning
Additional: Children welcome; ❤ dishes, vegan/other diets on request

Gay Hussar ✿

W1 2 Greek Street W1
Map no: D4
Tel: 0171 437 0973
Chef: Lazlo Holecz
Cost: Alc £25, fixed-price L £16.
H/wine £9.50. Service inc
Credit cards: ⬛ 📇 📇 📇 OTHER
Times: Last L 2.30pm/D 10.45

All around, terrace cafes and trendy eating places come and go, yet the Gay Hussar resolutely plods on. It is a popular haunt, noted for an old-fashioned style of service and setting. Look for Hungarian dishes ranging from pressed boar's head to cold fillet of pike and creamed beetroot salad

Seats: 70. Air conditioned
Additional: Children welcome; children's portions. ✪ dishes
Directions: Of Soho Square. Nearest Tube – Tottenham Court Road

Gilbert's ✿✿

SW7 Exhibition Road SW7 2HF
Map no: A2
Tel: 0171 589 8947
Chef: Akim Kalsau
Proprietor: Julia Chalkley
Cost: Fixed-price L £12.50/D £17. H/wine £11.50 ❢ Service exc
Credit cards: ⬛ 📇 📇 📇 OTHER
Times: Last L 2pm, last D 10pm. Closed Sat L, Sun & Bhs, 1 wk at Xmas, 2 days at Easter
Menus: Fixed-price L & D, pre-theatre
Seats: 30. Air-conditioning
Additional: ✪ dishes

☺ *Confident British cooking with character and appeal in a personally-run restaurant*

After feeding the mind at the South Kensington museums, a meal at this small, friendly restaurant near the Tube station should refresh the body satisfactorily. Proprietor Julia Chalkley now has an assistant chef but her influence can still be seen on the menu and in the cooking. Standards remain high, resulting in honest and appealing dishes. Typical of first courses is the ravioli of wild mushrooms with home-made pasta chosen at a recent inspection meal. Alternatives may include grilled aubergine, sweet red pepper and goats' cheese. A main course of tender and moist braised smoked ham came with spinach and a Madeira sauce that had a deft, light touch. Sauté of calves' liver with tarragon and confit of guinea fowl with chestnuts and bacon have also been recommended. The menu is a set-price two or three-course meal, with puddings costing extra. On this occasion a boozy bread pudding was a little disappointing; chocolate tipsy cake and sticky toffee pudding were better choices. To complement the food, a short but nicely balanced wine list is offered.

Directions: Bottom end of Exhibition Rd. Nearest Tube: South Kensington

Chillies were one of the earliest plants to be cultivated in the pre-Columbian New World. Archaeological evidence suggests that they were used at least 8,000 years ago to impart flavour and spiciness to food. The Mayans used 30 different varieties of chilli and recent evidence shows that the Aztecs used them in almost every dish. Today chillies are grown throughout the world. The characteristic for which chillies are best known is their heat. The fiery sensation is caused by capsaicin, a potent chemical that survives both cooking and freezing. As well as causing a burning sensation, this substance triggers the brain to produce endorphins, natural pain killers that promote a sense of well-being and stimulation. Also, capsaicin is a natural decongestant. The hottest chilli in the world is probably the Scotch bonnet chilli (so named because its shape resembles a Highlander's cap). A single Scotch bonnet has the fire power of 50 jalapeno chillies. Grown in the Caribbean it is an essential ingredient in Jamaican jerk dishes. When handling chillies you should wear rubber gloves. Wash your hands with soap afterwards and take care not to touch your face, or eyes. If your hands start to sting after handling chillies, rub them with a little toothpaste.

Gloucester Hotel ❀

☺ *Major refurbishment has recently been completed at this purpose-built South Kensington hotel. Modish Brit-meets-Med food is served in the restaurant, where choices may include chargrilled baby squid with corn cake and a red chilli dressing, and braised beef with country vegetables and parsley dumplings*

Directions: Turn right out of Gloucester Road Tube (2 mins). Entrance on Courtfield Rd close to Cromwell Rd

SW7 4-18 Harrington Gardens
SW7 4LH
Map no: A1
Tel: 0171 411 4212
Chef: Mark Edwards
Proprietor: CDL.
Manager: Neil Armishaw
Cost: Alc £22. H/wine £9.95 ♥
Service inc
Credit cards: 🖪 💳 💳 🖭
Times: Noon-last L 3pm, last D
10.45pm
Menus: A la carte, fixed-price L
& D, pre-theatre, bar menu
Seats: 155. No-smoking area,
air-conditioning
Additional: Children welcome,
children's portions; ♥ dishes,
vegan/other diets on request

Good Earth Restaurant ❀

☺ *Frequently crowded Chinese that's far from run-of-the-mill. The lengthy menu covers most regions. Soft shell crab with spiced salt and peppercorns, bang-bang chicken, steamed sea bass with spring onions and ginger, mustard chicken Mandarin and aubergine in garlic sauce, have all been particularly enjoyed*

Seats: 100. Air conditioned
Additional: Children welcome; ♥ menu
Directions: On Mill Hill Circus

NW7 143-145 Broadway
Mill Hill NW7
Map no: D3
Tel: 0181 959 7011
Chef: Ah Chiu
Proprietor: Joe Chan.
Manageress: Jenny Siu
Cost: Alc £18 H/wine £8 Service
exc
Credit cards: 🖪 💳 💳 🖭 OTHER
Times: last L 2.30pm./D
11.15pm Closed 24-27 Dec

Gopal's Restaurant ❀

☺ *A consistent standard of cooking makes Gopal's one of the best Indian restaurants in London. The menu includes such wonderful dishes as steamed chicken cooked on the bone in a sealed pot, prawns with yoghurt and coconut sauce, and Indian cottage cheese cooked with chopped tomatoes, onions and coriander seeds*

Menus: A la carte
Seats: 50. Air-conditioning
Additional: Children welcome, children's portions on request;
♥ dishes
Directions: Off Oxford St & Shaftesbury Ave

W1 12 Bateman Street
W1V 5TD
Map no: D4
Tel: 0171 434 0840
Chef: N P Pittal
Proprietor: N P Pittal
Cost: Alc £14.95 Service exc
Credit cards: 🖪 💳 💳 OTHER
Times: Last L 3pm, last D
11.15pm

Goring Hotel ❀❀

An imaginative approach to classical European cooking in a stylish hotel with a country house atmosphere

SW1 Beeston Place
Grosvenor Gardens SW1
Map no: C2
Tel: 0171 396 9000
Chef: John Elliott
Proprietor: George E Goring.
Manager: William A Cowpe
Cost: Fixed-price L £22.50/D
£27.50. H/wine £15 ▼ Service
exc
Credit cards: ▦ ▦ ▦ ▦ OTHER
Times: 12.30pm-last L 2.30pm,
6pm-last D 10pm
Menus: Fixed-price L & D, pre-
theatre, bar menu
Seats: 70. Air conditioned. No
cigars/pipes in restaurant
Additional: Children welcome;
children's portions, ✿ dishes,
vegan/other diets on request

The real strength of this Victoria-based hotel with a distinct country house atmosphere is its commitment to customers, and this is nowhere more evident than in the newly refurbished restaurant. Here a willing and courteous team of staff – many of them long-serving – provide professional service to match the dedicated approach of those in the kitchen. John Elliott's fixed-price three-course menus include some very imaginative treatments of classic British/European cooking. Tagliatelle with Paris mushrooms might be followed by salmon fishcakes on a fine spinach and sorrel sauce, then a perfectly cooked roast lamb with a herb crust; puddings include a well made prune and Bramley apple tart served with an Armagnac crème brûlée. Tempting appetisers like warm artichoke provençale or deep-fried cheese puffs precede the meal, and home-made chocolate truffles accompany the excellent espresso coffee that ends it. A list of over 200 bins offers a good selection of classic premier cru-classe Bordeaux, as well as Burgundies and Californian, in amounts varying from magnums to half bottles.

Directions: Between Buckingham Palace & Grosvenor Gardens, two minutes from Victoria Station

Great Nepalese Restaurant ❀

☺ *The bland street beside Euston Station hides a real find. Nepalese dishes are this popular restaurant's strength, but everything it does is noted for both the freshness of the raw materials and the well-made sauces. Try boneless chicken, deep-fried and served with tomato pickle, and 'sahi korma', lamb with special spices*

Menus: A la carte, fixed-price
Seats: 48
Additional: Children welcome, children's portions; ✿ /vegan dishes
Directions: 150 yds from E side of Euston Station

NW1 48 Eversholt Street
NW1 1DA
Map no: D5
Tel: 0171 388 6737/5935
Chef: M Miah
Proprietor: G P Manandhar
Cost: Alc £12.50, fixed-price
L/D £10.95. H/wine £6.55
Service exc
Credit cards: ▦ ▦ ▦ ▦
Times: Noon-last L 2.30pm,
6pm-last D 11.30pm. Closed
25/26 Dec

Greek Valley Restaurant ❀❀

Good value Greek Cypriot cooking in a homely setting

The Bosnics maintain a cosy and informal atmosphere in their popular restaurant. The food is standard Greek cooking although Peter Bosnic adds his own variations to dishes. *Carte* and set-price menus are offered, and the spring and summer specials (Monday to Thursday only) are particularly good value for money. Effie Bosnic supervises the restaurant and is helpful in explaining all dishes fully. On a recent visit, our inspector tried shish kofte, lightly spiced, home-made minced lamb sausages. Moussaka offered a slight variation on the traditional recipe, layers of vegetables being substituted for purely aubergines, except that the result was a little dull and disappointing. Puddings are limited: baklava, ice-cream and a good example of kataifi (shredded pastry and syrup). Familiar favourites include dolmades, beef stifado and kleftico, but there are less well-known dishes such as haloumi (salty Cyprus cheese, grilled) and 'gharithes yiouvetsi' – prawns in tomato sauce. The reasonably priced wine list consists mostly of Greek and Cypriot wines.

Directions: Off Abbey Rd in St John's Wood, nr Saatchi Gallery. Main roads Finchley Rd NW3 & Maida Vale

NW8 130 Boundary Road
NW8 0RH
Map no: GtL C3
Tel: 0171 624 3217
Chef: Peter Bosnic
Proprietors: Peter & Effie Bosnic
Cost: *Alc* £11.50, fixed-price D £7.95 (Mon-Thur). H/wine £6.50 Service exc
Credit cards: ▨ ▥
Times: 6pm-last D midnight. Closed L, Sun
Menus: *A la carte*, fixed-price, ❶
Seats: 62. Air-conditioning
Additional: Children welcome, children's portions & menu; ❶ dishes, vegan/other diets on request

The Greenhouse ❀❀❀

Best of British – plus a few foreigners – on Gary Rhodes home ground

W1 27a Hays Mews W1X 7RJ
Map no: C3
Tel: 0171 499 3331
Chef: Gary Rhodes
Proprietor: David Levin
Cost: *Alc* £27. H/wine £10.50 ❢
Service exc
Credit cards: ▨ ▥ ▧ ▨
Times: 12.15-last L 2.30pm, 7pm-last D 11.15pm. Closed Sat L & Bhs
Menus: *A la carte*
Seats: 100. Air-conditioning
Additional: Children welcome, children's portions; ❶ dishes, vegan/other diets on request in advance

Tucked away in the centre of Mayfair may be a paradox, but Hay's Mews is exactly that. The fact that it can take two weeks notice to secure a reservation is testimony to the huge following TV chef Gary Rhodes has gained. Whilst our Gary might not be at the stove as often as visitors would wish, the food presented is carefully constructed and largely embodies the ethos that British is best. A signature dish of braised oxtail, is never off the menu, and the salmon fish cakes remain equally popular. One dish which has achieved celebrity status in its own right, since it was illustrated on the cover of Gary's first book, is smoked haddock with Welsh rarebit on a tomato and chive salad. Other old favourites are given a shot in the arm and brought into the nineties – baked cod with Gruyère cheese and spinach, or peppered roast lamb with a caper

and mint jus, for instance, but there are also a few foreigners such
as Caesar salad and beef carpaccio with fresh Parmesan. A recently
sampled dish of mushroom risotto with sautéed black pudding was
sensational; the creamy, delicious rice given an earthy twist by the
offal. Sometimes, though, the juggling of ingredients can miss the
mark slightly, and a main course of pan-fried halibut with noodles
in anchovy cream sauce and crispy Bayonne ham was spoilt by the
insipid sauce. A tender chicken breast served on a bed of braised
pearl barley with lemon and thyme had more harmonious flavours,
but the thyme did tend to dominate. Pastry work was a revelation,
and our inspector ate an unforgettable bread and butter pudding
scented with nutmeg. A velvety, smooth chocolate tart with crisp
pastry was also spot on. The wine list is well chosen, and prices
start at £10.50 for 'Le Vin de Levin', owner David Levin's own
wines from Touraine.

Directions: Behind Dorchester Hotel just off Hill St, nr Berkeley Sq

Green's Restaurant & Oyster Bar ❀❀

*The best of traditional British, and some inspired modern interpretations,
served in club-like surroundings*

A solid, old fashioned sort of place, deeply comfortable with
reassuring food. What else could it be, with shepherd's pie served
every Monday, faggots and pease pudding on Tuesday, steak and
kidney pie on Wednesday, and so on. But the cooking is not all
retrospective. Salmon tartare with yoghurt and chervil dressing,
grilled tuna steak with marinated grilled vegetables, and roast
chicken breast with spaghetti of vegetables and tarragon jus, reveals
a kitchen with a lively awareness of what is fashionable. Starters
range from squid and oyster risotto, native oysters, and quail's eggs
to smoked cod's roe, and smoked eel fillets. Other quintessential
British dishes (for the traditionalists) are available every day. Look
out for bangers and mash with crispy bacon and onion gravy, calves'
liver and bacon with mashed potato, and mixed grill. There is a
small choice of puddings – redcurrant cheesecake and lemon tart,
for example, as well as ice-creams and sorbets. British cheeses are
supplied by Paxton & Whitfield in nearby Jermyn Street. The wine
list has been carefully selected and includes some reputable bins
and wines of the month.

SW1 36 Duke Street
St. James's SW1Y 6DF
Map: D3
Tel: 0171 930 4566
Chef: Michael Hirst
Proprietor: Simon Parker-
Bowles.
Manager: Nick Boddington
Cost: *Alc* £27, H/wine £10 ❢
Service exc
Credit cards: 🔲 🔳 🔳 🔳
Times: noon-last L 2.45, 6pm-
last D 11pm. Closed Sun eve,
Dec 25, 26 & 31
Menus: *A la carte*
Seats: 70. Air conditioned
Additional: children welcomed;
❶ dishes, other diets on request

Directions: near Fortnum & Mason, opposite Cavendish Hotel

Halcyon Hotel ❀❀❀

*The Room at The Halcyon, an elegant modern restaurant offering elegant
modern cuisine*

Essentially a large townhouse, situated on Holland Park Avenue,
this hotel opens into a splendid, welcoming foyer with fresh flowers,
fine pictures and antique furnishings. The lower ground floor has a
small lounge bar, popular with local media people, and an elegant
modern restaurant. This is The Room, where chef Martin Hadden
capably prepares his imaginative modern dishes.
   An early spring meal started with smooth foie gras terrine. It was

W11 81 Holland Park W11 3RZ
Map no: GtL C3
Tel: 0171 221 5411
Chef: Martin Hadden
Proprietor: Halcyon Hotel
Corp Ltd.
Manager: Jérôme Poussin
Cost: *Alc* £32.50, fixed-price L
£24/D £30. H/wine £9.50 ❢
Service exc
Credit cards: 🔲 🔳 🔳 🔳

well balanced by crisp green beans and tart baby spinach, and came with good brioche. Other options included pan-fried langoustines accompanied by celeriac purée and truffle, and roast pigeon with a morel sausage, bacon and sage. For the main course sea bass was chosen. This was served with an intense scallop mousse, soft confit of fennel, trimmed asparagus and beurre blanc, again a balanced dish with no unnecessary frills. A separate vegetarian menu is available, with three starters and main courses, and dishes such as baked goats' cheese crottin with fresh tomato coulis, and millefeuille of artichoke and celeriac with chargrilled vegetables and a truffle sauce.

Dessert was less successful. A plum tart with an undercooked puff pastry base, served with a robust plum sauce and an understated cardamom ice-cream. Bread, coffee and petits fours were all first class, demonstrating the closest attention to detail. The friendly team of restaurant staff and the short but serious wine list contribute well to the pleasure of a meal here.

Directions: 200 metres up Holland Park Ave from Shepherds Bush roundabout. 2 mins walk from Holland Park Tube

Times: Last L 2.30pm, last D 10.30pm. Closed Sat L
Menus: A la carte, fixed-price L & D, bar menu, 7 course Gastronomic
Seats: 55. Air-conditioning
Additional: Children's portions; ❤/vegan dishes

The Halkin Hotel ❀❀❀

An innovative modern approach to classical Milanese cooking at this stylish hotel restaurant

SW1 Halkin Street
Belgravia SW1X 7DJ
Map no: C2
Tel: 0171 333 1000
Chef: Stefano Cavallini
Proprietor: Thierry Tollis
Cost: Alc £39, fixed-price L £32 (3 courses)/D £32.50. H/wine £15 ❗ Service inc
Credit cards: 🂱 🔳 🔳 🖳 OTHER
Times: 12.30-last L 2.30pm, 7.30pm-last D 11pm. Closed Sat/Sun L
Menus: A la carte, fixed-price L & D, bar menu
Seats: 40-50. Cigars and pipes not allowed in restaurant, air-conditioning
Additional: Children welcome, children's portions; ❤ dishes

A smart international crowd is served by a smart international staff in the coolly elegant restaurant at the Halkin Hotel. The young chef, Stefano Cavallini, is a protégé of the highly regarded Milanese chef Gualtiero Marchesi. He strives to match technical skill with dishes that are based on modern thought and experimentation. Occasional lapses in execution, dull flavours and incorrect temperature, for example, detract marginally from the end product. In the evening the five menu headings offer a choice of four courses, with a separate vegetarian section. Dishes sampled this year included an exceptional appetiser, a salad of langoustine and asparagus with a delightful shellfish vinaigrette served with sun-dried tomatoes, lemon and olives. Foie gras with Castelluccio lentils provided a wonderful contrast between the earthy lentils and the delicately pan-fried goose liver. A main course of gratinated saddle of lamb comprised a selection of best end, with a dense basil and parsley crust, and sweetbreads, kidneys and brains, all lightly cooked with crisp coatings. The dish was simply presented with a richly flavoured timbale of aubergine and tomato set in a heavily seasoned lamb jus. When making a choice from the dessert menu, it is advisable to overlook the cost and opt for 'di tutto un po', a selection of Italian desserts which may include the forceful mascarpone and cream-based tiramisu. The wine list covers Italy in some depth and there is also a short, top class selection of Bordeaux.

Directions: Between Belgrave Sq & Grosvenor Place. Access via Chapel St into Headford Place & left into Halkin St

The Hampshire 🏵🏵

A theatre-land hotel serving straightforward British/European cooking in comfort and style

The Hampshire hotel enjoys one of the best locations in London: right on Leicester Square in the heart of the West End. Its restaurant is called, rather aptly, 'Celebrities', popular with theatregoers and luvvies rather than the teeming masses queuing for the Square's various cinemas. Comfortable decor, professional service, and eye-catching menus, including *carte*, set price and pre-theatre options set the tone. Sensible raw produce is utilised in sensible proportions and pleasant combinations, typified by an excellent first course of lightly roasted scallops served with a ragout of coral and ceps. Real flavour burst from the venison cutlets (from a Norfolk farm) served with good spätlzi and perfectly cooked spinach. Sauces, though good, are second division in comparison to the quality of the meat. Desserts from the trolley are competent. Though the wine list has a corporate feel, there is an adequate variety to please most tastes and pockets.

Directions: S side of Leicester Sq on corner with St Martin's St

WC2 Leicester Square
WC2H 7LH
Map no: D4
Tel: 0171 839 9399
Chef: Colin Button
Proprietor: Edwardian Hotels.
Gen. Manager: P N Proquitte
Cost: Alc £40, fixed-price
L £19.50 (3 course)/D £27.50.
H/wine £14 Service inc
Credit cards: 🆇 🖩 🖾 📇
Times: 12.30-last L 2.30pm,
6pm-last D 11pm
Menus: A la carte, fixed-price L
& D, pre-theatre, banquet parties
Seats: 65. Air-conditioning
Additional: Children welcome,
children's portions on request;
🟊 dishes, vegan/other diets on
request

Harbour City 🏵

☺ *A lively restaurant in the heart of China Town which offers a special dim sum menu (12 noon-5pm) with a bewildering but appetising choice. Several set dinners and party menus are also available. Saké and a few Oriental wines are listed from an inexpensive international choice*

Times: Noon-last L 5pm, last D 11.30pm. Closed Xmas day
Menus: A la carte, fixed-price D
Seats: 160. Air-conditioning
Additional: Children welcome; 🟊 dishes, other diets on request
Directions: Nearest Tube: Leicester Square & Piccadilly

W1 46 Gerrard Street W1
Map no: D3
Tel: 0171 439 7859
Chef: Hing Lee
Proprietor: Harbour City
Restaurant
Cost: Alc £10.50, fixed-price
L from £1.60 (1 course)/D
£10.50. ⦿ Service exc
Credit cards: 🆇 🖩 🖾 📇 OTHER

Hilaire 🏵🏵🏵

Stylish South Ken restaurant with boldly confident, unfussy seasonal cooking

The style is European, robust and traditional. Both the daily changing fixed-price and *carte* menus offer serious dishes of great clarity, lacking all superflous frills. Typically, head chef/proprietor Bryan Webb marries luxury ingredients with rustic ones; oysters

SW7 68 Old Brompton Road
SW7 3LQ
Map no: A1
Tel: 0171 584 8993
Chef: Bryan Webb
Proprietor: Bryan Webb and
Dick Pyle.
Manager: Bernard Esseul

'au gratin' with laverbread and Stilton, escalope of salmon with asparagus and samphire salad, griddled fillet of John Dory with pea mash, dill and mustard. Offal is well presented – calves sweetbreads with mashed potato and olives, or tongue with mustard and caper sauce, for example. In a range of other dishes, such as potato pancakes, smoked eel and horseradish cream, chargrilled swordfish with spinach, chilli and pancetta, or baked artichokes with goats cheese, Mittle Europe meets the Med.

An early spring inspection meal began with smooth, intensely flavoured foie gras and duck live parfait, accompanied by toasted, buttery brioche. A dish of home-made tagliatelle with fresh morels (just in season) was quite outstanding, the pasta perfectly cooked 'with bite'. Almost transluscent roast cod with white beans, radicchio and lemon vinaigrette displayed fine judgement in timing and understanding of textures and taste balance. An old-fashioned oxtail faggot was also much savoured for its richly flavoured meat, set on a light, red wine jus and served with good creamed potatoes. Both main courses came with spinach, celeeriac purée and sweetly braised leeks with Gruyère and mozarella cheese. Other main courses might include fillet of lamb with tapenade and wild garlic, or veal cutlet with braised chicory and sage and Parmesan crust. Simply presented puddings, such as white and dark chocolate terrine, fresh apricot and almond tart and blood orange sorbet, are also recommended. British farmhouse cheeses come from Neal's Yard.

Directions: On N side of Old Brompton Rd about half way between South Kensington Tube and junction with Queensgate

Cost: *Alc* £28-£38, fixed-price L £20.50 (3 courses)/D £32.50 (4 courses). H/wine £10.20 ♥
Service exc
Credit cards: 🟦 🟫 🟫 🟦 OTHER
Times: 12.15-last L 2.30pm, 6.30-last D 11.30pm. Closed Sun, Sat L & Bhs
Menus: *A la carte*, fixed-price L & D, post-theatre
Seats: 60. Air-conditioning
Additional: Children welcome, children's portions; ♥ dishes, other diets on request in advance

Hogarth Hotel ❀

☺ *A pleasant hotel in the heart of Kensington serving sound food. A summer inspection meal consisted of tortellin with crab mousse and lime jus, followed by noisette of lamb with a port and rosemary sauce. Desserts include a brandy snap basket with an exotic fruit sorbet*

Directions: Nearest Tube – Earls Court

SW5 33 Hogarth Road Kensington SW5 0QQ
Map no: A1
Tel: 0171 370 6831
Chef: Andrew Tortice
Proprietor: Marston Hotels. Manager: G S Breese
Cost: *Alc* £16.70, fixed-price L/D £14.95 (3 courses). H/wine £8.95 ♥ Service exc
Credit cards: 🟦 🟫 🟫 🟦
Times: Noon-last L 1.45pm, 6pm-last D 9.30pm
Menus: *A la carte*, fixed-price L & D, pre-theatre, bar menu
Seats: 40. No-smoking area, air-conditioning
Additional: Children welcome, children's portions & menu; ♥ dishes, vegan/other diets on request

Holiday Inn Mayfair ❀

A smart, modern hotel in a great central location, just minutes from Piccadilly, Bond Street and the Royal Academy. The restaurant is stylish, the walls decorated with hand painted murals, and an international theme runs through both the menu and the wine list. Cooking is fair

W1 3 Berkeley Street W1
Map no: C3
Tel: 0171 493 8282
Chef: Barry Brewington
Proprietors: Holiday Inn.
Restaurant
Manager: Nathan Middlemiss
Cost: *Alc* from £22.50, 2 course "Quick Lunch" £8.95, fixed-price L £15.75 /D £19.50 (4 course). H/wine £14 ❢ Service exc.
Times: noon-last L 3pm, 5.30pm-last D 11pm.
Closed Sat L
Menus: *A la carte*, fixed-price L & D, pre-theatre, bar menu
Additional: children welcome; children's menu, ❤ dishes, vegan/other diets on request

Directions: Between Piccadilly and Berkeley Square, nearest Tube Green Park

Hotel Conrad ❀❀

A fashionable establishment producing food with a light touch that refuses to compromise on quality

Chelsea Harbour SW10 0XG
Map no: GtL C2
Tel: 0171 823 3000
Chef: Peter Brennan
Proprietors: Conrad Hotels.
General Manager: Doreen Boulding
Cost: *Alc* £33, fixed-price L £16.50/D £22.50. H/wine£15.50 Service exc
Credit cards: 🁢 🁢 🁢 🁢
Times: noon-last L 2.30pm, 6pm-last D 10.30pm
Menus: *A la carte*, fixed-price L & D, pre-theatre, Sun brunch, bar menu
Seats: 45. Air conditioned

Both architecturally and aesthetically modish Chelsea Harbour's Hotel Conrad currently offers just a brasserie supplemented by a lounge service of more informal dishes. This should be changed by 1996 as refurbishment and repositioning are due to add more space to both: a restaurant will replace the old brasserie which will become the lounge and secondary eating area. Meanwhile, the cooking continues to be modern with a strong European flavour and a determined emphasis on offering healthier and lighter sauced dishes. The menu is short but balanced and varied, although, apart from one or two seasonal dishes such as game, it doesn't appear to change its repertoire too much. Typically, pasta and pulses feature alongside more salad-based dishes, spiced and herbed dressings alongside more robust saucing. Both a wild mushroom and Parmesan risotto, and a warm scallop tomato and basil salad, prove that taste and texture can be enjoyed without too many calories or fats, although this doesn't prevent some dangerous looking desserts being offered, such as a warm chocolate treacle tart with fudge sauce and crème fraîche!

Additional: children welcome; children's menu, ❶ dishes, vegan/other on request

Directions: Chelsea Harbour, overlooking marina

Hotel Inter-Continental ❀❀❀

Exceptional cooking, plus soufflés savoury and sweet in the aptly named Le Soufflé

Centrally located, overlooking Hyde Park Corner, this large modern hotel provides smart facilities and a high standard of service to an international clientele. Le Soufflé is the elegant, discreetly lit restaurant, in the brilliant hands of Peter Kromberg for some twenty years. He and his team produce some very fine cooking indeed, and, given the name of the restaurant, it is no surprise to discover that soufflés are the speciality of the house, the *carte* offering maybe two out of a dozen dishes as starters, such as hot asparagus soufflé with smoked eel, crème fraîche and horseradish, or Gruyère cheese soufflé with a poached egg in the middle, served with a salad and cheese soldiers. Around five sweet soufflés are listed on the dessert menu (from a choice of nine items), including a particularly light, seasonal creation along with more decadent examples – perhaps hot Grand Marnier soufflé with chocolate truffles served with an iced nougatine and lime soufflé. To balance, there is also a range of low fat, high fibre dishes available at each stage of the meal, marked with a healthy heart symbol. These might include a main course of lightly poached free-range chicken suprême, filled with young vegetables, five spice sauce and tagliatelle noodles. Vegetarian options are also available, such as baked spring vegetables in a cep mushroom and truffle cream. In addition to the *carte*, there is a fixed-price lunch menu and a set 'Choix du Chef' of four or seven courses. A well designed wine list complements the food, with a page of wines by the glass, recommended bottles and an index.

W1 1 Hamilton Place
Hyde Park Corner W1
Map no: C2
Tel: 0171 409 3131
Chef: Peter Kromberg
Proprietors: Inter-Continental.
Manager: Josef Lanser
Cost: *Alc* £ 40, fixed-price
L £27.50 / D £37.50 (4 courses),
H/wine £15 ❢ Service exc
Credit cards: ◼ ▦ ▦ 🌄 OTHER
Times: 12.30-last L 3.30pm (Sun
noon-4pm), 7.30pm-last D
10.30pm (Sat 11.15pm). Closed
Sat L, Sun D, 2 wks after
Christmas
Seats: 80. No-smoking area. No
pipes. Air conditioned
Menus: *A la carte*, fixed-price
L & D, bar menu
Additional: Children permitted;
❶ dishes, vegan/other diets by
arrangement

Directions: on Hyde Park Corner. Nearest Tube – Hyde Park Corner

The Hothouse ❀❀

Interesting warehouse conversion serving French inspired food

Colourful wall hangings and ethnic-style cotton tablecloths contrast strikingly with exposed brickwork at this warehouse conversion that also takes in bare timbers and stripped floors. Swedish chef Christian Sanderfelt has put together a menu which is French in inspiration with Mediterranean overtones. The cooking tries hard, although sometimes the results are a mixed bag. At a meal in June, for instance, a timbale of lobster and sweetbread wrapped in grilled aubergine was chosen. In a firm mousseline, studded with lobster meat and chunks of calves' sweetbreads, the flavours worked well together, set off by a drizzled gazpacho purée, tomato coulis and a

E1 78-80 Wapping Lane E1
Map no: GtL D3
Tel: 0171 488 4797
Chef: Christian Sanderfelt
Proprietor: Nigel Fenner-
Fownes.
Manager: John Masterson
Cost: *Alc* £20, fixed-price L / D
£12.50 (2 course). H/wine £9.50
❢ Service 12.5% inc
Credit cards: ◼ ▦ ▦ OTHER
Times: noon-last L 3.30pm, last
D 11pm Closed Bhs

tarragon flavoured oil, yet seared gravad lax, although fresh with a lovely crispened skin and tangy mustard and parsley puréed sauce, was a tad overcured, thus a bit salty. A heavy hand with the salt marred seabass with seafood croquet and tomato and broadbeans. Desserts may include fresh vanilla and pear terrine with honey tea sauce. The pleasant but slow service would improve with a little staff training.

Directions: 2 mins walk Wapping Tube, 5 mins taxi Tower Hill/ St. Catherine's Wharf

Menus: *A la carte,* fixed-price L & D, bar menu
Seats: 100. Air conditioned
Additional: children welcome; ✿ dishes, children's portions, other diets on request

Hudson's Restaurant ✿

☺ *The waitresses wear appropriate costume in this 'Victorian Dining-room', and the style of cooking is simple. A meal here might consist of saffron mussels with white wine and cream, followed by roast guinea fowl, and fruit compote with honey ice-cream*

Menus: *A la carte,* fixed-price L & D, pre-theatre **Seats:** 50
Additional: Children welcome, children's portions; ✿ dishes, vegan/other diets on request
Directions: Left towards Regents Park (Baker St N side), next to Sherlock Holmes Museum

NW1 239 Baker Street
NW1 6XE
Map no: B4
Tel: 0171 935 3130
Chef: Peter Lattimore
Proprietor: Linda Piley
Cost: Alc £18.25, fixed-price L/D £16.50 (3 courses). H/wine £9.25 Service exc
Credit cards: 🔳 🔳 🔳 🔳 OTHER
Times: 10.30am-last L 2.30pm, last D 10.30pm. Closed Xmas day

Hyatt Carlton Tower Hotel ✿✿

A fine modern hotel serving everything from light meals to flamboyant French cuisine

SW1 Cadogan Place SW1X 9PY
Map no: B2
Tel: 0171 235 1234
Chef: Bernard Gaume
Proprietor: Hyatt Carlton Tower Hotel.
Gen Manager: Michael Gray
Cost: Fixed-price L £23.50/D £29.50. H/wine £14.50 Service exc
Credit cards: 🔳 🔳 🔳 🔳
Times: 12.30-last L 2.45pm, 6.30pm-last D 11.15pm
Menus: *A la carte,* fixed-price L & D
Seats: 150. Air-conditioning
Additional: Children welcome, children's portions; ✿ dishes, vegan/other diets on request

Towering above the heart of Knightsbridge, the higher floors of this busy international hotel offer splendid views over London. Service is courteous and efficient, particularly in the Chinoiserie Lounge, where light meals and refreshments are served. The popular Rib Room offers good straightforward dishes featuring prime cuts of meat, while upstairs in the Chelsea Room, chef Bernard Gaume presents menus of more flamboyant French cuisine. High quality ingredients and cooking skills were evident at a recent dinner. Marked out as a highlight was a light and fluffy mousseline of crab. Both main courses – baked turbot and a fillet of duck on a bed of green lentils – were correctly cooked, displaying a good combination of flavours and textures. A dessert trolley is supplemented by hot puddings, which included a raspberry soufflé. Despite good flavour this proved rather moist and heavy but the meal ended on a high with good espresso and petits fours.

Directions: From A4 (West Brompton Rd) to Knightsbridge Tube station turn right into Sloane St and next left onto Cadogan Place

The Hyde Park Hotel 🏵🏵

Stately Knightsbridge hotel undergoing considerable refurbishment

This great Edwardian hotel, now one of Forte's British flagships, is sited between the bustle of Knightsbridge and the relative tranquillity of Hyde Park. The Restaurant on the Park looks out over the latter, and offers a short, Italian-influenced menu. It is not to be confused with Marco Pierre White's Restaurant, in the former grill room in the basement (see entry). Our inspection meal, however, was of variable quality, in need of a lighter touch throughout. An appetiser of beef carpaccio was tender but lacked flavour and was underseasoned, and home-made ravioli was adequate in texture, but laden with a heavy potato and mushroom filling. Another starter, a tomato and fontina cheese pie was far better constructed, served with a mushroom salad. Main courses fared no better with sea bass of a disappointingly poor quality, and fillet of lamb with a crude thyme-infused sauce. An almond and apple tart was simply dry and uninspired. Espresso, at least, was sound. It should be said that, not long after our inspection, the kitchen was due to be closed for refurbishment – a prospect which may have had an effect on the quality of the dishes sampled.

Directions: Located at junction of Sloane St & Knightsbridge

SW1 66 Knightsbridge
SW1Y 7LA
Map no: B2
Tel: 0171 235 2000
Chef: Antonio Fallini
Proprietor: Forte.
Manager: Paolo Biscioni
Cost: *Alc* £30, fixed-price
L £25/D £36. H/wine £19 ♥
Service inc
Credit cards: 🔳 ▨ ▨ ▨ OTHER
Times: 7am-last L 2.30pm, last
D 11pm
Menus: *A la carte*, fixed-price L
& D, pre-theatre, bar menu, one
hour business lunch
Seats: 60. No-smoking area, air-
conditioning
Additional: Children welcome,
children's portions & menu;
♥ dishes, other diets on request

Imperial City 🏵

A popular Chinese restaurant beneath the Royal Exchange. The menu is short but is a fair introduction to an assortment of regional Chinese dishes. Hong Kong style prawns and scallops, braised red pork casserole, Shanghai style, spicy Szechuan dan dan noodles, and Peking braised lamb are typical examples

Times: 11.30am-last D 8.30pm. Closed Sat, Sun, Xmas, 1 Jan & Bhs
Seats: 180. Air conditioned
Additional: Children welcome; ♥ dishes
Directions: Royal Exchange is off Cornhill. Nearest Tube – Bank

EC3 Royal Exchange
Cornhill EC3
Map no: G4
Tel: 0171 626-3437
Chef: K L Tan
Proprietor: Thai Restaurants Ltd.
Manager: Nick Lee
Cost: Fixed-price L/D £13.90 (3
courses), £18.90, £24.80. Wine
£8.50 ♥ Service exc
Credit cards: 🔳 ▨ ▨ ▨ OTHER

Indian Connoisseurs 🏵

☺ *Good value Indian and Bangladeshi cooking is served at this cosy little restaurant. Standard tandoori and biryani dishes feature but regional seafood, and game, in season, have their place on the menu. Meat and vegetarian thalis (set meals) are worth exploring*

Menus: *A la carte*, fixed-price L & D, ♥ **Seats:** 46. No-smoking area,
Air conditioning **Additional:** ♥ dishes, vegan/other diets on request
Directions: Off Praed St close to BR Paddington. Nearest Tubes:
Paddington & Edgeware Road. Buses 15,7,23,27,36, opp St Mary's
Hospital

W2 8 Norfolk Place W2
Map no: A4
Tel: 0171 402 3299
Chef: Kabir Miah
Proprietor: Azizur Rahman
Cost: *Alc* £12.50, fixed-price
L £6.95/D £9.50. H/wine £5.95
Service exc
Credit cards: 🔳 ▨ ▨ ▨
Times: Noon-last L 2.30pm,
6pm-last D 11.55pm. Closed
Xmas day

Interlude de Chavot 🏵🏵🏵

A blandly decorated, but quietly excellent and very welcome addition to the London scene

Spend a little time with Eric Chavot, an alumnus of the Marco Pierre White school of haute cuisine, and you will be treated to technically accomplished cooking that is, for the most part, sublime. The premises are blandly decorated to resemble a suburban sitting-room and there is nothing to distract one's attention from the food. This is firmly French in conception, although the MPW influence is apparent, and the menu reminiscent of The Canteen's. It is in English, but the odd word of French culinary jargon is thrown in for the sake of confusion. However, the seven dishes listed at each course are all at the same price. No concession is made to vegetarianism.

Foie gras and chicken parfait is perfectly smooth and served with impeccable brioche; plump and succulent poached oysters are served on a bed of scrambled egg with a light and frothy velouté. Main courses have been less precisely executed. Rump of lamb provençale with an olive and pepper jus was marred by an over salted red pepper concealed beneath stacked slices of nicely pink meat. Roasted leg of rabbit stuffed with squid was marginally overcooked, but accompanied by a superb risotto of pearl barely that was fragrant with fresh herbs. Desserts include a crème brûlée with praline that was stunning and an extraordinary chocolate 'soup' with a scoop of spiced brown bread ice cream floating in a crisp little chocolate boat. Details, like the crusty bread rolls, espresso coffee and the petits fours served with it, are commendable. Early criticism of the service, under the smiling direction of Elaine Emmanuel, has evidently been taken to heart since the waiters now move with unobtrusive grace and appear to have acquired the knack of anticipating every request. An utterly conventional wine list includes a virtuous selection of half bottles.

Directions: Oxford Street end of Charlotte Street. Tubes – Tottenham Court Road, Goodge Street

W1 5 Charlotte Street W1
Map no: C4
Tel: 0171 637 0222
Chef: Eric Crouillere-Chavot
Proprietors: Eric Crouillere-Chavot, Claire Emmanuel and Marco Pierre White

The Ivy 🏵🏵🏵

A buzzing restaurant serving an imaginative range of international dishes

A seriously fashion conscious theatre-land restaurant loved by the luvvies – The Ivy is under the same ownership as Le Caprice, and attracts a similar following; it also takes orders till midnight. Apart from the stained glass latticed windows, the exterior is discreet, giving little indication of the activity within. It is essential to book: tables can be turned over as often as three times a night. The interior combines traditional features, a staffed cloakroom, wood panelling and leather seating, with bold modern paintings. Likewise, the menu has a classical layout but eclectic content. A typical selection of starters might include potted shrimps on toast, New England scallop and clam chowder, and the delicious 'torta Milanese' sampled at a test meal – a moulded risotto fried until golden and served with wild mushrooms and garlic butter. This was followed by sea bass with a rather heavy herb crust and a Jerusalem artichoke purée, fashionably described as mash. Calves' liver, sausages and mash, and salmon fishcakes with sorrel sauce are among the most popular dishes and are therefore permanent features of the seasonal menu. Vegetables, ordered separately, are

WC2 1 West Street Covent Garden WC2H 9NE
Map no: D3
Tel: 0171 836 4757
Chefs: Des McDonald (head chef) and Mark Hix (executive chef)
Proprietors: Jeremy King and Christopher Corbin
Cost: *Alc* £24.75-£38, fixed-price Sat/Sun brunch £14.50. H/wine £8.75 ❣ Service exc
Credit cards: 🂠 ▨ ▨ 🂱 OTHER
Times: Noon-last L 3pm, 5.30pm-last D midnight. Closed 24-28 Dec & Bhs
Menus: *A la carte*, fixed-price Sat/Sun brunch
Seats: 100. Air-conditioning
Additional: Children welcome; ❶ dishes, vegan/other diets on request

worth checking out – pumpkin and parsnip are roasted with cumin, or a panache of minted beans. For dessert, a combination of iced berries and a warm white chocolate sauce was a real winner. Espresso is excellent, tea is by Fauchon and there are chocolate truffles. Service is generally animated and informed, if rushed on occasions. The recommendation of a 1993 Leeuwin Estate Margaret River Riesling from an intelligent and well chosen wine list was much appreciated.

Directions: Nearest Tube: Leicester Square & Covent Garden

Jimmy Beez ❀❀

☺ *Good value food in a lively atmosphere with live music at weekends*

At the Cambridge Garden end of Portobello Road, this small, plain restaurant is gaining in popularity. During the week it attracts a young, trendy crowd, and local families at weekends who come for the brunch menu. In addition to serving meals all day, with the dinner menu coming into force at 6pm, the place offers a good variety of seasonally influenced dishes. On a recent visit the meal started with good bread served with tapenade given an extra bite with Parmesan cheese. A goats' cheese tarte tatin was simple but had a great honesty of flavour. Excellent calves' liver, cooked nicely pink on a bed of spinach, was carefully but simply prepared; also recommended was the fried spinach with sesame seeds.Puddings are a delight: a light, not too sweet sticky toffee pudding, especially so. Simple though this restaurant is, it has a lively, informal atmosphere, and is well worth a visit especially for those who appreciate uncomplicated, value-for-money dining.

Directions: From Notting Hill Tube – 1.5 miles down Portobello Rd, from Ladbroke Grove – 2 min walk up Oxford or Cambridge Gdns

W10 303 Portobello Road W10
Map no: GtL C3
Tel: 0181 964 9100
Chef: William Panton
Proprietor: James Breslaw
Cost: Alc £20, fixed-price L £12/D £20. H/wine £8 Service exc
Credit cards: ▨ ▥ ▨ 🔄 OTHER
Times: 11am-last L 6pm, last D 11pm. Closed 10 days at Xmas
Menus: A la carte, fixed-price L & D, Sat & Sun brunch (11-6pm)
Seats: 72. No-smoking area, air-conditioning
Additional: Children welcome, children's portions; ❂ dishes, vegan/other diets on request

Jin ❀

☺ *A bright, modern, South Korean restaurant in the heart of Soho with an informal atmosphere. An interesting menu centres around do-it-yourself barbecues set within each table, such as barbecued sirloin marinated in soy sauce. Also recommended is chicken with mushrooms, peppers and potatoes in a rich wine sauce*

Menus: A la carte, fixed-price D, ❂ **Seats:** 50. Air-conditioning **Additional:** Children welcome; ❂ dishes, vegan/other diets on request
Directions: Five mins walk from Tottenham Court Road or Leicester Square tube stations

W1 16 Bateman Street W1
Map no: D4
Tel: 0171 734 0908/0856
Chef: Mr Lee
Proprietor: Tony Wee
Cost: Alc £15, fixed-price D £19.50. H/wine £7.50 Service inc
Credit cards: ▨ ▥ ▨ 🔄
Times: Noon-last L 2.30pm, 6pm-last D 11pm. Closed Sun & 25/26 Dec, 1 Jan

Kai Mayfair ❀❀

Exotically named dishes of diverse Chinese provenance at this smart long-established restaurant

Expect to confront dishes named 'The Encirclement of the Sleeping Phoenix', 'Harmony in Four' and 'Buddha Jumps Over The Wall' at this long-established Chinese restaurant. Fortunately, all is explained in a sub-text to each dish on a menu which takes in several regional

W1 65 South Audley Street W1
Map no: C3
Tel: 0171 493 8988/8507
Chef: Vincent Looi
Proprietor: Bernard Yeoh
Cost: Alc £40. H/wine £13 ❢ Service inc
Credit cards: ▨ ▥ ▨ 🔄 OTHER

Kai Mayfair

Times: Last L 2.30pm, last D
11.30pm
Menus: *A la carte*, fixed-price
L, ❂
Seats: 110. Air-conditioning
Additional: Children welcome;
❂ dishes

styles of Chinese cooking. Recent refurbishment has taken the
décor at this rather expensive restaurant to a new high, which
complements the formal service, professionally performed by
attentive waitresses wearing smart uniforms of Chinese-style
trousers and jackets. The *carte* include selections of hot and cold
starters, abalone, shark's fin, seafood, beef and lamb etc. Terrine of
steamed chicken (The Encirclement of the Sleeping Phoenix) and
soft shelled crab are typical starters, while a speciality main course
is duck in orange sauce; Peking duck is also available. There is an
international wine list which includes a section of establishment
recommendations.

Directions: Marble Arch onto Park Lane situated behind Dorchester, or
Oxford St into N Audley St, pass American Embassy into S Audley St

Kalamara's ❀

☺ *Now open for lunch as well as dinner, this popular Greek restaurant
offers a varied carte of dips, salads and seafood to start, along with
vegetarian choices and main courses of either seafood or meat. A few
traditional sweets, such as baklava and halva, and a short list of Greek
wines complete the picture*

Menus: *A la carte*, fixed-price D **Seats:** 96
Additional: Children welcome, children's portions; ❂ dishes,
vegan/other diets on request
Directions: Nearest Tube: Bayswater

W2 76-78 Inverness Mews
W2 3JQ
Map no: GtL C3
Tel: 0171 727 9122
Chef: Kamm
Proprietor: F Ridha.
Manager: W Basilico
Cost: *Alc* £20, fixed-price D £16
❢ Service inc
Credit cards: 🅐 🅑 🅒 🅓
Times: Noon-last L 2.30pm,
6.30pm-last D midnight. Closed
Sun & Bhs

Kastoori ❀

*A vegetarian restaurant, run by the Thanki family, who prepare a varied
menu of Indian, Gujarati and Kathihwadi dishes. Meals suitable for
vegans are clearly denoted, and the interesting menu offers a good variety
of starters, Indian breads, curries, dhosas, and a range of specials, plus
three thalis (set meals)*

Menus: Fixed-price, ❂
Seats: 82. Air-conditioning
Additional: Children welcome, children's portions on request;
❂ dishes, vegan/other diets on request
Directions: Between Tooting Bec & Tooting Broadway tube stations

SW17 188 Upper Tooting Road
SW17 7EJ
Map no: GtL C2
Tel: 0181 767 7027
Chef: Manos Thanki
Proprietor: D Sthankiya
Cost: H/wine £6.95
Credit cards: 🅐 🅑
Times: 12.30-last L 2.30pm,
6pm-last D 10.30pm. Closed
Mon/Tue L & Xmas day, one wk
mid Jan

Ken Lo's Memories of China ❀

☺ *Enjoying impressive views over the river and marina at Chelsea Harbour, this stylish Chinese restaurant offers a wide choice. Dumplings filled with pork and spring onion and served with rice vinegar and shredded ginger dip, and roasted lamb with hoisin sauce, spring onion and iceberg lettuce leaves are recommended*

SW10 Chelsea Harbour
SW10 0XD
Map no: GtL C2
Tel: 0171 352 4953
Chef: Tim Tang
Cost: Alc £20, fixed-price L £8. H/wine £10.50 Service inc
Credit cards: 🂠 ▦ ▦ ⬛
Times: Noon-last L 2.30pm, 7pm-last D 10.45pm
Menus: Multi-course Chinese menu, bar menu
Seats: 110. Air-conditioning
Additional: Children welcome

Directions: Down King's Rd, turn left at Lots Rd

Ken Lo's Memories of China Restaurant ❀

The late Ken Lo's original London restaurant set the tone for the design-led Chinese restaurants of today. A loyal following still enjoy the lemon chicken with crisp batter and tangy sauce, Cantonese lobster broth, and stir-fried Chinese greens with garlic

SW1 67 Edbury Street
SW1V 0NZ
Map no: C2
Tel: 0171 730 7734

Chef: Kam Po But
Proprietor: Franco Zanellato
Cost: Alc £25, fixed-price L £15.25/D £26.80. H/wine £10.50 Service inc
Credit cards: 🂠 ▦ ▦ ⬛
Times: Noon-last L 2.30pm, 7pm-last D 11.15pm. Closed Bhs
Menus: A la carte, fixed-price L & D
Directions: At the junction of Ebury Street and Eccleston Street. Nearest Tubes – Sloane Square & Victoria

Kensington Park Hotel ❀

A bright, modern hotel where the Cairngorm Restaurant serves some sound cooking. A spring meal here included a light pastry case filled with scrambled eggs and asparagus tips, followed by a rosette of beef with shallots and olive potatoes, with frozen mango parfait for dessert

Times: 6pm-last D 10pm. Closed Sun/Mon & Aug, 26-30 Dec
Menus: A la carte, fixed-price D
Seats: 40. Air-conditioning
Additional: ✿ dishes, vegan/other diets on request
Directions: Nearest Tube – Kensington High Street

W8 16-32 De Vere Gardens
W8 5AG
Map no: A2
Tel: 0171 937 8080
Chef: Patrick Riddler
Proprietor: Thistle Hotels.
Rest Manager: Christian Franzelin
Cost: Alc £30, fixed-price D £19.95. H/wine £12.75 ❢
Service exc
Credit cards: 🂠 ▦ ▦ ⬛

Kensington Place ❀❀

Popular, fashionable restaurant with innovative modern cooking

Kensington Place still retains its popularity and the buzz created when all the tables are full is truly exciting. The young staff are as fashion conscious as their clientele, and with the minimalist decor which features high-tech service stations, there is a trendy feel to the place. Rowley Leigh continues to produce a harmonious blend of classical and modern dishes. A starter of fish soup with croûtons and rouille is a perennial favourite and provides a contrast to such innovative dishes as griddled scallops and pea purée and mint vinaigrette. Cooking skills are of a high level. A warm salad of smoked eel with bacon was a good example of intelligent use of materials with the smoked fish enhanced by the crisp bacon. Occasionally, timing can miss the mark slightly, and a succulent dish of brill with sea kale, scallops and buerre blanc was spoiled by rather tired new potatoes. There is always a vegetarian dish, and the Mediterranean was evident in baked artichoke and peppers with truffle paste and mozzarella. The menu changes daily but revolves around a core of seasonally influenced dishes. The wine list is short with wines chosen to complement the style of cooking at affordable prices.

Directions: 150 yds before junction of Kensington Church Street & Notting Hill Gate

W8 201/205 Kensington Church Street W8 7LX
Map no: GtL C3
Tel: 0171 727 3184
Chef: Rowley Leigh
Proprietors: Nick Smallwood and Simon Slater
Cost: Alc £25, fixed-price L £13.50. H/wine £9.75 ❢ Service exc
Credit cards: 🅴 🅳 OTHER
Times: Noon-last L 3pm, 6.30pm-last D 11.45pm (10.15pm Sun). Closed 5 days at Xmas
Menus: A la carte, fixed-price L
Seats: 140. Air conditioning
Additional: Children welcome, children's portions; ❤ dishes

L'Accento ❀

The bright waistcoats of the waiters make a cheerful contrast to the stark brown mural on one side of the restaurant. The food is well executed and honest. The main menu, which changes monthly, offers basil tagliolini with lobster, ossobucco, and calves' liver with balsamic vinegar. There is a weekly-changing set menu

Menus: A la carte, fixed-price, pre-theatre
Seats: 75. Air-conditioning
Additional: Children welcome, children's portions & menu; ❤ dishes, other diets on request
Directions: Off Westbourne Grove. Nearest Tube: Bayswater – Queensway

W2 16 Garway Road W2 4NH
Map no: GtL C3
Tel: 0171 243 2201/2664
Chef: Roberto Porceddu
Proprietors: Giovanni Tomaselli and Roberto Porceddu
Cost: Alc £25, fixed-price L/D £10.50. H/wine £7.95 Service exc
Credit cards: 🅴 🅳
Times: 12.30-last L 2.30pm, last D 11.30pm. Closed Bhs

Laicram ❀❀

An hospitable local Thai restaurant with a comprehensive menu

Unobtrusively tucked in a small side street around the corner from Blackheath station, this unassuming Thai restaurant has such a reputation that's its wise to book well in advance. It's not hard to see why, as the place is welcoming and the service cheerful, plus there's a comprehensive menu of Thai specialities that are well explained. 'Tom kha gia' is a wonderful broth of galingale, root herbs, lemon grass and chillies with fresh chicken, all tempered with coconut milk. Soups are one of the strengths of the kitchen, seafood another. 'Pat ped talay' is a stir-fried and highly-spiced mixture of prawns and squid, crab claws, mussel and big flakes of white fish. The standard is good, but portions tend to be on the small side.

SE3 1 Blackheath Grove Blackheath SE3
Map no: GtL E2
Tel: 0181 852 4710
Chef: Amnury Suttwat
Proprietor: Somchitt Dhirabutra
Cost: H/wine £7.50
Credit cards: 🅴 🅳
Menus: A la carte
Times: Midday-Last L 2.30pm, 6pm-Last D 11.30pm. Closed Bhs
Seats: 50
Additional: Children welcome. ❤ *menu; Vegan/other diets on request*

Unusually, there's a sweet trolley dispensing fresh fruit salads and Thai sweetmeats such as 'met kanoon', made with coconut.

Directions: Off the main shopping street, in a side road near the Post Office. Opposite the station

L'Altro 🏵🏵

Modern, accurate, no-nonsense Italian cooking with vibrant flavours

Whilst tapas bars are in danger of becoming played out, L'Altro offers, instead, a lunchtime antipasto bar. This includes dishes such as baby artichokes al gratin with Parmesan, sautéed spinach with wild mushrooms and sausage, and grilled ciabatta with mixed peppers, roast garlic and olive oil. The lunch menu also expands to include dishes such as home-made ravioli with spinach and ricotta in butter, sage and Parmesan sauce, baked sea bass with fresh herbs, and baby chicken cooked with spicy sauce and rosemary potatoes. The dinner menu runs along parallel lines, in terms of recipes and ingredients – sweetbreads sautéed with lentils and rice in a rosemary and white wine sauce, spaghetti lobster, skewered scallops with pine nuts and rucola pesto, and roast quail filled with fennel sausages on a bed of polenta. Typical Italian desserts are budino al cioccolato, zabaglione and panna cotta in caramel sauce. Decorated with trompe l'oeil frescoes and bare tables packed tightly together, the restaurant can be noisy and jostling at times, but the modern Italian regional menu works well, from the giant foccacia to the new wave all-Italian wine list.

Directions: From Notting Hill Gate, straight down Kensington Park Rd. From Ladbroke Grove tube, turn right, 2/3 blocks, left at Westbourne Park Rd, 1st right is Kensington Park Rd

W11 210 Kensington Park Road
Notting Hill W11 1NR
Map no: GtL C3
Tel: 0171 792 1066
Chef: Massimo Bianchi
Proprietor: Kathryn Phillips
(Manager)
Cost: *Alc* £30. H/wine £8.90
Service exc
Credit cards: 🔲 📰 🎫 💷 OTHER
Times: 12.30-last L 3pm,
7.30pm-last D 11pm. Closed
Sun D & Xmas, Easter & Bhs
Menus: *A la carte* D, antipasto
L menu
Seats: 45. No pipes or cigars,
air-conditioning
Additional: Children's portions
on request, ❤ dishes

The Landmark Hotel 🏵🏵

Bright modern food in a centrally located hotel with the added bonus of striking 19th-century Gothic architecture

NW1 222 Marylebone Road
NW1 6TQ
Map no: GtL C3
Tel: 0171 631 8000
Chef: Roger Peters
Proprietor: Landmark
Cost: *Alc* £40, fixed-price
L £21.50/D £33. H/wine £22 ♥
Service exc
Credit cards: 🔲 📰 🎫 💷
Times: Noon-last L 3pm, 7pm-
last D 11pm. Closed Sat L
Menus: *A la carte*, fixed-price
L & D,
Seats: 88. No-smoking area, no
pipes, air-conditioning
Additional: Children welcome;
❤ dishes, vegan/other diets on
request

A new chef, a new kitchen brigade, new management and staff in the Dining Room, and a new name have brought a fresh approach to the former Regent Hotel. Ralph Porciani walks on the wild side of modernism, brightly coloured sauces are a hallmark, and ingredients tumble over themselves on the plate in a jumble of textures and flavours. Pumpkin ravioli is set on a grainy, jet black prune and squid ink sauce, garnished with arugula leaves dressed with oil, dill, tomato concasse, and a very good, finely-oiled brunoise of celeriac, onion and basil; lean spring lamb is served with a colourful turban of sliced courgettes and carrots filled with risotto, and set on a luminous orange and cardamom sauce. Some flavours lack vitality, and there is a feeling that a simpler approach would be more successful, though there is no doubting the talent behind it all. Puddings are accomplished – a well-constructed crème brûlée with a fresh raspberry coulis is recommended. Good Colombian coffee and petits fours. The wine list features a strong Italian section; French wines are by the glass. Every Friday night there is dinner dancing.

Directions: Directly opposite Marylebone BR & Tube stations

The Lanesborough Hotel ❀❀❀

Refined international cooking at the Conservatory restaurant of this fashionable London hotel

The former St George's Hospital, lavishly redeveloped to become one of the city's most fashionable hotels, the Lanesborough is a fine listed building situated on Hyde Park Corner between Hyde and Green Parks. Public areas are not grand in scale, but they are exquisitely furnished and a host of attentive and smartly dressed staff provide correct service. The Conservatory Restaurant is a lovely setting for Paul Gayler's innovative cooking – one sits under a glass canopy among enormous urns filled with potted plants and fresh flowers.

The lunch menu offers appetisers, typically soups, a terrine of foie gras, and deep-fried Cornish scallops, plus a section of salads, pasta and vegetarian dishes, some of which are available as a starter or main course. Main courses range from fish and chips with tartare sauce to spice roasted duckling with honey and ginger, plus a selection of dishes from the grill. The good menu range comprises a *carte* for each meal, daily set menus, Sunday brunch, and a weekly vegetarian set meal. Light and vegetarian dishes are clearly denoted throughout. At an early spring dinner our inspector began with a generous Caesar salad with grilled chicken, followed by a thick cut of baked cod with root vegetables. A well risen lemon soufflé was served with coconut ice-cream. Good coffee came with petits fours. The extensive wine list has a comprehensive French selection and plenty of half bottles and wines by the glass.

Every meal is available here, including breakfast with specials such as devilled kidneys and black pudding with hash brown potato strudel, and huevos rancheros with chorizo sausage, guacamole and spicy red salsa. Afternoon tea is served here too, featuring the traditional Russian samovar.

Directions: On Hyde Park Corner. Nearest Tube – Hyde Park Corner

SW1 Hyde Park Corner
SW1X 7TA
Map no: C2
Tel: 0171 259 5599
Chef: Paul Gayler
Proprietor: Rosewood Hotels.
Manager: Geofry Gelardi
Cost: *Alc* £24.50-£51.50, fixed-price L £22.50 (3 courses)/D £28.50. H/wine £15 ♥ Service inc
Credit cards: 🅰 💳 💳 💳
Times: Breakfast 7am-noon, noon-last L 2.30pm, last D midnight
Menus: *A la carte*, fixed-price L & D, ♥ , bar menu, breakfast, tea
Seats: 106. No cigars or pipes at breakfast
Additional: Children welcome, children's portions & menu; ♥ dishes, vegan/other diets on request

Langan's ❀❀

Still a place to go to be seen, but the kitchen is coasting on its culinary reputation

To dismiss this glitzy institution as a tourist trap is to miss the point of what remains a fixture of fashionable metropolitan life. Of its three founding fathers, as depicted on the menu by David Hockney, Peter Langan has passed on and Michael Caine and Richard Shepherd have other business interests demanding their attention. Some of the lustre may have rubbed off and some of the thunder of the old days, when Peter Langan's presence was so keenly felt, may have been stolen by the arrival on the scene of contenders like Quaglino's, but this 200 seater remains as packed as it has been for the past 20 years. The long list of reinterpreted British dishes and brasserie staples that once seemed innovative is now reassuringly familiar, and the standard of the cooking is consistently OK. Still, people don't necessarily come here for the food, but come to be seen consuming it. Langan's remains one of the capital's most glamorous salons.

Directions: Stratton Street is about half-way along Piccadilly. Nearest Tube – Green Park

W1 Stratton Street W1
Map no: C3
Tel: 0171 491 8822
Chefs: Ron Smith and Dennis Mynnot
Proprietors: Richard Shepherd and Michael Caine
Cost: Alc £23. H/wine £8.25. Service charge 12.5%. Cover charge £1
Credit cards: 🅰 💳 💳 📄
Times: 12.30-Last L 2.30pm, 7pm-Last D11.45pm. Lunch not served Sat. Closed Sun, BHs, Easter and Xmas
Menu: A la carte
Seats: 200. No restriction on smoking. Air conditioned
Additional: Children welcome; ❶ dishes

The Lansdowne ❀

☺ *Bare floorboards, stripped tables and bright vases of flowers add to the convivial pub atmosphere. A daily-changing menu features hearty bowls of soup, crisp interesting salads and generous portions of pasta. Look out for black pudding, apples and mashed potato, or duck terrine with onion, prune and sultana relish*

Menus: A la carte, fixed-price Sun L
Seats: 70
Additional: Children not permitted at D; ❶ dishes
Directions: Over footbridge from Chalk Hill Tube, left down Gloucester Ave

NW1 90 Gloucester Ave NW1
Map no: GtL C3
Tel: 0171 483 0409
Chefs: Amanda Pritchett and Simon Green
Proprietor: Amanda Pritchett and Simon Palmer
Cost: Alc £15, fixed-price Sun L £15. H/wine £8 ❗
Credit cards: None taken
Times: Noon-last L 2.30pm, last D 10pm. Closed Mon L & Dec 24-Jan 2

La Tante Claire ❀❀❀❀❀

Superb French cooking, including some of the finest dishes in London, created by a dedicated chef

'There are few chefs of the standing of Pierre Koffmann who actually cook and attend each service of each day that the restaurant is open,' wrote one inspector this year. TV junketings or lavish art-house cookery books are not for M. Koffmann. His Chelsea restaurant has a calm, measured air, the decor is understated, the effect light and airy, tables are reasonably spaced and staff are unhurried and correct. It is the food that is all important.
Pierre Koffmann's cooking reflects his native Gascony, his technique is exact, and certain signature dishes such as the 'pied de cochon aux morilles' that so influenced a younger Marco Pierre White, always appear on the menu. Dishes are deceptively simple in description, giving perhaps a hint of the directness of the style but not of the depth that distinguishes each dish.

SW3 68 Royal Hospital Road SW3 4HP
Map no: B1
Tel: 0171 352 6045
Chef: Pierre Koffmann
Proprietor: Pierre Koffmann. Manager: Bruno Bellemère
Cost: Alc £61, fixed-price L £26. H/wine £13.50 Service inc
Credit cards: 🅰 💳 💳 📄
Times: Last L 2pm, last D 11pm. Closed Sat/Sun & 3 wks in Aug, 10 days at Xmas
Menus: A la carte, fixed-price L
Seats: 43. Air-conditioning
Additional: Children welcome; ❶ /other diets on request

La Tante Claire

This was evident at a lunch in April. Dishes chosen included a well conceived and brilliantly balanced, but plainly titled 'ravioli de langoustines et bouillon épicé', and an 'assiette canardière aux deux sauces', which was in fact a combination of slices of duck breast, a confit of the leg, a duck sausage, and pieces of duck wrapped in filo pastry. Vegetables formed an integral part of the dish, crisp mange tout, creamy pomme purée, fine pasta cooked al dente and leaf spinach. A signature dish of 'soufflé pistachio avec sa glace' was deliciously moist, had a superb flavour of pistachio with the ice-cream set inside the well-risen soufflé.

Crème de cresson, confit of duck with cabbage and tarte frangipane with prunes could form a set lunch that is outstanding value at £26 for those three courses, plus good, freshly baked bread, amuse-gueule, excellent espresso and petits fours of which the tiny tarte au citron and the chocolate truffle are highly recommended. The comprehensive wine list is entirely French and includes some first-class vintages, some excellent regional wines from Gascony and beyond, and a decent range of half bottles.

Directions: Between Embankment & Sloane Sq, near Army Museum

Launceston Place ®®

Modern cooking for a loyal local clientele in a smart residential area of South Kensington

A sound neighbourhood place, a sister restaurant to Kensington Place, where both the Mediterranean and Britain provide the kitchen with inspiration. Add to that the friendly and willing service, with the team taking a close interest in their customers' enjoyment, and you have an idea of why Launceston Place is popular. The *carte* offers a good range of choices and a typical meal could kick off with crostini and carpaccio of beef, artichokes and Parmesan, enhanced by pesto and a powerful truffle oil, or poached egg with black pudding and crispy bacon and mustard sauce. Then a roast lobster of 'excellent quality', served with crisp chips 'that actually tasted of potato', and home-made mayonnaise, or deep-fried lamb's sweetbreads with morels. The dessert menu is a collection of nursery favourites, often tweaked a little to fit the modern European style. Examples might be apple fritters with Armagnac anglaise or rhubarb and raisin bread and butter pudding

1A Launceston Place W8
Map no: A2
Tel: 0171 937 6912
Chef: Derek Francis
Proprietors: Nick Smallwood and Simon Slater
Cost: *Alc* £25, fixed-price L & D £16.50. H/wine £9.75 ᵠ Service exc
Credit cards: ▨ ▦ ▦ OTHER
Times: 12.30pm-last L 2.30pm (3pm Sun), 7pm-last D 11.30pm. Closed Sat lunch & Sun evening
Menus: *A la carte*, fixed-price L & D, late supper
Seats: 85. Air conditioned
Additional: Children permitted; children's portions, Ⓥ dishes, vegan on request

with custard. Bread is from Sally Clarke. The wine list is sensibly pitched.

Directions: Just south of Kensington Palace. Between Gloucester Road and High Street Kensington Tubes

Laurent ❀❀

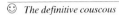

☺ *The definitive couscous*

Laurent serves, arguably, the best couscous in London. If it tastes home-made, then that is just what it is; the homely, front-room restaurant has been a family-run affair for over twelve years. Basically, this is a one item menu – couscous comes in various permutations, from the most basic with vegetables, up to couscous Royal with vegetables, lamb and a mixed grill of lamb chop, brochette and merguez. Alternatively, there is chicken or fish couscous. The latter was much enjoyed on our most recent visit. Fresh halibut steak on the bone was braised with onion, carrots and courgettes in a lightly spiced sauce, and served with excellent fresh cracked wheat couscous flavoured with cumin and caraway seeds. Try not to miss, however, the home made spicy merguez sausages, or the single starter, 'brique à l'oeuf' – lightly cooked egg in crispy filo pastry. Watch out for some very hot harissa sauce, which looks harmless but can inflict serious damage! Desserts are ice-cream, crêpes Suzette or a well-made crème brûlée. Coffee is in the Arab style, richly flavoured and slightly sweet. North African wines are the recommended choice, otherwise drink the mint tea.

Directions: Junction with Cricklewood Lane

NW2 428 Finchley Road
NW2 2HY
Map no: GtL C4
Tel: 0171 794 3603
Chef: Laurent Farrugia
Proprietor: Laurent Farrugia
Cost: *Alc* £12 Service exc
Credit cards: ⬛ ▦ ▦
Times: Last L 2pm, last D 11pm. Closed Sun & first 3 wks in Aug
Menus: *A la carte*
Seats: 36
Additional: Children welcome, children's portions; ❂ dishes

Le Boudin Blanc ❀❀

☺ *Simple decor, brisk service and French bistro food attracts a lively following*

Shepherd's Market may have a dubious image, but this all-day bistro-café on two floors does a lot to dispel the sleaze. Chefs tend to change frequently, however, and whilst the quality of ingredients remains good, cooking skills can be inconsistent. The menu is French, mostly along the lines of moules marinières, snails, onion soup, medallions of monkfish sautéed with tarragon and aniseed butter, and confit of duck with lentils. The eponymous boudin blanc, or white pudding, is served grilled with red cabbage. A delicate, soufflé-like moule tart started our inspection meal well, brightened with saffron and a piquant dressing. Roasted ham knuckle, erroneously billed as pork shank, was, alas, killed by salt; haricot beans would have been a good match if they had not been hard. Layers of passion fruit and chocolate mousse were uneven in texture, but the flavours were brought out by a smooth fruit coulis. A selection of reasonably priced, predominantly French wines is available, and the remarkable value-for-money, two-course, daily blackboard special remains a huge success despite, or maybe because of, the cramped seating and noisy music.

Directions: Off Curzon St, Park Lane

W1 5 Trebeck Street
Mayfair W1Y 7RH
Map no: C3
Tel: 0171 499 3292
Chef: Thierry Aubugeau
Proprietor: Le Boudin Blanc Ltd
Cost: *Alc* £18.50, fixed-price
L/D £8.95 ❢ Service exc
Credit cards: ⬛ ▦ ▦ OTHER
Times: 11am-11pm. Closed Dec 25/26 & Jan 1
Menus: *A la carte*, fixed-price
L & D
Seats: 75. Air-conditioning
Additional: ❂ dishes

Le Café du Jardin ⬡

☺ *A popular brasserie-style restaurant where French and Italian inspired dishes are the order of the day. Recently enjoyed has been the 'risotto al funghi', which had a good selection of wild mushrooms, 'confit de cuisse de canard' – braised duck with a red wine sauce – and a dark and white chocolate mousse cake*

Additional: Children permitted; ❂ dishes
Directions: On the corner of Wellngton Street and Tavistock Street. Nearest Tube – Covent Garden

WC2 28 Wellington Street WC2
Map no: E3
Tel: 0171 836 8769
Chef: Tony Howarth
Proprietors: Tony Howarth and Robert Seigler
Cost: Alc £22, pre-theatre D £9.50. H/wine £8.95. Service inc
Credit cards: 🅰 🅱 🅲 🅳

Le Café du Marche ⬡

☺ *This bustling French brasserie uses upstairs as a grill room at lunch time. The short fixed-price menu offers sound cooking. Inspection yielded a tender, moist fillet of pork with mushroom and chestnut sauce, and lemon tart with a fluffy, tangy filling and fruity strawberry coulis*

Menus: Fixed-price L & D
Seats: 100. No pipes allowed, air-conditioning
Additional: Children welcome, children's portions; ❂ dishes, other diets on request
Directions: From Smithfield Market onto Charterhouse St, through gate and into Charterhouse Mews

EC1 Charterhouse Square EC1
Map no: F4
Tel: 0171 608 1609
Chef: Simon Cottard
Proprietor: C K Graham-Wood
Cost: Fixed-price L/D £19.75. H/wine £8 Service exc
Credit cards: 🅰 🅱 OTHER
Times: Noon-last L 2.30pm, 6pm-last D 10pm. Closed Bhs & 1 wk at Xmas

Le Caprice ⬡⬡⬡

A place to see and be seen, and to sample outstanding modern brasserie dishes

Just off Piccadilly, sharing the same street as the Ritz, is this smart, ultra fashionable restaurant; a single room in mirrored monochrome with a bar, counter and crisp linen-swathed tables. Service is carefully choreographed and the atmosphere is great, animated enough until the clock chimes 8pm when it reaches a crescendo with the arrival of the glitterati, the luvvies and the pianist.

The cooking is modern brasserie in style, with some Oriental influences, the menu concise, just one sheet with some handwritten daily additions. Eastern hors d'oeuvre is an interesting starter – crisp, irregularly shaped onion bhajis, sweet tomato salsa, filo-wrapped king prawn, tangy roasted seaweed and smoked chicken. Fish features prominently with salmon fishcake on a bed of spinach with sorrel sauce, deep fried cod with chips and minted pea purée, and seared wild salmon with roasted cucumbers and tapenade salad. Other choices could be Mexican griddled chicken salad with guacamole, piquillio peppers and chorizo sausage, and Chateaubriand with woodland mushrooms and a Madeira and tarragon jus.

Popular puddings include a perennial coffee brûlée, served in a large cup and saucer with plain custard on top of a robust coffee créme, with a crisp sugar lid. Wines are from Europe and the New World, and the list includes several half bottles and a section of wines by the glass.

Directions: Nearest Tube: Green Park. Arlington St runs beside the Ritz, Le Caprice is at the end

SW1 Arlington Street SW1A 1RT
Map no: C3
Tel: 0171 629 2239
Chefs: Mark Hix and Tim Hughes
Proprietors: Jeremy King and Christopher Corbin.
Manager: Jesus Adorno
Cost: Alc £15-£34. H/wine £8.75
Credit cards: 🅰 🅱 🅲 🅳 OTHER
Times: Noon-last L 3pm, 6pm-last D midnight
Menus: A la carte, ❂
Seats: 70. Air-conditioning
Additional: Children welcome; ❂ dishes, vegan/other diets on request

Le Gavroche ❀❀❀❀❀

An English institution serving classic French food in the grand style

Le Gavroche has become an English institution. The basement dining-room projects the stereotype image of an English gentlemens' club; solid comfort expressed in dark wood, green leather and softly lit lamps. Yet it is French to the core. Institutions have a tendency to reject change and this is perhaps why it has taken several years for Michel Roux to change the formula of the menu to reflect his own personal style. It is still played safely. Young Michel has not embraced the Mediterranean diet and several signature dishes created by father Albert remain in a section entitled 'Hommage à Mon Père', soufflé Suissesse, l'assiette du boucher, and omelette Rothschild amongst them.

The new style has had a mixed reception. 'Ragoût de langoustines et pied de cochon à la grain moutarde' was a daring combination which failed to come off. Slightly pappy, small langoustines were combined with slices of gelatinous trotter and batons of fennel making an interesting combination of textures, but the flavours were all overpowered by the well-executed grain mustard sauce. Far better was the 'rillettes de lapin' complemented by a crisp celeriac remoulade and a sweet compôte of prunes, all gutsy but harmonious flavours. A 'choucroute de la mer au genièvre' comprised a selection of first-rate fish and shellfish: langoustines, turbot, lobster, mussels and red mullet, cooked to perfection with a nest of choucroute perfumed with juniper; yet the fish had difficulty competing with the acidity of the cabbage, with only the mullet winning through. Banana soufflé with sauce caramel was light, still moist within and flavoured with a banana liqueur, topped with caramelised banana, with sliced banana underneath. A delicious caramel sauce was poured inside.

Canapés are generously sized – more than a mouthful – the cheeseboard is exceptional, the espresso superb, as are the petits fours. The set-price lunch remains the best value in town. Initially it may seem more expensive than other restaurants in the top league, the £37 is inclusive of coffee, petits fours, a choice of mineral water (French, of course) and a half bottle of wine. The wine is selected by sommelier Thierry Tomasin to complement the weekly changing menu and from a choice of five on a recent visit there was a superb 1992 St Aubin 1er cru, 'La Chatenière' and a 1975 St Emilion, Château Bellevue Mondotte. The wine list in general makes wonderful reading but the mark ups are high.

Directions: From Park Lane, into Upper Brook Street (one-way), Le Gavroche is on the right. Nearest Tube – Marble Arch

W1 43 Upper Brook Street
W1Y 1PF
Map no: B3
Tel: 0171 408 0881/499 1826
Chef: Michel Roux
Proprietor: Le Gavroche Ltd.
Manager: Silvano Giraldin
Cost: Alc £80, fixed-price
L £37/D £75 (6 courses). H/wine
£16.50 ¶ Service inc
Credit cards: ▨ ▦ ▰ ▣ OTHER
Times: Last L 2pm, last D 11pm.
Closed Sat/Sun & Xmas-New
Year, Bhs
Menus: A la carte, fixed-price
L & D
Seats: 60. Air-conditioning
Additional: ◑ dishes, vegan/
other diets on request

Leith's Restaurant ❀❀❀

Begun in 1969 by Prue Leith this well loved restaurant has been taken over by sympathetic new owners

Prue Leith's original concept of quality with style still holds firm at this well established restaurant. It was purchased from Prue Leith in the summer of 1995 by an association of Caroline Waldegrave and Sir Christopher Bland (who own Leith's School of Food & Wine), existing chef Alex Floyd and managing director Nick Tarayan. As we go to press a few changes are anticipated. For instance the hors d'oeuvre trolley will disappear, but a plated

W11 92 Kensington Park Road
W11 2PN
Map no: GtL C3
Tel: 0171 229 4481
Chef: Alex Floyd
Proprietor: Alex Floyd, Sir
Christopher Bland, Caroline
Waldegrave and Nick Tarayan
Cost: Alc £33.50-£44.50,
fixed-price D £26.50. H/wine
£14.50 ¶
Credit cards: ▨ ▦ ▰ ▣ OTHER

Leith's Restaurant

Times: 7pm-last D11.30pm
(10pm Sun), Tue-Fri L. Closed
Aug Bh, 4 days at Xmas
Menus: *A la carte*, fixed-price
D, **❂**
Seats: 75. Air-conditioning
Additional: No children under 7,
children's portions on request;
❂ dishes, vegan/other diets on
request

selection will be available as a starter. The restaurant had already
been redesigned into several smart dining areas, illuminated by
pools of light from the ceiling and appointed with gleaming
silverware, fresh flowers and crisp white linen. Fun paintings adorn
the walls, and the overall comfort is enhanced by air conditioning.

Alex Floyd offers a weekly fixed-price two-course menu and a
seasonal *carte*, and guests are welcome to mix and match between
the two. Wherever possible, fresh organically grown produce is
used, and vegetarian dishes, guaranteed to contain no gelatine or
meat stocks, are clearly marked. At a recent meal a cup of warm
golden shellfish consommé and,some delightful home-made bread
made a promising start, backed up by a chicken liver tartlet with
a light chicken mousse attractively garnished with dressed salad.
The main course was a memorable pan-fried sea bass with poached
scallops and a courgette galette on a rather salty tomato coulis,
textured with finely chopped peppers. There is a good choice of
first class desserts, and the selection of well kept cheeses is worthy
of consideration. Helpful comments inform the lengthy and
reasonably priced wine list.

Directions: 500 yds N of Notting Hill Gate

Le Meridien Piccadilly ❀❀❀

A creative collaboration of two accomplished chefs results in fine French
food presented in grand style

Situated a stone's throw from Piccadilly Circus, this city centre hotel
has many attractions, not least of which is the choice of restaurants.
Chief among them is the Oak Room where the style is formal with
a full team of restaurant staff. The menus are devised in
consultation with Michel Lorain of the renowned La Côte St
Jacques. He comes over from Joigny around four times a year.
A new head chef is now in place, Dominique Zunda, late of the
Meridien, New Orleans, and in July our inspector went along to
sample his cooking.

The meal had all the hallmarks of an accomplished classically
trained chef – and brigade. An appetiser of guinea fowl roulade
was a decently sized mouthful of balanced meat and herb flavours.
White saddle meat of young rabbit, moist and perfectly timed,
served with boned breadcrumbed frogs' legs on a light pan jus
with an outer circle of pungent wild mushrooms was simple and

W1 21 Piccadilly W1V 0BH
Map no: C3
Tel: 0171 465 1640
Chef: Domenique Zunda
Proprietor: Le Meridien - Forte.
Manager: Jean Quero
Cost: *Alc* £60, fixed-price
L £24.50/D £28 (3 courses).
H/wine £15.50 **❢** Service exc
Credit cards: ▨ ▥ ▤ ▨ OTHER
Times: Noon-2.30pm, last D
10.30pm. Closed Sat L, Sun &
1st wk Jan, 3 wks Aug
Menus: *A la carte*, fixed-price
L & D
Seats: 45. Cigar & pipes in bar
only, air-conditioning
Additional: Children welcome;
❂ dishes

Le Meridien Piccadilly

effective. Grilled turbot with white and pink peppercorns, summer vegetables and a lemon grass nage demonstrated the same finesse. Pudding was picturesque – a stunning display of pear fanned 360 degrees around its light sablé base. Beneath it a rather shy crème patisserie and around it some raspberry coulis. The accompanying vanilla ice-cream, reassuringly pock-marked with tiny black spots, contained small pieces of candied walnut.

Extras were all on form, fresh white and brown rustic rolls, frothy, strong espresso and delicate petits fours. The lengthy wine list, heavily slanted in favour of Burgundy and Bordeaux, is prefaced by a fulsome selection from California.

Directions: On the north side of Piccadilly close to Piccadilly Circus. Nearest Tube – Piccadilly Circus

Le Meridien Westbury ❀

The convivial Polo restaurant provides very comfortable surroundings in which to enjoy some lively, if slightly over elaborate, cooking with a pronounced Mediterranean feel. A typical dish might be roasted loin of pork with potato cake, red onion relish, green cabbage and roasted garlic

Times: 12.30-last L 2pm, 6pm-last D 10.30pm
Menus: A la carte, fixed-price L & D, pre-theatre, bar menu
Seats: 60. Air-conditioning
Additional: Children welcome, children's portions; ❂ /vegan dishes
Directions: Nearest Tubes – Bond Street & Green Park

W1 Bond Street W1A 4UH
Map no: C3
Tel: 0171 629 7755
Chef: Geoff Balharrie
Proprietor: Le Meridien Hotels.
Manager: Andrew Buchanan
Cost: Alc £29, fixed-price L £15/D £22.50. H/wine £15
Service exc
Credit cards: 🄰 💳 💳 🄿

Le Mesurier ❀❀

A popular lunchtime-only restaurant with a short menu of modern French cooking

Le Mesurier may not have the best of addresses, but the terraced townhouse in Old Street has an intimate feel. Indeed, the lunchtime-only restaurant has certainly stood the test of time. Chef/proprietor Gillian Enthoven offers a short handwritten *carte*, with three items listed at each of three courses. The cooking is modern, individual and has a pronounced French accent. Starters might offer smoked salmon and cucumber salad, hot and sour pickled prawns, and a twice baked goats' cheese soufflé. To follow

EC1 113 Old Street EC1V 9JR
Map no: F5
Tel: 0171 251 8717
Chef: Gilliam Enthoven
Proprietor: Gillian Enthoven
Cost: Alc £25. H/wine £9
Service exc
Credit cards: 🄰 💳 💳 🄿 OTHER
Times: Last L 3pm, dinner party bookings only. Closed Sat/Sun & 1 wk at Xmas, 3 wks at Aug
Menus: A la carte
Seats: 20

Le Mesurier

Additional: No children;
❶ dishes, other diets on request

there could be breast of chicken with cheese sauce, fillet of beef
with parsley profiterole, and Dover sole with a white wine, cream
and mushroom sauce. Tempting desserts include passion fruit
soufflé, hot fudge sundae, and pancakes with home-made lemon
curd. Alternatively there is an assortment of French cheeses, all
followed by an unlimited supply of coffee. Appropriate to the style
of the establishment, the wine list offers 20 reasonably priced wines.

Directions: Nearest Tube: Old Street. 100 yds ahead is St Lukes
Church – entrance next to it

Lemonia 🏵

☺ *A friendly, casual atmosphere can be found at this popular Greek
restaurant. Expect dishes such as stuffed vine leaves, spiced sausages, and
diced lamb baked in an earthenware dish with onions and herbs. Desserts
are popular pastry confections strong on honey, nuts and spices*

Menus: A la carte
Seats: 150. Air-conditioning
Additional: Children welcome, children's portions; ❶ dishes, other
diets on request
Directions: Nearest Tube: Chalk Farm. Nr Primrose Hill & London
Zoo

NW1 89 Regent's Park Road
NW1 8UY
Map no: GtL C3
Tel: 0171 586 7454
Chefs: A Evangelm and
Mr Khaud
Proprietor: A Evangelm
Cost: Alc £18, fixed-price
L £7.95/D £10.50. H/wine £9.25
❗ Service exc
Credit cards: 🔲 🔲
Times: Noon-last L 3pm, 6pm-
last D 11.30pm. Closed Sat
L, Sun D & 25/26 Dec

Le Petit Max 🏵🏵

*Small is beautiful – delightful French food and atmosphere in tiny Surrey
restaurant*

Don't be fooled by the sign above the door which reads 'Bonzo's
Café Bistro'. This is the right place – petit being the word. It's so
small, dining-room and kitchen merge into one, and you have to
negotiate the latter in order to use the facilities. But, small is
beautiful, and with the ever convivial Max Renzland and his
brother Mark describing the dishes as they cook to order, the
results are good enough to make you forget the squeeze.
Remember to bring your own wine, or buy from the shop next door,
as the place is unlicensed. Our inspector kicked off with duck
confit, puy lentils, pickled cabbage blanched in balsamic vinegar
and a savoury, creamy sauce constructed from roast garlic, chicken

Hampton Wick
Map no: GtL B1
Tel: 0181 977 0236
Chef: Max Renzland
*Proprietors: Max Renzland &
Mark Renzland*

stock and mustard. This was followed by roast fillets of Cornish sea bass, served with a classic velouté sauce, spinach, spiced red cabbage and olive oil mash. The chef's speciality, tarte à la crème, is well recommended, alongside tarte tatin, and crème brûlée with raspberries. All the details, from the freshly sliced baguette to the black olives, Charentais butter and cafetière coffee are suitably Gallic.

Directions: On the A310 Teddington Road, by Hampton Wick Station

Le Pont de la Tour ❀❀

A lively riverside restaurant with an interesting choice of food and wine, particularly seafood

Spectacular views of Tower Bridge and the Tower of London and St Katherine's Dock draw the crowds. In summer a canopied terrace comes into its own. Whether inside or out, it's a cool place to be seen, which makes for an interesting atmosphere, but be prepared for service which can be a bit rushed. The food is good, though. Lunch is fixed-price and there is a fairly extensive evening *carte*. The Mediterranean is the predominant influence. Bread comes from the restaurant's own bakery and dishes include langoustine mayonnaise, or rare grilled duck breast with pork rillettes, french beans and plum chutney. Oysters are a popular choice, perhaps served with champagne sabayon and matchstick frites, or there could be grilled Dover sole and 'pigeonneau de Bresse aux truffes en bouillon'. The dessert menu returns to Britain to rework a Yorkshire treacle tart with Jersey clotted cream, but there is also a more exotic apricot and cardamom sorbet. Espresso is excellent. The range of the wine list is exceptional, with a sound selection of house wines.

SE1 36d Shad Thames SE1 2YE
Map no: G3
Tel: 0171 403 8403
Chef: David Burke
Proprietors: Sir Terence Conran, Joel Kissin and David Burke.
Manager: Patrick Fischnauer
Cost: *Alc* £55.60, fixed-price L £26.50. H/wine £11.60 ♥
Service inc
Credit cards: ▧ ▦ ▨ ▨
Times: Noon-last L 3pm, 6pm-last D midnight. Closed Sat L & Good Fri, 4 days at Xmas
Menus: *A la carte*, fixed-price L, pre-theatre, bar menu, ♥
Seats: 105 + 66 outside
Additional: ♥ dishes

Directions: SE side of Tower Bridge

Les Associés ❀❀

A popular, welcoming and authentic French bistro in Crouch End

Chef Marc Spinder has returned to the kitchen of this small but estimable and thoroughly French bistro in Crouch End. It was here that our inspector enjoyed a well-prepared meal that offered few surprises, but was sound in all departments. A duck salad included succulent slices of tasty breast on a bed of crisp leaves, with a light, raspberry-flavoured sauce and was followed by roasted monkfish, wrapped in cabbage leaves, with a cream-based sauce and served with a small selection of well-cooked vegetables including parmentier potatoes, mange tout, carrots, broccoli and baby sweetcorn. For dessert, a selection of three mousses – chocolate, passion fruit and raspberry, with three separate fruit coulis, which was deemed 'delicious'. The short wine list is exclusively French and reasonably priced. The room looks like someone's home and the welcome is warm, the service pleasant.

172 Park Road N8
Map no: B5
Tel: 0181 348 8944
Chef: Gilles Charvet
Proprietors: Gilles Charvet and Didier Bertran
Cost: *Alc* £27, fixed-price L £15.95. H/wine £9.80. Service inc
Credit cards: ▧ ▨
Menu: *A la carte*
Times: 12.30-Last L 2pm, 7.30pm-Last D 10pm. Closed Sun, Mon, and Aug
Seats: 38
Additional: Children welcome, children's portions/menu.
♥ dishes/other diets on request

Directions: Half-way along Park Road, opposite the swimming pool. Nearest Tube – Finsbury Park

L'Escargot ❀❀❀❀

Soho institution offering a varied selection of classic French dishes with a modern slant

W1 Greek Street W1V 5LQ
Map no: D4
Tel: 0171 437 2679/6828
Chef: Garry Hollihead
Proprietor: J Lahoud
Cost: *Alc* £36.50, fixed-price L £25/D £34. H/wine £14.50 ❢ Service exc
Credit cards: 🔳 📰 📰 📰
Times: 12.30-last L 2.15pm, last D 11pm. Closed Sun/Mon & Dec 24/25, Jan 1
Menus: *A la carte*, fixed-price L & D
Seats: 36. Air-conditioning
Additional: ❂ dishes, vegan/other diets on request

Part of the Soho scene since 1927, this famous restaurant had a rebirth in the early 90's. It now offers a bustling (particularly in the evening) street level bistro, and a quieter, intimate restaurant on the first and second floors. The former has bare boards, cream walls hung with large modern paintings, red banquettes, slick service and a largely French brasserie menu.

The restaurant on the other hand is almost Edwardian in style, with formally dressed, attentive staff. Here the menu remains rooted in French classic tradition with Mediterranean overtones. Michael Gray is responsible for the consistent standards. Recent reports have suggested that the cooking is currently on form, with flavours spot on, perfectly partnered and technically accomplished.

Dinner in June kicked off with escabeche of salmon with a tangy, slightly acidic, warm marinade flavoured with saffron, coriander seeds and herbs, and textured by tomato and carrots. Roast duck with endive and parsley jus was chosen as a main course. Tender duck breast came with a confit of the leg ('lovely glazed skin'), sweet, braised endive and a fresh tasting parsley jus. Dramatic presentation and sound skills were displayed with a dessert of craqueline. A thin layer of eggy sponge topped with a light, creamy mousse was wrapped in a crisp craqueline circular mould and topped by orange and aniseed sorbet, and surrounded by a concentrated orange sauce. The only niggle was that the aniseed flavour was too subtle. A set lunch at £21.50 for two courses has included an excellent boudin noir set on soft onions and topped with caramelised apples, and sea bream 'en papillote' with provençale herbs, accompanied by a simple but well executed buerre blanc and boiled potatoes garnished with chives. High-quality bread, unsalted Normandy butter, rich, strong espresso and good petits fours do not let the side down.

The wine list is long, mainly French and can be pricey. For bottles around the £20 mark, French regional wines and non-French producers provide the solution.

Directions: Tube to Leicester Sq, walk up Charing Cross Rd. Into Soho/Compton St, walk along Greek St. Next to Prince Edward Theatre

Les Saveurs ❀❀❀❀❀

Discreet setting for some stunning food, amongst the best in the capital

W1 37a Curzon Street W1A 7AF
Map no: C3
Tel: 0171 491 8919
Chef: Joël Antunès
Proprietor: Fujikoshi UK Ltd.
Manager: Frederic Serol
Cost: Alc £42, fixed-price
L £22.50 (3 courses)/D £38.
H/wine £15 ❢ Service exc
Credit cards: 🅰 💳 💳 💲 OTHER
Times: Noon-last L 2.15pm,
7pm-last D 10.30pm. Closed
Sat/Sun & 2 wks end Aug, Dec
24-Jan 10
Menus: A la carte, fixed-price
L & D
Seats: 50. No pipes allowed,
air-conditioning
Additional: ♥ dishes

There is little hype or fanfare about the entrance; it could be mistaken for a private club or even associated with the Curzon cinema next door. Yet the cool, muted basement dining-room is both elegant and light and makes a sophisticated setting for Joël Antunès equally sophisticated cooking. The base is classical France – he is a native of Montpelier and has trained with some of France's finest, including Joel Robouchon – but a stint at Bangkok's Oriental Hotel has given a pronounced Far Eastern influence (although this year's reports suggest that this has somewhat abated). The style is simple, and accuracy of seasoning, respect of raw materials, and final execution are near faultless. Joël Antunès stands up to the best.

Dinner in June commenced with aperitifs with mini gougère, black olive palmier and sesame pastry crisp and was followed by an amuse-gueule of cod brandade served in a baby tomato with a streak of balsamic vinegar across the plate. A first course of raw mackerel was rolled in a vibrant marinated tomato, and served with dressed leaves and a quennelle of rich sauce tartare – flavours were exhilarating, a cross between Japan and the Mediterranean. The main course was rabbit. Two tiny trimmed racks, the sautéed liver and kidney and saddle rolled in bacon, served with roasted garlic and placed on a rich Parmesan risotto. Inspired touches included a tiny wun tun filled with a mince of rabbit meat and foie gras, a cinnamon flavoured crisp and a rosemary infused sauce. Overall, 'a fabulous dish' – complete in taste, texture and imagination with no jarring notes. By contrast, a dessert of al dente peaches with red currants and raspberries in champagne seemed not entirely finished after such perfection.

The short, daily-changing lunch menu at £22.50 for two courses and the four-course dinner menu at £38.00 both represent excellent value. Service, led by sommelier Claude Douard, is smooth and well coordinated, but too many of the staff did not command English well enough to explain the dishes properly at our last visit. The extensive wine list is predominantly French with many classics but few bargains. It is among the 'vins etrangers' and the lesser known French regional wines that reasonably priced bottles are to be had.

Directions: Between Hyde Park & Green Park (Mayfair area). Next to the Curzon Cinema

Lexingtons ❀❀

Modish Brit meets Med cooking at this trendy Soho restaurant

Bare wooden tables and bold modern art create a strong contemporary look and Harriet Arden and Martin Saxon work hard to produce an atmosphere that is relaxed and cheerful. Chef Andy Farquharson cooks a manageable *carte* of modern British food with a strong Mediterranean bias. Slow baked peppers on toasted crostini, seared salmon with rocket and Parmesan salad, crusted cod with sun-dried tomato risotto, and roast rump of lamb with Mediterranean vegetables, for example, leave no doubt as to where the inspiration lies. Puddings range from chocolate brownies, through lemon, mango and raspberry sorbet to banana burnt cream. The set dinner of two courses and coffee for £10 is excellent value, and vegetarians are well catered for. The wine list is international in scope and offers a reasonable selection of half bottles and wines by the glass.

Directions: Nearest Tubes: Oxford Circus & Piccadilly Circus

W1 45 Lexington Street
W1R 3LG
Map no: D3
Tel: 0171 434 3401
Chef: Andy Farquharson
Proprietors: Harriet Arden and Martin Saxon
Cost: *Alc* £25, fixed-price D £10. H/wine £9 ● Service exc
Credit cards: 🌑 ▆ ▆ 🌑
Times: Noon-last L 3pm, 6pm-last D 11pm. Closed Sat L, Sun & Bhs, 1 wk at Xmas
Menus: *A la carte*, fixed-price D, pre-theatre
Seats: 50. Air-conditioning
Additional: Children welcome, children's portions; ● dishes, vegan/other diets on request in advance

Lindsay House ❀❀

The emphasis is on sound English cooking at this popular restaurant useful for theatregoers

W1 21 Romilly Street W1
Map no: C3
Tel: 0171 439 0450
Chef: Paul Hodgson
Proprietor: Roger Wren.
Manager: Ian Townsend
Cost: *Alc* £25, fixed-price L £14.75 (3 courses). H/wine £9.50 Service exc
Credit cards: 🌑 ▆ ▆ 🌑
Times: 12.30-last L 2.30pm, 6pm-last D midnight (10pm Sun). Closed Dec 25/26
Menus: *A la carte*, fixed-price L
Seats: 35. No pipes allowed, air-conditioning
Additional: Children welcome, children's portions; ● dishes, vegan/other diets on request

This bastion of traditional English cooking stands firm amidst the polyglot throng of Soho restaurants. Liver and bacon, braised oxtail and ox-cheek, and English burnt cream, are amongst the no-frills, home-grown elements on the menu. However, since we are all Europeans now, the menu also includes plenty of dishes such as grilled goats' cheese salad, roast breast of duckling with ginger and Armagnac, fillets of Dover sole with crab and herb mousse, and pears poached in orange, Grand Marnier and Sauternes.

A mixed game terrine of venison, hare, pigeon and truffles, with Cumberland sauce, should have been the works, but surprisingly lacked real gamey flavour on our visit. A main course of roast fillet of lamb had tender slices of lightly cooked meat served on a bed of delicious wild mushrooms, accompanied by a deep tarragon and mint sauce. Chocolate and pistachio terrine, garnished with fresh summer fruits, made an excellent dessert. The thoughtfully chosen wine list includes some fine clarets and Burgundies, plus a short selection of New World wines. Note that the restaurant usefully opens at 6pm for the benefit of theatregoers.

Directions: Off Shaftesbury Ave, nearest tube: Piccadilly Circus

The London Hilton on Park Lane 🏵🏵🏵

Stunning views across London from the 28th floor restaurant complemented by fashionable modern British cooking

Even from the far end of Hyde Park, the sixties tower block looks quite impressive, as it rises above the the trees. From those same upper floors the views across the city, especially at night, are stunning, definitely among the best in the capital. The rooftop Windows Restaurant, refurbished a few years ago with cherry oak panelling, muted creams and beiges and cool marble requires booking well in advance for one of the coveted window tables. The well thought-out, balanced menus, developed by executive chef David Chambers, are interpreted by Jacques Rolancy whose classical style is executed with a lightness of touch which marks his cooking as something special.

A lunchtime visit during Wimbledon fortnight yielded a perfect, summer dish of lobster and baby squid salad with green Dijon mustard dressing – the warmed lobster and squid providing a contrast to the watercress, chervil and frizée salad with a tapenade-style dressing. A cappuccino of white beans flavoured with truffle was unusually light, transforming a potentially robust soup into something more fashion conscious. A simply described sauté of calves' liver with a shallot and vinegar sauce was in fact two thick slices of perfectly cooked liver laid on a bed of crushed potatoes, morels and diamonds of mange tout. Puddings, alas, come from a gleaming silver trolley and are inclined to be rather cakey, not out of place for afternoon tea but a little heavy to finish a meal. Our inspector, a big chap, found it difficult to finish a chocolate and hazelnut gâteau layered with praline cream. The wine list is a serious document with serious Park Lane prices.

Directions: Nearest Tube: Hyde Park Corner. Restaurant on 28th floor of hotel

W1 22 Park Lane W1A 2HH
Map no: C3
Tel: 0171 493 8000
Chef: Jacques Rolancy
Proprietor: Hilton International.
Manager: Rudi Jägersbacher
Cost: *Alc* £48.50, fixed-price L £35.95/D £44 (5 courses). H/wine £14 ❢ Service exc
Credit cards: ▨ ▩ ▦ ▣ OTHER
Times: Breakfast 7am-10.30am, noon-last L 2.30pm, 7pm-last D 11pm (midnight Fri/Sat). Closed Sat L, Sun D
Menus: *A la carte,* fixed-price L & D, bar menu
Seats: 110. No pipes allowed, air-conditioning
Additional: Children welcome except at D; ❷ dishes, other diets on request

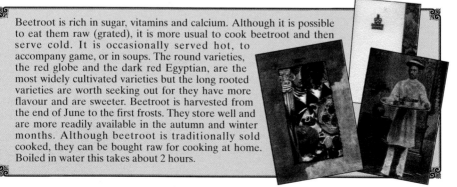

Beetroot is rich in sugar, vitamins and calcium. Although it is possible to eat them raw (grated), it is more usual to cook beetroot and then serve cold. It is occasionally served hot, to accompany game, or in soups. The round varieties, the red globe and the dark red Egyptian, are the most widely cultivated varieties but the long rooted varieties are worth seeking out for they have more flavour and are sweeter. Beetroot is harvested from the end of June to the first frosts. They store well and are more readily available in the autumn and winter months. Although beetroot is traditionally sold cooked, they can be bought raw for cooking at home. Boiled in water this takes about 2 hours.

London Marriott Hotel ❀

A purpose-built hotel in the heart of Mayfair. The restaurant offers contemporary British cooking. An inspection meal revealed skill and flair in a good terrine of duck served with minted apricot marmalade, and a succulent darne of salmon with crab crust and a subtle mustard cream sauce

W1 Grosvenor Square
W1A 4AW
Map no: C3
Tel: 0171 493 1232
Chef: Simon Traynor
Proprietor: Marriot Hotels.
Rest manager: Sarah James
Cost: *Alc* £32, fixed-price
L £24.50/D £12.50 (4.30-6.30pm). H/wine £14.50 ¶
Service exc
Credit cards: 🌑 ▨ ▨ ▨ OTHER
Times: 7am-last D 10.30pm.
Closed Bhs D unless full
Menus: *A la carte*, fixed-price
L, Sunday lunch buffet, pre-theatre
Seats: 75. No-smoking area, air-conditioning
Additional: Children welcome, children's portions; ❂ dishes, vegan/other diets on request

Directions: From Oxford St turn into Duke St opposite Selfridges. Main entrance on corner of Duke St & Grosvenor Square

The Lowndes Hotel ❀❀

☺ *An all-day hotel brasserie with above average food and cooking*

SW1 21 Lowndes Street
SW1X 9ES
Map no: B2
Tel: 0171 823 1234
Chef: Schilo van Coevorden
Proprietors: Hyatt International.
Manageress: Ms Danielle Van
Der Loos
Cost: Fixed-price L & D £13.50.
H/wine £10.50 ¶ Service exc
Credit cards: 🌑 ▨ ▨ ▨
Times: 7.30am-last D 11.15pm
(all day dining)
Menus: *A la carte*, fixed-price
L & D, bar menu, promotional
menus

Knightsbridge, Sloane Street, Kings Road – they are all right on the doorstep of Brasserie 21, the bar and restaurant of Belgravia's Lowndes Hotel. The modern European *carte* reads well, and most of the 11 starters are available as main courses (the exceptions are the soups). A typical example would be a stir fry of vegetables with penne and black olives which as a starter is £5.75 and as a main course is £8.75. The *carte* changes every two to three months and a daily fixed-price menu is offered alongside. All food is freshly prepared and cooked with serious care. At inspection, one of the first courses was an impressive red onion broth, with a creamy

Stilton cheese topping. This was followed by a shellfish soufflé with lobster sauce and a timbale of wild rice. Desserts can disappoint, as a dry, overcooked warm pear tartelette indicated, but probably an alternative, such as apple ravioli with marzipan parfait, would have been a better choice. Most of the 40-plus wines are young vintages with some good Chileans.

Seats: 35 Air conditioned
Additional: Children welcome; children's menu, ❷ dishes, vegan/other diets on request

Directions: Knightsbridge Tube, from Sloane Street take first left into Lowndes Square, located on the bottom right hand corner

Mamta ❀

☺ *Good quality vegetarian food can be enjoyed at this Indian restaurant in the Fulham Road. Diners can choose from a wide selection of chef's specials – thalis, and assorted vegetable, bread and rice dishes. The 'pani puri' – crisp puris filled with potato and chick peas – are recommended*

Menus: fixed- price L & D **Seats:** 40
Additional: children welcome; children's portions, ❷ menu, vegan on request
Directions: near Munster Road – nearest Tube Parsons Green

SW6 692 Fulham Road SW6
Map no: A1
Tel: 0171 371 5971
Chefs: M Daudbai and D Kamdar
Proprietor: Darshan Kamdar
Cost: Fixed-price L £ 4.95 / D £7.25, H/wine £6.95
Credit cards: 🟦 ▨ ▨ ▨
Times: 12.30pm- last L 2.15pm, 6pm-last D 10.30pm. Closed Dec 25/26/31

Mandarin Kitchen ❀❀

☺ *Popular Cantonese restaurant specialising in fish and seafood dishes*

Seafood is the speciality at this bustling, busy Chinese restaurant. The plain, white walls and smoked glass mirrors form an unremarkable backdrop for the many family gatherings and business meals that take place here. Nearly everyone comes for the fine, Scottish wild lobsters, baked and served with ginger and spring onion, or garlic and chilli. Market prices vary, but they're not over-priced, and a lobster for two usually works out at around £25.00. A bed of soft noodles is an essential side order to soak up the cooking juices. Other seafood specialities include sea bass, scallops, carp and Dover sole, as well as lesser known Chinese fish such as pomfret and yellow croaker. Live crabs are baked with garlic, green pepper and onion in black bean sauce, roast eel fillets are served with garlic and chilli, and Pacific oysters stewed with pork and mushrooms. There is plenty of meat choice as well, including excellent aromatic crispy duck, roast veal chop in mandarin sauce, and diced chicken and cashew nuts in yellow bean sauce. The wine list provides a standard European range, but sake, served hot, is the popular choice. Service, from uniformed staff, is swift and efficient.

Directions: Opposite Queensway Tube station, a few yards from Bayswater Tube station

W2 14 Queensway 3RX
Map no: C3
Tel: 0171 727 9012/9468
Chef: Mr Man
Proprietor: Helen Chenng (Manager)
Cost: Alc £12, fixed-price L/D £8.90. H/wine £7.50 ❗ Service exc
Credit cards: 🟦 ▨ ▨ ▨ OTHER
Times: Noon-last D 11.30pm. Closed Dec 25/26
Menus: A la carte, fixed-price L & D, ❷
Seats: 110. Air-conditioning
Additional: Children welcome; ❷ /vegan dishes

Mas Café ❀❀

☺ *Unconventional atmosphere and main-stream Med food*

The location, near Westbourne Terrace and Ladbroke Grove, might be less than salubrious, but this is a great place for people-watching. There's a bouncer on the door, the customers are a mix of local Rastafarians and well-heeled young execs, and the lingo roams between colloquial city-speak and Rasta rap. Strange and hip the

W11 6-8 All Saints Road W11 1HA
Map no: GtL C3
Tel: 0171 243 0969
Proprietors: I Alexander and D Stacey
Cost: Alc £15. H/wine £9 ❗ Service exc
Credit cards: 🟦 ▨ OTHER

atmosphere may be, but the food is surprisingly serious, and sensibly priced. Dishes typically show influences from Provence, Italy and North Africa – couscous with merguez sausage, pan-fried gnocchi with spinach and garlic, and duck confit with lentils, for example. Beef stifado, rabbit with mustard sauce, boned quails with honeyed onions, rosemary lamb chops with balsamic vinegar, and mixed fish cassoulet with Pernod and dill are amongst the main dish repertoire. Potatoes are usually cooked with rosemary and garlic, or dauphinoise. Puddings are mostly French, such as Normandy pear tart, chocolate parfait with vanilla sauce and orange crème renversée. A short but good wine list is not overpriced, and includes some quality bottles such as a Chablis 1er cru Montee de Tonnerre 1993 at £19.50.

Times: 6am-last D 11.30pm. Closed daytime L Mon-Fri & Bhs
Menus: *A la carte*, Sat brunch, bar menu
Seats: 170. No-smoking area
Additional: Children welcome, children's portions; ❶ dishes, other diets on request

Directions: Between Ladbroke Grove & Westbourne Park Tube station. Parallel to Portobello Rd

Matsuri ❀

A flamboyant restaurant featuring cocktail and Sushi bars with a wide range of dishes on offer. Look out for steamed egg curd in a pot, textured with fresh prawn and sliced mushrooms, or duck with bean sprouts, broccoli and baby corn. Sashimi is good. Crêpes with ice-cream, Grand Marnier and pineapple is for dessert

Menus: *A la carte*, fixed-price L & D, pre-theatre
Seats: 133. Air-conditioning
Additional: ❶/vegan dishes
Directions: From Green Park tube station down Piccadilly, turn right into St James, 1st left into Jermyn St, 1st right into Bury St

SW1 15 Bury Street SW1
Map no: D3
Tel: 0171 839 1101
Chef: Kanelino Takase
Manager: Shigemi Matsuda
Cost: *Alc* £26, fixed-price L £33 (8 courses)/D £53.50 (10 courses). H/wine £15.25 Service exc
Credit cards: 🔳 💳 💳 💳 OTHER
Times: Noon-last L 2.30pm, 6pm-last D 10pm. Closed Sun & Bhs

May-Fair Inter-Continental ❀❀

Stylish modern British food that knows how to keep it simple

W1 Stratton Street W1A 2AN
Map no: C3
Tel: 0171 915 2842
Chef: Michael Coaker
Proprietor: Mayfair Inter-Continental London.
Manager: Richard Griggs
Cost: *Alc* £30, fixed-price L £22.50/D £29.50. H/wine £10 ❶ Service exc
Credit cards: 🔳 💳 💳 💳 OTHER

Hidden away, yet just off Piccadilly, this popular, well-run hotel also has a smart restaurant, Le Chateau, serving contemporary British food. Dishes are well considered, and there is nothing too fussy or pretentious. Red mullet comes with spinach, calves' liver with black pudding and onion fondue, and a tender beef fillet, on our visit, was well matched with celeriac, oxtail and truffled mash. Nage of lobster and scallops showed off the first-class ingredients well. A little round apple sponge cake with a quenelle of cinnamon ice-cream, was simply delicious. A good selection of French and British cheeses is admirably given its own menu, and featured cheeses include Golden Cross, an unpasteurised goats' milk cheese from East Sussex, Keen's Cheddar, Brie de Meaux and Reblochon. Sunday jazz lunches have become something of an institution, and the three or four course menu (£20 and £23 respectively) ranges far and wide with dishes as diverse as roast rib of beef, medallions of monkfish with potato pancakes, grilled lemon chicken with spinach and forest mushrooms, and the 'Prime American Steak Breakfast' of steak, eggs, bacon and hash browns.

Directions: From Hyde Park Corner turn left off Piccadilly just before Green Park tube station

Times: Last L 2.30pm, last D 10.30pm. Closed Sat L & Aug
Menus: A la carte, fixed-price L & D, bar menu
Seats: 65. Air conditioning
Additional: Children welcome, children's portions on request; **𝟙** dishes, other diets on request

McClements 𝓮𝓮

☺ *French provincial-style dishes are a popular feature of this upmarket bistro*

Food straight from the French classical repertory – though not without a modern flourish or two – is the mainstay of this restaurant. The two McClements operations have merged – into the premises of the former McClements Bistro. John McClement, who has established a good local reputation over the years, has now changed his cooking style, paring it to the bone and discarding any elaboration. The daily-changing fixed-price menu is short and to the point, making up in execution what it lacks in description; everything, from breads to balanced sauces, is prepared with a confident hand. A recent inspection meal, for example, began with seared scallops accompanied by a sweet white wine sauce in which the flavours of wine, cream and stock were finely blended, and the rack of lamb which followed was served with a wonderful array of al dente vegetables. The choice of desserts might be limited to one hot and one cold, plus cheese, but these, like the good petits fours that come with coffee, are all of excellent quality. A straightforward wine list consists of mainly French varieties and offers a minimal choice of half bottles.

Directions: In a small parade of shops next to Twickenham station

2 Whitton Road
Twickenham
Map no: GtL B2
Tel: 0181 744 9598
Chef: John McClements
Proprietor: John McClements
Cost: Fixed-price L £10 (2 course) D £ 16 (3 course) H/wine £ 9 **❢** Service exc
Credit cards: 🅴 🖭
Times: midday-last L 2.30pm, 7pm-last D 11pm. Closed Sun.
Menus: fixed-price L & D
Seats: 45 Air conditioned
Additional: children welcome over 3; children's portions, **𝟙** dishes, other diets on request

Mijanou 𝓮𝓮

Cosy little French restaurant with sophisticated cooking

You have to ring to gain admittance into this intimate little restaurant, which has a romantic air all too rare these days. Sonia Blech uses excellent ingredients to create dishes with good, clean flavours. At lunch, there is a short set menu, but the evening sees her natural creativity at full rein with the seven course 'Menu Degustation', as well as a *carte*. At a recent meal, the terrine of calves' sweetbreads, liver and fillet displayed a subtle blend of flavours and textures, although the Fine de Bourgogne sauce did not quite have the strength of flavour to make it a 'perfect marriage'. Expertly cooked saddle of venison was tender and full of gamey flavour, and skilfully teamed with a sauce of elderberries and gin, accompanied by a crisp tatin of apple and shallots. Pepper

SW1 143 Ebury Street SW1 9QN
Map no: C1
Tel: 0171 730 4099
Chef: Sonia Blech
Proprietors: Neville & Sonia Blech
Cost: Alc £32.50, fixed-price L £15/D £25. H/wine £10.50 **❢** Service exc
Credit cards: 🅴 🖭 🖭 🖭
Times: Noon-last L 2pm, 7pm-last D 11pm. Closed Sat/Sun & 2 wks at Xmas, 3 wks Aug, 1 Wk Easter
Menus: A la carte, fixed-price L & D

crusted wild boar with ragoût of Toulouse sausages, lentils and spätzle would have been improved with a sauce, as the overall combination was a touch dry. Fromage blanc and prune ice-cream floating in a sea of Armagnac was a sensational end to the meal. The wine list is extensive, with all wines cleverly number coded to match the dishes.

Directions: Ebury Street is between Sloane Square and Victoria Station. Nearest Tube – Sloane Square

Seats: 30. No-smoking area, air-conditioning
Additional: Children's portions;
❤ dishes, other diets on request

Mims ❀❀

☺ *French/Mediterranean cooking with a light touch in a friendly and informal setting*

Mims is a lively shop-fronted restaurant with something of the boulevard café about its happy atmosphere and relaxed, friendly service. Chef and co-proprietor Ismail Al-Sersy offers a short fixed-price lunch and dinner menu, each of two or three courses, with seven starters and five main courses and desserts. The cooking is essentially French with lots of Mediterranean flavours. Starters might include langoustine with green leaves, basil, chives and lemon dressing, and chicken liver parfait with deep fried pancakes. Typical main courses are fillet of beef with buttered vegetables and garlic jus and grilled grey mullet with grilled courgette salad. Dark chocolate gâteau, bread and butter pudding and apple tart are among the traditional desserts. There is a list of popular wines with plenty available by the half bottle and the glass.

Directions: On East Barnet Road, opposite Sainsbury's

63 East Barnet Road
New Barnet EN4 8RN
Map no: C4
Tel: 0181 449 2974
Chef: Ismail Al-Sersy
Proprietors: Ismail Al-Sersy and Moustafa Abouzahrah
Cost: Fixed-price L £13.50/D £19. H/wine £9.50 Service exc
Credit cards: ▨ ▨ OTHER
Times: Closed Mon, Sat L & 1 wk at Xmas, 1 wk Aug
Menus: Fixed-price L & D
Seats: 40
Additional: Children over 6 welcome, children's portions;
❤ dishes, other diets on request

Ming ❀❀

☺ *Informal, North Chinese restaurant with unusually interesting dishes*

W1 35-36 Greek Street
W1V 5LN
Map no: D4
Tel: 0171 734 2721/437 0292
Chef: Jack Chang
Proprietor: Christine Jan
Cost: Alc £12-£19.50, fixed-price L £10/D £19.50 (5 courses). H/wine £8.25 Service exc
Credit cards: ▨ ▨ ▨ ▨ OTHER
Times: Noon-last D 11.45pm. Closed Sun & Dec 25/26, Bhs from 5pm
Menus: A la carte, fixed-price L & D, pre-theatre, ❤
Seats: 70. Air-conditioning
Additional: Children welcome;
❤ dishes, vegan/other diets on request

The virtues of Northern Chinese cooking sometimes get overlooked in the general mass of Cantonese-style restaurants. The most intriguing dishes at Ming come from the seasonal menu. In February, there were warming dishes such as duck and aubergine hotpot, whilst April, for example, saw garoupa steak in sauce, kohlrabi with shredded lean pork, and 'Thousand Ounces of Gold on Jade' or, more prosaically, imitation fish fingers with green vegetables. May featured a number of unusual Taiwanese specialities. There is also a short list of Ming Bowls, one-dish meals based on rice or noodles. Other specialities include Beijing fish soup, Tibetan garlic lamb, slow-cooked Empress beef and soft-shell crabs. On our most recent visit, dishes sampled included succulent, steamed scallops with soy sauce and fresh ginger, and beef Ming style, diced meat with fresh coriander served with onion-flavoured pancake 'wraps'. The fish mousse lost something in translation – the fillet of fish was set in egg white with a garnish of preserved vegetables. Battered and fried cauliflower spiked with salt and chilli, was eagerly devoured. Mantou, or Northern Chinese bread, comes steamed or wok grilled.

Directions: Off Shaftesbury Ave, behind Palace Theatre

Mitsukoshi ⌘⌘

Utterly correct service and authentic cuisine at popular West End Japanese restaurant

Proof of Mitsukoshi's authenticity, if any were required, would be the constant numbers of Japanese diners. In addition to the main dining-room, with its stark modern decor and laquered black tables, there are a range of private salons, some with traditional low tables and cushions. The menu rotates around an excellent range of set menus, which offer examples of classic techniques, such as sashimi, sushi, tempura and one-pot 'nabemono' dishes cooked at the table. The helpful staff are always delighted to assist the uninitiated in choosing a balanced meal, and the service is very polite in true Japanese style. Ingredients are always of excellent quality, often imported directly from Japan. Fish is very good, and the sashimi dishes are bright and exquisitely fresh. The chef makes his own dashi stock from kelp and bonito tuna, and this is the base for many soups and sauces, such as the delicious miso soup flavoured with fermented soy beans, tofu and wakame seaweed. A particular speciality, which must be ordered a day in advance, is the Kaiseki menu, a multi-course banquet considered by many to be the pinnacle of Japanese cuisine.

Directions: One minute's walk from Piccadilly Circus

SW1 14-20 Regent Street
SW1Y 4PH
Map no: C3
Tel: 0171 930 0317
Chef: Jiro Shimada
Proprietor: Izumi Kudo
Cost: Fixed-price L £20/D £30 ❢
Service exc
Credit cards: ◼ ▦ ▦ ▣ OTHER
Times: Noon-last L 2pm, last D 9.30pm. Closed Sun & Bhs, Dec 25-Jan 2
Menus: A la carte, fixed-price L & D, pre-theatre
Seats: 80. Air-conditioning
Additional: Children over five permitted; ❶ dishes

Miyama ⌘

Japanese embassy staff are regular visitors for one-pot dishes cooked at the table such as 'shabu-shabu' or 'sukiyaki', or for a range of well-prepared sushi. Traditional Japanese set meals are perhaps the best introduction for the uninitiated: a 'tonkatsu' meal includes deep-fried tofu in batter and breaded pork escalope

Seats: 65. No pipes. Air conditioning
Additional: Children welcome; ❶ menu; Vegan on request
Directions: Nearest Tube – Green Park

W1 38 Clarges Street W1
Map no: C3
Tel: 0171 499 2443
Chef: F Miyama
Proprietors: F Miyama and T Miura
Cost: Alc £17, fixed-price L £11-£18; fixed-price D £32-£40.
Service charge 15%
Credit cards: ◼ ▦ ▦ ▣ OTHER
Times: Last L 2.30pm/D 10.30pm. Closed Sat and Sun lunch

Monkey's ☺☺

Good fish dishes on a French-style menu in popular restaurant with a welcoming atmosphere

Monkey's takes its name from the anthropomorphic period cartoons on the menu cover, a conceit that happily is not reflected in the menu. The only nuts in sight here are the chestnuts with the sautéed mignon of venison, and the pine nuts in a marinated chicken salad. The daily changing, French-style menu specialises in fish dishes, and interesting recipes include terrine of brill, salmon and sea scallops, mille-feuille of salmon and chives, stuffed fillet of sea bass and red pepper sauce, and fried monkfish with lentils and Pernod sauce. Meat and game dishes include roast Bresse pigeon and wild mushrooms, and calves' liver and bacon. Luxury ingredients are not stinted; try the lobster ravioli, or the foie gras which comes either in a terrine or as a warm salad. For the well-heeled, there is Sevruga caviar at £60 a throw. However, there is also a good-value lunch menu that features various regular plats du jour, such as beef Stroganoff on Fridays.

Directions: Corner of Cale St & Markhay St, five mins from Sloane Sq off Kings Rd

SW3 1 Chelsea Green SW3 3QT
Map no: B1
Tel: 0171 352 4711
Chef: Thomas Benhay
Proprietor: Thomas Benhay
Cost: *Alc* £35-£55, fixed-price L £15/D £35 (5 courses). H/wine £11 Service exc
Credit cards: ▨ ▧ OTHER
Times: 12.30-last L 2.30pm, 7.30-last D 11pm. Closed Sat/Sun & 2 wks Easter, last 3 wks Aug
Menus: *A la carte*, fixed-price L & D
Seats: 45. No pipes allowed, air-conditioning
Additional: Children welcome, children's portions; ❷ dishes, vegan/other diets on request

The Montcalm ☺

Named after an 18th-century General celebrated for his dignity and style, the Montcalm exemplifies those rare and welcome qualities. The cooking has an international ring to it, and includes some authentic Japanese dishes. Ingredients are fresh and of good quality, and the flavours are robust

Great Cumberland Place W1
Map no: B4
Tel: 0171 402 4288
Chef: Gary Robinson
Proprietor: Nikko Hotels.
Manager: Gerhard Schaller
Cost: Alc dinner £32, fixed-price L £14.50 (1 course), £17.50, £19.50/D £19.50 (inc wine).
Wine £12 ❗ Service exc
Credit cards: ▨ ▧ ▧ ▣ OTHER
Times: Last L 2pm/D 10pm. Closed Sat L, Sun
Seats: 60. No-smoking area. Air conditioned
Additional: Children welcome. ❷ dishes; Vegan/other diets on request. Pianist Fri/Sat evenings

Directions: Great Cumberland Place is north of Marble Arch. Nearest Tube – Marble Arch

> 'Alla cacciatora' means cooked the hunter's way, and originates from central Italy. Dishes cooked in this manner contain meat, game or poultry which is first sautéed, then cooked slowly with onions, celery, carrots, mushrooms, tomatoes, wine and herbs.

The Mountbatten ❀

Situated in the heart of Covent Garden, the Mountbatten has an elegant feel. The Ad Lib restaurant often features live music. A simple menu incorporates a decent choice, including traditional British favourites. Look out for well-prepared fisherman's pie and treacle tart

Times: *Last L 2.30pm/D 11.30pm*
Seats: *65. No-smoking area. Air conditioned*
Additional: *No children after 8pm.* ✪ *dishes; Vegan/other diets on request*
Directions: In Covent Garden, next to Seven Dials

Monmouth Street
Seven Dials
Covent Garden WC2 9HD
Map no: D3
Tel: 0171 836 4300
Chef: Keith Walker
Proprietors: Radisson Edwardian
Cost: *Alc* £25, fixed-price L/D
£15.50, £19.50. Service exc
Credit cards: 🅾 💳 💳 💳

Mulligans of Mayfair ❀❀

An authentic Irish pub with hearty food in the heart of Mayfair

Still the only remotely authentic Irish restaurant in central London, a little bit of Dublin in Mayfair, Mulligan's looks like a grand old Victorian boozer, with glass partitions dividing the popular lounge bar on the ground floor. There's an oyster bar that dispenses plump specimens freshly flown in from the Emerald Isle and, downstairs in the basement dining-room, there's a variety of traditional dishes, like braised beef with boxty, and Irish stew with colcannon. There is always a great selection of Irish Farmhouse cheeses. Pints of that famous black Liffy water are the best accompaniment, but the wine list includes some good clarets and Burgundies.

Directions: Situated between Burlington Gardens and Clifford Street, just north of Piccadilly

13-14 Cork Street W1X 1PF
Map no: C3
Tel: 0171 409 1370
Chef: *Seamus McFadden*
Proprietor: *Mulligans*
Cost: *Alc £22.50; H/wine £5.95 (half bottle). Service inc*
Credit cards: 🅾 💳 💳 💳
Times: *12.30-last L 2.30pm, 6.30pm-last D 11pm. Closed Sat lunch, Sun, Xmas*
Additional: *Children welcome; children's portions;* ✪ *dishes*

Museum Street Café ❀❀

A popular, simple little café with short fixed-price menus of imaginative modern cooking, including many dishes from the chargrill

Owners Gail Koerber and Mark Nathan have a straightforward approach to food, wine and service at this bright little café. While their cooking is simple they achieve some well-balanced flavours which make for enjoyable dishes. Short fixed-price menus of either two or three courses are offered for lunch and dinner. The lunch selection changes daily and the dinner menu weekly. There is a choice of two starters, which could include salad with grilled aubergine, feta cheese, tomatoes and garlic croûtons, and the soup of the day, perhaps salmon and coconut with coriander, lime and chilli. The emphasis is on chargrilling for the main courses. A test meal sampled chargrilled loin of veal with roasted red onions and salsa verde, or there could be seared tuna with sherry and cayenne mayonnaise. Vegetables – perhaps french beans, Savoy cabbage, carrots and broccoli – are carefully cooked and well seasoned. Desserts include Elizabeth David's black fruit fool with walnut drops, or a delicious white chocolate buttermilk tart with rhubarb compote. Alternatively, one can finish with cheese from Neal's Yard Dairy. A few inexpensive red and white wines are listed, in keeping with the style of the menu.

Directions: Museum Street is off Bloomsbury Way – near British Museum – nearest Tubes – Tottenham Court Road & Holborn

47 Museum Street WC1
Map no: D4
Tel: 0171 405 3211 / 3212
Chefs: Mark Nathan and Gail Koerber
Proprietors: Mark Nathan and Gail Koerber
Cost: Fixed-price L £15 /D £21. H/wine £8 ❗ Service exc.
Credit cards: 🅾 💳 💳 OTHER
Menus: Fixed-price L & D
Times: 12.30pm-last L 2.30pm, 6.30pm-last D 9.30pm. Closed Sat, Sun, Bhs,Christmas, 2 wks Summer
Seats: 35. No smoking
Additional: Children permitted; ✪ dishes/other diets on request

Naughts 'n' Crosses ✿

Colourful with fresh flowers, plants and curtains, this is a smart modern restaurant. The cooking is Franco-British with a detectable Oriental influence. A typical meal might include smoked chicken and pepper pancake with mustard cream sauce, rack of lamb with Madeira sauce, and Caledonian cream parfait

77 The Grove
Ealing W5 5LL
Map no: GtL B3
Tel: 0181 840 7568
Chef: Anthony Ma
Manager: Jorgen Kunath

Directions: Nearest Tube – Ealing Broadway

Neal Street Restaurant ✿✿✿

Wild mushrooms, truffles and pasta are the key elements at this ever popular, mould-breaking Italian restaurant in Covent Garden

WC2 26 Neal Street WC2H 9PS
Map no: D4
Tel: 0171 836 8368
Chef: Nick Melmoth-Coombs
Proprietor: Antonio Carluccio
Cost: *Alc* £37. H/wine £12.50
Service exc
Credit cards: ▨ ▤ ▨ ▨
Times: 12.30-last L 2.30pm, 7.30pm-last D 11pm. Closed Sun & Bhs, 1 wk at Xmas
Menus: *A la carte*
Seats: 65. Air-conditioning
Additional: Children welcome; ❶ dishes, vegan/other diets on request

There is a reassuring consistency and quality to the cooking in this restaurant, a temple to the twin delights of mushrooms and pasta. Through television and books, these two ingredients have been indelibly linked with the smiling face of Antonio Carluccio, who has dedicated many years to tracking down every sort and size of fungi. A selection of fresh mushrooms are displayed in a basket by the entrance, waiting to be cooked as starters with a few herbs and a little lemon juice. Other first courses might include truffled endive salad or wild mushroom soup, with main courses also leaning heavily in the same direction – pappardalle with funghi, chicken scallopine with shitake and oyster mushrooms, and sautéed veal kidney with morels and red wine. Mushroom eating, however, is not compulsory, and a range of other good, robust Italian dishes includes seafood antipasto, stuffed calamari on rocket, and entrecôte with freshly grated wild horseradish.

An inspection meal started with black olives and marvellous focaccia topped with crushed sea salt. Of the four speciality pastas, black angels hair with seafood and bottarga was particularly fine. A correctly cooked, handsome piece of turbot was simply served with two types of mushrooms, honey fungus and Judas ear, enlivened with a hint of chilli. From an all-Italian dessert choice, a pear poached in honey, saffron and spices delivered an intense flavour, enhanced by a Grappa-laden cream sauce. Espresso is rich and strong, served with Carluccio's own brand of chocolate. Afterwards, the temptation to visit the adjacent delicatessen, run by Priscilla Carluccio, is hard to resist.

Directions: Nearest Tube: Covent Garden. Just N of where Shelton St crosses Neal St

Nico at Ninety ✿✿✿✿✿

Stunning, near faultless cooking from one of our greatest chefs

W1 90 Park Lane W1A 3AA
Map no: B3
Tel: 0171 409 1290
Chefs: Nico Ladenis and Paul Rhodes
Proprietors: Nico & Dinah-Jane Ladenis
Cost: Fixed-price L £29/D £57 (3 courses). H/wine £18 ❢ Service inc
Credit cards: ▨ ▤ ▨ ▨
Times: Closed Sat L, Sun & Bhs, 10 days at Xmas, 4 days Easter

The restaurant may be part of Grosvenor House Hotel but it has its own smartly canopied entrance from Park Lane. The dining-room is elegant, stylish, with a prosperous air and a feeling of solid comfort enhanced by well-spaced large tables and very comfortable chairs. Yet there is a pleasing lack of pretension. The service – and there is lots of it – is accessible, informative, welcoming; the menu reads with astonishing simplicity in straightforward English with not one jot of French culinary jargon to complicate matters. It does justice to Nico Ladenis's inspired cooking where technique and intelligence come through. Complexity has never been his favoured route, instead light but true use of flavours is a hallmark of food that is continually evolving.

The current repertoire of dishes shows considerable finesse. The selection of starters can be strong on fish with grilled scallops and baby spinach leaves, or crispy salmon with ginger and teriyaki sauce. Fish main courses have their own section, offering perhaps, steamed sea bass with an olive crust and basil purée or fillet of John Dory with a sweet and sour Oriental sauce. Offal makes an appearance in veal sweetbreads with Parma ham and morels.

A spring meal produced a report loaded with superlatives. A superbly cooked risotto of ceps came bursting with flavour, its neighbour, a ragout of scallops and lobster with leeks was of equal quality. Both a succulent fillet of turbot topped with a crust of fried potatoes and accompanied by a smooth delicate sauce and breast of maize-fed chicken cooked in goose fat and served with morels and foie gras pancakes revealed contrasts of taste and texture which were remarkable. Lemon tart was 'a masterpiece', the assiette of desserts just as stunning with every piece exquisitely presented. Lunch is a bargain at £29 for three courses including service and tax. This encompasses a choice of some seven or eight dishes at each stage. Marinated salmon with celeriac remoulade and leeks could be followed by roast best end of lamb with gratin potatoes, and poached pears with crispy almonds and chocolate sauce.

The wine list is high on quality, but pricey. Affordable drinking is to be had from a short list that is entitled 'An interesting selection of wines to merit your attention'. They should. They are all in the region of £20-£25.

Directions: Next to Grosvenor House Hotel

Nico Central ❀❀❀

Characteristic Nico establishment with simple but sophisticated food

It takes a slightly more adventurous type of tourist to stray away from the umbilical cord of Oxford Street, but those who do will be well rewarded at this small, elegant restaurant, just off Oxford Circus. Like its sister restaurant, Simply Nico, the formula marries simple but imaginative ideas with commendably consistent cooking, and the place is much patronised by the local business community. Set price two and three course menus are realistically priced, and include some ever-green favourites plus hallmark extras such as good olives, fine bread, excellent chips and Nico's signature creamy, puréed potatoes. The two restaurants share many dishes and, typically, one might expect to find soufflé of Stilton with walnut and pear, smoked trout mousse with smoked salmon and brioche, ragoût of chicken with wild mushrooms, fricassé of guinea fowl with tarragon, and braised ox-tongue with beetroot, Madeira and spinach. A little joke is to serve mushy peas with fillet of cod or deep-fried hake.

Recent inspection meals have praised the bold crab ravioli with tangy spring onion mayonnaise, the light and fluffy fillet of brill, nicely baked with a crust of fresh croûtons and simply served with provençale vegetables, and boudin blanc sausage of chicken and foie gras, packed with colour and flavour and served with a caramelised apple galette. Saucing is highly skilled, as demonstrated by a superb béarnaise sauce. Luscious desserts include hot ginger and walnut sponge with toffee sauce, and nougat glace with blackcurrant coulis.

Menus: *A la carte*, fixed-price L & D
Seats: 80. No pipes allowed, air-conditioning
Additional: Children under 6 not permitted; ❂ dishes

W1 35 Great Portland Street W1N 5DD
Map no: C4
Tel: 0171 436 8846
Chef: Andre Garrett
Proprietors: Nico & Dinah-Jane Ladenis.
Manager: Jean-François Girard
Cost: Fixed-price L £23.50 (3 courses)/D £26. H/wine £12.
❗ Service inc
Credit cards: 🂠 🖭 🖭 🂠
Times: Noon-last L 2pm, 7pm-last D 11pm. Closed Sat L, Sun & Bhs, 10 days at Xmas
Menus: *A la carte*, fixed-price L & D
Seats: 55. No pipes allowed, air-conditioning
Additional: Children over 10 permitted; ❂ dishes, vegan/other diets on request

A superb tarte tatin with home-made vanilla ice-cream quite entranced one of our seasoned inspectors. Excellent espresso coffee comes with chocolate truffles. Attentive service is provided by a keen, on-the-ball young team.

Directions: 5 mins walk from Oxford Circus Tube station, Oxford St end of Gt Portland St

Nicole's ❀❀

Bring your best handbag to this sleek, fashion conscious modern restaurant in the basement of Nicole Farhi

It takes a brave man to eat here unaccompanied at lunchtime, if he is not to feel hemmed in by a sea of designer handbags, designer shopping bags and designer plastic bags. Unlike dinner, when candlelit peace and quiet prevails, lunchtimes are all hustle and bustle, as fashionable New Bond Street shoppers, having shopped till they've dropped, recover their strength with a soupçon of smoked haddock chowder, a morsel of grilled brill with wild mushroom and leek butter, and, yes, perhaps just a mouthful of duck confit with white bean purée. Rhubarb beignets with ginger ice-cream, warm pear brûlée tart, and caramelised apple pudding with custard, however, are a major hazard to the hips.

The cooking style is modern European, and uses plenty of organic ingredients. Chef Annie Waite trained at Clarke's, and her cooking is coherent, concise and fatally tempting. Our inspector thoroughly enjoyed the risotto of the day, textured with red onion and rocket. The seared calves' liver with caramelised shallots came with maize polenta and fresh spinach cooked in olive oil, all of which were made for each other.

Directions: Turn off Regent St into Conduit St – at 1st junction turn left into New Bond St. Entrance 50 metres on right

W1 158 New Bond Street W1
Map no: D4
Tel: 0171 499 8404
Chef: Annie Wayte
Proprietor: N F Restaurants Ltd.
Manager: Philippe Larmaz
Cost: *Alc* £25. H/wine £9.50 ❢
Service inc
Credit cards: 🄰 🄱 🄲 🄳 OTHER
Times: 10am-last L 3.30pm, last D 10.45pm (6pm Sat). Closed Sun
Menus: *A la carte*, bar menu, breakfast, afternoon tea
Seats: 68. No-smoking area, air-conditioning
Additional: Children's portions on request; ❶ dishes, vegan/other diets on request

The Nosh Brothers ❀

☺ *The Nosh brothers, Nick and Mick, offer reasonably priced modern British cooking at this Fulham Road restaurant. Expect dishes such as fresh seafood Nosh platter, chicken in filo pastry stuffed with garlic and spinach and served with lemon butter sauce, and banana and poppyseed cake with hot chocolate sauce*

Menus: *A la carte*, fixed-price D
Seats: 75. Air-conditioning
Additional: Children welcome; ❶/vegan dishes
Directions: Fulham Rd between Munster Rd & Parsons Green Lane

SW6 773 Fulham Road SW6
Map no: E3
Tel: 0171 736 7311
Chefs: Nick & Mick Nosh
Proprietor: Marek
Cost: Fixed-price D £10 (Mon-Thur). H/wine £8.50 ❢ Service inc
Credit cards: 🄰 🄲 OTHER
Times: 7.30pm-last D 11pm. Closed Sun & Dec 25, Jan 1

> 'A la parisienne' describes classic styles of presentation that are typical of the repertoire of Parisien restaurants. Fish or shellfish 'à la parisienne' is a cold dish made with mayonnaise and accompanied by artichoke hearts garnished with a mix of small diced vegetables in mayonnaise, stuffed hard boiled eggs and/or cubes of aspic. Soup 'à la parisienne' is made with leeks and potatoes, finished with milk, and garnished with chervil leaves.

Odette's ❀❀❀

Fascinating clientele, stylish surroundings with interesting food, exceptional wine and reasonable prices

The clientele at Odette's is as exotic as the ingredients in the dishes, and it is difficult to say which is the more interesting. The ground floor restaurant is well established and there is an informal wine bar downstairs serving a less complicated menu. The restaurant is grand – its walls completely covered with gilt-framed mirrors of all shapes and sizes. Round tables are swathed in white linen, topped with tall white candles, polished glass and silverware, and finished with vast white lilies arranged with contorted Chinese willow. Short but interesting, the menu offers five or so choices at each course, including vegetarian dishes. The meal begins with excellent black olives and cheese-flavoured friandises, followed by home-baked bread. Pan-fried lambs' brains with sorrel and egg could be followed by fillet of beef with braised red cabbage and cinnamon or broad bean and pea risotto with basil and Parmesan. A May inspection meal included a wonderful dish of tartare of scallops in buckwheat pancakes stacked to form a gâteau, with tomato providing a contrasting texture. The main course, new season lamb, was served with a powerful turnip and potato cake in a thin lamb stock sauce. Fresh, barely cooked spinach in olive oil and nutmeg was 'delightful'. Best of all, though, was the almond and pistachio panna cotta with chocolate sauce. The balance of flavours was near-perfect. An exceptional wine list makes a serious effort to deliver flavours worthy of the food, and at fair prices; half bottles are well represented. Well-paced service adds to a memorable experience.

Directions: Nr Primrose Hill. Nearest Tube: Chalk Farm

NW1 130 Regents Park Road
NW1 8XL
Map no: GtL C3
Tel: 0171 586 5486/8766
Chef: Paul Holmes
Proprietor: Simone Green.
Manager: John Mason
Cost: Alc £22, fixed-price L £10.
H/wine £10.95 ❗ Service exc
Credit cards: 🅰 📧 🆔 💳
Times: 12.30-last L 2.30pm,
7pm-last D 11pm. Closed Sun
pm & Bhs, 2 wks at Xmas
Menus: A la carte, fixed-price
L, bar menu
Seats: 60. Air-conditioning
Additional: Children welcome,
children's portions; ❂ dishes,
vegan/other dishes on request

Odin's Restaurant ❀❀

☺ *Enjoyable, uncomplicated cooking in a popular restaurant comfortably distant from the West End's brasher parts*

Hundreds of original oil paintings cover the walls, serving to remind visitors of one of the two of the late Peter Langan's special interests. His presence is still strong as, glass replenished and ready to drink, he stares out from both the menu and wine list. Richard Shepherd and Michael Caine are joint proprietors, Dieter Schultz is still the manager and Shaun Butcher continues to maintain an impressive standard of uncomplicated cooking. At Odin's uncomplicated means just that, as examples like roast pigeon with red lentils, mushroom spring roll with curried chick peas and tomato salad prove. The daily menu is determined by market fresh produce and on an inspection visit steamed mussels, cooked in white wine and cream, were tried. Although the flavour wasn't the best, the sauce was good. Roast rack of tender, pink English lamb with split peas and mint sauce was accompanied by fresh vegetables cooked just right. A favourite dessert with a long pedigree is Mrs Langan's chocolate pudding. Wines are predominantly French, with a notable selection of red Bordeaux and domaine-bottled white Burgundies. The house wines available by the glass should not be overlooked either.

Directions: At Marylebone High Street end of Devonshire Street. Nearest Tubes – Baker Street, Regents Park, Great Portland Street

27 Devonshire Street W1
Map no: C4
Tel: 0171 935 7296
Chef: Shaun Butcher
Proprietors: Michael Caine and
Richard Shepherd
Cost: Alc £23. Wine £8.50.
Service inc
Credit cards: 🅰 📧 🆔 💳 OTHER
Menu: A la carte
Times: 12.30-last L 2.30pm,
7pm-last D 11.30pm. Closed
Sat, Sun
Seats: 60. Air conditioned
Additional: ❂ dishes

The Old Delhi ❀

☺ *An Indian restaurant with a wine list that includes premier cru claret at £295 is somewhat out of the ordinary and this jewel-like establishment on a corner near Edgware Road is a cut above your average tandoori. Well-made familiar staples include proper biryanis and there is a strong Iranian influence*

Cost: Alc £20. H/wine £8 (half bottle). Service inc
Credit cards: ⬛ 💳 💳 💳
Seats: 56
Additional: Children welcome; ✿ dishes
Directions: In Kendal Street, off Edgeware Road. Nearest Tube – Marble Arch

W2 48 Kendal Street W2
Map no: B3
Tel: 0171 724 9580
Chef: Ram
Proprietors: Jay Shaghaghi, Hasser

Olde Village Bakery ❀

☺ *This 16th-century building, once the village bakery, is now a tea shop offering a serious lunch and dinner service in a relaxed atmosphere. The daily-changing menu might feature chicken and pistachio nut terrine with balsamic dressing, or a confit of rabbit leg with a thick sage and onion jus*

33 High Street
Pinner
Middlesex HA5 5PS
Map no: GtL A4
Tel: 0181 868 4704
Chef: Phillip Scarles
Proprietors: Susan & Kevin Davies
Cost: Alc £20, fixed-price L & D £10. H/wine £8.99 ! Service exc
Credit cards: ⬛ 💳 💳 💳 OTHER
Times: 10am-last L 3pm, last D 10pm. Closed 1st wk Jan (open Jan 1)
Menus: A la carte, fixed-price L & D, ✿
Seats: 60. No-smoking area, no pipes or cigars
Additional: Children welcome, children's portions; ✿ dishes, vegan/other dishes on request

Directions: From Northwood A404, turn right at Pinner Green into Bridge St. 2nd left is High St

Olivo ❀❀

☺ *Inspired Italian food with a Sardinian bias served in a stylish setting*

Modern blue and yellow decor, distinctive wooden seats and smartly uniformed staff suggest an image-conscious restaurant. It is, but the food clearly comes first. Fish is a staple – gurnard fillets may appear, for example – and on a recent occasion there was sweet, tender cuttlefish served in an olive oil and garlic sauce finished off with a visually appealing pool of black ink vinaigrette – 'near faultless'. Unhappily, a beef escalope, with a simple tomato sauce and cold, hard, roast potatoes, was wide of the mark, but another main course displayed an inspired combination of earthy lentils with lambs' kidneys. The reasonably priced, weekly-changing lunchtime menu offers a short choice of enjoyable desserts such as

SW1 21 Eccleston Street SW1
Map no: C2
Tel: 0171 730 2505
Chef: Sandro Mella
Proprietor: Mauro Sanna. Manager: J L Journade
Cost: Alc D £20.50, fixed-price L £15.50. H/wine £9 ! Service exc
Credit cards: ⬛ 💳 💳 OTHER
Times: noon-last L 2.30pm, 7pm-last D 11pm. Closed Sat L, Sun, BHs, 1wk Aug
Menus: A la carte D, fixed-price L

apple flan, coffee mousse or traditional Sardinian 'sebada', a warm pastry shell filled with cheese, dressed with honey. Dinner menus change nightly. The wine list is partisan and a selection of grappas is available for those who like a drink with a kick.

Directions: From Buckingham Palace Road, opposite Victoria Station, turn into Eccleston Street. Olivo is on the left

Seats: 43 Air conditioned
Additional: children welcome over 5; children's portions, other diets on request

Oriental House ❀

☺ *Oriental House offers Cantonese cooking, from both fixed price menus (for a minimum of two persons), and a carte. Dishes include seafoods such as pan fried squid with green pepper and black bean sauce, or meat and poultry choices like beef in satay sauce, or grilled chicken Peking style*

Menus: A la carte, fixed-price D, ❖
Seats: 56. Air-conditioning
Additional: Children welcome; ❖ dishes, vegan/other dishes on request
Directions: Nearest Tube: Earl's Court

SW5 251 Old Brompton Road SW5 9HP
Map no: A1
Tel: 0171 370 2323
Chef: Ying-Ho Wong
Proprietor: Chi-Kin Lau
Cost: Alc £18. H/wine £9.80
Service inc
Credit cards: ▨ ▨ ▨ OTHER
Times: 6pm-last D 10.45pm.
Closed Mon & Bhs

Orsino ❀

☺ *There is a relaxed, informal atmosphere at this simple but fashionable restaurant which features uncomplicated Italian food. A selection of pizza and pasta is supported by modish dishes such as grilled tuna with roast tomato and white beans, or pork chops with porcini, rosemary and polenta*

Menus: Fixed-price L
Seats: 100. No-smoking area, cigars & pipes discouraged
Additional: Children welcome; ❖ dishes
Directions: Off Holland Park Ave

W11 119 Portland Road W11
Map no: GtL C3
Tel: 0171 221 3299
Chef: Anne Kettle
Manager: Nick Guerreri
Cost: Fixed-price L £13.50.
H/wine £10.50 Service exc
Credit cards: None taken
Times: Noon last D 10.45pm.
Closed Dec 24/25

Parmesan cheese or 'parmigiano reggiano' originated in the area that formed the Duchy of Parma, between Parma and Reggio Emilio. Locals will tell you that the cheese has been made there for over 2,000 years but whether this is so or not, it was an established favourite by the 14th century; Boccaccio referred to it in the 'Decameron'. Nowadays 'parmigiano reggiano' is made in the provinces of Parma, Reggio Emilia, Bologna, Modena and Mantua. The method of making Parmesan has remained unchanged through the centuries. Small cheese factories produce four to six cheeses a day using milk from local cows. The milk is partially skimmed and the whey from the previous batch is added to help the fermentation. The cheese is curdled with calves' rennet, shaped, and salted for 25 days. The shapes weigh between 30-35kg and it takes 16 litres of milk to make each kilogram of cheese. The cheeses are matured for different periods of time and are named by their age. 'Parmigiano nuovo' is less than one year old, 'parmigiano vecchio' is one and half to two years old, and 'parmigiano stravecchio' is two years old or more. A good Parmesan is hard, yellow, crumbly in texture and has a rich, fruity and slightly salty taste. The best cheeses are manufactured from the middle of April to the beginning of November. Parmesan should never be bought already grated, for once the cheese has been grated it looses some of its flavour.

Orso ❀❀

Highly popular basement Italian restaurant with cooking of considerable brio

Orso is well established as one of the most accomplished Italian restaurants in this part of town. Skilful timing and preparation of organic ingredients define an evolving menu that changes twice daily. Flavours can be exciting, as in a thin pasta of crab, courgettes and chopped tomato, or tender calves' liver sautéed in olive oil and white wine with sage. A cross-section of appetisers on a July day included fried courgette flowers filled with sun-dried tomatoes, ricotta and basil, a salad of tuna, red onion, cherry tomatoes and white beans, and potato and argula soup. A separate pizza section offered, amongst others, one with Gorgonzola, Parma ham, spinach and onions. First courses featured leek and ricotta ravioli with sage and butter, and risotto with courgettes, lemon and mint. Entrées included veal kidneys with Marsala and shallots, and grilled rabbit with tomato, green olives and oregano. A short list of vegetables typically comes dressed with olive oil and lemon. There are some good Italian cheeses including pecorino with pear, but desserts are otherwise limited to such things as strawberry and mascarpone mousse or pear and raspberry torte.

Directions: 1 block in from the Strand, 2 blocks down from Royal Opera House

WC2 27 Wellington Street WC2E 7DA
Map no: D3
Tel: 0171 240 5269
Chef: Martin Wilson
Proprietor: Orso Restaurants Ltd.
Manager: Linda Thorne
Cost: *Alc* £24, fixed-price L £13.50 (Sat/Sun). H/wine £10.50 Service exc
Credit cards: None taken
Times: Noon-last D midnight. Closed Dec 24/25
Menus: *A la carte,* fixed-price L (Sat/Sun)
Seats: 110. No-smoking area, cigars & pipes discouraged, air-conditioning
Additional: Children welcome; ❤ dishes

Osteria Antica Bologna ❀❀

☺ *Hearty Italian peasant food in a cosy, candlelit, hospitable trattoria*

Presentation remains rustic and flavours honest at this unpretentious trattoria which has ridden the wave of early popularity and settled into its role as a friendly local purveyor of crostini and tiramisu. There are two small and densely packed rooms that are particularly cosy in the evening when they gleam with candlelight and resound with the low murmur of people enjoying themselves. Regulars may simply opt for a quick bowl of pasta and a salad, but to investigate the menu more thoroughly, 'bruscetta calabrese' – topped with tomatoes, chilli and rocket – is the almost obligatory starting point. There is a strong selection of antipasti which, at our last visit, included fried courgette and barley cakes with a red pepper sauce, and tender strips of octopus with cannellini beans, radicchio, and a warm potato salad. Meaty main courses might be goat stew in a tomato and almond sauce, served with chunky polenta, or balls of lean lamb in a tangy tomato sauce. There are some great wines on an all Italian list, but those on a restricted budget will do just as well with a jug of house wine.

Directions: Off Battersea Rise, between Wandsworth and Clapham Commons

23 Northcote Road SW11
Map no: GtL C2
Tel: 0171 978 4771
Chefs: *Aurelio Spagnuolo and Raffaele Petralia*
Proprietors: *Rochelle Porteous and Aurelio Spagnuolo*
Cost: *Alc £15, fixed-price lunch £7.50. H/wine £6.90. Service exc. Cover charge 60p*
Credit cards: 🟦 ▦ ▨ 🔲 OTHER
Menus: *A la carte, fixed-price lunch*
Times: *Mon-Fri Midday-last L 3pm, 6pm-last D 11pm (11.30pm Fri); Sat Midday-11.30pm; Sun 12.30-10.30pm. Closed 10 days Xmas/New Year*
Seats: *75. Air conditioned*
Additional: *Children welcome; children's portions.* ❤ *dishes; Vegan on request*

  ☺ This symbol means a good meal for £25 or less per person.

  ❤ This symbol means a vegetarian choice is always offered.

Overton's ❀❀

Popular restaurant with a short, modern menu and well-supervised professional service

Overton's has the air of a gentleman's club, particularly at lunchtime, and even more so since it returned to the style and standard of food with which it was formerly associated. Chef Nigel Davies offers a short but well-balanced menu, which includes a good selection of fish dishes. Typical starters could be terrine of rabbit, chicken livers and pistachio with apple chutney, pan-fried scallops with Savoy cabbage, peppers and Alsace bacon, and fettucini with wild mushrooms, roquette and Parmesan. As a main course, our inspector chose pan-fried brill, tomato fondue and herb brioche crust, but although the fish itself was excellent, the crust lacked the flavour with which to complement it. Other dishes on the menu included grilled sea bass with black beans, spring onions and ginger risotto, and magret of duck, red cabbage, caramelised onions and Calvados. Dessert of the day may be spotted dick (a bit stodgy on our sampling), or something similar, plus a short selection of others. The wine list is well chosen and reasonably priced. Helpful and attentive staff are well drilled by the quietly efficient restaurant manager, John Pombo.

Directions: Off Piccadilly. Nearest Tube – Green Park

SW1 5 St James's Street
SW1A 1EF
Map no: C3
Tel: 0171 839 3774
Chef: Nigel H Davies
Proprietor: Overtons Restaurant Ltd
Cost: Alc £27.35. H/wine £10.50 ❢ Service inc
Credit cards: 🖪 🖿 🖾 💷 OTHER
Times: Closed Sat/Sun & Bhs, 10 days at Xmas
Menus: A la carte, bar menu
Seats: 54. No pipes allowed, air-conditioning
Additional: Children over 8 welcome, children's portions; ❷ dishes, other dishes on request

Park Lane Hotel ❀❀

A smart brasserie serving cooking in the modern style to an international clientele

The Park Lane was built in the 1920s, but there is little feel of the Art Deco era in the Brasserie on the Park which favours a more modern decor, and an upmarket feel. Staff are attentive, warm and friendly but could show more attention to small details, such as checking that the bread baskets are not served with dry, stale pieces of baguette. The menu has much to offer, is modern in approach, but the cooking can, on occasion, lack balance and direction. An inspection meal yielded a starter of linguine with wild mushrooms that had a too strong balsamic vinegar taste, scallops served with masses of chopped leeks on a buttery white wine and cream sauce flecked with diced red peppers, and clafoutis – soft pastry tart filled with batter pudding mixture mixed with Morello and glacé cherries – served with thin crème anglaise. Rich, full-flavoured espresso is served with chocolate creams.

Directions: Nearest Tubes – Hyde Park Corner, Green Park

W1 Piccadilly W1X 8BX
Map no: C3
Tel: 0171 499 6321
Chef: Jon Tindau
Proprietor: Clive Carr
Cost: Alc £28, fixed-price L £19.50/D £29. H/wine £16 ❢ Service inc
Credit cards: 🖪 🖿 🖾 💷 OTHER
Times: Last L 2pm/D 10.30pm. Closed Sat L, Sun, Bhs
Seats: 60. No-smoking area. Air conditioned
Additional: Children welcome; children's portions; ❷ dishes; Vegan/other diets on request

Partners Brasserie ❀❀

Popular brasserie with carefully cooked fresh food. A good choice includes an excellent, inexpensive set menu

The well-proven format of this popular neighbourhood brasserie, sister restaurant to Partners in Dorking, has been maintained by new chef Rebecca Jones. If anything, she has added an adventurous, eclectic style to the modern recipes, which can result in some memorable moments. Starting off with home-made warm bread

23 Stonecot Hill
Sutton SM3 9HB
Map no: GtL C1
Tel: 0181 644 7743
Chef: Rebecca Jones
Proprietor: Andrew Thomason
Cost: Alc £17.50, fixed-price L/D £10.95. H/wine £7.95 Service exc
Credit cards: 🖪 🖿 🖾 💷 OTHER

rolls, our inspector chose the beautifully cooked sauté of chicken livers, followed by roasted fillet of Cornish cod with herb crust and an onion jus. Vegetables were stir-fried and matched the main dish well. The crème brûlée was not completely cooked through but, despite the slip, the richness and flavour were still apparent. Other dishes from the eclectic range include chicken satay with spicy peanut dip, roast breast of duck glazed with honey and crushed peppercorns and, from the chargrill, tiger prawns with garlic butter or liver and bacon with mash and onion gravy. Check for daily specials. Sensibly priced wines from around the world include house Cuvée Lupe Cholet available by the glass or bottle. The Partners Dining Club is worth exploring for privilege card special benefits.

Times: Last L 2pm, last D 9.30pm. Closed Sun/Mon
Menus: A la carte, fixed-price L & D
Seats: 30. Air-conditioning
Additional: Children welcome, children's portions; ◐ dishes, other dishes on request

Directions: On A24 near Woodstock Pub

Pearl of Knightsbridge ❀❀

☺ *Smart, upmarket Cantonese Chinese on Knightsbridge Green opposite Harrods*

Predominantly Cantonese food with a few Peking dishes is served in this smart, modern Chinese restaurant, popular with the well-heeled Knightsbridge set. Cooking is sound and the fixed-price lunch is excellent value, and there is a set menu for two or more people at dinner. Starters may include mixed hors d'oeuvre or phoenix tail prawns, while main courses include a good range of fish, poultry and meat dishes. Our inspector sampled the crispy aromatic duck with all the works – thin pancakes, shredded spring onions and cucumber, and a good plum sauce, sautéed beef with excellent black bean sauce garnished with mixed vegetables, and 'eight treasures' which consisted of crisp, pan-fried assorted vegetables, well seasoned and served with cashew nuts and mushrooms. Fragrant boiled rice was moist and fluffy.
The wine list is not extensive, but then jasmine tea is probably the best accompaniment. Staff are friendly and professional.

SW1 22 Brompton Road SW1
Map no: B2
Tel: 0171 225 3888
Chef: Hong Cheong
Proprietor: Anna Lam
Cost: A la carte £20, fixed-price £12.75. Service exc. Cover charge £2
Credit cards: 🔳 🔳 🔳 🔳
Menus: A la carte, fixed-price lunch and dinner
Times: Midday-last L 3pm, 6pm-last D 11.30pm. Closed Xmas
Additional: Children welcome; ◐ dishes

Directions: On the north side of Brompton Road at the junction with Knightsbridge. Nearest Tube – Knightsbridge

The Peasant ❀❀

Rustic Mediterranean food in laid-back former pub

Two years on, the hype has died down, the pace is more measured, and the quality of the cooking more accurate. The style is boldly simple, reflected in the design of the former pub, stripped bare to highlight eye-catching features such as a mosaic floor, bevelled glass and colourful murals. Based around an Italian core, the menu takes in all the Med, and is decided collectively by the staff. Slices of rustic bread are perfect for dipping into a bowl of clean, fresh olive oil poured at the table, and original and faintly exotic flavours arose, on our visit, from a romesco sauce of dried red peppers, tomatoes and pine nuts, served with a mozzarella cheese, basil and aubergine 'sandwich'. Other starters might include wild rocket and potato soup or baby octopus marinated with lemon, parsley and Parmesan. Main courses bring roast rabbit with garlic and spring greens, tagine of lamb with courgettes, potatoes, thyme and sesame seeds, and Italian veggie dishes such as spinach, walnut and

EC1 240 St Johns Street EC1
Map no: F4
Tel: 0171 336 7726
Chef: Enrico Sartor
Proprietors: Craig Schorn
Cost: Alc £20
Times: 12.30pm-last L 2.30pm, 6.30pm, last D 10.45pm. Closed Sat L, Sun
Additional: Children welcome; ◐ dishes

Gorgonzola cannelloni. Sea trout baked with chermoula had a pungent green herb and cumin crust, but was not perhaps the best choice of fish to be given this treatment.

Directions: Nearest Tube – Farringdon

The People's Palace ❀❀

☺ *Mezzanine dining on a vast scale, with an ever-improving menu shaped by Gary Rhodes*

Gary's Rhodeshow continues apace, this time at the Royal Festival Hall. The People's Palace is a massive, lofty room with gracious lines, dominated by the expanse of window overlooking the Thames, and the menu offers his classic British dishes with a modern interpretation, at very reasonable prices. The sixty bin wine list, which is all available by the glass and half-carafe, is arranged into traditional, European and New World wines, with the house wine, Le Vin de Levin at £9.00. The very formal service adds to the sense of occasion, but in no way detracts from the relaxed atmosphere. The food is good. Our inspector enjoyed a silky smooth chicken liver parfait with a contrasting grape chutney, followed by baked cod on oyster mushrooms, cabbage and thyme, served skin side up. The bread and butter pudding was simply exquisite, light and full of rich vanilla flavour. Equally good was the apple and almond tart with clotted cream. Other dishes bring in wider European influences, such as beef carpaccio with spiced marinated aubergines, grilled goats' cheese crostini, chargrilled breast of chicken with creamed tarragon noodles, and collar of bacon with sauerkraut and mustard sauce.

Directions: Level 3 of the Royal Festival Hall

SE1 Royal Festival Hall
Southbank SE1
Map no: E2
Tel: 0171 923 9999
Chef: Gary Rhodes
Proprietors: David & Joseph Levin
Cost: *Alc* £16, fixed-price L/D £13.50 (3 courses). H/wine £9.00 Service exc
Credit cards: 🔲 📷 💳 💳 OTHER
Times: Last L 3pm, last D 11pm.
Menus: *A la carte*, fixed-price L & D
Seats: 185. Air conditioning.
Additional: Children welcome, children's portions; ❂ dishes, other dishes on request

Percy's ❀❀

Genuinely eclectic cooking in singular restaurant run by dedicated husband and wife team

66/68 Station Road
North Harrow HA2 7SJ
Map no: Gtl B4
Tel: 0181 427 2021
Chef: Tina Bricknell-Webb
Proprietors: Tony & Tina Bricknell Webb
Cost: *Alc* £21.75-£27.75, fixed-price L £10. H/wine £9.80 ❗ Service exc

Pure talent fuels the cooking at this unique restaurant set in a bland Greater London suburb, talent that has not been shaped or refined by professional training. Whether or not one regards the latter as a straight-jacket or needy discipline, there is no doubt that Tina Bricknell-Webb has considerable native ability and a free-ranging mind. Great care is taken by Tina, and husband Tony, to source ingredients, and a regular supply of vegetables and salads come from their own farm in Devon. The short menu changes frequently, and is supplemented by the freshest of fresh fish; a recent meal of John Dory was faultlessly timed, matched with an excellent lime and tarragon béarnaise sauce. For starters, there might be a fish, noodle and vegetable chowder or warm chicken liver salad, and other main courses might include breast of chicken wrapped in smoked bacon with lightly spiced mango and coconut cream sauce and fresh coriander, or grilled organic Aberdeen Angus fillet steak with shitake mushrooms, thyme and peppercorn jus. Desserts include a precisely executed, tangy and rich lemon tart, accompanied by an unusual rosemary ice-cream which, after initial doubts, made a surprisingly good match.

Credit cards: 🔲 🔳 🔳 🔳 OTHER
Times: Noon-last L 3pm, 6.30pm-last D 10.30pm. Closed Sun/Mon & Dec 27-Jan 3
Menus: *A la carte*, fixed-price L
Seats: 70. No smoking
Additional: Children over 10 welcome, children's portions by arrangement; ✪ dishes, vegan/other dishes on request

Directions: Opp North Harrow tube station

Persad Tandoori 🏵

In a busy suburban shopping centre this smart little Indian restaurant offers a carte featuring tandoori, biryani and pilau dishes. Set meals and some Persian dishes complete the picture. To finish, various fruits are offered along with a couple of Indian sweets

Menus: *A la carte*, Sun buffet **Seats:** 42
Additional: Children welcome, children's portions & menu; ✪ dishes, vegan dishes on request
Directions: In the High Street

36 High Street Ruislip HA4 7AN
Map no: GtL A4
Tel: 01895 630102/676587
Chef: Abdul Khair Ali
Proprietor: H R Choudhury
Cost: *Alc* £40 (4 courses), fixed-price L £3.40. H/wine £6 ▮ Service inc
Credit cards: 🔲 🔳 🔳 🔳
Times: Noon-last L 2.30pm, last D 11.45pm. Closed Xmas day

Pied à Terre 🏵🏵🏵🏵

Stark, minimalist setting for some bold, innovative modern cooking

W1P 34 Charlotte Street W1P 1HJ
Map no: C4
Tel: 0171 636 1178
Chef: Richard Neat
Proprietors: Richard Neat and David Moore
Cost: *Alc* £42.50, fixed-price L £19.50/D £42.50. H/wine £14 ▮ Service inc
Credit cards: 🔲 🔳 🔳 🔳 OTHER
Times: 12.15-last L 2.15pm, 7.15pm-last D 10.30pm. Closed Sat L, Sun & 2 wks at Xmas, New Year, last 2 wks Aug
Menus: *A la carte*, fixed-price L & D
Seats: 40. Air-conditioning
Additional: Children welcome; ✪ dishes, vegan/other dishes on request

It is a functional room: stark white walls, tables close packed. In contrast, Richard Neat's cooking is innovative and bold, his individual style perfected over the years by stints with some of the great chefs – in Paris, Joël Robuchon; in England, Raymond Blanc and Marco Pierre White. Some feel that Neat's food is now at the cutting edge of originality. Certainly, amuse-gueules of snails cooked three times in milk and covered with a fine chicken mousseline studded with finely chopped girolles, and casseroled lambs' tongues with red wine, show he is not afraid to experiment with the unusual, both ingredients and combinations.

Flavours are gentle rather than assertive, which does not stop the overall dish being exciting. Praise has come for mille-feuille of artichokes with langoustines and purée of salt cod, garnished with baked seaweed and for moist, firm-textured duck breast, baked with rösti potato and confit of gizzard, and served on buttered lentils. Offal makes frequent appearances, salad of pig's head, crispy trotter, brains and gherkins, for example, but that is tempered on the same menu with some unashamed luxury such as braised foie gras. The clever touch is to achieve balance – in a classic aspect of French cooking in which the refined is combined with earthy rusticism – with saucisson and choucroute. Fish is cooked with the same sense of originality. Fillets of sole come with crab, orange, and celery tagliatelle, sea bream with almond paste, confit salsify and red peppers. Nor do standards fail at the dessert stage. Dark bitter chocolate pavé, soufflé, and black cherry sorbet proved to be a rich dark fondue layered with sponge and set in a chocolate cup, topped with the sorbet and fresh mint, served with a separate chocolate soufflé and caramel ice-cream.

The set-price lunch menu is excellent value at £16.50 for two courses. Deep-fried rock oysters with olive oil hollandaise and red wine sauce could be followed by roasted lamb chump, sweetbread and kidney with rosemary juice and pea purée. Espresso coffee is dark and rich and comes with superb petits fours. The wines are mostly French with a token showing from the rest of the world, but there is a decent selection of bottles under £20, and some reasonably priced halves.

Directions: S end of Charlotte St just over Goodge St

Poons 🏵🏵

☺ *Lively, modish West End Chinese with some fine classic dishes*

Poons retains its brightness and young, cosmopolitan clientele. The cool, white interior is offset with blonde wood and brightly coloured, abstract Chinese tree paintings. It is not the place to go for a quiet night, though, as the inexpensive menu draws the crowds, with set meals starting at £14 for two. Note no credit cards are accepted. Few restaurants do the ubiquitous Peking duck as well as Poons. This is the real thing – thin, floury pancakes, moist meat and delicious crisp duck skin, served separately on prawn crackers, only let down by dull plum sauce. Poons is equally renowned for its wind-dried meat, which can be sampled in many variations, including an intriguing 'chicken sandwich', composed of pork in sweet wine sauce layered between slices of chicken. Fish dishes, on the other hand, can sometimes be under par – fried squid, strongly laced with garlic, was too heavily salted, and steamed scallops in the shell not in perfect order, despite the powerful accompanying sauce of soy and corn oil with spring onions and chilli seeds. Jasmine tea is, of course, de rigueur.

Directions: Opposite Swiss Centre (NCP) car park. Nearest Tube: Leicester Square

WC2 4 Leicester Square
WC2 7BL
Map no: D4
Tel: 0171 437 1528
Chef: Yuan Jin He
Proprietor: W N Poon.
Manager: Lesley Hau
Cost: *Alc* £18, fixed-price L/D
£14. H/wine £6.50 Service exc
Credit cards: 🂠 🂡 🂢 🂣 OTHER
Times: Noon-last D 11.30pm.
Closed Dec 24-27
Menus: *A la carte*, fixed-price
L & D
Seats: 120. Air-conditioning
Additional: Children welcome;
❶ dishes

Quaglino's ❀❀

Theatrical Conran brasserie with a legendary name, where cooking represents a triumph of quality over scale

As popular as on the day it opened, this one-time ballroom, converted into a 21st-century brasserie by Sir Terence Conran, simply fizzes with excitement, as tout-le-monde make an entrance down the central staircase. Giant columns, a mezzanine floor with bar overlooking the vast dining-room, and eye-catching fittings all give the impression of an ocean-going liner on party night. The menu, like the clientele, is cosmopolitan, and leans towards a lottery-winning European peasant-style of cooking . Lightly seared in the pan, foie gras with watercress and caramelised apple slices proved an excellent starter. Of the two salads sampled, the eponymous 'Quaglino's' was simple but effective, with creamed Parmesan and thinly sliced pecorino, whilst a chargrilled aubergine and pepper salad held its texture well. Scallops with spinach and ginger exemplified the best skills of the kitchen, as did a dish of braised beef with red wine and creamed parsnips. Desserts range from sophisticated prune and Armagnac parfait to school puds such as hot treacle pudding and custard. Espresso coffee is good, but our tea-lover was rewarded with a cup of not-too-hot-water and a tea bag! Despite the crowds, service is attentive and speedy, with no suggestion of pressure on table occupancy.

Directions: Bury St runs parallel with St James's, and is adjacent to Jermyn St

SW1 16 Bury Street SW1Y 6AL
Map no: C3
Tel: 0171 930 6767
Chef: Martin Webb
Proprietors: Sir Terence Conran, Joel Kissin and Tom Conran.
Manager: Eric Garnier
Cost: *Alc* £35.40, fixed-price L £12.95 ❗ Service inc
Credit cards: 🅾 🔲 🔲 🖃
Times: Noon-last L 3pm, 5.30pm-last D 1am (Mon-Thur), 2am (Fri/Sat), 11pm (Sun) Closed 3 days at Xmas
Menus: *A la carte*, fixed-price L, pre-theatre, bar menu
Seats: 338. Air-conditioning
Additional: ❂ dishes

Quality Chop House ❀❀

'Quality' and 'civility' are the watchwords of this unique establishment which offers a varied and reasonably priced daily menu

'Progressive working class caterer' is proclaimed on the window of Quality Chop House; a restaurant full of surprises. It has tables for six, which you might well have to share, narrow wooden bench seats and bottles of sauce on the side. Service is crisply efficient as befits an establishment that can serve meals at speed. The daily printed menu provides a startling range of dishes spanning many countries, but majoring in Mediterranean influences, with the odd Oriental and traditional British flourish. For example, bang-bang chicken might be followed by corned beef hash, or warm asparagus and pecorino by Toulouse sausages, mash and onion gravy. A recent meal comprised roasted vegetables and goats' cheese salad, then duck, slowly roasted, to give a crisp fragrant skin and moist meat, on a bed of dressed lettuce with french beans and potato cake. Desserts range from ices or fromage frais with exotic fruits to treacle pudding or caramel cheesecake. There is a 30-bin wine list, and a good choice of teas and coffees. Sunday brunch offers eggs Benedict, grilled T-bone steak, and a jug of bloody Mary or bucks fizz.

Directions: On the left-hand side of Farringdon Road, just before it meets Rosebery Avenue. Nearest Tube – Farringdon or Kings Cross

EC1 94 Farringdon Road EC1
Map no: E4
Tel: 0171 837 5093
Chef: Charles Fontaine
Proprietor: Fiona McIndoe
Cost: *Alc* from £13.50. H/wine £9 ❗ Service exc
Credit cards: None
Times: noon-last L 3pm (4pm Sun), 6.30pm (7pm Sun)-last D 11.30pm. Closed Sat lunch, Dec 24-Jan 3 approx
Menus: *A la carte*, Sun brunch
Seats: 48. Air conditioned
Additional: Children welcome; children's portions, ❂ dishes, other diets on request

Quincy's ❀❀

Uncomplicated, well-cooked dishes using fresh seasonal produce

Quincey's succeeds where other similar establishments fail, because of simple, unpretentious values. David Philpott's cooking is honest and correct, and his short, well-balanced, monthly changing, set-price menu offers daily specials plus a fish dish of the day. His careful approach extends to extras such as fresh wholemeal bread and unsalted butter, and canapés along the lines of chicken mousse on toast. On our visit, chilled vichyssoise was rather thin, lacking in body and flavour, but the main course of grilled rabbit with mashed potatoes, lemon butter and capers had tender and flavoursome meat. French beans and fresh spinach were good accompaniments. A pear tart with marzipan and home-made chocolate ice-cream had excellent fruit and light pastry. Other dishes typical of his style might include sweetbread ragoût with carrots and orange, fillet of beef with cep fumet and rösti, and rhubarb compote with panna cotta. Ones with a touch of originality include a collation of duck appetisers, chartreuse of pigeon with juniper, and coulibiac of winter fruits and rice pudding.

Directions: Situated between Hendon Way & Cricklewood Lane on the Finchley Rd

NW2 675 Finchley Road
NW2 2JP
Map no: GtL C4
Tel: 0171 794 8499
Chef: David Philpott
Proprietor: David Wardle
Cost: Fixed-price D £24. H/wine £9 Service exc
Credit cards: ⬛ 🟦 🟦
Times: 7pm-last D 10.30pm. Closed Sun/Mon & 1 wk at Xmas
Menus: Fixed-price D
Seats: 30. Air-conditioning
Additional: Children welcome, children's portions; ❂ dishes, other dishes on request

RSJ The Restaurant on the South Bank ❀❀

Committed, modern Anglo-French food at sunny culinary oasis on the South Bank

The dreary location leaves a certain amount to be desired, but the popularity of the place testifies to the demand that exists from nearby office workers, theatregoers, media folk and assorted luvvies. Food combinations are interesting but not outlandish, techniques simple but sophisticated, and the cooking generally shows an eye for current trends without following them blindly. Dishes worth sampling include chilled watercress soup with an oyster Chantilly, roast woodland pigeon with penne pasta, cèpes, smoked bacon, shallots and pigeon jus, pan-fried scallops with anchovy salsa and warm potato salad, and roast guinea fowl with broad beans, mushrooms, dauphinoise potatoes and foie gras sauce. Some of the vegetarian options look suspiciously like non-vegetarian ones minus key ingredients, but those complete in their own identity include wild asparagus tart with spinach, sorrel and leek with fresh herbs, and focaccia served with roast provençale vegetables, basil oil and Parmesan shavings. A dessert of roast banana and pecan strudel with fudge sauce and maple ice-cream, would tempt all persuasions.

Directions: On the corner of Coin Street and Stamford Street. Near National Theatre and LWT Studios

SE1 13a Coin Street SE1 8YQ
Map no: E3
Tel: 0171 928 4554
Chef: Ian Stabler
Proprietor: Nigel Wilkinson
Cost: Alc £24, fixed-price L/D £15.95. H/wine £9.75 ❗ Service inc
Credit cards: ⬛ 🟦 🟦 OTHER
Times: Noon-last L 2pm, 6pm-last D 11pm. Closed Sat L, Sun & Bhs
Menus: A la carte, fixed-price L & D
Seats: 40. Air-conditioning
Additional: Children welcome, children's portions; ❂ dishes, other dishes on request

A classic sauce vierge is based on butter and lemon juice and is traditionally served with asparagus, leeks and other boiled vegetables.

The Radisson Edwardian Hotel ❀

The pick of the hotels hard by Heathrow airport, The Radisson is a strikingly modern building which contains Henley's Restaurant. Here a French chef strives to produce British food for a corporate clientele. This may not sound inspiring, but our inspector enjoyed seafood salad, roast duck, apple and black pudding, and a well made pear tart

Directions: On the A4, eastbound side

Bath Road, Hayes
Greater London UB3 5AW
Map no: GtL A3
Tel: 0181 759 6311
Chef: Jean-Claude Sandillon
Cost: *Alc* £31, fixed-price L & D
£16.75/£28
Credit cards: ■ ■ ■ ■ OTHER
Times: Last D 11.30pm

Rani ❀❀

A vegetarian Indian restaurant that specialises in the subtle flavours and simple ingredients of Gujarat

N3 7 Long Lane
Finchley N3 2PR
Map no: GtL C4
Tel: 0181 349 4386/2636
Chef: Sheila Pattni
Proprietor: Jyotimbra Pattni
Cost: *Alc* £17, fixed-price D
£13. H/wine £8.60 Service exc
Credit cards: ■ ■ ■ OTHER
Times: 6pm-last D 10.30pm.
Closed Xmas day
Menus: *A la carte,* fixed-price D
Seats: 90. No-smoking area
Additional: Children welcome,
children's menu; ❶ dishes,
vegan dishes on request

One of the best vegetarian Indian restaurants in the country, Rani serves authentic Gujarati cooking. Vegetarianism is the norm in this part of north-west India, and spices are used to bring out the subtle flavours of simple ingredients such as fresh vegetables, yoghurt, rice, wheat and pulses. Here in London, chef Sheila Pattni replicates the skilful balancing of flavours in some very enjoyable dishes. The menu provides a good choice, but some of the dishes are quite filling so one needs to order with care. Starters include generously sized samosas, which are well worth trying; and 'dhal vada', spiced black lentil fritters dipped in yoghurt sauce. There is a choice of curries, such as mixed vegetable, black-eyed beans, and cauliflower and pea, plus a special curry of the day. Diners are also invited to design their own set meal. The menu is immensely helpful – a braille version is available and there are symbols to denote ingredients that may cause problems to certain individuals. Finally, there are some tempting desserts: 'Rani Nutty Delight', and 'bundi' – saffron flavoured gram flour drops. A short list of 12 reasonably priced wines is also offered.

Directions: 5 min walk from Finchley Central station

Ransome's Dock

*An eclectic range of good value dishes served in the informal
surroundings of a modern riverside restaurant*

Friendly informality is the note struck at this modern riverside
restaurant, which has an outside terrace for summer dining.
Another feature is an artesian well which allows the restaurant
to produce and bottle its own brand of mineral water. The cooking
is simple and succinct, and good value dishes are offered from a
monthly *carte*. The range is eclectic, with starters such as Thai
chicken noodle soup, Swiss chard and Gruyère filo pastries, and
Morecambe Bay potted shrimps appearing on the same menu.
Our inspector's choice, sautéed scallops with spring onions and
ginger with a soy flavoured beurre blanc, was much appreciated, as
was the main course, veal and Parmesan meatballs with pappadelle
ribbon pasta, artichoke and a delightful olive and tomato sauce.
The dessert was claimed as 'one of the best soufflés this year', a hot
prune and Armagnac soufflé with an Armagnac crème anglaise.
The wine list is a testament to Martin Lam's dedication to quality.
It is an interesting list with a house selection, wines by the glass,
special purchases and bin ends, skilfully ordered by type, flavour
and ascending price.

Directions: between Albert and Battersea Bridges – nearest Tube –
Sloane Square

SW11 35-37 Parkgate Road
Battersea SW11
Map no: GtL C2
Tel: 0171 223 1611 & 924 2462
Chef: Martin Lam
Proprietors: Martin and Vanessa
Lam
Cost: *Alc* £25, fixed-price L
£11.50 (2 course) H/wine
£10.15 ❢ Service exc
Credit cards: 🌑 🍷 🍷 💷 OTHER
Times: all day from noon-last D
11pm (12pm Sat). Closed Sun
eve, Christmas
Menus: *A la carte* D, fixed-price
L, Sat & Sun brunch
Seats: 65. Air conditioned
Additional: Children welcome;
children's portions; ❶ dishes;
vegan/other diets on request

Rasa

*Authentic South Indian food with interesting and original flavours in up
and coming part of Stoke Newington*

Rasa is completely 'green', in that it is both strictly vegetarian and
non-smoking. The South Indian cooking relies on subtle spicing.
There is almost no use of oil, and vegetables are usually steamed
rather than fried so that they retain both texture and flavour. The
list of starters could more aptly be described as snacks; the cashew
nut pakoras are round patties bound with chickpea flour then
lightly fried, and the 'masala vadai' is a spiced lentil version; both
come with a fresh coconut chutney. All the home-made chutneys
are streets ahead of the norm and another popular one is lemon,
garlic and ginger with black mustard seeds. The specialities are
memorable – steamed rice pancakes called 'appams' are served
with a comforting white potato curry with fresh coconut milk, and
the 'moru kachiathu' is a sweet, mild curry of ripe mangoes and
green bananas. Rice may be given a kick with flavourings of lemon,
coconut and tamarind. There are lots of interesting drinks including
fresh Keralan lime juice and soda, large bottles of Cobra lager, very
sweet mango lassi, and even an Indian sparkling wine.

Directions: Bus no 73 from Oxford St, Angel, Kings Cross, Euston. BR
from Liverpool St to Stoke Newington High St

N16 55 Stoke Newington
Church Street N16
Map no: GtL D4
Tel: 0171 249 0344
Chef: Moorkoth Kymar
Proprietor: Das Padmanabhan
Cost: *Alc* £20 Service exc
Credit cards: 🌑 🍷 🍷 💷
Times: Noon-last L 2.30pm,
6pm-last D 11pm. Closed Dec
25/26
Menus: *A la carte*, ❶
Seats: 42. No smoking,
air-conditioning
Additional: Children welcome,
children's portions & menu;
❶ dishes, vegan dishes on
request

Rocket or arugula is a Mediterranean herb that has been
popular since Roman times. It enhances any salad, as it
has a pungent, peppery taste, and is used as an alternative to wilted spinach.

Red Fort ❀❀

Metropolitan Moghul food that has much to interest

It is still hard for many, accustomed to neighbourhood curry house prices, to adjust to the fact that Indian restaurants of quality now charge high prices. Moghul cuisine, with its Persian influences, involves considerable time and skill if correctly done, and the Red Fort succeeds intermittently. The short menu includes starters such as 'shimla mirch', capsicum stuffed with spiced vegetables baked in the tandoori oven, and Sula lamb, a classical smoked kebab of lamb from Rajasthan. Main courses include 'murgh jaipuri', a red-hot dish of chicken cooked with whole spices and chillies, and 'boal dopiaza', chunks of Bangladeshi fish cooked with medium hot spices and onions. Other dishes are built around hare, venison, quail and pomfret fish. Thin, hard nan bread gave a poor initial impression on our visit, but chicken tandoori was well marinated, freshly cooked, moist and tender but 'murgh hara', chicken marinated in spiced yoghurt, was dry and lacked flavour. On the other hand 'gosht pasanda naawabi' had good quality meat served in a sauce which included almonds and cashew nuts,

W1 77 Dean Street W1V 5HA
Map no: D4
Tel: 0171 437 2115
Chef: Naresh Mattha
Proprietor: Amin Ali
Cost: Alc £25. H/wine £8.95
Service exc
Credit cards: ▨ ▤ ▨ ▨ OTHER
Times: Noon-last L 2.30pm,
6pm-last D 11.30pm
Menus: A la carte, pre-theatre
Seats: 120. Air-conditioning
Additional: ❂ dishes

Directions: In between Oxford St & Shaftesbury Ave. Nearest Tube: Piccadilly Circus or Tottenham Court Road

The Restaurant ❀❀❀❀❀

The enfant terrible of haute cuisine partners the grand old lady of British hotels

Genius is no respecter of personality, and love him or loathe him, Marco Pierre White has a talent that only the most churlish – or those who have been barred entrance – would deny. The man has an ego as towering as the stately pile of the Hyde Park Hotel, under which his restaurant burrows and labours. The young Turk may be getting on a bit now, but he stays ahead of the game with a combination of chutzpah, bragadaccio, obsessive single-mindedness and outrageous talent. One wonders where he goes from here. That does not matter – what does is that he continues to wring every last ounce of flavour out of each ingredient, and in doing so, push back the boundaries of creative cuisine.

The setting is just right – luxurious, individual but surprisingly restrained. Tables are swathed in white linen which billow down to the coir matting floor covered with oriental rugs. Lunchtime eating is still a bargain, and only a degree of choice is sacrificed; quality is never compromised.

A small amuse-bouche comprises two small slices of marinated salmon flecked with fleur de sel, or an oyster fritter with a sharp beurre blanc. The starter sampled on our visit was a magnificent marinière of shellfish and calamaris scented with basil with crisp-fried squid topping a delicate liquid of mussels, clams and scallops. 'Bressoles of squab pigeon mouginoise', with confit of garlic, pomme fondante and fumet of truffles, unfolded to reveal exquisite layers of pigeon breast, truffles and sweet garlic and chicken mousse, all wrapped in a thin crêpinette, and set on a disc of Savoy cabbage with tiny turned carrots and turnips.

The traditional pre-pudding appetiser was a miniature crème caramel with marinated raisins, intensely flavoured with vanilla and caramel. The pudding itself was a Marco signature dish, 'Pyramide'

SW1 Hyde Park Hotel
66 Knightsbridge SW1X 7LA
Map no: B2
Tel: 0171 259 5380
Chef: Marco Pierre White
Managers: Nicholas Munier and Jean Coltard
Cost: Alc £76, fixed-price L £29.50 ▼ Service exc
Credit cards: ▨ ▤ ▨ ▨ OTHER
Times: Noon-last L 2.15pm,
7pm-last D 11pm
Menus: A la carte, fixed-price L
Seats: 60. No pipes allowed, air-conditioning
Additional: ❂ dishes, vegan/other dishes on request

– four triangles of croquante surround a sharp and delicious passion fruit sorbet, inside of which was a praline parfait. The accompanying passion fruit sauce was studded with pink grapefruit and orange segments. Petits fours arrive at the same time – a lavish selection.

Directions: Nearest Tube: Knightsbridge

Restaurant 192 ❀

Modern European cooking at this popular bistro, provides starters such as gazpacho or chicken liver terrine, followed by baked salmon with roasted fennel and aromatic vegetables or tagliatelle with artichokes and pesto. Desserts include banana toffee pancakes and chocolate truffle cake

Times: 12.30-last L 3pm, 7pm-last D 11.30pm
Menus: A la carte, fixed-price L **Seats:** 100. No-smoking area
Additional: Children welcome, small portions on request; ❖ dishes, other dishes on request in advance
Directions: 5 mins from Ladbroke Grove Tube station, 10 mins walk from Notting Hill Tube station. Close to 52 bus route

W11 192 Kensington Park Road W11 2ES
Map no: GtL C3
Tel: 0171 229 0482
Chef: Albert Clarke
Proprietors: Anthony Mackintosh and Partners.
Manager: Anna Hugo
Cost: Alc from £20, fixed-price L £9.50. H/wine £8.90 ❢ Service exc
Credit cards: 🅰 💳 💳 📄 OTHER

Rhapsody ❀

Argentinian chef/patron Alberto Portughesis is on a one man mission to popularise South American cuisine in Shepherds Bush. The menu is market led, but expect cheesey empanadas, spicy black bean soup and beef that tastes like it's been culled from the pampas. Don't miss the pumpkin pudding with dried fruits, nor the excellent Latino wine list

Additional: Children permitted; ❖ dishes
Directions: Off Rockley Road at Shepherds Bush

W14 25 Richmond Way W14
Map no: GtL C3
Tel: 0171 602 6778
Chef: Alberto Portugheis
Proprietors: Alberto Portugheis
Cost: Alc £20. Wine £8. Service charge 12.5%
Credit cards: 🅰 💳 💳 📄
Times: Midday-last L 2.30pm, 7pm-last D 10.30. Lunch not served Sat. Closed Sun

Ristorante L'Incontro ❀❀

Though not cheap, this smart restaurant on the edge of Chelsea offers a worthwhile opportunity to sample modern Italian cooking at its most genuine

SW1 87 Pimlico Road SW1
Map no: C1
Tel: 0171 730 3663 / 6327
Chef: D Minuzzo
Proprietor: Mr I Santini
Manager: Gino Santini
Cost: Alc £34.50, fixed-price L £17.50 £16.80. H/wine £16.50. Cover charge £1.50, service exc

A place to see and be seen, rather than a gourmet Mecca, this Chelsea-chic Italian restaurant nevertheless provides careful, caring service and a range of dishes so popular with its regulars that changes are rarely made. The owner is proud of his Venetian roots and endeavours to implement this north-eastern influence. Antipasti of bean and pasta soup, fish mousse, and scallops precede the pasta that is made on the premises and served with different sauces – artichoke or anchovy and onion, for example – and main dishes include cuttlefish in ink sauce with polenta or langoustines with lime. The employment of a succession of young chefs trained in Milanese kitchens can result in inconsistencies; both seasoning and flavouring could be out of balance. Intending customers should be aware that a dinner for two might quickly reach three figures, boosted by cover and service charges. Lunchtime provides a more affordable option, the one-dish meal offering an alternative to those of two or three courses and even the house wine is more reasonably priced; other prices on a predominantly Italian wine list could certainly make the unprepared wince.

Directions: From Lower Sloane Street, left into Pimlico Road, the restaurant is on the right. Nearest Tube – Sloane Square

Credit cards: 🂠 ▦ ▦ 🅿 OTHER
Times: 12.30pm-last L 2.30pm, 7pm-last D 11.30pm/10.30pm Sun Closed Sat & Sun L, some Bhs, Dec 25/6
Menus: A la carte D, fixed-price L, one dish L
Seats: 65.(+ 40 in Piano Bar) Air conditioned
Additional: children welcome; ❂ dishes, children's portions/ vegan/other diets on request

Ritz Hotel ❀❀❀

De luxe food and wine to match the pedigree of this legendary London hotel

One could not better the siting of a hotel which occupies a prime position in Piccadilly, next to Green Park. The lush, overblown decor which makes the Ritz so special, really works in the dining-room, where a grandiose trompe l'oeil sweeps across the ceiling and light pours in from windows looking onto the park.

The cooking of David Nicholls continues to develop, with some exciting new dishes being introduced. On a recent inspection, our inspector singled out for special praise the Chinese-style scallops, lobster and langoustine ravioli, the warm foie gras with Calvados and grape onion compote, and crab cakes with green cabbage. Roasted sweetbreads with truffles and buttered noodles, however, lacked edge. As well as appetisers of an unusual baked sea bass with soy sauce reduction and baked spaghetti noodles, there is also a complementary sorbet, perhaps fruit and Cointreau with mint. Raspberry soufflé was the high spot of our meal – light, beautifully textured and well-risen, it was served with three mini-pots of crème brûlée, fresh raspberries, and crème fraîche. Coffee was disappointingly poor.

The lunch menu features a daily trolley speciality such as roast rib of Scottish beef with Yorkshire pudding, or the Ritz mixed grill with rösti potatoes. Many popular dishes, such as grilled Dover sole, poached salmon or pan-fried calves' liver and bacon, are always available. The wine list is highly impressive listing over three hundred classic bins including Jereboams and many Magnums. As well as prestige champagnes, there are fine 1ère grand cru classe Bordeaux, and some fine Burgundies.

Directions: Nearest Tube – Green Park

W1 150 Piccadilly W1V 9DG
Map no: C3
Tel: 0171 493 8181
Chef: David Nicholls
Proprietor: Trafalgar House/Mandarin Oriental.
Gen Manager: Brian Williams
Cost: Alc £40-£60, fixed-price L £29/D £49. H/wine £16.50
Credit cards: 🂠 ▦ ▦ 🅿 OTHER
Times: Last L 2.30pm, last D 11.15pm (10.30 pm Sun)
Menus: A la carte, fixed-price L & D, pre-theatre, bar menu
Seats: 120. No pipes allowed, air-conditioning
Additional: Children over 5 welcome, children's menu (Sun L); ❂ dishes, vegan/other diets on request

> **Ossetra** caviar has small, even eggs of a golden yellow to brown colour, and it is quite oily. But it is considered by many to be the best.

Riva 🏵🏵

Authentic northern Italian cooking, big on flavour, generously portioned and reasonably priced

One of the best Italian restaurants in town, Riva specialises in dishes from the north, particularly Lombardy and the Veneto. Authentic flavours and reasonable prices are part of the appeal, along with friendly service supervised by the owner, Andrea Riva. A successful inspection meal began with a good selection of country breads and a starter of 'stuzzichini' – a ramekin of cheese fondue served with good polenta crisps, slices of chargrilled aubergine with a filling of melted taleggio, little cakes of salt cod, and potato fritters. This was followed by 'coniglio farcito', crispy roast rabbit sliced and stuffed with excellent cotechino (spicy Italian sausage), served with great spätzli and decent spinach. There is a section of dishes served as a starter or main course; perhaps spaghetti with clams, tomatoes and dried mushrooms, or 'gnocchi alle noci', pumpkin and spinach dumplings with walnuts and gorgonzola. From an extensive dessert menu with the ubiquitous tiramisu, panna cotta and gelati, our inspector plumped for 'sbrisolona', a biscuity almond crumble soaked in vin santo and served with mascarpone. There is a short list of interesting Italian wines.

Directions: Junction of Church Rd with Castelnau Rd. Entrance in Castelnau Rd

SW13 169 Church Road
Barnes SW13 9HR
Map no: GtL C3
Tel: 0181 748 0434
Chef: Franceso Zanchetta
Proprietor: Andrea Riva
Cost: Alc £22. H/wine £9.75 ❢
Service inc
Credit cards: 🆇 🆇 🆇 OTHER
Times: Noon-last L 2.30pm,
7pm-last D 11pm. Closed Sat L
& Bhs, Xmas, Easter, 2 wks in
Aug
Menus: A la carte
Seats: 50. Air-conditioning
Additional: Children welcome,
children's portions; ❶ dishes,
vegan/other dishes on request

River Café 🏵🏵🏵

Confident, coherent and uncompromising cooking in Thames-side Tuscan outpost

The River Café leads where others try to follow. Few match up to the standards, though, set by the highly successful cooking partnership of Rose Gray and Ruth Rogers. The forthright Italian menu changes twice daily, and is constructed from the best ingredients to be found this side of Lucca. The restaurant has been completely redesigned and enlarged. With its minimalist cobalt decor, impressive reflective panels and wall clock hologram, it could now be described as an ultra-fashionable warehouse or upmarket Teutonic works canteen. Service, however, is most attentive, and as all the staff are involved in the preparation of the food, their product knowledge is excellent.

No butter comes with the ciabatta, but extra virgin olive oil can be requested. Our visit began with a delightful fritto misto of calves' brains, lambs' sweetbreads, Swiss chard, capers and sage, perfectly deep-fried in a light egg and flour batter, not disimilar to a tempura. This was followed by turbot baked in sea salt. A neatly cut fillet was served at room temperature, topped with a fine aïoli blended with ground almonds. A magically fresh mixed salad of artichoke hearts, broccoli tops and crisp, green beans was expertly seasoned and dressed with oil and wild garlic. Classic lemon tart was quite memorable for its light and slightly crisp shortcrust pastry, tangy citrus filling and caramel top.

Espresso coffee is authentically rich. The wines are all Italian, apart from half bottles of champagne, and several are available by the glass. One bottle particularly enjoyed was the Sauvignon bianco 'Le Speranze' 1993 (Geoff Merril-Veneto). There are also wines

W6 Rainville Road
Hammersmith W6 9HA
Map no: GtL C3
Tel: 0171 381 8824
Chefs: Rose Gray, Ruth Rogers
and Theo Randall
Manager: Giles Boden
Cost: Alc £32. H/wine £9.50 ❢
Service inc
Credit cards: 🆇 🆇 🆇 OTHER
Times: 12.30-last L 3pm,
7.30pm-last D 9.30pm. Closed
Sun D & Bhs, Xmas-New Year
Menus: A la carte
Seats: 98 + 50 outside
Additional: Children welcome,
children's portions; ❶ dishes,
vegan/other dishes on request

specially selected to go with desserts and cheese. The Reserve list has limited quantities of some fine vintage wines, including a Barolo 1961 G Conterno, from the Piemonte at £145.

Directions: Off Fulham Palace Rd. Junction of Rainville Road and Bowfell Road

Royal China ⊛⊛

Super-smart Chinese restaurant with theatrical decor and some unusual dishes

The Putney Royal China shares a menu with its sister restaurant in Queensway (see following entry) and features equally striking black and gold lacquer decor. Prices are for the well-heeled, but there are various set price menus to consider as well. The extensive *carte* is largely Cantonese, with a few additional Szechuan and Peking dishes, including the famous Peking duck. There are also an unusually high number of fish dishes, such as Royal China fish (stir-fried Dover sole off the bone, replaced on the original bone) and sautéed fillet of eel with spicy salt. Fresh lobster can be prepared in any one of six different ways. Dishes tested by our inspector, on our last visit, included Dragon King rolls, seasonal pieces of seafood (mostly prawns) wrapped in rice paper, and tender steamed chicken in lotus leaf with Chinese mushrooms. Double cooked Szechuan pork had a tangy sauce of peppers and bamboo shoots. Details were careless – freshly cooked rice was moist and lumpy, and the jasmine tea weak, with scant flavour.

Directions: Between Queensway & Bayswater Station. Next to Queens ice skating rink

W2 13 Queensway W2 4QJ
Map no: GtL C3
Tel: 0171 221 2535
Chefs: Wai-Hung Lo and Simon Man
Proprietor: Playwell Ltd.
Manager: Kenny Hall
Cost: Alc £15-£25, fixed-price D £22-£28. H/wine £8.50 ⦀
Service exc
Credit cards: ▨ ▤ ▨ ▨ OTHER
Times: Noon-last L 5pm, last D 11pm. Closed Dec 23-25
Menus: A la carte, fixed-price D
Seats: 100. Air-conditioning
Additional: Children welcome; ⦿ dishes, vegan/other dishes on request

Royal China ⊛⊛

Glitzy, upmarket Cantonese restaurant

If you choose wisely, this restaurant is capable of providing an exceptional Chinese meal, which no doubt accounts for its popularity with many affluent Asian families. The decor is dazzlingly dramatic, in black and gold, and the menu has become increasingly refined with a wider choice of seafood and luxury dishes. It is, however, the more off-beat items, such as seafood hot pot and roasted chicken with monk bean flavour, which continue to attract the most interest. An inspection meal started with wonderful, fresh, steamed scallops with garlic and a sauce of scallions and soy sauce. Fragrant yam duck proved warm and moist, full of succulent meat, contrasting with the dry texture of the yams. From the chef's Speciality menu came the winter-warming, robust dish of stewed pork with eggplant. Not everyone, however, will care for the amount of MSG obviously used in the cooking. The short wine list has some good vintage French and Italian wines, but saki and Tiger beer are also available. The uniformed staff, it must be said, sometimes seem a bit too keen in their obvious efforts to induce customers to spend more and more money.

Directions: Travelling north from the traffic lights in Putney High Street, Chelverton Road is 2nd left. Nearest Tube – East Putney

SW15 3 Chelverton Road Putney SW15
Map no: GtL C2
Cost: Alc £26, Set menus £20, £26. Service charge 15%
Chef: Siew Wing
Proprietors: Playwell Ltd
Credit cards: ▨ ▤ ▨ ▨
Menus: A la carte, set menus, Seafood Gourmet, Dim Sum
Times: Midday-last L 4pm, 6.30pm-last D 11.30pm
Additional: Children welcome

Royal Lancaster Hotel ❀

Located on the first floor of this large hotel, La Rosette Restaurant provides a formal setting for the enjoyment of generous portions of dishes such as sautéed calves' liver with red onion gravy, or grilled grey mullet with pimento coulis

Menus: A la carte, fixed-price L & D
Seats: 65. No-smoking area, air-conditioning
Additional: Children welcome, children's portions; ✿ dishes, vegan/other dishes on request
Directions: Next to Hyde Park & Lancaster Gate tube station

W2 Lancaster Terrace W2 2TY
Map no: A3
Tel: 0171 262 6737
Chef: Nigel Blatchford
Manager: Majidel Ghazel
Cost: Alc £30, fixed-price L £22.50 (3 courses)/D£35.75.
H/wine £20 Service exc
Credit cards: 🔲 🔳 🔳 🔳 OTHER
Times: 12.30-last L 2.30pm, 6.30-last D 10.45pm. Closed Sat L, Sun

Royal Westminster ❀

Good fresh produce and interesting sauces feature in the imaginative cooking available here. Dishes might include horn of John Dory with white crabmeat and chives, and strawberry samosa – crisp pastry filled with strawberries and ice-cream served with a strawberry sauce

Times: Last D 10.30pm. Closed L all week, and Sun D
Additional: Children's menu; high chairs; ✿ dishes
Directions: Close to Victoria Station

SW1 49 Buckingham Palace Road SW1
Map no: C1
Tel: 0171 834 1821
Chef: Bruce Smith
Proprietor: Mount Charlotte Thistle
Cost: Alc £26
Credit cards: 🔲 🔳 🔳 🔳

Rules ❀❀

The seasonal menus of this long-established restaurant take maximum advantage of good fresh produce, including Scottish game

Still very popular, especially with those wishing to dine before going to the theatre, this bustling restaurant serves an extensive range of traditional British food. A speciality is game, obtained from the owners' Scottish estate. Pheasant, partridge, wild duck, teal and a small selection of furred game all appear on a menu which not only includes such old favourites as steak and kidney pie and roast beef with Yorkshire pudding but also nostalgic desserts like spotted dick and treacle sponge with custard. The honest cooking of Neil Pass and his team is thoroughly enjoyable, their careful preparation making the best possible use of quality produce. The reasonably priced wine list, though short, provides enough variety to complement the interesting range of dishes featured on the *carte*. The only disappointments are coffee – served by the cup, none too warm and of an inferior blend – and service, which can be hurried and lacking in finesse. The pre-theatre menu offers excellent value for money, and weekend lunches are also good value.

Directions: Maiden Lane is parallel with the Strand. Nearest Tubes – the Strand, Covent Garen

WC2 35 Maiden Lane Covent Garden WC2
Map no: D3
Tel: 0171 836 5314
Chef: Neil Pass
Proprietor: John Mayhew.
Manager: Ricky McMenemy
Cost: Alc £24.50, afternoon 2 course £7.95, pre-theatre D & Sat/Sun L £12.95 (2 course)
H/wine £8.75 Service exc
Credit cards: 🔲 🔳 🔳 🔳 OTHER
Times: Noon-last D 11.15pm, afternoon meals 3pm-5pm Mon-Fri Closed Xmas
Menus: A la carte L & D, afternoon meals, pre-theatre D, Fixed-price Sat/Sun L
Seats: 140. Air conditioned
Additional: Children welcome; ✿ dishes, children's/other dishes on request

Sabras ❀❀

One of the better vegetarian Indian restaurant in London offering top-quality home-cooking

To encourage customers to his bright, colourful restaurant, Hermant Desai offers a number of business schemes including membership of the Sabras club, which gives a 10% discount on

NW10 Willesden High Road NW10
Map no: GtL C3
Tel: 0181 459 0340
Chefs: Hemant & Nalinee Desai
Proprietor: Hemant Desai

meals. The cooking is shared by Hermant and his wife Nalinee, and is a good example of Indian home-cooking, the most striking aspect being the freshness of the flavours. The menu reads well and includes a selection of hot and cold appetisers, such as 'pani puri' – crisp puff pastry filled with potato, chick peas, spiced tamarind, and date and pepper water. Jumbo dhosas are filling but are worth the experience. Smaller vegetable dishes include 'Kashmiri kofta' balls made from assorted vegetables and various flour and spices, fried and served in a nutty lentil sauce.

Directions: Nearest Tube: Willesden Green

St George's, The Heights ✿✿

As we went to press the hotel informed us that Adam Newell was leaving, to be replaced by Nick Evenden, sous chef from the Café Royal. It is understood that the style of cooking will remain broadly the same at The Heights where the cooking on our last visit was described as follows.

It is a chastening experience to go to a restaurant where the staff are better dressed than the customers, so it is best to be warned before braving the Armani-clad ranks at The Heights. However, should one fall below sartorially satisfactory standards, the young and enthusiastic staff will be discreet, and the exciting and innovative food should restore all inner harmony. Tucked away in Langham Place, just a short walk from Regent Street, the restaurant occupies the 14th floor of this special Forte hotel. Decorated in minimalist fashion, it boasts spectacular views over the city and, as a consequence, window tables are much in demand. The distinctive cooking style succeeded in marrying flavours in startling ways. However, outré ingredients make one reach for the diners' dictionary: breast of cannette, roasted mahi mahi and cups of ristretto and macchiato and the like frankly need elucidation, unless the diner is to feel pig-ignorant as well as badly dressed. Tarts in various guises, fresh anchovy or red mullet with tapenade and rouille, have been high-powered starters. Main courses may include a fair number of game and poultry dishes; pot roasted pigeon comes with shallot tarte Tatin, medallion of rabbit with herb risotto and baby beetroot, and chicken two ways – fricassée of corn-fed chicken with peas and broad beans, and breast of black-legged chicken with pearl barley and truffle oil. Puddings can be stunning, as in a chocolate and pear brûlée with raisin madeleines.

Directions: Langham Place is N end of Regent Street

W1 Langham Place W1N 8QS
Map no: C4
Tel: 0171 636 1939
Chef: Nick Evenden
Proprietor: Forte Hotels
Cost: Alc £30, fixed-price L £19.50. H/wine £9 Service inc
Credit cards: ◪ ▦ ▦ 🖭 OTHER
Times: Noon-last L 2.30pm. Closed Sat L, Sun & 1st 2 wks Aug, 10 days at Xmas
Menus: A la carte, fixed-price L, bar menu
Seats: 80. No pipes or cigars, air-conditioning
Additional: Children welcome, children's portions; ✿ dishes, other dishes on request

St John ✿✿

☺ *Back to basics with a fundamentalist carnivores' menu at City restaurant*

Cry, 'Where's the beef?' at this former meat and fish smokehouse close to Smithfield Market, and you're likely to end up with a bit more than you bargained for, especially the unmentionable bits. A leaping porker illustrates the menu which is uncompromising, indeed almost austere, in style. The food is fin de siècle – both of them. Victorian working class staples, such as jellied tripe, whelks, oysters, roast marrowbone and stuffed lamb's heart are reinvented

EC1 26 St John Street EC1
Map no: F5
Tel: 0171 251 0848
Chef: Fergus Henderson
Proprietor: Trevor Gulliver
Cost: Alc £20. H/wine £8.50 ▮ Service exc
Credit cards: ◪ ▦ ▦ 🖭 OTHER
Times: Last L 3pm, last D 11.30pm. Closed Xmas/New Year & Bhs
Menus: A la carte, bar menu

for 20th-century middle class consumption. The faint-hearted, however, are accommodated with Mediterranean working class dishes of rabbit, spinach and olives or cod, potato and saffron. Culinary historians will have a field day – jugged hare and mash, brawn, mince and tatties, and boiled beef and carrots all have a tale to tell. The daily menu bluntly lists dishes individually, and one-course meals can be taken, although the cooking is good enough to make one want to spend more. Our inspector thoroughly appreciated the roasted bone marrow with parsley, puy lentils and vinaigrette salad, followed by a whole, succulent roast pigeon set on a white pickled cabbage flavoured with juniper berries.

Directions: 3 mins walk from Farringdon Tube & BR stations. The restaurant is 100 metres from Smithfield Market on N side

Seats: 100
Additional: Children welcome; ❤ dishes

St Quentin Brasserie ❀❀

☺ *French brasserie with a genuine taste of cuisine bourgeoise*

This is not the place to choose for an intimate little rendezvous à deux. Busy and bubbling, with tables packed close together, this Parisian style brasserie caters for different needs. The standard of cooking is reliably high, with well-made and cleanly flavoured French dishes. Classics of the genre include Bayonne ham with celeriac, baked snails with garlic, duck liver terrine, lamb shank with red wine sauce, lemon tart and crème brûlée. A wholesome fish soup with garlic and croûtons was built on a good stock base, the fish puréed with potato and herbs. Although the main course, on our inspection, was an unorthodox version, the chef's interpretation of pig's trotters stuffed with foie gras was nonetheless tasty and enjoyable, served on a bed of crisp french beans and shallots. A tarte Tatin was disappointing, the flaky pastry overcooked and hard. The wine list offers a good selection of French wines, with a few good vintage clarets and Burgundies. Although service is attentive, at times it can feel rather hurried.

Directions: Nearest Tube: South Kensington. Opposite Brompton Oratory

SW3 243 Brompton Road
SW3 2EP
Map no: B2
Tel: 0171 589 8005
Chef: Nigel Davis
Proprietor: Savoy Plc.
Manager: Garnier
Cost: Alc £20.50, fixed-price L/D £9. H/wine £8.90 ❢ Service exc
Credit cards: ▧ ▨ ▨ ▨ OTHER
Times: Noon-last L 3pm, 7pm-last D 11pm
Menus: A la carte, fixed-price L & D, pre-theatre
Seats: 85. Air-conditioning
Additional: Children welcome, children's portions; ❤ dishes, other dishes on request

Salloos ❀❀

In one of Belgravia's quiet streets a first-class Pakistani restaurant with the highest standards of cooking

Kinnerton Street was once a slum. The converted, prettified houses would be unrecognisable to the cow-keeper, purveyors of asses' milk and wheelwright who lived here 150 years ago. Salloos has been established for a number of years, and it goes from strength to strength. The menu does not alter and still offers interesting Pakistani dishes, including some of the owner's own unique recipes. One, for example, is 'shahi kofta', an adaptation of chicken meatballs in a subtle sauce. Or there is 'haleem akbari', a delicate dish from the days of the Moghal emperors, made of shredded lamb cooked in whole wheat germ, lentils and spices, chicken 'karahi', a speciality from the Khyber, and 'palak gosht' a typical Punjabi dish of diced young lamb with spinach cooked in onions, and mild, freshly ground spices. Meat quality here is high and great care is taken to blend spices to ensure nothing emerges with harsh

SW1 62-64 Kinnerton Street
SW1
Map no: B2
Tel: 0171 235 4444 / 6845
Chefs: Abdul Aziz and Humayun Khan
Proprietors: Mr & Mrs F Salahuddin
Cost: Alc £27.50, fixed-price L £16, fixed-price D £25 (4 course) H/wine £12.50. Cover charge £1.50, service 15% exc
Credit cards: ▧ ▨ ▨ ▨ OTHER
Times: noon-last L 2.30pm, 7pm-last D 11.15pm. Closed Sun
Menus: A la carte, fixed-price L & D
Seats: 65. Air conditioned

flavours. Basmati rice is cooked in lightly spiced lamb stock known as yakhni. The standard of service remains high and is usually supervised by one of the daughters of the family.

Directions: nr. Hyde Park Corner – take first left into Wilton Place, first right opposite Berkeley Hotel. Nearest Tube – Knightsbridge

Additional: Children permitted (over 6 after 8pm); ❂ dishes, vegan/other diets on request

Samratt ❂

A smart modern, Indian restaurant just off Putney High Street. A comprehensive menu includes particularly good examples of popular dishes such as chicken tikka masala and lamb badam pasanda. Herbs and spices are well balanced and the sauces are well made

Menus: *A la carte* **Seats:** 78. No-smoking area
Additional: Children welcome; ❂ dishes
Directions: Off Putney High Street, 5 mins walk from Putney Bridge

SW15 18/20 Lacy Road SW15
Map no: GtL C2
Tel: 0181 788 9110
Chef: Abdul Hashim
Proprietor: Satyendra Nath Datta
Credit cards: 🔳 🔳 🔳
Times: Noon-last L 2.30pm, 6pm-last D 11.30pm. Closed Xmas/Boxing Day

San Lorenzo Fuoriporta ❂

A stylish establishment sporting a bright, contemporary Italian look. Standard antipasti, pasta, and pizza, appear alongside such modish dishes as raw tuna with rucola, spaghetti with smoked salmon and ricotta cheese, and grilled boar cutlets with rosemary and beans

Menus: *A la carte*, fixed-price L **Seats:** 120 (180 summer)
Additional: Children welcome, children's portions; ❂ dishes, vegan/other dishes on request
Directions: Bottom of Wimbledon Hill Rd, turn right into Worple Rd, then 1st right into Worple Mews

SW19 Worple Road Mews SW19
Map no: GtL C2
Tel: 0181 946 8463
Chef: Elizio
Proprietor: Ghigo Berni
Cost: *Alc* £30, fixed-price L £17.50. H/wine £10.50 Service exc
Credit cards: 🔳 🔳 🔳 🔳 OTHER
Times: Noon-last L 2.45pm (3.15pm Sun), 7pm-last D 10.45pm. Closed Bhs

Santini ❂❂

Venetian dishes are the speciality of this Italian restaurant, with some particularly good seafood

SW1 29 Ebury Street SW1W 0NZ
Map no: C1
Tel: 0171 730 4094/8275
Chef: Giuseppe Rosselli
Proprietor: I Santin
Cost: *Alc* £30.50, fixed-price L £18.30 (3 courses). H/wine £13.50 Service exc
Credit cards: 🔳 🔳 🔳 🔳 OTHER

A popular little restaurant handy for Victoria Station. Giuseppe Rosselli offers a fixed-price lunch menu, a *carte* and additional Venetian specialities which provide a good choice of dishes. Antipasti may include stuffed courgette flowers (in season), a grilled vegetable platter, seafood salad, and carpaccio. The pasta is good especially fresh ravioli with ricotta and spinach, pappadelle with artichoke sauce, and tagliatelle in a creamy shellfish sauce. Monkfish with green peppers, tomato and garlic, and squid stewed in white wine and herbs and served with polenta, and veal escalopes with fresh orange sauce, or chicken breast cooked in a lemon, mustard and herb sauce, are typical main courses. Desserts, cheese and fresh fruit are offered from the trolley to finish. The wine list is predominantly Italian, with a few French wines.

Directions: On corner of Ebury St & Lower Belgrave St, just 2 mins walk from Victoria Station

Times: 12.30-last L 2.30pm, 7pm-last D 11.30pm (10.30pm Sun). Closed Dec 25/26 & some Bhs
Menus: A la carte, fixed-price L
Seats: 65. No pipes allowed, air-conditioning
Additional: Children welcome, children's portions on request; ✿ dishes

The Savoy ❀❀❀

High powered, international hotel restaurant with a distinguished hand at the helm

WC2 Strand
Map no: E3
Tel: 0171 836 4343
Chef: Anton Edelmann
Proprietor: The Savoy Group plc
Cost: Alc £38.50, fixed-price lunch £26.50, fixed-price dinner £31 (Sun-Thu), £37 (Fri, Sat). H/wine £14.75. Service inc
Credit cards: ▩ ▨ ▨ ▨
Menus: A la carte, Sunday Family lunch, fixed-price lunch and dinner
Times: 12.30-last L 2.30pm, 6pm-last D 11.30pm
Seats: 140. No pipes. Air conditioned
Additional: Children welcome; children's portions. ✿ menu; Vegan on request

This world famous hotel remains a steady ship, and The River Restaurant continues to showcase chef Anton Edelmann's considerable skills. Menu scrutiny is a formidable task, but everything is precisely translated from the French, except for 'frivolités', which perhaps speaks for itself. The backbone *carte* ranges between scallops on a lobster ragoût, fillet of turbot filled with crab meat and herbs to chateaubriand for two. Wild mushrooms feature in at least four dishes. One of these, a seafood ravioli with wild mushrooms, had an intense, pungent flavour and lightly creamed sauce topped with swirling strands of deep-fried seaweed. A main course fillet of top-quality lamb was tender and pink, served on a bed of puréed aubergines with chopped ratatouille. The dessert nearly stole the show. Spring fruit soup was a kaleidoscope of colours, shapes and textures, served with a smooth lemon yoghurt ice-cream under a spun sugar web.

The set dinner does not lack for interest either, although dishes are in a less elaborate mode – cream of lentils with smoked duck, fillet of veal, veal kidney and sweetbreads with seasonal vegetables, and crêpes suzette with Grand Marnier. One particularly commendable idea is the seasonal menu Edelmann creates together with River Restaurant sommelier Werner Wissmann. Each of the five courses of the no choice, set meal is matched with a glass of pre-selected wine from the legendary Savoy Cellars. On our visit, only the restaurant service was a shade off the mark, with four separate waiters unsure of dishes on the menu – a surprising slip for somewhere so consummately professional.

Directions: From Embankment Tube, you can walk east through the riverside gardens to the hotel, or see following entry

Savoy Grill ❀❀❀

Even the ubiquitous "bangers and mash" take on new respectability here – prepared with the expertise one naturally associates with this renowned hotel

The exceptionally popular wood-panelled Grill Room of this world-famous restaurant is always busy – and particularly so at lunch, when such traditional favourites as the daily roasts are avaialble. Predictably, the luxuries are there, but they appear alongside dishes down-to-earth enough to please the most plebeian soul. A starter of green pea and ham soup, for example, or black pudding with bacon and a poached egg provides an alternative to new season's asparagus or Beluga caviar, and these might be followed by farmhouse sausages with creamed potatoes, Lancashire hotpot, steak or cutlets. These mainly English 'plats du jour' and grills are complemented, however, by a more adventurous list of dishes which are predominantly French (though some modernism is detectable). Smoked eels with quails' eggs, chive dressing and sweet pepper salsa, for example, might be followed by pan-fried sea bass and red mullet with noodles and Niçoise vegetables, then fillet of beef with parsnip gratin and a truffle sauce. The standard and complexity of desserts is illustrated by a delicious "soupe de fruits" sampled by an inspector on the most recent visit – seasonal fruits in a delightful kaleidoscope of colours, shapes and textures being served with smooth lemon yoghurt ice-cream under a delicate spun-sugar web. The theatre menu (available from 6-7pm) provides a limited range of hors d'oeuvres and entrées plus some plats du jour; a few desserts are listed, but – in view of time constraints – guests are invited to forego this course and return after the performance for coffee and pastries in the Thames Foyer. A comprehensive wine list shared with the traditional first-floor River Restaurant offers good value for money, though it predictably includes some expensive items.

WC2 Strand
Map no: E3
Tel: 0171 836 4343
Chef: David Sharland
Proprietor: Savoy.
Manager: Angelo Maresca
Cost: *Alc* £45, pre-theatre £27-£29.75. H/wine £15.70 ▮
Service exc
Credit cards: ▨ ▨ ▨ ▨ OTHER
Times: last L 2.30pm, pre-theatre 6pm-7pm. last D 11.15pm.
Closed Sat L, Sun, Aug, Bhs
Seats: 100. No pipes. Air conditioning
Menus: *A la carte*, fixed-price pre-theatre menu
Additional: Children over 12 permitted; ❂ dishes, vegan/ other diets on request

Directions: between Charing Cross and The Aldwych. The hotel is set back from the Strand in a courtyard

The Selfridge Hotel ❀❀

Professional approach pleases both businessmen and tourists alike

The upgrading of this popular hotel, so well located for shopping trips, continues steadily. There are two restaurants, a brasserie for casual meals, and the more formal Fletchers. Here chef Mark Page cooks in the modern British style, and his short, set price menu and *carte* is lifted out of the ordinary by skilful preparation and well-balanced flavours. His selection of starters includes tarte tatin of cèpes and tarragon, roast wood pigeon and beetroot salad, and calves' sweetbreads and leek terrine with parsnip crisps, the latter dish a good mix of mousse and meat with delicious baby leeks. Our inspector selected expertly-made, rolled fillets of Dover sole filled with lobster mousse as a main course, from a choice which also

W1 Orchard Street W1H 0JS
Map no: B4
Tel: 0171 408 2080
Chef: Mark Page
Proprietor: Mount Charlotte Thistle.
Manager: Andrew Hickey
Cost: *Alc* £23.30, fixed-price L £16.95/D £24.50 (4 courses). H/wine £12 ▮ Service exc
Credit cards: ▨ ▨ ▨ ▨ OTHER
Times: 12.30-last L 2.30pm, 6.30pm-last D 10.30pm. Closed Sat L, Sun & Bhs, last 2 wks Aug

included blanquette of John Dory and mussels, braised lamb shank with artichoke and sweet garlic, and roast breast of duckling with a foie gras and potato galette. There is an interesting selection of desserts such as cinnamon mousse with green apple sorbet or a fine pear and apple terrine topped with crisp caramel.

Directions: Entrance on Duke Street, off Oxford Street, behind Selfridge store. Nearest Tube – Bond Street

Menus: A la carte, fixed-price L & D, pre-theatre, bar menu
Seats: 54. No-smoking area, air-conditioning
Additional: Children welcome, children's portions; ❂ dishes, vegan/other dishes on request

Shaw's ❀❀

A smart South Kensington restaurant with an imaginative approach, specialising in game and fish

A new venture for the Atkins who have taken over the former Chanterelle premises after their success at Farleyer House in Aberfeldy, Scotland. Everything is made on the premises, and Frances Atkins wants to specialise with game and fish, using her already well-established contacts north of the border. An inspection meal yielded freshly baked, warm bread rolls, then smoked haddock mousse with bacon skewers and deep-fried capers. The mignons of venison and beef which followed came on a rösti potato with red cabbage, wild mushrooms and a juniper-scented jus; vegetables could have had more impact, but the dish as a whole was well thought out. To finish treacle tart is highly recommended and the hot soufflé is well worth the wait. Service has been found to be a little uneven, with some staff still finding their feet, but Bill Atkins's personal and skilful involvement more than compensates. The wine list was composed by Master of Wine John Casson with the modern-style cooking very much in mind. A post-theatre supper menu is also available.

Directions: by Cranley Mews, 5 mins Gloucester Rd. Tube

SW7 119 Old Brompton Road SW7
Map no: A1
Tel: 0171 373 7774
Chef: Paul Lengronne and Frances Atkins
Proprietor: The Atkins Restaurant Co. Ltd
Cost: fixed-price L £17.50 (Sun £19.50) /D £29.95, H/wine £10 ❢ Service inc L, exc D
Credit cards: 🄲 🄼 🄼 🄼 OTHER
Times: noon-last L 2pm/3.30pm Sun, 7pm-last D10pm, last S 11.30pm Closed Xmas, N/Year, Easter, last 2 wks Aug
Menus: Fixed-price 2/3 course L & D, post-theatre Supper
Seats: 44. Air conditioned
Additional: children welcome; ❂ dishes, other diets on request

Shepherds ❀❀

Traditional favourites as well as more modish cooking in a sophisticated setting close to the Tate Gallery

Contemporary decor is fitting for a sophisticated restaurant just a stone's throw from the Tate Gallery. Very much in the Langan mould, Shepherds attracts a fashionable crowd with a menu which offers all the old favourites – with new dishes added from time to time – at very good prices. At a summer inspection, home-made, pan-fried black pudding with a good pork-blood taste and a crumbly onion and oatmeal texture, was served with sound, peppery bubble and squeak and a very good sticky white onion jus. Grilled fillets of fresh mackerel followed, with a subtle sauce of blended English mustard. Vegetables were fresh – well-cooked paysanne of carrots, shredded greens with bacon and new Jersey Royal potatoes, which had a good flavour. The only disappointment came with dessert, a spicy apple pie which was overcooked, the pastry soggy, and the custard sauce bland. Espresso is strong and slightly bitter. The wine list includes a good list of non-vintage champagne. There is also a special bar counter menu.

Directions: Near Tate Gallery and Westminster Hospital. Nearest Tube – Pimlico

SW1 Marsham Court
Marsham Street SW1
Map no: D2
Tel: 0171 834 9552
Chef: James Rice
Proprietors: Michael Caine and Richard Shepherd
Cost: Fixed-price lunch and dinner £16.95 (2 courses), £18.95. H/wine £9.50. Service charge 12.5%
Credit cards: 🄲 🄼 🄼 🄼 OTHER
Menu: Fixed-price carte
Times: 12.30pm-last L 2.45pm, 6.30pm-last D 11.30pm. Closed Sat, Sun, Bhs
Seats: 90, 14 Bar, 30 Private Room. Air conditioned
Additional: Children welcome; ❂ dish

Simply Nico ✿✿✿

☺ *High-class simplicity with all the Nico trademarks*

Despite the attractions of the various House of Commons dining-rooms, the proximity to Westminster means that Simply Nico has become a popular spot for politicians, as well as members of the banking world. Anyone hoping for an indiscreet tip or nugget of overheard gossip, though, is likely to be disappointed, as the tables are rather too close for private confidences. The cooking, however, fully compensates; like its sister, Nico Central, the cooking is defined by bold textures, rich flavours and honest ideas. Attentive service, by a young team, is both charming and properly professional.

The fixed-price menu offers excellent value-for-money, and a recent inspection meal praised a delicious crab gratin with fresh pasta and first-class lobster sauce, followed by escalope of brill baked with glazed sweet onion sauce on a tasty confit of spinach and mushrooms. Typically imaginative starters include gâteaux of salt-cod with new potatoes, escalope of salmon with chive velouté, and pressed guinea-fowl and foie gras terrine. Chargrilled rib-eye of beef with, perhaps, béarnaise sauce or horseradish cream, is available as a main course supplement, but, otherwise, there may be best end of lamb with couscous, wing of skate with roast artichokes, or confit of duck with honey, black pepper crust and coarse salt. Perennial favourites include fish soup with rouille and croûtons, and tender oxtail in red wine sauce. As ever, there is the option of chips or excellent puréed potatoes. For pudding, a divinely smooth chocolate marquise with tangy orange crème anglaise or terrine of prune and Armagnac ice-cream, should gird the loins of those rushing off to run the country.

Directions: Nearest Tube: St James's Park. 7 mins walk from Victoria Station. Rochester Rd is parallel to Victoria St (S bound)

SW1 48a Rochester Row
SW1P 1JU
Map no: D2
Tel: 0171 630 8061
Chef: Tim Johnson
Proprietors: Nico & Dinah-Jane Ladenis.
Manager: Julian Robinson
Cost: Fixed-price L £24 (3 courses)/D £26. H/wine £12 ❢
Service inc
Credit cards: ◼ ▦ ▦ ▣
Times: Noon-last L 2pm, 7pm-last D 11pm. Closed Sat L, Sun & Bhs, 10 days at Xmas
Menus: Fixed-price L & D
Seats: 45. No pipes allowed, air-conditioning
Additional: Children over 10 welcome; ❶ dishes, vegan/other dishes on request

Simpsons in the Strand ✿✿

Great British institution still serving Great British food

Nothing can match the roast beef and Yorkshire pudding at Simpson's. The aura of tradition alone gives it extra savour, plus the knowledge that little has changed at this famous English eating house since it was established in 1828. The menu, or 'Bill of Fare', illustrated by a brilliant Bateman cartoon, entertains and informs with facts and figures, such as their staggering daily consumption of beef, lamb and duck. Classic dishes include steak and kidney pie, home-made potted shrimps, quails' eggs with haddock and cheese sauce, and roast saddle of lamb from the trolley, with or without bubble and squeak. At lunch, there is a daily special such as Lancashire hot pot (Monday) or fish cakes with parsley sauce (Friday). A number of hallowed English puddings are offered such as Simpson's famous treacle roll and steamed chocolate sponge. Savouries include Welsh rarebit and Angels on Horseback. Breakfasts are another great Simpson's institution – salmon kedgeree, grilled kippers and pig's nose with parsley and onion sauce are time-honoured ways to kick-start the day, not to mention the cholesterol-defying 'Ten Deadly Sins', the fry-up to end all fry-ups.

Directions: Nearest Tube: Charing Cross. In the middle of the Strand between Charing Cross & Waterloo Bridge. Next to the Savoy Hotel

WC2 100 Strand WC2R 0EW
Map no: D3
Tel: 0171 836 9112
Chef: Tony Bradley
Proprietor: Savoy Group.
Manager: Brian Clivaz
Cost: Alc £25-£30, fixed-price L/D £10. H/wine £12 ❢ Service exc
Credit cards: ◼ ▦ ▦ ▣ OTHER
Times: Last L 2.30pm, last D 1am (Tue-Sat), 11pm (Mon), 9pm (Sun). Closed Dec 25/6, Jan 1, Good Friday
Menus: A la carte, fixed-price L & D, pre-theatre, bar menu
Seats: 350. No-smoking area, air-conditioning
Additional: Children's portions Sun; ❶ dishes, vegan/other diets on request

Singapore Garden Restaurant 🏵🏵

South East Asian dishes in generous numbers at one of north west London's more animated restaurants

With Swiss Cottage and the Finchley Road just round the corner one can be spoilt for choice in this area when it comes to eating out. The Lim family have built up a loyal clientele in a relatively short time, drawn by the animated atmosphere and by the fact that the mainly Chinese menu is extended by the inclusion of Singaporean and Malay dishes. A striking feature is the freshness of a wide variety of fish, meat and poultry dishes. Barbecued spare ribs, crispy aromatic duck, and chicken in a paper bag are familiar choices. Look out for Szechuan crispy beef (thin pieces of spiced meat fried with sliced carrots), soya bean crab (a mix of brown and white meat with soya sauce), and Ayam curry (small, tender and moist pieces of chicken breast served with a mild curry sauce). The service is hurried but not dismissive, and staff will gladly explain what the less obvious dishes are. There is a short, rather dull, wine list; Singaporean Tiger beer is the thing to drink, or even chendol, strips of jelly in coconut milk and syrup.

Directions: Off the Finchley Road in Swiss Cottage. Nearest Tube – Swiss Cottage, exit Belsize Road

83 Fairfax Road NW6 4DY
Map no: GtL C4
Tel: 0171 328 5314
Chef: S K Lim
Proprietors: The Lim family and Mrs Lin Toh
Cost: Alc £20, fixed-price lunch and dinner £16. H/wine £8.50. Service exc
Credit cards: 🅰 🔳 🔳 💷 OTHER
Menus: A la carte, fixed-price lunch and dinner
Times: Midday-last L 2pm, 6pm-last D 10pm (10.30pm Fri and Sat). Closed 5 days at Xmas
Seats: 100. Air conditioned
Additional: Children welcome; ⓥ dishes; other diets on request

Snows-on-the-Green 🏵🏵

☺ *Popular alternative to the BBC canteen with brightly flavoured dishes that pack a punch*

Sebastian Snow's uncomplicated formula works well, and he has built a loyal regular following, especially from the BBC. The *carte* lists Mediterranean and modern British dishes, and the set lunch offers wonderful value for money with either two courses for £12.50, or three courses for £15.50. Dishes are gutsy and combinations bold. Typical feisty starters from a summer menu included smoked eel, poached egg, bacon and frisée, and penne with chorizo and chicken livers. Flavours do not hide their light under a bushel, and there is a great sense of confidence about main course dishes such as roast red snapper with flageolet beans, rosemary and mash, chargrilled squid with crispy vegetables and pimento salsa, peppered duck breast with turnip and prunes, and fricassée of chicken with foie gras, morels and linguine. For dessert, try classic lemon tart or mascarpone mousse cake. The short, but well-constructed, wine list, mostly domaine and estate bottled, well matches this style of cooking. Aproned staff provide prompt, efficient service but tables are so close, one would be hard pressed to keep a secret here.

Directions: Nearest Tube: Hammersmith & Shepherds Bush Green. Opposite Brook Green, half way up Shepherds Bush Rd

W6 166 Shepherds Bush Road Hammersmith W6 7PB
Map no: GtL C3
Tel: 0171 603 2142
Chefs: Sebastian Snow and Gina Cariria
Proprietor: Sebastian Snow. Manager: L Gage
Cost: Alc £20, fixed-price L £15.50 (3 course). H/wine £10 Service exc
Credit cards: 🅰 🔳 🔳 OTHER
Times: Noon-last L 3pm, 7pm-last D 11pm. Closed Sat L, Sun D & Bhs, 10 days at Xmas
Menus: A la carte, fixed-price L
Seats: 65. Air-conditioning
Additional: Children welcome, children's portions; ⓥ dishes, other dishes on request

> Frittata is an Italian omelette, but closer in style to the slow-cooked, firm set, flat Spanish tortilla than the creamy, moist, oval-shaped French omelette. In a frittata other ingredients can be added to the eggs before cooking: grated cheese, prosciutto, onions and herbs.

Soho Soho ❀

Enjoy the bustling atmosphere while sampling some of the Provencal and Mediterranean inspired dishes on offer at this popular French restaurant. Dishes could include tartlet of grilled scallops with slices of Bayonne ham, or wild boar stewed in red wine with bacon and juniper berries

Menus: A la carte, fixed-price D, pre-theatre, bar menu
Seats: 65. No-smoking area, air-conditioning
Additional: Children welcome; ❤ dishes, vegan/other dishes on request
Directions: Nearest Tube: Tottenham Court Road & Leicester Square

W1 11 Frith Street W1V 5TS
Map no: D4
Tel: 0171 494 3491
Chef: Laurent Lebeau
Proprietors: Laurence Isaacson and Neville Abraham
Cost: Alc £35, fixed-price D £15.95 (3 courses). H/wine £9.75 ❗ Service inc
Credit cards: ▨ ▩ ▧ ▨ OTHER
Times: Noon-last L 2.45pm, last D 11.45pm. Closed Sun & Bhs, Xmas Day

Sonny's ❀❀

Four-in-one gastronomic establishment, comprising café, bar, restaurant and food shop, in fashionable Barnes

The designer decor at Sonny's manages to be both minimalist and attractive; at lunchtime it draws young execs from the entertainment industry, whilst dinner is usually full of 'Barnes Stormers' and neighbourhood regulars. A change of chef has not diminished the high standard of cooking, and the style remains Med meets modern Brit. A boned leg of rabbit with cannellini beans, served with a fine gravy based on chicken stock, was particularly memorable. Fresh, tender and accurately roasted, it was set on some wilted spinach leaves and fleshy white beans. Our inspector strongly recommends the cream and butter mashed potato to mop up the gravy. A white fish soup lacked coral richness, but was light and tasty, blended with saffron, garlic and tomato paste, and garnished with a paprika aïoli and croûtons. Walnut tart and apple sorbet made an excellent clean-tasting dessert. One less welcome item, though, is the charge made for the chocolate truffles to go with the Colombian coffee. Young and refreshing wines from France and the New World have been carefully selected, and many are available by the glass.

Directions: From Castelnau end of Church Road, on left by shops

SW13 94 Church Road Barnes SW13 0DQ
Map no: GtL C3
Tel: 0181 748 0393
Chef: Peter Harrison
Proprietor: Rebecca Mascavenhas
Cost: Alc £25.20, fixed-price L £13.50. H/wine £8.75 ❗ Service exc
Credit cards: ▨ ▩ ▧
Times: Noon-last L 2.30pm (3pm Sun), 7.30pm-last D 11pm. Closed Sun pm
Menus: A la carte, fixed-price L, café menu
Seats: 100. No pipes or cigars, air-conditioning
Additional: Children welcome; ❤ dishes, vegan/other dishes on request

The Square ❀❀❀

Generally sound modern cooking in traditional St James' meeting-place

The Square serves 'sunshine food', according to owner Nigel Platts-Martin, and that indeed is a broadly accurate label. The stylish St James' restaurant continues to increase in popularity, and still sticks true to its mix of Mediterranean sunshine dishes with a hint of West Coast sunshine thrown in as well. The boldly coloured square panel and closely set tables help create a sociable atmosphere, enjoyed by customers from all walks of life. Chef Philip Howard keeps the menu short but interesting, with about six to eight freshly selected dishes on the lunch and evening *cartes*. Plenty of fish and white meat is used to create admirable numbers such as seared new season's wild salmon with asparagus salad. However, one starter sampled was more redolent of British damp than azure skies – wet foie gras and chicken liver parfait was surrounded by a lightly dressed salad which included dried meat, croûtons, lardons, french beans and

SW1 32 King Street St James's SW1Y 6RJ
Map no: C3
Tel: 0171 839 8787
Chef: Philip Howard
Proprietor: Nigel Platts-Martin, Philip Howard.
Manager: John Davey
Cost: Alc L £35/D £45. H/wine £13.75 ❗ Service exc
Credit cards: ▨ ▩ ▧ ▨ OTHER
Times: Noon-last L 3pm, 6pm-last D 11.45pm. Closed Sat/Sun L & 5 days at Xmas
Menus: A la carte
Seats: 65. Air-conditioning
Additional: Children welcome; ❤ dishes, vegan/other dishes on request

tasteless tomatoes. The sun broke through intermittently with a main course of fresh, roasted scallops on a bed of sweet tomatoes, although the seafood was practically overwhelmed by copious amounts of basil and olive oil. Pesto noodles were nicely cooked but, again, it was no contest against a strongly flavoured tapenade. An unbroken front was restored with roast rabbit, set on a creamy potato compote with rich onion gravy. Desserts shone brightly with a fine caramel and vanilla flavoured crème brûlée, and a delicious assiette of chocolate – light white chocolate mousse, chocolate marquise, small chocolate sponges and banana sorbet. Unsatisfied chocoholics can top up with the chocolate truffles which partner the filter coffee. The wine list is comprehensive, with a bias to French reds, and there are two sommeliers on duty at any one time to assist with selection.

Directions: From Piccadilly Circus walk down Piccadilly, turn left at corner of Fortnum & Mason store down Duke St, St James, walk to end of street, turn left into King St. Entrance on right

Stafford Hotel ❀

A discreet, small hotel in a quiet cul-de-sac behind Green Park with a clubby atmosphere. The restaurant is traditional in terms of service and style, but the menu has moved with the times, offering, for example, terrine of smoked salmon, leeks and goats' cheese, and tuna with lyonnaise potatoes and basil infused oil

Menus: *A la carte,* fixed-price L & D, bar menu
Additional: children welcome; children's portions, ✪ dishes, vegan/other diets on reques
Directions: off St James's Street between Pall Mall & Piccadilly

SW1 16-18 St James's Place
SW1
Map no: C3
Chef: Armando Rodriguez
Proprietor: Daniel Thwaites
Brewery, Director Terry Holmes
Cost: *Alc* £30, fixed-price L
£22.50 / D £25.50. H/wine £14
❢ Service inc
Credit cards: 🖸 💳 💳 💳 OTHER
Times: 12.30pm-last L 2.30pm,
6pm-last D 10.30pm/9.30pm
Sun Closed Sat L

The Star of India ❀

A long established South Kensington restaurant whose menu roams the Indian sub-continent. Staple dishes such as tikkas and tandooris are supplemented by the likes of 'lal maas', a traditional Rajasthani speciality of lamb cooked with dried red chillies and Ajmeri red chilli paste

Menus: *a la carte,* fixed-price L & D
Seats: 96 **Additional:** ✪ dishes
Directions: Nearest Tube – Gloucester Road

SW5 154 Old Brompton Road
SW5 0BE
Map no: A1
Tel: 0171 373 2901
Chef: Vineet Bhatia
Cost: *Alc* L £20/D £23, fixed-price L £13.50/D £16. H/wine £8.25
Credit cards: 🖸 💳 💳 💳
Times: Last L 2.45pm, last D 11.45pm

Stephen Bull Bistro ❀❀

☺ *A bright, contemporary bistro flourishing on the fringe of the City*

This smart and appealing place has led the gastronomic revival around Smithfield and continues to prosper, offering straightforward cooking and a well put together wine list at sensible prices. The staff must have to be pretty fit to flit around the two-tiered layout, which is decorated in a simple, modern (some might say sparse) style, with furnishings that are functional (some might say uncomfortable), and lithe enough to weave between tables with barely adequate elbow room between them. There is a strong selection of seafood featuring such delicacies as Irish oysters, ceviche of scallops, sushi, crab and lobster, plus a full supporting

EC1 71 St John Street EC1 4AN
Map no: E5
Tel: 0171 490 1750
Chef: Steven Carter
Proprietor: Stephen Bull
Restaurants.
Manager: April Manley
Cost: *Alc* £16-£20. H/wine
£9.50 ❢ Service exc
Credit cards: 🖸 💳 💳
Times: Noon-last L 2.15pm, last
D 11pm. Closed Sat L, Sun &
Bhs, 1 wk at Xmas

Stephen Bull Bistro

Menus: *A la carte*
Seats: 125. No pipes or cigars,
air-conditioning
Additional: Children welcome,
children's portions; ❶ dishes,
vegan/other dishes on request

menu. Among the starters, a chicken liver parfait, which according to our inspector was 'very intense' is a particular winner. Three fish and three meat main course options might include baked cod served with a sort of Mediterranean mashed potato, studded with black olives, or a slightly chewy bavette steak garnished with a sautéed aubergine, mushrooms and pine nuts. The first rate wine list is not over-long, nor over-priced, and offers plenty of choice

Directions: Half way between Clerkenwell Rd & Smithfield Market

Stephen Bull Restaurant ❀❀❀

A popular restaurant for those who like to combine culinary delectation with a heightened sense of style

In a plain white walled room with black chairs, oak-finished floors, and contemporary lighting, Stephen Bull offers meals of imagination, confidence and sensitivity. There are many takers, for when one inspector visited at lunchtime on a cold January day the room was full and the decibel level high, creating a great atmosphere. The menu is short but superbly crafted. Well balanced, accurate and palate-pleasing compositions are cooked in an unpretentious manner; sauces are only introduced to the ingredients when they bring new dimension to the flavour or texture.

The appetite is sharpened with "delicious", crisp cheese biscuits, leading on to a choice of starters which tend not to be too heavy. A gravadlax-style thick fillet of salmon was dressed lightly with ginger, avocado and vinegar, topped with oiled leaves and an innocuous but powerful portion of horseradish cream, creating an "exciting sensation to all the taste buds". This was followed by a salmis of game, thick rough cut chunks of succulent squab, guinea fowl and wild duck sauced with a well-defined shiny meat jus, big braised shallots, and meaty 'pied de mouton'. The whole production was a successful amalgam of the smoky, the rich and the subtle. Unfortunately, although the creamy banana crème brûlée had good flavour, it was a little thick in its crust, and too runny underneath. Good espresso to finish however. The very sound wine list focuses on France but New World producers are represented and there is a decent selection of half bottles.

Directions: Off Marylebone High St, 75 yards down on the left. Nearest Tube – Bond Street

5-7 Blandford Street W1H 3AA
Map no: B4
Tel: 0171 486 9696
Proprietor: Stephen Bull,
Cost: *Alc* £23-27, H/wine £11
❗ Service exc
Credit cards: ▨ ▧ ▧
Times: 12.15pm-last L 2.15pm,
6.30pm-last D 10.45pm. Closed
Sat L, Sun, Bhs, 1 wk Christmas
Menus: *A la carte* L & D
Seats: 55 Air conditioned
Additional: Children welcome;
children's portions, ❶ dishes,
vegan/other diets on request

The Stepping Stone ❀❀

On the site of the former L'Arlequin, innovative modern cooking in stylish surroundings

It is a big step from The Stables in Barnes to Queenstown Road, where so many famous chefs have made their London debut. For Gary and Emer Levy the move could prove to be a milestone. The restaurant has a bright new contemporary design and divides into two areas – one non-smoking – to provide a relaxed and informal atmosphere. The cooking is modern and fairly innovative, and initial reports have been promising. The menu is well explained, including the daily specials, and items to watch out for are the home-made pasta and sausages, fish of the day, and wild rice cakes sautéed with field mushrooms and spinach. Inspectors have also recommended the granary bread, griddled scallops with sesame oil, soy, ginger, spring onion and coriander and pan-fried calves' liver with a well made celery remoulade set on fresh sorrel leaves. Desserts are all home-made and a well constructed crème brûlée was notable for its rich flavour and light caramel crust. There is a good selection of Belgian beers and an interesting selection of wines from around the world, some available by the glass and half bottle.

Directions: From Lavender Hill/Wandsworth Road crossroads, head north up Queenstown Road towards Chelsea Bridge. Restaurant on left after half a mile

SW8 123 Queenstown Road
SW8
Map no: GtL C2
Tel: 0171 622 0555
Proprietors: Gary & Emer Levy

Suntory Restaurant ❀❀

Long established and well patronised expense-account Japanese restaurant

Suntory is one of the oldest Japanese restaurants in London, and attracts a loyal corporate and social clientele. Furnished and decorated in traditional style, there is a choice of dining-rooms, a large Teppanyaki room with griddle tables, an open-plan bar and several small private salons. Chef Kato San has been here for a number of years, and his cooking is consistently reliable, using good quality ingredients and fresh produce. In addition to the main *carte* featuring sushi, one-pot, broiled, fried and braised dishes and so on, there is a wide range of set lunch menus, including the Shoukado, a beautifully arranged Japanese lunch box. Simplest choice is the daily, no-frills £15 lunch – Tuesdays, for example, offers chicken and egg on rice, deep-fried tofu and miso soup. Several set meals peak with the £69.40 Special Teppanyaki meal, which includes clam dobin-mushi soup, sashimi, scallops and King prawns, steak, and foie gras amongst its numerous courses. Wines are varied, with some good claret, and the house Grand Bateau Bordeaux 1989 at £18.

Directions: At the bottom of St James's Street, opposite St James's Palace. Nearest Tube – Green Park (turn right after Ritz Hotel)

SW1 72 St James's Street
SW1A 1PH
Map no: C3
Tel: 0171 409 0201
Chef: K Kato
Manager: K Hamamoto
Cost: *A/c* from £35, fixed-price L £35 (4 courses)/D from £49.80 (5 courses). H/wine £14 Service inc
Credit cards: 🎴 💳 💳 💳 OTHER
Times: Noon-last L 2pm, 6pm-last D 9.30pm. Closed Sun & Easter, Xmas
Menus: *A la carte*, fixed-price L & D, pre-theatre
Seats: 120. Air-conditioning
Additional: Children over 5 welcome L; ❶/vegan dishes

> Coriander is an aromatic umbelliferous plant used as both a herb (the fresh leaves) and a spice (the dried seeds). The taste of each is different, and one cannot be substituted for the other in a recipe.

Supan Thai Restaurant ✿

☺ *Simple, fresh decor complements the cooking at this Thai restaurant which has a strong local following. The menu offers no surprises but dishes are prepared with care and might include fish cakes with sweet chilli sauce, green chicken curry, or chargrilled beef salad with cucumber and onions*

Menus: *A la carte,* ✪
Seats: 60. No pipes or cigars, air-conditioning
Additional: Children welcome; ✪ dishes
Directions: Just off Harrow Rd – Junction of Elgin Ave

W9 4 Fernhead Road W9
Map no: B3
Tel: 0181 969 9387
Chef: K Thavisin
Proprietor: A Piempreecha
Cost: Alc £12. H/wine £7.25
Service exc
Credit cards: ▨ ▧ OTHER
Times: 12.30-last L 2.15pm,
6.30-last D 10.45pm (10.15pm
Sun). Closed Dec 25/6

Swallow International Hotel ✿

A large, purpose-built hotel on the busy Cromwell Road. All-day meals are available in the Fountain Brasserie, and Blayneys offers dinner cooked in a modern British-style with oriental overtones, for example, stir-fried strips of steak and prawns with a lemon and lime butter sauce

Cromwell Road SW5
Map no: A2
Tel: 0171 973 1000 Ext 2670
Chef: David Date
Proprietors: Swallow.
Manager: Nicky Glenton
Cost: Alc £25, fixed-price D
£18.95 (4 courses) H/wine £10 ▮
Service exc
Credit cards: ▨ ▧ ▧ ▨ OTHER
Times: 6pm-last D 11pm.
Menus: A la carte D, fixed-price
D, pre-theatre, L bar menu
Seats: 70 Air conditioned.
No-smoking area
Additional: Children welcome;
children's menu, children's
portions, ✪ dishes, other diets
on request

Directions: West side of the Cromwell Road, 3 mins Earl's Court tube

Sweetings ✿

This lively City restaurant opens for lunch only. The cooking is traditionally British and fresh fish from Billingsgate is a speciality. Look out for home-made fish pies, and the Mercia oysters which sell out quickly each day. Guinness and Black Velvet are served in silver tankards

Seats: 65. Air conditioned
Menus: A la carte, bar menu
Additional: Children permitted; children's portions
Directions: Corner of Queen Victoria St. & Queen St. close to Mansion House Tube

EC4 39 Queen Victoria Street
EC4
Map no: F3
Tel: 0171 248 3062
Chef: Paul Magson
Proprietor: Mrs P Needham.
Manager: Mrs S Cross
Cost: Alc £25, H/wine £10.95 ▮
Service exc
Credit cards: None taken
Times: 11.30am-3 pm Closed
Sat, Sun, Dec 25-Jan 2

Rillettes can be of pork, rabbit, goose, or poultry.
The meat is cooked in lard, pounded to shreds, potted and
preserved in the fat and usually served as an hors d'oeuvre.
Rillettes are always served cold.

Tabaq ❀

☺ *An informal restaurant named after a large serving dish used in India and Pakistan. The menu offers lambs' brains cooked to chef Manzoor Ahmed's own recipe, for example. Other dishes include 'palak methi', a Punjabi delicacy of spinach cooked with new potatoes and herbs, and a lightly marinated shish kebab murgh*

SW12 47 Balham Hill
South Clapham SW12 9DR
Map no: GtL C2
Tel: 0181 673 7820
Chef: Manzwr Ahmed
Proprietor: Mushtaq Ahmed
Cost: Alc £18.50, fixed-price L
£9.25. H/wine £7.25 Service exc
Credit cards: 🔲 🔳 🔳 🔳 OTHER
Times: Noon-last L 2.45pm,
6pm-last D 11.45pm. Closed
Sun
Menus: A la carte, fixed-price L
Seats: 50. No-smoking area
Additional: Children welcome,
children's portions; ◑ dishes,
vegan/other dishes on request

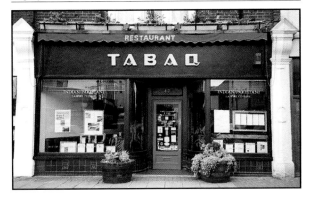

Directions: On the S Circular. Nearest Tube: Clapham South

Tamarind ❀❀

Upmarket North Indian restaurant with subtle, contemporary interior design

Designer Emily Todhunter has used slate, stone and wood in the cool, sleek interior of Tamarind to stunning effect – the hard materials are highlighted by splashes of colour from silk saris adorning the walls, and the glass-fronted kitchen is dominated by two free-standing Tandoor ovens. Amongst the appetisers on the classic Indian menu are 'aloo chaat anarkali', a sour-sweet potato and tomato salad with chopped onion and pomegranate seeds, and pan-fried spicy chicken livers. Main dishes obviously include a wide number of tandoori ones, such as spiced chicken drumsticks and pomfret tandoori (whole Indian ocean fish on the bone). Curries feature the ever-popular lamb rogan josh plus 'murgh adraki', chicken served in the karahi. Only 'jhinga zaikedar', a fiery dish of prawns, tomatoes, onions and peppers disappointed with a harsh, sharp flavour and a worrying lack of prawns. 'Dal burkhari' is a Tamarind special, well-flavoured but a little thin on our sampling. As well as the short but good wine list, there are freshly squeezed juices, organic yoghurt drinks and a knock-out selection of cocktails such as 'Imli' – tamarind juice, dark rum, orange juice and soda.

W1 20 Queen Street
Mayfair W1X 7PJ
Map no: C3
Tel: 0171 629 3561
Chef: Atul Kozhhar
Proprietor: Indian Cuisine Ltd.
Gen Manager: Rasinder Soor
Cost: Alc £32, fixed-price L
£13.50. H/wine £11 ❗ Service
inc
Credit cards: 🔲 🔳 🔳 🔳
Times: Noon-last L 3pm, 6pm-
last D 11.45pm. Closed Xmas &
Easter
Menus: A la carte, fixed-price L
Seats: 90. Air-conditioning
Additional: Children welcome;
◑ dishes

Directions: From Green Park Tube station walk to Half Moon St, turn left on Curzon St, 1st right is Queen St

---

Rösti is a Swiss speciality from Berne. It is quite simply a potato cake made from layers of finely sliced or grated potato, fried until golden.

Tatsusu ✿✿

A wide range of authentic Japanese cooking in busy City restaurant

Tatsusu is much patronised by Japanese City gents, and standards have to be high to meet their exacting requirements. The success of the place is shown by the ever-busy Sushi bar and Teppanyaki counters, as well as the main traditional restaurant on the lower floor, for which reservations are essential. The cooking is authentic, freshly prepared and benefiting from the chef's own primary and secondary dashi. In the past, our inspector has thoroughly enjoyed three kinds of sashimi, comprising 'sake' (salmon), 'hirame' (turbot) and the much sought-after 'hamachi' (yellowtail). The repertoire spans all the traditional grilled, braised, fried, one-pot, tofu and egg dishes. Try the 'chawan-mushi', steamed egg curd with chicken, vegetables and shrimp, served in a chawan cup, or the 'dobin-mushi', a soup cooked in the dobin pot. Also praised has been the 'yu-dofu', boiled emulsified beancurd in citrus and 'soy ponzu' sauce, and the fragrant miso soup with kelp and undisturbed, fermented bean paste. The 'ebi tempura', or prawns, should not be missed. Service is attentive and efficient, although communication at times can be an awesome task for those less than fluent in Japanese.

Directions: Ground floor of Broadgate Circle

EC1 32 Broadgate Circle
EC1M 6BT
Map no: G4
Tel: 0171 638 5863
Chefs: Mr Yamanaka and Mr Maehara
Manager: Nicholas Stern
Cost: ▮ Service inc
Credit cards: ▧ ▩ ▨ ▩ OTHER
Times: Last L 2.30pm, last D 9.45pm. Closed Sat/Sun & Bhs
Menus: *A la carte,* fixed-price, ♥
Seats: 130. No cigars or pipes, air-conditioning
Additional: Children welcome, children's portions & menu; ♥ dishes, vegan/other dishes on request

The Thai Garden ✿

☺ *An interesting vegetarian and fish restaurant, offering a good choice of set menus. Our inspector enjoyed a prawn satay with peanut sauce, crisp vegetables in sweet vinegar, pomfret fish with pepper and chilli topping, and an aubergine and mixed vegetable curry with coconut sauce*

Menus: *A la carte,* fixed-price L & D, ♥ **Seats:** 32. No-smoking area
Additional: Children welcome in early evening; ♥/vegan dishes
Directions: Nearest tube: Bethnal Green. 2nd left on Roman Road exit

E2 249 Globe Road E2 0JD
Map no: GtL D3
Tel: 0181 981 5748
Chef: K Duff
Proprietor: Suthinee Hufton
Cost: *Alc* £15, fixed-price L £7.50/D £21. H/wine £6.50
Service exc
Credit cards: ▧ ▩
Times: Noon-last L 2.45pm, 6pm-last D 10.45pm. Closed Sun & Bhs

Thailand ✿

☺ *A Thai/Lao temple of excellence in a jaded part of south-east London*

An unassuming restaurant, sandwiched between 'takeaways', in a parade of shops opposite Goldsmiths' College. Since its early days this 'little gem of a restaurant' has done a steady trade with students, locals and other regulars from all over London. The dining room is tiny, seating 25 at a push, so booking is essential. On busy nights service can be slow, but those in the know order starters straightaway, and then deliberate over the wide choice of Thai and Laotian main courses, largely based around seafood, chicken, beef and pork. Thai favourites include starters of succulent chicken and pork satay, better-than-average fish cakes with green beans, chilli paste, herbs and spices, and spiced crabmeat and chicken wrapped in spinach or cabbage leaves. A section featuring strong chilli sauces, includes pounded catfish with garlic, fish sauce and lime juice. There are nine different rice dishes, including steamed Lao sticky rice which helps diffuse the heat of Laotian char-grilled beef, with its tangy lime, onion and chilli dressing. To drink there is

SE14 14 Lewisham Way
New Cross SE14
Map no: GtL D3
Tel: 0181 691 4040
Chef: Gong Cambungoet
Proprietor: Mrs G Herman
Cost: *Alc* D £20, fixed-price D £20 (for parties). H/wine £8.50. Service exc
Credit cards: ▧ ▩
Times: 6pm-last D 11pm. Closed Sun, Mon, Dec 25/6, Jan 1
Seats: 25. Air conditioned
Additional: children permitted (no infants) ♥ dishes

Singaporean Tiger beer, a short and reasonably priced selection of wines and a staggering collection of malt whiskies, introduced by the patron's Scottish husband.

Directions: Opposite Goldsmiths College, 5 mins from New Cross and New Cross Gate Tubes

Thistells ❀

☺ *Chef/patron Sami Youssef's cooking remains consistently good at this friendly restaurant. Dishes might include fast fried liver with Eastern spices, which is a speciality, stuffed peppers with watercress sauce, or grilled trout with an almond and white wine sauce*

Menus: A la carte, fixed-price L & D, bar menu **Seats:** 35
Additional: Children welcome, children's portions; ❂ dishes, vegan/other dishes on request
Directions: Nearest BR: East Dulwich. Bus Nos 184, 185, 37, 176

SE22 65 Lordship Lane SE22
Map no: GtL D2
Tel: 0181 299 1921
Chef: Sami Youssef
Proprietor: Sami Youssef
Cost: Alc £15.98, fixed-price L/D £9.95. H/wine £7.50
Service exc
Credit cards: 🂠 🂡 🂢 5
Times: Noon-last L 2.30pm, last D 10.30pm. Closed Sun D

Tui ❀

☺ *Plain white walls contrast with black furnishings in this simple Thai restaurant where tables, bright with fresh flowers and white cloths, are set close together. Dishes include hot Thai soup made with chicken stock, lime leaves, coriander and sliced galingale, and barbecued, marinated pork and beef served with a peanut sauce*

Menus: A la carte, fixed-price L **Seats:** 56. No pipes or cigars
Additional: Children welcome L; ❂ dishes
Directions: Five mins walk from South Kensington tube station in direction of V&A Museum on Cromwell Rd. Entrance on corner of Thurloe Place & Exhibition Rd

SW7 19 Exhibition Road
SW7 2HE
Map no: A2
Tel: 0171 584 8359
Chefs: Mr & Mrs Kongsrivilai
Proprietor: E Thapthimthong
Cost: Alc £20, fixed-price L £10. H/wine £8.25 Service exc
Credit cards: 🂠 🂡 🂢 🂣 OTHER
Times: Noon-last L 2.30pm (2.50pm Sun), 6.20pm-last D 10.50pm (7pm-10.20pm Sun). Closed Bhs & 5 days at Xmas

Turners ❀❀❀

High-profile chef with an individual style of cooking

SW3 87-89 Walton Street
SW3 2HP
Map no: B2
Tel: 0171 584 6711
Chef: Jonathon Bibbings
Proprietor: Turners.
Manager: Richard Fletcher

Chef/Patron Brian Turner is not too grand to muck in and help out with the service, and can frequently be found out front, giving a helping hand and chatting to the regulars. There is both a lunch and

dinner menu du jour, as well as a French-style *carte*. The former are particularly good value, and a three course lunch for £13.50 might include a warm salad of grey mullet with tomatoes and chives, grilled loin of pork with wild mushrooms and Madeira sauce, and timbale of white chocolate and raspberries. As might be expected, given the address, the atmosphere is very fashionable, and the smart interior is decorated with designer co-ordinated fabrics. Tables are a little close together, however, and the air conditioning does not always adequately cope with drifting cigarette smoke.

The menu reflects that day's market produce, but long-standing favourites such as crab sausage in parsley sauce, and roast rack of English lamb with herbes de Provence, remain as popular as ever. Our inspector chose juicy and tender slices of prime duck breast served with a glace de viande textured with mixed wild mushrooms and whole green peppercorns. Vegetables were crunchy and full of flavour, and served with a butter sauce. Desserts are equally good – upside down banana tart with toffee ice-cream, or 'bavarois au citron vert', a luscious lime cream flavoured with citrus zest, served with fruit coulis and unusual pommes sèchées, deep-fried crisp slices of apple. The wine list has some unique Sassicaia vintage wines from the award-winning Tenuta San Guido in Northern Italy, and the fine Chablis collection is also well worthy of note, with most of the principal growers represented.

Directions: Directly behind Harrods, through Walton Place into Walton St. Towards the Fulham Rd end

Cost: *Alc* £41.70, fixed-price L £13.50 (3 courses)/D £26.50 (3 courses). H/wine £13.50 ⬤
Service inc
Credit cards: 🔲 🔳 🔳 💳 OTHER
Times: Last L 2.30pm, last D 11pm, Sun D 6pm-8.30pm.
Closed Sat L & Bhs, Dec 25-30
Menus: *A la carte*, fixed-price L & D
Seats: 55. No pipes allowed, air-conditioning
Additional: Children welcome, children's portions; ⬤ dishes, vegan/other dishes on request

The Two Brothers ❀

Friendly, family-run fish and chip place with a strong local following. Simple meals are perfectly cooked and include a good choice of fish, as well as succulent moules mariniére in a light cream sauce, jellied eels and home-made fish soup. Choose the 'excellent' bread and butter pudding for dessert

Seats: 90. No smoking. Air conditioned
Additional: Children permitted (no babies or push chairs after 6.30pm). children's portions
Directions: 2 mins Finchley Central tube

297 Regents Park Road, Finchley
Map no: GtL C3
Tel: 0181 346 0469
Proprietors: Leon and Tony Manzi
Cost: *Alc* from £13.30. H/wine £8.85. Service exc
Credit cards: 🔲 🔳 🔳 OTHER
Times: Noon-last L 2.30pm 5.30pm-last D 10.15pm. Closed Sun and Mon, Bhs except Good Fri, last 2 weeks Aug

Vasco & Piero's Pavilion Restaurant ❀❀

Genuine Italian regional cooking at modest prices

Italian regional food may just have been discovered elsewhere, but it has always been the backbone of this friendly, Italian Soho restaurant. Daily-changing, set-price menus, drawn from a defined repertoire, offer marvellous value-for-money. A real flavour of Italy comes through with starters such as black bean and pasta soup, bruschetta with calamari and mussels, and antipasto misto of frittata, grilled zucchini, tomato and mozzarella. Main course dishes typically include grilled breast of pigeon with Marsala and mushroom sauce, grilled lamb cutlets on garlic crostini, and calves' liver with sage. Carpaccio may be served cold with slices of pink lamb, or warm with sturgeon, basil, oregano and capers. The home-made pasta is much recommended – black pappardelle with fresh

W1 15 Poland Street W1V 3DE
Map no: D4
Tel: 0171 437 8774
Chef: Vasco Matteucci
Proprietor: Vasco Matteucci
Cost: *Alc* L £27, fixed-price D £13.95. H/wine £8.50 ⬤ Service exc
Credit cards: 🔲 🔳 🔳 💳
Times: Noon-last L 3pm, 6pm-last D 11pm. Closed Sat/Sun & Bhs
Menus: *A la carte* L, fixed-price D, special Sat D menu 6/year
Seats: 52. No pipes allowed, air-conditioning

salmon, for instance, or tortelloni stuffed with guinea fowl, sea bass or asparagus. Delicious salmon and caper fishcakes with avocado salsa are another regular favourite. Desserts include a properly made panna cotta with caramel and strawberries. The well-chosen list of Italian regional wines is a good match for the cooking.

Directions: On corner of Great Marlborough St & Noel St. From Oxford Circus tube station walk towards Tottenham Court Rd, Poland St is on right just passed M & S. Entrance half way down Poland St

Additional: Children welcome; ❶ dishes, vegan/other dishes on request

The Veeraswamy ❀❀

London's oldest and most famous Indian restaurant, still proudly going strong after all these years

This venerable Anglo-Indian restaurant still commands the best view of Regent Street from its elevated position, but book early if you want a coveted table by the window. Buffet lunches are as popular and as good value as ever. New chef Jude Henry Lobo is from Goa, so the Goan chicken and Goan fish curry should have authentic flair. Mint, unusually, flavoured a starter of soft, tender scallops served on buttery nan bread, with a separate mint and yoghurt sauce. The Delhi snack/starter of 'alu tikka' consisted of mixed potato and cottage cheese with fresh coriander. 'Sikand raan' arrived dramatically, with flaming rum on top of tandoori lamb baked with almonds, dried fruit and fresh coriander. Less thrilling, was 'murgh makhani', chicken breast in butter and tomato sauce, the latter made with a well known brand of tomato paste. Indian sweets feature in the short dessert list, or else try the sweet cinnamon-flavoured Masala tea, which cleanses the palate most efficiently. Extras, such as popadums, mango chutney, lime pickle and basmati rice are all good. A short wine list contains mostly French wines with a few New World wines, as well as an Indian sparkling champagne.

Directions: Entrance near junction of Swallow St & Regent St, located in Victory House. Entrance in Swallow St

W1 99/101 Regent Street
W1R 8RS
Map no: C3
Tel: 0171 734 1401
Chef: Henry Lobo
Proprietor: Sarova Hotels.
Manager: Aidan Fahy
Cost: Alc £25, fixed-price L £12.95/D £16.95. H/wine £11 ❗
Service exc
Credit cards: 🅽 🈺 🈹 🄿 OTHER
Times: Noon-last L 2.30pm, last D 11pm. Closed Sun & Bhs, Xmas, Jan 1
Menus: A la carte, fixed-price L & D, pre-theatre, buffet L Mon/Sat
Seats: 115. No-smoking area, air-conditioning
Additional: Children welcome; ❶/vegan dishes

Veronica's ❀❀

Enterprising themed British restaurant with well-researched dishes

It is refreshing to find a restaurant that looks to British heritage for inspiration. Veronica's bravely bucks the trend for European peasant food, and specialises in old English dishes and traditional British cooking. The historical/regional theme of the menu changes every 4–6 weeks, as does the decor in the front part of the restaurant. Additional space is also given over to exhibits by local artists. Our most recent visit coincided with a Victorian phase. Sausage N'Benton proved to be a 19th-century recipe for sage and veal sausages served with 'Benton' sauce of horseradish and mustard. Having sampled an admittedly excellent portion of their 'famous' twice-roasted duck, our inspector was still none too clear just how the end result differed from the single roasted variety. Victorian chocolate trifle, was based on Mrs Beeton's liqueur-soaked chocolate sponge, with raspberries, cream and home-made custard. A non-Victorian interest in healthy eating is indicated by various symbols on the menu – an attention to detail which is

W2 3 Hereford Road
Bayswater W2 4AB
Map no: GtL C3
Tel: 0171 229 5079/221 1452
Chefs: Antonio Feliccio and Veronica Shaw
Proprietor: Philip Shaw
Cost: Alc £22.50, fixed-price L/D £11.50. H/wine £9.50 ❗
Service exc
Credit cards: 🅽 🈺 🈹 🄿 OTHER
Times: Noon-last L 2.30pm, 7pm-last D midnight. Closed Bhs & 2 days at Xmas
Menus: A la carte, fixed-price L & D, pre-theatre, ❶/vegan
Seats: 60

perhaps explained by Veronica Shaw's previous existence as a headmistress.

Directions: Nearest Tube stations: Bayswater, Queensway & Nottinghill Gate. Herefore Road runs parallel to Queensway in between Bayswater Rd and Westbourne Grove

Wagamama

This modern Japanese fast-food place offers some of the best value-for-money around. Bookings are not accepted, tables are shared, but queues move quickly, and the atmosphere is vibrant. Look out for chicken based dumplings flavoured with cabbage, pak-choi, chives, water chestnuts and garlic, boiled then finished on a hot grill stone

Seats: 104. No pipes or cigars, air-conditioning
Additional: Children welcome; ❶ dishes, other dishes on request
Directions: Nearest Tube: Tottenham Court Road. Walk down New Oxford St, left up Bloomsbury St, 1st right. From British Museum, right down Coptic St, right down Streatham St

WC1 4 Streatham Street
WC1A 1JB
Map no: D4
Tel: 0171 323 9223
Proprietor: Wagamama Ltd
Cost: Fixed-price L/D £6.80.
H/wine £6.90 Service exc
Credit cards: None
Times: Noon-last D 11pm
(10pm Sun). Closed Dec 24-Jan 2
Menus: *A la carte*, fixed-price L & D

Additional: Children welcome, children's portions; ❶ dishes, vegan/other dishes on request

The Waldorf Hotel

Renowned for its Palm Court tea dances, the hotel has benefited from a multi-million pound refurbishment. Contemporary cooking in the restaurant has struck a chord with a growing following, but traditionalists can still enjoy the excellent plain grills. Expect fricasée of scallops, and lamb, garlic confit and creamy leeks

Directions: Nearest Tube: Covent Garden

WC2 Aldwych WC2B 4DD
Map no: E4
Tel: 0171 836 2400
Chef: Philippe Pichon
Proprietor: Forte.
Cost: *Alc* £41, fixed-price L/D £26.50
Credit cards: 🄰 🄱 🄲 🄳 OTHER
Times: Last D 10.30pm

Waltons

Smart English restaurant that remains ever popular

This much favoured, traditional English restaurant has had a change of chef, but the style of the menu and cooking remains unaltered. Their famous salmon and crab timbale heads the list of

SW3 121 Walton Street
SW3 2HP
Map no: B2
Tel: 0171 584 0204
Chef: John Coxon
Proprietor: Roger Wren.
Manager: Michael Mayhew
Cost: *Alc* £35, fixed-price L £14.75/D £21. H/wine £9.50 Service exc
Credit cards: 🄰 🄱 🄲 🄳
Times: 12.30-last L 2.30pm (2pm Sun & Bhs), 7.30pm-last D 11.30pm (7pm-10pm Sun & Bhs). Closed Dec 26
Menus: *A la carte*, fixed-price L & D, post-theatre
Seats: 75. No pipes allowed, air-conditioning
Additional: Children welcome, children's portions; ❶ dishes, vegan/other dishes on request

starters, which also includes pigeon and grilled pepper terrine, and smoked haddock and leek tartelette. Principal dishes range from grilled calves' liver and bacon, to baked slice of Scottish salmon, and grilled fillet steak with home-made chips. A winter inspection meal started with a sauté of succulent scallops, served with an unusual peach dressing on salad leaves that complemented the shellfish surprisingly well. The main course, rack of Southdown lamb with herb crust, was tender and lightly cooked, but the rosemary jus was rather sparse. Walton's apple and Calvados tart made a fine dessert, but the accompanying cinnamon custard could have been more generously portioned. The particularly good wine list includes some fine clarets and Burgundies. Traditional Sunday lunch is always popular, and the After-Theatre menu, at £21 for two courses, is worth staying out late for.

Directions: Nearest Tube: South Kensington. Off Brompton Road

The Washington ❀

The hotel's restaurant, Madison's offers a straightforward, short, fixed-price menu, and a carte, as well as an all-day menu available in the lounge. Food is freshly prepared. In the restaurant look out for king prawns with a Thermidor sauce, or perhaps a daily special such as Madison's flambé

Menus: A la carte D, fixed-price D, bar menu
Seats: 100. Air conditioned
Additional: Children welcome; children's portions, ❷ dishes, vegan on request
Directions: Nearest Tube – Green Park

W1 5-7 Curzon Street W1
Map no: C3
Tel: 0171 499 7000
Chef: Nicholas Patten
Proprietor: Sarova Hotels.
Manager: Fiona Sheeny
Cost: Alc £27, fixed-price D £19.95 H/wine £11.95 ❢ Service inc
Credit cards: 🜚 ▨ ▨ 🔳
Times: 5.30pm-last D 10pm

West Lodge Park Hotel ❀

Extensive grounds, including a fine Arboretum, surround this early William IV Regency-style country house. The Cedar restaurant provides a daily fixed-price menu, from one course to three, offering dishes such as a delightful fresh salmon ravioli served with a saffron cream and mushroom sauce

Menus: A la carte, fixed-price L & D
Seats: 75. No smoking in dining room
Additional: Children permitted; children's portions, ❷ dishes, vegan/other diets on request
Directions: 1 mile S of M25 exit 24 on the A111; 1 mile from Cockfosters & Hadley Wood stations

Cockfosters Road
Hadley Wood
Barnet EN4 0PY
Map no: GtL C5
Tel: 0181 440 8311
Chef: Peter Leggat
Proprietor: Beale's Ltd.
Manager: Peter Beale
Cost: Fixed-price L £17.95/D £20.95/£222.75 w/e H/wine £10.75. Service exc
Credit cards: 🜚 ▨ ▨ OTHER
Times: 12.30-last L 2pm/D 9.45pm. Closed 27-29 Dec

The White House ❀

It began life as an apartment block in the 30s, and was one of the most exclusive addresses in London. Now a stylish hotel, places to eat include an open-all-day garden café, the Wine Press wine bar, and the more formal restaurant, which offers international cooking of a sound standard

Additional: ❷ dishes
Directions: Opposite Regents Park

NW1 Albany Street NW1 3VP
Map no: C5
Tel: 0171 387 1200
Chef: Lovell Clinton
Proprietor: Stephen Paramor
Cost: Fixed-price L & D £12.75/22.75
Credit cards: 🜚 ▨ ▨ 🔳 OTHER
Times: Last D 11.15

The White Tower 🏵🏵

Identify with the rich and famous as you, like them, enjoy the range of authentic Cypriot and Greek dishes offered by this traditional West End restaurant

If you enjoy celebrity-spotting, a meal at this popular, bustling restaurant in the West End could pay added dividends – though the quality of the food itself ought to be sufficient attraction. Owners Mary Dunne and George Metaxeas have worked hard with chef Ken Whitehead to create an interesting *carte* (supplemented by 'specials') of tasty, wholesome and soundly cooked dishes, mainly Cypriot or mainland Greek in origin, though some French influence is detectable. A starter of taramasalata or 'mezedes a la Greque', for example, might be followed by either the traditional moussaka or chicken Anastassia, the plump chicken gently poached, cut into thin slices and presented on a bed of pilaff rice. The choice of desserts, though limited, includes baklava, and Greek coffee is served with Turkish delight. Greece figures prominently, too, on the short but interesting and very reasonably priced wine list. Well supervised service is both efficient and professional.

Directions: nearest Tubes Tottenham Court Road, Goodge Street

W1 1 Percy Street W1
Map no: D4
Tel: 0171 636 8141/2
Chef: Ken Whitehead
Proprietor: The Restaurant Partnership P.L.C.
Managers: Mary Dunne and George Metaxas
Cost: *Alc* £35-£40. H/wine £10.50. Service exc. Cover charge £2
Credit cards: 🔲 🔲 🔲 🔲 OTHER
Times: Last L 2.30pm,/D 10.30pm. Closed Sat L, Sun, Bhs
Menu: *A la carte*
Seats: 80. Partially air conditioned
Additional: children permitted (over 6 L,10 D) children's portions, 🟊 dishes

Wilson's 🏵🏵

☺ *A blast from the bagpipes and a plate of haggis are just some of the attractions at this friendly, good value restaurant serving food with a Scottish slant*

At Wilson's there is always the possibility that diners will be greeted by owner Bob Wilson with a tune from his bagpipes – he is always willing to oblige – and this will give some indication of the friendly and relaxing atmosphere of this popular restaurant. Then there may be the chance of pursuing the Scottish theme with a plate of haggis, mashed potatoes and swede (as a starter or main course). The accomplished cooking offers a simple fixed-price lunch menu and a more adventurous *carte* at dinner – both representing good value for money. The selection of starters might include Gruyère and anchovy tartlet, finnan haddock pudding, or chicken liver and pork pâté with red onion marmalade. These could be followed by strips of beef fillet with port and wild mushroom sauce, or roasted escalope of salmon with dill butter sauce. Vegetables and salad are charged separately. Some interesting desserts are offered, such as Manchester pudding, a firm light custard with raspberry jam topped with meringue, and Athol Brose, a concoction of toasted oats, heather honey, malt whisky and cream. A selection of some 22 wines is listed, including a few half bottles. The wines are mostly French and reasonably priced.

Directions: On the corner of Blythe Road and Shepherds Bush Road, 7 mins Goldhawk Rd/Hammersmith/Shepherds Bush Tubes

W14 236 Blythe Road W14
Map no: GtL C3
Tel: 0171 603 7267
Chef: Robert Hilton
Proprietor: Bob Wilson.
Manager: Tony Jimenez
Cost: *Alc* £16.50, fixed-price L £10, H/wine £8.95 ▮ Service exc
Credit cards: 🔲 🔲
Times: Last L 2pm/D 11pm. Closed Mon
Menus: *A la carte*, fixed-price L
Seats: 44. Air conditioned
Additional: Children welcome; children's portions, 🟊 dishes, vegan/other diets on request

> Sevruga caviar has small light to dark grey eggs and comes from the smallest sturgeons, which are the most prolific. It is also the cheapest of the three types of caviar available.

Wiltons ●●

Busy fish restaurant with a sensible, old-fashioned air and reliable, uncomplicated food

Wiltons is as much a part of Jermyn Street as the bespoke gentlemens' outfitters. Since 1742, it has been noted for oysters, fish and game, and the jaunty, top-hatted young lobster about town on the 20s style menu cover sets the timeless tone. Fish still dominates, and although there are modern recipes such as roast monkfish with herb crust and chargrilled tuna on the daily specials, part of the joy of Wiltons is in finding dishes long forgotten elsewhere. Real turtle soup, native oysters, lobster – Mornay, Thermidor and Newburg, Dover sole in one of seven ways from Véronique to Waleska, anchovies on toast and gulls' eggs are amongst the pleasures. Resolutely, there is not a vegetarian dish in sight, if one discounts melon, asparagus and Welsh rarebit. There are a few grilled meat choices such as fillet steak and lambs' kidneys, and desserts run along equally safe tracks with sherry trifle and pear Belle Hélène. A well balanced wine list complements the food with a number of fine clarets and Burgundies, plus a short selection of New World wines. Service is attentive and professional, but with a friendly touch.

Directions: On the corner of Walton Street and Draycott Avenue, just off Brompton Road. Nearest Tube – South Kensington

SW1 55 Jermyn Street
SW1Y 6LX
Map no: C3
Tel: 0171 629 9955
Chef: Ross Hayden
Manager: Robin Gundry
Cost: Alc £50, fixed-price L £19.75. H/wine £13.50 Service exc
Credit cards: 🔲 🔲 🔲 🔲
Times: Last L 2.30pm, last D 10.30pm. Closed Sat & Bhs
Menus: A la carte, fixed-price L, pre-theatre, bar menu
Seats: 90. No pipes allowed, air-conditioning
Additional: ♥ dishes, vegan/other dishes on request

The Windmill on The Common ●

☺ *A public house since 1729, the Windmill is a popular, busy establishment. There is an extensive range of bar food, and the small, wood-panelled restaurant offers an interesting menu of carefully cooked dishes – halibut with prawn sauce is particularly recommended*

Times: Last L 2.30pm, 7pm-last D 10pm. Closed Sun D
Menus: A la carte, Sun L, bar menu **Seats:** 30. Air-conditioning
Additional: Children welcome, children's portions; ♥ dishes, vegan/other dishes by arrangement:
Directions: Nearest Tubes: Clapham Common or Clapham South

SW4 Southside
Clapham Common SW4 9DE
Map no: GtL C2
Tel: 0181 673 4578
Chef: Andrew Paice
Proprietor: Youngs Brewery. Managers: Richard & Heather Williamson
Cost: Alc £18.50, fixed-price L £13.50 (Sun). H/wine £7.80 Service exc
Credit cards: 🔲 🔲 🔲 🔲 OTHER

Yumi ●●

A well-established restaurant offering a comprehensive selection of Japanese cuisine

This well-established Japanese restaurant may lack the stylistic elegance of some London establishments, but it has a welcoming atmosphere and dinner guests can usually depend upon the personal attention and sympathetic guidance of the proprietor, Mr Ousumi. Should you be reluctant to sit cross-legged on tatami mats, there are conventional Western tables on the ground floor and a small sushi bar on the first floor. A range of set menus provide a balanced and carefully prepared introduction to the cuisine. Our inspector enjoyed the selection of sashimi, although the brill was a bit chewy and yellow tail tuna was unavailable. Chawan mushi – a kind of custard with morsels of chicken and kelp – was fine, as was the miso soup. King prawn tempura were succulent, 'yu-dofu' – casseroled tofu – delicately flavoured, and gohan rice suitably sticky

W1 110 George Street W1
Map no: B4
Tel: 0171 935 8320
Chef: M Sato
Proprietors: T Osumi
Cost: Alc £30; fixed-price lunch £15.80; fixed-price dinner £26. H/wine £9.50. Service 12.5%. Cover charge
Credit cards: 🔲 🔲 🔲 🔲 OTHER
Menus: A la carte, fixed-price lunch and dinner, Banquet dinner, pre-theatre
Times: 12.30pm-last L 2pm, 5.30pm-last D 10pm. Closed Sat lunch, Sun, Bhs
Seats: 76. No cigars or pipes. Air conditioned

and served with crisp pickles. Service is smiling, though occasionally confused. To drink, there are several French wines, although Kirin beer may be more appropriate.

Additional: *Children permitted (over 9)*

Directions: A few yards east of the junction of George Street with Gloucester Place. Nearest Tube – Marble Arch

Zen Central ֍֍

Varied range of dishes in ultra-modern, stylish Chinese restaurant

Zen interiors are known for their sleek, modern design and the central restaurant is no exception. It is essential to book, particularly on a Sunday night, when many Chinese come to dine.

Popular dishes, in both senses, include crispy aromatic duck or lamb, sweet and sour pork fillet, and Szechuan crispy shredded beef. At the luxury end, there is lobster, braised abalone, roasted Kwantung suckling pig, and double-boiled fluffy shark's fin. The gourmet hors d'oeuvre include crab meat and coriander croquettes and Peking ravioli. Prawns and scallops come together in a rich, sea spice sauce, and chicken in a subtle lemongrass one; fresh spinach is enlivened with chilli, ginger and an almost cheesy beancurd sauce. The tropical fruit platter is a good way to cleanse the palate, but a refreshingly different choice is the chilled honey melon tapioca pudding. The cooking, however, is not without its flaws, such as overcooked special fried rice and seafood lacking in flavour. A calm, contemplative frame of mind must be adopted when paying the bill – prices are very steep. That, no doubt, is the secret of Zen.

W1 20-22 Queen Street
W1X 7PJ
Map no: C3
Tel: 0171 629 8103/629 8089
Chef: Wai Hung Ho
Proprietor: Zen Garden Group.
Manager: William Lee
Cost: *Alc* £25, fixed-price L £28 (4 courses)/D £42 (6 courses).
H/wine £12 Service exc
Credit cards: ■ ▦ ▦ ▣ OTHER
Times: Noon-last L 2.30pm, 6.30pm-last D 11.30pm. Closed Dec 24-27
Menus: *A la carte*, fixed-price L & D
Seats: 90. No pipes or cigars, air-conditioning
Additional: ❤ dishes, vegan/other dishes on request

Directions: Off Berkeley Square/Curzon Street

Zen Garden ֍֍

The latest addition to the Zen group of Chinese restaurants

W1 15-16 Berkeley Street
W1X 5AE
Map no: C3
Tel: 0171 493 1381
Chef: Cheung Hong
Proprietor: Zen Garden Group.
Manager: Joe Sham
Cost: *Alc* from £25, fixed-price D £28-£40. H/wine £12 Service exc
Credit cards: ■ ▦ ▦ ▣ OTHER
Times: Noon-last L 2.30pm, 6pm-last D 11.30pm. Closed Xmas wk
Menus: *A la carte*, fixed-price D
Seats: 120. Air-conditioning
Additional: Children welcome; ❤ dishes

A Mayfair restaurant, formerly the Empress Garden, has been completely revamped. The effect is lighter, yet retains a luxurious feel – chandeliers, colourful silk costumes on the walls – commensurate with the prices. This is not your average Chinese. However, ingredients are first-class and handled with care and understanding. Hong Cheung, from Tiger Lee on the Old

Brompton Road, offers an adventurous list to supplement the more standard menu. Red braised oxtail in a clay pot is one such speciality, a fragrant, rich stew flavoured with tangerine peel and stat anise. Fish cheek features more than once, maybe braised with spring onion and ginger, or as a broth with tofu providing a textural contrast. Steamed egg with fresh crab meat again displayed the Chinese fondness for unusual textures. Dim sum is available at lunchtime and Sunday is a favourite with families.

Directions: Off Berkeley Sq, opp Mayfair Hotel. Nearest Tube: Green Park

ZENW3 ❀❀

A health-conscious Chinese restaurant on bustling Hampstead High Street which offers a particularly good vegetarian selection

Strikingly different in design, this Chinese restaurant features a decor where the only splashes of colour are provided by flowers or paintings. Slick, well drilled service is similarly minimalist, and on busy nights there may be long delays for which neither apology nor explanation is forthcoming – a regrettable circumstance in view of the 12% service charge. The menu claims to offer healthy, evolved and delectable dishes entirely free of monosodium glutamate, and vegetable dishes such as sautéed spinach in a chilli and beancurd sauce or an intensely flavoured sea spice aubergine are certainly excellent. Reactions were mixed, though, on the occasion of a recent visit: quick-fried scallop stuffed with mashed shrimp in peppercorn salt was fresh and tasty, but the scallop content was negligible and a dipping sauce would have added interest; similarly, steamed sea bass, though of good quality and accompanied by a fragrant, subtle tangerine sauce, was overcooked. Sake and shaoshing represent the Far East on a wine list which includes labels from the New World as well as Europe.

Directions: 2 mins down hill from Hampstead Tube next to P.O.

NW3 83 Hampstead High Street NW3
Map no: GtL C4
Tel: 0171 794 7863/4
Chef: Kwok Lee Tangt
Proprietor: Zen Garden Group.
Manager: Dicken Chow
Cost: *Alc* £25, fixed-price L £11.50, D £26.50 (5 courses) H/wine £10. Service exc 12.5%
Credit cards: 🟥 💳 💳 💳
Times: Midday-last D 11.15pm. Closed Xmas
Menus: *A la carte*, fixed-price L & D
Seats: 140. Air conditioned
Additional: Children welcome;
❤ dishes, vegan on request

Chillies were one of the earliest plants to be cultivated in the pre-Columbian New World. Archaeological evidence suggests that they were used at least 8,000 years ago to impart flavour and spiciness to food. The Mayans used 30 different varieties of chilli and recent evidence shows that the Aztecs used them in almost every dish. Today chillies are grown throughout the world. The characteristic for which chillies are best known is their heat. The fiery sensation is caused by capsaicin, a potent chemical that survives both cooking and freezing. As well as causing a burning sensation, this substance triggers the brain to produce endorphins, natural pain killers that promote a sense of well-being and stimulation. Also, capsaicin is a natural decongestant. The hottest chilli in the world is probably the scotch bonnet chilli (so named because its shape resembles a Highlander's cap). A single scotch bonnet has the fire power of 50 jalapeno chillies. Grown in the Caribbean it is an essential ingredient in Jamaican jerk dishes. When handling chillies you should wear rubber gloves. Wash your hands with soap afterwards and take care not to touch your face, or eyes. If your hands start to sting after handling chillies, rub them with a little toothpaste.

Zoe ❀❀

☺ *Good West End meeting place with consistent cooking in the Mediterranean mode*

Who is Zoe? What is she? It's a question to ponder, or not, at this lively bar, café and restaurant near Oxford Street, where chef Conrad Melling offers a range of interesting Mediterranean inspired dishes. Country breads, hallmark of any Anthony Worrall-Thompson operation, arrive with roasted chilli and garlic oil, fava bean purée and sweet aubergine with poppy seed paste. On our inspection, this was followed by not-so-warm spinach salad with pan-fried oysters, pancetta and sweet peppers. Calf's liver was well handled, and served with a pretty spicy tomato and balsamic chutney, tasty jus and deep-fried pumpkin of disappointingly dry texture. The freshly prepared harlequin soufflé was worth the wait for its chocolate and fruit flavour. To finish, house espresso is rich and slightly bitter. There is a concise, seasonal list of wines selected by Berkmann Wine cellars, and some good quality, good value house wines from the Georges Duboeuf stable. The staff are friendly and helpful, although at times elusive, and their knowledge about what they are serving could be sharpened up.

Directions: Nearest Tube: Bond Street. Entrance at junction of Barret St & James St

W1 St Christophers Place W1
Map no: C4
Tel: 0171 224 1122
Chef: Troy Reid
Proprietor: Zen Group
Cost: *Alc* £20, fixed-price L & D £10. H/wine £8.45 ❗ Service exc
Credit cards: ◨ ▨ ▨ ▨ OTHER
Times: Noon-last D 2.30pm, 6.30pm-last D 11.30pm. Closed Sun & Bhs, Xmas
Menus: *A la carte*, fixed-price L & D, function menus for parties of 12+
Seats: 200. No-smoking area, air-conditioning
Additional: Children welcome, children's portions; ❶ dishes, vegan/other dishes on request

Parmesan cheese or 'parmigiano reggiano' originated in the area that formed the Duchy of Parma, between Parma and Reggio Emilio. Locals will tell you that the cheese has been made there for over 2,000 years but whether this is so or not, it was an established favourite by the 14th century; Boccaccio referred to it in the 'Decameron'. Nowadays 'parmigiano reggiano' is made in the provinces of Parma, Reggio Emilia, Bologna, Modena and Mantua. The method of making Parmesan has remained unchanged through the centuries. Small cheese factories produce four to six cheeses a day using milk from local cows. The milk is partially skimmed and the whey from the previous batch is added to help the fermentation. The cheese is curdled with calves' rennet, shaped, and salted for 25 days. The shapes weigh between 30-35kg and it takes 16 litres of milk to make each kilogram of cheese. The cheeses are matured for different periods of time and are named by their age. 'Parmigiano nuovo' is less than one year old, 'parmigiano vecchio' is one and half to two years old, and 'parmigiano stravecchio' is two years old or more. A good Parmesan is hard, yellow, crumbly in texture and has a rich, fruity and slightly salty taste. The best cheeses are manufactured from the middle of April to the beginning of November. Parmesan should never be bought already grated, for once the cheese has been grated it looses some of its flavour.

FLETCHERS
RESTAURANT

ENGLAND
AVON

ALVESTON, Alveston House Hotel ✿

☺ *Choose from an extensive carte or the fixed-price menu in Quincey's. The food is enjoyable with top marks for pan-fried chicken livers, and five spice beef with peppers*

Times: Open 12.30, Last L 1.45pm/D 9.30pm **Menus:** *A la carte,* fixed-price L/D, bar menu **Seats:** 75. No-smoking area
Additional: Children welcome, children's portions; ✿ dishes, vegan/other diets on request
Directions: On the A38, 3.5 miles N of the M4/M5 junction

Alveston
Bristol BS12 2LJ
Map no: 3 ST68
Tel: 01454 415050
Chef: Ian Maycock
Proprietor: Blaydon Hotels.
Manager: Julie Camm
Cost: *Alc* £20.25, fixed-price
L/D £15.25. Wine £8.75 ▮
Service inc
Credit cards: 🖎 🎟 🎟 🖾 OTHER

BATH, Bath Spa Hotel ✿✿

Well located, stylish Georgian hotel where some bright ideas on the modern menu are revealed

Sydney Road BA2 6JF
Map no: 3 ST76
Tel: 01225 444424
Chef: Jonathan Fraser
Proprietors: Forte.
Rest. Manager: Simon Roberts
Cost: *Alc* £23-£32, fixed-price
Sun L £16.50 H/wine £17.50 ▮
Service exc
Credit cards: 🖎 🎟 🎟 🖾 OTHER
Times: 7pm-last D 10pm, noon-last Sun L 2pm
Menus: *A la carte* D, fixed-price Sun L, pre-theatre, bar menu
Seats: 80. Air conditioned. No smoking in dining room
Additional: Children welcome, children's menu; ✿ menu, vegan/other diets on request

If location were all, the Bath Spa would score top marks. An imposing Georgian property, it has a delightful garden and enjoys an elevated position overlooking the city. A former nurses' home, it was reopened as a Forte hotel in 1990. There is a choice of dining areas – the colonnaded Alfresco for light snacks, and the Vellore, in the old ballroom, for more formal meals. A spring inspection meal produced a mixed report, with comments on lack of balance and poor timing. A warm liver parfait was overpowered by a sticky, too sweet, plum sauce. Salmon was succulent enough, but failed to deliver the promised tang of lemon grass and coriander; vegetables were lukewarm. It was all the more disappointing since the modern international menu shows some bright ideas, such as set meals built around a duck or seafood theme. Young visitors – surprisingly for such a smart hotel, families are genuinely welcome – should be well satisfied with the yummy childrens' menu which features a range of junior (non-alcoholic) cocktails.

Directions: From A4 turn left signposted A36 Warminster, right at mini roundabout & pass fire station, turn left into Sydney Place

BATH, Cliffe Hotel ❀

☺ *Built in the 1830s, the Cliffe Hotel is set in three acres of terraced gardens and overlooks the Avon valley. The menu offers a pleasing balance of dishes, and features some good vegetarian cooking. At a recent meal the spring onion and Roquefort tartlet was excellent. For dessert try the creamy tiramisù*

Menus: *A la carte*, fixed-price L, bar menu
Seats: 30. No smoking in dining room
Additional: Children welcome, children's menu; ❶ dishes, other diets on request
Directions: From A36 take B3108 (Bradford-on-Avon), turn right before railway bridge, follow to Limpley Stoke. Hotel on brow of hill

Crowe Hill
Limpley Stoke BA3 6HY
Map no: 3 ST76
Tel: 01225 723226
Chef: Richard Okill
Proprietors: Barbara & Richard Okill (Best Western)
Cost: *Alc* £17, fixed-price L £15 H/wine £8.45 Service inc
Credit cards: 🔲 🔲 🔲 🔲 OTHER
Times: 12.30-last L 2pm, last D 9.30pm

BATH, Clos du Roy ❀❀

Smart city-centre restaurant offering memorable French cooking at reasonable prices

1 Seven Dials
Saw Close BA1 2EN
Map no: 3 ST76
Tel: 01225 444450
Chef: Philippe Roy
Proprietor: Philippe Roy
Cost: *Alc* £25.20, fixed-price L £11.35/D £14.50. H/wine £8.35 Service inc
Credit cards: 🔲 🔲 🔲 🔲 OTHER
Times: Noon-last L 2.30pm, 6pm-last D 11.30pm.
Closed Dec 25
Menus: *A la carte*, fixed-price L & D, pre-theatre
Seats: 80
Additional: Children welcome, children's menu; ❶ dishes, vegan/other diets on request

In 1992, an award-winning French chef returned from nearby Box to the city where he had built his reputation with the first Clos du Roy. Philippe Roy wanted to create a restaurant which, in his own words, was 'rooted firmly in the best traditions of French cuisine', but which offered 'a new, exciting and satisfying experience'. It was challenging, but within nine months he was up and running again in Seven Dials. The spacious, curved dining room opening out on to a balcony is a good location for the wide choice of lunch and dinner menus, including a five-course surprise banquet. Starters worth trying might be sole terrine stuffed with fresh herbs served on a tomato coulis, or pan-fried 'chevrelle' on a bed of marinated vegetables with a raspberry dressing. The French provincial style comes through loud and clear with main courses such as cassolette of chicken livers with a sage jus, and 'aiguillette' of sirloin served with a Bordelaise sauce. Desserts come from the skilled hands of pâtissier Alain Dubini. Two sampled were traditional lemon tart served with a vanilla crème anglaise, and feuilleté of fresh fruits served with a warm Cointreau sabayon.

Directions: Next door to the Theatre Royal, under the wrought-iron dome of the Seven Dials centre

BATH,
Combe Grove Manor Hotel ❀❀

Stylish, modern English country house cooking served in an elegant setting

Brassknocker Hill
Monkton Combe BA2 7HS
Map no: 3 ST76
Tel: 01225 834644
Chef: Paul Mingo-West
Proprietors: Jack Chia Group.
Manager: Antonio Parrilla
Cost: *Alc* £31, fixed-price
L £16.50/D £25. H/wine £9.50 ▪
Service inc
Credit cards: ▨ ▨ ▨ ▨ OTHER
Times: Last L 2.30pm, last D
9.30pm
Menus: *A la carte*, fixed-price
L & D, bar menu
Seats: 60. No smoking in dining
room
Additional: Children welcome,
children's menu; ❂ dishes,
other diets on request

The Romans knew a thing or two about where to hang their helmets, which is why they chose Brassknocker Hill. In the 18th century it was chosen again, this time for Combe Grove Manor, together with its 82 acres of gardens and woodland, and views of the White Horse of Westbury, 16 miles away. The listed house is decorated and furnished in the Georgian style, the same dynasty of monarchs also providing the name of the elegant main restaurant. The menu offers some interesting starters, such as mussel consommé lightly flavoured with orange and star anise, chicken and ham ballottine garnished with pickled baby vegetables, and ravioli of local goat's cheese coated in a sweet shallot and butter sauce. Suprême of salmon rolled in oats, pan-fried and flamed in whisky could make for a main course to talk glowingly about, and loin of lamb, carved around a pastry case of lamb's offal with a tomato and basil sauce, is a stylish dish. In the less formal atmosphere of the Manor Vaults, the dishes are lighter and cheaper, but even cod is deep fried in beer batter to elevate it from humble fish and chips. The wine list is short and predictable, but reasonably priced.

Directions: Two miles south of Bath on A36; turn sharp right at traffic lights up Brassknocker Hill

BATH, ## Garlands Restaurant ❀❀

A well-run, congenial little restaurant specialising in French and English cooking

Beau Nash encouraged fashionable society to 'take the waters' in Bath; it did so in droves. These waters, from Britain's only hot spring, in the famous Roman Baths and Pump Room, can still be sampled today. Nearby, in a city appropriately awash with good restaurants, Tom and Jo Bridgeman have created a restaurant noted for its bright but cosy, relaxed atmosphere, with bold prints decorating the walls and fresh flowers adorning the tables.

7 Edgar Buildings
George Street BA1 2EE
Map no: 3 ST76
Tel: 01225 442283
Chef: Tom Bridgeman
Proprietor: Tom Bridgeman
Cost: *Alc* £21.95, fixed-price
L £10.50 (2 courses). H/wine
£9.95 ▪ Service exc
Credit cards: ▨ ▨ ▨ ▨
Times: Noon-last L 2.15pm.
Closed Mon, 3 days Xmas

A set-price menu and a short *carte* are available. Judging by inspectors' reports the cooking is generally on target but can occasionally miss the mark. A dinner which started with cured salmon with prawns and fromage frais signalled an enjoyable meal, but its accompanying salad was dull (watercress must be kept fresh). English calves' liver, with grain mustard and sage, was overcooked, dry and lacked flavour, but the vegetables were crisply cooked and well seasoned. The early promise of good things to come was honoured by dessert, a mango cheesecake, with a crisp biscuit base and a light, fruity filling.

Menus: *A la carte* L, fixed-price L
Seats: 28.
Additional: Children welcome; children's portions; ❷ dishes; other diets on request

Directions: City centre – from Circus go S down Gay Street, 1st left along George Street, restaurant on left at lights

BATH, **Haringtons Hotel** ✿

8/10 Queen Street BA1 1HE
Map no: 3 ST76
Tel: 01225 461728
Proprietor: D Pow

Situated on a cobbled street close to the theatre, the popular and lively restaurant at Haringtons operates long opening hours making it ideal for theatregoers. The range of dishes may include chicken liver parfait with apricot chutney, breast of chicken with a port and tarragon sauce, and almond and apricot tart

Directions: City centre, behind Queens Square

BATH, **The Hole In The Wall** ✿✿

☺ *An imaginative, wide choice of dishes in the modern British style is available in the rejuvenation of Bath's most famous restaurant*

16 George Street BA1 2EH
Map no: 3 ST76
Tel: 01225 425242
Chefs: Adrian Walton
Proprietors: Chris & Gunna Chown
Cost: *Alc* £19.50, fixed-price L £9.50 (2 course). H/wine £10 ❢ Service exc
Credit cards: ▨ ▩ ▨ OTHER
Times: Noon-last L 2pm, 6pm-last D11pm. Closed Sun, BH Mons, Xmas
Menus: *A la carte*, fixed-price L, pre-theatre
Seats: 70. Air conditioned. No-smoking rooms

George Perry-Smith, the father of modern British cooking, put The Hole In The Wall on the culinary map in the 60s. Since then the place has gone through various owners and cooking styles. It is now owned by Chris Chown (of Plas Bodegroes, in Pwlhelli) and some of the dishes on the menu pay homage to the Perry-Smith tradition. The charming restaurant remains the same: one cellar dining-room is lightened by the judicious use of mirrors to get the best from the available light; the other area is heavily beamed. Choosing food is a simple business. At lunchtime there is a two-course, fixed-price menu, while in the evening there is a three-course *carte* which costs £19.50 whatever the selection. There are a dozen or more choices at each stage. A typical meal could be escabeche of skate with herb bread, wild mushroom and Parmesan lasagne with truffle sauce, Wedmore strudel with a chilli dip, or daube of beef Bourgignonne with horseradish dumplings, and cinnamon biscuit of rhubarb and apple with elderflower custard. About 20 of the wines on the world-ranging list come by the glass, with slightly fewer available in half bottles.

Additional: Children permitted. ☻ dishes, other diets by arrangement

Directions: Town centre: George Street is at top end of Milsom Street

BATH, Lansdown Grove Hotel ❀

This family-run hotel occupies an elevated position with good views across the city. A capable team in the kitchen produce enjoyable dishes which however could be improved by a less cluttered presentation and combination of flavours. Expect chicken liver parfait, red pepper mousse and fillet of beef with a piquant sauce

Lansdown Road BA1 5EH
Map no: 3 ST76
Tel: 01225 315891
Proprietor: Aubrey Jackman

CLOSED

Directions: Up Lansdown Hill. Right after passing Camden Crescent

BATH, New Moon Restaurant & Brasserie ❀❀

☺ *A combined restaurant/brasserie with a kitchen that roams the world for inspiration*

The New Moon is part of the Seven Dials complex and overlooks a small courtyard with a fountain – an irresistible draw for tourists. The Brasserie menu runs through the day until 7pm, when the dinner *carte* takes over. From the brasserie a few examples give a good idea that the kitchen is in tune with the times: chargrilled fish and poultry, imaginative salads, plus Oriental, Californian and Mediterranean influences. The style is familiar: flour tortilla, refried beans, guacamole, sour cream and salsa, chargrilled Italian vegetables with lemon and anchovy mayonnaise, wild boar mustard and chilli sausages with creamed potatoes and apple compôte. There are daily specials as well. For dinner, some of the brasserie dishes are retained as starters or main courses, but dishes exclusive to the *carte* are roast breast of guinea fowl stuffed with a toasted almond mousseline, caramelised shallots and a lemon and thyme jus, seared tuna steak on puy lentils with a wasabi and soy butter. Interesting desserts include banana and coconut bavarois with rum anglaise, and chilled bitter chocolate pavé with lime glaze. The wine list offers 30 or so wines, of which about half are French.

Seven Dials
Saw Close
Map no: 3 ST76
Tel: 01225 444407
Chef: Nicholas Peter
Proprietor: Michael Tweedie
Cost: Alc £17, fixed-price L £7.95. H/wine £8.90 ₮
Service exc
Credit cards: 🞵 ▨ ▨ OTHER
Times: 11am-last L 3pm/D 11pm; closed Dec 25/6
Menus: A la carte, fixed-price L, pre-theatre, brasserie menu
Seats: 70. No-smoking area
Additional: Children welcome before late eve, children's portions; ☻ dishes, vegan/other diets on request

Directions: Next to Theatre Royal, on the left set back in the Seven Dials courtyard

Ginger originated in southeast Asia and is widely cultivated in hot countries for its spicy, aromatic rhizomes. It was much appreciated in the Middle Ages, as a flavouring and as a sweetmeat, but had fallen out of use in Europe by the 18th century, except in cakes, puddings and confectionery. Currently, ginger (especially fresh ginger) is having something of a revival, used extensively in both savoury and sweet dishes.

BATH, No 5 Bistro ❀❀

☺ Sound, decent quality cooking can be sampled in a relaxed atmosphere at this city centre bistro

A lovely relaxing atmosphere infuses this city centre bistro. The decor works well: polished wood floors, bright continental prints and posters, and numerous plants. Steve Smith cooks and Charles Home looks after front-of-house. At lunchtime the aim is to provide light meals; in the evening the choice is more extensive, with typical bistro-style dishes such as guinea fowl sausage with sweet and sour sauce, or roast Barbery duck. An inspection meal yielded excellent salmon rösti fishcakes with a lime, coriander and butter sauce, followed by a rich duck confit cassoulet – with the duck confit an excellent complement to the spicy sausage. For dessert there was a good, lightly steamed walnut and date pudding and an intensely flavoured chocolate brûlée. Espresso coffee is good. The wine list offers a good choice and reasonable prices, but on Mondays and Tuesdays diners may bring their own wine (no corkage). On Wednesday, a special 'Fish Feast' menu is offered.

Directions: 30 yards from Pulteney Bridge towards Laura Place

5 Argyle Street BA2 4BA
Map no: 3 ST76
Tel: 01225 444499
Chef: Steve Smith
Proprietors: Steve Smith and Charles Home
Cost: *Alc* £18. H/wine £7.45 ¶ Service inc
Credit cards: ▨ ▥ ▦ ▣ OTHER
Times: Noon-last L 2.30pm, 6.30pm-last D 10pm (Fri 10.30pm, Sat 11pm) Closed Sun, Mon L, Dec 25-29
Seats: 35
Additional: Children welcome, children's portions; ❂ dishes, other diets on request
Bring Your Own wine Mon & Tue eves – no charge

BATH, Olive Tree at the Queensberry Hotel ❀❀

A contemporary bistro in the heart of Georgian Bath offering modestly-priced modern cooking

Russell Street BA1 2QF
Map no: 3 ST76
Tel: 01225 447928
Chefs: Stephen Ross, Matthew Prasse and Jamie Wilmot
Proprietors: Stephen & Penny Ross
Cost: *Alc* £27; fixed-price L £9.50 & £10.50/D £18 (Sun £16.50) H/wine £11.50. Service exc
Credit cards: ▨ ▥ ▦
Times: Last L 2pm, last D 10pm. Closed Sun L & Xmas week
Menus: *A la carte* D, fixed-price L & D
Seats: 45. No smoking
Additional: Children welcome, children's portions; ❂ dishes; vegan/other diets on request

Stephen and Penny Ross's delightful Bath stone townhouse was built by John Wood, architect of the famous Royal Crescent and Circus nearby. The building is now a small, quiet, luxury hotel with the popular bistro-style Olive Tree restaurant in the basement. An open, airy feel is achieved by crisp white table-cloths and light-coloured floor tiles. Stephen Ross and his team have been well recognised for many years; here their style has evolved into a lighter, more modern approach, with the focus on the best ingredients cooked with appropriate garnishes. Seafood bruschetta, pigeon breasts with oranges and coriander, and shoulder of lamb with rosemary and root vegetables, come from a regularly changing menu, and there are daily dishes as well. An inspection meal

yielded warmed seafood on a bed of leeks and green beans, tender, pink, sliced Gressingham duck with a delicious plum compôte and tangy jus, creamy gratin dauphinoise, and some very al dente mange tout and carrots. To finish, a pretty, soft fruit terrine in sweet muscat jelly, on a crisp fruit brunoise with quenelles of blueberry sorbet. Strong cafetière coffee arrives with some 'good' fudge. The short wine list comes from the best suppliers and is fairly priced. Staff are friendly and willing.

Directions: 100yds north of Assembly Rooms in Lower Lansdown

BATH, Popjoys &

Once the home of Juliana Popjoy, Beau Nash's mistress, this house now features a pleasant ground-floor brasserie. Follow a mousse-filled smoked salmon cornet by griddled rump of lamb with apricot fritters and a red wine sauce, then take your pick from a short but tempting selection of desserts

Seats: 38. No pipes
Additional: Children welcome; ❂ dishes; Vegan/other diets on request
Directions: Centre of Bath, immediately beside the Theatre Royal

Beau Nash House
Saw Close BA1 2EN
Map no: 3 ST76
Tel: 01225 460494
Chef: John Simpson
Proprietor: Malcolm Buhr
Cost: Alc £25. H/wine £7.90.
Service exc
Credit cards: ▨ ▨ ▨
Times: Last D 10.30pm. Closed Mon

BATH, The Priory Hotel &&

Admirable French cooking in a semi-rural enclave a mile from the city centre

The city has grown up around the Priory since it was built in 1835, but has not encroached upon its two acres of gardens, terrace and croquet lawn. Decorations and furnishings are in a style the original owner would still recognise, but the outdoor swimming pool would require him to do a double-take. There are three- or four-course lunch and dinner menus, and a three-course *carte*. At dinner, a sensible balance of fish, meat and game means that it would be possible to start with cold, thinly sliced bresaola, garnished with baby leeks and parmesan, or hot crab and ginger ravioli with a sweet pepper and chive sauce. The main course could be fillet of John Dory with mustard and tarragon sauce, roast best end of Welsh lamb with a herb crust, served with a tomato and garlic jus, or braised quail served on a bed of wild mushrooms and foie gras. A vegetarian could choose fresh home-made egg pasta with sun-dried tomatoes, shitake mushrooms and parmesan. There are also daily specials, an example being leek and celeriac soup, roast breast of guinea fowl with apple and brandy sauce and a choice from the dessert menu. The only wines to be given tasting notes are the house varieties. Many of the others have reputations that precede them, especially among the clarets.

Directions: At the top of Park Lane, on west side of Victoria Park, turn left into Weston Road; 300 yards on left

Weston Road BA1 2XT
Map no: 3 ST76
Tel: 01225 331922
Chef: Michael Collom
Manager: Thomas Conboy
Cost: Alc £32; fixed-price L from £12.50/D £24-£28. Wine £11 ❢
Service inc
Credit cards: ▨ ▨ ▨ ▨ OTHER
Times: Last L 1.45pm, last D 9.15pm
Menus: A la carte, fixed-price L & D
Seats: 75. No smoking in dining room
Additional: Children welcome, children's portions; ❂ menu, vegan/other diets on request

We endeavour to be as accurate as possible but changes in personnel and data can occur in establishments after the Guide has gone to press.

BATH,
Rajpoot Tandoori Restaurant ❀❀

☺ *Unusual Indian dishes, as well as the ubiquitous, from a restaurant that takes its food seriously*

'Europeans wrongly believe Indian food is harmful to the digestive system', says the foreword to the menu. 'On the contrary', it continues, 'spices have medicinal and antiseptic qualities, and are full of iron.' That being so, what better way to take your medicine? Tandoori, Mughlai and Bengali dishes are all available, most being quite familiar to regular patrons of Indian restaurants, but some are not encountered very often. For example, heron tikka, which requires a double-take to discover that it is marinated venison cooked in the tandoor. 'Rezala' is a typical ceremonial lamb dish, 'kacchi akhni' is a Rajpoot biryani speciality and chicken 'indrupuri' is a mild dish involving Tia Maria, fresh cream and apricots. 'Tandoori machlee' (marinated trout, gently spiced, barbecued over charcoal), lamb roghan josh (spiced with herbs and cashew nuts) and chicken 'shashlik' (diced, marinated and barbecued with onion, tomato, capsicum and mushrooms) all received a good report at inspection. Only a vegetable dansak let the side down by being a little over spiced and overpoweringly lime-sharp. Service is friendly and attentive.

Directions: Near city centre, by Pulteney Bridge

Rajpoot House
4 Argyle Street BA2 4BA
Map no: 3 ST76
Tel: 01225 466833/464758
Chefs: H Zeraguai and M Ali
Proprietors: Ahmed Chowdhury & Mahmud Chowdhury
Cost: *Alc* £14.50, fixed-price D £15. H/wine £8.00. Service inc
Credit cards: ▨ 🔳 🔳 🔳 OTHER
Times: Midday-last L 2.30pm, 6pm-last D 11pm (11.30pm Sat). Closed Xmas
Menus: *A la carte*, fixed-price dinner
Seats: 90. Air conditioned
Additional: Children welcome, children's portions; ❤ menu; other diets on request

BATH, **Royal Crescent Hotel** ❀❀❀

Apparently simple but technically assured dishes in modern style are the hallmarks of this restaurant in a pleasant garden setting

16 Royal Crescent BA1 2LS
Map no: 3 ST76
Tel: 01225 319090
Chef: Steven Blake
Proprietors: Queens Moat. Manager: Simon Coombe
Cost: *Alc* £38; fixed-price L £18.50/D £33.50. H/wine £11.75 ♥ No service charge
Credit cards: ▨ 🔳 🔳 🔳
Times: 12.30pm-last L 2pm, 7pm-last D 9.30pm Daily
Menus: *A la carte* D, fixed-price L & D, pre-theatre, bar L menu
Seats: 60. Air conditioned. No smoking

Set in the centre of John Wood's splendid Regency terrace, distinguished from the residential sections flanking it only by two discreet planters bearing its name, The Royal Crescent serves some of the best food in Bath. The elegantly furnished cocktail bar and restaurant in fact form part of the Dower House, a short stroll across the garden from the main building. Here, chef Steven Blake offers a range of *carte* and fixed price menus which include good options for children, vegetarians and theatregoers. In line with the current fashion for simpler preparation, the English/French dishes contained in these are now less worked, and this has arguably heightened the overall enjoyment. Both a freshly made tortellini of foie gras with sweetbreads and a truffle dressing, for example, and a meunière of ray on a crab and spring onion rösti with ginger sauce were recently praised by our inspector. The cooking displays fine technical skills, a mastery of flavour combination and, importantly, an understanding of good buying. Dessert was equally accomplished – a casing of thick chocolate pastry proved an effective contrast to its excellent bitter orange filling, and the well made kumquat sauce that accompanied it. Extras, such as canapés (spring rolls, beef and pepper kebas and salmon in a crisp coating) and soft wholemeal rolls are all competently prepared. Both the New World and Europe are well represented in an informative wine list which ranges from reasonably priced house wines to vintage Burgundy and claret. Careful recruitment of staff and strong leadership ensure that guests can rely on receiving a warm welcome and the very best service – service charges being neither levied nor expected.

Additional: Children welcome, children's menu; ❶ menu, vegan/other diets on request

Directions: In city centre follow signs to Royal Crescent

BATH, Woods Restaurant ❀❀

Excellent value at innovative, lively restaurant near the Assembly rooms offering imaginative cooking with market-fresh menu

Kirk Vincent is a chef to watch. Self-taught, he has an evident passion for food, and is responsible for inventing all the dishes at Woods. Just away from the city centre, a shop-front exterior conceals the deceptively large, understated restaurant interior. A flexible lunch menu is available, supported by daily specials from the blackboard. At dinner, prices are fixed and range from £12 for three courses, to £19.95. A 'Happy Supper' menu is served between 6.30 and 7.30pm. A recent inspection meal started with smooth, richly flavoured duck liver parfait, served with home-made chutney. This was followed by a fillet of salmon which had been salted, then roasted to retain a slight crisp crust, matched perfectly by an olive oil mash and tomato and basil vinaigrette. Lemon tart had sufficient zest to cut through the cream, although the pastry could have been improved. All the base ingredients, such as sun-dried tomatoes, pesto, tapenade and sausages are made in-house, and espresso coffee is excellent.

9-13 Alfred Street BA1 2QX
Map no: 3 ST76
Tel: 01225 314812
Chefs: Kirk Vincent
Proprietors: David & Claude Price
Cost: *Alc* £19.95, fixed-price L £8-£11.45/D £12 (Mon-Fri), £19.95 (Sat). H/wine £9 ❢ No service charge
Credit cards: 🔲 ▭
Times: Last L 3pm D 11pm. Closed Sun D, Dec 24-26
Menus: *A la carte,* fixed-price D & Sun L, pre-theatre, bar menu
Seats: 120. No pipes or cigars in restaurant
Additional: Children welcome, children's portions; ❶ menu, vegan/other diets on request

Directions: Opposite the Assembly Rooms

BRISTOL,
Berkeley Square Hotel ❀❀

Interesting English cooking is served at this smart Georgian hotel close to the city centre

The elegant and peaceful square in which The Berkeley Square Hotel stands is close to the university, art gallery and the attractions of Clifton village. It is where the BBC filmed the 'House of Elliot', and is within easy reach of the city centre. Chef Dermot Gale continues to produce soundly cooked food, inspired by traditional

15 Berkeley Square Clifton B58 1HB
Map no: 3 ST57
Tel: 0117 9254000
Chef: Dermot Gale
Proprietors: Clifton Group. Manager: Sharon Love
Cost: *Alc* £15-£25, H/wine £8.75. Service exc
Credit cards: 🔲 ▭ ▭ ▱
Times: 7pm-Last D 9.45pm. Closed Sun

English dishes. At an inspection meal a leek and Stilton tart came 'bursting with flavour', and pears poached in red wine, served with crisp wafers of biscuit and amaretto ice-cream were delicious. Other recommended dishes have included chicken liver pâté with home-made chutney, Cumberland sausage with mash and shallot gravy, and sticky toffee pudding with butterscotch sauce. There is a solid air of well being about the place helped by a keen young team who provide the service in a cheerful, friendly manner; the only disappointment being that they lack sufficient knowledge of the dishes on the menu.

Menus: *A la carte* D, bar menu
Seats: 40
Additional: Children welcome, children's portions; ♥ menu, vegan/other diets on request

Directions: Top of Park Street turn left at traffic lights into Berkeley Square, hotel on right

BRISTOL, Bistro Twenty One ❀❀

21 Cotham Road South
Kingsdown BS6 5TZ
Map no: 3 ST57
Tel: 0117 942 1744
Chef: Alain Dubois
Proprietor: Alain Dubois
Cost: *Alc* £19.25, fixed-price L & D £12.95. H/wine £7.95. Service exc
Credit cards: ▨ ▨ ▨ ▨ OTHER
Times: Last L 2.30pm, last D 11.30pm. Closed Sunday
Menus: *A la carte* dinner, fixed-price L & D, pre-theatre
Seats: 70
Additional: Children welcome, children's portions; ♥ dishes; vegan/other diets on request

☺ *Sophisticated yet honestly flavoured dishes and informal efficiency are the hallmarks of this upmarket bistro*

A firm favourite in the city for some time, Alain Dubois' welcoming bistro provides relaxed, congenial surroundings and friendly but unobtrusive service as well as admirable food. Quality is its hallmark, a combination of first-rate basic ingredients and depth of cooking producing a set-price menu and *carte* of dishes which, despite their sophistication, manifest both honest flavours and robust textures. Starters include a rich fish soup with rouille, filo parcels of crab with coriander or a full-flavoured game pâté, these perhaps followed by guinea fowl with a well reduced juniper sauce, best end of lamb set off by ginger and honey sauce or a vegetarian option such as feuillete of wild mushrooms with a bold Madeira sauce. There will be market-fresh fish among the daily blackboard 'specials' – John Dory served simply with tarragon and cream sauce, perhaps, or the more innovative suprême of turbot with its bright saffron sauce. Al dente vegetables are served piping hot, the macaroons and truffles that accompany coffee are, like the puddings, home-made. A predominantly French wine list features some reasonably priced clarets.

Directions: Off the B4051 onto St Michael's Hill. First right into Horfield Rd (becomes Cotham Rd South). In front of Sports Centre

BRISTOL, Harveys ❀❀❀

12 Denmark Street BS1 5DQ
Map no: 3 ST57
Tel: 0117 927 5034
Chef: Paul Dunstane
Proprietors: John Harvey & Sons.
Manager: Ramon Farthing
Cost: *Alc* £30.50, fixed-price L £16.50 /D £29 (4 courses), surprise gourmet D £38. H/wine £12 ❢ Service inc
Credit cards: ▨ ▨ ▨ ▨ OTHER
Times: Noon-last L 1.45pm, 7pm-last D 10.30pm. Closed Sat L, Sun, BHs

As well as figuring prominently on the wide-ranging wine list, Harveys wines form the basis of an interesting museum collection

In contrast to the prestigious restaurant's setting – the domed, whitewashed medieval cellars adjoining Harveys Wine Museum – its *carte* and fixed-price menus are distinctly contemporary in style. The range of British dishes presented by executive chef Ramon Farthing is soundly based on classical combinations of flavours and techniques. On a cold evening in November, our inspector began his meal with lightly cooked slices of calves' liver layered with fresh pasta and creamed leeks and accompanied by a delicately flavoured Madeira sauce; this was followed by loin of lamb so lightly cooked as to be still blue, set on a bed of creamed potatoes strongly flavoured with spring onions, surrounded by flageolet beans and bacon and served with rosemary sauce. The delicious hot gooseberry

Harveys

Menus: *A la carte* fixed-price
L & D, pre/post theatre, surprise
gourmet D
Seats: 120. Air conditioned
Additional: Children over 8
permitted; ❶ menu,
vegan/other diets on request

soufflé that concluded the meal was light and fluffy, its tartness offset by a smooth white chocolate sauce. A separate menu identifies the characteristics and provenance of a range of English and Irish cheeses which include such regional specialities as Cornish Yarg (a moist cows' milk cheese covered in nettles) and Cashel – the creamy blue-veined product of Tipperary. An interestingly annotated wine list is, as one would expect, extensive enough to complement every choice and please the most discerning palate. The lunch menu is slanted to the needs of businessmen, being designed for service within the hour, but diners should allow themselves time to enjoy these unique surroundings – their vastness made welcoming by the clever use of rich soft furnishings and bright lighting – and to explore the interesting underground museum.

Directions: City centre off Unity Street at bottom of Park Street, opposite City Hall and Cathedral; follow signs for Harveys Wine Museum

BRISTOL, Henbury Lodge ❀

Characterful, privately-run hotel which dates from 1760. The dining-room opens out onto well-tended gardens. Simple cooking characterises the short, fixed-price menu. Look out for salad of fresh tuna with roast peppers, tomato and balsamic vinegar dressing, or grilled lamb cutlets with home-made red currant jelly

Station Road BS10 7QQ
Map no: 3 ST57
Tel: 0117 950 2615
Proprietor: D L Pearce

Directions: 4.5 miles NW of City centre, off A4018

BRISTOL, Howards Restaurant ❀❀

☺ *This charming restaurant's honest French and English cooking is ample reward for a foray into Bristol's docklands*

Honest, quality cooking combines with a warm, informal atmosphere to make this delightful Georgian bistro in Bristol's docklands the ideal choice for any occasion. Head chef David Short offers a seasonal *carte* of English and French dishes which is well supported by an equally inviting blackboard selection of additional fresh fish specialities and vegetarian/vegan options. Complimentary herb bread, served hot and crispy, will whet your appetite as you study these menus.

1A-2A Avon Crescent
Hotwells BS1 6XQ
Map no: 3 ST57
Tel: 0117 926 2921
Chef: David Short
Proprietors: Christopher &
Gillian Howard
Cost: *Alc* £20, fixed-price
L £13.00/D £15.00. H/wine
£7.50 Service exc
Credit cards: 🟦 📷 💳 💷
Times: Last L 2.30pm, last D
11pm. Closed Sun,

Howards Restaurant

Menus: A la carte, fixed-price
L & D, individual requirements
Seats: 65. No-smoking area
Additional: Children allowed;
❶ menu, Vegan/other diets on
request

On a cold, wet day in winter, an inspector enjoyed a main course
of succulent beef fillet, attractively flanked by colourful purées of
carrot, parsnip and spinach and served with a port wine sauce. The
seafood starter that preceded the beef was, on this occasion, rather
disappointing – the scallops appearing rather jaded and the prawns,
though huge and succulent, lacking flavour – but home-made bread
rolls had a good yeasty flavour, and vegetables were cooked
perfectly. The bread and butter pudding that followed was
accompanied by a smoothly subtle Cointreau cream. An extensive,
predominantly French wine list also includes some New World bins.

Directions: 5 mins. from City centre following for M5/Avonmouth.
On the dockside over small bridge, close to *SS Great Britain*

BRISTOL, **Hunt's Restaurant** ❀❀

*In the heart of the commercial centre, a place to recharge the batteries by
English cooking with French connotations*

Like other British cities devastated by wartime bombing, Bristol
also lost much of its past. St John's Arch in the old city wall
survived, as did the neighbouring 18th-century building housing
Andrew and Anne Hunt's simple, relaxed restaurant. Andrew was
previously a catering lecturer and before that executive chef at
Harveys of Bristol, so he knows his stuff. Starters range from an
inexpensive sorrel soup with cream and croûtons, to dearer, but still
good value, Cornish scallops with bacon, white wine and wild
thyme. Most of the main courses are about £14 or £15, with an even
balance between meat and fish. Maize-fed French guinea-fowl
comes with apples, Calvados and sweet marjoram, monkfish
americaine is cooked with brandy, cayenne, tomato and fresh
tarragon, and spiced plums accompany Hereford Trelough duck
breast. Desserts like marquise of chocolate, coffee and bean sauce
are available 'off the peg', as it were; others, such as hot cranberry
and Cointreau soufflé, and Normandy apple and almond tart with
butterscotch sauce, require about fifteen minutes notice to the
kitchen. The all-French house wine selection is well chosen; most of
the rest on a disciplined list are also French.

Directions: City centre, 25 yds from St John's Arch

26 Broad Street BS1 2HG
Map no: 3 ST57
Tel: 0117 9265580
Chefs: Andrew Hunt and Haydn
Neal
Proprietors: Andrew & Anne
Hunt
Cost: Alc £25, fixed-price
L £10.95 (2 course) £12.95.
H/wine £9.50 Service inc
Credit cards: ⊠ ▨ ▨ OTHER
Times: Last L 2pm, last D 10pm
Closed Sat L, Sun, Mon
Menus: A la carte, fixed-price L
Seats: 40
Additional: Children welcome,
children's portions; ❶ dishes,
vegan/other diets on request

BRISTOL, Jarvis Grange Hotel ❀

☺ *Eighteen acres of woodland surround this soundly managed hotel. Enjoyable cooking is served in the Woodlands Restaurant: perhaps rack of lamb baked in hay with a Madeira sauce, or fillet of red mullet with mussels. Fresh asparagus with a smooth butter sauce or prawn and cucumber soufflé are typical starters*

Menus: A la carte, fixed-price L & D, bar menu
Seats: 70. No smoking in dining room
Additional: Children welcome, children's menu; ❂ dishes, other diets on request
Directions: From Winterbourne High Street take B4057, first right on B4427 in 1 mile

Northwoods
Winterbourne BS17 1RP
Map no: 3 ST57
Tel: 01454 777333
Chef: Theo Guy
Proprietors: Jarvis Hotels.
Gen. Manager: Greg Ballesty
Cost: Alc £22.40, fixed-price
L £14.95/D £17.95. H/wine
£9.25
Credit cards: ▨ ▨ ▨ ▨ OTHER
Times: 12.30-last L 2pm, 7pm
(Sat 7.30pm)-last D 9.45pm.
Closed Sat L

BRISTOL, Markwicks Restaurant ❀❀

French provincial and modern English dishes, with fish a speciality, in striking surroundings

43 Corn Street BS1 1HT
Map no: 3 ST57
Tel: 0117 926 2658
Chefs: Stephen Markwick and
Sara Ody
Proprietors: Stephen & Judy
Markwick
Cost: Alc £26.70, fixed-price
L £16/D £21.50. H/wine £11.50
Service exc
Credit cards: ▨ ▨ ▨
Times: noon-last L 2pm, 7pm-
last D 10.30pm approx. Closed
Sat lunch, Sun, BHs, Xmas,
Easter, 2 wks Aug
Menus: A la carte, fixed-price
L & D
Seats: 40. No-smoking rooms
Additional: Children welcome,
children's portions; ❂ dishes,
vegan/other diets on request

Now well established on the city's eating-out scene, Stephen and Judy Markwick's basement restaurant lies under the Commercial Rooms, near the famous covered market. There are three dining-rooms, one with a striking black and white tiled floor dating back to the building's days as a safe deposit vault, one with unusual electric bunches of grapes decorating the ceiling and tables, while the panelled one is for private parties. Fish is a speciality and, in addition to the *carte* and fixed-price lunch and dinner menus, there is another featuring the daily catch. All the dishes look great in print, but just occasionally an extra ingredient tends to complicate rather than contribute, an example being the pesto coating a crisp goat's cheese, spinach and saffron tart. Too many herbs and powerful spices also submerged an otherwise splendid selection of fish in a Mediterranean bourride with a rouille already red chilli-based itself. Some of the desserts are imaginative, such as hot plum soufflé with poppy seed ice-cream. The wine list is well annotated with honest comments. Service, under the direction of Judy Markwick, is charming.

Directions: Top end of Corn Street beneath Commercial Rooms

BRISTOL, **Marriott Hotel** ❀

Lower Castle Street BS1 3AD
Map no: 3 ST57
Tel: 0117 929 4281
Chef: Joe Beaver
Proprietor: Marriott.
Manager: Jane Dowle
Cost: Alc £19.95, H/wine
£12.95 Service exc
Credit cards: 🅴 💳 💳 🅿 OTHER
Times: 7pm-last D 11.45pm

☺ *The carte at Le Chateau Restaurant is supplemented by regular visits from guest chefs from around the world. Otherwise, a typical meal might include wild mushroom fricasées in a filo basket, or marinated salmon salad, followed by honey curried swordfish or pan-fried duck breast in black cherry wine sauce*

Menu: A la carte D
Additional: Children permitted; ❂ dishes, vegan/other on request
Directions: In the city centre at the old market, opposite the Castle ruins

BRISTOL, **Orchid Restaurant** ❀

98 Whiteladies Road
Map no: 3 ST57
Tel: 0117 9238338
Chef: M Lau
Proprietor: Margaret Dullah
Cost: Alc £15; fixed-price
L £8/D £14. Wine £7.50.
Service exc
Credit cards: 🅴 💳 💳 OTHER
Times: Last L 2.30/D 11.30.
Closed Mon lunch

A Singaporean restaurant combining the subtleties of Chinese, Thai and Indonesian cooking. The wide range of dishes are brightly served with honest textures and flavours. A recent meal included 'cendawan istemewa' – mushrooms filled with prawns and water chestnuts – and fresh steamed bass with ginger and spring onions

Seats: 80. No pipes or cigars. Air conditioned
Additional: Children welcome; ❂ menu; Vegan/other diets on request

BRISTOL, **Restaurant Lettonie** ❀❀❀❀

9 Druid Hill
Stoke Bishop BS9 1EW
Map no: 3 ST57
Tel: 0117 968 6456
Chef: Martin Blunos
Proprietor: Siân Blunos
Cost: Fixed-price L £17.95/D
£23.50. H/wine £10.50
Service exc
Credit cards: 🅴 💳 💳 🅿 OTHER
Times: Last L 2pm/D 9pm.
Closed Sun, Mon, 2 weeks Aug,
Xmas
Menus: Fixed-price L & D
Seats: 24
Additional: Children welcome,
children's portions; ❂ dishes,
Vegan/other diets with notice

A stylish, up-market restaurant serving modern French cooking, incongruously set in a suburban shopping parade

The bland, suburban parade of shops rewards closer inspection. Here is a high-flying restaurant, one of the best in Bristol. Martin Blunos is a talented chef, offering two styles of fixed-price menus in the evening – one a limited choice supper menu, the other giving a more extensive choice. Lunch is good value. Quality shines through in a style of cooking that has a light touch and is thoughtful and assured. Offal has long been a favourite, whether pigs trotter with Madeira sauce, or calves' sweetbreads, pan-fried with caraway and served with a caraway cream. The Mediterranean influence is acknowledged too, in the likes of pan-fried red mullet with potato raviolis and a truffle oil dressing, or steamed stuffed fillet of red bream with a warm olive oil dressing.

A superlative dinner in early summer commenced with a light dish of artichoke heart filled with a delicate chicken and asparagus mousse wrapped in a spinach leaf; the whole was garnished with morels, baby asparagus and a 'lovely oak smoked butter'. The main course of baked cod with a crusty top and langoustine cream delighted with its intense flavours. Vegetables were an intrinsic part of the dish, mainly young spring vegetables with some very lightly breadcrumbed choux potato balls. A wonderful dessert of rich, dark chocolate marquise was accompanied by a very smooth and light cinnamon sorbet. A simpler style is apparent in the supper menu where fish soup, duck and mallard terrine with pickled pumpkin, and roast skirt of beef on a parsnip purée with a red wine sauce stand out for simple, clear flavours and an uncomplicated approach. Puddings can include prune and Armagnac parfait with banana, mascarpone and peach vinegar ice-cream with raspberries, and apple and caramel mousse with poached apple. The wine list has strong French overtones but the New World gets an airing; half bottles are particularly good.

Directions: Across Clifton Downs (away from the City) in a small row of shops at bottom of hill

BRISTOL, **Rodney Hotel** ❀❀

A hotel restaurant with a relaxed atmosphere, where the staff have a ready smile for customers. Popular with businessmen and tourists alike

Rodney Place
Clifton BS8 4HY
Map no: 3 ST57
Tel: 0117 973 5422
Proprietor: S Riley

The Marguerite Restaurant in the Rodney Hotel is part of an attractive, listed, 18th-century terrace. It features a concise, selective *carte* offering a varied choice of dishes including an interesting vegetarian selection. At a recent inspection meal an attractively presented starter of mille-feuille of mushrooms and asparagus spears in a creamy shallot and basil sauce, was followed by noisettes of fresh lamb, not over-trimmed, cooked to the very shade of pink asked for, on a minted jus with freshly cooked vegetables. The vegetables – crisply cooked ratatouille, minted new potatoes, mange-touts, baby corn and julienne of carrot – all tasted natural. The meal was completed with two slabs of rich chocolate mousse, lightly flavoured with rum and served with crème anglaise.

Parmesan cheese or 'parmigiano reggiano' originated in the area that formed the Duchy of Parma, between Parma and Reggio Emilio. Locals will tell you that the cheese has been made there for over 2,000 years but whether this is so or not, it was an established favourite by the 14th century; Boccaccio referred to it in the 'Decameron'. Nowadays 'parmigiano reggiano' is made in the provinces of Parma, Reggio Emilia, Bologna, Modena and Mantua. The method of making Parmesan has remained unchanged through the centuries. Small cheese factories produce four to six cheeses a day using milk from local cows. The milk is partially skimmed and the whey from the previous batch is added to help the fermentation. The cheese is curdled with calves' rennet, shaped, and salted for 25 days. The shapes weigh between 30-35kg and it takes 16 litres of milk to make each kilogram of cheese. The cheeses are matured for different periods of time and are named by their age. 'Parmigiano nuovo' is less than one year old, 'parmigiano vecchio' is one and half to two years old, and 'parmigiano stravecchio' is two years old or more. A good Parmesan is hard, yellow, crumbly in texture and has a rich, fruity and slightly salty taste. The best cheeses are manufactured from the middle of April to the beginning of November. Parmesan should never be bought already grated, for once the cheese has been grated it looses some of its flavour.

BRISTOL, **Swallow Royal Hotel** ✹✹

Top quality French cooking in one of Bristol's finest locations

College Green BS1 5TA
Map no: 3 ST57
Tel: 0117 925 5100
Chef: Michael Kitts
Proprietors: Swallow.
Manager: Philip Sager
Cost: *Alc* £20, fixed-price
L £12.50 (2 course)/D £19.
H/wine £9.50 ❢ Service inc
Credit cards: ◩ ▦ ▦ ▣ OTHER
Times: 12.15pm-last L 2.30pm,
7pm-last D 10.30pm
Menus: *A la carte,* fixed-price
L & D, snacks
Seats: 150. Air conditioned
No-smoking area
Additional: Children welcome,
children's menu; ❧ dishes,
vegan/other diets on request

Overlooking the road climbing up from Broad Quay, the impressively restored Swallow stands in one of the city's most commanding locations. The cathedral is next door and the uninspiringly named, but quite imposing, Council House is opposite. Inside, an elegant drawing room leads from the spacious marbled lobby, and there is a choice of two restaurants. The Terrace is the more informal, while the Palm Court is open for dinner only, Monday to Saturday. It is here, in what was once the ballroom, that chef Michael Kitts and his team deliver the sort of dishes that seem appropriate to such grand surroundings, and where a harpist's soothing plinks and plunks echo three nights a week. An inspection meal began with an appetiser of chicken and duck brawn served with caper, parsley and egg dressing. Crab and lemon broth with tiny pasta shells, known as conchigliette, was served with basil croûtes on the side. Then, before the grey mullet, came a palate-refreshing kiwi fruit sorbet; the fish was accompanied by a saffron-flavoured seafood risotto, garnished with mussels. It was served with an odd selection of vegetables including ratatouille, carrots and a spiced vegetable bhaji. A slightly mismatched pecan tart with blueberry ice cream followed.

Directions: City centre, next to the Cathedral

Beetroot is rich in sugar, vitamins and calcium. Although it is possible to eat them raw (grated), it is more usual to cook beetroot and then serve cold. It is occasionally served hot, to accompany game, or in soups. The round varieties, the red globe and the dark red Egyptian, are the most widely cultivated varieties but the long rooted varieties are worth seeking out for they have more flavour and are sweeter. Beetroot is harvested from the end of June to the first frosts. They store well and are more readily available in the autumn and winter months. Although beetroot is traditionally sold cooked, they can be bought raw for cooking at home. Boiled in water this takes about 2 hours.

CHELWOOD, **Chelwood House Hotel** ⊛

☺ *A charming country house hotel in a sympathetically transformed 300-year-old building, owned by Rudi and Jill Birk. Rudi's Bavarian origins are never forgotten, with dishes such as herrentopf (strips of beef fillet in a rich paprika and mushroom sauce, with spätzle) featuring regularly with local game and fish*

Seats: 30. No smoking in dining room
Menus: A la carte D, fixed-price Sun L
Additional: Children permitted; children's portions, ○ dishes; vegan/other diets on request
Directions: On A37 between Clutton and Pensford, 200 yds from Chelwood roundabout

Bristol BS18 4NH
Map no: 3 ST66
Tel: 01761 490730
Chef: Rudi Birk
Proprietor: Rudi Birk
Cost: Alc D £22, Sun L £13.50; H/wine £9.50. Service inc
Credit cards: ⬛ ▦ ▦ ▣
Times: Last D 9pm, last Sun L 1.30pm. Closed Mon-Sat L, Sun D, 2 wks after Xmas

HINTON CHARTERHOUSE,
Homewood Park Hotel ⊛⊛⊛

Exciting menus from new chef Stephen Morey promise well for the future

Hinton Charterhouse
Bath BA3 6BB
Map no: 3 ST75
Tel: 01225 723731
Chef: Stephen Morey
Proprietors: Frank Gueuning
Cost: Alc £35, fixed-price L £17.50/D £28.50. H/wine £12.50. Service inc
Credit cards: ⬛ ▦ ▦ ▣ OTHER
Times: 12.15pm-last L 2pm, 7.15-last D 10pm
Seats: 65. No smoking in dining room
Menus: A la carte; fixed-price L & D, bar menu
Additional: Children welcome, children's portions; ○ dishes

Service is totally professional and dishes are very attractively presented in the pretty restaurant of this elegant but unpretentious Georgian mansion between Bath and Warminster. Anglo-French cooking is modern in style, and Homewood Park has a good reputation for the use of quality fresh ingredients. New chef Stephen Morey – who was head at Gravetye Manor and then spent six months at Woolley Grange – appears equally committed to the use of quality produce, and his menus are inspiring; it seems hardly fair to identify minor disappointments in his cooking skills, since he had only been at the restaurant for four days at the time of our inspector's visit. Certainly a lightly pan-fried foie gras augured well for things to come – bursting with taste and served with a stunning cider-based reduction – and a well made prune and mascarpone tart held promise.

Directions: 5 miles south-east of Bath off A36, turning marked Sharpstone

HUNSTRETE,

Hunstrete House Hotel ❀❀❀

Inventive menu with well-judged cooking of high quality, fresh ingredients

Chelwood BS18 4NS
Map no: 3 ST66
Tel: 01761 490490
Chef: Robert Clayton
Proprietors: Arcadian International.
Manager: Richard Carr
Cost: *Alc* £34-£40, fixed-price L £15/D £29.50 H/wine £11.75
❗ Service exc
Credit cards: 🔲 ▆▆ ▆▆ OTHER
Times: Last L 2pm, last D 10pm Closed Sat L
Menus: *A la carte*, fixed-price L & D, pre-theatre
Seats: 50. No smoking in dining room
Additional: Children welcome, children's portions on request; ❷ dishes, vegan/other diets on request

Set on the edge of the Mendip Hills, near Bath, this 18th-century house has an enviable location. A vista of rolling fields and woodlands unfolds beyond the manicured gardens, although the lovely Italianate dining-room actually overlooks the internal courtyard. The days of long, complicated hotel restaurant menus are now, thankfully, on the way out, but not many have the courage to present one as concise as Hunstrete. There may be only five choices per course, but chef Robert Clayton and his small brigade achieve consistently high results and the short but well-balanced menu still manages to include a wide range of influences. Carpaccio, quails eggs, couscous and rocket are typical ingredients in a menu constructed with an awareness of metropolitan trends. The even shorter lunch menu may also feature dishes from the evening *carte*.

For starters, sea scallops may be served roasted with asparagus, pea purée and mint dressing, or as a delicious warm salad with sweet artichokes and risotto of lobster and trout. A roasted fillet of beef with purée of swede had a slightly over intense port and green pepper sauce, but the quality and the flavour of the beef were true. Typical other main courses may be pork tenderloin stuffed with prunes with summer cassolette, rösti potatoes and Calvados sauce, or feuilleté of pan-fried brill with mussels in a creamy ginger and saffron sauce. From a choice which included orange tart, cinnamon ice-cream and chocolate sauce, and a trio of raspberry desserts, Robert's divine apple and pear crumble with ace butterscotch sauce managed to warm the heart of one of our seasoned inspectors – no mean feat. The classical wine list also features a good choice of New World wines.

Directions: On A368 – 8 miles from Bath; from Bristol take A37 (Wells) turn left at Chelwood Bridge onto A368. Restaurant is 1.5 miles on left

MIDSOMER NORTON,
Country Ways Hotel ❀

☺ *English cooking with a modern slant from a well-balanced menu.*
Soups feature daily in a selection of competitively-priced starters. Main
dishes include fillet of salmon with hollandaise, fillet steak with green
peppercorn sauce, and aubergine, tomato and risotto in filo pastry with
a herb and tomato sauce

Menus: *A la carte* L & D
Seats: 20. No smoking in dining room
Additional: Children permitted; ❂ dishes, vegan/other diets on
request
Directions: Left off A37 onto A362 to Midsomer Norton, 1st right,
hotel next to Golf course

Marsh Lane BS18 5TT
Map no: 3 ST65
Tel: 01761 452449
Chef: Janet Richards
Proprietor: Janet Richards
Cost: *Alc* £20. H/wine £8.50.
No service charge
Credit cards: 🅴 ▧ 🅿 OTHER
Times: Last L 1.45pm, last D
8.45pm Closed Sun D, 1 wk
Xmas

NAILSEA, Howard's Bistro ❀

Wednesday evenings are themed – Thai or Italian, for example.
Other nights it's mainly French auberge-style. Daily-changing
blackboard starters include spinach and cream cheese pancake, or pot-
roasted shoulder of lamb and cassoulet, breast of pheasant, or noisettes
of monkfish poached with mussels

Menus: Fixed-price D & Sun L
Seats: 40. No-smoking area
Additional: Children welcome, children's portions; ❂ dishes,
vegan/other diets on request
Directions: In Nailsea old village near new West End shopping
precinct

2 King's Hill BS19 2AU
Map no: 3 ST47
Tel: 01275 858348
Chef: Christopher & Gillian
Howard
Proprietors: Christopher &
Gillian Howard
Cost: Fixed-price D £12.50/Sun
L £10 (Childen £3.50) H/wine
£7.25 ❗ Service exc
Credit cards: 🅴 ▧ ▧ 🅿
Times: Last D 10.30pm, last Sun
L 3pm Closed Sun D, Mon, BHs

PETTY FRANCE, Petty France Hotel ❀

Set in the beautiful Cotswold countryside, the Petty France attracts
a strong local following for its modern, eclectic cooking. Choices from
a weekly-changing carte could include fresh mussels in ginger wine,
or English sautéed calves' liver. A decent selection of English cheeses
is also available

Badminton GL9 1AF
Map no: 3 ST78
Tel: 01454 238361
Chefs: Jason & Jacqui Burton
Proprietor: Consort.
Manager: W J Fraser
Cost: *Alc* £18-£35, fixed-price
Sun L £13.95 H/wine £9.95 ❗
Service exc
Credit cards: 🅴 ▧ ▧ 🅿
Times: Last L 2pm/D 9.30pm
daily
Menus: *A la carte*, fixed-price
Sun L, bar menu
Seats: 80. No smoking in dining
room
Additional: Children over 2
welcome; ❂ menu, vegan/other
diets on request

Directions: On the A46, 5 miles north of the M4 junction 18

RANGEWORTHY, **Rangeworthy Court**

☺ *An imposing mid-1600s manor house offering interesting English cooking, such as half a well-roasted duck with ginger and blackcurrant sauce, pan-fried pigeon breast, and fillet of beef with Stilton and red wine sauce. Also, look out for lamb cutlets Italienne, or sea bass with mussels, poached in wine and orange juice. Vegetarian menu too*

Church Lane
Wotton Road BS17 5ND
Map no: 3 ST68
Tel: 01454 228347
Chefs: Peter Knight and David Organ
Proprietors: Lucia & Mervyn Gillett
Seats: 52
Times: Last L 1.45pm/D 9pm (Sat 9.30pm)
Cost: Alc £18; fixed-price L £11.50/D £16. Wine £8.50. Service inc
Credit cards: 🔲 🔲 🔲 🔲
Additional: Children welcome; children's portions/menu; ♥ dishes; Vegan/other diets on request

Directions: Signposted off B4058, down Church Lane

THORNBURY,
Thornbury Castle Hotel ❀❀

A unique ruined castle turned hotel provides an impressive setting for English dishes in the modern idiom

Bristol BS12 1HH
Map no: 3 ST69
Tel: 01454 281182
Chef: Steven Black
Proprietors: The Baron of Portlethen (Pride of Britain)
Cost: Fixed-price L £16.50 & £18.50 /D £31. H/wine £12.50. No service charge
Credit cards: 🔲 🔲 🔲 🔲 OTHER
Times: Noon-last L 2pm, last D 9.30pm (10pm Fri & Sat, 9pm Sun) Closed 2 days early Jan
Menus: Fixed-price L & D
Seats: 60. No smoking in the dining room

The 16th-century castle was never finished; the Duke of Buckingham lost his head, and then it was appropriated by Henry VIII. Now Thornbury is a stunning country house hotel, surrounded by vineyards, gardens and high walls, with distant views over the River Severn into Gloucestershire and Wales. There are impressive, richly decorated public rooms, with heraldic shields, tapestries, suits of armour and fine antique furniture, and staff provide a level of service that befits the grandeur of the surroundings. Steven Black is in charge of the kitchen, producing daily changing fixed-price menus. Dishes sampled this year have included a subtly flavoured wild mushroom risotto, and monkfish with crispy leeks and a smooth chive sauce. Other examples could include grilled fillet of red snapper with shi-take mushrooms and ginger sauce, or pan-fried calves' liver on a bed of creamed potato with a caramelized onion sauce. Traditional desserts include treacle tart with clotted cream, or a light butterscotch pudding with rich sauces of butterscotch and vanilla.

The wine list includes a good selection of half bottles, and wines from the castle's own vineyard.

Additional: Children over 12 permitted; ✔ menu, other diets by arrangement

Directions: Bear left at bottom of High Street into Castle Street. The entrance is to left of St Mary's Church

WESTON-SUPER-MARE,
Commodore Hotel ❀

Overlooking the sands at Keystoke, the Commodore's Alice's Restaurant (after the Malibu original) sticks to a policy of good value for money. Dishes like chicken Caribbean, English game pie, or suprême of salmon are typical. Sweets from the trolley are not for the diet-conscious

Beach Road
Sand Bay
Kewstoke BS22 9UZ
Map no: 3 ST36
Tel: 01934 415778
Chef: David Williams
Proprietor: John Stoakes
Seats: 82. No-smoking area
Times: Last L 2.30pm/D 9.30pm

Cost: Alc £15. H/wine £6.95. Service exc
Credit cards: 🟦 🟨 🟥 🔲
Additional: Children welcome; children's menu/portions; ✔ menu; other diets on request
Directions: 1.5 miles north of Weston-super-Mare along the coast toll road

BEDFORDSHIRE

FLITWICK, Flitwick Manor Hotel ❀❀❀

Smart country house hotel with upmarket menu

Church Road MK45 1AE
Map no: 4 TL03
Tel: 01525 712242
Chef: Duncan Poyser
Proprietor: Mazard Hotel Management.
Manager: Sonia Banks
Cost: Fixed-price L £20.95/D £37.50. H/wine £12.90 ❢ Service exc
Credit cards: 🃏 💳 💳 💳 OTHER
Times: Last L 1.45pm/last D 9.30pm
Seats: 40. No smoking in dining room
Menus: Fixed-price L & D, Terrace menu
Additional: Children permitted (over 8 at dinner), children's portions; ❂ dishes

The 17th-century manor house sits in the middle of acres of lovely grounds, ideal for pre- or post-prandial walks, croquet and tennis. After an aperitif in the lounge, sympathetically furnished in period style, the elegant decor of the dining-room provides a suitable setting for chef Duncan Poyser's choice of seasonally evolving menus. Dinner starts with a few simple appetisers, good, home-made bread and creamy, unsalted butter. On our last visit, a starter of aubergine roulade filled with potato and duck confit, accompanied by a fondant of goats' cheese and salad, proved an enjoyable starter; the novel combination of flavours worked well and ingredients were correctly seasoned and stylishly arranged. A fine main course of steamed brill had firm, well-flavoured fish accompanied by tender, new season asparagus and a captivating asparagus sauce. Turned carrots and broccoli flowers were additional decorations on the plate. A hot hazelnut soufflé with a light rum sauce arrived golden brown and well-risen, but was slightly undercooked. Excellent petits fours, but weak cafetière coffee rounded off the pricey £37.50 three-course, fixed-price menu. Service, by young staff, was efficient if not particularly polished.

Directions: On A5120, two miles from M1 junction 12

LEIGHTON BUZZARD, The King's Head ❀

Genteel, 17th-century timbered restaurant featuring English and international cuisine. Traditional specialities include braised oxtail, roast Aylesbury duckling and medallions of beef fillet flamed at the table with brandy, cream and green peppercorns. Fresh looking desserts are served from the trolley

Seats: 55. No smoking in restaurant. Air conditioned
Menus: *A la carte*, fixed-price L/D, special weekday L
Additional: Children permitted; ❂ dishes, vegan/other diets on request
Directions: Ivanhoe is on B458 between Leighton Buzzard and Tring

Ivinghoe LU7 9EB
Map no: 4 SP92
Tel: 01296 668388/668264
Chef: Patrick O'Keeffe
Proprietors: Forte Plc.
Manager: Georges De Maison
Cost: *Alc* £27.55, fixed-price L £13.25 & £21.25/D £21.25. H/wine £14.50. Service optional
Credit cards: 🃏 💳 💳 💳 OTHER
Times: Last L 1.45pm/D 9.30pm

WOBURN, **The Bell Inn** 🏵

☺ *The Bell Inn is a charming mixture of Tudor, Georgian and Victorian architecture. A good range of freshly cooked meals is offered and can be eaten either by candlelight in the beamed restaurant or in the pub atmosphere of the village bar. Try the grilled goats' cheese with bacon and shredded rosemary*

34 Bedford Street MK17 9QR
Map no: 4 SP93
Tel: 01525 290280
Chef: Grant Huntley
Proprietor: Tim Chilton (Best Western)
Cost: Fixed-price L/D £17.95. H/wine £10.50. Service exc
Credit cards: ⬛ 💳 💳 💳 OTHER
Times: Noon-last L 2.30pm, 7pm-last D 9.30pm. Closed Dec 25
Seats: 40. No-smoking area
Menus: Fixed-price L & D, bar menu
Additional: Children welcome, children's portions; ✪ dishes, vegan/other diets on request

Directions: Northern end of the main street in Woburn, 5 minutes from M1 junction 13

WOBURN, **Paris House Restaurant** 🏵🏵

Black and white mock-Tudor restaurant in grounds of Woburn Park, with French-orientated food and wine

Occasional careless streaks can, at times, mar the otherwise reliable cooking at this attractive timbered restaurant. A short set *carte* might not set the pulse racing, but it is balanced and sensibly not over-ambitious. First courses may include country pâté and pickles, smoked salmon roulade filled with cream cheese and dill, or salad of Cajun prawns, but our test wing of skate with nut brown butter and capers came a little over cooked. Its appeal was lessened further by the curious addition of a single cherry tomato and a pyramid of stale puff pastry. The coq au vin main course was more successful, correctly made and served with fresh noodles, baby carrots and turnips. Other main courses also draw from the French classics – steamed salmon in champagne sauce, roast rack of lamb with aubergines and tomato, and entrecôte chasseur, for example. Cherry tart and cherry sabayon had a good filling, poor pastry and a sabayon which rapidly lost its volume. The unusually structured wine list has detailed tasting notes, and is heavily weighted towards French bins, although there is a sprinkling of New World wines.

Woburn Park MK17 9PQ
Map no: 4 SP93
Tel: 01525 290692
Chef: Peter Chandler
Proprietor: Peter Chandler
Cost: Alc £38, fixed-price L £23/D £38 H/wine £10 ¶ Service exc
Credit cards: ⬛ 💳 💳 💳 OTHER
Times: noon-last L 2pm, 7-last D 9.30pm. Closed Sun D, Mon, Feb
Seats: 45+14 (private room). No pipes or cigars in restaurant
Menus: A la carte D, fixed price L & D
Additional: children welcome (must book at D); children's portions, ✪ dishes, other diets on request

Directions: on the A4012, 1.5 miles out of Woburn towards Hockcliffe, through huge archway

'Alla parmigiana' means the way it is made in Parma. As the name suggests it includes Parmesan and prosciutto although the latter is an optional ingredient.

BERKSHIRE

ASCOT, **Jade Fountain** ❀

☺ *Conventional menu at well-established Chinese restaurant. Tried and tested dishes include crispy duck, chicken with cashew nuts, sizzling beef and sweet and sour prawns*

Times: Noon-last L 1.45pm, 6pm-last D 10.15pm. Closed Xmas
Seats: 90. Air conditioned
Menus: A la carte, fixed-price D
Additional: Children over 2 welcome; children's portions, ❂ dishes, vegan/other diets on request
Directions: Town centre, a corner site in the middle of Sunninghill High Street

38 High Street
Sunninghill SL5 9NE
Map no: 4 SU96
Tel: 01344 27070
Chef: C K Lee
Proprietors: H F Man, Jade Fountain Ltd.
Manager: S Chiu
Cost: Alc £15-£20, fixed-price D £21 (4 courses). H/wine £8
Service exc
Credit cards: 🟦 🟦 🟦 🟦

ASCOT, **The Royal Berkshire Hotel** ❀❀

An excellent debut for a chef with a sound pedigree whose food is firmly in the modern idiom

The view across the lily pond to the tree-framed, bow-fronted Queen Anne house is attractively captured in the water colour on the menu cover. The Churchill family lived here for a while but, after purchase and much extending by Hilton International, it is now a busy country hotel with a popular leisure club and well regarded restaurant. Jean-Claud MacFarlane (ex-Bell Inn, Aston Clinton) made a favourable impression on one inspector who was impressed by the skill and care shown in the preparation of various dishes. That Spring dinner started with a faultless panache of seafood, mostly shellfish, with spiced basil sauce, followed by tender, grilled medallions of beef fillet, cooked exactly as ordered, served on crisp potato rösti, with horseradish jus and lightly cooked baby vegetables. Buttery shortcake with sliced fresh strawberries and whipped cream completed the meal. The repertoire is wide taking in the likes of asparagus charlotte with tarragon and lemon dressing, Dover sole grilled, meunière or Grenobloise, and flamed exotic fruit pancakes with coconut ice-cream.

Directions: M4 exit 10 or A30 follow A329 through Ascot. Hotel is on the left after 1.5 miles. From M3 exit 3 take A322

London Road SL5 0PP
Map no: 4 SU96
Tel: 01344 23322
Chef: Jean-Claud MacFarlane
Proprietors: Hilton Hotels.
Manager: Simon Pearce
Cost: Alc £40, fixed-price L £16-£22, fixed-price D £32. H/wine £14.95 ▮ Service inc
Credit cards: 🟦 🟦 🟦 🟦 OTHER
Times: Noon-last L 2pm/D 9.30pm
Seats: 45. No-smoking area
Menus: A la carte, fixed-price L & D, bar menu
Additional: Children welcome, children's menu; ❂ menu, vegan/other diets on request

BRACKNELL, **Coppid Beech Hotel** ❀❀

Modern eclectic cooking from a successful restaurant, leisure and business centre with a distinct Swiss look

Coppid Beech stands next to a dry ski-slope and the Alpine imagery is emphasised by peaks and glacier sculpturing, wooden shutters and balconies. The hotel also boasts a bier keller and brasserie. The restaurant, Rowans, offers a fixed-price menu which changes twice weekly and a *carte* which changes from time to time. Neil Thrift produces simple, appealing and balanced dishes. Starters such as ragout of herb gnocchi with asparagus, cheese fondue, and tempura fried prawns and rocket salad with a lime and chilli dressing, are typical openers. Main courses could include roasted

John Nike Way RG12 8TF
Map no: 4 SU86
Tel: 01344 303333
Chef: Neil Thrift
Proprietor: Alan Blenkinsopp
Cost: Alc £35, fixed-price L £17.50/D £25. H/wine £12.50 ▮ Service exc
Credit cards: 🟦 🟦 🟦 🟦 OTHER
Menus: A la carte, fixed-price L & D, Sunday L, bar menu, monthly regional speciality menus

Coppid Beech

Times: 7.00am-last L 2.30pm,
last D 10.30pm
Seats: 100. No-smoking area.
Air conditioned
Additional: Children welcome,
children's menu; ❂ menu,
vegan/other diets on request

whole lobster with Thai spices, lemon grass and noodles, osso buco
of monkfish with squid pasta, orange oil and baby fennel, hot-pot of
venison with sage and onion sausages and braised red cabbage,
summer vegetable on piccalilli with prunes and white onion mousse,
or tian of lamb with a gratin of turnip, fondant potatoes and green
peas. Grills are also available. There are wine promotions from
specific vineyards, such as Thames Valley, whose wines can be
sampled before ordering. Staff are friendly and responsive.

Directions: From M4 junction 10, follow A329(M) to first exit.
At roundabout take first exit to Binfield, hotel 300 metres on right

BRAY, Monkey Island Hotel ❂

*The hotel is set in well-tended grounds on an attractive island and the
Pavilion Restaurant offers ambitious cooking with enjoyable results.
An interesting, varied menu offers dishes such as crab soufflé, roast loin
of lamb with sautéed kidneys in a grain mustard and rosemary jus, and
lemon tart with clotted cream*

Menus: A la carte, fixed-price L & D, bar menu
Seats: 90. No-smoking area
Additional: Children welcome, children's menu; ❂ dishes, vegan/
other diets on request
Directions: M4 exit 8/9, A308 (Windsor) 1st left to Bray, 1st right into
Old Mill Lane, hotel at end

Bray-on-Thames SL6 2EE
Map no: 4 SU97
Tel: 01628 23400
Chef: Ian Butcher
Proprietor: N G H Group.
Manager: N Holdsworth
Cost: Alc £31, fixed-price
L £18.50/D £25 H/wine £12.60
Service exc Cover charge £1.30
Credit cards: 🔲 🔲 🔲 🔲
Times: Last L 2.30pm, last
D 9.30pm Closed Sat L
(26/12/95-3 wks for refurb)

BRAY, Waterside Inn ❂❂❂❂❂

*Probably the most stunning restaurant with rooms in the country, where
the outstanding modern French cooking is perfectly complemented by the
Thames-side setting*

Of course the Waterside Inn is special whatever time of the year,
but to enjoy it at its best pick a sunny lunchtime – to secure a
window seat it is wise not to leave the booking to chance. The
ceiling to floor windows of the restaurant fully exploit the view, and
when the weather is kind, visitors can enjoy aperitifs on the terrace
or in one of the intimate summer houses. A further option is the
electric launch that for a (fat) fee plies the Thames, although this
tends to be more popular post eating.

Ferry Road SL6 2AT
Map no: 4 SU97
Tel: 01628 20691
Chef: Michel Roux, Mark
Dodson Head Chef
Proprietor: Michel Roux
Cost: Alc £65, fixed-price L £29
(£37 w/ends), fixed-price D
£65.50 (5 course), H/wine £25 ❗
Service inc
Credit cards: 🔲 🔲 🔲 OTHER

Michel and Albert Roux bought the Waterside in 1972, and in the last eight years Michel Roux has been joined by Mark Dodson, who now heads the kitchen. Menus evolve slowly, which means they are not always in tune with the seasons. The cooking is deeply rooted in French classic tradition, luxury items such as foie gras, truffles and lobster are part of the style, but then so is exploration of more interesting techniques and combinations, and it is fashion-conscious enough for sauces to be light, and flavours to be more individual.

Recent meals have featured fillets of tiny sardines, served escabeche-style as an appetiser, with onions, carrots and a vinegary marinade, with quail egg, a watercress purée and some lambs' lettuce; cappelletti of lobster perfumed with Jerusalem artichoke, served with langoustine tails and a buttery tomato coulis; sweet, pan-fried scallops which contrasted well with the bitterness of accompanying chicory leaves and a light butter sauce flavoured with cinnamon; smoked salmon combined with aubergine purée and glazed with a light sabayon; milk-fed shoulder and leg of lamb, 'meltingly tender', with a selection of baby vegetables and a fully flavoured lamb jus and sauce paloise. Desserts can include intensely worked walnut and chocolate, a silky pistachio brûlée and a pear sablé. Diego Masciago heads the smart, all French team front-of-house with terrific style, and, as the French menu lacks sub-titles, is happy to translate. The French-only wine list has all the famous names with prices to match. Should you wish to stay, the bedrooms are stylish, comfortable and en-suite.

Times: Noon-last L 2pm (2.30pm Sun), 7pm-last D 10pm. Closed Mon, Tue L, Sun eves (3rd wk Oct-2nd wk Apr) & closed for 5 weeks from Boxing Day
Menus: A la carte, fixed-price L & D
Seats: 75. No cigars in dining room
Additional: Children over 12 permitted; ❶ dishes, vegan/other diets on request

Directions: M4 exit 8/9 follow A308 towards Windsor, turn Left before M/way overpass for Bray. The restaurant is clearly signposted

COOKHAM, Cookham Tandoori ❀❀

☺ *Cosy cottage setting for freshly-spiced Indian food of a consistently good standard*

The pretty beamed and timbered cottage is more suited to a traditional tea-room than an Indian restaurant, but the distinct flavours and use of fresh herbs and spices outweigh the unlikely setting. Azad Hussein learnt to cook from his East Bengali family, so, as well as the standard kormas, bhunas and birianis, there are a number of Jhalfarezi dishes which use green chillis as incendiary devices for the unwary. A couple of dishes show a contemporary influence – Indian style mussels, for example, are cooked with white wine, methi leaves and coriander. King prawn shashlik, coloured red to liven up its appearance, is served spitting on a skillet with peppers, tomato and onion; the sweet-sour flavour comes from the use of honey, ginger and garlic. Another chef's special is 'nawab murgh stick', chunks of tender chicken breast skewered, marinated in butter, spiced and cooked with creamed coconut, almonds, and sultanas. Psychedelic-looking pilau rice is light and fluffy. The European wine list is short but has a few classy choices, and there is always Kingfisher lager for a more authentic match.

High Street SL6 9SL
Map no: 4 SU56
Tel: 01628 522584
Chef: Azad Hussain
Proprietor: Bashirul Islam and Faruk Ahmed
Cost: Alc £15-£20, fixed-price Sun buffet L £12.95. H/w inc £9.50 ❢ Service exc
Credit cards: ▨ ▩ ▧
Times: Noon-last L 2.30pm, 6pm-last D 11pm. Closed Dec 25/6
Seats: 80. No-smoking area
Menus: A la carte, Sun buffet L
Additional: Children permitted, children's portions on Sundays; ❶ dishes, vegan on request

Directions: In Cookham village which is between Maidenhead and Marlow

MAIDENHEAD, **Fredrick's Hotel**

The manifestation of its owner's dream, this restaurant has achieved a popularity which makes booking essential

Shoppenhangers Road SL6 2PZ
Map no: 4 SU88
Tel: 01628 35934
Chef: Claudio Notarbartolo
Proprietor: Frederick W Lösel
Cost: *Alc* £37-£54, fixed-price
L £19.50 (Sun £23.50)/D £28.50
H/wine £13 Service exc
Credit cards: 🆒 📧 💳 📠
Times: Last L 2pm, last D
9.45pm Closed Sat L, Dec 24-30
Menus: *A la carte,* fixed-price
L & D, lounge menu
Seats: 60. Air conditioned.
Additional: Children welcome,
children's portions; ◑ dishes,
vegan/other diets on request

Still as busy and popular as ever, this luxurious restaurant forms the hub of a red brick turn-of-the-century hotel set in leafy suburbia beside the manicured lawns of the golf club. The formal elegance of the dining-room's gold and white decor, chandeliers and candlelit tables is matched by attentive professional service, and a degree of formality is demanded of guests – men being required to wear jackets and ties. New chef Claudio Notarbartolo takes good quality local produce as the basis for his seasonally influenced daily-changing set-price menus of French/English dishes: carefully selected fresh vegetables, correctly cooked so that each retains its colour, flavour and texture, are particularly impressive. An enjoyable autumn dinner began with iced crudité delightful hot and cold appetisers and excellent home-baked bread. A simply composed but effective seafood à la Greque came next – the medley of lightly poached mussels, squid, red mullet, sole and scallops set on an oiled bed of leaves, asparagus and artichoke. The main course of mallard was slightly disappointing, its jus lacking in depth though the meat itself was deliciously gamey, but a classic tarte tatin was first-rate. The *carte* always includes a vegetarian option – spinach, mushroom and lentil gateau with fresh asparagus, for example – and a selection of ripe British and continental cheeses is available. Though not cheap, the wine list contains white Burgundies, fine clarets and excellent champagnes; New World labels appear alongside those from all the classic growing areas.

Directions: From A404M exit Cox Green, turn left at roundabout; from A308 take turning next to station bridge

Pistou is Provençal in origin. The word is derived from the Italian 'pestare' - to pound, and is made by crushing fresh basil with garlic and olive oil. It is traditionally served with a soup based on vegetables and vermicelli ('soupe au pistou'). Parmesan may be added to pistou. It is very similar to the Italian pesto, a speciality of Genoa, consisting of a thick sauce also made of fresh basil, garlic, olive oil and Parmesan.

MAIDENHEAD, Ye Olde Bell Hotel ✿

A hotel of character located in a small peaceful village. In addition, the restaurant is pleasantly appointed and has a relaxing atmosphere – look out for fillet of Dover sole served with a light sauce of white wine and cream, or pan-fried pork cutlets with glazed apples and Calvados sauce

Menus: A la carte, fixed-price L & D, bar menu
Seats: 70
Additional: Children welcome, children's menu; ❂ dishes, vegan/other diets on request
Directions: M4 exit 8/9 or M40 exit 4, just off A4130

Maidenhead SL6 5LX
Map no: 4 SU88
Tel: 01628 825881
Chef: David Perron
Proprietors: Jarvis Hotels
Cost: Alc £25; fixed-price L £14.95/D £18.95. H/wine £10.20. Service exc
Credit cards: ▨ ▦ ▧ ▨ OTHER
Times: Last L 2.30pm/D 9.30pm

NEWBURY,
Donnington Valley Hotel ✿

Straightforward dishes such as grilled Dover sole and Angus fillet steak are perhaps the best choice, as cooking can be uncertain and over-elaborate at times. French influences show in dishes such as pigeon wrapped in veal and herb farce, and salmon and scallop terrine. Californian wines come from their own winery

Seats: 120. Air conditioned. No smoking in dining room
Menus: A la carte, fixed-price L/D, carvery
Additional: Children welcome; ❂ dishes, vegan/other diets on request
Directions: On old Oxford Road, Donnington

Donnington RG14 3AG
Map no: 4 SU46
Tel: 01635 551199
Chef: Kelvin Johnson
Proprietor: Ian Leslie
Cost: Alc from £25, fixed-price L £15/D £17.50 H/wine £9.95 Service inc
Credit cards: ▨ ▦ ▧ ▨
Times: Noon-last L 2pm, 7pm-last D 10pm

NEWBURY, Foley Lodge Hotel ✿

The formal 'Wellingtonia' restaurant, in the Georgian part of Foley Lodge, serves a decent standard of modern cooking. A meal might begin with a vegetable and chicken liver terrine, followed by brill garnished with oysters. White chocolate mousse on a duo of dark chocolate and sauce anglaise could conclude the meal

Directions: On B4000, 300 yards from junction with A4

Stockcross RG16 8JU
Map no: 4 SU46
Tel: 01635 551199
Proprietor: Sarah Corbett

NEWBURY,
Jarvis Elcot Park Hotel ✿

A fine Georgian country house in a peaceful rural setting. Main courses might include pan-fried chicken suprême with grain mustard sauce, or mushroom stroganoff served on a bed of wild rice. The 'Jarvisaurus Junior Menu' offers the usual selection of meals for children

Menus: A la carte, fixed-price L & D, bar menu
Seats: 130. Air conditioned
Additional: Children welcome, children's menu; ❂ dishes; other diets on request
Directions: Off the A4, halfway between Newbury and Hungerford

Elcot RG16 8NJ
Map no: 4 SU46
Tel: 01488 658100
Chef: Davide Paulissch
Proprietors: Jarvis Hotels. Manager: Frank Adam
Cost: Alc from £22; fixed-price L/D £15, Sun L £9.95. H/wine £9.95 Service exc
Credit cards: ▨ ▦ ▧ ▨ OTHER
Times: 12.30-last L 2pm, 7.30pm-last D 9.30pm/Sat 10pm Closed some Sat L

NEWBURY, **Regency Park Hotel** ✿✿

A peaceful setting for some well-worked dishes reminiscent of the late 1980s

Bowling Green Road RG18 3RP
Map no: 4 SU46
Tel: 01635 871555
Chef: Martin Jeavons
Proprietor: Peter Hazlerigg
Cost: *Alc* £27.50, fixed-price
L £14.50/D £19.50. H/wine
£11.95 ♥ Service inc
Credit cards: ▨ ▩ ▩ ▨ OTHER
Times: Last L 2.30pm/D
10.30pm
Menus: *A la carte,* fixed-price
L & D, pre-theatre, bar menu
Seats: 70. Air conditioned
Additional: Children welcome,
children's menu; ♥ dishes,
vegan/other on request

The lack of distractions in such a quiet setting make the Regency Park Hotel a popular conference venue. The cooking presents luxuries intricately woven, and, although this sort of cooking has lost favour in the more straightforward 90s, Martin Jeavons takes pride in a menu compilation that harks back to the late 80s. Complex dishes such as mosaic of venison and pork fillet finished with orange salad and port wine jelly, and medallions of beef fillet with collops of lobster, woodland mushrooms and a rich lobster bisque were once at home on many a menu. On one hand the style is dated – and can be fussy and heavy handed – on the other hand inspection produced a trout mousse that was rich and delicate, topped with simply prepared langoustine tails sandwiched between brittle feuilleté wafers with sesame seeds and drizzled with virgin olive oil, lashings of green herbs and garlic. Other dishes from the menu could be steamed salmon with samphire, boulangère potatoes and a lemon and thyme jus, or roast wood pigeon with wild mushrooms and port wine sauce. For dessert, the toffee and banana crumble with English custard is sure to please, but it may be worth trying the chestnut charlotte, if only for the delicious mocha and vanilla sauce which accompanies it.

Directions: From Thatcham A4 turn right into Worthfield Road then left. The hotel is on the right

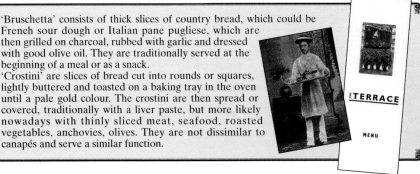

'Bruschetta' consists of thick slices of country bread, which could be French sour dough or Italian pane pugliese, which are then grilled on charcoal, rubbed with garlic and dressed with good olive oil. They are traditionally served at the beginning of a meal or as a snack.
'Crostini' are slices of bread cut into rounds or squares, lightly buttered and toasted on a baking tray in the oven until a pale gold colour. The crostini are then spread or covered, traditionally with a liver paste, but more likely nowadays with thinly sliced meat, seafood, roasted vegetables, anchovies, olives. They are not dissimilar to canapés and serve a similar function.

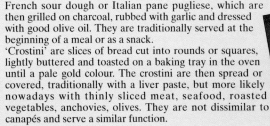

TERRACE

MENU

SHINFIELD,

L'Ortolan Restaurant ✿✿✿✿✿

Stunning, inventive cooking from one of Britain's top chefs, served in cool, fashionable surroundings

Church Lane RG2 9BY
Map no: 4 SU76
Tel: 01734 883783
Chef: John Burton-Race
Proprietor: John Burton-Race
Cost: *Alc* £49, fixed-price L £26
& £37/D £37 (not Sat)/Sun L
£28. H/wine £12.95 ❢ Service
exc
Credit cards: OTHER
Times: Noon-last L 2.15pm,
7.00-last D 10.15pm. Closed
Sun D, Mon, last 2 wks Aug, last
2 wks Feb
Menus: *A la carte,* fixed-price
L/D/Sun L
Seats: 60
Additional: Children welcome,
children's portions; other dishes
by arrangement

The red brick rectory sits in the country, surrounded by quiet and immaculately kept grounds. The decor is smart and cool: soft colours, masses of fresh and extravagant flower arrangements. This is the setting for a serious restaurant for serious diners; over the years John Burton-Race's style has evolved and consolidated. Flair and imagination there are in plenty with quality the main appeal. An inspector, commenting on a visit after an absence of some years, noted that the service was well paced and not as stiff as before, that the food was better: simpler and more precise. That meal produced escalope of foie gras, pan-fried then steamed on a bed of lentils spiked with lardons and baby onions with a frothy lentil cream that was memorable for its finesse and light touch, and a delicate tartlet of langoustines, the case lined with tender, bright green broad beans and set on a full flavoured lobster bisque, which was, in its contrasts of taste and texture, remarkable. Next came pot-roasted pigs trotters, served boned and filled with a delightfully light chicken mousseline spiked with ham, tongue, veal sweetbreads and morilles and served with a well-judged white wine Bercy sauce, and a superlative slice of seabass and langoustine, grilled, set on some good fennel and served with a chicken juice ('that really did taste of chicken') scented with rosemary. To finish, distinguished desserts of hot chocolate tart with white chocolate ice-cream and a perfect, light Grand Marnier soufflé.

A sense of balance is an essential component of the cooking, and is all the more marked by total confidence in technique and execution. Whether it is a reworking of a classic dish such as breast of Gressingham duckling, simply roasted, served with a caramelised citrus sauce and dressed with a lemon and orange marmalade, or a modish darne of John Dory marinated in ginger and cumin, dry roasted, and served on a potato galette and garnished with a salad, the quality of materials shines through. And it is always evident. 'Exquisite' canapés have included mini steak and kidney pie, salmon tartlet, and fish kebab, the cheese trolley has a stunning array of French cheeses in superb condition, bread is good, served with Echiré butter, and espresso is excellent. In fact, everything is excellent, apart from tables that are too close together but at a not 'over busy' lunch – 'guests were thoughtfully spaced at every other table'. As compensation, French staff are helpful and informed. The wine list is impressive in its scope and quality and, although some of the prices for the top quality wines are staggering, there is an excellent selection of half bottles.

Directions: M4 exit 11 & A33 (Basingstoke). At roundabout left to Three Mile Cross, left to Shinfield, right at Six Bells pub. L'Ortolan is up the hill on the left

SLOUGH, The Copthorne Hotel ❀

Only a short drive from Heathrow airport, the Copthorne attracts a largely business clientele. The Reflections Restaurant offers stylish, discreet surroundings in which to try modern, French-inspired dishes such as warm black pudding salad or Dover sole filled with spinach mousse

400 Cippenham Lane SL1 2YE
Map no: 4 SU97
Tel: 01753 516222
Chef: Graham Riley
Proprietor: Copthorne Hotels Ltd.
Manager: Patrick Maw
Cost: Alc from £18, fixed-price L £17.50/D £18. H/wine £12. Service inc
Credit cards: 🖸 📟 📟 💷 OTHER
Times: Noon-last L 2pm/D 10pm. Closed Sun & Bhs
Seats: 150. Air conditioned, no-smoking area
Menus: A la carte, fixed-price L & D, brasserie & bar menus
Additional: Children welcome, children's menu; ✪ menu, vegan/other diets on request

Directions: M4 exit 6 turn into Tunns Lane, take first left at roundabout into Cippenham Lane

SONNING, The French Horn ❀❀

Duck is a speciality and can be enjoyed overlooking a turn in the Thames

Aylesbury ducks roast on a spit before an open fire. Although duck is a speciality, a good range of fish (including two lobster dishes) is also available on both the *carte* and the interesting seasonal menu. The French Horn enjoys an idyllic setting by a turn in the Thames, and the professionally-run restaurant opens onto a covered terrace which overlooks the river and attractive grounds. New chef Gillie Company has joined from La Chouette in Dijon, bringing fresh enthusiasm to the kitchen. A typical meal might include whole scallops served with pasta, shallots and fresh tomatoes, followed by duck with apple sauce and sage stuffing, or perhaps calves' liver with spinach, mousseline potatoes and a rich bacon sauce. The dessert menu offers selections such as crème brûlée, tarte tatin and bread and butter pudding. The largely French wine list features an extraordinary range of first growth clarets, but there are some omissions elsewhere on the list and too few decent halves.

Sonning RG4 0JN
Map no: 4 SU77
Tel: 01734 692204
Chef: Giles Company
Proprietors: Emmanuel Family
Cost: Alc £35-40, fixed-price L £17.50/Sun L £33/D £28 (Sun-Fri) H/wine £10.50 Service inc
Credit cards: 🖸 📟 💷
Times: Last L 2pm/last D 9.30pm Closed Good Fri, Dec 26
Menus: A la carte, fixed-price L & D
Seats: 80
Additional: Children welcome, children's portions; ✪ dishes, vegan/other diets on request

Directions: M4 exit 8/9 & A4, village centre, on the river

STREATLEY, Swan Diplomat Hotel ✿✿

Enviable river views from hotel restaurant with modern French and British cooking

High Street RG8 9HR
Map no: 4 SU58
Tel: 01491 873737
Chef: Philip Clarke
Proprietor: Diplomat.
Manager: Janie Coppen-Garoner
Cost: Alc from £30, fixed-price
D £27.50/Sun Brunch £17.50.
H/wine £11. Service exc
Credit cards: ▨ ▧ ▧ ▨ OTHER
Times: 12.30pm-last Sun L 2pm,
7.30pm-last D 9.30pm Closed
L Mon-Sat, D Sun & Mon.
Brasserie closed L Sun only
Menus: A la carte D, fixed-price
D, Sun brunch, brasserie menu
Seats: 50. No cigars or pipes
Additional: Children welcome,
children's portions; ♥ menu,
vegan/other diets on request

In 1901 Havelock Ellis reputedly dedicated an ode entitled 'A Haven of Rest' to the then Swan at Streatley. This 'sweet nook', situated on an idyllic stretch of the Thames, still offers a restful waterside retreat for leisurely wining and dining. The modish menu at the Riverside Restaurant is written with a touch of hyperbole, but the cooking itself is sure-footed. Starters may include fricassé of woodland mushrooms flavoured with lemon thyme and blackberry vinegar, or pan-fried foie gras on toasted brioche, served with a rocket and lambs lettuce salad and balsamic vinegar sauce. A main course of steamed fillet of firm, very pink salmon came with a creamy vermouth sauce and monkfish rounds topped with herb crusts. Or there might be suprême of guinea fowl poached in chicken stock, scented with juniper, served on a bed of seasonal greens with a warm lentil vinaigrette, or saddle of wild rabbit roasted with thyme, garlic and lavender with a pink peppercorn sauce. A meringue and cream nest studded with exotic fruits, and served with raspberry coulis went down particularly well. Good English farmhouse cheeses, plus French ones from the Rungis Market, Paris.

Directions: Follow A329 from Pangbourne; on entering Streatley, turn right at traffic lights. The hotel is on the left before the bridge

WINDSOR, Aurora Garden Hotel ✿

Uncomplicated dishes in a short menu are cooked with commitment in this attractive restaurant overlooking a landscaped watergarden. Chicken suprême with a blue cheese sauce and crème caramel were both spot-on, as were a good selection of accurately cooked fresh vegetables

Seats: 45. No cigars or pipes
Additional: Children welcome; children's portions/menu; ♥ menu;
Vegan/other dishes on request
Directions: From the Castle turn left down High Street, then into Sheet Street. At the traffic lights straight on, turn right into Francis Road, 2nd exit of roundabout, 500 yds on right

14 Bolton Avenue SL4 3JF
Map no: 4 SU97
Tel: 01753 868686
Chef: Denton Robinson
Proprietor: Clare House.
Manageress: Josephine Currie
Cost: Alc £25; fixed-price
L/D £13.95. H/wine £8.50 ⬮
Service exc
Credit cards: ▨ ▧ ▧ ▨
Times: Last L 2pm/D 9pm.
Closed Xmas

WINDSOR, The Castle ֎֎

Food is uncomplicated but skilfully produced by chef Simon Furey and his team

High Street SL4 1LJ
Map no: 4 SU97
Tel: 01753 851011
Chef: Simon Furey
Proprietor: Forte Heritage.
Manager: Frank Tideman
Cost: Alc £30-£35, fixed-price
L £14.50 (2 course)/D £26.50
(3 course) H/wine £12 ♥ Service
inc
Credit cards: 🔳 💳 💳 💷
Times: Noon-last L 3pm, 6pm-
last D 10pm
Seats: 60. No smoking in dining
room
Menus: A la carte, fixed-price
L/D, bar menu
Additional: Children permitted;
♥ dishes, vegan/other diets on
request

A well-balanced and uncomplicated menu is offered in the
restaurant at The Castle. Care and skill go into the preparation
of the food, which features well-blended flavours and successful
sauces. At a meal taken in March, fresh home-baked bread was
sliced at the table and included olive, walnut and raisin, plain white,
and brown, all with a good texture and firm flavour. A starter of
salmon parfait comprised a light-textured parfait wrapped in
spinach leaf and smoked salmon, garnished with a creamy fromage
blanc. This was followed by noisette of lamb served on a mousse of
garden herbs, with a lamb jus; accompanying vegetables were fresh
and well timed, and included new potatoes, cauliflower, mange tout,
baby sweetcorn, carrots and broccoli. An enjoyable selection of
desserts offered the wide choice of iced maple parfait, sauce
caramel, chocolate torte with toffee sauce, lemon tart and home-
made sorbet. Good cafetière was served with home-made petits
fours.

Directions: In town centre, opposite Guildhall

WINDSOR,
Oakley Court Hotel ֎֎

A grand riverside setting for some quality modern cooking

The splendid neo-Gothic mansion stands in extensive grounds
which run down to the Thames. Gradual refurbishment does
nothing to disturb the peace and tranquillity of the setting, and
corporate entertaining is not intrusive. The Oakleaf Restaurant is
where Michael Croft's cooking mines a rich seam of fresh quality
produce; the Boaters serves more informal meals. Menus show a
keen awareness of what is fashionable: terrine of chargrilled
vegetables with a tomato and basil vinaigrette, crisp fried fillets of
red mullet with citrus fruits, ginger and coriander, or noisette of
lamb with black olive tapenade, rösti potatoes on a thyme and
garlic jus. Inspection yielded an excellent, delicate yet full flavoured
bourdin of scallop with asparagus, and a minestrone of scallops and

Windsor Road
Water Oakley SL4 5UR
Map no: 4 SU97
Tel: 01628 74141
Chef: Michael Croft
Proprietors: Queens Moat.
Manager: Oliver Sweeny
Cost: Alc £39.50, fixed-price
L £20/D £30. H/wine £14.10 ♥
Service inc
Credit cards: 🔳 💳 💳 💷 OTHER
Times: 12.30pm-last L 2pm,
7.30pm-last D 10pm
Seats: 70. Air conditioned.
No-smoking area
Menus: A la carte, fixed-price
L & D, pre-theatre, bar menu

langoustine tails with 'delicious' fresh pasta. Fillet of Scotch beef which followed, came with bright, al dente vegetables, excellent saucing and rösti potatoes, yet the beef itself was a little too dry and overpowered by a wild mushroom pâté. As compensation, a handsome chocolate marquise with coffee bean sauce concluded the meal.

Additonal: Children welcome, children's menu; ✪ dishes, vegan/other diets on request

Directions: Beside the Thames, off the A308 between Windsor and Maidenhead

YATTENDON, **Royal Oak Hotel** ❀❀

Stylish, up-to-the-minute cooking in an old English country inn

The archetypal English country inn, covered in wisteria and featuring polished wood tables, open log fires and a chequered quarry-tiled floor. The restuarant continues the theme, itself decorated in yellows and green in the style of a smart drawing-room. Service at the Royal Oak is polite and unstuffy, both in the bar and the restaurant. Liberal use of olive oil is a common feature of the menu produced by enthusiastic Scottish chef Robbie Macrae. At an inspection meal, an appetiser of lobster mousse was bound by a lovely tortellini and dribbled with a virgin olive oil dressing, whilst the rabbit stew was lathered in hot oil, alas, its flavour lost in the competition. For dessert, a prune and armagnac soufflé was golden and crusty, as near perfect as one could imagine. Other main courses available may include John Dory with a potato crust and tarragon velouté, or perhaps lightly spiced honey-glazed duck. The bar menu encompasses the usual bar meals, from ploughman's lunch to rump steak and chips, and the more adventurous dishes, such as artichoke à la grecque with couscous provençale.

The Square RG16 0UF
Map no: 4 SU57
Tel: 01635 201325
Chef: Robbie Macrae
Proprietor: Regal Hotels Plc.
Manager: Paul Marshall
Cost: *Alc* £25, fixed-price
L £19/D £25. H/wine £9.50 ❢
Service exc
Credit cards: ▨ ▩ ▩ ▩ OTHER
Times: 11am-last L 2.30pm, last
D 10pm
Menus: *A la carte*, fixed-price
L & D, bar menu
Seats: 65
Additional: Children permitted, children's menu; ✪ dishes, other diets on request

Directions: M4 exit 12 follow signs towards Pangbourne turn left for Yattendon: in the centre of the village

BUCKINGHAMSHIRE

ASTON CLINTON, **Bell Inn** ❀❀

Classical French and English cooking which reveal skill and a commitment to quality produce

Not many people know this: the A41 through Aston Clinton starts life as London's Baker Street and ends in the heart of Birkenhead. The Bell has stood on this road since the Duke of Buckingham used it as a coaching house, en route from the country seat at Stowe to his London house, now Buckingham Palace. There is an air of solidity, of nothing changing, about the place. Yet changes have occurred. As we go to press a new chef is being sought. The Bell has a reputation for finding the right person to maintain standards, and this is what we felt about the cooking on our last visit; a few modern touches have been injected into the classic French and traditional

Near Aylesbury HP22 5HP
Map no: 4 SP81
Tel: 01296 630252
Proprietor: Michael Harris.
Manager: George Bottley
Cost: *Alc* £24.95, fixed-price
L £10 (2 courses), fixed-price
D £15.95 (2 course). H/wine
£12.95 ❢ Service exc
Credit cards: ▨ ▩ ▩ OTHER
Times: 12.30pm-last L 1.45pm,
7.30pm-last D 9.45pm daily
Menus: *A la carte*, fixed-price
L & D, bar menu

Bell Inn

Seats: 120. Air conditioned.
No smoking in dining room
Additional: Children welcome,
children's menu; **V** menu,
vegan/other diets on request

English repertoire. Value-for-money is now a dominant theme,
especially the two-course lunch, but without sacrificing quality.
The famous Bell Inn smokies, pan-fried foie gras with crisp celeriac
and ginger wine sauce, roast woodland pigeon on puy lentils with
warm beetroot and truffle jus, give way to main courses of poached
fillet of salmon with baby vegetables, mussels, chive and vermouth
sauce, or roast pork fillet with a glazed poached pear and a rich
sherry sauce. A choice of three different wines by the glass for
each course features on the wine list.

Directions: In the centre of the village on the A41 4 miles from
Aylesbury. 10 mins M25 junction 20

AYLESBURY, Hartwell House Hotel ❀❀

*Grade I historic stately home with outstanding interior, but aspirational
food can be uneven*

Oxford Road HP17 8NL
Map no: 4 SP81
Tel: 01296 747444
Chef: Alan Maw
Proprietors: Historic House
Hotels.
Manager: Jonathan Thompson
Cost: Fixed-price L £24.50/
D £39.50. H/wine £11.50 ❢
Service inc
Credit cards: ▨ ▥ ▤ OTHER
Times: Last L 1.45pm/D 9.45pm
Menus: Fixed-price L & D,
Buttery

All too often a meal starts triumphantly, only to sag progressively
through the succeeding courses. Such, sadly, was the case with our
inspection meal at Hartwell House. A detailed 'Bill of Fare' offers
a three course, fixed-price dinner for a rather steep £39.50. Dishes
certainly sound good, if a bit elaborate, along the lines of feuilleté
of rabbit with baby asparagus and coriander butter sauce, and
medaillons of venison with sea scallops and glazed endive in a light

jus. A warm chicken sausage starter, with wild mushrooms and lentils on creamed potatoes, indeed proved stunning. However, the roast breast of Aylesbury duck, on a bed of spinach with a confit leg and a Calvados sauce, arrived dry and overcooked. The latter fault was echoed in a hot Amaretto soufflé – although the presence of the liqueur was unmistakeable, the dessert was heavy and disappointing. Staff were suitably professional, but failed to enquire whether everything was to our satisfaction during the course of dinner. An extensive wine list matches the affluent setting.

Seats: 138 (4 rooms).
No smoking in dining room
Additional: Children over 8 welcome; ♥ dishes, vegan/other diets on request

Directions: 2 miles from Aylesbury on the A418 (Oxford)

BURNHAM, Burnham Beeches Hotel ❀

A striking Georgian country house hotel which serves a monthly-changing menu of sound, seasonal cooking. Enterprising dishes could include pigeon and beetroot terrine. Desserts are a highlight, especially bread and butter pudding

Times: Last L 1.50pm/D 9.50pm. Closed Sat/BH, Mon lunch
Seats: 90
Additional: Children welcome; children's portions/menu; ♥ dishes; Vegan/other diets with prior notice
Directions: Off A355 via Farnham Royal roundabout

Grove Road SL1 8DP
Map no: 4 SU98
Tel: 01628 429955
Chef: Lawrence Bryant
Proprietors: Queens Moat Houses.
Manager: I Cullen
Cost: Fixed-price L/D £12.50-£22.50
Credit cards: 🌐 ▬ ▬ 💳

CHENIES, Bedford Arms ❀

A rural setting, yet close to junction 18 of the M25, is a plus for this attractive country inn. Tony Rocks offers an immense carte of classic dishes – Parma ham with melon, ragoût of salmon, turbot and sea bass with a white wine and tarragon sauce, and traditional dessert-trolley fare

Chenies WD3 6EQ
Map no: 4 TQ09
Tel: 01923 223301
Chef: Tony Rocks
Proprietor: Thistle.
Manager: Jean-Louis Jegard
Cost: *Alc* £31.50, fixed-price L £15/D £18.50 H/wine £11.50.
No service charge
Credit cards: 🌐 ▬ ▬ 💳 OTHER
Times: 12.30pm-last L 2.30pm, 7.30pm-last D 10pm
Closed Sat L
Menus: *A la carte,* fixed-price L & D, bar menu
Seats: 60. No-smoking area
Additional: Children welcome, children's menu; ♥ dishes, other diets on request

Directions: M25 exit 18/A404 towards Amersham, turn right to Latimer/Chenies, hotel is visible 200yds

DINTON, La Chouette ⊛⊛

Extrovert and entertaining chef/patron with some interesting Belgian specialities on the menu

The quintessentially English setting of the restaurant contrasts with the Continental ebullience of the Belgian chef/patron. On our visit the menu seemed almost redundant as the chef reeled off the list of starters and main courses, and only a brave person would disregard his advice. Nonetheless, Belgian dishes worth pursuing include veal kidneys cooked in the Liège style, fillet of salmon with bacon, and eels in green sauce. A meal of goose liver terrine, followed by duck breast with a morel sauce, showed a measure of skill and a sense of timing for the cooked items, including a profusion of fresh vegetables. In case they didn't already know, diners are left in no doubt that Belgium is famous for chocolate, and this ingredient indeed dominates the list of desserts enthusiastically described by M. Desmette. A hot chocolate soufflé, served in a flash, was well-timed and enjoyable in its simplicity. The wine list offers a mainly French selection, and the owner will readily suggest suitable bottles. If available, the fixed-price menu represents good value, otherwise the final bill may shock once the service charge has been added.

Directions: On the A418 at Dinton

Near Aylesbury HP17 8UW
Map no: 4 SP71
Tel: 01296 747422
Chef: Frederic Desmette
Proprietor: Frederic Desmette
Cost: *Alc* from £11.80, fixed-price L/D £10-£25 (£10-3 courses), H/wine £10. Service exc
Credit cards: ▧ ▥ ▧
Times: Noon-last L 2pm, 7pm-last D 9pm. Closed Sat L, Sun
Menus: *A la carte*, fixed-price L & D
Seats: 40. No cigars or pipes
Additional: Children welcome, children's portions; other diets on request

MARLOW, The Compleat Angler ⊛

Named after Izaak Walton's famous angling guide, this well-known, Thames-side hotel offers a simple, affordable fixed-price menu. A meal chosen from the more elaborate, and very expensive, carte could include terrine of foie gras, fillet of sea bass with tapenade, and mille-feuille with a raspberry mousse

Marlow Bridge SL7 1RG
Map no: 4 SU88
Tel: 01628 484444
Chef: Ferdinand Testka
Proprietors: Forte Grand.
Manager: David Warren
Cost: *Alc* £40, fixed-price L £22.95/D £29.50. H/wine £15
❢ Service inc
Credit cards: ▧ ▥ ▧ ▣
Times: Last L 2.30pm/D 10pm
Menus: *A la carte*, fixed-price L & D, bar menu
Seats: 96. No smoking in dining room
Additional: Children welcome, children's menu; ♥ menu, vegan/other diets on request

Directions: A404, centre of village on the south bank of the Thames by Marlow Bridge

TAPLOW, Cliveden Hotel ❀❀❀

A stately home setting, with corresponding prices, for a handsome choice of restaurants offering modern British or French cuisine

There is an inspiring approach to this magnificent former stately home, along the widest of gravel drives, past the Fountain of Love and through some of the finest gardens in the country. Public rooms reflect a range of moods and include two restaurants. The sumptuous Terrace Dining Room overlooks the famous parterre, with views of the Thames, and here guests enjoy superb cooking in the modern British style – simple dishes, many with a Mediterranean flavour. Examples might be fresh gnocchi with crayfish to start, then a choice of main courses, such as Pithivier of wild salmon; braised ham hock, thinly sliced, with pickled sauerkraut; and roast loin of lamb rolled in mustard and herbs with marinated chargrilled vegetables and couscous. Desserts include classics such as bread and butter pudding and crème brûlée. Not surprisingly in these surroundings, prices aren't cheap; vegetables and salads are charged separately and a £2.50 donation to the National Trust is added to each guest's bill. At lunch time, lighter meals are also available at the Pavilion leisure suite in the walled garden.

Waldo's is the intimate setting for chef Ron Maxfield's personal style of French cuisine. From a sophisticated and imaginative dinner menu our inspector sampled scallop mousse ravioli, with delicious baby langoustines and wild mushrooms in a creamy stock reduction, followed by tender and intensely flavoured mallard, sliced pink and served with leg confit, and a smooth Madeira reduction enriched with bitter chocolate and cut with raspberry vinegar. Dessert was a highlight: ginger soufflé with coconut ice-cream in a brandy snap basket wittily garnished with a chocolate palm tree. The wine list is also first rate, and advice from the helpful sommelier invaluable.

Directions: On the B476, 2 miles north of Taplow

Maidenhead SL6 0JF
Map no: 4 SU98
Tel: 01628 668561
Chef: Ron Maxfield
Proprietor: Cliveden Hotel.
Director/Manager: Stuart Wilson
Cost: *Alc* £55, fixed-price
L £28/D £ 36.50 H/wine £18 ♥
Service inc
Credit cards: 🆂 📷 📇 💷
Times: Last L 2.30pm, last
D 10.30pm (Terrace open daily,
Waldo's open for D Tue-Sat)
Menus: *A la carte,* fixed-price
L & D
Seats: 28 (Waldo's). Air
conditioned. 65 (Terrace).
No smoking in dining room
Additional: Children welcome,
children's menu; ♥ dishes,
vegan/other diets on request

'En papillote' describes a manner of cooking and serving. It is quite simply a way of wrapping food so that it is tightly enclosed in buttered or oiled greaseproof paper or aluminium foil and then cooked in the oven. The wrapping swells during cooking and the dish is served piping hot before the wrapping collapses. This preserves the flavour and is a method often employed with fish which requires a short cooking time.

A 'papillote' on the other hand, is a small decorative paper frill used to decorate the bone end of a lamb or veal chop, rack of lamb or chicken drumstick.

WOOBURN COMMON, **Chequers Inn** ✿

Busy village inn with a wide choice of dishes on both the carte and fixed-price menu. Most, such as venison in port wine and mushroom sauce, and iced parfait of walnuts and Grand Marnier, are carefully prepared

Kiln Lane HP10 0JQ
Map no: 4 SU98
Tel: 01628 529575
Chef: Mark Bentley
Proprietor: Peter Roehrig
Cost: *Alc* £25; fixed-price
L £14.95/D £17.95 H/wine £8
❢ Service exc
Credit cards: ▨ ▨▨ ▨▨ OTHER
Times: Last L 2.30pm/D 9.30pm
approx
Menus: *A la carte*, fixed-price
L/D, bar menu
Seats: 60
Additional: Children welcome;
♥ menu, vegan/other diets on
request

Directions: From High Wycombe, 2 miles along A40 turn left into Broad Lane, hotel 2.5 miles on right

CAMBRIDGESHIRE

BYTHORN, **Bennett's Restaurant** ✿

☺ *Relaxed pub restaurant with sound cooking and generous portions. Meat predominates, and fish dishes include home-pickled salmon. Daube of duck on Cumberland sauce was succulent, and a halibut steak with velouté sauce and dill nearly covered the plate. Traditional English puddings include almond tart*

Menus: *A la carte*, fixed-price L/D, bar menu
Seats: 50. No smoking in the dining room
Additional: Children welcome, children's portions; ♥ dishes, vegan/other diets on request
Directions: Off A14 at Bythorn, centre of village on right

The White Hart PE18 0QM
Map no: 4 TL07
Tel: 01832 710 226
Chef: Bill Bennett
Proprietor: Bill Bennett
Cost: *Alc* £22, fixed-price L £15
(4 courses)/D £22. H/wine £8.50
Service inc
Credit cards: ▨ ▨▨ OTHER
Times: Last L 2pm/D 10pm.
Closed Sun D, Mon

CAMBRIDGE,
Cambridge Garden Moat House ⌘

The hotel lies in its own grounds on the River Cam. Particular attention is given to the menu in Le Jardin restaurant where a wide range of modern and classical dishes combine exciting textures and flavours. In addition there are daily recommendations

Mill Lane CB2 1RT
Map: 5 TL45
Tel: 01223 259988
Chef: Alan Fuller
Proprietor: Queens Moat Houses Hotels.
Manager: Paul J Breen
Cost: *Alc* from £29.55, fixed-price L £9.99-£18.50/D £22.00, H/wine £11.95. Service exc
Credit cards: ▨ ▦ ▦ ▨
Times: 12.30pm-last L 2.30pm, 7.00pm-last D 9.45pm
Menus: *A la carte,* fixed-price L & D
Seats: 130
Additional: Children permitted, children's menu; ❂ dishes, other diets on request

Directions: City centre, from Trumpington Street past Fitzwilliam Museum turn left opposite signs to car park into Mill Lane

CAMBRIDGE, **Cambridge Lodge Hotel** ⌘

The professionalism of the restaurant operation is one reason for this hotel's popularity amongst visitors and locals. Another is the classical style cooking of chef Peter Reynolds. Specialities include roulade of pheasant and chicken topped with pine kernels, and peppered sirloin steak in a brandy flavoured peppered sauce

Menus: *A la carte,* fixed-price L & D, pre-theatre, bar menu
Seats: 74. No smoking in dining room
Additional: Children permitted before 8.30pm, children's portions; ❂ menu, vegan/other diets on request
Directions: One mile N of city on A1307

139 Huntingdon Road CB3 0DQ
Map no: 5 TL45
Tel: 01223 352833
Chef: Peter Reynolds
Proprietors: Sheila Hipwell and Darren Chamberlain
Cost: *Alc* £25; fixed-price L £14.95/D £19.95. H/wine £8.95. Service exc
Credit cards: ▨ ▦ ▦ ▨ OTHER
Times: Last L 1.45pm/D 9.30pm. Closed 27-31 Dec

CAMBRIDGE,
Midsummer House Restaurant ⌘⌘

Lovely location by the River Cam for stylish restaurant that continues to attract both town and gown

This well-established restaurant has had new owners, chef and staff during the last year, plus a few other changes. Although the conservatory and blue dining-room remain as smartly furnished as ever, the first floor is now given over to private dining and no longer used for pre-dinner drinks. The cooking is a mix of French classical and modern European, but occasionally dishes can get a little over-complicated. Quality ingredients are generally used to good effect, as shown in a summer starter of Scottish lobster and

Midsummer Common CB4 1HA
Map no: 5 TL45
Tel: 01223 69299
Chef: Anton Escalera
Proprietor: Crown Society.
Manager: J Teixeira
Cost: *Alc* £25.50-£38.50, fixed-price L £17-£36 (Sun £25)/D £24-£38 H/wine £15 ❢ Service inc
Credit cards: ▨ ▦ ▦
Times: Last L 2pm, last D 9pm
Closed Sat L, Sun D, Mon, Dec 26

Midsummer House Restaurant

Menus: *A la carte*, fixed-price
L & D
Seats: 40 (+14+6 private)
Additional: Children welcome,
children's portions; ❂ dishes,
vegan/other diets on request

chargrilled scallops presented in a choux pastry basket, surrounded by a brightly coloured red pimento coulis. The main course of langoustine ravioli, accompanied by Mediterranean vegetables, trumpet mushrooms and saffron and chervil nage, however, showed inconsistencies; flavourless langoustines, heavy pasta and superfluous, over-earthy mushrooms. A hot raspberry soufflé successfully graduated with honours, thanks to its golden appearance, intense fruit flavour and well-balanced sweetness. An accompanying ice-cream was rich, smooth and creamy.

Directions: Park (if possible) in Pretoria Road, off Chesterton Road, then walk across the footbridge to Midsummer House

DUXFORD, Duxford Lodge Hotel ❀❀

☺ *Modern French cooking with the warmth of the Mediterranean in an immaculately run hotel*

A neatly tended garden, a village centre setting, close proximity to the Duxford Imperial War Museum, and just a short distance from Junction 10 of the M11: this neat, red-brick hotel has much going for it. Public rooms are immaculately maintained, yet offer a relaxing and informal atmosphere, and the kitchen offers innovative but not outlandish cooking. The modern French cooking has a strong provençal touch in dishes such as a superlative warm tuna and tomato tart with pesto, applauded for depth of flavour as much as for the right balance of contrasting textures, and a 'lovely cut' of pan-fried turbot with olive oil, tomatoes, lemon juice, thyme and garlic. Tart tatin – 'cooked the way I like it, heavy on the caramelisation', which came with rich, hot caramel sauce, smooth and full flavoured, was not too sweet either. Coffee is an excellent Colombian, served with homemade petits fours. Service is enthusiastic and cheerful.

Directions: M11 exit 10, take A505 eastbound then 1st turning on right to Duxford; take right fork at T-junction, entrance 70yds on left

Ickleton Road CB2 4RU
Map no: 5 TL44
Tel: 01223 836444
Chefs: Ronald Craddock and
Patrick Tweedie
Proprietors: Mr R H & Mr S J
Craddock
Cost: *Alc* £21.25, fixed-price
L/D £16.65. H/wine £8.95
Service exc
Credit cards: 🏧 💳 💳 💳 OTHER
Times: Last L 2pm/D 9.30pm
Closed 26-31 Dec
Menus: *A la carte*, fixed-price
L & D, party menu
Seats: 36
Additional: Children welcome,
children's portions; ❂ dishes,
party menu, vegan/other diets on
request

Restaurant assessments are based on reports of visits carried out anonymously by the AA's Hotel and Restaurant Inspectors.

ELY,

Old Fire Engine House Restaurant ✤

☺ *Combining an art gallery and a restaurant, the Old Fire Engine is a popular place serving traditional old favourites enhanced by the quality of the local produce, especially seasonal game. Expect dishes such as salmon and mushroom au gratin, chicken breast in breadcrumbs with a fresh tarragon cream sauce, and Cambridge burnt cream*

Menu: *A la carte*
Seats: 36. No smoking in restaurant
Additional: Children welcome, children's portions; ♥ dishes, vegan/other diets prior notice
Directions: Just off A10 from Cambridge about 200yds west of Ely Cathedral

25 Saint Mary's Street CB7 4ER
Map no: 5 TL58
Tel: 01353 662582
Chef: Terri Kindred
Proprietors: Ann Ford and Michael Jarman
Cost: *Alc* £19.50. H/wine £7
❢ Service exc
Credit cards: ▨ ▨ OTHER
Times: Last L 2pm/D 9pm.
Closed Sun D, Bhs, 2 wks from Dec 24

FOWLMERE,

The Chequers Inn Restaurant ✤

☺ *Samuel Pepys once stayed at this fine 16th-century inn. Nowadays, modern visitors can expect sound Anglo-French cooking along the lines of ramekin of smoked haddock topped with egg, French magret duck breasts marinated with honey and cloves, and mille-feuille of fresh strawberries and Chantilly cream*

Additional: Children welcome, children's portions; ♥ dishes, vegan/other diets on request
Directions: On B1368 between Royston and Cambridge, accessible by A10 & A505

Near Royston SG8 7SR
Map no: 5 TL44
Tel: 01763 208369
Chef: Louis Gambie
Proprietors: Norman S Rushton
Cost: *Alc* £19.20, fixed-price L £14.25. H/wine £8.75. Service exc. Cover charge
Credit cards: ▨ ▨ ▨
Times: Last L 2pm/D10pm.
Closed Dec 25
Menus: *A la carte,* fixed-price L, bar menu
Seats: 30+24 (Conservatory)

KEYSTON, Pheasant Inn ✤✤

Enthusiastically run inn offering imaginative bar and restaurant food

Diners at this enchanting thatched village inn can choose to eat casually throughout the building, or with a degree of formality within the non-smoking restaurant – the Red Room – which provides large, highly polished tables and linen napkins. Chef Roger Jones offers the same menu wherever you choose to eat, based on modern British cooking. He concentrates on strong flavours and quality local produce, with fish being especially well represented. A recent meal started with home-made noodles and smoked salmon, courgette batons and fennel, all carefully bound by a smooth cream sauce. The main course of wood pigeon, served sliced around a centre mound of shredded carrot and chick peas set on a good port jus, had quite a distinct, almost earthy taste, well contrasted by the 'delightful' jus. A hot caramel soufflé pudding was full flavoured and moist, enhanced by a superb home-made Armagnac and prune ice-cream, while the rich cafetière coffee and petits fours were equally good. Poste houses continue to win awards for their selection of wines, and one can expect about 100 interesting wines of individuality and character, at every price range, along with helpful tasting notes.

Directions: Village centre, 12 miles from Huntingdon and Kettering off A14 signed Keyston

Huntingdon PE18 0RE
Map no: 4 TL07
Tel: 01832 710241
Chef: Roger Jones
Proprietors: Roger Jones (Huntsbridge Ltd)
Cost: *Alc* £20. H/wine £8.50 ❢ Service exc
Credit Cards: ▨ ▨ ▨ OTHER
Times: Last L 2pm, last D 10pm daily
Menus: *A la carte* L & D
Seats: 100. No smoking
Additional: Children welcome, children's portions; ♥ dishes, vegan/other diets on request

MELBOURN,
The Pink Geranium Restaurant

Highly popular restaurant with enterprising husband and wife owners and colourful, seasonal modern cooking

Think pink at this thatched and timbered cottage which nestles near the centre of the quiet village. The changing daily lunch and dinner menus and the seasonal *carte* are encouragingly short, and the young and dedicated kitchen brigade clearly enjoy working with ingredients such as fresh tuna, seared and served as an original salad niçoise, or globe artichokes paired with mushroom and corn salad. Main courses display well executed sauces, accompanied by an extra flourish or two, which stamp some character on the dishes; salmon, for example, with pimento butter sauce, or tender slices of lamb with a rich olive jus. Desserts do not disappoint, and a summer pudding, bursting with five varieties of berries, spelt summer through and through. The wine list reads like a roll call of French nobility, but there are also bottles from the New World. After dinner, repair to one of the comfy armchairs or sofas that occupy the ground floor and linger till going home time. A door-to-door chauffeur service, bookable in advance, is an admirable idea other restaurants would do well to copy.

Directions: On A10 between Royston and Cambridge. In the centre of the village, opposite the church

Station Road SG8 6DX
Map no: 5 TL34
Tel: 01763 260215
Chefs: Steven Saunders and Paul Murfitt
Proprietors: Steven & Sally Saunders
Cost: *Alc* £45, fixed-price L £18.95/D £29.95. H/wine £11.95
Times: Noon-last L 2pm,7pm-last D 9.30pm. Closed Sun D, Mon
Menus: *A la carte*, fixed-price L & D
Seats: 70. No smoking in the dining room
Additional: Children welcome, children's portions; ❂ menu, vegan/other diets on request

MELBOURN, ## Sheen Mill Restaurant

Rural setting for Anglo-French restaurant with a loyal following

This restored 17th-century watermill contains a large restaurant which has been nurtured for over ten years by an ex-London restaurateur. There is a peaceful atmosphere about the place, and nothing too racy about the menu, which offers a monthly changing fixed-price menu, a seasonally adjusted one, and a choice of over 100 wines. There is a professional, no-frills approach to the food, and an evening meal might start with French onion soup, terrine of calves' liver with onion confit, or a simply prepared leek and basil tartlet with faultless beurre blanc and chive sauce. Main courses offer something for everybody – medallions of beef with a tarragon mousse and a purée of shallots, perhaps, or grilled fillet of sea bass with sauce vièrge. A flambé section provides visual entertainment for those unlucky enough not to have a view over the mill pond. An inspection meal of tenderloin of pork, unfortunately, failed to live up to the name and suggested below par shopping skills. The veal-based jus, however, was well tempered with cream and grainy mustard. Desserts such as warm chestnut and Strega pudding with a vanilla custard, make for enjoyable eating.

Directions: Take 2nd exit on A10 Melbourn, Sheen Mill is 300yds on the right; from M11 exit 10 follow A505 to Melbourn

Station Road SG8 6DX
Map no: 5 TL34
Tel: 01763 261393
Chef: John Curtis
Proprietor: Mr & Mrs C G D Cescutti
Cost: *Alc* £25, fixed-price L £15.95/D £21.50. H/wine £8.50. Service exc
Credit cards: 🅱 💳 💳 🅿
Times: Noon-last L 2pm, 7pm-last D 10pm. Closed Sun D, Bhs
Menus: *A la carte*, fixed-price L & D, bar L menu
Seats: 100. No pipes or cigars, no-smoking area
Additional: Children welcome, children's portions; ❂ menu, vegan/other diets on request

Factual details of establishments in this Guide are from questionnaires we send to all restaurants that feature in the book.

SIX MILE BOTTOM,
Swynford Paddocks Hotel ☸

An elegant country house surrounded by well-tended gardens, grounds and paddocks. Patrick Collins produces an interesting menu of good Irish and French dishes. Specialities include petit fillet of beef topped with light goose liver pâté and wild mushroom sauce, and roast duckling with fresh cream and orange liqueur

Menus: *A la carte,* fixed-price D, bar menu **Seats:** 60. No smoking in dining room **Additional:** Children welcome, children's portions; ❤ dishes, vegan/other diets on request
Directions: On A1304 six miles south-west of Newmarket

Newmarket CB8 0UE
Map no: 5 TL55
Tel: 01638 570234
Chef: Patrick Collins
Proprietor: Qualitair Hotels.
Manager: Patricia Evans
Cost: *Alc* £20-£30, fixed-price D £22.95 (4 course). H/wine £10
Credit cards: ■ ■■ ■■ ■ OTHER
Times: Last L 2pm, last D 9.30pm. Closed between Xmas & N/year

WANSFORD, The Haycock Hotel ☸

The Haycock, a celebrated 17th-century coaching inn, is set in delightful grounds beside the River Nene. The pleasant restaurant offers essentially traditional English dishes using fresh ingredients wherever possible. Starters might include baked goats' cheese on toasted brioche, or a tasty terrine of chicken

Menus: *A la carte,* fixed-price L, bar menu **Seats:** 78
Additional: Children welcome, children's portions; ❤ menu, vegan/other diets on request
Directions: In village centre between A1 & A47

Wansford PE8 6JA
Map no: 4 TL09
Tel: 01780 782223
Chef: Richard Brandrick
Proprietor: Arcadian Int. UK.
Manager: Richard Neale
Cost: *Alc* £30 (inc wine), fixed-price L £14.95. H/wine £8.45 ❗
Service exc
Credit cards: ■ ■■ ■■ ■ OTHER
Times: Noon-last L 2pm, 7pm-last D 10pm

CHESHIRE

ALDERLEY EDGE,
Alderley Edge Hotel ☸☸

A restaurant in a beautiful house with large landscaped gardens providing well-presented, classic French cooking

Macclesfield Road SK9 7BJ
Map no: 7 SJ87
Tel: 01625 583033
Chef: Steve Kitchen
Proprietor: J W Lees & Co.
Manager: Ahmet Kurcer
Cost: *Alc* £27.75, fixed-price L £11.50/D £19.95. H/wine £11.95 ❗ Service exc
Credit cards: ■ ■■ ■■ ■
Times: last L 2pm/D10pm
Menus: *A la carte,* fixed-price L & D, bar L
Seats: 80. No pipes in restaurant. Air conditioned
Additional: Children permitted, children's portions; ❤ menu, vegan/other diets on request

Manchester's cotton kings built their homes well away from their grimy mills. This sandstone house, dating from 1850, is one of them, standing halfway up the 'Edge' overlooking the Cheshire Plain. An ambitious variety of eloquently described dishes prepared by the new head chef, Steve Kitchen (he has heard all the jokes), is available from several menus, including one for vegetarians. Complimentary appetisers, perhaps goats' cheese and vegetable terrine, introduce the repertoire. From the Winter/Spring Signatures *carte* perhaps chartreuse of lobster, scallop, brown shrimp and salmon with a saffron mayonnaise, or spiced chicken liver and mushroom feuilleté scented with truffles. A test main course produced an extremely good, tender breast of duck roasted in sweet spices with preserved vegetables, the deep-coloured sauce spot on. To finish, crêpe soufflé with a Grand Marnier sauce, or a classic lemon tart. The wine list is long, expensive and full of interest, with what is claimed to be the world's largest Champagne section.

Directions: A538 to Alderley Edge then the B5087 Macclesfield road

BOLLINGTON, Mauro's Restaurant

Enjoyable Italian cooking served in a setting reminiscent of a bright southern Italian restaurant

Vincenzo Mauro came here with his family from Capri 10 years ago. He brought a lot of Italy with him too; deep yellow walls are hung with pictures, terracotta fish and pots. Enzo and his son Alex are energetic hosts. A wide selection of hot and cold 'Caprese antipasti' is offered with pre-dinner drinks, including fresh chargrilled sardines, squid, anchovies, sun-dried tomatoes, marinated red peppers and home-made meat balls. Before you are escorted to your table, a superb pizzetti – lightly-fried dough filled with a rich tomato purée and covered with mozzarella – is presented to you. Among the wide selection of pasta main courses is 'orecchiette all' avocado (pasta with avocado, walnuts, basil and Parmesan). Fresh fish, chicken and meat dishes are also available. Whole sea bream, very fresh and delicately cooked, accompanied by crisp and fluffy sauté potatoes, spinach and mange-touts is heavily endorsed. From the pudding-laden trolleys come a rich, light and crumbly hazelnut and chocolate cake made to a secret recipe, and tiramisù. One hundred and forty grappas are available, as well as some excellent Italian wines from the balanced and well-presented wine list.

Directions: Situated on the main street of the village, at the Pott Shrigley end

88 Palmerston Street SK10 5PW
Map no: 7 SJ97
Tel: 01625 573898
Chef: Vincenzo Mauro
Proprietor: Vincenzo Mauro
Cost: *Alc* £17.50, Sunday
L £14.75. H/wine £8.50. Service exc
Credit cards: 🔲 📰 📰
Times: Noon-last L 2pm, last D 10pm. Closed Sat L, Sun (except first Sun of every month for Italian Sun L)
Menus: A la carte, fixed-price Sun L, lunchtime bar menu
Seats: 48. Air conditioned
Additional: Children welcome, children's portions; ♥ menu, vegan/other diets on request

Couscous has two meanings: the complete dish and the tiny granules of semolina with which it is usually made. The couscous concept is simple. Take a container with a perforated bottom, fill it with granules, and place it above a simmering stew. The grains will swell in the steam from the stew and at the same time be flavoured by it. When the two are served together the combination is wonderful, one of the highlights of Moroccan cooking. The dish itself is undoubtedly Berber, but the derivation of the word couscous is obscure. The favoured theory is that it is onomatopoeic, a verbal approximation of the hissing sound made as steam is forced through the holes of the 'couscoussier' into the grain.

BROXTON,

Broxton Hall Hotel ❀

☺ *Privately owned and personally run, Broxton Hall is an original Tudor house with many ancient features remaining. The restaurant itself enjoys views across the terrace and gardens, and offers an English menu with a French accent. In true country house style, all food is cooked on an Aga in the original kitchen*

Menus: A la carte L, fixed-price L & D, bar menu
Seats: 60. No pipes or cigars in restaurant
Additional: Children welcome L only, children's portions; ✿ dishes, vegan/other diets on request
Directions: On A41 halfway between Whitchurch and Chester, at Broxton roundabout

Whitchurch Road CH3 9JS
Map no: 7 SJ45
Tel: 01829 782321
Chefs: Jim Makin and Mark Dodd
Proprietors: Rosemary & George Hadley
Cost: Alc £18, fixed-price L £10.75/Sun £12.75/D £23.90 (5 course) H/wine £10.75. Service exc
Credit cards: 🅰 ▄ 🔤 ⯒
Times: Noon-last L 2pm, 6.30-last D 10pm. Closed Dec 25 & Jan 1

CHESTER,

The Chester Grosvenor Hotel ❀❀❀

Grand surroundings for classical French cuisine with generous use of luxurious ingredients

A marbled foyer, a sweeping staircase and a magnificent chandelier create a grand first impression at this traditional hotel. There is a graceful, understated style about the public rooms, which include a panelled library bar and the Arkle Restaurant, named after the legendary racehorse. With its highly polished tables and elegant appointments, the restaurant is a fitting setting for the skilled cooking of executive chef, Paul Reed. The seasonally-changing *carte* is written in French with English subtitles and features top quality British produce. This is supplemented by a couple of daily fish dishes and a six-course menu gourmand, while at lunch there is a shorter fixed price menu of two or three courses.

The food is based on classical principals but presentation is modern, and while there is a tendency towards gratuitous use of luxury ingredients the results are most enjoyable. A fillet of turbot came perched on a delicious truffle scented mash surrounded by girolle mushrooms, the highlight of an autumn meal, which also included a cushion of calves' sweetbreads with a strong, mustard flavoured herb crust and pickled vegetables. Other starters could be Landes duck liver with brawn and crackling salad, or a warm mousse of river pike with braised chicory and chilled oysters. These might be followed by pot-roasted Bresse pigeon with scented cabbage and a sweet garlic butter sauce, or Scottish beef fillet with flaked oxtails and celeriac fondants. Tempting desserts, such as double chocolate soufflé with pecan ice-cream, deserve careful consideration (an 'indulgence of summer desserts' may assist the indecisive), or there is the option of cheese or a savoury to finish. The wine list is excellent, with some useful sommeliers' recommendations; and lighter meals are also available in the hotel's popular brasserie.

Directions: City centre adjacent to the Eastgate Clock and Roman Walls

Eastgate Street CH1 1LT
Map no: 7 SJ46
Tel: 01244 324024
Chef: Paul Reed
Proprietors: Managing Director: Jonathan W Slater (Small Luxury Hotels of the World)
Cost: Alc £35-£55, fixed-price L £18-£37 (6 course) H/wine £10.50 ❢ Service exc
Credit cards: 🅰 ▄ 🔤 ⯒
Times: Noon-last L 2.30pm, 7pm-last D 9.30pm. Closed Sun D, Mon L, Dec 25/6, Jan 1-6
Menus: A la carte D, fixed-price L, pre-theatre, bar menu
Seats: 40. No cigars or pipes in restaurant. Air conditioned
Additional: Children welcome, children's menu; ✿ menu, vegan/other diets on request

CHESTER, **Crabwall Manor Hotel** ❀❀❀

An elegant manor house within view of the historic city offering imaginative modern dishes

Parkgate Road
Mollington CH1 6NE
Map no: 7 SJ46
Tel: 01244 851666
Chef: Michael Truelove
Proprietor: Julian Hook (Small Luxury Hotels of the World)
Cost: *Alc* £30, fixed-price Sun L (4 course) £15.50, H/wine £12.50. Service exc
Credit cards: 🅰 🔳 🔳 🔳 OTHER
Times: Noon-last L 2pm, 7pm-last D 10.00pm
Menus: *A la carte*, Sunday L
Seats: 95. Air conditioned
Additional: Children welcomed (half main course portion);
❤ dishes

This is an impressive former manor house with its distinctive turrets, Tudor origins and extensive grounds. Popularity with the business community is evident by the helicopter pad. Michael Truelove and his team take full advantage of available fresh produce to produce a repertoire with a classical base that has many resonances of modern British cooking. Results on the plate are impressively good. There's a certain degree of mix and match, as in grilled sea bass topped with red pepper confit set on a bed of pasta tagliatelle and a chicken stock reduction sauce, and roast sea scallops with deep fried leeks and liquorice sauce, or roast breast of duck with anise sauce garnished with a paupiette of its own confit, showing a hint of East-meets-West. Starters could include ravioli of scallops with Sauternes sauce, pea soup garnished with cod brandade, or panache of melon flavoured with mint.

One inspector commented favourably on a potage of fresh scallops with a light ginger sauce, and a robust braised lamb shank with lentils du pays and smoked bacon. Another meal produced lamb mousseline on a bed of spinach with crisp, fried leeks and a 'rich' sauce with lentils, 'succulent, flavoursome, tender' beef medallions with a sauce perigourdine and superb roasted pears with cinnamon ice-cream, fondue and butterscotch sauce. Other desserts could include lemon tart with orange syrup, or prune and frangipane tart. The wine list stretches out well beyond France and takes in an impressive selection of magnums and half bottles.

Directions: From M56 take A5117 then A540. Set back from the A540 north of Chester

CHESTER,
The Gateway To Wales Hotel ❀❀

☺ *Good taste, care and quality have gone into the creation of this modern, purpose-built hotel, some five miles west of Chester*

Welsh Road
Deeside CH5 2HX
Map no: 7 SJ46
Tel: 01244 830332
Chef: Nicholas Walton
Proprietor: Deborah K Harford-Corbett

The Gateway to Wales is not a bad description of this hotel which stands at the junction of a major route into Wales. Extensive leisure and conference facilities are a strong feature, and levels of service in both the hotel and restaurant are high. The cooking tries hard, sometimes missing the mark of flavour, but compensating for this with enthusiasm. This was the case with a pancake of Cornish crab and watercress on a lemon fish jus, which, despite being beautifully presented, was rather lacking in taste. A 'deliciously light' warm asparagus mousse wrapped in lightly steamed leeks on a good truffle cream sauce was judged to be more successful, as was a roast partridge with caramelised apple and an 'excellent' Welsh cider vinaigrette. Other main courses may include honey braised shank of pork, or loin of rabbit wrapped in a wild mushroom and chicken mousse with a chocolate scented sauce. Dutch apple flan with crème anglaise and vanilla ice-cream is typical of dessert.

Directions: Three and a half miles outside the city centre on A548 near the junction of the A550 and A494. Close to RAF Sealand

Cost: Alc £23 (5 course); fixed-price L £6.99 (2 course)/D £15.95 (4 course). H/wine £8.25. Service inc
Credit cards: 🔳 🔳 🔳 🔳 OTHER
Times: Last L 2.30pm, last D 9.30pm/9.00pm Sun
Menus: A la carte, fixed-price L & D, Sunday L, bar menu
Seats: 40. No smoking in dining room
Additional: Children welcome, children's menu; ❂ dishes, other diets on request

CHESTER,
Mollington Banastre Hotel ❀

☺ *Much extended Victorian residence with up-to-date conference and leisure facilities and handy for Chester and the motorway system. Expect chicken liver parfait, steamed seafood, scallops of venison on a tangy berry sauce. Good-value set lunch*

Seats: 80. No smoking in dining room **Additional:** Children welcome, children's menu; ❂ dishes, other diets on request
Directions: Bear left at end of M56 onto A5117, left at roundabout onto A540, the hotel is 2 miles on the right

Parkgate Road CH1 6NN
Map no: 7 SJ46
Tel: 01244 851471
Chef: Ron Knox
Proprietor: Managing Director: John Mawdsley (Best Western)
Cost: Alc £15-20, fixed-price L £12/D £22 (4 course) H/wine £9.95. Service inc
Credit cards: 🔳 🔳 🔳 🔳
Times: Last L 2pm/D 10pm
Menus: A la carte, fixed-price L/D, bar menu

HANDFORTH, Belfry Hotel ❀

Owned and run by the Beech family for nearly thirty years, the Belfry Hotel is a modern hotel with a pleasant split level restaurant. A recent inspection meal included lemon sole filled with fresh crab and set on a chive butter sauce, and finished with a creamy bread and butter pudding

Menus: A la carte, fixed-price L & D, bar menu **Seats:** 150
No-smoking area **Additional:** Children welcome, children's portions; ❂ menu, vegan/other diets on request
Directions: A34 to Handforth, at end of village

Stanley Road SK9 3LD
Map no: 7 SJ76
Tel: 0161 437 0511
Chef: Mark Fletcher
Proprietor: G A Beech
Cost: Alc £25, fixed-price L £14/D £16 H/wine £6.80 ❢ Service exc
Credit cards: 🔳 🔳 🔳 🔳
Times: Last L 2pm/last D 10pm
Closed Dec 26/7

HOLMES CHAPEL,
The Old Vicarage Hotel ❀

☺ *Visitors to this former rectory on the northern outskirts of town can look forward to some straightforward brasserie-style cooking based on sound produce. Expect cream of onion soup, tender loin of local lamb in a red wine sauce with apple and mint chutney, roulade of carrot and cauliflower, and crème caramel*

Additional: Children welcome; ❂ dishes, vegan available, other diets on request
Directions: 500 yds from Holmes Chapel centre on A50 Knutsford road

Knutsford Road CW4 8EF
Map: 7 SJ46
Tel: 01477 532041
Chef: Kenneth Howard
Proprietor: Luis Barbera
Cost: Alc £15.90, H/wine £7.80. Service inc
Credit cards: 🔳 🔳 🔳 OTHER
Times: Noon-last L 2.00pm, last D 10.00pm
Menus: A la carte, children's menu, ❂ dishes
Seats: 70

KNUTSFORD, **Belle Epoque** ✿

☺ *Long standing family-run restaurant set in an Edwardian building in one of Knutsford's main streets. Within, the Paris of the Belle Epoque is created. The brasserie menu makes excellent use of local ingredients. Look out for rabbit casserole with herb dumplings, or chargrilled tuna with tapenade*

Directions: Two miles off A50, 2 miles from M6 junction 19

60 King Street WA16 6DT
Map no: 7 SJ77
Tel: 01565 633060
Chefs: Graham Codd and David Mooney
Proprietors: Nerys Mooney.
Manager: Mark Walkden
Cost: *Alc* £16.50-£22. H/wine £10.50 ♥ Service inc
Credit cards: 🔳 🏧 🔳 🔳 OTHER
Times: Last L 2pm/D 10.30pm. Closed Sun & BHs
Menu: *A la carte*
Seats: 85. No-smoking room
Additional: Children permitted, children's portions; ✿ dishes, vegan/other diets on request

KNUTSFORD,
Cottage Restaurant & Lodge ✿

Housed in an attractive Cheshire brick building, the Cottage Restaurant is spacious, decorated with real character. An ambitious menu may include tartlet of smoked haddock with sun-dried tomatoes and spinach, and roast loin of Brecon lamb with green peppercorn sauce

Menus: Fixed-price L & D, early bird special (5.30-6.30pm)
Seats: 150. No-smoking area
Additional: Children welcome, children's portions; ✿ dishes, vegan/other diets on request
Directions: On A50 halfway between Knutsford and Holmes Chapel

Allostock WA16 9LU
Map no: 7 SJ77
Tel: 01565 722470
Chef: Brian Joy
Proprietors: C Lowe and F Fletcher
Cost: Fixed-price L £9.95/D £13.95 (2 course). H/wine £8.95 ♥ Service inc
Credit cards: 🔳 🏧 🔳 OTHER
Times: Last L 2pm, last D 9.30pm. Closed Sun D

KNUTSFORD, **Cottons Hotel** ✿

An appetising menu backed by careful and committed cooking ensures enjoyable results in the atmospheric hotel restaurant. Expect gnocchi with creamy pesto sauce, Cajun-style fish stew with crisp aubergine fritters, and a rich pecan and chocolate terrine

Menus: *A la carte*, fixed-price L & D, bar menu
Seats: 100. No-smoking area
Additional: Children welcome, children's portions; ✿ dishes, vegan/other diets on request
Directions: M6 exit 19/A556 (Stockport), R onto A50 (Knutsford) 1.5 miles

Manchester Road WA16 0SU
Map no: 7 SJ57
Tel: 01565 650333
Chef: Gary Jenkins
Proprietor: Shire Inns.
Manager: Mark Bowers
Cost: *Alc* £19.35-£30, fixed-price L £12.75/D £20 H/wine £8.95 No service charge
Credit cards: 🔳 🏧 🔳 🔳 OTHER
Times: Last L 2pm/last D 9.45pm/8.45pm Sun. Closed Sat L

KNUTSFORD, **The Longview Hotel** ❀

☺ *An end of terrace hotel with views across Knutsford Heath, the Longview serves a range of good value dishes.* Look out for chicken livers layered with aubergines on a bed of mixed leaves; red mullet coated in crab paste and wrapped in vine leaves, and lime mousse on a lovely plum and passion fruit purée

55 Manchester Road WA16 0LX
Map no: 7 SJ77
Tel: 01565 632119
Chefs: James Falconer-Flint and Yvonne Burke
Proprietors: Pauline & Stephen West
Cost: Alc £17.35. H/wine £7.95 ▌Service exc
Credit cards: 🆒 ▒ ▒ ▒
Times: 7pm-last D 9pm. Closed Sun & from Dec 24th-Jan 2nd

Menus: *A la carte*, bar menu (soups & sandwiches)
Seats: 38. Guests requested to refrain from smoking in dining room
Additional: Children permitted, children's portions; ❖ menu, vegan/other diets on request
Directions: On A50 Manchester road overlooking Knutsford Heath, 200yds from roundabout with A5033, just before the town square

KNUTSFORD, **The Toft Hotel** ❀

A restored 16th-century farmhouse, with a rustic restaurant featuring exposed brickwork. The emphasis here is on wholesome vegetarian cooking and Jean Davies' creative menu justifiably draws in the crowds at weekends. A typical dish might be artichoke and herb strudel with Gruyère cheese and chives

Menus: Fixed-price D, bar menu
Seats: 50. No smoking
Additional: Children over 10 permitted; ❖ menu
Directions: One mile south of Knutsford on the A50

Toft Road WA16 9EH
Map no: 7 SJ77
Tel: 01565 633470
Chef: Jean Davies
Proprietors: Jean & Tony Davies
Cost: Fixed-price D £17.50. H/wine £9.50 ▌Cover charge 10% for parties of 6. Service exc
Credit cards: 🆒 ▒ ▒ OTHER
Times: Last D 9.30pm
Open Thur-Sat D only

NANTWICH, **Churche's Mansion** ❀❀

☺ *A very old timber-framed house now soaking up the aromas of modern British, French and Mediterranean-style cooking*

A rich merchant built the house in 1577, and all the accoutrements of age can be seen in rich panelling, beams and a huge inglenook, and in the many reports of ghost sightings. The house is now a town-centre restaurant run by Amanda Latham and her father Robin. The lunch and dinner menus change monthly and both offer a remarkable choice of 10 or 11 dishes at every course. Even more remarkable is the near-total absence of duplication between these menus. The style reads well, but results on the plate can sometimes

Hospital Street CW5 5RY
Map no: 7 SJ65
Tel: 01270 625933
Chef: Graham Tucker
Proprietor: Amanda Latham
Cost: Fixed-price L £15.95/ D £25. H/wine £9.95. Service exc
Credit cards: 🆒 ▒ ▒ OTHER
Times: Last L 2.30pm, last D 9.30pm. Closed Sun D, Mon, 2nd wk Jan

involve a mix of too many flavours and ingredients that do not always work. At an inspection meal for example, creamed leeks did nothing for an otherwise adequate part-smoked salmon with scallops and asparagus with a star anise sauce. Much better was roast breast of Gressingham duck in orange, carrot and sweet herb sauce, with the leg diced and placed in a spiced filo parcel. Desserts are highly imaginative and the all-British cheeses are accompanied by notes on who makes them, and where. The good wine list sensibly recognises that a wide choice of halves is important.

Menus: Fixed-price L & D, bar lunch
Seats: 50. No smoking in the dining room
Additional: Children welcome Sat & Sun L (over 10 at D), children's portions; ♥ dishes, other diets by arrangement

Directions: M6 exit 16 & A500 – near town centre by roundabout off the Crewe/Stoke-on-Trent road

NANTWICH,
Rookery Hall Hotel ❀❀❀

An impressive setting for some sound, modern cooking

Worleston CW5 6DQ
Map no: 7 SJ65
Tel: 01270 610016
Chef: David Alton
Proprietors: Select Country Hotels Ltd.
Manager: Jeremy Rata
Cost: Fixed-price L £16.50/ D £28.50. H/wine from £12.45
Credit cards: ▨ ▩ ▩ ▣ OTHER
Times: Noon-last L 1.45pm, 7pm-last D 9.45pm
Menus: Fixed-price L & D
Seats: 30. No-smoking area
Additional: Children permitted before 8pm; ♥ dishes, vegan/other diets on request

The location of this impressive 17th-century country-house hotel is splendid: set within its own peaceful gardens and parkland of over 200 acres. Improvement and extension have changed the complexion of the place but private guests should not be unduly disturbed by any corporate shindig. David Alton cooks, producing modern British food with a style that is thoroughgoing; though flavours can on occasion be muted. Thus freshly made bread is sound, 'not startling', and a 'lovely' hot smoked salmon with crab and ginger beignets lacked the strong hit of ginger. Chosen at the same meal was poached brill on spinach with miniature vegetables and saffron sauce. This was more assured, with stunning presentation and wonderful aroma 'when the cloche was removed'. What impressed here was the relationship of all the ingredients, which melded well. Equal satisfaction has come from maize-fed Lancashire chicken with coriander tagliatelle, and a correctly made, very light peach and vanilla soufflé. Waitresses tend to be quiet and go through the motions of correct service. A good wine list is supplemented by an excellent cellar list with many fine wines.

Directions: On the B5074 north of Nantwich; situated 1.5 miles on right towards Worleston village

PRESTBURY, The White House ❀❀

A wide choice of dishes including lower fat choices is offered at this attractive village centre restaurant

The distinctive black and white restaurant in the centre of the village is one half of The White House, the other half being The Manor, where town house accommodation is provided. The restaurant has an intimate atmosphere created by the low ceiling, warm yellow walls and rich contrasting fabrics – fitting surroundings in which to enjoy chef proprietor Ryland Wakeham's skilful cooking. Service is professional and attentive, yet relaxed, and there is ample time to make one's choice from the menus in the small bar area. A wide variety of interesting dishes is offered, such as a delicious sauté of tender duck livers set around a potato pancake with warm goats' cheese and baby spinach, or ostrich satay with mange tout and tabbouleh, to ring the changes. A signature dish, enjoyed at an inspection meal, was grilled Cornish sea bass set on a smooth saffron mash with basil and sun-dried tomatoes, and spinach with nutmeg. The indecisive might like to conclude with a generous assortment entitled 'Le Grande Dessert'.

Directions: Village centre on A538 north of Macclesfield

Prestbury SK16 4HP
Map no: 7 SJ87
Tel: 01625 829376
Chefs: Ryland Wakeham, Mark Cunniffe and James Bagnall
Proprietors: Ryland & Judith Wakeham.
Manager: Phillip Harris
Cost: *Alc* £22.50, fixed-price L £11.95/D £16.50 H/wine £11(ltr) ❢ Service exc
Credit Cards: 🔲 🔲 🔲 🔲
Times: Last L 2pm, last D 10pm Closed Sun D, Mon L, Dec 25
Menus: *A la carte*, fixed-price L & D, bar menu
Seats: 70.
Additional: Children welcome, children's portions; ❤ dishes, vegan/other diets on request

PUDDINGTON, Craxton Wood ❀❀

Set in delightful grounds, a charming country-house hotel and restaurant offering sound French cooking

Parkgate Road L66 9PB
Map no: 7 SJ37
Tel: 0151 339 4717
Chef: James Minnis
Proprietor: Médard-Anthony Petranca
Cost: *Alc* £ 21.80-£32.50; fixed-price L & D £19.85. H/wine £12.85 Service inc
Credit cards: 🔲 🔲 🔲 🔲 OTHER
Times: Noon-last L 2pm, last D 10pm. Closed Sun and B/hols., last 2 weeks Aug & 1st week Sep
Menus: *A la carte*, fixed-price lunch and dinner
Seats: 85

Long service is a hallmark at the Petranca family's relaxed country-house hotel, surrounded by lawns, rose gardens and, at night, floodlit streams and woods. James Minnis has chalked up a good few years himself, and before coming here he cooked abroad. From his seasonal fixed-price menu (in French, with English sub-titles) comes this example of a Spring dinner – poached eggs served on a parfait of duck liver garnished with Madeira sauce, a main course of shallow-fried escalope of turkey, garnished with curry sauce on rice. Appearing on the *carte* were prawns fried in butter with garlic, ginger and julienne of leeks and carrots, roast loin of venison on sauerkraut served with a game sauce, or Dover sole fried in butter. The separate vegetarian menu, on which everything can be served as either a starter or main course, includes a medley of lettuces, avocado pear and grapefruit, and diced vegetables sautéed in olive oil with herbs and spices set in a filo basket. The wine list is very French, especially rich in Burgundies and Bordeaux.

Additional: Children welcome, children's portions; ♥ menu, other diets on request

Directions: Two miles from Wirral and Chester on A540

SANDIWAY, **Nunsmere Hall Hotel** ✿✿✿

A remarkable experience where both the setting and the food have an element of surprise

Tarporley Road CW8 2ES
Map no: 7 SJ67
Tel: 01606 889100
Chef: Paul Kitching
Proprietors: Malcolm & Julie McHardy
Cost: Alc £32, fixed-price L £19.50, H/wine £13.15
Service exc
Credit cards: 🁢 🁢 🁢 🁢 OTHER
Times: Noon-last L 2pm, 7pm-last D 10pm daily
Menus: A la carte D, fixed-price lunch, bar menu
Seats: 50. No smoking in the dining room
Additional: Children welcome (over 12 at D), children's portions; ♥ menu, vegan/other diets on request

Sir Aubrey Brocklebank, who built Nunsmere around 1900, masterminded the design of the Queen Mary, but died without seeing it completed. Son John (chairman of Cunard) encouraged the designing of the QE2. As shipbuilding had been in the Brocklebanks' blood since the 1700s, the 60-acre lake which almost surrounds the Hall should come as no surprise. Today's owners, Malcolm and Julie McHardy, have sympathetically extended and restored the place to its turn-of-the-century elegance.

Paul Kitching's cooking can be complex, but is soundly self-assured and he is not afraid of strong flavours or of experimenting with contrasting textures. From a repertoire that is inspired by France and the Mediterranean, seafood features prominently: cream of lobster bisque with herbs was noted for a distinctive taste, and steamed breast of chicken came with a robust crab and light curry sauce. Braised leg of duckling with creamed potatoes and black pudding, and poached farmhouse egg with deep-fried crispy spinach and morel mushrooms in a truffle cream sauce, roast whole squab with veal sweetbread and tarragon ravioli, roast loin of Cumbrian lamb with roasted garlic and aubergine wafers, or perhaps pan-fried Brixham scallops with lobster glaze and a herb beurre blanc are examples of an extensive range. The more conventional desserts include rich banana parfait with Amaretto and praline sauce, and a traditional lemon tart served with an orange sauce, or, for the indecisive, there is an assiette of desserts. Vegetarians have their own three-course menu and the Terrace Menu offers light meals overlooking the lawns. House wines are good, while the wide choice of half bottles will find favour. The main list is French, including a Connoisseur's Selection of about ten classic Burgundies and Bordeaux plus a wide-ranging gathering from elsewhere.

Directions: From Sandiway take the A49, one mile on left

TARPORLEY, The Wild Boar ❀

Originally a 17th-century hunting lodge, the Wild Boar is now an impressive hotel with an elegant restaurant. Main courses may include oven-baked saddle of venison scented with juniper, or a casserole of seafood with leeks and a dill sauce. For dessert the flambéed crêpe Suzette is worth trying

Menus: A la carte, fixed-price L & D
Seats: 70. Air conditioned
Additional: Children welcome, children's menu; ✿ menu, vegan/other diets on request
Directions: Two miles from Tarporley on A49 towards Whitchurch

Whitchurch Road CW6 9NW
Map no: 7 SJ56
Tel: 01829 260309
Chef: Andrew Griffiths
Proprietor: D G Woodward
Cost: Alc £35, fixed-price
L £13.50 (4 course)/D £19.50
(4 course) H/wine £9.90 ❢
Service exc
Credit cards: 🔳 🔳 🔳 🔳 OTHER
Times: Noon-last L 1.45pm,
7pm-last D 9.30pm

WARRINGTON,
Park Royal International ❀

☺ *This spacious, modern complex includes a large restaurant where a wide variety of dishes are available. Tom Rogers prides himself on making everything, including the ice-cream. Our inspector recently enjoyed the Scampi Bombay, tossed in butter with sliced banana and green grapes, lightly curried and served with rice*

Stretton WA4 4NS
Map: 7 SJ68
Tel: 01925 730706
Chef: Tom Rogers
Proprietor: n/a.
Manager: John Quine (Best
Western)
Cost: Alc £24, fixed-price
L £12.95, D £16.45. H/wine
£8.95 ❢ Service inc
Credit cards: 🔳 🔳 🔳 🔳 OTHER
Times: Noon-last L 2.30pm,
7pm-last D 10.00pm
Menus: A la carte, fixed-price
L & D, bar menu
Seats: 125
Additional: Children welcome,
children's menu; ✿ menu,
vegan available, other diets can
be accommodated

Directions: M56 exit 10, follow A49 towards Warrington, right towards Appleton Thorn at first set of lights, hotel 200yds on right

WILMSLOW, Stanneylands Hotel ❀❀

Traditional ingredients are handled in a modern way to produce fairly elaborate dishes in a formal hotel setting

Old-style formal but friendly service is characteristic of this attractive hotel, an extended red brick Edwardian residence in its own fine grounds. Menus are presented by the fireside in the cosy bar and meals are served in the panelled dining-rooms, where a harpist plays at dinner. Chef Matthew Barrett's food is quite elaborate with some interesting and unusual combinations. His menu is in three parts, with a *carte* offering some classical dishes such as smoked salmon, Dover sole and duck, with a meatless option such as pithivier of root vegetables and pulses on a white

Stanneylands Road SK9 4EY
Map no: 7 SJ88
Tel: 01625 525225
Chef: Matthew Barrett
Proprietor: Gordon Beech
Cost: Alc £35, fixed-price
L £13.50, D £25 (6 courses).
H/wine £10.50 ❢ Service exc
Credit cards: 🔳 🔳 🔳 🔳
Times: Last L 2pm/D 10pm.
Closed Dec 26-Jan 2
Menus: A la carte, fixed-price
L & D, pre-theatre, bar menu

wine butter sauce. Then there is a more experimental area of three daily items, the 'best from today's market', with more daring presentation and vegetables incorporated into the dish. From this section a main course of collops of monkfish baked with marinated Niçoise vegetables, grilled new potatoes and olive jus was sampled. Finally, there is a set six-course menu of 'interesting tastes and textures'. The highlight of the test meal, however, was a superb orange crème brûlée with Grand Marnier ice-cream.

Directions: Three miles from Manchester Airport. Minor road off B5166 at Styal to A34 between Wilmslow and Handforth. Bear right. Hotel is just after crossing river

Seats: 80. Partially air conditioned
Additional: Children welcome, children's menu; ❤ menu, vegan/other diets on request

CLEVELAND

EASINGTON, Grinkle Park Hotel ❁

Local produce, some grown in the hotel's own grounds, feature strongly on the various menus. Influenced by British modernism, the kitchen offers selections such as vegetable tartlet in a light curry sauce, rack of lamb in a rich sauce with rosemary, with summer pudding for dessert

Menus: A la carte, fixed-price L & D, bar menu
Seats: 80. No-smoking area
Additional: Children welcome; children's portions; ❤ dishes, other diets prior notice
Directions: Between Guisborough and Whitby off A171 or A174

Saltburn-by-the-Sea TS13 4UB
Map no: 8 NZ71
Tel: 01287 640515
Chef: Tim Backhouse
Proprietor: Bass.
Manager: Mrs Jane Norton
Cost: Alc £23, fixed-price
L £11.50/D £15.95. H/wine £9
Service exc
Credit cards: 🆇 ▦ ▦ 🄿
Times: Last L 1.45pm/D
9pm/9.30pm (Fri, Sat)

HARTLEPOOL, Krimo's Restaurant ❁

Mediterranean inspired food and a sea-front position combine to make Krimo's Restaurant extremely popular. Chef/owner Krimo Bouabda shows skill throughout his imaginative menu, which offers such dishes as mushroom paesano with a sage and cream sauce, or salmon steak gratin with a cheese crust topping

Times: Noon-last L 1.30pm, 7.30pm-last D 9pm. Closed Sun, Mon, Sat lunch, last 2 weeks Sept **Menus:** A la carte, fixed-price L & D
Seats: 56. Air conditioned **Additional:** Children over 8 welcome, children's portions; ❤ dishes, vegan/other diets on request
Directions: On A178 two miles from Hartlepool on the seafront

8 The Front
Seaton Carew TS25 1BS
Map no: 8 NZ53
Tel: 01429 266120
Chef: Krimo Bouabda
Proprietors: Krimo & Karen Bouabda
Cost: Alc £19, fixed-price L £6 (2 course)/D £13.95 (3 course). H/wine £7.50 Service exc
Credit cards: 🆇 ▦ OTHER

STOCKTON-ON-TEES, Parkmore Hotel ❁

Proximity to both the North Yorkshire Moors and the Yorkshire Dales is an added attraction for the Parkmore Hotel, a converted Victorian house set in its own grounds. Pleasing cooking – look out for terrine of game Weardale, baked duck breast in a sauce of lemon and honey with ginger, and banana meringue roulade

Menus: A la carte, fixed-price L & D, bar menu **Seats:** 65.
No smoking in dining room **Additional:** Children permitted, children's menu; ❤ menu, vegan/other dishes on request
Directions: On the A135 between Yarm and Stockton-on-Tees, almost opposite Eaglescliffe Golf Course

636 Yarm Road
Eaglescliffe TS16 0DH
Map no: 8 NZ41
Tel: 01642 786815
Chef: Dennis Ginsberg
Proprietor: Brian Reed (Best Western)
Cost: Alc £19.70; fixed-price
L £12.25/D £16.75. H/wine
£7.75 Service exc
Credit cards: 🆇 ▦ ▦ 🄿 OTHER
Times: Last L 2pm/D 9.45pm

CORNWALL & ISLES OF SCILLY

ALTARNUN, Penhallow Manor Hotel ✿

☺ *Daphne du Maurier visited Penhallow Manor, and featured it in her novel 'Jamaica Inn'. Imaginative dishes based on fresh local produce (and served in generous portions) are a strength. Expect cream of watercress soup, tomato and basil sorbet, and breast of chicken cooked with sherry and tarragon*

Seats: 30. No smoking in dining room **Additional:** Children over 12 permitted; ✿ dishes, vegan/other diets on request
Directions: From Launceston A30 8 miles; 1 mile after B3257 take slip road to Altarnun, hotel near the church

Penhallow PL15 7SJ
Map no: 2 SX28
Tel: 01566 82606
Chef: Julia Cubbidge
Proprietors: John & Julia Cubbidge
Cost: Fixed-price D £ 17.50 (4 courses). H/wine £7.50
Service exc
Credit cards: 🌣 💳 💳
Times: Last L 2pm, last D 8.30pm Closed Jan 4-Feb 10
Menus: Fixed-price D, L menu

BLACKWATER, Pennypots Restaurant ✿✿

Tiny restaurant with an increasingly large reputation for accomplished modern cooking

The pint-sized simply furnished 18th-century cottage happily no longer has to suffer the thunder of traffic from the A30, now the by-pass is in place. Kevin Viner's adventurous style of cooking derives from the modern British school. Twice baked cheese soufflé, ravioli of crab and langoustines, fillet of venison coated with bacon and hazelnuts on a prune and Cognac sauce with spiced pears, are typical of the genre. A recent test meal started with tiny appetisers of skewered Tandoori chicken, a crouton topped with smoked salmon and avocado in crème fraîche. At the table, an interesting selection of bread rolls was offered; basil bread, in particular, stood out. A good terrine of chicken liver pâté was served with a warm salad of mushrooms and hazelnut dressing, not a perfect pairing as the salad became soggy. After a complimentary sorbet, the main course of a duo of duck, the breast grilled with honey and cooked pink, and the leg confit just barely clinging to the bone, was served with a thin red wine sauce, well contrasted with segments of pink grapefruit. The selection of fresh vegetables included sweet potato cooked in cream and garlic. Desserts are a Pennypot strength and a vanilla crème brûlée with strawberries poached in Grand Marnier and a caramel syrup was well balanced and delicious.

Directions: Just off the A30, 0.75 mile from village centre

Truro TR4 8EY
Map no: 2 SW74
Tel: 01209 820347
Chef: Kevin Viner and Greg Laskey
Proprietors: Kevin & Jane Viner
Cost: Alc £24-£28.50. H/wine £7.95. Service exc
Credit cards: 🌣 💳
Times: 7pm-last D 9.30pm. Closed Sun, Mon, 4 wks in Winter
Menu: *A la carte* D
Seats: 30. No smoking in dining room until after 10pm
Additional: Children welcome; children's portions; ✿ dishes, other diets on request

CALSTOCK, Danescombe Valley ✿✿

Dinner in the tiny dining-room of one of Cornwall's great little country house hotels is a magical experience

The house, with its fine verandahs, bears a passing resemblance to one of Mississippi's old antebellum mansions. It was built in Georgian times for Lord Ashburton on one of the most beautiful stretches of the tidal River Tamar, in a spot known locally, and still understandably, as Hidden Valley. The traditional slate-floored bar, leading on to the terrace with its panoramic views of the river, is the natural meeting place before dinner. Italian-born Anna Smith's cooking relies entirely on local fresh produce to produce

Lower Kelly PL18 9RY
Map no: 2 SX46
Tel: 01822 832 414
Chef: Anna Smith
Proprietor: Martin & Anna Smith
Cost: Fixed-price D £30 (4 courses). House/w £8 ❢
Service inc
Credit cards: 🌣 💳 💳 💳 OTHER
Times: 7.30pm-Last D 8pm. Closed Wed, Thurs; Nov-March
Menus: Fixed-price dinner
Seats: 12

Danescombe Valley

Additional: Children over 12 permitted; no smoking in dining-room; ❂ dishes/other diets by prior arrangement

imaginative no-choice, four-course dinners. Although best described as modern British, her style is also influenced by her native country. A typical meal could consist of asparagus baked with Parma ham, baked marinated chicken breast with red pepper, sun-dried tomato and black olive sauce, fresh vegetables, and mascarpone and chocolate tart, or perhaps Italian omelette with herbs and salad, spiced duck breast roasted with honey and soy sauce, and ricotta and pear strudel. West Country unpasteurised farmhouse cheeses are served before dessert. The extensive wine list is a tribute to many hours of research and compilation by Martin Smith and includes a large number of Italian wines.

Directions: 0.5 mile west of Calstock village. Pass under viaduct. Turn right and follow road parallel to river 0.5 mile.

CONSTANTINE BAY, Treglos Hotel ❀

☺ *Under the same ownership for over 25 years, this attractive hotel is a short walk from the beach, overlooking the spectacular North Cornwall coastline. Local produce is a speciality, especially fresh fish, and choices may include Helford River oysters and tenderloin of beef with marmalade of onions and mushrooms*

Menus: A la carte, fixed-price L & D, bar menu, pre-theatre
Seats: 100. Air conditioned. No smoking in the dining room
Additional: Children permitted, children's menu; ❂ menu, vegan/other diets on request
Directions: Take B3276 (Constantine Bay). At Constantine Bay stores turn left, hotel 50 yds on left

Padstow PL28 8JH
Map no: 2 SW87
Tel: 01841 520727
Chef: Paul Becker
Proprietors: Jim Barlow (Crown Consort)
Cost: *Alc* from £20, fixed-price L £11.50 (6 course)/D £20 (7 course) Wine £8.50. Service inc
Credit cards: ▨ ▦
Times: Last L 1.30pm/D 9.15pm. Closed mid Nov-Mar

FALMOUTH, Greenbank Hotel ❀

☺ *Greenbank is ideally situated on the waters edge, and enjoys excellent views of the bay and surrounding hillside. The hotel's restaurant, Nightingales, offers an interesting, well balanced choice of carefully prepared dishes, perhaps breast of wood pigeon with a creamy leek and tarragon compote*

Menus: A la carte, fixed-price L & D, bar menu **Additional:** Children welcome, children's menu; ❂ dishes, vegan/other diets on request
Directions: 500yds past Falmouth Marina overlooking the water

Harbourside TR11 2SR
Map no: 2 SW83
Tel: 01326 312440
Chef: Paul Prinn
Proprietor: C N Gebhard
Cost: *Alc* £21, fixed-price L £9/D £15.95. H/wine £7.50. Service exc
Credit cards: ▨ ▦ ▦ ▣ OTHER
Times: Last L 2pm/D 9.45pm. Closed 24 Dec-14 Jan
Seats: 70. Air conditioned

FALMOUTH, **Penmere Manor Hotel** ❀

☺ *Consistent food is served in Penmere Manor's Bolitho's Restaurant. Choices from the daily-changing fixed-price menu or carte are varied; seafood features with fresh local lobster a highlight. Otherwise expect fresh mussels poached in cream, and medallions of fillet steak glazed with Stilton and cream*

Menus: A la carte D, fixed-price D, bar menu
Seats: 80. Air conditioned. No smoking in dining room
Additional: Children welcome, children's portions until 7.45pm; ❤ dishes, vegan/other diets on request
Directions: Turn off Hill Head roundabout towards Buddock 1 mile, then left into Mongleath road

Mongleath Road TR11 4PN
Map no: 2 SW83
Tel: 01326 211411
Chef: James Spargo and Richard Holland
Proprietors: Andrew Pope and Elizabeth Rose (Best Western)
Cost: Alc £24, fixed-price D £19 (4 course) H/wine £6.95 ❢
Service inc
Credit cards: 🔲 🔲 🔲 🔲 OTHER
Times: 7 pm-last D 9 pm daily
Closed Xmas

FALMOUTH, **Royal Duchy Hotel** ❀

☺ *Diners can choose from a variety of menus at the Royal Duchy, a fine seafront hotel with superb bay views. A recent meal included potted shellfish mousse wrapped in oak-smoked salmon, fennel and watercress soup, dill and honey-roasted gammon; with white chocolate terrine for dessert*

Cliff Road TR11 2QN
Map no: 2 SW83
Tel: 01326 313042
Chef: Desmond Turland
Proprietors: Brend Hotels. Manager: Darryl Reburn
Cost: Alc £15.95 min, fixed-price L £8.95/D £15.95. H/wine £7.95 ❢ Service exc
Credit cards: 🔲 🔲 🔲 🔲 OTHER
Times: 12.30-last L 2pm/D 9pm
Menus: A la carte, fixed-price L & D, bar lunches
Seats: 100. No-smoking area
Additional: Children welcome, children's menu; ❤ menu, vegan/other diets on request

Directions: Hotel is at Castle end of promenade

FOWEY,
Food for Thought Restaurant ❀❀

☺ *Beautifully cooked fresh local seafood is the speciality of this restaurant, located right on the quay*

An attractive building of Cornish stone with a beamed interior, this restaurant enjoys an excellent location on the quay. Not surprisingly, fresh local seafood, cooked to perfection by chef patron Martin Billingsley, is a feature. Try the scallop mousse with a carrot and Sauternes butter sauce, or a rendezvous of fresh fish and shellfish with a langoustine sauce. Viands, however, should not be overlooked, and another recommendation is breast of chicken filled with a mousse of wild mushrooms served with a sweetcorn pancake and a rather fierce tarragon sauce. Traditional puddings, all of

The Quay PL23 1AT
Map no: 2 SX15
Tel: 01726 832221
Chef: *Martin Billingsley*
Proprietor: *Martin Billingsley*
Cost: Alc £22, fixed-price dinner £16.95. H/wine £6.95
Credit cards: 🔲 🔲
Times: *7pm-Last D 9pm. Closed lunchtimes, Sun, Jan & Feb*
Menus: *A la carte, fixed-price dinner, Menu Exceptionel*
Seats: 38
Additional: *Children permitted;* ❤ *dish*

which are made on the premises, include bread and butter pudding, and sticky toffee pudding served with toffee sauce and Cornish clotted cream. A daily cheese selection is available as an alternative, and freshly brewed coffee comes with good petits fours. The house wine has been particularly well chosen, offering a choice of eight wines including Champagne. Car parking is restricted, so it is best to park in the town car park and walk down to the quay.

Directions: Walk down to the quay from the town centre car park

FOWEY, **Marina Hotel** ⚜

☺ *There is a superb view of the estuary from the waterfront restaurant of this small, family-run hotel. Locally caught fish is a speciality, but meat and game are equally good, especially as prime quality ingredients are combined to produce interesting dishes*

Menus: A la carte, fixed-price D, bar menu
Seats: 28. No smoking in dining room
Additional: Children permitted; ❤ dishes, other diets on request
Directions: In Fowey, drive down Lostwithiel Street, turn right into the Esplanade by Mace grocers. Hotel 50yds on left

The Esplanade PL23 1HY
Map no: 2 SX15
Tel: 01726 833315
Chef: Stephen Vincent
Proprietors: John & Carol Roberts
Cost: Alc £18, fixed-price D £16. H/wine £7.95. Service exc
Credit cards: 🔲 🔲 🔲 OTHER
Times: 11.30am-2pm, 7pm-last D 9pm. Closed Sun, Jan & Feb

GOLANT, **Cormorant Hotel** ⚜⚜

Delightful riverside hotel where fresh fish is a major draw

The small fishing village of Golant is a tranquil setting for this charming hotel, set high above the Fowey Estuary. Stunning views are to be seen from the full length picture windows in the public rooms. The food is good, too. Locally caught seafood is the order of the day, prepared with the freshest local produce. Lemon sole, brill and Dover sole are frequently available. The cooking has a distinctly French accent, but with an awareness of what is fashionable in modern British cooking. From a choice of fixed price menus starters such as scallop salad, fresh crab gratinée, moules marinière or brochette of king prawns and steak with a teriyaki sauce could be followed by salmon served on a bed of spinach with a tarragon sauce, pork tenderloin with ginger and pear sauce, fillet of sea bass with a fennel with Pernod and cream sauce, or sirloin steak au poivre. To finish, an exceptional bread and butter pudding studded with apricots marinated in Cognac. Service is caring.

Directions: Off A390 (Lostwithiel to St Austell) turn to Golant. Go right to end (almost to waters edge), entrance on right

Fowey PL23 1LL
Map no: 2 SX15
Tel: 01726 833426
Chef: Geoffrey Buckie and Gilles Gaucher
Proprietor: Sharon Buckle
Cost: Alc £30, fixed-price dinner £21.50 (4 courses), £29. Service exc
Credit cards: 🔲 🔲 🔲
Times: Midday-Last L 2pm, 7pm-Last D 9pm. Closed Jan
Menus: A la carte, light lunch, fixed-price dinner
Seats: 25. No smoking in restaurant
Additional: Children over 12 permitted; ❤ dishes; Vegan/other diets on request

> Ricotta is a by-product of cheese, made from whey, a watery milk residue. The two traditional 'ricotte' are 'piemontese' and 'romana', the latter being the one that is known in Britain. However, the 'ricotta romano' made for export, or made outside Italy, is made from the whey of cow's milk, whilst the genuine Italian 'romano' is made from the whey of ewe's milk that goes to make pecorino. The English 'ricotta' is quite acceptable for fillings and some desserts.

HELFORD, **Riverside Restaurant** ❀❀

Fish features strongly at this relaxed, creekside restaurant

On balmy summer evenings the atmosphere at the Riverside Restaurant is magical. Narrow lanes must first be negotiated before arriving at the cottage-style restaurant which sits by the side of a creek in the relaxed depths of Cornwall. Susie Darrel's starters and main courses are her strengths, and these could include steamed local mussels, lobster bisque or baked monkfish. Indeed, fish features strongly on the fixed-price menu, which is dependent on the local catch. The excellent vegetables are also local, and are always carefully cooked. A recent test meal started with an appetiser of large, garlicky prawns served hot. A folded pancake, filled with local scallops, lobster and clams accompanied by a well-balanced lobster sauce continued the meal in style. To follow, neatly trimmed west country lamb was chosen, served with a smooth red wine sauce with rosemary. A selection of English and French cheeses with grapes and dried apricots finished the meal. Edward Darrel's passion is his extensive wine list, featuring wines from both the New and Old Worlds and a good selection of half bottles.

Directions: The restaurant is clearly signposted in Helford village

Helford TR12 6JU
Map no: 2 SW72
Tel: 01326 231443
Chef: Susie Darrell
Proprietor: Susie Darrell
Cost: Fixed-price D £30 (4 course). H/wine £10 ▮ Service inc
Credit cards: None taken
Times: 7pm-last D 9pm
Menu: Fixed-price D
Seats: 30
Additional: Children permitted (over 12), children's high tea; other diets on request

HELSTON, **Nansloe Manor Hotel** ❀

☺ *This small 18th-century manor house stands in four acres of wooded grounds, surrounded by farmland. Local produce is used whenever possible, and all dishes are skilfully prepared using modern styles of presentation and spicing. The sweets, however, are more traditional, and come with bowls of Cornish clotted cream*

Menus: *A la carte* D, fixed-price Sun L, bar L
Seats: 30. No smoking in dining room
Additional: Children permitted (over 10); ♥ dishes, other diets on request
Directions: 300 yds from junction of A394 & A394 down a well-signed drive

Meneage Road TR13 0SB
Map no: 2 SW62
Tel: 01326 574691
Chefs: Martin Jones and Nick Tattersall
Proprietors: John & Wendy Pyatt
Cost: Alc £19, Sun L £11.50. H/wine £8.50. No service charge
Credit cards: ▨ ▨
Times: Last bar L 1.45pm (Mon-Sat), last Sun L 1.15pm/D 8.30pm

LISKEARD, **Well House Hotel** ❀❀❀

Modern British cooking, professionally prepared from quality local ingredients, in a country house setting

The restaurant at Well House is characterised by a professional approach in all areas. Careful shopping ensures a fine standard of ingredients with an emphasis on local produce. Fish from Looe is a feature, and our inspector enjoyed wonderful red mullet and scallops, which had abundant flavour and were served without too much elaboration. The bakery and vegetables reflect the same attention to detail which has secured the restaurant's reputation for good food. Chef Wayne Pearson presents a fixed-price dinner menu of two, three or four courses, producing dishes of outstanding quality. Typical examples from his daily dinner menu are starters of chicken liver and pink peppercorn parfait with kumquat chutney, and green bean and chorizo sausage salad with blue cheese dressing. These might be followed by steamed fillets of John Dory with an orange and dill cream sauce, or best end of lamb with

St Keyne PL14 4RN
Map no: 2 SX26
Chef: Wayne Pearson
Proprietor: Nick Wainford
Cost: Fixed-price L/D £19.95-£24.70. H/wine £8.50
Credit cards: ▨ ▨ OTHER
Times: Last L 1.30pm, last D 9pm
Menus: Fixed-price L & D daily
Seats: 32. No pipes or cigars
Additional: Children permitted (over 8 at D); ♥ dishes, vegan/other diets on request

Well House Hotel

ratatouille and rosemary jus. A selection of West Country cheeses with walnut bread is an optional course, and there is a tempting range of home-made puddings to finish. Marbled chocolate marquise is a favourite, served with orange and cardamom anglaise. The wine list has been refashioned and now offers a wider choice of New World wines and a decent selection of half bottles. The hotel's situation is idyllic, a country house with attractive gardens and mature grounds tucked away in the Looe Valley. Built by a tea planter with an understanding of Cornish light, the rooms are bright and airy, retaining much of their original refinement; and in the summer guests may also dine al fresco.

Directions: At St Keyne Church follow signs to St Keyne Well, the restaurant is 0.5 miles further

---

MARAZION,

Mount Haven Hotel ❀

The spectacular position overlooking St Michael's Mount is complemented by consistent cooking. Both the carte and the daily changing fixed-price menus are based on fresh local produce and offer a good choice, perhaps leek and cheddar cheese soup, and medallions of lamb with redcurrant and port sauce

Menus: A la carte D, fixed-price D & Sun L **Seats:** 50. No smoking **Additional:** Children permitted, children's portions; ❤ dishes, vegan/other diets on request
Directions: Leave A30 Penzance/Cambourne road at Marazion turning, go through the village to end of the built-up area

Turnpike Road TR17 0DQ
Map no: 2 SW53
Tel: 01736 710249
Chef: Simon Morley-Smith
Proprietors: John & Delyth James (Minotel)
Cost: Alc £15-£26, fixed-price D £17.50/Sun L £8.50. H/wine £8.50 Service inc
Credit cards: 🔳 🈺 🈺
Times: Noon-last L 2pm, last D 9pm (8.30pm Nov-Mar). Closed L Nov-Mar, Dec 23-28

'A la piémontaise' describes the various dishes of poultry, meat and fish that incorporate a risotto, usually accompanied by white Piedmont truffles. 'A la piémontaise' can also refer to dishes of the Piedmont region of northern Italy such as polenta, ravioli and macaroni that do not necessarily feature truffles. Pastries 'à la piémontaise' are usually based on another famous product of Piedmont - hazelnuts.

MAWNAN SMITH, **Trelawne Hotel** ✿

☺ *The fixed-price menu of this rural hotel offers modern British cooking prepared from fresh local produce. At inspection, quenelles of chicken liver pâté with pine nuts and lardons of bacon, and loin of lamb with diced mango and a duxelle of mushrooms, were enjoyed*

Directions: Three miles S of Falmouth on coast road to Mawnan Smith

Near Falmouth TR11 5HS
Map no: 2 SW72
Tel: 01326 250226
Chefs: Grant Mather and Nigel Woodland
Proprietor: G Paul Gibbons
Cost: Fixed-price L & D £22.50 (5 courses). H/wine £7.50. Service inc
Credit cards: 🆇 🖭 🖭 🖭
Times: Noon-last L 1.30pm, 7pm-last D 8.30pm. Closed Jan & Feb
Menus: Fixed-price L & D, bar menu
Seats: 36. No smoking
Additional: Children welcome (over 7 at D), children's portions; ❤ dishes, vegan/other diets on request

NEWBRIDGE,
The Newbridge Restaurant ✿

☺ *Located midway between Penzance and St Just, this roadside restaurant offers Italian cooking in a plant-filled conservatory. A typical meal could begin with tagliatelle in a cream sauce with mushrooms, mozzarella and garlic, followed by tender medallions of fillet steak cooked to order with a cream and Dolcelatte sauce*

Menus: A la carte D, fixed-price D
Seats: 54. No-smoking area.
Additional: Children welcome, children's portions; ❤ dishes, vegan/other diets on request
Directions: On A3071 in village of Newbridge

Newbridge TR20 8QH
Map no: 2 SW43
Tel: 01736 63777
Chefs: Sybil Anne & Hamish Blows
Proprietors: W & S A Blows
Cost: Alc £16, fixed-price D £17 (4 course). H/wine £7.50. Service exc
Credit cards: 🆇 🖭 🖭
Times: Last D 9.30pm. Closed Sun & Mon winter, 3 wks Nov

NEWQUAY, **Hotel Bristol** ✿

☺ *Overlooking the sea, this is a truly traditional family-run resort hotel. The kitchen prepares a short menu, but offers a reasonably varied choice. Look out for simple dishes such as cream of potato and leek soup, or roast duck, all cooked with care to retain the natural flavours*

Menus: A la carte, fixed-price L & D, bar menu **Seats:** 150
Additional: Children welcome (over 4 at D), children's menu; ❤ dishes, vegan/other diets on request
Directions: From A3058 follow signs for seafront hotels for 2.5 miles along Henver Road and Narrowcliff

Narrowcliff TR7 2PQ
Map no: 2 SW86
Tel: 01637 875181
Chef: Malcolm Jackson
Proprietors: The Young family
Cost: Alc £20, fixed-price L £10/ D £16.50. H/wine £8 Service inc
Credit cards: 🆇 🖭 🖭 🖭 OTHER
Times: Noon-last L 1.45pm, 7.15pm-last D 8.45pm

NEWQUAY, **Whipsiderry Hotel** 🏵

☺ *Imaginative French and English cooking is served at the Whipsiderry, standing in an elevated position overlooking Porth Beach. The menu may offer dishes such as chicken liver pâté flavoured with port, Provençal fish soup and poached Scottish salmon fillet with a light hollandaise*

Times: Last L 2pm/D 8.30pm Daily
Menus: A la carte, fixed-price L & D, bar menu
Seats: 50. No smoking in dining room
Additional: Children welcome, children's menu; ❤ menu, vegan/ other diets on request
Directions: B3276 (Padstow) turn R 0.5 mile from Newquay

Trevelgue Road
Porth TR7 3LY
Map no: 2 SW86
Tel: 01637 874777
Chef: Serge Ouggin
Proprietors: private.
Managers: Andy & Lisa Burbidge
Cost: Alc £12.95, fixed-price
L £10.95 (4 course)/D £14.95
(6 course) H/wine £6.95 ❢
Service inc
Credit cards: 🆒 ⚏

PADSTOW, **Old Custom House Inn** 🏵

☺ *A good range of traditional dishes are served in this former excise house, set in four 17th-century harbourside properties. A genial atmosphere prevails in both the inn and the separate restaurant. A reasonably-priced wine list with good European and New World selections is also available*

Menus: A la carte, fixed price L/D, Sun lunch, bar menu
Seats: 80. Air conditioned.
Additional: Children welcome, children's menu; ❤ dishes; Vegan/other diets on request
Directions: Follow one-way system into town, on the quayside, 2 minutes from harbourside car park

South Quay PL28 8ED
Map no: 2 SW97
Tel: 01841 532359
Chef: Guy Pompa
Proprietor: St Austell Brewery.
Manager: Linda Allen
Cost: Alc £15.00, fixed-price D
£10. H/wine £6.15. Service inc.
Cover charge
Credit cards: 🆒 ⚏ ⚏ 💳 OTHER
Times: Noon-Last L 2pm. 6.30-
Last D 9pm daily

PADSTOW,
St Petroc's House Restaurant 🏵🏵

Well-produced, good-value food in a lively informal atmosphere

Set in the fifth oldest building in Padstow, St Petroc's is very much an informal extension of the Seafood Restaurant, although it is rather a hilly walk away. Rick Stein cooks here on a couple of nights in the summer, but otherwise Paul Hearn and Paul Rippley run the show. The menu is short, changed frequently, and interesting. Cooking skills and quality of produce are good and include the likes of moules marinière, grilled local sausages with spring onion mashed potato and onion gravy, and chargrilled chopped lamb steak with tomato and coriander. An April inspection meal yielded 'garbure béarnaise' – a soup from south western France – which was packed with vegetables and flavoured with garlic, fresh herbs, haricot beans and duck confit. A fillet of haddock, which followed, had a lovely texture and was beautifully cooked, served with a sherry vinegar and butter sauce, and new potatoes and spring greens. For dessert, a light bread and butter pudding with an apricot glaze and a rich and creamy custard. The espresso is excellent.

Directions: Follow one-way around harbour, take first left, situated on the right

4 New Street PL28 8EA
Map no: 2 SW97
Tel: 01841 532 700
Chef: P Hearn
Proprietor: Rick Stein
Cost: Fixed-price L/D £14.95
(3 courses). H/wine £9.50 ❢
Service exc
Credit cards: 🆒 ⚏ OTHER.
Times: 12.30pm-last L 2.15pm,
7pm-last D 9.30pm. Closed
Mon; Dec 2-Dec 30 1995
Menus: Fixed-price L & D
Seats: 38
Additional: Children welcome, children's portions; ❤ dishes, other diets on request

PADSTOW,
The Seafood Restaurant ❁❁❁

Rick Stein's acclaimed restaurant still sets the pace for new wave fish cookery

The fish at The Seafood Restaurant, located bang on the quayside, comes straight off the boat, through the kitchen door and practically hurls itself straight into the pan. Little wonder then that Rick Stein, with access to such quality and with his superior cooking skills, has become established as a celebrity chef. He has the French understanding of simplicity when it comes to fish cookery – grilled queenies are served with noisette butter, hake with spring onion, mashed potato and morels. A whole Dover sole is seasoned with sea salt and lime, and cooked unskinned on the grill; local Padstow lobsters are grilled with fine herbes or served steamed with mayonnaise. Dishes are frequently given an intriguing East-West fillip by an unconventional use of spicing (mussels, cockles and clams masala, perhaps, or chargrilled fillets of Dover sole with coriander, cumin and chilli). Occasionally the unerring touch falters. Fillets of turbot with stir-fried spinach were nearly mugged by a tomato and coriander sauce.

Southern European influences are also evident in a classic fish and shellfish soup with rouille and Parmesan, hake with clams in green sauce, and chargrilled monkfish with a saffron and roasted red pepper dressing. Meat eaters, however, need not feel like the man in the Bateman cartoon: steak au poivre and squab with stir-fry cabbage and garlic chives may be on the menu. Desserts tend to the traditional with, for example, trifle, apple crumble tart and cinnamon ice-cream, or a light, perfectly spiced hot bread pudding with Armagnac. It's worth noting that at lunchtimes there is no minimum charge, so drop in for a bowl of moules or half a dozen Helfords on ice, as the fancy takes. Two other strings to the Stein bow are the sister bistro at St Petroc, and the well-stocked deli and bakery.

Directions: Situated on South Quay

Riverside PL28 8BY
Map no: 2 SW97
Tel: 01841 532485
Chef: C R Stein
Proprietor: C R Stein
Cost: *Alc* £33.45, fixed-price L £21.25/D £29.30. H/wine £9.50 ❢ Service exc
Credit cards: ⬛ ▦ OTHER
Times: Last L 2.15pm, Last D 10pm. Closed Sun, Dec 17-Feb 2
Menus: *A la carte*, fixed-price L & D
Seats: 75. Air conditioned
Additional: Children welcome (over 5 at D), children's portions; other diets to order

PENZANCE, Tarbert Hotel ❁

Daily fish specials add to the standard menu choices at this terraced Georgian house, located just off the town centre. Dishes might include venison pâté, duckling breast with apricot and brandy sauce, pan-fried grey mullet, Mediterranean prawns and large Cornish Megrim sole

Cost: *Alc* £16; fixed-price D £12.50. Wine £7.75. Service exc
Credit cards: ⬛ ▦ ▦ OTHER
Additional: Children permitted; children's portions; other diets on request
Directions: At top of Market Jew Street continue into Alverton Street. At traffic lights turn right into Clarence Street

11-12 Clarence Street
Map no: 2 SW43
Tel: 01736 63758
Chef: Phillip Thomas
Proprietors: Logis/Minotels. Managers: Patti & Jullian Evans
Seats: 32. No pipes or cigars in restaurant
Times: Last D 8.30pm. Closed 23 Dec-26 Jan

> Kir, the famous Burgundy aperitif based on cassis and dry white wine, is named after the late Canon Felix Kir, mayor of Dijon during the Second World War and hero of the Resistance.

POLPERRO, Claremont Hotel ❀

☺ *Situated near the centre of this popular fishing village, the Claremont provides friendly service in a relaxed atmosphere. The extensive choice of dishes may include crab bisque, fillet of sole with pieces of monkfish and salmon, and hazelnut meringue served with clotted cream. Puddings and pastries are all home-made*

Menus: A la carte, fixed-price D, seafood menu
Seats: 18.
Additional: Children welcome, children's menu; ❶ dishes, vegan/ other diets on request
Directions: Village centre

Fore Street PL13 2RG
Map no: 2SX25
Tel: 01503 272241
Chef: G Couturier
Proprietor: G Couturier (Logis of GB)
Cost: Alc £16, fixed-price D £11 H/wine £ 4.85 (0.5 l) ❢
Service inc
Credit cards: ▨ ▦ ▧ OTHER
Times: Last L 2pm/last D 8pm
Closed Sun, Oct 10- April 1

POLPERRO, The Kitchen ❀❀

☺ *A wide ranging menu, with vegetarian options and fish as a speciality, is offered at this friendly little restaurant*

A pretty candlelit cottage restaurant run by Ian and Vanessa Bateson. He cooks with a natural self-taught approach to quality fresh ingredients, all prepared to order, with seafood as a speciality. The *carte* offers a huge range of dishes with over a dozen starters, such as roast vegetables and noodle salad, gravad lax muffins, Cornish sausages, and soup of the day from the blackboard selection. A bewildering choice of main courses is divided between shellfish, poultry, meat, a serious vegetarian list, and daily specials – usually fresh fish. Dishes reflect an eclectic range of treatments with influences from around the world, and might offer crab dijonnaise (local baked white crabmeat with Dijon mustard and a cream sauce); chicken piri-piri (boneless breast of chicken baked with a hot chilli pepper paste); Aberdeen Angus rib steak cooked with Cajun spices, and a Brazil and cashew nut loaf. The minimum purchase per person is a main course, and to finish there is a choice of dessert or cheese.

Directions: Between the harbour & the car park

The Coombes PL13 2RQ
Map no: 2 SX25
Tel: 01503 272780
Chefs: Ian & Vanessa Bateson
Proprietors: Ian & Vanessa Bateson
Cost: Alc about £20. H/wine £8.90 ❢ Service exc
Credit cards: ▨ ▧
Times: 7pm-last D 9.30pm (later in Summer), Closed Sun, Mon/Tue low season, Nov-Easter
Menus: A la carte D
Seats: 24. No smoking in dining room
Additional: Children over 12 permitted; ❶ menu, other diets on request

POLZEATH, The Pentire Rocks Cornish Cottage Hotel ❀❀

A family-run hotel where the chef has a serious approach to cooking and the menu offers fresh local fish as a speciality

Clive and Christine Mason's well-run small hotel, overlooking a beautiful part of the North Cornish coast, continues to offer visitors a relaxed, informal atmosphere in which to enjoy a break by the sea. Chef Robert Windsor has recently taken over in the kitchen, and initial reports indicate sound cooking with a modern slant, based on a thoughtful, assured style, and influenced by fresh local produce. Fish is a speciality. A recent test meal started with a blanquette of scallops with Dublin Bay prawns in a creamy sauce with ginger and cucumber, which was followed by a robust carrot and orange soup. Although a roast breast of duck lacked the promised jasmine flavour it was still 'delicious'. Attention to detail is apparent in the careful cooking of vegetables, and in the choice of locally baked bread. Puddings include a gloriously flavoured hot

Wadebridge PL27 6US
Map no: 2 SW97
Tel: 01208 862213
Chefs: Carl Morrison and Robert Windsor
Proprietors: Clive & Christine Mason
Cost: Alc £20, fixed-price D £20 (5 course), Sun L £8.50. H/wine £8.50 ❢ Service exc
Credit cards: ▨ ▦ ▧ ▣ OTHER
Times: Noon-last L 1.30pm, last D 9pm. Closed Jan
Menus: A la carte & fixed-price D, Sun L, bar lunch menu
Seats: 40. No smoking in dining room

The Pentire Rocks
Cornish Cottage Hotel

Additional: Children welcome
(over 12 at D), children's menu;
❷ menu, vegan/other diets on
request

Grand Marnier soufflé accompanied by slices of orange in syrup
which is strongly recommended. Cafetière coffee comes with
handmade chocolates which unfortunately lack finesse.

Directions: From Wadebridge/Camelford pass the 'Bee Centre' and
take the right fork. The hotel is 300yds on the right

PORT GAVERNE, **Port Gaverne Hotel** ✿

☺ *An atmospheric 17th-century Cornish inn situated in a sheltered cove*
half a mile from the fishing village of Port Isaac. Fresh local fish is, of
course, a speciality. Menu selections may include Cornish crab soup, fresh
Port Isaac lobster, or roast breast of duck with an Armagnac sauce, for
meat eaters

Near Port Isaac PL29 3SQ
Map no: 2 SX08
Tel: 01208 880244
Chef: Ian Brodey
Proprietor: Midge Ross
(Hospitality Hotels of Cornwall)
Cost: *Alc* £18.50. H/wine £5.95
Service exc
Times: Last L 2pm/D 9pm
Closed Jan 6-Feb 17
Menu: *A la carte* L & D
Seats: 40. No smoking in dining
room
Additional: Children permitted
(over 7 at D); ❷ menu,
vegan/other diets on request

Directions: Signposted from B3314 2 miles from Delabole

Pissaladière is a speciality of the Nice region. The base
is either bread dough or shortcrust pastry spread with a
layer of onions, garnished with anchovy fillets and olives
and spread with pissalat - a purée of anchovies mixed
with cloves, thyme, bay leaf and pepper and olive oil -
before being cooked. It can be eaten hot or cold.

PORTHLEVEN, Critchards Restaurant ❀

The Harbour Road TR13 9JA
Map no: 2 SW62

☺ *Located in the centre of the village overlooking the harbour, this attractive restaurant specialises in local fish. Lobster, clams and oyster can be ordered with 24 hours notice (subject to availability), and other dishes may include woodland mushroom soup, and fillet of locally smoked haddock*

Tel: 01326 562407
Chef: Jo Critchard
Proprietors: Steve & Jo Critchard
Cost: Alc D £21, H/wine £8.60
Service exc
Credit cards: ▨ ▩ OTHER
Times: 6.30pm-last D 9.30pm.
Closed Sun, Jan, some dates Nov
& Dec

Menu: A la carte D (Seafood Rest)
Seats: 44. No smoking in dining room
dditional: Children over 5 welcome, children's menu; ❶ menu, vegan/other diets on request
Directions: Overlooking the harbour

PORTSCATHO, Gerrans Bay Hotel ❀

Gerrans TR2 5ED
Map no: 2 SW83

☺ *Traditional English food is served at this relaxed, family-run hotel in a pleasant village setting within walking distance of Portscatho beach. Fresh local produce features alongside home-grown herbs and may include avocado mousse, home-made tomato and red pepper soup, and rack of lamb with apricot and mint stuffing*

Tel: 01872 580338
Chef: Ann Greaves
Proprietors: Ann & Brian
Greaves
Cost: Fixed-price D £18
(5 course)/Sun L £9 (4 course).
H/wine £7.
Credit cards: ▨ ▩ ▩ OTHER
Times: Last L 1.30pm/last D 8pm
Daily. Closed Nov-Mar except
Christmas

Menus: Fixed-price D & Sun L, bar menu
Seats: 45. No smoking in dining room
Additional: Children welcome, children's portions; other diets to order
Directions: Off A3078, to Gerrans; the hotel is 100yds from Church

PORTSCATHO, Roseland House Hotel ❀

Rosevine TR2 5EW
Map no: 2 SW83

☺ *Roseland House stands in a cliff-top setting in six acres of terraced gardens, with a wooded path leading down to a secluded beach. Traditional English cooking includes dishes such as home-made celery and apple soup, seafood mornay, and tender roast Cornish spring lamb, with pear Belle Hélène for dessert*

Tel: 01872 580644
Chef: Mrs Carolyn Hindley
Proprietors: A D & C M Hindley
Cost: Fixed-price D £16.50 (6
course)/Sun L £9.50 (4 course).
H/Wine £4.50 (carafe) ❢ Service
exc
Credit cards: ▨ ▩
Times: Last L 2.30pm/D 8.30pm

Menus: A la carte L, fixed-price D, bar menu
Seats: 50. No smoking in dining room
Additional: Children welcome, children's menu; ❶ dishes, vegan/other diets on request
Directions: Off A3078, hotel signed on R 2 miles after Ruan High Lanes

PORTSCATHO, Rosevine Hotel ❀

Porthcurnick Beach TR2 5EW
Map no: 2 SW83

☺ *Quietly set in extensive mature gardens, this Georgian country house overlooks Porthcurnick beach. Traditional British, plus international dishes, are created by chef Ian Andrew Thomson Picken from fresh local ingredients, and dishes may include game soup, stir-fried pork with egg noodles, and fresh poached fillet of brill*

Tel: 01872 580206
Chef: Ian Andrew Thomson
Picken
Proprietors: R M & P A
Hearnden
Cost: Fixed-price D £16.50.
H/wine £6.75. Service exc
Credit cards: ▨ ▩
Times: Last L 1.45pm/D 8.30pm.
Closed Nov-Mar/Easter

Menus: Fixed-price D, bar menu
Seats: 50. No pipes or cigars in the restaurant
Additional: Children permitted, children's portions; other diets prior notice
Directions: After Ruan High Lanes take the 3rd L, 1 mile to sea

REDRUTH, Penventon Hotel ❀

☺ *Set in ten acres of grounds, this fine Georgian manor house offers an extensive choice in the 'dining galleries'. The long carte features Italian, French, British and Cornish sections, and fixed-price menus cover the same regions. Typical dishes may include chicken liver pâté, local crab, and prawn thermidor*

Redruth R15 1TE
Map no: 2 SW64
Tel: 01209 214141
Chef: Paul Naylor
Proprietor: David Pascoe & Family
Cost: *Alc* £17, fixed-price L £9.50/D £ 12.50-£13.95. H/wine £6.85 Service inc
Credit cards: ▨ ▨ ▨ OTHER
Times: Noon-last L 2pm/last D 9.30pm Daily
Menus: *A la carte,* fixed-price L & D, bar menu
Seats: 100. No-smoking area
Additional: Children welcome, children's menu; ❂ menu, vegan/other diets on request

Directions: On Redruth intersection of A30, 1 mile S of town centre

RUAN HIGH LANES,
The Hundred House Hotel ❀

☺ *Situated within a mile of the sea, and surrounded by unspoilt countryside, The Hundred House Hotel offers the best of Cornish produce, cooked in an assured manner. The main course is fixed unless by prior arrangement, but nevertheless includes dishes such as home-baked gammon with pineapple and Cumberland sauce*

Seats: 24. No smoking
Additional: Children over 10 welcome; other diets to order
Directions: On the A3078 at Ruan High Lanes

Truro TR2 5JR
Map no: 2 SW93
Tel: 01872 501336
Chef: Kitty Eccles
Proprietors: Mr & Mrs J M Eccles
Cost: Fixed-price D £21.50
Credit cards: ▨ ▨ ▨
Times: D 7.30pm. Closed Nov-Feb
Menus: Fixed-price D

SENNEN, The Land's End Hotel ❀❀

☺ *A dramatic cliff-top position ensures spectacular sea views from the Atlantic Restaurant where the food is imaginative and good*

This is the last hotel on the British mainland with magnificent views on a clear day of the Wolf Rock lighthouse, and the Scillies 28 miles away. Ann Long, well known locally for her cooking in her own restaurants, now controls the hotel and catering here. Under her supervision, Dorchester and Savoy-trained Alan Ward cooks in a modern eclectic style for the short, weekly-changing *carte,* influenced strongly by produce from the Atlantic waters on the doorstep, infused with ideas from the Mediterranean. Starters such as brill and prawn terrine wrapped in roasted seaweed and served on laverbread cream, duck liver mousse in pools of blackcurrant, or thinly sliced sirloin with Parmesan shavings on marinated wild mushrooms, and balsamic sun-dried tomato dressing, are

Sennen TR9 7AA
Map: 2 SW32
Tel: 01736 871844
Chef: Alan Ward
Proprietor: Manager: Richard Long
Cost: *Alc* £20.25, fixed-price Sun L £8.95. H/wine £7.80 Service exc
Credit cards: ▨ ▨ ▨ OTHER
Times: Last D 9.30pm/Sun 9pm; last Sun L 2pm
Menus: *A la carte* D, fixed-price D & Sun L, bar menu.
Seats: 75

representative of the imaginative style. For a main course, try pan-fried John Dory fillet served on sautéed spinach with thyme-scented butter, herb-crusted fillet of sea bass on a sorrel sauce, whole baby maize-fed guinea fowl with cranberry sauce, or mushrooms and walnut puff pastry parcel served on a spicy tomato sauce. It will be hard to resist a second trip to the more dramatic end of the A30.

Directions: A30 from Penzance, in Land's End complex

Additional: Children welcome, children's portions; ❂ dishes, vegan/other diets on request

ST AUSTELL, Boscundle Manor Hotel ❀

☺ *Fresh produce, including local fish, meat and dairy products, features in the cooking which is strongly traditionally English. Typical dishes served in the elegant dining-room might include smoked salmon, tender roast lamb with redcurrant jelly, and fresh fruit salad with clotted cream*

Menus: Fixed-price D
Seats: 20. No smoking in dining room
Additional: Children welcome, children's portions; ❂ dishes, other diets on request
Directions: Tregrehan signed 2m E of St Austell off A390

Tregrehan PL25 3RL
Map no: 2 SX05
Tel: 01726 813557
Chef: Mary Flint
Proprietors: Andrew & Mary Flint
Cost: Fixed-price D £22.50 (4 course). H/wine £9.50. Service inc
Credit cards: ▨ ▩ ▨
Times: Last D 8.30pm

ST AUSTELL, Carlyon Bay Hotel ❀

☺ *The 1930s hotel is set in sub-tropical gardens within extensive grounds and the restaurant itself commands fine views over Carlyon Bay; it is no surprise to find fresh fish on the menu. Look out for locally smoked seafood served with fresh Cornish crab, and rack of Cornish lamb roasted with honey and garlic*

Menus: Fixed-price L & D, bar menu
Seats: 150
Additional: Children welcome, children's menu; ❂ menu, vegan/other diets on request
Directions: A390 towards St Austell, take Charlestown Road at Mount Charles. Left into Church Road, over mini roundabout into Beech Road, right for Sea Road. Hotel 100m on the left

Sea Road PL25 3RD
Map no: 2 SX05
Tel: 01726 812304
Chef: Paul Leakey
Proprietors: Brend Hotels. Manager: Peter Brennan
Cost: Alc £22, fixed-price L £10.50, D £20 (5 courses). H/wine £7.95. Service exc
Credit cards: ▨ ▩ ▨ ▨ OTHER
Times: 12.30-last L 2pm, 7pm-last D 9pm

ST IVES, Chy-an-Dour Hotel ❀

☺ *Chef proprietor David Watson provides good quality continental-style dishes from a short fixed-price menu in the hotel dining-room. A typical meal could be sardine and lemon paté, a soup or sorbet, then a main course such as pork with apple cream and Calvados, with mixed forest fruits crème brûlée to finish*

Menu: Fixed-price D
Seats: 50. No smoking in dining room
Additional: Children over 5 welcome, children's portions; ❂ dishes, vegan/other diets on request
Directions: On A3074 into St Ives

Trelyon Avenue TR26 2AD
Map no: 2 SW54
Tel: 01736 796436
Chef: David Watson
Proprietor: David & Renee Watson
Cost: Fixed-price D £16.50 (4 course). H/wine £5.40. Service exc
Credit cards: ▨ ▩ OTHER
Times: Last D 8pm

ST IVES,
Pig 'n' Fish Restaurant ❀❀

A good choice of fresh fish and seafood dishes prepared in a variety of styles at this seaside restaurant

This is, uncompromisingly, a fish restaurant in a seaside setting, the kitchen revolving around the daily catch landed by the local fishing boats. Chef and co-proprietor Paul Sellars uses a variety of simple approaches, with French and Italian influences reflected in the menus. He previously worked with Rick Stein at the Seafood Restaurant, Padstow, as sous chef for seven years, and has been here in his own place for nearly two years. At a spring meal, the seafood soup had a good stock base, a substantial consistency and intense flavour, served with rouille, freshly grated Parmesan and croûtons. Fillet of brill came with a buttery Chardonnay sauce with a hint of basil, and the classic crème brûlée chosen for pudding had a good, even topping, a creamy texture and the fresh scent of vanilla pods. There might be the odd non-seafood dish, such as sliced duck breast with chicory and balsamic vinegar, and vegetarian dishes are available with prior notice. The short wine list is perfectly suited to the style of the restaurant, with some half bottles and wines by the glass.

Norway Lane TR26 1LZ
Map no: 2 SW54
Tel: 01736 794204
Chef: Paul Sellars
Proprietors: Debby & Paul Sellars
Cost: *A/c* £21-£27, fixed-price L/D £17.50. H/wine £9.50 ❢
Service exc
Credit cards: 🂱 🃏
Times: Last L 1.30pm/last D 9.30pm. Closed Sun, Mon, Nov-mid Feb
Menu: *A la carte,* fixed-price L & D
Seats: 30. No cigars or pipes
Additional: Children welcome, children's portions; other diets prior notice

Directions: 300yds from St. Ives Tate Gallery

ST IVES, Skidden House Hotel ❀

☺ *Dating back several centuries, this town-centre hotel has a distinctive, individual character. Enjoyable meals with a French flavour are served in the intimate dining-room; these may include smoked seafood platter, English fillet steak with pâté and Madeira wine sauce and sautéed wild mushrooms*

Skidden Hill TR26 2DU
Map no: 2 SW54
Tel: 01736 796899
Chef: Dennis Stoakes
Proprietor: Michael Hook (Logis of GB)
Cost: *A/c* £22.50; fixed-price D £17.50. H/wine £9.50. Service inc
Credit cards: 🂱 🃏 🃏 🃏 OTHER
Times: Last L 1.30pm/D 8.45pm
Menus: *A la carte,* fixed-price D, bar menu
Seats: 22. No smoking
Additional: Children permitted; ❤ menu, other diets on request

Directions: A30/A3074 St Ives, take 1st right after Station

We endeavour to be as accurate as possible but changes in personnel and data can occur in establishments after the Guide has gone to press.

ST MARTIN, St Martin's Hotel ❀❀

☺ *An imaginative choice of colourfully presented dishes is offered at this lovely island retreat*

Built in the late 1980s, this hotel was designed to resemble a cluster of cottages nestling into the hillside, by the water's edge. The Tean restaurant, benefiting from the glorious views, is further adorned with paintings by local artists of the island's produce and the fresh fish that feature so strongly in head chef Jonathan Cooke's menus. A summer meal might begin with a robust crab soup and some delicious bread rolls, followed by a kiwi fruit sorbet. The main course could be an attractively presented pudding of Cornish salmon with a brill mousse garnished with perfectly cooked asparagus, turned courgettes and tiny piles of puréed swede with an indulgent butterscotch sponge pudding to complete the meal, served with butterscotch sauce and crème anglaise, and accompanied by a crisp biscuit basket filled with lovely vanilla ice-cream. Cafetière coffee is served with excellent petits fours.

Directions: On the Island!

Isles of Scilly 0QW
Map no: 2 SW28
Tel: 01720 422092
Chef: Marc Bolger
Manager: Keith Bradford (Pride of Britain)
Cost: Fixed-price D £25 (4 course). H/wine £13 Service inc
Credit cards: 🔳 🔳 🔳 🔳 OTHER
Times: Last L 5pm/last D 9.30pm Closed Nov-Feb
Menus: Fixed-price D, bar menu
Seats: 60. No smoking in dining room
Additional: Children over 12 welcome, children's menu; ❶ dishes, vegan/other diets on request

ST MAWES, Idle Rocks Hotel ❀❀

Local fish is the speciality of the restaurant at this dramatically located harbour-side hotel

The Idle Rocks is a fine hotel occupying a superb location at the water's edge overlooking the sheltered harbour. Most of the public rooms, including the bar and waterside patio, are positioned to take full advantage of the magnificent view. Not surprisingly, the restaurant specialises in local fish, and the fixed-price menus offer imaginative dishes prepared from the very best of ingredients under the careful supervision of head chef Alan Vickops. A recent inspection meal began with a smooth duck pâté served with home-baked herb bread. This was followed by a grilled fillet of turbot on a bed of sliced potato with an oil-based sauce flavoured with sun-dried tomatoes. Lemon tart, chosen from a list of mouth-watering desserts, had a pleasant citrus flavour and was served with a less intense lemon jus. A courteous team of staff provide attentive service, and the relaxed atmosphere is in keeping with the character of this delightful fishing village.

Directions: Take the A3078 to St Mawes. Hotel is on the left as you enter the village. At waters edge

Tredenhan Road
Near Truro
Map no: 2 SW83
Tel: 01326 270771
Chef: Alan Vickops
Proprietor: E K Richardson
Cost: Fixed-price D £19.75 & £23.75. H/wine £9.25. Service exc
Credit cards: 🔳 🔳 🔳 OTHER
Times: Last L 2.30pm, Last D 9.15pm
Menus: Fixed-price D, Sun L, bar L menu
Seats: 60. No smoking in restaurant
Additional: Children welcome, children's portions & L menu; ❶ dishes, vegan/other diets on request

ST MAWES, Rising Sun Hotel ❀

☺ *Local seafood is strongly featured in the candlelit restaurant at this locally popular harbourside inn. Typical dishes include deep-fried brie with a raspberry and walnut vinaigrette and parcels of fresh halibut with leek, fennel and tomato accompanied by aïoli*

Times: Noon-last L 2.30pm, 6pm-last D 9.15pm
Menus: Fixed-price D & Sun L, Bistro, bar menu
Seats: 50
Additional: Children welcome, children's menu; ❶ dishes
Directions: On entering the village the hotel is on the right

Truro TR2 5DJ
Map no: 2 SW83
Tel: 01326 270233
Chef: Bill Jukes
Proprietor: St. Austell Brewery. Managers: Colin & Jacqueline Phillips
Cost: Fixed-price D £ 16.95/Sun L £9.95. H/wine £9.75 ❶ Service exc
Credit cards: 🔳 🔳 🔳 OTHER

ST MAWES, **The St Mawes Hotel** ✥

☺ *Situated on the seafront overlooking the harbour, the St Mawes offers home cooking making good use of local seafood. Cornish lobster can be enjoyed by prior arrangement, and other dishes offered might be mussels in garlic butter, prime whole Newlyn sole, or plaice and Scotch fillet or entrecôte steak*

Seats: 25. No cigars or pipes
Menus: Fixed-price L & D, bar menu
Additional: Children over 5 welcome, children's menu; ♥ menu, vegan/other diets on request
Directions: Opposite the Quay in centre of village

The Seafront TR2 5DW
Map no: 2 SW83
Tel: 01326 270266
Chef: Juliet Burrows
Proprietor: Clifford Burrows
Cost: Fixed price L £11.50 (2 course)/D £16. Wine £4.75 (0.5l). Service exc
Credit cards: ■■ ■■ ■■ OTHER
Times: Last L 1.45pm/D 8.15pm
Closed Dec-Jan

TALLAND BAY, **Allhays Hotel** ✥

☺ *Excellent views over Talland Bay, as well as a high standard of cooking, distinguish this friendly hotel. The set menu does not offer a choice of dishes but preferences, dislikes and dietary needs are taken into account. A typical main course might be lamb cutlets served on a bed of leeks*

Menus: Fixed-price D, bar menu (Res. only)
Seats: 14. No smoking
Additional: Children over 10 permitted; ♥ dishes, children's portions/vegan/other diets on request
Directions: Two miles from Looe on A387 towards Polperro

Near Looe PL13 2JB
Map no: 2 SX25
Tel: 01503 72434
Chef: Lynda Spring
Proprietors: Brian & Lynda Spring
Cost: Fixed-price D £14 H/wine £7.45 Service exc
Credit cards: ■■ ■■ ■■ ■■
Times: Last D 7pm Closed Dec 24-Jan 7

TALLAND BAY, **Talland Bay Hotel** ✥

A lovely country house set in extensive gardens overlooking Talland Bay. Traditional dishes with an international influence feature on a fixed-price menu – supplemented by carte dishes for an extra amount – and may feature linguine with flakes of salmon and prawns, and rack of Cornish lamb with a herb crust

Seats: 60. No smoking
Additional: Children over 5 welcome, children's portions & high tea; ♥ dishes, vegan/other diets on request
Directions: Follow A387 Polperro road from Looe, hotel is signed from crossroads

Near Looe PL13 2JB
Map no: 2 SX25
Tel: 01503 272667
Chef: Paul Isingswood
Proprietor: Barry & Annie Rosier
Cost: Alc from £28.25, fixed-price D £20/Sun. L £10.75. H/wine £8.50 Service exc
Credit cards: ■■ ■■ ■■ ■■ OTHER
Times: Last D 9pm/last Sun L 2pm. Closed Jan
Menus: A la carte, fixed-price D/Sun, L bar menu

TINTAGEL, **Trebrea Lodge Hotel** ✥

☺ *Unpretentious, well-prepared food is served at this beautifully preserved 18th-century manor house, set in large wooded grounds. A typical meal from the fixed-price menu might be roasted red pepper stuffed with tomato, fillet of wild salmon pan-fried with ginger, and glazed lemon tart*

Seats: 14. No smoking
Additional: Children over 8 welcome, children's portions; ♥ dishes, other diets on request
Directions: From Tintagel take Boscastle road, turn left at RC Church and right at top of lane

Trenale PL3 0HR
Map no: 2 SX08
Tel: 01840 770410
Chef: Sean Devlin
Proprietors: John Charlick and Sean Devlin
Cost: Fixed-price D £ 17.50 (4 course). H/wine £9 Service exc
Credit cards: ■■ ■■
Times: Last D 8pm Closed
Menus: Fixed-price D (no choice)

TRESCO, The Island Hotel ❀❀

Freshly caught seafood and an exquisite island setting combine to make this restaurant memorable

This island where visitors are greeted by a wealth of blooms and foliage is a very special place – and the hotel itself no less so. For some, the journey here will involve a trip by tractor/trailer "taxi" from the quay or heliport, but the meal makes any effort worthwhile. Chef Christopher Wyburne-Risdale is justifiably proud of his expertise with the freshest of seafood, Bryher crab and Tresco lobster proving particularly popular; dedicated carnivores, however, will probably succumb to the temptation of delicious Devonshire beef. In a charmingly decorated dining-room with spectacular views of the lighthouse on Round Island, Tean and St Helens, our inspector recently enjoyed a very tasty (if somewhat over-elaborate) starter of dressed salad leaves with tiger prawns and monkfish medallions in a provençal sauce with gravlax. This was followed by cream of wild mushroom and fennel soup, then a main course of brill with bacon lardons, button onions and mushrooms accompanied by a slightly bland thyme and champagne sauce.

Directions: Situated on north-eastern tip of island

Isles of Scilly TR24 0PU
Map no: 2 SW17
Tel: 01720 422883
Chef: Christopher R Wyburne-Risdale
Proprietors: Tresco Estate.
Manager: Ivan Curtis
Cost: Alc £33.65, fixed-price D £28.50 (5 courses). H/wine £9.95
Credit cards: ▧ ▨ ▨ OTHER
Times: Last L 2.15pm, Last D 9.30pm.
Menus: A la carte, fixed-price D, bar menu
Seats: 110. No smoking in dining room
Additional: Children welcome, children's menu; ❀ dishes, vegan/other diets on request

TRESCO, New Inn ❀

☺ *Beamed ceilings and a distinctly piratical feel make the restaurant at New Inn a charming place to eat. Imaginative menus take advantage of the variety of local seafood, but at a recent meal some fish dishes were overcooked. Try the smoked salmon roulade with asparagus*

Menu: Fixed-price D, bar L menu
Seats: 32. No smoking in dining room
Additional: Children welcome, children's menu; ❀ dishes, vegan/other diets on request
Directions: 250yds from the harbour (private island, contact hotel for details)

Isles of Scilly TR24 0QQ
Map no: 2 SW17
Tel: 01720 422844
Chef: Graham Shone
Proprietor: Tresco Estate.
Manager: Graham Shone
Cost: Fixed-price D £19. H/wine £6.95 ❢ Service exc
Credit cards: ▧ ▨ OTHER
Times: Last bar L 2pm, 7.30pm-last D 8.15pm

TREYARNON BAY, Waterbeach Hotel ❀

☺ *Wholesome cooking revealing skill and flair is a highlight of this hotel. A typical meal might include swede and herb soup, salmon mousse with lemon mayonnaise, and steak and stout pie with parsley potatoes, broccoli and glazed baby onions. The views towards the Cornish coast are glorious*

Menu: Fixed-price D
Seats: 45. No smoking in the dining room
Additional: Children welcome, children's portions; ❀ menu, other diets on request
Directions: Well signposted in Treyarnon Bay, 14 miles from Padstow

Padstow PL28 8JW
Map no: 2 SW87
Tel: 01841 520292
Chef: Mrs V Etherington
Proprietor: Mr A Etherington
Cost: Fixed-price D £12.50 (6 course). Wine £6.50. Service exc
Credit cards: ▧ ▨ OTHER
Times: Last D 8.15pm. Closed Oct-Mar

Anchoïade is an anchovy paste from Provence. It consists of a purée of anchovies mixed with crushed garlic and olive oil. It is usually served with raw vegetables, or spread thickly on slices of fresh bread, drizzled with olive oil, and browned in the oven.

TRURO, Alverton Manor Hotel ❀

Peacefully set in six acres of well-kept gardens and mature grounds, this former convent dates from around 1700. Modern British cooking is produced with enthusiasm and flair and served in the attractive candlelit restaurant. A well-chosen wine list of 76 bins accompanies the enjoyable food

Tregolls Road TR1 1XQ
Map no: 2 SW84
Tel: 01872 76633
Chef: Mike Smith
Proprietor: Manager Michael Bryant
Cost: *Alc* £24.65, fixed-price L £12.95 (3 courses)/D £19.50 (4 courses). Wine £8.25. Service exc
Credit cards: 🟦 ▆ 🔲 🔳 OTHER
Times: Noon-Last L 2pm. 7pm-Last D 9.30pm daily
Menu: *A la carte*, fixed price L & D, Sun lunch, bar menu
Seats: 40. No smoking in dining room
Additional: Children welcome, children's portions; ❷ dishes, vegan/other diets on request

Directions: From the Truro by-pass, take A39 to St Austell. Just past the church on the left

VERYAN, Nare Hotel ❀

Standing in grounds surrounded by National Trust land, the Nare Hotel enjoys some of the best uninterrupted sea views in Cornwall. The modern Anglo-French cooking features dishes such as oak-smoked Scottish salmon, and sautéed breast of Aylesbury duckling with blackcurrant sauce

Menus: *A la carte*, fixed-price L & D **Seats:** 70
Additional: Children welcome (over 8 at dinner), children's portions/L menu ; ❷ menu, vegan/other diets on request
Directions: Go through Veryan passing New Inn on left, continue for a mile to sea and hotel

Carne Beach TR2 5PF
Map no: 2 SW93
Tel: 01872 501279
Chef: Malcolm Sparks
Proprietors: Mr & Mrs T N Gray. Manager: Mrs D Burt
Cost: *Alc* from £29, fixed-price L £13/Sun L £15 (4 course)/D £27 (5 course). H/wine £9.75. Service exc
Credit cards: 🟦 🔳
Times: Last L 2pm/D 9.30pm Closed Jan 4-Feb 13

CUMBRIA

ALSTON,
Lovelady Shield Hotel ❀❀

A country house in a secluded valley offering an elegant dining environment

Probably little changed from when it was built in 1830, the secluded location of Lovelady Shield, under a wooded hillside and bordered by the River Nent, is only one of its assets. Others include the warm welcome of the Lyons, and their impeccable personal attention and hospitality. The dinner menu makes up for its limited choice by offering four or five courses. An inspection meal yielded good

Alston CA9 3LF
Map no: 12 NY74
Tel: 01434 381203
Chef: Barrie Garton
Proprietors: K S & M W Lyons
Cost: Fixed-price D £24.25 (4 course). H/wine £8.75. No service charge
Credit cards: 🟦 ▆ 🔳 🔲
Times: 7pm-last D 8.30pm. Closed Jan 4-Feb 4
Menus: Fixed-price D, bar L, Sun L by arrangement

Lovelady Shield Hotel

Seats: 30. No smoking in dining room
Additional: Children permitted (over 5), children's portions; ✪ dishes, vegan/other diets on request

pheasant terrine served with pine-nut oil, salad and a small portion of lavender jelly in a tart, followed by home-made soup, then pan-fried minute steak, with vegetables that distinctly lacked sparkle. Dessert was a let down. A less disappointingly soft wholemeal rhubarb and sultana crumble would have been appreciated so that even its pirouette round the microwave would have been forgiven. On the same Spring menu another choice might have been grilled fillet of Nile perch with stir-fried vegetables, moistened with a Chinese oyster condiment. Mr Lyons is enthusiastic about his carefully chosen wine list, and rightly so. Table service was meticulous.

Directions: Off the A689, 2.5 miles from East Alston; signposted at top of drive

AMBLESIDE, **Borrans Park Hotel** ⊛

☺ *Friendly, family-run hotel serving enjoyable home-cooked food based on fresh ingredients. Dishes include pea and mint soup, pork steaks with cream and mushroom sauce, and oatmeal crumble with mixed fruits. Service is geared to guests dining at the set time of 7pm. Cosy atmosphere with diners offered seconds*

Menus: A la carte D, fixed-price D **Seats:** 30. No smoking
Additional: Children permitted, children's menu; ✪ menu, vegan/other diets on request
Directions: On the A591 Coniston/Hawkshead road 0.5 mile past Waterhead traffic lights, opposite the Rugby Club

Borrans Road LA22 0EN
Map no: 7 NY30
Tel: 015394 33454
Chef: Katy Lewis
Proprietor: B W Lewis
Cost: Alc £16, fixed-price D £16. H/wine £7 ✦ Service inc
Credit cards: ▨ ▨▨ OTHER
Times: Last D 7pm

AMBLESIDE,
Nanny Brow Hotel ⊛

A fine looking country house with superb views over Brathay Valley. It all makes a delightful setting for a meal which might comprise of turnip and honey soup, apple and cider sorbet, breast of local wood pigeon in puff pastry, kumquat cheesecake, with a cheese platter to conclude

Menu: Fixed-price D **Seats:** 42. No smoking in dining room
Additional: Children permitted (over 12); ✪ menu, vegan/other diets on request
Directions: 1.50 miles from Ambleside on A593 to Coniston

Clappersgate LA22 9NF
Map no: 7 NY30
Tel: 015394 32036
Chef: Fred Fehlow
Proprietor: Michael W Fletcher
Cost: Fixed-price D £25.50 (5 course). H/wine £11.99 ✦ Service exc
Credit cards: ▨ ▨▨ ▨▨ ▨ OTHER
Times: Last D 8.45pm

AMBLESIDE, **Rothay Manor Hotel** ❀

☺ *Accurate flavours and distinctive seasoning are features of the cooking at Rothay Manor; an honest approach achieves quality without pretentiousness. Look out for wild mushrooms in a filo basket, cream of leek and potato soup and roast leg of lamb with rosemary and garlic*

Times: Last L 2pm (1.30pm Sun)/D 9pm. Closed Jan 3-Feb 11
Menus: Fixed-price L & D
Seats: 70. Air conditioned. No smoking
Additional: Children welcome, children's menu; ❶ menu, other diets on request
Directions: Quarter of mile out of Ambleside on the Coniston road

Rothay Bridge LA22 0EH
Map no: 7 NY30
Tel: 015394 33605
Chefs: Jane Binns and Colette Nixon
Proprietors: Nigel & Stephen Nixon
Cost: Fixed-price L £12, £14.50 (Sun)/D £26. H/wine £10. Service exc
Credit cards: 🂠 ▦ ▦ 🂡 OTHER

AMBLESIDE, **Wateredge Hotel** ❀

Set on the edge of Lake Windermere, with gardens stretching down to the water, the former fishermens' cottages make a delightful hotel. There is a commitment to the use of fresh produce throughout, from the home-baked bread to dishes such as tender roast loin of venison, or roast breast of goose with sweet and sour sauce

Menu: Fixed-price D
Seats: 50. No smoking. Partial air conditioning
Additional: Children permitted (over 7), children's portions; ❶ dishes, vegan/other diets on request
Directions: On A5075 Borrans Road opposite the Rugby Club

Borrans Road
Waterhead LA22 0EP
Map no: 7 NY30
Tel: 015394 32332
Chefs: Michael Cosgrove and Mark Cowap
Proprietors: Mr & Mrs Derek Cowap
Cost: Fixed-price D £25.90 (6 course). H/wine £11. Service exc
Credit cards: 🂠 ▦ ▦ OTHER
Times: 7pm-last D 8.30pm. Closed mid Dec-early Feb

APPLEBY-IN-WESTMORLAND,
Appleby Manor Hotel ❀

☺ *Guests may pick and mix between a daily-changing and three speciality fixed-price menus (which include vegetarian and health-conscious options). The cooking takes in locally caught rainbow trout, or cinnamon-roasted Gressingham duck, and all the desserts are home-made*

Roman Road CA16 6JB
Map no: 12 NY62
Tel: 017683 51571
Chef: Dave Farrar
Proprietor: Nick Swinscoe (Best Western)
Manager: Debbie Goldsmith
Cost: Alc from £19.95, fixed-price L/D £18.95. H/wine £9.95 No service charge
Credit cards: 🂠 ▦ ▦ 🂡 OTHER
Times: 12.30pm-last L 1.45pm, 7pm-last D 9pm. Closed Dec 24-26
Menus: A la carte, fixed-price L & D, bar menu
Seats: 70. No smoking in dining room
Additional: Children welcome, children's menu; ❶ dishes, other diets on request

Directions: M6 exit 38/B6260, through town, over bridge to T-junction, left, first right for 0.6 mile. From M6 exit 40/A66 (Brough), Appleby turn & immediate right for 0.5 mile

APPLEBY-IN-WESTMORLAND,
Tufton Arms Hotel ❀

The Conservatory Restaurant at this stylish country town hotel offers a variety of menus providing grills, pasta and home-cooked dishes to suit most tastes and budgets. Portions are generous, and a good crème brûlée has been a highlight of a recent meal

Market Square CA16 6XA
Map no: 12 NY62
Tel: 017683 51593
Chef: David Milsom
Proprietors: W D Milsom (Consort)
Cost: Alc £10.45-£25, fixed-price D £18.50. H/wine £7.95 ❢
Service exc
Credit cards: 🔳 🏧 🏧 💷 OTHER
Times: Last L 2pm/D 9.30pm
Menus: A la carte, fixed-price D, bar menu
Seats: 60. Air conditioned No-smoking area
Additional: Children welcome, children's portions; ❶ dishes, other diets with notice

Directions: In the centre of Appleby in the main street

BASSENTHWAITE,
Overwater Hall Hotel ❀❀

☺ *Sauces and desserts are particularly noteworthy at this isolated hotel where good quality cooking can be enjoyed*

Ireby CA5 1HH
Map no: 11 NY23
Tel: 017687 76566
Chef: Adrian Hyde
Proprietors: Adrian & Angela Hyde and Stephen Bore
Cost: Fixed-price D £15 & £19.95. H/wine £7.50. Service exc
Credit cards: 🔳 🏧
Times: 7pm-last D 9pm
Menu: Fixed-price D
Seats: 50. No smoking in restaurant

A beautifully isolated location is one reason for staying at this 19th-century country house hotel, set in eighteen acres of gardens and woodland with views of the fells. An excellent choice of British dishes with a French accent is another plus. High points are particularly good sauces and delicious home-made desserts, while an overall high standard of cooking is maintained. Starters may include chicken liver parfait and steamed asparagus glazed with an orange hollandaise sauce. For main course, fillets of salmon and brill in a watercress sauce or escalopes of veal sautéed with marsala and served with thyme jus and an onion marmalade are recommended. To finish, a choice of sweets and a selection of British cheeses. The carefully chosen wine list of 64 bins includes a selection of New World wines. Service is attentive and friendly, the atmosphere warm and relaxing.

Directions: Take the A591 from Keswick to Carlisle, after 6 miles turn right at the Castle Inn. Hotel is signposted after 2 miles

Additional: Children permitted, children's portions; ♥ dishes, other diets on request

---

BORROWDALE,

Borrowdale Gates Hotel ❀

☺ *A well-structured menu offers high quality cooking at this family-run hotel. A recent inspection meal yielded mousseline of scallops on a chervil and vermouth beurre blanc, followed by cream of chicken and asparagus soup, fillet of seabass on a capsicum sauce, and warm apple gratin with Mirehouse honey*

Menus: Fixed-price D & Sun L, bar L menu
Seats: 50. No smoking in dining room
Additional: Children welcome (over 7 at D), children's L portions; ♥ dishes, vegan/other diets on request
Directions: B5289 from Keswick, in Grange village turn right at double humpback bridge. Hotel quarter of a mile on right

Grange
Keswick CA12 5UQ
Map no: 11NY21
Tel: 017687 77204
Chef: Terry Parkinson
Proprietors: Mr & Mrs T H Parkinson
Cost: Fixed-price D £21.50 (4 course)/Sun L £13. H/wine £9 ! Service exc
Credit cards: 🖭 🖭 OTHER
Times: 12.15pm-last L 1.30pm, 7pm-last D 8.45pm. Closed Dec 6-18, Jan 3-Feb 3

BORROWDALE, **Borrowdale Hotel** ❀

☺ *Set in the beautiful Borrowdale valley, this traditional hotel mixes old English favourites with classic international cooking from a five-course fixed-price menu. Typical dishes might be poached plaice in a cream and mushroom sauce, seafood melody of scampi, scallops and prawns in a brandy and cream sauce, and sticky toffee pudding*

Menus: Fixed-price D/Sun L, bar menu **Seats:** 120. No-smoking area
Additional: Children welcome, children's menu; ♥ dishes, vegan/other diets on request
Directions: 3.5 miles S of Keswick on B5289

Keswick CA12 5UY
Map no: 11 NY21
Tel: 017687 77224
Chef: Peter Starauschek
Proprietor: Peter Fidrmuc
Cost: Fixed-price Sun L £10.50 (5 course)/D £15.50 & £18.50. H/wine £7.50 Service exc
Credit cards: 🖭 🖭 OTHER
Times: Last L 2pm, last D 9.15pm

BRAMPTON, **Farlam Hall Hotel** ❀❀

The honest flavours and textures of good local produce are skilfully preserved in a range of imaginative modern dishes

English cooking in the modern idiom forms the backbone of Barry Quinion's short but carefully structured daily-changing four-course dinner menu. At a recent inspection meal, the good texture of a roulade of salmon and halibut was enhanced by an intense watercress coulis, and this was followed by succulent best end of local lamb served on a bed of home-grown spinach with a rosemary and red wine sauce. Cheese was then offered before a selection of desserts which included an old-fashioned grape and brandy trifle with a vibrant flavour. A wine list which takes on board some good half bottles is worthy of mention, and staff – carefully supervised by the involved proprietors – successfully blend courtesy with

Hallbankgate CA8 2NG
Map no: 12NY56
Tel: 016977 46234
Chef: Barry Quinion
Proprietors: Quinion & Stevenson Families (Relais et Château)
Cost: Fixed-price D £28 (4 course). H/wine £28 ! Service exc
Credit cards: 🖭 🖭 🖭 OTHER
Times: Last D 8.30pm. Closed Dec 25-31
Menu: Fixed-price D
Seats: 40. No-smoking area

friendliness. Food is served at well spaced tables set with crisp linen, fine china and silver, the elegant dining room forming part of a delightful, historic country house dating in part from the late eighteenth century and set in beautiful landscaped gardens which feature an ornamental lake. Guests are encouraged to dine at 8pm, but the timing is not rigid.

Additional: Children permitted (over 5); ❂ dishes, other diets on request

Directions: 2.5 miles south east of Brampton on A689

CARTMEL, **Aynsome Manor Hotel** ❀

☺ *A lovely manor house set in open countryside offering memorable meals in an elegant candlelit dining-room. The five-course menu features well-produced English dishes. The kitchen is strong on soups and puddings, with main course choices including poached Scottish salmon and fillet of beef Wellington*

Menu: Fixed-price D & Sun L
Seats: 28. No smoking in dining room
Additional: Children permitted (over 5 at dinner), children's portions; other diets with notification
Directions: Leave A590 signed Cartmel. Hotel is 0.5 mile north of Carmel village on right

Grange over Sands LA11 6HH
Map no: 7 SD37
Tel: 015395 36653
Chef: Victor Sharratt
Proprietors: P Anthony and Margaret Varley
Cost: Fixed-price Sun L £10.95 (5 courses), D £18.50 (5 courses). H/wine £8. Service exc
Credit cards: ▨ ▬ ▩ OTHER
Times: last Sunday L 12.30 for 1pm, last D 8.30pm. Closed L Mon-Sat, Sun eve, & 2-26 Jan

CARTMEL, **Uplands Hotel** ❀❀❀

A friendly, well established hotel and restaurant serving reliable cooking in a relaxed atmosphere

A hillside overlooking Morecambe Bay is the location for this small hotel and restaurant, which stands in its own two acres of gardens. It is owned by Tom and Diana Peter who came to Uplands in 1985 after many years at John Tovey's Miller Howe in Windermere, where Tom learned many of his culinary skills. Although the menu proclaims itself to be 'in the Miller Howe manner', Tom has developed his own distinctive style, and the dishes are lighter than those of his mentor.

Di Peter looks after things front-of-house, creating a welcoming and informal atmosphere. The four-course fixed-price dinner menu offers a choice of starters and three main dishes, and there is always a home-made soup, such as fennel and almond, served with warm wholemeal bread. Options to start include smoked trout pâté served on cucumber and kiwi fruit salad, with natural yoghurt and herb dressing, or a hot salmon soufflé with watercress sauce. Main dishes sampled and appreciated include honey roasted duckling with green peppercorn sauce, and loin of lamb marinated in red wine, soya sauce and rosemary, and served with a redcurrant and caper sauce. Delicate vegetables were an integral part of the dish – carrots with ginger, French beans, purée of parsnip, creamed potatoes and grated beetroot.

There is a choice of around five desserts, perhaps banana, walnut and ginger farmhouse pie with warm butterscotch sauce, and a chocolate Grand Marnier mousse. About 40 wines are listed, with some good examples from South Africa and Australia and a reasonable number of half bottles.

Directions: 1 mile up road signed Grange opposite the Pig & Whistle pub in Cartmel

Haggs Lane LA11 6HD
Map no: 7 SD37
Tel: 015395 36248
Chef: Tom Peter
Proprietor: Diana Peter
Cost: Fixed-price L £14.50/D £26 (4 course). H/wine £8. No service charge
Credit cards: ▨ ▬ ▩
Times: Last L 1pm/last D 8pm Closed Jan 1-Feb 25
Menus: Fixed-price L & D
Seats: 28. No smoking
Additional: Children permitted (over 7 at D); ❂ dishes, vegan/other diets on request

CONISTON, The Old Rectory Hotel ❀

☺ *Sound standards of food and hospitality in this small, delightful, family-run hotel. The Anglo/French cooking will find much favour. Expect fillet of pork Normandy cooked in creamy cider and Calvados sauce garnished with apple rings, or chicken Marsala with toasted almonds*

Additional: Children welcome, children's portions; ❻ dishes; Vegan/other diets on request
Directions: 2.5 miles south of Coniston on the A593, just before Torver

Torver LA21 8AX
Map no: 7 SD39
Tel: 015394 41353
Chef: Carolyn Fletcher
Proprietors: Paul & Carolyn Fletcher
Cost: Fixed-price L £15.50, H/wine £8.25. Service exc
Times: Last D 7.30pm
Seats: 14. No smoking in dining room

CROOKLANDS, Crooklands Hotel ❀

Farming memorabilia and objets d'art decorate the Hay Loft restaurant at Crooklands, where generous portions are served from a reasonably-priced carte. A typical meal might be escalope of salmon with a red pepper and butter sauce, pigeon breast with shallots and red wine and home-made lemon and lime cheese-cake

Menus: A la carte, fixed-price Sun L, bar menu
Seats: 50. Air conditioned
Additional: Children welcome in Carvery, children's portions; ❻ dishes, vegan/other diets on request
Directions: 1.5 miles from M6 exit 36; 4 miles from Kendal A65

Near Milnthorpe LA7 7NW
Map no: 7 SD58
Tel: 015395 67432
Chef: Colin Scott
Proprietors: Neil & Hilda Connor (Best Western)
Cost: Alc £19, Carvery L £4.95/ Sun L £10.50. H/wine £7.95 ❣
Service inc
Credit cards: 🔳 💳 💳 💳
Times: Rest. 7pm-9pm Mon-Sat
Carvery open L/D Mon-Sun

CROSBY-ON-EDEN,
Crosby Lodge Hotel ❀

Good food, service and comfort are standard features at this charming country house hotel. The menu has an international flavour, but offers some traditional English dishes. Choose from the likes of grilled mussels with breadcrumbs, herbs and garlic, and chicken breast filled with Parma ham and asparagus

High Crosby CA6 4QZ
Map no: 12 NY45
Tel: 01228 573618
Chef: Michael Sedgwick
Proprietors: Michael & Patricia Sedgwick
Cost: Alc £27; fixed-price L £15.50/D £26. H/wine £10.90. Service exc
Credit cards: 🔳 💳 💳
Times: Noon-last L 1.30pm/D 9pm. Closed Dec 24-Jan 21
Menus: A la carte, fixed-price L & D, bar menu
Seats: 50. No smoking in dining room
Additional: Children permitted (over 5 dinner); ❻ dishes; children's portions & other diets on request

Directions: 3 miles from M6 exit 44 on A689 towards Carlisle Airport/Brampton. Right at Low/High Crosby sign, 1 mile on right

ELTERWATER, Langdale Hotel ❀

Looking out onto a water wheel and mill race, Purdys is the main restaurant of this hotel and country club. Imaginative dishes are attractively presented and may include duck confit, salmon cooked with lime, and profiteroles with home-made ice-cream. Staff are friendly, yet attentive and professional

Menu: A la carte D
Seats: 120. No smoking in dining room
Additional: Children welcome, children's menu; ❖ dishes, other diets on request

Ambleside LA22 9JD
Map no: 7 NY30
Tel: 015394 37302
Chef: David Rodgie
Proprietor: S & N – Langdale Hotel & Country Club.
Manager: David Fairs
Cost: Alc £27, H/wine £10 ❢
Service exc
Credit cards: 🅴 💳 💳 💳 OTHER
Times: Last D 9.45pm

ESKDALE GREEN, Bower House Inn ❀

☺ *A former farmhouse, now a character lakeland inn, which serves good quality country cooking in the attractive restaurant. The short menu offers the likes of smoked venison with gooseberry chutney, Aberdeen Angus sirloin steak, and grilled salmon with walnut and herb crust. Puddings are home-made*

Menus: A la carte, fixed-price D
Seats: 40. No smoking
Additional: Children welcome, children's portions; ❖ menu, vegan/other diets on request
Directions: From A595 follow signs to Eskdale Green

Holmrook CA19 1TD
Map no: 6 NY10
Tel: 019467 23244
Chef: Margaret Johnson and Paul Robinson
Proprietors: Derek & Beryl Connor
Cost: Alc from £18.50, fixed-price D £18.50. H/wine £6.50 ❢
Service exc
Credit cards: 🅴 💳 💳 OTHER
Times: 7pm-last L 2pm/ D 9pm

GRASMERE, Gold Rill Hotel ❀

☺ *An attractive hotel, situated in two acres of lawns and gardens, with wonderful views of the surrounding mountains and fells. A young and attentive staff serve excellent four-course evening meals in the ornate dining-room*

Menus: Fixed-price D, bar menu
Seats: 50. No smoking in dining room
Additional: Children over 5 welcome, children's portions; ❖ dishes, other diets on request
Directions: M6 exit 36 then A590/591: Red Bank Road in centre of village opposite St Oswalds Church. Hotel 200yds on left

Red Bank Road LA22 9PU
Map no: 11 NY30
Tel: 015394 35486
Chef: Ian Thompson
Proprietor: Paul Jewsbury
Cost: Fixed-price D £17.50 (4 course) H/wine £8.90 Service inc
Credit cards: 🅴 💳
Times: 7.30pm-8.30pm

Gressingham duck is a back cross of the white Aylesbury with the wild mallard - it is the latter which gives the slightly gamey flavour. Lunesdale duck is basically a superior Aylesbury with a bit less mallard, thus a less gamey flavour. Both cross-breeds have a high meat-to-bone ratio and a low fat content. Wild ducks have darker flesh because they use their muscles more than sedentary barnyard ducks, and their gamier flavour reflects a more naturally varied diet. Widgeon and teal, for example, often spend time on salt marshes and can have a pronounced fishy taste. Mallard is the most popular wild duck because it can be reared (like pheasant) ready to be shot when grown.

GRASMERE, **Grasmere Hotel** ❀

☺ *Paul and Gretchen Riley's Victorian hotel is just a couple of minutes walk from the village, yet lies sheltered in its own gardens which stretch down to the River Rothay. Everything is made on the premises, including the bread, and the hearty four-course dinners may feature roast duck and orange pie, or steak and kidney casserole*

Grasmere LA22 9TA
Map: 11 NY30
Tel: 015394 35277
Chef: Gretchen Riley
Proprietor: Paul Riley
Cost: Fixed-price D £ 15.50 (4 courses) H/wine £8.50 ❢ Service exc
Credit cards: 🔳 💳 💳 OTHER
Times: 7pm-last D 7.30pm. Closed Jan
Menu: Fixed-price dinner
Seats: 26. No smoking in dining room
Additional: Children over 8 permitted; ❤ menu, vegan/ other diets on request

Directions: Couple of minutes walk from village centre on river bank

GRASMERE, **Michael's Nook Hotel** ❀❀❀

Dinner at eight in a traditional country house setting

Ambleside LA22 9RP
Map no: 11 NY30
Tel: 015394 35496
Chef: Kevin Mangeolles
Proprietors: R S E Gifford
Cost: Fixed-price L £28.50 (4 course)/D £39.50 (5 course). H/wine £12. Service exc
Credit cards: 🔳 💳 💳 💳
Times: 12.30pm-last L 1pm, 7.30pm-last D 8.30pm
Menus: Fixed-price L & D daily
Seats: 45-50. No smoking in the restaurant
Additional: Children by arrangement; ❤ dishes, other diets by arrangement

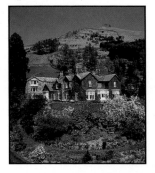

A Victorian country house hotel, Michael's Nook is set in beautiful gardens above Grasmere village. The owner, Reg Gifford, has a reputation as an antiques connoisseur, and the fine furniture, English prints, porcelain and rugs fit easily into the elegant surroundings. There are two dining rooms, one with gilt mirrors and oak panelling, the other richly decorated with red wall coverings and antique furnishings. Dinner, served at 8pm is a memorable meal and head chef Kevin Mangeolle's menus of modern British dishes are worthy of the highest praise. The options are a set-price five-course menu of chef's recommendations with several alternative dishes, a set seven-course gourmet menu, plus a four-course set-price lunch.

At a spring meal, a delicious turnip tarte tatin, both rich and light, with foie gras and a shallot sauce, was followed by creamed celeriac soup with ginger oil. The main course, roast leg of lamb filled with wild mushrooms on a bed of carrot and cabbage, was quite exquisite, with another delicate sauce. Alternatives could be a starter of mille-feuille of red mullet with mushroom and tomato dressing, and a main course of roast Gressingham duck garnished with a confit of leg, lentils and port sauce. The chef's recommendation for dessert might be vanilla crème brûlée served with glazed fruits and blueberry milkshake sauce, or a choice from the separate dessert menu. Chocolate dice on a pistachio sauce was a highlight of our inspector's meal, which concluded with British cheeses and fresh fruit. The wine list offers some good vintages, house wines, dessert wines and a good selection of half bottles. Smiling staff provide friendly and unobtrusive service.

Directions: A591, turn uphill at The Swan, bear left for 400 yds

GRASMERE, **Oak Bank Hotel** ❀

☺ *Located close to the village centre, with the River Rothay running past the garden, the Oak Bank offers mainly British cooking with some modern European influences. Dishes on the fixed-price menu might include smoked mackerel mousse, fennel and pear soup, and roast duckling with Lyth Valley damson sauce, with hazelnut gallette for dessert*

Menus: Fixed-price D, bar L menu **Seats:** 30. No smoking in dining room **Additional:** Children over 5 welcome, children's portions; ❶ dishes, vegan/other diets on request
Directions: off A591 in centre of village

Broadgate LA22 9TA
Map no: 11 NY30
Tel: 015394 35217
Chefs: Sharon Savasi
Proprietors: Attilio & Sharon Savasi
Cost: Fixed-price D £16.75 H/wine £1.60 glass. Service exc
Credit cards: 🆑 ☱ OTHER
Times: Last L 2pm, last D 8pm

GRASMERE,
White Moss House Hotel ❀❀

Genuine English dishes are transformed by a light modern touch

In the cottage restaurant of this charming little hotel looking out over the northern end of Rydal Water, Peter Dixon's culinary skills receive the highest praise. The five-course menu delivers, as promised, real English food cooked with lightness of touch in modern style. An excellent meal enjoyed by our inspector one May evening began with beautifully creamed fennel soup; this was followed by a superb dish of wild salmon poached with chervil and champagne, married with peat-smoked sea trout and served with caviar and dill sauce. The main course consisted of well-crisped mallard accompanied by a damson, port and Pinot Noir sauce and very good vegetables (a purée of salsify and celeriac proving particularly noteworthy). A selection of British cheeses preceded the sticky toffee pudding with pecan toffee sauce that rounded off the meal. The menu was complemented by an outstanding wine list providing over 200 choices. Family-style service is informal, however, and the atmosphere relaxed – circumstances no doubt particularly appreciated by those guests who have spent their day tramping the fells.

Directions: On A591 between Grasmere and Ambleside opposite Rydal Water

Rydal Water LA22 9SE
Map no: 11 NY30
Tel: 015394 35295
Chefs: Peter Dixon and Colin Percival
Proprietors: Peter & Susan Dixon
Cost: Fixed-price D £27.50 (5 course) H/wine £9.75 ❗ Service exc
Credit cards: 🆑 ☱
Times: D 8pm (one sitting). Closed Sun
Menu: Fixed-price D
Seats: 18. No smoking
Additional: Children welcome (no toddlers), children's portions; ❶ dishes/other diets on request

GRASMERE, **Wordsworth Hotel** 🏵

Artistically presented Anglo-French dishes are served in the stylish Prelude Restaurant at the Wordsworth Hotel, where the emphasis is very much on fresh seasonal produce. The hotel is attractively situated in landscaped gardens close to the churchyard where William Wordsworth is buried

Ambleside LA22 9SW
Map no: 11 NY30
Tel: 015394 35592
Chef: Bernard Warne
Proprietor: R A Gifford
Manager: Robin Lees
Cost: *Alc* £28, fixed-price
L £17.50/D £29.50 (both 4 course). H/wine £11.50. Service exc
Credit cards: 🔲 📧 📧 📧
Times: Last L 2pm/D 9pm
(9.30pm Fri/Sat)
Menus: *A la carte,* fixed-price L & D
Seats: 65. Air conditioned
No smoking in dining room
Additional: Children welcome, children's menu; ❶ menu, vegan/other diets on request

Directions: In the centre of Grasmere next to the Church

HOWTOWN, **Sharrow Bay** 🏵🏵🏵

A setting amid immaculate gardens on the shore of Lake Ullswater helps to make any visit to this restaurant a special occasion

Penrith CA10 2LZ
Map no: 12 NY41
Tel: 017684 86301/86483
Chefs: Johnnie Martin, Colin Akrigg, Philip Wilson and Robert Bond
Proprietors: Francis Coulson, Brian Sack, Nigel Lawrence and Nigel Lightburn
Cost: Fixed-price L £31.75 (4 course)/D £41.75 (5 course). H/wine £11.95 ❢ Service inc
Credit cards: None taken
Times: Last L 1.45, last D 8.45pm. Closed Dec, Jan, Feb
Menus: Fixed-price L & D
Seats: 65. No smoking in dining room

Sharrow Bay's world-wide reputation for outstanding hospitality is well deserved, and the food it serves will be no disappointment. Dining-rooms in contrasting styles offer a choice of surroundings – the Lakeside, with its splendid views of Ullswater, having an ambience quite different from that of the more intimate, wood-panelled Studio. Every meal here is an occasion, but none more so than the six-course dinner, its fixed-price menu of English dishes predominantly classical in style and generally unswayed by fashion – though the effect of modern influences is to be seen in such innovations as a starter of scallops with provençal vegetables, tarragon-dressed salad and a gazpacho sauce. Equally noteworthy elements of a meal enjoyed one warm summer evening were moist fillet of halibut with a light bonne femme sauce, a lime sorbet of expertly balanced acidity and sweetness, and extremely tender roast best end of lamb, cooked pink and served with a light, delicately flavoured courgette and leek mousse; the tangy lemon tart which followed was slightly overcooked on this occasion, however, and the petits fours which accompanied coffee were only average. An excellent, reasonably priced wine list offers an unusually large number of good wines by the glass as well as a wide choice of half bottles. Traditional growing areas provide such high points as three 1961 first-growth clarets, but the New World is also represented. Service is smoothly professional – though staff are also genuinely warm and willing to please.

Additional: Children permitted (over 12); other diets to order

Directions: Turn off A592 through Pooley Bridge, turn right (signed to Howtown), hotel 2 miles

KESWICK, **Brundholme Hotel** ❀

☺ *Herbs grown in the hotel's garden feature in the sound, modern cooking offered at this attractive country house. Dishes may include shellfish cassoulet with wild thyme and black tagliatelle, tomato and sorrel soup, and roast leg of lamb on a bed of sautéed parsnips*

Seats: 40. No smoking in dining room **Additional:** Children over 12 permitted; ❂ dishes, vegan/other diets on request
Directions: At A66 roundabout take exit to Keswick, first left after garage, next left again, hotel on right

Brundholme Road CA12 4NL
Map no: 11 NY22
Tel: 017687 74495
Chef: Ian Charlton
Proprietors: Ian Charlton and Suzy England
Cost: *Alc* £17.50 D. H/wine £9
Service exc
Credit cards: ◪ ▦ ▦
Times: Last L 1.30pm/D 8.30pm
Closed Dec-mid Feb
Menus: *A la carte* D

KESWICK,
Dale Head Hall Lakeside Hotel ❀

☺ *A friendly, informal place to stay. The 16th-century house has retained much of its original charm with plenty of oak beams and exposed stone. Traditional English dishes feature on the menu. Try the cream of fennel soup, sautéed fillet of sea bream, and leave room for the home made puddings. Good selection of local cheeses*

Thirlmere CA12 4TN
Map no: 11 NY22
Tel: 017687 72478
Chefs: Caroline Bonkenburg and Malcolm Mavin
Proprietor: Alan Lowe
Cost: Fixed-price D £24.50 (5 courses). H/wine £10.50 ❢
Service inc
Credit cards: ◪ ▦ OTHER
Times: Last D 8.30pm
Menu: Fixed-price D
Seats: 18. No smoking in dining room
Additional: Children permitted over 10. ❂ dishes

Directions: Halfway between Grasmere and Keswick, 400yds off A591 on shore of Thirlmere

KESWICK, Grange Hotel ✸

☺ *Five-course menus of sound British cooking are served in the restaurant of this Victorian converted house with a view out over the gardens and the distant fells. Fanned brest of smoked pigeon might be followed by a lemon sorbet, then Borrowdale trout. Farmhouse cheeses are an alternative to dessert*

Menus: Fixed-price D, pre-theatre
Additional: Children permitted (over 7); ❤ dishes, other diets on request
Directions: Take A591 towards Windermere for half a mile, first right, hotel 200 yds on right

Manor Brow
Ambleside Road CA12 4BA
Map no: 11 NY22
Tel: 017687 72500
Chef: Colin Brown
Proprietors: Duncan & Jane Millar
Cost: Fixed-price D £17.75 (5 course). H/wine £8.90 ❢ Service inc
Credit cards: 🔳 🔳
Times: Last D 8pm.
Closed Nov 6-Mar 9

KESWICK,
Swinside Lodge Hotel ✸✸

Well-presented food is offered on a set five-course menu at this Lakeland hotel

Newlands CA12 5UE
Map no: 11 NY22
Tel: 017687 72948
Chef: Chris Astley
Proprietor: Graham Taylor
Cost: Fixed-price D £24-£27.50 (5 courses) Service exc.
Unlicensed, no corkage charge
Credit cards: None
Times: Last D 7.30pm
Menus: Fixed-price D
Seats: 20. No smoking in dining room
Additional: Children permitted (over12); ❤ /other diets on request

What is lacking in choice is more than made up for in quality at this Victorian hotel, set in attractive gardens in the heart of Lakeland. Well presented, soundly cooked food is offered on a set five-course menu; a choice is only available for dessert, but guests are asked when they book if they have any particular dislikes. An inspection meal began with ricotta cheese tortellini served with smooth spinach mousse and a mild tomato and basil sauce, followed by celery and apple soup with floating pieces of Stilton-topped toast. As a main course a loin of lamb was chosen which proved to lack some of the sweetness expected of Welsh lamb but was served with a stuffed wild mushroom and a good selection of vegetables: ratatouille, honey-roast parsnips, green beans and dauphinoise potatoes. Desserts might include a light praline soufflé. There is a decent choice of English cheeses, and cafetière coffee comes with chocolate petits fours. The hotel does not hold a liquor licence, but guests may bring their own wine if they wish.

Directions: 3 miles south-west of Keswick. Take the A66 for Cockermouth, left at Portinscale, follow road to Grange

KIRKBY LONSDALE,
Cobwebs Restaurant ❀

Imaginative British cooking is served in the conservatory-style extension of this country house hotel A set four-course menu offers a choice of starters, and may include a duo of soups (a signature dish) and roast loin of lamb in a piquant sauce. Regional cheeses are featured

Menus: Fixed-price D
Seats: 25. No smoking in dining room
Additional: Children over12 permitted; ❂dishes, vegan/other diets on request
Directions: Take A65 east to Skipton – 8 miles into Cowan Bridge, turn left, restaurant 150yds on the left

Leck Cowan Bridge LA6 2HZ
Map no: 7 SD67
Tel: 015242 72141
Chef: Yvonne Thompson
Proprietor: Paul Kelly
Cost: Fixed-price D £28 (5 course). H/wine £9 Service inc
Credit cards: ◼ ▬
Times: 7.30pm-last D 8pm. Closed Sun, Mon, end Dec-mid Mar

MUNGRISDALE, **The Mill Hotel** ❀

A well-chosen wine list and a five-course fixed-price menu combine to provide an enjoyable meal at this charming hotel. Diners are presented with two choices of starter and main course (one vegetarain), and dishes may include braised venison pieces in red wine, or roast duckling in plum sauce

Near Penrith CA11 0XR
Map no: 11 NY33
Tel: 017687 79659
Chef: Eleanor M Quinlan
Proprietors: Richard & Eleanor Quinlan
Cost: Fixed-price D £21 (5 course) H/wine £9.75 ❢ Service exc
Credit cards: None
Times: 8.30am-last D 8pm. Closed Nov 1-Feb 20
Menu: Fixed-price D
Seats: 20. No smoking
Additional: Children welcome, children's portions; ❂ menu. vegan/other diets on request

Directions: Midway between Penrith & Keswick off A66, signs for Mungrisdale ; from M6 exit 40 take A66 (Keswick)

Beetroot is rich in sugar, vitamins and calcium. Although it is possible to eat them raw (grated), it is more usual to cook beetroot and then serve cold. It is occasionally served hot, to accompany game, or in soups. The round varieties, the red globe and the dark red Egyptian, are the most widely cultivated varieties but the long rooted varieties are worth seeking out for they have more flavour and are sweeter. Beetroot is harvested from the end of June to the first frosts. They store well and are more readily available in the autumn and winter months. Although beetroot is traditionally sold cooked, they can be bought raw for cooking at home. Boiled in water this takes about 2 hours.

NEWBY BRIDGE, **Lakeside Hotel** ❀

An old coaching inn retaining much of its original character and charm, uniquely situated on the shores of Lake Windermere. The cooking is usually consistent. Recent meals have included guinea fowl terrine, and petit tournedos of beef on a brioche croûton with bone marrow in a red wine jus

Ulverston LA12 8AT
Map no: 7 SD38
Tel: 015395 31207
Chef: Konrad Howlett
Proprietor: Neville R Talbot
Cost: *Alc* £25-£35, fixed-price
L £12.50/D £22.50 (5 courses),
H/wine £10.90 ❢ Service exc
Credit cards: ⬛ ▦ ▦ ▣ OTHER
Times: Last L 3pm/D 9.30pm
Menus: *A la carte*, fixed-price
L & D, bar menu
Seats: Lakeview 80, John
Ruskins 60. Air conditioned. No
smoking
Additional: Children welcome,
children's menu; ❷ menu,
vegan/other diets on request

Directions: From M6 exit 36 follow A590 to Newby Bridge, right over bridge and follow Hawkeshead Road for 1 mile

RAVENSTONEDALE, **Black Swan Hotel** ❀

☺ *Good food and real ales can be enjoyed at this traditional inn in a picturesque setting. The four-course fixed-price menu features dishes such as fresh asparagus spears with fresh cream and almonds, and locally farmed rainbow trout oven-baked in a paper parcel with herbs and white wine. Desserts are home-made*

Near Kirkby Stephen CA17 4NG
Map no: 7 NY70
Tel: 015396 23204
Chefs: Graham Bamber and
Mrs N W Stuart
Proprietors: G B & N W Stuart
Cost: *Alc* from £14.50, fixed-
price L £9.75, D £20 (4 course).
H/wine £9 ❢ Service exc
Credit cards: ⬛ ▦ ▦ ▣ OTHER
Times: Last L 2pm/ D 9.15pm

Menus: *A la carte*, fixed-price L & D, bar menu
Seats: 44. No smoking in dining room
Additional: Children welcome, children's portions; ❷ menu,
vegan/other diets on request
Directions: M6 exit 38/A685 (Brough) or from Scotch Corner towards
Kikby Stephen, then to Ravenstonedale

TEMPLE SOWERBY,
Temple Sowerby House Hotel ❀

☺ *Located in the centre of the village, but with extensive grounds to the rear, this former farmhouse features Georgian additions and is run in the style of a country house. The emphasis is on home-cooked dishes prepared from fresh produce, served from a daily-changing four-course menu in the attractive restaurant*

Near Penrith CA10 1RZ
Map no: 12 NY62
Tel: 017683 61578
Chef: David Rodgers
Proprietors: Cecile & Geoffrey
Temple
Cost: Fixed-price D £22
(5 course). H/wine £8 Service
exc
Credit cards: ⬛ ▦ ▦ ▣ OTHER
Times: Last L 2pm/D 9.15pm
daily

Menus: Fixed-price D, bar L menu
Seats: 50. No smoking in dining room
Additional: Children welcome, children's portion; ❷ dishes,
Vegan/other diets on request
Directions: On A66 5 miles E of Penrith in centre of village

THORNTHWAITE, **Thwaite Howe Hotel** ❀

☺ *Thwaite Howe occupies an elevated position with fine views across the valley to the distant fells. Country-house cooking is offered on a set five-course dinner menu, unfortunately only available to residents. At a March visit the sticky toffee pudding with butterscotch sauce was particularly enjoyed*

Menu: Fixed-price D
Seats: 16. No smoking
Additional: Children over 12 permitted; ❂ /other diets on request
Directions: From A66 3 miles W of Keswick; follow signs to Thornthwaite and the Gallery

Keswick CA12 5SA
Map no: 11 NY22
Tel: 017687 78281
Chef: Mary Kay
Proprietors: Harry & Mary Kay
Cost: Fixed-price D £15
(5 course). H/wine £7.95 Service exc
Credit Cards: None taken
Times: Last D 7pm. Closed Nov-Feb

ULVERSTON, **Bay Horse Inn** ❀❀

Creative cooking featuring home-baked loaves and fresh local fish is served in a conservatory restaurant

LA12 9EL
Map no: 7 SD27
Tel: 01229 583972
Chefs: Robert Lyons and Esther Jarvis
Proprietor: Robert Lyons
Cost: *Alc* D from £19, fixed-price L £14.50. H/wine £11.50 ❢
Service exc
Credit cards: ▨ ▦
Times: Last L 1.30pm/last D 8pm
Menus: *A la carte* D, fixed-price L, bar L menu
Seats: 50. No smoking in dining room
Additional: Children permitted (over 12); ❂ dishes, vegan/other diets on request

John Tovey inspired the transformation of the Bay Horse from a run-down pub to a stylish inn with a smart conservatory restaurant. Robert Lyons interprets the unique Tovey style with flair and ingenuity, producing quality cooking which, accompanied by an impressive wine list including a New World selection, attracts customers from a wide area. A typical meal might begin with a trio of home-baked mini-loaves (possibly granary, sun-dried tomato and onion, and leek, black olive and feta cheese). A refreshing starter of chilled tomato and basil soup with cream and roasted almonds could be followed by poached fillet of sea bass (caught off-shore and landed nearby) with fresh asparagus tops and a Noilly Prat and chive cream sauce, the latter chosen as a main course at a recent test meal. Reports complain that accompanying vegetables suffer the Tovey fate of being over-garnished, but this was made up for at inspection by an imaginative dish of light, deep-fried leek rings. A 'delicious' apple and strawberry farmhouse pie with fresh cream concluded the meal.

Directions: Leave A590 at sign for Canal Foot. Pass Glaxo Works

ULVERSTON, **Virginia House Hotel** ✿

☺ *Traditional British and modern-inspired cooking is available on the fixed-price and carte at this charming hotel. A typical meal might be smoked trout with a horseradish sauce, followed by fillet of pork with tequilla and red peppercorn sauce, with chocolate profiteroles filled with whipped cream to finish*

Seats: 35. No smoking in dining-room
Additional: Children welcome, children's portions; ❶ dishes, other diets with prior notice
Directions: Drive along A590. Follow signs to Town centre along one-way system. Queen Street is after Market Cross on one-way system, Virginia House Hotel is 400 yards after Market Cross

Queen Street LA12 7AF
Map no: 7 SD27
Tel: 01229 584 844
Chef: Alastair Sturgis
Proprietor: Patricia & Alastair Sturgis
Cost: *Alc* from £13.95, fixed price dinner £11 (2 courses), £13 (3 courses). House/w £7.50
❗ Service exc
Credit cards: 🔲 ■ 💳 💷 OTHER.
Times: 7pm- last D 8.45pm
Menus: *A la carte,* fixed-price dinner

WATERMILLOCK, **Leeming House** ✿✿

In a stunning setting, on the western shore of Ullswater, stands an elegant lakeside hotel offering a high standard of cooking

Near Penrith CA11 0JJ
Map no: 12 NY42
Tel: 017684 86622
Chef: Adam Marks
Proprietors: Forte Hotels. Manager: Christopher L Curry
Cost: *Alc* L £25.95, fixed-price Sun L £16.75/D £26.50 (3 course), £35.50.(5 course) H/wine £13.70 ❗ Service exc
Credit cards: 🔲 ■ 💳 💷 OTHER
Times: 12.30pm-last L 2.30pm (in Conservatory), last D 8.45pm
Menus: *A la carte* L, fixed-price Sun L, fixed-price D
Seats: 80. No smoking in dining room
Additional: Children welcome, children's menu; ❶ dishes; Vegan/other diets on request

Built as a private residence by a landowner from Co. Durham early in the 19th century, Leeming House was converted into a country house hotel in 1969. Trees from around the world have been planted in the 20 acres of woodlands and landscaped gardens which the magnificently mirrored dining room now overlooks. The kitchen is in the capable hands of Adam Marks who produces a fixed-price, three or six-course menu every day, comprising mainly modern French and English dishes. A ragout of Loch Duich scallops served in a basil hollandaise earned an inspector's praise. On a subsequent occasion, the choice of starters seemed rather ordinary – melon, avocado, fruit juices, prawn cocktail. Saddle of tender local venison, however, was good, accompanied by a thickish pepper sauce, spätzli, orange and red cabbage. A reasonable home-made plum frangipane followed. Other options might be pear and Calvados brûlée, or an all-English cheeseboard. The wine list is not extensive but quite adequate, and mainly French in content. General manager Christopher Curry's style is effective and discreet and this style is well reflected by his restaurant staff.

Directions: From M6 exit 40 A592 (Ullswater) then signs for Paterdale. Hotel is 2.5 miles along W shore of lake in Watermillock

WATERMILLOCK, **Old Church Hotel** ✿

☺ *A lovely hotel in a lakeside setting, the Old Church offers a short carte of English dishes. These might include parfait of chicken livers flavoured with herbs, spices and a splash of brandy; roast leg of Lakeland lamb, and an unusual white chocolate, and rum and raisin truffle cake with raspberry coulis*

Menus: A la carte D **Seats:** 20. No smoking in dining room
Additional: Children over 8 permitted; other diets on request
Directions: On A592 on lakeshore. M6 exit 40 5 miles

Penrith CA11 0JN
Map no: 12 NY42
Tel: 017684 86204
Chef: Kevin Whitemore
Proprietor: Kevin Whitemore
Cost: Alc £23.50, H/wine £9.75
Service inc
Credit cards: None taken
Times: Last D 8.30pm Closed Sun

WATERMILLOCK,
Rampsbeck Hotel ✿✿✿

Complex cooking in country house hotel on the edge of Lake Ullswater

Penrith CA11 0LP
Map no: 12 NY42
Tel: 017684 86442
Chef: Andrew McGeorge
Proprietors: T I & M M Gibb and M J MacDowall
Cost: Alc £ 34, fixed-price L £19.95/D £26 (4 course). H/wine £9. Service inc
Credit cards: ▨ ▱
Times: Last L 1.15pm/last D 8pm. Closed Jan 4-mid Feb
Times: 12pm-last L 1.45pm, 7pm-last D 8.30pm. Closed 4 Jan-mid Feb
Menus: A la carte, fixed-price L & D, bar L menu
Seats: 40. No smoking in dining room
Additional: Children permitted; ♥ menu, other diets on request

Whilst most hotels and restaurants nowadays include at least one or two vegetarian choices, few take the trouble to produce a special vegetarian dinner menu. Chef Andrew McGeorge's sample selection of feuilleté of creamed wild mushrooms and asparagus, and baked bell pepper with vegetable risotto and pimento sauce, could happily be ordered by any non-veggie guest.

As well as a four course, no-choice menu for £26, there is a more expensive dinner menu at £34, although the definition of four is rather elastic. The meal starts with canapés, then an appetiser of, perhaps, charred brochette of salmon and sole with couscous. This is confusing, as the starters on the menu are also called appetisers. Whatever their name, these first course dishes show typical dexterity, and a fondness for wrapping. Roast quail, for example, may be stuffed with wild mushrooms and sandwiched between pasta leaves, roasted saddle of rabbit is wrapped in air-dried ham and served with a natural cream jus scented with tarragon, poached boudin and Anna potatoes. You have to remind yourself this is only for starters. Take a breather with the mid-course sorbet, lemon grass, elderberry or rosemary, perhaps. After that, tuck into something along the multi-dimensional lines of saddle of Mansergh Hall lamb served with a thyme-flavoured jus, potato and garlic rösti, roasted button onions and sweetbreads – yes, wrapped in bacon. A main course of steamed fillet of bass was the highlight of our inspector's meal, stylishly garnished with home-made noodles, warm tomato and basil dressing and Dublin Bay prawns. At this point, most people solemnly swear to climb Scafell the next day, before going for broke with the chef's 'symphony' of desserts. Raspberry soufflé, however, seemed mostly made of egg white, but home-made raspberry ripple ice-cream was good.

Directions: M6 exit 40, signs to Ullswater; turn right at water's edge. Hotel is 1.25 miles on the right

WINDERMERE, **Beech Hill Hotel** 🏵🏵

☺ *Stunning views and superlative cooking go hand-in-hand at this lakeside hotel*

Situated three miles south of Bowness, Beech Hill boasts a series of terraced extensions, including a swimming pool, and grounds leading down to Lake Windermere. Its position is sufficiently elevated to provide a magnificent panoramic vista of the lake and distant peaks; indeed, the restaurant has breathtaking views. Chef David Swade has brought a new dimension to the cooking. He offers a four-course daily-changing menu which, at inspection yielded a superlative meal. Chicken liver parfait with Grand Marnier, toasted walnut bread and a shallot dressing was followed by steamed sea bass on a bed of cucumber spaghetti, with a cinnamon butter sauce and served with broccoli hollandaise, glazed carrot batons, courgettes provençale, baby corn, new potatoes and Byron potatoes, and hot raspberry soufflé to finish. Baked Atlantic salmon topped with creamed spinach, Parmesan cheese on an avocado and mint cream sauce or cannon of lamb, pan fried with basil, with wild mushrooms, baby grelotes and crayfish on a Marsala sauce, are examples of an adventurous approach. Attention to the smallest detail is sound with good home-baked bread, canapés and petits fours.

Directions: On A592, Newby Bridge 4 miles from Windermere

Newby Bridge Road
Cartmel Fell LA23 3LR
Map no: 7 SD49
Tel: 015394 42137
Chef: David Swale
Proprietor: Consort.
Manager: Philip Davis
Cost: Fixed-price L £10.50/D
£18.95 (4 course) H/wine £8.95
❗ Service exc
Credit cards: 🂠 ▦ ▦ 🂢 OTHER
Times: Last L 2pm, last D
9.30pm daily
Menus: Fixed-price L & D, bar menu
Seats: 100. No smoking in dining room
Additional: Children welcome, children's menu; ❶ dishes, vegan/other diets on request

WINDERMERE,
Burn How Garden House Hotel 🏵

☺ *Within walking distance of the town centre and Lake Windermere. The hotel dining-room overlooks beautiful gardens and offers traditional favourites such as chicken liver pâté, home-made cream of broccoli soup, and breast of Gressingham duck with a black cherry and port glaze*

Menus: A la carte, fixed-price D, bar menu
Seats: 40. No smoking in dining room
Additional: Children over 5 welcome, children's menu; ❶ dishes, other diets on request
Directions: First right approaching Bowness from Newby Bridge

Back Belsfield Road
Bowness LA23 3HH
Map no: 7 SD49
Tel: 015394 46226
Chef: Chris Adey
Proprietors: Michael Robinson (Best Western)
Cost: Alc £20, fixed-price D
£18.50, H/wine £10 Service inc
Credit cards: 🂠 ▦ ▦ 🂢 OTHER
Times: Last D 8.30-9pm

> Cassis is a liqueur with a rich, velvety fruit flavour that is made by macerating blackcurrants in spirit and sweetening the final result. It is a speciality of Dijon and the Côte d'Or and was first made commercially in 1841.

WINDERMERE, Cedar Manor Hotel ❀

☺ *Built in 1860 as a country retreat, Cedar Manor takes its name from a magnificent Indian cedar which stands in the grounds. The imaginative, daily-changing fixed-price menu includes choices such as seafood and mushrooms in a filo basket, wild strawberry sorbet, and boned leg of lamb filled with Cumberland sausage stuffing*

Directions: Situated on A591, quarter mile north of village

Ambleside Road LA23 1AX
Map no: 7 SD49
Tel: 015394 43192
Chef: Lynn Hadley
Proprietors: Lynn & Martin Hadley
Cost: Alc £20.50, fixed-price D £16.50 (4 course) H/wine £10.80. Service exc
Credit cards: ▨ ▨
Times: Last D 8.30pm. L by arrangement
Seats: 35. No smoking in dining room
Menus: A la carte, fixed-price D, children's high tea
Additional: Children over 6 welcome, children's portions; ❷ dishes, vegan/other diets on request

WINDERMERE,
Crag Brow Cottage Hotel ❀

An attractive cottage-style hotel with an informal and relaxing atmosphere. A great deal of care goes into the preparation of the food. Look out for smoked halibut with avocado and horseradish sauce, beef tournedos with red wine and Stilton sauce, and save room for the speciality sweet, Crêpe Crag Brow

Menus: A la carte, fixed-price D, Sun L, early eve D, bar L menu
Seats: 60. No smoking in dining room
Additional: Children welcome, children's portions; ❷ menu, vegan/other on request
Directions: In centre of Bowness, turn left at Lakeland shop

Bowness LA23 3BU
Map: 7 SD49
Tel: 015394 44080
Chef: John Mather
Proprietors: Peter & Anne Godfrey
Cost: Alc £25, fixed-price D £19.95 (5 courses) Sun L £9.95 (4 courses) H/wine £7.95. Service exc
Credit cards: ▨ ▨ OTHER
Times: Noon-last L 1.45pm, 6.30pm-last D 9pm

WINDERMERE,
Gilpin Lodge Hotel ❀❀

☺ *Caring owners provide an intimate setting for attractive food*

There are plans afoot to alter Gilpin Lodge, a delightfully intimate country house hotel which lies in twenty acres of grounds, east of Bowness. The possibility of a conservatory would offer greater flexibility for drinking and dining. But owner John Cunliffe is positive that this will not compromise the special atmosphere currently provided by the three small dining rooms. Here, chef Christopher Davies and his team offer a good choice of inventive dishes from an attractive five-course dinner menu; a chargrilled brochette of seafood on a bed of wild rice might be followed by

Crook Road LA23 3NE
Map no: 7 SD49
Tel: 015394 88818
Chef: Christopher Davies
Proprietors: Christine & John Cunliffe.
Manager: Richard Marriot
Cost: Alc L £12-14, fixed-price D £26 (4 course)/Sun L £14. H/wine £11.25 No fixed-price lunch, only Sunday ❢ No service charge
Credit cards: ▨ ▨ ▨ ▨
Times: Last L 2.30pm/D 8.30pm

mussel and chive soup, then roast Goosnargh duckling with a
sesame, honey and Grand Marnier sauce, whilst the Gilpin Lodge
bread and butter pudding could bring the meal to a pleasant close.
At a recent dinner, our inspector praised the canapés and selection
of home-made bread, but it was an 'outstanding' warm asparagus
and spinach mousse which stole the show from the roast rack of
early season lamb with a well reduced garlic sauce, and the slightly
over-sauced crêpe Suzette. The extensive wine list is reasonably
priced.

Directions: M6 exit 36 & A590/591 (Kendal), then B5284 for 5 miles

WINDERMERE,

Holbeck Ghyll Hotel ❀❀

*Elaborate menu handled with confidence at luxurious small Lakeland
hotel, once the hunting lodge of Lord Lonsdale*

The all-female kitchen uses good produce and considerable
technical skill in a rather fanciful, daily-changing menu. Dinners
start with canapés, followed by starters such as sauté of chicken
livers cooked with grapes and button mushrooms, finished with a
rich Armagnac sauce, or warm flakes of duck confit, French leaf salad with spring onion,
asparagus, citrus fruits and quails eggs with shallot dressing. A short
entrée course might feature soup or a lightly scrambled egg with
smoked salmon and herbs. Main courses have a French classic bias
– medallions of monkfish pan-fried in garlic and tarragon butter, on
a bed of julienne vegetables with a white wine sauce, for example.
Of greater interest, perhaps, are those dishes with a more
pronounced regional identity, such as roast loin of Cumbrian lamb
with redcurrants, rosemary, green lentils and roast potatoes, or a
traditional pot-roast of beef, slowly cooked in the Aga with
Yorkshire pudding, herb dumplings, roast parsnips and gravy.
Occasionally, flavours falter as in a dull fennel and courgette soup,
or the jus of a loin of pork served on a bed of sautéed white
cabbage. Desserts include a light coffee meringue.

Directions: 3 miles north of Windermere on A591, turn right into
Holbeck Lane. Hotel 0.5 mile on left

WINDERMERE, Langdale Chase Hotel ❀

Overlooking Lake Windermere, Langdale Chase is a magnificent Victorian country mansion with its own wooded grounds reaching to the water's edge. The kitchen's commitment to serious cooking is reflected in the well structured dinner menus which might include loin of venison with steamed cabbage and chestnut dumplings

Windermere LA23 1LW
Map no: 7 SD49
Tel: 015394 32201
Chef: Wendy Linders
Proprietor: Langdale Chase Hotel Ltd.
Manager: Thomas Noblett
Cost: Alc £24, fixed-price L £15 (3 courses)/D £23.50 (5 courses) H/wine £10.90 ❢ Service exc
Credit cards: 💳 💳 💳
Times: Last L 1.45pm/D 8.45pm daily
Menus: A la carte, fixed-price L/D, bar menu
Seats: 90. Air conditioned. No smoking in dining room
Additional: Children welcome, children's menu; ♥ dishes, vegan/other diets on request

Directions: On A591 3 miles N of Windermere, 2 miles S of Ambleside, on the lakeside

WINDERMERE, Lindeth Fell Hotel ❀

☺ *A comfortable Edwardian house which stands high above the town set in magnificent gardens and grounds; the dining-room enjoys superb views across the lake. Country-house cooking with modern presentation might offer fish mousse wrapped in smoked salmon, and roast rack of border lamb with tarragon sauce and port gravy*

Times: Last L 2pm/D 8.30pm. Open Mar-Nov
Menus: Fixed-price D & Sun L **Seats:** 36. No smoking in dining room **Additional:** Children permitted (pref. over 7 at dinner), children's menu; ♥ dishes, other diets on request
Directions: 1 mile south of Bowness on A5074 Lyth Valley Road

Upper Storrs
Park Road
Bowness LA23 3JP
Map no: 7 SD49
Tel: 015394 43286/ 44287
Chef: Diana Kennedy
Proprietors: Pat & Diana Kennedy
Cost: Fixed-price D £20 (5 course), Sun L £10 (3 course inc wine) H/wine £6 ❢ Service exc
Credit cards: 💳 💳

WINDERMERE,
Linthwaite House Hotel ❀❀

A graceful mansion set in magnificent grounds with elegantly presented food, good sauces, and consistent cooking

It's hard to imagine a more delightful setting, or indeed a better view, than that enjoyed by this fine Edwardian residence, which lies in fourteen acres of gardens and grounds, high above Lake Windermere. Faded Colonial is subtly blended with solid Victorian and, combined with the friendliness and attention of owner Mike Bevans and staff, a pleasant environment is offered in which to enjoy Ian Bravey's impressive modern cooking. Dinner may run to five courses, and may include starters such as a well-executed warm savoury pancake filled with crab and scallops with a saffron sauce,

Crook Road
Bowness LA23 3JA
Map no: 7 SD49
Tel: 015394 88600
Chef: Ian Bravey
Proprietors: Michael Bevans
Cost: Alc £ 25, fixed-price D £27 (4 course). H/wine £12.90 ❢ Service inc
Credit cards: 💳 💳 💳 OTHER
Times: Last L 2pm/D 8.45pm
Menus: A la carte L, fixed-price D, bar L menu
Seats: 45. No smoking in dining room

Linthwaite House Hotel

Additional: Children permitted (over 7 at dinner), children's portions; ❷ dishes, other diets on request

then correctly made Madeira consommé. This might be followed by a roast loin of lamb flavoured with garden sage and accompanied by a redcurrant and sage jus. The desserts may feature a smooth crème brûlée or rich home-made dark chocolate marquise, while cheese can be taken as, or instead of, an additional course. An enjoyable meal is complemented by a well balanced wine list, which provides splendid house wines, together with handy tasting notes.

Directions: On B5284 1 mile W of Golf Club

WINDERMERE, **Miller Howe Hotel** ❀❀

Acclaimed, good value English cooking from a Lakeland institution where dinner is an occasion

Rayrigg Road
Map no: 7 SD49
Tel: 015394 42536
Chefs: Christopher Blaydes
Proprietor: John Tovey
Cost: Fixed-price L £12.50, D £26. H/wine £16 Service exc
Credit cards: 🂫 📖 🂡 🂱 OTHER
Times: Last L 1pm/D 8pm. Closed early Dec-early Mar
Menu: Fixed-price lunch & dinner
Seats: 70. No smoking. Air conditioned
Additional: Children over 8 permitted; ❷ dishes, other diets on request

With an international reputation built up over 20 or so years, John Tovey's Miller Howe is now part of Lakeland's gastronomic heritage. The views over Lake Windermere far below, and across to the Langdale fells are feasts in their own right, especially for residents using the binoculars provided in their bedrooms. Dinner is a truly special occasion here. Guests meet for drinks and canapés at eight; half an hour later the lights are dimmed and the five-course dinner is served. No choice is offered. Bread is freshly baked each day and always contains something extra, such as tarragon and orange, or red pepper and onion. The menu is changed daily and, on an April evening, comprised braised ox tail with buttered mashed potato; marinated salmon, halibut and monkfish in reduced consommé aspic; marinated breast of local farm chicken stuffed with Dolcelatte; and, from the selection of desserts, banana, rum and toasted almond cheesecake. The style of cooking is not to everyone's taste. Dishes tend to be rather over endowed with different ingredients, with the result that flavours are neutralised and blended rather than standing out distinctively. Not a European wine to be seen, but a good selection from the New World.

Directions: On A592 between Windermere and Bowness

WINDERMERE,
Porthole Eating House ❀❀

Good Italian cooking and remarkable wines in a bustling, intimate atmosphere close to the lake

The Porthole is fortunate to be in a pedestrianised street and uses the pavement to great effect. In summer, so many aperitifs and light lunches are served al fresco that Ash Street more resembles Bowness-sur-Mer, than Bowness-on-Windermere. Owners Gianni and Judy Berton have a deservedly loyal following, so much so that on busy nights the Bertons happily cook from early evening until 11pm, and still have great difficulty turning anyone away. Little pizza rounds come with drinks, and family recipes from the Veneto and Tuscany feature on the *carte* and the list of individually priced specialities. Char and trout terrine, prawns poached in white wine and herbs, or delicious leek and goats' cheese mousse baked in a mould, for example, or there could be herb crusted salmon fillets in a tangy light juice, chicken saltimbocca, or fresh chicken breast wrapped in Parma ham served with a creamy sauce. Of the puddings, the home-made ice-creams are really smooth and creamy. The wine list is quite formidable – a serious distraction from the menu – with a great variety of classical French wines, plus a fine German selection.

Directions: In Bowness town centre near parish church

3 Ash Street
Bowness LA23 3EB
Map no: 7 SD49
Tel: 015394 42793
Chef: Mike Metcalfe
Proprietor: Gianni Berton
Cost: Alc £25. Wine £9.50.
Service exc
Credit cards: 🔳 💳 💳 💳
Times: 6pm-Last D 11pm.
Closed Tue, mid Dec
Menus: A la carte, fixed-price dinner and Sunday lunch (by request), pre-theatre
Seats: 40
Additional: Children welcome, children's portions; ❂ dishes; Vegan/other diets on request

WINDERMERE, Quarry Garth Hotel ❀❀

☺ *A charming country house hotel in secluded lakeside grounds where the cooking gets better and better*

Head chef Paul Maguire swapped North Hampshire for the Lake District. Even the AA, normally loyal to its Basingstoke base, would probably agree that Lake Windermere has the edge in scenic terms. Paul's standard of cooking is high and his four-course dinner menus, offering a choice of four starters, main courses and sweets, continue the Anglo-French style of his predecessor. Ragout of fresh salmon, terrine of chicken livers and home-made soups may feature among the first courses, followed by loin of lamb with a fresh herb crust, or pan-fried mignons of beef in a rich Madeira jus, served on a potato and celeriac rösti. Apple tart or bread and butter pudding with a cinnamon sauce anglaise are among the recommended sweets. Wines from Europe and the New World are helpfully grouped by taste. Well chosen staff assist owners Huw and Lynne

Troutbeck Bridge LA23 1LF
Map no: 7 SD49
Tel: 015394 88282
Chef: Huw Phillips
Proprietors: Huw & Lynne Phillips
Cost: Fixed-price dinner £21.50.
Wine £9.75. Service exc
Credit cards: 🔳 💳 💳 💳 OTHER
Times: Last D 9pm
Menus: Fixed-price dinner
Seats: 36. No smoking in dining room
Additional: Children permitted; ❂ dishes/other diets on request

Phillips with the attentive service. In an area bristling with good restaurants (just look through the neighbouring pages) Quarry Garth's star is in the ascendant, so booking is advisable.

Directions: On A591, 2 miles from Windermere travelling towards Ambleside

WINDERMERE, **Rogers Restaurant** ❀❀

☺ *Small, atmospheric restaurant set on two floors offering good value cooking*

Roger and Alena Pergl-Wilson have run their well established restaurant with unflagging commitment and enthusiasm for 14 years. The place is small and set on two floors, but it achieves the right degree of intimacy, and a relaxing atmosphere. Roger cooks. His style has its roots in France and has resisted the temptation to be fussy, thus allowing individual flavours to shine through. The set menu is keenly priced but for equally good value and wider choice the *carte* is preferable. Reports indicate that for reasons of economy raw materials are not as prime as previously offered. An inspection meal, for example, started well with a superb red pepper mousse with tomato salad and roasted herb butter, followed by a cream of mushroom soup. Then fillet of salmon came with sorrel sauce, the fish not the most flavoursome and the sauce insipid, though accompanying vegetables were fine. Bread and butter pudding did not quite reach heady heights either. You won't be alone in having difficulty reading the hand written menu; it is a bit of a standing joke.

4 High Street LA23 1AF
Map no: 7 SD49
Tel: 015394 44954
Chef: Roger Pergl-Wilson
Proprietors: Roger Pergl-Wilson
Cost: *Alc* £20, fixed-price D £15.75. H/wine £9.95 ❢ Service exc
Credit cards: 🄰 ▨ 🄳 💷
Times: 7pm-last D 9.30pm. Closed Sun, 1 wk summer & winter
Seats: 42. Air conditioned. No-smoking area
Menus: *A la carte* & fixed-price D
Additional: Children welcome, children's portions; ❂ dishes, vegan/other diets on request

Directions: Opposite the Tourist Office, close to the railway station

WITHERSLACK,
Old Vicarage Hotel ❀❀

Lovely location, atmospheric house, friendly hosts and pleasing food add up to a pleasant experience

Grange over Sands LA11 6RS
Map no: 7 SD48
Tel: 015395 52381
Chef: Stanley Reeve
Proprietors: Burrington-Brown and Reeve families (Fine Individual Hotels)
Cost: Fixed-price D £25 (4 course)/Sun L £13.50. H/wine £10 ❢ Service inc
Credit cards: 🄰 ▨ 🄳 💷 OTHER
Times: Last D 8pm/Sun L 1pm
Menus: Fixed-price D & Sun L
Seats: 40. No smoking in dining room
Additional: Children welcome, children's portions/high tea; ❂ dishes, vegan/other diets on request

Not surprisingly, the Old Vicarage Country House Hotel lies in a peaceful and secluded setting amidst gardens and woodland next to the church. Although it is well outside the village, however, it is only five minutes drive from the A590. Much of the Georgian house's character has been retained, and the three welcoming but small dining areas just manage to cope with a busy house. The four-course meal is carefully chosen, but offers a choice of starters and desserts only, as the main course is fixed. This might be roast leg of lamb with garden mint sauce, crab apple jelly and a rosemary and garlic gravy, or perhaps Gressingham duck with blackberry sauce. The starters might feature dishes such as Loch Fyne smoked salmon, home-made apple and celery soup, or an 'excellent' chicken liver terrine with damson sauce, whilst desserts could include orange marmalade meringue pudding, or red berry fruit pancakes. Each table is given their own cheeseboard with three cheeses in perfect condition, home-made oatcakes and proprietary biscuits. The wine list is good, but expensive, offering a large selection of half bottles at a price.

Directions: Off A590, Take turning in village signposted to church

DERBYSHIRE

ASHBOURNE, Callow Hall Hotel ❀❀

A lovely country house where a mix of modern and traditional British and French cooking can be enjoyed

Mappleton Road DE6 2AA
Map no: 7 SK14
Tel: 01335 343403
Chefs: David & Anthony Spencer
Proprietors: David, Dorothy & Anthony Spencer
Cost: *Alc* D £27.85, fixed-price D £29 (4 course)/Sun L £14.25. H/wine £9.50. Service exc
Credit cards: 🌑 💳 💳 💳
Times: Last D 9.15pm, last Sun L 1.30pm. Closed Sun D, Dec 25/6
Menus: *A la carte*, fixed-price D & Sun L
Seats: 70. No smoking

Callow Hall stands in 44 acres of neat gardens and grounds, surrounded by beautiful open countryside. It has been sympathetically restored by owners David, Dorothy and Anthony Spencer. Visitors can choose from the short, four-course fixed-price menu which changes daily to make the best use of fresh local produce, and the seasonally changing *carte* – both of which offer interesting selections. A typical starter might be sautéed calves' liver topped with sesame seeds with bacon, shallots and a port sauce, or fresh asparagus spears with Parma ham and hollandaise sauce. This could be followed by king scallops with grapefruit and Noilly Prat, and then roast guinea fowl with button onions, mushrooms, bacon, croûtons and a red wine sauce; vegetables are young and fresh. The selection of desserts might include tart tatin or rhubarb tart with custard, with coffee and petits fours to round off the meal.

Directions: 0.75 mile from Ashbourne: A515 (Buxton), sharp left by Bowling Green Pub, first right Mappleton Road

ASHFORD-IN-THE-WATER,

Riverside Country House Hotel ❀❀

Modern French and English cooking with a hint of the traditional served in an attractive riverside setting

Additional: Children welcome, children's portions; ❶ dishes, vegan/other diets on request

Fennel Street DE45 1QF
Map no: 7 SK16
Tel: 01629 814275
Chef: Simon Wild
Proprietors: Roger & Susan Taylor
Cost: *Alc* £25.50, fixed-price L £12.95 (2 course)/Sun L £16.95 (4 course), fixed-price D £29.50 (5 course). H/wine £11.50 Service inc
Credit cards: ▨ ▩ ▩ ▨ OTHER
Times: Last L 2.30pm/ D 9.30pm
Seats: 50 + 30. No smoking in dining room
Menus: *A la carte*, fixed-price L/ Sun L/ D, bar menu
Additional: Children welcome, children's portions; ❶ dishes, vegan/other diets on request

Run by enthusiastic owners Sue and Roger Taylor, this ivy-clad Georgian house stands in delightful mature gardens which front on to the river. A relaxing atmosphere prevails, whilst staff are friendly and attentive. The fixed-price dinner menu offers a selection of modern English and French cooking, with traditional influences, under the control of head chef Simon Wild. A typical meal could begin with an appetiser of marinated duck breast with green salad, followed by mild and creamy Welsh goats' cheese on pickled beetroot with salad and a walnut dressing. Baked fillet steak may be available as a main course – at an inspection meal this was served with mixed wild mushrooms and a Madeira sauce and accompanied by crisp french beans and broccoli and new potatoes. Desserts might include apples poached in elderflower syrup with a cinnamon pastry top and caramel sauce. The wine list offers a good selection.

Directions: On A6 1 mile N of Bakewell in Ashford village next to Sheepwash Bridge

> Cassolette is a small container with a short handle made of heatproof porcelain, tempered glass or metal, and is used to prepare certain hot main dishes, first courses, and cold puddings. The word is also applied to a variety of dishes that are served in cassolettes. Savoury cassolettes include ragouts; sweet cassolettes can include flavoured creams, custards and poached fruits.

BAKEWELL,
Croft Hotel ❀

☺ *Mr and Mrs Macaskill provide friendly, enthusiastic service in their delightful country hotel. The short menu gives no choice on the main course but this is compensated for by the use of good quality fresh produce and careful presentation. Try watercress soup, and roasted poussin stuffed with mushroom and bacon*

Seats: 25. No smoking in dining room
Additional: Children over 10 permitted; ❂ dishes, vegan/other diets on request
Directions: Take A6 from Bakewell, 1.75 miles turn right (A6020). After 0.75 miles left to Great Longstone. On right entering village

Great Longstone DE45 1TF
Map no: 8 SK26
Tel: 01629 640278
Chef: Lynne Macaskill
Proprietors: R A & L Macaskill
Cost: Fixed-price D £21.50 (4 courses). H/wine £8.15. Service inc
Credit cards: 🔳 🔳
Times: Last D 7.30pm

BAKEWELL,
Renaissance Restaurant ❀

A small, comfortably appointed restaurant, with most tables looking onto a walled garden (which provides herbs for the kitchen). Fresh produce features in dishes such as home-made boudin of scallop rolled in French herbs on a tomato and balsamic vinegar vinaigrette, and fresh salmon and halibut with a red pepper sauce

Directions: A6 from Derby. Bakewell roundabout take Buxton exit, first right. Bath Street is a one-way street in centre of town

Bath Street DE45 13X
Map no: 8 SK26
Tel: 01629 812687
Proprietor: Eric Piedaniel

BAKEWELL,
Rutland Arms Hotel ❀❀

Georgian charm in the home of the famous Bakewell Pudding. Mainly modern British cooking with French influences

Some of the world's great discoveries were accidental – gravity, penicillin, Bakewell Pudding. Bakewell Pudding? Yes, and in the kitchens of this very hotel, an 1804 coaching inn in the town centre, where Jane Austen may well have stayed while revising Pride and Prejudice. The Four Seasons Restaurant offers a high quality *carte* and fixed-price menu, with dishes such as king prawns with curly salad, and pan-fried foie gras on a bed of mushy peas with onion gravy, or main courses such as grilled fillet of beef with bearnaise sauce and asparagus, or steamed sea bream served with young leeks in a lobster sauce and salmon caviar. Vegetables are fresh and cooked al dente. Unsurprisingly, sweets include Bakewell Pudding, made to an allegedly still-secret recipe, created when a cook spread egg mixture on top of the jam instead of stirring it in; it is served with sauce anglaise. Dinner orders are taken in the Lounge Bar; guests are then escorted to their table where service is prompt and efficient.

Directions: A6 into Bakewell, Hotel in centre of town

The Square DE45 1BT
Map no: 8 SK26
Tel: 01629 812812
Chef: Peter Sanders
Proprietor: Peter Mason (Best Western).
Manager: Garven McKife
Cost: *Alc* £25, fixed-price L £10.50/D £17.50. H/wine £9 Service inc
Credit cards: 🔳 🔳 🔳 🔳 OTHER
Times: Noon-last L 2.30pm, 7pm-last D 9.30pm
Menus: *A la carte*, fixed-price L & D, bar menu
Seats: 50. No smoking
Additional: Children welcome, children's menu; ❂ dishes, vegan/other diets on request

BASLOW, **Cavendish Hotel** ❀❀

An elegant restaurant with sensational views, where an imaginative chef produces superb food

The mellow, stone-built house sits on the edge of the Chatsworth estate, ancestral home of the Dukes of Devonshire. It has unrivalled views across parkland to the great house itself. A flagstoned lobby with open log fires, fresh flowers everywhere, and proprietor Eric Marsh's collection of paintings and fine art in the drawing and dining rooms, all help to confirm the Cavendish's status as a serious country house hotel. Nick Buckingham presides over the kitchen and is noted for getting the best from the fresh local produce. An inspection meal opened well with a fine buttery pastry tartlet of cheese and mushroom with a light butter sauce. The first course, a leek and chicken terrine, was slightly overawed by a robust grain mustard sauce, but the gamey roast partridge which followed was set off well by an orange and cranberry gravy. Desserts scaled the heights with a vanilla parfait and rich chocolate sauce. The wine list, with some decent clarets, is really quite reasonable. For less formal dining there is a south-facing garden room serving café-style dishes.

Directions: In Baslow village on A619

Bakewell DE45 1SP
Map no: 8 SK27
Tel: 01246 582311
Chef: Nick Buckingham
Proprietor: Eric Marsh
Cost: Fixed-price L & D £27.95, H/wine £15.50. Service exc
Credit cards: ▨ ▧ ▧ ▨ OTHER
Times: 12.30-last L 2pm, 7pm-last D 10pm
Menus: *A la carte*, fixed-price L & D, all-day Garden Room menu
Seats: 50. No smoking in dining room
Additional: Children welcome, children's portions; ❂ menu, vegan/other diets on request

BASLOW, **Fischer's Restaurant** ❀❀❀

This elegant restaurant and its informal alternative, the good-value Café Max, are attractively housed in a fine Edwardian manor

Baslow Hall
Calver Road DE45 1RR
Map no: 8 SK27
Tel: 01246 583259
Chef: Max Fischer
Proprietors: Max & Susan Fischer
Cost: Fixed-price L £16.50 (2 courses), £19.50/D £36. H/wine £10.50 ❢ Service exc
Credit cards: ▨ ▧ ▧ ▨ OTHER
Times: Last L 2pm, last D 9.30pm Closed Sun D, Dec 25/6
Menus: Fixed-price L & D (*A la carte* in Café Max)
Seats: 40+25+12. No smoking in main dining room

A country house retreat exemplifying all that is superb in the genre, Fischer's at Baslow Hall offers hospitality at its warmest and most natural. The restaurant itself leads off a panelled hallway which doubles as a lounge, and here guests can relax in front of an open fire or enjoy a pre-dinner drink with delicious canapés. The menu is straightforward and refreshingly simple, descriptions of the imaginative European dishes being both accurate and honest. Chef/proprietor Max Fischer uses only the freshest of ingredients – langoustine and scallops, for example, coming live from Scotland – and his skilful, intelligent treatment of these produces tempting dishes which are remarkable for their clarity of flavour.
    A memorable dinner began with the surprisingly generous

appetiser of a softly poached egg nesting on a tangy thick onion confit coated with a creamy glazed hollandaise. Moist, softly textured scallops, lightly toasted to seal in their flavour, were served with vibrantly dressed chopped tomato and apple set around oiled lambs' lettuce. A main course of plump, tender, gamey duck breast came with batons of salsify on a buttered aubergine and shallot mix separated by a thick rösti. A rhubarb and stuffed prune panache coated by creamy, glazed custard sauce was set off by cinnamon-flavoured ice cream. Good cafetière coffee came with enjoyable home-made petits fours. The mainly European wine list offers some half bottles and house wines from £10.50.

Directions: On right of A623 (Stockport) as you leave Baslow towards Calver

Additional: Children permitted (over 12 at D in main room); ❤ dishes, vegan/other diets on request

BELPER, **Makeney Hall Hotel** ❀❀

A country house hotel with good choice of traditional French cuisine from seductively written menus

Milford DE56 0RU
Map no: 8 SK34
Tel: 01332 842999
Chef: Ronnie Wyatt-Goodwin
Proprietor: Sonia Holmes
Cost: *Alc* £30, fixed-price L £13 /D £19.50. H/wine £10.50. Service exc
Credit cards: ▨ ▩ ▩ ▨ OTHER
Times: Last L 1.45pm/D 9.45pm. Closed Sat L
Menus: *A la carte,* fixed-price L & D
Seats: 70
Additional: Children over 5 welcome, children's portions; ❤ menu, vegan/other diets on request

Makeney Hall is a country house hotel with a large restaurant divided between an airy conservatory and a richly panelled room with a splendid open fireplace. Here chef Ronnie Wyatt-Goodwin offers a good selection of dishes cooked in a traditional French style. A starter of local game terrine was particularly enjoyable, its richness balanced by a jelly of winter berries. Another option might be Mediterranean seafood soup perfumed with fennel and enhanced with yellow saffron. Fish is well represented, and a main course of monkfish and crab with a champagne sauce proved interesting, although the sauce was a touch over seasoned. Another main dish, fulsomely described in the eminently readable *carte,* is 'mignon of lamb enrobed in a cloak of spinach and game mousse served on a cake of potato and chervil brushed with a rosemary and redcurrant dew'. There are some wicked desserts such as 'pyramids of sheer chocolate indulgence resting on a flowing river of spearmint sauce garnished with rolls of ancient scripture', but for the Bramley apple soufflé we offer our inspector's personal testimonial 'it was golden in appearance with a good apple base and a more unusual custard filling'.

Directions: Join A6 north of Derby & turn right into Milford. Hotel is 0.25 miles

BUXTON, Lee Wood Hotel ❀❀

☺ *Imaginative modern British and French cooking with an emphasis on seafood are offered in the hotel's Garden restaurant*

13 Manchester Road SK17 6TQ
Map no: 7 SK07
Tel: 01298 23002
Chef: Sean Ballington
Proprietor: John Millican (Best Western)
Cost: Alc £21, fixed-price D £17.95/Sun L £12.95. H/wine £10.50 ❢ No service charge
Credit cards: ⬛ 🔳 🔳 🔳
Times: 12.15pm-last L 2pm, 7.15pm-last D 9.30pm
Seats: 80. No-smoking area
Menus: A la carte, fixed-price L/D, bar menu, pre-theatre
Additional: Children welcome, children's menu; ◑ menu, vegan/other diets on request

This friendly, comfortable, privately-run hotel is situated in attractive grounds overlooking the cricket ground. Although modernised, the Georgian charm of the building has been retained. The large, attractive conservatory-style Garden Restaurant is one such modern addition, and is the setting for chef Sean Ballington's enthusiastic modern British cooking. His frequently changing menus are priced by the number of courses taken. A meal in June featured sautéed chicken liver with smoked bacon and woodland mushrooms, served on salad with a light Oxford sauce. Turbot poached in white wine and placed on a bed of crab and prawns was chosen for the main course from a menu strong on fish. It was well constructed and served with interesting vegetables: sugar peas, turnip and okra. Puddings are made on the premises with summer pudding overflowing with red currants and blackberries a good choice for dessert. The wine list offers modest prices and some New World wines. the hotel's location is ideal for visitors to the Derbyshire Peak District.

Directions: North east on A5004, 300 metres beyond the Devonshire Royal Hospital

BUXTON,
Portland Hotel ❀

☺ *The Portland Hotel is ideally located opposite the Pavilion and its gardens, and features the Park Restaurant, a shaded conservatory offering a good range of freshly prepared and distinctively flavoured dishes, both sauced and more plainly cooked. Our inspector particularly enjoyed the liver pâté larded with bacon in a thin Seville orange sauce*

Seats: 100. No smoking in dining room
Menus: A la carte, fixed-price L & D, pre-theatre, bar menu
Additional: Children welcome, children's menu; ◑ menu, vegan/other diets on request
Directions: On A53 opposite the Pavilion Gardens & Opera House

32 St John's Road SK17 6XQ
Map no: 7 SK07
Tel: 01298 22462
Chefs: Brian Simmonds and Tony Bennett
Proprietors: Logis.
Managers: Brian & Linda Millner
Cost: Alc £22.50, fixed-price L £10.50/ D £18.50. H/wine £10 ❢ Service inc
Credit cards: ⬛ 🔳 🔳 🔳 OTHER
Times: 7am-last L 2pm/D 9.30pm

DERBY, Mickleover Court Hotel ❀

An impressive modern hotel on the outskirts of Derby. In the Avebury Restaurant there is a choice of menus, and dishes include celery and Stilton soufflé soup; steamed sea bass with sorrel sauce, and veal medallions with a mousse of Dublin Bay prawns

Menus: A la carte, fixed-price L & D, bar menu
Seats: 80. Air conditioned. No-smoking area
Additional: Children welcome, children's portions; ♥ dishes, vegan/other diets on request
Directions: From Mickleover take A516 (Uttoxeter) hotel is left of 1st roundabout

Etwall Road DE3 5XX
Map no: 8 SK 33
Tel: 01332 521234
Chef: Martin Clayton
Proprietor: Virgin.
Manager: Timothy Bramhall
Cost: Alc £25, fixed-price
L £14.50/D £19.50 H/wine
£10 ‼ Service inc
Credit cards: 🆕 🔜 🔜 🔜 OTHER
Times: Last L 2.30pm, last D 10pm daily

DOVERIDGE, The Beeches Farmhouse Hotel and Restaurant ❀

☺ Traditional farmhouse cooking served in intimate and elegant surroundings. Dishes are based on fresh ingredients: fillet of cod on a bed of spinach with parsley sauce, roast duck with rhubarb and caramel gravy, and, a regional favourite, Bakewell tart. A fine selection of British farmhouse cheeses is also available

Doveridge DE6 5LR
Map no: 7 SK13
Tel: 01889 590288
Chef: Barbara Tunnicliffe
Proprietors: Barbara & Paul Tunnicliffe
Cost: Alc £14.50. H/wine £7.25 Service exc
Credit cards: 🆕 🔜 🔜 🔜
Times: Last D 9.00pm. Closed Xmas Eve to 30 Dec
Seats: 70. Smoking allowed with coffee if other guests do not object
Menus: A la carte, Sun L, bar menu, pre-theatre
Additional: Children welcome (no highchairs after 8pm), children's menu; ♥ dishes, other diets on request

Directions: Turn off A50 (Uttoxeter–Derby) at Doveridge, down Marston Lane, (signed Waldley). At Waldley take 1st right then 1st left

'En papillote' describes a manner of cooking and serving. It is quite simply a way of wrapping food so that it is tightly enclosed in buttered or oiled greaseproof paper or aluminium foil and then cooked in the oven. The wrapping swells during cooking and the dish is served piping hot before the wrapping collapses. This preserves the flavour and is a method often employed with fish which requires a short cooking time.

A 'papillote' on the other hand, is a small decorative paper frill used to decorate the bone end of a lamb or veal chop, rack of lamb or chicken drumstick.

MATLOCK, **Riber Hall Hotel** ❀

Expect some imaginative modern British dishes at this beautifully restored Elizabethan manor house. An October menu featured mille-feuille of lobster and scallops, fillet of lamb with a herb stuffing, and coconut soufflé, and was complemented by a good wine list of predominantly French wines

Matlock DE4 5JU
Map no: 8 SK35
Tel: 01629 582795
Chef: Jeremy Brazelle
Proprietor: Alex Biggin
Cost: *Alc* £27; fixed-price
L £14.50/D £20 (4 course).
H/wine £12.50 Service exc
Credit cards: 🂠 📷 📠 💳 OTHER
Times: Last L 1.30pm/D 9.30pm
Seats: 75. No-smoking room
Menus: *A la carte,* fixed-price
L/D, bar menu, pre-theatre
Additional: Children welcome,
children's portions; ❤ menu,
vegan/other diets on request

Directions: One mile off A615 at Tansley

MELBOURNE,
The Bay Tree Restaurant ❀

Good fresh produce is used in the cooking at this beamed cottage restaurant, which provides an intimate and relaxed atmosphere in which to dine. A well-balanced menu offers dishes such as lobster ravioli, steak and kidney pie with a chive mash, and summer fruits and berries for dessert

Menus: *A la carte* L & D, fixed-price Sun L
Seats: 45. Air conditioned
Additional: Children welcome, children's portions; other diets on request
Directions: Town centre

4 Potter Street DE7 1DW
Map no: 8 SK32
Tel: 01332 863358
Chef: Rex William Howell
Proprietors: Rex William
Howell, Victoria Ann Talbott
Cost: *Alc* £30, fixed-price Sun
L £15.50. H/wine £9.50 ❢
Service exc
Credit cards: 🂠 📷 📠 OTHER
Times: Last L 2pm/3.30 Sun, last
D 9.45pm. Closed Sun D, Mon,
1st wk Jan, 3 wks Summer

RIDGEWAY,
The Old Vicarage Restaurant ❀❀❀

Civilised setting for creative, seasonal cuisine

This grand Victorian vicarage, with its comfortable sitting-room and peaceful dining-room, provides a perfect setting for Tessa Bramley's self-taught culinary skills. Although the service is formal, the atmosphere is friendly and relaxed, with Tessa's son Andrew keeping a watchful eye on the proceedings. A lunchtime inspection showed that creative skills still shine brightly, using the best of ingredients in interesting combinations.

Sophisticated canapés set the tone with mini pizzas and bagels, black olives and nuts. Home-made granary bread comes warm with

Ridgeway Moor S12 3XW
Map no: 8 SK48
Tel: 01142 475814
Chef: Tessa Bramley
Proprietors: Tessa & Andrew
Bramley
Cost: Fixed-price L & D £18.50-
£20, £35 (4 course). H/wine £12
Credit cards: 🂠 📷 📠 OTHER
Times: Last L 2pm, last D
10.45pm. Closed Sat L, Sun D,
Mon, Dec 26/7, 1st wk Jan
Menus: Fixed-price L & D
Seats: 50. No smoking in dining
room

The Old Vicarage Restaurant

Additional: Children welcome, children's portions; ❂ dishes, vegan/other diets on request

salted butter. A first course of mussels in a saffron and smoked salmon cream with soft, fluffy potato cakes were tantalisingly spiced with aubergine and cumin, although the mussels were a little overcooked. A fillet of English sea bass baked with spring onion, lemon grass and ginger with a soy butter sauce, showed skill at marrying tastes and textures. Less so, with 'poulet noir' on a creamy risotto with the livers served as a warm salad with raspberry vinaigrette. This was diminished by sloppy rice soaking up some of the accompanying sauce, and although each element had individual flavour, the total combination made for an overly heavy and rich dish. Other main courses might include pan-fried calves' liver with piroski and parsnip purée, or roast monkfish tail with deep-fried leek, pancetta and rhubarb butter sauce. Rhubarb was also the theme of our inspection pudding – rhubarb strudel with star anise and rhubarb sauce was lightly spoilt by overworked pastry, but the creamy, rhubarby ice-cream was superb. In addition to the restaurant, simpler, daily-changing dishes are served in the less expensive conservatory bistro. A selection of Tessa Bramley's seasonal recipes has now been published in a book entitled 'The Instinctive Cook'.

Directions: S/E of Sheffield off the A616 on B6054; follow sign for Ridgeway Cottage Industries, restaurant is 300yds on the left

DEVON

ASHBURTON, **Holne Chase Hotel** ❀

This hotel, set on the edge of Dartmoor surrounded by well-kept grounds and impressive views, offers modern English cooking which makes good use of local produce, especially vegetables from their own kitchen garden. Expect breast of chicken with a mushroom stuffing, and white chocolate bavaroise

Menus: *A la carte,* fixed-price L & D, bar L menu
Seats: 40. No smoking in dining room
Additional: Children welcome (L preferred), children's portions.
❂ dishes, vegan/other diets on request
Directions: Three miles north of Ashburton on Poundsgate road

Newton Abbot TQ13 7NS
Map no: 3 SX 77
Tel: 01364 631471
Chef: Jonathan Houndell
Proprietors: Kenneth & Mary Bromage
Cost: Alc £25, fixed-price L £14.50/D £21 (4 course). H/wine £7.75 Service inc
Credit cards: ▨ ▤ ▤ ▨ OTHER
Times: Last L 1.45pm, last D 9pm

AXMINSTER, **Fairwater Head Hotel** ❀

A welcoming Edwardian house set in its own well-tended gardens amidst unspoilt countryside, with panoramic views across the Axe valley. The attractive dining-room offers dishes to suit both simple and more adventurous tastes, prepared using fresh local produce. Desserts include an excellent rich chocolate and brandy mousse

Menus: *A la carte,* fixed-price L & D, Sun lunch **Seats:** 45. No smoking in dining-room **Additional:** Children welcome, children's portions; ❂ dishes, other diets on request
Directions: From Axminster or Lyme Regis take B3165 to Crewkerne. Hawkchurch village is signposted and hotel signs on approach to village

Near Axminster EX13 51X
Map no: 3 ST30
Tel: 01297 678 349
Chef: Ian Carter and Robert Renshaw
Proprietor: John & Judith Lowe, Harry & Rita Austin
Cost: *Alc* £25, fixed-price L £11, fixed-price D £ 18.50 (4 courses). H/wine £8
Credit cards: 🌑 💳 💳 💳
Times: Last L-2pm, last D-8pm. Closed Jan/Feb

BAMPTON, **Bark House Hotel** ❀❀

A former tannery set on the edge of Exmoor serving good quality cooking to resident diners

Named after the tannery which occupied this building in the 19th century, Bark House is set in pretty gardens in the beautiful Exe valley, close to the edge of Exmoor. The hotel makes an ideal base for exploring Exmoor, and the Devon, Somerset and Dorset coasts. The kitchen produces a range of imaginative dishes inspired by seasonal fresh ingredients, and served from a daily-set menu, although alternatives to the fixed courses are available on request. Fresh flavours are a key note. However, food is served at a set time and is only available to resident guests. A meal taken in October began with haddock bound with herbs and shallots and served warm on a bed of dressed green leaves, was followed by roast lamb, cooked pink, and served with a rich gravy, crispy roast potatoes and flageolet beans sautéed with herbs and garlic, and finished with a dessert of a rich home-made chocolate cake and fresh, good quality filter coffee. A friendly atmosphere prevails in the hotel under Pauline and Douglas West's enthusiastic management.

Oakford Bridge
nr Tiverton EX16 9HZ
Map no: 3 SS92
Tel: 01398 351236
Proprietors: Mr & Mrs West

Directions: 7 miles north of Tiverton on the A396

BARNSTAPLE,
Halmpstone Manor Hotel ❀❀

A range of fresh local produce is used at this rural hotel

Bishop's Tawton EX32 0EA
Map no: 2 SS53
Tel: 01271 830321
Chef: Mrs Jane Stanbury
Proprietor: Mrs Jane Stanbury
Cost: Fixed-price D £30 (6 courses). H/wine £9.50. Service inc
Credit cards: 🌑 💳 💳 💳
Times: 7.30pm-last D 9.30pm. Closed Nov & Jan
Menu: Fixed-price D
Seats: 24. No smoking
Additional: Children over 12 permitted; ❂ dishes, other diets on request

Halmpstone Manor lies in rural splendour. The beautifully panelled restaurant is an atmospheric setting for some sound Anglo-French cooking prepared from top quality produce: local beef, clotted cream, fresh soft fruits, as well as fish and shellfish from Brixham. The menu is set, but lack of choice is made up for by the quality of the cooking. Canapés such as quails' eggs or slices of salmon and broccoli tart may begin the five-course meal. A menu sampled in June commenced with fresh asparagus soup, followed by a crab and avocado salad, then fillet of beef, perfectly cooked and of excellent flavour, accompanied by a light sauce, although an accompanying onion confit was found to be too sweet and tended to overwhelm the beef, and the sauce. An attractive sweet trolley featured fresh raspberries, strawberries, meringues, and lemon mousse, and a chocolate roulade with crisp exterior and nice chewy inside. A choice of cheeses can also be taken as a separate course.

Directions: From Barnstaple take A377 to Bishop's Tawton. At end of village left for Cobatton for 2 miles; Sign on right

BOVEY TRACEY, Edgemoor Hotel ❀

☺ *A varied choice of carefully-prepared food draws the crowds at this locally popular hotel. Selections might include a warm salmon, monkfish and prawn puff pastry shell on a dry vermouth sauce and pan-fried calves' liver stuffed with onions, followed by a choice of desserts and filter coffee with fudge*

Haytor Road TQ13 9LE
Map no: 3 SX87
Tel: 01626 832466
Chef: Edward Elliott
Proprietors: Rod & Pat Day
Cost: Fixed-price L £12.75/D £18.25. H/wine £6.95 Service exc
Credit cards: 🟥 💳 💳 💳
Times: Noon-last L 1.45pm, 7pm-last D 9pm
Menus: Fixed-price L/D, bar menu
Seats: 40. No smoking in dining room
Additional: Children over 8 permitted, children's portions; ❂ dishes, vegan/other diets on request

Directions: One mile from Bovey Tracey on B3387 Haytor road

BRANSCOMBE, The Masons Arms ❀

☺ *A hugely atmospheric 14th-century inn situated half a mile from the sea and surrounded by stunning countryside. The menu reads well, is strong on local fish, game and meat, and offers the likes of lamb cutlets with a red and blackcurrant sauce. Service hits the right balance between being professional whilst remaining friendly*

Branscombe EX12 3DJ
Map:
Tel: 01297 680300
Chef: John Hayden
Proprietor: Murray Inglis
Cost: Alc £19, fixed-price Sun L £9.95. H/wine £8 Service inc
Credit cards: 🟥💳 OTHER
Times: Noon-2.30pm, 7pm-9.30pm

Menus: A la carte D, fixed-price Sun L **Seats:** 60. No-smoking area
Additional: Children welcome, children's menu; ❂ menu, vegan/other diets on request
Directions: 0.5 mile from sea on quiet road which runs through village

BROADHEMBURY, **Drewe Arms** ✿

☺ *Fish from Newlyn features strongly on the fixed-price blackboard menu at the Drewe Arms. Forming the focal point of the village, this is the epitome of an English country pub. Look out for hot chicken and bacon salad, John Dory with crab and lobster butter, hazelnut meringue with coffee cream. Booking is essential*

Seats: 35. No cigars or pipes in restaurant
Menus: A la carte, fixed-price L/D
Additional: Children welcome, children's portions; other diets on request
Directions: From junction 28 (M5), 5 miles on A373 Cullompton to Honiton

Broadhembury EX14 0NF
Map no: 3 ST10
Tel: 01404 841267
Chef: Kerstin & Nigel Burge
Proprietors: Kerstin & Nigel Burge
Cost: Alc £20, fixed-price L/D £17.95. H/wine £8.45. Service exc
Credit cards: None taken
Times: 11pm-last L 2pm, 6pm-last D 10pm

BURRINGTON,
Northcote Manor Hotel ✿

☺ *This stone-built, gabled manor house stands in twelve acres of charming grounds. An interesting selection of dishes is offered in the restaurant, featuring the likes of a delicious main course of beef with polenta, and an excellent pudding of finely glazed apple tart with meltingly smooth walnut ice-cream*

Directions: On A377 12 miles S of Barnstaple, opposite Portsmouth Arms pub

Umberleigh EX37 9LZ
Map no: 3 SS61
Tel: 01769 560501
Chef: Monika Spichtinger
Proprietors: Northcote Manor UK Ltd. Managing Director: Norbert Spichtinger
Cost: Alc £13-20, fixed-price D £18.50. (5 courses) H/wine £8.50 ¶ No service charge
Credit cards: ▨ ▨ ▨ ▨ OTHER
Times: Noon-last L 1.30pm, 7pm-last D 9.30pm. Closed Jan 3-Feb 28
Seats: 30. No smoking in dining room
Menus: A la carte L & D, fixed-price D
Additional: No children under 12; ❷ dishes/other diets prior notice

CHAGFORD, **Easton Court Hotel** ✿

☺ *Parts of this charming, non-pretentious hotel date back to the 15th century and within there is an intimate and comfortable atmosphere. Imaginative fixed-price, five-course menus feature local fish and game. Our inspector particularly enjoyed a dessert of meringues with whipped cream and fudge sauce*

Menu: Fixed-price D
Seats: 20. No smoking in dining room
Additional: Children over 12 permitted; other diets on request
Directions: On the A382 by the turning to Chagford

Easton Cross TQ13 8JL
Map no: 3 SX78
Tel: 01647 433469
Chef: Lynne Dan
Proprietors: Graham & Sally Kidson
Cost: Fixed-price D £22 (5 course). H/wine £7.75. Service exc
Credit cards: ▨ ▨ ▨
Times: 7pm-last D 8.30pm. Closed Jan

CHAGFORD, **Gidleigh Park** ✿✿✿✿

Serious cooking from a dedicated, talented chef, in one of the top country house hotels in the country

Newton Abbot TQ13 8HH
Map no: 3 SX78
Tel: 01647 432367
Chef: Michael Caines
Proprietors: Kay & Paul
Henderson (Relais & Chateaux).
Manager: Catherine Endacott
Cost: Fixed-price L £30-£40/
D £52.50 or £57.50. H/wine
£18 ● Service inc
Credit cards: 🔲 🔲 🔲 🔲 OTHER
Times: Last L 2pm, last D 9pm
daily
Menus: A la carte, fixed-price
L & D, bar menu
Seats: 35-40. No smoking in
dining room
Additional: Children welcome,
children's portions; ◐ dishes,
vegan/other diets on request

Michael Caines has an impeccable pedigree. His training with Raymond Blanc, Bernard Loiseau and Joel Robuchon has left him with a deep understanding of flavour and classical perfection of technique. He is also a man of formidable tenacity, overcoming serious injury, sustained in a car accident, to become the work horse around which the Gidleigh Park kitchen revolves. It is quite a combination.

Two menus are offered at dinner, a *carte* with around six choices per course, and a daily-changing 'Speciality Menu' which offers choice only at dessert. The latter features ideas that are likely to become Michael Caines' signature dishes, and a lentil and foie gras soup certainly falls into this category. It is done with a nod to Gordon Ramsey's cappuccino of langoustines. A light yet strongly flavoured lentil base, which was frothy on the surface, had foie gras (which had been seared then cubed) added to the soup at the very last minute. The liver remained pink and moist with no sign of further cooking in the liquid. Each taste of the foie gras created 'a taste explosion'. A middle course of ravioli of crab with ginger and lemon grass was a wonderful combination. There was no mousse or farce to bind the crab and this allowed the fresh flavours to shine through. The sauce, from sweated crab shells with brown meat, lemon grass and ginger, was a great accompaniment to the delicate pasta. A fondness for more humble ingredients in combination with luxuries is perhaps inherited from Raymond Blanc. A dish of stuffed leg of rabbit with buttered potatoes and lettuce was delightful, the leg boned and stuffed with rabbit livers scented with rosemary. Pastry work is also excellent, and a pistachio nut soufflé with pistachio ice-cream was worthy of Pierre Koffman.
Dishes on the *carte* have an appealing freshness. Salad of scallops and potatoes with truffle vinaigrette, or warm quail salad with crispy bacon, followed by red mullet with olives, tomato and fennel served with fennel cream sauce, or roast pigeon and potato galette, with pan-fried foie gras and Madeira sauce, are examples of the style. An indication of the level of dedication, and ambition, is the range of bread on offer; during an overnight stay, one inspector sampled eight varieties. Canapés are also well thought out: anchovy twists, cheese sablés, foie gras parfait and lamb fillet on creamed

vegetables and smoked salmon preceded our inspection meal. Of the wines it is sufficient to note that Paul Henderson's list is perhaps one of the two or three best in the country.

Directions: Chagford Square facing Webbers turn right, right fork, straight across crossroads into Holy Street. Restaurant in 1.5 miles

CHAGFORD, **Mill End Hotel** ✿

Sandy Park TQ13 8JN
Map no: 3 SX78
Tel: 01647 432282
Chef: Hazel Craddock
Proprietors: Nicholas Craddock
Cost: Alc £28.50; fixed-price
L £9.95-£15.00. H/wine £8.50.
Service exc
Credit cards: 🃏 💳 💳 💳 OTHER
Times: Last L 1.45pm/D 9pm.
Closed 5-15 Dec, 10-20 Jan
Seats: 40. No smoking

There is a relaxed atmosphere at this attractive former flour mill where the wheel still turns in the courtyard. Food is well prepared and enjoyable, especially the roasted Trelough duck with fresh sage, and the award-winning cheese selection is excellent

Additional: Children welcome, children's portions; ✿ dishes; Vegan/other diets on request. Live entertainment occasionally
Directions: From Exeter take A30 to Whiddon Down, turn south on A382 signposted Moreton Hampstead – do not turn into Chagford at Sandy Park, the hotel is at Dogmarsh Bridge

CHARDSTOCK, **Tytherleigh Cot Hotel** ✿

Axminster EX13 7BN
Map no: 3 ST30
Tel: 01460 221170
Chef: Patricia Grudgings
Proprietor: Frank Grudgings
Cost: Alc £24, fixed-price
L £14.95/D £18.95. Wine
£10.50 ▮ Service inc
Credit cards: 🃏 💳
Times: Last L 1.30pm/last D
9.30pm
Seats: 35. Air conditioned. No smoking in dining room.
Menus: A la carte, fixed-price L (non-resident by arrangement), fixed-price D
Additional: Children over 10 welcome, children's menu; ✿ dishes, other diets on request

Centred around a 14th-century former cider-house, this friendly hotel offers a range of good quality cooking in its conservatory restaurant. Dishes such as a fresh asparagus, noisettes of lamb with a herb crust, and bread and butter pudding are carefully prepared and served in a relaxed and informal atmosphere

Directions: In village centre one mile off A358 Chard/Axminster road

CHITTLEHAMHOLT, **Highbullen** ✿

Chittlehamholt
Umberleigh EX37 9HD
Tel: 01769 540561
Proprietor: Mr & Mrs Neil

A splendid Victorian mansion amid its own parkland and ancient, semi-natural woodland – ideal for bird-lovers and anglers. Light lunches are available in the bar or courtyard. Dinner in the restaurant could be fresh lobster and celery tart, grilled Oriental quail, or baked sea bass in lettuce with herbs

Directions: From Exeter A377 turn right onto B3226, left into village

CLAWTON, **Court Barn Hotel** ✿

☺ *The Victorian manor house set in five acres of grounds provides a gentle, relaxed atmosphere. The kitchen makes good use of local produce and from the five-course dinner menu one can choose robust dishes such as a chunky celery soup with Stilton, chicken roulade and a varied selection of puddings*

Clawton EX22 6PS
Map: 2 SX39
Tel: 01409 271219
Chef: Sue Wood
Proprietor: Robert Wood
Cost: Fixed-price L & D £16.50.
H/wine £8.25 ❢ Service inc
Credit cards: 🖸 ▦ ▦ ▣ OTHER
Times: Last L 1.30pm, last D
9pm. Occasionally closed in
winter
Menus: Fixed-price L & D, bar
menu
Seats: 35. No smoking in dining
room
Additional: Children welcome,
children's menu; ✆ menu,
vegan/other on request

Directions: Next to Church in Clawton 2.5 miles S of Holsworthy on A388

COLYFORD, **Swallows Eaves Hotel** ✿

☺ *A privately-run hotel set in the beautiful countryside of east Devon is the spot for some sound cooking. Fresh local produce features on the fixed-price menu which offers a decent choice of starters and dessert. Expect dishes along the lines of chicken breast stuffed with mushrooms with an orange sauce*

Seats: 16. No smoking
Additional: No children; other diets on request
Directions: In the centre of the village on the A3082

Swan Hill Road EX13 6QJ
Map no: 3 SY29
Tel: 01297 553184
Chef: Jane Beck
Proprietors: Jane & Jon Beck
Cost: Fixed-price D £18 (5
course) H/wine £8.50 ❢ Service
inc
Credit cards: None taken
Times: 7pm-last D 8pm. Closed
Jan

CROYDE, **Kittiwell House Hotel** ✿

☺ *A delightful, small, thatched hotel situated at the end of the village with a local reputation for food. Fresh produce is used to good effect with careful cooking seen in crab pastries with cream and brandy sauce, roast beef sirloin, and in the selection of vegetables. Sherry trifle is a wonderful, traditional dessert*

Menus: *A la carte,* fixed-price D & Sun L
Seats: 45
Additional: Children permitted, children's portions; ✆ dishes,
vegan/other diets on request
Directions: At top end of Croyde village

Croyde EX33 1PG
Map: 2 SS43
Tel: 01271 890247
Chef: David Rayner
Proprietors: Yvonne & James
Lang
Cost: *Alc* £18, fixed-price D
£15.90/Sun L £8.90. H/wine
£8.50 Service exc
Credit cards: 🖸 ▦ ▦ OTHER
Times: Noon-last L 2pm, 7pm-
last D 9.15pm. Closed Sun D,
mid Jan-mid Feb

DARTMOUTH,
Carved Angel Restaurant ❀❀❀

Home cooking elevated to the highest order in celebrated quayside restaurant

The Carved Angel has many other attributes other than good food; its location on Dartmouth's quayside, the bright, high-ceilinged dining room open to the working kitchen, and the accomplished service provided by a young staff who alternate kitchen and waiting duties. The latter results in a team which is both interested and knowledgeable about the food it serves. Joyce Molyneux has been at the Carved Angel for 21 years, and she is as passionate about her calling as ever. Not only has she long supported the produce of local farmers and fishermen, but all the restaurant pottery and glassware is made locally.

In the evening, a meal starts with a bowl of good olives and cheese straws and a selection of appetisers such as marinated stir-fried squid with chilli and lime, smoked salmon beignet and crab tart. A provençale fish soup was textured with vegetables and flaked fish and, as well as the usual Gruyère and croûtons, served with a fiery, fresh chilli rouille, rather like a salsa. Fried crab cakes were neatly made and set off in the American style with chopped guacamole. A middle cut of the freshest turbot was impeccably cooked and served on the bone, topped with a tangy orange and black olive butter. Braised fennel was full of real flavour, as were the new potatoes, chopped leeks, batons of celeriac and wilted spinach parcels. Other main course dishes might feature Dart salmon trout with rhubarb and white wine, breast of duck with pears, red wine and beetroot, and chargrilled guinea fowl with lemon and tarragon sauce and hazelnut noodles. For dessert, a chocolate pithivier, with vanilla ice-cream, had a rich gooey chocolate and almond filling, and an alternative dessert of Seville orange custard was perfect. There are lovely local cheeses, with flaky oat biscuits and home-made quince cheese.

Directions: Dartmouth centre, on the waters edge

2 South Embankment TQ6 9BH
Map no: 3 SX85
Tel: 01803 832465
Chefs: Joyce Molyneux and Nick Coiley
Proprietors: J Molyneux, N Coiley, M Matthews and D Shephard
Cost: *Alc* L £37.50, fixed-price L £29/D £45. H/wine £15
Service inc
Credit cards: OTHER
Times: Last L 1.45pm/D 9.30pm. Closed Sun, Mon, 6 weeks from Jan 2
Menus: *A la carte* L, fixed-price L & D, light L
Seats: 45. No smoking in dining room
Additional: Children welcome, children's portions; ❂ dishes, vegan/other diets on request

DARTMOUTH,
The Exchange Restaurant ❀❀

Inspired cooking in a smart, two-storey, brasserie-style restaurant in the heart of a town with a long nautical history

It must be difficult adjusting to cooking on dry land after eight years as a chef on a private yacht. But David Hawke has managed it and at least here in Dartmouth the sea is only metres away from his centuries-old restaurant, should he tire of being a landlubber. The restaurant is in two sections, partly at the rear on the ground floor, the rest a galleried area upstairs. The lunchtime selection is simple and salad-oriented, while the *carte* always reflects its owner's travels, and the Channel's proximity; at least one fish dish features daily. Interesting starters may include lightly spiced, devilled crab balls with aioli, scallops seared in sesame oil with fresh chillies, or black bean cakes with red pepper coulis and sour cream. To follow, pan-fried fillets of John Dory with capers, or pork fillet with orange, sweet pepper and rosemary, or perhaps lambs' kidneys sautéed with bacon and red wine, for example. Carefully sourced produce

5 Higher Street TQ6 9RB
Map no: 3 SX85
Tel: 01803 832022
Chef: David C Hawke
Proprietor: David C Hawke
Cost: *Alc* £22/24. H/wine £7.85
Service exc
Credit cards: ▨ ▨ OTHER
Times: 10.30am-last L 2pm/D 10pm. Closed Tue & Christmas
Menus: *A la carte*, fixed-price Sun L in winter
Seats: 50
Additional: Children permitted; ❂ dishes, vegan on request

includes organic duck breast, served, perhaps, with grapefruit, pink peppercorn and brandy sauce. For dessert, try the lemon syllabub. The Exchange operates brasserie-style, with relaxed informal service. The wine list is simple and reasonably priced.

Directions: In town centre near parish church

ERMINGTON, Ermewood House Hotel ✺

☺ *Traditional English cooking with a French accent, based on fresh local produce, is a feature at this friendly hotel overlooking the River Erme. Simple dishes reveal good strong flavours: broccoli and Stilton soup, breast of chicken with a tarragon and cream sauce, and chocolate truffle cake*

Seats: 22. No smoking in dining room
Additional: Children permitted; ♥ dishes; Vegan/other diets on request
Directions: Driveway to hotel off the A3121

Totnes Road PL21 9NS
Map no: 2 SX65
Tel: 01548 830741
Chef: Jack Mellor
Proprietors: Jack & Jennifer Mellor
Cost: Fixed-price D £17.50. H/wine £8.95 ♥ Service exc
Credit cards: ◪ ▨
Times: Last D 8.30pm. Closed Sun, Xmas and New Year

EXETER, Buckerell Lodge Hotel ✺✺

☺ *Skill and flair combine in the modern English/French dishes that make up this restaurant's tempting menus*

The air-conditioned restaurant of this pleasant family-run hotel near the city centre continues to please with its fixed-price three-course lunch and four-course dinner menus. Cooking is in the modern style, executive chef Melvin Rumbles bringing imagination as well as sound technique to the preparation of a range of French and English dishes. The prawn bisque served at a recent inspection meal was slightly lacking in flavour but the excellent beef which followed was accompanied by an intense sauce. A well executed liver dish looked equally appetising, while desserts included a good plum tart and chocolate truffle cake. Car parking is available nearby and the restaurant offers easy access to wheelchair users.

Directions: City centre on B3182/Topsham road. 200yds past County Hall

Topsham Road EX2 4SQ
Map no: 3 SX99
Tel: 01392 52451
Chefs : Melvin Rumbles and Robert Drakket
Proprietors: Bruce & Pat Jefford
Cost: Fixed-price L £14.95/D £19.95 (4 course) H/wine £9.95 Service exc
Credit cards: ◪ ▨ ▨ other
Times: Noon-last L 2pm/D 9.45pm
Menus: Fixed-price L & D
Seats: 60
Additional: Children welcome, children's portions; ♥ dishes, vegan/other diets on request

EXETER, Ebford House Hotel ✺✺

Interesting modern cooking using fresh local ingredients to create some robust dishes

Situated on the Exmouth road near Topsham, this pleasant Georgian hotel is noted for serving food that reflects the locality in its materials. Fresh local fish appear on a menu with a strong emphasis on home-baked bread, freshly made soups, sauces and puddings. An inspector reported glowingly on the quality of the ingredients used, particularly lamb which was 'cooked to perfection'. If there was a niggle it was that there can be a tendency to combine too many flavours in a dish; these do not always work. A typical meal might start with wild mushroom and guinea fowl terrine with tomato and chive vinaigrette, or pan-fried strips of chicken cooked with mixed herbs and brandy, followed by duck breast mille-feuille with glazed garlic and shallots and a plum

Exmouth Road EX3 0QH
Map no: 3 SX99
Tel: 01392 877658
Chefs: Mark Brimson and Paul Bazell
Proprietor: S Horton.
Manager: Carol McIntyre
Cost: Alc £20-£25, fixed-price L £12.95/D £18.50. H/wine £8.30 Service exc
Credit cards: ◪ ▨ ▨ OTHER
Times: Noon-last L 1.30pm, 6.30pm-last D 9.30pm. Closed Dec 24-28
Menus: A la carte, fixed-price L/D, bar menu, pre-theatre

Ebford House Hotel

Seats: 50. No smoking in dining room
Additional: Children welcome, children's menu; **❂** dishes, vegan/other diets on request

masala sauce, or pan-fried sirloin stuffed with Stilton and served with a wild mushroom and port wine sauce. Puddings are highly recommended. Don and Samantha Horton have worked hard to create a relaxed and friendly atmosphere.

Directions: On A376 Exmouth road near Topsham

EXETER, St Olaves Court Hotel ❀❀

Stylish modern English cooking is served in the candlelit restaurant of this Georgian hotel

Mary Arches Street EX4 3AZ
Map no: 3 SX99
Tel: 01392 217736
Chefs: Jason Horn and John Winstanley
Proprietors: R J & V Wyatt,
Cost: *Alc* £25-£29, fixed-price L & D £13.50. H/wine £10.50 ♥
Service exc
Credit cards: 🂡 🂢 🂣 🂤 OTHER
Times: Last L 2pm/D 9.30pm.
Closed Sat L, Sun L, Jan 2-9
Menus: *A la carte,* fixed-price L & D, pre-theatre, bar menu
Seats: 60. No smoking in dining room

One can be forgiven for thinking that time has stopped on entering this delightful, privately-run Georgian hotel: the old-fashioned feel of the place, the walled garden and the proximity to the cathedral all combine to create a tranquillity that is hard to shatter. Jason Horn – an Irish Young Chef finalist – is responsible for the imaginative modern English dishes served in the candlelit restaurant. A serious approach to cooking is reflected in the food, although less enthusiastic experimentation might improve the final result. A typical meal might begin with a beautifully presented terrine of leek and monkfish with a lemon and chive oil dressing, and continue with succulent oven-roasted chicken breast, filled with spinach and sliced onto a delicately flavoured grain mustard and sherry sauce. Dessert might be a rich chocolate pithivier with raspberry and orange ice-cream and a minted crème anglaise. Bread and petits fours are all made on the premises. The wine list complements the food, but is not over-extensive; some New World wines are included.

Directions: City centre, follow signs 'Mary Arches P'. Hotel is opposite

GITTISHAM, **Combe House Hotel** ❀❀

☺ *Impressive cooking in an exceptional Elizabethan manor house*

Co-owner John Boswell's lifetime involvement with racehorses is pretty evident. Pictures of his winners adorn the bar/lounge and some of his wife Therese's paintings, sculptures and murals are also displayed around the house, a fine Elizabethan manor. The beautiful grounds incorporate a stretch of fishing rights on the River Otter and a helicopter landing pad. The kitchen comes under Thérèse Boswell's jurisdiction and she supervises its activities very carefully. The food continues to impress – in fact, a late spring dinner was near-faultless. That particular meal began with a warm salad of succulent local scallops, sauteed in butter with garlic and mushrooms, then duck breast, with a piquant garlic, ginger and spring onion sauce, and ended with a smooth, delicious lemon tart with just the right amount of citrus flavour to cut through the smooth cream. There is a choice of short fixed-price menus or *carte* featuring country house-style cooking, together with a light lunch menu priced according to courses taken, and a fixed-price lunch on Sundays. The Boswells' son Mark owns a wine shop in nearby Ilminster and a selection from his stock comprises the wine list.

Directions: In Gittisham village off A30 & A303 south of Honiton

GULWORTHY, **The Horn of Plenty** ❀❀❀

Georgian house in the foothills of Dartmoor where the cooking lives up to its name

Additional: Children welcome, children's portions; ❂ dishes, vegan/other diets on request

Honiton EX14 0AD
Map no: 3 SY19
Tel: 01404 42756
Chef: Thérèse Boswell
Proprietors: John & Thérèse Boswell
Cost: *Alc* £18.50, fixed-price L £11.75/ D £18.50. H/wine £9 ❢ Service inc
Credit cards: OTHER
Times: Last L 2pm/ D 9.30
Menus: A la carte, fixed-price L & D, bar menu
Seats: 60
Additional: Children welcome, children's menu; ❂ dishes, vegan/other diets on request

Tavistock PL19 8JD
Map no: 2 SX47
Tel: 01822 832528
Chefs: Peter Gorton
Proprietors: Ian & Elaine Gatehouse
Cost: Fixed-price L £17.50/D £28.50. H/wine £11 Service exc
Credit cards: 🔲 🔳 🔳

Taking pot luck at The Horn of Plenty, a restaurant with rooms near Gulworthy, redefines the term. Monday dinners can be chosen from a shortened 'Pot Luck' menu at an inclusive £18.50 and such is

the quality and value, advance booking is now essential. Peter Gorton's cooking is as fine as the splendid views the 18th-century house commands over the Tamar Valley and, together with Kevin Bingham, he offers a good fixed-price menu, which includes a daily changing fish dish and speciality. The repertoire ranges far and wide, but is checked by a proper sense of restraint within each dish. Seasonal salad of pigeon, pine nuts and crispy bacon with a raspberry vinaigrette, roast rack of Devonshire lamb with a parsley crust and Madeira sauce, and pan-fried breast of duck marinated in Chinese spices, served with an orange and ginger sauce, are typical of the *carte*.

Canapés of hot salmon in filo pastry and duck liver started a winter inspection meal. The residual salt in an otherwise deliciously fresh first course of home-salted cod, on a bed of lentils with shallot butter sauce, slightly overpowered the flavour of the fish. Of the two main courses sampled, duck was tender and delicately flavoured, accompanied by rösti potatoes and set on a bed of celeriac. Although sole and prawns wrapped in a light tempura batter on a white wine sauce were equally enjoyable, a dipping sauce might have been a better choice, as the batter absorbed the sauce beneath. Vegetables were precisely cooked and seasoned. A dark, rich chocolate tart served with coconut sorbet kept up the standard, but the choice might equally well have been sticky toffee pudding with caramel sauce and clotted cream, or tulip horns filled with a white chocolate mousse and fresh strawberries. An extensive wine list offers depth and interest, and includes a good selection of halves.

Directions: 3 miles from Tavistock on A390. Turn right at Gulworthy Cross, then signed

Times: Last L 2pm/D 9.30pm. Closed Mon L
Menus: Fixed-price L & D
Seats: 50. No smoking in dining room
Additional: Children permitted (over 13 at D); ❂ dishes, vegan/other diets on request

HAYTOR, **Bel Alp House** ❂

Superb views across Dartmoor to the sea, and country-house cooking are features of this delightful Edwardian house. An alternative to the set choice menu is always available, and dishes may include smoked salmon parcel with prawns and mayonnaise, and honey-roasted duck breast on an orange sauce

Menu: Fixed-price D
Seats: 24. No smoking in dining room
Additional: Children over 6 welcome, children's early supper; ❂ dishes, other diets on request
Directions: 2.5 miles west of Bovey Tracey off B3387 to Haytor

Newton House TQ13 9XX
Map no: 3 SX77
Tel: 01364 661217
Chef: Sarah Curnoch
Proprietors: Roger & Sarah Curnoch
Cost: Fixed-price D £30 (4 course) H/wine £9. Service exc
Credit cards: ▨ ▨ OTHER
Times: Last D 8.30pm

HAYTOR, **Rock Inn** ❂

☺ *A delightful 16th-century inn with exposed beams, inglenook fireplaces and flagstone floors. Both the bar snack menu and the carte include interesting selections of fish, meat and game. Inspection yielded a decent beef in a red wine sauce, and lemon meringue pie*

Menus: A la carte, bar menu
Seats: 25. No smoking in dining room
Additional: Children welcome, children's portions; ❂ menu, vegan/other on request
Directions: In Haytor village on A3387, 3 miles from A382

Haytor TQ13 9XP
Map no: 3 SX77
Tel: 01364 661305
Chefs: Philip Hurrell and Steven Bowden
Proprietor: Christopher H H Graves
Cost: Alc £21.50 H/wine £7.25
Credit cards: ▨ ▨ ▨ OTHER
Times: Last L 2.15pm, last D 9.30pm

HOLBETON, **Alston Hall Hotel** ❀

Set in four acres of parkland, this Edwardian manor house offers a combination of modern and traditional dishes in the elegant Peony Room Restaurant. A March meal began with a roulade of smoked haddock with sole and smoked salmon, followed by lamb cutlets, and a dark chocolate and mocha mousse

Seats: 40. No smoking in dining room
Menu: Fixed-price D, bar menu
Additional: Children permitted (over 7 at dinner), children's menu; ❂ dishes, vegan/other diets on request
Directions: From A 379 take turning for Holbeton & bypass the village passing through Battilsborough Cross, hotel sign 0.75 mile on right

Alston PL8 1HN
Map no: 2 SX65
Tel: 01752 830555
Chef: Malcolm Morrison
Manager: Tim Pettifer
Cost: Fixed-price L £15/D £22 H/wine £10.95. Service exc
Credit cards: 🔳 🔳 🔳 🔳
Times: Noon-last L 1.45pm, 7pm-last D 9.30pm daily

HORRABRIDGE, **Overcombe Hotel** ❀

☺ *Overlooking Dartmoor, Overcombe Hotel provides a friendly home from home atmosphere. The short menu continues to please by offering carefully cooked dishes based on good quality ingredients. Freshly baked local granary bread is a plus, as is the robustly flavoured cream of spinach soup. Service is quiet and efficient*

Seats: 23. No smoking in dining room
Additional: Children welcome, children's portions; ❂ dishes; Vegan/other diets on request
Directions: Off the A386 past Yelverton roundabout travelling towards Tavistock. Take first left after sign Horrabridge

Near Yelverton PL20 7RN
Map no: 2 SX56
Tel: 01822 853501
Chef: Brenda J Durnell
Proprietors: Maurice and Brenda Durnell
Cost: Fixed-price D £12. Wine £8.25 litre. Service inc
Credit cards: 🔳 🔳
Times: Last D 7.30pm

ILFRACOMBE, **Elmfield Hotel** ❀

☺ *A range of well-prepared dishes are offered in the restaurant of this detached Victorian house. The carte and good-value fixed-price menu may feature dishes such as smoked salmon pâté, roast Ilfracombe lamb with mint sauce, and pork cooked with cider and apple; a good selection of desserts are also available*

Seats: 30. No smoking in dining room
Menus: A la carte, fixed-price D, bar L menu
Additional: Children permitted (over 8); ❂ menu, vegan/other diets on request
Directions: From Barnstaple on A361, at first lights left (Wilder Road), left next lights, left into Torrs Park. At top of hill on the left

Torrs Park EX34 8AZ
Map no: 2 SS54
Tel: 01271 863377
Chef: Ann Doody
Proprietors: Ann & Derek Doody
Cost: Alc £20, fixed-price D £11. H/wine £7.50 ♥ Service exc
Credit cards: 🔳 🔳
Times: Last bar L 1.45pm/last D 8pm Closed Nov-Mar

The sturgeon was still common in the river Gironde in France at the turn of the century and the present sturgeon fishery in the Gironde estuary is of some importance. Shortly after the First World War, Alfred Prunier (of the famous Paris restaurant) took a holiday in the region and recognised a neglected opportunity. He dispatched a knowledgeable Russian emigré and caviar has been produced there ever since. It is more lightly salted than the Russian and Iranian ones and is best eaten fresh in the region during June and July.

IVYBRIDGE,
Glazebrook House Hotel ❀

A delightful mid-Victorian house set in beautiful gardens on the southern edge of Dartmoor. The menu uses the best of local produce to create imaginative and well-balanced dishes. Look out for fresh mushroom soup, and tender venison medallions with a red wine and blackcurrant sauce

South Brent TQ10 9SE
Map: 3 SX65
Tel: 01364 73322
Chef: David Merriman
Proprietors: Sue & Laurence Cowley
Cost: Alc £25.50, fixed-price L & D £19.50. H/wine £8.95 Service inc
Credit cards: 🔳 🔳
Times: Last L 2.30pm, last D 9pm
Menus: A la carte, fixed-price L & D
Seats: 20. No smoking in dining room
Additional: Children permitted; ❂ dishes, vegan/other on request

Directions: Follow B&B signs from A38 at S. Brent to Glazebrook

KINGSBRIDGE,
Buckland-Tout-Saints Hotel ❀❀

A delightful Queen Anne manor house offering modern cooking prepared from fresh local produce

The mellow Queen Anne mansion is in an idyllic, secluded spot, surrounded by rolling Devon countryside. David Newland's short, fixed-price menu is product-led and the cooking is the sort favoured by country houses – light, avoiding the wilder aspects of modernism but not too obvious either. This translates as salmon and sole roulade, poached collops of monkfish with asparagus passata and sun-dried tomato, or sauté tenderloin of pork fillet with forest mushrooms and braised wild rice. An inspection meal taken in early summer indicated that the kitchen still required some fine-tuning. Tagliatelle with pieces of smoked chicken and a creamy pepper-based sauce was a little heavy and the accompanying sauce somewhat overpowering, and baked seabass came with an uninspiring white wine sauce, although the fish was delicately-flavoured and perfectly cooked. A good hot lemon and raspberry soufflé followed. The friendly staff offer attentive service.

Goveton TQ7 2DS
Map no: 3 SX74
Tel: 01548 853055
Chef: David Newland
Proprietors: John & Tove Taylor (Price of Britain)
Cost: Fixed-price L £14.50, fixed-price D £25. Service exc
Credit cards: 🔳 🔳 🔳 🔳
Times: Last L 1.45pm, Last D 9.30pm
Menus: Fixed-price lunch and dinner, Sun lunch
Seats: 54. No smoking in dining room
Additional: Children permitted; no babies at dinner; children's portions; ❂ menu

Directions: Two miles north-east of Kingsbridge, off the A381

Prices quoted in the Guide are based on information supplied by the establishments themselves.

LEWDOWN, Lewtrenchard Manor ❀❀

A 400-year-old manor house where the food is interesting, but never unnecessarily complicated

In the soft, green Devon countryside just below Dartmoor is the old stone manor house of Lewtrenchard, once the home of the Rev. Sabine Baring Gould, a hymn writer and novelist. Built around 1600, on the site of an earlier dwelling recorded in the Domesday Book, it is rich in ornate ceilings, oak panelling, carvings and large open fireplaces. James and Sue Murray run it, and Patrick Salvadori returned as head chef in 1994 to resume the devising and preparation of his unfussy, but excellent meals. An idea of his style may be gained from the short, six-item-per-course dinner menu. Starters might be pan-fried scallops with cucumber spaghetti and gazpacho sauce, fresh asparagus with a light Roquefort sauce and poached quails' eggs, or veal terrine studded with onions and herbs with a Cumberland sauce. For a main course, roast cutlet of new season's lamb with wholegrain mustard sauce, pork tenderloin wrapped in bacon, with a hint of garlic and a white wine sauce, or steamed fillet of wild salmon, with samphire and a light Noilly Prat sauce, might feature. All are accompanied by a selection of lightly cooked fresh vegetables.

Directions: Village centre, turn off A30 at Lewdown, signs for Lewtrenchard

Okehampton EX20 4PN
Map no: 2 SX48
Tel: 01556 783256
Chef: Patrick Salvador
Proprietors: James & Sue Murray
(Pride of Britain)
Cost: Fixed-price L £16/D £26.
H/wine £8.50 Service exc
Credit cards: 🂠 💳 💳 💳 OTHER
Times: Last L 1.45pm, last D 9.30pm daily
Menus: Fixed-price L & D, light L menu
Seats: 30. No smoking in dining room
Additional: Children welcome (over 8 at D), children's portions; vegan/other diets on request

LIFTON, Arundell Arms ❀❀❀

Stylish and vibrant cooking in welcoming, country pursuits hotel

Lifton PL16 0AA
Map no: 2 SX35
Tel: 01566 784666
Chefs: Philip Burgess and Nick Shopland
Proprietor: Anne Voss-Bark
(Best Western)
Cost: Fixed-price L £16.50/D £24.50 & £30.75. H/wine £9.75
❗ Service exc
Credit cards: 🂠 💳 💳 💳 OTHER
Times: Last L 2pm/D 9.30pm
Closed D Christmas
Menus: Fixed-price L & D, bar menu
Seats: 70. No smoking in dining room
Additional: Children permitted, children's portions; ♥ dishes, other diets on request

Popular for country sporting holidays, this hospitable old coaching inn, on the edge of Dartmoor, boasts 20 miles of fishing waters. It offers a congenial, rustic interior with attractive lounge and bar, featuring flagstone floors and log fires, and an elegant cream and apricot dining-room. One of the main strengths of the hotel is the cooking of Philip Burgess, who makes imaginative use of first-class seasonal produce, particularly fish and game. Tamar salmon, for example, comes either locally-smoked with cucumber pickle, or poached with cucumber, fennel purée and chervil and tarragon butter.

The short, sensible menu is basically English with French classical overtones. Typical dishes include braised oxtail with horseradish dumplings, root vegetables and Madeira, and roasted rack of English new season lamb with celeriac dauphinoise and mint and saffron sauce. Both a rich leek and wood mushroom tart with Gruyère cheese, and smooth pan-fried lambs' kidneys with creamy garlic dressing got our inspection dinner off to a flying start. A main course of fillet of Trelough duck, lightly glazed with honey and cooked pink with hints of ginger and lemon grass, scored highly. The fluffy fillet of Cornish sea bass, on a confit of shallots, garlic and wild mushrooms, ran a close second. Bright, colourful al dente vegetables accompanied. Iced poppy seed terrine had a lip-smacking butterscotch sauce, but caramelised rice pudding or English strawberry trifle would tempt equally. There is also a selection of local farmhouse cheeses, and a savoury, baked goats' cheese salad. Commendably, there is a separate mini list of 'Verre de Vin' preserved wines by the glass, as well as the balanced main list. Occasional gourmet events are worth looking out for, such as a Viennese Christmas and a spring festival gala dinner.

Directions: Just off A30 in village of Lifton

LIFTON, **Lifton Hall** 🏵🏵

Stylish hotel restaurant offering unusual and imaginative modern cooking

Gary and Mary Dodds acquired the hotel late in 1993 and since then have totally refurbished it. Dan's Bar has the character of a village inn and serves an interesting range of bar meals, but the real eating takes place in Herbs Restaurant. Here, under chef Christopher Hope, East meets West – eastern flavours, West Country produce, that is. There are modern British dishes as well. One of the first things to notice is the unusual home-made bread, with ingredients such as smoked bacon and blue cheese, or carrot and basil. Appetisers, or 'teasers' as they are known here, include the highly recommended crab in a creamy, oriental spiced sauce, served in a filo basket. A meal taken one spring day revealed slightly overcooked grilled scallops which had begun to toughen, and the separate flavours of turbot, wild salmon and monkfish didn't quite make their intended rendezvous. A white chocolate parfait was a picture – thin layers of crisply cooked puff pastry dusted with slightly caramelised icing sugar, either side of a creamy parfait sitting on a zabaglione-type sauce, and a strawberry coulis decorated with Alpine strawberries. The kitchen's style and presentation could be less complicated.

Directions: Leave A30 signposted Lifton Down/Tavistock. Hotel is 300yds from village on left

Lifton PL16 0DR
Map: 2 SX38
Tel: 01566 784863/784263
Chef: Christopher Hope
Proprietors: Mary & Gary Dodds
Cost: *Alc* £22, fixed-price L & D £19.80. H/wine £7.25 ♥ Service inc
Credit cards: 🔳 🔳 🔳 🔳 OTHER
Times: 7.30am-last D 9.30pm
Menus: *A la carte,* fixed-price L & D, bar menu
Seats: 30. No smoking
Additional: Children welcome, children's portions; ❶ dishes, other diets on request

The Japanese sukiyaki is a 'nabemono' dish, which simply means cooked at the table. The origin of 'nabemono' dishes dates from the time when religion banned the consumption of meat. Sukiyaki - which translates as 'grilled on a ploughshare' - developed in country districts when peasants used to cut birds and game into thin strips and grill them secretly in the fields. Nowadays, sukiyaki consists of wafer-thin slices of beef, pieces of vegetables, vermicelli or thin noodles and bean curd, sautéed in a pan at the table, with raw egg added before serving.

LIFTON,

Thatched Cottage Hotel ❀

Low beamed ceilings and inglenook fireplace produce a cosy atmosphere in this 16th-century thatched cottage. A good selection of home-cooked dishes are offered, ranging from fillet of trout with a white wine sauce to a hearty meal of roast beef and Yorkshire pudding. For dessert try the fruit crumble

Sprytown PL16 0AY
Map no: 3 SS74
Tel: 01566 784224
Chefs: Rita Willing and Victoria Bryant
Proprietors: G & R Willing, V. Bryant and J Purr
Cost: Alc £13.45, fixed-price D £19.50. H/wine £8.50 ! Service exc
Credit cards: ▨ ▩ ▩ ▨ OTHER
Times: Last L 2pm, last D 9.30 pm
Seats: 32. No-smoking area
Additional: Children permitted, children's portions; ❂ dishes, other diets on request
Menus: A la carte L, fixed-price D, weight watchers menu

Directions: From A30 at Stowford turn S on C493 2 miles to Sprytown Cross – straight ahead 100yds on right

LYMPSTONE,

River House Restaurant ❀❀

Informal restaurant with lovely estuary views serving fresh, soundly cooked food

The Strand EX8 5EY
Map no: 3 SX98
Tel: 01395 265147
Chef: Shirley Wilkes
Proprietors: Michael Wilkes
Cost: Alc L£18, fixed-price L & D £25.95 (2 courses), £29.50 (3 courses). H/wine £8.95 ! Service exc
Credit cards: ▨ ▩ ▩
Times: Noon-Last L 1.30pm, 7pm-Last D 9.30pm (10.30pm Sat). Closed Mon, Sun, 26-27 Dec, 1-2 Jan
Menus: A la carte lunch, fixed-price L and D, Sun L (private parties)
Seats: 34. No smoking in dining room
Additional: Children permitted (over 6); children's portions; ❂ dishes, Vegan/other diets on request

From the street, the River House appears as it might in any village street; all the houses hide the delightful estuary views which can be seen from the ground floor sitting room and the first floor restaurant. Relaxed and unpretentious, the establishment exhibits a large variety of local artists' work on the walls and great care is taken to provide a genial, homely atmosphere. Michael Wilkes provides the relaxed and informal service, whilst wife Shirley offers menus prepared from good local produce, particularly fish. Some vegetables, herbs, and fruit are produced on the Wilkes' own allotment, depending on the season. A delicious crab filled pancake served with a cheese sauce might be followed by a rack of lamb, cooked perfectly pink if requested, served with a superb amount of chopped rosemary and oregano in a smooth Madeira sauce. The selection of fresh vegetables is impressive, each having its own individual flavour. The desserts, including the ice-creams, are home-made, and attractively presented, although at a recent meal our inspector found the chocolate mousse somewhat lacking in taste. The reasonably priced wine list is predominantly French, with a few wines from other areas.

Directions: From the A376 (Exeter-Exmouth), follow signs for Lympstone. Through village, on right, near post office

LYNMOUTH, **Rising Sun Hotel** ❀❀

An ancient harbourside inn serving superb food based on local produce

Harbourside EX35 6EQ
Map no: 3 SS74
Tel: 01598 753223
Chef: David Lamprell
Proprietor: Hugo Jeune
Cost: Alc £23.50, fixed-price
L £21.50. H/wine £8.95. Service
exc
Credit cards: 🔲 🔲 🔲 🔲 OTHER
Times: Last L 2pm/D 9pm
Seats: 30. No smoking in dining
room
Menus: A la carte, fixed-price
L, bar L menu
Additional: Children permitted
(over 8 at D), children's
portions; ♥ menu, vegan/other
diets by arrangement

In a picturesque setting, overlooking the small harbour and the
East Lyn salmon river, the Rising Sun is an historic fourteenth-
century thatched smugglers inn, with all the appropriate charm and
character: crooked ceilings, thick walls, uneven oak floors. In the
oak-panelled restaurant, chef David Lamprell offers a variety of
superb dishes, specialising in local Exmoor game and seafood.
Starters such as fresh moules marinière with garlic, cream and
chives, or smoked leg of venison, sliced on a rich redcurrant and
Cassis sauce, served with toasted herb and cheese loaf, might be
followed by grilled fillets of local trout with a root ginger and
currant sauce, finished with chervil, or the suprême of Exmoor
duck, served with a confit of honey-glazed leg on a Calvados and
cream sauce. To finish, a choice from the daily pudding menu, or
a selection of local cheeses. There is a relatively short, but well
chosen wine list.

Directions: M5 exit 23 & A39 (Minehead) to Lynmouth, opposite the
harbour

LYNTON, **Chough's Nest Hotel** ❀

☺ *A spectacular cliff-side location is the setting for this beautiful stone-
built hotel. Expect a choice of soundly-cooked dishes, with Indonesian
food a speciality on the short fixed-price menu. A typical meal might
comprise lamb and mint soup, 'beef rendang' served with lime-flavoured
rice, and tiramisù for dessert*

Menus: Fixed-price D
Seats: 24. No smoking
Additional: Children over 6 welcome; ♥ dishes, other diets on
request
Directions: From Lynton Parish Church turn onto North Walk. Last
hotel on left

North Walk EX35 6HJ
Map no: 3 SS74
Tel: 01598 753315
Chef: Andrew Collier
Proprietor: Andrew Collier
Cost: Fixed-price D £13.50-£15
(5 courses). H/wine £5.10
Service inc
Credit cards: 🔲 🔲 🔲
Times: Dinner 7-8pm

Entries in this Guide are based on reports filed by our
team of professionally trained, full-time inspectors.

LYNTON, Combe Park Hotel ⊛

☺ *Located in a peaceful position at the head of Watersmeet Valley, this former hunting lodge offers traditional country-house cooking. Fresh local produce is used in dishes such as goujons of lemon sole in tartare sauce, pork fillet en croûte, and home-made meringue nests filled with strawberries and cream*

Seats: 20. No smoking in dining room **Menu:** Fixed-price D
Additional: Children over 12 permitted; ❂ dishes on request
Directions: At Hillsford Bridge, at junction of A39/B3223

Hillsford Bridge EX35 6LE
Map no: 3 SS74
Tel: 01598 52356
Chef: Mrs Shirley Barnes
Proprietors: Mr & Mrs Barnes
and Mr Walley
Cost: Fixed-price D £18 (5
course) H/wine £9 ❢ Service exc
Credit cards: None taken
Times: Last D 7pm. Closed Nov-
March

LYNTON, Hewitts Hotel ⊛⊛

Uncomplicated dishes made from fresh local ingredients at cliff-top hotel

Hewitts is not a place for those with vertigo. The splendid location, right on the edge of the cliff, commands a spectacular view over Lynmouth Bay and Countisbury Hill. It is a handsome house, built in the mid-Victorian era by Sir Thomas Hewitt for his new bride, who had also fallen in love with the view. From the main panelled hall, a magnificent staircase sweeps up to the galleried landing and stained glass windows. Nonetheless, the house has a friendly air, and service is helpful and efficient. Chef Robert Schyns offers a value-for-money set dinner, with well-prepared dishes that show a touch of Continental flair. At a recent test meal, a starter of well flavoured slices of chicken galantine was balanced with an onion and sultana confit. Lamb cutlets with redcurrant jus, cooked pink, were thankfully not overpowered by the accompanying Stilton mousse. Vegetables were colourful and soundly cooked. Chocolate mousse made a satisfying dessert.

Directions: North Walk off Lee Road

The Hoe
North Walk
Map no: 3 SS74
Tel: 01598 52293
Chef: Robert Schyns
Proprietor: Richard J Stagg
Cost: Alc £36.00; fixed-price
lunch £14.50; fixed-price
dinner £19.50. Wine £10.25 ❢
Service inc
Credit cards: ▧ ▨ OTHER
Times: Last L 2pm, Last D 9pm
Menus: A la carte, fixed-price
lunch and dinner, Sunday lunch,
bar menu
Seats: 30. No smoking in dining
room
Additional: Children permitted
lunch only (over 8); Children's
menu; ❂ menu; other diets on
request

LYNTON, Lynton Cottage ⊛

The view of Lynmouth Bay and the cliffs is something to savour from the terrace, drink in hand. Neither the starters nor the main courses are unnecessarily complicated, just simply-cooked dishes with broad appeal, from a choice of five which changes every day.

Menus: Bar menu L, fixed-price D **Seats:** 45 **Additional:** Children over 12 permitted; ❂ dishes, other diets on prior request
Directions: Situated in North Walk off main road through town

North Walk EX35 6ED
Map no: 3 SS74
Tel: 01598 752 342
Chef: Leon Balanche
Proprietor: John Jones
Cost: Fixed-price D £21.50.
H/wine £10.50
Credit cards: ▧ ▨ ▨ ▨ OTHER
Times: Last L-2pm
Last D-8.45pm

MARTINHOE, Old Rectory Hotel ⊛

Set in three acres of well-tended gardens some 500 yards from the North Devon coastal footpath, the Old Rectory offers stylish fresh food on a short fixed-price menu. Look out for smoked shellfish platter, cream of watercress soup and roast leg of lamb with juniper berries; puddings are particularly recommended

Menu: Fixed-price D **Seats:** 25. No smoking in dining room
Additional: No children; other diets on request
Directions: Right at Blackmore Gate onto A39 (Parracombe). Use Parracombe by-pass, take 3rd left at Martinhoe Cross

Parracombe EX31 4QT
Map no: 3 SS64
Tel: 01598 763368
Chef: Suzanne Bradbury
Proprietors: John & Suzanne
Bradbury
Cost: Fixed-price D £24. H/wine
£8.50 ❢ Service inc
Credit cards: None taken
Times: Last D 7.30pm

MARY TAVY,
The Stannary Restaurant ✿✿

Talented vegetarian cook with a creative way of blending flavours

The setting is an elegant 16th-century building with Victorian overtones. Alison Fife is a creative cook who has honed her skills over the years. By using prime quality raw materials, much of it organic, sometimes unusual, and combining them with subtle spicing, she produces strong old-fashioned flavours in dishes that show real flair and originality. Ingredients blend well together. An inspection meal produced a sweet corn tart filled with creamed corn and topped with baby cobs, followed by a filling Greek-inspired dish 'helios' – sun-dried tomatoes, sunflower seeds and quinoa wrapped in vine leaves. For dessert there were filo pastry triangles of muscatel grapes and a muscatel sauce. Other dishes, chosen from a menu which plunders the world for inspiration, could be Greek houmus or Indonesian coconut soup. Coffee is strong, served with home-made petits fours. The wine list offers a good choice.

Tavistock PL19 9QB
Map no: 2 SX57
Tel: 01822 810897
Chef: Alison Fife
Proprietors: Michael Cook and Alison Fife
Cost: Fixed-price D £30. H/wine £9 ❢ Service inc
Credit cards: ▨ ▨ ▨
Times: 7pm-last D 9.30pm. Closed Sun, Mon, (Tue/Wed, Jan-Easter), 3 days Xmas
Menu: Fixed-price D (exclusively vegetarian)
Seats: 20. No smoking in dining room
Additional: No children; ❂ menu, vegan/other diets on request

Directions: 4 miles north-east of Tavistock on A386 (Okehampton)

PARKHAM, **Penhaven House Hotel** ✿

A 17th-century rectory set in extensive gardens and woodlands whose kitchen offers a good balance of meat, fish and vegetarian dishes. Bread is made on the premises, fish caught locally, and many herbs and vegetables are home-grown. Choose from the daily-changing fixed-price menu or the extensive carte

Menus: *A la carte,* fixed-price L & D
Seats: 40. No smoking in dining room
Additional: Children over 10 permitted; ❂ menu, vegan/other diets on request
Directions: From A39 at Horns Cross, follow signs to Parkham, on entering village, after church on right take next left

Bideford EX39 5PL
Map no: 2 SS32
Tel: 01237 451711
Chef: Joseph Lindhorst
Proprietors: Maxine & Alan Wade
Cost: Alc £22, fixed-price L £8.95/D £13.95 (both 4 course). H/wine £9.50 Service inc
Credit cards: ▨ ▨ ▨ ▨
Times: Last L 1.45pm/D 9pm

In the Middle Ages, the word 'plum' meant virtually any dried fruit, hence names such as plum pudding and plum cake. The earliest cultivation of plums took place in Syria, and the fruit was first recorded by Roman authors in the 1st century AD. The Crusaders introduced the plum to western Europe. In 14th century England, Chaucer commented on a garden where plums grew and they were certainly a feature in the gardens of medieval monasteries. Greengages are considered the finest dessert plums. Thought to have originated in Armenia, they reached France in the 16th century during the reign of François I (the greengage is still known there as 'Reine Claude' after his wife). Sir Thomas Gage gave his name to the fruit when he introduced it to Britain in the 18th century.

PLYMOUTH,

Chez Nous Restaurant ❀❀❀

French to its very soul, this bistro serves fine food in a relaxed, informal atmosphere

13 Frankfort Gate PL1 QA
Map no: 2 SX45
Tel: 01752 266793
Chef: Jacques Marchal
Proprietors: Jacques & Suzanne Marchal
Cost: Fixed-price L & D £28.50. H/wine £10.50. Service exc
Credit cards: ❏ ▦ ▥ ▣ OTHER
Times: Last L 2pm, last D 10.30pm. Closed Sun, Mon, BHs, 3 wks Feb & Sept
Menus: Fixed-price L & D, pre-theatre
Seats: 28. No cigars or pipes
Additional: Children welcome; other diets prior notice

The red, white and blue of the tricoleur – the flag of chef Jacques Marchal's native France – predominate in the decor of this friendly bistro-style restaurant. An impressive selection of framed menus from the finest French restaurants provides both a further demonstration of national pride and a prompt to the gastric juices! Suzanne Marchal supervises front-of-house and is very happy to discuss the blackboard menu, tailoring meals to customers' preferences, while the atmosphere, though very much geared to the appreciation of fine food, is unpretentious and akin to eating "en famille" in France. Jacques makes optimum use of the freshest ingredients the market can offer; his cooking is carefully executed but unelaborate, allowing the produce to speak for itself.

A recently enjoyed starter of confit de canard au choux was typical, the duck leg served on a bed of cabbage and pine nuts with a Madeira flavoured jus. Other successful bourgeois dishes include a simple warm asparagus vinaigrette and a signature bouillabaisse which deliciously combines monkfish, scallops, salmon and turbot in a flavoursome fish and saffron broth; though the main ingredients are not typically Mediterranean, the traditional accompaniments of garlicky rouille, croûtons and Parmesan can bring a real touch of the sun to a chilly day in Plymouth. Offal is a favourite, too, both tongue and sweetbreads appearing regularly on the fixed-price menus. Desserts include a chocolate meringue with chestnut ice-cream, soft Italian meringue combining well with the rich chocolate ganache though the ice-cream itself may be a little lacking in flavour.

A superb range of cognacs, armagnacs and eaux de vie is offered with coffee and petits fours, and a predominantly French wine list featuring some top names also includes house wines starting at £10.

Directions: Frankfurt Gate is a pedestrianised street between Western Approach & Market Avenue

PLYMOUTH, Duke of Cornwall ❀

☺ *This sound Devonshire restaurant features carefully prepared British and European dishes. Fresh ingredients are used well, especially vegetables. Service in the restaurant is extremely polite and friendly and vegetarians are well catered for*

Menus: A la carte L & D, fixed-price Sun L, bar L menu **Seats:** 70-100. No-smoking area **Additional:** Children permitted, children's portions; ✿ dishes, vegan/other diets on request **Directions:** City centre, follow signs "Pavilions", hotel road is opposite

Millbay Road PL1 3LG
Map no: 2 SX45
Tel: 01752 266256
Chef: John Sergeant
Manager: Jeremy Palmer (Best Western)
Cost: Alc £17.95, fixed-price Sun L £9.95. Service exc
Credit cards: 🔳 🔳 🔳 🔳 OTHER
Times: Last L 2pm, last D 10pm. Closed Sat L

POUNDSGATE, Leusdon Lodge ❀

☺ *The restaurant of this solid Victorian stone-built residence is quite a find. For a start it is way off the beaten track, but peace and tranquillity and spectacular views across the eastern slopes of Dartmoor are a bonus. Expect Swiss cheese soufflé, breast of chicken with a Calvados cream sauce, and coffee and Tia Maria bavarois*

Menus: Fixed-price dinner **Seats:** 20. No smoking **Additional:** Children permitted, children's portions; ✿ dishes, other diets prior notice **Directions:** From A38 go through Poundsgate and after 400yds turn right (Leusdon), then follow signs to the hotel

Ashburton TQ13 7PE
Map no: 2 SX77
Tel: 01364 631304
Chef: Miranda Russell
Proprietor: Ivor Russell
Cost: Fixed-price D £21.50. H/wine £10.00 ❗ Service inc
Credit cards: 🔳 🔳
Times: Last D 8.45pm daily

SALCOMBE, Bolt Head Hotel ❀

Built in 1901, this wood-constructed hotel benefits from superb views of the estuary. Fresh local ingredients are used in the imaginative cooking; at a recent test meal poached pear filled with herbed cream cheese pâté, fillet of salmon in a pink peppercorn sauce, and tenderloin of pork were enjoyed

Menus: Fixed-price D/Sun L, bar menu **Seats:** 60 **Additional:** Children welcome, children's portion; ✿ dishes, other diets on request **Directions:** At Malborough follow signs for Sharpitor, hotel is above beach at South Sands

South Sands TQ8 8LL
Map no: 3 SX73
Tel: 01548 843751
Chef: John Gallagher
Proprietor: Colin Smith (Best Western)
Manager: Alan Messenger
Cost: Fixed-price L £7.75/D £23. H/wine £8.25 Service exc
Credit cards: 🔳 🔳 🔳 OTHER
Times: Last L 2.15pm, last D 9pm Closed Nov-Mar

SALCOMBE, Soar Mill Cove Hotel ❀❀

Local specialities, distinctive cooking and home baking are all features of the food at Soar Mill Cove

Distinctive, imaginative cooking can be enjoyed in the attractive setting of this well known Devon cove. Many local specialities are featured on the fixed-price three-course menu, cooked in chef Keith Makepeace's own particular style. Well-produced sauces are notable, although they can detract from the more subtle flavours of the main ingredients, and home baking is also a strength – as reflected in the inviting sweet trolley. A recent meal began with two finely crumbed crab cakes with a good strong flavour, accompanied by a creamy fish sauce with a slightly sweet but reasonably fishy taste. The breast of Gressingham duck which followed was a touch overcooked but came off the bone easily and satisfied; it was served with a tangy elderberry wine sauce and a marmalade of citrus fruit zest. A well-made apfelstrudel with ice cream and rum crème anglaise made a pleasant finish to the meal.

Soar Mill Cove
Salcombe TQ7 3DS
Map no: 3 SX73
Tel: 01548 561566
Chef: Keith Stephen Makepeace
Proprietor: Makepeace Family
Cost: Alc L £20, fixed-price D £32. H/wine £10.20 ❗ Service exc
Credit cards: 🔳 🔳 🔳
Times: Last L 2.30pm/D 9.30pm
Menus: A la carte light L, fixed-price D, bar menu
Seats: 48. No smoking
Additional: Children welcome (over 3 at D), children's menu; other diets on request

Soar Mill Cove Hotel

Directions: A381 to Salcombe, through village follow signs to sea

SALCOMBE, Tides Reach Hotel ✸

An attractive hotel run by the Edwards family for the past 27 years. The airy restaurant overlooks a pond complete with fish and ducks which makes for a pleasant setting. Chef Finn Ibsen offers modern British cooking, and makes full use of locally caught fresh fish, plus quality produce and ingredients

Menus: A la carte D, fixed-price D, bar menu **Seats:** 90. No smoking in dining room **Additional:** Children over 8 permitted; ❶ dishes, vegan/other diets on request
Directions: Take Cliff road towards sea and Bolt Head

South Sands TQ8 8LJ
Map no: 3 SX73
Tel: 01548 843466
Chef: Finn Ibsen
Proprietor: John Edwards (Partner)
Cost: Alc £30.50, fixed-price D £21.75 (4 course). H/wine £9.85
❢ Service inc
Credit cards: 🔲 🔲 🔲 🔲 OTHER
Times: 7pm-last D pm. Closed last wk Dec-3rd wk Feb

SIDMOUTH, Brownlands Hotel ✸

☺ *Peacefully set in its own beautifully kept grounds, this fine Victorian country hotel affords glorious views across the valley to the town and sea front. The elegant dining-room offers imaginative home-cooked food; at a recent meal, our inspector particularly enjoyed a dish of asparagus and mushroom*

Sid Road EX10 9AG
Map no: 3 SY18
Tel: 01395 513053
Chefs: Laurence J Barber and Janice May
Proprietors: Peter, Diane & Steven Kendall-Torry
Cost: Fixed-price Sun L £10.50/ D £18.95 (6 course). H/wine £7.95 Service inc
Credit cards: None taken
Times: Last Sun L 1.15pm/ D 8pm. Open Mar-Oct
Menus: Fixed-price D & Sun L
Seats: 40. Air conditioned. No smoking in dining room
Additional: Children permitted (over 8); ❶ dishes, vegan/other diets on request

Directions: Signposted, in Brownlands Road which is off Sid Road

SIDMOUTH, **Riviera Hotel** ✿

☺ *The Riviera is an impressive Regency building set on Sidmouth's esplanade, overlooking Lyme Bay. Familiar English and French dishes are offered in the restaurant along the lines of lobster bisque and steak Diane. Puddings, from the trolley, are home-made*

The Esplanade EX10 8AY
Map no: 3 SS64
Tel: 01395 515201
Chefs: Mark Leavers and
Christian Miquel
Proprietor: Peter S. Wharton –
Director
Cost: *Alc* £20.50, fixed-price
L £12 (5 course)/ D £20
(7 course). H/wine £ 8.95
❢ Service exc
Credit cards: ▨ ▩ ▨ ▨ OTHER
Times: Last L 2pm, 7pm-last D
9pm, Bar open all day
Menus: *A la carte,* fixed-price
L & D, pre-theatre, bar menu
Seats: 90. Air conditioned
Additional: Children welcome,
children's menu; ❶ dishes,
vegan/other diets on request

Directions: In the centre of the Esplanade overlooking Lyme Bay

SIDMOUTH, **Victoria Hotel** ✿

A new head chef has introduced an imaginative menu, with separate sections for vegetarians and those on special diets. Dishes which have shown a high degree of effort and skill include pan-fried fillet of beef with Madeira sauce and choux pastry gâteau with cream and strawberries

Esplanade EX10 8RY
Map no: 3 SS64
Tel: 01395 512651
Proprietors: Brend Hotels

Directions: At the western end of the Esplanade

SOUTH MOLTON, **Marsh Hall Hotel** ✿

☺ *Dating from the 17th century and featuring an impressive Victorian frontage, Marsh Hall stands in well-tended grounds close to the North Devon link. Local meat, plus herbs, fruit and vegetables from the hotel's gardens, are used to create dishes such as fresh tomato soup, and rack of lamb with redcurrants and rosemary*

South Molton EX3 3HQ
Map no: 3 SS72
Tel: 01769 572666
Chef: Judy Griffiths
Proprietors: Tony & Judy
Griffiths
Cost: Fixed-price D £18.50.
H/wine £8. Service inc
Credit cards: ▨ ▩ ▨ ▨
Times: Last D 8.30pm Open
every day

Menu: Fixed-price D
Seats: 24. No smoking in dining room
Additional: Children permitted (over 12); ❶ dishes/other diets on request
Directions: Off A361 signposted North Molton; first right, then right again

> The guinea pig, a cherished domestic pet in thousands of households in the Western world, is considered a delicacy in parts of South America. The animals were once reserved for the exclusive delectation of Inca nobility but nowadays are part of the staple diet of the inhabitants of the high Andes of Peru, Bolivia and Ecuador.

SOUTH MOLTON,

Whitechapel Manor Hotel ❀❀❀

Family managed Grade I Devon manor with a welcoming atmosphere and imaginative cooking

South Molton EX36 3EG
Map no: 3 SS72
Tel: 01769 573377
Chefs: Patricia Shapland and Martin Lee
Proprietors: John & Patricia Shapland (Pride of Britain)
Cost: Fixed-price D £28-£40/Sun L £19.50. H/wine £12 Service inc
Credit cards: ◼ ▨ ▨ ▨ OTHER
Times: Last L 1.45pm/D 8.45pm
Menus: Fixed-price D & Sun L, gourmet D Fri & Sat
Seats: 28. No smoking in dining room
Additional: Children welcome, other diets on request

Whitechapel Manor is located on the edge of Exmoor where the rich, red Devonshire soil makes the region so fertile and abundant. Martin Lee is well positioned to take advantage of all the fine, local fish, fowl and dairy produce. His Anglo-French menu may thus feature Cornish scallops sautéed with a veal jus, sirloin of Devon beef with roasted root vegetables and a full-bodied port wine sauce, or roast local partridge with Savoy cabbage, smoked bacon and a partridge and Madeira jus. There is always a splendid selection of South-Western cheeses, served with home-made walnut and raisin bread, oatmeal biscuits and a green salad.

Three or four-course dinners start with hot canapés, such as ratatouille tartlets, blue cheese shortcake and fishy filo parcels. Dishes which have been well received include tender roast quail with orange zest sauce, fillet of red mullet with a vibrant provençale sauce, confit of duck with crisp potatoes and shallots, and an excellent lobster mousse served with a prawn sauce. Although it tasted good, and was rare in texture, a breast of duck with lentils was somehow lacking in pinkness. Vegetables can sometimes be over blanched. Desserts, such as praline parfait and layers of dark chocolate mousse with puff pastry leaves and coffee bean sauce, handsomely bring up the rear. Warm caramelised apple tart had good pastry and a sharp apple flavour, balanced by caramel ice-cream. Service runs smoothly, and the conscientious young staff clearly take pride in their hotel.

Directions: From Tiverton take A361, Whitechapel signed at roundabout. Right after 0.75 mile

STAVERTON, Sea Trout Inn ❀❀

☺ *A country restaurant featuring careful French/English cooking*

Andrew Mogford's Sea Trout is a 15th-century inn, reposing quietly in the Dart Valley, a few miles upstream from the old town of Totnes. Bar areas are extensive and traditional in character, and main meals such as mixed grills are served. In the restaurant the

Staverton TQ9 6PA
Map: 3 SX76
Tel: 01803 762274
Chef: Ian Baillie
Proprietor: Andrew Mogford

Sea Trout Inn

Cost: *Alc* £16/20, fixed-price
L £9.50/D £17.50. H/wine £6.75
❗ Service exc
Credit cards: ◼ ◼ ◼
Times: Noon-last L 2pm, 7pm-
last D 9.30pm
Menus: *A la carte,* fixed-price
L & D, bar menu
Seats: 36
Additional: Children permitted,
children's portions; ✿ dishes,
other diets on request

carte always includes a home-made soup and half a dozen or so
other starters, such as gravad lax, poached scallops with asparagus,
and grilled field mushrooms filled with prawns, parsley and garlic
butter. Fish (from nearby Brixham) and meat – again locally sourced
– are pretty evenly balanced among the main courses: roast fillet of
monkfish, poached red snapper; sauté of pork tenderloin, poached
breast of chicken, a good choice of steaks, and chef's specials. If
everything is cooked with the care shown in a braised shoulder of
lamb with a medley of vegetables and garlic roast potatoes, no-one
will be disappointed. Some desserts, such as chocolate tart, are
accompanied by Devon clotted cream; others include Salcombe
Dairy speciality ice-creams. Farmhouse cheeses are from
Ticklemore's in Totnes. Eighty or so wines make up the wine list.

Directions: In village centre, from A38 turn onto A384 to Staverton

STOKE CANON, **Barton Cross Hotel** ❀

☺ *Charming, thatched country hotel with inglenook fireplaces and
heavily beamed ceilings that's handy for Exeter. The unusual galleried
restaurant is the setting for cooking that is strong on local produce.
Especially good is the home-made bread and the bread and butter pudding*

Huxham EX5 4EJ
Map no: 3 SX99
Tel: 01392 841245
Chef: Paul George Bending
Proprietors: Brian Hamilton
Cost: *Alc* £22.50, fixed-price
L £18.50. H/wine £9.00 ❗
Service exc
Credit cards: ◼ ◼ ◼ OTHER
Times: Last L 2pm, last D
9.30pm
Menus: *A la carte,* fixed-price
lunch
Seats: 40. No smoking in dining
room
Additional: Children welcome,
children's menu; ✿ menu,
vegan/other diets on request

Directions: 4 miles from Exeter off A396 Tiverton road; right at Stoke
Canon church towards Huxham for 0.25 mile

TAVISTOCK, Moorland Hall Hotel ❀

☺ *Chef Gillian Farr cooks eclectic British food in an informal and relaxed atmosphere. Guests enjoy the varied menus, cooked with special attention to the balance of flavours. Our inspector enjoyed a robust potato and leek soup, followed by noisettes of lamb with Cumberland sauce and a lovely crème brûlée*

Menu: Fixed-price D
Seats: 20. No smoking in dining room
Additional: Children welcome, children's portions/high tea; ❂ menu, other diets on request
Directions: Signposted from the centre of Mary Tavy on the A386

Brentnor Road PL19 9PY
Map no: 2 SX47
Tel: 01822 810466
Chef: Gill Farr
Proprietors: Mr & Mrs A R Farr
Cost: Fixed-price D £15
(5 course). H/wine £7.25 Service exc
Credit cards: ▨ ▨
Times: Last D 8pm. Reservations only

THURLESTONE, Heron House Hotel ❀

☺ *Heron House stands within fifty yards of an award-winning beach, and with RSPB land at the rear. A short, daily-changing fixed-price menu offers imaginative British cooking and may include selections such as home-made cream of vegetable soup, seafood crêpe with halibut, salmon and prawns, and lemon fritters*

Menus: Fixed-price D, bar snack L
Seats: 60. No smoking in dining room
Additional: Children permitted; ❂ dishes, vegan/other diets on request
Directions: From Kingsbridge take Salcombe road; ignore signs for Thurlestone, right for Hope Cove, straight on at crossroads, fork right at Galryston

Thurlestone Sands TQ7 3JY
Map no: 3SX64
Tel: 01548 561308
Chef: Pearl Rowland
Proprietor: Pearl F Rowland
Cost: Fixed-price D £ 16.95
H/wine £9.25. Service exc
Credit cards: ▨ ▨ OTHER
Times: Last D 8.45pm Open daily

THURLESTONE, Thurlestone Hotel ❀

Situated overlooking the South Devon coastline, Thurlestone Hotel offers modern British cooking. Fresh Salcombe crab with grapefruit may be followed by chicken liver salad, with venison with port and redcurrant sauce as a main course. A good choice of puddings is also available

Menus: Fixed-price L & D, bar menu
Seats: 120. Air conditioned. No-smoking area
Additional: Children welcome, children's menu; ❂ dishes, vegan/other diets on request
Directions: Village centre on A379 Kingsbridge/Plymouth road

Kingsbridge TQ7 3NN
Map no: 3 SX76
Tel: 01548 560382
Chef: Philip Hoskins
Proprietor: The Grose Family. Manager: Julie Baugh
Cost: Fixed-price L £15/ D £25
H/wine £8.95 ❢ No service charge
Credit cards: ▨ ▨
Times: 12.30pm-last L 2pm, 7.30pm-last D 9pm

'Bruschetta' consists of thick slices of country bread, which could be French sour dough or Italian pane pugliese, which are then grilled on charcoal, rubbed with garlic and dressed with good olive oil. They are traditionally served at the beginning of a meal or as a snack.
'Crostini' are slices of bread cut into rounds or squares, lightly buttered and toasted on a baking tray in the oven until a pale gold colour. The crostini are then spread or covered, traditionally with a liver paste, but more likely nowadays with thinly sliced meat, seafood, roasted vegetables, anchovies, olives. They are not dissimilar to canapés and serve a similar function.

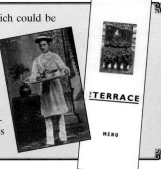

TORQUAY, The Imperial Hotel ✤

The Imperial stands in its own grounds with marvellous bay views. Its Regatta Restaurant offers imaginative dishes on a fixed-price menu and short carte, with selections such as terrine of salmon and asparagus in a herb jelly, contrefillet of beef with braised button onions, and peaches in a puff pastry lattice

Park Hill Road TQ1 2DG
Map no: 3 SX96
Tel: 01803 294301
Chef: Jonathan Binns
Proprietors: Forte Grand.
Gen. Manager: Charles Barker
Cost: *Alc* £40, fixed-price D
£32. H/wine £15.50 ▉ Service
exc
Credit cards: ▨ ▦ ▦ ▨ OTHER
Times: Noon-last L 2.30pm,
6pm-last D 9.30pm
Seats: 300. Air conditioned.
No-smoking area
Menus: A la carte, fixed-price D,
light L menu (Sundeck Rest)
Additional: Children welcome,
children's menu; ♥ menu,
vegan/other diets on request

Directions: Park Hill Road is off Torwood Street/Babbacombe Road, just north of the new harbour

TORQUAY,
Langtry's at The Osborne ✹✹

☺ *Adventurous cooking which strives for effect*

Hesketh Crescent
Meadfoot TQ1 2LL
Map no: 3 SX96
Tel: 01803 213311
Chef: Ken Rowe
Proprietor: Managing Director:
Barry Cole
Cost: *Alc* D £19.50, fixed-price
D £22.50 (4 courses & coffee).
H/wine £10.25 ▉ No service
charge
Credit cards: ▨ ▦ ▦ ▨ OTHER
Times: Last D 10pm (9.30pm
winter)
Menus: A la carte D, fixed-price
D, Sun L, bar menu

There is a new fashion amongst chefs for signature dishes. Once, this just meant something the kitchen happened to be particularly good at, then it became a shorthand for others to use in describing those dishes. Now it is something chefs award themselves. Thus, on an April menu, head chef Ken Rowe indicated by asterisks the following signature dishes: tartare of fresh salmon layered with cucumber soaked in yoghurt, served on a crisp sesame seed crouton with a sweet lemon dressing; boneless quail filled with pine nut and

thyme stuffing, accompanied by a timbale of bubble and squeak and a lightly fried quail's egg with a rich Madeira glaze; raspberry and nougatine parfait accompanied by fresh fruits and trio of fruit coulis. Non-signature dishes are described no less effusively, and are equally as intricate, with gastronomic fashion-victim ingredients galore – lavender, strawberry vinegar and lemongrass. Liquorice ice-cream, no doubt, has its fans, but others may prefer to stick with a trio of good regional cheeses. The *carte* changes monthly, and an across-the-board pricing structure means that all starters are priced at £3.25, main courses at £14, and desserts at £4.50.

Seats: 50. No smoking in restaurant. Air conditioned
Additional: Children welcome, children's menu; ❂ dishes, other diets on request

Directions: From Harbour (with harbour on right) turn left up Torwood St. Right at lights (Meadfoot Beach). Hotel straight in front

TORQUAY, Orestone Manor ❀❀

The imaginative use of the best that the surrounding countryside can provide has earned many loyal customers for this friendly hotel

Rockhouse Lane
Maidencombe
TQ1 4SX
Map no: 3 SX96
Tel: 01803 328098
Chef: Ashley Carkeet
Proprietors: Mike Staples
Cost: Fixed-price L £12.50/D £25.50. H/wine £9.50 Service inc
Credit cards: 🅰 ▦ ▦ 🅿 OTHER
Times: Last L 1.30pm, last D 8.30pm. Closed Jan
Menus: Fixed-price L & D, bar menu
Seats: 50. No smoking in restaurant
Additional: Children over 10 permitted; ❂ dishes, vegan/other diets on request

Warmth, conviviality and particularly attentive service must rank high among the attractions of this sympathetically restored Georgian country lodge. The same determination to provide the absolute best for guests is, however, also evident in chef Ashley Carkeet's ambitious Anglo-French fixed-price menus, his marketing ranging far and wide to ensure that only the freshest and best of raw materials are used. Fish comes direct from Brixham harbour, Somerset provides game (including venison), the Devon countryside, fruit and vegetables, and from the hotel's own garden, herbs. A supplementary list of additional daily choices takes optimum advantage of seasonal availability. One evening in early May it offered a starter of steamed salmon rolled around a prawn mousse and served with asparagus and baby gem lettuce. Soup was a cream of mushroom flavoured with spring onions and fresh herbs, seasonal salad leaves were served with a wild garlic and olive oil dressing, and grilled fillet of new season's lamb was topped with kidneys and accompanied by an apricot, tarragon and port sauce. An interesting wine list composed mainly of New World labels and young vintages accompanied the meal.

Directions: Off B3199 Torquay/Teignmouth coastal road; turn right on Watcombe Hill opposite Brunle Manor

TORQUAY, **The Table Restaurant** ❀❀❀

A tiny restaurant serving a high standard of cooking from an innovative modern British menu

Trevor and Jane Brooks have run The Table for the last eight years. Theirs is a pretty little restaurant housed on the ground floor of a Victorian property in the Babbacombe area of the town. Consistency and high standards are the driving forces behind the cooking style, with prime local produce inspiring the daily specials. Fish features strongly. The kitchen is minute, so it is amazing that such original dishes come out of it – all down to Trevor's ingenuity and dedication. Jane provides friendly and hospitable service to the five tables, taking the meal at a relaxed pace so that a visit to the restaurant should be regarded as the whole evening's entertainment. There is a short but interesting handwritten menu, priced for three courses, with a choice of three items at each stage. The meal commences with home-baked bread, which included slices of San Francisco sour bread on one occasion – a recipe gleaned from a recent trip to the USA. The starter, seared scallops, was served with local asparagus, a concassé of tomatoes and some spinach, an unusual dish full of natural flavours. Vegetables formed an integral part of the main course; the saddle of lamb was cooked pink as requested and served sliced with a spiced purée of aubergine, a small round of rösti potato, fine beans, sugar snap peas, baby corn and tiny sprigs of broccoli. There was also a dark jus with plenty of chopped tarragon. The dessert provided a splendid combination of taste and texture, a light, well risen chocolate soufflé served with banana praline ice cream. Wines are reasonably priced and listed by style rather than area, coming mainly from Europe.

Directions: B3189 (Torwood Street) from Torquay Harbour, 2 miles to Babbacombe

135 Babbacombe Road
TQ1 3SR
Map no: 3 SX96
Tel: 01803 324292
Proprietors: Mr & Mrs T Brooks
Chef: Trevor Brooks
Cost: Fixed-price D £28. H/wine £9.50 ❢ Service exc
Credit cards: 🖎 🖳
Times: Last D 10pm. Closed Sun & Mon, Feb 1-18 & Sept 1-18
Menu: Fixed-price D
Seats: 20. No smoking
Additional: Children permitted; other diets prior notice

TWO BRIDGES, **Prince Hall Hotel** ❀

New owners have taken over Prince Hall but former chef/patron Jean Claude Denat has remained as chef. The dishes are mainly French-influenced, based on fresh local produce, but Cajun specialities from Louisiana help to create some imaginative menus. Fresh Kumba fish soup which contains fresh fish, rice and whole shell prawns is recommended

Menu: Fixed-price D
Seats: 22 (inc 15 residents). No smoking in dining room
Additional: No children; other diets on request
Directions: From Two Bridges take B3357 Dartmeet Road; hotel is hidden 1 mile on the right

Yelverton PL20 6SA
Map no: 2 SX96
Tel: 01822 890403
Chef: Jean Claude Denat
Proprietor: Adam & Carrie Southwell
Cost: Fixed-price D £19.95 (4 courses). H/wine £8.25. Service exc
Credit cards: 🖎 🖳 🖳 🖳 OTHER
Times: Last D 8.30pm. Closed 4-6 weeks Xmas/New Year (phone to check)

WHIMPLE, **Woodhayes Hotel** ❀❀

Excellent quality cooking can be enjoyed in a relaxed, tranquil atmosphere

Set in four-and-a-half acres of grounds, this handsome Georgian country house is peacefully set on the edge of the cider-apple village of Whimple; yet it is conveniently close to the M5 and Exeter. A predominantly set menu offers seven courses (some

Exeter EX5 2TD
Map no: 3 SY09
Tel: 01404 822237
Chefs: Katherine & Michael Rendle
Proprietors: Frank & Katherine Rendle

Woodhayes Hotel

Cost: Fixed-price D £25 (7 courses). H/wine £10.50 ❢
Service inc
Credit cards: ▨ ▩ ▩ ▣ OTHER
Times: Last D 7.30pm for 8-ish
Seats: 16. No smoking
Menus: Fixed-price D (residents fixed-price L)
Additional: Children over 12 welcome; ✿ dishes, vegan/other diets on request

verbal choices are also available) of well-executed English and French dishes, from which superior quality fresh ingredients shine through. A January meal began with an appetiser of Parma ham and fresh pear, which was followed by piping hot carrot and orange soup flavoured with coriander. The fish course consisted of lightly steamed fillet of seabass with dressed salad leaves. A succulent sirloin of beef with a mild grainy mustard sauce formed the core of the meal, and was served with fresh spinach, roast parsnips and creamed potatoes. The selection of desserts included date pudding with toffee sauce, crème brûlée and home-made ice-creams, with local cheeses available to follow. Dinner is served in a relaxed and informal style in the elegant dining room, which is decorated with fresh flowers.

Directions: On A30 midway Honiton/Exeter. Straight down Whimple Road, first building on right

WINKLEIGH, Pophams ❀❀

☺ *A popular little eating place where the food is memorable*

A tiny cafe-cum-restaurant with seating for just ten and open only for lunch has become renowned in the West Country for both the quality of the cooking and its charm. More a delicatessen than a restaurant, it is set in the centre of the sleepy Devonshire village of Winkleigh, and is firmly on the map both for locals and those in the know who are passing through. Owners Melvyn Popham and Dennis Hawkes offer a warm welcome and a relaxed atmosphere, and visitors can watch Melvyn at work in the tiny open-plan kitchen. The blackboard menu offers plenty of choice at all three courses, and just about everything is cooked to order. Soups, home-made, of course, are popular. A recent inspection meal began with a rich chicken liver terrine served with a dressed salad and a smooth, spicy Cumberland sauce, was followed by a succulent roasted chicken breast with a crisp Parmesan coating, served with a creamy curry sauce. A rich lemon tart, and sticky toffee pudding with lashings of cream were stunning desserts.

Directions: In village centre, about 9 miles from Okehampton

Castle Street EX19 8HQ
Map no: 3 SS60
Tel: 01837 83767
Chef: Melvyn John Popham
Proprietors: Dennis Hawkes and Melvyn Popham
Cost: Alc £17. Un-licensed. No corkage charge. Service exc
Times: 9am-last L 3pm. Closed Sun, Dec 25, Feb
Menu: A la carte L
Seats: 10. Air conditioned. No smoking.
Additional: No children under 14; ✿ dishes; other diets on request

WOOLACOMBE, Little Beach Hotel ✿

☺ *Stunning views over Morte Bay from this comfortable hotel serving traditional English cooking from a short fixed-price menu. A recent five-course meal began with tomato stuffed with tuna, capers and cheese, and was followed by mushroom soup with barley and stout, lamb cutlets, treacle tart, and cheese and biscuits*

Menus: Fixed-price D, bar menu
Seats: 20. No smoking in dining room
Additional: Children permitted (over 7); ✪ dishes, other diets on request
Directions: From village centre 0.5 mile along seafront on right-hand side

The Esplanade EX34 7DJ
Map no: 2 SS44
Tel: 01271 870398
Chef: Mrs N B Welling
Proprietor: B D Welling
Cost: Fixed-price D £15 (5 course). H/wine £6.95
Service inc
Credit cards: 🔳 💳
Times: 12.30pm-last L 1.30pm, 7.17pm-last D 8pm. Closed Nov-Mar

WOOLACOMBE, Watersmeet Hotel ✿✿

English and French dishes in pleasant bayside setting

Spectacular views over the bay mark out this pleasant hotel. Two menus, 'Traditional English Fayre' and 'Watersmeet Dinner Menu', offer a good selection of dishes, ranging from plainly cooked to more imaginatively prepared food. A typical meal might begin with quenelles of smooth chicken liver pâté with a rich Cumberland sauce, served with a simple salad garnish. Seafood bisque could follow, with tranche of Devon salmon, oven-baked in Chardonnay and topped with a herb crust, as a main course. At a recent visit this was accompanied by a selection of vegetables which included carrots, french beans, almondine and new potatoes, and a filo pastry basket filled with peppers, mange tout and baby corn. For dessert, a white and dark chocolate terrine with caramel sauce. The well-balanced wine list offers a good range of wines from around the world. Service is notably friendly and attentive.

Directions: From A361 follow signs to Woolacombe, right at beach car park, 300 yards on right

Mortehoe EX34 7EB
Map no: 2 SS44
Tel: 01271 870333
Chefs: John Physick and Brian Wheeldon
Proprietors: Mr & Mrs Brian Wheeldon.
Manager: Neil Bradley
Cost: *Alc* £22.50, fixed-price D £25.50 (5 courses). H/wine £9.85 Service inc
Credit cards: 🔳 💳 💳
Times: Noon-last L 2.30pm, 7pm-last D 8.30/9pm. Closed Dec & Jan
Seats: 60. No smoking in dining room
Menus: A la carte, fixed-price D, bar L menu
Additional: Children over 8 welcome, children's portions/high tea; ✪ dishes, other diets on request

Entries in this Guide are based on reports filed by our team of professionally trained, full-time inspectors.

YARCOMBE,
The Belfry Hotel ❀

Devon EX14 9BD
Map no: 3 ST20
Tel: 01404 861234/861588
Chef: Jackie Rees

☺ *Originally the local school, the Belfry is made up of dressed flint and Portland stone and has a lot to offer in terms of character and hospitality. The choice of dishes served in the wood-panelled restaurant are based on fresh local produce. Baked ham with Dijon mustard and cider sauce is recommended*

Proprietors: Jackie & Tony Rees
Cost: Alc D £16.95, fixed-price D £12.75 (2 courses). H/wine £8.90 ¶ Service inc
Credit cards: ▩ ▥ ▥
Times: 7pm-last D 8.45pm. Closed last 2 weeks Nov & Feb

Menus: A la carte & fixed-price D **Seats:** 18. No smoking in dining room **Additional:** Children permitted; ❂ menu, vegan/other diets on request
Directions: On A30 7 miles E of Honiton in centre of Yarcombe

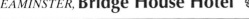

DORSET

BEAMINSTER, **Bridge House Hotel** ❀❀

3 Prout Bridge DT8 3AY
Map no: 3 ST40
Tel: 01308 862200
Chefs: Jackie Rae and Peter Pinkster

☺ *A small village hotel with a friendly, well-run restaurant offering skilfully prepared food*

Situated in the heart of picturesque Beaminster, Peter Pinkster's small, personally-run hotel dates back to the 13th century. Thick stone walls and beamed ceilings testify to its great age, while the attractive dining room opens into a conservatory and looks over the pretty walled garden. There is no *carte* but the fixed-price, two/three-course lunch menu is good value, as is the multi-choice dinner menu with a wide range of dishes, some with a supplement attached. On top of all that, there are daily recommendations, such as tender breast of pigeon, 'tasting just as it should', with a rich Madeira sauce. A representative selection of other possible main courses could be baked stuffed aubergine topped with cheese, rabbit braised with root vegetables, marinated monkfish kebab, fillets of John Dory with ginger and chive cream sauce, and fresh vegetable strudel on a butter sauce. For dessert there is home-made ice cream and sorbets, orange and Grand Marnier jelly, bread and butter pudding and warm pecan pie with vanilla ice-cream. A good wine list offers a small choice from all the popular countries and regions, with quite a few in half bottles.

Proprietor: Peter Pinkster (Virgin Hotel Marketing)
Cost: Fixed-price L £13.95/D £17.95. H/wine £8.45. Service exc
Credit cards: ▩ ▥ ▥ ▣ OTHER
Times: 12.30pm-last L 2pm, 7-last D 9pm
Menus: A la carte, fixed-price L & D, Sun L
Seats: 48. No smoking in dining room
Additional: Children permitted, children's menu; ❂ menu, other diets on request

Directions: On A3066 100yards down hill from the town square

BOURNEMOUTH, **Farthings** ❀

5/7 Grove Road BH1 3AS
Map no: 4 SZ09
Tel: 01202 558660
Chef: Ian Morton
Proprietor: Tom & Sheila Porteus

An old Victorian coach house now converted into a country house-style restaurant. The large French windows of the restaurant overlook a peaceful garden where most meals are served in the summer. The imaginative menu might include pan-fried escalope of pork or maybe a delicately flavoured smoked fish terrine

Cost: Alc £23, fixed-price L £10.95/D £18.50. H/wine £8.75 Service exc
Credit cards: ▩ ▥ ▥ ▣
Times: Last L 2pm, last D 10.30pm. Closed Sun D & Mon (Jan-Mar)

Menus: A la carte, fixed-price L & D, bar menu **Seats:** 30. No smoking in one dining room **Additional:** Children welcome, children's portions; ❂ menu, other diets on request
Directions: On roundabout, top of hill on Bath Road going from Pier to Lansdowne

BOURNEMOUTH, **Hotel Piccadilly** ⊛

☺ *A friendly, welcoming hotel with a loyal following due to the owner's commitment and care. The kitchen produces English dishes, mainly steaks, with generally pleasing results. At inspection a tender beef fillet was served with mushroom sauce, and good, fresh vegetables*

Bath Road BH1 2NN
Map no: 4 SZ09
Tel: 01202 556420
Chef: Wilfred Beckett
Proprietors: Marie & Don Cowie
Cost: *Alc* £20, fixed-price L £8.50/D £14.50. H/wine £7.95. Service exc
Credit cards: ▨ ▧ ▧ ▨ OTHER
Times: Last L 2pm/D 9pm
Menus: *A la carte*, fixed-price L & D, bar menu
Seats: 90. No smoking in dining room
Additional: Children welcome, children's menu; ◑ menu, vegan/other diets on request

Directions: Bath Road leads to the Pier, the hotel is near the Lansdowne roundabout

BOURNEMOUTH,
Langtry Manor Hotel ⊛

☺ *A family owned, and personally-run hotel, with a distinctly historic theme. The high-ceilinged dining-room sports a minstrel's gallery and has a warm, comfortable atmosphere. The kitchen produces good quality dishes, perhaps fish pâté, followed by lightly cooked beef medallions with a sherry sauce, and crisp, fresh vegetables*

26 Derby Road
East Cliff BH1 3QB
Map no: 4 SZ09
Tel: 01202 553887
Chef: Stuart Glanville
Proprietor: Pamela Hamilton Howard
Cost: Fixed-price D £19.75 (4 courses) H/wine £7.95. Service inc
Credit cards: ▨ ▧ ▧ ▨ OTHER
Times: 7pm-last D 9pm

Menus: Fixed-price D, bar snack menu
Seats: 100. No smoking in dining room
Additional: Children permitted, children's portions; ◑ dishes, other diets on request
Directions: On the East Cliff, corner of Darby and Knyveton roads

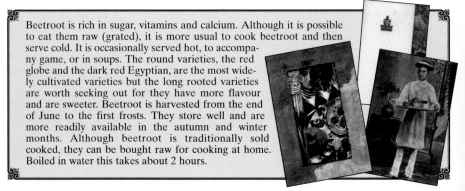

Beetroot is rich in sugar, vitamins and calcium. Although it is possible to eat them raw (grated), it is more usual to cook beetroot and then serve cold. It is occasionally served hot, to accompany game, or in soups. The round varieties, the red globe and the dark red Egyptian, are the most widely cultivated varieties but the long rooted varieties are worth seeking out for they have more flavour and are sweeter. Beetroot is harvested from the end of June to the first frosts. They store well and are more readily available in the autumn and winter months. Although beetroot is traditionally sold cooked, they can be bought raw for cooking at home. Boiled in water this takes about 2 hours.

BOURNEMOUTH, Queens Hotel ❀

☺ *The Queens Hotel is centrally located on the Eastcliff, close to the promenade. A mix of modern and traditional British dishes may include smoked salmon and cream cheese roulade, cream of celery and Stilton soup, and fillets of veal with a cream of mushroom sauce*

Directions: Follow signs to East Cliff, hotel is one road back from seafront

Meyrick Road
East Cliff BH1 3DL
Map no: 4 SZ09
Tel: 01202 554415
Chef: Will Summerell
Proprietors: Arthur Young Hotels.
Manager: David Burr
Cost: Fixed-price L £8.25/D £16.95. Wine £8.95. Service exc
Credit cards: 🂠 💳 💳 💷 OTHER
Times: 12.30pm-last L 1.45pm, 7pm-last D 8.45pm
Menus: Fixed-price L & D, bar menu
Seats: 200. Air conditioned
Additional: Children welcome, children's menu; ◐ menu, vegan on request, other diets by arrangement

BOURNEMOUTH, Royal Bath Hotel ❀❀

A commanding clifftop position for a premier seaside hotel serving carefully cooked Anglo-French food

The sea views are as splendid today as when the hotel was built 155 years ago, long before anyone spotted Bournemouth's potential for party political conferences. There are two main restaurants – the less formal Garden, and Oscars, which offers dishes in both classic and modern styles. An insistence on quality ingredients was evident from an inspection meal which began with an appetiser of quail's egg on a tiny potato pancake with a piquant chive sauce. Typifying the modern approach were warm fillets of fresh red mullet set on tender aubergine, served with a tangy sweet and sour tomato-based sauce. More traditionally, roast breast of grouse came with Savoy cabbage, a red wine sauce and an innovative mille-feuille of potato, crispy bacon and oyster mushrooms; an assembly which worked well and rendered the accompanying vegetables almost superfluous. Not quite so special was a clumsily made pecan nut tart with a poorly made ice-cream in a crisp brandy snap case. Also weak were the doughy, chewy home-made rolls. The wine selection is limited and might even be considered dull. In contrast, lively dinner dances take place on Saturday evenings.

Directions: Within the Royal Bath Hotel above the Pavilion and Promenade

Bath Road BH1 2EW
Map no: 4 SZ09
Tel: 01202 555555
Chef: Gerard Puigdellivol
Proprietors: De Vere.
Manager: A Lawson
Cost: Alc £45, fixed-price L £15.50/D £28.50. H/wine £10.75 ! Service inc
Credit cards: 🂠 💳 💳 💷
Times: Last L 2.15pm/D 10.15pm. Closed Sun, Bh Mon
Menus: A la carte, fixed-price L & D
Seats: 40. Air conditioned. No pipes or cigars
Additional: Children welcome, children's menu; ◐ dishes, vegan/other diets on request

BOURNEMOUTH,

Sophisticats Restaurant ❀

Classic international food cooked by chef Bernard Calligan.
The 'tried and trusted' menu offers such delights as Old English
venison pie. By popular demand the carte rarely changes, but the daily
specials differ and seasonal produce is put to good use. A beautifully rich
chocolate marquise is not to be missed

Menu: *A la carte* D
Seats: 34
Additional: Children permitted; ❂ dishes; other diets on request
Directions: One mile from town centre

43 Charminster Road BH8 8UE
Map no: 4 SZ09
Tel: 01202 291019
Chef: Bernard Calligan
Proprietors: B J Calligan and
J E Knight
Cost: *Alc* £23.70. H/wine £8.25.
Service exc
Credit cards: None taken
Times: 7pm-last D 9.30pm.
Closed Sun, Mon, 2 wks Jan,1
wk July

BRIDPORT, Bridge House Hotel ❀

☺ *An attractive property, dating back to the 18th century. Chef Simon*
Badger cooks enjoyable, fresh-tasting food. Look out for tomatoes and
mushrooms with olives in a sherry and cream sauce, served on a bed of
tagliatelli. There is a choice of fixed-price and carte menus

Menus: *A la carte* D, fixed-price D
Seats: 25. No smoking in dining room
Additional: Children welcome, children's portions; ❂ dishes, other
diets on request
Directions: From A35/A3066 roundabout into Bridport (East Street)
Hotel is 1st Georgian building on right

115 East Street DT6 3LB
Map no: 3 SY49
Tel: 01308 423371
Chef: Simon Badger
Proprietor: Simon Badger
Cost: *Alc* £16.50, fixed-price D
£14.50. H/wine £6.50. Service
exc
Credit cards: ▨ ▨ ▨
Times: Last D 9.30pm. Closed
Sun, Mon

BRIDPORT, Riverside Restaurant ❀❀

Seafood is an obvious choice at this lively restaurant with a waterside
setting

West Bay DT6 4EZ
Map no: 3 SY49
Tel: 01308 422011
Chefs: Neil Fanous, Michael
Mills and Janet Watson
Proprietors: Arthur & Janet
Watson
Cost: *Alc* £12.95-£25. H/wine
£10.95 (litre) ❢ Service exc
Credit cards: ▨ ▨ OTHER
Times: 11am-last L 2.30pm (later
on Sun), 6.30pm-last D
8.30/9pm. Fri & Sat Closed Sun
D, Mon (exc BHs), late Nov-
early Mar
Menu: *A la carte*
Seats: 70. No cigars or pipes
Additional: Children welcome,
children's portion; ❂ dishes

Approached by a wooden footbridge over the river, the Riverside
Restaurant is in a pretty waterside setting. The simple wooden
tables and bare floor boards create an unpretentious atmosphere
whilst the large paintings by local artists displayed on the walls add
colour. The gentle jazz and blues music usually played here is nearly
always lost in the lively buzz of satisfied customers. This is a
seafood restaurant, with influences from around the world, whose

menu appeals to all tastes and changes according to the daily catch. There might be anything from John Dory and sea bream to the ever popular cod in Guinness batter with home-made mushy peas and chips. At a meal in June the starters included a duck leg confit, brandade of cod with a salt cod dip and a very good, richly flavoured fish soup. A fillet of brill was perfectly cooked and served with a 'tasty' sorrel sauce and 'lovely crunchy' deep-fried spinach and fresh vegetables. Sweets range from the ubiquitous sticky toffee pudding to a creamy crème brûlée concealing large fresh strawberries.

Directions: In the centre of West Bay by the river

BRIDPORT, Roundham House ❀

Built as a gentleman's residence in 1903, Roundham House keeps its daily-changing, fixed-price menu simple. West Bay lemon sole, grilled sirloin steak, lambs' liver and bacon, roast breast of chicken and vegetable curry and rice are as complicated as it gets. The desserts are straight-talking too, plum and apple pie with custard, for example

Seats: 20. No smoking in dining room
Additional: ❂ dishes; other diets on request
Directions: From roundabout on A35 south of Bridport take road signposted West Bay, then 2nd turning on left into Roundham Gardens

Roundham Gardens DT6 4BD
West Bay Road
Map no: 3 SY49
Tel: 01308 422753
Chef: Betty Patricia Moody
Proprietors: Robert David Moody & Betty Patricia Moody
Cost: H/wine £7.50
Credit cards: 🄰 🄳 🄿 OTHER
Times: Last D 8pm. Closed Nov-Jan

BRIDPORT, Three Horseshoes Inn ❀

A blackboard menu and seperate pasta board list the choices at this bistro-style inn. Fish soup is richly flavoured and comes with mussels in their shells and large pieces of fish, or, for a main course, thick slices of wild duck might be enjoyed. There is a tempting selection of desserts

Additional: No smoking in restaurant. Children welcome
Directions: In the village of Powerstock, 5 miles north-east of Bridport

Powerstock DT6 3TF
Map no: 3 SY49
Tel: 01308 485328
Chef: Will Longman
Proprietors: Mr & Mrs Ferguson
Cost: Alc £30, Fixed-price L £10.50/D £12.50. H/wine £6.50 Service exc
Credit cards: 🄰 🄳 🄴
Times: Last L 2pm/D 10pm

CHRISTCHURCH,
Splinters Restaurant ❀❀

Some truly imaginative dishes at every course in a lovely old building with lots of nooks and crannies

Splinters sits in a quiet, cobbled corner of historic Christchurch, close to the beautiful 12th-century priory. Within, there's a choice of dining-rooms, all with gleaming wood-panelled walls. The upstairs lounge, with its Victorian fireplace, is used mainly for after-dinner coffee, and the entrance area, featuring Lloyd Loom furniture, serves as a bar/brasserie at lunch time. Eamonn Redden masterminds the menus using good quality local produce to produce dishes such as home smoked mussels in a 'delicious' soup, complemented by a hint of saffron, confit of duck with a perfectly crisped skin and 'excellent' spinach and leek timbale. Or there's a choice of curried parsnip soup with onion fritters, shrimp and oyster junket with a leek sauce and individual clafoutis of black pudding

12 Church Street BH23 1BW
Map no: 4 SZ19
Tel: 01202 483454
Chef: Eammon Redden
Proprietors: Timothy Lloyd and Robert Wilson
Cost: Alc £ 25, fixed-price L/D £14.50/£22.50. H/wine £10.40
❂ Service exc
Credit cards: 🄰 🄳 🄴 🄿 OTHER
Times: 10.30am-last L 2.30pm, 7pm-last D 10.30pm, Closed 2 weeks mid Jan
Menus: A la carte, fixed-price L & D, bar/brasserie menu
Seats: 40. (+ 22 private room)

and apple served with a sweet sage sauce. Main courses might be saddle of lamb stuffed with apricots and almonds, roast sea scallops with a strawberry and green peppercorn sauce, or Gruyère cheese and broccoli bread and butter pudding. For dessert how about mushroom ice-cream capped with sweet truffle meringue and cappuccino sauce?

Directions: Splinters is on left side of cobbled street directly in front of Priory Gates

CHRISTCHURCH,
Waterford Lodge Hotel ❀❀

Good home baking and and the imaginative use of local produce make a meal here a memorable experience

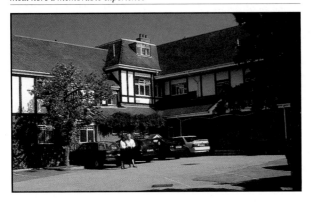

Additional: Children permitted, children's portions; ❶ dishes, other diets on request

87 Bure Lane BH23 4DN
Map:
Tel: 01425 272948
Chef: Ian Badley
Proprietors: Ian & David Badley (Best Western Hotels)
Cost: *Alc* £21.95, fixed-price L £13.95, fixed-price D (2 course) £16.95. H/wine £9.60 ❢ Service exc
Credit cards: ▨ ▥ ▥ ▣ OTHER
Times: Last L 1.45pm, last D 9pm daily
Menus: *A la carte,* fixed-price L & D
Seats: 40. No cigars or pipes
Additional: Children over 5 permitted, children's menu; ❶ dishes, vegan/other diets on request

Housed in a welcoming hotel on the edge of the village of Mudeford, close to the sea, this restaurant offers a *carte* and set-price menus of sound, carefully prepared English and French dishes based on local produce. An evening meal in early summer began with a crisp filo pastry case filled with crab and served on a complex salad containing asparagus, prawns and quails' eggs; the main course, a ballontine of pigeon, was filled with a delicious chestnut and parsnip purée – the slight sweetness of the stuffing providing an effective contrast to the rich flavour of the tender meat – and no less than six vegetables were served. The lemon tart which followed was a slight disappointment, its slightly firm filling lacking the expected intensity of flavour, but fresh filter coffee came with good home-made petits fours. Breads are baked on the premises and are 'more-ish'. A list of wines chosen for their quality, consistency and value-for-money includes some good vintages and a reasonable range of half bottles.

Directions: From A35 Somerford roundabout take A337 towards Highcliffe, next right to Mudeford, hotel on right

Factual details of establishments in this Guide are from questionnaires we send to all restaurants that feature in the book.

CORFE CASTLE, **Mortons House Hotel** ❀

*A sympathetically converted sixteenth-century Elizabethan manor
overlooking the village. The restaurant serves traditional English dishes. A
typical meal might be chicken liver parfait, followed by pot-roast English
poussin cooked in mead, with a choice of home-made puddings to finish*

East Street BH20 5EE
Map no: 3 SY98
Tel: 01929 480988
Chef: Christopher Button
Proprietors: Mr & Mrs David
Langford
Cost: Fixed-price L £15/D
£22.50 (6 course) /Sun L £9.50
(4 course). H/wine £10. Service
exc
Credit cards: 🆅 🆅 🆅 🆅
Times: Last L 2pm, last D
8.30pm
Menus: Fixed-price L & D, bar
L menu
Seats: 45+20. No smoking in
dining rooms
Additional: Children permitted,
children's portions; ❂ dishes,
other diets on request

Directions: In centre of village on A351

DORCHESTER, **The Mock Turtle** ❀❀

*Interconnecting rooms in a 17th-century town house make a delightful
setting for a sound menu, strong on fish*

There is no turtle soup, mock or otherwise, on the fixed-price
menus; new English cooking, instead, is the order of the day.
Modern methods and ingredients are in evidence – chicken breast
rubbed with Cajun spices and blackened in the pan, 'pink' duck
breast grilled and placed on a pool of crème de cassis sauce, and
black pudding served with Madeira sauce, burnt onion and apple
relish. Combinations sometimes sound a little forced, as in a
chicken and date terrine, or a prawn and bacon salad, but there are
plenty of more straightforward dishes such as chargrilled entrecôte
minute steak, fillet of beef Stroganoff, moules marinière and grilled
lamb cutlets milanaise. Fresh fish and seafood dishes stand out, and
daily specials may include whole grilled West country brill, ragout
of monkfish, lemon sole and king scallops or Portland crab bisque.
Similar dishes appear in the amazing value £10 two course lunch
menu. Pancakes, mousses, cream horns and savarins form the
backbone of the interesting dessert menu

34 High West Street DT1 1UP
Map no: 3 SY69
Tel: 01305 264011
Chef: Raymond Hodder
Proprietors: Raymond, Alan &
Vivien Hodder
Cost: Fixed-price L £10 (2
course)/D £19.50 H/wine £ 7.95
Service exc
Credit cards: 🆅 🆅 OTHER
Times: Last L 2pm, last D
9.30pm Closed Sat/Sun/Mon
L, Sun D, Dec 26/27, Jan 1
Menus: Fixed-price L & D
Seats: 55. No pipes or cigars in
dining room
Additional: Children permitted;
❂ dishes, vegan/other diets on
request

Directions: Town centre, top of High West Street

DORCHESTER, **Yalbury Cottage** ❀

*Picture postcard thatched cottage in the charming small village of Lower
Bockhampton. Local produce features on a menu that includes chilled
cucumber soup with a touch of fennel, game, meaty noisettes of lamb with
chicken and tarragon mousse and tarragon sauce, and lemon tart*

Lower Bockhampton
Dorchester DT2 8PZ
Map no: 3 SY69
Tel: 01305 262382
Proprietors: Derek & Heather
Furminger

Directions: Two miles east of Dorchester, off A35

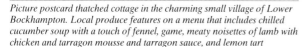

EVERSHOT, Summer Lodge ❀❀❀

The wide range of modern English dishes served in this attractive restaurant is securely based on good traditional ingredients

A Georgian dower house is the setting for this delightful, airy restaurant, the hotel's pleasant public rooms also including a bar and small lounge where canapés are served. Walls hung with unusual modern prints, an extensive collection of cheese dishes and windows overlooking the attractive gardens all vie for the attention of the guests seated at candlelit tables decked with fresh flowers. Chef Donna Horlock presents *carte* and fixed-price menus of modern English dishes ranging in style from a simple rabbit terrine with Cumberland sauce to thinly sliced smoked salmon with shallots and soured cream, from lamb steaks with spring vegetables to pan-fried breast of guinea fowl with sage noodles and lingonberries. One evening in early summer our inspector enjoyed a well balanced meal with no disappointments. Marinated olives provided a contrast to canapés of duck terrine, salmon mousse and cheese filo, and light-textured home-made rolls were served with unsalted butter. Ravioli filled with a lobster and crab mousse was accompanied by a sauce of langoustine, ginger and chives with grain mustard – a successful blend of flavours – this being followed by a pig's trotter stuffed with a coarse farce of the meat blended with fresh figs and prunes, set on good creamed potato and complemented by baby turnips, french beans, asparagus tips and a sauce of morels, cream and brandy. Kumquat tart, its bitter-sweet cream base topped with caramelised slices of the fruit, came with a light, crisp chocolate tuille filled with well made treacle ice-cream, and miniscule cups of filter coffee were flanked by Bendicks mints. A wide-ranging wine list contains examples from some of the world's best estates and offers a good choice of half bottles as well as a fine selection of sherries.

Directions: 1 mile W of A37 halfway between Dorchester and Yeovil, turn left in village

Evershot DT2 0JR
Map no: 3 ST50
Tel: 01935 83424
Chef: Donna Horlock
Proprietors: Nigel & Margaret Corbett (Relais & Chateaux)
Cost: A/c £35, fixed-price L £9.75/D £29.75(5 course). H/wine £12 Service exc
Credit cards: 🔳 🔳 🔳 🔳 OTHER
Times: Last L 2pm, last D 9pm daily
Menus: *A la carte,* fixed-price L & D
Seats: 50. No smoking until eating finished
Additional: Children welcome (not under 5 at D), children's portions; ❂ dishes, vegan/other diets on request

---

GILLINGHAM,
Stock Hill Hotel ❀❀❀

Gëmutlich welcome at tranquil and luxurious country house hotel with highly accomplished European cuisine

Stock Hill is the epitome of the English country house, quietly set in its own ten acres of grounds. The sumptuous and opulent drawing-room, full of antiques and objects, is complemented by an understated and elegant dining-room. Austrian-born chef Peter Hauser cooks in the grand European style, with confidence and authority. His excellent patisserie is not to be missed, and Viennese afternoon teas are a new introduction. Ingredients are always of tip-top quality, and may feature rarely found local items such as crayfish, sweetbreads and Cornish octopus. The walled kitchen garden provides plenty of home-grown produce.

This year, our inspection meal began with skilfully made canapés of ham, gherkins, egg and anchovy Jagerwecken, celery tart remoulade and Chinese rice with home-cured herrings. Lemon brioche with sesame seeds and wholemeal poppy seed bread struck a pleasingly original note. A refined sautéed starter of calves' liver

Stock Hill SP8 5NR
Map no: 3 ST82
Tel: 01747 823626
Chef: Peter Hauser and Lorna Connor
Proprietors: Peter & Nita Hauser
Cost: Fixed-price L £19/D £28 (4 course). H/wine £13.50 ❢
Service exc
Credit cards: 🔳 🔳 🔳
Times: Last L 1.45pm/D 8.45pm. Closed Mon L
Menus: Fixed-price L & D
Seats: 24-30. No smoking
Additional: Children over 7 welcome, children's portions; ❂ dishes, vegan/other diets on request

Stock Hill Hotel

with shallots, brandy and puff pastry was tender and full of flavour. Aga-roasted French cornfed guinea fowl had a light, moist texture; stuffed with an apple, it was served with a rosemary sauce flavoured with Madeira wine. This was additionally garnished with a nutmeg spiced potato purée, cream enriched carrot purée and broccoli topped with tarragon béarnaise sauce. Desserts matched expectations with a beautifully cooked and artistically presented apple and strawberry flan under a net of pulled sugar. Coffee comes with home-made peppermint creams and vanilla Kipferl. The descriptive wine list numbers around 80 good quality bins, with some interesting cru classe Bordeaux and domaine Burgundy amongst them. A notable dessert wine, Bonnezeaux Chateau des Gauliers 1947, would certainly be a wine to remember at £75, but a good selection of other pudding wines are available by the glass as well.

Directions: 3 miles off A303 on B3081

HIGHCLIFFE,

The Lord Bute Restaurant ☺☺

☺ *Smart little restaurant with unpretentious menu full of honest enthusiasm*

An appreciative local clientele frequent this attractive restaurant, once the gatehouse of Highcliffe Castle. The welcome is genuine, and the sensible, unpretentious meals good value for money. Much use is made of high-quality regional ingredients purchased locally. A main course of thinly sliced, sautéed pork with a delicious brown sauce was well finished with a dollop of cream and peppercorns; a starter of scallop and artichoke terrine with lemon mayonnaise has also been enjoyed in the past, as has a subtle lemon mousse served in a crisp, chocolate shell. Freshly cooked vegetables may include Brussels sprouts, carrots, green beans and both roast and new potatoes. The wine list is priced fairly, and there is a choice suited to most palates and pockets.

Directions: Follow the A337 to Lymington, situated opposite St Mark's churchyard in Highcliffe

Lymington Road BH23 4JS
Map no: 4 SZ29
Tel: 01425 278884
Chefs: Christopher Denley and Tim Hoyle
Proprietors: Christopher Denley, Stephen Caunter and Simon Denley
Cost: *Alc* £20, Fixed-price L £12.50/D £16.50. H/wine £9.95 Service exc
Credit cards: 🆒 💳 💳 💳
Times: Closed Sat lunch, Sun eve, Mon all day
Seats: 75-80. No pipes or cigars in restaurant
Additional: ❶ dishes. No children under 10

LYME REGIS, Kersbrook Hotel & Restaurant ❀

Pound Road DT7 3HX
Map no: 3 SY39
Tel: 012974 42596
Chef: Norman Arnold
Proprietor: Eric Hall Stephenson
Cost: *Alc* from £16.50, fixed-price L £5.50/D £16.50 (4 course). H/wine £8 ¶ Service exc
Credit cards: ◼ ▦ ▤ OTHER
Times: Last L 1.45pm/D 9pm

Every effort is made to please here; visitors may even request 'any traditional dish, or personal favourite'. Accordingly, the cooking is interesting and wide-ranging, with a large selection of fish choices such as traditional crab pâté. There is also a suitably good choice of speciality coffees

Menus: *A la carte,* fixed-price L & D, bar menu
Seats: 40. No-smoking room
Additional: Children permitted (over 12 at D); ♥ dishes,vegan/other diets on request
Directions: Town centre – go along main street (Pound Street) turn R at Car Park into Pound Road

MAIDEN NEWTON, Le Petit Canard ❀❀

Dorchester Road DT2 0BE
Map no: 3 SY59
Tel: 01300 320536
Chef: Geoff Chapman
Proprietors: Geoff & Lin Chapman
Cost: Fixed-price D £21.50. H/wine £10.95 ¶ Service exc
Credit cards: ◼ ▤
Times: 7pm-last D 9pm. Closed Sun, Mon, first wk Jan
Menu: Fixed-price D
Seats: 28. No cigars or pipes
Additional: Children permitted (pref. over 7); ♥ dishes

Successful husband and wife venture producing adventurous cooking

There is more to Le Petit Canard than just a pretty, intimate restaurant offering a warm, friendly atmosphere and charming service. Geoff Chapman's cooking is innovative and adventurous – there are not many places that list kangaroo on the menu. A recent meal impressed an inspector with its clarity of flavours and textures. It commenced with a light, airy goats' cheese soufflé served with mixed leaves and a sun-dried tomato dressing. Baked lemon chicken followed, well set off by a creamy pesto sauce and served with fresh, well-timed vegetables. As for the kangaroo, the small piece sampled was surprisingly a cross between well-hung beef and venison; it was rather liked. Less unorthodox choices off the short fixed-price menu might be lamb fillet brushed with hoi sin on a bed of beansprouts, or crispy ginger duck on garlicky Chinese greens. Puddings along the lines of passionfruit and pistachio Napoleon are difficult to resist. Lin Chapman is passionate about wines, and it shows in her enthusiastic wine list.

Directions: In the centre of Maiden Newton 8 miles from Dorchester

Rhubarb originated in northern Asia. It is botanically not a fruit but a vegetable, but is classed as a fruit since that is how it is normally eaten. The Chinese valued rhubarb medicinally, and it was so regarded when it arrived in Britain in the 16th century. Indeed, the first recipe for rhubarb did not appear until the late 18th century. Recipes for sweet pies and tarts followed in the 19th century, but it was Mrs Beeton who really popularised it with her extensive repertoire of recipes for rhubarb jams, rhubarb pudding, rhubarb tart and rhubarb wine. Rhubarb can be forced to provide fruit out of season which probably helped to increase its popularity in Victorian times. The normal growing season lasts from May to July, but early forced rhubarb (January - April) is tender, pink and delicious. By comparison, the unforced summer rhubarb can be coarse and sour. Early forced rhubarb makes a good accompaniment to fish, especially wild salmon.

POOLE, Harbour Heights Hotel ❀

Occupying a hill top, Harbour Heights enjoys spectacular harbour views. A good choice is offered on the daily set menu, carte and extensive vegetarian menu, and selections might include chicken and sweetcorn roulade, tiger prawns in filo pastry, and sautéed strips of beef with ginger

Seats: 300. No-smoking area
Additional: Children welcome, children's portions/menu; ❂ menu; other diets on request
Directions: Midway between Poole and Bournemouth, overlooking Poole Harbour and the Purbeck Hills

73 Haven Road
Sandbanks BH13 7LW
Map no: 4 SZ09
Tel: 01202 707272
Chef: Nino Satorello
Proprietor: Paul Shee
Cost: Alc £20; Sunday L £10.95; fixed-price D £15.50. Wine £8.95. Service exc
Credit cards: ▨ ▨ ▨ ▨ OTHER
Times: Last L 2pm/Last D 9.30pm

POOLE, Haven Hotel ❀❀

Waterfront dining in luxurious continental style

La Roche, the small dining-room, located to the right when approaching the main hotel restaurant, is popular at weekends, but tends to be unfairly neglected during the week. Chef Karl Heinz Nayler has well-honed professional skills, and shapes his short, neo-classical menu with Continental flair and imagination. Sauces are a basic building block – red wine sauce boldly matches oven-roasted fillet of turbot, and a Madeira sauce is the background for veal kidney served with a feuilleté of leek noodles. Fashionable ingredients are not neglected – terrine of pigeon and lentils, and red mullet soup are both attractive starters. Main courses demonstrate considerable technical complexity, as in marinated and braised oxtail off the bone, wrapped in filo pastry and presented with roast shallots and garlic red wine sauce. Glossy desserts include apple and Calvados soufflé, and brochette of marinated fruit which, typically, is set upon a bed of rice pudding, glazed with Grand Marnier sabayon and ringed by a cordon of raspberry coulis. Well over a hundred bins are listed, mostly by flavour and style, and there is also an excellent range of bin ends.

Directions: From Poole or Bournemouth follow signs to Sandbanks Peninsula

Banks Road
Sandbanks BH13 7QL
Map no: 4 SZ09
Tel: 01202 707333
Chef: Karl Heinz Nagler
Proprietors: F J B Hotels.
Managers: J G Butterworth and Christopher T Smith
Cost: Alc £30, fixed-price L £15/D £22. H/wine £9.75 ❢ Service exc
Credit cards: ▨ ▨ ▨ ▨
Times: Last L 2pm/D10pm. La Roche 7pm-10pm Mon-Sat
Menus: A la carte, fixed-price L & D, Brasserie, pre-theatre
Seats: Main restaurant 150. La Roche 30. No smoking in main restaurant
Additional: Children permitted, children's menu; ❂ menu, vegan/other diets on request

POOLE, **Mansion House Hotel**

☺ *Friendly hotel near Poole Quay with much improved menu and well patronised dining club*

Thames Street BH15 1JN
Map no: 4 SZ09
Tel: 01202 685666
Chefs: Gerry Godden
Proprietor: Robert Leonard.
Manager: Jackie Gooden
Cost: Fixed-price L £10-£17/D
£19.50. H/wine £11.50 ☕
Service exc
Credit cards: ▨ ▧ ▧ ▨
Times: Last L 2pm/D 9.30pm.
Closed Sat L, Sun D, BH Mon L
Menus: Fixed-price L & D, bar
menu
Seats: 85. Air conditioned.
No-smoking area
Additional: Children welcome
(no babies), children's portions;
❷ dishes, other diets by
arrangement

The Mansion House dining-club enjoys considerable local popularity, and hotel residents are able to enjoy temporary membership which brings them a 15% discount. The Club Dining Room, with its attractive cherry-wood panelling, offers good-value set menus. At first sight the *carte* seems over ambitious and worryingly long, listing about a dozen choices at each course, other than the dessert. A kitchen needs to be well drilled to cope with a fusillade of orders ranging from lightly braised tiger prawns in a cardamon and orange sauce with vegetable ribbons, to pan-roasted pigeon breasts on a bed of black pudding with red wine sauce. Recent inspection meals have praised the robust terrine of duck confit with a bright, spring onion vinaigrette, followed by an inventive combination of tender, pan-fried fillets of pork with Dorset air-dried ham and sage, finished with a Marsala sauce and served with gnocchi. A twice-baked cheese soufflé with roasted red pepper dressing, and leg of duck, slowly cooked in a red wine sauce flavoured with five spice, served with butter noodles, scored equally well.

Directions: Follow the signs for Poole Quay, left at Bridge, first road left is Thames Street

---

Salsify is a root vegetable of which there are two varieties: true salsify, which is white and thick and knobbly with numerous small tubers, and the black salsify, which is long, black, smooth and tapering. Black salsify is easier to peel and is cultivated for canning. Both the true and the black variety have a strong and slightly bitter taste and tender flesh. Both types are in season between October and March. The word salsify comes from the Catalan 'escorso', which means viper. The plant was noted in Catalonia as a treatment for snake bites.

POOLE, **Mez Creiz** ❀

☺ *An informal bistro specialising in locally caught shellfish. Mez Creiz is the name of the Breton fishing boat where the Italian proprietor learned his trade. The blackboard menu varies according to the catch but could include oysters from Weymouth and local flat fish, all offered at keen prices*

Seats: 38
Additional: Children welcome, children's portions
Directions: 200yds from the Quay which runs parallel to the High Street

16 High Street NH15 1BP
Map no: 4 SZ09
Tel: 01202 674970
Chef: Karen Brailsford
Proprietors: Karen Brailsford and Nick Dogana
Cost: Alc £13.50. H/wine £7.65. Service exc
Credit cards: ⬛ 🟦 🟥 🔲 OTHER
Times: Last D 10.30pm (11pm Sat). Lunch not served. Closed 2 weeks Xmas, Sun in winter

POOLE, **Salterns Hotel** ❀❀

An attractive hotel with panoramic views and a restaurant which continues to generate praise

38 Salterns Way
Lilliput BH14 8JR
Map no: 4 SZ09
Tel: 01202 707321
Chef: Nigel Popperwell
Proprietors: John & Beverly Smith (Best Western)
Costs: Alc £21, fixed-price L £15.50 (4 course)/D£25 (4 course). H/wine £9.50 ❗ Service exc
Credit cards: ⬛ 🟦 🟥 🔲
Times: Noon-last L 2pm, 7pm-last D 9.30pm
Menus: A la carte, fixed-price L & D, bar menu
Seats: 50. Air conditioned
Additional: Children permitted; ❶ menu, children's/other diets on request

Salterns is a hotel which goes from strength to strength. One of the best locations on the south coast helps; it overlooks a marina, Poole Harbour and Brownsea Island. Locally-caught fresh fish (and seasonal game) feature strongly on varied menus: grilled suprême of turbot on a bed of poached leeks with a Meaux mustard sauce, or pan-fried fillet of red mullet with home-made noodles and a balsamic vinegar sauce, for example. In recent months, starters of crayfish ravioli, warm salad of smoked haddock with mixed leaves and poached egg have drawn praise, as has a main course of steamed brill with a smooth langoustine sauce. From the dinner *carte* might come steamed suprême of chicken filled with salmon and crab mousse, served on a white wine and coriander sauce, pan-fried fillet of lamb with a lamb, mint and horseradish cream sauce, or medallions of prime beef fillet, served with a red wine and shallot sauce. Desserts include iced coconut mousse served with fresh fruit set on a rich orange sauce, and individual chocolate and raspberry tartlets set on a raspberry coulis. There is a fine wine list which also incorporates a selection of 22 Armagnacs going back to 1904.

Directions: From Poole take B3369 for Sandbanks; after 1.5 miles in Lilliput turn right (Salterns Way). Restaurant on right at end

POOLE, **Sandbanks Hotel** ✿

The Sandbanks Hotel provides a wide choice of dining; in addition to the set menu offered in the large main restaurant, there is a more intimate a la carte restaurant, La Mer, and even a children's restaurant. Most tastes can be accommodated, from vegan to dishes such as veal fillet, pan fried in butter

Menus: A la carte, fixed-price L & D, brasserie, children's restaurant
Seats: Alc restaurant 38, main restaurant 200. No smoking in dining rooms
Additional: Children welcome in main restaurant, children's menu; ❻ menu, vegan/other diets on request
Directions: From Poole or Bournemouth follow signs to Sandbanks Peninsula

15 Banks Road BH13 7PS
Map no: 4 SZ09
Tel: 01202 707377
Chef: Robert Jones
Proprietors: J G Butterworth (FJB Hotels).
Manager: John Belk
Cost: Alc £23.50, fixed-price L £14/D £17.75. H/wine £9.75 ❢
Service exc
Credit cards: 🅽 ▦ ▱ ▣
Times: Last L 2pm, last D 9.30pm. Sun no Alc service

POOLE, **The Warehouse Brasserie** ✿

☺ *An informal brasserie in a stylish quayside warehouse conversion. A wide choice of fish is available, with selections depending on the day's catch; meat, pasta and vegetarian dishes are also available. A typical meal might include twice-baked mushroom soufflé, monkfish with Provençal sauce, and steamed pudding*

Menus: A la carte L & D, bar L menu
Seats: 90. No pipes allowed
Additional: Children welcome, children's portions; ❻ dishes, vegan/other diets on request
Directions: End of High Street, 1st floor Newfoundland House, on the Quay

The Quay
Map no: 4 SZ09
Tel: 01202 677238
Chefs: D Ricketts and Edward Cox
Proprietor: D Ricketts.
Manager: Leigh Boulter
Cost: Alc £18-£20, H/wine £6.95. Service exc
Credit cards: 🅽 ▦ ▱ ▣ OTHER
Times: Last L 2.30pm/last D 10pm Closed Sat L (bar L open), Sun, Dec 26-Jan 11

SHAFTESBURY, **La Fleur de Lys** ✿✿

Modern English and French cooking in a friendly atmosphere

Good flavours, careful preparation and an unpretentious approach, are the hallmarks of this smart, first-floor restaurant with views over Blackmoor Vale. The menu offers a good choice, and charts a neat mid-course between the austerely simple and the over-elaborate. Starters may include pan-fried scallops coated in herb crumbs and served on grated ginger and carrot on watercress sauce, a salad of Parma ham with pink grapefruit, melon and raspberries in a raspberry dressing, and terrine of spring chicken with chicken livers, English veal and wild mushrooms. Main courses run along the lines of roasted fillet of sea bass with roasted fennel, served on a bed of spinach with Pernod sauce, and roast saddle of venison with apples, chestnuts and cranberries on a cranberry and red wine sauce. One of the most tempting of the classy desserts is coffee hazelnut beignets soufflés, served with a Tia Maria ice-cream and butterscotch sauce. The latter may also make an appearance alongside nougatine baskets filled with honey and pecan nut ice-cream and crystallized pecans.

Directions: Town centre, near the Post Office, on the main road

25 Salisbury Street SP7 8EL
Map no: 3 ST82
Tel: 01747 853717
Chefs: David Shepherd and Marc Preston
Proprietors: David Shepherd, Mary Griffin and Marc Preston
Cost: Alc £25, fixed-price L £12/D £19.95. H/wine £10
Service exc
Credit cards: 🅽 ▦ ▱ ▣
Times: Last L 2.30pm, last D 10pm Closed Sun D, Mon L
Menus: A la carte, fixed-price L & D
Seats: 40. No-smoking area
Additional: Children welcome, children's portions; ❻ dishes, other diets on request

SHAFTESBURY, Royal Chase Hotel ❀

☺ *This traditional hotel is handy for Hardy country, being just minutes from the A30. The Byzant restaurant offers a good choice of meals prepared from fresh ingredients. A sample meal might include a lightly flavoured galantine of pheasant, followed by a confit of salmon, with apricot tatin to finish*

Times: Noon-last L 2pm/D 9.30pm **Seats:** 74 (Byzant) + 30 (Country). No-smoking area; no cigars or pipes in restaurants **Menus:** A la carte, fixed-price L & D, bar menu **Additional:** Children welcome, children's menu; ❂ menu, vegan/other diets on request **Directions:** Set back from A30/A350 roundabout to east of town

Royal Chase Roundabout
SP7 8DB
Map no: 3 ST82
Tel: 01747 853355
Chef: Antony Sayers
Proprietors: George Hunt (Best Western).
Manager: Michael Ash
Cost: Alc £13.50, fixed-price L £10/D £18.50. H/wine £8.50 ❢
Service inc
Credit cards: 🔲 🔲 🔲 🔲 OTHER

SHERBORNE, Pheasants Restaurant ❀❀

Accomplished but not over-elaborate English cooking is the speciality of this High Street restaurant

The enjoyment of good English cooking is enhanced by a relaxed and friendly setting in this charming town house at the top of the High Street. Chef Neil Cadle offers both a set-price menu and a more extensive *carte* – the interesting dishes featured on both of them making optimum use of local produce and striking a nice balance between refined and more robust flavours. A vibrant gazpacho with garlic croûtons provided the start to a recent meal, and this was followed by superbly tender and appropriately gamey venison accompanied by a celeriac and fresh mango rösti and Madeira sauce. Desserts ranged from made-to-order bread and butter pudding, to a duo of white and dark chocolate ice-creams – delicious, though perhaps more like iced parfaits in texture – complemented by a huge brandy snap filled with cream and a mocha caramel sauce. Coffee, petits fours and mints are served in the comfortable, cosy lounge.

Directions: At the top of the High Street, A30 (Salisbury/Yeovil)

24 Greenhill DT9 4EW
Map no: 3 ST61
Tel: 01935 815252
Chef: Neil D Cadle
Proprietor: Andrew Overhill
Cost: Alc £23, fixed-price L £13.50/D £18.95 (4 course). H/wine £8.50 ❢ Service exc
Credit cards: 🔲 🔲
Times: Last L 2pm, last D 10pm. Closed Mon & 2 weeks mid-Jan
Menus: A la carte, fixed-price lunch & dinner
Seats: 40/45. No cigars or pipes
Additional: Children welcome; ❂ menu, vegan/other diets on request

STUDLAND, Manor House Hotel ❀

☺ *Situated off the Bridport to Weymouth coast road, this hotel features a fixed-price menu of two or three courses. Visitors could expect half a dozen grilled oysters béarnaise, and medallions of pork fillet, oyster mushrooms and Madeira sauce. Sweets are chosen from the trolley*

Swanage BH19 3AU
Map no: 4 SZ08
Tel: 01929 450288
Chef: David Rolfe
Proprietor: Richard Rose
Cost: Fixed-price L £6.85 (2 course), £7.85/D £18.50 (4 course) H/wine £7.95 Service exc
Credit cards: 🔲 🔲 🔲 OTHER
Times: Last L 2pm, last D 8.30pm Closed mid-Dec-Dec 27
Menus: Fixed-price L & D, bar menu
Seats: 80. No smoking in dining room
Additional: Children welcome, children's menu; ❂ dishes, vegan/other diets on request

Directions: In centre of village

STURMINSTER NEWTON,
Plumber Manor 🏵🏵

Relaxed country manor in lovely setting with careful, consistent cooking of good ingredients

The Prideaux-Brune family have opened the doors of their rural, family manor house to those in need of a breath of fresh air and a spot of rest and relaxation. Local squire, Richard Prideaux-Brune, is the welcoming host, and his brother Brian, a talented chef who continues to satisy an appreciative audience. He cooks with care, and uses good quality, fresh ingredients with a minimum of fuss. Boned and stuffed quail with wild rice in filo pastry, fillet of brill in a mustard sauce, and tender spring lamb with a garlic and herb crust, have all been praised. Fish is well-handled. Crab mousseline with scallops on a ginger sauce, and fillet of turbot with fennel and Pernod are good examples, and the extra fish course on the set menu is worth taking. Contemporary dishes include Aylesbury duck on a mango coulis, and carpeggio of smoked venison with basil and Balsamic dressing but, on the whole, the range is reassuringly familiar – beef Wellington, escalope of pork with prunes and brandy, smoked salmon paupiettes with smoked trout mousse and curried parsnip soup. Desserts usually include the popular sticky ginger pudding with warm butterscotch sauce.

Directions: At Sturminster Newton cross the packhorse bridge, right to Stalbridge (A357). First left to Hazelbury Bryan. Two miles on left opposite the Red Lion

Hazelbury Bryan Road
DT10 2AF
Map no: 3 ST71
Tel: 01258 472507
Chef: Brian Prideaux Brune
Proprietor: Richard Prideaux Brune (Pride of Britain)
Cost: Fixed-price D £20-£25 (3 courses), Sun L £17.50 H/wine £10 ● Service inc
Credit cards: 🅴 💳 💳 💷 OTHER
Times: Last L 2pm (Sun), Last D 9.30pm. Closed Feb
Menus: Fixed-price D, Sun L
Seats: 60. Smoking discouraged
Additional: Children welcome, children's portions; ♥ dishes; Vegan/other diets on request

SWANAGE, **The Cauldron Bistro** 🏵

A cheerful, well-run bistro, 'full of fun', offering a variety of simply prepared dishes such as roast halibut with celeriac and potato rösti. The adventurous should look out for the more unusual grilled wild boar and apple with sour cream and horseradish sauce, Caspian caviar, ostrich, bison and Eldon wild blue pork

Menus: A la carte, fixed-price D, Sun light L
Seats: 36. No cigars or pipes
Additional: Children welcomed, children's portions; ♥ menu, vegan/other diets on request
Directions: At lower end of the High Street opposite The Old Quay

5 High Street BH19 2LN
Map no: 4 SZ07
Tel: 01929 422671
Chef: Mr T Flenley
Proprietors: Margaret & Terry Flenley
Cost: Alc £19.00, fixed-price D £10.95 (2 courses) H/wine £7.75. Service exc
Credit cards: 🅴 💳 💳 💷 OTHER
Times: Last L 2pm/D 9.30pm. Closed Mon, Tues L (Summer), Tues (Winter), last 3 weeks Jan

> Wild rice is not a rice at all. It is the seed of an aquatic grass which comes from the northern United States. It was originally harvested by native American tribes. The seeds grow one by one up the stalk and resemble little black sticks. It is extremely expensive and is not uncommon to buy it mixed with brown rice.
> Perfumed rice is a long grain rice from Vietnam and Thailand which has a distinctive taste.

SWANAGE, **Grand Hotel** ❀

A personally-run hotel that stands to the east of Swanage, overlooking the bay. The restaurant catches the best of the sea views, and features fresh local produce. Look out for sea bream baked with green peppercorns, as well as Mediterranean influences such as roasted vegetables with saffron dressing

Burlington Road BH19 1LU
Map no: 4 SZ07
Tel: 01929 423353
Chef: Theresa Read
Proprietor: Mr Kingham
Cost: Fixed-price L £9.50/D £17.50. Service exc
Credit cards: ⬛ 💳 💳 💷
Times: Last D 9.30pm
Additional: Children welcome, ❶ dish

Directions: In a residential street on the cliff top

WAREHAM,
Kemps Hotel ❀

☺ *Kemps features a choice of menus – including vegetarian – all of which offer modern English cooking. A typical meal might start with a warm salad of wild and cultivated mushrooms, followed by pan-fried venison steak (or a choice from the fresh fish, available each day) with a home-made dessert to finish*

East Stoke BH20 6AL
Map no: 3 SY98
Tel: 01929 462563
Chef: Phil Simpkiss
Proprietors: Paul & Gill Warren
Cost: Alc £20, fixed-price D £18.95 (4 course). H/wine £8.25 Service exc
Credit cards: ⬛ 💳 💳 💷
Times: Last L 1.50pm/D 9.50pm
Closed Sat L

Menus: A la carte, fixed-price L & D, bar menu·
Seats: 60. No smoking in dining room
Additional: Children permitted, children's portions; ❶ menu, vegan/other diets on request
Directions: On A352 midway between Wareham and Wool

WAREHAM, **Priory Hotel** ❀❀

The vaulted cellars of this former priory make an attractive setting to enjoy modern English cooking

Dating from the 16th century, the former Lady St Mary Priory presents a classic English setting in peaceful gardens on the banks of the River Frome. *Carte* and fixed-price menus are offered in the vaulted cellars of the candlelit Abbots Cellars restaurant, or during warmer months in the Greenwood room which overlooks the terrace. Chef Michael Rust cooks modern English food with some flair and imagination, but a report on a recent meal suggested that by using less complicated combinations, balance and textures would be more in tune with each other. Dishes may include terrine of duck confit and foie gras flavoured with port wine and truffles, prime

Church Green BH20 4ND
Map no: 3 SY98
Tel: 01929 551666
Chef: Michael Rust
Proprietors: John Turner
Cost: Alc £35, fixed-price L £14.95/D £24.50. H/wine £10.50 Service exc
Credit cards: ⬛ 💳 💳 💷
Times: Last L 2pm/D 9.30pm daily
Seats: Greenwood 24, Cellar 48. No smoking in dining rooms
Menus: A la carte, fixed-price L & D, bar menu

fillet of beef with polenta, salsa verde and Burgundy wine jus served with caramelised shallots, and crème brûlée. The selection of farmhouse cheeses may include Jersey Blue, Somerset Brie and Dorset Blue Vinney, and cafetière coffee is served with home-made fudge and friandises. The carefully chosen wine list offers a good choice. Dinner service is professional and well turned out.

Additional: Children permitted; ♥ menu, vegan/other diets on request

Directions: Town centre between the church and the River Frome

WAREHAM, **Springfield Hotel** ❀

A family-run hotel set in attractive grounds. Fresh, good quality produce is used in the Anglo-French cooking, and an extensive choice of dishes is available. A meal might comprise smoked salmon, egg and asparagus pancake with a cheese sauce, breast of chicken stuffed with spinach, and lemon cheesecake

Menus: *A la carte,* fixed-price D, bar menu
Seats: 50. No smoking in dining room
Additional: Children welcome, children's menu; ♥ menu, vegan/other diets on request
Directions: Just off Wareham bypass outside Stoborough, signed Grange Road

Grange Road BH20 5AL
Map no: 3 SY98
Tel: 01929 552177
Chef: Andrew Cannon
Proprietor: C L Alford.
Manager: L Alford
Cost: *Alc* £18.50-£25, fixed-price D £15. H/Wine £8.50. Service inc
Credit cards: 🄰 🄼 🄼 🄿
Times: Last L 2pm/D 9pm (Sat 9.30pm)

WEST BEXINGTON, **Manor Hotel** ❀

☺ *This popular hotel, situated yards from Chesil Beach with wonderful sea views, can be dated to the Doomsday book. Chef Clive Jobson's cooking incorporates fine, quality ingredients, with which he creates imaginative food. Do not miss the extremely tempting and no doubt calorie-filled desserts*

Directions: Off signposted Bridport-Weymouth coast road (B3157)

Beach Road DT6 9DF
Map no: 3 SY58
Tel: 01308 897 616
Chef: Clive Jobson
Proprietor: Richard Childs
Cost: Fixed-price L £12.50/£14.40, fixed-price D £17.50/£20.50. House/w £7.55
Credit cards: 🄰 🄼 🄼 🄿
Times: Noon-last L 1.30pm, last D-9.30pm
Menus: Fixed-price L & D, Sun lunch
Seats: 60
Additional: Children welcome, children's portions; ♥ dishes, other diets on request

> A quenelle is a dumpling made with spiced meat or fish forcemeat bound with egg, fat and often a panada - a thick flour paste. The mixture is moulded into a small egg shape and poached in boiling water. The name comes from the German 'knödle' meaning dumpling.

WEYMOUTH, Perry's Restaurant ❀❀

☺ *Splendid harbourside setting for local seafood*

4 Trinity Road DT48TJ
Map no: 3 SY67
Tel: 01305 785799
Chefs: Andy Pike and Wayne Cramp
Proprietors: Raymond, Alan & Vivien Hodder
Cost: Alc £20, fixed-price L £12.50. H/wine £7.95. Service exc
Credit cards: ◼ ▩ OTHER
Times: Noon-last L 2pm, 7pm-last D 9.30pm. Closed Sat & Mon L, Sun D Oct-Easter, Dec 26/7, Jan
Menus: A la carte, fixed-price L
Seats: 55. (+20 Terrace, Summer)

In an attractive building overlooking the Old Quay, Perry's is a relaxed and friendly restaurant. In such a setting it is obvious that fresh fish should dominate, either on the menu or on the daily specials blackboard, and of course, crabs, lobsters, mussels, oysters, brill and sole all duly appear. Fish dishes are well prepared with the likes of fillet of cod with herb crunch topping, with a creamy butter sauce flavoured with Chardonnay and garnished with mussels a typical example. The short *carte* caters for meat eaters too. Desserts are highly recommended, especially the sticky toffee pudding and crème brûlée.

Additional: Children permitted; ✿ dishes, other diets on request
Directions: On south side of harbour – follow signs for Brewers Quay

WEYMOUTH, The Sea Cow ❀

A popular waterside restaurant, serving locally caught fish. Husband and wife, Terry and Sue Woolcock, do all the cooking and do ensure that meat eaters are amply catered for. Fresh skate with a lemon and wine butter sauce has been praised. The Woolcocks also run a successful dinner club

7 Custom House Quay DT4 8BE
Map no: 3 SY67
Tel: 01305 783524
Chef: Terence Woolcock
Proprietors: T M & S Woolcock
Cost: Alc £18-£23, fixed-price Sun L £8.95. H/wine £9.90 ltr ❢ Service exc
Credit cards: ◼ ▩
Times: Last L 2pm/D 10.15pm. Closed Sun D in winter, Dec 25, Jan 1
Menus: A la carte L & D, fixed-price Sun L, pre-theatre, bar menu
Seat: 120. No-smoking area
Additional: Children welcome, children's portions; ✿ dishes; vegan/other diets on request

Directions: On the Quay

WIMBORNE, **Les Bouviers** ❀❀

A smart cottage restaurant offering exuberant French cooking from a talented young chef

Oakley Hill
Merley BH21 1RJ
Map no: 4 SZ09
Tel: 01202 889555
Chef: James Coward
Proprietor: James Coward
Cost: *Alc* £25; fixed-price L
£7.50 (2 course)/D £23.95
(5 courses) H/wine £8.25 ▾
Service exc
Credit cards: ◼ ▦ ▤ ▨ OTHER
Times: Noon-last L 2pm, 7pm-last D 10pm. Closed Sat L
Menus: *A la carte,* fixed-price L & D, surprise menu
Seats: 65. No-smoking area
Additional: Children welcome, children's portions; ❶ menu, vegan/other diets on request

James Coward is the chef/proprietor – Coward is a corruption of cowherd, and that is what a 'bouvier' is in old French, hence the name. There is an extensive choice offered, with the blackboard Gourmand fixed-price menu running alongside an elaborate *carte*, and a 'Menu Surprise' comprising a minimum of seven courses with selected wines to accompany each one. Recent meals have included a successful twice-baked soufflé, served with watercress, slowly-poached assorted seafood (salmon, scallops, hake, sole, mussels and shellfish) with saffron pasta, and quails filled with ginger mousse. A steamed chocolate pudding skilfully enclosed a home-made white chocolate ice-cream and chocolate sauce. Other dishes have been found to be variable in quality. The exuberant cooking style is an extension of great enthusiasm and, while most dishes work well, in an attempt to be creative and innovative, some are a touch over-complicated with unnecessary contrasting flavours and textures. The mostly French wine list has a very good Burgundy section and some quirky descriptions. Wine service is efficient.

Directions: 0.5 miles south of A31 Wimborne by-pass on A349

WIMBORNE MINSTER,
Beechleas Hotel ❀❀

☺ *Subtle flavours are evident in the uncomplicated cooking served at Beechleas Hotel*

17 Poole Road BH21 1QA
Map no: 4 SZ09
Tel: 01202 841684
Chef: Paulina Humphrey
Proprietor: Josephine McQuillan
Cost: Fixed-price D £18.75.
H/wine £8.95. Service exc
Credit cards: ◼ ▦ ▤
Times: 7.30pm-last D 9.30pm.
Closed Sun, Mon, Dec 24-Jan 22
Seats: 25. No smoking in dining room
Menu: Fixed-price D
Additional: Children welcome, children's portion; ❶ dishes, vegan on request, other diets prior notice

Coherent, refined and uncomplicated cooking is served in the conservatory restaurant of this handsome Grade II listed Georgian house. Fresh ingredients include locally reared meat, free range poultry, and herbs from the hotel's garden. Everything is home-made – the breads, patisserie, and preserves are particularly worth a mention. At a meal in March, a starter of home-made liver pâté was pink and delicately-flavoured, blended with Cognac and port wine and served with fingers of wholemeal toast. A subtle cauliflower and Stilton soup followed. The main course of rack of lamb was served with a light jus with red wine and port, and came with a

Beechleas Hotel

selection of fresh, crisp vegetables. Dessert was a white and dark chocolate parfait – an iced home-made roulade with a dark chocolate sauce garnished with angelica whipped cream. Cafetière coffee was served with hand-made chocolate truffles. A carefully chosen wine list includes a good selection of domaine-bottled vintage Burgundy and cru classe Bordeaux.

Directions: On A349 at Wimborne

COUNTY DURHAM

BEAMISH, Beamish Park Hotel ❀

A high standard of cooking is maintained in the restaurant of this comfortable hotel. From the interesting fixed-price menu choose roast pigeon salad with bacon croûtons and raspberry vinaigrette, grilled breast of duck with honey, soy sauce and black pepper, and fresh strawberry shortbread tart

Beamish Burn Road
Marley Hill NE16 5EG
Map no: 12 NZ25
Tel: 01207 230666
Chef: Clive Imber
Proprietor: William Walker
Cost: Fixed-price D£14.95 (2 courses), £17.95. H/wine £8.95
Credit cards: 🟥 💳 💳 💳
Times: Last L (Sun only) 2pm, Last D 10pm. Closed Sun eve
Seats: 38. No smoking in dining room
Additional: Children welcome, ❤ dishes.

Directions: Just off A6076 Newcastle to Stanley road

DARLINGTON,
Hallgarth House Hotel ❀

A 16th-century stone-built house, now a pleasant hotel, set in 67 acres of grounds. Herbs from the walled garden feature in the cooking. Dishes such as pan-fried scallops, or poached breast of duckling are served in the romantic dining-room at candlelit mahogany tables

Coatham Mundeville DL1 3LU
Map no: 8 NZ21
Tel: 01325 300400
Chef: Kevin Hacking
Proprietor: Regal Hotel.
Manager: Ryhs Roberts
Cost: *Alc* £25, fixed-price L
£10.95/D £19.95. H/wine £8.95
Service inc
Credit cards: 🌑 ▦ ▩ 🔲 OTHER
Times: Last L 2pm/last D 9.30pm
Closed Sat L, Sun D
Menus: *A la carte,* fixed-price L
& D, bar menu
Seats: 70. No smoking in dining room
Additional: Children welcome, children's portions (& bar menu); ❂ dishes, vegan/other diets on request

Directions: A1(M) exit 59 (Spennyhook) & A167 (Darlington), take 1st left to Brafferton, hotel 200yds on right

DURHAM, **Royal County Hotel** ❀

A new chef has revitalised the cooking at this business-orientated hotel close to the cathedral. Dishes to try include salmon in pastry with cream sauce garnished with mussels, smooth duck liver parfait with tangy beetroot and red currant chutney, dressed leaves and toasted brioche, and fillet of sea bass with a tomato fondue

Directions: From the north, join A690. Follow City centre signs, left at first two roundabouts. Left at traffic lights, hotel on left

Durham DH1 3JN
Map no: 12 NZ24
Tel: 0191 386 6821
Chef: John Cruikshank
Proprietor: Neal Crocker
Cost: Fixed-price L £14/D £23.
Service exc
Credit cards: 🌑 ▦ ▩ 🔲 OTHER
Times: Last D 10.15pm

EBCHESTER, **The Raven Hotel** ❀

A modern hotel serving decent, well prepared and attractively presented food. At inspection, rack of lamb had 'excellent flavour' and a 'well matching' red wine and red currant sauce. Puddings are generally rich but well-made. Look out for the fresh orange trifle

Directions: On B6309

Ebchester
Map no: 12 NZ15
Tel: 01207 560367
Chef: Ray Valentine
Proprietor: Yearn Income Ltd.
Manager: R Young
Credit cards: 🌑 ▦ ▩ 🔲
Times: Last D 10pm

Balsamic vinegar is made from the cooked and concentrated must of the white grapes of the Trebbiano vine and aged in 12 kegs of different woods. By law it must be at least 10 years old. A deep, rich dark brown in colour, it is a full-bodied vinegar with an intense aromatic fragrance and a distinctive flavour which is at once both sweet and sour.

REDWORTH,

Redworth Hall Hotel ❀❀

☺ *Fine cooking from a choice of restaurants combined with the sheer pleasure of dining in one of the county's most beautiful houses*

Near Newton Aycliffe DL5 6NL
Map no: 8 NZ22
Tel: 01388 772442
Chef: Scott MacRae
Proprietor: Grand Heritage.
Manager: Brian Phillpotts
Cost: Alc £19.20, fixed-price L £11.50/D £16.95. H/wine £10.95 ❢ Service inc
Credit cards: 🄰 💳 💳 💳
Times: Noon-last L 2pm, 7pm-last D 10pm
Menus: A la carte, fixed-price L & D, bar menu
Seats: 24 (Blue Room), 85 (Conservatory Restaurant). No smoking in Blue Room
Additional: Children welcome, children's portions; ❶ menu, vegan/other diets on request

With its 25 acres of gardens and woodland, this impressive Elizabethan country manor looks every inch the part of a large, comfortable hotel. The kitchen displays a sound approach to food. Scott Macrae's cooking is up-to-date, and his menus are wide-ranging, with France and the Mediterranean as the main inspiration, lifted with oriental flourishes. A meal might begin with a nage of brill, salmon, sea scallops and mussels with sea vegetables and ozeki, followed by pan-fried duck breast marinated in honey and soya with braised fennel and a plum thyme sauce. A dinner in early spring kicked off with seared king scallops with lentil and coriander sauce, then an excellent roast loin of lamb set on a warm salad of spinach, oyster mushrooms and new potatoes dressed with a tarragon jus, with chocolate rosewater mousse with an orange blossom crème brûlée to finish. The extensive wine list is well balanced between France, with most major regions represented, and further-flung countries. Lighter meals may be taken in the Conservatory and include a carvery, chargrill and simple dishes such as Whitby cod, mushy peas and chips.

Directions: A1(M) exit 58/A68 (Carbridge); hotel is on the A6072 (off A68) near Newton Aycliffe

ROMALDKIRK, Rose & Crown Hotel ❀❀

☺ *An enthusiastically-run village inn where the strengths include hospitality, service and very good cooking*

Set in one of England's loveliest villages, the handsomely proportioned Rose & Crown dates back to 1733. From the outside it has probably changed very little and the interior, too, retains much of its 18th-century charm with beams, panelling and open fireplaces. What has changed is the fare. Christopher Davy cooks in a solid, reliable manner, inspired by the seasons and backed by fine local produce. Although still English in style, taste, methods and presentation reflect a light, modern approach. Potted pink trout

Romaldkirk DL12 9EB
Map no: 12 NY92
Tel: 01833 650213
Chefs: Christopher Davy and Dawn Stephenson
Proprietors: Christopher & Alison Davy
Cost: Fixed-price L £10.95, D £22 (4 courses). H/wine £8.50 ❢ Service inc
Credit cards: 🄰 💳 OTHER

with fresh herbs and a yoghurt sauce, sauteed Whitby woof (catfish) with prawns, capers and nut brown butter, pan-fried strips of beef fillet with green peppercorns and fresh noodles, or chargrilled breast of Lunesdale duckling with a Calvados sauce and caramelised apples, are just a few examples. A satisfactory winter dinner yielded queen scallops with bacon and mushrooms in a cheese sauce, served with home-baked bread, plaice with a well-judged vermouth sauce was 'fresh and had sweet flavour', and crisp meringues and home-made vanilla ice-cream finished the meal. The wine list is wide-ranging but descriptions are few.

Directions: On B6277 in the centre of the village, near the church

Times: Noon-last L 1.30pm, 7pm-last D 9pm. Closed Sun eve, Dec 25/6
Menus: Fixed-priced L & D, bar menu
Seats: 24. No smoking in dining room
Additional: Children permitted (pref. not late eve), children's portions; ✪ dishes/other diets on request

RUSHYFORD,
Eden Arms Swallow Hotel ✿

Comfortable, well-run roadside coaching inn dating from the 17th century. Martin Strangward offers some careful cooking which encompasses baked smoked mackerel in filo pastry with home-made horseradish sauce, and breast of chicken stuffed with mushroom and truffle mousseline

Rushyford DL17 0LL
Map no: 8 NZ22
Tel: 01388 720541
Chef: Martin Strangward
Proprietor: S Grant
Cost: Alc £19.50, fixed-price L £11.60/D £15.95. Service exc
Credit cards: ▨ ▧ ▨ ▨ OTHER
Times: Last D 10pm

Directions: On A167

EAST SUSSEX

ALFRISTON,
Moonraker's Restaurant ❀❀

A serious approach to cooking from a chef who takes pains with the production and presentation of food

This long-established restaurant, set in a 16th-century beamed and inglenooked cottage, is an integral part of Alfriston's High Street. Chef Mark Goodwin shows a dedicated approach to modern British cooking, and his short *carte* is supplemented on weekdays by two short, fixed-price menus. Typical dishes include cassoulet of beans and vegetables in a chilli sauce with wild rice, and grilled medallions of smoked ham in a light Stilton sauce. One inspector was impressed with a meal that began with a generous bowl of very hot carrot and coriander soup, and was followed by a grilled breast of Barbary duck served with a zesty ginger and lime flavoured jus, although the rather plain and uninteresting vegetables came in for some criticism. Balance was restored, however, by a rich, crisply topped raspberry mascarpone brûlée. Proprietor Norman Gillies runs a smoothly efficient front-of-house, providing attentive service; there are many regular customers. The wine list includes mainly recent vintages; house wine is served by the glass.

Directions: Alfriston is about 3 miles from Seaford, just off the A259. Moonrakers is on the right-hand side of the High Street

High Street BN26 5TD
Map no: 5 TQ50
Tel: 01323 870472
Chef: Mark Goodwin
Proprietor: Norman Gillies
Cost: *Alc* from £19.50, fixed-price D £16.95. H/wine £8.50. Service inc
Credit cards: 🔲 🔲 🔲
Times: Last D 9.45pm. Closed Sun eve, last 2 weeks Jan
Menus: *A la carte*, fixed-price D, Sun L
Seats: 48. No-smoking area
Additional: Children over 6 welcome, children's portions; ❂ dishes, vegan/other diets on request

BATTLE, Netherfield Place ❀❀

Both the modern British cooking and the selection of wines are impressive at this Georgian-style country house

The elegant 1920s Georgian-style country house is set in well-kept grounds; the kitchen garden supplies fresh fruit, vegetables and herbs to the restaurant. A five-course fixed-price menu and *carte* offer modern British cooking which, while well-prepared and enjoyable can, at times, be over-complicated, disrupting the flavours and balance of dishes. A meal might begin with appetisers

Netherfield TN33 9PP
Map no: 5 TQ71
Tel: 01424 774455
Chef: Michael Collier
Proprietors: Michael & Helen Collier (Pride of Britain)
Cost: *Alc* £28, fixed-price L £16/D £24 (5 course). H/wine £9.50 ❢ Service exc
Credit cards: 🔲 🔲 🔲 🔲
Times: Last L 2pm, last D 9.30pm/9pm Sun. Closed last wk Dec & first 2 wks Jan

in the drawing room – at a meal in March these included hot deep-fried egg and breadcrumbed mushrooms, mini-baked potatoes with chives and chicken liver pâté on toast. Starters might include home-made ravioli with goats' cheese and a fennel butter sauce, followed by a rosemary and gin sorbet. Roast breast of mallard duck set on puy lentils and spinach with a sage and shallot sauce may be among the main courses. The choice of desserts could include strawberry soufflé. Coffee comes with home-made petits fours. A classic wine list features 168 vintage bins, including impressive cru classe Bordeaux and domaine-bottled Burgundy; New World selections and half-bottles are also available.

Directions: M25 exit 5/A21 (Hastings) to A2100 for Netherfield; hotel is on the left after 1.5 miles

Menus: *A la carte*, fixed-price L & D
Seats: 60. No pipes or cigars
Additional: Children permitted (before 8pm) children's portions; ❂ dishes, vegan/other diets on request

BATTLE, Powdermills Hotel ❀

The candlelit Orangery Restaurant in this 18th-century manor house is the setting for chef Paul Webbe's modern Anglo-French cooking. Recommended have been the mousseline of salmon with mussel and chive sauce, ballotine of rabbit with smoked bacon and Dijon sauce, and caramelised Bramley flan with vanilla ice-cream

Seats: 100. No smoking in dining room
Additional: Children permitted at lunch, children's menu; ❂ menu, vegan/other diets on request
Directions: Through Battle towards Hastings, turn right into Powdermills Lane, the hotel is on the right after a sharp bend

Powdermills Lane TN33 0SP
Tel: 01424 775511
Map no: 5 TQ71
Chef: Paul Webbe
Proprietor: Julie Cowpland
Cost: *Alc* £21.50, H/wine £8.95. Service exc
Credit cards: ▨ ▨▨ ▨▨ ▨ OTHER
Times: Last L 2pm/D 9pm
Menus: *A la carte* L & D (fixed-price L & D residents only), library L menu

BRIGHTON, Black Chapati ❀❀

Atmospheric, minimalist restaurant serving some imaginative Asian cooking

The hippy trail to India gave Stephen Funnell a good basic understanding of the region's cooking, and he is now building imaginatively upon this. A combination of minimalist black furnishings and recipes from the Indian sub-continent is mirrored in the name of this unassuming little restaurant, tucked away just off Preston Circus. The food, described by Funnell and co-proprietor, Lauren Alker, as 'evolved Asian' is more eclectic than this might suggest. The kitchen produces a variety of innovative home-spun dishes which in some cases demonstrate real flair. Starters include roast sea bass with a salad of buckwheat noodles, crab soup with coriander and pork wuntun, and smoked duck with lentil salad and a sweet mustard sauce. Main course choice offers Korean fried beef with mushroom rice and kim chee salad, roast breast of duck with gingered Chinese cabbage, and vegetarian thali. Desserts are generally restricted to such standard items as crème brûlée and warm apple tart with cinnamon ice-cream. Carefully chosen beers and ciders – notably cidre Breton, which the chef claims as his favourite drink – provide an interesting alternative to the short wine list.

Directions: Directions are complex. Readers are advised to use a local map

12 Circus Parade
New England Road BN1 4GW
Map no: 4 TQ30
Tel: 01273 699011
Chefs: S Funnell and L Alker
Proprietors: S Funnell and L Alker
Cost: *Alc* £20, fixed-price L £8.95 H/wine £8.50. Service inc
Credit cards: ▨ ▨▨ ▨▨ OTHER
Times: Last L 2pm, Last D 10.30pm. Closed Sun eve, Mon, 1 week Xmas
Menus: *A la carte*, Sunday L, fixed-price L
Seats: 30
Additional: No children after 9pm, no babies; ❂ dish

BRIGHTON, **Brighton Thistle** ❀

A large, modern hotel on Brighton's seafront, overlooking the Victorian pier, with a large, spacious atrium at its heart – ideal for pre dinner drinks. The Noblesse restaurant serves elaborately conceived dishes such as pigeon wrapped in Parma ham, dressed on a bed of green lentils with honey and brandy sauce

Kings Road BN1 2GS
Map no: 4 TQ30
Tel: 01273 206700
Chef: Andrew Furrer
Proprietor: Thistle.
Manager: Luis Hermosilla
Cost: Fixed price L/D £16.50 / £23. H/wine £12.50 ❢ Service inc
Credit cards: 🅰 💳 💳 🖃
Times: Last L 2pm, last D 10pm. Closed Sun
Menus: Fixed price lunch and dinner
Seats: 40. Air conditioned
Additional: Children welcome, ♥ dishes, vegan/other diets on request

Directions: City centre

BRIGHTON, **The Grand** ❀

A conservatory overlooking the seafront, an elaborate formal room and a large, lighter room all form part of the busy King's Restaurant. Cooking is traditional with a French orientation. Trout mousse and beef in pink peppercorn sauce are typical offerings, with coconut mousse for dessert

Times: Last L 2.30pm (3pm Sun)/D 10pm **Additional:** Children welcome before 9pm: ♥ menu, vegan/other diets on request
Directions: On seafront by the Conference Centre

Kings Road BN 2FW
Map no: 4 TQ30
Tel: 01273 321188
Chef: Ivan Parnell
Proprietors: De Vere.
Manager: Richard Baker
Cost: Fixed-price L £16/D £24. H/wine £11.50 ❢ Service exc
Credit cards: 🅰 💳 💳 🖃

BRIGHTON, **Langan's Bistro** ❀❀

Consistently enjoyable food based on seasonally available fresh produce in this colourful restaurant

Langan's is located off the seafront, about halfway between the Marina and the Palace Pier. It has the feel of a French bistro. Quality cooking, from a daily-changing *carte* which alters to make use of the best market produce, distinguishes Mark Emmerson's cooking. His dishes combine subtle flavours, colours and textures, and results are consistent. A typical meal might include smoked salmon and avocado soufflé with a Parmesan lining and a light butter and chive sauce, or tail of monkfish with a tapenade jus, set on slices of aubergine. Vegetables are interesting – at a recent visit our inspector was particularly taken with parsnips marinated in sherry vinegar, port and veal stock. The selection of desserts may include tarte au citron, and iced praline parfait, or there's cheese as an alternative. A carefully chosen wine list features young vintage French wines from reputable producers

1 Paston Place
Map no: 4 TQ30
Tel: 01273 606933
Chef: Mark Emmerson
Proprietor: Nicole Emmerson
Cost: Alc £25-£28, fixed-price L £14.50. H/wine £8.80. Service exc Cover charge 75p
Credit cards: 🅰 💳 💳 🖃
Times: Last L 2.15pm, last D 10.15pm. Closed Sat L, Sun D, Mon, 1st 2 wks Jan, last 2 wks Aug
Menus: A la carte, fixed-price L
Seats: 45. Air conditioned
Additional: Children welcome, children's menu; ♥ dishes, vegan/other diets on request

Directions: Just off the seafront about halfway between the Palace Pier and the Marina

BRIGHTON, **Topps Hotel** 👀👀

Steak and kidney pudding is always available in the basement restaurant at Topps, which serves a range of English and French dishes

A straightforward and uncomplicated approach to cooking is producing some very satisfying results in the attractive basement restaurant of this Regency town house. The fixed-price menu includes two courses and coffee, with a selection of sweets available from £3.00. (The restaurant operates for dinner only and is closed on Sundays and Wednesdays.) Good quality English and French dishes retain freshness and flavour, and the selection always includes steak and kidney pudding. A typical meal might begin with a shell and white fish soup made with tomato and garlic stock and textured with fresh mussels, prawns and turbot followed by tender rack of lamb with a well-made white onion sauce, served with plain crisply fresh vegetables, with chocolate truffle parfait and marinated dried fruits for dessert. Meals are served in a friendly and informal atmosphere. The short wine list includes selections of New World wines and half-bottles, and the house French-bottled Cuvee de Ropiteau N/V is recommended for its good value.

Directions: In Regency Square which is opposite the West Pier

17 Regency Square BN1 2FG
Map no: 4 TQ30
Tel: 01273 729334
Chef: Pauline Collins
Proprietors: Paul & Pauline Collins
Cost: Fixed-price D £18.95 (2 courses), £21.95. H/wine £7.50
⍟ Service inc
Credit cards: 🆑 ▆▆ ▆▆ 🔲 OTHER
Times: Last D 9.20pm. Closed Sun, Mon, Xmas & Jan
Menu: Fixed-price dinner
Seats: 20
Additional: Children permitted; ⓥ dishes

BRIGHTON, **Whytes** 👀👀

Keenly priced modern dishes based on local ingredients, especially fish

A converted seafront fisherman's cottage is the setting for a restaurant which, naturally, makes good use of locally caught fish. A husband and wife operation, Ian Whyte cooks while Jane Whyte runs front-of-house with a warm and attentive approach to her customers. Ian's cooking is reliable, honest and uncomplicated; he has a natural flair for modern cooking which is evident in his skilfully produced fixed-price menu. This changes every six weeks and makes the most of fresh local produce, meat and game as well as fish. Roast fillet of lamb, cooked pink, comes with garlic and cumin, or there is fillet steak with stout and mushrooms, and perhaps chicken suprême wrapped in smoked bacon. The colourful selection of vegetables which accompany main courses are well timed, losing none of their natural flavours. For dessert, freshly made rum and Grand Marnier pancake with cream or crème brûlée round of the meal nicely. Coffee comes with chocolate truffles.

Directions: On the Brighton-Hove border, opposite the seafront. First right after the Norfolk Resort Hotel

33 Western Street BN1 2PG
Map no: 4 TQ30
Tel: 01273 776618
Chef: Ian Whyte
Proprietors: Ian & Jane Whyte
Cost: Fixed-price L £18.95, Fixed-price D £15.50 (2 courses), £18.95. H/wine £7.50. Service exc
Credit cards: 🆑 ▆▆ ▆▆
Times: 7pm-Last D 10pm. Closed Sun
Menus: Fixed-price D
Seats: 36. Smokers asked to consider other diners
Additional: Children permitted, ⓥ dishes

In the south of Italy, the best mozzarella is spun from the curd of water-buffalo milk. It is sometimes called 'bufalina' and it is superb cheese, eaten absolutely fresh and dripping with its own buttermilk - white, delicate, fresh and fragrant. It has a more defined taste and body than mozzarella made from cow's milk. The mozzarella sold in Britain with its whey in a plastic bag is a rubbery, neutral-tasting factory product, whose most appropriate use is as a binding agent because of its characteristic melting properties.

EASTBOURNE, **The Downland Hotel** ❀❀

A small hotel where hard work and a dedicated approach is paying off, especially in the restaurant

Better to work long and hard for yourselves rather than for other people, was Patrick and Stephanie Faulkner's rationale for buying the Downland in 1988. It was a sound move. Guests are, apparently, often surprised that a small hotel can offer food of such a high standard and, for this, Patrick modestly claims the credit, since he is the chef. The *carte* changes four times a year and there is a three-course fixed-price menu for half-board residents. A winter meal commenced with a light, well baked starter of spinach-wrapped puff pastry filled with chopped veal, served with a spiced tomato and onion concassee, flavoured with hazelnut oil, ginger and chilli. The main course on this occasion was baked fillet of fresh salmon, filled with cheese and served with sautéed whole fresh scallops, garnished with dill and limes. A fish fumet flavoured and blended with a lime hollandaise accompanied it. The selection of vegetables bordered on the astonishing – diced swede, carrots, haricots verts, yellow peppers, cauliflower mornay, broccoli and diced baked potato with herbs. Rounding the meal off, a suet sponge filled with banana and sultana, and a brandy and vanilla-flavoured double cream sauce. There are some good value French house wines on the short list.

Directions: On A2021 about half a mile from the town centre

37 Lewes Road BN21 2BU
Map no: 5 TV69
Tel: 01323 732689
Chef: Patrick Faulkner
Proprietors: Patrick and
Stephanie Faulkner
Cost: *Alc* £26, fixed-price D
£17.50. H/wine £8.50. Service
exc
Credit cards: 🅰 💳 💳 💳
Times: Last D 9pm (8.30pm
Sun). Closed 21 Dec-19 Jan
Seats: 35. No cigars or pipes
Additional: Children permitted
(over 7 at D); children's
menu/portions; ❤ menu,
vegan/other diets on request

EASTBOURNE,
Grand Hotel ❀❀

The spacious and gracious surroundings are a bonus for diners at Eastbourne's top hotel

The late playwright Dennis Potter's 'huge creamy palace', as he called it, is almost at the western limit of Eastbourne's three-mile promenade, just before the road begins its tortuous climb up to Beachy Head. Diners can eat on the terrace, in the Garden Restaurant or more formally in the Mirabelle, where ex-Lanesborough chef Mark Jones maintains standards with his enterprising cooking. In late September, an inspection meal began with a slightly unseasonal yellow cherry tomato gazpacho, followed by pistachio-studded duck liver and foie gras terrine, set on green leaves with a toasted brioche. An overpowering spinach and garlic stuffing accompanied a moist saddle of rabbit, with a good, light jus, roasted garlic cloves, chanterelles and an excellent timbale of endives. A lemon tart was respectably tangy. Staff in big hotels sometimes lack the spontaneity and confidence of their colleagues in smaller establishments, as can be the case at the Grand. Wines by the bottle or glass are reasonably priced.

Directions: On the seafront at the western end of town

King Edward's Parade
BN21 4EQ
Map no: 5 TV69
Tel: 01323 412345
Chefs: Neil Wiggins
Proprietors: De Vere.
Manager: Peter Hawley
Cost: *Alc* £30, fixed-price L
£18.50 / D £26.50. H/wine
£10.75 ❗ Service inc
Credit cards: 🅰 💳 💳 💳
Times: Last L 2.30pm / D 10pm.
Closed Sun, Mon, 1 week in Jan
Seats: 50. No smoking before
2pm or 9pm. No pipes. Air
conditioned
Menus: A la carte, fixed-price
L & D
Additional: Children welcome,
children's portions; ❤ menu,
vegan/other diets on request

EASTBOURNE, **Lansdowne Hotel** ❀

☺ *Traditional favourites cooked to a high standard at this hospitable hotel. Grilled sirloin of Scotch beef with a mushroom and red wine sauce, poached suprême of chicken in asparagus and cream sauce are typical examples. Cold buffets also available. Very warm, welcoming atmosphere*

King Edward's Parade BN21 4EE
Map no: 5 TV69
Tel: 01323 725174
Chef: George Thompson
Proprietor: n/a.
Manager: Tony Hazell (Best Western)
Cost: A/c £10.25, fixed-price D £14 (4 course)/Sun L £7.25 & £10.25 H/wine £8.50 Service inc (exc L)
Times: Noon-last L 2pm, 6pm-last D 8.30pm. Closed Jan 1-13
Menus: A la carte L, fixed-price L & D, pre-theatre, bar menu
Seats: 140
Additional: Children welcome, children's menu; ❤ menu, vegan/other diets on request

Directions: On B2103 seafront road opposite Western Lawns

FOREST ROW, **Ashdown Park Hotel** ❀❀

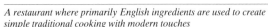
A restaurant where primarily English ingredients are used to create simple traditional cooking with modern touches

Wych Cross RH18 5JR
Map no: 5 TQ43
Tel: 01342 824988
Chef: John McManus
Proprietor: n/a Small Luxury Hotels.
Manager: Graeme C Bateman
Cost: A/c av. £30, fixed-price L £17 / D £27. H/wine £12.50. Service inc
Credit cards: 🔲 🔲 🔲 🔲 OTHER
Times: Last L 2pm / D 9.30pm (10pm Fri/Sat)
Menus: A la carte, fixed-price L & D
Seats: 100. Air conditioned. No pipes or cigars

The Ashdown Forest once covered much of south eastern England; now, it is largely reduced to heathland covering the central Weald. The mansion, built in the late 19th-century, was a convent (the ecclesiastical touches are still evident) and a training centre before becoming a hotel three years ago. In the large Anderida Restaurant, where a pianist plays most evenings, the atmosphere is formal but relaxed – no country house chintzes here. John McManus's style of cooking is a mix of simple, traditional-style dishes with a modern ring. Influences from Northern France and the Mediterranean are to be seen in dishes such as salad of avocado with baked goats' cheese and pesto, duo of mullet and sole with

saffron cream, and sirloin of beef with béarnaise sauce. An inspection meal hit the target precisely: duck terrine 'like a succulent rillette', then fillets of sea bass with a pungent, but not overstrong, warmed saffron vinaigrette. *Carte* desserts are supplemented on busy nights with a trolley carrying a varied, well-made selection such as a light, yet rich, Paris-Brest with a praline bavarois. The long wine list has been compiled by those who know their stuff – someone with a clear bias towards France.

Additional: Children welcome (over 7 at dinner), children's menu; ❶ dishes, vegan/other diets on request

Directions: From A22 at Wych Cross take Hartfield turning, hotel is 0.75 mile on the right

HAILSHAM, **The Olde Forge** ❀

☺ *Chef Jean Daniels offers an extensive carte and daily set menus of modern British cooking. The beamed former forge is small and comfortable, a delightful setting for her soundly cooked, interesting dishes. Recommended is Olde Forge pâté, and poached plaice in wine*

Times: Last D 9.30pm, last Sun L 2pm
Menus: *A la carte,* fixed-price D & Sun L
Seats: 24. No smoking in dining room
Additional: Children welcome, children's portions; ❶ menu, vegan/other diets on request
Directions: On A271 (Bexhill) 2.5 miles from A22, north-east of Hailsham

Magham Down BN27 1PN
Map no: 5 TQ50
Tel: 01323 842893
Chef: Jean Daniels
Proprietors: J P Bull.
Manager: Tracey Bull
Cost: *Alc* £16-£19, fixed-price D£13.95/Sun L £9.95. H/wine £8 Service exc
Credit cards: ▨ ▤ ▧ ▨ OTHER

HASTINGS & ST LEONARDS,
Röser's Restaurant ❀❀❀

The 'best cod in the south' comes not from a chippy but a high quality restaurant serving modern French cooking

Our inspector is nothing if not consistent. Last year he said Röser's was 'a restaurant I'd go out of my way for'; he still would. What he particularly makes a diversion for are super fresh seafood, home-smoked and home-marinated scallops, and what he still claims is probably the best cod in the south, crusted with salsa. Almost opposite Hastings pier, Röser's is essentially just an unassuming family restaurant, but one where chef Gerald Röser provides high standard modern French cooking.

A complimentary appetiser of a cup of golden guinea fowl consommé ('perfect for a cold March evening') was followed by a ragoût of mussels, scallops and langoustines in a chive and truffle sauce. The main course was roasted guinea fowl, corn-fed and tender, marinated in red wine and herbs and served with a rich glace textured with lardons of smoked wild boar bacon. The apple mille-feuille was crisply textured and layered with crème pâtissier and served with a fine butterscotch sauce. Other dishes which have been highly praised are wild boar sausages with a marjoram and port sauce, roasted scallops with a saffron sauce, and the grilled sea bass with coriander seeds, basil and tomato. Chef Röser works virtually single handed in the kitchen, ensuring that everything leaves it in a state of perfection. His wife Jenny takes care of the attentive, friendly service.

The award-winning wine list offers the chance to enjoy the best Chablis, cru classe Bordeaux and domaine-bottled Burgundy; there

64 Eversfield Place TN37 6DB
Map no: 5 TQ80
Tel: 01424 712218
Chef: Gerald Röser
Proprietors: Gerald & Jenny Röser
Cost: *Alc* £29.65, fixed-price L £16.95/D £19.95. H/wine £9.95 ❗ Service exc
Credit cards: ▨ ▤ ▧ ▨ OTHER
Times: Last L 1.45pm, last D 9.45pm. Closed 1 wk Jan, 2 wks Aug
Menus: *A la carte,* fixed-price L & D
Seat: 30. No cigars or pipes
Additional: Children welcome; ❶ dishes, vegan/other diets on request

is a good choice of vintage Château Petrus. There are also plenty of New World and good quality French regional wines. Special events, such as 'Rösers Game Dinner', are held from time to time.

Directions: Opposite Hastings pier

HERSTMONCEUX, Sundial Restaurant ❀❀

Mainly French and a little Italian cuisine freshly prepared and cooked to order at this auberge-style establishment

Hailsham BN27 4LA
Map no: 5 TQ81
Tel: 01323 832217
Chef: Giuseppi Bertoli
Proprietors: Giuseppi & Laure Bertoli
Cost: *Alc* £30-£35, fixed-price L £15.50/D £24.50. H/wine £10.75. Service exc
Credit cards: 🅂 💳 💳 🖼
Times: Last L 2.30pm, last D 9.30pm Closed Sun D, Mon, Xmas-Jan 20, last 3 wks Aug
Menus: *A la carte*, fixed-price L & D
Seats: 50 (+20 private room). No smoking in dining room
Additional: Children welcome, children's menu; ❶ dishes; other diets on request

For more than 27 years, Giuseppi and Laurette Bertoli have run their French-style auberge in a 17th-century roadside cottage; their commitment and attention to detail setting standards for others to follow. The restaurant has a friendly atmosphere and French-born Laurette takes great care over the service, offering complimentary appetisers in the bar. The choice of dishes is extensive, and as well as the *carte* there is a fixed-price lunch and dinner menu and the five-course 'Gourmandise Surprise'. The plats du jour are well worth trying, as are Giuseppi's personally advised additional recommendations. This year our inspector enjoyed home-made fetuccine filled with prawns and mushrooms and topped with lobster, followed by fillets of turbot filled with a light scallop mousse and served with a purée of celeriac and a lovely velouté sauce. Home-made desserts are plentiful, and are sometimes displayed on the restaurant buffet. There is also a lengthy wine list with some cru classe Bordeaux and domaine bottled Burgundy as well as regional wines from Italy and house wine by the pitcher.

Directions: In the centre of the village, on the A271

> Basil is an aromatic plant which originated in India. The name is derived from the Greek 'basilikos' meaning royal, for in ancient Greece basil was known as 'the royal herb', since only the sovereign 'basileus' was allowed to cut it (with a golden sickle). In most of the Mediterranean it was used chiefly as a perfume and insect repellent. The herb is strongly connected with Provence and Italy, especially Liguria, the region that invented pesto sauce.

HOVE, Quentin's ❀❀

Uncomplicated cooking with some Oriental influences in a restaurant that takes food seriously

An unassuming little restaurant with its simple decor, scrubbed tables and hard-backed chairs, and informal atmosphere. Quentin Fitch and his wife Candy are the minds behind a successful concept of uncomplicated cooking, good wines and attentive service; they have been rewarded with a strong local following. Quentin is self-taught, and his cooking style demonstrates a serious and dedicated approach, whilst both his monthly changing menu and blackboard specials offer a good choice and value-for-money. Dishes to look out for include chervil and sweet corn crabcakes with a tapenade toast, sautéed lambs kidneys with smoked bacon and Conference pears, grilled Indian-style chicken salad with minted yoghurt and lemon dressing, and a Thai-style mixed grill of seafood with a piquant peanut sauce, coriander rice and salad. Inspectors have also praised filo parcels of mushroom mousse with walnuts and marinated peppers, and pan-fried smoked cod cakes in an excellent lemon butter sauce.

42 Western Road
Map no: 4 TQ30
Tel: 01273 822734
Chef: Quentin Fitch
Proprietors: Candy & Quentin Fitch
Cost: Alc £16, fixed-price L £4.95 (1 course), fixed-price D by arrangement from £12.95. H/wine £8.50 ❗ Service exc
Credit cards: ◼ ▦ ▦ ▣
Times: Last L 2.30pm/D 10.30pm. L not served Sat. Closed Sun, Mon, last week Aug, 1st week Sep
Seats: 42. No pipes or cigars. Air conditioned
Additional: Children welcome. ◗ dishes; other diets on request

Directions: On the south side of Western Road between Brunswick Square and Palmeira Square

HOVE, Whitehaven Hotel ❀

The Rolling Clock restaurant, named after the 17th-century inclined clock that sits proudly on the mantelpiece, offers a menu which features seafood from around the world. Desserts are highly recommended, especially the chocolate cups filled with raspberry cream, served with a fresh strawberry coulis

Menus: Fixed price L & D, bar menu **Seats:** 35. Air conditioned
Additional: Children over 12 permitted, ◗ dishes, vegan/other diets on request
Directions: Central Hove, off Church Road opposite County Cricket Ground

34 Wilbury Road BN3 3JP
Map: 4TQ30
Tel: 01273 73117
Chef: Steve Grant
Proprietor: Independent.
Manager: David Mitchell
Cost: Fixed price L /D £9.95 / £14.50. H/wine £8.25. Service exc
Credit cards: ◼ ▦ ▦ ▣ OTHER
Times: Last L 2pm, last D 9pm. Closed Sun

JEVINGTON, Hungry Monk ❀❀

The restaurant that "invented" banoffie pie continues to serve an interesting range of imaginative French/English dishes

The sense of permanence and atmosphere of wellbeing that have been created in this delightful restaurant – now in its twenty-eighth year – must account in no small measure for its popularity. Loyal, and in many cases celebrated, guests seem drawn irresistibly to the safe haven of its antique-furnished lounges, candlelit oak-beamed dining room and terraced gardens. Attentive, friendly service is perfectly pitched, and a choice of some two hundred wines (helpfully coded by both taste and style) offers three pages of half bottles and good house wine from £8.90. Food quality must be the deciding factor in any restaurant's success, however, and this year sees no changes – the very successful partnership of Thai La Roche and Claire Burgess providing a consistently enjoyable range of dishes in French/English style. A main course of prune-stuffed rabbit wrapped in prosciutto, served roasted on a bed of flageolet

Polegate BN26 5QF
Map no: 4 TQ60
Tel: 01323 482178
Chefs: Claire Burgess and Thai La Roche
Proprietors: Nigel & Sue Mackenzie
Cost: Fixed-price L and D £20.90. Wine £8 ❗ Service charge for parties over 8
Credit cards: ▦
Times: Midday-Last L 2.15pm, Last D 10.30pm. L not served Mon, Sat. Closed Bhs (except Good Fri)
Menus: Fixed-price L and D
Seats: 40 (also 3 private dining rooms). No smoking

Hungry Monk

Additional: Children permitted (no children under 3 in main dining room); ❂ dishes; other diets on request

beans and accompanied by a creamed jus with fresh rosemary, could well be preceded by a light, well made Provençal onion tart and followed by banoffie pie – the recipe for the latter originating here in 1972. As a final flourish, dark and white chocolates are provided with the richly flavoured cafetière coffee that ends the meal.

Directions: Follow the A22 towards Eastbourne. Turn right on to the B2105. The restaurant is between Polegate and Friston

LEWES, Shelleys ❀

Chef Yannick Vuillemy provides imaginative meals in both modern and classic styles in this delightful town house hotel. Various menus tempt diners with dishes ranging from smoked salmon and beef to a pigeon salad with raspberry vinegar, or monkfish with thyme and fennel

Menus: *A la carte,* fixed-price L & D, bar menu
Seats: 60. No smoking in dining room
Additional: Children welcome, children's portions; ❂ dishes, vegan/other diets on request
Directions: Town centre

High Street BN7 1XS
Map no: 5 TQ41
Tel: 01273 472361
Chef: Yannick Vuillemey
Proprietor: Thistle.
Manager: Graeme Coles
Cost: *Alc* £27.50, fixed-price L £15/D £21.50 H/wine £10.50
❢ Service exc
Credit cards: 🂠 🖼 🖼 💳
Times: Last L 2.15pm/last D 9.15 pm

Gressingham duck is a back cross of the white Aylesbury with the wild mallard - it is the latter which gives the slightly gamey flavour. Lunesdale duck is basically a superior Aylesbury with a bit less mallard, thus a less gamey flavour. Both cross-breeds have a high meat-to-bone ratio and a low fat content. Wild ducks have darker flesh because they use their muscles more than sedentary barnyard ducks, and their gamier flavour reflects a more naturally varied diet. Widgeon and teal, for example, often spend time on salt marshes and can have a pronounced fishy taste. Mallard is the most popular wild duck because it can be reared (like pheasant) ready to be shot when grown.

MAYFIELD,
Rose & Crown Restaurant ❀

☺ *A charmingly unspoilt listed building facing south across the village green. In addition to the regular menus, the informal restaurant offers daily changing specials which take advantage of seasonal game and fresh local produce, particularly fish. Look out for gamekeeper's pie: venison, rabbit, pheasant etc, cooked in a rich claret gravy*

Fletchling Street TN20 6TE
Map no: 5 TQ52
Tel: 01435 872200
Chef: Mathew Hill
Proprietor: Labatt.
Manager: Sean McCory
Cost: *Alc* £14.90, fixed-price
Sun L £10.85 H/wine £8.10
❢ Service inc
Credit cards: ▨ ▩ OTHER
Times: Last L 2.30pm/last D 10pm
Menus: *A la carte,* fixed-price
Sun L, bar menu
Seats: 85. No-smoking area
Additional: Children welcome (not late eve), children's portions; ❶ dishes, vegan on request

Directions: Mayfield turn off A267 into village, then just off High Street

---

PEASMARSH, **Flackley Ash Hotel** ❀

☺ *A relaxed, friendly Georgian country hotel offering a short menu which takes full opportunity of the quality ingredients readily available. An inspection meal yielded chicken, pork and brandy terrine, breast of Barbary duck with green pepper sauce, and treacle pudding with syrup and crème anglaise*

Rye TN31 6YH
Map: 5 TQ82
Tel: 01797 230651
Chef: Dale Skinner
Proprietors: Clive & Jeannie Bennett (Best Western)
Cost: Fixed price L from £10.95, fixed price D £19.95. H/wine £9.95 Service inc
Credit cards: ▨ ▩ ▩ ▣ OTHER
Times: 12.30pm-last L1.45pm, 7pm-last D 9.45pm

Menus: Fixed price L & D, bar menu
Seats: 100. No smoking in dining room
Additional: Children welcome, children's menu; ❶ menu, other diets on request
Directions: 4 miles NW of Rye on A268

RYE, **Landgate Bistro** ❀

☺ *A good choice of modern British dishes, cooked to order, at this simple, well established bistro. Typical dishes are crab terrine, leek and Roquefort tart, ham in white wine and parsley aspic, 'Very Fishy Stew', a house standard, plus Gressingham duck with lime flavoured sauce, and leg-steak of English lamb with flageolet beans, tomatoes and garlic*

5-6 Landgate TN31 7LH
Map no: 5 TQ92
Tel: 01797 222829
Chef: Toni Ferguson-Lees
Proprietors: Toni Ferguson-Lees and Nick Parkin
Cost: *Alc* £16.50-£25, fixed-price D £15.50 H/wine £7.90 Service inc
Credit cards: ▨ ▩ ▩ ▣ OTHER
Times: 7pm-last D 9.30pm
Closed Sun, Mon, Xmas, 1 wk in Summer & Autumn

Menus: *A la carte* & fixed-price D
Seats: 30
Additional: Children permitted; ❶ dishes
Directions: From the High Street head towards the Landgate. The Bistro is in a row of shops on the left-hand side

RYE, **Mermaid Inn** ⊛

Rebuilt in 1420, this ancient inn is reputedly one of the oldest in Britain. It is highly atmospheric, especially the romantic, panelled dining-room. Although fresh fish is a speciality, our inspector was taken by the roast breast of pheasant and the crème caramel with Grand Marnier and orange that followed

Menus: *A la carte,* fixed-price L & D, bar menu
Seats: 60
Additional: Children permitted, children's portions; ❤ dishes; other diets on request
Directions: Town centre. Car park through archway

Mermaid Street TN317EU
Map no: 5 TQ92
Tel: 01797 223065
Chef: Brian Murray
Proprietors: Robert Pinwill and Judith Blincow
Cost: *Alc* from £20, fixed-price L £14.95/D £19 (4 course). H/wine £8.95 Service exc
Credit cards: ▨ ▩ ▩ ▨ OTHER
Times: Last L 2.15pm/D 9.30pm

UCKFIELD, **Hooke Hall** ⊛⊛

Northern Italian food served in the elegant atmosphere of an 18th century town house

250 High Street TN22 1EN
Map no: 5 TQ42
Tel: 01825 766844
Chef: Michelle Pavanello
Proprietors: Juliet & Alistair Percy
Cost: *Alc* £20-£25, fixed-price L £9.95 (2 course). H/wine £9.50. Service exc
Credit cards: ▨ ▩ ▩
Times: Last L 2pm, last D 9pm Closed Sat L, Sun,1 wk Feb
Menus: *A la carte,* fixed-price L
Seats: 32. No-smoking area
Additional: Children welcome, children's portions; ❤ dishes

Hooke Hall is an elegant, classic Queen Anne town house built in the early 18th century. Lovingly restored by its dedicated owners Alistair and Juliet Percy, the house now incorporates La Scaletta restaurant which is styled on Harry's Bar in London. Chef Michele Pavanello has produced an interesting menu which specialises in regional cooking from northern Italy. All the dishes use fresh ingredients, even the pasta is made on the premises, and the ready availability of seasonal produce affects what is on offer. Recent recommendations have included 'ravioli di stufato al burro montato', a fine ravioli with a rich meat filling served with butter sauce and fresh Parmesan cheese, and 'risotto ai funghi e tartufo', a creamy risotto served with mushrooms and truffle. Although the choice of desserts is a bit limited most are delicious, particularly the orange mousse with vanilla custard, dark chocolate chippings, icing sugar and a slice of fresh orange. The wine list offers a very good selection of Italian wines with most regions represented, whilst non Italian wines are also available including some by the glass.

Directions: Northern end of High Street

UCKFIELD,
Horsted Place Hotel ❀❀❀

Anglo-French cuisine formally served in gracious country house surroundings

An impressive Victorian gothic mansion in the heart of the Sussex Downs, providing a haven of gracious living. Sporting facilities are a feature of the hotel, but the culinary arts are equally well represented, from memorable breakfasts to superb cream teas served in the sumptuous drawing room. However, Allan Garth's seasonal *carte* and fixed-price menus are the primary attraction for the serious bon vivant. His dishes are British based, French inspired and presented in a refreshingly uncomplicated style. Dishes sampled this year have included a beautifully cooked rabbit confit served with flageolet beans and an excellent glace de viande, a tranche of poached wild Tayside salmon with shredded greens textured with pancetta, served with a carefully seasoned butter sauce and fresh vegetables. Gratin of rhubarb with a kirsch sabayon was a fine dessert.

There is a good menu choice: the *carte*, with about four items at each course; a daily fixed price lunch and dinner menu, plus a separate vegetarian menu. The latter offers two starters and two main courses, such as double baked goats' cheese soufflé with a walnut dressing, and tomatoes filled with lentils and carrots flavoured with turmeric and ginger, placed on a purée of sweet potato. Other options from the *carte* might be ballotine de foie gras with warm brioche toast and carpaccio de boeuf (thin slices of marinated beef with olives, pine nuts and pecorino cheese), among the starters. Main courses include coquilles St Jacques (pan-fried scallops with artichokes and tomatoes), and osso buco (braised shin of veal with root vegetables and Parma ham). Wines from around the world are listed, including reasonably priced French regional wines, and a recommended Domaine St Julien des Coteaux des Pezenas 1994.

Directions: Two miles south of Uckfield on the A26

Little Horsted TN22 5TS
Map no: 5 TQ42
Tel: 01825 750581
Chef: Allan Garth
Manager: Jonathan Ritchie
Cost: *Alc* £35, fixed-price L £14.95, fixed-price D £28.50.
H/wine £9.95 ♥ No service charge
Credit cards: 🂠 📠 🃏 🂡
Times: Midday-last L 2pm, 7.30pm-last D 9.30pm
Menus: *A la carte*, fixed-price L and D, Sunday L, pre-theatre
Seats: 40. No smoking in the dining room
Additional: Children over 8 permitted, children's portions; ♥ menu; other diets on request

WILMINGTON, Crossways ❀❀

Cheerful and charming country hotel and restaurant with good regional cooking and personal service

Crossways is a home from home – or, at least, an ideal one in which guests are encouraged to leave the kids behind. Fresh, local ingredients are reliably cooked in a monthly changing, fixed-price, four-course menu. In winter, game is much used, game pudding and game pie both include pheasant, rabbit, venison and pigeon, and game sausage is served with apricot relish. Other cold weather choices include traditional calves' liver and bacon, and chicken with wild mushrooms and chestnut stuffing. There is a daily fish dish, plus a home-made soup of the day. Hit the right season and you might be able to sample David Stott's famous hedgerow cheesecake that uses spinach, herbs and nettles from the hotel garden. Regular favourites include seafood pancake and crab noodle bake, but in summer there may also be tomato and herb summer pudding, new season Sussex lamb, and roast Gressingham duck served with gooseberry instead of cranberry and orange sauce. Generous

Wilmington BN26 5SG
Map no: 4 TQ42
Tel: 01323 482455
Chef: David Stott
Proprietor: David Stott
Credit cards: 🂠 📠 🃏 🂡
Times: Last D 8.45pm. Closed Sun and Mon, 24 Dec-24 Jan
Seats: 22

portions of vegetables are left on the table on a help-yourself basis. All the sweets, ice-creams and sorbets are home-made, and a short, well priced wine list includes an interesting selection of local English wines.

Directions: A27. Two miles west of Polegate

ESSEX

BRENTWOOD, **Marygreen Manor** ❀

A Tudor manor house provides the setting for an old-fashioned dining experience. The emphasis is on good timing and fresh flavours, best illustrated by dishes such as Jerusalem artichoke and broccoli soup, or chicken suprême with a mushroom and spinach filling in a tomato and carrot sauce

London Road CM14 4NR
Map: 5 TQ59
Tel: 01277 225252
Chef: Jack Rajubally
Proprietor: S P Pearson (Independent)
Cost: Alc £30, fixed price L & D £19.50-£25. H/wine £9.95 Service exc
Credit cards: 🟦 ▦ ▤ 🔲
Times: Last L 2.15pm/last D 10.15pm/9.30pm Sun
Menus: A la carte, fixed price L & D, bar menu
Seats: 120. No cigars or pipes
Additional: Children permitted, children's portions; ❂ dishes, vegan/other diets on request

Directions: 0.5 mile from M25 junction 28, 1 mile from Brentwood town centre

BROXTED, **Whitehall Hotel** ❀❀

Imaginative, modern English cooking in a delightful country manor house with impressive rural views

Much of Essex is splendid rolling farming country, strewn with pretty towns and villages. Broxted is one of those pretty villages, and Whitehall was originally its Elizabethan manor house. The period character of the original building is strongly reflected in the log-burning fires and timber-vaulted restaurant. Here Stuart Townsend presents menus full of modern touches. From the six-

Church End CM6 2BZ
Map no: 5 TL52
Tel: 01279 850603
Chef: Stuart Townsend
Proprietors: n/a.
Manager: Jonathan Linford
Cost: Alc £36.50, fixed price L £19.50/D £34. H/wine £12
❢ Service exc
Credit cards: 🟦 ▦ ▤ 🔲

Whitehall Hotel

Times: Last L 2.30pm, last D 9.30pm Closed Dec 26th-30th
Menus: *A la carte*, fixed price L & D
Seats: 40. No cigars or pipes
Additional: Children welcome, children's menu; ❂ dishes, vegan/other diets on request

course 'Menu Surprise' could come full-flavoured, home-made game sausage (hare, venison and pigeon) on a rösti of onions and chives in a hot beetroot sauce, then slices of salmon and spinach layered with puff pastry on a chive sauce, and finally a light, hot mango and honey soufflé. An alternative choice could be pan-fried langoustines with trompett mushrooms and a lobster cream sauce, loin of wild hare with an apple and celeriac rösti on a light port jus and, to finish, gratin of red fruits. The wine list runs from Alsace to South Africa and there is a good choice of halves, although only one is under £10.

Directions: From M11 junction 8 follow signs for Stansted Airport and then for Broxted

CHELMSFORD,
Pontlands Park Country Hotel ❀

Well-prepared dishes from a wide range of influences which take in France, Greece, Italy and Britain are offered at this well-tended, converted Victorian residence. Both carte and fixed-price menus are keenly priced and Sunday lunch is popular

West Hanningfield Road
Great Baddow CM2 8HR
Map no: 5 TL70
Tel: 01245 476444
Chef: Stephen Wright
Proprietor: Jason Bartella
Cost: *Alc* from £25, fixed-price L £14/D £18.50. H/wine £9.75 Service exc
Credit cards: ▨ ▨ ▨ ▨ OTHER
Times: Last L 2pm/D 10pm. Closed Sat L, Sun D, Dec 27-30
Menus: *A la carte*, fixed-price L & D, bar menu (by arrangement)
Seats: 100. Air conditioned. No-smoking area
Additional: Children welcome, children's menu; ❂ menu, vegan/other diets on request

Directions: A12 & A130 to Great Baddow, take first slip road and first left

COGGESHALL, **Baumann's** ❀❀

A relaxed, comfortable brasserie where European influences give an innovative twist to well established British dishes

4-6 Stoneham Street CO6 1TT
Map no: 5 TL82
Tel: 01376 561453
Chefs: Mark Baumann and Doug Wright
Proprietors: Baumanns
Cost: Alc £24, fixed-price L £9.95, Sunday L £13.95. H/wine £8.50 ‼ Service inc
Credit cards: ⊠ ▨ ▨ OTHER
Times: 12.30-last L 2pm, 7.30pm-last D 10pm. Closed Sun eve, Mon, 2 weeks Jan
Menus: A la carte, fixed-price L, Sunday L
Seats: 75. No pipes or cigars
Additional: Children welcome, children's portions: ❂ dishes; other diets on request

There is no sense of urgency about this comfortable brasserie. Decor, though attractive, is not designed to be statement making; chairs from local antique shops are set on bare wooden floor boards, walls are still hung with pictures from the Los Angeles restaurant of a former owner, and tables are clad in plain white linen. Mark Baumann heads the kitchen team that produces a range of basically British dishes enlivened by European influences: 'London Particular', for example, is a creamy pea soup scented with smoked ham and chive crème fraîche, sirloin of beef is served with a crushed tomato, mushroom and garlic provençale and grilled fillet of red mullet with tomatoes, pesto and cucumber spaghetti. Excellent use is made of traditional meats in dishes like rabbit cider hot-pot or roasted goose breast on a sage, onion and apple compôte, the daily selection of fish is Billingsgate's best, and desserts include rhubarb crumble deliciously partnered by cinnamon custard and an over-the-top English trifle with baked Tonbridge biscuits. The short wine list, organised by colour and characteristics, offers a broad-based choice.

Directions: In the centre of Coggeshall opposite the clock tower

COGGESHALL, **White Hart** ❀❀

A range of unashamedly rich Italian dishes in an ancient and typically English inn

An historic inn dating from 1420 which retains many original features – notably a bay from the town's guildhall, now incorporated in the comfortable first-floor Guild Room lounge. The beamed dining-room provides an attractive setting in which to enjoy chef Fausto Mazza's rich, traditional Italian cooking, his *carte* and fixed-price menus offering a range of dishes that are refreshingly honest in their sheer indulgence. Home-made pasta features strongly and can be the basis of a useful vegetarian option (as in canelloni al forno, stuffed with ricotto cheese then topped with a cream and fresh tomato sauce). Main courses often include

Market End CO6 1NH
Map no: 5 TL82
Tel: 01376 561654
Chef: Fausto Mazza
Proprietor: Mario Casella
Cost: Alc £29, Sunday L £14.95. Wine £9.25. Service exc
Credit cards: ⊠ ▨ ▨ ▨ OTHER
Menus: A la carte, Sunday L, bar menu
Times: Midday-last L 2pm, 7pm-last D 10pm. D not served Sun
Seats: 80

an excellent risotto, but our inspector chose suprême of guinea fowl served with a seasonally appropriate raspberry and Marsala sauce. Fish figures prominently; oak-smoked salmon on a leaf salad as a starter, mussels, scallops, squid and prawn in a risotto and monkfish tails with wild mushrooms and tarragon sauce among the main courses. Ice creams and sorbets predictably hold sway on the dessert menu, but the flambee trolley offers a more exciting alternative in crêpes Suzette, banana mocha or zablaglione. A mainly Italian wine list includes some French (and a very few New World) labels.

Additional: Children permitted, children's portions; ❂ dishes; other diets on request.

Directions: From the A12 towards Ipswich take the A120, left towards Braintree; at the B1024 crossroads turn left again

COLCHESTER, Martha's Vineyard ❀❀

American owner brings the taste of Ohio to a sleepy Essex village

A real find. Housed in a fifteenth-century cottage at the centre of a sleepy village on the Essex border, this unpretentious little restaurant is obviously thriving. Ohio-born Larkin Warrens starts each day by baking bread and making her own pasta – a true sign of commitment. The menu, kept sensibly short, is drawing more and more on American influences. Rabbit sausage is served with a mild Mexican mustard sauce, creamy savoury cheesecake has sun-dried tomatoes blended into its topping, and moist pan-seared chicken comes with tangy salsa Caribe – a memorable taste sensation comprised of papaya, coconut, lime juice and chillies. Vegetables (served on the main course plate) included good potato cakes and sautéed spinach at a recent inspection visit, with rhubarb and coriander seeds adding a new dimension to the light bread and butter pudding sampled on the same occasion. Prices are kept deliberately low, a three-course meal with coffee and a glass of wine probably costing less than £20. The wine list features a whole section of Californian reds, an admirable number of halves and a recommendable house Chardonnay from Napa Valley.

High Street
Nayland CO6 4JF
Map no: 5 TL92
Tel: 01206 2628888
Chef: Larkin Rogers
Proprietors: Larkin Rogers, Christopher Warren
Cost: *Alc* £18.50. H/wine £10.95. Service exc
Credit cards: 🄰 🄼
Times: 7.30pm-last D 9.30pm, Sun L 12.30-last L 2pm. Closed Sun, Mon, 2 weeks in winter, 2 weeks in summer
Menus: *A la carte*, Sunday L
Seats: 41. No smoking
Additional: Children welcome, ❂ menu

Directions: 6.5 miles north of Colchester, just off the A134, in the middle of Nayland High Street

DEDHAM, Le Talbooth Restaurant ❀❀

A popular restaurant serving interesting meals in a riverside setting

This is Constable country and the River Stour ambles past this atmospheric black and white house creating a classic English setting. The well established restaurant – linked to the nearby Talbooth Hotel – has a strong local following. However, inspectors' reports of the cooking are mixed. At a meal taken in winter linguine with assorted seafood was accompanied by a slightly over fiery tomato coulis and a dull saffron and clam cream, although the linguine itself was very good. A main course of poached fillet of lamb wrapped in chard and served in broth was highly enjoyable, though the vegetables ranged from good chard to bland carrots and poor potatoes. From a good choice of hot and cold puddings came a baked raspberry soufflé followed by decent cafetière coffee and

Colchester CO7 6HP
Map no: 5 TM03
Tel: 01206 323150
Chef: Henrik Iversen
Proprietor: Gerald M W Milsom
Cost: *Alc* £35, fixed-price L £15/D £19.95 H/wine £12.25 Service inc
Credit cards: 🄰 🄼 🄼 OTHER
Times: Noon-last L 2pm, 7pm-Last D 9pm
Menus: *A la carte*, fixed-price L & D
Seats: 80. No cigars or pipes in dining room

Le Talbooth Restaurant

Additional: Children permitted, children's portions; ❤ dishes, other diets with notice

well-made chocolates. The wine list is notable for its range and depth, and includes a decent selection of Italian and New World wines, as well as good quality Bordeaux and Burgundy.

Directions: 6 miles from Colchester: follow signs from the A12 to Stratford St Mary, restaurant on left before the village

FELSTED, **Rumbles Cottage** ❀

In addition to a carte, this small, converted cottage features interesting fixed-price menus on selected days: the 'Guinea Pig' and a pasta menu. Owner/chef Joy Hadley offers modern British cooking, but also includes dishes such as Circassian chicken, and lesser known cheeses from Britain and Ireland are a speciality

Seats: 50. Smoking discouraged
Additional: Children welcome, children's portions; ❤ dishes, vegan/other diets on request
Directions: In centre of village, approached by A120 or A130

Braintree Road CM6 3DJ
Map no: 5 TL62
Tel: 01371 820996
Chef: E Joy Hadley
Proprietor: E Joy Hadley
Cost: *Alc* £19.70-£23.95, fixed-price D £10 & £12.50/Sun L £12.50 H/wine £7.95 ❢ Service exc
Credit cards: 🔳 🔳
Times: Last D 9pm/Sun L 2pm Closed Sun D, Mon

GREAT CHESTERFORD,
The Crown House ❀

Hospitable, friendly atmosphere in this listed Tudor building. Chef John Pearman cooks fresh tasting home-made dishes which could be enjoyed in the pine-panelled dining-room or open-plan lounge area. Breakfast is served in the light conservatory. A relaxed and informal environment

Menus: A la carte, fixed-price L & D, pre-theatre
Seats: 60. No smoking in dining room
Additional: Children welcome, children's portions; ❤ dishes, other diets on request
Directions: On B1383 1 mile from Stump Cross close to M1 exits 9 or 10

Saffron Walden CB10 1NY
Map no: 5 TL54
Tel: 01799 530515
Chef: Philip Stowell
Proprietors: Coolisle Ltd.
Manager: Alan Phillips
Cost: *Alc* £19.50, fixed-price L £10.95/D £15. H/wine £7.50 Service inc
Credit cards: 🔳 🔳 🔳 OTHER
Times: Last L 2.15pm/ D 9.15pm

GREAT DUNMOW, Starr ✿✿

Consistent quality is appreciated at this smart brasserie restaurant

There is nothing outlandish or startling about this attractive, well looked after restaurant with rooms. Its smart brasserie atmosphere predictably appeals to a fairly conservative clientele. A limited lunchtime *carte* is supplemented by both blackboard specials and verbally described dishes of the day, a more elaborate set-price menu being offered in the evening. Proprietors describe cuisine as 'English with a French accent', which seems fair comment – a range of solid, no-nonsense staples more noteworthy for consistency than imagination being redeemed by vegetables and sauces in Continental style. Seared fresh tuna with a ratatouille and tapenade sauce, or crispy duck parcels with plum sauce and a julienne of cucumber, for example, might be followed by medallions of beef fillet layered with potato rösti and a béarnaise sauce, or roast stuffed guinea fowl enlivened by a fresh coriander sauce. Desserts change daily, ranging from steamed sponges and fruit in filo pastry to lighter -often chocolate-based – confections. An informal wine list covers the major growing districts of Europe and the New World; half bottles are listed separately, and house wines start at about £10.

Directions: At Junc 8 on the M11, take the A120 towards Chelmsford

Market Place CM6 1AX
Map no: 4 TL62
Tel: 01371 874321
Chef: Mark Fisher
Proprietors: Brian & Vanessa Jones
Cost: *Alc* L £22, fixed-price D £21.50, £32.50; Sun L £21.50. Wine £10.50. Service inc
Credit cards: ▨ ▧ ▨ OTHER
Menus: *A la carte* , fixed-price D, Sunday L
Times: Last L 1.30pm, Last D 9.30pm. Closed Sat L , Sun D and 1 week after New Year
Seats: 87. No smoking in dining room
Additional: . Children welcome, children's portions; ❶ menu, vegan/other diets on request

HARWICH, The Pier at Harwich ✿

Situated on the quayside, the Pier at Harwich is split in two: upstairs the Pier Restaurant, on the ground floor the more modestly priced and simpler-styled Ha'penny Pier. Unsurprisingly, both restaurants feature seafood as a speciality. Baked fillet of sea-trout on a bed of samphire with lime juice, butter and white wine is a typical offering

Times: Last L 2pm/D 9.30pm
Menus: *A la carte*, fixed-price L & D
Seats: 70+50. No cigars or pipes
Additional: Children welcome, children's menu; ❶ menu, other diets on request
Directions: On the quayside of old Harwich

The Quay CO12 3HH
Map no: 5 TM23
Tel: 01255 241212
Chef: C E Oakley
Proprietors: G M W Milsom.
Manager: C E Oakley
Cost: *Alc* £25, fixed-price L £12.50/D £16.50. H/wine £7.95. Service exc

Britain lies at the northern limit for growing asparagus and it grows slowly, due to the coolness of the soil. Although at the height of the season English asparagus is often more expensive than imported varieties, the slow growing results in a strong, intense flavour that makes the higher price worth while. It takes three years before a plant can be cut and about five years before it yields a full crop. Then each spear must be cut by hand. The season is short, about six weeks from early May to late June, after which the plant must be left to develop leaves, so that it can regenerate itself. Most native asparagus come from the Vale of Evesham in Herefordshire, Kent and Suffolk.

MANNINGTREE, **Stour Bay Cafe** ❀❀

A popular local restaurant with a chef from LA providing a touch of
West Coast cooking to a varied brasserie-style menu

A California-influenced brasserie in a small Essex town is, to say the least, unusual. Co-owner and chef Sherri Singleton left Los Angeles over six years ago and has now broadened her repertoire to include ideas from beyond the Golden State. The style reads well. Dishes are true to their description and surprisingly restrained in approach. Ingredients are undeniably fresh. The daily-changing menu revolves around a choice of four fish dishes preceded by half a dozen starters, and a selection of meat dishes which change less often. These might be a rich Louisiana duck and smoked sausage gumbo, lamb ragoût with tomatoes and white beans, or chargrilled, hoisin-marinated duck breast with fresh plum chutney. Fish could be grilled salmon fillet in tomato and orange sauce, chargrilled tuna with pepper aïoli, or seafood fricassée (poached pieces of monkfish, salmon, squid and mussels in a cream-based saffron and basil sauce). Freshly baked walnut bread comes 'hot from the oven'. Desserts are more brash sounding and typically North American – some sticky, some frozen and some just decadent. The wine list is California-heavy, but other New Worlds and France do get a look in.

Directions: Town centre (A137 from Colchester or Ipswich) – large green building in High Street

39-43 High Street CO1 1AH
Map no: 5 TM13
Tel: 01206 396687
Chef: Sherri Singleton
Proprietors: Sherri Singleton and David McKay
Cost: *Alc* £16-£18, fixed price Fri-Sun L £13.95. H/ wine £8.75
⦙ Service exc
Credit cards: 🆇 💳 💳
Times: Last L 2.15pm, last D 9.30pm/10pm Sat. Closed Mon-Thur L, Mon D, Sun D, Bhs
Menus: *A la carte* & three day fixed price L
Seats: 65 + private room. No smoking in dining room
Additional: Children welcome, children's portions; ✿ dishes, vegan/other diets on request

ROCHFORD, **Hotel Renouf** ❀

Within easy reach of the M25, the Hotel Renouf offers French and
English cooking from a 'Discovery of Taste' menu with suggested wines,
plus an extensive carte. A typical meal might include baby scallops with
ginger, coriander and leeks, and fillet of bass in pastry, while duck is a
particular speciality

Directions: From M25 exit 29, A127 into Rochford, reservoir on left, turn right at mini-roundabout, right again into car park

Bradley Way SS4 1BU
Map no: 5 TQ89
Tel: 01702 544393
Chef: Melvin & Derek Renouf
Proprietor: Derek J Renouf
Cost: *Alc* £27.75, fixed-price L & D £17.50. H/wine £9 **⦙** Service inc
Credit cards: 🆇 💳 💳 💳 OTHER
Times: Last L 1.45pm/D 9.45pm. Closed Dec 26-30
Menus: *A la carte,* fixed-price L & D
Seats: 45. Air conditioned
Additional: Children welcome, children's portions; ✿ dishes, vegan/other diets on request

SAFFRON WALDEN, **Saffron Hotel** ❀

This 16th-century building offers a comfortable and welcoming atmosphere in which to chose from the daily changing carte and set menus. Chef Nigel Few creates imaginative dishes along the lines of roulade of pork and venison wrapped in Parma ham served on a bed of sweet and sour cabbage

10-18 High Street CB10 1AY
Map no: 5 RL53
Tel: 01799 522676
Chef: Nigel Few
Proprietor: Debbie Ball
Cost: Alc £20, fixed-price L/D £13.50. H/wine £9. Service exc
Credit cards: 🃏 🃏
Times: Noon-last L 2pm, 7pm-last D 9.30pm Closed Sun D
Menus: A la carte, fixed-price L & D, bar menu
Seats: 52. Air conditioned. No smoking
Additional: Children welcome, children's portions; ❂ dishes, vegan/other diets on request

Directions: Town centre – in the High Street

SOUTHEND-ON-SEA, **Schulers Hotel** ❀

Undoubtedly the focal point of this hotel is the large restaurant, complete with sea facing views. Manfred Schuler hails from Lucerne and has enlarged the traditional English repertoire with Swiss dishes such as 'emince of veal Zurichoise'. He also bakes excellent home-made bread, including pretzel

Menus: A la carte, fixed-price L & D
Seats: n/a. No smoking
Additional: Children welcome, children's portions; ❂ menu, other diets on request
Directions: From A127 into Southend follow seafront signs, then Eastern Esplanade B1016 (east of pier)

161 Eastern Esplanade SS1 2YB
Map no: 5 TQ88
Tel: 01702 610172
Chef: Manfred Schuler
Proprietors: Manfred Schuler
Costs: Alc £18.25, fixed-price L/D from £8.75. H/wine £9.50 Service exc
Credit cards: 🃏 🃏 🃏 🃏 OTHER
Times: Last L 2pm/D 9.30pm Sat 10.30pm. Closed Sun D & Mon L, and 25/26 Dec

Tatin is the name given to an apple tart that is cooked beneath a lid of pastry, but served reversed, with the pastry on the bottom and the apple on top. Upside-down tarts, made with apples or pears, have a long tradition throughout the French Orléanais region and are a speciality of Solange, but the Tart Tatin, a delicious combination of caramelised apples cooked under a crisp, lightly risen puff pastry was made famous by the Tatin sisters who ran a hotel-restaurant in the village of Lamotte-Beuvron in the Loire valley at the beginning of this century. It is said that the Tatin sisters went for a long walk, forgetting they had left a pan of apples simmering in butter and sugar on the stove. When they returned the apples were caramelised. Tart Tatin was first served in Paris at Maxim's, where it remains a speciality.

WEST MERSEA, Le **Champenois** ✿

Simple, uncomplicated dishes with a hint of French: pâté and onion soup are provided along with snails and frogs' legs for authenticity. Main courses include skate wing with vermouth and rack of lamb. Deserts are a highlight with the selection varying daily, perhaps crème brûlée, apple flan or ice-cream

Menus: *A la carte,* fixed-price L & D
Seats: 45. No-smoking area. No cigars or pipes
Additional: Children welcome, children's portions; ✪ dishes, other diets on request
Directions: Drive through village, turning right at main Church

Blackwater Hotel
20-22 Church Road CO5 8QH
Map no: 5 TM01
Tel: 01206 383338/383038
Chef: R Roudesli
Proprietor: Mrs M Chapleo
Cost: *Alc* £19.55-£27.20, fixed-price L/D £17.50. H/wine £8.25
❢ No service charge
Credit cards: 🅴 🈸 🈺
Times: Last L 2pm/D 10pm. Closed Tue L, Sun D, first 3 wks Jan

WETHERSFIELD, **Dicken's** ✿✿

Mediterranean style is tailored to suit local taste in the kitchens of this pleasant restaurant overlooking the village green

A range of straightforward Mediterranean-style dishes has been capably adapted to suit local customer preferences at this pleasant restaurant overlooking the village green. Despite the apparent simplicity of cooking style, however, classic skill is evident, both in the balancing of ingredients to create true, robust flavours and in a talent for composition that leads naturally to attractive presentation. The dinner *carte* (supplemented by perhaps three daily 'specials' at each stage) offers traditional starters like bruschetta – roasted peppers, plum tomatoes and basil on grilled country bread – and the ever-popular fish soup with rouille and croûtons. Main course might include a choice between steamed fillet of brill on herb noodles and rack of lamb with a rosemary and olive jus. Desserts are more imaginative than many, crème brûlée being served with stewed plums and ginger, and brown bread ice-cream with caramelised pears. An excellent, keenly priced and predominantly French wine list includes classified clarets from 1970 and thoughtfully chosen house wines starting at £9.95.

Directions: Overlooking the green, in the centre of Wethersfield

The Green CM7 4BS
Map no: 5 TL73
Tel: 01371 850723
Chef: W John Dicken
Proprietor: W John Dicken
Cost: *Alc* £18, fixed-price L £8-£15. H/wine £8.75. Service exc
Credit cards: 🅴 🈸 OTHER
Times: Last L 2pm, Last D 9.30pm. Closed Mon, Tue, and Sun D
Menus: *A la carte,* Sunday L
Seats: 60. Smoking with consideration for other guests
Additional: Children welcome, children's portions; ✪ dishes, vegan/other diets on request.

GLOUCESTERSHIRE

BIBURY, Swan Hotel ✿✿

Dining here is a treat although the prices are as stately as the surroundings

Cirencester GL7 5NW
Map no: 4 SP10
Tel: 01285 740695
Chef: Guy Bossom
Proprietor: Heinz Sedlacek
Cost: Fixed-price lunch £17.50,
fixed-price dinner £37.50.
H/wine £12.50 ❢ Service inc
Credit cards: 🌑 💳 💳 💳 OTHER
Times: Midday-last L 2pm,
7.30pm-last D 9.30pm
Menus: A la carte, fixed-price
lunch and dinner, bar menu
Seats: 65. No smoking in dining-
room
Additional: Children welcome,
children's portions/menu;
❂ menu, vegan/other diets
on request

If a setting could be better than picture-postcard, the Swan is in it. The honey-coloured stone building sits solidly opposite gardens, a trout farm and the River Coln. The interior is all sumptuous fabrics and furnishings, fine period furniture and a few reproduction Rennie Mackintosh chairs. A swan motif is worked into the burgundy carpets, and even turns up in piped chocolate form on home-made langue-de-chat biscuits. Guy Bossom's daily-changing, fixed-price, five-course menu is available in the elegant, almost baroque, dining room, and Ian Lovering provides lighter meals in Jankowski's (Polish for swan, it seems) Brasserie, with its softened Mediterranean themes. Guy's bold style of cooking enables many flavours to meet successfully on the plate. A recent superlative inspection dinner started with a ravioli of basil mousse with red mullet in a green herb sauce, followed by baked brill with onion marmalade, and a crème brûlée 'as near to perfect as can be eaten anywhere'. Despite a low key wine list, which is not very clear and has some high price tags, this was a highly enjoyable meal.

Directions: On B4425 between Cirencester (7 miles) and Burford (9 miles). Beside bridge in centre of Bibury

BIRDLIP,
Kingshead House Restaurant ✿

Unpretentious and wholesome modern Anglo-French cooking is served in the oak-beamed restaurant at this 17th-century coaching inn. A July menu featured hot rabbit pâté in brioche, grilled goats' cheese on foccaccio with marinated aubergines, and steamed escalope of wild salmon with a sorrel sauce

Menus: A la carte L (inc Sun), fixed-price D & Sun L, pre-theatre, bar menu **Seats:** 34. Smoking restricted to after meal **Additional:** Children welcome, children's portions; ❂ dishes, other diets on request **Directions:** In Birdlip on the B4070

Birdlip GL4 8JH
Map no: 3 SO91
Tel: 01452 862299
Chef: Judy Knock
Proprietors: Warren & Judy
Knock
Cost: Alc from £12.50, fixed-
price D £24.50 (4 course)/Sun
L £16.50. H/wine £9.80 ❢
Service exc
Credit cards: 🌑 💳 💳 💳 OTHER
Times: Last L 1.45pm/D 9.45pm.
Closed Mon, Sat L, Sun D, Dec
26/7, Jan 1/2

BLOCKLEY, **Crown Inn** ❀

Imaginatively-prepared international dishes are served in the Coach House restaurant of this 16th-century village-centre inn. This might include shellfish and fish stew, game pie, and breast of guinea fowl in puff pastry, and a choice of home-made desserts

Menu: *A la carte* L & D, bar menu **Seats:** 40+40. No-smoking area
Additional: Children permitted, children's portions; ❂ dishes, vegan/other diets on request
Directions: A44 (Evesham) from Moreton-in-Marsh, first right after Burton-on-the-Hill

High Street GL56 9EX
Map no: 4 SP13
Tel: 01386 700245
Chef: Richard Smith
Proprietor: John Champion
Cost: *Alc* £25 approx. H/wine £9.50 ❢ Service exc
Times: Last L 2pm/D 9.30pm

BOURTON-ON-THE-WATER,
Dial House Hotel ❀

☺ *Located in the centre of a busy tourist village, this well-maintained hotel offers carefully prepared, uncomplicated dishes making good use of local produce. Dishes available on the carte may include warm goats' cheese salad, rack of English lamb with thyme and garlic, and sweet potatoes with mozzarella and avocado*

The Chestnuts
High Street GL54 2AN
Map no: 4 SP12
Tel: 01451 822244
Chefs: Steve Jones,
Proprietors: Lynn & Peter Boxall
Cost: *Alc* £19.50, fixed-price L £12.95. H/wine £9.50 ❢ Service exc
Credit cards: ▨ ▩ ▩ OTHER
Times: Noon-last L 2pm, 7pm-last D 9.15pm
Menus: *A la carte,* fixed-price L, bar menu
Seats: 30. No smoking in dining room
Additional: Children permitted lunch only, ❂ menu, vegan/other diets on request

Directions: Village centre, on A40/A429

BUCKLAND, **Buckland Manor** ❀❀❀

A country house restaurant that scores highly on every count, but the prices reflect the quality

The Buckland Manor estate dates from the seventh century. From any angle it is the archetypal Cotswold country house, with the church next door and far-reaching views over the Vale of Evesham. The gardens, which supply fresh produce, are splendid, the interior breathtaking, especially the restaurant which features dark wood tables, upholstered chairs and fine panelling. The high standards seen throughout the hotel are echoed in the kitchen where Martyn Pearn works on a monthly-changing *carte*. This is amply complemented by what must be one of the longest (and heaviest) wine lists to be found, with a very full selection of Bordeaux, Burgundies and sparkling wines. The well-crafted cooking is

Near Broadway WR12 7LY
Map no: 4 SP03
Tel: 01386 852626
Chef: Martyn Pearn
Proprietor: Roy Vaughan
Cost: *Alc* £41, fixed-price L £22.70. H/wine £9.50 ❢ Service inc
Credit cards: ▨ ▩ ▩
Times: Last L 2pm, last D 9pm
Menus: *A la carte,* fixed-price L, Sun L, bar menu
Seats: 40. No smoking in dining-room

Buckland Manor

Additional: Children over 12 permitted; ❂ dishes; Gentlemen are requested to wear jacket and tie in dining-room

basically English with French touches and hints of luxury along the lines of mousseline of Cornish scallops with Sevruga caviar and a light chive sauce, and home-cured duck ham, thinly sliced and served with a lambs lettuce salad topped with sautéed foie gras. An acknowledgement of modernism can be seen in dishes such as pot-roasted Deben duck breast on an Armagnac, cream and green peppercorn sauce, or blanquette of monkfish tails served in a rich cream sauce garnished with garlic fritters and shredded leeks. The latter, an inspection choice, came with a tarragon mousse which had absorbed too much of the 'offaly' taste of the enveloping caul, although the jus and the vegetables were finely judged. At the same inspection meal, maize-fed chicken ballotine lacked an intensity of flavour, as did the perfectly risen rhubarb soufflé with a smooth ice-cream made with ginger and Advocaat, although the taste of the liqueur was mysteriously absent.

Directions: Through Broadway, turn on to the B4632 (Cheltenham). After 1.5 miles left turn to Buckland. The Manor is through the village on the right-hand side

CHARINGWORTH,
Charingworth Manor Hotel ❀❀

A lovely old manor house set in rolling Cotswold countryside which makes a stylish setting for imaginative food

A snaking driveway leads up to the manor house which sits in a quiet location overlooking its 54 acres of open land. The 14th-century character of the building is wonderfully maintained throughout the hotel. In the kitchen, Matthew Laughton, who has been promoted from sous-chef, distinguishes himself with his inspired dishes on a monthly-changing, continually-evolving menu. They make interesting reading. Note a salad of squid stuffed with a risotto of its own ink with a black olive dressing and steamed salmon topped with smoked cods' roe soufflé in a sorrel butter. One very satisfactory meal took in spinach and nutmeg gnocchi with a ricotta cheese sauce, followed by lightly-seasoned braised shank of lamb served with minted couscous. Dessert was another example of the chef's inventiveness, an old-fashioned junket, pepped up by poached pears and honey. The wide-choice wine list includes a discriminating selection from Bordeaux. Formal wear is expected in the smart dining room.

Directions: From A429 Fosse Way take B4035 towards Chipping Campden, hotel is 3 miles on right

GL55 6NS
Map no: 4 SP13
Tel: 01386 593555
Chef: Mathew Laughton
Proprietor: English Rose Hotels.
Manager: Colin Heaney
Cost: *Alc* £31, fixed price
L £18.50. H/wine £12.95 ❢
Service inc
Credit cards: 🔲 🔲 🔲 🔲 OTHER
Times: 12.30-last L 2pm, 7pm-last D 9.30pm/10pm Fri & Sat
Menus: *A la carte*, fixed price L
Seats: 48. No smoking in the dining room
Additional: Children welcome, children's portions; ❂ menu, vegan/other diets on request

CHELTENHAM,
Cleeveway House Restaurant ❀❀

☺ *A quintessentially English country house hotel with a delightfully old fashioned approach to cooking*

The charming manor house which incorporates the Cleeveway House Restaurant was built in the early 18th century from golden Cotswold stone. Rose gardens, green lawns and flourishing borders now surround this small country house which offers meals along traditional lines. The menu sticks to favourites which were probably learnt when the chef was cooking in the 1960s at the Hole-in-the-Wall in Bath. An early summer meal might include cheese soufflé, Gressingham duck with mint, lime and honey sauce, and for dessert, poached pears in a well scented syrup with white wine. One inspector felt some dishes were let down by occasional poor timing, but did enjoy a chicken breast stuffed with cashew nuts which was coated in a rich, well combined mixture of tarragon, white wine and grain mustard. The wine list is weighted in favour of Burgundy and Bordeaux but the New World has some representation. A pleasant feature of the restaurant is the small opening in the dining room into the kitchen where the easy-going preparations can be observed.

Bishops Cleeve GL52 4SA
Map no: 3 SO92
Tel: 01242 672585
Chef: John Marfell
Proprietors: Susan & John Marfell
Cost: *Alc* £20, Sun L £14.50. H/wine £9 ▮ Service inc
Credit cards: ▨ ▨ ▨ OTHER
Times: Noon-last L 1.45pm, 7pm-last D 9.45pm. Closed Sun D, Mon L, Christmas week
Menus: *A la carte*, fixed-price Sun L
Seats: 38. Air conditioned
Additional: Children welcome, children's portions; ◑ dishes, other diets prior notice

Directions: from Cheltenham A435(Evesham), right at 2nd roundabout on Bishop's Cleeve bypass, 200 yards on left

CHELTENHAM, Golden Valley Hotel ❀

A popular business hotel offering well executed cooking expressed in bold textures and flavours. An imaginative menu offers dishes such as roast halibut with layers of salmon, wrapped in pastry and complemented by a robust ragoût of lobster, scallops and prawns. Puddings include a rich chocolate roulade

Gloucester Road GL51 0TS
Map: 3 SO92
Tel: 01242 23691
Chef: Ronnie Pharoah
Proprietor: Thistle & Mount Charlotte.
Manager: Mike Hughes
Cost: *Alc* £25, fixed price L £14.50/D £17.50 Mon/Thur, £25 Fri/Sun. H/wine £9.50 Service inc
Credit cards: ▨ ▨ ▨ ▨
Times: 12.30pm-last L 1.45pm, 7pm-last D 9.45pm/Sun 9.15pm
Menus: *A la carte,* fixed price L & D, bar menu in lounge
Seats: 120. Air conditioned
Additional: Children welcome, children's menu; ◑ menu, vegan/other diets on request

Directions: 2.5 miles from centre of Cheltenham on A40 (Gloucester), 1 mile M5 exit 11, towards Cheltenham, 2nd exit off first roundabout

CHELTENHAM, **Greenway Hotel**

One of Cheltenham's finest restaurants, in a beautiful location just to the south of the town

Shurdington GL51 5UG
Map no: 3 SO92
Tel: 01242 862352
Chef: Christopher Colmer
Proprietor: David A White
(Pride of Britain)
Cost: Alc £27.50, fixed-price
L £16/D£27.50. H/wine £11.75
! Service exc
Credit cards: ■ ■ ■ ■ OTHER
Times: Last L 2pm/last D
9.30pm. Closed Sat L
Menus: A la carte, fixed-price
L & D, light L (May-Oct)
Seats: 50. No pipes or cigars in
diing room
Additional: Children over 7
welcome, children's portions;
♥ dishes, vegan/other diets on
request

Little has altered here after a near-seamless change of ownership. Many of the original staff remain, well drilled in the art of looking after their guests. Also unchanged is the Elizabethan house, still ivy-clad, the gardens colourful with the Cotswolds rising behind. The restaurant has a conservatory extension at the rear of the building which overlooks a fish pond and some fine trees. Chef Christopher Colmer was a Roux Brothers scholar in 1995 and a runner-up in the Chef of the Year competition a year earlier. His cooking style is essentially British with French influences. It manifests itself on the regularly changing, fixed-price menu in starters such as roast Bresse pigeon with a beetroot and pearl barley risotto, and scallops with Gewürztraminer and fresh lime. Main courses include roasted Severn salmon with a Provençal vegetable galette and a red pepper and tomato fondue, saddle of Cotswold venison with swede and carrot dauphinoise and a blackberry scented sauce, sea bass with salmon mousseline, and corn-fed chicken breast with a butter bean and turnip sauce. The dessert section might offer lime and pistachio cheesecake, white chocolate and raspberry mousse or poached pear, lightly caramelised and served with an odd combination of toffee and scented lavender ice-cream. A middle of the road, worldwide wine list draws heavily on the established French grape producing regions.

Directions: 2.5 miles south of Cheltenham on A46 (Stroud)

CHELTENHAM,
Le Champignon Sauvage ❀❀❀

Bold, French terroir-style cooking and friendly service in a small, popular town restaurant

Le Champignon Sauvage continues to go from strength to strength. David and Helen Everitt-Matthias run an unassuming restaurant which brings customers back time and time again. David cooks, helped by one sous-chef, and Helen runs front-of-house with terrific

14 Suffolk Road GL50 2AQ
Map no: 3 SO92
Tel: 01242 573449
Chef: David Everitt-Matthias
Proprietor: David & Helen
Everitt-Matthias
Cost: Fixed-price L £17.50/D
£29.50. H/wine £9.50 ! Service
exc
Credit cards: ■ ■ ■ ■ OTHER

Le Champignon Sauvage

Times: Last L 1.30pm/last D
9.30pm. Closed Sat L, Sun,
Christmas, Easter
Menus: Fixed-price L & D
Seats: 30. Air conditioned
Additional: Children welcome,
other diets by request

style. Hand-painted cover plates are used in the boldly decorated dining room and chairs are also expressive, draped in tail-coat style covers. The cosy bar area features prints of the eponymous fungi and showcases the many awards David has received for his bold, innovative cooking.

There are two, three and four-course, set-price menus on which the dishes are listed in French (with English translations). Although French country-style is a description that covers most dishes, some influences from other parts of the world are detectable, giving an eclectic feel to the menu. A summer meal started with a wonderfully fresh, colourful trout dish, the lightly steamed fillet resting on a bed of baby vegetables, some richly flavoured tomato confit and an anchovy-scented bread jus of velvety texture and 'limpid clarity'. Stunning saucing continued into the main course, a North African-inspired, melt-in-the-mouth chump of Cinderford lamb in a thin coriander crust with cinnamon-spiced couscous, which revealed an ability to squeeze every last milligram of flavour from the high quality ingredients used. To finish, apricot walnut tart, served with some crunchy nougat glace, the various components complementing each other well: warm tart, iced nougat; smooth apricots, crunchy parfait. French wines are in pole position on the wine list, ahead of a reasonably international line-up. The half dozen house wines are modestly priced.

Directions: South of town centre, near Boys' College on A40 (Oxford). Please phone for exact details

CHELTENHAM, **Mayflower Chinese Restaurant** ❀

☺ *Cantonese Chinese with a high standard of cooking; hot and spicy dishes as well as the staple favourites. Look out for crispy seaweed, king prawn with ginger and spring onions and yung chow fried rice. Various selected set menus are provided alongside individual dishes*

Menus: *A la carte,* fixed-price L & D, pre-theatre
Seats: 80+50. Air conditioned
Additional: Children welcome, ❤ menu, vegan/other diets on request
Directions: Town centre opposite Eagle Star building

32-34 Clarence Street
GL50 3NX
Map no: 3 SO92
Tel: 01242 522426
Chefs: Mr C F Kong & Mrs M M Kong
Proprietors: The Kong Family
Cost: *Alc* £15.50, fixed-price L £6.50/D £19.50. H/wine £8.95 Service exc
Credit cards: ▨ ▤ ▨ ▨ OTHER
Times: Last L 1.45pm/D 10.45pm. Closed Sun L, Dec 24-27

CHELTENHAM, Regency House Hotel ❀

Original Victorian features have been carefully preserved at this professionally-maintained hotel. The enjoyable cooking has a French influence and the menu may feature dishes such as cheddar and smoked salmon soufflé, fillet of salmon with chives and ginger, and loin of lamb in a red wine sauce with redcurrant jelly

Seats: 16. No smoking in dining room
Additional: Children welcome at lunch; children's portions;
❶ dishes; other diets on request
Directions: Clarence Square is in Pitville just north of the town centre

50 Clarence Square GL50 4JR
Map no: 3 SO92
Tel: 01242 582718
Chef: Barbara Oates
Proprietor: John Oates
Cost: Fixed-price L/D £15.95.
H/wine £6.20 ❗ Service inc
Credit cards: 💳 💳 💳
Times: Last L 2pm/D 8pm
Closed 24 Dec-2 Jan

CHELTENHAM,
Restaurant On The Park ❀❀

Up and running again in fine style and serving genuinely interesting food

Last year we were unable to make a formal assessment because major changes had just taken place; now we can. The Restaurant on the Park is part of a Georgian townhouse hotel located on the Evesham Road overlooking Pitville Park. Starched linen and good table appointments go well with the high-ceilinged restaurant, where chef Eamonn Webster has been given a free hand to run his own operation. He provides a short selection of dishes from both *carte* and fixed-price menus. These feature a combination of traditional and modern dishes with good ingredients and some imaginative touches. A starter of deep-fried dates stuffed with Stilton sounds risky, but the sweet and salt flavours and soft texture were well balanced by a dice of dressed tomato. Fashionable Oriental and Mediterranean influences are evident in main courses such as Thai chicken breast marinated in green curry, lime, paw-paw and coconut milk; pigeon breast with garlic polenta, and poached sea bass with caramelised red cabbage. Desserts range from lemon tart with vanilla sauce to macadamia nut parfait with a blueberry sauce. The wine list is carefully chosen and includes good tasting notes and a fair number of half bottles.

Directions: A435 (Evesham) from Cheltenham centre, hotel at 3rd lights opposite Pittvale Park

38 Evesham Road GL52 2AH
Map no: 3 SO92
Tel: 01242 518898
Chef: Eamonn Webster
Cost: Alc £26, fixed-price
L £14.50/D £19.50 H/wine
£9.25 ❗ Service exc
Credit cards: 💳 💳 💳 💳
Times: Last L 2pm/last D
9.30pm/10pm Fri & Sat Closed
1 wk Jan
Menus: A la carte, fixed-price L
& D
Seats: 30. No-smoking area
Additional: Children welcome
(over 8 at D); ❶ dishes, vegan/
other diets on request

CHELTENHAM, Staithes Restaurant ❀❀

Well crafted and reasonably priced dishes, served in a pleasantly informal atmosphere, give this restaurant a wide appeal

The provision of a range of moderately priced dishes, simply cooked in a predominantly modern English-style and served in an upmarket bistro setting, has proved a winning formula. A menu based on staple local ingredients changes every two months or so, making the most of seasonal availability. It is geared to appeal to a middle range of tastes, the strength lying in the execution of the dishes, and this in turn depends on hard-worked basic skills. Winter starters might include parsnip and apple soup, creamy steamed mussels, or a caramelised bacon salad, these perhaps followed by main courses such as braised breast of chicken, salmon en croûte, or

12 Suffolk Road GL50 2AQ
Map: 3 SO92
Tel: 01242 260666
Chef: Paul Lucas
Proprietor: Heather & Paul
Lucas
Cost: Alc £15.80-£26.35.
H/wine £9.95 Service exc
Credit cards: 💳 💳 💳 💳 OTHER
Times: L by reservation only,
7.30pm (Sat 7pm)-last D 10pm.
Closed Sun, Christmas wk, Bh
Mon, two wks in summer
Menus: A la carte

halibut in vermouth sauce. Crisply steamed fresh vegetables are liberally doused in butter, while desserts include well-made versions of such old favourites as bread and butter pudding. Home-made petits fours have replaced the commercially produced chocolates that were previously served with coffee. The wine list represents most areas of the world.

Seats: 24. No smoking in dining room
Additional: Children by arrangement only, ❶ dish, other diets by arrangement

Directions: Close to Cheltenham Boys College; near junction of Suffolk Road with Bath Road, on S side of town

CHIPPING CAMPDEN,
Cotswold House Hotel ❀❀

Consistently well-balanced, modern eclectic cooking in a delightful country house hotel

An eclectic mix of modern cooking styles makes up the short seasonal *carte* and daily set-price menu. Carefully chosen fresh ingredients are consistently well-handled and effectively complemented by suitable, sometimes imaginative, garnishes, while such extras as bread rolls, canapés and petits fours are all made in the hotel's own kitchen. Dishes worthy of note have included a trio of seafood ravioli with lemon grass, an inviting ballotine of Barbary duck with orange and figs, succulent sea bass set on an exciting crab sauce, and beef fillet with bittersweet shallots. English and French country cheeses – served with walnut bread or fruit – provide an alternative to such temptations as gingerbread parfait with white chocolate or a gratin of strawberries and raspberries with citrus fruit. Cafetière coffee is served with home-made sweets. The thoughtfully selected and informative wine list is being revised, but presumably will offer a similar width of choice and range of half bottles.

The Square GL55 6AN
Map no: 4 SP13
Tel: 01386 840330
Chef: Raymond Boreham
Proprietors: Robert & Gill Greenstock
Cost: *Alc* £26.50 fixed price L £15.75, D £16.50. H/wine £10.50 No service charge
Credit cards: 🔵 💳 💳
Menus: *A la carte*, fixed price L & D
Times: Last L 2pm, last D 9.30pm. Closed 24-28 Dec
Seats: 35. No smoking in dining room
Additional: Children over 8 permitted, children's portions; ❶ dishes, vegan/others on request

Directions: 1 mile north of A44 between Moreton-in-Marsh and Broadway on B4081

CHIPPING CAMPDEN, Noel Arms Hotel ❀

☺ *A fair selection of dishes is included on the fixed-price menu including noisettes of local lamb surrounded by a medley of mushrooms garnished with turned vegetables. This town-centre inn has been welcoming visitors for more than six centuries*

Menus: *A la carte* D, fixed-price Sun L, bar menu **Seats:** 60
Additional: Children welcome, children's portions; ❶ dishes, other diets on request
Directions: Town centre

High Street GL55 6AT
Map no: 4 SP13
Tel: 01386 840317
Chef: Mark Finegan
Proprietor: Neil John
Cost: Fixed-price D £15.75 (2 course) & £17.75/Sun L £10.95. H/wine £9.95 ❢ Service exc
Credit cards: 🔵 💳 💳 💳 OTHER
Times: Last D 9.45pm/Sun L 3pm

> Ginger originated in southeast Asia and is widely culti-vated in hot countries for its spicy, aromatic rhizomes. It was much appreciated in the Middle Ages, as a flavour-ing and as a sweetmeat, but had fallen out of use in Europe by the 18th century, except in cakes, puddings and confectionery. Currently, ginger (especially fresh ginger) is having something of a revival, used extensively in both savoury and sweet dishes.

FLETCHER
RESTAURANT

CHIPPING CAMPDEN,
Seymour House Hotel ❀❀

A town centre hotel proudly declaring its newly acquired two-rosette skills

A former market centre for the Cotswold wool trade, Chipping Campden was once described by the historian G M Trevelyan as 'the most beautiful village now left on the island'. Parts of the mainly Georgian building go back to the early 1700s, including one of the few original malt houses left in England. In the Malt House Bar light, mainly Italian, meals are served while the main restaurant is run by John Heckles, formerly at Ilkley's Box Tree. By his own admission he is fond of cooking fish dishes, such as sea bass with three mushrooms (shitake, monkey head, oyster) in olive and white truffle oils. An Italian bias also shows through on the three-course, fixed-price restaurant menu in the shape of 'gnochetti verdi al dolcelatte' (prepared with potato and spinach), 'ravioli di pesce' (pasta parcels filled with fresh market fish with a roast salmon sauce) and 'filetto al piatto' (thin slices of Scottish beef placed on an extremely hot plate sizzling with olive oil). Evesham Vale kebabs are skewers of fresh, herb-flavoured vegetables served on saffron rice with a sweet and sour sauce. There is a choice of home-made desserts.

Directions: Town centre – along the High Street

High Street GL55 6AH
Map no: 4 SP13
Tel: 01386 840429
Chef: John Eccles
Proprietor: Romavtik Hotel.
Manager: Felice Tocchin
Cost: Alc £18.95-£29.50, fixed-price Sun L £14.50. H/wine £9.95 ltr Service exc
Credit cards: 🂠 🪙 🂠 OTHER
Times: Last bar L 2.30pm/D 10pm
Menus: A la carte D, bar L menu, fixed-price Sun L
Additional: Children welcome, children's portions; ❶ dishes, vegan/other diets on request

CIRENCESTER, **The Crown Of Crucis** ❀

☺ *A two-floored restaurant in a traditional Cotswold stone building which offers imaginative cooking that's excellent value-for-money. The choice of dishes could include medallions of pork served in a 'tasty' Madeira sauce, and there is a colourful display of home-made sweets*

Menus: A la carte, fixed price L & D, bar menu
Seats: 70. Air conditioned
Additional: Children welcome, children's menu; ❶ menu, vegan/other on request
Directions: 3 miles E of Cirencester on A417 to Lechlade

Ampney Crucis GL7 5RS
Map: 3 SP00
Tel: 01285 851806
Chef: Kevin Clark
Proprietor: R K Mills
Cost: Alc £15, fixed price L (2 course) £7.45, D (3 course) £14 H/wine £6.55 ❗ Service exc
Credit cards: 🂠 🪙 🂠 💳 OTHER
Times: Last L 2.30pm, last D 10pm; Closed Christmas day

COLN ST ALDWYNS, **The New Inn** ❀❀

☺ *Modern influences bring new life to traditional English dishes in the character setting of this old inn*

Born of a decree by Elizabeth I that there should be a coaching inn within a day's travel of every major town, the New Inn was old when Wren built St Paul's. Locals, as well as travellers, flock here today, however, lured largely by the skilfully executed dishes featured on the imaginative fixed-price menus. The predominant style is English, in some cases a triumphant reinterpretation of old English recipes, but the latest culinary trends are also detectable – in fish soup with rouille and croûtons, or grilled crottin cheese with endive. A typical meal might begin with air-dried tomatoes and crostini, followed by breast of chicken with pesto mash and beetroot sauce. Desserts can have a touch of the exotic, too: try the fruit and meringue gateau with Thai spices and mulled fruit syrup. An interesting range of cheeses includes cider-washed Celtic

Coln St Aldwyns GL7 5AN
Map: 4 SP10
Tel: 01285 750651
Chef: Tony Robson-Burrel

The New Inn

Proprietors: Brian & Sandra-Anne Evans
Cost: Fixed price Sun L £13.50, fixed price D £21. H/wine £8.75
❗ Service exc
Credit cards: ▨ ▦ ▨ OTHER
Times: Last Sun L 2.15pm, last D 9.30pm
Menus: Fixed price D and Sun L, bar menu
Seats: 40
Additional: Children welcome, children's portions; ❤ dishes, other diets on request

Promise, the soft Livarot from Normandy (traditionally circled by strips of sedge) and creamy blue Fourme d'Ambert, an ancient cheese from the Auvergne region.

Directions: 8 miles E of Cirencester between Bibury (B4425) and Fairford (A417)

GLOUCESTER,
Hatherley Manor Hotel

A 17th-century manor house hotel conveniently positioned just north of the city. Good use of quality produce is made on the more imaginative seasonal dishes. Recent inspection meals have praised the game terrine with fruit chutney, the robust roast pheasant with braised wild mushrooms and the home-made apple strudel

Down Hatherley Lane
GL2 9QA
Map no: 3 SO81
Tel: 01452 730217
Chef: Jerry Davis
Cost: Alc £21-£28, fixed-price L £9.75-£11.25/D £16.00
Credit cards: ▨ ▦ ▨ ▣ OTHER
Times: Last D 9.30pm

Directions: From Gloucester take A38 towards Tewkesbury. Take right turn signed Down Hatherley

GLOUCESTER, **Hatton Court** ✿

Set atop Upton Hill, this well maintained manor house offers sweeping views across the Severn Valley. The main restaurant is attractively positioned with eye catching picture windows, and offers a dedicated approach to cooking. The result is simply crafted, enjoyable meals based on seasonal ingredients. There is a wide selection of wines

Upton Hill
Upton St Leonards GL4 8DE
Map no: 3 SO81
Tel: 01452 617412
Chef: Dave Murphy
Proprietor: Hatton Hotel Group.
Manager: Colin Parcell
Cost: *Alc* from £23.45, fixed-price L £14.50/D £19.95.
H/wine £9.95 ❢ Service exc
Credit cards: 〓 〓 〓 ᴾ OTHER
Times: 12.30pm-last L 2pm.
7.30pm-last D 10pm
Seats: 80. No smoking in dining room
Additional: Children welcome, children's menu; ◐ menu, vegan/other diets on request

Directions: Three miles from Gloucester on B4037

LOWER SLAUGHTER,
Lower Slaughter Manor ✿✿✿

A country house hotel that lives up to expectations in every respect

Cheltenham GL54 2HP
Map no: 4 SP12
Tel: 01451 820456
Chef: Michael Benjamin
Proprietors: Audrey & Peter Marks
Cost: *Alc* £36, fixed-price
L £12.95 & £17.95/D £32.50.
H/wine £16 ❢ Service exc
Credit cards: 〓 〓 〓 ᴾ
Times: Last L 2pm (2.30pm Sun), last D 9.30pm (10pm Fri & Sat).
Closed 3 wks Jan
Menus: *A la carte,* fixed-price L & D

Audrey and Peter Marks' gracious, 17th-century, grade II listed manor house is well situated for exploring the unspoilt beauty of the Cotswolds. It stands in neatly kept gardens with a croquet lawn, putting green and tennis courts, beside the village church and the shallow Slaughter Brook. Within, the public rooms have been elegantly, lavishly furnished with stunning fabrics, comfortable seating and abundant fresh flowers. Service is professional and hospitable and guests are made to feel extremely welcome.
Head chef Michael Benjamin, who was previously at Gidleigh Park

in Devon, produces exciting dishes, wherever possible making full use of fresh local produce, as well as herbs from the garden, local honey and home-made preserves. The dinner *carte* offers a really wide choice at each course. At inspection roasted sweetbreads, served with a fricassée of wild mushrooms, globe artichoke and tomatoes in a richly flavoured reduction of the cooking juices, established a standard that remained high for the rest of the meal. A succulent fillet of beef, set on a bed of horseradish-flavoured mash and accompanied by a red onion confit and baby vegetables, showed how well powerful tastes and different textures can be balanced. The plate of four caramel desserts included a smooth crème caramel, hot soufflé, rice pudding and caramel ice-cream. The wine list has a selection of Californian and other New World bins worthy of special comment. Bordeaux and Burgundies are plentiful too.

Seats: 36. No smoking in dining room
Additional: Children over 10 permitted; ♥ menu, other diets with notice

Directions: Off the A429 signposted 'The Slaughters'. Half a mile into village on the right

LOWER SLAUGHTER,

Washbourne Court Hotel ❀❀❀

Unusual flavour combinations and skilful cooking characterise the food at this attractive Cotswold hotel

A quintessentially English village is the setting for this pretty hotel of honey-coloured Cotswold stone. It dates from the 17th century and stands in four acres of grounds alongside the River Eye. The atmosphere is one of professional efficiency coupled with natural friendliness, and the high point of any visit must be the delicious cooking of chef Stuart Macleod. Combining unusual flavours, he produces dishes of great technical skill using the best seasonally available produce. The daily changing 'Cotswold Market Menu', offers good value for money with a choice of three dishes at each course. These might include terrine of Cotswold pigeon with a crisp walnut salad; tenderloin of local pork encased in Parma ham and basil and set on a spicy tomato salsa, and chocolate marshmallow with a compote of summer fruit.

The *carte* showcases some signature dishes, and divides the main courses between fish, meat, and a vegetarian option. An inspection meal commenced with a gently warmed casserole of native oysters and water asparagus with a smoked salmon feuilleté and beurre blanc, and was followed by tender pot-roasted chump of Welsh lamb set on a lime and poppy seed dressing with a Swiss cheese and sage gnocchi – unexpected flavours perhaps, but executed with élan. The dish came with a base of onion marmalade and some baby leeks and carrots, plus a side plate of turned carrots, courgette, spinach mousse, dauphinoise potatoes and baby corn, and while this might demonstrate a lack of restraint, each element was sympathetically treated and accurately cooked. Soufflés are a speciality – a marmalade and malt whisky soufflé with cinnamon butterscotch sauce, was a model example. There is a comprehensive wine list with representation from around the world, including several half bottles.

Lower Slaughter GL54 2HS
Map no: 4 SP12
Tel: 01451 822143
Chef: Stuart McLeod and Anthony Duce
Proprietor: Michael Pender. Manager: Ahmet Ulun
Cost: *Alc* from £30, fixed-price D £25.95. H/wine £10.47 Service inc
Credit cards: ▨ ▩ ▤ OTHER
Times: Last L 2.30pm/D 9.15pm
Menus: *A la carte,* fixed-price D, light L menu
Seats: 36 (+40 on riverside terrace). No smoking in dining room
Additional: Children welcome (no babies); ♥ dishes, vegan/ other diets on request

Directions: Off A429 village centre by the river

MORETON-IN-MARSH,
Manor House Hotel ❀

Contemporary French and English carte, fixed-price and Sunday lunch menus. Chef Luc Gabbard produces simple but appealing dishes along the lines of pan-roasted guinea fowl, oven-baked trout, traditional lamb stew, or spinach and Ricotta cheese canneloni

Menus: A la carte, fixed-price L & D, bar menu
Seats: 50. No smoking in dining room
Additional: Children welcome, children's portions; ❤ menu, other diets on request
Directions: On the A429 (Fosse Way) – town centre

High Street GL56 0LJ
Map no: 4 SP23
Tel: 01608 650501
Chef: Daniel Giallombardo
Proprietor: Coraltrend Ltd.
Manager: Duncan Williams
Cost: Alc from £25, fixed-price L from £8.50/D £19.50. H/wine £10.50 ❢ No service charge
Credit cards: ▨ ▨ ▨ ▨ OTHER
Times: Last L 2pm/D 9.30pm

MORETON-IN-MARSH,
Marsh Goose Restaurant ❀❀

A spirit of daring results in genuinely inventive modern dishes in a Cotswold town restaurant

This is a smart restaurant in a smart Cotswold town run by smart staff in an accomplished and confident style. The confidence is undoubtedly born of success, and a solid track record in the kitchen. Sonya Kidney relies on '30 minutes of stress' each morning to devise the day's three menus and starts producing with the help of a small team. At lunchtime there is a set three course and reduced choice menu, while for dinner there is slightly more elaboration. There is nothing staid or traditional about the cooking, which, at a recent inspection, showed a fondness for matching meat with fish, as in slices of rare roast beef with marinated anchovies and a gently seasoned tarragon cream dressing, or delicate fillets of neatly folded lemon sole, with beetroot, crispy bacon, capers and saffron cream dressing. The ideas are inventive and the execution is polished. Vegetables might also be usefully off-beat. Desserts include poached pear and rhubarb with mascarpone and a light shortbread biscuit. Gutsy cooking is matched by thick, strong espresso and a thoughtful wine list.

Directions: In the High Street opposite the war memorial

High Street GL56 0AX
Map no: 4 SP23
Tel: 01608 652111
Chef: Sonya Kidney
Proprietor: Gordon Campbell-Gray
Cost: Alc L from £18, fixed-price L £13.50, fixed-price D £23. H/wine £8.50. Service exc
Credit cards: ▨ ▨ ▨
Times: 12.30-last L 2.30pm, 7.30pm-last D 9.45pm. Closed Sun D, Mon
Menus: A la carte L, fixed-price L & D, Sunday L
Seats: 60. No smoking in dining room
Additional: Children permitted, children's portions; ❤ dishes; other diets on request

PAINSWICK, **Painswick Hotel** ❀❀

Excellent fresh fish could well be the highlight of a meal at this delightful country house hotel

A Palladian building at the centre of the village, this hotel – once the home of wealthy rectors – still smacks of country house style with its range of public areas and individually decorated bedrooms. In fact, the atmosphere is friendly and unassuming and the surroundings just quirky enough to be interesting. The kitchen is one area that takes itself seriously. Callum Williams and his team maintain an absolute dedication to standards. The menu is straightforward (though not without some original twists). The excellence of the cooking lies in the uncomplicated preparation of fresh ingredients which include seafood from a saltwater tank and salmon smoked on the premises. A dinner enjoyed one evening this

Painswick Hotel

Kemps Lane GL6 6YB
Map no: 3 SO80
Tel: 01452 812160
Chef: Calum Williamson
Proprietor: S Moore.
Manager: Julia Robb
Cost: *Alc* £28, fixed-price
L £14.75, D £23.50. H/wine
£10.50 ! Service inc
Credit cards: ▨ ▨ ▨ OTHER
Times: 12.30-last L 1.45pm,
7.30pm-last D 9.30pm
Menus: *A la carte,* fixed-price
L & D
Seats: 60. No-smoking area
Additional: Children welcome,
children's portions; ❂ menu,
other diets on request

spring began with a warm salad of asparagus, mussels and prawns
with a tomato flesh brunoise garnish. The main course was a lightly
blackened fillet of plaice served on ratatouille and accompanied by
a side plate of crisp, well seasoned vegetables. Some half bottles are
included in a widely ranging wine list which also offers a good span
of prices.

Directions: Painswick is on A46, the Stroud/Cheltenham road.
The turning into Kemps Lane is just near the church

STONEHOUSE, Stonehouse Court ✿

*Traditional menus can be enjoyed in this country house atmosphere. Chef
Alan Postill creates his dishes from freshly prepared ingredients – many
of the herbs used are taken from the hotel's own kitchen garden. For
example, roast back of lamb wrapped in bacon with basil and red currant*

Menus: *A la carte,* fixed-price L & D, bar menu
Seats: 45. No cigars or pipes
Additional: Children welcome, children's menu; ❂ menu,
vegan/other diets on request
Directions: M5 exit 13/A419 (Stroud); 1.5 miles from Mway, 1 mile
from Stonehouse

Bristol Road GL10 3RA
Map no: 3 SO80
Tel: 01453 825155
Chef: Alan Postill
Proprietors: Arcadian.
Manager: Simon Courtenay-
Warren
Cost: *Alc* £28, fixed-price
L £12/D £16.75 (4 course).
H/wine £10.50 ! Service inc
Credit cards: ▨ ▨ ▨ ▨ OTHER
Times: Last L 2pm/D
9.30pm/9.45pm Fri & Sat

STOW-ON-THE-WOLD, Fosse Manor ✿

☺ *Cooking is a highlight in this hospitable, family-run hotel. A good
choice of temptingly described, imaginative dishes such as warm salad of
black pudding with crisp bacon, sauté potatoes and poached egg. Carte or
fixed- price dinners and Sunday lunches can be enjoyed in a very pleasant
atmosphere*

Menus: *A la carte,* fixed-price L, bar menu
Seats: 70. No smoking in dining room
Additional: Children welcome, children's menu; ❂ menu,
Vegan/other diets on request
Directions: One mile S of Stow on the A429 (Cirencester)

Cheltenham GL54 1JX
Map no: 4 SP12
Tel: 01451 830354
Chef: Mark Lawson Smith
Proprietors: B Johnson (Consort)
Cost: *Alc* £17.50, fixed-price
L £13.95. H/wine £10.95 (litre) !
Service exc
Credit cards: ▨ ▨ ▨ ▨ OTHER
Times: Last L 2pm/D 10pm.
Closed Dec 22-29

STOW-ON-THE-WOLD, **Grapevine Hotel** ✿

☺ *Good quality dishes prepared with care are the hall mark of this village-centre inn. Settle in the conservatory restaurant and choose prawn beignets on a tomato and shallot salad, or lamb noisettes on a bed of celeriac*

Sheep Street GL54 1AU
Map no: 4 SP12
Tel: 01451 830344
Chef: Michael James
Proprietor: Sandra (Sam) Elliott
(Best Western)
Cost: Fixed-price D £17.50/Sun
L £9.95. H/wine £9 ⦿ Service
exc
Credit cards: 🌑 💳 💳 💳 OTHER
Times: Last L 2.30pm/D 9.30pm.
Closed 24 Dec 24-Jan 11
Menus: Fixed-price D & Sun L,
bar menu
Seats: 50+20. No smoking in
dining room
Additional: Children welcome,
children's menu, ❂ menu,
vegan/other diets on request

Directions: Off A429 at Stow onto A436 (Chipping Norton), 150 yards on right facing small green

STOW-ON-THE-WOLD,
Old Farmhouse Hotel ✿

☺ *An enthusiastically run converted farmhouse, lying just outside Stow-on-the-Wold, where staff work hard to create a welcoming atmosphere. The restaurant serves hearty, country-style meals. These may include poached monkfish with a scallop, prawn and vermouth sauce or vegetable and Stilton pancakes*

Lower Swell GL54 1LF
Map no: 4 SP12
Tel: Freephone 0500 657842
Chef: Graham Simmonds
Proprietor: Erik Burger
Cost: Fixed price L (2 course)
£10.50, D (3 course) £15.95.
H/wine £8.50 ⦿ Service inc
Credit cards: 🌑 💳
Times: Noon-last L 2pm/D 9pm.
Closed 2 weeks Jan

Menus: Fixed-price L & D, bar menu
Seats: 30. No smoking in dining room
Additional: Children welcome, children's menu; ❂ dishes,
vegan/other diets on request
Directions: 1 mile W of Stow on the B4068

STOW-ON-THE-WOLD,
Wyck Hill House Hotel ✿✿✿

Stylish country house surroundings for a variety of English dishes with Mediterranean and exotic influences

There are panoramic views over the Windrush Valley from this early 18th-century country mansion, which is set in its own fine grounds. Comfortably furnished day rooms include an attractive cedar-panelled library, a clubby cocktail bar and a foyer lounge with deep-cushioned sofas and an open fire. The restaurant is of contrasting styles, ornate and traditional in the lofty inner room with its rich damask walls and central floral display, and rather more spartan in its conservatory extension. Hospitality remains a strength and under

Burford Road GL54 1HY
Map no: 4 SP12
Tel: 01451 831936
Chef: Ian Smith
Proprietor: Lyric.
Manager: Peter Robinson
Cost: *Alc* dinner £30-£36, fixed-price L £11.95 & £13.50.
H/wine £11.95. Service exc
Credit cards: 🌑 💳 💳 💳 OTHER
Times: Last L 2pm, last D
9.30pm Daily
Menus: *A la carte* D,
fixed-price L

the direction of manager Peter Robinson staff throughout the hotel provide particularly friendly and attentive service.

Chef Ian Smith continues to produce enjoyable, well presented and competently cooked meals, which begin with canapés and good home-made rolls. The menus offer a good range of dishes from the exotic and spicy to the simple and tasty, with a separate vegetarian choice. At an early spring meal our inspector, choosing from the fixed-price menu, plumped for a mousseline of sole wrapped in leeks, topped with scallops and accompanied by delicious wild mushrooms and a butter sauce; a successful starter, having more flavour than the main course, pavé of lamb with ratatouille, potato galette, tapenade and a fresh tomato coulis. The meal concluded with warm lemon tart served with honey ice-cream. The wine list is clearly presented and reasonably priced.

Directions: A424 (Burford) 1.5 miles from Stow

Seats: 70. No smoking. Air conditioned
Additional: Children welcome, children's portions; ❶ menu, vegan/other diets on request

TETBURY, Calcot Manor ❀❀

Choose from a skilfully executed range of modern European dishes in the timeless setting of a former abbey

Calcot GL8 8YJ
Map no: 3 ST89
Tel: 01666 890391
Chef: Edward Portlock
Proprietors: Richard Ball (Pride of Britain)
Cost: Fixed price L £17/D £25
Credit cards: ▨ ▩ ▩ ▩ OTHER
Times: Last L 2pm / D 9.30pm
Menu: Fixed price L & D, bar menu
Seats: 50. No smoking in dining room
Additional: Children welcome, children's menu; ❶ menu, vegan/other on request

The owners of Calcot Manor describe it as 'a place of tranquillity where the past is always present', and, since the Cistercian monks would have routinely fed and housed travellers, it is not inappropriate that this sprawling Cotswold building which once formed part of Kingswood Abbey is now a hotel. Times change, however, and today's fairly formal restaurant offers its guests fixed-price seasonal menus of dishes in modern European style. Head chef Edward Portlock, who has worked his way up in Calcot's kitchens, cooks with both skill and originality, bringing a delicate – sometimes even exotic – touch to robust local products. A recent inspection lunch began with a generous serving of smooth, chicken liver parfait; followed by leg and breast of poussin with a rich, clear sauce of wild mushrooms, then a deliciously light, subtly flavoured, hot pineapple soufflé. Locally baked flavoured breads are worthy of note for their quality and flavour. Service is pleasant, achieving the ideal balance of friendliness and professionalism. An extensive and usefully annotated wine list includes some New World labels.

Directions: 4 miles W of Tetbury on A4135 close to intersection with A45

TETBURY, Close Hotel ✿✿

Inventive combinations and interesting garnishes feature in a good choice of dishes with a British regional slant

A good choice of dishes from the *carte* and fixed-price menus is offered at this smart hotel restaurant. At a summer meal, canapés were served in the bar and garden, and our inspector's meal began with warm rolls and a pungent crab soup topped with a generous blob of herb butter and filled with small crabmeat tortellini. These complex garnishes were more successful than anticipated, particularly in the main course – slivers of pink duck breast fanned around a rich onion marmalade served with a lightly creamed sesame sauce. For pudding, a delicate yoghurt and citrus terrine came with vibrant spiced rhubarb compote. Alternative dishes might be Double Gloucester and ham tart as a starter, served with salad, and a choice of four vegetarian dishes available as either a starter or main course, such as layers of crisp aubergine with avocado mousse and a tomato oil. Other main courses are divided between fish and meat sections, typically, fillets of trout on herb pasta with caper and almond cream, and cannon of lamb with a rosemary crust and apricot gravy. There is also a good selection of wine, with several half bottles and wines by the glass.

Directions: Centre of Tetbury – M4 exit 17 or 18 follow signs

8 Long Street GL8 8AQ
Map no: 3 ST89
Tel: 01666 502272
Chef: Paul Welch
Proprietors: Virgin.
Manager: Sean Spencer
Cost: *Alc* from £29.50, fixed-price L £18.50/D £25.25.
H/wine £14 ❢ Service exc
Credit cards: 🂠 📷 📷 💳 OTHER
Times: Last L 2pm, Last D 9.45pm
Menus: A la carte, fixed-price L & D, bar menu
Seats: 36. Smoking restricted
Additional: Children over 6 permitted until 7pm, children's menu; ❻ dishes, vegan/other diets on request

TETBURY, Hunters Hall Inn ✿

☺ *A popular inn with an intimate little restaurant serving value-for-money meals. Fresh local produce is used to create dishes which may include robust soups, or fillet of salmon with a creamy blue cheese sauce and asparagus. To finish the meal leave room for the selection of home-made puddings*

Directions: On the A4135 4 miles W of Tetbury

Kingscote GL8 8XZ
Map no: 3 ST89
Tel: 01453 860393
Chef: Kevin Stokes
Proprietor: David Barnett-Roberts (Logis of Great Britain)
Cost: *Alc* £17. H/wine £7.75 ❢ Service not included
Credit cards: 🂠 📷 📷 💳 OTHER
Times: 11am-last L 2pm, 6pm-last D 9.45pm D
Menus: A la carte L & D, bar menu
Seats: 45. No-smoking area
Additional: Children welcome, children's menu; ❻ dishes, vegan/other diets on request

Rocket or arugula is a Mediterranean herb that has been popular since Roman times. It enhances any salad, as it has a pungent, peppery taste, and is used as an alternative to wilted spinach.

TETBURY, **Snooty Fox** ✿

The 16th-century coaching inn is ideally located in the centre of Tetbury, overlooking the town hall and the market place. Modern English cooking is served in the elegant oak-panelled restaurant, and there is an extensive choice from both the carte and fixed-price menus

Directions: Town centre opposite the Market Place

Market Place GL8 8DD
Map no: 3 ST89
Tel: 01666 502436
Chef: Stephen Woodcock
Proprietor: Hiscox family
Cost: Alc £25, fixed-price
L £14/D £18. H/wine £8.95
Service exc
Credit cards: 🃏 ▨ ▨ 💷 OTHER
Times: 12.30-last L 1.45pm,
7.30pm-last D 9.45pm/9.15pm
Sun & Bhs
Menus: *A la carte,* fixed-price
L & D, bar menu
Seats: 52. No smoking in dining
room
Additional: Children welcome
(over 5 dinner), children's
portions; ✆ menu, vegan/other
diets on request

TEWKESBURY,
Tewkesbury Park Hotel ✿

☺ *Standing in 176 acres of parkland, this hotel, built around an 18th century mansion, offers reasonably priced meals in either the Garden restaurant or the Pavilion. The highlight of a recent inspection meal was a darne of salmon topped with a nut crust, served on a bed of fresh spinach*

Directions: From M5 exit 9 /A438 (Tewkesbury), onto A38 passing the Abbey and in 500yds entrance to Lincoln Green Lane is on right

Lincoln Green Lane GL20 7DN
Map: 3 SO83
Tel: 01684 295405
Chef: Cliff Owens
Proprietor: Country Club Hotels.
Manager: Peter Bech
Cost: Fixed price L £13/D £18
Credit cards: 🃏 ▨ ▨ 💷
Times: Noon-last L 2pm
5.30pm; last D 10pm. Closed
Sat L
Menus: Fixed price L & D, bar
menu
Seats: 100. No smoking in
dining room
Additional: Children welcome,
children's menu; ✆ dishes,
vegan/other on request

UPPER SLAUGHTER,

Lords of the Manor 🏵🏵🏵

A grand name for a grand country house hotel and restaurant where a young chef's talent is a considerable attraction

GL54 2JD
Map no: 4 SP12
Tel: 01451 820243
Chef: Robert-Clive Dixon
Gen Manager: Richard Young
Cost: Alc £38, fixed-price L
£17.95, fixed-price D £29.50.
H/wine £12.95 ▮ Service inc
Credit cards: 🔲 🔲 🔲 🔲 OTHER
Times: Last L 2pm, Last D
9.30pm. Closed 2-11 Jan 1996
Menus: A la carte, fixed-price
L & D, Sunday L
Seats: 65. No smoking
Additional: Children welcome,
children's menu/portions.
♥ dishes, vegan/other diets
on request

Robert-Clive Dixon has been called a rising star among chefs.
His stellar ascent continues as his sometimes daring, but always
rewarding, cooking attracts customers to this ancient manor house
hotel and restaurant. The original part of the house dates from
1650, and for 200 years it was the parish rectory. The Victorians
added considerably to it but, because all their external facings were
also of mellow, yellow Cotswold stone, the 'new' blends well with
the old. The eight acres of gardens, parkland and lake are
considered to be one of the loveliest small estates in England.
Inside the house are all the quintessential period elements – low
ceilings, narrow passages, mahogany panelling and that special
atmosphere unique to big, old houses. Not to dress for dinner
would be a solecism.
   Choose from two and three-course, set-price lunch and dinner
menus, or the *carte*. The cooking is best described as country style
with a modern influence. Among the starters are French goats' milk
cheese from Sancerre with grilled peppers, olives, Parma ham and
french beans, fish soup with rouille, Gruyère and sippets, and
tagliatelle with wild mushrooms and white truffle oil dressing.
Main courses are prepared with the same degree of controlled
imagination. Fillet of turbot cooked on a broth of Savoy cabbage,
ham hock, salami and garlic, or roast Cornish lamb with warm cous
cous salad, plum tomatoes and anchovies, and daube of Scottish
beef with heart and a roast parsnip purée. The consistency of his
approach is apparent. Desserts include hot plum soufflé with vanilla
ice-cream, and chocolate and rose-water mousse with orange
blossom brûlée. The wine list leaves few countries unvisited, and
begins with descriptions of wines available by the glass, and house
recommendations.

Directions: Follow the sign towards The Slaughters off the A429.
The restaurant is located in the centre of Upper Slaughter

WINCHCOMBE, Wesley House ❀❀

A smart guest house-cum-restaurant with a European menu based on classical training and French experience

High Street GL54 5LT
Map no: 4 SP02
Tel: 01242 602366
Chef: Jonathan Lewis
Proprietors: Jonathan Lewis and Matthew Brown
Cost: Fixed-price L £12.50/D £22.50. H/wine £8.95 ⚑ Service exc
Credit cards: ▨ ▦ ▨ OTHER
Times: Last L 2.30pm, last D 9.30-10pm. Closed Sun D
Menus: Fixed-price L & D, bar menu
Seats: 50. No-smoking in dining room
Additional: Children welcome, children's portions; ❦ menu, vegan/other diets on request

John Wesley was once here, but there is no hint of his temperance at this inviting restaurant and guest house. The two owners have invested their many years experience in the hotel business to create this small, peaceful haven. There is a measured and well pitched style, based on chef Jonathan Lewis' classical training boosted by a three-month sabbatical in France. Dinner is slightly more elaborate. An inspection meal chosen from the reasonably-priced lunch menu included home-baked black olive brioche, an earthy pork and duckling terrine served with a raspberry dressing, and ballantine of chicken – unfortunately let down by a poorly executed sauce – and a beautifully light citrus-flavoured bread and butter pudding. The menu also offers several types of fish – brill, cod and plaice – from a supplier heartily endorsed by the chef. There is a serious wine list with a varied selection, and service is charming and assured.

Directions: In centre of Winchcombe on the main road

GREATER MANCHESTER

BURY, Normandie Hotel ❀❀❀

French cuisine with hearty flavours and some refinement is offered at this hotel in the foothills of the Pennines

Mother and son team Gillian and Max Moussa have created a gastronomic haven in the foothills of the Pennines. The Normandie, set high on a hillside over Bury with commanding views of Greater Manchester, is made up of a number of old buildings, with no common architectural theme, that in their day have been an inn, a French restaurant, and latterly, a hotel. Drinks are offered in the spacious lounge, and this gives guests the chance to pore over the two menus. The fixed price menu offers good value for money but chef Pascal Pommier's abilities are best reflected in the à la *carte* dishes. Strong, hearty flavours with refinement are characteristic, and a boudin blanc with chick peas proved an excellent marriage of

Elbut Lane
Birtle BL9 6UT
Map no: 7 SD81
Tel: 0161 764 1170
Chef: Pascal Pommier
Proprietors: Gillian & Max Moussa
Cost: *Alc* £24-£35, fixed-price L £15.60/D £18.95. H/wine £11.25 ⚑ Service inc
Credit cards: ▨ ▦ ▨ ▣ OTHER
Times: Last L 2pm, last D 9.30pm. Closed Sun, Mon L, 1 wk Easter, 2 wks after Dec 25
Menus: *A la carte*, fixed-price L & D

textures and flavours, the yielding boudin a contrast to the crunchy chick peas. Starters also include a home-made soup of ham and spring vegetables, and pan-fried scallops with a grain mustard sauce and roast potatoes. Among the main courses are steamed sea bass with soya sauce and spring onions, and fillet of beef with port sauce and wild mushrooms. Our inspector chose 'Magret de canette au cassis' – roast duck breast, served pink with an intensely flavoured cassis sauce – served with spinach and Anna potatoes. The sweet sauce was balanced by the earthy spinach and crunchy potato cake. Puddings are a highlight and there are several fruity options, such as pear bavarois, iced nougat with poached pineapple and white rum, and a banana soufflé with toffee ice-cream, which was a shining example of how this dish should be made.

The lengthy wine list represents an ongoing love affair for Max Moussa, who has a passion for wine. It features many classic names priced at a sensible level, and plenty of half bottles.

Directions: From M66 exit 2, turn right Wash Lane, right into Willow Street, right at B6222, left into Elbut Lane, up hill 1 mile

Seats: 45. No cigars or pipes
Additional: Children welcome, children's portions; ♥ dishes, vegan on request, other diets with notice

MANCHESTER, Holiday Inn Crowne Plaza ❀

A large, impressive hotel built in the grand style of the Edwardian era. The French Restaurant offers a carte of French-style cooking with a careful balance of flavours and textures. Try the char-grilled sirloin steak or the oxtail braised in whisky and served with butter beans and mange tout

Peter Street M60 2DS
Map no: 7 SJ89
Tel: 0161 236 3333
Chef: Bernard Farant
Proprietor: Holiday Inn.
Manager: Bruno Lucchi
Cost: Alc £38-£46, fixed-price D £32.50 (4 course) H/wine £10.50 ❢ Service exc
Credit cards: ⬛ 💳 💳 🏧
Times: 7pm-last D 11pm Closed Sun, Bhs
Menus: A la carte, fixed-price D
Seats: 40. Air conditioned
Additional: Children welcome, children's portions; ♥ dishes, vegan/other diets on request

Directions: City centre, heart of theatreland and close to Arndale precinct

MANCHESTER, Little Yang Sing ❀❀

☺ *A popular off-shoot of one of Manchester's more famous Chinese restaurants*

Little Yang Sing is a hugely popular Cantonese restaurant located on the edge of Manchester's bustling Chinatown. The extensive *carte* is supplemented by a long list of dim sum, which go down well

17 George Street M1 4HE
Map no: 7 SJ89
Tel: 0161 228 7722
Chef: Au Ting Chung
Proprietor: Christine Yeung
Cost: Alc £14, fixed-price L £8.95/D £15. H/wine £9 Service exc

with the local Chinese community. It is easy to be overwhelmed by the vast range of dishes on offer, but the helpful staff are pleased to help in constructing a tailor-made meal. There is also a wide choice of set dinners available in the evening. A recent lunch began with some dim sum, steamed chicken's feet with a black bean sauce, and a subtly spiced pork and brawn dumpling, and 'pak far' soup which was beautifully textured, marrying smooth beancurd with crisp vegetables. Do try some of the more unusual items, such as the rich and succulent braised spiced brisket dish with broccoli. A diner at another table was heard to remark, 'This is the best Chinese food in Britain.' While this is of course debatable, it would be hard to make such a judgment without first sampling this benchmark cuisine.

Directions: Behind Piccadilly Plaza on the corner of George and Charlotte Street, on Metrolink route

Credit cards: 🔳 💳 💳 OTHER
Times: Last L 5.30pm/D 11.15pm. Closed Xmas day
Menus: *A la carte,* fixed-price L & D
Seats: 90. Air conditioned. No smoking
Additional: Children welcome, children's menu; ❶ dishes, vegan/other diets on request

MANCHESTER, Market Restaurant ❀❀

Pleasant, informal restaurant opposite the old fish market serves something to please every taste

Relaxed and unpretentious though it is, this informal eating place has carved itself a real niche in the Manchester restaurant scene. A monthly-changing seasonal *carte* in modern British style includes six dishes at each course. Smooth chicken liver terrine with onion chutney or houmus with warm pitta bread, for example, might be followed by top rib of beef in a green peppercorn sauce or wild mushroom pancakes; Sweets are something of a speciality here, particularly as featured in the meetings of the Pudding Club, held on Tuesday evenings approximately five times a year and billed as 'ideal for those of us who read menus from the bottom upwards' – a light main course preceding five different puddings. Should your taste buds be titillated by the savoury, on the other hand, you will prefer the Starters Society meals, where you are free to sample as much as you care to of about 15 hot and cold dishes. On these occasions speciality beers supplement a main wine list which contains some organic and alcohol-free examples as well as a New World selection.

Directions: On the corner of Edge Street and High Street, close to Craft Village. Nearest Metro station – High Street

Edge Street
104 High Street M4 1HQ
Map no: 7 SJ89
Tel: 0161 834 3743
Chefs: Mary-Rose Edgecombe, Paul Mertz and Dawn Wellens
Proprietors: Peter & Anne O'Grady and Mary-Rose Edgecombe
Cost: *Alc* from £17.50. H/wine £4.75 ❗ Service exc
Credit cards: 🔳 💳 💳 💳 OTHER
Times: 6pm-Last D 9.30pm. Closed Sun, Mon, Tues, 1 week Xmas, 1 week Easter, 4 weeks Aug
Menus: *A la carte*
Seats: 40. Smoking not encouraged
Additional: Children welcome, children's portions; ❶ dishes, vegan/other diets on request

MANCHESTER,
Moss Nook Restaurant ❀❀

Though not cheap, this French restaurant in the grand manner provides an appropriate setting for a special occasion

One eats in style at this long-established and prestigious restaurant. Lace tablecloths are set with silver and fresh flowers, curtains are elaborately draped, and mirrors, ornate clocks and cherubs deck the walls. The atmosphere remains intimate, however, and there is neither condescension nor obsequiousness in the service provided by knowledgeable, and in most cases, long-serving staff. A wide-ranging *carte* in French classical style (changed quarterly, though some popular dishes may be carried over), is supplemented by the

Ringway Road M22 5WD
Map no: 7 SJ89
Tel: 0161 437 4778
Chef: Kevin Lofthouse
Proprietors: Pauline & Derek Harrison
Cost: *Alc* £35, fixed-price L £16.50 (5 courses), fixed-price D £29.50 (7 courses). H/wine £9.90 ❗ Service exc
Credit cards: 🔳 💳 💳 💳
Times: Last L 1.30pm, Last D 9.30pm. Closed Sat L, Sun, Mon, 2 weeks Xmas

'Menu Surprise', chef Kevin Loftman's personal selection of dishes being designed, it states, "to take you through an adventure of flavours and textures from canapés to coffee." Saucing is all important and comes in a variety of styles. At the time of our last visit, goujons of chicken which had been marinated in yoghurt and coriander were served with a rich garlic and butter sauce, and the fish course – grilled medley of fish and shellfish – was partnered by a light béarnaise. A shallot and Dijon mustard sauce then proved the perfect complement for fillet of beef. The predominantly French wine list is extensive and carefully researched; it includes some half bottles and house wine from £9.50.

Menus: *A la carte,* fixed-price L & D
Seats: 65. No pipes
Additional: No children under 12; ❂ dishes; other diets on prior request

Directions: Close to Manchester airport – at junction of Ringway with B5166

MANCHESTER,
Victoria & Albert Hotel ❀❀

Flamboyant and colourful dishes served in a refined atmosphere

Created from old warehouses by the River Irwell, the Victoria and Albert retains the exposed brick walls, wooden beams and iron pillars of another era. There are several restaurants and cafés within the hotel, but of particular note is the Sherlock Holmes Restaurant. Here John Benson-Smith and his team have produced a series of imaginative and exciting menus, including a huge selection of breakfast dishes and a special vegetarian selection. The food is colourful and flamboyant but underpinned by a sound classical technique. An example of this style might be the delicious turbot poached in champagne and chicken stock and served with spinach and a generous helping of wild mushrooms in a cream sauce. Other main courses might include chargrilled sirloin steak served with chips and mustard, or perhaps poached fillet of plaice with prawns and a parsley sauce, and from the vegetarian menu, chick pea and mushroom curry with herb rice. For dessert the selection of cheeses from the trolley are worth a mention, but for sheer indulgence try the sherry trifle with generous helpings of cream.

Water Street M60 9EA
Map no: 7 SJ89
Tel: 0161 832 1188
Chef: John Benson-Smith
Proprietors: Granada.
Manager: Jim Diamond
Cost: *Alc* £27, fixed-price L £17.50/D £35 (5 course). H/wine £12.75 ❗ Service inc
Credit cards: 🌑 📇 📧 💳
Times: Last L 2pm, last D 9.30pm. Closed Sat L, Sun, Bhs
Menus: *A la carte,* fixed-price L & D, pre-theatre, bar menu
Seats: 80. No-smoking area
Additional: Children permitted, children's menu; ❂ menu, vegan/other diets on request

Directions: Head for City centre and follow signs for Granada Studios Tour. Hotel is opposite

MANCHESTER, **Woodlands Restaurant** ❀

Converted from a private, Victorian house, Woodlands is still run by members of the proprietor's family. Of the fish and meat dishes offered, many are accompanied by rich sauces, such as the medallions of venison flamed with whisky and a tarragon cream sauce. Desserts, though not for slimmers, are a highlight

Times: Last L 1.45pm, last D 9.45. Closed Sat L, Sun, Mon. Open Sun L on last Sun of month
Seats: 36. No cigars or pipes
Additional: Children welcome, children's portions; ❂ dishes, vegan/other on request
Directions: From the M67 take A6017 to Ashton, after half a mile turn left at traffic lights, then right into B6169 Shepley Road. Woodlands is 200yds on the left

33 Shepley Road
Audenshaw M34 5DJ
Map no: 7 SJ89
Tel: 0161 336 4241
Chef: William Mark Jackson
Proprietors: Mr & Mrs Dennis Crank.
Manageress: Lesley Ann Jackson
Cost: *Alc* £25, fixed-price L & D £15.65. H/wine £8.25 Service exc
Credit cards: 🌑 📧
Menus: Fixed price L & D £15.95

MANCHESTER, Yang Sing 🏵🏵

Huge, atmospheric Chinese restaurant packed with Mancunians enjoying some of the best Cantonese food in the country

The Chinese are known for their love of children, and no-one need worry about bringing their offspring to this highly acclaimed Chinese restaurant. As the management are so fond of saying – of course, they welcome children, it is only the adults who ever cause problems. On the edge of Manchester's ever-burgeoning Chinatown, the Yang Sing still stands head and shoulders above the opposition, with talented chef Harry Yeung still firmly in control of the non-stop output of the huge basement restaurant. There are plenty of familiar items on the long menu, but there is also considerable scope for those who prefer a more adventurous eating experience. Fried, fresh and dried squid in black bean sauce, crispy roasted suckling pig, ox tripe with noodles in soup, and braised brisket with spices are amongst the more unusual dishes, along with 'specials' such as steamed pork pie with salted egg, and quick-fried chicken gizzards with cashew nuts. Dim sum include spicy meat and nut dumplings, fried crabmeat balls and steamed spare ribs, but a more comprehensive list is available between noon and 4.30pm.

Directions: Princess Street is a one way street leading from the Town Hall to the A57M and Wilmslow

34 Princess Street M1 4JY
Map no: 7 SJ89
Tel: 0161 236 2200
Chef: Harry Yeung
Proprietors: Yang Sing Restaurants Ltd
Credit cards: ◼ ▦ ▦
Times: Midday-last D 11pm. Closed Xmas day
Menu: *A la carte*
Seats: Restaurant 140, ground floor 110, main banqueting room 220. Air conditioned
Additional: Children welcome, ❶ dishes, vegan/other diets on request

MANCHESTER AIRPORT, Etrop Grange 🏵

Chef Hamish Reas produces a good choice of dishes based on fresh local produce in this pleasant hotel dating from the 18th century. Fixed-price dinners, Sunday lunch and bar menus are available. A typical dish could be filo parcel of beansprout, crisp vegetables and pimento on a light tomato sauce

Thorley Lane M90 4EG
Map no: 7 SJ88
Tel: 0161 499 0500
Chef: Hamish Deas
Proprietor: Regal. Manager: Kevin Pearson
Cost: Fixed-price L £16.50/ D £27.50. H/wine £10.95 Service inc
Credit cards: ◼ ▦ ▦ ▣ OTHER
Times: Last L 2pm/D 10pm
Menus: Fixed-price L & D, bar menu
Seats: 60. No-smoking area
Additional: Children welcome, children's portions; ❶ dishes, vegan/other diets on request

Directions: Off junct 5 of M56. At main airport roundabout, take first left (to Terminal 2), then first right (Thorley Lane), 200yds on right

RAMSBOTTOM,
The Village Restaurant

☺ *This informal bistro offers a limited choice menu which makes good use of local produce as well as ingredients from the excellent delicatessen in the basement. At a recent meal, our inspector particularly enjoyed the home-made winter vegetable soup, and the tender organic pork in a red wine and apple sauce*

16 Market Place BL10 9HT
Map no: 7 SD71
Tel: 0170 682 5070
Chef: Ros Hunter
Proprietors: Ros Hunter and Chris Johnson
Cost: Fixed-price L £10 (2 course), D & Sun L £17.50 (4 course). H/wine £8.95 ‼
Service exc
Credit cards: 🟦 🖼 💳 💳 OTHER
Times: Noon-last L 2.30pm/D 8pm. Closed Sun D, Mon, Tue
Seats: 40. No smoking
Menus: Fixed-price L & D
Additional: Children permitted; ✔ dishes, vegan/other diets on request

Directions: In the centre of the village – M66 exit 1 follow signs to Ramsbottom

ROCHDALE, French Connection

A moorland setting for contemporary Anglo-French cooking. The lunch-time bistro menu pays homage to regional specialities such as black pudding, although sometimes with imaginative variations: onion and cheese tart with Mozzarella, or tomato soup with roast garlic and saffron. A more extensive carte is available evenings

Edenfield Road
Cheesden
Norden OL12 7TY
Map no: 7 SD81
Tel: 01706 50167
Chef: Andrew Nutter
Proprietors: R S Nutter, K J Nutter & Andrew Nutter
Cost: Alc £22.50. H/wine £7.80. Service exc
Credit cards: 🟦 💳 OTHER
Times: Noon-last L 2pm, 7pm-last D 9.30pm. Closed Mon, Bh Mon, first 2 wks Aug
Menu: A la carte
Seats: 52. No smoking in dining room
Additional: Children welcome, children's portions; ✔ menu, vegan/other diets on request

Directions: On the A680 between Rochdale and Edenfield

STANDISH, **Kilhey Court Hotel** 🏵🏵

A hotel restaurant offering a good variety of imaginative and carefully prepared dishes

Kilhey Court is a large hotel set in 10 acres of gardens fringed by the Worthington lakes. Public areas include a permanent marquee, a weekend night club and a well equipped leisure centre and Italian-style restaurant. The split-level restaurant in the main hotel, however, is the place to enjoy the technical skills of head chef Gary Butcher who produces a range of imaginative dishes. At a summer meal, a first course of crispy confit of duck served on a simple bed of leaves with a black olive vinaigrette proved most enjoyable. This was followed by wonderfully fresh red mullet, a rather unnecessary salad of cherry tomatoes, and a good choice of well cooked vegetables – stuffed courgettes and baby turnips among them. Alternative main courses could be fillet of Pendle lamb with a peppercorn crust, loin of wild boar, or pan-fried duckling with marrowfat peas and a potato rösti. Delicious rhubarb summer pudding is one of a traditional selection presented to the table on a butler's tray. Service is professional and friendly, and good advice is readily available about the reasonably extensive wine list.

Directions: On A5106 at Worthington

Chorley Road WN1 2XN
Map no: 7 SD51
Tel: 01257 472100
Chef: Gary Butcher
Proprietors: T Bladon and R Bradshaw
Cost: *Alc* £28, fixed-price L £12.95/D £19.95
Credit cards: 🔳 🔳 🔳 🔳 OTHER
Times: Last D 9.45pm
Closed 25-26 Dec, 1 Jan

HAMPSHIRE

ALRESFORD, **Hunters** 🏵

Chef Michael Greenhalgh makes full use of local produce on a carte that changes seasonally. Main courses may include wild boar sausages with creamed potatoes and an onion and mustard confit, or rainbow trout on a bed of noodles served with a light cream sauce

Times: Last L 2pm/last D 10pm/early Sup 6.30pm-7.30pm. Closed 1 wk Christmas
Menus: *A la carte,* fixed-price L & D, early Supper
Seats: 30+75. No-smoking area
Additional: Children welcome, children's portions; ♥ menu, vegan/other diets on request
Directions: Off A31 – turn left in centre of Alresford

32 Broad Street SO24 9AQ
Map no: 4 SU53
Tel: 01962 732468
Chef: Michael Greenhalgh
Proprietor: Martin Birmingham
Cost: *Alc* £18.70-26.95, fixed-price L £9.95/D £15.95/early Supper £9.95 H/wine £8.95
❗ Service exc
Credit cards: 🔳 🔳 🔳 🔳 OTHER

BARTON-ON-SEA, **The Cliff House** 🏵

☺ *A cliff-top restaurant noted for straight-forward cooking, featuring home-made soups, pies, curries and traditional roasts on its good value carte and fixed-price menus. Typical dishes could be celery soup, chicken breast in Stilton sauce and lemon meringue pie. A loyal local following makes booking essential*

Menus: *A la carte,* fixed-price L & D, bar menu
Seats: 50. No smoking in dining room
Additional: Children welcome, children's portions; ♥ menu, vegan/other diets on request
Directions: Off A337 between Highcliffe and New Milton on far end of sea road

Marine Drive West BH25 7QL
Map no: 4 SZ29
Tel: 01425619333
Chefs: James Simpson, Martin Cooper and Daren Wooldridge
Proprietors: James Simpson
Cost: *Alc* from £16.90, fixed-price L £11.50/D £16.50, H/wine £9.95 ❗ Service exc
Credit cards: 🔳 🔳 🔳
Times: Last L 2pm/D 9pm

BASINGSTOKE,
Audleys Wood Hotel ☺☺

Ambitious food is served at this Victorian house, peacefully located in extensive grounds

Alton Road RG25 2JT
Map no: 4 SU65
Tel: 01256 817555
Chef: Christopher Cleveland
Proprietor: Mount Charlotte Thistle.
Manager: Robert Hunter
Cost: Alc £30, fixed-price L £17.95/D £20-£27. H/wine £13.85 ▌ Service inc
Credit cards: ▨ ▦ ▦ ▣
Times: Last L 1.45pm/D 9.45pm. Closed Sat L, Bhs L
Menus: A la carte, fixed-price L & D
Seats: 70. No-smoking area
Additional: Children welcome, children's portions; ✪ dishes, vegan/other diets on request

Surrounded by seven acres of well maintained grounds, this sympathetically extended Victorian residence retains much of the character of the original house with some fine dark wood panelling and handsome fireplaces. The striking restaurant, once the palm house and conservatory, with its unusual vaulted ceiling and small minstrels gallery, makes an agreeable setting for the enjoyable, carefully prepared and attractively presented food of chef Christopher Cleveland. The interesting daily-changing menu – three courses priced according to the main course selected – are supplemented by a more extensive seasonal *carte* which also includes some vegetarian options. The cooking is assured and flavours well defined and nicely judged, as exampled by ravioli of crab with spinach and coriander and a good saffron sauce. However, the highlight of a recent meal was a succulent breast of guinea fowl, served with fresh girolles, asparagus and a scattering of broad beans accompanied by a caramel flavoured Madeira sauce. A comprehensive wine list is offered, although the selection of half bottles is fairly modest.

Directions: M6 exit 6 & A339 (Alton) 1.5 miles from Basingstoke

BASINGSTOKE,
Basingstoke Country Hotel ☺

Interesting carte and good value fixed-price menus offer carefully prepared dishes – though they might benefit from being less complicated and concentrating on fewer flavours. At a recent meal lamb cutlets were beautifully cooked, and filo pastry parcels were enjoyable

Credit cards: ▨ ▦ ▦ ▣
Additional: Children welcome, children's portions; ✪ dishes, vegan/ other diets on request
Directions: On A30 between Nately Scures and Hook

Nately Scures
Hook RG27 9JS
Map no: 4 SU65
Tel: 01256 746161
Chef: Paul Haverson
Seats: 90. Air conditioned
Times: Last L 2pm/D 9.45pm
Cost: Alc £25, fixed-price L £11.50 (2 courses), £14.50/ D £19.50. H/wine £9.95 ▌ Service inc

BEAULIEU, **Beaulieu Hotel** ❀

Well-made tomato and orange soup, followed by a nicely-grilled darne of salmon with a saffron and prawn sauce, were highlights of a test meal at this well-run, small hotel. The setting, in the heart of the New Forest, is delightful

Menus: A la carte, fixed-price D & Sun L
Seats: 42. No smoking
Additional: Children welcome, children's menu; ❶ dishes, vegan/other diets on request
Directions: On the B3056 between Lyndhurst and Beaulieu, opposite the Railway Station

Beaulieu Road SO42 7YQ
Map no: 4 SU30
Tel: 01703 293344
Chef: G Ryan
Proprietor: Care Motels.
Manager: Bryan Davies
Cost: Fixed-price D £15/Sun L £8.95. H/wine £9.75 Service exc
Credit cards: 🔳 🔳 🔳 🔳
Times: Last D 8.45pm, last Sun L 1.30pm

BEAULIEU, **Montagu Arms Hotel** ❀❀

Picturesque hotel and restaurant in the centre of popular New Forest village

Think Beaulieu, and think vintage cars and New Forest ponies. Think, also, the Montagu Arms, where chef Simon Fennell makes the best use he can of local produce. His menu offers an interesting choice of dishes, plus a selection of grills. Appetisers, such as smoked salmon and mackerel roulade, are served in the bar, before one moves into the spacious, beamed restaurant. A recent starter of duck confit was served, unusually, with home-made piccalilli (shades of G. Rhodes). The bold, rich flavours, however, were marred by a burnt pancake wrapping. Breast of chicken was imaginatively filled with a light prune mousse and an apricot sauce. The accompanying rice timbale was a nice idea, but the spicing could have been more pronounced. But white chocolate soufflé proved a delicious end to the meal, with just the right degree of sweetness, balanced by the sharpness of a raspberry compote. Restaurant, and indeed, all the hotel staff serve with a smile. Overnight guests will appreciate, in addition, the irresistible shortbread served with early morning tea, and that breakfast includes such treats as scrambled egg and smoked salmon.

Directions: From Southampton take A326 (Fawley), follow signs to Beaulieu (B3054). The hotel is on the left as you enter the village

Place Lane
Map no: 4 SU30
Tel: 01590 612324
Chef: Simon Fennel
Proprietor: Green Close Ltd
Cost: Alc £35, fixed-price L £14.95, fixed-price D £23.90 (2 courses), £23.90.
H/wine £12.50 ❗ Service exc
Credit cards: 🔳 🔳 🔳 🔳 OTHER
Times: 12.30-last L 2pm, 7.30pm-last D 9.30pm (10pm Sat
Menus: A la carte, fixed-price L & D, Sun L
Seats: 80-100. No smoking in dining room
Additional: Children welcome, children's portions; ❶ dishes, vegan/other diets on request

BROCKENHURST,
Careys Manor Hotel ❀❀

Conveniently located country house hotel and leisure centre with diverse clientele

The much extended manor house, close to the M27, is popular with both business and leisure visitors. The three course £21.95 dinner menu offers a choice of four dishes at each course, but there are supplements attached to any further choice made from the *carte*. Dishes typical of the general smart-hotel-mode of cooking are roulade of salmon filled with sole and asparagus mousse on watercress sauce, lambs' sweetbreads and oyster mushrooms cooked with sherry sauce and served on toasted brioche, whole grilled Dover sole topped with artichokes, prawns and grapes glazed with herb hollandaise, and roast rack of lamb sliced onto

Brockenhurst SO42 7RH
Map no: 4 SU30
Tel: 01590 623551
Chef: Kevin Dorrington
Proprietor: Greenclose Ltd
Seats: 90. No smoking
Times: Last L 2pm/D 10pm
Cost: Alc £28.20-£37.40, fixed-price L £13.75/D £19.95
Credit cards: 🔳 🔳 🔳 OTHER
Additional: Children permitted, children's portions; ❶ menu, vegan/other diets on request

a bed of potato purée and spring onions with Madeira sauce. There is a selection of fresh vegetables and potatoes, or mixed seasonal salad with French, blue cheese or Thousand Island dressing. Chargrill dishes are a good choice, and include steaks, cutlets and Chateaubriand with béarnaise sauce. Lunch dishes are simpler – strips of smoked chicken bound in a basil dressing, perhaps, followed by lamb's liver with bacon and onion sauce.

Directions: On the A337 between Lyndhurst and Lymington

BROCKENHURST,
Le Poussin Restaurant ❀❀❀

A New Forest village setting for some wonderfully accurate and reasonably priced modern English cookery

Flawless cooking and impeccable service were experienced by our inspector on a recent visit to this family-run restaurant. It is located down a narrow alleyway off the high street (just wide enough to admit a modest car), which leads into a not too attractive courtyard that gets prettier around the entrance to Le Poussin. The interior is small and oblong, painted white with round tables set about the perimeter. Clever spot lighting, crisp white linens and the occasional thematic print transform the room, providing an excellent foil to the cooking. The atmosphere is quiet and respectful but by no means stuffy. The service is distinguished by its correctness and the food by its remarkable accuracy of flavour, balance and texture. Lunch is excellent value.

Each course offers two dishes and there is no impression that economies have been made to keep down the price. The meal begins with wonderful bread – at inspection, olive, and a crusted rosemary and sea salt – and delicious, complimentary canapés. Typical first courses could include creamed wild mushroom and potato soup, or a twice baked cheese soufflé, perfectly light and well risen, glazed and crusted, with a mature cheddar sauce. Among the main courses could be fillet of New Forest venison cooked rare with a rich red wine sauce, or fillet of sea bass lightly steamed with a good reduction sauce, finished with saffron and butter. Puddings can include poached pears glazed and set on a light caramel sauce with a really thin brandy snap basket filled with vanilla speckled ice-cream. The wine list is mainly French, but stretches to Australia. The Aitken's son is visiting Chile and Argentina this winter to introduce some lesser known wines.

Directions: Village centre through an archway between two shops

The Courtyard
Brookley Road SO42 7RB
Map no: 4 SU30
Tel: 01590 23063
Chef: Alex Aitken
Proprietors: Alex & Caroline Aitken
Cost: Fixed-price L £15/D £25. H/wine £10 ❢ Service exc
Credit cards: 🌑 🔳
Times: Last L 1.30pm/last D 9pm. Closed Sun D, Mon, Tue
Menus: Fixed-price L & D
Seats: 24. No smoking
Additional: Children welcome, other diets by request

BROCKENHURST, New Park Manor ❀❀

Ever improving menu demonstrates a serious approach to food at this New Forest hotel

Set in its own grounds overlooking open forest, this former hunting lodge has a peaceful and relaxing air. As well as an elegant bar/lounge, the wood-panelled, candlelit restaurant has an open log fire to add to the atmosphere in winter months. Chef Matthew Tilt continues to improve the standard of cooking and quality of ingredients, and offers a well-balanced, fixed-price, three-course

Lyndhurst Road SD42 7QH
Map no: 4 SU30
Tel: 01590 623467
Chef: Matthew Tilt
Proprietor: Karel Van Gelderen
Cost: Alc £35, fixed-price L £15/D £27. H/wine £9.50 ❢ Service exc
Credit cards: 🌑 🔳 🔳 🔳

menu alongside an Anglo-French *carte*. Sautéed langoustine and red mullet in a lemon and herb fumet, spilling from its cornucopia filo 'horn of plenty' is still recommended for its subtle flavours and textures. Our inspector was also highly pleased with the tender noisettes of lamb, lightly cooked with a herb and thyme crust, served with a redcurrant jus lié. Vegetables, such as turned carrots, green beans and the ubiquitous baby corn, are cooked al dente. Desserts are sensibly limited, and the 'citrus grove', a chilled fruit parfait served with a light orange sauce, was an enjoyable conclusion to the meal. The wine list, with its mini-descriptions, mixes New World with old.

Directions: Turn off the A337 between Lyndhurst and Brockenhurst and follow the hotel signs

Times: Last L 2.30pm/D 9.30pm
Menus: *A la carte*, fixed-price L & D
Seats: 45. No smoking
Additional: Children welcome, ♥ menu, vegan/other diets on request

BROCKENHURST, **Rhinefield House** ✿✿

Magnificent surroundings for a good variety of dishes from both English and French culinary traditions

Rhinefield Road SO42 7QB
Map no: 4 SU30
Tel: 01590 22922
Chef: Mark Wadlow
Proprietor: Virgin Hotels.
Manager: David London
Cost: *Alc* £23-£29.50, fixed-price L £14/D £19.95. H/ wine £10 ♥ Service exc
Credit cards: 🟦 💳 💳 💳 OTHER
Times: L 2pm, last D 10pm (Sun 9.30pm). Closed Sat L (bar L open)
Menus: *A la carte*, fixed-price L & D, bar menu
Seats: 40. No-smoking area
Additional: Children welcome, children's menu; ♥ menu, vegan/other diets on request

A forest hotel situated at the end of a long drive, Rhinefield House is a magnificent 19th-century building: an engaging mixture of Tudor and Gothic architecture with some fascinating features – a fireback dated 1653, and carvings by Grinling Gibbons and Aummonier. Most impressive among the public areas are the Alhambra Room with its pillars and mosaic floor – an exact copy of the palace of the same name in Granada and now part of the cocktail bar – and the Armada Restaurant with its carved wooden panelling. In the restaurant, chef Mark Wadlow offers a seasonally changing fixed-price menu in addition to the *carte*, and guests are welcome to mix and match between the two. Successful dishes sampled this year have included brioche with smoked haddock, and monkfish cassoulet with roasted red peppers and tomato, both strong on good fresh flavours. White chocolate ice-cream in a brandy snap basket formed a particularly delicious part of a platter of chocolate desserts, served on a raspberry coulis. A vegetarian option is always available, such as tian of aubergine and tomato set on a fennel cream, and there is an extensive and carefully selected wine list with some half bottles.

Directions: From Brockenhurst centre follow signs to Rhinefield. Hotel is on the left

BROCKENHURST,

Thatched Cottage Hotel 🏶🏶

A quintessentially English country cottage providing imaginative cooking

16 Brookley Road SO4 7RR
Map no: 4 SU30
Tel: 01590 623090
Chef: Michiyo Matysik
Proprietor: The Matysik Family
Cost: Fixed price D £24.50/Sun
L (2 course) £13. H/wine £9.50
❢ Service charge inc
Credit cards: 🖾 🖾 OTHER
Times: 12.30pm-last L 2pm
7.30pm-last D 9.30pm. Closed
Sun D, Mon L, month Jan
Menu: A la carte L, fixed-price
D & Sun L
Seats: 20. No smoking in dining
room
Additional: Children permitted
over 10, chidren's portions L
only; ❤/other diets on request

The Matysik family run this four hundred year old thatched house
with commendable style. It's but a short walk to the New Forest,
and visitors continue to be impressed by the food. Besides the usual
fixed-price menu are regular Celebration Menus which might
feature authentic Japanese dishes prepared by Japanese daughter-
in-law, Michiyo Matysik. The kitchen shows a serious, dedicated
approach, and uses the best quality ingredients enhanced by home-
grown vegetables, soft fruits and herbs. The three-course, fixed-
price menu is modern country house cooking along the lines of
nettle soup with a pastry cap, truffles and wild mushrooms, New
Forest venison strudel with cranberry jus, and chicken suprême
filled with goose liver parfait on a truffle cream sauce. A melange
of fresh steamed vegetables could include al dente cauliflower,
haricot vert, broccoli, baby corn and carrots. Rhubarb, orange and
strawberry terrine on a foam of vanilla and cinnamon, and
gratinated plum salad with a light Masala wine zabaglione are
typical desserts. The wines are divided between New World and
others, with a pricing policy that is not too painful.

Directions: on A337 in Brockenhurst, turning before level crossing

BROCKENHURST,

Whitley Ridge Hotel 🏶🏶

☺ *Freshly prepared food based on traditional home recipes are offered
at this forest hotel*

A part Georgian, part Victorian former royal hunting lodge,
this country house hotel is set in the heart of the New Forest,
surrounded by five acres of parkland and gardens complete with
freely roaming deer. The restaurant is an attractive room with its
own terrace, where guests can relax after dinner. Chef Karen
Mustey offers a seasonal *carte* plus a daily fixed-price menu.
Starters might include bresaola, home-cured topside of beef
set on crisp French lettuce and presented with ribbons of green

Beaulieu Road SO4 7QL
Map no: 4 SU30
Tel: 01590 622354
Chef: Karen Mustey
Proprietors: Rennie & Sue Law
Cost: Alc £22, fixed-price L
£11/D £19. H/wine £9.50 ❢
Service inc
Credit cards: 🖾 🖾 🖾 🖾 OTHER
Times: 7pm-last D 9pm. Sunday
L noon-last L 2pm
Menus: A la carte, fixed-price D,
Sun L, children's tea, bar menu
Seats: 40. No smoking in dining
room

Whitley Ridge Hotel

Additional: Children permitted, no under 7 at dinner; ❶ menu, vegan/other diets on request

peppercorn sauce; moules marinière, featuring Lymington mussels, and our inspector's choice, a home-made chicken liver pâté in a crisp filo basket served with a well balanced port and orange sauce. A main course of tender kidneys turbigo came with a delicious rich sauce and crisp fresh vegetables. Alternatives might be a choice from the varied vegetarian menu, such as deep-fried aubergine fritters with a chilli and coriander sauce; or, from the general menu, leg of venison, lamb cutlet, and poached fillet of brill, prepared according to traditional home recipes. To finish, try the summer pudding with all the fruit flavours marinated in brandy.

Directions: A337 (from Lyndhurst) turn left towards Beaulieu on B3055, approx 1 mile

BROOK, Bell Inn ❀

A skilful and innovative approach to cooking is taken by chef Malcolm Lugg at the Bell Inn, where freshly-prepared Anglo-French dishes are served. The menu may include game terrine with a juniper-flavoured Cumberland sauce (prepared from local game) and tartlet of lamb with a purée of sweet potato

Lyndhurst SO43 7HE
Map no: 4 SU21
Tel: 01703 812214
Chef: Malcolm Lugg
Proprietor: Brook Enterprises.
Manager: Gavin Scott
Cost: Alc £18-£30, fixed-price L £12.50/D £23.50. H/wine £8.75
Service exc
Credit cards: ▦ ▦ ▦ ▣ OTHER
Times: Last L 2.30pm/D 9.30pm

Menus: A la carte, fixed-price L & D, bar menu **Seats:** 50. No smoking in dining room **Additional:** Children welcome, children's menu; ❶ dishes, vegan/other diets on request **Directions:** M27 junction 1 (Cadnam) 3rd exit, signed Brook, 1 mile on right

BUCKLERS HARD,
Master Builders House Hotel ❀

☺ *A popular hotel in a picturesque village, noted for its efficiency and friendliness even under pressure. Skilful use is made of local produce to provide imaginative dishes involving fish and game. Look out for terrine of assorted seafood, or wood pigeon marinated in brandy with a peppercorn sauce*

Beaulieu SO4 7XB
Map no: 4 SU40
Tel: 01590 616253
Chef: Simon Berry
Proprietors: Gardner Merchant.
Manager: Chris Plumpton
Cost: Alc £15-£20, fixed price L/D £12.95. H/wine £9.75.
Service inc
Credit cards: ▦ ▦ ▦ ▣
Times: Noon-last L 2.15pm
7pm-last D 9.30pm

Menus: A la carte, fixed price L & D, bar menu **Seats:** 80. No smoking in Buffet bar **Additional:** Children welcome, children's menu; ❶ dishes, vegan/other diets on request
Directions: Bucklers Hard is signposted from Beaulieu

DENMEAD,

Barnards Restaurant ⊛⊛

☺ *Ever popular, personally-run restaurant with a reliable reputation for mainstream French food*

A restaurant that plays it safe is no bad thing. The menu at Barnard's may not win any prizes for cutting edge originality, but over the years chef/patron David Barnard has built up a well-deserved reputation for the consistent quality of his Anglo-French cooking. Sauces are a particular forte of the short, unpretentious *carte* and set menu; hollandaise spiked with tarragon vinegar and chopped shallots for fish, or coral flavoured lobster sauce for strips of fillet steak sautéed in butter. There is a daily changing fish dish, but other favourites keep their tried and tested place. Goats' cheese soufflé rolled in ribbed almonds, baked and served on a seasonal salad dressed in hazelnut vinaigrette is a regular starter, as is a smooth chicken liver pâté, and an omelette filled with creamy, smoked haddock. Desserts may include fresh grapes marinated in Cointreau, topped with a rich custard and glazed with demerara sugar, or home-made ice-creams and sorbets. A brasserie lunch menu, available Wednesday to Friday, features a range of lighter dishes, such as mussels in garlic and herb sauce, and fresh salmon fishcakes with tomato sauce.

Directions: Opposite village church; from A3M exit 3/B2150 (Waterlooville)

Hambledon Road PO7 6NU
Map no: 4 SU61
Tel: 01705 257788
Chef: David Barnard
Proprietor: David Barnard
Cost: Alc £25, fixed-price L/D £14.50. H/wine £8.50. No service charge
Credit cards: ■ ■ ■ ▣ OTHER
Times: Last L 1.45pm (Wed, Thur, Fri) last D 9.45pm (Tue-Sat) Lunch Closed Sun, Mon, 1 wk Aug, 1 wk Xmas
Menus: A la carte, fixed-price L & D
Seats: 40. No smoking in dining room
Additional: Children welcome, children's portions; ♥ dishes, other diets on request

EMSWORTH, **Julies Restaurant** ⊛⊛

☺ *Both an innovative approach and up-to-date trends are brought to bear on good fresh ingredients by this informal cottage restaurant*

A very friendly atmosphere pervades this tiny, 300 year old restaurant – a one-time fisherman's cottage which apparently boasts a resident ghost called Fred. Dedicated chef/proprietor Kevin Hartley works single-handed to produce the enjoyable range of Mediterranean-influenced continental dishes that make up the *carte* and fixed-price menus; results do not always conform exactly to menu descriptions, but ingredients are all fresh and the food is clearly cooked to order. Delicious wholemeal and olive bread rolls, dusted with flour and served hot, are particularly worthy of mention. A March inspection meal began with a mousse of Scottish salmon and sorrel, served hot with pieces of salmon, wilted sorrel leaves and tomato concasse in an egg-thickened cream timbale. A braised rolled loin of fresh local rabbit, layered with Savoy cabbage and home-smoked bacon and accompanied by a melange of colourful, crunchy vegetables. A semi-descriptive wine list offers 34 popular bins from around the world, including some half bottles.

Directions: At Emsworth town centre, first right after Emsworth Square – South Street. Go 100 yds down towards the Quay. Restaurant on left facing main car park.

30 South Street PO10 7EH
Map no: 4 SU70
Tel: 01243 370 534
Chef: Kevin Michael Hartley
Proprietor: Kevin Michael Hartley
Cost: Alc from £18, fixed-price L £8.95, fixed-price D £12.95. H/wine £8.95 ♦ Service exc
Credit cards: ■ ■ ■ ▣
Times: Noon-last L 2.30, last D 9.30. Closed 1 week Jan
Menus: A la carte, fixed-price L & D, Sun lunch (September-end March)
Seats: 26
Additional: ♥ dishes, other diets on request

Entries in this Guide are based on reports filed by our team of professionally trained, full-time inspectors.

EMSWORTH, 36 On The Quay ❀❀

A delightful harbour side restaurant serving soundly cooked, imaginative food

47 South Street PO10 7EG
Map no: 4 SU70
Tel: 01243 375592
Chef: Frank Eckermann
Proprietor: Raymond Shortland
Cost: Fixed-price L £19.55 /D
£29.95 (5 courses) H/wine
£11.50 Service exc
Credit cards: ⬛ 🚼 🚼 OTHER
Times: Noon-last L 1.45pm,
7pm-last D 9.45pm. Closed 2
wks Sept
Menus: Fixed-price L & D
Seats: 45. No-smoking area
Additional: Children over
11 permitted, ◐ dishes,
vegan/other diets on request

Perched on the harbour's edge at Emsworth, 36 On The Quay is a pretty restaurant with lovely views over the estuary. The marine setting is enhanced by the mass of white sails skimming across the water on race days, and by the salty sea breezes. Within, it is elegantly decorated in aquamarine and yellow pastels and feels like someone's front room with old portraits adorning the walls. Proprietor Raymond Shortland greets guests as they arrive and oversees the very professional service in the restaurant. The fixed-price menu, prepared by chef Frank Eckermann, provides an interesting choice, backed up by good canapés and homemade rolls. At a meal in May the daily special – skilfully prepared salmon and lobster boudin – was followed by roast guinea fowl with a rich Madeira sauce, braised red cabbage and gratin potatoes. Desserts might include lime and ginger soufflé or traditional bread and butter pudding with apple and brandy. Full flavoured filter coffee is served with an excellent selection of petit fours. The wine list is comprehensive, and offers a good range of price and vintages.

Directions: Last building on the right in South Street which runs from the Square in centre of Emsworth

EVERSLEY, New Mill Restaurant ❀❀

Modern British standards in polished restaurant on the river

A picturesque riverside setting in six acres on the Blackwater Race, makes this former 16th-century mill the ideal spot for discreet and special dining. The Grill Room offers a more informal alternative to the River Room Restaurant, which overlooks the river and waterside gardens occupied by Albert and Albertina, the house ducks. The menu is structured around a good, representative cross-section of modern classics and attempts nothing too adventurous or outré. Starters include Caesar salad, twice baked Caerphilly cheese soufflé and gravad lax of salmon with dill mustard sauce. Grilled monkfish with a herb crust and red pepper sauce, and half a Gressingham duck, with apple, cherry and cinnamon sauce, are typical of the main courses, all served with

New Mill Road RG27 0RA
Map no: 4 SU76
Tel: 01734 732277/723105
Chef: Stephen Read
Proprietor: n/a.
Manager: Anthony Finn
Cost: Riverside: Alc £28, fixed-price L £12.50/D £19.50.
H/wine £10 ❗ Service inc
Credit cards: ⬛ 🚼 🚼 💳 OTHER
Times: Last L 2pm, last D 10pm
Closed Sat L
Menus: *A la carte,* fixed-price
L & D, bar/grill room menu
Seats: 80 (Grill Room 36). No
pipes or cigars

New Mill

Additional: Children welcome, children's menu; ❶ dishes, vegan/other diets on request

fresh vegetables or mixed salad. Chargrill choices include marinated loin of tuna, served on a bed of salad niçoise, and calves' liver and bacon, with deep-fried onion rings. The wine list has been carefully and thoughtfully put together and, as well as a very good selection of vintage New and Old World wines, highlights 'Ten of the Best'.

Directions: From Eversley village take A327 (Reading), cross the river, turn left at cross roads into New Mill Road

FAIR OAK, **Noorani Restaurant** ❀❀

Consistent cooking at superior Indian restaurant

The intelligent use of fresh herbs and spices lifts this popular neighbourhood restaurant above the run-of-the-mill curry house norm. Basic raw ingredients, such as meat, are good and not stewed to oblivion. Duck, as well as chicken, features in a wide range of dishes, and imported fish gives extra interest. As well as the usual roll-call of tikkas and goshts, there are a number of unusual dishes including 'sally' lamb, a Parsi wedding dish made with tender lamb cooked with dried apricots in a spicy red masala sauce. The karai, a wok-like utensil, is used to cook a number of speciality dishes, using a pungent mix of ginger, garlic, tomatoes, onion and peppers. Vegetarian choice includes green peas with fresh cottage cheese and 'dum aloo Kashmiri' – small potatoes stuffed with potato, herbs and spices and cooked in a cashew nut paste sauce. Sundays and Mondays, there is an Indian hotel-style buffet. 24 hour notice is required for the two Noorani specials – whole leg of lamb, or fresh Bangladeshi fish, each marinaded for several hours in herbs and spices then, as the menu promises, 'served with a flourish'.

Directions: In village square opposite the war memorial

465 Fair Oak Road
Map no: 4 SU41
Tel: 01703 601901
Chefs: Helen Miah & Sanu Miah.
Manager: Anam Huque
Cost: *Alc* £12/18, buffet lunch (Sun, Mon) £5.95, fixed-price dinner £9.95. H/wine £6.95 ❢
Service exc
Credit cards: ▨ ▦ ▨ OTHER
Times: Noon-last L 2.30pm, last D 7.30pm. Closed 2 days Xmas
Menus: *A la carte*, buffet L Sun, Mon
Seats: 80. Air conditioned
Additional: ❶ menu

Pissaladière is a speciality of the Nice region. The base is either bread dough or shortcrust pastry spread with a layer of onions, garnished with anchovy fillets and olives and spread with pissalat - a purée of anchovies mixed with cloves, thyme, bay leaf and pepper and olive oil - before being cooked. It can be eaten hot or cold.

FAREHAM, **Lysses House Hotel** ❀

A popular restaurant offering a range of reliable dishes on its varied menus, with vegetarian and healthy eating options included. At a recent inspection meal rabbit and foie gras terrine with toasted brioche was followed by moist, succulent corn-fed chicken, and strawberry tart

Menus: A la carte, fixed-price L & D, bar menu
Seats: 60. Air conditioned. No smoking in dining room
Additional: Children welcome, children's portions; ❂ dishes, vegan/other diets on request
Directions: From M27 exit 11 follow signs to Fareham town centre; hotel is at top of High Street

51 High Street PO16 7BQ
Map no: 4 SU50
Tel: 01329 822622
Chef: Clive Wright
Proprietor: Colin Mercer.
Manageress: Nicola Stafford
Cost: Alc £23, fixed-price L
£13.95/D £18.50. H/wine £9.35
❢ Service inc
Credit cards: 🌑 🔳 🔲 🔲
Times: Last L 1.45pm/D 9.45pm.
Closed Sun, BHs

FAREHAM, **Solent Hotel** ❀

Friendly staff and a charming interior at this modern hotel offering carte, fixed-price, Sunday lunch and bar menus. Dishes may include steamed seafood with linguine, collops of Scottish venison or pithivier of brie de Meaux and aubergine. Finish with Belgian chocolate truffle torte

Times: Last L 2pm/last D 10pm. Closed Sat L, Bhs L
Menus: A la carte, fixed-price L & D, bar menu
Seats: 106. Air conditioned. No smoking in dining room
Additional: Children welcome, children's menu; ❂ dishes, vegan/other diets on request
Directions: M27 exit 9 signed Business Park, between Southampton and Portsmouth

Solent Business Park
Rookery Avenue
Whitely PO15 7AJ
Map no: 4 SU50
Tel: 01489 880000
Chef: Chris Taylor
Proprietors: Shire Inns.
Manager: Robert J Wade
Cost: Alc £23, fixed-price
L £13.95/D £20. H/wine £9.95
❢ Service inc
Credit cards: 🌑 🔳 🔲 🔲 OTHER

FORDINGBRIDGE,
Ashburn Hotel ❀

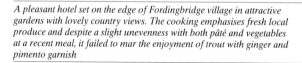

A pleasant hotel set on the edge of Fordingbridge village in attractive gardens with lovely country views. The cooking emphasises fresh local produce and despite a slight unevenness with both pâté and vegetables at a recent meal, it failed to mar the enjoyment of trout with ginger and pimento garnish

Seats: 50. No smoking
Additional: Children welcome, children's portions/menu; ❂ dishes, vegan/other diets on request
Directions: On the B3078

Damerham Road
Map no: 4 SU11
Tel: 01425 652060
Chef: Michael Belton
Proprietors: Minotels.
Managers: Mr & Mrs Robinson, Mr & Mrs Harman
Cost: Alc £25, fixed-price
L £8.50/D £12.95. Service exc
Credit cards: 🌑 🔳 🔲 OTHER
Times: Last L 1.45pm/D 9pm

FORDINGBRIDGE, **Hour Glass** ❀

☺ In winter, a roaring log fire adds to the atmosphere at this 13th-century thatched cottage. The set-price lunch menu is good value and in the evening a more extensive carte is introduced. Recommended are the chicken livers and lardons in a spicy dressing, and white chocolate and Cointreau mousse in coffee sauce

Menus: Fixed-price L & D   **Seats:** 42. No-smoking area
Additional: No children permitted, children's portions; ❂ dishes, vegan/other diets on request
Directions: On main A338 (Salisbury/Ringwood road) just outside Fordingbridge

Burgate SP6 1LX
Map no: 4 SU11
Tel: 01425 652348
Chef: J M Collins
Proprietors: J M Collins
Cost: Fixed-price L £10.95, fixed price D (4 course) £17.95.
H/wine £8.95. Service exc
Credit cards: 🌑 🔲 🔲
Times: Last L 1.30pm/D 9.45pm.
Closed Sun eve & Mon, 2 weeks Nov

FORDINGBRIDGE,

Lions Court Restaurant ☺☺

☺ *A modern touch is brought to classic French cooking in the kitchens of this charming hotel*

29 The High Street SP6 1AS
Map: 4 SU11
Tel: 01425 652006
Chef: Danny Wilson
Proprietors: Michael & Jenny Eastick
Cost: Alc £14.50-£20, fixed-price L £10.50/D £12.50. H/wine £7.90 Service exc
Credit cards: 🔲 🔲 🔲 OTHER
Times: 10am-last L 2pm, 7pm-last D 9.30pm. Closed Sun D, Mon, 2 wks Jan
Menus: Fixed-price L & D
Seats: 50. No smoking in lower dining room
Additional: Children welcome, children's portions; ☻ dishes, vegan/other diets on request

A beamed building dating from the 17th century provides the perfect setting for a restaurant where the enjoyment of good food is enhanced by a welcoming atmosphere and friendly service. Michael and Jenny Eastrick both regard customer care as a priority. Cooking is modern in style, but based on French classic dishes. Daniel Wilson shows his flair for innovation in menus that include light lunches and an early evening fixed-price deal as well as the main seasonal *carte*. The best of locally produced ingredients are used wherever possible – tender roast loin of venison served with juniper berries in a port wine reduction perhaps following whole roasted quail filled with chicken and thyme mousse and accompanied by a rich glace de viande textured with pistachio nuts. Vegetables are fresh and colourful, with good natural flavours. Home-made desserts range from rice pudding with a fruit compote to fresh pineapple with strawberries, kiwi fruit and black grapes. A descriptive list of wines from around the world offers both a connoisseurs' choice and a value-for-money house selection.

Directions: On A338, town centre, half way up High Street

FORDINGBRIDGE, Moonacre ☺☺

Exceptional value for money in country cottage with satisfying and coherent cooking

Chef/proprietor Barbara Garnsworthy takes a serious approach to food and her modern country cooking is based on developing real flavour from quality ingredients. She describes her style as English plus, and that well suits a repertoire that ranges from pigeon, hare and guinea fowl terrine with medlar jelly, to baked brie in filo pastry with pesto on rocket and mixed leaf salad, and chicken breast stuffed with bacon, mushrooms, tarragon and white wine. Fish features strongly – fillet of brill may be stuffed with a leek and prawn or crab meat mousse, Cornish pilchards grilled with garlic and herb butter, or fresh and smoked salmon combined in fishcakes

Alderholt
Map no: 4 SU11
Tel: 01425 653142
Chef: Barbara Garnsworthy
Proprietor: Barbara Garnsworthy
Cost: Alc £15.20, fixed-price D £11/Sun L £12. H/wine £7.50. Service exc
Credit cards: 🔲 🔲
Times: Last D 10pm, last Sun L 2pm, Closed Sun D, Mon, 2 wks Mar
Menus: A la carte, fixed-price D & Sun L

with sorrel and parsley sauce. There is a sensible short choice of three good cheeses, but it would be hard to pass by some of the excellent puddings, such as chocolate and brandy pot or coffee and walnut tart with crème fraîche. The thoughtfully chosen wine list is an able match for the food, with reputable growers, good house wines and very fair prices.

Directions: In Alderholt which is off the A338 south-west of Fordingbridge

Seats: 36
Additional: Children welcome, children's portions; ❂ dishes, other diets with notice

FORDINGBRIDGE, **Three Lions** ❀❀

As we went to press there were changes at the Three Lions. Mike Womersley, formally chef at Lucknam Park, in Wiltshire (where he achieved three AA rosettes) has taken over from Karl and June Wadstack as chef/proprietor. Early indications are that Mike is going to try and beat the the Wadstack's success (two AA rosettes for this pleasant village pub in the 1995 guide). The repertoire is market led with the blackboard still assuming a pivotal role, but any resemblance to typical chalked-up pub menus begins and ends with the wood they are made from. Simply described dishes include starters such as a salad of wild mushrooms, poached farm egg and balsamic dressing, or grilled sardines provençale, followed perhaps by sea bass with Oriental sauce, or braised and sautéed lamb and Madeira sauce. For dessert there is crème brûlée with tarragon, or fresh strawberries with vervain ice-cream and strawberry coulis.

Directions: Turn off A338 at Fordingbridge onto B3078 to Cadnam Road, then turn right into minor road to Stuckton

Map no: 4 SU11
Tel: 01425 652489
Chef: Mike Womersley
Proprietors: M & J Womersley
Cost: Alc £23.50. Wine from £8.95 ❢ Service exc
Credit cards: ▨ ▆ OTHER
Times: Last L 1.30pm, last D 9pm (9.30pm Sat). Dinner not served Sun. Closed Mon, Xmas, 2-3 wks end Jan/beg Feb
Menus: A la carte, blackboard
Seats: 55. Smoking not encouraged in dining room; no pipes or cigars. Air conditioned
Additional: No children under 14. ❂ dishes by arrangement

GRAYSHOTT, **Woods Place** ❀❀

A simple village centre restaurant offering European dishes in a relaxed atmosphere

Woods Place is easily found on the main parade in the village. It was once the butcher's shop which accounts for the Victorian tiled walls. The style is simple, relaxed. The cooking is eclectic, a strong European bias with Mediterranean overtones, bolstered by Swedish dishes from chef/patron Eric Norrgren's native country – notably Swedish hash, cubes of beef potato and onion topped with raw egg yolk, and Jansson's temptation, sliced potato baked with fish and cream. A summer meal began with gravlax – thick slices of salmon marinated in mustard and dill, with sun-dried tomato rolls and was followed by tender fillets of rabbit marinated in herbs and wrapped in crispy bacon with a thyme-flavoured sauce. Tarte tatin for dessert had good caramelised apples. Filter coffee was served with freshly made, citrus-flavoured shortbread. The wine list contains a simple selection of reasonably priced wines; a premium Swedish beer is also available.

Directions: A3 to Hindhead (from London) turn right onto B3002. Woods Place is 0.5 mile on left

Headley Road GU26 6LB
Map no: 4 SU83
Tel: 01428 605 555
Chef: Eric Norrgren
Proprietor: Dana & Eric Norrgren
Cost: Alc £21.30. H/wine £7.90 ❢ Service inc
Credit cards: ▨ ▆ ▆ ▨
Times: Noon-last L 2.30pm, 7pm-last D 11.30pm. Closed Sum, Mon
Menus: A la carte
Seats: 36
Additional: Children welcome, children's portions

Prices quoted in the Guide are based on information supplied by the establishments themselves.

HEDGE END, Botleigh Grange Hotel

A pleasant hotel set in beautiful grounds with a lake and wood, which offers an imaginative menu and professional, attentive service. Local suppliers are used wherever possible. Look out for monkfish ravioli, pheasant with chestnut and onion stuffing and a rich port sauce and try the rich chocolate sponge for dessert

Map no: 4 SU41
Tel: 01489 787700
Chef: Martin Nash
Proprietor: Best Western.
Manager: Philip Audrain
Cost: Alc £22, fixed-price
L £10.50/D £16.50.
H/wine £8.95 ¶ Service inc
Credit cards: ■ ■ ■ ■ OTHER
Times: Last L 2pm/D 10pm
Seats: 90. No smoking in dining room
Additional: Children welcome, children's menu/portions. Vegetarian dishes

Directions: On the A334, 1 mile from junc 7 of M27

HIGHCLERE,
Hollington Country House ❀❀❀

A relaxed, friendly country house restaurant with an ambitious and talented chef

Woolton Hill RG20 9XA
Map no: 4 SU45
Tel: 01635 255100
Chef: David Lake
Proprietors: John Guy
Cost: Alc £30-£40, fixed-price
L £16.75/D £28. H/wine £12 ¶
Service exc
Credit cards: ■ ■ ■ ■
Times: Last L 2pm, last D 9.30pm
Menus: A la carte, fixed-price
L & D
Seats: 50. No-smoking area
Additional: Children welcome, children's portions; ♥ dishes, vegan on request, other diets by arrangement

Gertrude Jekyll originally designed the gardens of the 1904 house which was restored and converted by the proprietors, John and Penny Guy, in 1992 to create a relaxing country home, rather than a formal hotel. The fixed-price menu changes every day and the *carte* ticks over with the seasons, but one can draw from either on a mix and match basis. Both rely on abundant supplies of quality local produce. David Lake, the young chef, is intent on building a strong reputation and if he continues to provide meals like the one experienced at inspection, he should succeed. A first course showed his flair – lamb sweetbreads and foie gras layered between discs of fine filo with savoy cabbage and served with a split sauce (oils and balsamic vinegar). The following large noisette of lamb, stuffed with a wonderfully crunchy leek was served on a bed of spinach with a well made rich veal jus, but perhaps too little of the advertised rosemary. There followed a rich, but not sickly, chocolate marquise wrapped in a thin layer of Genoise sponge, served with lightly whipped cream and poached plum.

Other choices from a spring *carte* convey the Hollington style – lightly pan-fried Hampshire trout fillets with a mushroom duxelle and a sweet Gewürztraminer sauce, confit of rabbit leg, and tian of layered Provençal vegetables cooked with olive oil and basil, accompanied by roasted tomatoes and pesto, wine-braised oxtail, boned and filled with cabbage, bacon and shallots, steamed fillet of turbot on a confit of leeks with braised fennel and a light vegetable nage. Among the desserts could be the English classic, Eve's

Pudding, a savarin of winter-stored fruits, or assiette of banana. The comprehensive range of Antipodean wines is probably unequalled in this country, but there are French and other European bottles too.

Directions: Take A343 (Andover) from Newbury. Follow signs for Hollington Herb Garden: restaurant is next door

HURSTBOURNE TARRANT,
Esseborne Manor 🏵🏵

Exciting cooking at this family-owned hotel with a cosy atmosphere and attentive service

Andover SP11 0ER
Map no: 4 SU35
Tel: 01264 736444
Chef: Nick Watson
Proprietor: Ian & Lucilla Hamilton (Pride of Britain)
Cost: *Alc* £27, fixed-price L £17.50. H/wine £12. No service charge
Credit cards: 🔲 🔲 🔲 🔲 OTHER
Times: Last L 2pm/D 9.30pm
Menus: *A la carte,* fixed-price L
Seats: 30. No cigars or pipes
Additional: Children over 12 permitted, 🌣 dishes, vegan/other diets on request

Down a short drive from the main road, nestling in the quiet of the North Wessex Downs, is the Georgian/Victorian farmhouse known as Esseborne Manor. The delightful restaurant offers an exciting array of dishes carefully prepared under the supervision of the new head chef Nicholas Watson. A starter of marinated scallops and red snapper was perhaps a little overpowered by a pungent balsamic vinegar sauce but a breast of gamey pheasant was complemented by a parsnip purée and a port wine sauce. The iced lemon and stem ginger parfait delivered all the promised flavours and served with a chestnut purée and rich chocolate sauce, proved the highlight of the evening. The wine list offers a good selection of New Worlds and half bottles.

Directions: On A343, 1 mile north of Hurstbourne Tarrant

LIPHOOK,
Nippon Kan at Old Thorns 🏵

Traditional teppan yaki counters provide the focal point of an authentic Japanese restaurant, part of the Old Thorns Golf Hotel. Rice dishes, sushi and a short carte offering popular options such as tempura and sukiyaki as well as a range of set menus with rice, miso soup and pickles

Times: 12.30pm-last L 2pm/D 8.30pm. Closed Mon; day after Bh Mons **Seats:** 36 **Additional:** Children welcome, children's portions/ menu **Directions:** Approx. 500 yards from Griggs Green exit off A3

Longmoor Road GU30 7PE
Map no: 4 SU83
Tel: 01428 724555
Chef: Mr T Suzuki
Proprietor: London Kosaido Co Ltd.
Cost: *Alc* from £28, fixed-price L £8.50. H/wine £8.95 ❢ Service inc
Credit cards: 🔲 🔲 🔲 🔲 OTHER

LIPHOOK,
Old Thorns Golf Course Hotel ❀❀

Smart international cuisine at Japanese golf hotel

Japanese golfers take their sport seriously, and nowhere more so than in this East meets West Japanese owned hotel, golf course and luxury leisure complex. The cuisine, as well as the fairways, are expected to be of the highest standard, and there are two first-class restaurants, one Japanese and one European. This year, in the latter, a short, seasonal *carte* has offered dishes such as a well-constructed brawn of pigeon and finely diced vegetables served with red cabbage and apple chutney, and a rather dry Scottish rib-eye steak with glazed foie gras, mushroom duxelle and a fine Madeira sauce. Most dishes have an international slant, such as haddock kedgeree, sautéed mushrooms with lemon and garlic topped with mozzarella, halibut torte sandwiched with smoked salmon and ginger, and trimmed lamb cutlets baked with a crust of basil, pine nuts and apricots. There is a good selection of desserts, some of which need more care in preparation. Some 60 bins from around the world include, at one end, some 1er Cru Classe Red Bordeaux, such as a 1976 Latour for £169, and at the other, a good value £8.95 house wine.

Directions: Approx. 500yds from Griggs Green exit off A3

Longmoor Road GU30 7PE
Map no: 4 SU83
Tel: 01428 724555
Chef: Geoff Sutton
Proprietor: London Kosaido Co Ltd
Cost: Alc £23.95, fixed-price D £20. H/wine £8.95 ❢ Service inc
Credit cards: ◪ 🎫 🎫 💷 OTHER
Times: Last L 2pm, 7pm-last D 9pm. Closed Sun night, Sat L
Menus: A la carte, fixed-price D, Sun lunch
Seats: 50
Additional: Children over 12 permitted; ❶ & vegan dishes, ❶ menu, other diets on request

LYMINGTON,
Gordleton Mill Hotel ❀❀❀

A converted mill house in the New Forest with an exciting choice of French Mediterranean cooking from a range of menus

The prestigious Provence Restaurant is a mainstay of this fine hotel, a converted 17th-century water mill by the water race in its own attractive gardens. Talented new chef/manager Toby Hill gained much of his experience at Le Manoir aux Quat Saisons. There is an excellent choice of menus, including the *carte*, a good value three-course menu du jour, and a menu gourmandise of six courses inclusive of wine (carefully selected to accompany each course), coffee and petits fours. Fresh fish and seafood feature

Silver Street
Hordle SO41 6DJ
Map no: 4 SZ39
Tel: 01590 682219
Chef: Toby Hill
Proprietor: W F Stone.
Managers: Toby Hill and Melanie Philby
Cost: Alc from £37, fixed-price L £15/D £45 (6 course inc wine). H/wine £13 ❢ Service exc
Credit cards: ◪ 🎫 🎫 💷 OTHER
Times: Noon-last L 2pm, 7pm-last D 9.30pm. Closed 2 wks Jan
Menus: A la carte, fixed-price L & D
Seats: 50 (6 terrace tables). Air conditioned. No smoking in dining room
Additional: Children over 7 permitted, children's portions; ❶ dishes, vegan/other diets on request

prominently, with supplies obtained daily, and the quality of the ingredients is enhanced by produce from the kitchen garden, which provides herbs, salads, berry fruits and vegetables.

At a recent inspection meal an impressive langoustine mousseline appetiser, wrapped in a spinach leaf and set on an olive oil vinaigrette, made a stunning first impression. The starter was succulent steamed langoustines set on a julienne of courgettes, garnished with firm-textured ravioli filled with fresh crab and tomato set on spinach leaves and served with a butter, tomato and garlic-oil sauce. The main course comprised tender pink slices of Norfolk duck breast, garnished with filo parcels of shallots and figs, and served with a refined jus flavoured with fresh chopped herbs. The dessert, 'pomme soufflé au sabayon de Calvados', was set in an apple with a cherry confit base, had a lovely soufflé top, with lashings of Calvados and was accompanied by an apple sorbet in an almond tulip. There is an impressive wine list with a big French section and vintage wines from all the principal growing regions of the world, including a fine collection of Hospices de Beaune from the 1960s, and a good selection of half bottles.

Gordleton Mill Hotel

Directions: Take A337 to Lymington, at railway bridge mini-roundabout go straight on then first right in 1.5 miles

LYMINGTON, **Stanwell House Hotel** ❀

An elegant restaurant which leads onto the hotel's gardens and offers skilfully prepared Anglo-French cooking. Good honest flavours and fresh ingredients feature strongly in dishes such as goats' cheese and leek tartlet and noisettes of lamb on a bed of pease pudding

Times: Last L 2pm/D 9.30pm
Seats: 60. No-smoking area. No pipes or cigars
Additional: Children welcome, children's menu/portions. ♥ dishes, vegan on request.
Directions: In the High Street

High Street
Map no: 4 SZ39
Tel: 01590 677123
Chef: Mark Hewitt
Proprietors: Arcadian International.
Manager: Andrew Woodland
Cost: Alc L £11/D £22.50.
Service exc
Credit cards: 🗅 🖭 🖼 💷 OTHER

LYNDHURST, **Crown Hotel** ❀

Located at a focal point in town is this 19th-century coaching inn offering quality cooking using locally supplied ingredients. Choose from a daily fixed-price menu or a seasonally changing carte. Try chicken liver salad, fillet of salmon with strips of smoked salmon, and apricot soufflé with iced ginger parfait

Seats: 80 **Additional:** Children welcome, children's menu; ♥ dishes, other diets on request
Directions: Follow one-way traffic system, opposite village church in High Street

High Street SO43 7NF
Map no: 4 SU30
Tel: 01703 282922
Chef: Paul Putt
Proprietors: Mr & Mrs Green (Best Western).
Manager: Jenny McDonald
Cost: Alc £28.50, fixed-price L/D £12.75 /£16. H/wine £9.50.
❢ Service exc
Credit cards: 🗅 🖭 🖼 💷 OTHER
Times: Last L 1.45pm/D 9.30pm

LYNDHURST, **Parkhill Hotel** ❀❀

An idyllically situated New Forest hotel offering an imaginative range of modern English dishes

Standing at the end of a long winding drive leading from the forest, this handsome 18th-century property is beautifully situated in its own grounds. The hotel continues to be improved under the

Beaulieu Road SO43 7FZ
Map no: 4 SU30
Tel: 01703 282944
Chef: Richard Turner
Proprietors: N M & G P Topham

ownership of Mr and Mrs Topham, and the interior is attractive and well furnished. Chef Richard Turner and his team offer a varied menu of modern English dishes, cooked with skill using good quality produce. Lemon sole and seafood soufflé made a favourable first impression at a recent test meal, served with a tomato and lime sauce. This was followed by an excellent saddle of lamb, though the combination of the accompanying honeyed parsnips and redcurrant sauce was perhaps a little too sweet. Hot chocolate pudding with superb pistachio sauce rounded off the meal. Alternative dishes could be marinated local freshwater trout served with warm sautéed tiger prawns and lemon dressing, and Cajun spiced chicken on a bed of black noodles with an orange and ginger sauce. A selection of dishes carved or presented at the table is also available, including chateaubriand lightly smoked over camomile leaves, and New Forest venison Diane, flambéed at the table in Cognac, with a mushroom and shallot cream sauce.

Cost: *Alc* from £28.50, fixed-price L £12.20/D £25.50 (4 course). H/wine £10.75
❗ Service exc
Credit cards: 🔳 🔳 🔳 🔳 OTHER
Times: Last L 2pm, last D 9.30pm
Menus: *A la carte*, fixed-price L & D, bar menu
Seats: 80. No smoking in dining room
Additional: Children welcome, children's menu; ❶ menu, vegan/other diets on request

Directions: From Lyndhurst take B3056 (Beaulieu). After 1 mile turn right at Parkhill sign; from Southampton take A35 (Lyndhurst)

MIDDLE WALLOP, Fifehead Manor 🏵🏵

An historic country house hotel deep in the heart of what a local brewery used to call the Strong Country

Wallop here simply means 'valley of the stream', not beer. Any disappointment in such a prosaic explanation can be more than offset by this lovely manor house, with foundations said to date from the 11th century. The low-ceilinged, beamed dining-room was probably the main hall of the medieval manor house and the remains of a minstrels' gallery are still visible. There are two set-price menus – lunch and dinner, with the latter offering a larger choice. Simplicity and saucing are the keynotes of what the proprietors call Mediterranean-style cooking, although honey and soy-glazed duck in a sesame sauce, fillet of lamb with a green peppercorn and parsley crust, and beef fillet with mixed wild mushrooms and a Madeira sauce would appear to carry passports from elsewhere. Market-fresh fish, such as prime turbot and salmon in a cucumber and chive butter sauce, is available daily. Desserts come with or without guilt-free tags. For example, lemon mousse with fresh strawberries and a lemon sorbet will slip down a treat, whereas warm blackberry, apple and almond tart with almond ice-cream, or trio of chocolate pudding will happily make a nonsense of any calorie-controlled diet. Fifty or so wines makes for a good choice.

Map no: 4 SU23
Tel: 01264 781565
Chef: Mark Robertson
Proprietors: Mr & Mrs Bishop-Milnes
Cost: Fixed-price L £19, £25/D £25 Service exc
Credit cards: 🔳 🔳 🔳 🔳
Times: Last L 2.15pm, Last D 9.15pm. Closed 2 weeks Xmas
Menus: Fixed-price lunch and dinner, Sunday lunch, pre-theatre, bar menu
Seats: 40. No smoking in dining room
Additional: Children welcome, children's portions/menu; ❶ dishes, vegan/other diets on request

Directions: On the A343, 5 miles south of Andover

MILFORD ON SEA, Rocher's Restaurant 🏵🏵

Typical little French restaurant transplanted to a pretty New Forest village

69/71 High Street SO41 0QG
Map no: 4 SZ29
Tel: 01590 642340
Chef: Alain Rocher
Proprietors: Alain & Rebecca Rocher

Chef/patron Alain Rocher single-handedly cooks a short, unashamedly French menu that changes daily, according to market supplies. Fans of true cuisine bourgeoise will enjoy a skilful range of dishes such as chicken livers with capers, avocado and smoked salmon fan with lemon sauce, noisettes of lamb with creamy garlic sauce, and pan-fried guinea fowl with coarse grain mustard sauce. Fish is well represented and deftly cooked; choose from the likes of sea bass scented with a delicate Noilly Pratt sauce, scallops with ginger sauce or the classic sole meunière. Desserts are equally mainstream – chocolate parfait with vanilla sauce, caramel and peppermint bavaroise, and freshly made crème brûlée. Cheeses, naturellement, are French. The large and interesting wine list shows a strong patriotic bent, and features some fine wines from the Loire, clarets and Burgundies. Amongst the de-luxe, special occasion choices are a 1981 Ch. Margaux 1er Cru Classe for £117, and an Hospices de Beaune Pommard Dames de la Charité 1985 for £86. There are, however, plenty of good, less expensive wines, including a decent number of halves.

Cost: Alc £23.50, fixed-price L £14.50, fixed-price D £16.50, £19.40, £22.90. Sunday lunch £13.50. H/wine from £8.50 Service exc
Credit cards: 🔳 ▨ 🔟 OTHER
Times: Sunday L noon-1.45pm, 7.15pm-Last dinner 9.30pm. Closed L (except Sun) Mon, Tue, 2 weeks June
Menus: Fixed-price dinner, Sunday lunch
Seats: 30. No cigars or pipes
Additional: No children under 10 (under 13 at dinner)

Directions: On the B3058, 3 miles south-west of Lymington

MILFORD ON SEA, **South Lawn Hotel** ❀

☺ *Peaceful hotel providing high standards of comfort and service, especially in the relaxing dining-room. The kitchen keeps faith with local produce. The sweet trolley is a further temptation laden with delicious home-made deserts and fresh fruit*

Lymington Road SO41 0RF
Map no: 4 SZ29
Tel: 01590 643911
Chef: David Gates and Ernst Barten
Proprietors: Ernst & Jennifer Barten
Cost: Alc £22, fixed-price L £10.25/£16.25, H/wine £13.60 ❢ Service exc
Credit cards: 🔳 ▨
Times: Last L 1.30pm/D 8.30pm Closed Dec 20-Jan 19
Menus: A la carte, fixed-price L & D
Seats: 80. No smoking in dining room
Additional: Children over 7 welcome, children's portions; ❶ dishes, other diets on request

Directions: Turn off A337 at Everton onto B3508, 0.5 mile on right

NEW MILTON,
Chewton Glen Hotel ❀❀❀

Imaginative menus with a classical base and modern influences at this top ranking hotel, health & country club

Ideally situated between the New Forest and the sea, this internationally renowned hotel is set in immaculate grounds and has one of the finest health and country clubs in Britain. Pierre Chevillard's cooking lives up to the superior surroundings – a handsome Palladian country house – drawing on both modern and classical traditions to present an eclectic range of dishes which, as one might imagine, are not cheap.
    A spring meal began with good canapés, and an appetiser of

Chewton Farm Road BH25 6QS
Map no: 4 SZ29
Tel: 01425 275341
Chef: Pierre Chevillard
Proprietor: Martin Skan (Relais & Chateaux/Leading Hotels)
Cost: Alc £45-£50, fixed-price L £23.50/D £39.50. H/wine £13 Service exc
Credit cards: 🔳 ▨ 🔟 OTHER
Times: Last L 1.45pm/last D 9.30pm
Menus: A la carte, fixed-price L & D Daily

Seats: 180. Air conditioned.
No smoking in dining room
Additional: Children over 7
permitted, ❂ dishes, vegan/
other diets on request

scrambled eggs with foie gras. Dishes tried this year have included ravioli of langoustines served with a fondue of cucumber in a brandy and coriander sauce, the dish a little overpowered by the flavour of orange zest in the sauce, and also a fricassé of scallops on a bed of lentils with crispy bacon and a sweet pepper coulis, an excellent combination of flavours and textures. A main course of emince of new season lamb, studded with garlic, came with an intensely flavoured gratin of courgette and tomato, plus a good lamb jus; and pavé of black Aberdeen Angus was served on a bed of creamed mousseron with a black pepper and brandy sauce. There is a selection of English and French farmhouse cheeses from the trolley and a tempting dessert menu including whisky crème brûlée with hazelnut shortbread, and peach tart topped with walnut crumble and accompanied by a wonderful pistachio ice cream. Mediterranean and oriental influences are evident in dishes such as early summer Italian salad with pesto and toasted goats' cheese, and sea bass with shiitake mushrooms, ginger and lemon grass. The wine list and wine service are both first class. Every country and region is represented, with full pages devoted to different vintages of some classic estates. There are also six pages of Champagnes and a good choice of half bottles.

Directions: On A35 (Lyndhurst) turn right through Walkford, then 2nd left into Chewton Farm Road

OLD BURGHCLERE,

The Dew Pond Restaurant ❀❀❀

The simplicity of this whitewashed restaurant complements the enjoyment of a good range of dishes notable for their natural flavours

Set in open countryside but easily accessible from Newbury, Basingstoke and Winchester, this charming restaurant was created from two 16th-century drovers' cottages. Within, the atmosphere is homely, the eating area semi-divided into two rooms like those of a private house, and a friendly staff provides both a warm welcome and helpful but unobtrusive service.

Chef/proprietor Keith Marshall offers interesting fixed-price menus of beautifully simple Anglo-French dishes, their natural flavours an accolade to the expert preparation of quality ingredients. On a recent visit the twice-baked Gruyère soufflé was perfect –

RG15 9LH
Map no: 4 SU45
Tel: 01635 27408
Chef: Keith Marshall
Proprietor: Keith Marshall
Cost: Fixed-price dinner £23.
H/wine £11. Service inc
Credit cards: ▨ ▧
Times: 7pm-last D 10pm.
Closed Sun D, Mon
Menus: Fixed-price dinner,
Sun lunch
Seats: 44.
Additional: ❂ menu, vegan/
other diets on request

The Dew Pond Restaurant

light, cheesy and served with a single cream and leek sauce. Rosy pink medallions of roe deer and a tiny tomato and basil tart melted in the mouth, a jus-based sauce lightly scented with ginger and juniper achieving just the right balance. Desserts are so tempting as to make choice difficult, but our inspector opted for a plated selection including a deliciously zesty lemon tart, a rich dark and light chocolate mousse with moist hazelnut sponge, a creamy iced nougat parfait and a light strawberry mousse in a brandy snap basket. The equally delectable chocolate truffles and caramel-dipped fresh fruit that accompanied Colombian infused coffee ended the meal on a high note. An extensive, good-value wine list contains some noteworthy labels.

Directions: Six miles south of Newbury. Take the Burghclere turn off A34 (Winchester), and follow signs for Old Burghclere

PORTSMOUTH & SOUTHSEA,

Bistro Montparnasse ❀❀

Welcoming high-street bistro with a lively, seasonal menu

The name may suggest pure cuisine bourgeois, but then, what's in a name? Gillian Scott's broad Euro-menu takes in dishes such as escalope of salmon with a mild curry cream with spiced lentils, confit of pork with spätzle and a beer sauce, as well as Alsace onion tart. One of her strongest influences is Italian, and over the last year, seasonal menus have featured brodetto, the Italian seafood stew, prosciutto and sautéed greens with warm balsamic vinegar dressing, and meatballs with lemon and Parmesan on wholewheat tagliatelle. Delicious Italian breads, served with olives and extra virgin olive oil, are made in-house. On a recent visit, however, the pizzetta with aubergine and pesto was light and tasty, if a bit short on the last item. Crispy breast of duck was rather overcooked, but served with an aromatic sauce of lemon grass and honey. An excellent Italian inspired dessert of olive oil sponge, flavoured with Sauterne and served with a compote of rhubarb, was refreshingly different. The wine list is predominantly French, although there are inclusions from Europe and the New World, and several half bottle choices.

Directions: Follow signs to D-Day Museum, then turn left into Castle Avenue the restaurant is at first junction

103 Palmerston Road
Southsea PO5 3PS
Map no: 4 SU60
Tel: 01705 816754
Chef: Gillian Scott
Proprietors: Peter & Gillian Scott
Cost: *Alc* £25, fixed-price D £12.50. H/wine £8.50 ❢ Service exc
Credit cards: ▨ ▤ ▨
Times: 7pm-last D 10pm (Tue-Sat). Closed Sun, Mon, Bhs
Menus: *A la carte* & fixed-price D
Seats: 40+25. No cigars or pipe
Additional: Children welcome, ❷ dishes, vegan/other diets on request

RINGWOOD,
Moortown Lodge Hotel ❀❀

Uncomplicated but delightful cooking in an attractive hotel restaurant

Ringwood is one of the gateways to the New Forest. This small, country-style hotel, situated just south of the town, has been owned and run by Bob and Jilly Burrows-Jones for about nine years. They know how to welcome and care for their customers: he maintains a solicitous presence out front while she cooks the short, four-course set menu (supplemented by a daily special). The cooking style is simple but based on sound technique and a fair degree of flair and imagination. On a recent visit the meal started with floating cheese island – a cheese soufflé – beautifully light and delicately flavoured, although, unfortunately, the sauce was quite bland. The main course, poussin in a rich wine sauce, came with a selection of fresh local vegetables. Dessert was a creamy ginger and Advocaat syllabub served with a macaroon. The wine list favours France, with a good choice of half bottles. Vegetarians are catered for on request. Local sausages served at breakfast are excellent and afternoon tea comes with home-made cake.

Directions: From Ringwood centre take B3347 towards Christchurch for about 1.5 miles

244 Christchurch Road
BH24 3AS
Map no: 4 SU10
Tel: 01425 471404
Chef: Jilly Burrows-Jones
Proprietors: Jilly & Bob Burrows-Jones
Cost: Fixed price D £14.95. H/wine £7.95. Service exc
Credit cards: 🔲 🔳 🔳
Times: 7pm-last D 8.30pm. Closed Sun, 2 weeks Jan
Menus: Fixed price D, gourmet dishes at weekend
Seats: 24. No smoking in dining room
Additional: Children welcome, ❷ dishes, vegan/other diets by arrangement

RINGWOOD,
Tyrrells Ford Country House ❀

An attractive country house which stands in ten acres of woodland and gardens. The smartly decorated restaurant offers a considerable choice of dishes, including a well-made liver pate, and a tender breast of chicken, agreeably cooked with a good pepper sauce and fresh vegetables

Avon BH23 7BH
Map no: 4 SU10
Tel: 01425 672646
Chef: n/a
Proprietor: n/a.
Manageress: Mrs. Collette Birkbeck (Best Western)
Cost: Alc from £21.10, fixed-price L £13.95 /D £17.95 (4 course). H/wine £8.95 Service exc
Credit cards: 🔲 🔳 🔳 🔳 OTHER
Times: 11am-last L 2pm/D 9.30pm
Seats: 120. No-smoking area
Menus: A la carte, fixed-price L & D, bar menu
Additional: Children welcome, children's portions; ❷ dishes, vegan/other diets on request

Directions: M27/A31 to Ringwood, B3347 south 3 miles to Avon

'Alla parmigiana' means the way it is made in Parma. As the name suggests it includes Parmesan and prosciutto although the latter is an optional ingredient.

ROMSEY,
Old Manor House Restaurant ❀❀❀

Italian cooking, including robust regional fare, based on quality
ingredients served in a beamed cottage restaurant

21 Palmerston Street SO51 8GF
Map no: 4 SU32
Tel: 01794 517353
Chef: Mauro Bregoli
Proprietor: Mauro Bregoli
Cost: *Alc* £25, fixed-price L &
D £17.50. H/wine £9.95 Service
exc
Credit cards: 🔳 ▦ ▦ OTHER
Times: Noon-last L 2pm, 7pm-
last D 9.30pm. Closed Sun D,
Mon
Menus: *A la carte*, fixed-price
lunch and dinner
Seats: 45. No cigars or pipes
Additional: Children welcome,
❻ dishes, other diets on request

A Tudor beamed cottage, standing opposite the entrance to the
Broadlands estate, this restaurant has a sophisticated atmosphere
which accurately reflects the serious intent in the kitchen. The
front-of-house is supervised by Esther Bregoli. The kitchen is the
domain of anglophile chef Mauro Bregoli, whose passion for fishing
and hunting is evident in the carefully sourced ingredients – locally
produced wherever possible. The most successful dishes are those
that draw on Mr Bregoli's Italian roots. A risotto of snails with
pesto, sampled early this year, was a delicious combination of
tender snails and rice. Starters also include home-smoked salmon
and bresaola, as well as popular salamis and hearty cotechino, a
spicy Italian sausage served hot with lentils, which show a command
of regional cookery contrasting with the more refined recipes often
featured.

Some dishes can miss the mark completely, with a tendency to
disguise rather than enhance the quality of the main ingredient. For
example, a superb fillet of brill was somewhat spoiled by an oily
potato crust. Other main course options might be pan-fried breast
of duck with a reduction sauce of honey and balsamic vinegar, and
boned pig's head stuffed with morels and served with borlotti beans
and red onion marmalade. Puddings include the familiar tiramisu
and zuppa inglese along with more unusual items such as lasagna of
two chocolates with an infusion of mint, and a crème brûlée
strangely flavoured with fennel and fresh herbs; the latter
ingredients were regarded as unnecessary as the custard was
excellent and stood alone without elaboration. Coffee is strong and
full flavoured, accompanied by good quality petits fours. It is worth
spending time perusing the magnificent wine list, which offers great
vintages from the best estates and some exceptional Italian wines.

Directions: Opposite the entrance to Broadlands Estate

Our inspectors never book in the name of the AA. They
disclose their identity only after the bill has been paid.

ROTHERWICK, Tylney Hall Hotel ❀❀

A fine country house hotel with an enviable record in providing very good food

Rotherwick RG27 9AZ
Map no: 4 SU75
Tel: 01256 764881
Chef: Stephen Hine
Manager: Rita Mooney
Cost: *Alc* £35, fixed price L
£19.50/D £28. H/wine £12.85.
Service inc
Credit cards: 🂾 📰 💳 💷 OTHER
Times: 12.30-last L 2pm, 7.30-
last D 8.45pm
Seats: 100
Additional: Children welcome,
children's menu; ❂ dishes,
vegan/other diets on request

There are 66 acres of woodland, lakes and rose gardens to wander
around (much of it laid out by Gertrude Jekyll) and from which to
look back at the imposing, 19th-century, red-brick mansion. Within,
there is a natural harmony between an old-fashioned style of
service and the modern eclectic cooking. Stephen Hine has been
the chef here for a long time and he and his team know instinctively
how to compile winning *cartes* and fixed-price lunch and dinner
menus. There is no denying the hard work and effort behind the
production of food in the kitchen; the style is refreshingly simple.
Sample dishes from one recent dinner included lobster terrine
served with vegetable vinaigrette, grilled sea bass with black pepper
and lime, complemented by a caraway and vermouth sauce and
'perfectly cooked' quail married well with an artichoke heart and
mushroom ragout, but rather underwhelmed by a Madeira sauce.
Desserts are standard trolley offerings but there are specials such as
iced praline nougat with a sauce of oranges, grapefruit and passion
fruit, or baked apple in filo pastry with cinnamon sauce. There is an
extensive wine list.

Directions: from M4 jnct. 11 take B3349 towards Hook, left to
Rotherwick at sharp bend, left again and left in village to Newnham,
1 mile on right; from M3 jnct. 5 take A287 to Newnham

SHERFIELD ON LODDON, Wessex House ❀

☺ *A pleasant hotel on the edge of the village offering sound cooking
based on fresh produce. At a recent meal, home-made vegetable soup,
chicken breast filled with Stilton, and sticky toffee pudding were heavily
endorsed. The fixed-price menu changes weekly*

Menus: *A la carte,* fixed price L & D
Seats: 80
Additional: Children welcome, children's portions; ❂ menu,
vegan/other diets on request
Directions: Off A33 Basingstoke–Reading road in Sherfield

Reading Road RG27 0EX
Map: 4 SU65
Tel: 01256 882243
Chef: Mr J Lado
Proprietor: Mr & Mrs H Hall
Cost: *Alc,* £16.25-£23.50, fixed
price L £10.95/D £10.95
(£14.95 Fri & Sat)
Credit cards: 🂾 📰 💳 💷
Times: Noon-last L 1.30pm,
6.30pm-last D 9.30

SILCHESTER, **Romans Hotel** ✦

Named, naturally, after the local ruins, this privately-run hotel is set in attractive gardens. Menus include a carte and a daily fixed-price, plus theme menus offering the likes of escalope of ostrich and caviar – complete with an accompanying choice of vodkas. Service is professional and attentive

Menus: A la carte, fixed price L & D, Sun lunch, bar menu
Seats: 40
Additional: Children welcome, children's portions; ✦ dishes on request
Directions: In the centre of the village

Little London Road RG7 2PN
Map no: 4 SU66
Tel: 01734 700421
Chef: Shelley May
Proprietor: Mr N Tuthill
Cost: Fixed-price L & D £13.95 (2 courses), £16.95 (3 courses). H/wine £8.90 ❢ Service exc
Credit cards: 🔲 🔲 🔲 🔲
Times: Last L 2pm, last D 9.30pm. Closed Sun D, Sat L, 24 Dec-2 Jan

SOUTHAMPTON,
De Vere Grand Harbour ✦

Fresh fish is a feature at this harbour hotel. Paupiettes of plaice filled with cockles and mussels, white wine stock with carrots and coriander has been highly recommended. Starters include the likes of chicken liver parfait and for desert, rum baba

Menus: A la carte, fixed-price L
Seats: 45. Air conditioned. No smoking in dining room
Additional: Children welcome, children's menu; ✦ dishes, vegan/ other diets on request
Directions: In 'old town' Southampton

West Quay Road SO15 1AG
Map no: 4 SU41
Tel: 01703 633033
Chef: David Hewlett
Proprietor: De Vere Hotels. Manager: Duncan Fisher
Cost: Alc £25.50, fixed-price £15.50. H/wine £10.75 Service exc
Credit cards: 🔲 🔲 🔲 🔲 OTHER
Times: Last L 2.15pm/last D 10.15pm Closed Sun, some Bhs

SOUTHAMPTON, **Golden Palace** ✦

☺ *A large, unpretentious city centre Chinese restaurant. It caters especially well for large parties and family groups. The lengthy carte offers all the standard favourites in large portions and at low prices. Meaty spare ribs, and beef with green peppers and black bean sauce are typical examples. The wine list offers popular European wines*

Seats: 80
Additional: Children welcome, ✦ menu, vegan on request
Directions: Above shops in pedestrian area near the Bar Gate

17a Above Bar Street
Map no: 4 SU41
Tel: 01703 226636
Chef: Tony Shek
Proprietor: David Lai
Costs: Fixed-price L £4.30 (£4.60 Sat). Service exc
Credit cards: 🔲 🔲 🔲 🔲
Times: Last D 11.45pm

SOUTHAMPTON, **Kuti's Brasserie** ✦

☺ *Spacious, modern and colourful restaurant with a relaxed, friendly, informal atmosphere. Cooking is standard North Indian with traditional tandoori dishes. Expect bhoona lamb tikka, rogan gosht and lamb badam pasana*

Menus: A la carte, fixed-price L & Sun D buffet
Seats: 30. Air conditioned
Additional: Children welcome, ✦ dishes, children's portions/vegan/ other diets on request,
Directions: In old part of City near Ocean Village and docks

37-39 Oxford Street
Map no: 4 SU41
Tel: 01703 221585/333473
Chefs: Romis, K, & Iqbal Miah
Proprietors: Chandra K Miah and others.
Managers: K & Anwar Miah
Cost: A la carte from £8.50, Sun D buffet £9.50 H/wine £7.50 ❢ Service exc
Credit cards: 🔲 🔲 🔲 🔲 OTHER
Times: Noon-last L 2.15pm, 6pm-last D 11.30pm Closed Dec 25/6

STOCKBRIDGE, **Peat Spade Inn** 🏵🏵

Simple English and European dishes carefully cooked and served by one dedicated professional

Longstock SO20 6DR
Map no: 4 SU33
Tel: 01264 810612
Chef: Julie Teresa Tuckett
Proprietor: Julie Teresa Tuckett
Cost: Alc £19.50-£25.50, fixed-price L/D £11.85 (2 courses), £16.50. H/wine £9.75 ❢ Service exc
Credit cards: 💳 💳
Times: Last L 2pm/D 10pm. Closed Sun D, Dec 25/26, 2/3 wks Feb-Mar
Menus: A la carte, fixed-price L & D
Seats: 30. No pipes
Additional: Children permitted, children's portions; ❤ dishes, vegan dish; other diets on request

A dedicated approach to cooking is evident at this small restaurant, tucked away in the charming village of Longstock. It is very much a one woman show, performed by Julie Tuckett, who manages to cook the food and serve it herself with only occasional help; expect to enjoy a leisurely meal of reasonably priced, simple English and European dishes. The ingredients used reflect careful shopping – seasonal local game may feature, for example. Inspection yielded a particularly enjoyable starter of tomato, aubergine and feta tart which proved to be fresh in flavour with an excellent pastry crust, and chargrilled breast of Barbary duck with a correctly cooked sauce based on the meat juices. The blackboard menu has a selection of dishes available as either a starter or main course, such as rillettes of pork, and a selection of substantial salads. Typical main courses from the *carte* are roast fillet of venison, and sautéed lambs' kidneys with Madeira. Puddings have a pronounced traditional slant – treacle tart, sticky toffee pudding, and sherry trifle. There is a short wine list featuring a choice of 16 wines available by the glass.

Directions: Longstock is one and a half miles north of Stockbridge, off A3057

SWAY, **String of Horses** 🏵

Classic French dishes are served in the restaurant of this delightful hotel on the fringe of the New Forest. Chicken liver timbale and lemon sole poached in white wine, with raspberry torte for dessert, formed the components of one inspection meal

Mead End Road
Sway
Map no: 4 SZ39
Tel: 01590 682631
Chef: Julio Frias Robles
Proprietor: Gillian A Reardon
Seats: 30. No smoking
Times: Last Sun L 2pm/Last D 9pm. Lunch served only on Sun, D not served Sun. Closed Mon, Tue

Cost: Alc from £20, Sun L £11.95, fixed-price D £17.95. H/wine £8.50 (litre). Service exc
Credit cards: 💳 💳 💳 💳 OTHER
Additional: Children permitted, over 14 at dinner; ❤ dishes; other diets on request
Directions: From village centre with Post Office on your left, cross Station bridge and take 2nd left, 350yds on left

WARSASH,
Nook and Cranny Restaurant ❀

In a sleepy hamlet, this 18th-century cottage has been converted into a popular restaurant. Sound cooking could include warm pigeon salad on mixed leaves with bacon and garlic croutons, 'soufflé suissesse', a twice baked cheese soufflé, and tarte au citron. The fixed-price menu offers good value

Menus: Fixed-price L & D
Seats: 50
Additional: Children welcome, children's portions; ❂ dishes, other diets on request
Directions: Turn off Warsash road into Fleet End Road, restaurant within 1 mile

Hook Lane
Hook Village SO31 9HH
Map no: 4 SU40
Tel: 01489 584129
Chef: Colin Wood
Proprietor: Colin Wood
Cost: Fixed price L £13.95 /D £16.95. H/wine £8.50 ▮ Service inc
Credit cards: ▨ ▨
Times: Noon-last L 1.430pm, 7pm-last D 9.30pm. Closed Sun, Mon; Dec 25-30

WICKHAM, **Old House Hotel** ❀❀

French regional cooking in a relaxed and friendly setting is offered at this elegantly appointed Georgian hotel

There is a rustic French character to the bar and restaurant of this privately owned Georgian hotel, which stands on the town's main square. This is also reflected in the menu, priced for two or three courses, with its French titles and comprehensive English descriptions. It offers some good fish, perhaps local sea bass served with an olive oil and garden herb sauce. Alternatively, there are starters such as duck rillettes, or coarse Barbary duck pate, or a twice baked soufflé of goats' cheese with a salad of sun-dried tomatoes, marinated olives, baby spinach and corn. Seasonal game can feature (with a warning to beware of shot); look out for dishes along the lines of fresh roasted partridge, served with cooking juices, flavoured with Cointreau and fresh orange, and garnished with brandy-soaked prunes. There could also be English fillet steak or Aberdeen Angus sirloin. Desserts, including a rich chocolate marquise with creamy pistachio sauce, are irresistible. The wine list favours France, though the New World is well represented. Service is particularly warm and friendly, creating the most hospitable of atmospheres.

Directions: In the centre of Wickham, 3 miles north of Fareham at the junction of A32 and B2177

The Square PO17 5JG
Map no: 4 SU51
Tel: 01329 833049
Chef: Nicholas Harman
Proprietors: Richard & Annie Skipwirth
Cost: Fixed-price L & D £25. H/wine £12.50. Service inc
Credit cards: ▨ ▨ ▨ ▨
Times: 12.30-last L 1.45pm, 7.30pm-last D 9.30pm. Closed Sun, Sat L Mon L, Bhs, 2 wks Christmas & Aug, 1wk Easter
Menus: Fixed-price L & D
Seats: 35. No cigars or pipes in dining room
Additional: Children welcome, children's portions; ❂ vegan, children's dishes on request

WINCHESTER, **Hotel du Vin** ❀❀

An impressive selections of wines accompanies the modern Mediterranean cooking at this attractive city centre town house hotel

A stylish town house hotel where the cooking is Mediterranean-inspired. The daily changing *carte* is complemented by daily wine selections from the main cellar list, chosen by the hotel's award-winning sommelier; the cellar list also changes on a frequent basis. At a meal taken in winter a plum tomato, grain mustard and Gruyère cheese tart was found to have excellent flavour, and a risotto was well constructed, strong on the advertised Parma ham. A main course of shank of lamb was tender and served rustic-style

14 Southgate Street SO23 9EF
Map no: 4 SU42
Tel: 01962 841414
Chef: James Martin
Proprietors: Messrs. Hutson and Basset
Cost: *Alc* £20-£25, fixed-price Sun L £19.50. H/wine £9.95 ▮ Service exc
Credit cards: ▨ ▨ ▨ ▨ OTHER
Times: Last L 1.45pm/last D 9.45pm

with flageolet beans and red peppers. Dessert included an excellent well-textured crème brûlée. A fixed-price Sunday lunch offers the likes of asparagus with melted butter and rock salt, followed by a traditional roast sirloin of beef with Yorkshire pudding and onion gravy, with perhaps plum and Armagnac tart with crème anglaise for dessert.

Directions: 2 mins from City centre – just off High Street

WINCHESTER, Hunters ❀❀

A setting near the heart of the ancient city with a good range of dishes cooked in modern style

Decorated with saucy Victorian photos and a favourite haunt of local barristers, this city restaurant is so popular that it fairly buzzes with activity, particularly at lunch times. The staff's calm, friendly demeanour ensures that the atmosphere always remains relaxed, however, and high standards of cooking are maintained – the interesting *carte* and fixed-price menu both catering as much for the health-conscious eater as the traditionalist. A starter of moules marinière sampled on a recent inspection visit was excellent, the mussels plump and the wine sauce light and creamy; this was followed by very good (though, on this occasion, overcooked) wild boar and apple sausages served with a rich, onion gravy and perfect creamed potatoes. Desserts ranged from sticky toffee pudding to a white chocolate bavarois, with a strawberry and champagne crème brûlée proving particularly delicious, its flavours all mingling in the cream and the topping slightly chewy in places. The sensibly priced wine list that accompanied the meal successfully covered both Europe and the New World.

Directions: towards top of the City just off High Street, 200yds from Theatre Royal & Library car park

Menus: *A la carte* L & D, fixed-price L
Seats: 45. No pipes or cigars
Additional: Children welcome, children's portions; ❂ dishes, other diets on request

5 Jewry Street SO23 8RZ
Map no: 4 SU42
Tel: 01962 860006
Chef: Alan Stubbington
Proprietor: David Birmingham
Cost: Alc £25, fixed price L £7.50 (2 course), fixed price D £13.50 (3 course). H/wine £8.95
❢ Service exc
Credit cards: ▨ ▩ ▩ ▨ OTHER
Times: noon-last L 2pm, last D 10pm. Closed Sun, Dec 24-30
Menus: *A la carte*, fixed price L & D, pre-theatre
Seats: 42 + private room 25. No smoking in dining room
Additional: Children welcome, children's portions; ❂ dishes, vegan/other diets on request

WINCHESTER,
Lainston House Hotel ❀❀

Enjoyable cooking in elegant, period setting

Acres of parkland and attractive gardens surround this splendid William and Mary mansion. The bar is panelled in carved cedar, and the serene dining-room has well-spaced tables and comfortable high-backed chairs. Dinner is by candlelight, and the stylish menu mixes new and classic ideas. Starters, for example, include green leaf salad of lobster and asparagus with saffron vinaigrette, terrine of beef and wild mushrooms served with Balsamic dressing, and chilled watercress soup with caviar cream. Saucing is one of chef Friedrich Litty's strengths; pan-fried sea bass is set on a bed of potato purée with marinated shallots and a red wine sauce, pan-fried fillet of pork comes with creamed potatoes, caramelised apples, julienne of celeriac and Calvados sauce, and fillet of beef with rösti potato, deep-fried onion rings, mange-touts, haricots verts and Madeira sauce. There is a hot dessert of the day, as well as others such as Grand Marnier crème brûlée and caramelized lemon

Sparsholt SO21 2LT
Map no: 4 SU42
Tel: 01962 863588
Chef: Friedrich Litty
Proprietor: Exclusive Hotels
Cost: Alc £36, fixed-price L £18.50/D £34.50.
H/wine £13 ❢ Service exc
Credit cards: ▨ ▩ ▩ ▨ OTHER
Times: 12.30-last L 2pm, 7pm-last D 10pm
Menus: *A la carte*, fixed-price L, gourmet dinner Fri/Sat, Sun L
Seats: 70. No cigars or pipes
Additional: Children welcome, children's portions; ❂ dishes; vegan/other diets on request

tart with orange sauce and whipped cream. Along with the full list, a number of special recommended wines are offered, selected with the evening's menu in mind.

Directions: Three miles from the centre of Winchester, off the A272 road to Stockbridge. Signposted

WINCHESTER, Old Chesil Rectory ⍟⍟

The food is modern in style, the building ancient; the combination of the two provides a memorable experience

1 Chesil Street SO23 8HU
Map no: 4 SU42
Tel: 01962 851555
Chef: Nicholas A Ruthven-Stuart and Nicola Saunders
Proprietors: Nicholas and Christina Ruthven-Stuart
Cost: *Alc* lunch £26.50, fixed-price L £9.25 (2 courses) H/wine £9.25 ❢ Service exc
Credit cards: ▦ ▦ OTHER
Times: Midday-last L 2pm, 6pm-last D 9.30pm. Closed Sun, Mon, 1 week Xmas, last week July, 1st week August
Menus: *A la carte*, fixed-price L, pre-theatre, bar menu
Seats: 60. No-smoking area
Additional: Children welcome, children's portions; ❶ dishes, vegan/other diets on request

The setting of this two-storey restaurant in one of the oldest buildings in the area – an erstwhile rectory dating from the 16th century – must in itself make eating here something that is not easily forgotten. Oak beams, wooden floors and exposed bricks and mortar establish a permanence that shrug off the minor changes that have taken place over the past four centuries. The food served is equally noteworthy in its own right, however, chef/proprietor Nicholas Ruthven-Stuart spurning any idea of an 'olde worlde', typically English echo of the surroundings and plumping rather for an eclectic collection of international dishes in modern style. Skill, flair and more than a touch of individuality have been brought to the formulation of the dinner *carte* and fixed-price luncheon menus, while a supplementary blackboard menu also allows optimum use of fresh seasonal produce in such dishes as cream of leek and watercress soup or sweet and sour herring salad. Domaine, estate and vintage wines all appear on a descriptive wine list featuring many of the reputable growers in both the Old and New Worlds.

Directions: From the centre of Winchester (King Alfred's statue) at the bottom end of The Broadway take the exit over the bridge. The restaurant is immediately in front on the mini roundabout

Pecorino is an Italian cheese produced in every region of central and southern Italy. It is made from sheep's milk and takes its name from 'pecora', the Italian for sheep. The pecorino we are most familiar with outside Italy is 'romano', a hard, pungent grating cheese from Rome.

WINCHESTER, Royal Hotel ✿

Very friendly, popular and welcoming hotel. Freshly cooked, well-made dishes such as tasty mackerel and salmon pâté, and tender breast of chicken filled with a light prawn mousse served with a delicate cream sauce and fresh vegetables. To follow one could choose a zesty lemon tart with crème fraîche

St Peter Street
Map no: 4 SU42
Tel: 01962 840840
Managers: Tony & Pamela Smith
Cost: Alc £25; fixed-price
L £12.25/D £17.50. H/wine
£9.25 ⁍ Service exc.
Credit cards: 🔳 💳 💳 🔳 OTHER
Times: Last L 12.30pm/D
9.30pm
Seats: 80. No smoking in dining
room
Additional: Children welcome,
children's portions; ❂ dishes

Directions: Take one-way system through Winchester, turn right off St George's Street into St Peter's Street. Hotel is on the right

WINCHESTER, Wykeham Arms ✿

☺ *Traditional pub food is done extremely well at this popular inn with a lively atmosphere. Expect ploughmans, steak pies, mushroom pâté, salmon and haddock fishcakes, smoked haddock in creamy cheese sauce with dauphinoise potato. Delightful bar divided into various eating areas*

Menu: A la carte L & D changes daily
Seats: 66. No-smoking in 3 out of 4 dining rooms
Additional: Children over 14 permitted ; ❂ dishes, other diets on request
Directions: South of Cathedral by Winchester College/end of Canon Street

73 Kingsgate Street SO23 9PE
Map no: 4 SU42
Tel: 01962 853834
Chef: Vanessa Booth
Proprietor: Graeme Jameson
Cost: Alc £17.25, H/wine £8.95
⁍ Service inc
Credit cards: 🔳 💳 💳 OTHER
Times: Last L 2.30pm, last D
9pm

HEREFORD & WORCESTER

ABBERLEY, **The Elms** ❀❀

Queen Anne house with aspirational cuisine

Evesham WR6 6AT
Map no: 3 SO76
Tel: 01299 896666
Chef: Graham Mairs
Proprietors: Queens Moat.
Manager: Shaun Whitehouse
Cost: Fixed-price D £24 and
£28.50. H/wine £12.95 ❢
Service inc
Credit cards: 🔳 🔳 🔳 🔳
Times: Last Sun L 2pm, last D
9.30pm/10pm Fri-Sat
Menus: Fixed-price D & Sun L,
bar menu
Seats: 60. No smoking in dining
room
Additional: Children welcome,
children's menu; ❶ dishes,
vegan/other diets on request

The Elms does its best to maintain standards. However, a seasonal menu offered by new chef Graham Mairs suffers from pretentious purple patches, with a surfeit of esoteric descriptive terms such as quadrini, coussin, menage and crystallis. Ingredients and techniques are equally modish; cappuccino of smoked haddock is glazed with saffron and whiskey sabayon, brogole of guinea fowl is poached in a lime and ginger emulsion, and bourride of skate braised through a tarragon and mustard seed braissage. No, we don't know what half of it means either, but it does detract from the quality of what is on the plate. A number of dishes carry a supplement, such as the rack of English lamb cooked in hay and aromatic herbs served with a wild mushroom glace, or the hot tea smoked Gressingham duck spiked in a cinnamon jus. Thankfully, there is a sensible dinner menu to turn to, with non-frightening dishes such as cauliflower and cumin soup, baked fillet of codling on slow-baked plum tomatoes and hot pancakes with orange sauce. Look out for the dessert crème 'Renate' with pomegranate syrup which the chef has dedicated to his mother.

Directions: On A443 between Worcester and Tenbury Wells. Not in Abberley village

BISHAMPTON, **Nightingale Restaurant** ❀

☺ *As one might expect from a part of the country which runs a pedigree herd of cattle, the relatively small set menu strongly features this local beef. Dishes such as pan-fried sirloin with mushrooms, or fillet with sage and Madeira cream account for almost half of the main course choices*

Menus: Fixed-price D (Business/party L by arrangement) **Seats:** 40.
No-smoking in dining room **Additional:** Children welcome,
children's portions; ❶ dishes, other diets on request
Directions: Off B4084 at Lower Moor or Fladbury; off A422 at
Flyford Flannel

Nightingale Farm WR10 2NH
Map no: 3 SO95
Tel: 01386 462521
Chefs: Peter Hornett and A C
Morris
Proprietors: H K & W A
Robertson
Cost: Fixed-price D £17.50.
H/wine £8.50. Service exc
Credit cards: 🔳 🔳
Times: Last D 9.05pm. Closed
Sun, Bhs, Christmas

BRIMFIELD, **Poppies Restaurant** ✿✿✿

Part of the old world Roebuck Inn, this village restaurant nevertheless has a vibrant modern style that is attracting guests from an ever-increasing area

Now well established as one of the top British women chefs, Carole Evans has put this bright, refreshingly informal little restaurant firmly on the gastronomic map. Bar meals include such traditional favourites as old-fashioned steak and kidney pie, while a short value-for-money set-price lunch menu and imaginative dinner *carte* of modern English dishes make excellent use of local produce. Shropshire blue cheese soufflé flamed with Herefordshire cider brandy, for example, or roast fillet of Herefordshire beef served on a horseradish purée, are supplemented by fish and seafood from Cornwall.

During the course of a recent inspection visit, smooth and delicious oxtail 'en gelée' was followed by baked fillets of turbot stuffed with mushrooms and tarragon and roasted on a julienne of vegetables, then a special bread and butter pudding with apricot sauce (just one of a mouthwatering selection of home-made desserts and ice-creams). An impressive selection of farmhouse cheeses offers guests the chance to try relatively unknown varieties like Old Worcester White (a hard but very rich and creamy cows' milk cheese), Malvern (lightly salted, smooth-textured and made from ewes' milk) and Hereford Hop (a full-fat semi-hard cheese made to a single Gloucester recipe and coated with hops for a tangy flavour).

An interestingly annotated, reasonably priced wine list based mainly on the traditional growing areas offers a very good choice of half bottles and some bin ends which are worthy of consideration.

Directions: 4 miles south of Ludlow in the village of Brimfield

The Roebuck
Ludlow SY8 4NE
Map no: 3 SO56
Tel: 01584 711230
Chef: Carole Evans
Proprietor: Carole Evans
Cost: *Alc* £35, fixed-price L £20. H/wine £12. Service inc
Credit cards: ▨ ▩ OTHER
Times: Last L 2pm, last D 9.30pm. Closed Sun, Mon,
Menus: *A la carte*, fixed-price L, bar menu
Seats: 40. No-smoking area. No pipes or cigars
Additional: Children welcome; ✪ dishes, other diets on request

BROADWAY, **Collin House Hotel** ✿

☺ *Charming, secluded country house hotel. Enjoyable, imaginative cooking includes crab and ginger soufflé with lemon grass sauce, and steak and kidney pudding in Guinness. The carte is backed up by daily blackboard specials based on fresh seasonal produce, and there is a light supper menu. Highly popular locally*

Seats: 24. No smoking in dining room
Menus: *A la carte*, fixed-price L & D, bar menu
Additional: Children welcome (but under 7 by prior arrangement), children's menu; ✪ dishes, vegan/other diets on request
Directions: North-west on A44 for 1 mile from Broadway, turn right at Collin Lane. The restaurant 300yds on right

Collin Lane WR12 7PB
Map no: 4 SP03
Tel: 01386 858354
Chefs: Mark Brookes and Antony Ike
Proprietor: John Mills
Cost: *Alc* £21, fixed-price L £6/D £21. H/wine £ 9.95 Service inc
Credit cards: ▨ ▩
Times: noon-last L 1.30pm / D 9pm Closed Dec 25-30

BROADWAY, **Dormy House Hotel** ✿✿

A good choice of light classical dishes from a range of menus at this stone-built former farmhouse

A converted 17th-century farmhouse, this attractive hotel is located in its own grounds high above the village of Broadway. Flagged floors, stone walls, beamed ceilings and open fires create a cosy country house atmosphere, though the elegant restaurant retains a

Willersley Hill WR12 7LF
Map no: 4 SP03
Tel: 01386 852711
Chef: Alan Cutler and Simon Boyle
Proprietor: Ingrid Philip-Sorensen.
Manager: David Field

certain formality. Classically trained chef Alan Cutler believes in making the best use of quality ingredients, and the various menus offer a wide range of carefully prepared and well presented dishes. Starters from the *carte* might include lobster and smoked salmon mousse set in a fish glaze with a watercress and lemon sauce, and braised boneless oxtail filled with a chicken and mushroom farce on a red wine sauce. Among the main courses, an Oriental influence is evident in the Thai bouillabaisse – a classical fish stew with a twist. Other options might be fillet of beef with deep-fried beetroot and celeriac crisps on a light cream and spring onion sauce, or a vegetarian dish of Provençal vegetables with cornmeal steamed pudding and a spicy tomato sauce. Desserts include hot caramel soufflé with praline ice-cream, and a trio of chocolate temptations. British farmhouse cheeses come with warm pecan and sultana bread.

Directions: Take Saintbury turn off A44, after 1 mile bear left at staggered crossroads

Cost: *Alc* from £36.50, fixed-price L £15 (2 course), £17/D £26.50 (4 course). H/wine £9.95 Service exc
Credit cards: 🔳 🔳 🔳 🔳 OTHER
Times: Last L 2pm, last D 9.30pm/9pm Sun. Closed Sat L, Dec 25/6
Menus: *A la carte*, fixed-price L & D, bar menu
Seats: 70/80. No-smoking area
Additional: Children permitted (no young children after 7.30pm), children's menu; 🅥 menu, vegan/other diets on request

BROADWAY, The Lygon Arms 🏵️🏵️

World famous Cotswold hotel in honey-pot tourist village

The facade of this celebrated hostelry is deceptive. Behind the mellow-stone street entrance stretches a large hotel with beautiful private gardens. Much extended, the old part still has most character with massive walls, flagstone floors and period antiques. In Winter, the fragrant scent of wood smoke permeates the air. A nostalgic sketch of a traffic-free bygone Broadway graces the cover of the menu. Inside, the *carte* features a superior mix of modern English and haute cuisine. Ingredients are classy and well-sourced, and combinations attractive. Layers of filo pastry, for example, are filled with Indian spiced Cornish crab, grilled scallops and coriander, and cannon of local lamb is wrapped in courgette with onion potato cakes and tarragon gravy. There are French classic references in dishes such as paupiettes of sole with a champagne and green pea sauce, traditional British favourites, such as roast rib of Scottish beef, and transatlantic influence in a choice of meat from the chargrill. Desserts are equally eclectic and include the intriguingly named 'Wait 'n See'. Allow time to study the deluxe, indexed wine list, but if price deters note there is also a good selection of half bottles.

Directions: In the centre of the High Street

High Street WR12 7DU
Map no: 4 SP03
Tel: 01386 852255
Chef: Roger Narbett
Proprietors: Savoy Group Plc.
Manager: Kirk Ritchie
Cost: Fixed-price L £20.50/D £32. H/wine £11 Service exc
Credit cards: 🔳 🔳 🔳 🔳
Times: Last L 2pm, Last D 9.15pm
Menus: *A la carte*, fixed-price L & D, pre-theatre, bar menu
Seats: 120. No smoking requested in dining room
Additional: Children welcome (over 5 at D), children's menu; 🅥 menu, vegan/other diets on request

The sturgeon was still common in the river Gironde in France at the turn of the century and the present sturgeon fishery in the Gironde estuary is of some importance. Shortly after the First World War, Alfred Prunier (of the famous Paris restaurant) took a holiday in the region and recognised a neglected opportunity. He dispatched a knowledgeable Russian emigré and caviar has been produced there ever since. It is more lightly salted than the Russian and Iranian ones and is best eaten fresh in the region during June and July.

BROMSGROVE,
Grafton Manor Hotel ❀❀

Bright, adventurous cooking from chef Simon Morris, whose family own and manage this peaceful country house hotel just off the Worcester Road

An extensive herb garden supplies the kitchen of 16th-century Grafton Manor, and Simon Morris makes imaginative use of all that grows there. Comfrey fritters may partner a terrine of witch sole with tarragon butter sauce, for example, or lovage will emphasise a Dijon mustard and honey sauce to go with roast fillet of pork, or marjoram flavour a pink prawn sauce served with fillet of lake pike, grilled with olive oil. Dinner prices are fixed according to the number of courses taken, and although basically modern British, Simon borrows from both Mediterranean and Indian cuisines as well. The latter is a special interest, and many of his dishes show a clever Anglo-Asian attitude to spicing. Grilled fillet of Scotch salmon is marinated in yoghurt, coriander and spices, and served with tomato and ginger chutney; sweetcorn soup is invigorated with cardamom and coriander, and breast of chicken stuffed under the skin with sausage meat infused with samba powder and curry leaves. For dessert, there may be Hyderabadi apricots served with mango and coriander sorbet, Grafton rhubarb and sweet cicely crème brûlée, or the little-known Worcestershire pear pudding.

Directions: Off the B4091, 1.5 miles south of Bromsgrove

Grafton Lane B61 7HA
Map no: 7 SO97
Tel: 01527 579007
Chef: Simon Morris
Proprietor: The Morris Family
(Pride of Britain)
Cost: Fixed-price L £20.50/D
£24.95 & £31.50 (4 course),
H/wine £10.50 ❢ Service inc
Credit cards: 🗪 🎫 🎫 💳 OTHER
Times: Last L 1.45pm, last D
9pm
Menus: Fixed-price L & D,
Seats: 45. No smoking in dining
room
Additional: Children welcome,
children's portions; ❤ menu,
vegan/other diets on request

BROMSGROVE, Pine Lodge Hotel ❀

Varied choices on the fixed-price menus and carte include vegetarian dishes and grills. Chef Mark Higgins creates soundly prepared and presented dishes for the two restaurants in this modern hotel. Look out for pigeon breast baked with lentils and smoked bacon and a red wine sauce. Very friendly and cheerful atmosphere

Menus: A la carte, fixed-price L & D, bar menu **Seats:** 100. Air conditioned **Additional:** Children welcome, children's menu; ❤ dishes, vegan/other diets on request
Directions: On A448 Kidderminster road 1 mile W of Bromsgrove centre

Kidderminster Road B61 9AB
Map no: 7 SO97
Tel: 01527 576600
Chef: Mark Higgins
Proprietor: Andrew Weir Hotels.
Manager: Patrick J Martin
Cost: Alc £20-£25, fixed-price L
£13.75/D £16.25 H/wine £8.95
Service inc
Credit cards: 🗪 🎫 🎫 💳 OTHER
Times: Last L 2pm/last D 10pm
(9.30pm Sun) Closed Sat L

CHADDESLEY CORBETT,
Brockencote Hall Hotel ❀❀

☺ *Impressive English country house surroundings for appetising French cooking*

An impressive country house hotel, Brockencote Hall is set in 70 acres of landscaped grounds, with its own lake, dovecote and gatehouse. The cool elegance of the dining room provides the perfect atmosphere for classic French cuisine from the kitchen of chef Didier Philipot. A choice of fixed-price menus is offered, from which guests can mix and match, and there is an additional selection of 'Les Simples' for guests who prefer lighter food more simply presented. The general menu might start with crunchy layers of brick pastry filled with pan-fried woodland pigeon and wild

Kidderminster DY10 4PY
Map no: 7 SO87
Tel: 01562 777876
Chef: Didia Philidot
Proprietors: Alison & Joseph
Petitjean
Cost: Fixed-price L £17.50/D
£22.50. H/wine £12.40 Service
inc
Credit cards: 🗪 🎫 🎫 💳 OTHER
Times: Last L 1.30pm, last D
9.30pm. Closed Sat lunch
Menus: Fixed-price lunch and
dinner, Sat L
Seats: 75. No smoking in dining
room

Brockencote Hall Hotel

Additional: Children welcome, children's portions; other diets on request

mushrooms, or six Loch Fyne oysters served warm with salpicons of vegetables on croûtons with a light saffron butter sauce. Typical main courses are meli-melo of monkfish and scallops with a green peppercorn and lime butter sauce, and roast rump of lamb topped with tomato and courgette flowers and served with a natural lamb jus scented with garden herbs. Desserts include passion fruit crème brûlée with a brunoise of exotic fruit in a ginger syrup, and bitter chocolate tart, cooked to order, and served warm with toffee ice-cream. The wine list is comprehensive with some excellent bin ends always to hand.

Directions: The village is on the A448 between Kidderminster and Bromsgrove

CORSE LAWN,
Corse Lawn House Hotel ⊛⊛

An attractive village green setting for a character hotel with fine food, including a vegetarian menu

An elegant Grade II Queen Ann property, Corse Lawn House is set back off the village green overlooking an ornamental pond, providing character surroundings with a relaxed atmosphere. One of the hotel's strengths is the worthy cooking of Baba Hine who presides in the kitchen, ably backed by an enthusiastic team. It is very much a family operation, and Denis Hine is in charge front-of-house, aided by son Giles. Recent inspection meals have praised a dish of smooth crab sausage set off by a fresh tomato sauce and chick peas; a bright fillet of hake presented with king prawns, chives and tomato; best end of lamb with a lentil crust, and a fresh blackberry tart served with elderflower ice-cream. There is a good choice of dishes from both fixed-price and *carte* menus, including a serious vegetarian menu with five starters and main courses, such as French onion tart with hollandaise sauce followed by aubergine fritters with tomato sauce and wild rice. An alternative venue for meals is the Simply Corse Lawn bistro, which offers an imaginative range of dishes in a less formal atmosphere. A comprehensive classical wine list is also available.

Directions: Village centre, on B4211 5 miles south-west of Tewkesbury

Corse Lawn GL19 4LZ
Map no: 3 SO83
Tel: 01452 780771
Chef: Baba Hine
Proprietors: Baba, Denis & Giles Hine
Cost: Alc £25-£35, fixed-price L £15.95/D £23.50. H/wine £7.50 ♥ Service inc
Credit cards: 🖪 🖩 🖩 🖳
Times: Last L 2pm, last D 10pm
Menus: A la carte, fixed-price L & D, bar menu
Seats: 50
Additional: Children welcome, children's portions; ♥ menu, vegan/other diets on request

EVESHAM, **The Evesham Hotel** ✤

☺ *Set back from the river in extensive mature gardens, the Evesham offers a good range of imaginative dishes featuring honest textures and flavours. A typical meal might begin with grilled Loch Fyne queen scallops, followed by breast of duckling with a blackberry sauce, with a coffee and rum jelly for dessert*

Coopers Lane WR11 6DA
Map no: 4 SP04
Tel: 01386 765566 or
FREEPHONE 0800 716969
Chef: Ian Mann
Proprietor: Jenkinson Family
Cost: *Alc* £19, buffet L £6.65.
H/wine £9.60 Service inc
Credit cards: 🔳 🔳 🔳 🔳 OTHER
Times: Last L 2pm, last D
9.30pm
Menus: *A la carte,* buffet L
Seats: 55. Smoking not
encouraged. No cigars or pipes
Additional: Children welcome,
children's menu; ❂ dishes,
other diets on request

Directions: Coopers Lane is off the road alongside the River Avon

EVESHAM, **The Mill At Harvington** ✤✤

A splendidly sited hotel restaurant specialising in seasonal country cooking

For centuries the people of Harvington have worked the fertile fields in the flood plain of the River Avon, and in the mid-1700s they built a malting mill for their barley. Later it became a bread mill and the cast-iron bakery oven doors can still be seen in this fine Georgian building, now transformed into an hotel. The restaurant is sunny in the summer, with flowers and views across the garden to the river. Menus are changed frequently to take advantage of the freshest seasonal foods, particularly those from the Vale of Evesham. There was a good atmosphere for a meal taken in late autumn, when when early, open log fires were already flickering against the elegant decor. First, there was chicken and asparagus terrine, smooth and well-textured; next, a walnut-coated, tender rack of lamb, trimmed very lean, with a beer sauce; finally, an estimable hot butterscotch pudding. Lunch, which may be taken on the terrace (weather permitting), may be chosen from a very good value menu, with several dishes, such as grilled goats' cheese salad, pasta and pesto and black pudding, available as either a starter or a main course. The wine list is set out in two ways – one according to taste, the other price – and there are some excellent notes on grape varieties.

Directions: Turn south off B439, opposite Harvington village, down Anchor Lane

Anchor Lane WR11 5NR
Map no: 4 SP04
Tel: 01386 870688
Chef: Jane Greenhalgh with Bill
Downing and John Hunter
Proprietors: Simon & Jane
Greenhalgh
Cost: Fixed price L £13.95 / D
£21.50. H/wine £8.95 ❢ No
service charge
Credit cards: 🔳 🔳 🔳 🔳 OTHER
Times: Last L 1.45pm/D 8.45pm.
Closed 24-29 Dec
Seats: 40. No smoking in dining
room
Menus: Fixed price L & D, bar
menu
Additional: Children permitted,
children's portions on request;
❂ dishes, vegan/other diets on
request

EVESHAM, **Nightingales Hotel** ❀

A former farmhouse, now a friendly, delightful, family-run hotel offering a good selection of dishes based on fresh produce. Aberdeen Angus beef features on the menu and may be served with poivre sauce and a selection of vegetables. Delicious desserts such as chilled rum and sultana rice pudding

Seats: 36. No smoking
Additional: Children welcome; ❂ dishes
Directions: Junction 5 of M5, Evesham road

Bishampton WR10 2NH
Map no: 4 SP04
Tel: 01386 462521
Chef: Angela Robertson-Morris
Proprietor: Mrs Robertson
Cost: Fixed-price D £18.50
Credit cards: 🟦 🟥
Times: Last D 9pm

EVESHAM, **Riverside Hotel** ❀❀

A good standard of cooking based on quality ingredients at this riverside restaurant with rooms

Offenham Road WR11 5JP
Map no: 4 SP04
Tel: 01386 446200
Chef: Rosemary Willmott
Proprietors: Vincent Willmott
Cost: Fixed-price L £16.95/D £21.95. H/wine £8.95 ❢ Service inc.
Credit cards: 🟦 🟥 OTHER
Times: 2pm/D 9pm. Closed Sun D, Mon, 1st wk Jan
Menus: Fixed-price L & D, bar menu
Seats: 45. No smoking in dining room
Additional: Children welcome, children's portions; ❂ dishes/vegan on request

Initially difficult to find but well worth the effort, this hotel is tucked away between Evesham and Offenham, perched above the river in an area of outstanding beauty. Run very much as a restaurant with rooms, it is a friendly establishment with the emphasis firmly on food. The dining-room with its river views is the hub of the house and the setting for Rosemary Willmott's commendable cooking. The daily menu offers a good seasonal balance with some imaginative ideas, all based on quality local ingredients. There are about eight options at the first two courses, with starters such as home-potted Morecambe Bay shrimps in spiced butter, crisp calamares in tempura batter with spicy tomato salsa, and our inspector's choice, a generous portion of rich duck liver and brandy paté. This was followed by steamed fillet of sea bass, with a good roundness of flavour, served with a simple fresh crab and prawn sauce. Other main courses, including roast rack of lamb with a herb crust, were again full of flavour and well presented in a simple style. The dessert choice is more limited, with options such as home-made rhubarb ice-cream and rich chocolate truffle torte.

Directions: 2 miles from town centre on B4510 (Offenham). At end of narrow lane marked 'The Parks'

LEDBURY, **Feathers Hotel** 🏵

☺ *The striking Elizabethan black-and-white building offers satisfying food in the spacious Fuggles Bar. A typical meal might comprise of home-made soup, followed by medallions of beef with black pepper and thyme, with sticky toffee pudding to finish. Staff are friendly and courteous*

High Street HR8 1DS
Map no: 3 SO73
Tel: 01531 635266
Chef: Mr J M Capaldi
Proprietor: David Elliston
Cost: *Alc* £15, H/wine £7.75
❗ Service exc
Credit cards: 💳 💳 💳 💳 OTHER
Times: Noon-2pm, 7pm-9.30pm
Menus: *A la carte*
Seats: 60
Additional: Children welcomed; children's portions on request, 🅥 dishes, vegan/other diets on request

Directions: Ledbury is on A449/A438/A417 and hotel is prominent on main street

LEDBURY,
Hope End Hotel 🏵🏵

Fresh local produce including much from the hotel's own grounds features in the cooking at the Hope End – situated in a hidden valley

The house lies at the end of a winding track which takes you through gentle hills, parkland and verdant pasture and into a courtyard where chickens stray. English eccentricity does for the rest with Turkish minarets, turrets and domes – added to the property in the early 19th century by the father of Elizabeth Barrett Browning, whose childhood home this was. Pagodas, hidden seats and a lake are to be discovered in the grounds. The Hegartys grow most of their fruit, vegetables and herbs, and Patricia Hegarty's cooking makes the most of these with an intuitive understanding of fresh accurate flavours, balance and attractive presentation. A short but well balanced set menu offers dishes such as timbale of rice, chicken and cardamom with a contrasting sorrel dressing, pheasant braised in cider and served with an apple puree, and home-made fig ice-cream (from their own hot-house figs). Bread and preserves are all made on the premises. The wine list offers about 150 European and New World wines.

Directions: From the centre of town, take B4214 Bromyard road, then first right after railway bridge, signed. Entrance on left

Hope End HB8 1JQ
Map no: 3 SO73
Tel: 01531 633613
Chef: *Patricia Hegarty*
Proprietors: *Patricia & John Hegarty*
Cost: *Fixed-price dinner £30. H/wine from £8. No service charge*
Credit cards: 💳 💳 OTHER
Times: *Last D 8.30pm. Closed mid Dec to 1st week in Feb*
Menus: *Fixed-price dinner*
Seats: *24. No smoking in dining room*
Additional: *No children under 12.* 🅥 *dishes*

FLETCHER RESTAURANT

LEOMINSTER,
The Marsh Country Hotel ❀❀

First-rate food and idyllic surroundings are the twin attractions of an historic but homely hotel

Eyton HR6 0AG
Map no: 3 SO45
Tel: 01568 613952
Chef: Jacqueline Gilleland
Proprietors: Jacqueline & Martin Gilleland
Cost: Fixed price L & D £19.95. H/wine £9.75 ❢ Service inc.
Credit cards: ▧ ▦ ▦ ▨
Times: Last D 9pm, last Sun L 2pm Closed early Jan
Menus: Fixed price D & Sun. L
Seats: 24. No smoking in dining room
Additional: Children permitted over 12; ❷ dishes, other diets on request

Unspoilt countryside – its picturesque black and white villages, forests and rolling hills reminiscent of a bygone age – surround this beautiful, tranquil timbered home. The ground floor is dominated by a heavily beamed, flagstoned medieval hall, and off this leads the very elegant buttercup yellow dining room where an extremely well balanced set menu is served. Chef Jacqueline Gilleland makes effective use of fresh produce in a range of English dishes retaining honest flavours and textures. Fish comes from Newlyn, while the hotel garden provides vegetables and some fruit (the rest being supplied by a local orchard). In the course of a recent inspection, a light flaky pastry tart of courgettes and rosemary preceded roast duck with a pot of spinach. Vegetables are tailored to each dish's main ingredient, creating a harmonious whole. Desserts include skilful interpretations of such classics as tarte tatin or a mulberry compote. The level of cooking exhibits an accuracy and depth of flavour. The accompanying wine list is both varied and appropriate.

Directions: Two miles N/W of Leominster. Follow signs for Eyton and Lucton

MALVERN, Colwall Park Hotel ❀

A sedate, country hotel set at the foot of the Malvern hills noted for its warmth and friendliness – guests are always made to feel welcome. The restaurant offers a menu of daily changing dishes which, at inspection, featured poached haddock with Welsh rarebit, followed by roast breast of chicken in a rich cream sauce

Menus: Fixed-price L & D, bar menu
Seats: 36. No smoking requested
Additional: Children welcomed; children's & ❷ dishes, vegan on request, other diets with prior notice
Directions: Centre of village on B4218 between Ledbury and Malvern

Colwall WR13 6QG
Map: 3 SO74
Tel: 01684 540206
Chef: Peter Botteril
Proprietors: Basil & Elizabeth Frost (Logis)
Cost: Fixed-price L £13.50 /D £22.50. H/wine £8.75 Service exc
Credit cards: ▧ ▦ ▦
Times: Last L 1.45pm, last D 9pm/8.30 Sun. Closed first wk Jan

MALVERN,
The Cottage in the Wood Hotel ✿

Lovely, family-run country house hotel which boasts outstanding views and a friendly atmosphere. Seasonal produce enhances the well-executed dishes with honest textures and flavours: bright scallop with seaweed, fillet of lamb with tomato and basil sauce, and 'scrumptious' pecan pie

Holywell Road
Malvern Wells WR14 4LG
Map no: 3 SO74
Tel: 01684 575859
Chefs: Kathryn Young and Dominic Pattin
Proprietors: John & Sue Pattin
Cost: Alc £25-£28, fixed-price L £9.95/Sun £12.95. H/wine £11. No service charge
Credit cards: ⬛ ⬛ ⬛ OTHER
Times: Last L 2pm/D 9pm
Menus: A la carte, fixed-price L, bar menu
Seats: 50. No smoking in dining room
Additional: Children permitted; children's portions; ✿ dishes, vegan/other diets on request

Directions: Signed turning 3 miles south of Great Malvern off A449

MALVERN, Holdfast Cottage ✿

Set in two acres of grounds just outside Malvern, this small hotel offers a short but interesting daily-changing fixed-price menu. Food is prepared with care and attention, and may include dishes such as tomato, onion and red wine soup, escalopes of pork flavoured with sage and lemon, and warm treacle and apple tart

Little Malvern WR13 6NA
Map no: 3 SO74
Tel: 01684 310288
Chef: Jane Knowles
Proprietors: Stephen & Jane Knowles
Cost: Fixed-price D £17 (4 course). H/wine £8.95 ▮
Credit cards: ⬛ ⬛
Times: Last D 9pm

Menu: Fixed-price D
Seats: 24. No smoking in restaurant
Additional: Children welcome, children's portions; ✿ dishes, other diets on request
Directions: On A4104 midway between Welland and Little Malvern

Béarnaise sauce is a hot, creamy sauce made from egg yolks and vinegar beaten together over a low heat and mixed with butter. The sauce is traditionally served with grilled meats or fish. Some dishes are called 'à la béarnaise' even though they are not accompanied by the sauce. These are inspired by the regional cooking of Béarn, dishes such as daubes, poule au pot and game confit with ceps. The association between béarnaise sauce and Béarn (the birthplace of Henri IV) is probably due to the fact that it was first made in the 1830's in a restaurant in Saint-Germaine-en-Laye called the Pavillon Henri IV. Various other sauces are derived from béarnaise sauce: sauce paloise is béarnaise sauce with mint; sauce valoise is béarnaise sauce mixed with meat glaze.

ROSS-ON-WYE, Chase Hotel ❀

All the specialities of this richly productive area are brought to the tables of this elegant but informally welcoming restaurant. Typical dishes could include rillette of salmon with salsa verde and olive bread, seared ducks' livers with rösti potato and balsamic vinegar, and chocolate leaves with mascarpone cheese and cherries

Gloucester Road HR9 5LH
Map no: 3 SO52
Tel: 01989 763161
Chef: Ken Tait
Proprietors: John & Ann Lewis
Cost: Alc £23, fixed-price
L £12.50. H/wine £8.55 ❢
Service exc
Credit cards: 🃏 💳 💳 💳 OTHER
Times: Last L 1.45pm, last D
9.45pm Closed L Bhs
Menus: A la carte, fixed-price
L, pre-theatre, bar menu
Seats: 60
Additional: Children welcome,
children's portions; ❤ dishes,
vegan/other diets on request

Directions: From town centre follow B4260 towards Gloucester, hotel 200yds on right

ROSS-ON-WYE, Pengethley Manor ❀❀

A charming hotel offering a good choice of dishes from fixed-price and vegetarian menus

Ross-on-Wye HR9 6LL
Map no: 3 SO52
Tel: 01989 730211
Chef: Ferdinand Van der Knaap
Proprietors: Mrs G A Wisker
Cost: Alc £28, fixed-price L
£16/Sun L £13.80/D £24 (4
course). H/wine £12.75 Service
exc
Credit cards: 🃏 💳 💳 💳 OTHER
Seats: 48
Times: Last L 2pm, last D
9.30pm
Additional: Children welcome,
children's portions; ❤ menu,
other diets on request

The Wisker's have put in a lot of care and attention at their lovely old Georgian manor. The extensive grounds are a delight, public rooms have an elegant, tasteful look and service is attentive. To stimulate the appetite amenities include a heated swimming pool and a trout lake. The cooking is sound. Chef Ferdinand Van-Der-Knapp provides *carte* and fixed-price menus based on fresh ingredients and sound technique. A May inspection meal kicked off with a woodland mushroom terrine, nicely balanced with an onion and cassis marmalade. This was followed by a well-made seafood cascade which included pan-fried Dublin Bay prawns, scallops, a roulade of crab meat and a garlic butter sauce and came with an amazing array of vegetables – fine beans wrapped in bacon, mange-tout with flaked almonds, duchesse potatoes, and carrots and cauliflower in a white wine and Stilton sauce. A light pancake of black cherries with Grand Marnier finished the meal. Attention is paid to minor details: crusty bread and petits fours are good and coffee is a decent cafetière.

Directions: A49 (Ross-on-Wye to Hereford road); 2nd turning on right after Peterstow Common; 10 mins from M50

ROSS-ON-WYE, **Peterstowe** ✱✱

An interesting selection of English/French dishes in modern style has its success firmly rooted in top quality fresh ingredients

Peterstow HR9 6LB
Map no: 3 SO52
Tel: 01989 562826
Chef: Andrew Poole
Proprietors: Mike & Jeanne Denne
Cost: *Alc* £19.50-£29, fixed-price L £12.50/D £24.50. H/wine £9.50 Service inc
Credit cards: 🄰 💳 💳 💳 OTHER
Times: Last L 2pm, last D 9pm daily
Menus: *A la carte*, fixed-price L & D
Seats: 40. No smoking in dining room
Additional: Children welcome (over & at D), children's portions; ❂ dishes, vegan/other diets on request

Delightfully situated in 28 acres of woodland and pasture beside the Hereford road, this country house hotel continues to provide an excellent level of friendly, attentive service. Food standards remain high, too. Chef Andrew Poole has created an interesting *carte* and fixed-price menus of modern English/French dishes which derive maximum advantage from quality fresh, often local, produce. Warm lamb salad, for example, is based on fillets of Welsh lamb from just over the border, pan-fried and served with Provençal vegetables, dressed salad leaves and crispy leeks, Herefordshire beef comes with parsnip crumble, baby carrots, cocotte potatoes and a red wine sauce, and breast of Deben duck is presented on a bed of cabbage with pearl barley risotto, a red onion and coriander parcel and lemon grass sauce. Desserts include a raspberry torte accompanied by a confit of the same fruit, and a selection of British cheeses is served with fresh fruit as well as walnut bread. The predominantly French wine list contains both a connoisseurs' collection and a separate list of half bottles.

Directions: On A49 in village, next to the Church, 3 miles from Ross-on-Wye

ULLINGSWICK,
Steppes Country House ⊛⊛

A tranquil old farmhouse serves a wide-ranging but fairly simple range of dishes in its welcoming little dining-room

Charming and unique, this quaint 17th-century country house hotel is tucked away in a quiet hamlet on the road from Gloucester to Leominster. Thanks to the owners' hard work, many original features of the farmstead have been preserved in the stone-floored, beamed main building. Guests are assured of a warm welcome, particularly in the attractive little dining-room where Tricia Howland presents an eclectic four-course dinner *carte* of fairly simple dishes based on first-class produce. Gravad lax with dill sauce could be followed by lamb fillet with a rich Cumberland sauce, and tempting desserts are complemented by a highly regarded cheese board featuring mainly English varieties and including some rarities too fascinating to ignore – surely you owe it to yourself to sample Stinking Bishop? The house gourmet dinner, an artistically presented set-price meal available only to guests who have booked leisure breaks, will appeal to those who like adventurous cooking; many hours of careful preparation ensure an excellent balance of colour, aroma, flavour and texture.

Directions: Off the A417 Gloucester to Leominster road

Nr Hereford HR1 3JG
Map no: 3 SO54
Tel: 01432 820424
Chef: Tricia Howland
Proprietors: Henry & Tricia Howland
Cost: *Alc* £25, fixed-price D £22.50 (4 course). H/wine £7.50 Service inc
Credit cards: ▨ ▨ ▨ OTHER
Times: Last D 8.30pm (Booking essential)
Menus: *A la carte* D, fixed-price D, bar L menu
Seats: 12. No smoking in dining room
Additional: Children over 12 welcome; ◑ dishes, vegan/other diets on request

WALTERSTONE,
Allt-yr-Ynys Hotel ⊛

Queen Elizabeth I is reputed to have once been a guest at this 16th-century house, set in sixteen acres of grounds. The short carte of carefully prepared dishes may feature the likes of crab and prawn salad, roast rack of local lamb on a cake of rösti potato and warm treacle tart

Directions: 7 miles NE of Abergavenny, off A465

Abergavenny HR2 0DU
Map no: 3 SO32
Tel: 01873 890307
Chef: J W G Mannifold
Proprietor: Mr & Mrs Mannifold
Credit cards: ▨ ▨ ▨ ▨ OTHER

WEOBLEY, Ye Olde Salutation Inn ⊛⊛

Modern Anglo-French cooking making a tremendously popular and successful appearance

All the quintessential ingredients of great age – exposed beams and timbers, open log fires and uneven floors – are here. And so they should be, since this former cider and ale house and adjoining cottage are over 500 years old. The chef, Mark Green, is self-taught. The only fixed-price meal is Sunday lunch, otherwise everything is selected from the three-course *carte*. Sample starters might be baked quails' egg tartlet filled with creamed leeks and smoked Cheddar cheese, or home-cured gravad lax with honey and coarse-grain mustard.

Main courses, all served with lightly steamed vegetables or salad, could include fillet of salmon with fresh pasta noodles on a light mussel cream, roast loin of lamb in a mild peppercorn crust, with a light mint-scented sauce, or tenderloin of pork layered with pan-fried apple on an orange & cider cream. Vegetarian dishes are available. All the desserts are home-made, including lemon soufflé,

Market Pitch HR4 8SJ
Map no: 3 SO45
Tel: 01544 318443
Chef: Mark Green
Proprietor: Mr & Mrs C Anthony
Credit cards: ▨ ▨ ▨ ▨ OTHER
Times: Last D 9.00 pm

chocolate torte and bread and butter pudding. The wine list is modestly priced with some good value bin-ends. Owners Chris and Frances Anthony run a friendly, informal house.

Directions: Down hill into village, take first right, then second right

WORCESTER, **Brown's Restaurant**

An 'eclectic' cooking style, say the owners of this converted mill on the banks of the Severn

What was once functional, probably barely-noticed industrial architecture, today helps to attract customers to Brown's. The Tansleys have run this converted corn mill on the banks of the Severn for 15 years. Its enormously high ceilings and iron girders are softened by vanilla-coloured brick and modern paintings. An interesting mezzanine floor, where drinks may be taken in the evening, also serves as an overflow dining area. Despite a rather soft and dull starter of ravioli of Parmesan, feta and spinach, the food is good. Favourable main courses have included rabbit sausage set on a bed of lentils, and fresh grilled halibut with a warm fennel and red pepper salsa. Puddings are also good, especially a deliciously powerful gingerbread ice-cream set on a sweet but sharp rhubarb sauce with caramelised bananas. The more ambitious set-price dinner menu includes smoked haddock with hollandaise and a concassée of tomatoes, followed by spatchcock of quail with sage and couscous. A well-stocked wine list could do with a more consistent approach to tasting notes.

Directions: City centre, along River Bank, car park opposite

The Old Cornmill
South Quay
Map no: 3 SO85
Tel: 01905 26263
Chef: W R Tansley and Kevin Powles
Proprietors: P M Tansley and Richard Hill
Cost: Fixed-price L £16/D £30 (4 course). H/wine £ 9.90
Service inc
Credit cards: 🔲 🔲 🔲 🔲 OTHER
Times: Last L 1.45pm, last D 9.45pm Closed Sat L, Sun D, Bh Mons, 1 wk from Dec 24
Menus: Fixed-price L & D
Seats: 80. No-smoking area
Additional: Children over 8 welcome, children's portions; dishes, other diets on request

WORCESTER, **Fownes Hotel** ❀

Close to the city centre, this former Victorian glove factory has been converted into a stylish modern hotel. Well-presented dishes, served in the King's Restaurant, might feature fresh mussel brioche, pheasant with chestnuts, shallots and white port sauce, and honey ice-cream with a compote of raspberries

City Walls Road WR1 2AP
Map no: 3 SO85
Tel: 01905 613151
Chef: John Holden
Proprietor: Mr Swire
Cost: Alc £23, fixed-price L £8.95/D £14.95. H/wine £9.50. Service inc
Credit cards: 🔲 🔲 🔲 🔲 OTHER
Times: Last L 2.30pm/D 9.45pm. L not served Sat
Seats: 50. No pipes
Additional: Children welcome, children's portions/menu; dish; vegan/other diets on request

Directions: Beside A 38 inner ring road, 100yds from the Commandery and the Cathedral

HERTFORDSHIRE

BISHOP'S STORTFORD,
The Mill Restaurant ❀

Little Hallingbury CM22 7QT
Map no: 4 TL52
Tel: 01279 726554
Credit cards: ▨ ▨ ▨

Well-executed and attractively presented food inspired by fresh produce is served in this 19th-century mill conversion by the canal. The carte is supplemented by a good value fixed-price menu in the evening. Look out for oatmeal fishcakes, duck breast with coriander and leeks, and glazed pear with chocolate mousse

---

Directions: Off A1060 to Hatfield Heath

ELSTREE, Edgwarebury Hotel ❀❀

Barnet Lane WD6 3RE
Map no: 4 TG19
Tel: 0181 953 8227
Chef: Christopher Fisher
Proprietor: Country Club.
Manager: Tomas Perez
Cost: Fixed-price L & D £24.50
(5 course). H/wine £9.95 ❢
Service exc
Credit cards: ▨ ▨ ▨ ▨ OTHER
Times: Last L pm/last D pm
Closed
Menus: Fixed-price L & D
Seats: 26. No smoking in dining room
Additional: Children welcome;
❶ dishes, vegan/other diets on request

An outer suburban fringe hotel restaurant providing modern British cooking

---

Looking for all the world like a black and white timbered transplant from Cheshire, the Edgwarebury continues the Tudor theme inside, with big stone fireplaces, carvings and oak beams. There are two restaurants, one informal, catering more for conference delegates, and the Cavendish, offering good variety on its five-course, set-price menu as well as views of the ten acres of natural woodland outside. Dinner began well with canapés of freshly-made chicken liver, haddock and egg filo parcels, but the cabbage and sesame seed tartlet starter with smooth, tender slices of black pudding on top, left a hard-to-shift flavour of stale oil. Grilled grouper was moist and fresh, although a victim of too much pepper, and the accompanying samphire tasted as if extra salt had been added to its water. Side dishes included tomato and basil vinaigrette with shallots, and expertly-cooked buttered broccoli. Lemon tart, although good in texture, suffered from an overdose of zest. It must be said, though, that overall the meal was enjoyable and just needed a more delicate touch in places.

Directions: Access from M1 exits 4 & 5, M25 exits19 & 23, Barnet Lane is signed Elstree & Aldenham

HEMEL HEMPSTEAD,
The Bobsleigh Inn ❀

*Herbs from the kitchen garden feature in the international cooking.
Look out for dishes such as fricassee of wild mushrooms with roasted
garlic, smoked bacon and shallots and monkfish roasted in crushed black
peppercorns set on sea asparagus in a cucumber and lemon sauce*

Menus: *A la carte*, fixed-price L & D, bar menu **Seats:** 80
Additional: Children permitted, children's portions; ♥ menu,
vegan/other diets on request
Directions: From Hemel Hempstead take A4251 past station, turn
left at Swan (B4505 to Chesham), 1.5 miles on left

Hempstead Road
Bovingdon HP3 0DS
Map no: 4 TL00
Tel: 01442 833276
Chef: Stuart Ambury
Proprietors: Celia Derbyshire
and Arthur Rickett
Cost: *Alc* from £23, fixed-price L
£14.95/D £18.95. H/wine
£10.50 Service inc
Credit cards: 🔳 🔳 🔳 🔳 OTHER
Times: Last L 2pm, last D
9.30pm. Closed Bh Mons, Dec
26-Jan 6

ST ALBANS, The Noke ❀

*A good range of both modern and traditional dishes are served at this
extended 19th-century hotel. Friendly and professional staff attend in the
restaurant, where a meal might begin with a sweet pepper terrine, followed
by pan-roasted halibut with a fennel butter sauce, and lemon tart for dessert*

Watford Road AL2 3DS
Map no: 4 TL10
Tel: 01727 854252
Chef: Andrew Sticking
Proprietors: Thistle.
Manager: Gerard L Virlombier
Cost: *Alc* from £27, fixed-price
L £18.50/D £ 22. H/wine £11
Service exc
Credit cards: 🔳 🔳 🔳 🔳
Times: Last L 2pm, last D 10pm.
Closed Sat L
Menus: *A la carte*, fixed-price L
& D, bar menu
Seats: 90. Air conditioned.
Smoking on request only
Additional: Children welcome,
children's portions; ♥ menu,
vegan/other diets on request

Directions: On A405, Watford road; from M25 exit 21A, first
roundabout left hand turning

ST ALBANS,
Sopwell House Hotel ❀❀

*Modern English and international cooking with some vegetarian choices
in a conservatory-style hotel restaurant*

The grace, colour and style of this hotel reflect a time when the
house and the surrounding land were owned by the Mountbatten
family. The Magnolia Conservatory Restaurant is the showpiece
setting for new head chef Paul Harrison's cooking. Here, the choice
of menus includes a *carte*, a three-course fixed-price dinner menu
and a two or three course traditional English lunch. A choice of
vegetarian dishes is also offered, such as cassoulet of mushrooms in
a light biscuit basket, and 'horns of plenty', puff pastry horns filled
with a puree of leek and pea, served with new season asparagus.

Cottonmill Lane AL1 2HQ
Map no: 4 TL10
Tel: 01727 864477
Chef: Paul Harrison
Restaurant Manager: David
Williams (Best Western)
Cost: *Alc* £30 (Rest.) £15
(Brasserie). fixed-price L £16.95
/ D £19.50. H/wine
£9.75/£11.75 ❢ Service exc
Credit cards: 🔳 🔳 🔳 🔳 OTHER

Sopwell House Hotel

Times: 12.30pm-last L 2.30pm,
7.30pm-last D 10pm. Closed Sat
L Sun D, Bhs. Brasserie 7am-
10pm every day
Menus: *A la carte,* fixed-price
L& D, Rest. & Brasserie menus
Seats: 100 Rest. 60 Brasserie (Air
conditioned) No-smoking areas
Additional: Children welcome,
children's menu; ❂ dishes,
vegan/other diets on request

An inspection meal comprised duck and chicken terrine with green
herb sauce, followed by an enjoyable salmon en croûte with chive
cream sauce accompanied by fresh-tasting vegetables. The pudding,
lemon tart, was disappointing, and it was felt that banqueting
demands can, on occasion, detract from the quality of the
restaurant food. For an informal alternative, there is the hotel's
Bejerano's Brasserie, with a diverse menu ranging from bagels and
baked potatoes, and salads and steaks, with good vegetarian and
children's selections, fish and grills.

Directions: On London road from St Albans follow signs to Sopwell,
over mini-roundabout, hotel on left

TRING, **Rose & Crown Hotel** ❀

☺ *Located in the centre of town, this Tudor-style hotel was built at
the turn of the century to accommodate guests of the Rothschild family.
The restaurant serves well-prepared English dishes, and selections
might include a smooth terrine of chicken livers, followed by roast
breast of local duckling*

High Street HP23 5AH
Map no: 4 SP91
Tel: 01442 824071
Chef: Greig Barnes
Proprietor: Chris & Alison
Wilson
Cost: *Alc* £13-22 fixed-price
L £9.95/D £17.95 (4 course).
H/wine £7.95 ❢ Service exc
Credit cards: ▨ ▥ ▧ ▨ OTHER
Times: Noon-last L 2pm, 7pm-
last D 10pm
Menus: *A la carte,* fixed-price L
& D, bar menu
Seats: 60. No-smoking area
Additional: Children welcome
(not Sat D), children's menu;
❂ dishes, vegan/other diets on
request

Directions: Centre of Tring on B4635, easy access M1/M25/M40

WARE, **Hanbury Manor** ✿✿✿

A Jacobean-style mansion strong on leisure activities and conferences
offering classic French cooking in the Zodiac Restaurant

Thundridge SG12 0SD
Map no: 5 TL31
Tel: 01920 487722
Chef: Rory Kennedy
Proprietors: Country Club.
Manager: Richard McKevitt
Cost: *Alc* from £35, fixed-price
L £19.50 /£26 Sun, fixed-price
D £25. H/wine £13 ▪ Service inc
Credit cards: ◪ ▦ ▦ ▨ OTHER
Times: Noon-last L 2.30pm,
7pm last D 10.30pm. Closed
Mon but Conservatory open
Menus: *A la carte*, fixed-price L
& D, bar menu
Seats: 48 Rest.(+ 32
Conservatory) No smoking in
dining room
Additional: Children welcome
(over 8 at D in main Restaurant)
children's menu; ❂ menu,
vegan on request

Hanbury Manor has extensive leisure facilities which draw in
golfers and the conference crowd. They probably prefer the light
and airy Conservatory for lunch, and Vardon's, which is open all
day, for informal meals. But the Zodiac room is different. It is not
home to simple cooking, nor is it especially cheap. Albert Roux of
Le Gavroche is a consultant, with Rory Kennedy the executive
chef. Every menu is translated into French, including the prices and
VAT (IVA), and there is an exuberance in composition and
presentation that some find over-worked. Luxury items can feature:
foie gras terrine with braised pork and warm brioche, hot
mousseline of chicken, celeriac and caviar, and roast Scottish
lobster Viennoise with a 'sauce crustaces'. Soufflé Suissesse, a
stalwart of Le Gavroche's menu, makes an appearance, but has
been 'rather ordinary'. Modern trends are also acknowledged:
ravioli of goats' cheese with basil, pesto and pine kernels, saute of
chicken with grilled aubergines, Morteaux sausage, confit of garlic
and tarragon cream, or escalope of tuna with potato and garlic,
orange confit and sauce vierge.

One inspection meal included well-made canapes of mozzarella
with pesto, goujon of sole and 'a sort of lobster mousse', and an
unexciting rump of lamb served with a quite sticky sauce and
orange and basil confit – 'the strands of orange beat the flavour of
the basil'. The highlight of a May meal was some wonderfully
flavoured English asparagus, innovatively matched with plump
oysters in a light chervil sauce. Desserts have disappointed. Mint
and chocolate mousse with vanilla cream had no special merit with
the mint tasting rather synthetic. The smartly uniformed staff are
generally friendly and willing, but the service at times can be a little
starchy and erratic.

Directions: On the A10, just past the sign for Ware N, 12 miles N of
M25 exit 25

HUMBERSIDE

BEVERLEY, **The Manor House** ✿✿

Fresh local ingredients are the inspiration behind the food served at this country house hotel

Walkington HV17 8RT
Map no: 8 TA03
Tel: 01482 881645
Chef: Derek Baugh
Proprietor: Derek Baugh
Cost: *Alc* £27.50, fixed-price D £15
Credit cards: ▨ ▦ OTHER
Times: Last D 9.15pm

Derek and Lee Baugh are steadily building up a sound following at their small hotel set in extensive grounds. The restaurant extends from the elegant dining-room into a conservatory overlooking the garden. Two fixed-price menus offer imaginative, well-designed dishes, based on local produce and sound technique. Good saucing was notable in a dish of nine queenies which came in various guises: lobster mousseline, a light tempura with crispy cabbage, sage-crumbed, Mornay, white wine. A smooth, fine blend of broccoli soup was followed by pan-fried calves' livers – 'not too cruelly force fed, pink by origin rather than by cooking' – which came with buttered fried onions and greenback bacon, and served with a marvelously glossy jus; accompanying vegetables were plain but flavoursome. Desserts are imaginative but also include the usual traditional favourites of crème brûlée and bread and butter pudding. A good wine list is provided to complement the cooking.

Directions: 4 miles south west off the B1230

CLEETHORPES, **Kingsway Hotel** ✿

Traditional service has been professionally maintained for four generations by the Harris family at their seafront hotel. Classic French and British dishes are prepared in a reliable manner although, on occasion, the cooking can be uneven. Otherwise, look for straightforward food but perfectly pleasing

Kingsway DN35 0AE
Map no: 8 TA30
Tel: 01472 601122
Chef: Ivor Trushell
Proprietor: John Harris
Cost: *Alc* £22.80, fixed-price L £12.35 (3 courses)/D £15.95 (3 courses. H/wine £8.75
Service exc

Credit cards: ▨ ▦ ▦ ▨ OTHER
Times: 12.30pm-last L 2pm, 7pm-last D 9pm. Closed 25-26 Dec
Seats: 80. No smoking in drawing room
Additional: Children welcome, children's portions; ✿ dishes
Directions: At junction of A1098 and sea front

HULL, **Cerutti's Restaurant** ⊛

Splendid views over the Humber estuary are enjoyed from Cerutti's first floor dining-room. The menu features locally caught fish cooked with some good ideas and lots of enthusiasm. The halibut fromage in a Dijon mustard and cream sauce has been particularly enjoyed

Times: Noon-last L 2pm, last D 9.30pm. Closed Sat L, Sunday, Bhs & 1 wk Xmas
Seats: 36
Additional: Children welcome; ✿ / vegan dishes
Directions: Follow signs for Fruit Market and Corporation Pier

10 Nelson Street HU1 1XE
Map no: 8 TA02
Tel: 01482 328501
Chef: Tim Bell
Proprietor: A J Cerutti
Cost: *Alc* £21.95. H/wine £10.95. Service exc
Credit cards: 🔳 💳

WILLERBY, **Willerby Manor Hotel** ⊛

☺ *A good choice of reliably cooked dishes are offered on the various menus of this traditional restaurant. At inspection, a ravioli of smoked cod was particularly enjoyed. Look out for terrine of pressed leeks and baby vegetables, and steamed venison pudding with a light blackberry sauce*

Seats: 60 **Menus:** *A la carte*, fixed-price L & D
Additional: Children welcome: children's portions; ✿ dishes, vegan/other diets on request
Directions: Off the A1105 west of Hull, just off main street of Willerby

Well Lane HU10 6ER
Map no: 8 TA03
Chef: Adam Richardson
Proprietor: Alexandra Townend
Cost: *Alc* £20, fixed-price L £12 / D £14. H/wine £7.85
Times: Last L 2pm, last D 9.30pm. Closed Sat L, Sun D, Bhs, Christmas-N/year

WINTERINGHAM,
Winteringham Fields ⊛⊛⊛

Provincial cooking from Switzerland and France in a tranquil countryside setting

Winteringham DN15 9PF
Map no: 8 SE92
Tel: 01724 733096
Chef: Germain Schwab
Proprietors: Germain & Annie Schwab
Cost: *Alc* £41, fixed-price L £17.50/D £20. H/wine £12 ❢ Service inc
Credit cards: 🔳 💳 💳 OTHER
Times: Noon-last L 1.30pm, 7.30-last D 9.30pm. Closed 2 wks Xmas, 1st wk Aug
Seats: 36. No smoking in dining room
Menus: *A la carte*, fixed-price L & D

The lure of Winteringham Fields is such that city pressures can be swapped in an instant for peace and tranquillity. Elegant and comfortable surroundings – this was once the home of the Marquis of Lincolnshire – in a quiet rural village, are the irresistible setting for cooking which chef/proprietor Germain Schwab describes as a contrast of bitterness and sweetness. Indeed, visitors are drawn by his mainly Swiss and French provincial cooking which relies on the very best seasonal produce available. Simplicity is a keynote, as can be seen in sea bass steamed over fish stock, sauce from the juices, with spinach, or noisettes of Yorkshire farmed venison, pan-fried with juniper berries, and the cooking shows accuracy and restrained inventiveness. The modern movement is skilfully acknowledged in dishes such as darne of hake with black ink noodles and clam ravioli, and gateaux of spiced wild rabbit and foie gras with sweet and sour sauce.

An inspection meal commenced with a flow of appetisers which included a small red pepper and orange soup, served in the lounge, and a brochette of mushroom and Stilton. A tuna sashimi was also interesting. A 'quite superb' crusted salmi of wood pigeon with black truffles was softly tender, the pastry topping the lightest imaginable, and the flavours clean and fresh with a hint of sweetness. The daily fish special of skate wings in a cider sauce with new potatoes was seaside fresh and very enjoyable. The only off note of the whole evening was a crème brûlée that was 'far too sweet', and with orange zest and coffee essence, 'unnecessarily complicated'. The cheese board was a real delight – 30-plus varieties including some real rarities. The wine list is very satisfactory with some excellent choices in the Swiss and Australian sections, and includes a wide range of half bottles.

Directions: Village centre, off the A1077, 4 miles S of Humber Bridge

Additional: Children welcome, ❤ dishes, vegan/other diets on request

ISLE OF WIGHT

SEAVIEW, **Seaview Hotel** ❀❀

Good modern cooking with plenty of fresh fish and local produce in a seaside hotel restaurant

Seaview overlooks the harbour in a pretty seaside village with sands, rock pools and clinker-built dinghies, and is owned by the charming Nicola and Nicholas Hayward. They believe in polished, unstuffy service and great food. Charles Bartlett changes the *carte* and set-price menus regularly, but some dishes remain constant, especially those based on fish. A memorable inspection dinner began with sauteed chicken livers with shallots in a sweet reduced gravy, followed by 'brilliant' white fillet of sea bass set on a creamy basil-flavoured sauce, topped with shredded root vegetables. Vegetables can be unusual – mashed beetroot and Parmesan-crusted potatoes, for instance. Other main courses could include roasted chicory and tomatoes with a tomato and tarragon sauce, lambs' kidneys sauteed with fino sherry, wholegrain mustard and served with long-grain rice, and breast of French duck, roasted with caramelised onions and orange and peppercorn chutney. Puddings include steamed treacle pudding with local cream, floating islands topped with almonds and crème anglaise, or the savoury Welsh rarebit. The wine list lacks detail but is sensibly priced.

Directions: In High Street near seafront

High Street PO34 5EX
Map no: 4 SZ69
Tel: 01983 612711
Chef: Charles Bartlett
Proprietors: Nicholas & Nicola Hayward
Cost: *Alc* £20.75, fixed-price Sun L £9.95. H/wine £7.85. No service charge
Credit cards: 🅰 💳 💳 💳 OTHER
Times: 12.30pm-last L 1.45pm, 7.30pm-last D 9.30pm. Closed Sun D except Bhs
Menus: *A la carte*, Sunday L, bar meals
Seats: 36. No-smoking until dining over
Additional: Children over 5 welcome, children's menu; ❤ dishes, vegan/other diets on request

KENT

ASHFORD, **Eastwell Manor** ❀❀❀

Classical cooking with a modern slant in a stunning setting that was once the haunt of royalty

Boughton Lees TN25 4HR
Map no: 5 TR04
Tel: 01233 219955
Chef: Ian Mansfield
Proprietor: Queens Moat Houses.
Manager: Petra Billson
Cost: *Alc* £36.50, fixed-price
L £19.50 /D £28.50. H/wine
£14.25 ❢ Service exc
Credit cards: 🂠 💳 💳 💳
Times: 12.30-last L 2pm,
7.30pm-last D 9.45pm
Seats: 80. No smoking in dining room
Menus: *A la carte*, fixed-price
L & D, bar menu
Additional: Children permitted;
children's menu; ❶ dishes,
vegan/other diets on request

Kings and Queens have been regular visitors in the past to this lovingly cared for manor house. Indeed, little has changed over the centuries with the exception of the odd injection of modern luxury. This applies especially to the clubby, oak-panelled dining-room where the highlight of any visit is testing out the growing reputation of chef Ian Mansfield. He has settled in well and has built up a network of suppliers that satisfy his intent to provide dishes with as much natural flavour as possible. Texture is also preserved, and seasoning cannot be faulted, even an occasional foray into the Far East comes off handsomely. This was illustrated by a crab and ginger ravioli, chosen at a recent meal, which was 'wondrously matched' with a cardomom scented sauce.

The style of cooking is classical with a modern slant. A seasonal menu offers half a dozen starters and main courses, with choices like salad of smoked squab pigeon breast, confit leg, beans and cabbage, or herb-crusted lamb loin, ratatouille and black olive polenta. A shorter, cheaper fixed-price menu might tempt with marinated sea trout, pasta salad and basil oil, or red mullet with Niçoise vegetables and a smooth bouillabaisse sauce, or breast of chicken with a sweetcorn and basil broth and spring vegetables, or tart of red goat cheese with a red pepper sauce. Desserts can include hot fondant chocolate with mint chocolate ice-cream, oranges in clove syrup and a caramel ice-cream, and 'jellie' of seasonal berries and red wine with mascarpone sorbet. The lengthy wine list provides a carefully chosen selection of fine and good value wines from all the best growing regions of the world.

Directions: M20 exit 9 follow A251 Faversham, Hotel on L after Kennington, or from Canterbury A28 to Ashford L turn to Boughton Lees

BRANDS HATCH, **Brandshatch Place** ❀❀

A good selection of menus offers beautifully presented English dishes in the pleasant surroundings of a Georgian country house hotel

Talented, self-taught chef Mark Cheesman is reaching new heights in his cooking. An inspector was impressed by choices from a 'Speciality Spring Menu', which ran alongside the *carte* and fixed-price menu, and offered exceptional value-for-money. Home-made bread was followed by a delicious ballotine of guinea fowl filled with dried fruit and bacon which had been washed in a sherry and sultana jus. The main course was an assiette of local lamb which included noisette of lamb with a herb crust, a pastry bouchée filled with sweetbreads and wild mushrooms, and roast kidneys set on a rich onion marmalade. Desserts are equally tempting, and the strawberry mousse with crystallised limes, English berry fruits and a delightful raspberry coulis was a highlight of the meal. There is also a selection of fine cheeses and a semi-descriptive list of wines, grouped by style, with a good choice by the glass. Brandshatch Place is close to Brands Hatch motor racing circuit and within easy reach of London.

Directions: Off the A20; M25 exit 3 follow signs for Circuit then Fawkham, 2nd turning on right after M/way bridge

Fawkham DA3 8NQ
Map no: 5 TQ56
Tel: 01474 872239
Chef: Mark Cheesman
Proprietor: Arcadian Int.
Manager: Yvonne Colgan
Cost: Alc £30, fixed-price L £15.95/D £19.95. H/wine £11.10 ❗ Service exc
Credit cards: ■ ■ ■ ■ OTHER
Times: Noon-last L 2pm, 7pm-last D 9.30pm. Closed Sat L, Dec 26
Seats: 60. No smoking in dining room
Menus: A la carte, fixed-price L & D
Additional: Children welcome, children's menu; ❂ menu, vegan/other diets on request

BROADSTAIRS, **Royal Albion Hotel** ❀

☺ *Established in 1886, the Marchesi Brothers is a cheerful, family-run restaurant (within the Royal Albion) with great sea views. Fixed-price and carte menus offer dishes such as home-made fish soup with a Provençal rouille, salmon fishcakes with a prawn, cream and white wine sauce, and rich apricot crème brûlée*

Menus: A la carte, fixed-price L & D
Seats: 65. No-smoking area
Additional: Children welcome, children's portions; ❂ dishes, other diets on request
Directions: Town centre – down High Street, turn right into Albion Street 50 yards on right

Albion Street CT10 1LU
Map no: 5 TR36
Tel: 01843 862481
Chef: Steven Watson
Proprietors: John, David & Peter Rodger.
Manager: David Rodger
Cost: Alc £22, fixed-price L £10.95/D £12.50 H/wine £8.50 ❗ Service inc
Credit cards: ■ ■ ■ OTHER
Times: Last L 2pm, last D 9.30pm Closed Sun D, Dec 27-30

CANTERBURY, **County Hotel, Sullys** ❀❀

Close to everything worth seeing, a hotel restaurant serving good international food

Medieval streets, ancient houses and Canterbury Cathedral are all on the hotel's doorstep but, behind the mock-Tudor facade, in the kitchen of Sullys Restaurant, there is heritage of a different kind. Recent arrival François Garcin is a chef whose career resumé stretches from London's Walton Street to the Hotel Martinez in Cannes, via Cairo's Nile Hilton. He offers seasonal speciality and weekly-changing fixed-price menus at lunch and dinner. It was the Spring version of the former that seduced an inspector one evening: a faultless fresh foie gras and truffle charlotte with crystal-clear port jelly, poached brill, served with a peppercorn mignonette and shallot butter sauce; some disappointingly plain and unexciting vegetables marginally weakened the impact but honour was restored with a plum and whisky pancake soufflé with apricot

High Street CT1 2RX
Map no: 5 TR15
Tel: 01227 766266
Chef: François C Garcin
Manager: J B Penturo
Cost: Fixed-price L £16/D £19.50, seasonal special L/D £25.50 H/wine £10.50
Credit cards: ■ ■ ■ ■ OTHER
Times: Last L 2.30pm, last D 10pm
Menus: Fixed-price L & D, Seasonal special L & D
Seats: 60. Air conditioned
Additional: Children welcome, children's portions; ❂ menu, vegan/other diets on request

coulis. From the other menu, green asparagus and Parma ham gratinated with hollandaise, veal Chartreuse with a cider sauce, and warm strawberry feuilleté with green peppercorn and caramel sauce, could have been an alternative meal worth trying.
There is an interesting selection of wines, including a good showing from Italy and some creditable domaine-bottled Burgundies.

Directions: City centre – Hotel car park via Stour Street, High Street is pedestrianised

CANTERBURY, Ristorante Tuo e Mio ❀

☺ *A long established, family-run restaurant with eye-catchingly light decor. Menus contain much familiar Italian food, with dishes such as 'scaloppina al funghetto', veal with wild mushroom sauce, or a special of the day, swordfish with salsa verde. Desserts include tiramisu, and the espresso is wonderfully strong*

Menus: A la carte, fixed-price L
Seats: 70. No cigars or pipes
Additional: Children welcome, ❤ dishes, other diets on request
Directions: Opposite King's School

16 The Borough CT1 2DR
Map no: 5 TR15
Tel: 01227 761471
Chefs: M Orietti and Y Mula
Proprietors: R P M Greggio
Cost: Alc £16-£20, fixed-price L £13 (4 course). H/wine £7.50 ❢
Service inc. Cover charge 50p
Credit cards: ▨ ▨ ▨ ▨ OTHER
Times: Last L 2.30pm/D 10.45pm. Closed Mon & Tue L, last 2 wks Feb, last 2 wks Aug

CRANBROOK,
Kennel Holt Hotel ❀

An attractive hotel set in stunning gardens. Two lovely lounges and a characterful restaurant, all with beams, log fires and wood panelling, add to the appeal. The fixed-price menu offers straightforward homely, cooking. Try the aubergine, courgette and Parmesan torte, duck breast with perigourdine sauce, and the lemon tart for dessert

Goudhurst Road TN7 2PT
Map no: 5 TQ73
Tel: 01580 712032
Chef: Neil Chalmers
Proprietor: Neil & Sally Chalmers
Cost: Fixed-price L / D £20.
H/wine £10 Service exc
Credit cards: ▨ ▨ ▨ ▨ OTHER
Times: 12.30pm-last L 1.30pm/last D 9pm. Closed Mon, Sat L, Sun D
Menus: Fixed-price L & D
Seats: 25. No smoking in dining room
Additional: Children welcome, children's portions; ❤ dishes, other diets on request

Directions: On A262 1 mile from A229 crossroad, 3 miles from Goudhurst towards Cranbrook

> Pink peppercorns are, in fact, not a peppercorn at all. They are the processed berry of a South American relative of the poison ivy. They are toxic if eaten in large quantities.

DEAL, Dunkerleys Restaurant ❀

Fish is a speciality at this seafront restaurant. The uncomplicated menu offers simple but enjoyable dishes, complemented by a short list of inexpensive wines. A meal in May featured chilled haddock vichyssoise, baked seabass on a bed of mushroom and sliced onions, and poached pear with a gratin of sabayon

Menus: *A la carte* L & D, fixed-price L
Seats: 40. Air Conditioned. No-smoking area
Additional: Children welcome, children's portions/Sun L menu; ❂ dishes, vegan/other diets on request
Directions: Turn off A2 onto A258 to Deal – 100 yds before Deal Pier

Deal CT14 7AH
Map no: 5 TR35
Tel: 01304 375016
Chefs: Ian Dunkerley and Stephen Harvey
Proprietor: Ian Dunkerley
Cost: *Alc* £20-£30, fixed-price L £9.50. H/wine £7.95 ❢ Service exc
Credit cards: ▨ ▨ ▨ ▨ OTHER
Times: Last L 3pm, last D10 pm Closed Mon L

DOVER, Wallett's Court ❀❀❀

A manor house hotel with an almost medieval flavour to the menu with its emphasis on hearty game dishes

A Grade II listed Jacobean manor house, Wallett's Court has some fine original features, including a carved porch, an ancient staircase, oak beams, moulded plaster fireplaces, a 17th-century wall painting and a priest hole. It stands in delightful grounds, open to the sea air and not far from the clifftops. The Oakley family and their polite staff create a welcoming and relaxed atmosphere, particularly in the evening when the hotel centres on the restaurant. Christopher Oakley learnt his professional cooking skills with the Roux brothers, in the early days when he was head chef at Le Poulbot in the City. He continues to cook to a very high standard with no slavish following of fashion, and flavours stand out confidently.

The fixed-price menu changes monthly and starters include straightforward soups and more substantial dishes such as spinach pancakes, filled with smoked haddock and served with a saffron sauce, and a 'Huntsman's Platter' – local game terrine and smoked Barbary duck breast with Cumberland sauce. There is a traditional English, almost medieval, feel to the menu with ingredients such as wild boar, pigeon, venison and quail, sitting happily alongside a combination of feta cheese, olives and Spanish tomatoes. Main courses generally range from locally caught fish probably served in a cream sauce and garnished with a concasse of tomatoes and baby cucumbers, to a rich game casserole with red wine and wild woodland mushrooms. Desserts are good, with bread and butter pudding a speciality. There is also a modestly priced wine list with wines from around the world, some available by the half bottle or glass.

Directions: From A2 take A258 (Dover/Deal) 1st right to St. Margaret's hotel is on the right

West Cliffe CT15 6EW
Map no: 5 TR34
Tel: 01304 852424
Chef: Christopher Oakley
Proprietors: Christopher & Lea Oakley & Family
Cost: Fixed-price D £21/£25 (5 course). H/wine £11 ❢. Service exc
Credit cards: ▨ ▨
Times: 7pm-Last D 9pm. Closed Sun, Dec 24-27
Menus: Fixed-price D
Seats: 40. No smoking in dining room
Additional: Children welcome, children's portions; ❂ dishes; other diets by arrangement

EDENBRIDGE,
Honours Mill Restaurant ❀❀

A former water mill serving good quality cooking in the first floor restaurant

Old working parts and props create decorative interest in the downstairs section of this former water mill. The restaurant is on

87 High Street TN8 5AU
Map no: 5 TQ44
Tel: 01732 866757
Chef: Martin Radmall
Proprietors: Neville, Duncan & Giles Goodhew

the first floor: all (very) low beams, fresh flowers and an intimate atmosphere. Carefully presented food with a pronounced leaning towards haute cuisine is Martin Randall's ambitious style. A test meal began with an appetiser of freshly baked onion tartlets dusted with paprika; followed by a well-constructed terrine of red mullet set in a sole mousse with a bright yellow saffron sauce. Then sausage of lambs' sweetbreads blended with morrel mushrooms came served on a bed of puy lentils with a richly flavoured jus. Only a dark chocolate marquise disappointed: chocolate mousse wrapped in liqueur-flavoured Genoise sponge and served with a thin but very grainy coffee sauce. Almond petits fours were better made. A good choice of French regional wines is included in the reasonable wine list.

Directions: Town centre, southern end of High Street, just north of the bridge

Cost: Fixed-price L £ 15.50 & £32.75/Sun L £ 23.50, fixed-price D £32.75 (£26 Tues Fri). H/wine £10.10 Service inc
Credit cards: 🔳 📧 📧
Times: Last L 2pm, last D10pm. Closed Sat L, Sun D, Mon, 2 wks after Xmas
Menus: Fixed-price L & D, Sunday lunch
Seats: 36. No cigars or pipes
Additional: Children permitted, children's portions; other diets by arrangement

FAVERSHAM, **Read's Restaurant** ✿✿✿

Reliable cooking based on sound skills and outstanding produce in a class restaurant in a rural Kent village

The Pitchfords have been at Read's for a long time; long enough to establish what must now be a fine reputation for an uncomplicated, straightforward and consistently high standard of cooking. The building is another matter. A converted 1960's supermarket, there is a blandness about the place that no amount of work can hide, although a recent extension now offers a bar area with an open-air terrace overlooking the gently undulating Belmont Valley.

David Pitchford uses the best quality ingredients available in his reliable recipes and the results on the plate are outstanding. (The evening menu reveals more of the range of cooking than lunch, and this is reflected in a higher price.) A reworking of traditional ideas takes in current modern practices: up-to-the-minute herbs and spices, and thin slivers of vegetables can be intergral parts of a dish, and offal features occasionally. Fillet steak with black pudding, bacon and honey-glazed onions, and new season's Romney Marsh lamb with broad beans and a sauce of sweet Kentish herbs gives something of an idea of the style. There is nothing innovative, nothing shocking, just well thought out ideas, prepared with sound technique.

An inspection lunch yielded a fine chicken liver parfait served with plain melba toast and a salad of mixed leaves, followed by escalope of fresh salmon with a 'superior' butter sauce and fresh, new season's asparagus with plain haricot vert, mange tout, chateau potatoes, and sliced courgette with garlic tomato and herb sauce. Pudding was sliced, juicy, fresh pineapple cooked in butter and served with a refined caramel sauce and pineapple sorbet. Service throughout is relaxed and attentive, a tribute to Rona Pitchford's front-of-house skills. The wine list boasts over 250 bins from most of the major wine-producing areas of the world, including some very rare and expensive, but the modestly-priced house wine is also worth trying.

Directions: M2 exit 6 turn left onto A2, then left into Brogdale Road, signposted Painters Forstal 1.5 miles S Faversham

Painters Forstal ME13 0EE
Map no: 5 TR06
Tel: 01795 535344
Chef: David Pitchford
Proprietors: David & Rona Pitchford
Cost: *Alc* £34, fixed-price L £15.50 / D £25 H/wine £12 ❢
No service charge
Credit cards: 🔳 📧 📧 💳 OTHER
Times: Last L 2pm / D10pm. Closed Sun, Mon, 2 weeks Aug/Sept
Seats: 40 + 20. private
Menus: *A la carte,* fixed-price L & D
Additional: Children welcome, children's menu. ❶ dishes, other diets on request

HYTHE, **The Hythe Imperial Hotel** ✿

A seafront hotel set in extensive grounds is the setting for a meal in the Princes Restaurant. Bread and pastries, made on the premises, are particularly noteworthy. Otherwise, low marks for duck confit and fillets of sole filled with crab meat, but high marks for a well-made, and enjoyable, tiramisu

Seats: 200. No smoking in dining room. Air conditioned
Menus: *A la carte,* fixed-price L & D, bar menu
Additional: Children welcome, children's menu; ✔ dishes,
vegan/other diets on request
Directions: M20 exit 11 /A261 to Hythe follow signs to Folkestone, R into Twiss Road opposite Bell Inn, towards sea front & Hotel is on L

Princes Parade CT21 6AE
Map no: 5 TR13
Tel: 01303 267441
Chef: David Lintern
Proprietors: Marston.
Manager: David Nott (Best
Western)
Cost: *Alc* £25, fixed-price L
£15/D £20. H/wine £10.95 ❢
Service inc
Credit cards: 🔳 🔳 🔳 🔳 OTHER
Times: 12.30-last L 2pm,
7.30pm-last D 9pm

LITTLEBOURNE, **The Bow Window Inn** ✿

☺ *Oak beams, candlelight and a good choice of dishes from the carte and daily specials board make eating at this charming inn a pleasurable experience. A test meal yielded leek and salmon mille-feuille, rack of New Zealand lamb with a good-flavoured demi-glace, followed by home-made apple pie*

Directions: In centre of village

50 High Street CT3 1ST
Map no: 5 TR25
Tel: 01227 721244
Chefs: Darren Ball and Aaron
Golfinch
Proprietors: Lynn & Paul
Thurgate
Cost: *Alc* £13, fixed-price Sun L
£8.25 H/wine £5.90 ❢ Service
inc
Credit cards: 🔳 🔳 OTHER
Times: 11am-last L 2, 6pm-last
D 9.30pm
Seats: 40
Menus: *A la carte* L & D, fixed-price Sun L
Additional: Children over 12
permitted; ✔ dishes, vegan/
other diets on request

LITTLEBOURNE, **King William IV** ✿

☺ *Reliable, honest English cooking can be enjoyed in the warm, friendly atmosphere of this old village inn. A daily changing carte includes dishes such as vine leaves stuffed with mushrooms and bacon, fillet of salmon in puff pastry, and chocolate and pistachio nut terrine with raspberry coulis*

Menus: *A la carte* L & D, bar menu
Seats: 40. No smoking in dining room
Additional: Children welcome, ✔ dishes, other diets by
arrangement
Directions: On A257 3 miles E of Canterbury

4 High Street CT3 1ST
Map no: 5 TR25
Tel: 01227 721264
Chef: R W Steinmetz
Proprietors: Mr & Mrs Steinmetz
Cost: *Alc* from £15. H/wine £8 ❢
Service exc
Credit cards: 🔳 🔳 🔳 OTHER
Times: Noon-last L 2pm, 7pm-
last D 9pm Closed Sun D

MAIDSTONE, **Tanyard Hotel** ❀

Tanyard is set in ten acres of landscaped hillside and gardens and the attractive candlelit restaurant offers an interesting range of modern British cooking. At a February inspection, crab and spring onion parcels were followed by steamed salmon, cod and prawns with a leek mousse, with banana cheesecake to finish

Wierton Hill
Boughton Monchelsea ME17 4JT
Map no: 5 TQ85
Tel: 01622 744705
Chef: Jan Davies
Proprietor: Jan Davies
Cost: Fixed-price L £16.50/D
£25 (4 course). H/wine £9
Service exc
Credit cards: 🗖 🖃 🖃 🖭 OTHER
Times: last L 1.45pm/last D
11pm Closed Christmas, 2 wks
in winter
Menus: Fixed-price L & D
Seats: 28. No smoking in dining
room
Additional: Children over 6
permitted; ❂ dishes, other diets
with notice

Directions: Turn off B2163 at Cock Pub nr Boughton Monchelsea

ROCHESTER,
Bridgewood Manor Hotel ❀❀

Maidstone Road ME5 9AX
Map no: 5 TQ76
Tel: 01634 201333
Credit cards: 🗖 🖃 🖃 🖭

Friendly, accommodating business hotel serving some very good food indeed

A modern business-orientated hotel, ideally placed for the M2 and M20. The cooking is of a good standard, especially the fine saucing noted at an inspection meal in June. This commenced with a choice of bread, presented then sliced at the table. The first course of rabbit pieces in a crisp, light pastry case, was good, and was followed by fresh sea bass with an intense shellfish jus, an open langoustine ravioli, and bright tomato fondue, and accompanied by a vegetable spaghetti and new potatoes. 'A complex and enjoyable dish.' Dessert was a white chocolate and pistachio terrine, the two tastes well balanced, the texture smooth, set on a sharp cherry compote. Appetisers and petits fours were also of a good standard. The wine list is very thorough, with a good number of halves and wines by the glass. Drinks may be taken in the bar, which being a hotel can be busy, but inspectors' reports have noted that staff are genuinely attentive to guests' needs. The decor of the hotel exudes an air of quality, enlivened by fresh flowers and attractive fabrics.

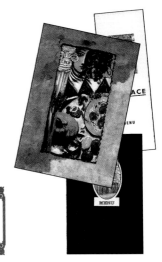

Directions: Adjacent to roundabout on A229

> Coriander is an aromatic umbelliferous plant used as both a herb (the fresh leaves) and a spice (the dried seeds). The taste of each is different, and one cannot be substituted for the other in a recipe.

ROYAL TUNBRIDGE WELLS, **Cheevers** ❀❀

☺ *Originality and dedication combine to achieve some exciting results at this well established restaurant*

Chef and co-proprietor Timothy Cheevers has stuck to an effective formula over the years with a simple but continually evolving menu. However, his cooking is currently achieving new highs, resulting in fine food prepared with considerable flair. The home-baked bread is a wonderful start to the meal, followed by dishes such parfait of calves' liver with toasted brioche, and fettucine with wild mushrooms. A main course of sea bass and fennel was very enjoyable, served with a pungent tomato and garlic coulis. Well seasoned, fresh and colourful vegetables accompany each dish, and there is a good selection of home-made desserts to choose from. The tarte au citron is recommended, and the parfait of two chocolates with a coffee cream sauce. The wines have been carefully selected to complement the food, and the house Chardonnay Carcasonne, available by the glass, is well worth a try. Service is attentive and efficient, personally provided by the other half of this successful partnership, Mr Martin Miles.

Directions: From the railway station, the restaurant is halfway down the High Street on the right

56 High Street
Map no: 5 TQ53
Tel: 01892 545524
Chef: Timothy Cheevers
Proprietors: Timothy Cheevers and Martin Miles
Cost: *Alc* £19, fixed-price D (Fri, Sat) £25. H/wine £8.95 ❢ Service exc
Credit cards: 🔳 🔳 🔳 OTHER
Times: Last L 2pm/1.45pm Sat, last D 10.30pm. Closed Sun, Mon, 1 wk Xmas
Menus: *A la carte* L & D (Tue, Wed, Thur), fixed-price dinner Fri/Sat
Seats: 32. Air conditioned
Additional: Children welcome, children's portions

ROYAL TUNBRIDGE WELLS,

Royal Wells Inn ❀❀

An individual hotel of great character serving modern Anglo-French cooking

Mount Ephraim TN4 8BE
Map no: 5 TQ53
Tel: 01892 511188
Chef: Robert Sloan
Proprietors: Robert & David Sloan (Consort)
Cost: *Alc* £25 aprox, fixed-price L £10.50/D £19.50 (£17.50 Tue-Thur). H/wine £9.75 ❢ Service inc
Credit cards: 🔳 🔳 🔳 💷 OTHER
Times: Last L 2pm, last D10pm Closed Sun, Mon D, Dec 25/6
Seats: 40
Additional: Children welcome, children's portions; ❤ dishes, other diets on request

The Royal Wells Inn is a distinctive Victorian edifice which dominates a hilltop overlooking the town. It has been in the Sloan family for 25 years. Two sons have taken over responsibility for the management and instigated improvements to the interior. A major focus of the hotel is the elegant front-facing conservatory restaurant which offers a daily fixed-price menu and the main *carte*. A winter inspection meal began with a simple but effective starter of squid served with olive oil, garlic and chilli, followed by heart warming, full-flavoured braised leg of lamb with flageolet beans, tomato and basil. Alternatives could be spinach and ricotta beignets with anchovy hollandaise, and roast marinated pork fillet with sage and apple. To conclude, there are desserts such as lemon pie, chocolate marquise, and a Baileys and marscapone cheesecake, or a savoury such as Scotch woodcock. For a less formal meal, the hotel has a cheerful brasserie serving simpler food.

Directions: Situated 75yds from the juction of the A21 and A264

ROYAL TUNBRIDGE WELLS, **Spa Hotel** ✿

Professional silver service sets the tone in the impressive crystal-chandeliered restaurant of this 18th-century country mansion. Fresh seafood, well-executed sauces and enjoyable patisserie are particularly good here, and typical dishes might be brochette of scallops and smoked bacon and medallions of beef on a celeriac pancake

Menus: A la carte, fixed-price L & D, bar menu
Seats: 76. No smoking in dining room **Additional:** Children welcome, children's menu; ✿ dishes, vegan/other diets on request
Directions: On A264 leaving Tunbridge towards E. Grinstead

Royal Tunbridge Wells TN4 8XJ
Map no: 5 TQ53
Tel: 01892 520331
Chef: Edward Heasman
Proprietor: Richard Goring (Best Western).
Manager: Andrew Salter
Cost: Alc £25.50, fixed-price
L £15.50/D £14 H/wine £8.75
❗ Service exc
Credit cards: 🔳 🔳 🔳 🔳 OTHER
Times: Last L 2pm, last D
9.30pm Closed most BHs

ROYAL TUNBRIDGE WELLS,
Thackeray's House Restaurant ✿✿✿

The former home of the novelist William Makepeace Thackeray, now a stylish restaurant, where modern British cooking is served

85 London Road TN1 1EA
Map no: 5 TQ53
Tel: 01892 511921
Chef: Bruce Wass
Proprietor: Bruce Wass.
Manager: Mark Slaney
Cost: Alc £30-35, fixed-price
L £12 (2 course) / D £22.50
(3 course) H/wine £11.75 ❗
Service exc
Credit cards: 🔳 🔳 OTHER
Times: 12.30-last L 2.30pm,
7pm-last D 10pm. Closed Sun
D, Mon, 5 days at Xmas
Seats: 50. No pipes or cigars
Menus: A la carte, fixed-price
L & D
Additional: Children welcome,
children's menu, ✿ menu

Thackeray's house, where the novelist lived in the mid-19th century, has been Bruce Wass's domain for a decade. The restaurant dining-room on the ground floor is stylish; crisp linen, subdued colour scheme, a lounge for drinks on the first floor, and in the basement, a popular bistro. The restaurant *carte* and fixed-price menus (excellent value for lunch) grasps current fashions for dishes such as fresh sardine salad, crab and sweet pepper vinaigrette, roast grey mullet with capers and pine nuts, and Gressingham duck with sweet and sour onions and Cassis sauce, but inspectors' reports are mixed, with comments about insipidity in with the more general praise.

One inspection meal kicked off with duck liver and heart terrine with onion marmalade. It was beautifully constructed but lacked an exciting flavour, although the onion marmalade was excellent, cooked in Cassis. Red mullet fillets, which followed, were excellent, served with a rich fennel-butter sauce, textured with dill, but accompanying vegetables were disappointing, namely under-cooked shredded cabbage, and poorly prepared new season's potatoes, although the sweetly flavoured and well-glazed carrots did partly compensate. The highlight of this meal was an apricot, walnut, ginger and toffee pudding, served with a sound caramel sauce. Other dishes which might be offered on the fixed-price menus include starters like nettle and spinach soup, or goats' cheese with fennel, roast tomato, crispy fried artichoke and rocket salad, while a main course choice might be rump of lamb with pesto jus. Service can sometimes be a bit hurried and disinterested. The wine list boasts a very good house selection. The Domaine de Labette Vin de Pays 1993 is particularly good value.

Directions: At corner of London Road/Mount Ephraim Road overlooking the Common, 2 mins from hospital

SEVENOAKS, **Royal Oak Hotel** 🌸

A well-established High Street hotel which has retained much of the look of a 17th-century inn. A recent inspection meal consisted of a full-flavoured liver and mushroom terrine, salmon darne with a pesto sauce, and a warming traditional bread and butter pudding

Seats: 70. Air conditioned. No smoking in dining room
Menus: *A la carte*, fixed-price L & D, bar menu **Additional:** Children welcome, children's portions; ✿ menu; other diets pre-book
Directions: M25 exit 5; at far end of High Street, opposite Sevenoaks school, walking distance from the town centre

Upper High Street
Map no: 5 TQ55
Tel: 01732 451109
Chef: James Butterfill
Proprietors: Brook Hotels.
Manager: Lisa Butterfill
Cost: *Alc* £23-£31, fixed-price L £10.95/D £13.95. H/wine £8.95
♥ Service exc
Credit cards: 🔳 🔳 🔳 🔳
Times: Last L 2pm/D 10pm
Closed Sat L

SISSINGHURST, **Rankins** 🌸🌸

Serious, modern British cooking in a charming English village setting

The Rankins' small, personally-run restaurant is set in an unassuming but historic terrace on the only through road through Sissinghurst. Hugh Rankin takes his cooking seriously. Dishes are based on well sourced produce with an eye to what is currently in fashion. In other words Mediterranean features happily on a menu with up-dated British cooking: couscous with a Mediterranean style bean stew, finished with parsley and garlic purée, and cod and leek crumble, are examples of the style. A typical meal could be fresh fettucine with roast red pepper and tomato sauce with shaved Parmesan, followed by deep-fried duck breast with cognac, cream and green peppercorn sauce, with lemon drenched pudding to finish. The short wine list is sound on price but could be better annotated; there is a decent list of half bottles.

Directions: Village centre, on right on A262 (Ashford)

The Street TN17 2JH
Map no: 5 TQ73
Tel: 01580 713964
Chef: Hugh Rankin
Proprietors: Hugh & Leonora Rankin
Cost: Fixed-price D £22.95/Sun L £19.95. H/wine £7.80. Service exc
Credit cards: 🔳 🔳
Times: Last D 9 pm, last Sun L 1.30pm Closed Sun D, Mon, Tue
Menus: Fixed-price D & Sun L
Seats: 26
Additional: Children permitted, children's portions; ✿ dishes, other diets on request

WESTERHAM, **Kings Arms Hotel** 🌸

☺ *A delightful town-centre Georgian hotel that is a popular local landmark. The bar is cosy, the lounge inviting and ably-prepared food could include baked crab Thermidor, pan-fried breast of duck in a blackcurrant sauce, and broccoli and cream cheese pie, with fresh strawberry torte for dessert*

Menus: *A la carte*, Terrace menu **Seats:** 60. No cigars or pipes **Additional:** Children welcome, children's portions. ✿ dishes, vegan/ other diets on request
Directions: On A25, in the centre of Westerham

Market Square TN16 1AN
Map no: 5 TQ45
Tel: 01959 562990
Chef: Terry Howland
Proprietor: Consort.
Manager: K Lindsay Eaton
Cost: *Alc* from £18.50. H/wine £9.75 Service inc
Credit cards: 🔳 🔳 🔳 🔳 OTHER
Times: Last L 2.30pm, last D 10pm.Closed between Xmas & N/Year

WHITSTABLE,
Whitstable Oyster Fisher Co 🌸

☺ *A casual atmosphere and simple cooking are attractive features of this popular, shore-front fish restaurant. Locally caught fish features on the daily-changing blackboard menu. Go for native oysters, scallops in white wine and cream or baked halibut with Gruyère and mustard*

Seats: 150 **Cost:** *Alc* £15. H/wine £9 ♥ Service exc
Credit cards: 🔳 🔳 🔳 🔳 OTHER **Additional:** Children welcome, children's portions; ✿ dishes, other diets on request

Horsebridge Beach
Map no: 5 TR16
Tel: 01227 276856
Chefs: Nikki Billington and Chris Williams
Proprietors: Whitstable Oyster Fishery Co
Times: Last L 2pm/D 9pm. Closed Xmas, New Year's Day

LANCASHIRE

BILLINGTON,
Foxfields Hotel ✿

The presentation of food is first-class in this modern commercial hotel. In addition, good use is made of herbs. Rich flavours predominate in modern Anglo-French dishes, and flexibility is offered with options from carte, fixed-price and chef's specials menus

Whalley Road BB7 9HY
Map no: 7 SD73
Tel: 01254 822556
Chef: Peter Desmet
Proprietors: Lyric Hotels.
Manager: Stuart Chirnside
Cost: Alc £22, fixed-price L £11.95/D £14.50. H/wine £9.95. Service exc
Credit cards: ▨ ▨ ▨ ▨ OTHER
Times: Last L1.45pm, last D 9.30pm Closed Sat L
Menus: A la carte, fixed-price L & D, bar menu
Seats: 90. Air conditioned. No-smoking area
Additional: Children welcome, children's portions; ✪ menu, vegan/other diets on request

Directions: From A59 follow sign for Whalley, hotel is 0.5 mile on right

BLACKBURN, Millstone Hotel ✿

☺ *Situated at the village cross-roads, this former coaching inn draws a good local following to its Millers Restaurant. The varied menu is supplemented by blackboard specials, and a meal might include fish soup with aïoli and Parmesan, lamb shank with lentils, root vegetables and a red onion compote, and tiramisu with mascarpone*

Church Lane
Mellor BB2 7JR
Map no: 7 SD62
Tel: 01254 813333
Chef: Mark Wilkin
Proprietors: Shire Inns.
Manager: Anthony Whiteley
Cost: Alc £20, fixed-price L £13.50/D £20. H/wine £10.45
❢ Service exc
Credit cards: ▨ ▨ ▨ ▨ OTHER
Times: Last L 2pm/D 9.30pm
Menus: A la carte, fixed-price L & D, bar menu
Seats: 34. No smoking in dining room
Additional: Children welcome, children's menu; ✪ dishes, vegan on request

Directions: Three miles west of Blackburn at the juction of Mellor Lane and Church Lane

BLACKPOOL, September Brasserie ✿✿

A brasserie restaurant close to the prom living up to its claim to provide creative eclectic food

15-17 Queen Street FY1 1PU
Map no: 7 SD33
Tel: 01253 23282
Chef: Michael Golowicz
Proprietor: Michael Golowicz
Cost: *Alc* L £13/D £22, fixed-price D £15.95. H/wine £2 glass
❚ Service exc
Credit cards: ▨ ▩ ▩ ▨ OTHER
Times: Last L 2pm, last D 9.30pm. Closed Sun, Mon, 2 wks Summer & Winter
Menus: *A la carte* L & D, fixed-price D
Seats: 40. Air conditioned
Additional: Children permitted; children's portions; ◐ dishes, other diets on request

Blackpool may not generally be associated with the culinary arts, but this oasis of good food is situated just a stone's throw from the famous promenade, occupying first floor premises above a town-centre hairdresser. The menu is changed monthly to make the most of fresh seasonal ingredients; daily blackboard specials increase the choice, and add good-value business lunches. Dishes range from up-market bangers and mash to breast of local cock pheasant stuffed with teal and spinach. Among the starters there might be spinach and barley soup with wild mushrooms and seaweed, or pan-fried chicken livers with chopped bacon and garlic with a good bite of chilli. Particularly intriguing main courses are free-range Canadian bison braised with lentils du pays and coriander, and roast saddle of wild rabbit with Dublin Bay prawns and lemon grass. Our inspector went for the pink and gamey breast of mallard with Cassis (difficult to detect) and well flavoured sautéed mushrooms. To finish there might be brandy snap discs with chestnut Ameretto cream, or British farmhouse cheeses. The wine list has a selection from most French regions as well as New World wines

Directions: 200 yards from the promenade, adjacent to the Cenotaph

GISBURN Stirk House Hotel ✿

Skilful handling of fresh produce can be discerned in the cooking at Stirk House. A daily-changing fixed-price menu and carte offer dishes such as smoked loin of lamb, gazpacho soup and trout Wellington with a duxelle of mushroom. This might be followed by brown bread and butter ice-cream in an almond cup

Menus: *A la carte*, fixed-price L & D, children's, pre-theatre, bar menu, Sun L
Seats: 80. No smoking. Air conditioning
Additional: Children welcome; children's menu; ◐ menu, vegan dishes, other diets on request
Directions: West of village on A59, Clitheroe Road

Gisburn BB7 4LJ
Map no: 7 SD84
Tel: 01200 445581
Chef: Keith Blackburn
Manager: David Raistrick
Cost: *Alc* £20, fixed-price L £8.95 (3 course)/D £18 (5 course). H/wine £9 Service inc
Credit cards: ▨ ▩ ▩ ▨
Times: Last L 2pm, last D 9.30pm

LANGHO, **Northcote Manor** ✿✿

A country house hotel with a smartly decorated restaurant and an enviable reputation for fine food

Langho BB6 8BE
Map no: 7 SD73
Tel: 01254 240555
Chef: Nigel Haworth
Proprietors: N Haworth and C Bancroft
Cost: *Alc* £26-£40, fixed-price L £20
Credit cards: 🌑 ▨ ▨ 🅿
Times: Last D 9.30pm

Craig Bancroft and Nigel Haworth have every right to be pleased with their achievements since they came here 11 years ago. Nigel, who trained in Switzerland and at Gleneagles, and head chef William Reid, produce modern British versions of traditional dishes, including seasonal specialities and some from the home patch. Proudly wearing the red rose are home-potted Morecambe Bay shrimps, rich black pudding from Bury, topped with moist, flaky pink trout and a sharp mustard and watercress sauce, and delicate, oak-smoked salmon from Fleetwood with chopped shallots, parsley and capers – all grouped together as 'tiny Lancashire delicacies'. Main courses sampled included appetising fresh grilled red mullet with oysters, softly braised leeks and forest mushrooms, and lightly seared scallops with pungent shavings of tête de moine cheese (which rather overpowered the more subtle flavour of the scallops). The more expensive 'Chef's Gourmet' menu offers dishes such as whole roast fillet of Angus beef on spinach and celeriac with oysters, shallot sauce, parsley pesto and purée potatoes. Puddings are very good, especially sticky toffee pudding.

Directions: From M6 take A59, follow signs for Clitheroe. At first traffic lights left onto Skipton/Clitheroe road for 8 miles. Left into Northcote Road. The hotel is on the right

Couscous has two meanings: the complete dish and the tiny granules of semolina with which it is usually made. The couscous concept is simple. Take a container with a perforated bottom, fill it with granules, and place it above a simmering stew. The grains will swell in the steam from the stew and at the same time be flavoured by it. When the two are served together the combination is wonderful, one of the highlights of Moroccan cooking. The dish itself is undoubtedly Berber, but the derivation of the word couscous is obscure. The favoured theory is that it is onomatopoeic, a verbal approximation of the hissing sound made as steam is forced through the holes of the 'couscoussier' into the grain.

LONGRIDGE,
Paul Heathcotes Restaurant 🏵🏵🏵🏵

A remarkable chef/proprietor with an impeccable background cooking stylish modern food

104-106 Higher Road PR3 3SY
Map no: 7 SD63
Tel: 01772 784969
Chefs: Paul Heathcote and Andrew Barnes
Proprietor: Paul Heathcote
Cost: *Alc* £35.40, fixed-price L £22.50 (4 course) / D £36 (6 courses). H/wine £12 ❢ Service inc
Credit cards: 🔳 🏧 🏧 🏧 OTHER
Times: Last L 2pm (Fri & Sun), last D 9.30pm (Tue-Sun). Closed Mon
Menus: *A la carte* D, fixed-price D / Fri & Sun L
Seats: 60. No smoking in dining room
Additional: Children welcome, ❶ dishes, vegan/other diets on request

Paul Heathcote is proud of his roots. A Lancashire lad, he has firmly established himself in this gastronomically unfashionable part of the North of England, bringing together his prestigious training at the Manoir aux Quat'Saisons, Connaught and Sharrow Bay into a style of modern British cooking that also incorporates traditional northern ingredients; even the bread can include black pudding. Another plus is the earthiness, honesty, and realistically (large) sized portions at affordable prices. The gourmet fixed-price menu and *carte* both show curiosity and enthusiasm. Materials are of a high standard, especially the fowl from nearby Goosnargh and the fish, and the predominant style is to treat every dish at its own face value. Pigs trotter filled with ham hock and sage, served with a tartlet of pea purée and onion sauce sits next to pressed terrine of lamb, broad beans, tomato and tarragon with olive oil, served with a salad of sun-dried tomatoes and olives, or open ravioli of braised snails and turkey with parsley butter and turkey juices. Main courses range from a simple roast lamb with hot-pot potatoes, roast shallots, braised leeks and rosemary scented juices, to the more complicated baked fillet of halibut with dried citrus fruit and tortellini of lobster and scallops with orange butter sauce.

An inspection meal commenced with a robust confit of duck leg, with a pease pudding and a Madeira sauce, followed by a sweet, smooth parsnip and chestnut soup. For main course, a medley of fresh fish was chosen. Salmon, seabass, turbot, halibut, brill and mussels were offset by 'a lovely' herb scented liquor; winter root vegetables were an intrinsic part of the dish. Dessert did not disappoint: an exceptional bread and butter pudding with the top slightly caramelised, and accompanied by a sauce anglaise and compote of apricots won the battle between creamed rice pudding scented with hazelnut oil and served with caramel ice-cream or mille-feuille of strawberries layered between crisp chocolate biscuits and served with dark chocolate sorbet. The wine list complements the food well by dipping into most countries.

Directions: Follow signs for Golf Club & Jeffery Hill. Higher Road is beside White Bull Pub in Longridge. Heathcotes 0.5 mile on right

PRESTON,
Broughton Park Hotel ❀❀

A well-established country house restaurant strong on seasonally changing menus featuring skilfully prepared and imaginatively presented French/English dishes

Garstang Road
Broughton PR3 5JB
Map no: 7 SD52
Tel: 01772 864087
Chef: Neil McKevitt
Proprietor: Country Club.
Manager: Paul Le Roi
Cost: Alc £30, fixed-price L
£13.25/D £18.95. H/wine £9.95
❢ Service exc
Credit cards: 💳 💳 💳 💳 OTHER
Times: Noon-last L 1.45pm,
7pm-last D 9.45pm /8.45pm Sun
Closed L Sat & Bh
Menus: A la carte, fixed-price L
& D
Seats: 60. No smoking in dining
room
Additional: Children welcome,
children's menu; ❤ dishes,
vegan/other diets on request

Guests are assured of a cordial welcome and attentive service in the delightful Courtyard Restaurant of this extended Victorian country house. They can also be confident of enjoying an above-average meal, for Neil McKevitt continues to exhibit both skill and flair in his interpretation of the traditional, seasonally-changing dishes featured on *carte* and fixed-price menus. The fresh, quality produce on which he bases his French/English style of cooking brings distinct textures and flavours to recipes ranging from salt cod ragoût with new potatoes and Catalan pesto, to roast saddle of lamb with an artichoke and chestnut stuffing, courgette and tomato tart and thyme juices. Desserts are particularly good. A selection of British and French cheeses is served with celery, fruit and nuts, and coffee comes with home-made chocolates as well as petits fours. Smoking is allowed in the lounge, where Havana cigars are on sale, though it is not permitted in the restaurant itself.

Directions: On A6 five miles N of Preston, 0.5 mile from M6 exit 32

PRESTON, Heathcotes Brasserie ❀❀

☺ *A modern, lively restaurant where the atmosphere buzzes and the superb food is good-value*

In a leafy, lawyer-and-stock-broker Preston square, Paul Heathcote has opened his second restaurant: a cool, design-conscious brasserie featuring a two dimensional mural, moulded white plastic chairs and mineral water in Heathcote's own-label bottles. The ambiance is busy, the service attentive. The food, cooked by Max Gnoyke (Heathcote's sous chef for the last three years), shows an awareness of what is currently fashionable in that it includes all the trademarks of modern British cooking, including offal. Mediterranean influences are there, of course, exemplified by bread and aïoli – instead of butter – served at each table. An enjoyable lunch began with a deliciously smooth, rich pressed terrine of ham

23 Winkley Square
Map no: 7 SD52
Tel: 01772 252732
Chef: Max Gnoyke
Proprietor: Paul Heathcote.
Manager: Andrew Morris
Cost: Alc £17.50, fixed-price
L £8.50 (2 course) & £10.50/Sun
L £13.50, children's menu
£4.95. H/wine £10.25 ❢ Service
exc
Credit cards: 💳 💳 OTHER
Times: Last L 2.15pm, last D
10.30pm
Menus: A la carte, fixed-price L,
bar menu

hock and chicken liver, accompanied by apricot chutney. Next came well-executed ox cheek and oxtail, braised in red wine until tender, and set on a bed of rich mashed potato. Alternative main courses might include fish and chips, smoked haddock and poached egg, or lobster Thermidor. Finally, another classic for pudding, a crème brûlée, perfectly set off by a base of sharp blackcurrants.

Seats: 90+70 (Seafood bar). No cigars or pipes
Additional: Children welcome, children's menu; ❤ dishes, vegan/other diets on request

Directions: Town Centre

RAWTENSTALL, **The Rose Restaurant** ❀

A Victorian house in a little mill town, artistically elegant in period style and rose-patterned fabrics. The menu features both British and international dishes, such as frogs' legs provençale, duck roasted en casserole, boned roast quail with root vegetables and red wine sauce, and first-class bread and butter pudding

Waterfoot BB4 7AR
Map no: 7 SD82
Tel: 01706 215788
Chef: Lee Martin Page
Credit cards: 🔳 🔳
Times: Last L 2pm, last D 9.30pm. Closed first wk Jan, last wk Jul

Directions: In town centre, off A681

SLAIDBURN, **Parrock Head** ❀

☺ *Good cooking is apparent in selections from the daily-changing fixed-price menu: mushroom and Madeira soup, slices of pork loin with an apricot and mustard sauce, chocolate parfait with a mocha sauce. But composition of dishes can be uneccessarily fussy; a simpler approach would be better*

Clitheroe BB7 3AH
Map no: 7 SD75
Tel: 01200 446614
Chefs: Vicki Umbers and Dale Thornber
Proprietor: Richard and Vicky Umbers
Cost: Fixed-price L £13.50/D £17.50. H/wine £7.50 ▮ Service exc
Credit cards: 🔳 🔳 🔳 🔳
Times: Last D 9pm

Menu: Fixed-price D, bar menu
Seats: 35. No smoking in dining room
Additional: Children over 8-10 welcome, children's menu; ❤ dishes, vegan/other diets on request
Directions: Take B6478 to Slaidburn; from village take Woodhouse Lane to N Wier; 1 mile on left

THORNTON, **The Victorian House** ❀❀

☺ *Simply presented, uncomplicated modern cooking informally served in an elaborately decorated Victorian-style restaurant*

Didier and Louise Guerin's Victorian villa is decorated throughout in Victorian style, with dark papered walls, heavy drapes, period lighting and lace. The contrast between the formal atmosphere thus created and the Didier Guerin's modern cooking is really striking. His style is based on allowing the natural taste and texture of ingredients to shine through. At lunchtime, a wide choice of dishes is available from the good-value bistro menu served in the conservatory.

Our inspection meal began with meaty crab and salmon terrine accompanied by a rich home-made basil mayonnaise. A beautifully simple dish of home-made gnocchi with a fresh tomato sauce followed. The highlight of the meal was pan-fried tuna fish served on a bed of boulangère potato with an avocado and tomato salsa, the taste and texture of the fish providing an effective contrast to the potato and salsa. A dessert of tangy rhubarb and vanilla cream tart was also appreciated. Other choices could include sautéed lambs' kidneys served with Dijon mustard and a purée of

Thornton FY5 4HF
Map no: 7 SD34
Tel: 01253 860619
Chefs: Didier Guerin
Proprietors: Mr & Mrs Didier Guerin
Cost: *Alc* £9.50, fixed-price D £21 (4 courses). H/wine £9.50 Service inc
Credit cards: 🔳 🔳 OTHER
Times: Last L 1.30pm, last D 9.30pm.
Closed Sun, last 2 wks Jan
Seats: 60
Additional: Children over 6 welcome, children's portions; ❤ / vegan dishes

potato, celeriac and bacon, or Thai-style chicken. There is also an interesting wine list with some attractive prices.

Directions: Take Kirkham exit off M55, follow A585 towards Fleetwood, take Thornton exit at roundabout, continue towards Fleetwood, turn right at Church

UPHOLLAND, **Holland Hall Hotel** ❀

☺ *Holland Hall Hotel, and its themed Churchill's restaurant, is an extended 17th-century listed building. A good selection of home-made breads – including fruit, onion and wholemeal – complement a wide choice of dishes such as twice-baked cheese soufflé, and trio of seabass, Tay salmon and lemon sole in a light saffron batter*

Menus: *A la carte,* fixed-price D, bar menu
Seats: 56. No-smoking area
Additional: Children welcome, children's portions; ❿ dishes, vegan/other diets on request
Directions: 2 mins from M6 junction 26 overlooking Deanwood Golf Course

6 Lafford Lane WN8 0QZ
Map no: SD50
Tel: 01695 624426
Chef: J Nugent
Proprietor: T Rathbone
Cost: *Alc* £18, fixed-price D £15.95. H/wine £7.95 ❢ Service exc
Credit cards: 🆒 💳 💳 💳
Times: Noon-last L12.30 pm, last D 10.30pm

WRIGHTINGTON, **High Moor Inn** ❀❀

Culinary skill is reflected in an enthusiastic modern menu in a stark moorland setting

For ten years now High Moor has been building on its local reputation. Though there have been a couple of changes of chef in recent years, visitors have always been sure of a warm welcome and an enjoyable meal. Appetites in this part of the country are healthy, thus there is a set-price menu for two, three and four courses, and in addition, there are canapés in the lounge and a tasting course which may be home-made sorbet, or – served on a recent visit – creamy white onion and woodland mushroom soup. One section of the menu is devoted to fish which can be served either as a starter, second, or main course, and there are always daily specials. Grey mullet is served on a bed of beansprouts with a red pepper purée and delicately flavoured saffron sauce. Roast rib of beef with béarnaise sauce is a favourite with couples at weekends and another favourite is best end of lamb with a fragrant tian of aubergine, tomatoes and spinach and a light garlic cream. Vegetables can be superfluous and over complicated: courgettes with roasted red peppers, carrot and coriander mousse and broccoli polonaise, could be one evenings selection. Staff are well trained.

Directions: From M6 exit 27 follow sign Parbold, after Hospital R into Robin Hood Lane, 1st L into Highmoor Lane

High Moor Lane WN6 9QA
Map no: 7 SD51
Tel: 01257 252364
Chefs: Darren Wynn and Lee Conroy
Proprietors: James J Sines and John Nelson
Cost: *Alc* £13.90-£22.40 fixed-price L £11/D £11.50 H/wine £8.25 ❢ Service exc
Credit cards: 🆒 💳 💳 💳 OTHER
Times: Noon-last L 2pm, 5.30pm-last D 9.30pm
Seats: 100. Air conditioned
Additional: Children welcome, children's portions; ❿ dishes, vegan/other diets on request

Caviar is the egg of the female sturgeon. After removal, they are washed, sieved, put in brine, drained and finally packed into tins. The former Soviet Union and Iran are the principal producers. In previous centuries the sturgeon was fairly common in European waters. Such large quantities were taken when they entered rivers to spawn that nowadays there are few.

LEICESTERSHIRE

BLABY, **Time Out Hotel** ✿

☺ *The recently refurbished restaurant forms the focal point of the Time Out Hotel and offers a range of popular, classical dishes. At inspection, chicken liver pâté was served with a toasted brioche, and rack of lamb came with wholegrain mustard and béarnaise sauce. Home-made rum and raisin ice-cream was for dessert*

Directions: Off the A426

Enderby Road LE8 4GD
Map no: 4 SP50
Tel: 0116 278 7898
Chef: Mark Turner
Cost: Fixed-price L £10.50/ D £15.95
Credit cards: 🔲 🔲 🔲 🔲 OTHER
Times: Last D 10pm

EAST MIDLANDS AIRPORT,
Donington Thistle ✿

A modern hotel, convenient for East Midlands Airport, offering an imaginative carte and varied fixed-price menus. A much enjoyed inspection meal kicked off with galantine of duck filled with leeks and orange, then veal fillets on a potato cake in pepper sauce, and finished with strawberry mousse

Directions: At East Midlands International Airport, 2miles from junction 24 of M1 and 1 mile from M1/A42 interchange

Castle Donington DE74 2SH
Map no: 8 SK42
Tel: 01332 850700
Chef: Phillip O'Hagan
Cost: *Alc* £22-£36, fixed-price L £10.95/D £18
Credit cards: 🔲 🔲 🔲 🔲

HINCKLEY, **Sketchley Grange Hotel** ✿

☺ *A varied selection of English and international dishes are served in the Willow Restaurant of this extended country house. The good quality food is served in a professional and attentive manner, and a meal could comprise king scallops en croûte, galantine of roasted grouse and a berry crème brûlée*

Directions: From M69 exit 1 take B4109, at mini roundabout turn left, then first right

Sketchley Lane
Burbage LE10 3HU
Map no: 4 SP49
Tel: 01455 251133
Chef: Colin Bliss
Proprietor: Nigel Downe
Cost: *Alc* £19.95, fixed-price L £11.75/D £17.50 (4 course). H/wine £8.95. Service inc
Credit cards: 🔲 🔲 🔲 🔲 OTHER
Times: Last L 2.30pm, last D 9.45pm
Menus: *A la carte,* fixed-price L & D, bar menu
Seats: 90. Air conditioned. No smoking in dining room
Additional: Childen welcome, children's menu; ♥ menu, vegan/other diets on request

LEICESTER, **Belmont House Hotel** ❀

Set in a quiet Victorian conservation area, Belmont House's Cherry Restaurant offers a decent standard of international cooking. The varied selection may include king scallops with orange zest and grated ginger, medallions of beef in a port wine sauce served on a rösti, and chocolate crème brûlée

Menus: A la carte, fixed-price L & D, bar menu
Seats: 60
Additional: Children welcome, children's portions; ❂ dishes, vegan on request
Directions: Head for railway station, first right off A6 heading south

De Montfort Street LE1 7GR
Map no: 4 SK50
Tel: 0116 254 4773
Chef: Mark Crockett
Manager: James Bowie (Best Western)
Cost: Alc £22.50, fixed-price L £12.95/D £17.50. H/wine £10.75 ❢ Service exc
Credit cards: 🌑 ▦ ▨ 🖭 OTHER
Times: Last L 2pm/D 10pm. Closed Sat L, Bh Mons

LEICESTER, **The Tiffin** ❀

An airy restaurant offering eastern cooking in a western setting where food is cooked to order to produce a perfect balance of distinctive flavours. Fresh ingredients are used in a wide variety of dishes including sizzling chicken chilli, 'dahl masala' and tomato 'raita'. Very popular at lunchtime so book ahead

Directions: Head for railway station, first right off A6 heading south

1 De Montfort Street LE1 7GE
Map no: 4 SP60
Tel: 0116 247 0420
Chef: Mohammed Ali
Proprietor: Pravin Parmar
Credit cards: 🌑 ▦ ▨ 🖭 OTHER
Times: Last L 2pm/ last D 11pm. Closed Sun, 24-26 Dec

MARKET HARBOROUGH, Three Swans Hotel ❀

Charles I was one former visitor to this fine old coaching inn. Fair cooking includes mushroom soup, sliced chicken marinaded in soya sauce and root ginger with bamboo shoots, bean sprouts and water-chestnuts, salmon en croûte with white wine, cream and tomato sauce, and a rich white chocolate mousse in a chocolate cup

Seats: 85. Air conditioned
Menus: Fixed-price L & D
Additional: Children over 8 welcome, children's portions; ❂ menu, vegan/other diets on request
Directions: Town centre – prominent in High Street

21 High Street LE16 7NJ
Map no: 4 SP78
Tel: 01858 466644
Chef: Richard Payne
Manager: Josef Reissmann (Best Western)
Cost: Fixed-price L £12.95/D £18.95 (4 course). H/wine £10.85 ❢ Service exc
Credit cards: 🌑 ▦ ▨ 🖭 OTHER
Times: 11am-last L 2.15pm, 7pm-last D 10pm. Closed Sun D

MELTON MOWBRAY, **Stapleford Park** ❀

A relatively short menu is offered at Stapleford Park, but the range of cooking includes Tex Mex, modern British and classic French. Notable aspects at an April meal were the fresh-baked rosemary loaf, the Caesar salad, and the bread and butter pudding

Menus: A la carte L & D, bar menu
Seats: 50. No smoking in dining room
Additional: Children welcome; ❂ dishes, other diets on request
Directions: Follow Melton ring road A607 (Grantham) onto B676, 4 miles turn right signed Stapleford

Stapleford LE14 2EF
Map no: 8 SK71
Tel: 01572 787522
Chef: Malcom Jessop
Manager: Mark Scott
Cost: Alc £30, H/wine £12.50 Service exc
Credit cards: 🌑 ▦ ▨ 🖭
Times: Last L 2.30pm, last D 9.30pm, 10.30pm Fri & Sat

NORMANTON, Normanton Park Hotel ❀

☺ *The recently restored Georgian stable block is all that remains of the original Hall and estate. The Orangery Restaurant is the setting for the well-prepared, predominantly modern British cooking. Look out for ravioli of Norfolk crab, braised breast of chicken in a pimento and asparagus sauce, and individual summer pudding*

Menus: A la carte, fixed-price L & D, bar menu **Seats:** 80
Additional: Children welcome, children's menu; ❂ menu, vegan/other diets on request
Directions: South shore of Rutland Water near Edith Weston

Rutland Water
South Shore LE15 8RP
Map no: 4 SK90
Tel: 01780 720315
Chef: Paul Huxtable
Proprietor: Daniel Hales
Cost: Alc £20, fixed-price L/D £14.95. H/wine £7.50 ❢ Service inc
Credit cards: ▨ ▩ OTHER
Times: Last L 2.30pm/D 9.45pm

OAKHAM, Barnsdale Lodge ❀

Freshly cooked dishes with an international flavour are served at this popular roadside farmhouse which overlooks Rutland Water. A meal might begin with roast baby beetroots with goats' cheese and fresh herbs, followed by Rutland trout served with a whisky and kipper butter, and chocolate tiramisu for dessert

Menus: A la carte, fixed-price Sun L , bar menu, pre-theatre
Seats: 59+50 outside.No-smoking area **Additional:** Children welcome, children's menu; ❂ dishes; vegan/other diets on request
Directions: On the A606 (Oakham-Stamford) 2 miles outside Oakham

The Avenue
Rutland Water LE15 8AH
Map no: 8 SK80
Tel: 01572 724678
Chef: Robert Knowles
Proprietor: Robert Reid
Manager: Graham Marsh
Cost: Alc £18-£35, fixed-price Sun L £13.95. H/wine £7.95
Credit cards: ▨ ▩ OTHER
Times: Last L 2pm/D 9.45pm

OAKHAM, Hambleton Hall ❀❀❀❀

Outstanding modern British cooking in a secluded, luxurious setting

Hambleton LE15 8TH
Map no: 8 SK80
Tel: 01572 756991
Chef: Aaron Patterson
Proprietors: Tim & Stefa Hart
Cost: Alc £50, fixed-price L & D £29.50. H/wine £17 ❢ Service inc
Credit cards: ▨ ▧ ▩ ▣
Times: 12.30pm-last L 2pm, 7pm-last D 9.30pm
Menus: A la carte, fixed-price L & D, snack menu
Seats: 60. No cigars or pipes

The lane ambles through a sleepy village which nestles on the shores of Rutland Water before arriving at Hambleton Hall. Built in Victorian times as a hunting lodge, today the place oozes luxury as a country house hotel. The comfortable rooms, originally designed by Nina Campbell, and public areas share the same impeccable aesthetic quality. Flowers abound. Chef Aaron Petterson invests a lot of effort in his cooking. He is constantly aiming to perfect his skills and the general consensus is that a meal at Hambleton Hall is well worth the detour.

Current trends are well represented: ravioli of crab, ginger and

coriander with soya-roasted scallops and lemongrass scented juice, braised pigs trotter filled with morels, onions and sweetbreads with a Madeira sauce, pot roasted calves' sweetbreads with a watercress and black truffle sauce, and simply roasted loin of spring lamb with a mille-feuille of aubergine, fondant potatoes, tapenade and rosemary scented juice.

Some of the dishes are almost too elaborate. An inspection meal, for instance, kicked off with an exquisite terrine of foie gras with a salad of artichokes, green beans, leeks and hazelnuts, loosely bound by a truffle flavoured, soft-jellied bouillon reduction which added depth to the dish. This was followed by Norfolk pigeon, cooked en cocotte, with a Gewürztraminer infused jus, baby turnips, petit pois, lentils, braised green cabbage and bacon lardons, sweet red cabbage, morels and chanterelles. Although perfectly executed with distinct, clearly individual flavours, the dish was confused 'all in all a little too much'. After that a chocolate soufflé with a pistachio sabyon and a ball of banana and vanilla ice-cream, although very good 'failed to sustain interest'. The overall view was that there was a tendency to over embellishment, too much striving to perfect contrasts of textures and taste.

Attention to detail, however, is admirable. Freshly made bread comes in brown, white and olive, 'amuse bouche' could be a delicious hot gazpacho bouillon with morsels of lobster, and petits fours are excellent. Thirty 'wines of the moment' that are drinking particularly well, introduce a thoughtful, thoroughly laid out wine list that reveals a balanced attitude towards France and the rest of Europe, and the New World. Half bottles are particularly well represented.

Directions: From A1 take A606 Oakham road. One mile before Oakham turn left to Hambleton village. Restaurant is on the right off the main street

Additional: Children welcome, children's portions; ❷ menu, vegan/other diets on request

OAKHAM, **Whipper-in Hotel** ❀

Modern English food is served in the candlelit restaurant of this market town coaching inn. The varied menus are complemented by a well-chosen, if pricey, wine list. Typical dishes might be smoked chicken and avocado salad, poached collops of monkfish, and white chocolate mousse in a dark chocolate cup

Menus: A la carte, fixed-price L & D, bar menu **Seats:** 50. No-smoking area **Additional:** Children welcome, children's portions; ❷ dishes, other diets on request
Directions: Town centre on the right in the Market Place

Market Place LE15 6DT
Map no: 8 SK80
Tel: 01572 756971
Chef: David Tofiluk
Proprietor: David Tofiluk (Brook Hotels)
Cost: Alc £27, fixed-price L £10.95/D £14.95. H/wine £8.95 Service exc
Credit cards: 🖪 🖼 🖭
Times: Last L 2.30pm, last D 9.30pm

QUORN, **Quorn Country Hotel** ❀

Delicate and varied cooking in the modern style, served in the hotel's Shires Restaurant, retains natural flavours and is complemented by subtle sauces. Expect mille-feuille of smoked and fresh salmon, roast Gressingham duck with an orange sauce and chocolate crème brûlée

Times: Last L 2.30pm, last D 9.30pm Closed Sat L
Menus: A la carte, fixed-price L & D, bar menu
Additional: Air conditioned. No-smoking area. Children welcome, children's menu; ❷ dishes, vegan/other diets on request
Directions: Village centre, on A6

Quorn LE12 8BB
Map no: 8 SK51
Tel: 01509 415065
Chef: David Wilkinson
Proprietor: J N Brankin-Frisby (Virgin Marketing).
Manager: Tom Redhead
Cost: Alc £22.50, fixed-price L £14.95/D £18.95 H/wine £9.25
❗ No service charge
Credit cards: 🖪 🖼 🖭 🖺

QUORN, **Quorn Grange** ✿

Imaginative cooking complements the elegant marbled restaurant of this country house hotel. Fresh good quality ingredients are used to create dishes such as crab and lobster bisque, stuffed guinea fowl with a passion fruit-flavoured jus, and bread and butter pudding. Service is professional yet relaxed

Menus: *A la carte,* fixed-price L & D
Seats: 60. No-smoking area
Additional: Children welcome, children's portions; ♥ menu, vegan/other diets on request
Directions: Turn off B591 Quorn High St into Wood Lane signed Switherland

88 Wood Lane LE12 8DB
Map no: 8 SK51
Tel: 01509 412167
Chef: Gerard Stacey-Midgley
Proprietor: E Jeremy Lord.
Manager: Gary Bland
Cost: *Alc* £24, fixed-price L
£9.85 (2 course)/D£15.95.
H/wine £10.20 Service inc
Credit cards: 🔳 💳 💳 💳 OTHER
Times: Last L 2pm/D
9.30pm/10pm wk end. Closed
Dec 26-28

STRETTON, **Ram Jam Inn** ✿

An old inn which has been sympathetically converted and is particularly popular with travellers on the A1. The menu is short but offers modern cooking, supplemented by imaginative daily specials. Try roasted pork fillet, red cabbage and chutney, and treacle tart with praline ice-cream

Great North Road LE15 7QX
Map no: 8 SK92
Tel: 01780 410776
Chef: Nick Davies
Proprietor: Tim Hart
Cost: *Alc* £18
Credit cards: 🔳 💳 💳 💳 OTHER
Times: Last D 10pm
Closed 25 Dec

Directions: On northbound carriageway of A1

'Carpaccio' is a truly modern Italian dish, created at Harry's Bar in Venice in the early 1960's. Arrigio Cipriani named it after the famous painter Carpaccio because there was an exhibition of his work in Venice at the time, and Cipriani felt that the reds in the paintings reflected the red in the dish. Carpaccio is very thinly sliced fillet of beef, dressed with a small amount of mayonnaise, flavoured with a little mustard and a drop of brandy and tabasco with enough cream to make the sauce of a fluid consistency. The carpaccio currently fashionable in British restaurants is in fact a derivation of 'carne all'abese': raw meat, either sliced or minced, dressed with olive oil and lemon juice and covered with shavings of truffle or Parmesan, extended these days to include thinly sliced tuna, salmon, venison and even wild boar.

UPPINGHAM, Lake Isle Hotel 🏵

A small townhouse hotel in Uppingham High Street, serving food that stands out for its sheer simplicity. The kitchen keeps faith with seasonal produce, perhaps a timbale of sole and spinach with a white wine and vermouth sauce, tartlets of crab, pheasant and venison pie, or leg of lamb with a 'gutsy' mint gravy

High Street East LE15 9PZ
Map no: 4 SP89
Tel: 01572 822951
Chefs: David Whitfield and Tim Balflour
Proprietor: Claire Whitfield.
Manageress: Nicola Goden
Cost: Fixed-price L £13.50/D £21 H/wine £8.95 ¶ Service exc.
Credit cards: 🌑 📠 📠 📠
Times: Last L 1.45pm (Sun 2pm). Last D 10.30pm (Sat 10pm). Closed Mon L
Seats: 40. No pipes or cigars
Menus: Fixed-price L & D
Additional: Children permitted, children's portions; 👶 menu; other diets on request

Directions: Entrance via Reeves Yard to rear of Restaurant

LINCOLNSHIRE

BECKINGHAM,
Black Swan Restaurant 🏵🏵

☺ *Standards remain consistent at this riverside inn, though the menu, with its new eclectic flavour, is constantly updated*

A long established riverside inn, the Black Swan keeps pace with the times by updating its menu and pricing policies. However, the sound cooking of quality produce by chef/proprietor Anton Indans remains constant. At lunchtime the menu now ranges from soups and sandwiches to grilled escalopes of salmon with a saffron sauce, which can be eaten in the bar or in the garden. Dishes have taken on a more modern, eclectic flavour, with French provincial, Mediterranean, Californian, and Pacific rim influences: as can be seen in starters such as garlic sautéed black tiger prawns served with a mixed leaf and omelette salad with a chilli and red pepper dressing, and clear beef consommé with chive dim sum. Among the main courses there could be Thai-spiced chicken, guinea fowl casserole, magret of duck, and a roast loin of lamb garnished with a minted fine bean and lentil cassoulet with home-made lamb sausage. Soufflés and parfaits feature on the dessert menu, with a selection of home-made ice-creams. Alternatively, an English cheeseboard is offered.

Hillside LN5 0RF
Map no: 8 SK85
Tel: 01636 626474
Chef: Anton Indans
Proprietors: Alison & Anton Indans
Cost: Alc £19.50, H/wine £8.20. Service exc
Credit cards: 🌑 📠
Times: Last L 2pm, last D 10pm. Closed Sun D, Mon, Dec 25, 1 wk Feb, 2 wks Aug
Menus: A la carte, bar menu
Seats: 35. No smoking in dining room
Additional: Children welcome, children's portions; 👶 dishes, special diets on request

Directions: 5 miles from Newark, A17 (Sleaford), 1st right & right again in village

GRANTHAM, **Harry's Place** ⊛⊛⊛

Original and lovingly prepared food in intimate, private setting

Small is beautiful – and they don't come much smaller than this. The location is unremarkable, on the outskirts of Grantham, but Harry's Place is exceptional, both for the fact that the elegant, fuschia-pink dining-room of Harry and Caroline Hallam's Georgian home has only three tables, but for the serious, dedicated cooking on offer. Harry cooks. Although not formally trained he prefers to work and experiment by himself. The repertoire is fairly limited, and dishes tend to reappear with slight variations, depending on market availability. Each course offers two choices, but Harry regularly travels far and wide to source the best ingredients. Scallops, for example, come from the Orkneys and grouse from Yorkshire. Wholemeal bread is perfectly baked, as befits a man whose family were bakers. First courses include fish soup with anchovy and saffron rouille, Filey crab terrine with dill mayonnaise, and one of Harry's own inventions – sautéed chicken livers served chilled and enrobed with sherry and black pepper jelly, Cumberland sauce and green salad. Another innovative starter, which sometimes turns up as a main course, is escalope of wild River Dee salmon, lightly cooked in a Sauterne Noilly Prat and chive sauce. For our main course, French free-range, corn-fed chicken roasted with lemon, thyme, ginger, coriander and Parma ham, proved to be another excellent dish full of abundant flavours. Other main courses might be loin of roe deer in tarragon, white wine and Madeira sauce, or local lamb roasted with rosemary, lavender, white wine and Calvados. Both a tarte au citron and pithivier of toasted almonds and mincemeat were served with vanilla ice-cream, each dessert accurate and finely tuned.

Directions: On the B1174 two miles north-west of Grantham

17 High Street
Great Gonerby NG31 8JS
Map no: 8 SK93
Tel: 01476 61780
Chef: Harry Hallam
Proprietors: Harry & Caroline Hallam
Cost: *Alc* £27.50-£39. H/wine £18.50 ¶ Service exc
Credit cards: 🔳 🔤
Times: Last L 2pm, last D 9.30pm. Closed Sun, Mon, BHs, Dec 25/6
Menus: *A la carte* L & D
Seats: 10. No smoking
Additional: Children welcome (not under 5); other diets on request

LINCOLN, **Wig & Mitre** ⊛

Situated in the heart of old Lincoln, the Wig & Mitre offers a variety of dishes from a number of menus, all of which can be mixed and matched. The cooking is predominately English with international influences, and features dishes such as roast saddle of rabbit with mushrooms and bacon in a white wine sauce with thyme

29 Steep Hill LN2 1LU
Map no: 8 SK97
Tel: 01522 535190
Chefs: Paul Vidic and Peter Dodd
Proprietors: Michael & Valerie Hope
Cost: *Alc* £12-£24. H/wine £9.10 ¶ Service inc
Credit cards: 🔳 🔤 🔤 💷 OTHER
Times: Open 8am-11pm food all day Closed Dec 25
Menus: *A la carte,* bar menu
Seats: 60
Additional: Children welcome, children's portions/menu by arrangement; ♥ dishes, vegan/other diets on request

Directions: Close to Cathedral, Castle and car park at top of Steep Hill

LOUTH, **Kenwick Park Hotel** ❀❀

Pleasant golfing hotel with extensive leisure facilities where one can work up an appetite for some sound modern cooking

Louth LN11 8NR
Map no: 8 TF28
Tel: 01507 608806
Chef: Paul Harvey
Proprietor: Mr Dowie

Kenwick Park is a much extended Georgian mansion set in the 500 acre Kenwick Park Estate. Excellent leisure facilities include a leisure centre with a large swimming pool, squash court and gymnasium. Not surprisingly, as the place overlooks a golf course, the restaurant is called Fairways. An inspection meal started with a sweet pepper soup with strips of beef, Oriental style. This was followed by a good looking breast of honey-glazed duck served with a rich plum sauce and well timed vegetables that were both crisp and full of flavour. For dessert, iced praline parfait was excellent. It came with a well made coffee sauce with coffee beans. The wine list offers about 80 well chosen bins which include a good selection of New World wines and half bottles. The Keepers Bar is designed as a conservatory to maximise the views over the golf course.

Directions: Take A631 from Market Rasen

STAMFORD,
George of Stamford Hotel ❀

Visitors can eat in the cobbled courtyard in the summer months, under trellises and hanging baskets. Good quality produce is used in the imaginative, well-prepared dishes, which may include spicy Thai crab cake with a lime leaf and coconut sauce, and breast of pigeon on a bed of black pudding polenta

St. Martin's PE9 2LB
Map no: 8 TF00
Tel: 01780 55171
Chefs: Chris Pitman and Matthew Carroll
Proprietor: Lawrence Hoskins. Manager: Chris Pitman (Poste)
Cost: _Alc_ £27.40, fixed-price L £16.50-£19.50. H/wine £8.75
Times: Last L 2.30pm/D 10.30pm

Seats: 250
Menus: _A la carte,_ fixed-price L, bar menu
Additional: Children welcome, children's portions; ❂ dishes, vegan/other diets on request
Directions: From the A1 take B1081 to traffic lights, hotel is on the left

Rhubarb originated in northern Asia. It is botanically not a fruit but a vegetable, but is classed as a fruit since that is how it is normally eaten. The Chinese valued rhubarb medicinally, and it was so regarded when it arrived in Britain in the 16th century. Indeed, the first recipe for rhubarb did not appear until the late 18th century. Recipes for sweet pies and tarts followed in the 19th century, but it was Mrs Beeton who really popularised it with her extensive repertoire of recipes for rhubarb jams, rhubarb pudding, rhubarb tart and rhubarb wine. Rhubarb can be forced to provide fruit out of season which probably helped to increase its popularity in Victorian times. The normal growing season lasts from May to July, but early forced rhubarb (January - April) is tender, pink and delicious. By comparison, the unforced summer rhubarb can be coarse and sour. Early forced rhubarb makes a good accompaniment to fish, especially wild salmon.

SUTTON ON SEA,
Grange & Links Hotel ❀

There's a warm welcome for guests at this popular golfing hotel which has benefited from extensive refurbishment. The attractive restaurant offers good home-cooking with fresh fish and steaks featuring on the menu. A lively bar is also on hand

Directions: From Sutton on Sea follow signs to Sandilands

Sea Lane
Sandilands LN12 2RA
Map no: 9 TF58
Tel: 01507 441334
Chef: Tina Harrison
Proprietor: Ann Askew
Cost: Alc £25, fixed-price
L £13.50/D £16.50.
H/wine £8 ♥ Service exc
Credit cards: 🔲 🔲 🔲 🔲 OTHER
Times: Last L 1.30pm/D 8.45pm
Menus: A la carte, fixed-price L
Seats: 100
Additional: Children welcome,
children's portions/menu;
♥ menu, vegan/other diets
on request

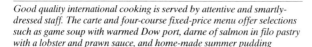

MERSEYSIDE

BIRKENHEAD, **Beadles** ❀

In the centre of Oxton old village, this relaxed and informal restaurant has been run by Ray and Bea Gott for over eighteen years. Sound cooking includes warm Thai duck salad, baked cod with a herb crust, and rhubarb crumble. Vegetables are locally supplied or taken from the garden

Menus: A la carte D
Seats: 34. Smoking permitted only after coffee served
Additional: Children over 7 permitted; ♥ dishes, other diets on request
Directions: Centre of village

5 Rosemount
Oxton L43 5SG
Map no: 7 SJ38
Tel: 0151 653 9010
Chef: Bea Gott
Proprietors: Roy & Bea Gott
Cost: Alc £22. H/wine £7.
Service exc
Credit cards: 🔲 🔲 OTHER
Times: Last D 9pm. Closed Sun
Mon, 2 wks Feb & Aug/Sep

BIRKENHEAD, **Bowler Hat Hotel** ❀

Good quality international cooking is served by attentive and smartly-dressed staff. The carte and four-course fixed-price menu offer selections such as game soup with warmed Dow port, darne of salmon in filo pastry with a lobster and prawn sauce, and home-made summer pudding

Menus: A la carte, fixed-price L & D, bar menu
Seats: 110. Air conditioned. No smoking area
Additional: Children permitted until 7.30pm, children's portions;
♥ menu, vegan/other diets on request
Directions: M53 exit 3 (Birkenhead), left at 3rd lights (Holm Lane) to T junction, 200yds on left

Talbot Road
Oxton L43 2HH
Map no: 7 SJ38
Tel: 0151 652 4931
Chef: Ian Carruthers
Proprietor: D Solomon.
Manager: Ian Carruthers
Cost: Alc £27.50, fixed-price
L £11.95/D £17.50.
H/wine £9.35 ♥ Service inc
Credit cards: 🔲 🔲 🔲 🔲 OTHER
Times: Last L 2.30pm, last D
10pm Closed Sat L

BIRKENHEAD, **Capitol** ❀

☺ *A local Chinese with a sound reputation, offering Cantonese, Peking and Szechuen dishes. Banquets include one devoted to seafood, another is all vegetarian. The various dining areas are attractively decorated with paintings by Chinese artists, available for sale*

29 Argyle Street
Hamilton Square L41 6AE
Map no: 7 SJ38
Tel: 0151 647 9212
Chef: Yan Tam
Proprietor: Steve Tam
Cost: *Alc* £13.75, fixed-price
L £5.50/D £12.95 H/wine £7.95.
Service inc
Credit cards: 🟦 ▓ ▩ OTHER
Times: Last L 2pm, last D
11.30pm. Closed Dec 25/6
Menus: *A la carte,* fixed-price L
& D, pre-theatre
Seats: 80. Air conditioned
Additional: Children welcome,
children's menu; ✪ menu,
vegan/other diets on request

Directions: Town centre, at the corner of Hamilton Square

SOUTHPORT, **Royal Clifton Hotel** ❀

An imposing promenade hotel where decently prepared food can be chosen from either the carte or the daily changing fixed-price menus. At a recent inspection, duck and pork liver terrine was followed by fresh turbot with a butter and blue Curaçao sauce and butterfly prawns, with home-made apple pie to finish

Promenade PR8 1RB
Map no: 7 SD32
Tel: 01704 533771
Chef: Mark Conlon
Proprietor: Crown House Hotels
(Best Western)
Credit cards: 🟦 ▓ ▩ 🔲

Directions: On the Promenade

ST HELENS, **Chalon Court** ❀❀

Business orientated modern hotel with expense account menu

The ultra-modern, commercial hotel is immediately distinguished by its striking glass facade. The restaurant offers a daily changing 'Speciality' menu and *carte* choice. Orders are taken in the bar, where appetisers, such as quails eggs, are served. On our inspection, a starter of fresh asparagus came wrapped in smoked ham and curled up in rather dry puff pastry, embellished with a bit of salad. A sharp sorbet of rhubarb and diced fruit salad followed. The main course was neck of lamb, a cut normally only found in a domestic setting, but here attractively presented in a rich sauce of its own juices, with fennel and tarragon. Other main courses are along more stereotyped hotel lines, such as poached suprême of salmon stuffed with crab mousse, and pan-fried strips of beef and chicken fillet with shallot and red wine confit and tarragon cream sauce. A bread and butter pudding demonstrated a novel variation on the theme –

Linkway West WA10 1NG
Map no: 7 SJ59
Tel: 01744 543444
Chef: John Branagan
Proprietors: Celebrated Hotels.
Manager: Jeremy Roberts
Cost: *Alc* £24.95, fixed-price
L £7.95 (2 course)/D £14.95 &
£19.95. H/wine £9.50. Service
inc
Credit cards: 🟦 ▓ ▩ 🔲 OTHER
Times: Last L 1.45pm, last D
9.45pm
Menus: *A la carte,* fixed-price L
& D, bar menu
Seats: 64. Air conditioned. No
smoking in dining room

brown and white layers with exotic fruit, served ice-cold with a warm custard. Details, such as fresh coffee, good petits fours and bread, are all as they should be.

Directions: M62 exit 7 and linkway to St Helens. Hotel is on right approaching town centre

THORNTON HOUGH, **Thornton Hall** ❀❀

Business orientated hotel with unusually smart food

Although the impressive country house hotel stands in seven acres of grounds and gardens in a rural location, easy access to the M53 and major industrial areas makes it suitable for many business needs. Staff are pleasant and helpful, and show courtesy under pressure. Meals have impressed with flair and careful cooking, as our inspector discovered. After simple canapés and soft, fresh rolls, a starter of warm quail salad was served with rosemary, Charlotte potatoes, smoked bacon and endive, all heightened with a sharp balsamic dressing. Superb grilled sea bass came with shallots, leeks and a mild basil butter sauce. Other dishes, from the spring-summer menu, which caught the eye, included corn and mussel chowder with a Brie turnover, roasted Norfolk duck breast in a passionfruit glaze accompanied by a confit wun tun, and roulade of wild Irish sea salmon with chervil on a Merlot sauce with artichoke tempura. Desserts are equally exotic; individual bittersweet chocolate and raspberry charlotte set upon an eau de vie scented English cream, and quenelles of maple syrup mousse and a sesame case with a honey blossom ice and tuille butterfly.

Directions: Junction 4 of M 53 onto B5151. Turn right at first cross road onto B5136 signposted Thornton Hough. Hotel approx 1 mile on left

Additional: Children welcome, children's menu; ❶ menu, vegan/other diets on request

Thornton Hall Hotel
Neston Road
Wirral L63 1JF
Map no: 7 SJ38
Tel: 0151 336 3938
Manager: Colin Fraser
Cost: *Alc* £25, fixed-price L £9, fixed-price D £17.95. H/wine £9.50 ❶ Service inc
Credit cards: ▨ ▨ ▨ ▨ OTHER.
Times: 12.30pm-last L 2pm, 7pm-last D 9.30pm (10pm Sat)
Menus: *A la carte,* fixed-price L (weekdays only) & D, Sun lunch
Seats: 50
Additional: Children welcome, children's portions; ❶ & vegan dishes

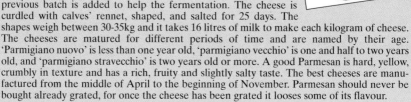

Parmesan cheese or 'parmigiano reggiano' originated in the area that formed the Duchy of Parma, between Parma and Reggio Emilio. Locals will tell you that the cheese has been made there for over 2,000 years but whether this is so or not, it was an established favourite by the 14th century; Boccaccio referred to it in the 'Decameron'. Nowadays 'parmigiano reggiano' is made in the provinces of Parma, Reggio Emilia, Bologna, Modena and Mantua. The method of making Parmesan has remained unchanged through the centuries. Small cheese factories produce four to six cheeses a day using milk from local cows. The milk is partially skimmed and the whey from the previous batch is added to help the fermentation. The cheese is curdled with calves' rennet, shaped, and salted for 25 days. The shapes weigh between 30-35kg and it takes 16 litres of milk to make each kilogram of cheese. The cheeses are matured for different periods of time and are named by their age. 'Parmigiano nuovo' is less than one year old, 'parmigiano vecchio' is one and half to two years old, and 'parmigiano stravecchio' is two years old or more. A good Parmesan is hard, yellow, crumbly in texture and has a rich, fruity and slightly salty taste. The best cheeses are manufactured from the middle of April to the beginning of November. Parmesan should never be bought already grated, for once the cheese has been grated it looses some of its flavour.

PLETCHERS
RESTAURANT

NORFOLK

BLAKENEY, Morston Hall ❀❀

Friendly, courteous service and good quality cooking are the strengths of this country house restaurant

A 17th-century coastal house, Morston Hall has been sympathetically renovated to create a comfortable small country house hotel with a relaxing atmosphere. The young proprietors, Tracy and Galton Blackiston and Justin Fraser, provide a cheerful and genuinely caring service. Galton Blackiston and his team create increasingly imaginative, good quality dishes for a set, four-course dinner served at 8.00 pm, with guests gathering before-hand for a drink in the conservatory. A recent inspection meal began with superbly cooked asparagus with wild mushrooms in a pastry case, followed by pan-fried peppered monkfish which was delightfully meaty and fresh and complemented by a sharp lemon and anchovy dressing. Marinated chicken on a bed of aubergine purée with a Marsala sauce was a particularly successful main course, accompanied by a selection of well-judged vegetables. A light full-flavoured banana soufflé served with port, poached pear and pistachio ice-cream made an interesting finish. Wines from all the major grape varieties worldwide feature on the restaurant's extensive list.

Directions: On A149 (King's Lynn/Cromer) 2 miles west of Blakeney in the village of Morston

Holt NR25 7AA
Map no: 9 TG04
Tel: 01263 741041
Chef: Galton Blackiston
Proprietors: Galton & Tracy Blackiston and Justin Fraser
Cost: Fixed-price D £24.50/Sun L £15. H/wine £9 ❢ Service inc
Credit cards: 🅴 💳 💳
Times: Last D 7.30pm for 8pm, last Sun L 12.30 for 1pm Closed Jan-Feb
Menus: Fixed-price D & Sun L
Seats: 40. No smoking in dining room
Additional: Children welcome; ❶ dishes, vegan/other diets on request

BURNHAM MARKET, Hoste Arms Hotel ❀

☺ *A fashionable inn in a delightful village, run with devotion and style. Its flag-stoned bar (serving real ale) leads into a dining-room – all waxed-panelling and white linen – which hovers between the sophisticated and the casual, where chef Glenn Purcell offers a diversified fixed-price menu*

Menus: A la carte, fixed-price D, bar menu
Seats: 40. Air conditioned. No smoking area
Additional: Children welcome, children's portions; ❶ dishes, vegan/other diets on request
Directions: In the centre of the village

The Green PE31 8HE
Map no: 8 TF84
Tel: 01328 738777
Chef: Glen Purcell
Proprietor: Paul Whittome.
Manager: Fiona Lyne
Cost: Alc £17.50, fixed-price D £17.50. H/wine £7.50 ❢ Service exc
Credit cards: 🅴 💳 OTHER
Times: Last L 2pm, last D 9pm

DISS, Salisbury House Restaurant ❀❀

☺ *Enjoyable, unfussy food skilfully prepared and served with care in a relaxed country home atmosphere*

Set in mature gardens on the fringes of Diss, the Victorian Salisbury House exudes a homely and tranquil atmosphere Chef/proprietor Barry Davis offers a monthly-changing *carte* of modern Anglo-French dishes based on sound quality produce. For example, a fish course always features with most of the fish coming from nearby Lowestoft. An inspection meal began with a full-flavoured, creamy textured asparagus mousse served with a powerful tomato vinaigrette. Mousses appear at each course – a special feature of the cooking; mousseline of salmon in a chive sauce was the fish choice

84 Victoria Road IP22 3JG
Map no: 5 TM18
Tel: 01379 644738
Chef: Barry Davies
Proprietor: Barry Davies
Cost: Fixed-price D £18.50 (2 courses), £22, £27 (4 course). H/wine £8.55. Service exc
Credit cards: 🅴 💳
Menus: Fixed-price D (L by appointment Tue-Fri)
Times: Last D 9.15pm. Closed Sun, Mon, 2 wks Aug 1 wk Xmas

Salisbury House Restaurant

Seats: 36. No smoking in dining rooms
Additional: Children welcome, children's portions; other diets on request

at inspection, for example. Main course was lamb fillet coated in thyme and set on a bracing sauce lifted by balsamic vinegar and brown sugar. Vegetables are presented imaginatively; in this instance carrot julienne with ginger and courgettes with almonds. For pudding, three options are offered (plus cheeses) and the predominantly French wine list presents a quite extensive selection. Finally, coffee or tisane is accompanied by freshly-made petits fours.

Directions: On A1066 (Thetford/Scole) 0.25 mile east of Diss town centre

ERPINGHAM, Ark Restaurant ֍֍

☺ *A family run, friendly place for unpretentious but discerning dining*

A restored flint cottage with stripped pine furniture and understated decor is the informal setting for some wonderfully straightforward cooking. Sheila and Becky Kidd offer a short daily-changing menu, reflecting both what is in season locally and their imaginative approach to food. Recent first courses, for example, have featured coriander mushrooms, grilled local goats' cheese in vine leaves and pork, and chicken liver and chard pâté. Main courses offer a choice between fish and meat, with perhaps ragoût of turbot, or tender spring lamb braised in a cream sauce thickened with aubergine purée. Vegetables are simply prepared and fresh tasting; vegetarian dishes interesting and unusual. For pudding, there is a good selection of the traditional: sticky toffee pudding, rhubarb crumble, lifted occasionally with exotic flourishes along the lines of star anise crème brûlée, and orange and mango in rosemary scented juice. The wine list includes some reasonably-priced house bottles and a wide selection of halves.

Directions: Just off A140 4 miles north of Aylsham

The Street NR11 7QB
Map no: 9 TG13
Tel: 01263 761535
Chefs: Becky & Sheila Kidd
Proprietors: Sheila & Michael Kidd
Cost: *Alc* £21.25, fixed-price D from £16.75 (2 course)/Sun L £12.25 (3 course). H/wine £8 ▮ Service exc
Credit cards: None taken
Times: Last D 9.30pm, last Sun L 2pm Closed Sun D, Mon D
Menus: *A la carte* D, fixed-price D & Sun L
Seats: 36. No smoking in dining room
Additional: Children welcome, children's portions; ❶ dishes, vegan/other diets with prior notice

In the 19th century oysters were considered to be a poor man's food and vast quantities were consumed. Pollution and disease have depleted the population of native oysters - they have a higher mortality rate and take twice as long to grow as Pacific or rock oysters - hence the higher price

GREAT YARMOUTH, **Imperial** ❀

The hotel's Rambouillet Restaurant serves locally-landed fish and shellfish, as well as dishes based on chicken, sirloin and fillet steak, lamb and duckling, from a daily-changing menu. Other items, such as boeuf bourguignonne, omelette Arnold Bennett, grills and even fish and chips are available every day, together with a vegetarian selection

North Drive NR30 1EQ
Map no: 5 TG50
Tel: 01493 851113
Chefs: Roger Mobbs and Stephen Duffield
Proprietor: Nicholas Mobbs
Cost: Alc £19, fixed-price L £8.50/D £14.50. H/wine £9.50 ♥ Service exc
Times: Last L 2.30pm, Last D 10pm
Menus: A la carte, fixed-price L & D
Seats: 70. Air conditioned
Additional: Children welcome, children's portions; ♥ menu, other diets on request

Directions: Situated on the seafront 100 yds north of the Britannia Pier

GRIMSTON,
Congham Hall Hotel ❀❀

A beautiful restaurant offering quality cooking and charming service in a beguiling historic home

Lynn Road PE 32 1AH
Map no: 9 TF72
Tel: 01485 600250
Chef: Jonathan Nicholson
Proprietors: Christine & Trevor Forecast
Cost: Alc £24, fixed-price D £24 & £32 (4 course)/Sun L £15. H/wine £11.50 ♥ Service exc
Credit cards: 🂠 ▥ ▥ ▣
Times: Last L 2pm, last D 9.30pm Daily
Menus: A la carte L & D, fixed-price D & Sun L, bar L menu
Seats: 50. No smoking in dining room

Surrounded by immaculately kept grounds, Congham Hall is a delightful Georgian manor turned country house hotel. The kitchen garden provides most of the herbs and vegetables. Visitors are immediately made to feel welcome by a dedicated small team of staff led by proprietors Christine and Trevor Forecast, who all help create a relaxing environment throughout the public rooms. These include the attractive Orangery restaurant, where, beneath glass skylights and hanging plants, guests can choose from chef Jonathan Nicholson's fixed -price menus. Particularly enjoyable on a recent inspection meal was a first course of confit duck roulade with foie gras parfait. This was followed by a main course of steamed tranche of brill with a promising langoustine mousseline. The rich, fruity flavour of a hot raspberry soufflé was well complemented by a smooth vanilla ice-cream. Most of the world's major producing areas feature on the lengthy wine list.

Additional: Children over 12 permitted; ❶ dishes, vegan/other diets on request

Directions: A149/A148 roundabout N/E of King's Lynn, take A148 (Sandringham), after 100 yards right to Grimston, then on left after 2.5 miles

HETHERSETT, **Park Farm Hotel** ✸

☺ *A sound level of commitment to presenting good food is evident at this country hotel built around a Georgian farmhouse. Regularly changing set-price menus and a carte offer a wide range of dishes, such as our sample meal choices of salmon cressonnière followed by mixed berry crumble*

Heathersett NR9 3DL
Map no: 5 TG10
Tel: 01603 810264
Chef: Peter Rogers
Proprietors: Mr & Mrs P G Gowing & Mr D Gowing
Cost: *Alc* from £18, fixed-price L £10.25 /D £14.75. H/wine £8.25 ❶ Service exc
Credit cards: 🔳 ▨ ▨ ▨ OTHER
Times: Last L 2pm, last D 9pm
Menus: *A la carte,* fixed-price L & D, bar menu
Seats: 60. Air conditioned. No smoking in dining room.
Additional: Children welcome, children's menu; ❶ menu, vegan/other diets on request

Directions: 5 miles south of Norwich on B1172 (the old A11)

HOLT, **Yetman's** ✸✸

The young chef at this charmingly informal country restaurant makes excellent use of fresh local ingredients in her daily-changing menus

A real find in rural Norfolk; a smart, white-painted building with a pastel yellow interior which neatly fits the conventional mould of well-established restaurants. What makes it unusual however, is an informal style of service which is uniquely personal. A contemporary theme runs through the daily-changing menu which offers four choices at each course, and Alison Yetman is fortunate in having a ready supply of fresh local ingredients. Meals are simply but carefully crafted: all the flavours are there in such dishes as pink, perfectly roasted loin of lamb with apricot stuffing and a citrus mint sauce, chargrilled grey mullet with olive oil and baked red peppers, and aubergines cooked three ways (marinated, puréed or as a salad). Well-timed vegetables retain both taste and texture, home-made breads are good, and guests with a sweet tooth

37 Norwich Road NR25 6SA
Map no: 9 TG03
Tel: 01263 713320
Chef: Alison Yetman
Proprietors: Alison & Peter Yetman
Cost: Fixed-price D & Sun L £23.50/Sat L £18.75. H/wine £10.75 ❶ Service exc
Credit cards: None taken
Times: Last D 9pm, last Sat & Sun L 2pm Closed Tue, Mon in Winter
Menus: Fixed-price D & w/end L
Seats: 32. No smoking in dining room

will enjoy desserts like lemon and pecan roulade or an almond basket filled with cinnamon ice-cream and a compote of black cherries. The wine list includes a few carefully chosen French examples as well as drawing widely from across the New World.

Directions: Village centre

KING'S LYNN, Rococo ❀❀

A chic Old Town restaurant serving modern British food

This is an intimate, smart restaurant. On arrival visitors are settled into a comfortable, colourfully decorated lounge, the walls covered with large oil paintings. Cooking is good, based on sound skills and quality produce. An evening inspection meal yielded good, fresh scallops, lightly seared and served with bright yellow saffron noodles in a well-made white port sauce. Tender duck confit with a red wine and honey reduction and caramelised shallots, followed. The sweetness of the dish was nicely balanced and the duck was crisp and tender and accompanying vegetables were fresh, simply prepared and had a good bite. A good blend of smooth rich chocolate marquise and lavender and gin flavoured ice-cream rounded off the meal. Cooffee is good, served with delicate petits fours. Lunch includes a simple, quick menu; this supplements the monthly changing two or three course set menu which offers a nicely balanced selection of seasonally inspired dishes.

Directions: Follow signs to The Old Town, next to Tourist Information

Additional: Children welcome, children's portions; ❂ dishes, other diets on request

11 Saturday Market Place
PE30 5DQ
Map no: 9 TF62
Tel: 01553 771483
Chef: Nick Anderson
Proprietors: Nick & Anne Anderson
Cost: Alc £28, fixed-price L £13/D £25.50. H/wine £9.50
❢ Service exc
Credit cards: 🅱 🆎 🆎 OTHER
Times: Last L 2pm, last D 10.pm
Closed Sun, Mon L, Dec 25-30
Menus: A la carte, fixed-price L & D, bar menu, pre-theatre
Seats: 40. No-smoking area
Additional: Children welcome, children's portions; ❂ dishes, vegan/ other diets on request

NORWICH, Adlard's Restaurant ❀❀❀

Dedicated French and British cooking in unpretentious small restaurant

The dark green interior of Adlards remains a favourite haunt. Chef/proprietor David Adlard is equally in evidence both sides of the swing door, ferrying plates to and from the kitchen. He also continues to demonstrate his accomplished cooking skills through set-priced menus at dinner and lunch. The latter, in particular, offers great value for money, and is flexible enough to accommodate anyone wanting just one course. Lunch see a suitably lighter style. A May menu, for example, included mackerel escabeche with frisée salad, cod poached in a court bouillon with parsley aïoli and Tunisian orange cake with sour cream. All main courses, day and evening, come with an appropriate carbohydrate – chicken fricassée with basmati and wild rice, fillet of beef with chips, Lunesdale duck with pommes fondant, noisette of lamb with gratin dauphinoise, and so on. A lunchtime inspection started with a warm confit of tender, well-flavoured duck, with a dressed salad, home-made apple chutney and crispy croûtons. The main course was worth the wait – a plump, moist chicken breast with asparagus nage and spears, although the rösti of pasta, in all honesty, did little to enhance it. The meal ended with an old favourite, pear with cassolette of prune and Earl Grey ice-cream.

The evening menu stretches to take in increasingly refined dishes such as tuna in spiced marinade, with grilled sea scallop and vegetable vermicelli and ginger butter sauce; roast squab pigeon with pear tarte tatin, creamed potatoes with olive oil and game

99 Upper St Giles Street
NR2 1AB
Map no: 5 TG20
Tel: 01603 633522
Chefs: David Adlard and Aiden Byrme
Proprietor: David Adlard
Cost: Fixed-price L £13.50 (2 course) & £16.50/D £31 & £34 (4 course) £32. H/wine £9 Service exc
Credit cards: 🅱 🆎 🆎 OTHER
Times: Last L 1.45pm, last D 10.30pm. Closed Sun D, Mon L, 1 wk after Xmas
Menus: Fixed-price L & D
Seats: 40. Smoking restricted
Additional: Children welcome, children's portions; other diets on request

sauce; roast sea bass with braised fennel and crab ravioli, sauce americaine and tagliatelle. Coffee is fresh and mellow, and comes with delicious petits fours. The terrific back-to-front wine list is well priced, with plenty of half bottles – and, for once, a positive virtue is made of the decidedly non-plonkish house wine.

Directions: City centre; 200 yards behind the City Hall

NORWICH, **Brasted's** ❀❀

8-10 St Andrews Hill NR2 1AD
Map no: 5 TG20
Tel: 01603 625949
Chef: Adrian Clarke
Proprietor: John Brasted

A well-established restaurant coming up to date with a new look and lighter choices on the menu

Cost: *Alc* £25, fixed-price
L £8.50 (2 course) & £12.50.
H/wine £9.50 Sevice exc
Times: Last L 2pm, last D
9.30pm (unless booked). Closed
Sun, Bhs
Menus: *A la carte*, fixed-price L,
pre-theatre
Seats: 22
Additional: Children permitted,
children's portions; ❂ dishes,
other diets on request

There is something reassuring about the sense of continuity at this gentle city-centre restaurant, where service is managed by a cheerful, long serving member of staff with occasional help from the gregarious owner, John Brasted. Yet recent changes have brought renewed vigour to the place. The decor is more refined with dark, boldly-striped material draped on the walls contrasting with crisp white linen tablecloths, and the menu has been up dated, allowing for lighter ingredients and new, clearly indicated vegetarian dishes. Certain favourites have been retained by popular demand, such as cheese parcels served with home-made apple and thyme jelly. There is a wide range of starters: steamed asparagus with butter, Sevruga caviar with blinis, and 'salmon extravaganza' – a presentation of various salmon dishes. Beef stroganoff is a main course speciality, alongside rabbit pie, and pork loin chop grilled with wild mushrooms and finished with crème fraîche. Among the vegetarian dishes is a warm tart of fresh tomatoes, cheese and pesto sauce. The wine list has an enthusiast's touch, covering mainly France, some areas in great detail.

Directions: City centre, close to the Castle & Cathedral, between London Street and St Andrews Street

NORWICH, **By Appointment** ❀

27-29 St George's Street
NR3 1AB
Map no: 5 TG20
Tel: 01603 630730
Chef: Timothy David Brown
Proprietors: Timothy David
Brown and Robert Culyer
Cost: *Alc* £24.25, H/wine £9
‼ Service exc
Credit cards: 🔳 🔳 OTHER
Times: Last D 9.30pm. Closed
Sun, Mon

Entered through the rear via the kitchen, this fifteenth-century property conveys a charmingly intimate atmosphere. The personally-run restaurant offers a large carte of sound dishes such as fillet of beef, filled with a duxelle of tomatoes and mushrooms, wrapped in puff pastry, with a fresh garden mint and mustard sauce

Menus: *A la carte* D **Seats:** 40. No smoking in dining room
Additional: Children over 12 permitted, children's portions;
❂ dishes, other diets by arrangement
Directions: City centre, from St Andrews Hall, down St Georges Street, into Colegate then first right into Courtyard

NORWICH,
Greens Seafood Restaurant ❀❀

82 Upper St Giles Street
NR2 1LT
Map no: 5 TG20
Tel: 01603 623733
Chef/Proprietor: *Dennis*
Crompton
Cost: *Alc* £28, fixed-price
£12.50

Superb seafood at a restaurant offering special facilities for theatregoers

Excellent seafood makes up the majority of the menu but, to cater for all tastes, meat dishes such as duck and steak are also offered.

The freshness of raw materials is important, evident in an inspection main course of sea-bass stuffed with a fish mousse. The clear flavour of bass was ably enhanced by a tarragon sauce and a garnish of scampi tails. The kitchen's confidence was also demonstrated by an excellent home-cured salmon which accompanied a tomato and Gruyère tart. On the same inspection visit a pudding of poached pear encasing an apple mousse and presented on a cassis sauce proved a successful combination of flavours. Diners hoping to attend the nearby Maddermarket Theatre or Theatre Royal may interrupt their meal, take in a performance, and return to finish their meal.

Directions: Near St John's RC Cathedral

Credit cards: ▨ ▧
Times: Last L 2.15pm/D 10.30pm Closed Sat L, Sun, Mon, 10 days Xmas, 2 wks mid-Aug and Bhs
Menus: A la carte, fixed-price
Seats: 48
Additional: Children permitted (over 6)

NORWICH, **Marco's Restaurant** ❀❀

Authentic Italian food and an award-winning, all-Italian wine list at a popular city-centre restaurant

You will search in vain for pizza or lasagna on the menu at this Italian restaurant. Chef proprietor Marco Vessalio leaves them to the big Italian chains, preferring to concentrate on lesser known dishes from around the regions. The wines are totally Italian, which Marco feels is appropriate as he is serving all-Italian food, and the list, representing almost all the regions of Italy, was a regional winner of the 1994 Italian Wine List Of The Year award. The comprehensive *carte* offers a good range of antipasti: mushroom gratinée with fresh herbs, garlic and Fontina cheese, or specially cured wild boar (bresaola) served with buffalo mozzarella and an olive oil and lemon juice dressing. In a regional round up of main courses – all served with fresh vegetables or salad – there is a Genoese fish speciality comprising halibut, monkfish, sea bass, king prawns, garlic, herbs, wine and tomato; chicken breast, sage and Parma ham from Rome; and medallions of venison 'alla piemontese'. Among the zabaglione, gelati and sorbeti, there are some less than Italian-sounding desserts – summer pudding and bread and butter pudding – but these are, of course, presented in Italian style.

Directions: City centre: from market place facing Guildhall, turn right then left into Pottergate

17 Pottergate NR2 1DS
Map no: 5 TG20
Tel: 01603 624044
Chef: Marco Vessalio
Proprietor: Marco Vessalio
Cost: Alc £25, fixed-price L £14. H/wine £9.50. Service exc
Credit cards: ▨ ▧ ▧ ▨
Times: Last L 2pm, last D 10pm. Closed Sun, Mon, last 2 wks Sept
Menus: A la carte, fixed-price L
Seats: 22. No smoking in the dining room
Additional: Children welcome, children's portions; ❂ dishes, other diets on request

NORWICH, **Pinocchio's Restaurant** ❀

☺ *A warm ambiance is enlivened by background jazz at this pine-furnished brasserie which serves Italian food. New wave leanings are evident in some of the dishes, though many – lasagna, fritto misto, and lamb and butterbeans – are reassuringly traditional. Straightforward kitchen skills ensure success*

Menus: A la carte, fixed-price L & D daily specials, pre-theatre
Seats: 100. No-smoking area
Additional: Children welcome, children's portions; ❂ dishes, vegan/other diets on request
Directions: From City centre follow Castle Meadow to traffic lights, 1st left into Bank Plain; leads to St Andrew's and St Benedict's Streets, restaurant on the right

11 St Benedicts Street NR2 4PE
Map no: 5 TG20
Tel: 01603 613318
Chef: Pino Longordo
Proprietors: Nigel & Jane Raffles.
Manager: Christopher Parker
Cost: Alc £16, L daily specials under £5/D £6.95. H/wine £7.25 ▮ Service exc
Credit cards: ▨ ▧ OTHER
Times: Last L 2pm, last D 11pm/10.30pm Sun. Closed Sun L, Dec 25/6

NORWICH, St Benedicts Restaurant ❀

☺ *This well-established bistro continues to please with its simple formula, serious food and cheerful service. The menus, chalked up on blackboards, offer modern-style eclectic cooking which makes the best use of seasonally available produce. Enjoyable dishes have been venison sausages and vegetable tempura*

Seats: 42 No cigars or pipes
Menus: *A la carte*, pre- & post theatre meals, daily dishes
Additional: Children welcome, children's portions;
❷ dishes, vegan/other diets on request
Directions: At City end of St. Benedicts: nearest car park Duke Street

9 St Benedicts NR2 4PE
Map no: 5 TG20
Tel: 01603 765377
Chef: Nigel Raffles and Edward Hipkiss
Proprietors: S J & N Raffles
Cost: *Alc* £16, daily specials £3.95-£9.50 H/wine £7.25 ❢
Service exc
Credit cards: ▨ ▨ ▨ ▨ OTHER
Times: Noon-last L 2pm, 7pm-last D 10-10.30pm

NORWICH, Sprowston Manor ❀❀

Accomplished and imaginative cooking in a stylish and hospitable country house hotel setting

New chef Paul Linsell brings flair and originality to bear in his modern British cooking. The highlight of a recent inspection meal was a delightful delice of fresh salmon. A superior cut, admirably fresh, it combined a well-balanced flavour with a melt-in-the-mouth texture, and was accompanied by a judiciously sharp, contrasting sauce. Noisettes of saddle of lamb was chosen as a main course. These proved to be really tender and full-flavoured, arranged on a spring onion galette, served with a velvety red wine and rosemary jus. Eclectic influences are to be seen in first courses of calamari with olives, and wild mushroom soup, and in the interesting sauces which accompany many typical main courses: orange and tarragon sauce with breast of turkey, and a crevette, champagne cream sauce served with pan-fried plaice. Puddings are not as yet a strength, though a firm, but ripe, poached pear in red wine syrup was very sound, as was a rich dark chocolate mousse specked with chocolate chips. There is an extensive wine list. Service is caring and genuinely hospitable.

Directions: Take A1151 (Wroxham) & follow signs to Sprowston Park

Sprowston Dale NR7 8RP
Map no: 5 TG20
Tel: 01603 410871
Chef: Paul Linsell
Proprietor: John Cotter (Best Western)
Cost: *Alc* £35, fixed-price L £18.50/D £20 H/wine £9.95 ❢
No service charge
Credit cards: ▨ ▨ ▨ ▨ OTHER
Times: Last L 2.30pm, last D 10pm Daily
Menus: *A la carte*, fixed-price L & D, bar menu
Seats: 120. No smoking in dining room
Additional: Children welcome, children's menu; ❷ dishes, vegan/other diets on request

THETFORD, Martine's ❀

☺ *An informal, simple restaurant where the cooking is homely and competent. Although occasional flourishes such as couscous add spice, pheasant breast and fish pie are typical dishes. The wine list is of particular interest as chef/proprietor Martine Greslon knows her grapes and offers a well researched selection*

Menus: *A la carte* L & D, fixed-price Thur pasta D, special D eves
Seats: 30+20. (+20 Garden). No-smoking area
Additional: Children welcome, children's portions; ❷ dishes, other diets on request
Directions: Old A11 (Norwich), turn right before Fire Station, follow one-way to car park on right

17 St Giles Lane IP24 2AE
Map no: 5 TL88
Tel: 01842 762000
Chef: Martine Greslow
Proprietor: Martine Greslow
Cost: *Alc* £16, fixed-price Thur D £ 6.50. H/wine £7.95 ❢
Service exc
Credit cards: ▨ ▨ ▨ OTHER
Times: Last L 2pm, last D 9.30pm Closed Sun, Mon, 1 wk Aug, 1 wk after Xmas

TITCHWELL, Titchwell Manor Hotel ❀

The fresh seafood at this coastal hotel can be recommended for its simple preparation. Cromer crab with crisp salad and local mussels poached in white wine are typical first courses, followed by fillet of sea bass or queen scallops. A choice of dining areas is offered

Times: Last L 2pm, last D 9.30pm
Seats: 45. No smoking in dining room
Additional: Children welcome, children's menu; ♥ menu, vegan/other diets on request
Directions: On the A149 coast road between Brancaster and Thornham

Brancaster PE31 8BB
Map no: 9 TF74
Tel: 01485 210221
Chefs: Roger Skeen, Peter Bagge and Adam Wright
Proprietors: Margaret & Ian Snaith
Cost: *Alc* £25, fixed-price L £10.95/D £18.95 (4 course). H/wine £10.75 Service exc
Credit cards: 🟦 🟦 🟦 🟦 OTHER

WELLS-NEXT-THE-SEA,
Moorings Restaurant ❀❀

Fresh fish feature in imaginative dishes meticulously prepared by the talented Carla Phillips

6 Freeman Street NR23 1BA
Map no: 9 TF94
Tel: 01328 710949
Chef: Carla Phillips
Proprietors: Carla & Bernard Phillips
Cost: *Alc* £20.25. H/wine £7.95 ▮ Service exc
Credit cards: None
Times: Last L 1.30pm, last D 8.30pm. Closed Tue, Wed, Thur L, 2 wks Jun& early Dec
Menus: *A la carte* L & D
Seats: 35. No smoking in the dining room
Additional: Children welcome, children's portions; ♥ menu, vegan/other diets on request

New Yorker Carla Phillips combines local ingredients with recipes garnered from all over the world. Her unassuming restaurant – run with husband Bernard – trawls Norfolk for the best produce available; fish makes a major contribution, and vegetables are a strength. Hand-written menus are full of detail and annotations, and recipes are readily supplied, plus a list of suppliers, thus turning the presentation of a meal into a personalised service. The flavours of the dishes speak for themselves: a spicy fish soup, sampled on an inspection visit, had a delicate charm. Other starters may range from home-smoked sea trout to marinated goats' cheese. Main courses display thought and attention to detail, evident in the brill steamed over fennel, served on an aubergine purée and coated with a Niçoise sauce. Vegetable can include stuffed courgette flowers. Puddings are traditional, along the line of French apple tart, trifle, and pecan pie; cheeses are predominantly British. The atmosphere is relaxed, service informal and the local reputation strong.

Directions: Off A149, a few yards from the Quay

WYMONDHAM, **Number Twenty Four** ❀

24 Middleton Street NR18 0BH
Map no: 5 TG10
Tel: 01953 607750
Chef: Richard Hughes
Proprietors: Richard & Sue Hughes
Cost: Fixed-price L £5 (1 course)/D £16.95.
H/wine £7.95 ❢ Service inc
Credit cards: ▧ ▨

☺ *Good food cooked in upbeat, confident fashion comes at affordable prices at Richard Hughes' cheerful tea shop. Chicken 'Japanese style' and Thai influenced dishes appear on a menu based on seasonal regional produce. A studied list of wines is also offered*

Times: Last L 2.30pm, last D 9.30pm. Closed Sun, Mon, Tue D, Dec 24-30 **Menus:** Fixed-price L & D
Seats: 60. No smoking before 9.30pm **Additional:** Children welcome, children's portions; ❶ menu, vegan/other diets on request
Directions: Town centre opposite War Memorial

NORTHAMPTONSHIRE

CASTLE ASHBY, **Falcon Hotel** ❀

Castle Ashby NN7 1LF
Map no: 4 SP85
Tel: 01604 696200
Chef: Neil Helks
Proprietors: Neville and Josephine Watson (Best Western)
Cost: Alc £23, fixed-price L/D £19.50. H/wine £8.35 Service exc
Credit cards: ▧ ▨ ▨ OTHER
Times: Last L 2pm, last D 9.30pm

Hot asparagus with roasted red peppers, and feuilleté of asparagus with wild mushrooms and thyme from a seasonal asparagus menu, supplement the fixed-price and carte selections at this 16th-century country inn. Other choices might be foie gras with sweetcorn pancake and grilled venison cutlet with Cumberland sauce

Seats: 55 **Additional:** children permitted (not under 8 at D), children's portions; ❶ dishes, vegan/other diets on request
Directions: From A428 Northampton-Bedford road turn of at Castle Ashby sign, hotel ahead

HELLIDON,
Hellidon Lakes Hotel ❀

Daventry NN11 6LN
Map no: 4 SP55
Tel: 01327 62550
Chef: Edward Stephens
Proprietors: G S & J A Nicoll
Cost: Alc £25, fixed-price L £12.95/D £17.95. H/wine £9.95 Service exc
Credit cards: ▧ ▨ ▨ ▨ OTHER
Times: Last L 2.30pm, last D 9.30pm

The spacious restaurant of this modern hotel has lovely views from its elevated position overlooking the adjoining golf course. Edward Stephens cooks Anglo-French dishes with a reputation for generous portions whether you choose from the daily-changing set-price menu or the carte

Menus: A la carte, fixed-price L & D, bar menu **Seats:** 80
Additional: Children permitted at L, over12 at D, children's portions; ❶ dishes, other diets by arrangement
Directions: 1.5 miles off A361 at Charwelton, follow signs Golf Club

HOLDENBY,
Lynton House Hotel ❀❀

The Croft NN6 8DJ
Map no: 4 SP66
Tel: 01604 770777
Chef: Carol Bertozzi
Proprietors: Carol & Carlo Bertozzi
Cost: Alc £21.25 (4 course), fixed-price L £12.50-£17.75. H/wine £9.75 ❢ Service exc
Credit cards: ▧ ▨ ▨

Reliable Anglo-Italian cooking in an old English country rectory

The look is English, with pink cloths, button-back repro Queen Anne chairs and pastoral prints, but the accent is unmistakably Italian. Carlo Bertozzi and his English wife Carol, offer a menu which has a heavy, but not exclusive, Italian slant. Starters may include antipasto, ricotta and spinach tortelloni, pan-fried sardines and aubergines filled with pepper, onions and olives. This is

Lynton House Hotel

Times: Last L 1.45pm, last D
9.45pm. Closed Sat L, Mon L,
Sun
Menus: *A la carte*, fixed-price L
Seats: 45. No-smoking area
Additional: Children over 6
welcome, children's portions;
🍲 dishes

followed by a sorbet or soup, such as the classic 'pasta e fagioli' –
pasta, bean and ham soup. Amongst the main courses, small squid
stuffed with prawns and pesto, cooked in virgin olive oil and lemon,
and fresh salmon cooked with cream, Dolcelatte and coriander
leaves, catch the eye for originality. More familiar choices would be
calves' liver with onions, or breast of duckling with a black cherry
and Cognac sauce. Italian desserts are well represented with
tiramisu, budino of soft fruit with Amaretto coulis, and fritella or
pancake with poached peach, lemon and Aurum orange liqueur.
The wine list is a worthy one, and boasts a good selection of new
vogue Tuscan wines. Tips are neither sought nor included.

Directions: M1 exits 18 & 15A, on Church Brampton/East Haddon
road, follow the signs for Holdenby House Gardens

HORTON,
French Partridge Restaurant 🌸🌸

Enjoyable and uncomplicated food in reliable, personally-run, country
restaurant

David Partridge cooks in a straightforward, slightly old-fashioned
style. Occasional attempts to keep up with modern times are not
always too successful, viz a pleasant but curiously constructed
chicken liver and Parma ham crostini, and a fish stock-based salsa
verde to accompany poached hake. The four-course, set dinners
follow a regular pattern. Starters, along the lines of smoked
haddock chowder, game pâté with spicy plum sauce or melon with
ginger wine, are followed by a fish or cheese entrée, such as
haddock fillet with lemon juice, or hot cheese soufflé. Chicken Kiev
and braised oxtail in red wine sauce are typical of the four main
course choices, but our inspector plumped for tender, braised
young rabbit with home-made tagliatelle and tomato cream sauce.
The accompanying stir-fried medley of vegetables could have been
crisper, but retained their individual flavours well. As well as half
a dozen desserts, such as crêpes Suzette, fresh strawberry pavlova
and an excellent, traditional Bakewell pudding, there are savouries
such as mushrooms or soft herring roes on toast. In our experience,
service can, at times, be painfully slow.

Horton NN7 2AP
Map no: 4 SP85
Tel: 01604 870033
Chef: D C Partridge
Proprietors: D C & M Partridge
Cost: Fixed-price D £23. H/wine
£10.50. Service inc
Credit cards: None taken
Times: 7.30pm-last D 9pm
approx. Closed Sun, Mon
Menu: Fixed-price D
Seats: 45. No smoking in dining
room
Additional: Children permitted;
🍲 dishes, other diets on request

Directions: On B526,village centre, 6 miles from Northampton

KETTERING, **Kettering Park Hotel** ❀

The hotel's Langberrys restaurant produces lively, interesting modern cooking, in keeping with the contemporary setting. Two menus offer a good selection of innovative dishes, including on a recent visit, a tender lamb shank with lentils and root vegetables. The prompt table service is impressive

Menus: Last L 1.45pm/D 9.30pm. Closed Sat L
Seats: 90. No smoking in dining room
Additional: Children welcome, children's portions; ❶ dishes, vegan/other diets on request
Directions: South of Kettering at the intersection of the A509 and A14

Kettering Parkway NN15 6XT
Map no: 4 SP87
Tel: 01536 416666
Chef: Darren Winder
Proprietor: Shire Inns.
Manager: Gordon Jackson
Cost: Alc £25-£30, fixed-price
L £12.95/D £21. H/wine £9.95
Credit cards: ▨ ▨ ▨ ▨ OTHER
Times: Last L 1.45pm, last D
9.45pm Closed Sat L, BHs L

ROADE, **Roadhouse Restaurant** ❀

A smart restaurant serving honest, uncomplicated cooking prepared from sound, well-sourced staple ingredients. A short lunchtime and succinct dinner menu provide choices such as chicken liver parfait with raisin and pear chutney, and baked fillet of salmon in breadcrumbs

Menus: A la carte D, fixed-price L
Seats: 40
Additional: Children permitted, children's portions; other diets prior notice
Directions: Take A508 (Milton Keynes), L at the George Inn, 300yds on the left

16 High Street NN7 2NW
Map no: 4 SP75
Tel: 01604 863372
Chef: Christopher Kewley
Proprietors: Christopher & Susan Kewley
Cost: Alc £24, fixed-price L £15.
H/wine £9.50. Service inc
Credit cards: ▨ ▨ ▨ OTHER
Times: Last L 1.45pm/D 9.30pm.
Closed Sun, Mon.

TOWCESTER,
Vine House Restaurant ❀❀

Well-executed cooking, including modern interpretations of traditional English classics, can be enjoyed in this tranquil setting

The old village of Paulersbury, two miles south of Towcester, makes a pleasant setting for a meal at the Vine House. Marcos Springett cooks very well indeed. He makes sound use of seasonally available produce and this is reflected in his daily-changing menus. Lunch is a good-value, fixed-price affair, and there is a more extensive choice in the evening. He is inspired by traditional English dishes and his modern interpretations are imaginative. Steak and kidney sausages, or wild rabbit sausages are made on the premises. A typical meal might begin with traditional potted beef and horseradish with mustard sauce, and continue with fillet of sea trout on a bed of cauliflower purée, served with chive sauce and lightly cooked baby broad beans. For dessert, cinnamon double cream crème brûlée, or hot apricot bread pudding served with vanilla pod custard and homemade ice-cream might be offered. The well-chosen wine list includes a number of fine wines and a short selection of New World wines.

Directions: 2 miles S of Towcester, signposted from the A5

100 High Street
Paulerspury NN12 7NA
Map no: 4 SP64
Tel: 01327 811267
Chef: Marcus Springett
Proprietors: Marcus & Julie Springett
Cost: Fixed-price L £13.95/D £19.50/£23.50 Fri & Sat. H/wine £9.95. Service exc
Credit cards: ▨ ▨
Times: Last L 2pm/D 10pm.
Closed Sun. Mon L
Menus: Fixed-price L & D
Seats: 45. No-smoking area. No pipes or cigars
Additional: Children welcome, children's portions; other diets 24 hours notice

NORTHUMBERLAND

ALNWICK, **Blackmores** ❀

John Blackmore offers refreshingly unfussy cooking in his small, cosy restaurant. There is a carte and daily changing specials and portions are generous. The fish mousse with king prawns is highly recommended, as are the puddings. Attention is paid to such details as homemade bread and petits fours

Seats: 28. No smoking in dining room
Additional: Children over 5 welcome, children's portions; ❂ menu, vegan/other diets on request
Directions: Follow signs for Castle, park & walk down 'Narrowgate' – 200 yds

Narrowgate NE66 1NL
Map no: 12 NU11
Tel: 01665 604465
Chef: John Blackmore
Proprietors: John & Penny Blackmore
Cost: Alc £20.75-£27.50, fixed-price D £18.50. H/wine £8.50. Service inc
Credit cards: 🔲 🔲 🔲 🔲
Times: Last D 9pm. Closed Sun, Mon

BERWICK-UPON-TWEED, **Funnywayt'Mekalivin** ❀❀

Honest but tongue-twisting name for exemplary, one-woman restaurant

Tucked away in a narrow street in the old part of town, Elizabeth Middlemiss's restaurant continues to fly the flag for honest, authentic British cooking. The shop frontage is easy to miss, especially in the dark, but once inside you'll find an inviting little restaurant. Tables are solid and sensibly sized, there are newspapers to read and plenty of bric-a-brac to comment on, including a post office letter box built into the wall. The daily-changing dinner menu runs to five courses and offers a choice for desserts only. A typical meal may start with potato, leek and onion soup with lovage, followed by courgette soufflé, then tarragon chicken as a main course. A chocolate roulade with Seville oranges and Cointreau cream might precede a selection of local cheeses accompanied by home-made oatcakes. Elizabeth excels in delicious pastries and sponges, with soufflés not far behind. Lunch is now self-service from a buffet selection, and offers a similar standard of cooking at give-away prices. The tireless proprietor also offers three bedrooms on a b&b basis.

Directions: From the main street go down Hide Hill and turn into Bridge Street. The restaurant is half way along on the left

41 Bridge Street TD15 1EF
Map no: 12 NT95
Tel: 01289 308827
Chef: Elizabeth Middlemiss
Proprietors: Elizabeth & Robert Middlemiss
Cost: Alc lunch £10, fixed-price dinner £22.50. H/wine £8.25 ❢
Service inc
Credit cards: 🔲 🔲 OTHER
Times: 11.30am-last L 2.30pm, last D 8.30pm. Closed Sun, Mon
Menus: A la carte, fixed-price dinner, pre-theatre
Seats: 36. No smoking in dining room
Additional: Children welcome, ❂ menu; other diets on request

BLANCHLAND, **Lord Crewe Arms Hotel** ❀

Dating from medieval times, this historic hotel is the focal-point of a fine conservation village. Flagstone floors and vaulted ceilings are features and the dining-room sports twin fireplaces, crisp linen and silverware. This is the setting for Ian Press's assured English cooking presented in splendid four-course dinners

Additional: Children welcome, children's portions; ❂ menu, vegan/other diets on request
Directions: 10 miles south of Hexham on B6306

Nr Consett DH8 9SP
Map no: 12 NY95
Tel: 01434 675251
Chef: Ian Press
Proprietors: Alexander Todd, Peter Gingell and Ian Press
Cost: Alc £28. fixed-price L £14.50. H/wine £10.50. Service exc
Credit cards: 🔲 🔲 🔲 🔲 OTHER
Times: Last Sun L 2pm. Last D 9.15pm
Seats: 50

CORNHILL-ON-TWEED,
Tillmouth Park Hotel ❀

TD12 4UU
Map no: 12 NT83
Tel: 01890 882255
Chef: David Jeffrey
General manager: Charles Carroll
Cost: Fixed-price D £23.50
Credit cards: 🅰 💳 💳 💳 OTHER
Times: Noon-last L 2pm, 7.30pm-last D 8.45pm
Menus: A la carte, fixed-price D

Set in mature grounds, this late Victorian country house is located close to the Scottish border. The restaurant overlooks the gardens and serves fine cooking with honest flavours based on fresh local produce. Quenelles of smooth chicken liver pâté might be followed by tender spring lamb

Seats: 80 **Additional:** ♥ dishes, other diets on request
Directions: 4 miles from Coldstream on A698 heading towards Berwick

HEXHAM, **Black House Restaurant** ❀

Dipton Mill Road NE46 1RZ
Map no: 12 NY96
Tel: 01434 604744
Chef: Hazel Pittock
Proprietors: Christopher & Hazel Pittock
Cost: Alc £18-£25. H/wine £9.75. Service exc
Credit cards: 🅰 💳
Times: Last D 9.30pm. Closed Sun, Mon

A fine country house setting for Hazel Pittock's imaginative, attractive dishes. Typical of the carte is loin of venison with a spiced sloe gin and redcurrant sauce. Starters and puddings are equally interesting and on selected Fridays a set menu consists of these courses only

Menu: A la carte D & Sun L on last Sun of month **Seats:** 28.
No smoking in dining room **Additional:** No children under 14;
♥ dishes, other diets by arrangement
Directions: From Hexham/Priestpopple take Eastgate turning, after 0.25 mile fork right to crossroads, Restaurant on left

LONGHORSLEY,
Linden Hall Hotel and Health Spa ❀

Morpeth NE65 8XF
Map no: 12 NZ19
Tel: 01670 516611
Chef: Keith Marshall
Manager: Julia Marshall
Cost: Fixed-price L £17.50/D £24.50. H/wine £11.25 ❗ Service inc
Credit cards: 🅰 💳 💳 💳 OTHER
Times: Last L 2pm, last D 9.45pm

The Dobson Restaurant at Linden Hall features Anglo-French cooking professionally served by polite and hospitable staff. A recent inspection meal consisted of venison terrine, followed by fillet of sea bass, and a selection of orange desserts, including a tart, parfait and mousse

Seats: 75. No smoking in dining room **Additional:** Children welcome (under 12 until 7pm), children's menu; ♥ menu, vegan/other diets on request
Directions: 7 miles N of Morpeth on A697 (Coldstream), 1 mile after Longhorsley

POWBURN, **Breamish House Hotel** ❀❀

Alnwick NE66 4LL
Map no: 12 NU01
Tel: 01665 578266
Chefs: Alan & Doreen Johnson and Debbie Lowrie
Proprietors: Alan & Doreen Johnson
Cost: Fixed-price D £21.50 (5 course)/Sun L £13.50 (4 course). H/wine £6.20 (half carafe) Service exc
Credit cards: 🅰 💳 OTHER
Times: D 7.30pm for 8pm, Sun L 12.30 for 1pm
Menus: Fixed price D & Sun L
Seats: 30. No smoking in dining room
Additional: Children over 12 welcome; other diets to order

☺ *Enjoyable food is served in the elegant dining-room of this intimate, relaxed country house hotel*

Breamish House stands at the end of a long drive, a pleasant 17th-century former farmhouse in a classic English setting. A welcoming atmosphere prevails and Doreen Johnson cooks five-course dinners based on well-tried favourites prepared with confidence and a spirit of adventure. Understatement and good value are key notes. Warm mushroom mille-feuilles, light and crisp with 'a lovely cream sauce between the layers', roast beef served with a nicely flavoured gravy, superb Yorkshire pudding and fresh vegetables, made noteworthy by the outstanding quality of the beef, and a smooth textured red berry trifle with lashings of sherry made a May meal highly enjoyable. Coffee is rich and strong.

Directions: Village centre, on the A697

NORTH YORKSHIRE

APPLETON-LE-MOORS,
Appleton Hall Hotel ❀

☺ *The Victorian country house hotel stands in its own grounds on the edge of the village and is noted for a relaxed atmosphere and attentive, willing service. The fixed-price menu is based on the sound cooking of English inspired dishes; presentation is a strength*

York YO6 6TF
Map no: 8 SE78
Tel: 01751 417227
Chef: Robert Meynell
Proprietor: Graham Davies
Cost: Fixed-price D £18.95/Sun
L £11.95. H/wine £7.50. Service
exc
Credit cards: ■ ▨ ▨ OTHER
Times: Last D 8.30pm, last Sun
L 1pm
Menus: Fixed-price D & Sun L
Additional: Children over12
permitted; other diets by
arrangement; no smoking in
restaurant

Directions: 1.5 miles off A170 2 miles E of Kikbymoorside

ARNCLIFFE, **Amerdale House Hotel** ❀

A former manor house whose restaurant provides a daily-changing fixed-price menu. Four courses, based on good quality produce, might include buttered eggs with smoked salmon, spinach and goats' cheese tart, breast of Barbary duck, and apple and raspberry crème brûlée

Menu: Fixed-price D **Seats:** 25. No smoking in dining room
Additional: Children welcome, children's portions; ♥ dishes, other
diets on request
Directions: On edge of village

Littondale Skipton BD23 5QE
Map no: 7 SD97
Tel: 01756 770250
Chef: Nigel Crapper
Proprietors: Paula & Nigel
Crapper
Cost: Fixed-price D £24 (4
course). H/wine £ 9.90 Service
exc
Credit cards: ■ ▨
Times: 7.30pm-last D 8.30pm

ASENBY, **Crab and Lobster** ❀❀

Eye-catching pub/brasserie/restaurant with extensive menu strong in fish

It's hard to miss the mustard-coloured thatched cottage, hung with
lobster pots and fishing nets. Inside, it may look a bit like Steptoe's
yard, but once you squeeze past the wonderful mix of oddities, the
rewards are plentiful. An unusually long and varied menu offers a
plethora of choices, including a great variety of fresh fish from the
nearby North-East ports. Roast monkfish with crisp calamari and
jus marinière, lobster thermidor, halibut chunks with spinach and
sauce soubise, Scotch beef fillet, Parmesan polenta and salsa verde
are a few of the main courses from which our inspector chose lamb
shank in herb jus, generous enough for two. A first course of crab

Dishforth Road YO7 3QL
Map no: 8 SE37
Tel: 01845 577286
Chef: Michael Pickard
Proprietor: David & Jackie
Barnard
Cost: *Alc* £20-£25, fixed-price
L £13.75. H/wine £8.50
Service exc
Credit cards: ■ ▨ ▨ OTHER
Times: Last L 2.30pm, last D
9.45pm Closed Sun D, Dec 25

cakes on truffle sauce was also much enjoyed. Other starters may be Provençal fish soup and rouille, salad of seared tuna niçoise or tagliarini of mussels à la mouclade. The even longer brasserie menu bears a number of similarities, but also includes homelier items such as fish pie with cheese potato crust, beef en daube with parsnip mash and, naturally, Crab and Lobster bisque. Puddings are not to be missed, either – try the lemon tart. It's delicious.

Directions: Leave A1 for A19 at Dishforth, 3 miles turn left for Asenby

Menus: *A la carte,* fixed-price L, bar menu, Sun BBQ
Seats: 120.
Additional: Children permitted, children's portions; ♥ menu, vegan/other diets on request

---

ASKRIGG,
King's Arms Hotel ❀❀

In the heart of a national park, a village inn offering renowned good food

Market Place DL8 3HQ
Map no: 7 SD99
Tel: 01969 650258
Chef: John Barber
Proprietors: Liz & Ray Hopwood
Cost: *Alc* £13.50, fixed-price L £12.50/D £25. H/wine £8.75 ❢ Service exc
Credit cards: ▨ ▧ ▦ OTHER
Times: Noon-last L 2pm, 6.30pm-last D 9pm (Sun 7pm-8.30pm)
Seats: Restaurant 30+Grill 40. No-smoking
Menus: *A la carte,* fixed-price L & D, bar menu
Additional: children permitted in Grill, children's portions, ♥ dishes; vegan on request

The Kings Arms is the fine old stone inn made famous by the TV series 'All Creatures Great and Small'. It is a pleasure to stay there. The bars are full of character, provide real ales and decent meals, while the panelled restaurant does full justice to John Barber's careful cooking which features much local produce. The four-course menu may be short but each dish is well described. Starters could include avocado wrapped in bacon, a warm salad of black pudding cocktail, lacquered by a Dijon vinaigrette, or full-flavoured chicken liver parfait with port sauce. For a main course there could be chicken breast filled with a light apricot mousseline and Pernod sauce, feuillete of calf's liver with crème Cassis sauce, or fillet of turbot with a herb nut filling. A simple caramelised rice pudding enlivened with compote of rhubarb, or a rich bread and butter pudding, make a satisfying finish. Service is friendly and attentive.

Directions: M6 exit 37 & A684: in centre of village

BILBROUGH,
Bilbrough Manor Hotel ❀❀

Attention to detail, Brideshead surroundings and some delicious cooking

Colin and Susan Bell are justifiably proud of their beautiful manor house situated just off the A64, near York and run the hotel with a

York YYO2 3PH
Map no: 8 SE54
Tel: 01937 834002
Chef: Andrew Jones
Proprietors: Susan & Colin Bell
Cost: *Alc* from £22, fixed-price L £14.50 (inc wine)/D £25, £30. H/wine £11.95 ❢ Service exc

pride and a passion. The supremely comfortable drawing room, well stocked library with wonderful views over the grounds and the open fires all create a relaxed atmosphere. New chef Andrew Jones is a very capable cook, though occasionally too ambitious. Our inspector found the starter of Roquefort terrine wrapped in smoked venison with a prune sauce a confusing medley of flavours. However, the main course was excellent. The right balance was achieved with the finest Scotch beef in a cream, brandy and peppercorn sauce accompanied by crisp vegetables. A light, well made blackcurrant soufflé with ginger ice-cream and fresh fruit was a pudding not be missed. The wine list covers just about every wine growing country in the world. Particularly note-worthy was the home smoked haddock for breakfast the following morning.

Credit cards: ⬛ 🟦 🟦 🟦
Times: Last L 2pm, last D 9.30pm
Menus: *A la carte*, fixed-price L& D, pre-theatre, bar menu, menu exceptioniel
Seats: 80. No-smoking in dining room
Additional: Children over 10 permitted Sun L; 🟣 menu, vegan/other diets on request

Directions: Off A64, in main street past the Church

BOLTON ABBEY,
Devonshire Arms Hotel ❀❀

Good quality cooking is served in beautiful surroundings

Skipton BD23 6AJ
Map no: 7 SE05
Tel: 01756 710441
Chef: Gavin Beedham
Proprietors: Duke & Duchess of Devonshire (Small Luxury Hotels).
Managing Director: Martin C G Harris
Cost: Fixed-price L £16.95/D £30 (4 course) H/wine £10.95
❗ Service inc
Credit cards: ⬛ 🟦 🟦 🟦 OTHER
Times: Last L 2pm, last D 10pm daily
Menus: Fixed-price L & D, bar menu
Seats: 70. No smoking in dining room
Additional: Children (12+) welcome, children's menu; 🟣 dishes, vegan/other diets on request

British country house cooking with a light imaginative twist is served in this fine hotel, owned by the Duke and Duchess of Devonshire. The setting is magnificent: attractive grounds and surrounded by lovely rolling countryside. The kitchen cooks to a high standard and produces a varied menu in the modern style, although a test meal report was mixed, indicating that some fine-tuning is required to achieve a better clarity of taste and balance. At this particular meal a starter of wood pigeon, bacon and truffle terrine with sherry vinaigrette was nicely presented and contained some well cooked tender wood pigeon, but the individual flavours were difficult to identify and somewhat subdued. The main course of salmon and scallop tournedos with horseradish and leek risotto and a shallot beurre blanc had a good flavour but suffered from the fish being slightly overcooked, which made the dish too heavy. A highly enjoyable tangy lemon tart for dessert came with raspberry purée. Most wine growing regions are represented on the wine list, and there's a reasonable selection of half bottles.

Directions: On the B6160 to Bolton Abbey, 250yds north of A59 roundabout junction

BUCKDEN, **Buck Inn** ❀

☺ *Beautifully situated in the village centre and surrounded by superb Dales scenery, this typical Georgian coaching house offers open fires, stone floors and wooden beams. Only the best available produce is used in the cooking. Desserts include a tempting caramelised orange and Cointreau tart, served with piped cream*

Seats: Restaurant 40, Dining Room 40. No smoking
Additional: Children welcome, childrens menu/portions where possible; ❶ dishes
Directions: In centre of village

Near Skipton
Map no: 7 SD97
Tel: 01756 760228
Chef: Marco Cording
Proprietors: Roy, Marjorie & Nigel Hayton
Cost: Alc £17. H/wine £6.50. Service exc
Credit cards: ▨ ▩
Times: Midday-last L 2.30pm, 7pm-last D 9pm

CRATHORNE, **Crathorne Hall Hotel** ❀❀

Quality and hospitality are the watchwords at this delightful Edwardian country house hotel

Step back in time and enjoy the period elegance and a warm welcome at this Edwardian country house hotel. Set in beautiful extensive grounds just off the A19 and near Teeside Airport, Crathorne Hall Hotel is the perfect place to relax. Glowing wood panelling, an impressive fireplace, flower-filled rooms and a beautiful drawing-room are just some of the beguiling details which won over one inspector. The seduction was completed by a menu of traditional as well as more original English cookery which fully complemented the Hall's historic charm. Phillip Pomfret has now established himself in the kitchen. An inspection meal yielded a superb, airy apple-smoked cheese soufflé, followed by succulent baked monkfish tail resting on a bed of spinach and Parma ham and coated in the lightest of tomato sauces – a perfect match, served with a side dish of some ten vegetables. A slightly disappointing crème brûlée clouded dessert. The wine list favours award-winning vintages both from France and the New World.

Directions: From A19, take junction signposted Crathorne and follow signs to Crathorne. Hotel entrance is on left-hand side on way into village

Crathorne Hall Hotel
Yarm TS15 0AR
Map no: 8 NZ40
Tel: 01642 700398
Chef: Philip Pomfret
Proprietor: Virgin Hotels
Cost: Alc £22.75, fixed-price L £14.50, fixed-price D £22.75 (4 courses). H/wine £11.25
❢ Service inc
Credit cards: ▨ ▩ ▨ ▣ OTHER
Times: Noon last L 2pm, last D - 10pm
Menus: A la carte, fixed-price L & D, Sun lunch, bar menu
Seats: 60
Additional: Children welcome, children's menu; ❶ & vegan dishes, other diets on request

ESCRICK, **The Parsonage Hotel** ❀

Once the local parsonage, this is now a well-managed hotel noted for friendly and attentive service. The kitchen features Anglo-French cooking which is both well-prepared and presented. Look out for pork fillets with apricot and almonds, or steak sautéed with onions and mushrooms, and bananas flamed in Bacardi

Seats: 40. No smoking in dining room
Menus: fixed-price L & D, bar L menu
Additional: Children welcome, children's portions; ❶ dishes, vegan/other diets on request
Directions: In village centre, on A19 S of York

Main Street
Map no: 8 SE64
Tel: 01904 728111
Chef: Martin Griffiths
Manager: Peter Taylor
Cost: Fixed-price L £9.50/D £18.50 (4 course). H/wine £8.95. Service exc
Credit cards: ▨ ▩ ▨ ▣ OTHER
Times: Noon-last L 2pm, 7pm-last D 9.30pm

Prices quoted in the Guide are based on information supplied by the establishments themselves.

GOATHLAND, **Mallyan Spout Hotel** ❀

This delightful hotel is found amidst superb scenery in the moorland village of Goathland. Enjoyable dishes include pork with mushroom, prune and cream sauce, and local produce is used as much as possible. Service is warm and friendly

Seats: 60. No smoking area
Additional: Children permitted (over 6 at dinner), children's portions; ❤ dishes, vegan/other diets on request
Directions: Off A172 (Pickering/Whitby) in village, opposite church

Whitby YO22 5AN
Map no: 8 NZ80
Tel: 01947 86486
Chefs: David Fletcher and Martin Skelton
Proprietors: Peter & Judith Heslop
Cost: Alc £18.50-£26, fixed-price L £12.50/D £18.50. H/wine £8.50. Service exc
Credit cards: 🟦 💳 💳 💳 OTHER
Times: Last L 2pm, last D 9pm

GRASSINGTON,
Grassington House Hotel ❀

☺ *Grassington House dates from the 18th century and stands in the centre of the town's cobbled square. Warm, attentive service is a keynote, especially in the delightful dining-room. Cooking is of a good standard and the frequently varied menu offers a sound selection on all courses. Soups and desserts are all home-made*

Menus: A la carte L & D, bar menu
Seats: 45. Smoking discouraged
Additional Children welcome, children's menu; ❤ dishes, vegan/other diets on request
Directions: In centre of village, 9 miles from Skipton (B6265)

5 The Square BD23 5AQ
Map no: 7 SE06
Tel: 01756 752406
Chefs: Joseph Lodge and Keith Anderson
Proprietors: Gordon & Linda Elsworth
Cost: A la carte £14.50. H/wine £7.95 ❢ Service exc
Credit cards: 🟦 💳 OTHER
Times: Last L 2pm, last D 9pm

HARROGATE,
Balmoral Hotel ❀❀

Old world charm and peaceful retreat within easy walking distance of bustling city centre

Franklin Mount HG1 5EJ
Map no: 8 SE35
Tel: 01423 508208
Chef: Graham Fyfe
Proprietors: Keith & Alison Hartwell
Cost: Fixed-price D £18 & £25.50 (4 course). H/wine £8.80. Service inc
Credit cards: 🟦 💳 💳 OTHER
Times: 7pm-last D 9.30pm daily
Menus: Fixed price D
Seats: 45. No smoking in dining room

A friendly smile and a charming suite with a four poster bed are just part of the welcome in this successfully run hotel. Spacious rooms and lovely antiques create a mellow comfortable environment. Proprietors, Alison & Keith Hartwell have ensured that service and food go from strength to strength. Two choices of menu are offered. Not surprisingly, the modern English cooking kicks off with some delicious dim sum in the bar. Our inspector enjoyed mushrooms in a bacon quiche and a mustard sabayon sauce – though there were unfortunately signs of microwaving. However, quality was restored by a main course of breast of duck with truffle, shallot and wild mushrooms and a well reduced Madeira sauce. The meat was pink and tender and served with a well-timed selection of vegetables. A tangy lemon tart with a sauce anglaise was the perfect dessert. Good strong coffee and an assortment of petits fours rounded off an enjoyable inspection meal.

Additional: Children permitted, children's portions; ✿ menu, vegan/other diets on request

Directions: Follow signs for Conference Centre, 100 yds past on right

HARROGATE,
The Boar's Head Hotel ✿✿

☺ *In the picturesque village of Ripley an historic hotel which was once a famous inn on the Leeds to Edinburgh Coaching run*

Ripley HG3 3AY
Map no: 8 SE35
Tel: 01423 771888
Chef: David Box
Manager: Paul Tatham
Cost: *Alc* £24.75. H/wine £8.95
❗ Service exc
Credit cards: ◪ ▦ ▰ OTHER
Menus: *A la carte* L & D, bar menu
Times: Last L 2pm, last D 9.30pm
Seats: 40. No smoking in dining room
Additional: Children welcome, children's menu; ✿ dishes, vegan/other diets on request

Standing in the cobbled market square is The Boar's Head, part of the Ripley Castle estate, restored by Sir Thomas and Lady Ingilby three years ago. Many of its portraits and pictures come from the castle and add to the country house feel. Comfort and an old fashioned ambience are the watchwords. There are two menus, and the inspection meal from the *carte* hit a high note, kicking off with marinated chicken livers in a rich wine sauce with diced nuts and pine kernels. It was served with crisp deep-fried almond potatoes and was a 'super starter'. An excellent main course of tender rich venison followed, flavoured with a deep-red wine sauce and accompanied by Savoy cabbage and good plain vegetables, with asparagus getting top marks. Only the Calvados soufflé disappointed, being set in an apple which was not fully cooked. The wine list is extensive and includes a wide selection of half bottles.

Directions: On A61, 3 miles north of Harrogate

HARROGATE, **Dusty Miller** ❀❀

A bow-fronted house in a Nidderdale village offering good food in the classical style

Dusty Miller used to be an antique shop, and vestiges of that trade can still be seen from the paintings of local characters by John A Blackmore on the walls. It is a popular restaurant of ten years standing, and with Harrogate only a few miles away, has found favour with a conference attending, expense account clientele. Cooking is classical. Chef Brian Dennison's menus are not extensive, and items such as crisp roast duckling with Dubonnet and redcurrants, or Nidderdale lamb with herbs are usually available. There is also a fish of the day. An inspection meal turned up a terrine of game, venison, grouse and wood pigeon breast which, though cooked very red (and thus not to everyone's taste) was well-executed and full of flavour. Next came fresh, delightfully sweet-tasting turbot with a lovely chive sauce, and fresh vegetables cooked al dente. About 50 wines feature on the hand-written wine list. Service is friendly and attentive.

Directions Take Rippon Road out of Harrogate for 6 miles, then Pately Bridge Road for 6 miles

Summerbridge HG3 4BU
Map no: 8 SE35
Tel: 01423 780837
Chefs: Ben South and Brian Dennison
Proprietor: Brian Dennison
Cost: Alc £30, proprietor's menu £24 (3 courses), late dinner £9.90 (main course only)
Credit cards: 🔳 🔳 🔳
Times: Last D 11pm. Closed 24/25 December, 2 weeks August
Seats: 28
Additional: Children over 10 permitted

HARROGATE, **Grundy's Restaurant** ❀

☺ *A stylish restaurant offering modern British cooking from the carte, and a particularly good value fixed-price menu. A typical meal might be cashew nut, cream cheese and herb pâté, followed by grilled fillet of fresh salmon with a watercress cream sauce, and raspberry mousse*

Seats: 40. No cigars or pipes **Additional:** Children permitted; children's portions, ♥ dishes, vegan/other diets on request
Directions: Close to Royal Hall: from Leeds direction turn R at traffic lights in town centre & R at next lights, 40yds. on R

21 Cheltenham Cres HG1 1DH
Map no: 8 SE35
Tel: 01423 502610
Chef: Val Grundy
Proprietors: Val & Chris Grundy
Cost: Alc D £15.65-22.70, fixed-price D £12.95. H/wine £8.50 ❢ Service exc
Credit cards: 🔳 🔳 🔳 OTHER
Times: 6.30pm-last D 10pm. Closed Sun, Bhs, 2 wks Jan- Feb, 2 wks Jul/ Aug

HARROGATE, **La Bergerie** ❀❀

The food is a triumph in this defiantly Gallic restaurant

Standing in a side road in Mount Parade, off the centre of town, this terraced house is a little touch of France in Harrogate. From the cosy lounge with photographs of herded sheep to the stylish dining-room, everything breathes France. Chef/owner Jacques Giron specialises in the dishes of south-western France, all produced with flair and first-rate skills. The seasonally changing menu may include roast pigeon breast served on a bed of courgettes with a neatly balanced wine and cognac sauce, followed by salmon with a Riesling and cream sauce, or best end of lamb with braised lettuce and served with a provençale herb sauce. The list of home-made puddings could cause agonies of choice, two examples being marquise of chocolate with a confit of walnuts and vanilla sauce, or tarte tatin au vin – an upside-down, pan cooked apple pie with red wine, French-country style. Not surprisingly, the robust wine list is totally dedicated to France and includes a range of half bottles.

Directions: From one-way system 1st left onto Cheltenham Mount and 1st right into Mount Parade

Harrogate HG1
Map no: 8 SE35
Tel: 01423 500089
Chef: Jaques Salvador Giron
Proprietor: Jaques Salvador Giron.
Manager: Simon Wade
Cost: Fixed-price L /D £14.50, £16.50 (4 course). H/wine £7.90 Service exc
Credit cards: 🔳 🔳
Times: Last L 2.30pm, last D 11pm Closed Sun, BHs
Menus: Fixed-price L & D, pre-theatre
Seats: 35. No smoking area
Additional: Children welcome, children's portions; ♥ dishes, vegan/other diets on request

HARROGATE, **Millers, The Bistro** ❀❀❀

Classic cooking in a bright and bustling bistro setting

Simon Gueller has established a fine reputation for sophisticated European food over the last few years. He chooses his ingredients with care, and cooks them meticulously. Flavours are crisp and clean, unhindered by extraneous or distracting elements. Freshly delivered fish is always prominent on the short, precise menu, usually cooked in a correct Franco-Italian style. Mediterranean fish soup, ink risotto, or roast tuna fish with tomatoes, olives and saffron may be for starters, followed by roast sea bass with olive pomme purée and sauce vierge, or cod viennoise with sabayon of grain mustard and gratin dauphinoise. Francophile meat dishes include terrine of pork knuckle and foie gras, fillet of beef with snails and béarnaise sauce, and breast of chicken with sauce 'bois boudran' and braised celery heart. A recent inspection meal included ballotine of salmon and lobster with carrots and truffles, served just at the right temperature to bring out the combined flavours, followed by a superb piece of local lamb, roasted with olives and set on creamed parsley with herb jus and fondant potatoes. Crème brûlée was a perfect demonstration of how it should be done, with a light, crisp top, burnt caramel taste and rich and creamy texture. Lunches are a shorter version of the dinner menu, and include a reasonably priced two courses. There is a well-chosen wine list, and service is attentive and delightfully friendly.

Directions: Town centre, just to the west of Parliament Street (A61) near the Cenotaph

1 Montpelier Mews
HG21 2TG
Map no: 8 SE35
Tel: 01423 530708
Chef: Simon Gueller
Proprietors: Simon & Rena Gueller
Cost: Fixed-price D £23. H/wine £8.95 ! Service exc Cover charge £1
Credit cards: ▨ ▧ ▨ OTHER
Times: Noon-last L 2pm, 7pm-last D 9.30-10pm Closed Sun, Mon, Dec 25- Jan 4, 2 wks Aug
Menus: *A la carte* L, fixed price D
Seats: 40
Additional: Children welcome, children's portions; other diets on request

HARROGATE, **Nidd Hall** ❀

An elegant Georgian manor house set in 45 acres of grounds which include a lake used by guests for fishing or boating. Modern cooking includes codling pan fried in olive oil, fricasée of rabbit, and beef carpaccio with Parmesan shavings, all served in the lovely restaurant

Nidd HG3 3BN
Map no: 8 SE35
Tel: 01423 771598
Chef: Jeremy Collar
Proprietor: Leisure Holdings.
Manager: Stephen Watson
Cost: Fixed-price L & D £21.50 (2 course) & £26.50. H/wine £12.50 Service inc
Credit cards: ▨ ▧ ▨ ▨ OTHER
Times: Last L 2pm, last D 10pm Closed Sat L
Menus: Fixed-price L & D, bar menu
Seats: 40
Additional: Children welcome, children's portions; ♥ dishes, vegan/other diets on request

Directions: On B6165 between Ripley & Knaresborough

HARROGATE, **Studley Hotel** ❀

Sound cooking in the hotel's Le Breton Room includes a nice mix of chargrilling and more classical offerings. Value for money is assured with dishes such as tagliatelle with wild mushroom sauce, fresh Whitby cod with grain mustard sauce, and savoury apple tart for dessert

28 Swan Road HG1 2SE
Map: 8 SE35
Tel: 01423 560425
Chef: Michel Boulineau
Manger: P Whardall

Directions: Close to Conference Centre, near the entrance to Valley Gardens

HARROGATE, **White House Hotel** ❀❀

☺ *Simple but effective cooking in delightful Victorian town house*

10 Park Parade HG1 5AH
Map no: 8 SE35
Tel: 01423 501388
Chef: Jennie Forster
Proprietor: Jennie Forster
Cost: Alc £18.50, fixed-price L £14.95. H/wine £8.95. Service exc
Credit cards: ▨ ▨ ▨ ▨ OTHER
Times: Last L 1.30pm, last D 9pm
Menus: A la carte, fixed-price L
Seats: 29. No smoking in dining room
Additional: Children welcome, children's portions; ❂ dishes, vegan/other diets by arrangement

Inspired by a Venetian villa, the 19th century White House was built by a former Mayor of Harrogate and 'doctor of water cures'. Now a restaurant with rooms, it is also the home of chef/proprietor Jennie Forster and, in keeping with the spa setting, many dishes are healthily easy on the waistline. It's not, however, a kill-joy menu, and there are quite a number of naughty but nice things as well. The menu is scattered with apt quotations, along the lines of Mae West's 'Too much of a good thing can be wonderful', and there are five choices at each course. Starters might include smoked venison with fresh fruit and grilled goats' cheese on mixed leaves with gooseberry sauce, but our inspector opted for the terrine of the day, finding it moist and meaty, neatly accompanied by a good Cumberland sauce. Fresh local produce figures large in the main courses, perhaps chicken in brandy sauce with wild mushrooms, or fillet of beef in a rich, red wine sauce, both of which have been excellent. Jennie's speciality, lemon tart, lived up to its reputation, but other good blow-the-calories choices might be chocolate marquise, sticky toffee pudding or British cheeses.

Directions: Opposite Christchurch, parallel with A59 close to Wetherby/Skipton junction

HELMSLEY, **Black Swan** ❀

Market Place YO6 5BJ
Map no: 8 SE68
Tel: 01439 770466
Chef: Nigel Wright
Proprietors: Forte.
Manager: Steven Maslen

The Black Swan, situated at one end of the market square, was originally an Elizabethan coaching inn. The elegant restaurant, overlooks a pleasant garden, and offers traditional dishes which change little from year to year due to their popularity. Sussex chicken, leek pie and roast fillet of turbot with lobster sauce, are prime examples

Cost: *Alc* £30, fixed-price L £15 /D £26.50. H/wine £13 ❗ Service inc
Credit cards: ▨ ▨ ▨ ▨ OTHER
Times: 12.30pm-last L 2pm, 7.30pm-last D 9.30pm
Seats: 75 No smoking in restaurant
Menus: *A la carte,* fixed-price L & D
Additional: Children welcome, children's menu; ❶ menu, vegan/other diets on request

Directions: In centre of village – A170 from Scarborough or Thirsk

HELMSLEY, **Feversham Arms Hotel** ❀

1 High Street YO6 5AG
Map no: 8 SE68
Tel: 01439 770766
Chefs: Martin Steel and Linda Barker

Attractive hotel rebuilt in Yorkshire stone on the site of an earlier inn by the Earl of Feversham in 1855. Some rooms have four poster beds, others have luxurious bathrooms with hand painted baths. The elegant Goya restaurant is noted for its food, particularly fish specialities

Managing Director: Gonzalo Aragues y Gaston
Cost: *Alc* from £20, fixed-price L £12 (4 course)/D £20 (4 course) H/wine £9.50 Service exc
Credit cards: ▨ ▨ ▨ ▨ OTHER
Times: Last L 2.30pm, last D 9.30pm daily

Menus: *A la carte,* fixed-price L & D, bar menu
Seats: 44. Smoking discouraged in dining room
Additional: Children welcome, children's menu; ❶ dishes, vegan/ other diets on request
Directions: 200 yds north of Market Place

HETTON, **Angel Inn** ❀❀

Skipton BD23 6LT
Map no: 7 SO95
Tel: 01756 730263
Chefs: Denis Watkins and John Topham

Easy-going pub/brasserie/restaurant with high-quality, carefully prepared food. Booking essential

Proprietors: Denis & Juliet Watkins and John Topham
Cost: *Alc* £22.95, fixed-price L £17/D £22.95. H/wine £8.90 ❗ Service exc

The Angel Inn has long been pulling in the crowds, well before the current vogue for pub dining swept the metropolis. An interesting and well-balanced choice is always on offer, including a daily fish dish. Cooking is eclectic, with familiar dishes given an unexpected spin here and there. Recent starters have included brandade of smoked chicken with green bean salad, and Loch Fyne smoked salmon with a chilli, red pepper and tomato ice-cream. Wood pigeon with grilled polenta, roast garlic and thyme sauce, and pan-fried breast of Oriental chicken marinated in Thai spices with a home-made spring roll, typify the broad canvas. A number of dishes are shared with the bar/brasserie menu, which expands to include ever-popular dishes such as Caesar salad, gravad lax, salmon en croûte and calves' liver with sweet cured bacon, bubble

Credit cards: ▨ ▨ ▨
Times: Last L 2pm, last D 9.30pm. Closed 3rd wk Jan
Menus: *A la carte,* fixed-price L & D, bar brasserie
Seats: 55+65 (Brasserie). Air conditioned. No smoking area

Additional: Children permitted, children's portions; ☯ dishes, vegan/other diets on request

and squeak and red wine sauce. Sweets and puddings largely play safe with the likes of sticky toffee pudding and caramel sauce, Summer pudding and home-made rice pudding. The overwhelming, well-priced wine list is regularly updated, and there is a fine selection of wines by the glass.

Directions: In village centre, B6265 (Rylestone) from Skipton bypass

HOVINGHAM, **Worsley Arms Hotel** ❀❀

☺ *A friendly hotel in a chocolate-box village with a bright new chef*

York YO6 4LA
Map no: 8 SE67
Tel: 01653 628234
Chef: Rodney Yorke
Manager: A Euan Rodger
Cost: Fixed-price L £14.50/D £21.50 H/wine £9.50 ! Service inc
Credit cards: 🜲 💳 💳 OTHER
Times: Last L 2pm, last D 9.30pm
Menus: Fixed-price L & D, bar menu
Seats: 45. No pipes or cigars in dining room
Additional: Children welcome, children's portions; ☯ dishes, vegan/other diets on request

Nestling along the B1257, Hovingham presents a quintessentially English scene: a chocolate box village with obligatory neighbouring castle – in this instance, Castle Howard. Such a slice of pretty rural England might intimidate lesser hotels but the effortless charm of the Worsley Arms more than complements its beautiful surroundings. Some of the well furnished bedrooms are located in bijoux cottages across the road. New chef, Rodney Yorke, formerly of Gleneagles, is quickly making his mark with some excellent food. From the uncomplicated *carte* our inspector enjoyed a moist, fresh chicken roulade filled with black olives and Parma ham. The main course was a bright white timbale of monkfish with two sauces – tomato and chive and a Chardonnay. Both were well made and the flavours were bright and clear. Accompanying vegetables were full of natural flavour and colour. The dessert of crème brûlée had a lovely thickish texture and the top was thin and crisp. Excellent coffee, but served with commercial sweets.

Directions: On B1257 midway between Malton and Helmsley

KIRKBYMOORSIDE,
George and Dragon Hotel ❀

17 Market Place YO6 6AA
Map no: 8 SE68
Tel: 01751 433334
Chef: Alan Dyson
Proprietors: Mr & Mrs Colling
Cost: *Alc* £17, Sun lunch £10.90
Credit cards: ▨ ▩ ▦ OTHER
Times: Noon-last L 2pm,
6.30pm-last D 9.15pm
(Sun 7pm-9.15pm)
Menus: *A la carte,* Sun L
Seats: 80

Both bar meals and restaurant dinners at this 17th-century hotel are worth seeking out; the hotel also boasts an award-winning wine list. A tender beef fillet with Diane sauce made a strong centrepiece at our inspection meal, but a lemon tart was pretty dull. Welcoming staff are a credit to the hard-working owners

Additional: Children welcome; ❷ dishes, other diets on request
Directions: In centre of town

KNARESBOROUGH, Carriages ❀

89 High Street HG5 0HL
Map no: 8 SE35
Tel: 01423 867041
Chef: Bruce Grey
Proprietor: Jon Holder
Cost: *Alc* £16.50. Service exc
Credit cards: None taken
Times: Last L 2.15pm, last D
9.30pm Closed Sun, Dec 25/6

☺ *A friendly, unassuming wine bar, offering excellent cooking prepared from only the best available produce. The decor promotes an intimate atmosphere in which to enjoy dishes such as a delightfully fresh pan-fried scallop tart with saffron butter, and Mrs Applebee's Cheshire pink from the cheeseboard*

Menus: *A la carte,* bar menu
Seats: 22+Garden. No cigars or pipes
Additional: Children permitted, children's portions; ❷ dishes, other diets by arrangement

KNARESBOROUGH,
Dower House Hotel ❀

Bond End HG5 9AL
Map no: 8 SE35
Tel: 01423 863302
Chef: Stuart Mein
Proprietors: Nic Davies (Best Western)
Cost: *Alc* £25, fixed-price
L £10.75/D £18.50. H/wine
£7.95 Service exc
Credit cards: ▨ ▩ ▦ ▨
Times: Last L 1.45pm/last D
9.30pm, children's menu
5.30pm-6.30pm

A family-run Grade II listed hotel where the emphasis is on prompt, efficient service. The Terrace Restaurant overlooks attractive gardens and is noted for the competent cooking of modern British dishes. At inspection, duckling dressed with hazelnuts and fennel was particularly good

Menus: *A la carte,* fixed-price L & D, bar menu,
Seats: 120. No smoking in dining room
Additional: Children welcome, children's menu/portions; ❷ menu, vegan/other diets on request
Directions: At Harrogate end of Knaresborough High Street

Pissaladière is a speciality of the Nice region. The base is either bread dough or shortcrust pastry spread with a layer of onions, garnished with anchovy fillets and olives and spread with pissalat - a purée of anchovies mixed with cloves, thyme, bay leaf and pepper and olive oil - before being cooked. It can be eaten hot or cold.

MALTON, **Burythorpe House Hotel** ❀

☺ *A lovely family-run Georgian country house hotel featuring good value home cooking based on local produce. Look out for fresh fish from Whitby. Also noteworthy is a hot, airy tomato soufflé, as well as noisettes of lamb with a piquant onion and nutmeg sauce*

Menus: A la carte, fixed-price L & D
Seats: n/a. No smoking area
Additional: Children welcome (over 7 after 7pm), childrens menu; ❶ dishes, vegan/other diets on request
Directions: On edge of Burythorpe village, 4 miles south of Malton

Burythorpe YO17 9LB
Map no: 8 SE77
Tel: 01653 658200
Chef: S M Austin
Proprietors: Mr & Mrs Austin
Cost: Alc £18, fixed-price
L £9.95/D £15.25 (4 course).
H/wine £8.75 ❗ Service exc
Credit cards: ▨ ▨
Times: By reservation only, last
L 1.30pm, last D 9.30pm

MALTON, **Newstead Grange** ❀

☺ *Well tended gardens provide much of the fresh produce used in the solid, traditional cooking at this elegant Georgian house. A fixed-price, four-course menu offers good food but no choice of dishes. A typical meal could consist of smoked trout pâté, roast leg of lamb, and French apple flan. Open to residents only*

Menus: Fixed-price D
Seats: 16. No smoking in dining room
Additional: Normally reidents only; children over 11 permitted; other diets on request
Directions: On the Beverley road

Norton YO17 9PJ
Map no 8 SE77
Tel: 01653 692502
Chef: Pat Williams
Proprietors: Pat & Paul Williams
Cost: Fixed-price D £14.50 (4 course)
Credit cards: ▨ ▨
Times: D served at 7.45pm

MARKINGTON, **Hob Green Hotel** ❀

☺ *A delightful country house set in 870 acres of farm and woodland, overlooking the rolling Yorkshire dales. Service is good and the atmosphere is one of peace and tranquillity. Modern British cooking might include fresh crab and avocado Thermidor, noisettes of lamb with a herb crust, and crème brûlée*

Menus: A la carte L & D, fixed-price Sun L, light L menu
Seats: 40. No cigars or pipes in dining room
Additional: Children permitted L only, children's menu; ❶ dishes, other diets on request
Directions: One mile from village of Markington off A61

Harrogate HG3 3PJ
Map no: 8 SE26
Tel: 01423 770031
Chef: Andrew Brown
Proprietor: Gary Locker (Best Western)
Cost: Alc £20, fixed-price Sun
L £11.95. H/wine £9.75. Service exc
Credit cards: ▨ ▨ ▨ ▨
Times: Last L 1.45pm, last D 9.30pm

MIDDLEHAM, **Millers House Hotel** ❀

☺ *An attractive, hospitable Georgian house, set back from the village square, offering sound, wholesome cooking based on fresh local produce. Kidneys in a light curry sauce, local lamb 'full of flavour', and rhubarb crumble with a light and creamy custard, made up one enjoyable inspection meal*

Menu: Fixed-price D
Seats: 30. No smoking in dining room
Additional: Children over 10 permitted; ❶ menu, vegan & other diets on request
Directions: A1 & A684 (Leyburn) to Middleham – off the village square

Middleham DL8 4NR
Map no: 7 SE18
Tel: 01969 622630
Chefs: Judith Sunderland and Chris Seal
Proprietors: Crossley & Judith Sunderland
Cost: Fixed-price D £19.50.
H/wine £5.15 ❗ No service charge
Credit cards: ▨ ▨ OTHER
Times: Last D 8.30pm

MOULTON, **Black Bull Inn** ✿

For 20 years, Mr and Mrs Pagendam have run this old village inn that now incorporates a conservatory extension, and a Pullman railway car. Varied carte and set price menus major on fresh fish dishes, imaginatively served, and complemented by a wine list featuring some reasonably priced bottles

Seats: 100. Air conditioned areas
Additional: Children over 7 permitted; ✿ dishes, vegan & special diets on request
Directions: Off the A1, a mile south of Scotch Corner

Map no: NZ20
Tel: 01325 377289
Chef: Stuart Birkett
Proprietors: G H & A M C Pagendam
Cost: Alc £24, Sunday L £15, fixed-price L £13.75. H/wine £7.25. Service exc
Credit cards: ▨ ▨ ▨
Times: Midday-last L 2pm; last D 10.15pm. Closed Sun evening & 24-27 Dec

NORTHALLERTON,
Solberge Hall Hotel ✿

Lovely views of the surrounding countryside can be enjoyed in the Garden restaurant, where good quality food is served. Dishes on the varied menu make good use of local produce and may include Wensleydale venison sausages, salmon and asparagus in filo pastry and a smooth chocolate and orange cream

Seats: 70. No smoking in dining room
Additional: Children welcome, not very young children at dinner; children's portions; ✿ menu; other diets on request; pianist Sunday lunchtimes
Directions: 2 miles south of Northallerton, turning right off the A167

Newby Wiske
Map no: SE39
Tel: 01609 779191
Chef: Peter Wood
Proprietor: Michael Hollins. General Manager: Linda Mercer
Cost: Alc £25, fixed-price L £10-£15/D £19.50. H/wine £9.95. Service exc
Credit cards: ▨ ▨ ▨ ▨ OTHER
Times: Last L 2pm, last D 9.30pm

NUNNINGTON,
Ryedale Lodge Restaurant ✿

Once the local village railway station, this attractive building was lovingly converted by Janet and Jon Laird. She cooks and he runs front-of-house. Expect crab and lobster tart, home-made vegetable soup, roast loin of lamb with tangy/sweet redcurrant, orange and mint sauce and crème brûlée

Additional: Children welcome, children's menu; ✿ menu, vegan/other diets on request
Directions: 1 mile due west of Nunnington village

Nunington Y06 5XB
Map no: 8 SE67
Tel: 01439 748246
Chef: Janet Laird
Proprietors: Jon & Janet Laird
Cost: Fixed-price £26.75 (5 course). H/wine £9 ! Service exc
Credit cards: ▨ ▨
Times: 7.30pm-last D 9pm
Menu: fixed-price D
Seats: 30+20 Conservatory. No smoking in dining room

PATELEY BRIDGE,
Sportsman's Arms Restaurant ✿

Nestling in the small village of Wath, this mellow 17th-century building radiates warmth and welcome, with a cosy lounge, log fires and attractive restaurant. Cooking, in the hands of patron/chef Ray Carter, features such local ingredients as Nidderdale trout and Whitby turbot

Seats: 50. No smoking in dining room
Additional: Children welcome, children's portions; ✿ dishes, vegan/other diets on request
Directions: 2 miles north of Pateley Bridge on minor road

Wath-in-Nidderdale
Map no: 7 SE16
Tel: 01423 711306
Chefs: Ray Carter and Chris Williamson
Proprietors: Jane & Ray Carter
Cost: H/wine £9.50. Service exc
Credit cards: ▨ ▨
Times: Midday-last L 2.30pm, 7pm-last D 10pm. Closed Xmas Day

PICKERING, **Forest & Vale Hotel** ❀

An extensive range of food is offered at this delightful hotel, where staff are extremely caring and helpful and the atmosphere is friendly and relaxed. Our inspector enjoyed a smooth chicken liver parfait, followed by Whitby sole topped by a light, succulent lobster mousse, with raspberry pavlova to finish

Menus: A la carte, fixed-price L & D, bar menu
Seats: 50. No cigars or pipes
Additional: Children welcome, children's menu; ❶ menu, vegan/other diets on request
Directions: In Pickering on junction of A170 & A169

Malton Road YO18 7DL
Map no: 8 SE78
Tel: 01751 472722
Chef: Tony Spittlehouse
Proprietors: Paul Flack (Consort)
Cost: Alc £25, fixed-price L £9.55/D £15.95. H/wine £9. Service exc
Credit cards: 🂠 🂡 🂢 🂣
Times: Last L 2pm, last D 9pm

PICKERING, **Fox & Hounds** ❀

Pleasant country restaurant serving soundly cooked food. Inspection produced an enjoyable light savoury tart of Bayonne ham and asparagus with a tangy apricot chutney, tender rib-eye steak with a well made red wine sauce and lemon tart for dessert

Menus: A la carte, fixed-price L
Seats: 60. No smoking in dining-room
Additional: Children welcome, children's menu/portions; ❶ menu, vegan and other diets on request
Directions: In centre of Sinnington

Main Street
Sinnington YO6 6SQ
Map no: 8 SE78
Tel: 01751 431577
Chef: Russell Moore
Proprietors: Mr & Mrs Bradley
Cost: Alc £15. H/wine £7.15
Service exc
Credit cards: 🂠 🂡
Times: 11.45am-last L 1.45pm, 6.30-last D 9pm

ROSEDALE ABBEY, **Milburn Arms Hotel** ❀❀

Local produce, home-grown herbs and a selection of Yorkshire cheeses all feature on the menu at this country hotel-cum-village pub

Pickering YO18 8RA
Map no 8 SE79
Tel: 01751 417312
Chef: Andrew Pern
Proprietor: Terry Bentley
Cost: Alc £20 approx, fixed-price Sunday L £8.75. H/wine £7.95 Service exc
Credit cards: 🂠 🂡 🂣
Times: 7pm-last D 9.30pm, noon-last Sun L 2pm
Menus: A la carte D, fixed-price Sun L, bar menu
Seats: 60. Air conditioned. No smoking in dining room.
Additional: Children welcome (over 5 at D), children's menu; ❶ menu, vegan/other diets on request

A charmingly-run village inn where the North Yorkshire moors provide the peaceful setting and the kitchen the soundly prepared dishes with a regional accent. Dinner in early June commenced with an onion and Gruyère quiche, offered as a taster. Grilled black pudding with sauté of onions, apple sauce and garlic, served on a croûton with a light cider sauce, came with a poached quail egg, and was found to have a good contrast of textures and flavours.

Medallions of local venison with bubble and squeak and traditional Yorkshire sauce was based on sound quality meat, tender and succulent, 'with a subtle but not strong game flavour'. Accompanying vegetables came in north country portions: baked potato with onion, Cheddar and cottage cheese topping, french beans, red cabbage, shredded leak and broccoli. To finish, a light steamed date sponge with toffee sauce. Other reports have commentated favourably on well-presented home-made ravioli of fresh Whitby crab with coriander, and wild boar casserole with red wine and juniper berries and a parsley and black pudding dumpling.

Directions: In village centre, 3 miles W of A170 at Pickering

SETTLE, **Royal Oak Hotel** ❀

☺ *Owned and run by the Longrigg family, this town centre hotel offers a good choice of English dishes. Honey-baked guinea fowl, skewered, roasted langoustines, and strips of chicken in ginger with a lime and orange sauce appear amongst the quality steaks and home-made puddings*

Menus: *A la carte,* fixed-price D & Sun L, bar menu
Seats: 36. No smoking area
Additional: Children welcome, children's menu; ❤ menu, vegan/other diets on request
Directions: Town centre, in north-west corner of Market Square

Market Place BD24 9ED
Map no: 7 SD86
Tel: 01729 822561
Chef: Gary Sustr
Proprietors: W B Longrigg
Cost: *Alc* £15, fixed-price D £12.50/Sun L £11.95. H/wine £7 Service inc
Credit cards: ▨ ▨
Times: Last L 2pm, last D10pm. Closed Xmas Day evening

SKIPTON, **Randell's Hotel** ❀

☺ *The Trans-Pennine Waterway passes at the back of this large, purpose-built hotel, overlooked by the aptly named Waterways Restaurant. Competent cooking produces spicy stir-fried beef with peppers, and salmon en croûte served with plain but nicely cooked vegetables. Look out for Osbourne pudding for dessert*

Keighley Road
Snaygill
Skipton BD23 2TA
Map no: 7 SD95
Tel: 01756 700100
Chef: Malcom Whybrow
Proprietor: United Hotels.
Gen Manager: Paul Burroughes
Cost: Fixed-price D £15.95. H/wine £9.95 Service inc
Credit cards: ▨ ▨ ▨ ▨ OTHER
Times: Last D 10pm, L Sun only
Menus: Fixed price dinner, Sun L, children's, bar menu
Seats: 70. No smoking in restaurant. Air conditioned
Additional: Children permitted; children's menu/portions; ❤ menu, vegan/other diets on request

Directions: On A629 a mile from Skipton centre, beside trans-Pennine waterway

STADDLE BRIDGE,
McCoys (Tontine Inn) ❀❀

Idiosyncratic restaurant and bistro with cooking to match

The eccentric atmosphere will charm connoisseurs of the genre. This is not the only attraction, however, and its popularity stems equally from the skillful cooking of the eponymous brothers. The menu is similar in both the mirror-lined restaurant and the informal cellar bistro, in a style which simply reflects the mood of the moment. That said, there will be plenty to choose from, especially for fish and seafood fans. Recent starters have included langoustine ravioli, Irish oysters and scallops with caviar beurre rouge. Tuna, monkfish, halibut, sea bass and salmon all featured as main courses on the same menu, along with roast guinea fowl with mushroom farce and red wine sauce, and chicken 'Jo-Jo' – breast of chicken, vermouth, crème fraîche and mushrooms. Chargrilling is a favoured technique; steaks come as they are, or with poivre and béarnaise sauces, grilled vegetables with Scottish smoked salmon and citrus mayonnaise. Puddings make liberal use of the liqueur bottle, and a good choice includes Cointreau ice-cream and prunes and, to quote, 'Thin, thin, oh so very thin layers of puff pastry, crème pâtissière and strawberries'.

Directions: At the junction of the A19 & A172

Northallerton DL6 3JB
Map no: 8 SE49
Tel: 01609 882671
Chef: Tom McCoy
Proprietors: McCoy Bros
Cost: Alc £30. H/wine £10.45
Service exc
Credit cards: 💳 💳 💳 💳 OTHER
Times: Last L 2pm, last D 10pm.
Bistro open L daily; Rest. closed
Sun, Mon, Dec 25/6, Jan 1
Menu: A la carte
Seats: 60+70 (Bistro). Air
conditioned
Additional: Children welcome,
children's portions ; ❷ menu

THIRSK,
Sheppard's Hotel ❀

A cleverly converted farmhouse, Shepherd's is a delightful, family-run hotel where efficient service is a keynote. The bistro dining-room and small restaurant offer an extensive range of interesting dishes, prepared using the best produce. At inspection chicken breast in peanut and ginger sauce was well liked

Seats: Restaurant 40+Bistro 75. No pipes in dining areas
Menus: A la carte D, fixed-price D & Sun L
Additional: Children welcome, children's portions; ❷ menu, vegan/other diets on request
Directions: 0.5 from Thirsk off A61 Thirsk/Ripon road towards Sowerby

Front Street YO7 1JE
Map no: 8 SE48
Tel: 01845 523655
Chef: William C Murray
Proprietors: Olga & Roy
Sheppard
Cost: Alc Restaurant £25/Bistro
£16, fixed-price Sun L £10.75
H/wine £9.95 (litre) No service
charge
Credit cards: 💳 💳 OTHER
Times: Last L 2pm, last D 10pm.
Rest closed Sun, Mon. Bistro
open 7 days

YORK, Ambassador ❀

☺ *An elegantly furnished hotel which stands in its own grounds and is convenient for both the racecourse and the city. The kitchen produces soundly prepared dishes along the lines of king prawns in garlic and herb butter, or roast breast of duckling with baby caramelised turnips and rich Madeira sauce*

Menus: A la carte, fixed-price D/Sun L (by arrangement only), pre-theatre bar snacks
Seats: 75. No smoking in dining room
Additional: Children welcome, children's menu; ❷ dishes, vegan/other diets on request
Directions: On A1036 near racecourse

125 The Mount YO2 2DA
Map no: 8 SE65
Tel: 01904 641316
Chef: Robert McQue
Proprietor: Consort.
Manager: John Milburn
Cost: Alc £19.50, fixed-price D
£17/Sun L £ 9.95 H/wine £9.95
Service exc
Credit cards: 💳 💳 💳 OTHER
Times: Last D 9.30pm, last Sun
L 2pm

YORK, **Dean Court Hotel** ❀

☺ *A delightful 19th-century hotel, situated right in the heart of the city, popular with locals and tourists alike. The quality of the cooking is high, and fresh produce is used in dishes such as poached scallops in ginger, and collops of beef with herbs and mushroom crust with whisky and shallot sauce*

Directions: City centre, directly opposite York Minster

Duncombe Place YO1 2EF
Map no: 8 SE65
Tel: 01904 625082
Chef: John Egan
Manager: David Brooks
Cost: Fixed-price L £12.50/D
£18.50. H/wine £9.75 ❢ Service exc
Credit cards: 🅰 💳 🚃 💷 OTHER
Times: Last L 2pm, last D
7.30pm
Menus: Fixed-price L & D, pre-theatre
Seats: 60. No smoking in dining room
Additional: Children welcome, children's menu; ❤ menu, vegan/other diets on request

YORK, **The Grange Hotel** ❀

Within easy walking distance of the city centre, this comfortable Regency hotel is known for attentive and friendly service. The Ivy Restaurant yielded, at inspection, superb scallops and freshly made apple tart. Less formal meals are available in the Brasserie

Times: Last L 2pm, last D 10pm. Closed Bhs L
Menus: A la carte, fixed-price L & D
Seats: 55
Additional: Children welcome, children's menu; ❤ dishes, other diets on request
Directions: On A19 north of York 2 miles from junction with A1237

Clifton YO3 6AA
Map no: 8 SE65
Tel: 01904 644744
Chef: Christopher Falcus
Manager: Andrew Harris
Cost: Alc £25, fixed-price
L £13/D £23. H/wine £9.50.
Service inc
Credit cards: 🅰 💳 🚃 💷 OTHER

YORK, **Kilma Hotel** ❀

A former Victorian parsonage has been converted into a well furnished, comfortable modern hotel. It stands in its own grounds within easy walking distance of the city. Quality cooking includes latticed salmon mousse, wild mushroom soup, chicken brest filled with scampi and summer pudding

129 Holgate Road YO2 4DE
Map no: 8 SE65
Tel: 01904 658844/625787
Chef: Christopher Betteriddge
Proprietor: Richard Stables

YORK, **Melton's Restaurant** ❀❀

A popular restaurant where the chef/patron has established a reputation for sound cooking

An unpretentious restaurant where Michael Hjort has been holding the torch for fair eating for some time. Dishes are uncomplicated and tastes are fresh and clear with only the best of fresh produce used in the cooking. An inspection meal kicked off with good, fresh

7 Scarcroft Road YO2 1ND
Map no: 8 SE65
Tel: 01904 634341
Chef: Michael Hjort
Proprietors: Michael & Lucy Hjort

walnut and raisin bread, and escabeche of mackerel with ginger, mixed with olive oil, carrots and onions; it was 'a good starter'. Mutton steaks with red wine and shallots 'was really very good' with flavours being distinct and fresh tasting. Vegetables were part of the dish and comprised of 'crunchy' french beans and 'lovely' gratin dauphinoise. A well made and fairly light ginger sponge topped with 'quite superb' full flavoured sherry custard, rounded off the meal. The *carte* is revamped monthly and the set menus (Monday to Thursday) are also available as lunch and early dinner menus all week. Specials are added most days. The well chosen wines cover most styles. The list also includes excellent Adnams Broadside and Samuel Smiths Imperial Stout, as well as Belgian fruit beers.

Directions: From centre head S across Skeldergate Bridge, opposite Bishopthorpe Road car park

Cost: *Alc* £23, fixed-price L £13.90/D £19.50 & £28.50 (w/end 5 course). H/wine £9.20 ❗ Service inc
Credit cards: ▨ ▧ OTHER
Times: Last L 2pm, last D 10pm. Closed Sun D, Mon L, 3 wks from Dec 24, last wk Aug
Menus: A la carte, fixed-price L & D, pre-theatre
Seats: 40. No smoking room
Additional: Children welcome, children's menu; ❶ dishes, vegan/other diets on request

YORK, **Middlethorpe Hall Hotel** ❀❀

Luxurious and discreet dining in beautifully restored 17th-century mansion

Bishopthorpe Road YO2 1QB
Map no: 8 SE65
Tel: 01904 641241
Chef: Andrew Wood
Proprietors: Historic House Hotels.
Manager: Stephen Browning
Cost: Gourmet £33.95, fixed-price L £12.50/D £25.95. H/wine £11.50 Service inc
Credit cards: ▨ ▧ ▧ OTHER
Times: Last L 1.45pm, last D 9.45pm
Menus: Gourmet, fixed-price L & D
Seats: 60. No smoking in dining room
Additional: Children over 8 permitted; ❶ menu, vegan/other diets on request

The immaculate William III country house stands only a mile and a half from the city centre, close by the race-course. It has been carefully furnished, with public rooms filled with antiques, fine pictures and lush floral arrangements. The two panelled dining-rooms have a hushed elegance, and overlook the quiet gardens. Andrew Wood is now in control of the kitchen, and has shown himself capable of producing some fine dishes in the two set-price menus offered. Nonetheless, there were a few niggles with our inspection meal, taken from the considerably more expensive 'Gourmet' menu. A stew of scallops, with poached baby vegetables would have been even better had the coral not been removed, and although the cannon of lamb, spiked with pesto and served with couscous and olive gravy, had top-notch meat, the power of the pesto intruded on the overall flavour. Vegetables were crisp and vibrant, and an apple and pear tart with cinnamon custard made a good end-piece. Dishes on the standard dinner menu, however, sound not dissimilar – which may lead one to query how much the extra price brings added value.

Directions: 1.5 miles S of York beside the racecourse

YORK, **Monkbar Hotel** ✿

☺ *Attractively-presented dishes making good use of local produce are served at this busy hotel. Our inspector recently enjoyed a tuna roulade followed by sea scallops julienne with red pimento, and noisettes of lamb with port wine sauce on a wild mushroom mousse. A grainy crème brûlée was the only disappointment*

York YO3 7PF
Map no: 8 SE65
Tel: 01904 638086
Chef: Gerard Dowd
Proprietor: Consort.
Manager: Roberto Ramirez
Cost: Fixed-price D £14.95
H/wine £8.95 Service exc
Credit cards: 🟦 ▰ ▰ 🔲 OTHER
Times: Last L pm/last D pm
Closed

Menus: *A la carte,* fixed-price D, bar menu, pre-theatre
Seats: 80. No smoking in dining room
Additional: Children welcome,children's menu, ❂ dishes, vegan/ other diets on request
Directions: Easily accessible from inner ring road and A64

YORK, **Mount Royale** ✿

Within walking distance of the Minster, this family-owned hotel is filled with objets d'art, paintings and antiques. Local ingredients are handled well and carefully presented, although a duo of beef and pork fillet, on our inspection, lacked flavour. A novel idea is to show dishes to diners before taking their orders

The Mount YO2 2DA
Map no: 8 SE65
Tel: 01904 628856
Chef: Karen Brotherton
Proprietor: Oxtoby Family
Cost: Alc £26.50, fixed-price
D £26.50 (4 course) H/wine £10
❢ Service exc
Credit cards: 🟦 ▰ ▰ 🔲 OTHER
Times: Last L 3pm, last D
9.30pm

Menus: *A la carte,* fixed-price D, light L menu
Seats: 80. No smoking area
Additional: Children welcome, children's menu; ❂ dishes, other diets on request
Directions: On the Mount – main route heading W from City centre

YORK, **19 Grape Lane Restaurant** ✿✿

Modern English food without fuss or complication in a historic timbered building in the shadow of the Minster

In a beautiful timbered house down a narrow cobbled street, 19 Grape Lane has an appropriate wealth of character and original features. Tables are provided on two floors, the upper one being for smokers. A warm welcome awaits from hard-working proprietors Gordon and Carolyn Alexander. Chef Michael Fraser has been in control of the kitchen for about nine years and his various menus, a *carte,* a fixed-price and a daily-changing blackboard, always provide plenty of interest. Mainly hot and cold salad dishes and snacks are

19 Grape Lane YO1 2HU
Map no: 8 SE65
Tel: 01904 636366
Chef: Michael Fraser
Proprietors: Gordon & Carolyn
Alexander
Cost: Alc £18.70-£26.95, fixed-price L £12.50. H/wine £8.95 ❢
Service exc
Credit cards: 🟦 ▰

served at lunchtime. Food is refreshingly unpretentious, is competently cooked and translates into traditional dishes with imaginative touches. Dinner could begin with duck and pistachio nut terrine wrapped in bacon and served with a crisp salad, continue with oregano-flavoured baked cod with a Cheddar topping and a tangy tomato sauce, and finish with a straightforward bread and butter pudding with vanilla custard, or sticky toffee pudding. Well-priced wines from all over the world feature on the wine list.

Directions: Turn right in front of Minster down Petergate, take 2nd right into Grape Lane

YORK, **The Town House Hotel** ❀

☺ *Just a short walk from York's ancient city walls is the Town House – several Victorian terraced houses converted into a comfortable hotel. The Grapevine Restaurant offers regional specialities such as Yorkshire pudding and black pudding alongside dishes from further afield*

Menus: *A la carte,* fixed-price D, pre-theatre, bar menu
Seats: 50.
Additional: Children welcome, children's menu; ❂ dishes, vegan/ other diets on request
Direction: 10 mins walk from City Centre on A59 (Harrogate)

YORK, **York Pavilion Hotel** ❀

☺ *An elegant restaurant overlooking gardens serves modern British cooking from a daily changing fixed-price menu backed up by a seasonally changing carte. A recent inspection meal featured raviolette of calves' liver, mille-feuille of pork with a sage and shallot stuffing, and roasted pear with butterscotch sauce*

Seats: 95 (in 3 rooms). No smoking in dining room
Menus: *A la carte,* fixed-price L & D, pre-theatre, bar menu
Additional: Children welcome, children's menu; ❂ dishes, vegan/other diets on request
Directions: On A19 (Selby) 0.5 mile inside York outer ring road

Times: Last L 1.45pm, last D 9.pm/10pm Sat Closed Sun, Mon, Dec 25/7, 3 wks Jan-Feb, last 2 wks Sept
Menus: *A la carte,* fixed-price L, light L menu
Seats: 34. No-smoking area, no pipes or cigars
Additional: Children permitted, over 5 at D, children's portions; ❂ dishes, vegan/other diets on request

98-104 Holgate Road YO2 4BB
Map no: 8 SE65
Tel: 01904 636171
Chef: Neil Cook
Proprietor: Richard A Hind
Cost: Fixed-price D £12.50 H/wine £8.25 ❢ Service exc
Credit cards: ▨ ▧
Times: 4.30am-last D 9.30pm Closed Dec 24-Jan 1

45 Main Street
Fulford YO1 4PJ
Map no: 8 SE65
Tel: 01904 622099
Chef: Sean Harris
Proprietors: Andrew & Irene Cossins (Best Western)
Cost: Alc £23.95, fixed-price L £9.95/D £17.95 (4 course) H/wine £10.95 Service inc
Credit cards: ▨ ▧ ▨ OTHER
Times: Last L 2pm, last D 9.30pm

Rhubarb originated in northern Asia. It is botanically not a fruit but a vegetable, but is classed as a fruit since that is how it is normally eaten. The Chinese valued rhubarb medicinally, and it was so regarded when it arrived in Britain in the 16th century. Indeed, the first recipe for rhubarb did not appear until the late 18th century. Recipes for sweet pies and tarts followed in the 19th century, but it was Mrs Beeton who really popularised it with her extensive repertoire of recipes for rhubarb jams, rhubarb pudding, rhubarb tart and rhubarb wine. Rhubarb can be forced to provide fruit out of season which probably helped to increase its popularity in Victorian times. The normal growing season lasts from May to July, but early forced rhubarb (January - April) is tender, pink and delicious. By comparison, the unforced summer rhubarb can be coarse and sour. Early forced rhubarb makes a good accompaniment to fish, especially wild salmon.

NOTTINGHAMSHIRE

LANGAR, **Langar Hall** ❁

Straightforward cooking using fresh ingredients can be enjoyed in the attractive pillared dining-room where evening meals are taken by candlelight. The carte offers the likes of twice-baked cheese soufflé, and wood pigeon breasts with cabbage and truffle sauce

Langar NG13 9HG
Map no: 8 SK73
Tel: 01949 860559
Chefs: Christopher Green and Toby Garratt
Proprietor: Imogen Skirving
Cost: *Alc* £20-£30. H/wine £9.50. Service exc
Credit cards: 🔳 🔳 🔳 🔳
Times: Last L 2pm, last D 9.30pm/10pm Fri-Sat. Closed Sun, Dec 25-30
Menus: A la carte L & D
Seats: 34+16. No smoking room
Additional: Children welcome, children's portions; ❷ dishes, vegan/other diets on request

Directions: Off A46 & A52, village centre, behind the church

NOTTINGHAM, **Forte Crest** ❁

Conveniently situated in the city centre, opposite a National Car Park, this modern hotel offers commendable food standards. During the course of a recent meal, collops of monkfish in a mussel and saffron sauce were preceded by pork and goose liver pâté en croûte then followed by an excellent chocolate parfait

Saint James's Street NG1 6BN
Map no: 8 SK53
Tel: 0115 947 0131
Manager: Mr Sullivan

Directions: City centre

NOTTINGHAM, **Ginza** ❁

☺ *A well established Japanese restaurant noted for popular tepanyaki dishes. Various set meals include a suki yaki and a tempura set meal; the latter including light, crisply battered king prawns, aubergine and sweet potato, Japanese pickled vegetables, sweet pickled seaweed and chopped jelly fish*

Menus: A la carte, fixed-price L & D
Seats: 120.
Additional: Children welcome, (children's portions Sun only); ❷ dishes, vegan/other diets on request
Directions: From city centre follow A60 (Mansfield) just past Sports Ground and Moat House

593-595 Mansfield Road NG5 2FW
Map no: 8 SK53
Tel: 0115 969 1660
Chef: Roy Cheung
Proprietor: Derek Hung
Cost: *Alc* £15, fixed-price L £8 (£10.50 Sun)/D £15 & £25 H/wine £7.75 Service inc
Credit cards: 🔳 🔳 🔳 🔳 OTHER
Times: Last L 2pm, last D 11pm Closed Bhs L, Dec 25/6 L

NOTTINGHAM, **Sonny's** ❀❀

Animated modern brasserie with bang-up-to-date menu

Set in the smart part of town, amidst the interior design and fashion shops, this lively and unaffected brasserie continues to thrive on an eclectic, winning formula. With some six or seven starters and main courses to play with, chef Graeme Watson delivers deceptively simple dishes that depend on sound, underlying technical skills. Thus, a potentially bland chicken breast is transformed into a Mediterranean delight, served with its own braised jus, puy lentils and tasty, sage flavoured polenta. Contemporary methods such as chargrilling, items like salsas, and ingredients along the lines of saffron, goats' cheese and duck breast are all much in evidence. Starters include haddock soufflé, seared pigeon salad with a saffron vinegar marinade and home-made linguine with sun-dried tomatoes, oyster mushrooms and pine nuts. Main courses might feature loin of lamb with black-eyed bean and coriander salsa, chargrilled salmon with cucumber and mint relish, or rib of beef for two. Crisp french fries and a great Caesar salad are perennials and, for dessert, crème brûlée is authentically crisp and creamy. The modern wine list has laid-back tasting notes, plenty of half bottles and fair prices.

Directions: City centre, close to Market Square and Victoria Centre

3 Carlton Street
Hockley NG1 1NL
Map no: 8 SK53
Tel: 0115 947 3041
Chef: Graeme Watson
Proprietor: Rebecca Mascarenhas.
Manager: Arten Janmaat
Cost: *Alc* £25 av. H/wine £8.95
Service exc
Credit cards: 🔳 🔳 🔳
Times: Last L 2.30pm, last D 10.30pm (11pm Fri & Sat,10pm Sun). Closed Dec 25/6, Jan 1
Menus: *A la carte*
Seats: 80. No cigars or pipes. Air conditioned
Additional: Children permitted; ❶ dishes, vegan/other diets on request

---

OXFORDSHIRE

ADDERBURY, **Red Lion** ❀

☺ *A popular coaching inn offering modern home cooking and enjoyable food in a relaxed and informal atmosphere. Particularly recommended dishes have included salmon terrine and lamb provençale. Much of the fish on the menu comes from the proprietor's own Cornish fishing boats*

Menus: *A la carte* L & D, fixed-price Sun L, bar menu
Seats: 50. No smoking area
Additional: Children welcome, children's menu; ❶ menu, vegan/ other diets on request
Directions: On main Banbury/Oxford road, opposite village green

Oxford Road OX17 3LU
Map no 4 SP52
Tel: 01295 810269
Chef: Peter Caven
Proprietors: Michael & Andrea Mortimer
Cost: *Alc* £20, fixed-price Sun L £10.95. H/wine £7.10 ❗ Service inc
Credit cards: 🔳 🔳 🔳 🔳 OTHER
Times: Last L 2.30pm, last D 10pm

BURFORD, **The Bay Tree** ❀

Good modern English cooking from a choice of menus is found in an elegant setting, overlooking a meticulously kept walled terrace and garden. Try warm salad of bacon and black pudding topped with a poached egg and parsley dressing, and medallions of beef with braised shallots and a rich Madeira and cracked pepper jus

Menus: *A la carte*, fixed-price D, bar menu
Seats: 45. No smoking in dining room
Additional: Children welcome, children's portions on request; other diets on request
Directions: Off main street in centre of Burford

12-14 Sheep Street OX18 4LW
Map no: 4 SP21
Tel: 01993 822791
Chef: Ted Turner
Proprietor: R Halsley.
Manager: Ruth Brown
Cost: *Alc* £27.50, fixed-price D £22.50. H/wine £9.95 Service exc
Credit cards: 🔳 🔳 🔳 🔳
Times: Last L 2pm, last D 9.30pm/9pm Sun

BURFORD, **Inn For All Seasons** ✿

☺ *A lovely 16th-century coaching inn with a warm and friendly atmosphere, efficient, informal service and generous portions of good food. Fresh produce features. At inspection a starter of Wiltshire ham terrine studded with green peppers served with a sweet home-made lime pickle was well liked*

The Barringtons OX18 4TN
Map no: 4 SP21
Tel: 01451 844324
Chef: Matthew Sharp
Proprietor: Matthew Sharp
Cost: *Alc* £15.75, fixed-price D £15.75. H/wine £8.50 ❢
Service inc
Credit cards: 🌑 💳 OTHER
Times: Last L 2.30pm, last D 10pm Closed Dec 25/26
Menus: *A la carte*, fixed-price L & D, bar menu
Seats: 30. No smoking in dining room
Additional: Children welcome, children's menu; ❶ dishes, vegan/other diets on request

Directions: On A40 (Cheltenham) 3 miles from Burford

CHADLINGTON, **The Manor** ✿

A charming, personally-run country house hotel where home-grown vegetables and herbs feature on the short but perfectly balanced menu. At a recent meal, pumpkin soup, terrine of pork and venison, whole grilled red mullet, and a tangy lemon tart, all showed freshness and accuracy of flavour

Menus: Fixed-price D
Seats: 20. No smoking in dining room
Additional: Children permitted, children's portions; other diets with notice
Directions: In village centre, beside the Church

Oxford OX7 3LX
Map no: 4 SP32
Tel: 01608 676711
Chef: Chris Grant
Proprietors: David & Chris Grant
Cost: Fixed-price D £ 25 (5 course). H/wine £9 Service inc
Credit cards: 🌑 💳
Times: Last D 8.30pm

CHARLBURY, **The Bell Hotel** ✿

This cosy inn, popular with locals, has as its focal point a charming lounge bar with a huge inglenook and flagstoned floor. There is a Spanish flavour to the menu, inspired by manager Juan Claramonte's Catalan origins. Fillets of salmon cooked in white wine sauce and crème brûlée Catalan style are recommended

Menus: *A la carte*, fixed-price L & D, bar menu
Seats: 30. No smoking in dining room
Additional: Children welcome; ❶ dishes, other diets on request
Directions: Charlbury centre, turn off A44 (Cheltenham) 7 miles from Burford

Church Street OX7 3PP
Map no: 4 SP31
Tel: 01608 810278
Chefs: Salvador Fernandez, Andrew Minchin and Calvin Heath
Manager: Juan Claramonte
Cost: *Alc* from £12.50, fixed-price L/D £15 H/wine £6.75 ❢
Service exc
Credit cards: 🌑 💳 💳
Times: Last L 2.15pm, last D 9.15pm daily

CLANFIELD, **Plough at Clanfield** ❀❀

16th-century village inn in perfect picture postcard setting

Bourton Road OX18 2RB
Map no: 4 SP20
Tel: 0136 781 0222
Chef: Darren Lake
Proprietors: Hatton Hotels.
Manager: P Knight
Cost: *Alc* £23.95 or £28.95,
fixed-price L £15/D £19.50.
H/wine £9.95 ❢ Service exc
Credit cards: 🔲 🔲 🔲 🔲 OTHER
Times: Last L 2pm, last D
9.30pm (10pm Fri & Sat)
Menus: *A la carte*, fixed-price L
& D, bar menu
Seats: 30. No smoking in dining
room
Additional: Children permitted,
children's portions; ❤ dishes,
other diets on request

The Plough is in a classic English setting: roses and wisteria, tumble over the Cotswold stone; within, there is a beamed interior and the relaxed atmosphere of a country inn. There are three set menus of ascending price offered here – house, epicure and gastronomic – although there is little otherwise to distinguish them. Dishes sound tempting enough, though, with aspirational ideas such as ravioli of lambs' sweetbreads with morel sauce, and pan-fried fillet of beef with braised lentils, smoked bacon and red wine jus. An inspection meal yielded duck terrine with tea cake-like brioche and sweet Cumberland sauce, pan-fried brill with a herb crust, served on a bed of surprisingly robust ratatouille, with a chive beurre blanc but few signs of the advertised olives. To finish, an English burnt cream with a clean vanilla flavour.

Directions: Village centre, on A4095

DEDDINGTON, **Dexter's** ❀❀

Enthusiastic and confident cooking in a simply understated setting

A decor that is smart yet has a rustic simplicity makes a comfortable setting for straightforward cooking at this pleasant restaurant. There is a brief menu for lunch in addition to the *carte* which might offer a regularly-changing choice of six dishes per course. While most of these appeal to robust tastes, the menu might also offer more subtle dishes such as Thai fish soup. At a recent inspection meal, that particular dish proved to be a delicate and measured combination of flavours and contained three types of fish: tuna, salmon and halibut. This preceeded plainly cooked new season lamb chops; vegetables and puddings are prepared in a similarly uncomplicated style. The short and thoughtful wine list offers a reasonable choice. Service is both informed and informal.

Deddington OX15 0SE
Map no: 4 SP43
Tel: 01869 338813
Chef: Jane Dexter Harrison
Proprietor: Jane Dexter
Harrison.
Manager: Leigh Gooding
Cost: *Alc* £23.50, fixed-price
Sun L £15.95. H/wine £9 ❢
Service exc
Credit cards: 🔲 🔲 🔲 OTHER
Times: Last L 2pm, last D 10pm.
Closed Mon
Seats: 30. Smoking restricted in
dining room
Additional: Children welcome;
❤ dishes, others on request

Directions: Village centre, A4260 from Banbury; left at lights

DEDDINGTON, **Holcombe Hotel** ❀

See entry at end of Oxfordshire, page 495

DORCHESTER-ON-THAMES,
White Hart Hotel ❀❀

Confident, competent cooking which attracts locals and visitors in numbers

A heavily-beamed, 17th-century coaching inn in a charming Thameside village of winding lanes and fashionable shops. The place induces a feeling of well-being, from both the setting and the food. The relaxed and animated atmosphere can be largely attributed to a loyal local following who come here daily to meet, and to business people and tourists. One bistro-style *carte* covers both bar and restaurant, from a light snack to a substantial three-course lunch or dinner. Chef Tony Baker's cooking is confident, his flavours true and unfussy, and he produces good, satisfying dishes at affordable prices. These qualities were clearly evident in an inspection meal which commenced with potted duck and chicken liver parfait with home-made apple chutney, was followed by pan-fried breast of duck and venison sausages, served with creamed potatoes and a robust, but complementary, redcurrant sauce, and finished with sticky toffee pudding.

Directions: In village centre

High Street
Map no: 4 SU59
Tel: 01865 340074
Chef: Jon Wills
Proprietors: Raceoak.
Managers: Mr & Mrs Jack Bradley
Cost: *Alc* from £19.65, fixed-price L £9.50 (2 courses), £13.50/D £13.50. H/wine £8.95. Service inc
Credit cards: 🅴 📷 📷 📷 OTHER
Times: Last L 2pm, last D 9.30pm. Closed Xmas Day
Menus: *A la carte*, fixed-price, Sunday lunch, bar menu
Seats: 35
Additional: Children welcome, children's portions; ❦ dishes; other diets on request

GORING, The Leatherne Bottle ❀❀

Expect the unexpected in extravagantly creative menu with assertive flavours, in glorious Thameside setting

Oxon RG8 0HS
Map no: 4 SU68
Tel: 01491 872667
Chefs: Keith Read and Clive O'Connor
Proprietors: Annie Bonnet and Keith Read
Cost: *Alc* £27 approx.
H/wine £ 10.50 ❦ Service exc
Credit cards: 🅴 📷 📷
Times: Last L 2pm/2.30pm Sat & Sun, last D 9pm/9.30pm Sat/8.30pm Sun Closed Dec 25
Menus: *A la carte* L & D
Seats: 60. Air conditioned
Additional: Children permitted; ❦ dishes, other diets on request

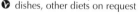

The Leatherne Bottle's stunning Thameside setting is the place to head for, especially in fine weather. The food is modern and unusually exciting, the menu full of surprises, and makes liberal use of spices and herbs from the wonderful garden. Fresh salad niçoise is made with chargrilled tuna fillet, quail's eggs, baby tomatoes, lemon balm and fresh marinated anchovies, whole Cornish brown crab is steamed with warm ginger and red clover, and roast local suckling pig marinated with lemon leaves, ginger, coriander and lemon thyme and served with crisp crackling and nasturtiam and courgette flower pasta. The creative cooking sets out to rock the taste-buds boldly, and oriental techniques and ingredients meet Western ones in a sort of United Nations of flavour. Lambs' brains

are pan-fried crisp with ground lemon grass and roast sesame seeds, and served with chargrilled ciabatta, chickweed and lemon thyme jelly; local maize-fed guinea fowl, off the bone, is roasted slowly in its own juices with galangale, lemon leaves and lemon thyme. Texture pairings, too, provoke – a dish of smoked salmon and spring nettle ice cream with smoked halibut, crispy spring roll and salmon caviar olive oil, for example, makes every mouthful an adventure.

Directions: M4 exit 12/M40 exit 6, signed off B4009 Goring–Wallingford

GREAT MILTON, Le Manoir Aux Quat'Saison ❀❀❀❀❀

A fine 15th-century English manor house setting for stunning French cooking by an undisputed master

'A visit to Raymond Blanc's celebrated hotel must rate as one of the greatest pleasures in life', observed one inspector recently. The mellow-stoned, 15th-century manor house which stands in grand gardens beside the church in a quiet country village close to Oxford represents a classic English setting. But this very personal operation is French and every aspect of a meal, or even a stay here, bears Raymond Blanc's unique stamp. His tireless efforts in the pursuit of perfection include two acres of grounds allotted just for the growing of vegetables, herbs and salad leaves. Breakfast, too, is a memorable event, with 'fabulous' Viennoiseries (croissant, brioche etc) baked on the premises and served with outstanding home-made preserves.

The heart of the hotel is the kitchen, and it is here that Raymond Blanc and head chef Clive Fretwell create seasonal menus where imagination and technique are as important as simplicity is the keynote. For example, a dinner in May commenced with an amuse-gueule of deep-fried mille-feuille of aubergine layered with an intensely flavoured garlicky aubergine caviar set on a basil purée. Lightly cooked, delicately flavoured lambs' sweetbreads followed, served with green, white and water asparagus, morels and a Gewürztraminer jus; quite a lively juxtaposition of texture and taste but balanced well by the freshness of the asparagus. Five of the tiniest fillets of red mullet came highly seasoned with a creamy textured and richly flavoured squid ink risotto, a squid tube filled with crab meat, braised baby fennel, and an artichoke heart; a powerful fishy jus with olive oil was served separately – an outstanding combination of vibrant flavours, all perfectly matched. An individual cider and Calvados mousse contained caramelised apple and came with a beautifully made, fresh tasting apple sorbet which was layered between dried apple; an apple and vanilla sauce further heightened the lovely, clean flavours.

Other dishes recommended this year have included a superb 'theme of wild salmon' which featured a pyramid of salmon en gelée with caviar and salmon roe, beetroot marinated salmon, gravad lax and seared salmon with a cucumber cream sauce, and a stunning, earthy dish of veal kidneys with snails, parsley butter and an Hermitage wine sauce. The wine list can be as stunning as the food, with breathtaking prices to match. As compensation, there are some 100 bottles under £30 and a good range of half bottles.

Directions: From M40 junction 7 follow A329 towards Wallingford. In 1 mile turn right, signposted Great Milton Manor

Church Road OX44 7PD
Map no: 4 SP60
Tel: 01844 278881
Chef: Raymond Blanc
Proprietor: Raymond Blanc Restaurants Ltd
Cost: *Alc* £75, fixed-price L £29.50 (3-courses). D Menu Gourmand £65 (8 courses). H/wine £20 ♥ Service inc
Credit cards: 🆇 💳 💳 💳 OTHER
Menus: *A la carte*, Menu Gourmand, fixed-price lunch Sun L, children's
Times: Last L 2pm, last D 10.15pm
Seats: 120. No smoking in restaurant. Air conditioned
Additional: Children welcome, children's menu; ♥ menu, vegan/other diets on request

HENLEY-ON-THAMES, **Red Lion Hotel** ❀

☺ *Situated besides the River Thames, this 16th-century ivy-clad coaching inn overlooks the Royal Regatta course. A modern, imaginative style of cooking is the keynote here, and a recent inspection meal included a well-made escalope of salmon with pistou and a fresh tomato sauce*

Times: 12.30pm-last L 2pm, 6.30pm-last D 10pm
Seats: 80.
Additional: Children welcome, children's menu; ❷ dishes, vegan/other diets on request
Directions: On the right when entering Henley by the bridge

Hart Street RG9 2AR
Map no: 4 SU78
Tel: 01491 572161
Chef: Emil Forde
Proprietors: Miller Family (Durrant's Hotel).
Manager: R S Buscwell
Cost: *Alc* £22, fixed-price D/Sun L £18.50. H/wine £10.75.
Service inc
Credit cards: 🂠 🂠 🂠 OTHER

HORTON-CUM-STUDLEY,

Studley Priory Hotel ❀❀

Change of chef augurs well at this large Elizabethan manor

Oxford OX33 1AZ
Map no: 4 SP51
Tel: 01865 351203
Chef: Trevor Bosch
Manager: Mark Bright
Cost: Fixed-price L/D £22.50.
H/wine £10.70.
Credit cards: 🂠 🂠 🂠 🂠 OTHER
Times: Last L 1.45pm, last D 9.30pm
Menus: Fixed-price, bar L menu
Seats: 60. No smoking in dining room
Additional: Children welcome (over 5 at dinner), children's portions; ❷ menu, vegan/other diets on request

When Hamlet told Ophelia to take herself off to a nunnery, it was probably somewhere like Studley Priory that Shakespeare had in mind. Only six miles from Oxford, this former Benedictine nunnery was founded in the 12th century, and extended when Henry VIII dissolved the monasteries and it passed into private hands. A friendly, professional welcome now awaits guests, and the imaginative cuisine of new chef Trevor Bosch makes dining here a treat. The new-look menu features meals priced according to the main course taken. Well-conceived dishes include woodland pigeon stuffed with aubergine confit, terrine of veal sweetbreads and kidneys, and ravioli of lobster and vegetable spaghetti garnished with sautéed King scallops. Our inspection meal started with the ubiquitous Caesar salad, here served with garlic croûtons, smoked pancetta and mixed leaves; the dressing, however, needed to be more emphatic. A well-executed grilled loin of new season's lamb with basil and Madeira jus was pleasingly paired with pommes dauphinoise and chargrilled ratatouille vegetables. Pudding was a banana crème brûlée.

Directions: At top of hill in the village

KINGHAM,
The Mill House Hotel ❀❀

☺ *Relaxed and friendly welcome in Cotswold stone hotel in rural village*

Chipping Norton OX7 6UH
Map no: 4 SP22
Tel: 01608 658188
Chef: Stephen Lewis
Proprietors: John & Sheila Parslow.
Manager: Stephen Ellis
Cost: *Alc* £19.95, fixed-price L £12.95/D £19.95. H/wine £10.70 ❢ Service exc
Credit cards: 🂠 🖾 🖾 🖳 OTHER
Times: Last L 2pm, last D 9.30pm
Menus: *A la carte*, fixed-price L & D, bar menu
Seats: 70. No smoking in dining room
Additional: Children over 5 welcome; ❂ menu, vegan/other diets on request

Over the past years, the former mill has been lovingly restored and extended, whilst still retaining the original character of the building. It is now a charming, small hotel set in seven acres of gardens, bordered by a trout stream, where Head Chef Mark Robbins continues to provide imaginative and well-balanced set price menus. Several dishes, such as roast whole quail, baron of lamb and coffee soufflé, carry a supplementary charge. At a recent test meal the chicken terrine was well flavoured with dill, studded with pink and green peppercorns, wrapped in smoked bacon and served with glistening salad leaves. A main course of poached breast of chicken filled with a mousse of smoked bacon and chervil was served with a Dijon and mustard cream sauce. Vegetables were precisely and crisply cooked, retaining their natural flavours. An original, hot strudel of banana, apple and fudge completed the meal, and was served with some delicious home-made vanilla and chocolate ice-cream. Coffee and three kinds of fudge are served in the lounge which has French windows leading onto a sunny terrace.

Directions: On B4450, on southern outskirts of Kingham village

MIDDLETON STONEY,
Jersey Arms Hotel ❀

☺ *The kitchen here makes a determined effort to create fresh-tasting food, offered from an imaginative menu. The cooking style is simple, there can be an occasional spot of unevenness, but on the whole soundly prepared dishes could include leek and Stilton soup, and saddle of rabbit with redcurrant sauce*

Bicester OX6 8FG
Map no: 4 SP52
Tel: 01869 343234
Chef: Douglas Parrott
Proprietor: Donald Livingston
Cost: *Alc* £19.50. H/wine £9.25 Service exc
Credit cards: 🂠 🖾 🖾 🖳 OTHER
Times: Last L 2pm, last D 9.30pm Closed Sun D

Menus: *A la carte* L & D, bar menu
Seats: 50. Smoking restricted in dining room
Additional: Children welcome, children's portions; ❂ dishes, other diets on request
Directions: On B430, 3 miles from Bicester, 10 miles N of Oxford

MINSTER LOVELL,
Lovells at Windrush Farm ❀❀

Quietly elegant setting for restaurant with a dedicated approach to food

Minster Lovell OX8 5RN
Map no: 4 SP31
Tel: 01993 779802
Chef: Marcus Ashenford
Proprietors: Mark Maguire and Norma Cooper
Cost: Fixed-price L £14.50 (Sun £17.50-4 course)/D £29.50 (7 course) H/wine £ 12 ❢ Service exc
Credit cards: 🟦 ▨ ▨ ▨
Times: Last L 2pm, last D 9.15pm. Closed Sun D, Mon, Jan
Menus: Fixed-price L & D
Seats: 18. No smoking in dining room
Additional: Children welcome; children's portions/other diets by arrangement

Seven courses, these slim-line days, tend to be the exception rather than the rule. Happily the £29.50 set dinner at Lovells has sensible portion control, although the regimented pattern of all diners being shown to their tables and served at the same time, can lead to late night dining. Set lunches offer a more restrained three courses for £14.50. The kitchen shows singular enthusiasm for their task, which whilst entirely commendable, could benefit from greater restraint; at times, the variety of competing, over-elaborate tastes can bewilder as much as engage. A recent meal started with a busy combination of seared scallops with pepper confit, spinach and a Gewürztraminer cream sauce with ham, leek and tomatoes. This was followed by a tender and mildly flavoured venison steak, served on a rösti potato bed with a light, runny Madeira sauce. A trio of desserts was a bewildering array of plum soufflé, almond and honey ice-cream, and lemon curd ravioli. Along the way, there are canapés, appetisers, soup and a 'Pre Dessert', such as chocolate tart with mandarin sorbet, to limber up with before hitting the real thing!

Directions: From the Witney–Minster Lovell road, take the first turning to the Old Minster

MOULSFORD,
Beetle & Wedge Hotel ❀❀❀

A truly delightful eating experience, whether in the informal Boathouse or the more sophisticated Dining Room

Ferry Lane OX10 9JF
Map no: 4 SU58
Tel: 01491 651381
Chef: Richard Smith
Proprietors: Kate & Richard Smith
Cost: Alc £25-30 (in Boathouse), fixed-price L £21.50/D £35/Sun L £27.50 (in Dining Room). H/wine £11.50 ❢ Service exc
Credit cards: 🟦 ▨ ▨ ▨ OTHER
Times: 12.30-last L 2pm, 7.30-last D 10pm. Closed 25 Dec. Dining Room closed Sun eve & Mon

An absolute gem of a place, nestling on the banks of the Thames, part country house and part upmarket inn is the former home of Jerome K Jerome, and the source of inspiration for 'Three Men in a Boat'. The experience is quintessentially English, whether dining in the rustic, beamed Boathouse on the waterfront, or in the sophisticated Dining Room where all tables have wonderful views of the river. The menus in either place have a strong British undertow, with enough awareness of what is currently in fashion to keep them in the swim of mainstream modernism. Thus the Boathouse serves food in a lively, informal atmosphere, and real ales are on tap. Here the menu caters for all tastes, with fish, seafood, a variety of meats and a good vegetarian choice; there is also a charcoal grill for dishes such as calves' kidneys and black pudding with grain mustard sauce, and escalope of salmon hollandaise. In the Dining Room starters include hot Stilton soufflé with wild mushroom sauce, and sauté of pigeon breast and duck livers with spring onions and garlic, while main course choices could be fillet of hare with button onions, wild mushrooms and foie gras, or steamed fillet of halibut with mussels, saffron and cumin sauce. Service in both places is spontaneous and caring.

Inspection yielded sautéed squid set off with crunchy beansprouts, finely diced tomato, and spring onions. Roast pheasant followed, gamey and tender, harmoniously cooked with caramelised shallots and served with a cream and brandy sauce. Dessert comprised big fluffy doughnut balls coated in cinnamon sugar and served with a ramekin of smooth, sharp lemon curd. In all, a faultless meal. There are no halves on the wine list, but bottles under £20 can be ordered by the glass.

Directions: In village turn towards river via Ferry Lane

Seats: Dining Room 40, Boathouse 60. No smoking in Dining Room
Menus: *A la carte*, fixed-price L & D
Additional: Children welcome, children's portions on request; ❶ dishes, vegan/other diets on request

OXFORD, **Bath Place Hotel** ❀❀

Cottage style restaurant tucked away down a cobbled city alley serving neo-classical dishes with a European slant

The hotel is fortunate to occupy the three sides to an end of alley, which it utilises to great effect. On sunny days, it feels almost continental, filled with tubs and hanging baskets. The cooking, however, aspires to a certain degree of grandeur in the *carte*, set menus and the 'menu surprise', an eight course tasting menu. Typical first dishes might include a warm salad of wood pigeon breasts, orange and tomato, dressed with walnut oil, terrine of chicken, lambs sweetbread, cèpes and pistachio nuts with a compote of kumquats, or tartare of Scottish salmon with dill, lemon, cream and garnish of Baltic caviar, cucumber and red pepper coulis. Main courses are in the same complex vein, as demonstrated by an essay in lamb cookery – roasted best end plus pan-fried offal, set on a bed of lamb casserole with a white wine, tomato and tarragon sauce. Alternatively, roast breast of French 'Poulet Noir' chicken comes with wild asparagus and wild mushrooms in a Madeira sauce. For pudding, try frozen glacé fruit nougat with a red fruit sauce, or a plate of miniature chocolate desserts with chocolate sorbet and chocolate sauce.

Directions: City centre, opposite Holywell Music Room between Hertford & New College

4 & 5 Bath Place
Holywell Street OX1 3SU
Map no: 4 SP50
Tel: 01865 791812
Chef: Jeremy Blake O'Connor
Proprietors: Kathleen & Yolanda Fawsitt
Cost: *Alc* £33-£47, fixed-price L £14.50 (2 course), £17.50 (Sun L £19.50)/D £24.50 (5 course). H/wine £10.50 ❢ Service exc
Credit cards: 🅲 💳 💳
Times: Last L 2pm/2.30 Sun, last D 10pm/10.30pm Fri & Sat/9.30 Sun
Menus: *A la carte*, fixed-price L & D
Seats: 32. Air conditioned. No smoking in dining room
Additional: Children welcome, children's portions; ❶ menu, vegan/ other diets on request

OXFORD,
15 North Parade Restaurant ❀❀

☺ *A cool, modern restaurant, tucked away in the northern outskirts of Oxford, offering good, imaginative cooking*

Thanks to a flood, the opportunity arose to move the kitchen from the basement to the back of the restaurant, open-plan style, which

15 North Parade Avenue
OX2 6LX
Map no: 4 SP50
Tel: 01865 513773
Chef: Sean Wood
Proprietor: Georgina Wood
Cost: *Alc* £19, fixed-price L £12/D £15 H/wine £9.75 ❢ Service exc

now adds an extra dimension to the decor. This might be best described as modern Italianate with bold colours. Other changes have introduced two chefs to the kitchen, one the owners's son. It has been suggested that Oxford was reluctant to take to a bold bistro-style of cooking and this may explain why, despite the impression given by the seasonally-based *carte* and fixed-price menus, the result shows signs of a restraining hand, almost watered down. For example, mussels, with celery and leek, had lost their sea flavour, and a sauce with flageolet beans was understated. The *carte* offers a choice of four courses from three sections which might include potted partridge with spiced cranberry, crab ravioli in a lemon grass fumé, or baked salmon with soy, ginger and coriander. Bread is baked on the premises. There is a short, balanced selection of Old and New World wines. Service is overseen in a caring, genial fashion by the owner, Georgina Wood.

Directions: Off the Banbury road, turning opposite Cavendish Lodge hotel

Credit cards: ◼ ▦ OTHER
Times: Last L 2pm, last D 10.30pm. Closed Sun D, Mon, BHs, 2 wks Aug
Menus: *A la carte*, fixed-price L & D
Seats: 60/90. No smoking room
Additional: Children welcome, children's portions; ❂ dishes, vegan/other diets on request

OXFORD, **Liason** ❁

A popular Chinese restaurant specialising in freshly made dim sum. Other dishes on an extensive menu include clay pot dishes such as braised fresh fish with oyster sauce, sizzling platters of hot and fierce chicken cooked with green pepper, and Cantonese and Beijing set dinners

29 Castle Street
Map no: 4 SP50
Tel: 01865 242944
Cost: *Alc* £30, fixed-price £14.80. H/Wine £8.50.
Credit cards: ◼ ▦ ▦ ▣
Times: Midday-last L 2.45pm, 6pm-11.15pm. Closed Xmas

Directions: The restaurant is behind the main shopping centre

OXFORD, **Munchy Munchy** ❁❁

☺ *Exciting South-East Asian food with plenty of zest and punch*

The name may sound like a Eurovision song contest entry, but the food transcends the giggles. The minimalist decor is striking with bold orange and gold jungle murals, pine tables and chairs, and a noise-bouncing quarry tiled floor. The daily changing range of dishes is eclectic, drawing from the cuisines of Thailand, Malaysia, Indonesia and China, although the bed-rock style is Sumatran 'Padang'. Amongst the most successful dishes are the down-home ones with robust, highly spiced sauces and gutsy flavours. Our inspector enjoyed a meltingly tender duck with Szechuan red

6 Park End Street OX1 1HH
Map no: 4 SP50
Tel: 01865 245710
Chef: Ethel Ow
Proprietors: Tony & Ethel Ow
Cost: *Alc* £12. Service exc
Credit cards: ◼ ▦ OTHER
Times: Last L 2pm, last D 10pm Closed Sun, Mon
Menus: *A la carte* L & D
Seats: 60. No-smoking area

peppers, star anise and mint in a tahini sauce. Other choices might include Indonesian oyster omelette with almonds, leeks and coriander seeds, or chicken with paprika, juniper berries, fennel seeds and mint in coconut milk. Vegetables are also treated with care, and aromatic long-grain rice is correctly cooked. Desserts are limited to ice-cream, sorbet or fresh fruit. Although there is a short selection of wines, the best accompaniment is a cool Asian beer or one of the unusual Chinese teas.

Directions: West of city centre, between Nuffield College & the station

Additional: Children welcome (over 6 Fri-Sat), children's portions; ◐ dish

OXFORD, **Whites** ❀❀

Original dishes cooked with élan in centrally located restaurant cum wine shop

Turl Street QX1 3DH
Map no: 4 SP50
Tel: 01865 793396
Chefs: Christopher Bland and Bertrand Faucueux
Proprietor: Michael White
Cost: *Alc* £31.50, fixed-price L £12.95/D £29.50 & £38.50 (both inc glasses of selected wine. H/wine £14 ❢ Service exc
Credit cards: ▨ ▤ ▤ ▣ OTHER
Times: 12.30pm-last L 2pm, 6.30pm-last D 10pm. Closed Sun D, Sun during University vacations, 1 wk Xmas/NYr
Menus: *A la carte,* fixed-price L & D
Seats: 40. No-smoking area
Additional: Children over 6 permitted; ◐ dishes, vegan/other diets by arrangement

The damson decor and reproduction Mackintosh straight-backed chairs give a bold sense of style to the restaurant, matched by an air of almost unrestrained gusto that bursts forth from the kitchen. Two sensibly priced set menus include a glass of wine with each course, a highly attractive proposition that rather puts the seasonally changing menu in the shade. For example, a roast fillet of salmon, topped with a fig tapenade and a coriander pesto sauce, was confidently served with a deep 1988 Médoc. Other dishes sampled have included a starter of guinea fowl mousse, attractively encased in a Chinese cabbage leaf, marginally marred by an undercooked interior, and a main course of moist turbot, with a cream-based watercress and mussel sauce, though the latter showed little sign of the advertised star anise. Desserts are pretty special, and a full-flavoured tarte tatin has won much praise. Rich espresso coffee delivers a mighty kick. The interesting wine list is mainly French, drawn from the vaulted cellar wine shop below the restaurant where, amidst a well laid out selection of bottles, is the heart-stopping sight of a £6000 methuselah of Romanée-Conti.

Directions: City centre, next to Jesus College, opposite Exeter College

SHIPTON-UNDER-WYCHWOOD, Lamb Inn ✿

A well established, traditional village inn with a loyal following. Country dishes are cooked with zeal, with emphasis on fresh local ingredients. A typical menu may include smoked Welsh venison, Cotswold pie, fillet of pork with Brie and apple, or roast lamb with rosemary and garlic

Menus: Fixed-price D & Sun L, bar menu
Seats: 30. No smoking in dining room
Additional: No children under 14; ❂ dishes, other diets on request
Directions: In village centre

High Street OX7 6DQ
Map no: 4 SP21
Tel: 01993 830465
Chef: Robin Bancroft
Proprietor: Mr L Valenta
Cost: Fixed-price D £21
(4 course)/Sun L £14.95.
H/wine £8.75 Service exc
Credit cards: 🔳 🔳 🔳
Times: Last L 2pm, last D
9.30pm. Closed Mon, Dec 25/6

SHIPTON-UNDER-WYCHWOOD,
Shaven Crown Hotel ✿

☺ *The renovated medieval hospice within the setting of a terraced courtyard with a lily pond at its centre is idyllic. Here, interesting Anglo-French cooking is served. Look out for rack of garlic and rosemary lamb, and pork with prunes, juniper berries and Pernod*

Menus: Fixed-price D & Sun L, bar menu (L & D)
Seats: 30. No smoking in dining room
Additional: Children welcome (over 5 in Rest), children's portions; ❂ dishes, other diets on request
Directions: On A361, village centre, 4 miles N of Burford

OX7 6BA
Map no: 4 SP21
Tel: 01993 830330
Chef: Stanley Rider
Proprietors: Trevor & Mary Brookes
Cost: Fixed-price D £14.95
(2course), £18.50/Sun L £11.95
(2 course) & £14.95. H/wine £8
Service inc
Credit cards: 🔳 🔳
Times: Last D 9.30pm, last Sun L
1.45pm Closed Dec 25 (except bar)

STONOR, Stonor Arms ✿✿✿

A relaxed, informal inn-cum-country house with a well-earned reputation

Near Henley-on-Thames
RG9 6HE
Map no: 4 SU78
Tel: 01491 638345/638866
Chefs: Stephen Frost and
Amanda Beeden
Proprietors: Stonor Hotels.
Manager: Stephen Frost
Cost: Alc £22, fixed-price D
£29.50. H/wine £8.95. Service
exc
Credit cards: 🔳 🔳 🔳 OTHER
Times: Last L 2pm, last D
9.30pm
Seats: 40+20 No cigars or pipes
Menus: A la carte, fixed-price D,
bar menu
Additional: Children welcome,
children's portions; ❂ dishes,
vegan/other diets on request

Stonor Arms lies in the middle of a one-street village of picturesque cottages and farms, surrounded by rolling hills and meadow. In May, when the late sun is dappled and casts a honeyed glow, and the wisteria hangs like tendrils from the eves against the whitewashed walls, it is the quintessential English country scene of jigsaws and old-fashioned chocolate boxes. But there is nothing old-fashioned about this inn-cum-country house. The rustic and rather genteel shabbiness is tempered by contemporary wall coverings, designer fabrics and collectibles of boating artifacts and prints, and the food is good.

Under the auspices of Stephen Frost, a modern eclectic style of cooking, in either the Stonor Restaurant or the more informal Blades Brasserie which is housed in the conservatory, is offered. Reports suggest that when Stephen Frost is absent from the stove enthusiasm overtakes balance and judgement, and this was the case at a recent inspection. Cornish scallops were not successfully sealed, and were a bit flabby, their flavour muted. Nevertheless, an accompanying coriander and shallot dressing on a mound of wonderful green leaves 'from the same supplier as the Manoir aux Quat'Saisons' was superb. Duck breast was pink and juicy, served with a finely-judged reduction, just slightly marred by a very pithy and rather bitter lime julienne. An accompanying filo parcel containing home-made chutney and foie gras appeared to be completely devoid of the latter. Chocolate pithivier served with a rich crème fraîche ice- cream was more successful. Then there is good, heartstopping espresso. The wine list is fine both for the depth and quality of the wines and for their vintages, but the house selection is probably the best value, with an excellent Cosme-Palacio Hermanos white Rioja for around £16. Service remains friendly and attentive and, like everything else here, extremely professional.

Directions: In centre of village

THAME, **Spread Eagle Hotel** ✸

Expanded considerably since its days as a coaching inn, this attractive hotel offers decent food. Each change of menu introduces a particular theme, and our inspector sampled mussel and watercress soup, duckling with apple sauce and a spot-on crème brûlée from the Normandy menu

Times: Last L 2pm/2.30 Sun, last D 10pm/9pm Sun Closed Bhs, Dec 28-30
Menus: A la carte, fixed-price L & D, bar menu
Seats: 64.
Additional: Children welcome, children's menu; ♥ dishes, vegan/other diets on request
Directions: Town centre

Cornmarket OX9 2BW
Map no: 4 SP70
Tel: 01844 213661
Chef: Michael Thomas
Proprietors: D M L Barrington (Best Western)
Cost: Alc £24.95, fixed-price L £17.45/D £19.95 H/wine £8.90 ❢ Service inc
Credit cards: 🟦 🟦 🟦 🟦 OTHER

WANTAGE, **Foxes** ✸

An intimate, personally-run restaurant featuring a choice of frequently changing fixed-price menus. A meal might start with marinated tuna fish, followed by loin of wild boar, with a selection of homemade desserts such as a fruit tuille basket. Cheeses come from Wells Stores

Menus: Fixed-price L & D
Seats: 30/35. No smoking in dining room
Additional: Children permitted; ♥ menu, vegan/other diets on request
Directions: Just off market place on A338 Newbury/Reading road

8 Newbury Street OX12 8BS
Map no: 4 SU38
Tel: 01235 760568
Chef: Karen Sweeney
Proprietors: Karen Sweeney and Nicholas Offen
Cost: Fixed-price L £13 approx, D £ 23.95, £18.95 (2 course) H/wine £10 ❢ Service exc
Credit cards: 🟦 🟦
Times: Last L 1.30pm, last D 9.30pm. Closed Sun & Mon (unless pre-booked), Sat L, Jan

> Restaurant assessments are based on reports of visits carried out anonymously by the AA's Hotel and Restaurant Inspectors.

WESTON-ON-THE-GREEN,
Weston Manor Hotel ❀

Bicester OX6 8QL
Map no: 4 SP51
Tel: 01869 350621
Chef: Andrew Cunningham
Proprietor: Dudley Osborn
Cost: Fixed-price L £16.75/D £25.50. H/wine £12.95. Service exc
Credit cards: 🔲 🔲 🔲 🔲
Times: 12.30pm-last L 2.15pm, 7.30pm-last D 9.30pm.

This stone mansion, set in beautifully maintained gardens, offers enjoyable cooking. Guests eat in an amazing baronial hall, where a varied menu of mainly French inspired cooking provides an interesting choice. A delicious pudding of fruit shortbread with Grand Marnier parfait has been praised

Menus: Fixed-price L & D, bar menu
Seats: 40.
Additional: Children welcome, children's menu; ❤ dishes, vegan/other diets on request
Directions: M40 exit 9 (Oxford) 2 mins, in village centre

WOODSTOCK, **Bear Hotel** ❀

Park Street OX20 1SZ
Map no: 4 SP41
Tel: 01993 811511
Chef: Ian Morgan
Proprietor: Forte Heritage.
Manager: Philip Barton
Cost: Fixed-price L £14.95 (2 course) £16.95/£18.50 Sun/D £25.95 H/wine £13.50 ❗ Service inc
Credit cards: 🔲 🔲 🔲 🔲 OTHER
Times: Last L 2.30pm, last D 10pm daily
Menus: Fixed-price L & D, bar menu
Seats: 90. No smoking in dining room
Additional: Children welcome, children's menu; ❤ dishes, vegan/other diets on request

A town centre hotel that has evolved gently from its 13th century origins. Historic resonances abound, with an ivy-clad exterior, and beamed ceilings within. The food is imaginative and well-presented. Look out for braised oxtail with root vegetables, confit of duck with Chinese spices, and roast pear with pistachio sauce

Directions: At end of High Street by the gates of Blenheim Palace

WOODSTOCK, **The Chef Imperial** ❀

22 High Street OX20 1TF
Map no: 4 SP41
Tel: 01993 813593
Chef: P C Wong
Proprietor: Alan Shek
Cost: Alc £15-£20, fixed-price L £7.50/D £15-£20. H/wine £8.50. Service exc
Credit cards: 🔲 🔲 🔲
Times: Last L 2.30pm, last D 11.59pm. Closed Dec 25-27

☺ *The only Chinese restaurant in Woodstock offers Peking and Szechuan cuisine, including a 'Leave-it-to-us Feast', for inexperienced visitors. A wide choice of dishes is available, from appetisers such as minced quails wrapped in lettuce, to fresh lobster, stir-fried with ginger and spring onions*

Menus: A la carte, fixed-price L & D
Seats: 100. Air conditioned. No-smoking area
Additional: Children welcome, ❤ menu, vegan/other diets on request
Directions: Town centre

WOODSTOCK, **Feathers Hotel** ❀❀

A lively range of interesting food that is based on sound ingredients is offered at this town centre hotel

There is a strong sense of individuality about the Feathers – a succession of town houses with winding staircases, low portals, and creaking sounds to boot. This is reflected in the large, wood-panelled restaurant, which is the focal point of the establishment. David Lewis has an open-minded approach and draws on locally supplied produce, and seasonal game from a nearby estate, for inspiration. The result is fresh tasting, well-cooked meals with a seasonal bias. Smoked salmon prepared in three ways, chargrilled, tartare and mousse, with alternatives such as duckling terrine with orange and pistachio, or goats' cheese and aubergine gâteau, then perhaps main courses of chargrilled tuna and scallops with soya and ginger, or a full-flavoured saddle of hare accompanied by a rich mini rösti and a purée of swede, are sound examples of the repertoire. Dessert could be white chocolate and ginger mousse with rhubarb, or blueberry tartlet with coconut ice-cream or a twice-baked chocolate soufflé with fresh strawberry compote.

Directions: Town centre

Market Street OX20 1SX
Map no: 4 SP41
Tel: 01993 812291
Chef: David Lewis
Proprietor: Tom Lewis
Cost: Alc £ 34.65, fixed-price Sun L £19.50 H/wine £10.75 ❢
Service exc
Credit cards: 🔳 🔳 🔳 🔳 OTHER
Times: Last L 2.30pm, last D 9.30pm
Menus: A la carte L & D, fixed-price Sun L, bar menu
Seats: 60. Air conditioned
Additional: Children welcome; children's portions/other diets on request

WOODSTOCK, **Marlborough Arms** ❀

☺ *A charming, welcoming hotel which offers some sound English dishes. There is a set menu plus a lengthy carte, offering the likes of poached salmon fillet with a creamy dill sauce, braised knuckle of gammon, cod and chips, bangers and mash and white onion sauce, and steamed sultana pudding and custard for dessert*

Menus: A la carte, fixed-price L & D, bar menu
Seats: 80.
Additional: Children welcome, children's portions; ❷ dishes, vegan on request, other diets with notice
Directions: Town centre

Oxford Street OX20 1TS
Map no: 4 SP41
Tel: 01993 811227
Chef: Patrick Crasby
Proprietor: Goldstream Ltd.
Manager: Mike Davis
Cost: Alc £15-£20, fixed-price L £9.95/D £13.95 H/wine £9.85
Service exc
Credit cards: 🔳 🔳 🔳 OTHER
Times: Last L 2pm, last D 10pm. Closed Sat L

DEDDINGTON, **Holcombe Hotel** ❀

A popular, friendly inn, built in the 17th century of Cotswold stone. The restaurant offers menus featuring both French and English cuisine. Our inspector enjoyed his starter of stuffed mushrooms, then baked haddock with chervil cream sauce and fresh raspberry trifle to finish

Seats: 50. No-smoking area
Additional: Children welcome; ❷ dishes, other diets on request
Directions: In village centre on A4260 by traffic lights

High Street OX15 0SL
Map no: 4 SP43
Tel: 01869 338274
Chef: Alan Marshall
Proprietors: Mr & Mrs C Mahfoudh
Cost: Alc £25, fixed-price L £14.50, £21.50/D £25.50. H/wine £10.50
Credit cards: 🔳 🔳 🔳 OTHER
Times: Last L 2.15pm, last D 10pm. Closed 1-12 Jan

'Brandade' is a speciality of Languedoc and Provence. In its basic form it is a purée of salt cod, olive oil and milk, but in the Toulon and Marseilles areas crushed garlic was added and this has become the standard recipe. Nowadays potato purée is also included. The word is derived from the Provençal verb 'brandar' meaning to stir.

SHROPSHIRE

BRIDGNORTH,
Haywain Restaurant ❀❀

☺ *Back with its original owner, and with a new chef, this smart restaurant is going from strength to strength*

This secluded cottage-style restaurant is tucked away near the River Severn. Its cosy charm and friendly welcome make it well worth the journey. New chef, Carl Withey, trained for several years in France. A fixed-price menu offers up to seven courses. There are five choices of main course with, for example, paupiette of sole, or salmon with artichokes. Rabbit, lamb and beef also feature. Our inspector started with a delicious thick nettle soup, followed by juicy rosettes of lamb served with a sharp but surprisingly complementary damson sauce, and a selection of fresh vegetables. An open glazed apple tart made a good finish, followed by a small cheese selection. There is also an extensive cold menu with a selection of salads, smoked and fresh meats, crab and various fish which has proved popular. The wide ranging wine list offers some forty bins.

Directions: 1 mile off A442 in village on river bank between Bridgnorth and Kidderminster

Hampton Loade WV15 6HD
Map no: 7 SO79
Tel: 01746 780404
Chef: Paul Lacey
Proprietor: David R Browning
Cost: Fixed-price D £15.50, £25 (7course)/Sun L £11.95 (5 course). H/wine £6.95 ❢
Service inc
Credit cards: 🔲 🔲 🔲 🔲
Times: Last D 9.30pm, last Sun L 2.30pm. Closed Sun D, Mon
Menus: Fixed-price D & Sun L
Seats: 50. No smoking in dining room
Additional: Children welcome, children's portions; ❶ dishes, vegan/other diets on request

CHURCH STRETTON,
Mynd House Hotel ❀

☺ *Set in a sleepy hamlet, the Mynd House Hotel is relaxed and friendly. The food is good too – a typical meal might include carrot soup, fillet of red bream, and apricot tartlets. Fixed price menus and an extensive wine list are also available*

Menus: A la carte D, fixed-price D
Seats: 12/30. No smoking in dining room
Additional: Children welcome; ❶ dishes, other diets on request
Directions: Village centre, 0.5 mile off A49 on B4370 (Little Stretton)

Little Stretton SY6 6RB
Map no: 7 SO49
Tel: 01694 722212
Chef: Janet Hill
Proprietors: Robert & Janet Hill
Cost: Alc £18.95, fixed-price D £25 (5 course) H/wine £8.50
Service inc
Credit cards: 🔲 🔲 🔲 OTHER
Times: 7.30pm-last D 9pm
Closed Jan, 2wks Summer

CLEOBURY MORTIMER,
Redfern Hotel ❀

☺ *A modern hotel offering reliable home cooking; bread is freshly made and there are the likes of duck liver salad, rack of lamb with a spinach crust, and bread and butter pudding, to make a satisfying meal. Hospitality is warm and welcoming and the atmosphere informal and relaxed*

Menus: A la carte, fixed price L & D, Sun lunch **Seats:** 30
Additional: Children welcome, children's menu; ❶ & vegan dishes, other diets on request
Directions: In Cleobury Mortimer on A4117 midway (11 miles) between Kidderminster and Ludlow

DY14 8AA
Map no: 7 SO67
Tel: 01299 270 395
Chef: Richard Redfern and Jamie Bailey
Proprietor: Jon Redfern
Cost: Alc £19.50, fixed-price L £4.95 (3courses), fixed-price D £15.95 (5 courses). H/wine £6.95 ❢ Service inc
Credit cards: 🔲 🔲 🔲 🔲 OTHER.
Times: Noon-last L 2pm, 7.30-last D 9.30pm

DORRINGTON,
Country Friends Restaurant ❀❀

A long-established village restaurant serving a small but balanced selection of modern eclectic cooking

A fine black and white timber-framed house, situated in lovely grounds in the middle of the village, is the setting for some cooking that is well on course. Pauline and Charles Whittaker run this as a family affair, she maintaining a presence out front, he in the kitchen. The short, but well-balanced menu is changed every six weeks or so, and from it diners may choose two, three or four courses at set-prices. Fresh fish features according to availability and, at lunchtime, a blackboard selection of lighter meals is offered. Sampled on recent visits were calves' liver accompanied by onions, bacon strips and Cassis sauce, a trio of smoked, marinated and roast salmon, slices of good-tasting duck breast on a bed of bean sprouts and other oriental vegetables, and succulent and 'perfectly flavoured' fillet steak. Puddings include vanilla bavarois with a strawberry coulis, a rich trio of chocolates and even Welsh rarebit. All this, together with the savoury quiche tartlets served with pre-dinner drinks in the lounge, and the strong coffee and petits fours afterwards, made for pleasant experiences. The wine list lacks descriptions, but there is a decent selection of half bottles.

Directions: On A49 in centre of village

Shrewsbury SY5 7JD
Map no: 7 SJ40
Tel: 01743 718707
Chef: Charles Whittaker
Proprietors: Charles & Pauline Whittaker
Cost: Fixed-price L & D £21.50 (2 courses), £24.85. H/wine £9.50 Service exc
Credit cards: 🔳 🔳 🔳 OTHER
Times: Last L 2pm, last D 9pm. Closed Sun except last Sun in month, Mon, 2 weeks Jul
Menus: Fixed-price L & D, bar men
Seats: 40. No smoking in dining room
Additional: Children welcome; ❂ dish; other diets on request

LUDLOW, **Dinham Hall Hotel** ❀

☺ *A Georgian town house close to Ludlow Castle is the setting for a daily-changing, fixed-price, four-course menu. A superb rack of lamb in a port wine jus was the highlight of a recent inspection meal. Look out for a smooth mango and coconut crème brûlée for dessert*

By the Castle SY8 1EJ
Map no: 7 SO57
Tel: 01584 876464
Chef: Scott Dickson
Proprietor: J P Mifsud
Cost: Alc £14 (2 course), fixed-price D £19.50 (4 course). H/wine £ 10.50 Service exc
Credit cards: 🔳 🔳 🔳 ⯒ OTHER
Times: Last L 2pm, last D 9.15pm daily
Menus: A la carte L, fixed-price D & Sun L
Seats: 30. No smoking in dining room
Additional: Children welcome, children's portions; ❂ dishes, vegan/other diets on request

Directions: Town centre, off Market Place, by the Castle

LUDLOW, **The Feathers at Ludlow** ❀

A reasonable standard of cooking is to be had in the restaurant of this impressive timber-framed inn dating from the 17th century. Typical dishes might include mushroom and white wine soup, pan-fried duck breast with redcurrent and sage sauce, and strawberry mousse for dessert

Menus: *A la carte*, fixed-price L & D, bar menu
Seats: 60. Air conditioned. No smoking in dining room
Additional: Children welcome, children's portions; ❂ dishes, other diets on request
Directions: Town centre

Bull Ring SY8 1AA
Map no: 7 SO57
Tel: 01584 875261
Chef: Philip Woodhall
Proprietor: O Edwards.
Managers: Mr & Mrs Peter Nash
Cost: Alc £24, fixed-price L £13/D £ 19.50 (4 course)
H/wine £9 ❗ Service exc
Credit cards: 🔲 🔲 🔲 🔲 OTHER
Times: Last L 2pm, last D 9pm daily

LUDLOW,
The Merchant House ❀❀❀

☺ *Small-town restaurant where Shaun Hill concentrates on doing what he most enjoys – cooking*

62 Lower Corve Street
Map no: 7 SO57
Tel: 01584 875438
Chef: Shaun Hill
Proprietors: Shaun & Anja Hill
Cost: Fixed-price D £ 25.
H/wine £11.50 Service inc
Credit cards: 🔲 🔲 🔲 OTHER
Times: Last L 2.30pm, last D 9.30pm. Closed Sun, Mon, 1 wk summer & winter
Menus: Fixed-price L & D
Seats: 24. No smoking in dining room
Additional: Children permitted

Drawn to the attractive, historical town of Ludlow, simply because he liked it, celebrated chef/patron Shaun Hill has made an instant hit locally with the honesty and quality of his style of cooking. It is certainly a major move from the rarefied air of Gidleigh Park to the more humble, homely surroundings of The Merchant House, but at least it's a place to call his own. At the time, his decision was regarded a bit like the other Mr Hill announcing he was to become a bus driver, but it's the sort of move many a high-pressured, high-profile chef would love to have the courage to make.

Converted from a private house in a quiet street, the little two-room restaurant has exposed timbers, freshly painted white plaster walls and some interesting, if rather gloomy, oil-paintings. The menu is short and sweet; three choices at each course means being able to cope alone in the kitchen, buying daily from local markets. The style is simpler, but still direct and robust in flavour. On the night our inspector visited, the mood was Mediterranean, with a starter of grilled red mullet with ginger, garlic and tomato setting the tone. Saddle of wild boar with dill is a favourite Hill combination; vegetables, such as broad beans, peas, asparagus, salsisfy and spinach strewn rather than surgically arranged around the plate. Other choices might have been calves' sweetbreads and kidneys with a potato and olive cake, or roast corn-fed pigeon with

fresh goats' cheese gnocchi. Puddings are first-class with a raspberry crème brûlée matching all expectations. The service is friendly and relaxed, led by Anja Hill and local ladies. The wine list offers a good choice at realistic prices.

Directions: Town centre next to Unicorn pub

LUDLOW, Oaks ✿✿

In the relaxed atmosphere of this oak-panelled restaurant you can enjoy a well produced and varied selection of modern English dishes

Well positioned at the lower end of this bustling little market town, Oaks forms part of an impressive seventeenth-century building which retains such original features as the oak panelling from which the restaurant derives its name. A friendly, relaxed atmosphere prevails, particularly in the small lounge bar where Mrs Adams chats cheerfully to customers as she hands out menus and serves a delicious range of canapés which includes skewered pork and an interesting selection of sushi. Her husband, meanwhile, is busy in the kitchen, engaged in the preparation of a varied *carte* of modern English dishes firmly based on seafood and good local produce. A first course of pan-fried monkfish tails with squid and a bouillabaisse sauce – served with absolutely delicious, warm, home-made bread made from locally-ground organic flour – was followed by delicately home-smoked loin of spring lamb with a sweet rosemary sauce, but an alternative main course might have been chosen from a daily-changing fish menu which includes (subject to market availability) sea bass, hake and halibut. Service is relaxed, and the value-for-money wine list offers a fair number of half bottles.

Directions: 2 mins from town centre, opposite old livestock market

17 Carve Street
Map no: 7 SO57
Tel: 01584 872325
Chef: Ken Adams
Proprietor: Ken Adams
Cost: *Alc* £22, fixed-price Sun L £12.50. H/wine £10 Service exc
Credit cards: 🔲 🔲
Times: Last D 10pm. Closed Mon, 2 wks Feb
Menus: *A la carte*, fixed-price Sun L
Seats: 30. No smoking in dining room
Additional: Children permitted, children's portions; ♥ dishes, vegan/other diets on request

MARKET DRAYTON, Goldstone Hall ✿✿

☺ *A fine 17th-century country house hotel which was for many years the seat of Shropshire squires*

Set in impressive gardens and mature woodland, just off the A529 Goldstone Hall is a jewel of Tudor architecture. Beams, exposed timbers and open fires abound and many rooms have original panelled walls. The Hall also has good facilities for business meetings and for functions. Chef Simon Smith had only started a few days prior to our inspection, but looks set to push high standards even higher. The daily changing *carte* is short but uses fresh produce as it comes available. Our inspector enjoyed a fresh home made roll with a balanced starter of sauté new potatoes, artichoke pieces and mushrooms with a few crisp salad leaves. The poached salmon which followed was firm with a subtle, delicate taste and was accompanied by an imaginative sauce of samphire and basil. Though the side dish of vegetables was disappointingly dull, standards reasserted themselves with dessert – a dark and white chocolate mousse with an attractively presented dark and white chocolate sauce.

Directions: From A529 4 miles S of Market Drayton, follow signs for Goldstone Hall Gardens

Goldstone TF9 2NA
Map no: 7 SJ63
Tel: 01630 661202
Chef: Simon Smith
Proprietors: John Cushing and Helen Ward
Cost: *Alc* £19.50, fixed-price L £15.45. H/wine £8.95 ♥ Service inc
Credit cards: 🔲 🔲 🔲 🔲 OTHER
Times: Last L 2.30pm, last D 10.30pm daily
Menus: *A la carte*, fixed-price L
Seats: 60. No smoking in dining room
Additional: Children permitted, children's portions; ♥ dishes, vegan/other diets on request

NORTON, **Hundred House Hotel**

The bustling restaurant of this creeper-clad Georgian inn serves a good selection of quality cooking. An inspection on St David's Day produced some well-cooked traditional Welsh dishes; food on the regular carte may include fish soup with croûtons and saffron rouille, and home-cured breast of duck on a bed of chive potatoes

Shifnal TF11 9EE
Map no: 7 SJ70
Tel: 01952 730353
Chef: Stuart Philips
Proprietors: Henry Silvia, David & Stuart Phillips
Cost: Alc £20-£27, fixed-price Sun L £13.95. H/wine £1.55 glass ! Service exc
Credit cards: ▨ ▨ ▨ OTHER
Times: Last L 2.30pm, last D 10pm daily
Menus: A la carte, fixed-price Sun L, bar menu
Seats: 60.
Additional: Children welcome, children's portions (& bar menu); ✆ dishes

Directions: On A 442 midway between Telford and Bridgnorth

OSWESTRY, **Wynnstay** ▨▨

Elegant surroundings, professional service and imaginative cooking in modern style make a meal here something to remember

Well positioned at the centre of the historic market town, this long established hotel – a Georgian house with its own 200-year-old crown bowling green – features the elegant Camellia Restaurant where chef Les Simpson's skills are matched by attentive professional service. A successful summer meal began with a deliciously creamy salmon terrine wrapped in thin slices of smoked salmon and accompanied by home-made horseradish mayonnaise. An intermediate course of distinctively flavoured watercress soup then preceded the main course – a very tender cannon of lamb encased in light filo pastry and served on a bed of celeriac purée with a mint beurre blanc. This proved extremely successful, though both poached codling with tomato hollandaise and a selection from sea bass, brill, scallops and monkfish with a saffron rice timbale looked equally tempting. There is also a good choice of desserts, the menu ranging from home-made apple pie to a rich, creamy crème brûlée. The wine list is fun and offers a short selection of popular wines.

Church Street SY11 2SZ
Map no: 7 SJ33
Tel: 01691 655261
Chef: Les Simpson
Proprietor: B Woodward
Cost: Alc £35, fixed-price L £12.50, £15/D £15.95, £17.95. Service exc
Credit cards: ▨ ▨ ▨ ▨ OTHER
Times: Last D 9.30pm
Menus: A la carte, fixed-price L & D
Additional: ✆ dishes

Directions: In centre of town, opposite church

> Celeriac is a variety of celery grown for its bulbous whitish root. It is sold without leaves and resembles a white, heavy ball which can weigh as much as 1kg. It is available from mid-September to the end of April, but is at its best in autumn.

SHIFNAL, **Park House** ❀

Situated in spacious grounds and offering elegant public areas with high ceilings and chandeliers, this hotel still bears signs of its 17th-century origins as two country houses. Here one might enjoy such modern dishes as mousseline-coated smoked salmon served with an avocado and white wine fish sauce

Menus: *A la carte,* fixed-price L & D
Directions: Junction 4 of M54, through Shifnal, take right-hand fork at small roundabout, follow road round Park House on left

Park Street TF11 9BA
Map no: 7 SJ71
Tel: 01952 460128
Chef:
Proprietor: MacDonald Hotels
Cost: *Alc* £30, fixed-price L £9.50, £11/D £16. Service exc
Credit cards: ◼ ▦ ▩ ▨ OTHER
Times: Last D 10.30pm

SHREWSBURY,
Albright Hussey Hotel ❀❀

Atmospheric hotel with an ancient pedigree noted for cooking that is bang up-to-date

The black and white timbered building dates from Tudor times; the red brick extension was added at the beginning of the 17th century. This is an atmospheric hotel, set in landscaped gardens with an original moat crossed by a stone bridge. Within, there is a wealth of oak panelling, with beams and huge open fireplaces. The French *carte* with English subtitles offers a good choice. A duet of home-made pasta with mixed seafood infused with fresh tomatoes and basil jus, or a light rock fish soup flavoured with saffron and Gruyère cheese might precede chicken breast filled with ham and walnut mousse served on a Jacqueline sauce, or boned honey glazed duck roasted and served on a casserole of warm lentils with a tangerine and Armagnac sauce. For dessert, passion fruit soufflé served with a warm fruit coulis and langue de chat biscuit, or a hot apple flan served on a praline anglaise with cinnamon and Calvados ice-cream show the range. The wine list majors in French, but other European and New World wines get a showing. There is a short but reasonably priced selection of half bottles.

Directions: On A528 (Wem) 2 miles from centre of Shrewsbury

Ellesmere Road SY4 3AF
Map no: 7 SJ41
Tel: Bomere Heath 01939 290571/290523
Chefs: Nigel Huxley and Nick Shingles
Proprietor: Franco Subbiani
Cost: *Alc* from £22.50, fixed-price L £12.50/D £22.50 (5 course). H/wine £9.50 ❗ Service exc
Credit cards: ◼ ▦ ▩ ▨ OTHER
Times: Last L 2.15pm, last D 10.15pm
Menu: *A la carte,* fixed-price L & D
Seats: 94. No smoking requested
Additional: Children welcome, children's portions; ✿ menu, vegan/other diets on request

TELFORD, **Holiday Inn** ✤

An eclectic mix of dishes appears at the hotel's Courts Restaurant with both Japanese and healthy eating appearing on the carte. Expect scallop-flavoured broth with courgette and straw mushrooms, steamed sea bass on continental parsley garnished with Japanese ginger and seaweed, and sticky toffee meringue

Menus: *A la carte*, fixed-price L & D, bar menu
Seats: 100. No smoking area
Additional: Children welcome, children's menu; ❤ dishes, other diets on request
Directions: M54 exit 4 follow signs town centre until Hotel sign

St Quentin Gate TF3 4EH
Map no: 7 SJ60
Tel: 01952 292500
Chef: John MitchelL
Manager: James Ford (Holiday Inn)
Cost: *Alc* £18/19, fixed-price L £10.95/D £15.95 H/wine £8.75 Service inc
Credit cards: 🔳 🔳 🔳 🔳 OTHER
Times: Last L 3pm, last D 10pm daily

TELFORD, **Madeley Court Hotel** ✤✤

An impressive manor house of Elizabethan origins, in a lakeside setting, with an interesting selection of dishes

Map no 7 SJ60
Tel: 01952 680068
Chef: Paul Davies-Clarkson
Credit cards: 🔳 🔳 🔳 🔳
Additional: Children welcome, ❤ dishes.

Open fires, panelled walls and a marvellous, spiral oak staircase set the scene in the sympathetically restored Grade I listed Elizabethan manor house. The great hall, now the main restaurant, is much older, dating back to the 13th century. Chef Paul Davis-Clarkson produces short, regularly changing menus and is not afraid to roam the world picking up such ideas as banana and curry soup accompanied by miniature poppadoms. A recent meal produced a delicious, tender shank of lamb garnished with shallots and fresh herbs and good, fresh vegetables. Desserts are mostly fruit-based, and work well with the likes of caramel mousse and poached fruits. There is also a decent selection of fine traditional cheeses. Canapes, bread and coffee all show attention to small details. The Brasserie in the undercroft is ideal for more informal dining. In both places smartly uniformed staff provide friendly and attentive service, very much in keeping with the style of the place.

Directions: Take A442 towards Kidderminster, continue into single carriageway, turn left at roundabout with ornamental mine shaft

WORFIELD, **Old Vicarage Hotel** ❀❀❀

A talented young chef demonstrating his skills in a pleasant corner of Shropshire

Worfield WV15 5JZ
Map no: 7 SO79
Tel: 01746 716497
Chef: John Williams
Proprietor: Peter Iles
Cost: Fixed-price D Mon-Thu £21.50/Fri-Sat £26.50, Sun L £13.50 H/wine £12 ❢ Service exc
Credit cards: 🔲 🔲 🔲 🔲
Times: Last L 2pm, last D 9pm. Closed Sat lunch
Seats: 50. No-smoking area
Menus: Fixed-price D & Sun L
Additional: Children permitted (not under 8 at dinner), children's menu; ✿ dishes, vegan/other diets on request

A converted country parsonage in an attractive corner of Shropshire is the setting for the fine cooking of John Williams. He has settled in well and his frequently-changing fixed-price menus are enhanced by the realistic evidence of the judicious use of the freshest possible ingredients. Produce from the local countryside features strongly, with glazed cannon of new season's lamb with spring onion mash and thyme scented jus and glazed sirloin of Hereford beef with tomato fondue and crispy celeriac. Fish is there, too, perhaps a duo of Cornish mullet with buttered leeks and wild mushroom and chive butter sauce, and there is always a serious vegetarian offering which might include fine tart of creamed leeks, wild mushrooms and goats' cheese.

A recent meal began with a light seafood sausage served on mixed leaves with a simple cream and chive sauce which had quite a sharp kick to it. Glazed suprême of chicken, stuffed with a tarragon mousse with wild mushrooms, was well-prepared and presented but the predominant flavour of the mousse was more of Stilton than tarragon. The vegetables were brightly coloured and clearly garden fresh, with a decent carrot purée and skilfully-made dauphinoise potato. Puddings are interesting with choices like poppy seed and Bushmills whiskey parfait with coffee ice-cream and caramel sauce, or marmalade sponge pudding with whipped cream and fresh mint anglaise; the sampled classic lemon torte was highly praised. The cheese board, which is offered as an additional course, is stunning, with a good selection of traditional and new hand-made British farmhouse cheeses including Teifi, a gouda-type cheese with mustard seed, and St Illtyd, a cheddar cheese blended with Welsh wine, garlic and herbs. The wine list covers the main growing regions, and there is an exceptionally good selection of halves.

Directions: From Wolverhampton take A454 Bridgnorth road, from M54 exit 4 take A442 towards Kidderminster

SOMERSET

AXBRIDGE, **The Oak House Hotel** ❀

☺ *Honest English dishes are prepared from quality produce at this village-centre hotel. Fresh textures and flavours are retained in dishes such as garlic mushrooms stuffed with fresh crab meat, tenderloin of pork cooked in Somerset cider, and home-made bread and butter pudding with custard*

The Square BS26 2AP
Map no: 3 ST45
Tel: 01934 732444
Chef: Martin Ball
Proprietors: Peter & Pat Cook
Cost: Fixed-price L /D £13.50
H/wine £6.75 Service exc
Credit cards: ▨ ▩ ▩
Times: Last L 2.15pm, last D 9.15pm daily
Menus: Fixed-price L & D, bistro menu
Seats: 60. No smoking area
Additional: Children (not under 10) permitted, children's portions; ✿ dishes, vegan/other diets on request

Directions: On east side of town square, 2 miles W of Cheddar on A371

BECKINGTON, **Woolpack Inn** ❀❀

A delightful village inn with a friendly atmosphere and a solid reputation for good food

The Woolpack Inn continues to offer high standards of comfort and cooking. Set in the heart of Beckington, a delightful village on the borders of Somerset, Avon and Wiltshire, this is a relaxed, informal 16th-century coaching-inn, with an attractive, flagstoned bar area, an ingelnook fireplace and various 'cosy' dining areas. The *carte*, which changes throughout the year, offers an interesting choice and is supported by a selection of blackboard specials, including fresh fish. Chef David Woolfall has a light touch and is a stickler for well prepared dishes. An inspector was impressed by a 'faultless' cheese and broccoli souffle, and by the gently steamed fillet of fresh halibut which was served with a Provençale sauce. Puddings might include treacle and apple tart, served with lashings of clotted cream. The wine list is comprehensive with good descriptions. Proprietors Martin Tarr and Paul Toogood maintain a strong presence and genuinely enjoy the company of their guests.

Near Bath BA3 6SP
Map no: 3 ST85
Tel: 01373 831244
Chef: David Woolfall
Proprietors: Martin E W Tarr and Paul A Toogood
Cost: *Alc* £22-£28. H/wine £8.50 ❗ Service exc
Credit cards: ▨ ▩ OTHER
Times: Last L 2pm, last D 10pm/9pm Sun
Menus: *A la carte* L & D, bar menu
Seats: 60. No smoking area
Additional: Children welcome, children's portions; ✿ dishes, vegan/other diets on request

Directions: Village centre, just off A36 near junction with A361

Ossetra caviar has small, even eggs of a golden yellow to brown colour, and it is quite oily. But it is considered by many to be the best.

BRUTON, Truffles Restaurant ✤✤

An intimate restaurant with open beams, a cosy air and in the winter a roaring log fire

Having gathered a wealth of experience in larger establishments, Denise and Martin Bottrill moved here eight years ago and have never looked back. The fixed-price menu changes monthly and offers a choice of five dishes for each course. An inspection in May revealed a delicate starter of guinea fowl and mushroom terrine but with an over dominant ratatouille chutney. A more subtle choice would be the filo basket filled with softly scrambled eggs with finely diced smoked salmon served with a smooth butter sauce and chives. The main course of crisp breast of duck cut by brandy flavoured jus and fresh stoned halved cherries was happily devoured. Garlicky sauté new potatoes with chopped parsley, seared courgette and aubergine and crunchy mange tout, accompanied. The wine list includes a wide half bottle selection and dessert wines are available by the glass. A midweek supper menu offers excellent value.

95 High Street BA10 0AR
Map no: 3 ST63
Tel: 01749 812255
Chef: Martin Bottrill
Proprietors: Denise & Martin Bottrill
Cost: Fixed-price L £13.50/D £20.95 H/wine £8.50 ❢ Service exc
Credit cards: ▨ ▨ OTHER
Times: Last L 2pm, last D 9.30pm Closed Sun D, Mon
Menus: Fixed-price L & D
Seats: 20. Smoking discouraged
Additional: Children over 5 welcome, children's portions; ✿ menu, other diets on request

Directions: Bruton centre, at start of one-way system, on left

CASTLE CARY, George Hotel ✤

An archetypal English inn dating from the 15th century with an attractive panelled restaurant overlooking the town's market place. Local produce features on the menu; look out for locally reared Barrow boar, a popular dish. Otherwise, chicken liver parfait, escalope of pork with sweet apple and sage sauce show the range

Market Place BA7 7AH
Map no: 3 SY63
Tel: 01963 350761
Chef: Martin J Barrett
Proprietors: Mrs Sparkes

Directions: Off A371, in centre of town

DULVERTON, Ashwick House Hotel ✤

Built in 1901, this attractive Edwardian house stands in six acres of grounds above the Barle valley. Fresh local ingredients are used in dishes such as mushroom and coriander soup, smoked fish soufflé and fillet of pork with spinach and sorrel. A choice of starters and sweets are available on the otherwise set menu

Dulverton TA22 9QD
Map no: 3 SS92
Tel: 01398 23868
Chef: R Sherwood
Proprietor: R Sherwood
Cost: Fixed-price D £22.75. H/wine £10. Service exc
Credit cards: None taken
Times: Last D 8.30pm, last Sun L 1.45pm
Menus: Fixed-price D & Sun L
Seats: 35. No-smoking in dining room
Additional: Children permitted (over 8 at D); other diets with prior notice

Directions: Off B3223 Lynton road, turn left after second cattle grid

DUNSTER, **Exmoor House Hotel** ✤

☺ *A quaint and cosy family-run hotel which has a charming, homely atmosphere. The evening meal is served in the candlelit dining-room. The short menu offers simple, well cooked wholesome meals such as apple and parsnip soup followed perhaps by lamb in apricot sauce*

Menu: Fixed-price D **Seats:** 24. Exclusively non-smoking
Additional: No children under 12; children's portions; ♥ dishes; other diets on request
Directions: To Dunster on A396, off High Street, 75 yds from church

12 West Street TA24 6SN
Map no: 3 SS94
Tel: 01643 821268
Chef: Phyl Lally
Proprietors: Brendan Lally
Cost: Fixed-price D £15
(4 course). H/wine £7.90.
Service inc
Credit cards: 🂠 💳 💳 💳 OTHER
Times: Last D 8pm. Closed Nov-Jan

EXEBRIDGE, **Anchor Inn Hotel** ✤

☺ *A small village inn overlooking the River Exe which has strong rustic appeal. Local ingredients are used to create decent food that has an old fashioned ring to it. Salmon steak with Pernod sauce, or scampi Thermidor, are typical dishes, followed by a home-made pudding. Generous portions are appreciated*

Menus: A la carte, fixed-price D, bar menu **Seats:** 35. No-smoking area **Additional:** Children welcome (until 7pm), children's menu; ♥ dishes, other diets on request
Directions: M5 exit 27, through Tiverton to Exebridge

Dulverton TA22 9AZ
Map no: 3 SS92
Tel: 01398 23433
Chef: David Lynn
Proprietors: John & Judy Phripp
Cost: Alc £11.95, fixed-price D £18.95 (4 course) H/wine £6.95
Service exc
Credit cards: 🂠
Times: Last L 2pm, last D 9.30pm daily

EXFORD, **Crown Hotel** ✤✤

☺ *A new chef brings flair and imagination to a hotel restaurant in the middle of Exmoor*

Park Street TA247PP
Map no: 3 SS83
Tel: 01643 831554
Chef: Simon Whiteley
Proprietor: Michael Bradley
Cost: Fixed-price D £ 22/Sun L £15. H/wine £9.75 ❢ Service exc
Credit cards: 🂠 💳 💳 OTHER
Times: Last D 9.30pm, last Sun L 2pm
Menus: Fixed-price D & Sun L, bar menu
Seats: 32. No smoking area
Additional: Children welcome, children's portions; ♥ dishes, vegan/other diets on request

Recent refurbishment has turned the Crown into a comfortable hotel and it is a well-deserved new entry. Recent inspections have praised the terrine of Cornish crab, or better still, a bright brochette of baby tuna, moist, freshly flavoured with pancetta, with braised young leeks and a good ginger dressing. Such imaginative flourishes made a lively impression, and were followed through with sea-bass roasted with chicken juices, and thinly sliced fillet of venison, cooked pink, with a richness of flavour, a red wine reduction and a subtle quince mousseline with a dash of bitter chocolate. An accompanying celeriac pear and currant gratin added to the dish. The flair and ambition at work is obvious. Tempting, rich

puddings might include tangy, robust lemon tart with raspberry coulis; alternatively, there is a decent cheese board to explore.

Directions: Village centre facing the green

HOLFORD, Combe House Hotel ❁

☺ *A traditional country house hotel set amid the Quantock Hills is, surprisingly, a converted tannery, complete with water wheel. A short, but imaginative menu offers the likes of pan-fried Barbary duck, or lambs' sweetbread with a brandy, Madeira, and cream sauce. The home-made puddings are highly recommended*

Menus: Fixed-price D, Bar L menu
Seats: 40. No smoking in dining room **Additional:** Children welcome, children's portions; other diets on request
Directions: 0.5 mile from A39, turn up lane between garage & Plough Inn, then left at fork to Holford Combe

Bridgwater TA5 1RZ
Map no: 3 ST14
Tel: 01278 741382
Chef: Lynn Gardner
Proprietor: Richard Bjergfelt
Cost: Fixed-price D £ 15.75
(4 course). H/wine £7.50
Service exc
Credit cards: ■ ■ ■
Times: Last Bar L 2.30pm, last D 8.30pm Closed Nov 1-mid Mar

MINEHEAD, Periton Park Hotel ❁❁

☺ *A little gem of comfort and tranquillity offering attractive seasonal menus with good choices*

Neatly tucked away on the edge of Exmoor National Park, this building dates from 1875 and still retains a 19th-century air, despite modern facilities such as a helicopter pad. The Hunts share the cooking, although Angela takes the leading role for dinner with her series of seasonal three-course set menus using the best local produce available. From our inspection reports, smooth, smoked mackerel, trout and salmon terrine, fillet of sea bream with a coriander and olive oil dressing, moist, pan-fried medallions of Exmoor venison and local Gressingham duck with a delicate Cointreau-laced sauce, have all stood out. Aubergine galette – layers of aubergine, tomato, onion and ricotta cheese, with a tomato and herb sauce – has also been commended. Rich, home-made puddings include lemon tart with fresh cream and Marsala-soaked trifle with raspberry jam. If you prefer, coffee can be taken in the book-lined drawing room in front of the log fire. Bagborough wine from the nearby Quantocks appears on the reasonably priced, descriptive wine list.

Directions: Off A39 signposted Porlock & Lynmouth. Hotel about 1 mile on left

Middlecombe TA24 8SW
Map no: 3 SS94
Tel: 01643 706885
Chef: Angela Hunt
Proprietors: Angela & Richard Hunt (Logis of GB)
Cost: Fixed-price D £20. H/wine £8.25. Service inc
Credit cards: ■ ■ ■ OTHER
Times: 7pm-last D 9pm
Menus: A la carte, fixed-price D
Seats: 24. No smoking in dining room
Additional: Children over 12 permitted; ♥ dishes, other diets prior notice

MONTACUTE, Kings Arms Inn Hotel ❁

☺ *A 16th century building, constructed in traditional Ham stone, which has mellowed well over the years. In contrast, the elegant dining room offers guests a modern and innovative menu where choice may include pan-fried calves liver with onion marmalade or asparagus, goats' cheese and mushroom strudel*

Menus: A la carte L & D, bar menu **Seats:** 22. No smoking in dining room **Additional:** Children welcome, children's portions; ♥ dishes, other diets on request
Directions: Just off A303 via A3088 ; in village centre, next to church

Bishopston TA15 6UU
Map no: 3 ST41
Tel: 01935 822513
Chef: Graham Page
Proprietors: Karen & Jonathan Arthur
Cost: Alc £19. H/wine £8 ❢
Service exc
Credit cards: ■ ■ ■
Times: Midday-last L 2pm, 7pm-last D 9.30pm. Closed 25-26 Dec

MONTACUTE, The Milk House ❀❀

Emphasis on organic food at relaxed restaurant in picture-book village

Ethical considerations aside, the use of organic produce also results in food with a good, clean, natural flavour. At The Milk House, vegetables are garden-fresh, the wine list has a strong organic section, and the menu shows a conscience when it comes to ingredients such as pork, guinea fowl and fish. Pre-dinner drinks and coffee are served in the two lounges, one of which has a blazing log fire and deep armchairs, whilst the other is set aside for smokers. The dining-room of the 15th-century building is furnished with antiques, but is nonetheless informal and relaxing. There are two vegetarian main courses, one of which will be suitable for vegans. Non-dairy spreads and soya cream are available on request. The style of Lee Dufton's cooking is mainly, but not exclusively, French provincial; starters may include warm goats' cheese salad, smoked salmon roulé or marinated mushrooms, followed by breast of Barbary duck with sweet and sour red cabbage, pine nut fricadelle with fennel sauce or the fish dish of the day. It's as easy to sin on the puddings here as anywhere else, especially when they include chocolate and chestnut mousse-cake and sticky toffee pudding.

Directions: Follow National Trust signs to Montacute House – in the square opposite

The Borough TA15 6XB
Map no: 3 ST41
Tel: 01935 823823
Chef: Lee (Elizabeth) Dufton
Proprietors: Lee & Bill Dufton
Cost: *Alc* £25, fixed-price D £22 /Sun L £12.50 H/wine £9.50 ❗
Service inc
Credit cards: ▨ ▨
Times: 7.30pm-11.30pm Sun L Summer only Closed Mon, Tue, 2 wks Xmas & Summer
Menus: *A la carte*, fixed-price D & Sun L in Summer
Seats: 30. No smoking in dining room
Additional: Children welcome (not Babies), children's portions; ❷ dishes, vegan/other diets on request

NUNNEY, The George at Nunney ❀

Situated in the centre of this ancient Saxon village, the 17th-century hotel has a relaxed atmosphere created by a friendly team of local staff. Imaginative combinations of flavours and textures feature in the cooking, which may include such dishes as flamed lambs' kidneys, and Somerset meat loaf with a rich onion gravy

Menus: *A la carte*, fixed-price L & D, bar menu
Seats: 50.
Additional: Children welcome until 8pm, children's portions; ❷ dishes, vegan/other diets on request
Directions: A361 Frome–Shepton Mallet – 0.25 mile N, opposite medieval castle

11 Church Street BA11 4LW
Map no: 3 ST74
Tel: 01373 836458
Chefs: Caroline Filder, Mark Humphreys and Andrew Smith
Proprietor: David & Majorie Page
Cost: *Alc* £16, fixed-price L £6.95/D £ 12.50 H/wine £8 ❗
Service exc
Credit cards: ▨ ▨
Times: Last L 2.15pm, last D 10pm daily

PORLOCK, The Oaks Hotel ❀

Standing overlooking the pretty village of Porlock, this elegant Edwardian house serves good quality food in a relaxed atmosphere. The four-course menu offers selections such as cream of watercress soup, monkfish with lime and ginger, tenderloin of pork stuffed with mushrooms and walnuts, and sherry trifle

Menu: Fixed-price D
Seats: 24. No smoking in dining room
Additional: Children over 8 permitted, children's portions; other diets on request
Directions: From Minehead, as you enter Porlock, at the bottom of Dunstersteepe Road on the left

Doverhay TA24 8ES
Map no: 3 SS84
Tel: 01643 862265
Chef: Anne Riley
Proprietor: Tim Riley
Cost: Fixed-price D £22 (4 course). H/wine £8.50 Service inc
Credit cards: ▨ ▨ ▨ OTHER
Times: 7pm-last D 8.30pm. Closed Jan & Feb

SHEPTON MALLET,
Bowlish House Restaurant ❀

An intimate restaurant, personally-run by a husband and wife team, offering quality cooking in the modern British style. A typical meal might start with spinach soufflé in a tomato sauce, followed by honey-glazed duck breast on a strawberry and pink peppercorn sauce, with an apricot and kirsch crème to finish

Menus: Fixed-price D & monthly Sun L
Seats: 24. No smoking area
Additional: Children welcome; ❶ dishes, children's portions/vegan/other diets on request
Directions: 0.25 mile from town centre on A371 Wells road

Bowlish BA4 5JD
Map no: 3 ST64
Tel: 01749 342022
Chef: Linda Morley
Proprietor: Bob Morley
Cost: Fixed-price D £ 22.50.
H/wine £8.95 ❗ Service exc
Credit cards: 💳 💳 💳
Times: Last D 9.30pm , last Sun L 1.30pm Closed Sun L except 1st Sun of month, 1 wk Autumn & Winter

---

SHEPTON MALLET, Shrubbery Hotel ❀

☺ *Town centre hotel with a cosy restaurant. A varied choice of dishes in the two or three course, set menu may include mushrooms with butter and mustard sauce, rack of lamb with rosemary gravy, and orange and Cointreau gateau. On the whole dishes are soundly cooked, but seasoning can sometimes be heavy-handed*

Seats: Restaurant 36, Bistro 40. No smoking in dining room
Additional: Children welcome, children's menu/portions; ❶ menu; other diets on request; live entertainment
Directions: On main A361 through town, next to police station

Commercial Road BA4 5BU
Map no: 3 ST64
Tel: 01749 346671
Chefs: Jon Dors, Stephanie Ward and Hamish Curwen-Reed
Proprietors: Stephanie Ward and Hamish Curwen-Reed
Cost: *Alc* £16.50, fixed-price D £10.95. H/wine £7.50 ❗ Service exc
Credit cards: 💳 💳 OTHER
Times: Last L 2.15pm, last D 10pm

SHIPHAM,
Daneswood House Hotel ❀❀

☺ *Impressive Edwardian country house with breathtaking views over the Bristol Channel*

Cuck Hill BS25 1RD
Map no: 3 ST45
Tel: 01934 843145
Chefs: John Dawson and Elise Hodges
Proprietors: David & Elise Hodges
Cost: Fixed-price L/D £22.95. H/wine £8.95 Service inc
Credit cards: 💳 💳 💳 💳 OTHER
Times: Last L 2pm, last D 9.30pm Closed Sun D
Menus: Fixed-price L & D
Seats: 45. Smoking area
Additional: Children welcome, children's portions; ❶ dishes, vegan/other diets on request

Owners David and Elise Hodges have made many improvements over the years to this delightful hotel while retaining many original features. The bedrooms are individually decorated and visitors would particularly like the cottage suites which have a spacious sitting-room and bathroom on the ground floor with the bedroom above. The fixed-price menu changes daily and might offer piping hot cream of vegetable soup with chunky vegetables and croûtons. Medallions of locally reared wild boar can be enjoyed as a main course and though at inspection it arrived slightly pink, it had a robust flavour served with a neatly complementing Madeira sauce. The French and English menu offers an eclectic mix which might include roast rack of lamb with a fresh herb crust scented with garlic and lemon grass or papillote of perch, cooked in foil with strips of peppers, root vegetables and white wine. There is also a reasonable vegetarian selection. The wine list offers a predominantly European choice.

Directions: On A38 Bristol/Bridgwater, just outside the village

SIMONSBATH,
Simonsbath House Hotel ❀

☺ *A 17th-century house, set in the wilds of Exmoor, is the background for some imaginative cooking. A short menu is served, the choice of dishes based on fresh local ingredients. Look out for courgette and dill soup, beef medallions with shallot, mustard and beer sauce, and rich chocolate mousse*

Menu: Fixed-price D
Seats: 26. No-smoking in dining room
Additional: Children over 10 permitted; other diets on request
Directions: Situated on B3223 in the village

Minehead TA24 7SH
Map no: 3 SS73
Tel: 01643 831259
Chef: Sue Burns
Proprietors: Sue & Mike Burns
Cost: Fixed-price D £21.50 (5 course). H/wine £8.25. No service charge
Credit cards: 🌑 📰 🔜 💷
Times: 7pm-last D 8.30pm. Closed Dec & Jan

STON EASTON, Ston Easton Park ❀❀❀

A splendid 18th-century country house setting for imaginatively conceived and elaborately presented dishes

Bath BA3 4DF
Map no: 3 ST65
Tel: 01761 241631
Chef: Mark Harrington
Proprietors: Peter & Christine Smedley
Cost: *Alc* from £38.50, fixed-price L £26, fixed-price D £38.50 (4 courses). H/wine £14.50 ❢ Service inc
Credit cards: 🌑 📰 🔜 💷 OTHER.
Times: Last L-2pm, last D-9.30pm (10pm Fri & Sat)

A Palladian mansion set in classical parkland, created by Humphrey Repton, Ston Easton Park has been extensively restored to recapture its 18th-century splendour. It is now a country house hotel with quality period furnishings throughout and beautifully decorated public rooms. There are two dining-rooms, one available for private parties, and the restaurant where classical cooking with modern French influences is served. Head chef Mark Harrington has established a well deserved reputation for his carefully prepared and elaborately presented dishes. His imaginative *carte* and daily set-price menus take full account of freshly available produce, some from the hotel's own garden.

Dinner begins with a complimentary hors d'oeuvre and home-made bread rolls. Starters might include feuilletté of globe artichoke, comprising feta cheese, artichoke and sun-dried tomatoes baked in filo pastry, or a dish of king scallops roasted in lemon oil and presented with a huge mound of crispy fried vegetables with a soya dressing. Fillet of sea bass, as a main course, was baked on a bed of roast peppers and thyme to provide an enjoyable combination of flavours. There is always a vegetarian option on the *carte*, such as baked wholemeal tartlet of goats' cheese, avocado and crème fraîche, while a meatier dish (fish and fowl predominate) could be gateau of maize-fed chicken studded with Parma ham and tomatoes and baked in a light brioche and puff pastry crust. Apple and mincemeat tart is recommended, served with home-made cinnamon ice-cream. The lengthy wine list offers no house wines but begins with bottles at the cheaper end (around £14.50), and includes some halves.

Directions: On A37 from Bristol to Shepton Mallet, about 6 miles from Wells

Menus: *A la carte,* fixed-price L & D, Sun lunch
Seats: 40, No smoking in dining-room
Additional: Children over 7 permitted, children's portions; ❤ dishes, other diets on request

TAUNTON, **Castle Hotel** ❀❀❀❀

A talented chef gives English dishes a modern slant in a historic castle

Castle Green TA1 1NF
Map no: 3 ST22
Tel: 01823 272671
Chef: Philip Vickery
Proprietor: Kit Chapman.
Manager: Andrew Grahame
Cost: Fixed-price L £17.90/D £20.90. H/wine £9.70 ❢ No service charge
Credit cards: 🔲 🔳 🔳 🔳 OTHER
Times: 12.30pm-last L 2pm, 7.30pm-last D 9pm daily
Menus: Fixed-price L & D
Seats: 70. No smoking in dining room
Additional: Children welcome, children's portions; ❤ dishes, other diets on request

It is a genuine castle (of Norman origin) and the wisteria draped façade makes a striking first impression. Within, the odd tapestry and heavy stonework in the public areas keep up the image. But the town centre location is unusual – although visitors will be delighted that there is parking right at the entrance – and the style of the place is far removed from that of the country house hotel; there is more of an immediacy here. The Castle's strength lies in the kitchen. Philip Vickery continues to develop his modern British style of cooking which owes as much to an adaptive understanding of Mediterranean and Far Eastern themes as to English seasonal variations.

The menu remains short. Execution of dishes such as seared salmon with a spice crust, couscous and spring onion crème fraîche, and ravioli of braised aubergines with spring cabbage and pepper oil, show a willingness to work with daring combinations; this does not always come off. A meal in early summer began with fried wing of skate with beetroot vinaigrette, rocket and saffron mayonnaise. The tang of the mayonnaise was too acidic, overpowering the fish, especially when taken in combination with the lightly acidulated batons of beetroot. It all lacked that essential balance of flavours. Braised corn-fed duck with star anise, green ginger and lemongrass was also tried. The 'moist, juicy' duck was of 'good flavour', enhanced by a spicy reduction. However, the flavours of ginger and lemongrass did not really come through and it was served with wilted spinach, new potatoes, baby onions, fennel and artichoke, which added little to a dish that had pronounced Oriental overtones. An individual delicate pastry tart filled with rhubarb and topped with a nutty crumble recalls that a reworking of traditional English puddings are a speciality here. It came with an imaginatively conceived lemon-curd ice-cream. Another dessert that has pleased has been a delicate baked egg custard tart with nutmeg ice-cream. Dishes can be strikingly presented, and lunchtime offerings of grilled sirloin steak with tomatoes, chips and mushrooms, or steamed spiced lamb pudding with braised cabbage and mashed potatoes are welcome simply on the premise that everyone wants an old favourite once in a while. Bread is baked on the premises and includes a sweet-flavoured caraway and buttermilk roll, and petits fours are good. The New World has a good showing on a wine list that begins with a short list of table wines priced between £10 and £14, before getting down to serious business, and prices, in France. Half bottles are well represented.

Directions: Town centre follow directions for Castle & Museum

TAUNTON,

Farthings Hotel ❀❀

☺ *Pretty family-run Georgian hotel, dominated by its popular and busy restaurant*

Hatch Beauchamp TA3 6SG
Map no: 3 ST22
Tel: 01823 480664
Chefs: Neil McKellar
Proprietors: David & Marie Barker (Logis)
Cost: Fixed-price L £10.50/D £17.50, £19 (4 course). H/wine £7.95 ❢ Service exc
Credit cards: 🔲 🔲 🔲 🔲 OTHER
Times: Last L 1.30pm, last D 8.30pm daily
Menus: Fixed-price L & D, bar menu

Farthings can be found snuggling in the peaceful village of Hatch Beauchamp, off the A358 from Taunton. Owners Mr and Mrs Baker have created a relaxed and friendly atmosphere. Each bedroom is uniquely decorated with an en suite bathroom and many thoughtful extras like fresh flowers, books and magazines. However, it is the restaurant which demands most attention and there is a healthy non resident trade who enjoy the two dining-rooms as well as the small comfortable lounge and gardens. A reasonable fixed-price menu might include a thick warm watercress soup with a sabayon of herbs, followed by generous succulent medallions of pork served with a jus of the cooking juices and Calvados, although on our visit the promised hint of cinnamon needed prompting. The dish was garnished with caramelised sliced plums and apples. Vegetables were simply cooked and full of flavour. Dessert was a lemon tart, the filling smooth and tangy. The wine list draws from around the world.

Directions: Village centre, just off A358 between Taunton (M5 exit 25) & Ilminster

Seats: 40. No smoking in dining room
Additional: Children welcome until 7pm, children's portions; ❶ dishes, vegan/other diets on request

TAUNTON, Nightingales ❀❀

☺ *A small, cosy restaurant set in an old farm with many traditional features and much character*

Nightingales is worth a detour. Currently, dinner only is served on two nights a week, with lunch on Sundays, but the short, fixed-price menu changes fortnightly, and offers an eclectic mix of well-made Mediterranean and Oriental influenced food. Dinner in early summer started with savoury hors d'oeuvre of fresh salmon and mayonnaise tartlets and home-made cheese straws. Freshly baked bread rolls accompanied a full-flavoured mushroom soup which had a superb cheese soufflé floating on top. The fresh roast fillet of salmon which followed had a tomato concasse with a lively but subtle flavour and was accompanied by side dishes of crunchy, al dente vegetables. Dessert was a wonderfully thick dark chocolate mousse with fruity raspberry ice-cream. Strong coffee comes with home-made petits fours. The wine list is predominantly French.

Directions: From M5 exit 25 take A358 (Ilminster), Restaurant is 4 miles at bottom of hill on left after traffic lights

Bath House Farm
Lower West Hatch TA3 5RH
Map no: 3 ST22
Tel: 01823 480806
Chefs: Sally Edwards and Margaret Barlow
Proprietors: Margaret & Jeremy Barlow
Cost: Fixed-price D £18.50/Sun L £12.50. H/wine £8.50 Service exc
Credit cards: 🔳 💳
Times: Last D 9.30pm, last Sun L 2.30pm Open Fri D, Sat D, Sun L Closed last wk Oct
Menus: Fixed-price Fri/Sat D & Sun L
Seats: 40. No smoking in dining room
Additional: Children welcome, children's portions; ❶ dishes, vegan/other diets on request

WELLS, Ancient Gate House Hotel ❀

☺ *The building is of 14th-century origin and boasts an unrivalled position in the cathedral close. Oak beams and panelling give the interior a distinctive English charm. As a contrast, the restaurant specialises in Italian cooking. A variety of traditional trattoria staples are on offer, from a range of popular pasta to more adventurous Fisherman's risotto*

Menus: A la carte, fixed-price L & D, bar menu
Seats: 45.
Additional: Children welcome, children's portions; ❶ dishes, vegan/ other diets on request
Directions: On the Cathedral Green in Sadler Street leading to Market Place

Sadler Street BA5 2RR
Map no: 3 ST54
Tel: 01749 672029
Chef: Vincenzo Ferro
Proprietor: Franco Rossi
Cost: Alc £15.50, fixed-price L £6.20/D £13.75 H/wine £8.90 Service exc
Credit cards: 🔳 💳 💳 OTHER
Times: Last L 2pm, last D 10.30pm daily

WELLS, **The Fountain** ❀

☺ *Do not be misled by first impressions; above the pub is an attractive, informal restaurant furnished in country pine. The kitchen gets a big E for endeavour, energy and enthusiasm, with a wide range of dishes such as Poole mussels with wine, cream and garlic, terrine of salmon, braised duckling and guinea fowl casserole*

Seats: 30. No pipes in restaurant
Additional: Children welcome, children's menu/portions; ❤ menu, vegan/other diets on request
Directions: In city centre at junction of A371 & B3139, 50 yds from Cathedral

1 St Thomas Street
Map no: 3 ST54
Tel: 01749 672317
Chef: Julie Pearce
Proprietors: Adrian & Sarah Lawrence
Cost: Alc £12.50, fixed-price L £5.50 (2 courses), £7.50. H/wine £6.75 ❢ Service exc
Credit cards: ▨ ▤ ▤ OTHER
Times: 11am–last L 2pm, 6pm–last D 9.30pm. Closed 25 & 26 Dec

WHEDDON CROSS,
Raneleigh Manor Country House ❀

Guests are asked their preferences when they book a meal at this comfortable Victorian hotel, the main course being set. Home-cooked dishes are imaginative. On a recent visit, stir-fried prawns with mushrooms and cashew nuts were followed by moist breast of chicken with a honey and mustard sauce

Minehead TA24 7BB
Map no: 3 SS93
Tel: 01643 841484
Chef: Mrs Piper
Proprietors: Mr & Mrs Piper

WILLITON, **Curdon Mill** ❀

A pleasant mill conversion that has retained some of the original water mill workings in the first floor restaurant. Consistent cooking relies on fresh local produce with likely dishes including chicken liver pâté, steak and kidney pudding and chocolate and pear filo tart. A relaxed atmosphere prevails

Times: Last D 8.30pm, last Sunday L 2.30pm
Seats: 50. No-smoking area
Additional: Children permitted, children's portions; ❤ menu, vegan/other diets on request
Directions: On the Stogumber road (A358)

Yellow TA4 4LS
Map no: 3 ST04
Tel: 01984 56522
Chefs: Daphne Criddle and Lorraine Seldon
Proprietors: Richard & Daphne Criddle
Cost: Fixed-price D £19.50, Sunday L £11.50. H/wine £7.80 ❢ Service inc
Credit cards: ▨ ▤

WILLITON, **White House Hotel** ❀❀❀

A pretty period property with a dinner-only restaurant serving good food prepared with skill and originality

Dick and Kay Smith have provided excellent standards of food, wine and hospitality for over 28 years. The restaurant is an attractive room with whitewashed walls and shuttered windows, and only dinner is served when the hotel is open from mid May until the end of October. The fixed-price three-course menu offers modern British dishes with French, Mediterranean and Californian influences. The approach to fine ingredients is simple, and flavours are wonderfully fresh and clear.

An early summer meal began with a robust red pepper and tomato soup served with well made bread rolls, followed by a crêpe aux fruit de mer – a lightly gratinated crab, prawn and mushroom-filled pancake napped with a cheese sauce. Other options were grilled breast of wood pigeon thinly sliced on a hot beetroot salad, and a pâté of duck livers, garlic, Armagnac and thyme, served with

Long Street TA4 4QW
Map no: 3 ST04
Tel: 01984 632306
Chefs: Dick & Kay Smith
Proprietors: Dick & Kay Smith
Cost: Fixed-price D £27.50. H/wine £9.50 ❢ Service exc
Credit cards: No cards taken
Times: Last D 8.30pm
Menus: Fixed-price D
Seats: 26. No smoking in dining room
Additional: Children welcome, children's portions; ❤ dishes

a confit of red onions, monbazillac jelly and toasted brioche. Main courses include a creamy fish stew with monkfish, haddock, bacon, potato, onions and sweetcorn, and our inspector's choice, succulent local spring lamb, which came with a minty béarnaise sauce and some carefully cooked vegetables. Delice au chocolat completed the meal, a chocolate mousse set on a brandied chocolate sponge, but equally tempting was the 'sablé aux fraises', the French version of strawberry shortcake. The wine list is Dick Smith's hobby and his passion is evident (how many hotels can boast a bottle of 1949 Chateau D'Yquem). The list is mainly French with a few New World wines and a good selection of half bottles.

Directions: On the A39 in the centre of village

WINSFORD, **Royal Oak Inn** ✤

Dating from the 12th century, this thatched inn is set in the centre of the picturesque village of Winsford, on the edge of Exmoor National Park. The traditional English dishes offered may include watercress and onion soup, breast of chicken filled with brie and wrapped in bacon, and old-fashioned trifle for dessert

Menus: Fixed-price L & D, bar menu
Seats: 34. No smoking in dining room
Additional: Children welcome, children's portions; ❤ dishes, other diets on request
Directions: From M5 exit 27 take A396 (Minehead) 20 miles turn left to Winsford, then left in the village

Minehead TA24 7JE
Map no: 3 SS93
Tel: 01645 381455
Chef: Kevin Smokum
Proprietor: Charles Steven
Cost: Fixed-price L £14.50/D £22.50 H/wine £8.50 Service exc
Credit cards: 🔲 🔲 🔲 🔲
Times: Last L 1.30pm, last D 9pm daily

WITHYPOOL, **Royal Oak Inn** ✤

A charming little inn with a cosy atmosphere where one can eat in congenial surroundings. Care goes into the cooking which makes good use of seasonal produce. Dishes can include local venison steak with port wine sauce, and homemade chocolate meringue with Cointreau flavoured cream

Withypool TA24 7QP
Map no: 3 SS83
Tel: 0164 383 1506
Chef: Peter Norris
Proprietor: Michael Bradley
Cost: Alc £26, fixed-price D £20/Sun L £13.50 H/wine £10.50 ❗ Service exc
Credit cards: 🔲 🔲 🔲 🔲 OTHER
Times: Last L 2pm, last D 9.30pm Closed Dec 24-26
Menus: A la carte, fixed-price L & D, bar menu
Seats: 32
Additional: Children welcome (not babies), children's portions; ❤ dishes, vegan/other diets on request

Directions: Off B3223 between Dulverton and Simonsbath

WITHYPOOL, **Westerclose Hotel** ❀

Set amidst beautiful moorland scenery the hotel's Barle Restaurant offers imaginative food using homegrown organic produce in the vegetarian dishes. Look out for pan-fried butternut, red onions and field mushrooms, with chilli, cumin, fresh tagliatelle and crème fraîche. Venison, steaks and lamb feature

Menus: *A la carte* L & D, fixed-price D, bar menu
Seats: 25. No smoking in dining room
Additional: Children welcome (over 6 at D), children's menu;
❷ dishes, other diets with notice
Directions: Off B3223 between Dulverton and Simonsbath, signed in village

Minehead TA24 7QR
Map no: 3 SS83
Tel: 01643 831302
Chefs: Joanna Foster and Edward Nuttal
Proprietors: Ben, Joanna & Mrs R P Foster, Blue Walshe
Cost: *Alc* £16.50, fixed-price D £19, £22 (4 course). H/wine £7.95 Service exc
Credit cards: 💳 💳 💳
Times: Last L 2.30pm, last D 9.15pm Closed Mon D, Dec 30-Mar 1

WIVELISCOMBE,
Langley House Hotel ❀❀

A delightful, small family-run hotel, dating from the sixteenth century, nestling in the Brendon Hills

Langley House is an oasis of informality and comfort just outside Wiveliscombe. Great care has been lavished both on the 4 acre garden and the house itself. Husband and wife team, Peter and Ann Wilson (he cooks, she manages) provide a very personal service and have won plaudits both for the decor and cooking. There is no choice on the menu until the pudding stage. At inspection appetising samplers included a simple but effective starter of fanned dessert pear served in a nutty walnut oil dressing with a small rosette of herb cheese, and a delicate fillet of sea bream topped with Provençal breadcrumbs with some lightly sweated leeks and a thinnish butter sauce was a great success. Also notable was a roasted fillet of Somerset new season lamb, cooked pink and served with ratatouille, although the flavour of the pepper scented tomato coulis tended to dominate. The wine list draws from around the world.

Directions: Off B3227 0.5 mile from Wiveliscombe on Langley Marsh road

Langley Marsh TA4 2UF
Map no: 3 ST02
Tel: 01984 623318
Chef: Peter Wilson
Proprietors: Peter & Anne Wilson
Cost: Fixed-price D £24.50, £28.50 (4 course). H/wine £9.50 ❢ Service inc
Credit cards: 💳 💳 💳
Times: 7.30pm-last D 8.30pm
Menu: Fixed-price dinner
Seats: 18. No smoking in dining room
Additional: Children welcome (over 10 at D), children's menu;
❷ dishes, other diets on request

WOOKEY HOLE, **Glencot House** ❀

Glencot House is a unique hotel, crammed full with antiques and ornate furnishings, giving it a distinct charm. From an imaginative menu, a recent inspection meal included terrine of rabbit followed by rack of lamb with a mustard crust. The overall atmosphere is that of a private country house

Menus: *A la carte,* fixed-price D, bar menu
Seats: 24. No smoking in dining room
Additional: Children welcome, children's menu; ❷ dishes, vegan/other diets with prior arrangement
Directions: From Wells follow signs to Wookey, turn left 150yds after pink cottage on brow of hill

Wells BA5 1BH
Map no: 3 ST54
Tel: 01749 677160
Chef: Danny Cannon
Proprietor: Mrs J Attia
Cost: *Alc* £18.50, fixed-price D £22.50 H/wine £8.30 ❢ Service exc
Credit cards: 💳 💳
Times: D 6.30-8.30pm. Closed Xmas

YEOVIL, Little Barwick House 🏵🏵

A listed Georgian house surrounded by well tended gardens offering a haven of peaceful informality and honest hospitality

Barwick Village BA22 9TD
Map no: 3 ST51
Tel: 01935 23902
Chef: Veronica Colley
Proprietors: Veronica & Christopher Colley (Logis GB)
Cost: Fixed-price D £16.90 (2 course), £22.90, £24.90 (4 course). H/wine £9.60. Service exc
Credit cards: 🔳 🏧 🔤
Times: 7pm-last D 9pm/9.30pm Sat Closed Sun (except Res), Xmas
Menus: Fixed-price D
Seats: 40. Air conditioned. No smoking in dining room
Additional: Children welcome, children's portions; ♥ dishes, other diets on request

This charming country house is tucked away in sleepy Barwick village just off the A37 Yeovil to Dorchester road. Attractively furnished bedrooms, a comfortable lounge with flop-about-in sofas and armchairs and the de rigueur open fire, all almost as irresistible as the food. Chef Veronica Colley, part owner with her husband Christopher, obviously enjoys creating the daily-changing menus using local produce. The essence here is on fresh natural flavours, cooked and served with uncluttered care. A hugely enjoyed inspection dinner started with a distinct creamed smokie (flaked Finnan haddock baked in a little pot with cream, topped with cheese) followed by a breast of Barbary Duck served finely sliced with a light jus of orange, fresh ginger and onion accompanied by a selection of fresh vegetables. An iced gâteau Diane light in texture and full of flavour completed the meal. The wine list includes a strong selection from France but New World wines get a look in. Dessert wines are available by the glass.

Directions: Turn off A371 Yeovil/Dorchester opp Red House pub, 0.25 mile on left

YEOVIL, Yeovil Court Hotel 🏵

This popular hotel, situated on the western fringes of town, has a friendly and relaxed air about it. Staff are eager and conscientious and guests will find a cheerful atmosphere. Recent inspections have commented favourably on field mushrooms filled with a light chicken and Stilton mousse, baked with garlic butter

Menus: *A la carte,* fixed-price L , bar menu
Seats: 50. No cigars or pipes in dining room
Additional: Children welcome, children's menu; ♥ dishes, other diets on request
Directions: On A30, 2.5 miles west of Yeovil

West Coker Road BA20 2NE
Map no: 3 ST51
Tel: 01935 863746
Chef: Howard Mosley
Proprietor: Brian Devonport
Cost: Alc £13-£19, fixed-price L £10. H/wine £7.90 ❢ Service inc
Credit cards: 🔳 🏧 🔤 💳 OTHER
Times: Last L 1.45pm, last D 9.45pm Closed Sat L, Sun D, BHs, open Dec 25

SOUTH YORKSHIRE

BARNSLEY, **Armstrongs Restaurant** ❀❀

☺ *Good value dining and a famous pudding single out this town centre restaurant*

Standing opposite the majestic town hall, this well-established restaurant offers interesting modern British cooking. Good use of many Mediterranean ingredients, and recipes, is evident, in conjunction with a more subtle Oriental approach. An excellent good-value menu is offered between 7 and 8 p.m. (Tuesday to Friday) with a greater choice of more sophisticated and serious dishes later in the evening. Lunches tend to be lighter in style, taken from a shorter menu. An inspection lunch sampled a local favourite of sesame seed coated salmon escalope; the flavour of the fish contrasting well with a red wine and soy sauce. Noisettes of lamb, the main course, provided an even greater flavour contrast, combined with olives and dried Moroccan lemon on a basil jus. To finish, a butterscotch meringue pudding for which the restaurant is known, lived up to its reputation.

Directions: M1 exit 37; in the town centre by the Town Hall

6 Shambles Street S70 2SQ
Map no: 8 SE30
Tel: 01226 240113
Chef: Nick Pound
Proprietor: Nick Pound
Cost: Alc £17, fixed-price D
£12.95. H/wine £8.95. Service exc
Credit cards: 🃏 📧 📧 OTHER
Times: Last L 2pm, last D
9.30pm Closed Sat L, Sun, Mon
Menus: A la carte L & D, fixed-price early D (7pm-8pm exc Sat)
Seats: 60
Additional: Children welcome, children's portions; ❦ dishes, vegan/other diets on request

CHAPELTOWN, **Greenhead House** ❀❀

Immensely popular local restaurant in pretty period stone house. Booking is essential

It is now ten years since Neil and Anne Allen started turning this old stone house into a restaurant. They have succeeded. The loving care given to the house and garden is well evident – recently they redecorated the dining-room in restful green and white creating a cottage feel that is immediately complementary to the earthy country cooking. The four-course meal price is governed by the main dish and there is a varied choice of four or five items for each course. A meal in June opened with a cebiche of salmon, marinated in lemon and orange, followed by a beautiful cauliflower soup with Gruyère cheese and lovage, which was perfectly balanced. Baby guinea fowl marinated in oil and thyme, was next. Grilled, its juices sweetened with Sauterne, it was a memorable dish. A finale of a rum rich chestnut cake with a burnt sugar top, just introduced, was an instant success and likely to become a fixture on the menu.

Directions: M1 exit 35 follow signs to Chapeltown, over two roundabouts, Restaurant is on right

84 Buncross Road S30 4SF
Map no: 8 SK39
Tel: 0114 2469004
Chef: Neil Allen
Proprietors: Neil & Anne Allen
Cost: Fixed-price D £27.50,
£29.50 (4 course). H/wine £9.95
❦ Service exc
Credit cards: 🃏 📧
Times: Last D 9pm. Closed Sun, Mon, Tue, 2 wks Easter, 2 wks mid-Aug, Dec 26-Jan 1
Menu: Fixed-price D
Seats: 34. No smoking in dining room
Additional: Children permitted (not under 7), children's portions; other diets with notice

Mille-feuille in its classic 19th-century French form is thin layers of the lightest puff pastry separated by layers of cream, jam or any other filling with the top covered with icing sugar. This idea was then extended to savoury dishes with fillings of fish or shellfish, but nowadays chefs interpret mille-feuille as anything layered. This could be thin slices of apple, aubergine, celeriac, filo, you name it, as long as it arrives in an artistically arranged pile.

CHAPELTOWN,

Staindrop Lodge Hotel ❀

A hospitable hotel, well suited to the business guest, with a restaurant holding a good reputation for imaginative British cooking. Both a carte and fixed-price menu are available, which change fortnightly. The restaurant staff are very cheerful and their service is efficient

Lane End S30 4UH
Map no: 8 SK39
Tel: 0114 2846727
Chef: John P Olerenshaw
Proprietors: Mark & Sue Bailey
Cost: *Alc* £21.50, fixed-price L £10/D £17.90 (4 course) H/wine £8 Service exc
Credit cards: 🔲 🔲 🔲 🔲 OTHER
Times: Last L 1.45pm, last D 9.30pm Closed Sat L, Sun D, Mon L, Dec 26, Jan 1
Menus: *A la carte*, fixed-price L & D
Seats: 70. No pipes or cigars in dining room
Additional: Children welcome, children's portions; ❤ dishes, vegan/other diets on request

Directions: M1 exit 35/A629, 0.5 mile from Chapeltown, following signs to High Green

ROTHERHAM, Swallow Hotel ❀

This well-presented modern hotel offers Anglo-French cooking with some traditional regional specialities. Both fixed price menus and a carte are offered. Particularly recommended has been a starter of scallops with bacon and peppers in a butter sauce

Menus: *A la carte*, fixed-price L & D, bar menu
Seats: 100. Air conditioned. No smoking area
Additional: Children welcome, children's menu; ❤ dishes, vegan/other diets on request
Directions: M1 exit 33 – 2 miles from Rotherham centre on A630

West Bawtry Road S60 4NA
Map no: 8 SK49
Tel: 01709 830630
Chef: Alan McGilveray
Manager: Ed Schofield
Cost: *Alc* £30, fixed-price L £12.95 £9.95 Sun)/D £16.95 (4 course) H/wine £10.25 Service exc
Credit cards: 🔲 🔲 🔲 🔲 OTHER
Times: Last L 1.45pm/ Sun 2pm, last D 9.45pm/9.15 Sun L

Britain lies at the northern limit for growing asparagus and it grows slowly, due to the coolness of the soil. Although at the height of the season English asparagus is often more expensive than imported varieties, the slow growing results in a strong, intense flavour that makes the higher price worth while. It takes three years before a plant can be cut and about five years before it yields a full crop. Then each spear must be cut by hand. The season is short, about six weeks from early May to late June, after which the plant must be left to develop leaves, so that it can regenerate itself. Most native asparagus come from the Vale of Evesham in Herefordshire, Kent and Suffolk.

SHEFFIELD, **Charnwood Hotel** ✸

Originally a Georgian mansion, Charnwood is now a well established hotel. In addition to Leo's, a brasserie, there is a more formal restaurant, Henfrey's, offering dishes which display a strong modern European bias combined with a more classical approach; try the particularly enjoyable larded potato terrine

10 Sharrow Lane S11 8AA
Map no: 8 SK38
Tel: 0114 2589411
Chef: Murray Chapman
Proprietor: Mr & Mrs C J King
Cost: *Alc* Henfreys £26/Brasserie £16, fixed-price L/D £12.
H/wine £8.95. Service exc
Credit cards: 🔳 💳 💳 💳 OTHER
Times: Henfrey's 7pm-last D 9.30pm Closed Sun, Mon.
Brasserie 7am-11pm open 7 days
Seats: Henfrey's 28.
Brasserie 50. Air conditioned

Menus: *A la carte* D Henfrey's & Brasserie, fixed-price L & D Brasserie, pre-theatre, bar menu   **Additional:** Children welcome, children's menu; ❤ menu, vegan/other diets on request
Directions: M1 exit 33 & A621. 1.5 miles south-west of city centre, off London Road

SHEFFIELD, **Harley Hotel** ✸

A centrally located hotel, popular with business clients, which prides itself on providing a good choice of imaginative, modern dishes. Fashionable combinations, such as wood pigeon with mango, or lamb with garlic and aubergine purée, show the flair of the chef. Quality fresh produce is used

Menus: *A la carte*, fixed-price L & D, bar menu   **Seats:** 55. Air conditioned   **Additional:** Children over 12 permitted; ❤ dishes, vegan/other diets on request
Directions: 0.5 mile from centre, junction of West Street (A57) & Hanover Street (Inner City Ring Road)

334 Glossop Road S10 2HW
Map no: 8 SK38
Tel: 0114 2752288
Chef: Ian Morton
Proprietor: A C Womack
Cost: *Alc* £15-£30, fixed-price L £9.50 (2 course)/D £15.50
H/wine £11 ▮ Service exc
Credit cards: 🔳 💳 💳 💳
Times: Last L 2.15pm, last D 9.45pm Closed Sat L, Sun, Bhs

STAFFORDSHIRE

WATERHOUSES, **Old Beams** ✸✸✸

An award-winning village restaurant with rooms features first-rate modern English cooking

Wedgwood pottery is – predictably, in view of the area – very much in evidence throughout this attractive, beamed house dating from 1746. Service that combines genuine charm with professionalism creates a relaxed atmosphere, and food is excellent – the *carte* and

Leek Road ST10 3HW
Map no: 7 SK05
Tel: 01538 308254
Chef: Nigel Wallis
Proprietors: Nigel & Ann Wallis
Cost: Fixed-price L £10.95 (2 course), £17.50/D £18.50 & £35. H/wine £15.75 ▮ No service charge

supplementary plats du jour offering a choice of modern British dishes that makes decisions difficult. All the extras maintain the same superb standard: home-made bread rolls are first-class, and an appetiser of turbot, crab mousseline and ginger beurre blanc served before a recent inspection meal was, indeed, very appetising. The starter, a hot soufflé of lobster and scallop, had the consistency and texture of a floating island; though slightly undercooked, it was outstandingly tasty, complementing seared scallops with a restrained saffron olive oil dressing. A well made, if perhaps not entirely necessary, palate-freshener of rhubarb sorbet followed, then the very tender and juicy stuffed leg and saddle of a farmed rabbit – amusingly accompanied by its tiny rack – with excellent tarragon jus and attractively presented vegetables. Charlotte of white peaches with an effective cappuccino of vanilla, though marginally heavy, was enjoyable, and good espresso coffee came with quality fudge and chocolate petits fours. An outstanding wine list includes a half bottle of Zind Hubrecht Pinot Gris Vieilles Vignes 1992.

Directions: On A523, Leek to Ashbourne road

Credit cards: 🔲 🔲 🔲 🔲 OTHER
Times: Last L 1.45pm, last D 9.30pm. Closed Sat L, Sun D, Mon
Menu: Fixed-price L & D
Seats: 40. No smoking in dining room
Additional: Children permitted; ❤ dishes, vegan/other diets on request

---

SUFFOLK

ALDEBURGH, **Regatta Restaurant**

☺ *One of a trio of busy restaurants owned by Robert Mabey. Modern eclectic cooking is the keynote, as seen in dishes such as Mediterranean fish soup, Thai-style chicken breast with king prawns and steamed rice, and glazed fillet of beef with horseradish gravy and chips. Puddings are a strong point.*

Menus: Fixed-price L & D, bar menu **Seats:** 80. No smoking area
Additional: Children welcome, children's menu; ❤ dishes, other diets on request
Directions: Town centre, bright yellow paintwork

171 High Street IP15 5AN
Map no: 5 TM45
Tel: 01728 452011
Chef: Robert Mabey
Proprietor: Robert Mabey
Cost: Alc £18.20. fixed-price L £8.95, £6.95 (2 course).
H/wine £7.50 Service exc
Credit cards: 🔲 🔲 🔲 🔲
Times: Last L 2pm, last D 10pm
Closed Mon & Tue in low season

BURY ST EDMUNDS, **Angel Hotel** ❀❀

Well located town-centre hotel with professional polish to the cooking

The creeper-covered building, close to the Cathedral, has been providing food and shelter since the Middle Ages. Meals are well prepared and professionally turned out by Chef des Cuisines Denis Groualle. A typical four-course evening meal may start with chicken and pistachio terrine, followed by quenelle of fresh fruit sorbet, medallions of pork fillet garnished with courgettes and tomato coulis, and iced Grand Marnier parfait with strawberry sauce, but there is a choice of three dishes at each course. The *carte* is more aspirational, and is structured on the French classics. First courses include warm fricassée of snails and vegetables with shallot dressing, and salad of smoked duck breast and foie gras moistened with balsamic; main courses show a range of high-class skills from pan-fried sea bream served on spinach with asparagus and shellfish bisque, to breast of Deben duck accompanied by braised Savoy cabbage and wild mushrooms, finished with a seed mustard sauce.

Directions: Town centre, close to Tourist Information

Angel Hill IP33 1LT
Map no: 5 TL86
Tel: 01284 753926
Chef: Denis Groualle
Proprietor: Mary Gough.
Manager: G Skinner
Cost: Alc £25.35, fixed-price L £13.95/D £19.95 (4 course)
H/wine £9.25 ❗ Service exc
Credit cards: 🔲 🔲 🔲 🔲
Times: Last L 2pm, last D 10pm
Closed Sat L
Menus: A la carte, fixed-price L & D, pre-theatre, bar menu
Seats: 40. No smoking in dining room
Additional: Children welcome, children's portions; ❤ dishes, vegan/other diets on request

BURY ST EDMUNDS, **The Priory Hotel** ✿

Simple yet skilfully cooked dishes are prepared and served in this pleasant hotel. The choice can include a tasty starter of chicken liver terrine with red pepper marmalade, and a well balanced lamb with port and red currant sauce

Menus: *A la carte*, fixed-price L & D **Seats:** 30. No smoking area
Additional: Children welcome, children's portions; ✿ dishes, vegan/other diets on request
Directions: Off A14 at Bury West exit, left on slip road for 1 mile, right at mini roundabout, left at lights, hotel on left

Tollgate IP32 6EH
Map no: 5 TL86
Tel: 01284 766181
Chef: Didier Piot
Proprietor: Mr & Mrs Cobbold (Best Western)
Cost: *Alc* £24.50, fixed-price L/D £17.50 H/wine £9.75 Service exc
Credit cards: ▨ ▩ ▨ ▨
Times: Last L 2pm, last D 9.30pm

BURY ST EDMUNDS,
Ravenwood Hall Hotel ✿

A magnificent sixteenth-century hall set in extensive gardens and woodlands. The cosy, intimate restaurant offers traditional cooking based on local produce and home-smoked fish and meats, home-preserved fruits and vegetables; try the smoked chicken sausages, served on a bed of leeks with a fresh herb sauce

Rougham IP30 9JA
Map no: 5 TL86
Tel: 01359 270345
Chef: David White
Proprietor: Craig Jarvis
Cost: *Alc* £24.95, fixed-price L /D £16.95 H/wine £9.50 ❢
No service charge
Credit cards: ▨ ▩ ▨ ▨ OTHER
Times: Last L 2pm, last D 9.30pm daily
Menus: *A la carte*, fixed-price L & D, bar menu
Seats: 45. No-smoking area
Additional: Children welcome, children's menu; ✿ dishes, vegan/other diets on request

Directions: 3 miles east of Bury St Edmunds off A14 (formerly A45) signposted Rougham

EARL STONHAM,
Mr Underhills Restaurant ✿✿✿

Individual cooking from enthusiastic husband and wife team in small, country restaurant

In the restaurant world, the relentless pursuit of the new can often lead to ill-conceived gimmickry – but, if a dish works, why not retain it within a repertoire? The question arose at Mr Underhills when, inadvertently, our inspector ordered a meal virtually identical to that chosen last year. Happily, he was able to report, quality remains consistently high. Duplication, however, need not be a problem for regular guests, as the no-choice menu is discussed on booking so alternatives, including vegetarian ones, can be arranged.

Norwich Road IP14 5DW
Map no: 5 TM15
Tel: 01449 711206
Chef: Christopher Bradley
Proprietors: Christopher & Judy Bradley
Cost: Fixed-price D £29/Sun L £24. H/wine £10.10 Service exc
Credit cards: ▨ ▩
Times: Last D 8.45pm, last Sun L 1.30pm, Closed Sun D, Mon, Bhs (open Dec 25)
Menus: Fixed-price D & Sun L
Seats: 24. No smoking in dining room

The formula may not allow for much adventure, but it does permit Christopher Bradley to produce excellent dinners demonstrating creativity in the use of flavours and textures. Judy Bradley organises the front-of-house, and together they go to great lengths to source the best ingredients possible, making a point of using local produce when available.

Although they know what to expect in advance, diners are presented with their own personalised copies of the night's menu, charmingly illustrated by a cartoon of the Bradleys in full flow. Favourite dishes likely to make a reappearance include roasted smoked haddock with tomato and sherry vinegar dressing, and fillet of beef with tarragon essence. Our suitably summery inspection meal started with a good selection of locally made bread. A warm salad of tender asparagus was a real winner, dressed with a combination of broad beans and asparagus purée and a basil vinaigrette. Breast of Barbary duck with garden herbs, was served with the marinated, slow-cooked leg alongside. The accompanying jus was subtly perfumed with a potpourri of thyme, lavender, rosemary and caramelised honey. A hot chocolate tart was to die for: a light, chocolate crust (no pastry), filled with melted, intensely rich, dark chocolate, set on a vanilla sauce and served with smooth, caramel ice-cream.

Directions: On A140, 300 yds south of the junction with the A1120

Additional: Children welcome, children's portions; other diets on request

FRESSINGFIELD, **Fox & Goose Inn**

Good food simply presented in an eclectic range of styles at this friendly village restaurant

The Fox & Goose may well be mistaken for a pub in its quiet setting beside the village pond. Indeed, within, the welcome is friendly and informal. A comprehensive selection of dishes is offered from lunch menus and *carte*. The range of cooking is certainly eclectic, from exotic eastern dishes to traditional British fare, but regardless of style the philosophy is the same – the freshest quality ingredients simply prepared and presented. The additional blackboard specials are equally diverse, including, on one occasion, calves' liver parfait with home-made zucchini pickles and toasted ciabatta; Caribbean fish stew with ginger, chilli, squid, salmon, hake and coriander; and crispy baked cod with spicy tomato.

At a summer meal our inspector enjoyed a warm starter of scallops and squid with pancetta, served with sweet charred tomato, salsa dressing and grilled polenta. A livelier main course of an eclectically matched Thai-style guinea fowl pot-au-feu was a meal in itself, the flavour of the tender guinea fowl clearly identifiable along with those of broccoli, baby spinach, spring onion and fresh noodles. For dessert, citrus curd tart was refreshingly different, a balanced combination of lemon, lime and orange in a smooth curd encased in golden pastry.

This is an enterprising establishment, offering a children's menu with options such as chicken on a stick with peanut sauce, and home-made sausage with chips or mash; a bar menu with a selection of simple dishes in starter or main course portions; and special theme evenings throughout the year. For those who are not driving (and you can only arrive by car) there is a splendid wine list.

Directions: A140 & B1118 (Stradbroke) left after 6 miles – in village centre by the church

Nr Diss IP21 5PB
Map no: 5 TM27
Tel: 01379 586247
Chefs: Ruth Watson, Brendan Ansbro, James Perry and Max Dougall
Proprietor: Ruth Watson.
Manager: Tim O'Leary
Cost: A/c £23, fixed-price L £13.50. H/wine £8.50
Service exc
Credit cards: No cards taken
Times: Last L 2.15pm, last D 9.30pm Closed Mon, Tue, 2 wks July & Xmas/NYear
Menus: *A la carte* D, fixed-price L, bar menu
Seats: 50
Additional: Children welcome, children's menu; ♥ menu, vegan/other diets on request

HINTLESHAM,
Hintlesham Hall Hotel ❀❀❀

Grand country house surroundings for a good choice of modern English cooking

Ipswich 1P8 3NS
Map no: 5 TM04
Tel: 01473 652334
Chef: Alan Ford
Proprietors: (Small Luxury Hotels).
Manager & Director: Timothy Sunderland
Cost: *Alc* £30, fixed-price L £18.50/D £24. H/wine £12.50 ▮
Service inc
Credit cards: 🖪 🖼 🖭 💷 OTHER
Times: Last L 1.45pm, last D 9.30pm
Menus: *A la carte,* fixed-price L & D
Seats: 100. No smoking in dining room
Additional: Children welcome (over 10 at D); ♥ menu, vegan/other diets on request

An impressive Tudor house with an elegant Georgian façade, Hintlesham Hall is set in 170 acres of grounds, with an 18-hole golf course, a leisure centre and a herb garden. Country house charm and comfort pervade the public areas, including the three lovely lounges, but the main dining room with its double height ceiling is soberly decorated, making more of a feature of chef Alan Ford's carefully presented dishes. The seasonally changing menus provide a good choice of balanced dishes, and are not unreasonably priced considering the splendour of the setting.

Starters include a light but full flavoured smoked haddock and green peppercorn roulade, and escalope of foie gras surrounded by braised oxtail and topped with a morel tortellini. An 'in between' course is offered, generally salad, soup or sorbet dishes, such as chicken and coriander consommé, and melon and white wine granite. Typical main courses are tender medallions of venison served with a rounded redcurrant jus, and a pigeon dish comprising roast and confit of pigeon set around a crisp filo gateau layered with braised vegetables. A vegetarian dish is always available, on this occasion oyster mushroom, spinach and caramelised onion ravioli glazed with a light chive sauce. Vegetables are simply and effectively cooked, and desserts demonstrate the same serious approach, though a disappointing vanilla cheesecake proved rather too gelatinous. Other options might be a hot apple and Calvados soufflé with its own sorbet, frozen rhubarb crumble, summer pudding terrine, or white and dark chocolate charlotte. There is an extensive wine list, well laid out and annotated in a helpful forthright manner.

Directions: 5 miles W of Ipswich on the A1071 Hadleigh road

> Rocket or arugula is a Mediterranean herb that has been popular since Roman times. It enhances any salad, as it has a pungent, peppery taste, and is used as an alternative to wilted spinach.

IPSWICH, **Belstead Brook Hotel** ❀

Belstead Brook lies in extensive gardens and woodlands, on the site of a Saxon settlement. The restaurant offers a wide choice of dining, including vegetarian, diabetic and 'gluten free' menus. Our inspector recently enjoyed a good main course of guinea fowl, wrapped in Savoy cabbage

Menus: A la carte, fixed-price L & D, bar menu **Seats:** 80. No smoking area **Additional:** Children's portions; ✿ dishes **Directions:** From A12/14 Ipswich exit follow signs for Pinewood, at 3rd roundabout take Belmont road, right at T jnctn & left at next T

Belstead Road IP2 9HB
Map no: 5 TM14
Tel: 01473 684 241
Chef: John Gear
Proprietor: (Best Western).
Manager: Patrick Mauser
Cost: Alc £25, fixed-price L & D £16.50 H/wine £9.75 ❢ Service inc
Credit cards: ▨ ▨ ▨ ▨ OTHER
Times: Last L 2pm, last D 10pm Closed Sat L

IPSWICH, **Kwoks Rendezvous** ❀

Modern, centrally located Chinese, specialising in Peking and Szechuan dishes. Fresh, balanced flavours shine through in dishes such as Shanghai spicy beef – a cold dish of thinly sliced beef with a spicy soya sauce – chicken with celery, and fried noodles with prawns and shredded beef

Seats: 50 No smoking area **Menus:** A la carte, fixed-price L & D **Additional:** Children welcome, children's portions; ✿ menu **Directions:** From Civic Drive towards Novotel, left into St Peter Street and then St Nicholas Street. Kwoks is opposite public car park

23 St Nicholas Street IP1 1TW
Map no: 5 TM14
Tel: 01473 256833
Chef: Thomas Kwok
Proprietor: Thomas Kwok
Cost: Alc £15-£25, fixed-price L & D £14.95-£16.95 (4 courses), H/wine £7.95 Service exc
Credit cards: ▨ ▨ ▨
Times: noon-last L 1.45pm, 6.30pm-last D 10.45pm. Closed Sun, Bhs, 2 wks Spring

IPSWICH, **Marlborough Hotel** ❀❀

Modern interpretations of classical French cooking are offered from a good-value menu at this refurbished hotel restaurant

Henley Road IP1 3SP
Map no: 5 TM14
Tel: 01473 257677
Chef: Simon Barker
Proprietor: Robert Gough (Best Western)
Cost: Alc £26, fixed-price L £14.65/D £17.15 H/wine £ 9.15 ❢ Service exc
Credit cards: ▨ ▨ ▨ ▨ OTHER
Times: Last L 2pm, last D 9.30pm
Menus: A la carte, fixed-price L & D, bar menu
Seats: 50. No smoking in dining room
Additional: Children permitted; ✿ dishes, vegan/other diets on request

An appealing new look, with bolder fabrics and colour schemes, has been given to the restaurant at the Marlborough Hotel, which is located to the north of the town in a quiet residential area. In these refreshed surroundings, Simon Baker continues to offer good value fixed-price menus alongside the *carte*. Dishes are based on modern interpretations of classical French cooking and almost everything is made on the premises, including the bread rolls and the petits fours. Starters might include warm chicken tikka salad, or a venison and guinea fowl terrine with cranberry vinaigrette, but the highlight of an inspection meal was a trout mousseline served with fresh scallops and scampi on a saffron sauce. Main courses range from pan-fried fillet of salmon with prawns in a herb and lemon butter, to peppered

venison, roasted and sliced onto a bed of creamed potato with a Cognac jus. The wine list has representation from around the world and offers a good choice of wines by the half bottle and by the glass.

Directions: Take the A12/14 (Felixstowe & Yarmouth), right at lights at brow of hill, hotel is 500yds on right

IPSWICH,
The Old Boot House Restaurant ❀❀

A former pub now a thriving restaurant drawing on local produce

Located on the peaceful fringe of the village of Shotley, proprietors Ian and Pamela Chamberlain offer a warm welcome in relaxing and informal surroundings. Ian's selection of dishes are mostly modern British in style while his cooking is unpretentious and prepared with care. A recent inspection meal for example, began with a mouth watering combination of Cromer crab and farmhouse cheddar omelette. This was followed by baked breast of chicken filled with Mediterranean vegetables and wrapped in Parma ham. Tender new potatoes and a range of crisp spring vegetables accompanied. Pudding was a very good example of crème brûlée – with a confident texture and flavour, topped with crisp caramel. Other dishes offered could include a starter of crisp baked spinach scallop and bacon tartlet, followed by tenderloin of lamb and mint pea casserole. The short wine list includes New World wines, and is well chosen to complement the style of the dishes.

Directions: 7 miles SE of Ipswich on B1456, through Chelmondiston, and 0.25 mile beyond Shotley sign on right.

Shotley IP9 1EY
Map no: 5 TM14
Tel: 01473 787755
Chef: Ian Chamberlain
Proprietors: Ian & Pamela Chamberlain
Cost: Alc from £16.25, fixed-price Sun L £10.50 (2course), £12.95. H/wine £7.50 ❢ No service charge
Credit cards: 🂠 🂡
Menus: A la carte L & D, fixed-price Sun L, bar L menu
Times: Last L 1.45pm, last D 9pm (flexible) Closed Sun D, Mon
Seats: 45. No smoking in dining room
Additional: Children permitted (early D preferred), children's portions; other diets booked in advance

IPSWICH, **Orwell House** ❀

A modest, comfortable family-run restaurant where fish features heavily on the menu. Seafood croustade, roast king scallops with garlic, coriander and bacon, fillet of brill, or lobster thermidor are balanced by honey-roast duck, and breast of chicken in coconut milk with green curry

4A Orwell Place IP4 1BB
Map no: 5 TM14
Tel: 01473 230254
Chef: Jonathan King
Proprietors: Rosemary & Derek King
Cost: Alc £15-£30, fixed-price L/D £9.95. H/wine £7.95 ❢ Service exc
Credit cards: 🂠 🂡 🂢 🂣 OTHER
Times: Last L 2pm, last D 9.30pm Closed Sat L, Sun
Menus: A la carte, fixed-price L & D, pre-theatre, bar menu
Seats: 60. No smoking in dining room
Additional: Children welcome, children's menu; ❖ dishes, vegan on request

Directions: E of town centre, opposite St Pancras Church and Cox Lane car park

IPSWICH, St Peter's Restaurant ❀❀

An informal brasserie atmosphere in this user-friendly restaurant that genuinely welcomes children

An appreciation of fresh food and a friendly, cheerful ambience are much in evidence at this corner restaurant. Within, it is all varnished pine and tiled floors with blackboards bearing descriptions of modern brasserie dishes dotted around. First courses might include mushrooms and leeks à la Greque, mussels with garlic and herb butter or, tried on an inspection visit, a warm escalope of smoked salmon with dill sauce. Main courses have included Chinese grilled chicken with black bean sauce, and baked halibut with shallots, white wine sauce and noodles. The short wine list is supplemented by a few house selections; there is, in addition, a wine bar at one end of the restaurant, serving light meals. There are a baby changing facilities in the ladies room.

Directions: On outskirts of town centre, corner of St Peter's Street and Star Lane, near St Peter's Church

35-37 St Peter's Street IP1 1XP
Map no: 5 TM14
Tel: 01473 210810
Chef: Robert Mabey
Proprietor: Robert Mabey
Cost: Fixed-price L £8.95/D £25. H/wine £7.50 Service exc
Credit cards: 💳 💳 💳 💳 OTHER
Times: Last L 2pm, last D 10pm Closed Sun, Mon
Menus: Fixed-price L & D, pre-theatre, bar menu
Seats: 85. No-smoking area
Additional: Children welcome, children's portions; ❤ dishes, vegan/other diets on request

IXWORTH, Theobalds Restaurant ❀❀

Consistently good cooking in traditional English country cottage setting

68 High Street IP31 2HJ
Map no: 5 TL97
Tel: 01359 231707
Chef: Simon Theobald
Proprietors: Simon & Geraldine Theobald
Cost: Fixed-price D £25.50-28.50/Sun L £16.95 Service exc
Credit cards: 💳 💳
Times: Last L 1.30pm, last D 9.30pm Closed Sat L, Sun D, Mon, 1 wk Aug
Menus: *A la carte* wkday L, fixed-price D & Sun L
Seats: 36. No smoking whilst others eating
Additional: Children welcome (over 8 at D), children's portions; ❤ dishes, other diets on request

Simon Theobald takes obvious pride in his cooking, and it reflects in the skilful way he prepares his dishes. Combinations of ingredients show a degree of imagination that whets the appetite – tournedos of hare served with red wine sauce laced with raspberry vinegar and bitter chocolate, roast fillet of turbot stuffed with tomatoes and served with a white port and chive sauce, fillet of lamb sautéed with artichokes and rosemary and sherry sauce. Game appears regularly in season – roast partridge with roast chestnuts and port sauce, for example, or pheasant and walnut terrine with quince jelly and toasted brioche. He also has the confidence to play it straight with dishes such as twice baked cheese soufflé, Chateaubriand with tarragon hollandaise, or grilled wing of skate with spinach and buttered lemon sauce. Desserts also have a glossy appeal – chocolate truffle cake with coffee bean sauce, or iced mandarin and nougat mousse on a marzipan base with chocolate sauce.

Directions: 7 miles from Bury St Edmunds on A143 Bury/Diss road

LAVENHAM, **The Swan** ❀

A classic Elizabethan inn serving traditional English dishes based on fresh seasonal ingredients. The lovely surroundings create a warm and relaxing atmosphere in which to enjoy dishes such as pheasant breast covered in a fresh herb and garlic crust, roast leg of lamb with rosemary, and liver and bacon

High Street CO10 9QA
Map no: 5 TL94
Tel: 01787 247477
Chef: Andrew Barrass
Proprietor: Forte Heritage.
Manager: Michael Grange
Cost: Fixed-price L £14.95/D £21.55. H/wine £12.75 ❢
Service exc
Credit cards: 🔲 📷 📟 💷 OTHER
Times: Last L 2pm, last D 9.30pm daily
Menus: Fixed-price L & D, bar menu
Seats: 70. No smoking in dining room
Additional: Children welcome, children's portions; ❤ dishes, vegan/other diets on request

Directions: In main street of village, A1141 (Bury/Hadleigh)

LONG MELFORD,
Chimneys Restaurant ❀❀

A popular country restaurant set in a beautiful 16th-century house

Sitting by the large inglenook fireplace in this friendly, informal restaurant, diners are faced with a wonderful problem of choice. The kitchen has compiled an exciting selection of modern English dishes to make any decision an agonising one. Should it be parfait of chicken livers with orange salad, or timbale of flaked salmon bound in crème fraîche? This could be followed by roulade of sole and sea trout with chives. The *carte* has a wider choice: rich Mediterranean fish soup, or fillet of lamb with wild mushrooms in a lattice flaky pastry. Nor is dessert any easier. Caramel and almond tart with fresh egg custard, or chilled passion fruit soufflé with mango sauce are just two of the choices. To finish, a strong blend of cafetière coffee with home-made fudge and petits fours. The wine list is reasonably priced.

Hall Street CO10 9JR
Map no: 5 TL84
Tel: 01787 379806
Chef: Jason Schroeder
Proprietor: Samuel Chalmers.
Manager: Wayne Messenger
Cost: *Alc* £27, fixed-price L £15.50. H/wine £9.85 Service exc
Credit cards: 🔲 📷 📟 💷
Times: Last L 2.30pm, last D 9.30pm Closed Sun D
Menus: *A la carte*, fixed-price L
Seats: 50. Air conditioned
Additional: Children welcome, children's portions; ❤ dishes, vegan/other diets on request

Directions: On main street of Long Melford village

> Mille-feuille in its classic 19th-century French form is thin layers of the lightest puff pastry separated by layers of cream, jam or any other filling with the top covered with icing sugar. This idea was then extended to savoury dishes with fillings of fish or shellfish, but nowadays chefs interpret mille-feuille as anything layered. This could be thin slices of apple, aubergine, celeriac, filo, you name it, as long as it arrives in an artistically arranged pile.

LONG MELFORD, **Countrymen Restaurant At The Black Lion Hotel** ❀

A well-kept, family-run hotel, occupying an idyllic site close to the 15th-century church. Stephen Errington transforms fresh produce into robust, unfussy dishes, offering perhaps, straightforward grilled lamb cutlets with fresh rosemary alongside fricassée of game in a creamy, soft green, peppercorn sauce

The Green CO10 9DN
Map no: 5 TL84
Tel: 01787 312356
Chef: Stephen Errington
Proprietor: Stephen Errington
Cost: *Alc* from £18.75, fixed-price L /D £13.25. H/wine £8.75
❢ Service exc
Credit cards: ▨ ▩ ▩ OTHER
Times: Last L 2pm, last D 9.30pm Closed Sun D, Mon
Seats: 50. No-smoking area
Additional: Children welcome, children's menu; ❤ dishes, other diets on request

Directions: On the green in the centre of the village

LONG MELFORD,
Scutchers Restaurant ❀

☺ *Friendly and easy going bistro with a menu that holds no surprises, but delivers honest food prepared by an experienced hand. Look out for a fresh tasting crab terrine, skate wings stuffed with salmon mousse, and medallions of venison in a black pepper sauce*

Westgate Street CO10 9DP
Map no: 5 TL84
Tel: 01787 310200/310620
Chef: Nicholas Barrett
Proprietor: Nicholas Barrett
Cost: *Alc* from £15. H/wine £7.75 ❢ Service exc
Credit cards: ▨ ▩ ▩
Times: Last L 2pm, last D 9.30. Closed Sun

Additional: Children welcome, children's portions; ❤ dishes; other diets on request
Directions: About one mile from Long Melford on the road to Clare

NEWMARKET, **Heath Court Hotel** ❀

This pleasant modern hotel has a lovely warm and relaxed atmosphere and friendly welcoming staff. Bertie's Brasserie offers traditional British cooking in an informal and lively environment. Dishes include duck terrine with caramelised oranges

Moulton Road CB8 8DY
Map no: 5 TL66
Tel: 01638 667171
Chef: Paul Rolt
Proprietor: Stephen Gross
Cost: *Alc* £18.92 av. H/wine £9.50 Service exc
Credit cards: ▨ ▩ ▩ ▨ OTHER
Times: Last L 2pm, last D 9.45pm Closed Sat/BH L (bar menu open)

Menus: *A la carte* L & D, bar menu
Seats: 70. No smoking area
Additional: Children welcome, children's menu; ❤ dishes, vegan/other diets on request
Directions: Top of High Street at start of the Gallops, signs for Moulton

ORFORD, **Butley Orford Oysterage** ✦

Local support is evident at this starkly simple restaurant.
Fresh seafood is prepared by a team of village ladies with a minimum
of fuss. The smokehouse at the rear provides all the excellent smoked
fish and oysters come from a private bed on Butley Creek. Otherwise
expect skate with brown butter, or griddled squid

Seats: 95
Additional: Children welcome, children's portions
Directions: In market square, next to town hall

Market Square IP12 2LH
Map no: 5 TM45
Tel: 01394 450277
Chefs: J Knights and J Pinney
Proprietors: Pinney & Pinney
Cost: Alc £18. H/wine £8.
Service exc
Credit cards: None taken
Times: Midday-last L 2.15pm,
last D 9pm. Closed 25 & 26 Dec

SOUTHWOLD,
The Crown at Southwold ✦

The focal point of this restored Georgian inn continues to be its well
regarded bar and restaurant, partly for the quality of its wines and beers.
The daily menus roam the world for inspiration, offering the likes of
steamed green lipped mussels on tagliatelle with fresh tarragon, and
grilled Suffolk duckling with crispy noodles

Seats: 22. Air conditioned. No smoking in restaurant **Menus:** fixed-
price L & D, bar menu **Additional:** children welcome, children's
portions; ❶ dishes, vegan/other diets with advance notice
Directions: Take A1095 off A12; at top of High Street, just before
Market Place

90 High Street IP18 6DP
Map no: 5 TM57
Tel: 01502 722275
Chef: Richard Pye
Proprietors: Adnams.
Manager: Anne Simpson
Cost: fixed-price L £15.50 D
£19.95. H/wine £8.40 ❶ Service
exc
Credit cards: 🟦 ▥ ▥ 🟦 OTHER
Times: 12.30pm-last L 1.30pm,
7.30pm-last D 9.30pm. Closed
2nd wk Jan

SOUTHWOLD, **Swan Hotel** ✦

There is a lovely, timeless character about this town hotel-cum-local
landmark – log burning fires are inviting and cosy, and the restaurant is
elegant. Dishes are simply crafted using good technique and fresh local
ingredients. With gentle charm, good service and intentions, this is a place
for decent food

Menus: Fixed-price L & D, bar L **Seats:** n/a. No smoking area
Additional: children permitted (over 5 at D); ❶ dishes, vegan/other
diets on request
Directions: Turn off A12 to Southwold, along High Street to Market
Place, hotel on left

Market Place IP18 6EG
Map no: 5 TM57
Tel: 01502 722186
Chef: Robert Brummel
Proprietor: Adnams.
Manager: Carole Wilkin
Cost: fixed-price L £14.50/D
£18.95/Sun L £16.95. H/wine
£ 6.95 ❶ Service exc
Credit cards: 🟦 ▥ ▥ 🟦 OTHER
Times: last L 1.45 (2.30pm Bar
L) , last D 9.30pm. Closed L Jan-
Mar

SUDBURY, **Mabey's Brasserie** ✦✦

A modern brasserie in Gainsborough's birthplace with tempting
blackboard menus and good value specials

Chef/proprietor Robert Mabey now looks after three East Anglian
brasseries. He can't be in three places at once, so the cooking was in
new hands when we last visited. There were differences – a tad less
self-confidence – but the modern, split-level restaurant remained as
informal and relaxing as before. There is an open galley kitchen,
and seasonal menus, including keenly priced daily specials, are
written on blackboards. One inspector found the won ton parcels
with chicken and ginger a bit dull, but on the whole the food was
found to be well prepared, direct and fresh. Examples include
grilled duck breast with green peppercorn sauce, and poached

47 Gainsborough Street
CO10 7SS
Map no: 5 TL84
Tel: 01787 374298
Chef: Robert Mabey
Proprietor: Robert Mabey
Cost: Alc £18, fixed-price L
£8.95, £6.95 (2 course). H/wine
£7.50 Service exc
Credit cards: 🟦 ▥ ▥ 🟦 OTHER
Times: Last L 2pm, last D 10pm
Closed Sun, Mon
Menus: Fixed-price L & D, pre-
theatre, bar menu
Seats: 40. No-smoking area

escalope of salmon with sorrel sauce. Any waywardness in the starters was virtually forgotten by the time desserts appeared. Summer pudding was fruity and tingling, served with a fresh crème anglaise. Other tempters might be crème brûlée, enlivened here with lime and honey, or blackcurrant sorbet with diced pears. The 40-or-so-bottles wine list offers mainly French and New World with the occasional guest, such as one from a fellow Suffolk restaurateur's vineyard in Provence.

Additional: Children welcome, children's menu; ❶ dishes, vegan/other diets on request

Directions: 150yds from Market Hill, next to Gainsborough House Museum

WOODBRIDGE, **Captain's Table** ❀

A pink painted cottage houses this long-established restaurant. Seafood features strongly. While the carte remains fairly fixed, and the set price menu varies depending on the day's catch, simplicity is the byword for the construction of all dishes, sauces and vegetables

3 Quay Street IP12 1BX
Map no: 5 TM24
Tel: 01394 383145
Chef: Tony Prentice
Proprietor: Tony Prentice
Cost: Alc £20, fixed-price L & D £11.95. H/wine £9.55. Service inc
Credit cards: 🔲 🔲 🔲 🔲 OTHER
Times: Last L 2pm, last D 9.30pm Closed Sun, Mon, 1st 2 weeks Feb

Seats: 46. No smoking in dining room
Additional: Children permitted, children's portions; ❶ dishes, vegan dishes by arrangement; other diets on request
Directions: Quay Street is opposite the cinema. The restaurant is 100yds on left

SURREY

BAGSHOT, **Pennyhill Park Hotel** ❀❀❀

An elegant setting and elaborately presented dishes are the hallmarks of this intimate restaurant

London Road GU19 5ET
Map no: 4 SU96
Tel: 01276 471774
Chef: Karl Edmunds
Proprietor: Exclusive Hotels. Manager: Dermot Fitzpatrick
Cost: Alc £35, fixed-price L £18.99/ ❶ £28. H/wine £14.25 ❶ Service inc
Credit cards: 🔲 🔲 🔲 🔲 OTHER
Times: Last L 2.30pm, last D 10.30pm
Menus: A la carte, fixed-price L & D, bar menu
Seats: 45. No smoking in dining room
Additional: Children permitted, children's menu; ❶ dishes, vegan/other diets on request

Surrounded by flagged terraces and formally laid out gardens, this creeper-clad hotel is a fine Victorian manor house set in 120 acres of private land bordering the Crown Estate. Though the magnificent interior displays a wealth of fine paintings and tapestries, the Latymer Restaurant – despite its impressive timbered ceiling – retains an intimate atmosphere. Chef Karl Edmunds' imaginative *carte* and fixed-price menus offer an appetising and balanced range of French/English dishes in traditional style; saucing is particularly noteworthy, though the presentation of vegetables can be over-elaborate. In the course of a autumn dinner, an assortment of chilled melon balls was followed by layers of succulent scallops with spinach and wafer-thin rösti on a creamy chive butter sauce; the main course was duck, served in a deep, rich jus with Parisienne vegetables, and pudding was excellent – an orange cheesecake and orange yoghurt ice-cream ball set on a marmalade-style purée. Fish figures prominently (smoked haddock, for example, being baked in puff pastry and served on a bed of diced beetroot and cucumber ribbons), and a traditional dish of the day is served from the silver trolley. An exceptionally good, predominantly French wine list ranges from interesting house wines at £15 to a Chateau Haut Brion 1959 at £325.

Directions: On A30 between Bagshot and Camberley

BRAMLEY, **Bramley Grange Hotel** ❀❀

A well-managed roadside hotel restaurant with a kitchen dedicated to producing a good standard of cooking

Horsham Road GU5 0BL
Map : 4 TQ04
Tel: 01483 893434
Chef: David Skan
Proprietor: (Mazard Hotel Management).
Manager: Dawn Hale
Cost: *Alc* £20-£25, fixed-price L/D £13.50. H/wine £9.95 ❢ Service inc
Credit cards: ▨ ▨ ▨ OTHER
Times: Last L 2.30pm, last D 9.30pm Closed Sat L
Menus: *A la carte*, fixed-price L & D, bar menu
Seats: 60. No-smoking area
Additional: Children welcome, children's portions; ❶ dishes, vegan/other diets on request

A mock-Tudor hotel set is secluded grounds with a wooded hillside for a backdrop. David Skan is an important contributor to the hotel's success; by producing dishes to a high standard, he demonstrates a serious and dedicated approach. There is a seasonal *carte* supplemented by a three-course daily set-menu, plus a special option called 'Around the World in Seven Dishes'. Fresh, quality ingredients were a highlight of a winter visit which yielded a light timbale of sole, with mussels, crab and prawns, served with a creamed saffron fumet, slightly dry but tender fillets of beef layered with foie gras mousse, with a well-flavoured brandy and truffle glace de viande. Vegetables, alas, lacked seasoning and were 'very plain and unexciting'; dauphinoise potatoes were a little dry. On the other hand, French apple tart with Chantilly cream and sliced fresh strawberries was 'worth the wait'. The wine list looks good with 75 or so bins including a good showing from the New World, and vintage French country wines.

Directions: Village centre, 2.5 miles from Guildford on A281 (Horsham)

BRAMLEY, **The Garden Restaurant** ❀

An intimate restaurant, located in the centre of the village, offering simple prepared food from a short, fixed-price menu. Typical dishes may include mussel crêpe with fish stock and cream sauce, steamed leg of lamb in mustard and onion sauce, and French bread and butter pudding

Menus: Fixed-price D & Sun L
Seats: 30. Air conditioned
Additional: children welcomed, children's portions; ❶ dishes, vegan dishes/other diets on request
Directions: On A281 3 miles south of Guildford

4a High Street GU5 0HB
Map no: 4 TQ04
Tel: 01483 894037
Chef: Peter Hirth
Proprietor: Peter Hirth
Cost: Fixed-price D £12.95/Sun L £10.95 (4 course)H/wine £8.50 ❢ Service inc
Credit cards: ▨ ▨ ▨ OTHER
Times: Open Fri/Sat D & Sun L only. Closed Mon-Thur

CAMBERLEY, Frimley Hall ✿

Enjoyable cooking is offered on well balanced carte and fixed-price menus in the smart restaurant of this comfortable, well-run hotel. A good choice is available and includes some interesting dishes: red mullet on rocket leaves with a coriander dressing, and braised rabbit in a cider, lavender and chervil sauce

Menus: A la carte, fixed-price L & D, Sun lunch, bar menu
Seats: 120. No smoking in dining-room
Additional: Children welcome, children`s menu; ✪ & vegan dishes, other diets on request
Directions: Close to Junction 3 of the M3

Frimley Hall
Portsmouth Road GU15 2BG
Map no: 4 SZ96
Tel: 01276 28321
Chef: Marc Legros
Proprietor: Forte Heritage
Cost: Alc £25.50, fixed-price
L £15.95, fixed-price D £19.95.
House/w £10.70 ❢Service inc
Credit cards: 🔳 📰 📰 💷
Times: Last L - 3pm, last D - 10pm

CLAYGATE, Le Petit Pierrot Restaurant ✿✿

This popular cosy restaurant continues to plough an excellent furrow

The draped fabrics on the walls and ceiling add to the intimacy of this small French restaurant. Chef/patron Jean-Pierre offers reasonable set-price menus at both lunch and dinner. His skilful cooking might include starters of grilled goats' cheese on seasonal leaves with hazelnuts or Provençal style squid with tomato, coriander and olive oil. Our inspector enjoyed a 'terrine de rouget aux herbs fraîches' – succulent red snapper with the right balance of herbs served with a beurre blanc sauce. 'Noisettes de chevreuil aux marrons' followed. The lightly sautéed pieces of venison were served with chestnuts and a tantalising poivrade sauce. Other main courses might include poached salmon with a green pea and white sauce or pan-fried calves' liver, stuffed with mango and ginger and served with a port sauce. There is a short selection of desserts and our inspector tried a pleasantly sweet crème brûlée with apple, cinnamon and Calvados. There is a well balanced list of French wines, reasonably priced with a few good clarets and Burgundies.

Directions: Village centre, 1 mile from Esher

4 The Parade KT10 0NU
Map no: 4 TQ16
Tel: 01372 465105
Chef: Jean Pierre Brichot
Proprietors: Jean Pierre and Annie Brichot
Cost: Fixed-price L £16.85, £9.95 (2 course)/D £18.95. H/wine £8.95 Service exc
Credit cards: 🔳 📰 📰 💷
Times: Last L 2.30pm, last D 10.30pm Closed Sat L, Sun
Menus: Fixed-price L & D
Seats: 32. Air conditioned
Additional: Children over permitted; ✪ dishes, other diets with notice

CLAYGATE, Les Alouettes ✿✿

A smart modern restaurant on the outer London/Surrey border, now a firm favourite with locals

Claygate is one of those outer London villages straddling the imaginary line which divides muddy front-wheel drive, off-road vehicles, from clean ones. The High Street still retains a distinctly rural appearance as it ambles along, at one point turning through 90 degrees. It is on this corner that the attractive gabled building, now housing Les Alouettes – meaning skylarks – stands. Inside, the lighting is comfortably subdued, with strategically placed mirrors creating an illusion of additional space. On a warm summer evening it was cool enough indoors to feel at ease with cold, warm and even hot dishes, beginning with a salad of warm goats' cheese from Chavignol, wrapped in brick pastry with pears, pine kernels and a walnut dressing, and thinly sliced tuna slices, marinated in olive oil, lime and herbs, served with a creamy fromage frais-filled tomato. Juicy pan-fried scallops served in their own shell were stabilised on the plate by a bed of salt, and crispy roast duck, served off the bone with caramelised pears and a rich ruby-coloured cassis sauce was,

High Street KT10 0JW
Map no: 4 TQ16
Tel: 01372 464882
Chef: Eric Bouchet
Proprietor: Steve Christov
Cost: Alc £26.50, fixed-price L £15.50/D £19.50. H/wine £11 ❢ Service exc
Credit cards: 🔳 📰 📰
Times: Last L 2pm, last D 9.30pm/10pm Fri-Sat Closed Sat L, Sun D, Mon
Menus: A la carte, fixed-price L & D
Seats: 70. Air conditioned
Additional: Children welcome, children's portions; ✪ dishes, other diets with notice

like everything else, prepared and cooked to impress. The desserts are as impressive as the main courses, and the wine list shows all the signs of compilation by an expert. Vegetarians have a separate menu.
Directions: On main A244 in Claygate

CRANLEIGH, **La Barbe Encore** ❀

The relaxed and informal atmosphere here is in keeping with a typical French bistro. Whilst the menu is not large, it is well balanced, offering daily specials such as 'morue pochée au lait, lentilles et citron' – cod poached in milk and served with lentils in cream with a little lemon juice

Times: Noon-last L 2pm, 7pm-last D 10.30pm. Closed Mon, Sun D
Seats: 60. No-smoking area. No cigars or pipes
Additional: Children welcome, children's portions on request; ❶ dishes, vegan/other diets on request
Directions: Horsham end of High Street between Hospital & Library

High Street GU6 8AE
Map no: 4 TQ03
Tel: 01483 273889
Chef: Jean Pierre Bonnet
Proprietors: Jean Pierre & Ann Bonnet
Cost: Fixed-price L £19.95/D £23.95. H/wine £9.25 ❢ Service exc
Credit cards: 🂠 🏧 ᙇ OTHER

DORKING, **Partners West Street** ❀❀

Partners West Street has been gaining in reputation ever since it was opened by Andrew Thompson and Tim McEntire in 1990

The 16th-century building, with its beams and nooks and crannies and two separate dining rooms, provides an intimate atmosphere. A recent inspection meal began with the lightest of cheese straws, followed by a starter of warm salad of crispy duck confit and duck livers on a firm fresh green salad, which was delicious. But it was the restaurant's own lobster sausages on ratatouille with a fresh basil sauce that stole the show. The lobster mousse had a firm texture and excellent taste. For the main course, seared medallion of sea bass on a bed of saffron noodles with crispy fried vegetables and a sweet and sour sauce was made with the freshest of fish. Roast fillet of English lamb was pink and very tender while the basil mousse topping really brought out the flavour. The goats' cheese sauce which accompanied the dish sounded potentially disastrous but in the event was an accomplished meat jus with the merest hint of goats' cheese. From the desserts list came a home-made mint ice-cream in a chocolate coat. The mainly French wine list has a dozen half bottles and some English wines from local vineyards including a recommended dessert wine from Leatherhead.

Directions: Town Centre – Guildford end of High Street

2, 3 & 4 West Street RH4 1BL
Map no: 4 TQ14
Tel: 01306 882826
Chefs: Tim McEntire and Paul Boyland
Proprietor: Andrew Thomason
Cost: Alc £27, fixed-price L £11.95/D £15 H/wine £10.95 Service exc
Credit cards: 🂠 🏧 ᙇ 🂡 OTHER
Times: Last L 2.30pm, last D 9.30pm Closed Sat L, Sun D
Menus: A la carte, fixed-price L & D
Seats: 45. No smoking in dining room
Additional: Children welcome, children's menu; ❶ dishes, other diets on request

EAST HORSLEY, **Jarvis Thatchers Hotel** ❀

Set in its own grounds, Thatchers is an extended timbered 1930s house. The fixed-price menu and carte both offer straightforward grills, mixed with more elaborate dishes. Typical dishes include salmon, soundly cooked calves' liver and a banoffee tart for dessert

Seats: 50-80
Additional: Children welcome, children's portions; ❶ dishes, vegan/other diets on request
Directions: On main road through village

Epsom Road KT24 6TB
Map no: 4 TQ05
Tel: 01483 284291
Chef: Paul O'Dowd
Proprietor: Jarvis Hotels
Cost: Alc £32, fixed-price L £14.50/D £19.50 H/wine £9.40. Service exc
Credit cards: 🂠 🏧 ᙇ 🂡 OTHER
Times: 12.30pm-last L 2pm, 7.30pm-last D 9.30pm

EGHAM, **Runnymede Hotel** ❁

The Runnymede's large, attractive restaurant caters for an international clientele and offers cooking of a cosmopolitan flavour. Dishes include cutlet of pork from a 'genuinely free-range farm' in Wiltshire, grilled with quince glaze and dauphinoise potatoes

Menus: Fixed-price L & D, bistro menu **Seats:** 120. Air conditioned
Additional: Children welcome, children's portions; ❂ dishes, vegan/other diets on request
Directions: On A308 Windsor road from M25 junction 3

Windsor Road TW20 0AG
Map no: 4 TQ07
Tel: 01784 436171
Chef: Laurence Curtis
Manager: Sue Crowley
Cost: Fixed-price L £16.95/D £22.50 H/wine £11.75 Service exc
Credit cards: 🟦 💳 💳 💳
Times: Last L 2.15pm, last D 9.45pm

EPSOM, **Le Raj** ❁❁

☺ *Creative and innovative Bangladeshi cooking from a dedicated chef*

211 Firtree Road KT17 3LB
Map no: 4 TQ26
Tel: 01737 371371
Chef: Enam Ali
Proprietor: Manager: Tipu Rahman
Cost: *Alc* £20. H/wine £7.50 Service exc
Credit cards: 🟦 💳 💳 💳
Times: Last L 2.15pm, last D 10.30pm Closed Dec 25/26
Menus: *A la carte* L & D
Seats: 50. Air conditioned
Additional: Children welcome; ❂ dishes, other diets on request

One inspector felt that his meal at Le Raj was 'one of the best Indian meals for a long time'. High praise indeed for chef Enam Ali. Using traditional cooking techniques he has adapted well-known recipes to create his own unique signature and style. Everything is cooked to order and garam masala, cultured yoghurts and breads are made on the premises. At inspection dishes sampled included fresh crisp samosas which were lightly fried and filled with chopped, crunchy vegetables. Equally delicious was 'pakura' – shredded onion and green pepper, battered with garum flour lightly spiced and deep fried. The chicken tikka was fresh, succulent and marinated with spices then lightly grilled on charcoal and garnished with allumette of grilled onion. An additional dish of 'sag ghost' – fresh spinach cooked in ghee with fresh lean lamb was delicately flavoured with spices and garnished with allumette of potato. There is a reasonable range of wines but no half bottles.

Directions: Off the A217, near the racecourse

ESHER, **Good Earth Restaurant** ❁❁

☺ *Top of the range Chinese restaurant with smart, contemporary decor*

Most of the main regions of China are represented in the menu at this popular restaurant, where the cooking is lifted out of the ordinary by interesting combinations of textures, and skilful use of

14-18 High Street KT10 9RT
Map no: 4 TQ16
Tel: 01372 462489
Chef: Mr Tang
Proprietors: Robert Cheung and Wesley Lau

spices and seasoning. Some of the more unusual dishes on the menu include deep-fried quail in peppercorns and spiced salt, Peking sliced lamb and cucumber clear soup, and Dover sole in rice wine sauce. The menu helpfully indicates which are hot and spicy dishes, and there is an excellent vegetarian choice including double-braised Winter bamboo shoots and Chinese mushrooms, 'Monks Casserole' in a clay pot, and faked yellow fish in hot, piquant sauce (actually made from split peas, mushrooms and spring onions). Honey-barbecued ribs with spicy sauce, lettuce-wrapped crispy lamb with tangy yellow plum sauce, sizzling salmon steak with black bean sauce and shredded beef mandarin with sticky orange sauce, have all been well recommended. The experienced proprietors, Robert Cheung and Wesley Lau, personally greet and seat guests, all the staff are very polite, and the freshly cooked dishes arrive without delay.

Directions: Sandown Park end of the High Street

Cost: *Alc* £17.50, fixed-price L £12 (2 course)/D £ 17.50. H/wine £8 Service exc
Credit cards: 🆇 🔳 🔳 🔳
Times: Last L 2.15pm, last D 11pm Closed Dec 24-27
Menus: *A la carte*, fixed-price L & D
Seats: 90. Air conditioned
Additional: Children welcome; ❷ dishes, vegan on request

EWELL, **C'est la Vie** ❀

☺ *Delightful, beamed farmhouse-style restaurant offering traditional French cooking. An inspection meal yielded well made fish soup, medley of fresh fish: scallops, prawns, scampi and salmon in a saffron cream sauce and lemon tart for dessert*

Menus: *A la carte*, fixed-price L & D
Seats: 42 (main rest), 20 (private dining room)
Additional: ❷ dishes, other diets on request
Directions: Centre of High Street

17 High Street KT17 1SB
Map no: 4 TQ26
Tel: 0181 394 2933
Proprietor: Clive Lane
Cost: *Alc* £18.50, fixed-price L £6.50 (2 courses), £14.75 (4 courses), fixed-price D £14.75 (4 courses)
Times: Noon-last L 2.30pm, 7pm-last D 10pm. Closed Sun D

GODALMING, **Inn on the Lake** ❀❀

☺ *Intelligent and well-judged cooking at convivial country house inn*

Ockford Road GU7 1RH
Map no: 4 SZ96
Tel: 01483 415 575
Chef: Neil O`Brien
Proprietor: Amberley Catering Group
Cost: *Alc* £18, fixed-price L/D£16.50. House/w £8.75 ❢ Service exc
Credit cards: 🆇 🔳 🔳 🔳
Times: Noon - last L 2pm, Last D - 10pm. Closed Xmas night
Menus: *A la carte*, fixed-price L & D, Sun lunch, bar menu
Seats: 75
Additional: Children welcome, children`s portions; ❷ & vegan dishes, other diets on request

Combining a popular country inn with a serious, high quality restaurant and hotel can be difficult. The Inn on the Lake, however, encompasses all needs in a building of Tudor origins, with ever-increasing modern extensions and adaptations. The inn features a good range of real ale and bar meals, whilst the Lake View Restaurant offers more formal and sedate surroundings. New chef Neil O'Brien's dishes are freshly prepared and skilfully cooked, using the best quality ingredients. Recommendations include a number of old favourites, such as calves' liver and bacon with melted onions and mashed potatoes, traditional bubble and squeak glazed with Cheddar cheese, and sticky toffee pudding with butterscotch sauce. Our inspector appreciated a starter of marinated salmon with poached quails eggs, served with a creamy, sweet mustard and dill sauce. Equally enjoyable was a tender, pink roast rack of lamb set on crispy aubergine cakes with a nage of sliced Provençal vegetables. Amongst a good selection of vegetables, red cabbage and dauphinoise potatoes stood out. The overall standard of the meal was well maintained by an egg custard tart garnished with mint and kiwi fruit.

Directions: Follow A30 through Bagshot. Take A325 (Portsmouth Road). Past Esso Petrol Station take fifth turn on right into Conifer Drive (leading to Lime Avenue). Turn right and follow signs for Frimley Hall Hotel.

GUILDFORD, **The Angel** ❀❀

Enjoy an accomplished meal in the atmospheric surroundings of the Crypt Restaurant

91 High Street GU1 3DP
Map no: 4 SU94
Tel: 01483 64555
Chef: Anthony O'Hare
Proprietor: Hazel Smith
Cost: *Alc* £23.50, fixed-price L £8.50 (2 courses), £10.95/D £14.50. H/wine £8.75. Service exc
Credit cards: ▨ ▨ ▨ ▨ OTHER
Times: Midday-last L 2.30pm, 7pm-last D 10.30pm
Seats: 42
Additional: Children welcome, children's menu/portions; ❂ dishes, vegan by arrangement; other diets on request

Ever since the sixteenth century, travellers have been made welcome at this charming High Street coaching inn which still retains many original features and all its character. The candlelit, flagstoned and vaulted Crypt Restaurant – one outcome of extensive improvements undertaken recently – boasts tapestry-hung walls and polished wooden tables set with crisp white linen and gleaming cutlery. It is an effective showplace for the talents of chef Anthony O'Hare. A typical meal might begin with home-made lobster and basil ravioli served with a brandy sauce, garnished with langoustine tails and topped with an allumette of deep-fried leek and carrot; this could be followed by tender mignons of lamb, set on rösti potato and accompanied by Madeira-flavoured red wine glace de viande and a selection of fresh, al dente vegetables, then poached pear with figs and Mirabelle sauce. Petits fours are offered with cafetière coffee (an excellent Colombian/Kenyan blend). Lunchtime visitors should note that the High Street is closed to traffic between 11am and 4pm.

Directions: In town centre (one-way street)

GUILDFORD, **The Manor** ❀

A good choice of typically English dishes which, though fairly unoriginal, demonstrate a sound degree of culinary skill, is served in a pleasant setting. Look out for soft-textured chicken liver pâté, tender, pink, honey-roast rack of lamb, and a deliciously moist bread and butter pudding with a rich, spicy flavour

Newlands Corner GU44 8SE
Map no: 4 SU94
Tel: 01483 222624
Chef: Ian Penn
Proprietor: Peter Davies
Cost: *Alc* £25, fixed-price
L £14.50/D £17.50
H/wine £9.50 ♪ Service exc
Credit cards: 🖃 🖃 🖃 🖃 OTHER
Times: Last L 2.30pm, last D
10pm
Menus: *A la carte*, fixed-price L
& D, Sun Jazz Brunch, bar menu
(not Sun)
Seats: 45
Additional: Children permitted,
children's portions; ♥ menu,
other diets by arrangement

Directions: M25 exit 10, A3 (Ripley) to W Clandon, up hill on A25

HASLEMERE, **Fleur de Sel** ❀❀❀

Good, classic French cooking from a chef/co-proprietor with an assured hand

23/27 Lower Street GU27 2NY
Map no: 4 SU94
Tel: 01428 651462
Chef: Michel Perraud
Proprietors: Michel &
Bernardette Perraud
Cost: *Alc* £26, fixed-price
L £16.50/D £26. H/wine £9.90.
Service exc
Credit cards: 🖃 🖃 🖃 OTHER
Times: Last L 2pm, last D 10pm.
Closed Sat L, Sun D, Mon, 3 wks
Summer
Seats: 50. No-smoking area
Menus: *A la carte*, fixed-price L
& D

The restaurant's joint-owner, Michel Perraud, is an accomplished chef. Trained at the Waterside in Bray, then employed as head chef at London's Le Cordon Bleu cookery school, M Perraud now oversees the creation of good, classical food without any frills. Starters might include mousseline of duck liver with toasted almonds or a finely flavoured hake and turbot terrine with tomato butter sauce. There is a leaning towards fish dishes on the menu such as salmon with tomato and orange sauce, turbot with a fish mousse or pan-fried Dover sole. However, game, poultry and meat also feature. At a recent meal thick slices of lamb fillet with mild bordelaise demi-glace sauce were served with pommes galette, crisp beans and hearty red beetroot. The simple desserts are crafted by a practised hand and may include such delights as crème brûlée with rhubarb or warm apple tart with cinnamon ice cream. The wine list is chauvinistic, centred on lesser Bordeaux and Burgundies with a few provincials.

Additional: Children welcome, children's portions; ❂ dishes; other dishes by arrangement

Directions: In the town centre turn right at top of High Street

HASLEMERE, Lythe Hill Hotel ❀❀

A delightful setting and skilled French cuisine make any meal here an occasion to remember

Petworth Road GU7 3BQ
Map no: 4 SU94
Tel: 01428 651251
Chef: Roger Clarke
Manager: Kevin Lorimer
Cost: *Alc* from £32, fixed-price D £22.50/Sun L £17.50. H/wine £11.75 Service exc
Credit cards: ⬛ ⬛ ⬛ OTHER
Times: Last D 9.30pm, last Sun L 2.15pm Closed Mon
Menus: *A la carte* D, fixed-price D/Sun L
Seats: 60. No smoking in dining room
Additional: Children welcome, children's portions; ❂ dishes, vegan/other diets on request

From its hillside setting this listed building – parts date from about 1457 – overlooks a peaceful lake and woodland. It offers two places to eat: the hotel dining-room and the restaurant Auberge de France. The latter is largely the achievement of chef Roger Clarke; he has cooked here for over fifteen years, and continues a long tradition of providing *carte* and fixed-price menus of interesting, classically based French dishes cooked with flair and professionalism. As a first course to a recent dinner, for example, our inspector enjoyed tiger bay prawns in a lemon, garlic and light soy sauce, dressed round a potato nest of assorted leaves; this was followed by a fillet of sea bass encrusted with pine nuts and served on a celeriac purée with a red wine reduction meat jus. The highlight of the meal, however, was a tender, full flavoured cannon of sliced pink lamb noisettes set around an aubergine and courgette gâteau and accompanied by the same red wine sauce, puréed carrots, duxelle of mushrooms and almondine potatoes. A wine list of some 140 bins includes both classic vintages and New World labels; there is a good range of house wines.

Directions: 1 mile east of Haslemere on B2131 off A286

HERSHAM, **The Dining Room** ❀

Little changes at this popular restaurant whose small rooms have a cosy relaxing atmosphere. Simple, classical English dishes include beef and ale pie, and game and tattie mash (a rich stew of venison, wild boar and rabbit). A short list of some 22 inexpensive wines complements the cooking style

Menus: *A la carte* L & D
Seats: 90. No-smoking area
Additional: Children welcome, children's portions/Sun menu; ❂ dishes, other diets on request
Directions: Off the village green, off A244 (Walton-on-Thames)

10-12 Queens Road KT12 5LS
Map no: 4 TQ16
Tel: 01932 231686
Cost: *Alc* £19. H/wine £7.50
Service exc
Credit cards: ▨ ▦ ▭
Times: Last L 2pm/2.30 Sun, last D 10.30pm Closed Sat L, Sun D, BHs, 1 wk Xmas

HERSHAM, **Ristorante San Marco** ❀

A bright, cheerful Italian restaurant serving familiar trattoria-style dishes: 'mozzarella tricolore', sirloin steak with green pepper sauce. 'Fegato alla Veneziana' features English calves' liver and not Dutch. Good cappuccino and a short list of Italian wines

Directions: Opposite Hersham Green

17 Queens Road KT12 5ND
Map no: 4 TQ16
Tel: 01932 227412
Chef: M Mongiovi
Proprietors: Jacques & Lisa Troquet

HORLEY, **Langshott Manor** ❀❀

Nothing is too much trouble in this gem of a family-run hotel – a beautiful sixteenth-century timber-framed manor house set in stunning grounds

Since taking over in 1986, the Noble family have given the 400 year old house a remarkable lease of life. Great care has been lavished on the building and the immaculate gardens to create a peaceful oasis only a short drive from Gatwick airport and the centre of London. The bedrooms are a mix of modern comforts and antiques – in keeping with the traditional ambience. The chef is Christopher Noble who produces a short and uncomplicated menu. A starter of coarse pork pâté and a main course of red mullet fillets with olive, tomato and chervil with fresh vegetables, were simple and savoury. The dessert, a rich, full cream crème brûlée, though slightly overcooked with an over caramelised crust, did slip down well. Breakfast was a highlight with an excellent fresh fruit salad and a full works English breakfast.

Directions: From A23 Horley, take Ladbroke Road turning off Chequers Hotel roundabout, 0.75 mile on right

Ladbroke Road RH6 9LN
Map no: 4 TQ24
Tel: 01293 786680
Chef: Christopher Noble
Proprietors: Geoffrey & Patricia Noble
Cost: Fixed-price D £25. H/wine £10.50 Service exc
Credit cards: ▨ ▦ ▭ ▣
Times: 7pm- last D 9.30pm Closed Xmas 5 days
Menus: Fixed-price D, bar menu
Seats: 14. No smoking in dining room
Additional: Children permitted if resident; ❂ dishes

NUTFIELD, **Nutfield Priory** ❀❀

A magnificent property high on Nutfield Ridge serving an imaginative range of modern English dishes

An extravagantly conceived Victorian folly turned comfortable country house hotel, Nutfield Priory provides the characterful setting for a good selection of wholesome English cooking. Cloisters Restaurant offers a choice of fixed-price and *carte*, along with a well balanced and reasonably priced wine list. A winter meal, chosen from the *carte*, commenced with roast sea scallop with

Redhill RH1 4EN
Map no: 4 TQ35
Tel: 01737 822066
Chef: Stephen Cane
Proprietor: Arcadian.
Manager: Cordelia Judd
Cost: *Alc* £30, fixed-price L £16/D £19.50 H/wine £11.50
❢ Service exc
Credit cards: ▨ ▦ ▭ ▣ OTHER

rocket and prosciutto, served with a balsamic dressing, followed by pot-roasted wild rabbit with home-dried tomatoes and essence of basil. The rabbit had a good gamey flavour and came with an equally well flavoured gravy sauce. A trio of English desserts concluded the meal – bread and butter pudding, treacle pudding and apple charlotte – served with a light sauce anglaise. Another feature is the imaginative vegetarian choice: gâteau of Provençal vegetables with pesto sauce, followed by tian of vegetable marrow with a casserole of forest mushrooms surrounded by beetroot sauce. Cheeses are also taken seriously, with a whole page of the menu devoted to the restaurant's selection, listed in order of strength from Cornish Yarg to Stilton.

Directions: On A25 1 mile east of Redhill

Times: Last L 2pm, last D 9.30pm Closed Sat L, Dec 26-30
Menus: *A la carte*, fixed-price L & D
Seats: 60. No smoking in dining room
Additional: Children welcome, children's portions; ❻ dishes, other diets on request

REIGATE, **Bridge House Hotel** ❀

Traditional British dishes are served in the restaurant of this popular hotel. Recommended dishes include grilled sardines with fresh herbs, garlic and lime, fresh monkfish steak with a white wine ginger and butter sauce, and a delicious zabaglione to finish. The panoramic views over Reigate valley are lovely

Reigate Hill RH2 9RP
Map no: 4 TQ25
Tel: 01737 246801
Chef: Mark Fagg
Proprietor: n/a
Manager: G Codo
Cost: *Alc* £30, fixed-price L £16/D £20 (£24 Sat) H/wine £9.85 Service exc
Credit cards: 🂠 ▦ ▨ ▨
Times: Last L 2.15pm, last D 10.30pm Closed BH(Mon)
Menus: *A la carte*, fixed-price L & D
Seats: 200
Additional: Children welcome, children's portions; ❻ dishes, vegan/other diets on request

Directions: .25 mile from M25 exit 8 on A217 towards Reigate

Antoine Augustin Parmentier (1737 - 1813). A military pharmacist and French agronomist who was an enthusiastic propagator of the potato. Although the potato had been cultivated in France since the 16th century, the French regarded the potato as unwholesome and indigestible, food for cattle and the poor. But, as a prisoner-of-war in Westphalia, Parmentier discovered the nutritional value of the vegetable, for it was highly prized by the local population. He encouraged the spread of the potato throughout France through booklets describing its cultivation and uses. For a time the potato was known as the 'parmentier' in his honour and he gave his name to various dishes based on potatoes, including a potato garnish for lamb and veal, a cream of potato soup, scrambled eggs mixed with sautéed cubes of potato, eggs cooked in nests of potato purée and omelettes filled with diced fried potatoes.

REIGATE, **The Dining Room** 🏶🏶

A popular venue for modern British cooking with lots of Mediterranean flavours

This restaurant was packed with enthusiastic diners at the time of our last visit, waited on by sharply dressed staff in white shirts, bright ties and aprons. There is a choice of menus, a fixed-price two-course affair for lunch or dinner (vegetables and puddings charged extra) and a *carte* offering five dishes at each of three courses. The cooking is modern British with some Mediterranean influences. An enjoyable test meal began with appetisers of warm cheese feuilletés, three Italian-style breads, and a slightly overdone twice-baked soufflé of goats' cheese. This was followed by roasted sea bass with aïoli, accompanied by a pepper-laced escabeche of carrots, and grilled potatoes. Dessert comprised caramelised pears and a purée set on a pastry base with a croustade topping of filo leaves, served with a gentle sorbet. The delicious petits fours are recommended – candied orange peel, mini florentines and dark and white truffles – served with strong, fresh espresso. Reservations however, were expressed about the service which could have been both better timed and better informed. There is a short wine list developed in conjunction with Bibendum with some half bottles.

Directions: Town centre, left-hand side of one-way system, parking opposite, on 1st floor

59a High Street
Map no: 4 TQ25
Tel: 01737 226650
Chef: Anthony Tobin
Proprietor: Paul Montalto
Cost: *Alc* £30, fixed-price L/D £13.95 (2 course) H/wine £8.50 Service exc
Credit cards: 🔳 💳 💳 💳 OTHER
Times: Last L 2pm, last D 10pm Closed Sun, Xmas, Easter, end Aug
Menus: *A la carte*, fixed-price L & D
Seats: 50. No smoking in dining room
Additional: Children welcome; ♥ dishes, children's portions/ other diets on request

RIPLEY, **Michels Restaurant** 🏶🏶🏶

Innovative dishes and complex combinations are characteristic of the dishes at this French restaurant

A beautiful Georgian house in Ripley High Street, owned and run by Erik and Karen Michel. They first met at design school in France and their artistic talents are evident in the restaurant's striking decor. The regularly changing menu not only demonstrates Erik's skill with flavours but also his love of colour. Dishes such as langoustine tails resting on a bed of red cabbage with a coriander sauce, and succulent monkfish tails with a quite acidic red wine sauce and cheese-flavoured hollandaise were vibrant both visually and in taste. A less successful dish was a combination of foie gras terrine with lentils wrapped in cabbage and served with a concasse of tomato

13 High Street GU23 6AQ
Map no: 4 TQ05
Tel: 01483 224777
Chef: Erik Michel
Proprietors: Erik & Karen Michel
Cost: *Alc* £35, fixed-price L £19/D £21 (4 course). H/wine £8.50 Service exc
Credit cards: 🔳 💳 💳
Times: Last L 1.30pm, last D 9pm Closed Sat L, Sun D, Mon
Menus: *A la carte*, fixed-price L & D
Seats: 45. No smoking until after dinner
Additional: Children welcome; ♥ dishes, other diets on request

with a walnut dressing – so complex that the foie gras was lost.

Other interesting options from the fairly pricey menu are starters of seared sea-dived scallops in a butter sauce flavoured with hops and served with barley, and ravioli of pig's trotter with green asparagus and truffle juice. Main dishes include loin of Hampshire hog slightly smoked and presented with a purée of garden peas; and duck breast with Chinese cabbage cooked with lime, served with a sesame galette and a duck gravy flavoured with peanut oil. Desserts, both unusual and appetising, might offer warm honey and orange soufflé served between orange pancakes, and a pastry case filled with goats' milk curd flavoured with rosewater, and accompanied by a blueberry salad.

Directions: In village centre, off A3

SOUTH GODSTONE,

La Bonne Auberge Restaurant ❀❀

Soundly cooked meat and game dishes are the speciality of this pleasant French restaurant

Tilburstow Hill RH9 8JY
Map no: 5 TQ34
Tel: 01342 893184
Chef: Martin Bradley
Proprietor: Antoine Jalley
Cost: *Alc* £28, fixed-price L £15/D £18.90. H/wine £9.50 Service inc
Credit cards: 🆑 📧 📧 📧 OTHER
Times: Last L 1.45pm, last D 10pm Closed Sun D, Mon, Bhs
Menus: *A la carte,* fixed-price L & D
Seats: 70. No-smoking area
Additional: Children welcome, children's portions; ❷ dishes, other diets on request

In a charming country house just outside the village, chef Martin Bradley continues to offer fine French cooking. Both skill and imagination are revealed in the dishes featured on his interesting set-price menu and *carte*: stuffed loin of rabbit accompanied by a redcurrant dressing, for example, might precede flash-cooked king scallops served with clams cooked in brandy and pasta made in the hotel's own kitchen, then a mousse of fresh fruits set on a full-flavoured coulis. A selection of quality French cheeses provides an alternative to the dessert trolley, and a choice of coffee (filter, espresso and decaffeinated), tea or a tisane, together with home-made chocolate fudge, rounds off the meal. Some one hundred and thirty different wines make up a list which contains hock and champagne as well as premier clarets and Burgundies and good examples from the Loire, Rhône and Beaujolais regions. Welcoming owners who profess 'a philosophy of continual improvement' ensure that the highest standards are maintained, and an efficient all-French staff is capable of providing informed advice as well as attentive service.

Directions: M25 exit 6 – A22 (Godstone) turn right after Bell pub

STOKE D'ABERNON,
Woodlands Park Hotel ✿✿

A beautiful 19th-century mansion where good food and facilities ensure popularity

Woodlands Lane KT11 3QB
Map no: 4 TQ15
Tel: 01372 843933
Chef: Nigel Beckett
Proprietors: Select.
Manager: Michael Dickson
Cost: *Alc* £31, fixed-price
L £12.50 (£14 Sun)/D £15.
H/wine £10.50 ♥ Service exc
Credit cards: 🖃 🖾 🖼 🖃
Times: Last L 2pm, last D
9.30pm Closed Sat L, Sun D
Menus: *A la carte*, fixed-price
L & D, bar menu
Seats: 35.
Additional: Children welcome,
children's menu; ♥ dishes,
vegan/other diets on request

Edward VII and Lily Langtry were once entertained in this striking mansion. Nowadays, visitors have the choice of two restaurants, casual dining in Langtry's Bar and Brasserie and the more formal Oak Room Restaurant. In the latter, chef Nigel Beckett offers a good range of menus including a good value three-course 'Chef's Special' at £15.00. Fish dishes are a particular strength and possible choices might include layered mousse of sole and lobster, or peppered monkfish. Our inspector was delighted with an appetizer of poached salmon with a delicate chive sauce textured with tomato concasse. Home-made bread rolls – onion, walnut, Shropshire Blue, Sesame and Tomato – accompanied a vibrant fish provençale soup with chopped crunchy vegetables. Stuffed saddle of rabbit rolled with fresh spinach was the main course, served with a full flavoured 'glace de viande'. For dessert, a passion fruit mousse with a lovely red berry coulis, feathered with cream, was deliciously fruity. Aromatic coffee, petits fours and a stroll around the extensive grounds, to finish. All this only moments from the M25.

Directions: On the A245 Cobham–Leatherhead road

WEYBRIDGE, **Oatlands Park Hotel** ✿

Enjoy dinner in a candlelit setting at the beautifully decorated Broadwater restaurant – which takes its name from the lake which the hotel overlooks. From the carte or fixed-price menu choose dishes such as spinach and Parmesan tart, or roast honey-glazed lamb. Leave room for impressive trolley of home-made sweets

Menus: *A la carte*, fixed-price L & D, bar menu
Seats: 120
Additional: Children welcome, children's portions; ♥ dishes, vegan/other diets on request
Directions: Along High Street to top of Monument Hill, turn left into Oatlands Drive, 1/3 mile on left

146 Oatlands Drive KT13 9HB
Map no: 4 TQ06
Tel: 01932 847242
Chef: John Hayes
Manager: Stephen Craner
Cost: *Alc* £21-£26, fixed-price
L £16/D £18.50. H/wine £10.95
Service exc
Credit cards: 🖃 🖾 🖼 🖃
Times: 12.30pm-last L
2pm,7.30pm-last D10pm.
Closed Sat L, BHs L

WEYBRIDGE, **The Ship** ❀

This popular and long established town centre hotel offers both modern and classical French cuisine. Recent recommendations have included baked fillets of sea bass with saffron noodles and sweet pepper sauce, and medallions of beef fillet with wild forest mushrooms and a very tasty port wine sauce

Monument Green KT13 8BQ
Map no: 4 TQ06
Tel: 01932 848364
Chef: Stephen Santin
Proprietor: Mount Charlotte Thistle.
Manager: Simon Scarborough
Cost: Alc £22.50, fixed-price L £13.75. H/wine £ 11.45
Service exc
Credit cards: ▨ ▨ ▨ ▨
Times: Last L 1.45pm, last D 9.45pm Closed Sat L, BHs L
Menus: A la carte, fixed-price L, bar menu
Seats: 45. Air conditioned. Smoking discouraged
Additional: Children welcome, children's portions; ❷ dishes, vegan/other diets on request

Directions: Town centre – from M25 exit 11, or A3 exit 10

TYNE & WEAR

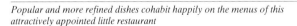

BOLDON, **Forsters Restaurant** ❀❀

Popular and more refined dishes cohabit happily on the menus of this attractively appointed little restaurant

Small but smart, this value-for-money restaurant stands in the shopping area of a village some eight miles east of Newcastle. There has been a gradual change of emphasis over the past few years; chef/proprietor Barry Forster has shifted slightly from his regular style to attract a wider clientele, and this is reflected in more diverse carte and fixed-price menus on which the occasional up-market dish rubs shoulders with popular choices. Full bodied French onion soup offers an alternative to such starters as ripe Ogee melon with prawn Marie Rose or a Swiss cheese soufflé, while desserts range from the ubiquitous sticky toffee pudding to home-made white and dark chocolate ice cream. Though tempted by grilled pork cutlets with crispy fried onions and a mustard seed sauce, our inspector chose as his main course grilled fillet of salmon filled with crab meat, asparagus and chive butter sauce; the crab could, perhaps have been regarded as slightly redundant, but the salmon itself was enjoyable and the hollandaise-style sauce effectively sharp. Service remains friendly and the atmosphere relaxed, current changes obviously meeting with the approval of customers.

2 St Bedes
Station Road NE36 0LE
Map no: 12 NZ36
Tel: 0191 519 0929
Chef: Barry Forster
Proprietor: Barry Forster
Cost: Alc £22, fixed-price D £16. H/wine £7.65. Service exc
Credit cards: ▨ ▨ ▨ ▨
Times: 7pm-last D 10pm. Closed Sun, Mon, BHs, 1 wk May & Sept
Menu: A la carte, fixed-price D
Seats: 28. No cigars or pipes
Additional: Children permitted, children's portions on request; ❷ dishes

Directions: In village of East Boldon, just off A184 Newcastle–Sunderland road

GATESHEAD, **Eslington Villa Hotel** ❀❀

In a quiet residential area, a restaurant noted for its warmth and carefully produced, good tasting food

Overlooking the Team Valley, the elegant Eslington Villa is run by Melanie and Nick Tulip and their dedicated staff. Ian Lowrey's cooking is robust with a distinct modern slant, although it also looks to the English past for inspiration. From the two or three-course fixed-price menu there might feature shellfish risotto or terrine of fresh salmon and sole with herb mayonnaise. The *carte* may go further afield with the likes of king prawn tempura and chilli ginger sauce, or stick to home shores with grilled Scottish scallops and fresh herbs, and a creamy butter or pork and chicken liver terrine served with a Cumberland sauce. Main courses range from supreme of pheasant wrapped in Parma ham, and poached fillet of salmon with cucumber butter, to grilled calves' liver with an onion marmalade and mustard sauce. Delicious puddings include warm sticky toffee pudding with butterscotch sauce, and lemon meringue tartlet served with raspberry coulis. The wine list ranges the world; house wines are from France and Australia.

Directions: Off A1(M) along Team Valley, turning right at Eastern Avenue, then left into Station Road

8 Station Road,
Low Fell NE9 6DR
Map no: 12 NZ26
Tel: 0191 487 6017
Chef: Ian Lowery
Proprietors: Melanie & Nick Tulip
Cost: *Alc* £26, fixed-price L £14.45/D £19.95 H/wine £8.95 ❗ Service exc
Credit cards: ▨ ▧ ▧ OTHER
Times: Last L 2pm, last D 11pm Closed Sat L, Sun D
Menus: *A la carte*, fixed-price L & D
Seats: 55. No smoking in dining room
Additional: Children welcome, children's portions; ❤ dishes, other diets on request

NEWCASTLE UPON TYNE, **Cafe 21** ❀❀

☺ *New wave, Mediterranean-style offshoot of pace-setting city centre restaurant*

A suburban shopping precinct may seem an unlikely location for Terry Laybourne's less formal addition to 21 Queen Street, but it works well. The simple, compact interior has a no-frills decor, paper tablecloths, and menus chalked up on blackboards. Everything is reasonably priced, but the fixed-price lunch, in particular, offers tremendous value. Typical evening starters might be marinated warm herrings with salad or fish soup, with crispy duck confit and butter beans, chargrilled tuna or navarin of lamb with seasonal vegetables as main courses. Home-made desserts feature warm chocolate tart, passionfruit cheesecake or the inevitable sticky toffee pudding. A leek and potato soup, drizzled with truffle oil, was smooth and sophisticated, followed, on our inspection, by pan-fried salmon with buttered risotto, the salmon beautifully succulent under a crispy skin. Lunch time omelettes looked superb, as did the pan-fried cod with peas and chips. Service is very attentive, and staff establish easy rapport with the surprisingly cosmopolitan customers.

Directions: Left at 2nd roundabout after Airport, right at next roundabout, left at next to Middle Drive, continue to roundabout and turn left, restaurant 200yds

Ponteland NE20 9PW
Map no: 12 NZ 26
Tel: 01661 820357
Chef: David Kennedy
Proprietor: Terence Laybourne. Manager: Paul Scott
Cost: *Alc* £16-£20, fixed-price L £13.50, £11 (2 course). H/wine £7 ❗ Service exc
Credit cards: ▨ ▧ ▧ ▣ OTHER
Times: Last L 3pm, last D 10.30pm Closed Sun, Mon
Menus: *A la carte*, fixed-price L
Seats: 38
Additional: Children welcome, children's portions; ❤ dishes, vegan/other diets on request

A quenelle is a dumpling made with spiced meat or fish forcemeat bound with egg, fat and often a panada - a thick flour paste. The mixture is moulded into a small egg shape and poached in boiling water. The name comes from the German 'knödle' meaning dumpling.

NEWCASTLE UPON TYNE,
The Copthorne ❀

Situated on the banks of the Tyne in the centre of the city, the Copthorne serves international cooking in its 'Le Rivage' restaurant. At a meal in May our inspector sampled a warm salad of pigeon with mushrooms and the sole Waleska; both were enjoyable, though vegetables were unnecessarily fussy

The Close,
Quayside NE1 3RT
Map no: 12 NZ 26
Tel: 0191 222 0333
Chef: Abulahamed Afia
Proprietor: Copthorne.
Manager: Stefan Drechsler
Cost: "Rivage" Alc £25,
fixed-price D £27.50 (4 course)
Service inc
Credit cards: 🔲 🔲 🔲 🔲 OTHER
Times: Last L 230pm, last D
10.30pm Closed Sun (Rivage
Only)
Menus: A la carte, fixed-price

L & D, bar menu
Seats: Rivage 34, Boaters 120.
Air conditioned. No-smoking
area
Additional: Children welcome,
children's menu; ❂ dishes,
vegan/other diets on request

Directions: From north side of Tyne Bridge turn left into Mosley Street, left at traffic lights into Dean Street and at bottom of hill turn right at roundabout, continue to find hotel on left

NEWCASTLE UPON TYNE, Courtneys ❀❀

Cosy, yet stylish in its own way, a small restaurant serving a wide range of international dishes

Beneath the Tyne Bridge, allegedly the inspiration for the one spanning Sydney Harbour, lies a small split-level restaurant. Its *carte* and daytime-only, fixed-price, two/three-course menu is more than capable of stimulating the taste buds, but so too is the daily-changing blackboard menu which many diners find no need to venture past. This was the case during a lunchtime visit which kicked off with a commendable cheese and ham soufflé, followed by suprême of salmon teriyaki with stir-fried vegetables. Then came marinated fillet of chargrilled salmon with a soya and sake sauce – a process which can also be done with duck, if preferred. An individual apple strudel from the *carte* was correctly cooked to order. Other starters are Maryland-style crab cake, poached egg on a muffin, dressed with smoked salmon, avocado and a hollandaise sauce, and home-made soup. Beef fillet with a sherry and truffle sauce, fillet of monkfish with scallops in a vermouth and chive sauce, and Toulouse sausage with a lentil gravy and basil mash are among the main courses. Vegetarians have a good choice, including vegetable stroganoff and tomato and aubergine gratin. There is a short but adequate wine list.

Directions: Bottom of Dean Street on right before roundabout at Quayside

5-7 The Side NE1 3JE
Map no: 12 NZ 26
Tel: 0191 232 5537
Map no: 12 NZ26
Tel: 0191 232 5537
Chef: Michael Carr
Proprietors: Michael & Kerensa
Carr
Cost: Alc £22.75, fixed-price
L £15, £13 (2 course). H/wine
£10 Service exc
Credit cards: 🔲 🔲 🔲 OTHER
Times: Last L 2pm, last D
10.30pm Closed Sat L, Sun
Menus: A la carte, fixed-price L
Seats: 26. Air conditioned
Additional: Children welcome,
children's portions; ❂ dishes,
vegan/other diets on request

NEWCASTLE UPON TYNE,

Fishermans Lodge Restaurant ❀❀

A highly recommended, mainly seafood restaurant, in a peaceful spot just outside the city

Fishermans Lodge is situated in the peace and quiet of Jesmond Dene, a deep wooded valley deceptively close to the city centre. Fish and seafood from North Shields fish quay are the focal points of the *carte*, fixed-price and bar lunch menus, but meat and game make a showing. At times the cooking can be strikingly artistic, as can be seen in braised and roast lamb shank with leek pudding and Madeira sauce, chargrilled fillet of beef with bacon lardons and mushroom sauce, lightly oak-smoked salmon with coriander sauce, but can also be uneven. At inspection a mild flavoured duck parfait 'that just melted in the mouth' made an impressive starter but escalopes of monkfish, with a white wine sauce with tomato and tarragon, generously topped with lobster, was found to have fennel rather than tarragon as the dominant flavour, and the cream sauce lacked depth. Aubergine gâteau filled with cucumber, and a creamed leek tartlet were poor. A toffee and banana crumble didn't quite come off – it was really just a pastry case with a crumble lid and the banana slices were hard and dry. The wine list is lengthy and reasonably international in scope.

Directions: 2.5 miles from City centre, off A1058 (Tynemouth) road at Benton Bank, middle of Jesmond Dene Park

Jesmond Dene,
Jesmond NE7 7BQ
Map no: 12 NZ 26
Tel: 0191 281 3281
Chef: Steven Jobson
Proprietors: Franco & Pamela Cetoloni
Cost: *Alc* £32, fixed-price L £17.80/D £26.50 (4 course). H/wine £10 Service exc
Credit cards: 🅰 📧 📧 📧 OTHER
Times: Last L 2pm, last D 11pm Closed Sat L, Sun
Menus: *A la carte*, fixed-price L & D, bar menu (Summer only)
Seats: 60 (+2 private rooms). No smoking in dining room
Additional: Children permitted (over 10 at D), children's portions; ❂ dishes, vegan/other diets on request

---

NEWCASTLE UPON TYNE,

Fishermans Wharf ❀

A long established city restaurant now benefitting from being in the hands of a former fish wholesaler. He ensures that only the best supplies of fish and game are used in the kitchen. Fish soup is a 'meal in itself', lemon sole Walenska comes garnished with collops of lobster and truffle, or there's lobster thermidor

Menus: *A la carte*, fixed-price L & D, pre-theatre **Seats:** 50. Air conditioned. No-smoking area **Additional:** Children welcome (not toddlers), children's portions; ❂ dishes, vegan/other diets on request **Directions:** From north side of Tyne bridge, turn left into Mosley Street, left into Dean Street and left again into The Side

15 The Side NE1 3JE
Map no: 12 NZ 26
Tel: 0191 232 1057
Chef: Simon Tennet
Proprietor: Alan Taylor
Cost: *Alc* £35, fixed-price L £15.75, £10 (2 course)/D £22.75. H/wine £ 11 Service exc
Credit cards: 🅰 📧 📧 📧 OTHER
Times: Last L 2pm, last D 11pm Closed Sat L, Sun

NEWCASTLE-UPON-TYNE,

Swallow Hotel ❀

Situated in the centre of the city, this modern hotel offers panoramic views of Newcastle from its sixth-floor restaurant. A daily-changing menu and a carte yield dishes such as scallops with ginger and aromatic vegetables and tender shank of lamb with a garlic and mint jus. Monthly dinner dances are held

Menus: *A la carte*, fixed-price L & D
Additional: No-smoking area ❂ dishes
Directions: City centre

Newgate Street NE1 5SX
Map no: 12 NZ26
Tel: 0191 232 1057
Chef: Stephen Gray
Proprietor: Swallow
Cost: *Alc* £25, fixed-price L £10.95/D £17.95. Service exc
Credit cards: 🅰 📧 📧 📧 OTHER
Times: Last D 9.30pm

NEWCASTLE UPON TYNE,

21 Queen Street ❀❀❀

A smart city restaurant below the famous Tyne Bridge brings an innovative touch to classically based French cuisine

Though the street itself is quiet, this well established and elegant restaurant is set in the lively quayside area of the city. Its discreet entrance leads on to a smart lounge, done in tones of mauve and green, and here you can relax with drinks and canapés while you choose your meal.

Terry Laybourne's good-value set-price lunch menu changes weekly, the one offered at dinner less frequently, but the fact that there are always at least half a dozen market specials avoids monotony. Several of the modern, French-influenced dishes – notably the thin tomato tart with pistou and a friture of garden herbs, or medallions of Kielder venison with sour cherries, grapes, walnuts and sauce Grand Veneur – remain popular; they are virtually permanent fixtures. Like much of the food offered they are classically inspired, but fashion also plays its part, decreeing such innovative twists as the use of lemon oil with grilled scallops and the accompaniment of best end of lamb by a parsley, garlic and olive oil mash. An autumn visit offered an abundance of wild mushrooms, simply fricaséed and delicious either on their own or partnering a delicate chicken and foie gras mousseline with an intense truffle jus. Only the finest fish is served, and braised truffle was topped with a medley of shellfish which included mussels, cockles, scallops, lobster and an oyster. Sticky toffee pudding with butterscotch sauce remains popular, but the dessert list also includes such temptations as chocolate extravaganza – a wealth of different textures and flavours juxtaposed in chocolate truffle topped with white chocolate mousse, a smooth iced chocolate parfait and a dramatic central cup of dark chocolate filled with orange crushed ice. The fairly priced selection of wines is good, though all are fairly young.

Directions: Queen Street runs parallel to and just behind Newcastle Quay – almost under the Tyne Bridge on north side of river

21 Queen Street,
Quayside NE1 3UG
Map no: 12 NZ 26
Tel: 0191 222 0755
Chef: Terence Laybourne
Manager: Nicholas Shottel
Cost: Alc £27.20, fixed-price
L £15, £13 (2 course). H/wine
£11.80 ❢ Service exc
Credit cards: 🔲 🔲 🔲 🔲
Times: Last L 2pm, last D
10.45pm
Menus: A la carte, fixed-price L
Seats: 70. No pipes in dining
room
Additional: Children welcome;
❤ dishes, children's portions/
vegan/other diets on request

NEWCASTLE UPON TYNE,

Vermont Hotel ❀❀

The former County Hall offers a choice of dining, though the Blue Room is recommended for a memorable meal

A smart hotel – one of the city's newest – the Vermont was once the County Hall, an imposing building just off the northern side of the High Level Bridge right in the city centre. It has two restaurants and bars as well as a separate bar/bistro. The Brasserie is open all day and provides a good choice of dishes, but the Blue Room offers a truly memorable dining experience. An inspection meal kicked off with superb canapés and a selection of home-baked bread. The starter, loin of lamb marinated in soya sauce and sesame seeds, was thinly sliced and set on crispy vegetables and soya dressed salad. To follow, sautéed scallops and salmon came with a good chive sauce, pea sized pieces of root vegetable, for added bite, and an excellent home-made tagliatelli topped with caviar. Dessert comprised lightly

Castle Garth NE1 1RQ
Map no: 12 NZ26
Tel: 0191 233 1010
Chef: Stephen Waites
Proprietor: Taz Group.
Manager: Nicky Hislop
Cost: Fixed-price D £ 27.50.
H/wine £11.50 ❢ Service inc
Credit cards: 🔲 🔲 🔲 🔲 OTHER
Times: 7pm-last D 11.30pm
Closed Sun, Mon
Menus: Fixed-price D
Seats: 75. Air conditioned.
No-smoking area
Additional: Children permitted,
children's portions; ❤ dishes,
vegan/other diets on request

Vermont Hotel

poached pears sliced onto a lemon curd tart served with cinnamon ice-cream. This first-class meal scarcely needed the additional 'surprise' dishes – the foie gras that arrived before the starter and a sorbet prior to the main course. The comprehensive wine list has a good selection of half bottles.

Directions: City centre, by the Castle and swing bridge

WARWICKSHIRE

ABBOT'S SALFORD,

Salford Hall Hotel ❀❀

Good quality British cooking is offered at this 15th-century establishment, set in its own grounds

Parts of Salford Hall date from the late 15th century. Simply crafted dishes with a focus on natural flavours are a feature of the well-executed modern British cooking offered on the weekly changing fixed-price menu and seasonal *carte*. Escalope of fresh Scottish salmon baked in filo pastry with orange butter, or roast loin of venison with damsons and a sloe gin sauce are typical examples of the cooking style. At a meal taken in March a brace of lightly sautéed wood-pigeon breasts served with a parsnip and bacon rösti cake and a red wine and tarragon sauce was well liked. For dessert there could be fig crème brûlée or British cheeses. Coffee comes with home-made fudge. Service is by courteous and professional staff, and the extensive wine list is supplemented by a short selection of suggested wines.

Directions: On the A439 8 miles west of Stratford-upon-Avon

Evesham WR11 5UT
Map no: 4 SP05
Tel: 01386 871300
Chef: Rob Bean
Proprietors: Charter Hotels Ltd
Cost: Fixed-price L £14.95
(3 courses)/D £18.95, £27.50.
H/wine £10.95
Credit cards: 🗠 🌅 🔤 💷
Times: Last L 2.00pm, last D 9.45pm
Seats: 50. No smoking in dining room
Additional: Children permitted; ❷ dishes

ALDERMINSTER, **Ettington Park Hotel** ✿

A Gothic Victorian mansion, set in 40 acres of mature grounds, is the backdrop for Christopher Hudson's well executed, seasonal dishes. An inspection meal yielded good, lightly grilled sea bass with a simple cream and saffron sauce and, a light-textured plum pudding parfait with dark chocolate sauce

Stratford-upon-Avon CU35 8BS
Map no: 4 SP25
Tel: 01789 450123
Chef: Christopher Hudson
Cost: Fixed-price L £16/
D £29.50. Service exc
Credit cards: 🆇 💳 💳
Times: Last D 9.30pm

Directions: 5 miles south of Stratford

ATHERSTONE, **Chapel House Hotel** ✿✿

Exact flavours and carefully-prepared dishes are features of the cooking at this attractive hotel

Friar's Gate CV9 1EY
Map no: 4 SP39
Tel: 01827 718949
Chef: Gary Thompson
Proprietors: Pat & David Roberts
Cost: Alc £22, fixed-price D £24
(4 course). H/wine £9.95 Service
inc
Credit cards: 🆇 💳 💳 💳 OTHER
Times: 7pm-last D 9.30pm
Closed Sun D, Dec 25/26
Menus: A la carte & fixed-
price D
Seats: 50
Additional: Children over 10
permitted; other diets on request

Friendly hospitality and decent cooking welcome visitors to Chapel House which stands hard by the church and boasts a well-tended walled garden. The cooking is traditional country house, carefully prepared with attention to small details: canapés are good as are the well-made petits fours. Choose from the *carte* or a four-course fixed-price menu. A meal taken in February was noteworthy for accurate flavours though mistiming meant that some vegetables were slightly overcooked. The meal began with veal and smoked bacon terrine, was followed by baked cod in a parsley butter sauce, with chocolate and Amaretto mousse for dessert. Sunday lunch menus and vegetarian dishes are available by arrangement. The short, conservative wine list includes a world-wide selection but majors in French wines. Staff are friendly and professional.

Directions: Town centre

'Pithiviers' is a large round puff-pastry tart filled with an almond cream. It is a speciality of Pithiviers, in the Orleans region, and is traditionally served on Twelfth Night, when it contains a dried broad bean. The town is also famous for another tart, also made of puff pastry, but this time filled with crystallised fruit and covered with white fondant icing. Nowadays, modern chefs interpret pithiviers in various ways, in both savoury and sweet dishes.

BARFORD, **The Glebe at Barford** ❀

A former rectory dating from the 1820s, and now converted into a popular conference venue, has been further enhanced by the efforts in the kitchen under head chef Andrew Wheeler. Menus change seasonally and show care in preparation and emphasis on simple flavours

Seats: 80. Air conditioned **Additional:** Children welcome. Children's menu/portions; ❶ menu, vegan/other diets on request
Directions: In village centre, near the church

Church Street CV35 8BS
Map no: 4 SP26
Tel: 01926 624218
Chef: Andrew Wheeler
Manager: David Jones
Cost: Fixed-price D £14.95, Sunday L £12.50. H/wine £9.50. Service exc
Credit cards: 🔲 ▦ ▩ ▨ OTHER
Times: 11.30am-last L 2.30pm, last D 10pm

CLAVERDON, **Ardencote Hotel** ❀

An extensive leisure centre plus a trout lake with its specially themed lodge and shop is the driving force behind this converted Victorian residence. Palms is an informal restaurant offering a menu with a broad, international appeal along the lines of haddock and gravad lax with chive and honey sauce, and kleftico with ratatouille

Menus: *A la carte*, fixed-price L & D, bar menu **Seats:** 50. Air conditioned **Additional:** Children welcome, children's menu; ❶ dishes, vegan/other diets on request
Directions: Follow Claverdon signs from Henley in Arden, 1 mile from village green on road to Shrewley

Lye Green Road CV35 8LS
Map no: 4 SP16
Tel: 01926 843111
Chef: Anthony Morgan
Proprietor: Walker Homes.
Manager: Andrew Walker
Cost: Alc £26.50, fixed-price L £17, £14.50 (2 course)/D £17.50, £19.50 (4 course). H/wine £ 9.75 Service exc
Credit cards: 🔲 ▦ ▩
Times: Last L 2pm, last D 9.30pm daily

HENLEY-IN-ARDEN,
Le Filbert Cottage Restaurant ❀❀

Classic French cooking in a quintessential English setting

In the centre of a classic English village is a cottage restaurant that is very Olde England. Within, there are oak beams and quarry-tiled floors, and French cooking. The food is simple, honest and colourful with fresh textures and individual flavours. An inspection meal began with a 'deliciously fresh' Cornish crab bisque flavoured with Cognac. The main course comprised of delicate fillets of Cornish brill, lightly poached and served with a mustard and herb sauce, and came with fresh al dente vegetables. Other dishes available on the *carte* could be 'escargots bourguignon', 'noisettes d'agneau' with a piquant cassis sauce or 'filet de boeuf au poivre noir'. For dessert try the light-textured home-made crème caramel with smooth vanilla sauce. The wine list features a good range of French wines and includes some fine vintages.

Directions: Town centre, A3400 at junction of High Street and Station Road

64 High Street B95 5BX
Map no: 4 SP16
Tel: 01564 792700
Chef: Maurice-Jean Gaudens Ricaud
Proprietor: Maurice-Jean Gaudens Ricaud
Cost: Alc £25. H/wine £9 Service exc Cover charge
Credit cards: 🔲 ▦ ▩
Times: Last L 1.30pm, last D 9.30pm Closed Sun, Mon
Menus: *A la carte* L & D
Seats: 30. No smoking in dining room
Additional: Children over 7 welcome; other diets prior notice

KENILWORTH, **Restaurant Bosquet** ❀❀

A popular town centre restaurant producing consistently high standards of French cooking

Located close to the centre of town, this traditional French restaurant has a loyal local following due to consistent cooking. At a recent inspection, a decent starter of terrine of scallops and pike served with a rich butter, shallot and white wine sauce kicked

97a Warwick Road CV8 1HP
Map no: 4 SP27
Tel: 01926 52463
Chef: Bernard Lignier
Proprietors: Bernard & Jane Lignier
Cost: Alc £28, fixed-price L/D £21 H/wine £11 Service exc
Credit cards: 🔲 ▦ ▩ OTHER

off the meal. The main course of saddle of lamb was well-timed and tender and came with a fines herbes and breadcrumbs crust and light sherry-flavoured jus. Vegetables included a rich ratatouille, french beans, mange tout and dauphinoise potatoes. Lemon tart had a good lemon flavour but slightly overcooked pastry; lime sorbet and a raspberry purée accompanied. Other dishes available on the short menus might be lamb with truffles, breast of duck with a spicy sauce, fillet of beef in red wine and squab pigeon wrapped in cabbage. Canapés and petits fours open and close the meal. The all-French wine list offers a full range of clarets and Burgundies.

Directions: In main street of Kenilworth

Times: Last L 1.15pm, last D 9.15pm Closed Sun, Mon, 4 wks Jul/Aug
Menus: A la carte, fixed-price L & D,
Seats: 26. No pipes in dining room
Additional: Children welcome, children's portions; ❂ dishes, other diets on request

---

ROYAL LEAMINGTON SPA,
Lansdowne Hotel ❀

☺ *Fresh ingredients are used in the accurately-flavoured dishes at this city centre Georgian hotel. The varied selections usually include Aberdeen Angus beef, as well as dishes such as tomato, onion and celery soup, sole fillets with lemon herb butter and buckwheat blinis with a sweet berry compote*

Menus: Fixed-price D **Seats:** 24. No smoking in dining room
Additional: Children over 5 permitted, children's portions; other diets on request **Directions:** Town centre, corner of Clarendon Street and Warwick Street, near The Parade

87 Clarendon Street CV32 4PF
Map no: 4 SP36
Tel: 01926 450505
Chef: Lucinda Button
Proprietors: David & Gillian Allen
Cost: Fixed-price D £17.95. H/wine £7.95 No service charge
Credit cards: ▨ ▨
Times: 6.30pm-last D 8.30pm Closed Sun D, Dec 25/26 & 31

ROYAL LEAMINGTON SPA,
Mallory Court Hotel ❀❀❀

Modern French cuisine from a choice of three fairly expensive menus at this manor house hotel

A squat, lovingly restored 1920's manor house set within orderly gardens, Mallory Court is an immaculately kept hotel. Proprietors Allan Holland and Jeremy Mort prefer to retain the ambience of a formal private house, so there is no bar, but there are two bright lounges with fine rugs, open fires and floral displays. The elegant oak-panelled dining room is the focus of the establishment.

Chef Stephen Shore has proved himself to be a worthy successor to Allan Holland. At a recent meal the dishes showed a sure touch and precision of execution from beginning to end. There is a broad choice of dishes from three separate menus – all on the expensive side – a carte, fixed price menus for lunch and dinner and a £60 set six-course gourmet menu. The cooking is modern French, with starters such as twice baked cheese soufflé Suissesse with a salad of herbs, bacon and croûtons; and lobster and fennel ravioli. Venison medallions were served with artichoke mousse as a main course, and other options could be feuilletté of roasted monkfish and spinach with a shellfish cream, or pink roasted suprême of Gressingham duck with a spiced rillette of the leg. To finish there might be pear and almond tart with poached blueberries, as sampled at a test meal, and a plate of three chocolate and pecan desserts. The wine list is mainly French with some emphasis on California in the New World section.

Directions: 2 miles S of Leamington off the B4087 towards Harbury

Harbury Lane
Bishop's Tachbrook CV33 9QB
Map no: 4 SP36
Tel: 01926 330214
Chef: Stephen Shore
Proprietors: Allan Holland and Jeremy Mort (Relais & Chateaux)
Cost: Alc £43.75-£53.25, fixed-price L £23.50, £19.50 (2 course)/D £ 30. H/wine £14.25 ❢ No service charge
Credit cards: ▨ ▨ ▨ ▨ OTHER
Times: Last L 2pm, last D 9.45pm daily
Menus: A la carte, fixed-price L & D, pre-theatre
Seats: 50. No cigars or pipes in dining room
Additional: Children over 9 welcome, children's portions; ❂ dishes, vegan/other diets on request

ROYAL LEAMINGTON SPA,
Regent Hotel ❁

Housed in the former wine cellar of this historic hotel, Vaults Restaurant offers a range of traditional favourites prepared with classically-trained technical skills. Appetising choices on the menu are complemented by an impressive wine list

Additional: Children permitted; ❤ dishes; no-smoking area
Directions: In town centre near Royal Priors Shopping Centre

77 The Parade CV32 4AX
Map no 4 SP36
Tel: 01926 427231
Chef: Roland Clark
Proprietor: Mrs Cridlan
Cost: Alc £15.25, fixed-price £24
Credit cards: 🆇 ▦ ▦ ▣
Times: Noon-last L 2pm, 7pm-last D 10pm

STRATFORD-UPON-AVON,
Alveston Manor Hotel ❁

A popular, traditional hotel offering good cooking from set lunch and dinner menus. Our inspector recently enjoyed a salmon and sole terrine and breast of chicken in Madeira sauce, with a Baileys cheese-cake for dessert. A good choice of farmhouse cheeses made at individual dairies is also available

Clopton Bridge CV37 7HP
Map no: 4 SP25
Tel: 01789 204581
Chef: Anthony Morrin
Proprietor: Forte.
Manager: Anne Marie Brennan
Cost: Alc from £26, fixed-price L £13.95/£23.50 H/wine £13 Service exc
Credit cards: 🆇 ▦ ▦ ▣ OTHER
Times: Last L 2pm, last D 9.30pm
Menus: A la carte, fixed-price L & D, bar menu
Seats: 100. No smoking before 10pm
Additional: Children welcome (early D requested), children's menu; ❤ dishes, vegan/other diets on request

Directions: On S side of River Avon, 5 mins walk from theatre and town centre

STRATFORD-UPON-AVON, The Arden ❁

Occupying an enviable position in the centre of Stratford by the waters edge, this popular hotel offers bright and well-executed dishes in its elegant restaurant. At a recent meal a smooth asparagus mousse was followed by lamb fillet in a light pastry with leaf spinach and a reduced port wine sauce

Menus: A la carte, fixed-price L & D, pre-theatre, bar menu
Seats: 70. No smoking in dining room
Additional: Children welcome, children's portions; ❤ dishes, other diets on request
Directions: On Waterside opposite Royal Shakespeare and Swan Theatres

Waterside CV37 6BA
Map no: 4 SP36
Tel: 01789 294949
Chef: Mark Gilberthorpe
Proprietor: Thistle.
Manager: Fred Trivett
Cost: Alc £26.70, fixed-price L £12.50/D £19.25 (4 course). H/wine £9.25 Service exc
Credit cards: 🆇 ▦ ▦ ▣
Times: Last L 2.30pm, last D Mon-Thurs 9.30pm, 10pm Fri-Sat

STRATFORD-UPON-AVON,
Billesley Manor Hotel ❀❀❀

Cooking of classic style with a modern twist is offered at this Elizabethan manor house hotel

Stylish public rooms with an abundance of wood panelling, carved fireplaces and ornate plasterwork create a delightful setting in which to enjoy the commendable cooking of chef Mark Naylor. The Elizabethan manor is set in 11 acres of grounds complete with topiary gardens, and William Shakespeare is reputed to have been a regular visitor.

Classic Anglo/French cooking with modern touches is offered from a choice of menus. An inspection starter of puff pastry with fillets of John Dory and a Chablis sauce was light and delicate yet full of flavour. Other starters might be wild mushroom, sweet pepper and tomato risotto, and confit of smoked duck, foie gras and shallots with apple and balsamic chutney, followed by a complimentary water ice or consommé. Principal dishes, accompanied by competently cooked vegetables, include rich medallions of venison with a robust glazed orange and cinnamon sauce. Other daily options are the fresh fish of the day, a choice from the separate vegetarian menu, or the silver carving trolley – a special roast dish carved at your table. Puddings that come with enthusiastic recommendations are the prune and Armagnac soufflé or the warm pear tart with hazelnut ice-cream. Those not prepared to wait for a hot dessert might try glazed iced honey nougat with mango.

Directions: On the A46, 3 miles west of Stratford-upon-Avon

Alcester B49 6NF
Map no: 4 SP25
Tel: 01789 279955
Chef: Mark Naylor
Proprietor: Queens Moat.
Manager: Peter Henderson
Cost: Alc £30+, fixed-price
L £18 (4 course)/D £27.50
(4 course). H/wine £10.75
Service exc
Credit cards: 🔲 💳 💳 💳
Times: Last L 2pm, last D
9.30pm/10pm Fri-Sat daily
Menus: A la carte, fixed-price
L & D, bar menu
Seats: 80. No cigars or pipes in
dining room
Additional: Children permitted,
children's menu; ❶ dishes,
vegan/other diets on request

STRATFORD-UPON-AVON,
Shakespeare Hotel ❀

Changes have taken place in the kitchen at this 17th-century town centre hotel since a new chef and team took over. Good quality, fresh ingredients are used to produce well-presented dishes such as homemade pasta with wild mushrooms, and tender chicken breast with Madeira sauce

Additional: Children welcome, children`s menu; ❶ & vegan dishes other diets on request
Directions: From Motorway Junction 15, follow signs to town centre. Go round one-way system up Bridge Street. At roundabout turn left. Hotel is 200yds on left-hand side

Chapel Street CV37 6ER
Map no: 4 SP25
Tel: 01789 294 771
Chef: Richard Walton
Proprietor: Forte Heritage
Cost: Fixed-price L £14.95,
fixed-price D £25.95
Credit cards: 🔲 💳 💳 💳 OTHER.
Times: 12.30pm-last L 2pm,
6pm- last D 9.30pm
Menus: Fixed-price L & D,
Sun lunch, lounge menu
Seats: 92. No smoking in
dining-room

STRATFORD-UPON-AVON,
Stratford House Hotel ❀

☺ *Located only 100 yards from the Royal Shakespeare Theatre, Stratford House provides sound choice and some consistent cooking in their conservatory restaurant. Look out for chicken liver pâté, and darne of salmon with cucumber spaghetti and a lemon butter sauce*

Menus: A la carte, fixed-price L, bistro menu, pre-theatre **Seats:** 45
Additional: Children welcome, children's portions; ❶ dishes, vegan/other diets on request
Directions: Town centre, 100 yds from Royal Shakespeare Theatre

Sheep Street CV37 6EF
Map no: 4 SP25
Tel: 01789 268288
Chef: Dennis Hemsworth
Proprietor: Sylvia Adcock
Cost: Alc £16.50, fixed-price
L £4.95. H/wine £8.50 ❢ Service
exc
Credit cards: 🔲 💳 💳 💳 OTHER
Times: Last L 3.30pm, last D
9.30pm Closed Sun D, 4 days
Xmas

STRATFORD-UPON-AVON,
Welcome Hotel ❀❀

A good range of well-prepared dishes including vegetarian and grill selections are available at this golfing hotel

A rural setting with unrestricted views over its own golf course, and just a mile from Stratford, makes the Welcombe a popular hotel. Well-executed food is provided in generous portions and cooked from good quality produce. A sample lunchtime menu featured marinated new potatoes with sliced breast of guinea fowl, casserole of pheasant, pigeon, hare and rabbit served in a mille-feuille pastry case with slices of tender venison, and a duo of chocolate parfait with crème anglaise for dessert. Evening menu options could be smoked chicken and oyster mushroom cappuccino soup or ravioli of shellfish, followed by mignons of beef with a sun-dried tomato and black olive crust set on a morel and grain mustard sauce, or perhaps whole Dover sole from the grill selection. Apple beignets with a cinnamon and hazelnut ice-cream might be among the desserts, with coffee and petits fours concluding the meal.
A relatively extensive and varied wine list includes a short selection of New World wines.

Directions: On A439 1 mile from town centre

Warwick Road CV37 0NR
Map no 4 SP36
Tel: 01789 295252
Chef: Michael Carver
Manager: Brian Miller
Cost: *Alc* £35, fixed-price
L £18.50/D £27.50. H/wine
£13.50 ❢ Service inc
Credit cards: 🆇 🆇 🆇 🆇 OTHER
Times: Last L 2pm, last D
9.45pm daily
Menus: *A la carte*, fixed-price
L & D, pre-theatre, bar menu
Seats: 60.
Additional: Children welcome, children's menu; ❶ dishes, vegan/other diets on request

WISHAW, **The Belfry** ❀❀

Both traditional and modern Anglo-French cooking are served in formal surroundings at this popular leisure hotel

Lichfield Road B76 9PR
Map no: 7 SP19
Tel: 01675 470301
Chef: Eric Bruce
Proprietor: De Vere.
Manager: Mike Maloney
Cost: *Alc* £34, fixed-price
L £15.95/D £27.50 (4 course).
H/wine £ 12.50 ❢ Service inc
Credit cards: 🆇 🆇 🆇 🆇
Times: Last L 2pm, last D 10pm
Closed Sat L, Sun D
Menus: *A la carte*, fixed-price
L & D, bar menu
Seats: 80. Air-conditioned.
No-smoking area

Golfers and sports enthusiasts are prominent among the visitors to this large hotel. Classical and modern Anglo-French cooking is served in the French restaurant which is run in a formal manner by attentive, smartly uniformed staff. An April meal began with canapés and an appetiser of Japanese beef, which was unfortunately rather heavy and sweet and uninspiring. A medley of seafood followed, which came with a rondelle of vegetables, spinach and salmon caviar and a wild mushroom sauce. Noisettes of English lamb on a bed of red onions and shallots garnished with a wild mushroom soufflé and a light rosemary jus formed the main course and were served with a standard selection of vegetables. Hot sticky toffee pudding finished the meal. The restaurant boasts red terra-cotta walls, beams, alcoves and well-appointed tables and has its own cocktail lounge reserved for diners. The wine list is fairly basic.

Additional: Children welcome, children's portions; dishes, vegan/other diets on request

Directions: At junction of A446 & A4091, 1 mile NW of M42 exit 9

WEST MIDLANDS

BALSALL COMMON, Haigs Hotel ❀❀

A small, privately-run hotel offering decent British food with a good measure of brio

Kenilworth Road CV7 7EL
Map no: 7 SP27
Tel: 01676 533004
Chefs: Paul Hartup and John Haynes
Proprietors: Jean & John Cooper
Cost: Alc £24, fixed-price Sun L £11.75/D £16.50. H/wine £8.75 Service exc
Credit cards: 🔳 ⚅ OTHER
Times: 7.30pm-last D 9pm/9.30pm Fri-Sat, last Sun L 2pm Closed Dec 26-Jan 4
Menus: A la carte, fixed-price D & Sun L
Seats: 60. No smoking in dining room
Additional: Children welcome, children's portions; dishes, vegan/other diets on request

Two years ago we called Haigs Hotel one of the best kept secrets in the West Midlands. With its refreshing warmth and hospitality, and remarkably good food, it can still make that claim. Enthusiastic new owners have taken over, well aware that they have high standards to maintain. In the kitchen, Paul Hartup continues to cook imaginative and varied food, and has an assured hand in saucing. He's a dab-hand with bread as well. A winter visit to the hotel's Poppies Restaurant produced a moist and well flavoured game terrine with red wine chutney, pan-fried rabbit sauced with a delicious mustard cream, shallots and bacon, and ended with a tangy, smooth-textured lemon tart. The wine list is small but varied and with only a modest mark-up. Those staying overnight might like to know that they do a pretty good breakfast.

Directions: On A452 4 miles N of NEC/Airport on left just before village centre

BALSALL COMMON, Nailcote Hall ❀❀

French classical cooking can be enjoyed in an attractive rural setting at this 17th-century hotel

Built in 1640, with a Georgian wing added in 1780, this timbered country house hotel stands in eight acres of mature grounds and

Nailcote Lane
Berkswell CV7 7DE
Map no: 7 SP27
Tel: 01203 466174
Chef: Aiden Callaghan
Proprietor: R W Cressman

gardens. French classical cooking is served in the formally appointed Oak Room. Typical starters could be pigeon, quail and tender pieces of pheasant with a red wine sauce in a golden pastry case, or oak-smoked Scotch salmon with a home-made vegetable piccalilli. This might be followed by calves' liver with a red onion marmalade, or loin of lamb with a mousse of foie gras and truffle and a rich Madeira sauce, served with bright fresh al dente vegetables. Tarte au citron with a fresh raspberry sauce could finish the meal. At inspection high standards of cooking were noted, with dishes prepared from first class produce and displaying honest textures and flavours. Service is by attentive, friendly and professional restaurant staff. The wine list features 95 bins covering France, Germany and Italy as well as some New World selections.

Directions: On B4101 Balsall/Coventry, 10 mins from NEC/Airport

Cost: Alc £24.50 (£26.50 Fri-Sat), fixed-price L £17.75/D £24.50. H/wine £10.75 Service inc
Credit cards: 🗚 🖭 🎫 💷
Times: Last L 2pm, last D 9.30pm Closed Sat L, Sun D
Menus: A la carte, fixed-price L & D, pre-theatre, bar menu
Seats: 30. No smoking in dining room
Additional: Children welcome; ❷ dishes, vegan/other diets on request

BIRMINGHAM, Chung Ying Garden ✿

☺ *Enjoyable Chinese restaurant serving authentic Cantonese dishes – with a great dim-sum selection – in the heart of China Town, near the Hippodrome Theatre. Try steamed scallop in soy and ginger, duck stuffed with corn and shrimp and hot, spicy king prawns*

Menus: A la carte, fixed-price D
Seats: 350. No-smoking area
Additional: Children permitted; ❷ dishes, other diets on request
Directions: City centre, off Hurst Street, near the Hippodrome Theatre

17 Thorp Street B5 4AT
Map no: 7 SP08
Tel: 0121 666 6622
Chef: Mr Wong
Manager: Ming Fang
Cost: Alc £12, fixed-price D £16. H/wine £9.50 Service exc
Credit cards: 🗚 🖭 🎫 💷 OTHER
Times: Noon-midnight (11pm Sun) Closed Sun

BIRMINGHAM, The Copthorne ✿

The Copthorne offers a combination of modern and classical dishes on the carte of Goldsmith's restaurant. Expect home-made smoked duck sausage on a parsnip and apple chutney and fillet of English beef on a fried potato cake with caramelised onions, and lemon tart with a honey and cinnamon cream

Menus: A la carte, bar menu
Seats: 46. No-smoking area
Additional: Children welcome, children's menu; ❷ dishes, vegan/other diets on request
Directions: City centre

Paradise Circus B3 3HJ
Map no: 7 SP08
Tel: 0121 200 2727
Chef: Martin Davies
Proprietor: Copthorne.
Manager: Stephen Price
Cost: Alc £. H/wine £ 9.95 ❗
Service exc
Credit cards: 🗚 🖭 🎫 💷 OTHER
Times: 7pm-last D 10pm Closed Sun, Bh Mons, Dec 25

BIRMINGHAM, Jonathans' Hotel ✿

With Victorian themes and decor, an extensive carte selection, and two 'gourmet' set menus, Jonathans' offers a broad selection. Dishes include game terrine with apricot chutney, and Parson Woodforde's Yorkshire fillet – stuffed fillet steak served in a Yorkshire pudding

Menus: A la carte, fixed-price L & D, pre-theatre
Seats: 200. No-smoking area
Additional: Children welcome, children's portions; ❷ dishes, vegan/other diets on request
Directions: From M5 exit 2 take A4123 (Birmingham), 1.5 miles on left

Oldbury B68 0LH
Map no: 7 SP08
Tel: 0121 429 3757
Chef: Graham Bradley
Manager: David Leatham
Cost: Alc £26, fixed-price L £5/D £24.60 (6 course) H/wine £11.90 ❗ Service exc
Credit cards: 🗚 🖭 🎫 💷 OTHER
Times: Last L 2pm, last D 10.30pm daily

BIRMINGHAM, **Shimla Pinks** ✿

A fashion-conscious Indian restaurant decorated with huge minimalist paintings, where the waiters dress uniformly in black. Traditional dishes have been similarly updated; fresh ingredients, herbs and spices are brought together in an innovative menu that echoes the decor

Times: *Midday-last L 2.30pm, 6pm-last D 11pm. Closed Sat & Sun lunch, 25-26 Dec* **Seats:** *165. Air conditioned* **Additional:** *Children welcome, children's portions;* ❂ *dishes, vegan/other diets on request* **Directions:** In city centre, near the ICC & opposite Novotel

214 Broad Street B15 1AY
Map no 7 SP08
Tel: 0121 633 0366
Chef: *Ganesh Shresta*
Proprietor: *Dhalinal & Pannum*
Cost: *Alc £15, fixed-price L £6.95/D £12.95 (2 courses), £14.95. H/wine £7.95* ❢ *Service exc*
Credit cards: 🔳 🔳 🔳 🔳 OTHER

BIRMINGHAM, **Swallow Hotel** ✿✿✿

Classical Mediterranean cookery stylishly presented in an attractive hotel restaurant

Five Ways
Edgbaston B16 8SJ
Map no: 7 SP08
Tel: 0121 452 1144
Chef: Jonathan Harrison
Proprietor: Swallow.
Manager: Brendan Carr
Cost: *Alc £38, fixed-price L £20.50, £17.50 (2 course)/D £25, £30 (4 course). H/wine £15.50* ❢ Service inc
Credit cards: 🔳 🔳 🔳 🔳 OTHER
Times: Last L 2pm, last D 9.30pm Closed Sat L
Menus: *A la carte,* fixed-price L & D, pre-theatre, lounge menu
Seats: 60. Air conditioned
Additional: Children welcome, children's menu; ❂ dishes, other diets on request

One of the best hotels in the city, the Swallow goes from strength to strength under new general manager Brendan Carr. He has a dedicated team who manage to combine a genuine willingness to please with professionalism and a sense of style. The smart marbled lobby leads to a series of small but comfortable day rooms and a choice of two restaurants. Langtry's is for informal meals, whilst the Sir Edward Elgar restaurant offers a totally different dining experience with Mediterranean menus, highly trained staff and live pianist.

Here meals might begin with an appetiser of wonderfully light mousseline of salmon and langoustine with a vegetable nage. This could be followed by a carefully constructed foie gras dodine layered with sweet apple confit and complemented by a lovely salad with celery leaves, egg and truffle. There were vibrant Mediterranean flavours in a dish of roasted cod with aubergine gateau and a combination of tomato and pesto sauces; however, the accompanying couscous cake did nothing to commend the grain. The French patissier is clearly very talented, producing a range of enterprising desserts and a trolley of home-made breads. The test meal concluded with a light iced coffee nougat and pistachio sauce presented in a dark chocolate cup set on delicious praline. There is also an extensive wine list with some good vintage champagnes, a selection of half bottles and wines by the glass.

Directions: City end of the A456, at the Five Ways roundabout

COVENTRY,
Brooklands Grange Hotel ❀

Behind the Jacobean facade there lies a thoroughly modern and comfortable business hotel, noted for its service. The food is good with straightforward grills served alongside fresh-flavoured crab cakes, and spicy, tender, plump Thai-style chicken

Additional: Children's menu; ❤ dishes, vegan/other diets on request; live entertainment **Seats:** 60. No cigars or pipes. No-smoking area
Directions: On A4144; on right, at Allesley roundabout

Holyhead Road
Map no: 4 SP37
Tel: 01203 601601
Chef: Stuart Hope
Manager: Lesley Jackson
Cost: *Alc* £25.55, fixed-price L/D £16.95. Service exc
Times: Midday-last L 2pm, 7pm-last D 10pm. Closed for lunch Sat & Bhs

HOCKLEY HEATH,
Nuthurst Grange Hotel ❀❀❀

Wide appeal is assured at this hotel restaurant

David and Darryl Randolph have created a wonderfully relaxing environment at Nuthurst Grange for the enjoyment of good food and wine. The cooking is inspired, assured and full of depth and flavour. The menu mix and pricing policy ensures a wide choice, and both light and hearty, traditional and modern dishes are featured. There is a good-value fixed price menu and a more ambitious selection priced per course. It is perfectly acceptable to order a main dish and coffee, or go the whole hog with four courses. Breads and appetisers are good, especially a 'sensuous' fish roulade. The likes of tomato and mozzarella tart with basil, and pease pudding with smoked goose breast appear among the starters. Our inspectors have particularly enjoyed the fresh-tasting crab and red pepper fish cakes, and a traditional dish of braised oxtail with thyme gravy. Sautéed chicken livers were also sampled, served on a bed of crisp green leaves liberally dosed with a spicy balsamic dressing, sweet shallots and croûtons, producing a memorable sensation of contrasting flavours and textures. Puddings range from passion fruit parfait to Eton mess, and the meal concludes with coffee and petits fours. The wine list includes plenty of bottles under £16.

Directions: Off A3400 0.5 mile south of Hockley Heath, turning at notice-board into Nuthurst Grange Lane

Nuthurst Grange Lane B94 5NL
Map no: 7 SP17
Tel: 01564 783972
Chef: David Randolph
Proprietor: David Randolph
Cost: *Alc* £45, fixed-price L from £16.50, fixed-price D from £19.50. H/wine £9.95 ❢ Service discouraged but discretionary
Credit cards: 🃏 💳 💳 💳 OTHER.
Times: Noon-last L 2pm, 7pm-last D 9.30pm. Closed Sat lunch
Menus: *A la carte,* fixed-price L & D, Sun lunch
Seats: 50 (+ private rooms). No smoking in dining-room
Additional: Children welcome, children`s portions; ❤ dishes, other diets by request

MERIDEN, Forest of Arden ❀

A golfing hotel and country club standing in 400 acres of rolling country-side. The attractive split-level restaurant has something of a Mediterranean feel and offers enjoyable modern cooking

Maxstoke Lane CV7 7HR
Map no: 4 SP28
Tel: 01676 522335
Chef: Glyn Windross
Proprietor: Michael O'Dwyer
Cost: Fixed-price L/D £19.50.
H/wine £10.95. Service inc
Credit cards: 🆇 💳 💳 💳
Times: 12.30-last L 2pm, 7pm-last D 9.45pm. Closed Sat lunch
Seats: 130. No smoking in dining room
Additional: Children welcome, ♥ menu, vegan/other diets on request; pianist Sunday lunchtime

Directions: From M42 jnct 6, take A45 (Coventry) after Stonebridge island, then left (Shepherds Lane), 1.5 miles on left

MERIDEN, Manor Hotel ❀

Georgian manor house sympathetically extended into a comfortable modern hotel. Although close to Birmingham Airport and the NEC, the setting is a quiet village. The Regency Restaurant offers chicken liver parfait, suprême of salmon filled with prawn mousse and lobster béarnaise. Less formal meals available in the Triumph Bar and Buttery

Directions: In centre of village

Main Road CV7 7NH
Map no: 4 SP28
Tel: 01676 522735
Chef: Peter Griffiths
Cost: *Alc* £35, fixed-price L & D £13.95, £16.95. Service exc
Credit cards: 🆇 💳 💳 💳
Times: Last D 10pm

SOLIHULL, Solihull Moat House ❀❀

Consistent and enjoyable food in a hotel in a Birmingham suburb

The large, modern purpose-built hotel is situated in the fashionable Birmingham suburb of Solihull and boasts landscaped gardens and a spacious car park.The hotel's Brookes Restaurant serves predominantly modern British food with a French accent, although some traditional English dishes make an appearance. Consistent cooking features dishes in which individual flavours are easily discernable. Guests can choose from an extensive selection which includes a 'healthy options' range and a good choice of vegetarian dishes. A meal could begin with an appetiser of Italian meats, followed by a timbale of oak-smoked salmon filled with scrambled egg and served with a champagne and chive butter sauce. Ballotine of chicken filled with sweetbreads and served with a white cabbage and bacon fricassée might be available as a main course, accompanied by a good selection of carefully-prepared vegetables; passion fruit delice served on a blackcurrant purée could conclude the meal.

Directions: Follow signs to Town centre and Conference Centre, 3rd turn at roundabout (Homer Road)

61 Homer Road B91 3QD
Map no: 7 SP17
Tel: 0121 633 9988
Chef: Barrie Corrick
Proprietor: Queens Moat.
Manager: Brian Dunne
Cost: *Alc* from £25, fixed-price L £12.50/D £16.75. H/wine £10.15 Service inc
Credit cards: 🆇 💳 💳 💳
Times: Last L 2pm, last D 10pm Closed Sat L
Menus: *A la carte*, fixed-price L & D, bar menu
Seats: 80. No-smoking area
Additional: Children welcome, children's menu; ♥ dishes, vegan/other diets on request

SUTTON COLDFIELD, **New Hall** ❀❀

Sound imaginative cooking in the fine restaurant of this ancient manor house hotel

Walmley Road B76 1BX
Map no: 7 SP19
Tel: 0121 378 2442
Chef: Simon Radley
Proprietors: Thistle Country
House (Small Luxury Hotels).
Managers: Ian & Caroline Parkes
Cost: Fixed-price L £18.50/D
£30. H/wine £11.95 ❢ Service
inc
Credit cards: 🖪 📰 🖼 🖃
Times: Last L 2pm, last D 10pm
daily
Menus: Fixed-price L & D, pre-
theatre
Seats: 60. No smoking in dining
room
Additional: Children permitted,
children's portions; ❤ dishes,
vegan/other diets on request

An 800-year-old country house, New Hall has been sympathetically
extended and converted into a charming hotel, set in 26 acres of
gardens including a moat, trout lake and yew walk. Many
architectural features have been retained, such as 16th-century oak
panelling, Flemish glass and Elizabethan plaster work. Public areas
include an elegant drawing room and a panelled dining room where
Simon Radley offers some fine cooking. Imaginative dishes from
the extended fixed-price menu might be cassoulet of duckling with
haricot beans and spiced sausage, a soup of watercress and oysters,
and salmon from the New Hall smokehouse. For main course,
succulent rack of lamb served with a julienne of vegetables, garlic
fritters and basil pasta, or rabbit with sweet onions and beer, and to
finish, dark and white chocolate mousse with a hazelnut sabayon.
The separate vegetarian menu of two starters and main courses
might have chargrilled asparagus with tomato compote and
tapenade, followed by a pine nut pastry with goats' cheese and
crushed dauphinoise. There is a worthy wine list with a wide choice
by the glass.

Directions: On the B4148 E of Sutton Coldfield, near Walmley, close
to M6/M42 junction

WALSALL, **The Fairlawns at Aldridge** ❀

*Daily blackboard fish specials supplement the reliably cooked English
dishes at The Fairlawns. Look out for brochette of salmon and monkfish
chargrilled with bacon, best end of English lamb roasted with garlic and
rosemary, and steamed sultana and suet pudding, all served in a friendly
and relaxed atmosphere*

Menus: *A la carte*, fixed-price L & D, bar menu
Seats: 70. No smoking before 2.30pm & 10.30pm
Additional: Children welcome, children's portions; ❤ menu,
vegan/other diets on request
Directions: Outskirts of Aldridge, 400yds from crossroads of A452
(Chester Road) & A454 (Little Aston Road)

78 Little Aston Road
Aldridge WS9 0NU
Map no: 7 SP09
Tel: 01922 55122
Chef: Todd Hubble
Proprietor: John Pette
Cost: *Alc* from £23.50, fixed-
price L £12.95 (2 courses),
£15/D £21. H/wine £9.95
❢ Service inc
Credit cards: 🖪 📰 🖼 🖃 OTHER
Times: Last L 2pm, last D 10pm
Closed Sun D, Bhs

WEST SUSSEX

AMBERLEY, **Amberley Castle** 🏵🏵

An impressive ancient building dripping with character but, at the time of going to press, a succession of chefs leaves the kitchen in a state of flux

Half ruin, half restored, an outstanding building that has stood for over 900 years, Amberley Castle makes a magnificent hotel. White peacocks, suits of armour, and a croquet lawn within the moat, are all entirely appropriate features of this extraordinary place, and even the proprietor's Pyrennean mountain dog is dwarfed by the massive 14th-century castle walls. In the Queen's Room restaurant, an impressive baronial dining-room with barrel-vaulted ceiling and lancet windows, smart dress is required and booking essential. An inspection meal began with a mousse of fresh asparagus served with lightly boiled quails' eggs and a garlic-laced ravigote sauce. The main course comprised sautéed loin of new season lamb sliced onto Anna potatoes with broad beans and a thick reduction sauce with a bracing tarragon flavour. For pudding, a tartlet filled with crème pâtissière, topped with raspberries and strawberries and served with a good Drambuie ice-cream. The extensive wine list provides authoritative notes on grape varieties and regions mainly from France. Breakfast is 'a sumptuous affair'.

Arundel BN18 9ND
Map no: 4 TQ01
Tel: 01798 831992
Chef: n/a
Proprietor: Martin Cummings (Small Luxury Hotels)
Cost: Alc £40+, fixed-price L £16.50/D £25.50. H/wine £13.50 ▮ Service inc
Credit cards: 🗠 📰 ⚏ 🖭
Times: 12.30pm-last L 2pm, 7.30pm-last D 9.30pm
Menus: A la carte; fixed-price L & D
Seats: 40. No smoking in dining room
Additional: Children permitted; ❷ dishes, vegan/other diets on request

Directions: Off the B2139 between Amberley and Houghton villages

ARUNDEL, **Burpham Country Hotel** 🏵

☺ *Tucked away in a peaceful village at the base of the South Downs, this delightful little hotel features a charming dining room serving imaginative interpretations of conventional dishes. A starter of smoked chicken and avocado crêpe, for example, might be followed by carefully prepared rack of lamb accompanied by rösti potatoes*

Arundell BN18 9RJ
Map no: 4 TQ00
Tel: 01903 882160
Chef: Marianne Walker
Cost: Fixed-price D £16.50 Service exc
Credit cards: 🗠 📰
Times: Last D 8.45pm

Directions: 3 miles northeast off A27

ARUNDEL, **George & Dragon** 🏵🏵

☺ *Sussex Downs pub with capable kitchen that delivers well prepared dishes*

The name of this remote country pub might stir the heart of every true-blooded Englishman, but the menu is predominantly French. Soufflés of goats' cheese, quennelles of halibut, salmon en croûte and breast of magret duckling grilled pink, have an unmistakable provenance. British heritage is not forgotten, however, with dishes such as lambs' kidneys in a port and whole grain mustard sauce (albeit served with coriander mayonnaise), fresh fanned pear with Stilton, walnut and celery on a poppy seed cream, calves' liver fried with onion, garlic and fresh chives, and roast rib of prime Scotch beef served for Sunday lunch. Other dishes are of a more polyglot nature – smoked chicken salad with orange, blush grapefruit and citrus dressing, wild mushroom ravioli and suprême of chicken with avocado filling and cream and lemon chive sauce. Desserts come

Burpham BN18 9RR
Map no: 4 TQ00
Tel: 01903 883131
Chefs: Kate Holle, David Futcher and Gary Scott
Proprietors: Tennants. Managers: James Rose and Kate Holle
Cost: Fixed-price D £15.95 (2 courses), £18.95/Sun L £15.50. H/wine £8.95 ▮ Service inc
Credit cards: 🗠 📰 ⚏ OTHER
Times: 7.15pm-last D 9.45pm, last Sun L 1.45pm Closed Sun eve
Menus: Fixed-price D & Sun L, bar menu

from the trolley. The wine list covers a number of European and New World countries, and is reasonably priced. There is also a good choice of real ales in the bar.

Directions: 2.5 miles off A27 1 mile E of Arundel signed Burpham

Seats: 40. No cigars or pipes in dining room
Additional: Children over 10 permitted (L only); ❂ dishes, oter diets prior notice

ARUNDEL, **The Swan Hotel** ❀

☺ *Located in the centre of Arundel, this charming hotel offers modern Anglo-French cooking noted for fresh flavours and good timing. Recommended dishes include chicken mousse with tarragon, and fillet of lamb with a redcurrant glaze on a beurre noir galette potato*

Menus: A la carte, fixed-price L & D, bar menu
Seats: 50
Additional: Children welcome until 8pm, children's portions; ❂ dishes, other diets on request
Directions: Town centre

27-29 High Street BN18 9AG
Map no: 4 TQ00
Tel: 01903 882314
Chef: Michael Collis
Proprietors: John Ryan and Stephen Lowson
Cost: Alc £18, fixed-price L /D £10.95. H/wine £8.25 ❢
No service charge
Credit cards: 🖾 🔳 ☰ 🔲 OTHER
Times: Last L 2.30pm, last D 9.45pm daily

ASHINGTON, **Mill House Hotel** ❀

A friendly atmosphere is assured at this quietly located hotel, suprisingly near the A42 Worthing to Horsham road. In the candlelit Millers Restaurant, chef Victor Hardy offers some worthy dishes, such as duck and chicken terrine, fillet of salmon with a mustard and herb crust, and home-made warm pear and almond tart

Directions: Off A24 (northbound)

Ashington RH20 3BZ
Map no: 4 TQ11
Tel: 01903 892426
Chef: Victor Hardy
Proprietor: Mrs Y Shute
Cost: Alc £30, fixed-price L £12.95/D £14.95. Service inc
Credit cards: 🖾 🔳 ☰ 🔲
Times: Last D 9pm

ASHINGTON,
The Willows Restaurant ❀❀

☺ *Broad, international menu offers something for all tastes*

The 15th-century farmhouse is set in pleasant, well-kept gardens, and the set-price dinner and Sunday lunch menus are good value-for-money, with an extensive range of well-cooked international dishes to select from. There are around 10 starters and 14 main courses, and amongst the former, safe bets would be smoked salmon cornets filled with fresh prawns, home-made cheese and spinach gnocchi, grilled Dover sole, roast duck with sage and onion stuffing and apple sauce, and steaks cooked plain, with peppercorns or tarragon butter. More up-tempo dishes would include smoked chicken breast salad with warm creamed puy lentils and roast garlic, deep-fried Mediterranean prawns in tempura batter with a spicy duo of salads, and pan-fried pork fillet with fresh noodles and a tomato and basil jus. Vegetarians are far from forgotten, and have their own multi-choice menu – baked Ashington goats' cheese on a toasted croûton served on a bed of marinated peppers and pine nuts, to start with, perhaps, followed by a selection of vegetables tossed in a spicy peanut sauce, served on a spaghetti of cucumber surrounded with a vegetable and chilli sweet and sour sauce.

Directions: Village centre (now by-passed by A24) midway between Horsham and Worthing

London Road RH20 3JR
Map no: 4 TQ11
Tel: 01903 892575
Chef: Carl Illes
Proprietors: Carl & Julie Illes
Cost: Fixed-price D £ 18.95/Sun L £16.50. H/wine £8.95 Service exc
Credit cards: 🖾 🔳 ☰
Times: Last D 9.30pm, last Sun L 2pm Closed Sun D, Mon
Menus: Fixed-price D & Sun L
Seats: 28. Smoking limited
Additional: Children permitted; ❂ dishes, vegan on request, other diets prior notice

BILLINGSHURST, The Gables ❀❀

Absolutely fresh produce is handled with skill and ingenuity

The setting is 'olde worlde' and essentially English, with its low oak beams and inglenook fireplace, but cooking here is both modern in style and recognisably touched by a strong international influence. Imaginative fixed-price menus are changed every three weeks, in line with seasonal availability of ingredients – chef Nicky Illes personally selecting the best and freshest of produce from the London markets. Daily specials, home-made soups and home-baked speciality breads are all excellent, and original touches raise quite simple dishes from the ordinary; pâté de foie gras and duck liver, for example, is served with a compote of blackcurrants and toasted walnut bread, while a crayfish and mussel risotto comes with saffron cream sauce. More traditional but well executed choices include chargrilled calves' liver with back bacon and a rich Madeira and sage sauce, and medallions of pan-fried venison with spätzle and a rich port and shallot sauce. Wines from around the world include fine domaine-bottled Burgundy and a good selection of cru-classe Bordeaux.

Parbrook RH14 9EU
Map no: 4 TQ02
Tel: 01403 782571
Chef: Nicholas Illes
Proprietors: Nicholas & Rebecca Illes
Cost: Fixed-price L £17.50/D £20.75. H/wine £8 ❢ Service exc
Credit cards: 🔳 🔳 🔳
Times: Last L 1.30pm, last D 9pm/10pm Fri-Sat Closed Sat L, Sun D, Mon
Menus: Fixed-price L & D
Seats: 50
Additional: Children welcome (not Fri-Sat D); ❤ dishes, vegan/other diets by arrangement

Directions: On the A29 just south of Billingshurst

BOSHAM, The Millstream Hotel ❀

A charming hotel which enjoys a picturesque setting with a former millstream running alongside the lawns. Cooking is sound and enjoyable. An inspection meal produced chicken parfait, venison 'glace de viande' and an English apple tart for dessert

Bosham Lane PO18 8HL
Map no: 4 SU80
Tel: 01243 573234
Chef: Bev Boakes
Manager: Jeremy Rodericks
Cost: Fixed-price L £12.75/D £17.25. H/wine £9.15 Service exc
Credit cards: 🔳 🔳 🔳 🔳 OTHER
Times: Last L 2pm, last D 9.30pm daily
Menus: Fixed-price L & D, bar L menu, pre-theatre
Seats: 80. No smoking in dining room
Additional: Children welcome, children's portions; ❤ menu, vegan/other diets on request

Directions: Off A259, in village on right towards the quay

BRACKLESHAM,
Cliffords Cottage Restaurant ❀❀

Friendly and informal cottage restaurant run by husband and wife team

The low-beamed ceilings and open log fire of this cosy cottage is quintessentially English, but the cooking is a thoughtful mix of

Bracklesham Lane PO20 8JA
Map no: 4 SZ89
Tel: 01243 670250
Chef: Tony Shanahan
Proprietors: Brenda & Tony Shanahan

British and French, at reasonable prices. Tony and Brenda Shanahan offer both fixed-price menus and a *carte*; interestingly, the former is written in plain English, the other in plain French (with more elaborate translations). Both, however, are distinguished by good use of fresh produce, careful preparation and consistent standards of cooking. A three-course set dinner may include a warm salad of chicken livers and crispy bacon, avocado mousse with smoked salmon and prawns, roast rack of lamb with herb crust, and venison steak with braised red onions. Sautéed, garlic or parsleyed potatoes come with a selection of fresh vegetables. On the *carte*, there are escargots, lobster thermidor, scampi and fillet steak garni from which to make a classic Franglais choice. Desserts look both ways across the Channel – pancakes in one direction, bread and butter pudding, the other.

Cost: *Alc* £25, fixed-price D £16.95/Sun L £12. H/wine £8.95 Service exc
Credit cards: 🔲 🔲 🔲 🔲
Times: Last D 9.30pm, last Sun L 1.30pm Closed Mon
Menus: *A la carte*, fixed-price L & D
Seats: 30. Air conditioned
Additional: Children over 5 permitted at Sun L, children's portions; ❂ dishes, other diets on request

Directions: On B2179 Birdham/Blacklesway road

CHICHESTER,
Comme Ça Restaurant ❀❀

A popular, personally-run restaurant serving French provincial cooking

French provincial cooking is served at this popular restaurant, located close to the Festival Theatre. (Theatregoers are offered pre and post theatre dining.) Good quality local produce is used in the well-constructed dishes. A meal in February began with 'pâtés au saumon, crevettes et aneth' – fresh tagliatelle cooked with salmon, prawns and dill. This was followed by pan-fried calves' liver cooked with sage butter and bacon with broccoli mousse, mange tout, baby corn, new potatoes and dauphinoise potatoes. The dessert of 'tarte au Metropan' was a highlight of the meal; prepared from a Normandy recipe, it had a fresh light pastry and appropriately sweet filling. Coffee with a home-made chocolate truffle and an almond friandise concluded the meal. The restaurant is personally run by chef-patron Michel Navet and Jane Owen-Navet, who ensure attentive service is provided. An interesting wine list features French and Australian house wines, domaine-bottled Rhône wines and a recently added selection of New World wines.

Broyle Road PO19 4BD
Map no: 4 SU80
Tel: 01243 788724/536307
Chef: Michel Navet
Proprietor: Michel Navet
Cost: *Alc* £25.30, fixed-price L £17.25/D £16.25. H/wine £8.95 Service exc
Credit cards: 🔲 🔲 🔲 OTHER
Times: Last L 2pm, last D 10.30pm/after theatre Closed Sun D, Mon
Menus: *A la carte*, fixed-price L & D, pre/post-theatre, bar menu
Seats: 90. No smoking in dining room
Additional: Children welcome, children's menu; ❂ menu, vegan/other diets on request

Directions: On the A286 near Festival Theatre

CHICHESTER, Confucius ❀

☺ *Situated just off the town centre, this family-run restaurant is furnished in a traditional Hong Kong style. The food is enjoyable and freshly prepared, featuring good quality ingredients; dishes may include steamed scallops served in the shell with ginger and spring onions, and deep-fried duck with a plum sauce*

Seats: 66. Air conditioned **Additional:** Children welcome, children's portions; ❂ dishes, vegan/ other diets on request
Directions: Town centre, off South Street

2 Cooper Street PO19 1EB
Map no: 4 SU80
Tel: 01243 783158
Chef: Koon Hung Li
Proprietor: Koon Hiun Lee
Cost: *Alc* £16, fixed-price L £5/D £13.50. H/wine £8 Service exc
Credit cards: 🔲 🔲 🔲 🔲
Times: Last L 1.45pm, last D 10.45pm
Closed Sun, Bhs, Xmas

Entries in this Guide are based on reports filed by our team of professionally trained, full-time inspectors.

CHICHESTER, **The Droveway** ❀❀

Anglo-French cuisine presented in a variety of guises

The two-course express lunch menu for only £10, must be one of Chichester's best buys, particularly when the choice includes dishes such as rib eye of pork, mille-feuille of salmon with tarragon, sticky toffee pudding and a fine selection of farmhouse cheeses served with celery and biscuits. It is worth returning with time to spare, however, to enjoy more fully the careful Anglo-French cooking of chef/patron Jonas Tester. The regularly changing 'menu du jour' goes in for French provincial classics, such as haddock mornay and ragoût of beef and mushrooms, whilst the *carte* aims for more upmarket haute cuisine. Papillon of asparagus and smoked ham, Florentine of eggs in puff pastry, tournedos 'au poivre' and papilotte of sea bass are all typical of the range. One starter, coquilles St Jacques 'Buerehiesel', is credited to the renowned Strasbourg restaurant of that name. Desserts include charlotte au chocolat and caramel and banana défendu.

Directions: City centre, 1st floor, corner of Southgate and Old Market Avenue

30a Southgate PO19 1DR
Map no: 4 SU80
Tel: 01243 528832
Chef: Jonas Tester
Proprietors: Jonas & Elly Tester
Cost: Alc £27, fixed-price L £10 (2 course), D £19.50. H/wine £11.50 ❢ Service exc
Credit cards: 🔳 🔳 🔳 OTHER
Times: Last L 2pm, last D 10pm Closed Sun, Mon
Menus: A la carte, fixed-price
Seats: 40. No-smoking room
Additional: Children welcome, children's portions; ❶ menu, vegan/other diets on request

CHICHESTER, **The Ship Hotel** ❀

☺ *A range of soundly cooked dishes is available from the carte and fixed-price menus in the hotel's Murray's Restaurant. Look out for home-made chicken liver pâté with pistachio nuts in puff pastry, and poached fillet of pork with pink peppercorn sauce. Desserts can be uninspiring*

Menus: A la carte, fixed-price L & D, pre-theatre, bar menu **Seats:** 54. No smoking in dining room **Additional:** Children welcome, children's portions; ❶ dishes, vegan/other diets on request
Directions: From Festival Theatre roundabout, turn towards shopping centre. Hotel is on left

North Street PO19 1NH
Map no: 4 SU80
Tel: 01243 778000
Chef: Robin Castle
Proprietor: First Secured Hotels. Managers: Peter & Colleen Cook
Cost: Alc £20, fixed-price L £10.50, £8.50 (2 course)/D £15.50. H/wine £8.75 Service exc
Credit cards: 🔳 🔳 🔳 OTHER
Times: Last L 2pm, last D 9.30pm daily

CHILGROVE, **White Horse Inn** ❀❀

☺ *A magnificent wine list with food to match in a peaceful rural setting*

The White Horse Inn nestles almost alone in a beautiful downland valley A nearby forge has been converted to provide accommodation for those who wish to experience the delights of the White Horse's celebrated wine list of well over 2,300 bins. Barry and Dorothea Phillips have managed to retain a comfortable pub atmosphere even though Neil Rusbridger's excellent cooking has given the inn a well-deserved reputation and large clientele. In the restaurant bacon and tomato soup, in which good bacon stock was evident, was sampled alongside a fresh, firm red mullet with pesto sauce. Spring lamb, for main course, was tender, slightly pink and served with a tomato concasse and an orange, mint and lamb jus; its neighbour an excellent calves' liver came with a restrained Madeira sauce. The accompanying onion marmalade was perhaps a shade vinegary. Both dishes were accompanied by good vegetables. For dessert, a rich smooth chocolate marquise served with chocolate beans and a coffee sauce. The cheese selection was a plate of five well-kept cheeses, one of which was local. The White Horse has two wine lists, one for connoisseurs. They make fascinating reading, so ensure you arrive in plenty of time to study them.

Map no: 4 SU81
Tel: 01243 535219
Chef: Neil Rusbridger
Proprietor: Barry Phillips
Cost: Alc £18.50, fixed-price L £17.50/D £23 (4 course). H/wine £11.50 ❢ Service exc
Credit cards: 🔳 🔳 🔳 OTHER
Times: Last L 2pm, last D 9.30pm Closed Sat L
Menus: A la carte, fixed-price L & D, bar menu
Seats: 70. Air conditioned
Additional: Children permitted; ❶ dishes, vegan/other diets on request
Directions: On the B2141 between Chichester and Petersfield

CLIMPING, **Bailiffscourt Hotel** ✿✿✿

A fabulous 30s folly serving an inventive repertoire of Anglo-French cooking with a new, less complicated approach

Climping B17 5RW
Map no: 4 TQ00
Tel: 01903 723511
Chef: Simon Rogan
Proprietor: Anne Goodman
Cost: *Alc* £35-£40, fixed-price
L £17.50/D £29.50. H/wine
£10.95 Service exc
Credit cards: 🖃 🖃 🖃 🖃 OTHER
Times: Last L 2.15pm, last D
9.45pm/10pm Fri-Sat
Menus: *A la carte*, fixed-price
L & D, bar menu
Seats: 50. No smoking in dining room
Additional: Children welcome, children's menu; ❶ dishes, vegan/other diets on request

Bailiffscourt is not all it may seem. The beautifully preserved medieval manor house was actually painstakingly put together just 60 years ago using centuries old materials to create this wonderful deception. To complete the effect two woods were uprooted from the Sussex Downs and replanted around the house, and the 15th-century gatehouse was moved, piece by piece, from North Sussex.

The kitchen, under the leadership of Simon Rogan produces interesting, elaborate dishes, such as a fillet of bass with aubergine confit, clam pistou, berrichone potatoes and an oyster jus, or pot au feu of lamb with sweetbread ravioli, braised courgette flower and a thyme bouillon. Generally these creations succeed, though there has been a degree of waywardness, and some dishes can deliver a bewildering variety on the plate.

However, recent reports indicate a modification of style, and new menus have been introduced, described by Simon Rogan as 'leaning to the theory that optimum ingredients should be cooked without complication to produce a perfect dish with the correct flavours'. Examples from the new *carte* are assiette of home-smoked salmon with caviar Chantilly; pavé of Angus beef with a potato and celeriac crust, grilled artichokes and claret sauce, and a dessert of croustillants of caramel. A separate vegetarian menu is also available. There is a lengthy wine list with a French core and international representation.

Directions: W of Littlehampton off the A259, signposted Bailiffscourt

COPTHORNE, **The Copthorne** ✿

Exposed brick walls and old beams feature in the intimate Lion d'Or restaurant at this former 16th-century farmhouse. Highlights on an extensive carte and daily-changing fixed price menu include chicken liver parfait and sea-bass given an Oriental treatment with a soy-based sauce

Menus: *A la carte*, fixed-price L & D, bar menu **Seats:** 60.
No-smoking area **Additional:** Children welcome, children's portions;
❶ dishes, vegan/other diets on request
Directions: A264 (East Grinstead) 3rd exit off roundabout

Copthorne Way RH10 3PG
Map no: 5 TQ33
Tel: 01342 714971
Chef: Richard Duckworth
Proprietor: Copthorne.
Manager: Paal Borresen
Cost: *Alc* £25, fixed-price
L £18.50/D £22.50. H/wine
£11.95 ❗ Service inc
Credit cards: 🖃 🖃 🖃 🖃
Times: Last L 1.30pm, last D
9.30pm Closed Sat L, Sun

COPTHORNE,
The Copthorne Effingham Park ❀

West Park Road RH10 3EU
Map no: 5 TQ33
Tel: 01342 714994
Chef: Kevin Lindsay
Proprietor: Copthorne Restaurant
Manager: Andrew Aitken
Cost: *Alc* £25-£30, fixed-price
L £15.50. H/wine £11.95
Service exc
Credit cards: 🔳 🔳 🔳 📳 OTHER
Times: Last L 2pm, last D 10pm
Closed Sun, Bhs

An effort is made to produce imaginative freshly-prepared food in the Wellingtonia restaurant at the Copthorne. Everything is home-made, and the Anglo-French cooking features dishes such as ravioli of forest mushrooms and spinach in a brandy sauce, and fish in a pastry case with a chive and white wine sauce

Menus: A la carte, fixed-price L
Seats: 60. Air conditioned. No smoking in dining room
Additional: Children welcome, children's menu; ❂ dishes, vegan/other diets on request
Directions: From M23 exit 10 take A264 (East Grinstead) straight on at first roundabout, signed at second roundabout

CRAWLEY,
Holiday Inn London-Gatwick ❀

Langley Drive
Map no: 4 TQ23
Tel: 01293 529991
Chef: David Woods
Proprietor: Holiday Inn.
Manager: Alan Murphy
Cost: *Alc* £23, fixed-price D
£9.95 (1 course)-£16.95, dinner
dance £18.50, dinner disco
£14.95, Sunday L £14.95.
H/wine £9.95 ◕ Service exc
Credit cards: 🔳 🔳 🔳 📳
Times: 7pm-last D 9.30pm, Sun
L12.30pm-2pm. Closed Bh
Mons

Busy, modern airport hotel with all-day coffee shop and the more formal Colonnade Restaurant, where the emphasis is on straightforward techniques and honest flavours. Despite the good intentions, execution sometimes falls short. Look out for seafood gâteau, a good hot weather dish; lemon tart fell below par

Seats: 100. No-smoking area. Air conditioned
Additional: Children welcome, children's menu/portions; ❂ menu, vegan/other diets on request; dinner disco every Friday, dinner dance 1st Saturday of month
Directions: At junction of A23 & A264, Tushmore roundabout

CUCKFIELD, Ockenden Manor ❀❀

Ockenden Lane RH17 5LD
Map no: 4 TQ32
Tel: 01444 416111
Chef: Geoff Welch
Proprietor: Mr & Mrs Goodman.
Manager: Mr Kerry Turner
Cost: *Alc* £35, fixed-price
L £18.50, £15.50 (2 course)/D
£29.50 (£32.50 Sat), H/wine
£10.50 Service inc

Quality fresh produce is used in the imaginative dishes served at this 16th-century manor house

Set in mature grounds and well-kept gardens, the Ockenden Manor dates in part from the early 16th century. The restaurant is atmospheric with stained-glass windows and an embossed ceiling.

An innovative and professional approach to cooking is taken by chef Geoff Walsh. Consistent standards are maintained by keeping faith with fresh produce, especially seafood from Newhaven and game from the Balcombe estate. A meal could begin with field mushrooms and roasted wood pigeon with a tarragon chicken mousse and a truffle and Madeira sauce. A typical main course could be poached fillet of Scotch salmon served with a spring onion butter flavoured with ginger, and a molleux of bitter chocolate served with home-made ice-cream, crème anglaise and toffee sauce for dessert. An outstanding wine list features 175 bins and includes classic vintage red Bordeaux. Service is professional and attentive and the atmosphere in the hotel relaxed and welcoming.

Directions: Village centre, off main street

Credit cards: ▨ ▨ ▨ ▨ OTHER
Times: Last L 2pm, last D 9.15pm
Menus: *A la carte*, fixed-price L & D
Seats: 45. No smoking in dining room
Additional: Children permitted (over 5 at dinner), children's portions; ✿ dishes, other diets if advised

EAST GRINSTEAD,

Gravetye Manor Hotel ❀❀

Immensely civilised setting where the return of a chef has revitalised the cooking

East Grinstead RH19 4LJ
Map no: 5 TQ33
Tel: 01342 810567
Chef: Mark Raffan
Proprietor: Peter Herbert (Relais & Chateaux)
Cost: *Alc* £35, fixed-price L £22 (Sun £28)/D £28. H/wine £15.50
❗ Service inc
Credit cards: ▨ ▨ OTHER
Times: Last L 2pm, last D 9.30pm Closed Dec 25 D except res
Menus: *A la carte*, fixed-price L & D
Seats: 50. No smoking in dining room
Additional: Children over 7 permitted, children's portions; ✿ dishes; other diets with notice

Chef Mark Raffan has come back to his former roost, bringing with him a return to traditional country house cooking. At the time of our inspection, his *carte* had not yet been introduced, so our choice was from the fixed-price menu, but was none the worse for that. Courgette flowers stuffed with lobster mousse pepped up with red pepper, made an attractive starter, served in a small pool of what was described as bouillabaisse jus, but bore more resemblance to a bisque. Coq au vin, with fresh tagliatelle, was, perhaps, an unusual inclusion in a summer menu, and had a more pedestrian flavour with somewhat overcooked meat. A textbook raspberry charlotte was served with a refreshing yoghurt glaze and raspberry coulis. Strong espresso partnered some fresh and exciting petits fours, including a frozen one of raspberry sorbet inside white chocolate. Note that prices on the menu, and on the extensive, archival wine list are plus VAT, a practice which does seem to bump up the cost of a meal.

Directions: Off B2028 2 miles SW of East Grinstead

EAST GRINSTEAD,
Woodbury House Hotel ❀

French and English country house cooking is served from the carte and fixed-price menu at Woodbury House. Wild mushrooms in puff pastry and pot-roast rack of lamb scored high marks at inspection but saucing was uneven. Baked lemon and rum pie for dessert, and decent petits fours come with coffee

Menus: *A la carte*, fixed-price L & D, bar menu
Seats: 45
Additional: Children welcome, children's menu; ❷ dishes, vegan/other diets on request
Directions: On A22 between East Grinstead and Forest Row

Lewes Road RH19 3UD
Map no: 5 TQ33
Chef: C Parker-Brooks
Proprietor: Nick G E Richards
Cost: *Alc* £20-£25, fixed-price
L £15/D £17.50 H/wine £10 ❢
Service exc
Credit cards: 🃏 💳 💳 🃏 OTHER
Times: Open 11am-11pm daily

GOODWOOD,
Goodwood Park Hotel ❀

Part of the Goodwood estate, this sprawling hotel combines both golf and country club for both leisure and conference purposes. Dukes Restaurant offers a formal approach to dining, whilst the Waterbeach Grill is open all day for more informal meals

Directions: Off the A27, following signs for Goodwood House, then signs for Golf & Country Club

Chichester PO18 0QB
Map no: 4 SU80
Tel: 01243 775537
Chef: Michael Oliver
Proprietor: Country Club.
Manager: Jonathan Orr-Ewing
Cost: *Alc* £19-£30, fixed-price
L £12.75/D £18.50.
H/wine £9.95 ❢ Service exc
Credit cards: 🃏 💳 💳 🃏
Times: Last L 2pm, last D
9.30pm Closed Sat L
Menus: *A la carte*, fixed-price
L & D, bar menu
Seats: 90. No smoking in dining room
Additional: Children welcome, children's portions; ❷ dishes, vegan/other diets on request

HORSHAM, **Random Hall Hotel** ❀

☺ *The candlelit Tudor-style restaurant of this late 16th century hotel serves imaginative modern British cooking The three-course fixed-price menu includes salmon fishcakes on a dill and cucumber cream sauce, and breast of duck with an orange and cranberry sauce among the choices*

Menus: *A la carte*, fixed-price L & D, pre-theatre, bar menu
Seats: 36. No-smoking area
Additional: Children over 5 welcome, children's portions; ❷ dishes, vegan/other diets on request
Directions: On A29, just outside Slinfold, 4 miles W of Horsham

Stane Street
Slinfold RH13 7QX
Map no: 4 TQ13
Tel: 01403 790558
Chef: Jonathan Gettings
Proprietors: Nigel & Kathy Evans
Cost: *Alc* £18.35, fixed-price
L £12.95 £9.95 (1 course)/D
£16.95. H/wine £ 8.95
❢ Service inc
Credit cards: 🃏 💳 💳 OTHER
Times: Last L 2pm, last D 10pm
Closed Dec 27-30

HURSTPIERPOINT, Boles ❀

Hurstpierpoint BN6 9PU
Map no: 4 TQ21
Tel: 01273 833452
Chef: Anne-Michele Bole
Proprietor: Anne-Michele Bole
Cost: Alc £15-£22, fixed-price
Sun L £10.95/special D £15.95.
H/wine £6.95 Cover charge 25p
Service exc
Credit cards: 🖾 🖾 🖾
Times: Last L 2pm, last D
9.30pm Closed Sat L

☺ *Anne-Michele Bole has worked extensively in Europe and has now brought her knowledge of European cooking to this small West Sussex village. A monthly changing menu could include stuffed poussin with Calvados and apples, or poached fillet of sea bass with a spinach sauce. The short wine list is reasonably priced*

Menus: A la carte, fixed-price Sun L & D specials **Seats:** 45.
No-smoking area **Additional:** Children welcome; ❂ dishes, children's portions/other diets on request
Directions: Town centre halfway along High Street

LANCING, Sussex Pad Hotel ❀❀

Old Shoreham Road
BN15 0RH
Map no: 4 TQ10
Tel: 01273 454647
Chef: Paul Hornsby
Proprietor: Wally Pack
Cost: Alc £16.50, fixed-price
L/D £16.50, £14 (2 course).
H/wine £9.66 Service exc
Credit cards: 🖾 🖾 🖾 🖾 OTHER
Times: Last L 2pm, last D 10pm
daily
Menus: A la carte, fixed-price L
& D, bar menu
Seats: 45. No smoking in dining
room
Additional: Children welcome,
children's portions; ❂ dishes,
vegan/other diets on request

☺ *A friendly, well-run hotel restaurant where fresh fish is a highlight*

With Shoreham Airport opposite, Lancing College close by, and the chalk bulk of the South Downs behind, the Sussex Pad's spacious lounge/bar/conservatory makes a popular meeting place, open all day for meals and light refreshments. The smaller, plush Ladywells Restaurant operates within more formal parameters. Fresh fish direct from Shoreham Harbour is the star of the show. Crab soup, lobster and peach salad, grilled langoustine coated with Cajun spices, grilled Dover sole, and black bream baked with spring onion, ginger, dry sherry and soya sauce, are handled with flair by chef/partner Paul Hornsby. The fish theme is picked up in the restaurant decor; owner Wally Pack is a former underwater fishing world champion, and all his trophies are on display. One inspection meal produced mussels cooked in wine and served with whole peppercorns, salmon, tomato and fish fumet, set on a bed of spinach leaves with rösti potato, some fine braised fennel and a timbale of basil and tomatoes. Desserts include bread and butter pudding with freshly grated nutmeg and a crème anglaise. There is a well chosen selection of young vintage wines.

Directions: On the A27 by Lancing College, opposite Shoreham airport

LOWER BEEDING,
Jeremy's at The Crabtree ❀❀

Brighton Road RH13 6PT
Map no: 4 TQ22
Tel: 01403 891257
Chef: Jeremy Ashpool
Proprietors: Jeremy & Vera
Ashpool.
Manager: Nick Wege
Cost: Alc £21.50, fixed-price
Sun L £14.95. H/wine £9.95
❗ Service inc
Credit cards: 🖾 🖾 OTHER
Times: Last L 2pm, last D
9.45pm. Closed Sun eve
Menus: A la carte, fixed-price
Sun L, mid-wk specials, bar
menu
Seats: 40. No-smoking area
Additional: Children permitted;
❂ dishes

☺ *Fresh modern cooking from a talented, self-taught chef*

The Crabtree is an unusual combination of architectural styles. A 17th-century, timbered cottage, with log-burning fire in a large inglenook, and a much later, more formal addition forming the front of the building, which is the aspect that visitors first see. The restaurant spills over several rooms in both these areas. The food, cooked by self-taught chef, Jeremy Ashpool, is modern and relies on an imaginative use of herbs and spices. The menu changes daily. There is plenty of fish on offer, and poached fillets of salmon and brill with asparagus, samphire and ginger butter sauce were greatly appreciated although it was felt that the ginger was too subtle. Grilled spiced spring lamb with bulgar wheat and cardamom and coriander sauce seemed somewhat overwhelmed by the marinade and did not have much of a lamb flavour. Starters of grilled fillet of skate with anchovy, tarragon and caper topping and toasted goats' cheese with olives and pine kernels were delightfully presented, as were the deserts of banana and yoghurt biscuit cake and home-made praline ice-cream. The latter was full of nuts and accompanied by a piquant raspberry sauce. The wine list has a selection of about 50 wines and the pub specialises in a good selection of beers, not least, the excellent local brew by King & Barnes.

Directions: 4 miles SE of Horsham on A281 Brighton road

LOWER BEEDING, **South Lodge Hotel** 🏵🏵

Beautifully restored Victorian house in an impressive position overlooking the South Downs

Sometimes the old adage that simple is best, is forgotten in the modern hotel kitchen. It's something chef Tim Neal would do well to consider, given the over-elaborate recipes and curious combinations to which his Anglo-European menu is at times prone. The partly-panelled restaurant is certainly elegant, with candles, crystal chandeliers, white linen and bone china settings. A plus is the ample leg room at table. After a generous, if not always tip-top, selection of appetisers and some dry bread rolls, chargrilled scallops had an enjoyable smokey flavour, served on couscous with a spicy gazpacho sauce. Confit of goose, which was tough, came with a creamy morel sauce and overcooked mushroom risotto. Garnished with turnips, carrots and brocolli with hollandaise, the whole concoction needed a radical rethink. Yet butterscotch soufflé, served with pistachio ice-cream, was light and well-risen. There is a well-chosen selection of world wines, with the house Armando Martino 1991 VQPRD Aglianico del Vulture much praised.

Brighton Road RH13 6PS
Map no: 4 TQ22
Tel: 01403 891711
Chef: Timothy Neal
Proprietors: Exclusive Hotels.
General Manager: David French
Cost: *Alc* £35, fixed-price L £16 (£18.50 Sun)/D £25.00, £32 (5 course). H/wine £13.50 ❢
Service exc
Credit cards: 🟦 🟦 🟦 🟦 OTHER
Times: Last L 2pm/3pm Sun, last D 10pm/10.30pm Fri-Sat
Menus: *A la carte*, fixed-price L & D, bar menu
Seats: 40. No smoking
Additional: Children welcome, children's menu; ❶ menu, vegan/other diets on request

Directions: At junction of A279 (Horsham) and A281, turn onto the Cowfold/Brighton road. Hotel is 0.5 mile on right

MIDHURST, **Angel Hotel** 🏵🏵🏵

A good choice of modern English food with Mediterranean flavours

Conviviality and popularity are hallmarks of old coaching inns, and the 16th-century Angel is no exception. One of its main attractions is the pretty, blue and yellow restaurant, offering a fixed-price two or three-course lunch menu and four-course dinner menu in addition to the *carte*. The same food is also served in the less formal brasserie. Starters range from Parma ham with Parmesan shavings and radicchio to deep fried Brixham squid with chilli. One inspector sampled tender knuckle of ham terrine served with three home-made chutneys, peach, red cabbage and pepper and onion, followed by a fresh flavoured brill boudin with a light mousse filling and delicate herb coating, accompanied by a bright Provençal sauce. Alternatives might be fillet of lamb en croûte with a rosemary jus, or pasta with pine kernels, peperonata and smoked mozzarella. Among the puddings, apple tatin with vanilla ice-cream is a favourite, but strawberry crème brûlée is recommended, served warm, with a good creamy vanilla flavour, fresh sliced strawberries and fine crisp topping.

North Street GU29 9DN
Map no: 4 SU82
Tel: 01730 812421
Chefs: Peter Crawford-Rolt and Andrew Stephenson
Proprietor: Peter Crawford-Rolt
Cost: *Alc* £25, fixed-price L £12.50 (2 courses), £14.50/D £17.50 (4 course). H/wine £10.50 ❢ Service exc
Credit cards: 🟦 🟦 🟦 🟦
Times: Last L 2.30pm, last D 10pm
Menus: *A la carte*, fixed-price L & D, pre-theatre, bar menu
Seats: 60 +50. No pipes or cigars in dining room
Additional: Children welcome, children's menu; ❶ dishes, vegan/other diets on request

Directions: Town centre, junction of A286 and A2721

MIDHURST, **Southdowns Hotel** ❀

☺ *Enjoy beautiful views across the downs from Southdowns, an attractive, privately-owned hotel located in the depths of the Sussex countryside. A high standard of cooking offers the likes of richly flavoured chicken liver parfait with plum confit, and fillet of salmon with a well-made pesto*

Trotton GU31 5JN
Map no: 4 SU82
Tel: 01730 821521
Chef: Peter Broomhead
Proprietors: R Lion and
D Vedovato
Cost: Fixed-price L £12.95, £10
(2 course)/D £ 19.95. H/wine
£10.55 ❢ No service charge
Credit cards: 🆇 🈸 🈺 🈴
Times: Last L 2pm, last D
9.30pm
Menus: Fixed-price L & D, bar
menu
Seats: 70. Air conditioned.
No-smoking area
Additional: Children welcome,
children's menu; ❶ dishes,
vegan/other diets on request

Directions: Just off A272 Petersfield road

MIDHURST, **Spread Eagle Hotel** ❀❀

A charming old inn with bags of character serving stylish, imaginative food in a bright, modern style

No one will question the age. The inn, built around 1430, sports enough heavy oak beams set in low ceilings, and log burning fires, for there to be no mistaking its antiquity. In the restaurant, beneath beams hung with Christmas puddings of years past, Ken Jelfs (ex-Gleneagles) continues to provide an ever-interesting choice of dishes. There are influences from France and the Mediterranean which translate into a style of modern British cooking which delivers excellent terrine of wood pigeon and rabbit on a bed of raw beetroot and orange with pumpkin seeds and olive oil dressing, as well as 'superb' roasted sweetbreads served with a buttered vegetable sauce. Other dishes coming in for praise this year have included warm mousseline of chicken with Stilton cheese in a 'delightful' mushroom sauce, fillet of sole stuffed with a mousse of salmon studded with salmon caviar and house smoked salmon with a chive sauce. Desserts range from chocolate and pear tart, to a warm date and ginger pudding with a caramelised ginger sauce. The wine list dips into each country, with France coming off best. There is a good selection of cru-classe Bordeaux and domaine-bottled Burgundies.

South Street GU29 9NH
Map no: 4 SU82
Tel: 01730 816911
Chef: Ken Jelfs
Proprietors: Anne Goodman.
Manager: Pontus Carminger
Cost: Fixed-price L £12.95 (2
course), £16.50/D £25. H/wine
£9.75. Service exc
Credit cards: 🆇 🈸 🈺 🈴 OTHER
Times: Last L 2.15pm, last D
9.30pm
Menus: Fixed-price L & D, bar
menu
Seats: 60. No smoking in dining
room
Additional: Children welcome,
children's portions; ❶ dishes,
vegan/other diets on request

Directions: Town centre, corner of South and West Streets

Restaurant assessments are based on reports of visits carried out anonymously by the AA's Hotel and Restaurant Inspectors.

PETWORTH, **L'Amico** ❀

☺ *The conservatory of an old farmhouse is the unlikely venue for some fine Italian cooking. Authentic ingredients, such as oil from Gino Tecchia's family farm near Livorno, give his dishes a traditional flavour. Home made pasta, fresh sardines, lamb marinated with herbs and fresh figs have all been praised*

Times: 7pm-last D 10pm; lunch also served. Closed Sun eve & all day Mon
Directions: To the east of the town

Grove Lane
Map no 4 SU92
Tel: 01798 343659
Chef: Gino Tecchia
Proprietors: Gino & Barbara Tecchia
Cost: Alc £20, fixed-price £12.75, £15.50. H/wine £8.75. Service exc

PULBOROUGH, **Chequers Hotel** ❀

☺ *A relaxing hotel with lots of personal touches that offers very acceptable cooking and a warm welcome. Home grown herbs could feature in the likes of carrot and chive soup, or there could be suprême of chicken with lemon sauce, and pear flan with apricot sauce to finish*

Menus: Fixed-price L & D, pre-theatre, all-day coffee shop
Seats: 28 (+19 Coffee shop). No smoking in dining room
Additional: Children welcome, children's portions; ❤ dishes, vegan/other diets on request
Directions: A29 just N of Pulborough, turn right opposite Church

Church Place RH20 1AD
Map no: 4 TQ01
Tel: 01798 872486
Chef: Gavin Swonnel
Proprietor: John Searancke (Minotel)
Cost: Fixed-price L £8.50/ D £16.95. H/wine £ 8.75 ❢ Service exc
Credit cards: 🔳 🈵 🈺 💳
Times: Last L 2pm, last D 9.30pm Closed Sat L

PULBOROUGH,
Stane Street Hollow Restaurant ❀❀

☺ *Local produce and home-smoked meats feature in the international cooking at this 16th-century establishment*

Codmore Hill RH20 1BG
Map no: 4 TQ01
Tel: 01798 872819
Chef: René Kaiser
Proprietors: René & Ann Kaiser
Cost: Alc £22, fixed-price L £13.50, £10.50 (2 course). H/wine £13 Service exc
Credit cards: 🔳 🈵
Times: Last L 1.30pm, last D 9.15pm Closed Sun D, Mon, Tue, 2 wks late May & Oct
Menus: A la carte, fixed-price L & D
Seats: 30. No smoking in dining room

International cooking, including dishes from the chef's native Switzerland, are prepared from fresh local ingredients at this 16th-century farmhouse. Fresh fish is supplied from Brixham and partridge and rabbit from local farmers, while much of the fruit and herbs used are home-grown; in addition, the chef smokes his own ham, salmon and chicken, and ducks and chickens are kept for their eggs. The standard of cooking is consistent. Starters might include fish mousse flavoured with smoked fish layered with fresh spinach, served in a puff pastry case with a light curry sauce. Typical main courses might be home-smoked ham topped with a mushroom and herb duxelle and a slice of Swiss cheese and baked in puff pastry, or roast fillet of pork served with a cider sauce with apples, capers and thyme. The choice of desserts may include an 'Assiette René' – a platter giving smaller portions of four desserts. The wine list includes an extensive range of vintage wines from reputable growers, a very good half-bottle selection and some Swiss and New World wines.

Directions: N of Pulborough on A29 at Codmore Hill

STORRINGTON,
Manleys Restaurant ❀❀❀❀

Sophisticated classical French cooking in a charming, personally-run restaurant

Additional: Children welcome, children's portions; ❂ dishes, vegan/other diets with notice

Manleys Hill RH20 4BT
Map no: 4 TQ01
Tel: 01903 742 331
Chef: Karl Löderer
Proprietor: Karl Löderer
Cost: *Alc* £35, fixed-price L £19.60, fixed-price D £28.50. House/w £13.50 ❗ Service not inc
Credit cards: 🔲 ▦ ▦ 💳 OTHER.
Times: Noon- last L 1.30pm, 7pm- last D 8.45pm (later on Sat). Closed Mon
Menus: *A la carte,* fixed-price L & D, Sun lunch
Seats: 48
Additional: Children welcome, children's portions; ❂ dishes, other diets on request

The former school house, set on the edge of town, has been run by the Löderer family for nearly twenty years. Karl Löderer cooks classical French dishes but reveals his Austrian background in dishes such as 'zigeuner speiss mit speck kartoffeln' – fillet of beef, veal, and lamb on a skewer with a piquant marinade, served on lyonnaise potatoes, and in the stunning dessert 'salzburger nockerln', a lemon and orange flavoured soufflé cooked in honey and rum. The cooking is sophisticated and remains resolutely classical, avoiding the wild side of modernism, but is not averse to adapting some of the better ideas. Thus a grilled breast of duck is served with 'orientale' spices on a bed of white cabbage flavoured with ginger, sliced sautéed veal comes with home-made pasta flavoured with pesto and mushrooms and grilled sea bass with Provençal-style squid.

Fish dishes are particularly good. An inspection meal commenced with pan-fried local scallops with home-made pasta, a chiffonade of vegetables and langoustine sauce, which was both succulent and perfectly cooked, and salmon and sole turban with a fish soufflé. Other dishes tried included terrine of home-smoked chicken and guinea fowl with pistachios and a potato and cucumber salad, venison steak, 'beautifully tender', accompanied by a red wine, shallot and mushroom sauce with griotte cherries and croquette potatoes, and finished with crème brûlée, and profiteroles with Grand Marnier cream and chocolate sauce. The pretty, light restaurant always has fresh flowers on the tables and is presided over by Mrs Löderer and her daughter Francesca, who provide a friendly, professional service. Austria gets a look in on a wine list dominated by France, with some German representation; the rest of Europe is ignored and the New World is confined to Australia.

Directions: On the main A283 just east of Storrington

STORRINGTON, Old Forge ❀❀

A beamed cottage restaurant offering innovative cooking based on fresh produce and home-grown vegetables

6a Church Street RH20 4LA
Map no: 4 TQ01
Tel: 01903 743402
Chefs: Clive Roberts
Proprietors: Clive & Cathy Roberts
Cost: *Alc* £25, fixed-price L £14.50/D £20.50. H/wine £9.50
❢ No service charge
Credit cards: 🔳 🔳 🔳 🔳 OTHER
Times: Last L 1.30pm, last D 9pm Closed Sat L, Sun D, Mon, Tue L, 1 wk Spring, 2 wks Oct
Menus: *A la carte*, fixed-price L & D
Seats: 36. Smoking restricted
Additional: Children welcome, children's portions; ❶ dishes, vegan/other diets on request

An old beamed cottage off the High Street, on the west side of the village, is the setting for some modern British cooking. Clive Roberts' innovative, interestingly-constructed dishes are all freshly cooked and individually prepared from top quality produce, including some home-grown vegetables. Breads, patisserie and ice-creams are all home-made. A typical menu may include dishes such as freshly steamed English asparagus served with a timbale of smoked trout wrapped in smoked salmon, and ragoût of veal kidneys with spring onions and smoked bacon, set on a bed of fresh noodles seasoned with ginger and chives. Desserts such as crisp filo leaves layered with rhubarb and orange and choux buns filled with pear caramel ice-cream set on a dark chocolate sauce may be offered. At an inspection meal, fresh water shrimp and tenderloin of pork were particularly enjoyed, as were the selection of fresh vegetables, including home-grown kohlrabi. The wine list is well described, features some good vintages, and has an outstanding New World selection.

Directions: On a side street in the village centre

TURNERS HILL, Alexander House ❀❀

Straightforward cooking is served in this attractive 17th-century country house

East Street RH10 4QD
Map no: 4 TQ33
Tel: 01342 714914
Chef: Tim Kelsey
Proprietor: International Hotels. Manager: Sarah Varcoe

Situated one mile east of Turners Hill village, this former 17th-century farmhouse is now a well-established, stylish country house hotel. Straightforward, uncomplicated cooking features traditional

English and classical French dishes. The choice available from the *carte*, fixed-price and vegetarian menus may include wild mushrooms in puff pastry on a bed of spinach with a truffle and Madeira sauce, and local fresh lobster grilled with a hot butter or light cheese sauce. An April meal began with simple canapés of cream cheese, prawn mini-tartlets and paprika salami on croûtons, was followed by a well-textured chicken liver parfait on a citrus salad and a main course of well-executed sole roulade with salmon, mussels and a white wine sauce. To finish, tarte Normande with a crème anglaise had a mild apple flavour and some sultanas, though no hint of the advertised cloves. Coffee came with a selection of house petits fours.

Directions: 1 mile east of Turners Hill on the B2110

WEST CHILTINGTON,
Roundabout Hotel ✿

This long-established hotel sits quietly in the Sussex countryside. A recent test meal reflected some sound cooking skills with a particular flair for home-made soups, terrines and puddings being displayed. Chicken and apricot terrine and steamed fillet of turbot with fresh pasta were especially enjoyed

Menu: *A la carte*, fixed-price L & D
Directions: 1.75 miles south via A293

Cost: *Alc* £40, fixed-price
L £18.75/D £24.95. H/wine
£14.50. Service exc
Credit cards: 💳 🏧 🔲 💳 OTHER
Times: Last L 2pm, last D
9.30pm/9pm Sun
Menus: *A la carte*; fixed-price
L & D, bar menu
Seats: 55. No smoking in dining
room
Additional: Children over & welcome, children's portions;
❤ menu, vegan/other diets on
request

Pulborough RH20 2PF
Map no: 4 SZ11
Tel: 01798 813838
Chef: David Iles
Proprietor: R Begley
Cost: *Alc* £22.25, fixed-price
L £16.25/D £20.25
Credit cards: 💳 🏧 🔲 💳
Times: Last D 9pm

WEST YORKSHIRE

BRADFORD, **Restaurant Nineteen** ✿✿✿

An appetising choice of imaginative modern British dishes at this fine suburban restaurant

The cooking is as good as ever. Restaurant Nineteen, a restaurant with rooms, occupies a substantially built suburban house in a leafy part of Bradford. Attention to detail is evident, not just in Stephen Smith's cooking, but in the house itself. Recently, the lounge was been completely refurbished to complement the elegant dining room.

Stephen Smith is an accomplished and imaginative chef and his dishes never fail to delight. A thoroughly enjoyable meal, began with good bread and sautéed chicken in three spices, which came with noodles and a creamy mushroom sauce. This was followed by fillet of brill with an unusual fish and herb sausage floating on a delightful herb cream sauce. Vegetables included deep green chopped spinach and crunchy mange tout. To finish, home-made Amaretto ice-cream with a warm compote of apricots was pronounced 'just perfect'. Full flavours are also promised in a dish of oxtail sausages with horseradish potatoes, and a more delicate fillet of salmon wrapped in seaweed, lightly steamed and served

19 North Park Road
Heaton BD9 4NT
Map no: 7 SE13
Tel: 01274 492559
Chef: Stephen Smith
Proprietors: Robert Barbour and
Stephen Smith
Cost: *Alc* £26.95, fixed-price D
£25. H/wine £12.50 Service exc
Credit cards: 💳 🏧 🔲 OTHER
Times: Last D 9.30pm/10pm Sat
Closed Sun, Mon, 1 wk Xmas,
1 wk May/June, 2 weeks
Aug/Sep
Menu: *A la carte* D,
fixed-price D
Seats: 34. No cigars or pipes in
dining room
Additional: Children permitted;
other diets on request

with ginger and spring onions. Mediterranean influences are evident in main courses of chicken breast roasted with goats' cheese and served with prosciutto and plum tomatoes, and fillet of beef with polenta and bacon chips. An enticing choice of desserts offers twice baked orange soufflé with vanilla custard, and mascarpone cheesecake with strawberries. The well balanced wine list provides plenty of choice, even for the most discerning.

Directions: Take A650 (Manningham Lane) from Bradford, left at Manningham Park gates, right into North Park Road, 350 yds on left

DEWSBURY, Healds Hall Hotel ☺

☺ *Good quality modern British cooking is served at this converted 18th-century house. Dishes available on either the carte or fixed-price menu might include saddle of rabbit stuffed with a wild duck and pistachio mousse, and medallions of venison and wood pigeon*

Menus: A la carte, fixed-price L & D, bar menu **Seats:** 40. No smoking in dining room **Additional:** Children welcome, children's portions; ♥ dishes, vegan/other diets on request **Directions:** On A62 Leeds/Huddersfield near M1 exit 40 & M62 exits 26/27

Liversedge WF15 6JA
Map no: 8 SE22
Tel: 01924 409112
Chef: Philip McVeagh
Proprietor: Thomas Harrington.
Manager: M C Gray
Cost: Alc £18, fixed-price
L £9.75/D £15.95
H/wine £7.95 Service exc
Credit cards: 💳 OTHER
Times: Last L 2.30pm, last D
9.30pm

HALIFAX, The Design House ☺☺

Down-to-earth staff provide good old fashioned Yorkshire hospitality in a modern fun setting

Part of a large converted mill, surrounded by offices and an art gallery, this restaurant is stylish and modern – plain colours predominate. The cooking is sound, modern British to the core, and very good value-for-money, especially the set-price lunch menu. A recent inspection meal kicked off with a well-made aubergine and caramelised onion tart that looked smart and tasted delightful. Another testimony to chef David Watson's skill was the flakey-textured Whitby cod, obviously from that day's market, served on light and creamy mashed potatoes with diced tomatoes and topped with pesto butter – a very effective presentation. A feather-light sponge made the tangy Eve's pudding memorable, and very strong and rich coffee was a fitting conclusion to a very enjoyable meal.

Directions: Dean Clough is on the outskirts of town, it is signposted and the restaurant is near Gate Five

Dean Clough HX3 5AX
Map no: 7 SE02
Tel: 01422 383242
Chef: David Watson
Proprietor: John Leach
Cost: Alc £20, fixed-price
L £9.50 (2 courses) Service exc
Times: Noon-last L 2pm,
6.30pm-last D 10.30pm.
Closed Sat L, Sun, 25, 26 Dec
Menus: A la carte, fixed-price L
Additional: Children welcome;
♥ dishes

HALIFAX, Holdsworth House Hotel ☺☺

Fresh natural flavours and textures are retained in the international cooking at Holdsworth House

Set in its own grounds three miles from Halifax town centre, this well-cared for 17th-century house retains much of its original charm. The restaurant is located in the older part of the house, and features beams and wood panelling. A well-balanced range of dishes are offered on the fixed-price menu and *carte* and cooked to retain fresh natural flavours and textures. The predominately modern English cooking offers dishes along the lines of langoustine ravioli on a soya butter sauce, and asparagus and truffle mousse

Holmfield HX2 9TG
Map no: 7 SE02
Tel: 01422 240024
Chef: Eric Claveau
Manager: G S Norris
Cost: Alc £25, fixed-price
L £12.50/D £19.50 (4 course).
H/wine £9.50. Service inc
Credit cards: 💳 OTHER
Times: Last L 2.30pm, last D
9.30pm Closed Sat L
Menus: A la carte, fixed-price
L & D

Holdsworth House Hotel

Seats: 70. No-smoking area
Additional: Children welcome,
children's portions; ❶ dishes,
vegan/other diets on request

bound in leek and served with Morels mushrooms, followed
perhaps by pigeon roasted with rosemary and Cassis and garnished
with a shallot and potato mille-feuille, or pan-fried king scallops
on a salad of chargrilled vegetables and balsamic vinegar.
At inspection, Camembert onion tartlet with home-made
apple chutney, steamed scallops with a soy and ginger sauce,
and a well-made apple and custard tart, formed the components
of a particularly enjoyable meal.

Directions: From Halifax take A629 (Keighley), 2 miles turn right at
garage to Holmfield, hotel 1.5 miles on right

HALIFAX, **The Imperial Crown** ❀

*Chef Michael Ricci is attracting a strong following with his very good
cooking. A test meal in the wood-panelled Wallis Simpson Restaurant
produced tender pan-fried scallops, chump of lamb with a simple
rosemary-scented jus, and a perfect crème brûlée for dessert – the top
brittle and the texture creamy*

Menus: A la carte D, fixed-price D, pre-theatre   **Seats:** 45
Additional: No children; ❶ dishes, vegan/other diets on request
Directions: Opposite Halifax railway station

42/46 Horton Street HX1 1BR
Map no: 7 SE02
Tel: 01422 342342
Chef: Michael Ricci
Proprietor: Christopher Turczak
Cost: Alc £20, fixed-price D
£14.50 H/wine £ 9.95 ¶ Service
exc
Credit cards: ⬛ ▨ ▨ ▨ OTHER
Times: 7pm-last D 10pm Closed
Sun

HAWORTH, **Weavers Restaurant** ❀❀

*Good solid cooking in a popular, two-storey restaurant set in a cobbled
street*

 The weavers who used to live in this row of cottages would feel at
home even now: the ceilings remain low, the walls are still stone and
they would probably recognise the bric-a-brac. It is the scale of the
Brontë industry which attracts so many visitors to this charming
Pennine village, and as a result to the restaurant, which would
amaze them. The kitchen is certainly switched on to current trends
that take in a smoked Ribblesdale cheese wrapped with air-dried
ham, 'baked to perfection' and served with a warm potato salad,
monkfish skewer with a light, spicy sauce, sliced, smoked goose
breast with mango and apricot, and tender, pan-fried calves' liver
with gin and lime sauce (which went well with the meat) and bubble
and squeak. It is also tuned in to more homely old favourites such

15 West Lane BD22 8DU
Map no: 7 SE03
Tel: 01535 643822
Chefs: Colin & Jane Rushworth
Proprietors: Colin & Jane
Rushworth
Cost: Alc £20-£25, fixed-price
D/Sun L £9.95 (2 courses)
£11.95. H/wine £8.25 ¶ Service
exc
Credit cards: ⬛ ▨ ▨ ▨ OTHER
Times: Last D 9.15pm, last Sun
L 1.45pm Closed Sun (except
L in Winter), Mon, 2 wks July,
2 wks Xmas
Menus: A la carte D, fixed-price
Sun L in Winter

as East Coast fish bake, traditional wild rabbit pie, and Pennine meat and potato pie. Sweets are equally good: chocolate and marshmallow brownies, sticky toffee pudding, and meringues. Despite all their years here, owners Colin and Jane Rushworth are full of enthusiasm, and they and their staff know how to offer good Yorkshire hospitality.

Directions: Haworth centre, by Brontë Museum car park

HUDDERSFIELD, **Bagden Hall** ❀

Forty acres of splendid grounds, which now include a nine-hole golf course, surround Bagden Hall. Quality cooking is the order of the day with a wide range of well-presented English and French dishes. The fixed-price menu is good value and staff are friendly and helpful

Times: Last L 2pm, last D 10pm Closed Sat L **Menus:** *A la carte*, fixed-price L & D, bar menu **Seats:** 49. No-smoking area **Additional:** Children permitted, children's portions; ♥ dishes, vegan/other diets on request **Directions:** On A36 Denby Dale road

Wakefield Road
Scissett HD8 9LE
Map no: 7 SE11
Tel: 01484 865330
Chef: Jeremy Hanson
Manager: Charles Storr
Cost: *Alc* £22.50, fixed-price
L £8.95 (2 course) £10.75/D
£15.95 (4 course). H/wine
£8.25 Service exc
Credit cards: 🔳 💳 💳 💳 OTHER

HUDDERSFIELD, **The Lodge Hotel** ❀

A fine, family-run Victorian hotel, set back from the road, which has the atmosphere of a country house. The kitchen has a solid reputation for competent, modern cooking. An extensive choice of dishes is available, all based on quality produce

Menus: Fixed-price L & D **Seats:** 60. No smoking in dining room **Additional:** Children permitted, children's portions; ♥ dishes, vegan/other diets on request **Directions:** M62 exit 24 signed Huddersfield, left at 1st lights (Birkby Road), right after Nuffield Hospital, 100yds on left

48 Birkby Lodge Road HD2 2BG
Map no: 7 SE11
Tel: 01484 431001
Chefs: Kevin & Garry Birley
Proprietors: Kevin & Garry Birley
Cost: Fixed-price L £11.95/D
£21.95 (4 course) H/wine £9.95
❢ Service exc
Credit cards: 🔳 💳 💳
Times: Last L 1.45pm, last D
9.45pm Closed Sun D, Dec 25
27, Jan 1

HUDDERSFIELD,
The Weavers Shed Restaurant ❀❀

Justifiably popular and successful restaurant with skilful and imaginative cooking of high quality, fresh ingredients

Do not miss the Yorkshire pudding with onion gravy at this down-to-earth restaurant, which still offers good, old-fashioned Yorkshire hospitality. The converted weavers' mill atmospherically echoes the past with open stone walls, flagstone floors and masses of textile memorabilia. Ian McGunnicle and Stephen Jackson cook in an emphatically modern British manner, using produce from their own garden wherever possible. The lunch menu is excellent value, and booking, especially for dinner, is strongly urged. The home-made treacle bread, which started our inspection, was moist and fresh, served with a wedge of creamy butter. Seared scallops were truly delicious, and the sauce Nero (squid ink and fish velouté) tasted first-rate and looked dramatic. A poached chicken main course was packed with flavour and was well matched by a light tomato and truffle sauce.

Directions: M62 exits 23/24 & A640, just outside Golcar village, 3 miles W of Huddersfield

Knowl Road
Golcar HD7 4AN
Map no: 7 SE11
Tel: 01484 654284
Chefs: Ian McGunnigle, Stephen Jackson and Robert Jones
Proprietor: Stephen Jackson
Cost: *Alc* £25, fixed-price
L £10.95. H/wine £8.95 ❢
Service exc
Credit cards: 🔳 💳 💳 OTHER
Times: Last L 2pm, last D 10pm
Closed Sun, Mon, Bhs, 2 wks Jan
& July/Aug
Menus: *A la carte* L & D, fixed-price L
Seats: 40
Additional: Children welcome, children's portions; ♥ dishes, vegan on request, other diets with prior notice

Seats: 45. Air conditioned. No smoking in dining room. **Additional:** Children welcome, children's portions; ♥ dishes, vegan/other diets on request

ILKLEY, **Box Tree Restaurant** ❀❀❀

Classical French style tempered by a modern awareness of healthier options is the strength of this elegant restaurant's cooking

With chef Thierry Le Prêtre-Granet (late of Whitechapel Manor) at its helm, this well established restaurant is once again enjoying a period of stability. Part of an eighteenth-century farmhouse west of the town centre, it recalls the charm of a bygone age in the wealth of fine art and objets d'art displayed in both the cocktail bar and dining areas. Tradition is reflected, too, in the warm and genuinely attentive service provided from the moment that one rings the doorbell to gain admittance. Food is based upon a fusion of classical French and modern English cooking, its style tempered by the healthier approach to eating which is so prevalent today. A recent winter inspection meal was preceded by canapés in the bar, then an appetiser of smoked salmon mousse wrapped in a slice of smoked salmon – all, like the bread rolls, light and freshly made. An attractive, expertly crafted terrine of pigeon and partridge with lentils was then followed by an artistically presented dish of pheasant and wild mushrooms garnished with shredded cabbage, turned carrots and finely diced potatoes and turnips and accompanied by a memorable Madeira-flavoured meat jus. Apple tart with caramel ice-cream proved first-class, and a choice of fruit or leaf teas offered an alternative to the selection of freshly ground speciality coffees. A predominantly French wine list ranges from vintage champagne (Krug Clos de Mesnil 1979 at £260, for example) to house wine starting at £9 a bottle.

Directions: On A65, on the Skipton side of Ilkley near the Church

27 Church Street LS29 9DR
Map no: 7 SE14
Tel: 01943 608484
Chef: Thierry Le Prêtre-Granet
Proprietor: Mme H L K Avis
Cost: Fixed-price L £22.50, fixed-price D £29.50. H/wine £9
❗ No service charge
Credit cards: 🖎 ▨ ▨
Times: Last L 2.30pm, last D 10pm. Closed Sun D, Mon, last 2 wks Jan
Menus: *A la carte* L, fixed-price L & D
Seats: 50. No smoking in dining room
Additional: Children permitted at L, children's portions; ❶ dishes, vegan/other diets on request

ILKLEY,
Rombalds Hotel ❀

Located on a quiet side road between the moor and the town, Rombalds serves classical cooking prepared with care in its attractive restaurant. Dishes offered might include a trio of seafood terrine with a dill and lemon sauce, chicken véronique, and white chocolate mousse with a strawberry purée

Menus: *A la carte,* fixed-price L & D, bar menu
Seats: 35. No smoking in dining room
Additional: Children welcome, children's portions; ❶ dishes, vegan/other diets on request
Directions: From A65 lights in town, turn up Brook Street, left at top, then immediately right into Wells Road, 600yds on left

11 West View
Wells Road LS29 9JG
Map no: 7 SE14
Tel: 01943 603201
Chef: Stephen Davies
Proprietors: Jill & Ian Guthrie
Cost: *Alc* £24, fixed-price L £9.95/D £12.95 H/wine £9
❗ Service exc
Credit cards: 🖎 ▨ ▨ ▨ OTHER
Times: Last L 2pm, last D 9.30pm. Closed Dec 27-31

LEEDS, **Brasserie Forty Four** ❀❀

Food in this lively and popular canalside restaurant has a distinct Mediterranean imprint

Michael Gill has firmly staked his claim in this smartly revitalised part of the city where the Leeds & Liverpool Canal meets the River Aire. Brasserie Forty Four is part of a waterside conversion that incorporates the stylish 44 The Calls next door. The brasserie itself is big, popular and fun. Booking is utterly essential. In the kitchen,

42-44 The Calls LS2 7EW
Map no: 8 SE23
Tel: 0113 234 3232
Chef: Jeff Baker
Proprietor: Michael Gill.
Manager: Steve Ridealgh
Cost: *Alc* £20.70, fixed-price L/D £8.75 (2 courses) & L £14.50. H/wine £9.45 ❗
Service exc

Jeff Baker offers a fashionable brasserie menu which changes on a regular basis. An inspection meal commenced with fresh, crisp pancakes filled with full flavoured diced duck breast with a well-matched plum and cucumber sauce. Cumin and lemon spiced lamb, which followed, was excellent, as was the accompanying tomato sauce. Fresh vegetables were 'plain and simple and having a lovely bright sheen to them'. Only the dessert sounded an off note, a somewhat ordinary upside-down pineapple cake 'which did not live long in the memory'. Coffee is good. The wine list covers many countries and supports the menu well. Staff are smartly dressed, keen, and look after their customers carefully.

Directions: From Crown Point Bridge, left past Church, left into High Court Road. On the riverside

Credit cards: ▨ ▨ ▨ ▨ OTHER
Times: Last L 2pm, last D 10.30pm/11pm Fri & Sat Closed Sun, Bhs, Xmas 4 days
Menus: *A la carte*, fixed-price L & D
Seats: 95. Air conditioned. No-smoking area
Additional: Children permitted; ✪ dishes, vegan/other diets on request

LEEDS,
Haley's Hotel ✿✿

A smart suburban restaurant for civilised dining

Shire Oak Road
Headingley LS6 2DE
Map no: 8 SE23
Tel: 0113 278 4446
Chef: Jon Vennel
Proprietor: John Appleyard. Manager: Moira Snap
Cost: *Alc* £22.95, fixed-price Sun L £13.95. H/wine £10.15 Service inc
Credit cards: ▨ ▨ ▨ ▨ OTHER
Times: Last D 9.45pm, last Sun L 2pm Closed Sun D
Menus: *A la carte* D, fixed-price Sun L
Seats: 45. Air conditioned
Additional: Children welcome until 8pm, children's portions; ✪ dishes, vegan/other diets on request

Shire Oak Road sounds leafy, and lo! so it is. Haley's opened here in 1990 in an elegantly restored Victorian house in the residential suburb of Headingley. There are two comfortable lounges filled with antiques and deep armchairs. Chef Jon Vennell, under John Appleyard's ownership, is doing much towards maintaining the professional feel of the restaurant. The monthly changing menu offers a mixed bag that might take in ravioli of lobster and leek, Yorkshire pudding filled with pan-fried chicken livers, fillet of beef with rösti potatoes, Thai-style chicken and herb pancakes filled with ratatouille. Inspection turned up a simple starter of smoked haddock mixed with fluffy mashed potato and served in a baked potato skin, followed pink, pan-fried saddle of lamb in a puff pastry feuilleté with a deeply flavoured wholegrain mustard sauce. Desserts range from rich chocolate mousse, iced Grand Marnier soufflé, to a caramelised tart Tatin with soft, tangy apples. About 50 wines from all over the world are available. Service needs to improve, though.

Directions: On A660 (Leeds/Otley) in Headingley between Lloyds and Midland banks

LEEDS, **Leodis Brasserie** ☻☻

☺ *Spacious old warehouse restaurant that has emerged as one of Leed's dining hot spots*

In a spacious converted warehouse on the River Aire, in a now trendy part of Leeds, Leodis is one of the town's fashionable eating spots, bustling with diners at both lunch and dinner. Steven Kendell offers a mixed bag of '90s culinary influences: Mediterranean, European rustic and modern interpretations of traditional English dishes. It is his confidence in the making of these diverse dishes, complemented by strong presentational skills, that make it all work. Flavours, in particular, are not at all masked and really do stand out in their own right. Choice can be difficult. An inspection meal produced croustade of mushrooms with a poached egg and hollandaise sauce that was deep in flavour and with the egg still 'perfectly soft', followed by 'tender' fillet of beef on good brioche toast, with a bold tasting red wine and mushroom sauce. Crème brûlée was judged to be a fine example with its thick, creamy texture and exact topping. Vegetables, although very fresh, can be on the raw side of al dente. The excellent bread is baked on the premises. There's a well-balanced wine list and service is very friendly and attentive.

Directions: From City square follow M/way sign, turn left by Hilton Hotel onto Sovereign Street, 100yds on left

Victoria Mill
Sovereign Street LS1 4BJ
Map no: 8 SE23
Tel: 0113 242 1010
Chefs: Steven Kendell and Nick Male
Proprietors: Martin Spalding and Steven Kendell
Cost: *Alc* from £15.55, fixed-price L/D £11.95. H/wine £8.95 Service exc
Credit cards: ▨ ▩ ▨ ▨ OTHER
Times: Last L 2pm, last D 10pm/11pm Fri & Sat Closed Sun
Menus: *A la carte*, fixed-price L & D
Seats: 100. Air conditioned
Additional: Children welcome, children's portions; ❂ dishes, vegan/other diets on request

LEEDS, **Olive Tree** ☻

☺ *Bouzouki music enlivens George and Vasoulla Psarias' Greek restaurant. They are justifiably proud of dishes such as 'kleftico' (lamb cooked slowly in the oven with olive oil and fresh oregano) or the self-indulgent dessert 'stafidhopitta' – crisp filo pastry filled with sultanas, orange liqueur and a hint of cinnamon*

55 Rodley Lane LS13 1NG
Map no: 8 SE23
Tel: 0113 2569283
Chefs: George Psarias and Andreas Lacovou
Proprietors: George & Vasoulla Psarias
Cost: *Alc* £16.25, fixed-price L/D £9.95 H/wine £7.95 Service exc
Credit cards: ▨ ▩ ▨ OTHER
Times: Last L 2.30pm, last D 11.30pm Closed Dec 25, Jan 1
Menus: *A la carte*, fixed-price L & D
Seats: 150
Additional: Children welcome, children's portions; ❂ dishes, vegan/other diets on request

Directions: On Rodley roundabout, outer ring road (A6120), n/w of city

RIPPONDEN,
Over The Bridge Restaurant ❀

Millfold HX6 4DJ
Map no: 7 SE01
Tel: 01422 823722
Chefs: Susan Tyer, Pam Stewart and Ian Beaumont

☺ *Honest and reliable British cooking is served at this popular restaurant, which stands beside the hump-backed bridge. A meal might begin with cassoulet of duck, chicken and ham with fillet of salmon with rhubarb, spring onions and ginger to follow, and a choice of desserts and British cheeses to conclude*

Proprietor: Ian Beaumont.
Manager: Stuart Wood
Cost: Fixed-price D £22.50
H/wine £ 9.50 ♥ Service inc
Credit cards: 🗃 ▥ ▥

Menus: Fixed-price D
Seats: 45.
Additional: Children permitted, children's portions; ♥ dishes, vegan/other diets on request
Directions: A58 Ripponden, in village centre by Church

Times: Last D 9.30pm Closed Sun

ROTHWELL, Oulton Hall Hotel ❀

Rothwell Lane LS26 8HN
Map no: 8 SE32
Tel: 0113 821000
Chef: Steve Collinson

Classically inspired cooking dominates the menu at this splendid mansion set in formal gardens. Dishes might include mille-feuille of duck livers, rich game consommé and pan-fried fillet of Scottish beef with hazelnut mousseline. A good vegetarian selection is also available and service is efficient and attentive

Proprietor: De Vere
Manager: M Thaw
Cost: *Alc* £30, fixed-price L £11 (Sun £12.50)/D £19.95 H/wine £9.50 ♥ Service inc
Credit cards: 🗃 ▥ ▥ ▣

Menus: *A la carte,* fixed-price L & D, bar menu
Seats: 140. No smoking in dining room
Additional: Children welcome, children's menu; ♥ dishes, vegan/other diets on request
Directions: M62 Junction 30, follow signs to Rothwell

Times: Last L 2pm/3pm Sun, last D 10pm Closed Sat L

WAKEFIELD, Swallow Hotel ❀

Queens Street WF1 1JU
Map no: 7 SE32
Tel: 01924 372111
Chef: Barry Gell

City centre hotel with a spacious, first-floor restaurant where short, frequently changing menus are carefully cooked and, occasionally, show unexpected flair. Whole grilled plaice, topped with mozzarella and paprika, and shellfish, mushrooms and garlic in a pastry case have been enjoyed this year. The young, smartly uniformed staff try encouragingly hard

Proprietor: Swallow
Cost: *Alc* £8, fixed-price D £14.50. Service exc
Credit cards: 🗃 ▥ ▥ ▣

Directions: City centre

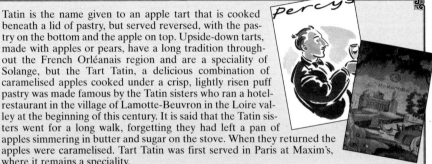

Tatin is the name given to an apple tart that is cooked beneath a lid of pastry, but served reversed, with the pastry on the bottom and the apple on top. Upside-down tarts, made with apples or pears, have a long tradition throughout the French Orléanais region and are a speciality of Solange, but the Tart Tatin, a delicious combination of caramelised apples cooked under a crisp, lightly risen puff pastry was made famous by the Tatin sisters who ran a hotel-restaurant in the village of Lamotte-Beuvron in the Loire valley at the beginning of this century. It is said that the Tatin sisters went for a long walk, forgetting they had left a pan of apples simmering in butter and sugar on the stove. When they returned the apples were caramelised. Tart Tatin was first served in Paris at Maxim's, where it remains a speciality.

Percy's

WETHERBY, **Wood Hall Hotel** ✸

Set overlooking open parkland and woods leading down to the River Wharf, Wood Hall offers modern British cooking in its elegant dining room. Expect confit of duck and smoked bacon, saddle of wild boar with a casserole of beetroot and chocolate marquise. A well-scripted wine list is also offered

Trip Lane
Linton LS22 4JA
Map no 8 SE44
Tel: 01937 587271
Chef: Stephanie Moon
Proprietor: Country Mansion.
Manager: Stephen Davenport
Cost: *Alc* £30, fixed-price
L £15.95 (£13.95 Sun)/
D £26.95 H/wine £10.95 ❢
Service exc
Credit cards: 🟦 🔳 🔳 🔳 OTHER
Times: Last L 2pm/2.30pm Sun,
last D 10pm
Menus: *A la carte*, fixed-price
L & D
Seats: 70. No smoking in dining
room
Additional: Children over 6
welcome, children's portions;
❷ menu, vegan/other diets on
request

Directions: In village, take turning opposite the Windmill pub signed Wood Hall and Linton

WILTSHIRE

ALDBOURNE, **Raffles Restaurant** ✸✸

Classic cooking served in comfortable surroundings

Tucked away next to the village green in the charming village of Aldbourne, this smart restaurant is indeed named after Horning's gentleman thief. Chef/patron James Hannan trained at the Ritz, and this background is perhaps reflected in the preference for technically well-executed classical dishes served in a traditional yet comfortable setting, which features polished dark wood, heavy linen and Villeroy and Bosch china. A summer lunch started with a delicious salad with poached egg and oak smoked bacon, the toothsome, slightly sweet bacon contrasting well with the refreshing bitterness of the leaves. A main course of duck breast with red and green cabbage reflects Mr Hannan's love for earthiness and classic flavour combinations. The selection of puddings is one which will warm the heart of the nostalgic – bread and butter pudding, apple strudel, and crème brûlée are to the fore. These old favourites remain eternally popular, and they are made with panache here. The wine list is well chosen, and features some well known names.

The Green SN8 2BW
Map no: 4 SU27
Tel: 01672 540700
Chef: James F Hannan
Proprietor: James F Hannan
Cost: *Alc* £17.50. H/wine £8.95.
Service exc
Credit cards: 🟦 🔳 🔳 🔳
Times: Last L 2pm, last D 10pm
Closed Sat L, Sun D, Mon L, Aug
28-Sept 10, Dec 25-30
Menus: *A la carte* L & D
Seats: 38. No cigars or pipes
Additional: Children welcome,
children's portions; ❷ dishes,
other diets on request

Directions: On B4192 between exits 14 & 15 of M4

BOX,
Box House Hotel 🏵🏵

A good choice of food and wine is available at this Georgian mansion, situated between Bath and Cheltenham

Standing in the village of Box between Bath and Cheltenham, this handsome Georgian mansion is surrounded by well-tended walled gardens. The modern English cooking features dishes with strong, distinct flavours and diners choose from a fixed-price menu or *carte*. Smoked salmon terrine served with a tomato coulis, pan-fried pigeon breasts garnished with croûtons and lardons, roast leg, thigh and saddle of rabbit on a bed of onion confit with a sage sauce or steamed fillet of brill served on a bed of leeks with a dugleré sauce, are examples of the style. Typical desserts might be Dutch apple tart served with crème anglaise and warm Christmas pudding strudel. The restaurant is popular with non-resident diners. The wine list of over sixty bins includes wines from Tasmania, Chile and Mexico as well as more established New and Old World producers.

Directions: In village, on the A4 (M4 exit 18 & A46)

London Road
Map no: 3 ST86
Tel: 01225 744447
Chef: Darren Francis
Proprietors: Charles Tull
Cost: Alc £17.50-£30, fixed-price L/D £12.50. H/wine £9.50 Service exc
Credit cards: 🟥 ▨ ▨ ▨
Times: Last L 2pm, last D 9.30pm daily
Menus: A la carte, fixed-price L & D
Seats: 60
Additional: Children welcome, children's menu; ✪ dishes, vegan/other diets on request

BRADFORD ON AVON,
Woolley Grange 🏵🏵🏵

Mediterranean influences add piquancy to the honest flavours and textures that are this restaurant's strength

Woolley Green BA15 1TX
Map no: 3 ST86
Tel: 01225 864705
Chef: Peter Stott
Proprietors: Nigel & Heather Chapman
Cost: Fixed-price D £28/Sun L £17 H/wine £10.50 ♥ Service inc
Credit cards: 🟥 ▨ ▨ ▨ OTHER
Times: Last L 2pm, last D 10pm Closed Sat L
Menus: Terrace L menu, fixed-price D & Sun L, bar menu
Seats: 54. No smoking in dining room
Additional: Children welcome, children's portions; ✪ dishes, vegan/other diets on request

A delightful Jacobean house overlooking equally attractive gardens, Woolley Grange continues to strengthen its restaurant's reputation for fine food. New chef Peter Stott presents fixed-price lunch and dinner menus in country house style, the success of his honest and apparently simple dishes based firmly in the natural flavours and textures of first-rate fresh produce. Chilled lovage soup with sour cream and chives, warm fillets of eel on creamed potatoes and fried ox tongue with mixed leaves and mustard fruits would surely have seemed familiar to the original inhabitants of the house – as would roasted forerib of beef, rack of lamb and guinea fowl, braised ham hock or poached salmon. Innovative touches have been introduced, however: blackened bream fillet comes with

a tomato chilli salsa and fried calves' liver with avocado as well as the expected sage. Starters are perhaps less traditional than the main courses, the Mediterranean influence clearly obvious in such choices as crostini of goats' cheese with tapenade and pesto, bresaola with chargrilled vegetables, Parmesan and truffle oil or sun-dried tomato risotto with shaved Parmesan. Puddings, too, range from poached pears with port and claret jelly to warm chargrilled peaches with Amaretto and walnut biscotti. An eclectic selection of cheeses, available either as an alternative to dessert or an extra course, might include varieties as diverse as Cashel Blue, St Nectaire and Waterloo. The well presented, interestingly annotated and wide-ranging wine list includes a short, continually changing selection of rare, high quality and good-value one-offs.

Directions: Village centre, off the Bath road, 1 mile N/E of Bradford

CASTLE COMBE, **Castle Inn** 🏵🏵

☺ *Historic Castle Combe is an appropriate setting for this 12th-century inn, which serves both traditional and modern British cooking*

Chippenham SN14 7HN
Map no: 3 ST87
Tel: 01249 783030
Chef: Simon Walker
Proprietor: Hatton Hotels.
Manager: Craig Bicknell
Cost: Fixed-price L £12.50/
D £17.50. H/wine £10 ♦ Service
inc
Credit cards: 🔳 🔳 🔳 🔳 OTHER
Times: Last L 2pm, last D
9.30pm
Menus: Fixed-price L & D, bar
menu
Seats: 26+ 20. No-smoking area
Additional: Children welcome,
children's portions; ♥ dishes,
other diets on request

Located in the market place of historic Castle Combe, this ancient inn originated in the 12th century and still retains many period features. Traditional and modern British dishes are offered in Oliver's Restaurant, prepared by Simon Walker (ex-Angel at Chippenham). Three to five courses can be chosen from the fixed-price menu, which may feature dishes such as asparagus salad with quails' eggs and roquette, crisp filo tart of scrambled egg and smoked salmon and casserole of guinea fowl in a red wine and wild mushroom sauce. A rich dark chocolate and rum pot with shortbread, or Bakewell tart might be among the desserts. At a July inspection it was felt that the kitchen needed some fine tuning: a soup was thinly flavoured and lacked seasoning; lamb came with a rather uninspiring sauce. The wine list has a good content and selection of half-bottles.

Directions: In village centre, M4 exit 17 & A420 (Chippenham)

CASTLE COMBE, **Manor House Hotel** ⚜⚜

Good quality food is served in an attractive setting with fresh produce supplied by the kitchen garden and orchards

The drive to Manor House passes a weir and sweeps over a small bridge before reaching the parkland surrounding the hotel. The immediate grounds feature Italianate gardens, as well as a kitchen garden and orchards which supply produce to the hotel kitchen. After such an entrance it is no surprise to find a real country house atmosphere prevailing. The cooking, though sound, requires more attention to detail, especially where seasoning is concerned. A meal in May featured a good selection of canapés, which were followed by cheese and chive soufflé served on a bed of citrus fruit. An orange and anise sorbet formed an intermediate course, then came a tranche of salmon with a chopped smoked salmon and chive sauce. Our inspector was particularly impressed by the dessert of iced tiramisu decorated with spirals of caramel. The accompanying wine list includes a wide range of bins from around the world.

Directions: Off B4039 near centre of village, signposted from market cross

Map no: 3 ST87
Tel: 01249 782206
Chef: Mark Taylor
Proprietor: Exclusive Hotels. Manager: Martin J Clubbe
Cost: *Alc* £44, fixed-price L £16.95/D £32 (4 course). H/wine £16.50. Service exc
Credit cards: 🟦 💳 💳 💳
Times: Last L 2pm, last D 10pm
Menus: *A la carte,* fixed-price L & D, pre-theatre, bar menu
Seats: 70. No smoking in dining room
Additional: Children welcome, children's menu; menu, vegan/other diets on request

CHIPPENHAM, **Stanton Manor Hotel** ⚜

Stanton Manor stands in extensive woodlands and gardens, including a kitchen garden supplying some of the fresh produce used in the kitchen. Dishes could include mussel pâté on a Pernod mayonnaise, pan-fried escalope of Scotch salmon with a green peppercorn and brandy sauce and deep-fried rose water ice-cream

Menus: *A la carte,* fixed-price L & D, bar menu
Seats: 30. No smoking in dining room
Additional: Children welcome, children's portions; ❶ dishes, vegan/other diets on request
Directions: In village centre, next to Church. M4 exit 17 & A429 (Cirencester)

Stanton St Quintin SN14 6DQ
Map no 3 ST97
Tel: 01666 837552
Chef: Tony Ashton
Proprietors: Philip & Elizabeth Bullock
Cost: *Alc* £23, fixed-price L/D £18, £15 (2 course). H/wine £9.50 No service charge
Credit cards: 🟦 💳 💳 💳
Times: Last L 2pm, last D 9.30pm Closed Sat L

COLERNE, **Lucknam Park** ⚜⚜⚜

A stylish Georgian hotel offering soundly prepared English cooking in an idyllic setting

Elegance and style combined with first class professionalism are the hallmarks of Lucknam Park, a fine English hotel with Georgian charm. Tucked away in a quiet Wiltshire hamlet just fifteen minutes from the city of Bath, the hotel enjoys a reputation for its idyllic setting and graceful architecture. The dining room is large with a trompe l'oeil ceiling of a cloudy sky and some enormous oil portraits displayed on the walls.

Strong clean flavours and superb technique combine to create a masterful menu here, which is based on sound modern English-style cooking and uses organic ingredients wherever possible. Starters include glazed scallops and langoustines with a spinach mousseline, and wing of skate simmered in white wine and served with a radish salad and a dressing of spiced oils. Main courses may feature roast loin of venison with gnocchi and tomato confit or perhaps baked fillet of sea bass with an intense red wine sauce. Carefully chosen

Colerne SN14 8AZ
Map no: 3 ST87
Tel: 01225 742777

Lucknam Park

Chef: Michael Womersley
Managing Director: Robert Carter
Cost: *Alc* £42.50, fixed-price
L £24.50. H/wine £15.50 ‼
Service inc
Credit cards: 🆒 🈺 🈺 🈺 OTHER
Times: Last L 2.30pm, last D
9.30pm daily
Menus: *A la carte* D (Set Price),
fixed-price L
Seats: 80. No smoking in dining room
Additional: Children permitted
(over 12 at D); ❶ dishes, vegan
dishes on request

vegetables accompany each dish, and fine local produce is used throughout. One inspector enjoyed a tender Trelough duck with sautéed foie gras and a sauterne sauce. This was followed by mille-feuille of poached pear with cinnamon ice-cream and macaroon biscuits. Other desserts might include blackberry and apple soufflé or hot chocolate pudding with vanilla sauce and caramelised fruits.

Hospitality at Lucknam Park is of a very high standard. In particular the talented sommelier is more than willing to offer advice in choosing from the lengthy, impressively French wine list. The classic regions get fair representation but prices are high; there are some dozen bottles under £20. Half bottles are available and there is a section of other European and New World wines.

Directions: Turn off A4 2 miles from Bath for Batheaston and left for Colerne, left again at crossroad, entrance 0.25 mile on left

CRUDWELL, Mayfield House Hotel ✿

☺ *Good value imaginative dishes are prepared from fresh produce at Mayfield House, located on the edge of the Cotswolds a few miles north of Malmesbury. Young chef Mark Bullows produces good home-made mushroom soup with tarragon, and fillet of lamb cooked to order with a rosemary and mint sauce*

Menus: Fixed-price L & D, bar menu **Seats:** 45. No smoking in dining room **Additional:** Children welcome, children's menu; ❶ dishes, vegan/other diets on request **Directions:** Village centre, on A429 between Malmesbury and Cirencester

Malmesbury SN16 9EW
Map no: 3 ST99
Tel: 01666 577409
Chef: Mark Bullows
Proprietors: Max Strelling and Chris Marston
Cost: Fixed-price L /D £15.95. H/wine £7.25 Service exc
Credit cards: 🆒 🈺 🈺 🈺
Times: Last L 2pm, last D 9pm daily

FORD, White Hart Inn ✿

☺ *Set beside the River Bybrook in the village of Ford, this 16th-century village inn serves sound English cooking in a relaxed and informal atmosphere. Expect pan-fried sweetbreads with noodles and cream on a garlic croûton, brochette of monkfish, basil, orange and redcurrant, and blackcurrant crumble with custard*

Menus: *A la carte,* fixed-price L & D, bar menu **Seats:** 100. No-smoking area **Additional:** Children welcome, children's portions; ❶ dishes, vegan/other diets on request
Directions: In village centre, 10 mins from Bath, M4 exit 17 or 18

Chippenham SN14 8RP
Map no 3 ST87
Tel: 01249 782213
Chefs: Lee Owen, Jon Todd, Tony Farmer and Steven Perkins
Proprietors: Mr & Mrs C Phillips
Cost: *Alc* £16, fixed-price L £5/D £12. H/wine £7.50 Service exc
Credit cards: 🆒 🈺 🈺 🈺 OTHER
Times: Last L 2pm, last D 9.30pm daily

HINDON, **Lamb at Hindon Hotel** ❀

☺ *Freshly cooked food makes use of local meat and game, and the cooking may feature dishes such as baked whole quail with a bacon, pigeon and walnut stuffing, and grilled brill fillets with a lemon and tarragon sauce. The stone-built house dates from the 17th century and is set in this immensely picturesque village*

Menus: *A la carte* L, fixed-price D & Sun L, bar menu
Seats: 40. No smoking in dining room
Additional: Children welcome, children's menu; ❻ dishes, vegan/other diets on request
Directions: In village centre, 1 mile off A303 & A350

Salisbury SP3 6DP
Map no: 3 ST93
Tel: 01747 820573
Chef: David Sammons
Proprietors: John Croft
(Minotel/Logis)
Cost: Fixed-price D £18.95.
H/wine £ 6.95 ❗ Service inc
Credit cards: ⬛ 💳 ⬜ OTHER
Times: Last L 2pm, last D
9.30pm daily

INGLESHAM,
Inglesham Forge Restaurant ❀

☺ *Traditional cooking is produced with skill at this cottage restaurant. Classic dishes such as fillet steak au poivre and poached salmon hollandaise may be available, and a meal could comprise seafood gratinée, rack of lamb with a thyme sauce and crème brûlée*

Additional: Children welcome, children's portions; ❻ dishes, vegan/other diets on request
Directions: In village centre

Swindon SN6 7QY
Map no: 4 SU29
Tel: 01367 252298
Chef: Manuel Gomez
Proprietor: Manuel Gomez
Cost: *Alc* £20-£22. H/wine
£9.50 ❗ Service inc
Credit cards: ⬛ 💳
Times: Last L 2pm, last D
9.30pm Closed Sun
Menus: *A la carte* L & D
Seats: 30. No pipes or cigars in dining room

MALMESBURY, **Knoll House Hotel** ❀

Imaginative dishes prepared from fresh ingredients and presented in a modern style at this extended Victorian hotel. Expect applewood-smoked pheasant salad glazed with walnut-oil vinaigrette, or oven-roasted mallard with sliced goose sausage, green lentils and a Madeira sauce

Menus: *A la carte* L & D, bar menu
Seats: 36. No smoking in dining room
Additional: Children welcome, children's menu; ❻ dishes, vegan/other diets on request
Directions: On the B4042 Swindon road

Swindon Road SN16 9LU
Map no: 3 ST98
Tel: 01666 823114
Chef: T Herbert
Proprietor: Simon Haggarty
Cost: *Alc* £25. H/wine £9
Service exc
Credit cards: ⬛ 💳 ⬜ OTHER
Times: Last L 1.45pm, last D
9.30pm

MALMESBURY, **Old Bell Hotel** ❀❀

☺ *Ancient hotel with a modern look*

The wisteria-clad hotel, one of England's oldest, serves high-quality, modern food. A short, mainstream menu is given a lift with some unusual ingredients and methods, such as home-smoked quails or guinea fowl poached in a white wine stock with a herb sausage and root vegetables. Although there is a nod to the Mediterranean with fish dishes such as grilled monkfish with aubergine baked with Provençal vegetables, meat is cooked more to yeoman tastes. Roast leg of lamb with garlic and rosemary is carved from the trolley, roast beef served with Yorkshire pudding and horseradish for Sunday lunch, and ham hock honey-roasted with glazed parsnips, carrots and leeks. Billy Bunter desserts include cold caramel soufflé with nut brittle and warm treacle tart with vanilla ice cream. The Great Hall serves lighter meals such as Welsh rarebit grilled with

Abbey Row SN16 0BW
Map no: 3 ST98
Tel: 01666 822344
Chef: Daren Barclay
Proprietors: Nicholas Dickinson
and Nigel Chapman
Cost: Fixed-price D £18.50 (4 course)/Sun L £12.50. H/wine
£10 ❗ Service inc
Credit cards: ⬛ 💳 ⬜ OTHER
Times: Last L 2pm, last D
9.30pm daily
Menus: Fixed-price D & Sun L
Seats: 60. No cigars or pipes in dining room

Wiltshire ham, salad niçoise with fresh tuna, salad of chicken livers with avocado and bacon, and salmon and coriander fishcakes with curry mayonnaise. Carefully chosen wines are listed by grape variety, making for an easy, user-friendly guide.

Additional: Children welcome, children's menu; ❂ dishes, other diets on request

Directions: Off A429, centre of Malmesbury next to the Abbey

MARLBOROUGH, **Harrow Inn** ❀

SN8 3JP
Map no: 4 SU16
Tel: 01672 870871
Chef: Luis Lopez
Proprietor: Harrow Inn Ltd
Cost: Alc £15
Credit cards: ▨ ▩
Times: Last L 2pm, last D 9pm. Restaurant closed Mon
Seats: 20. No smoking

This charming village pub offers a range of traditional dishes such as steak pie, spotted dick and rice puddings, cooked with an understanding and use of fresh ingredients that lifts them above the norm. The short wine list concentrates on the native wines of Luis Lopez, the Spanish chef/landord

Additional: Children welcome: ❂ dishes
Directions: Junction 14 of M4. A4 from Hungerford to Marlborough, 1 mile from Hungerford

MARLBOROUGH, **Ivy House Hotel** ❀

High Street SN8 1HJ
Map no: 4 SU16
Tel: 01672 515333
Chef: David Ball
Proprietors: David Ball and Josephine Scott
Cost: Alc from £24, fixed-price L £10.95, £8.95 (2 course)/ D £16.50, £14.50 (2 course). H/wine £7.50 Service exc
Credit cards: ▨ ▩ ▩
Times: Last L 2pm, last D 9.30pm daily

Built in 1707 as the Marlborough Academy for boys, this ivy-clad Grade II residence offers modern English cooking. Typical dishes might be chicken liver parfait, rack of lamb with a port and rosemary sauce and sticky toffee pudding. The interesting wine list includes New World wines

Menus: A la carte, fixed-price L & D, bar menu
Seats: 55. Air conditioned. No-smoking area
Additional: Children welcome, children's portions; ❂ dishes, vegan/ other diets on request
Directions: Town centre in main street

MELKSHAM, **Beechfield House Hotel** ❀

Beanacre SN12 7PU
Map no 3 ST96
Tel: 01225 703700
Chef: TBA
Proprietor: Macdonald Hotels. Manager: Lorna Bryden
Cost: Fixed-price L £9.95/D £19.95 (4 course). H/wine £9.95 Service exc
Credit cards: ▨ ▩ ▩ ▣ OTHER
Times: Last L 2pm, last D 9.30pm Closed Sat L

☺ *Fruit and vegetables used in the kitchen are grown in the extensive grounds surrounding Beechfield House. The modern English cooking might feature venison pâté, grilled lamb cutlets on a hazelnut and aubergine casserole, and profiteroles with vanilla cream in white chocolate sauce*

Menus: Fixed-price L & D, bar menu
Seats: 30. No smoking in dining room
Additional: Children welcome, children's portions; ❂ dishes, vegan/ other diets on request
Directions: In the village, on the A350 Melksham/Chippenham road

'Pithiviers' is a large round puff-pastry tart filled with an almond cream. It is a speciality of Pithiviers, in the Orleans region, and is traditionally served on Twelfth Night, when it contains a dried broad bean. The town is also famous for another tart, also made of puff pastry, but this time filled with crystallised fruit and covered with white fondant icing. Nowadays, modern chefs interpret pithiviers in various ways, in both savoury and sweet dishes.

MELKSHAM, **Shaw Country Hotel** ❀

☺ *A decent selection of dishes is offered in this 16th-century, creeper-clad hotel. The predominantly modern cooking may include dishes such as garlic and chive potato rösti crowned with goats' cheese, or loin of venison marinated in red wine and gin with wild mushroom sauce and home-made apricot and almond chutney*

Menus: A la carte, fixed-price L & D, bar menu **Seats:** 40.
No smoking in dining room **Additional:** Children welcome, children's menu; ❶ dishes, vegan/other diets on request **Directions:** 1 mile north-west of Melksham on A365, from M4 exits 17 or 18

Bath Road
Shaw SN12 8EF
Map no 3 ST96
Tel: 01225 702836/790321
Chefs: Nicholas & Paul Lewis
Proprietors: J T & C M Lewis
Cost: Alc £16.95, fixed-price
L £9.95/D £13.95. H/wine
£7.50 Service exc
Credit cards: 🗾 🖼 🖭 🏧 OTHER
Times: Last L 2pm, last D
9.30pm Closed Sat L

MELKSHAM, **Toxique** ❀❀

☺ *A farmhouse restaurant where the welcome is genuine and the food is sound*

Peter Jewkes is an architect and wine buff, Helen Bartlett an interior designer and chef. They have brought their various talents together to create Toxique, a restaurant set in a delightful, 17th-century stone-built farmhouse. Candles in flowerpots on the tables, unframed pictures and a relaxed style all suggest a welcoming informality, and that, of course, is the intention. Success means that Helen now has permanent help in the kitchen, and this has enabled her to extend her repertoire and make the menu more interesting. There is no *carte* but the fixed-price, three-course menu changes regularly. Fish, meat and game (in season) are always included and vegetarians are catered for on request. At one meal, a brioche filled with an abundance of calves' liver, with a sweet flavoured, pleasantly textured Madeira sauce, was followed by fillet of beef with a sweetish Armagnac sauce, turned carrots, turnip, caramelised onion and garlic, all on sliced potatoes flavoured with horseradish, and then, to finish, filo pastry filled with sliced red plums and franzipan. The extensive, largely French wine list describes everything well.

Directions: Take Calne road from Melksham centre, 0.3 mile turn into Forest Road. Restaurant is on left after 0.75 mile

187 Woodrow Road SN12 7AY
Map no 3 ST96
Tel: 01225 702129
Chef: Helen Bartlett
Proprietors: Helen Bartlett and Peter Jewkes
Cost: Fixed-price L £14 (2 course), £17/D £28. H/wine £9.75. Service inc
Credit cards: 🗾 🖼 🖭 OTHER
Times: Last D 10, last Sun L 2pm. Closed Sun D, Mon, Tue
Menu: Fixed-price D & Sun L
Seats: 35. No smoking in dining room
Additional: Children welcome, children's portions; ❶ dishes, vegan/other diets on request

PURTON,
The Pear Tree at Purton ❀❀

A former vicarage built in mellow stone and set in well-tended grounds offers an impressive menu in a conservatory restaurant

Inspectors' reports on this pleasant, rurally situated former vicarage have noted the quality of the supplies to the restaurant kitchen. The raw materials are interpreted in a modern style with influences extending beyond Britain. An inspection lunch yielded smoked haddock, leek and potato soup, made memorable by the use of undyed haddock, followed by stir-fried salmon with egg noodles, red onion and apple and a tomato concasse. Accompanying vegetables included baby leeks, carrots, mange tout, haricots verts and cabbage. At lunch throughout the week there is always a traditional British pudding offered, along the lines of a jam roly poly with apricot jam which impressed our inspector. Other recommended dishes have been terrine of duck, apple and juniper berries, grilled fillet of

Church End SN5 9ED
Map no: 4 SU08
Tel: 01793 772100
Chef: Catherine Berry
Proprietors: Francis & Anne Young
Cost: Fixed-price L £17.50 (Sun £12.50)/D £27.50 (4 course).
H/wine £11 ❢ Service exc
Credit cards: 🗾 🖼 🖭 🏧 OTHER
Times: Last L 2pm, last D 9.30pm Closed Sat L
Menus: Fixed-price L & D
Seats: 60. No pipes or cigars in dining room
Additional: Children welcome, children's portions; ❶ dishes, vegan/other diets on request

The Pear Tree at Purton

Scotch beef and hot chocolate soufflé with white chocolate ice cream. Good espresso. The wine list is well-explained.

Directions: From M4 exit 16 follow signs to Purton, turn right at grocers, 0.25 mile on right

REDLYNCH,
Langley Wood Restaurant ❀

☺ *A small country house, dating back to the seventeenth century, situated in five acres of its own wooded grounds. Personally-run, the hotel offers a short, regularly changing carte, which relies upon fresh, local produce. Dishes include leg of English lamb roasted with garlic and rosemary, served with orange sauce*

Salisbury SP5 2PB
Map no: 4 SU22
Tel: 01794 390348
Chef: Sylvia Rosen
Proprietors: David & Sylvia Rosen
Cost: *Alc* £22, fixed-price Sun L £13.75. H/wine £8.50 Service exc
Credit cards: 🅰 📧 💳 📇
Times: Last D 11pm, last Sun L 2pm Closed Sun D, Mon, Tue
Menus: *A la carte* D, fixed-price Sun L
Seats: 30. No smoking in dining room
Additional: Children welcome, children's portions at L; ❷ dishes, other diets with notice

Directions: In village, between Woodfalls and Landford

REDLYNCH, Les Mirabelles ❀❀

New Forest restaurant à la Française

It's hard to know whether to describe Les Mirabelles as a chalet or a log cabin. Either way, the wooden building seems an unlikely

Forest Edge Road
Nomansland SP5 2BN
Map no: 4 SU22
Tel: 01794 390205
Chef: Eric Nicola
Cost: *Alc* £20-£25

setting for such an unmistakeably French restaurant. Outside, there may be New Forest ponies on the cricket pitch but, inside, there are little French figurines on the tables and French music in the background. As well as a generous *carte*, daily specials are chalked up on a board. On our inspection, pâté Lorain was skillfully made, the tender chunks of pork lightly flavoured with thyme, wrapped in puff pastry and served hot. The main course was a beautiful piece of turbot, perfectly cooked and served with a red pepper sauce. Vegetables were fresh and nicely cooked, with the exception, ironically, of watery French beans. A fondant chocolat is a 'cooked mousse' which is allowed to remain liquid in the centre; this was a superb example, rich in flavour and served with a sharp, apricot sauce. The wine list offers a variety of French and New World wines at reasonable prices, with a selection of halves and a choice of French or Australian house wine.

Directions: Between A36 and B3078. Ring for directions

Credit cards: ▨ ▧ OTHER
Times: Last L 2pm, last D 9.30pm.
Closed Sun D, Mon
Seats: 40. Non-smoking area
Additional: Children welcome;
❿ dishes

ROWDE, **George & Dragon** ❀❀

☺ *Imaginative modern cooking served in an informal pub atmosphere*

Run by Tim and Helen Withers, the George and Dragon enjoys a reputation for good restaurant food in an informal pub atmosphere. The quality and interest of the dishes on the hand-written menus and blackboards reflect Tim's two years at the Carved Angel and his cooking skills remain impressive. A recent inspection meal started with a coarse terrine of turbot and lobster, accompanied by a herb mayonnaise. A compote of honey and rhubarb proved to be a lively contrast to the breast and leg of duck, which was cooked until tender with a crispy skin. Vegetables, whilst simply presented, were full of flavour and definitely enjoyable. The selection of puddings included bread and butter pudding, tart blackberry and apple crumble and gooseberry and elderflower fool. A changing sea food menu of fresh market fish may also be available and might offer monkfish with cucumber, mustard and crème fraîche or perhaps steamed cod with mussels and crab sauce. The confident wine list with bottles from both the New and Old Worlds completes the extremely reasonably priced menu at this popular restaurant.

Directions: On the A342 Devizes–Chippenham road

High Street SN10 2PN
Map no: 3 ST96
Tel: 01380 723053
Chef: Tim Withers
Proprietors: Tim & Helen Withers
Cost: *Alc* £19.50, fixed-price L £10, £8.50 (2course). H/wine £7.75 ❢ Service exc
Credit cards: ▨ ▧ OTHER
Times: Last L 2pm, last D 10pm Closed Sun, Mon L, (Bar open Sun & Mon L), Dec 25/6, Jan 1
Menus: *A la carte*, fixed-price L, bar menu (same as Restaurant)
Seats: 35. Smoking discouraged in dining room
Additional: Children welcome, children's portions; ❿ dishes, other diets with notice

SALISBURY, **Milford Hall Hotel** ❀

Modern British cooking with a pronounced Oriental influence is offered on a well-balanced menu at this pleasant hotel within easy walking distance of the city centre. Enjoyable dishes could include broccoli and Stilton tart, feuilleté of salmon and crab in a lobster sauce, and profiteroles with cream and dark chocolate sauce

Menus: *A la carte*, fixed-price L & D, bar menu
Seats: 70+25. No smoking in dining room
Additional: Children welcome; ❿ dishes, other diets on request
Directions: At junction of Castle Street, A30 ring rd & A345 (Amesbury), less than 0.5 mile from Market Square

206 Castle Street SP1 3TE
Map no: 4 SU12
Tel: 01722 417411
Chefs: William Cully and Peter Roberts
Proprietors: Graham Fitch and Pam Bruford
Cost: *Alc* £18-£20, fixed-price L £9.95/D £13.50 H/wine £8.95 Service exc
Credit cards: ▨ ▧ ▧
Times: Last L 2pm, last D 9.30pm daily

SWINDON, **Blunsdon House Hotel** ❀

☺ *Traditional cooking is served in a formal fashion in the Ridge Restaurant at Blunsdon House. Reworked classic dishes feature strongly on the menu, served with rich and slightly heavy sauces, and may include king scallops in a fish velouté, and fillet of beef 'Blunsdon' garnished with wild mushrooms, foie gras and truffle*

Menus: A la carte, fixed-price L & D, bar menu
Seats: 70. Air conditioned. No-smoking area
Additional: Children's menu; ❤ dishes, vegan/other diets on request
Directions: 3 miles north of town centre. From A419 take turning signposted Broad Blunsdon, then first left

Blunsdon SN2 4AD
Map no: 4 SU18
Tel: 01793 721701
Chef: Elisley Haines
Proprietor: John Clifford (Best Western)
Cost: Alc £17.50, fixed-price L £10.75/D £11.75.
H/wine £9.50 Service inc
Credit cards: 🔲 🔲 🔲 🔲 OTHER
Times: Last L 2pm, last D 10pm
Closed Sat L

SWINDON, **Chiseldon House Hotel** ❀❀

Flair and imagination inform the menus at this tranquil country house hotel in three acres of lawned garden

A Grade II listed former manor house, Chiseldon has been tastefully converted into a comfortable hotel with a friendly home-from-home atmosphere. The Orangery Restaurant is a suitable setting for chef John Farrow's interesting, seasonally biased menus. A first course of creamy vegetable soup accompanied by fresh-from-the-oven rolls made a successful start to a sample meal. This was followed by succulent roast sirloin of beef, its flavour enhanced by a smooth and tangy red wine and mustard sauce. Vegetables were fresh and crisp but a crème brûlée to finish could only have benefitted from a more brittle burnt sugar topping. Staff are pleasant and the atmosphere here relaxed.

Directions: On B4006

Chiseldon SN4 0NE
Map no: 4 SU18
Tel: 01793 741010
Chef: John Farrow
Proprietor: SKC Leisure Ltd
Cost: Alc £38, fixed-price L £14.95/D £22.95. Service exc
Credit cards: 🔲 🔲 🔲 🔲 OTHER
Menus: A la carte, fixed-price L & D

TEFFONT MAGNA,
Howard's House Hotel ❀❀❀

Appetising modern British cooking in the fresh, country-style restaurant of a converted village manor house

Teffont Evias SP3 5RJ
Map no: 3 ST93
Tel: 01722 716392/716821
Chef: Paul Firmin
Proprietors: Jonathan Ford and Paul Firmin
Cost: Alc £23.85-£31.50, fixed-price Sun L £17.50. H/wine £12 Service exc
Credit cards: 🔲 🔲 🔲 🔲
Times: Last L 2pm, last D 9.30pm
Menus: A la carte, fixed-price Sun L
Seats: 35. No smoking in dining room
Additional: Children welcome, children's menu; ❤ dishes, other diets on request

Howard's House, a 300-year-old manor house restored and converted into a charming hotel, is set in lovely grounds in the beautiful Nadder valley. Chef and co-owner Paul Firmin offers a sensibly-sized *carte* of modern cooking which takes some inspiration from France and the Far East. On the menu this is translated into the likes of boudin noir with red onions, apple and Calvados jelly, or steamed mussels with lemon grass, star anise and coriander. There is also an intelligent adaptation of traditional British dishes – rack of lamb is served with its own steamed suet pudding of kidneys and with sage and onion gravy.

For one dinner, breast of pigeon 'tender pink' and seared with a sliver of foie gras, was encased in good puff pastry and served on a nicely clarified truffle-flavoured sauce, but a bourride of fish, excellent monkfish, good bass, and decent red mullet, was slightly overpowered by the intense use of saffron. An attractively marbled white and dark chocolate parfait completed the meal, served with a good raspberry coulis. Quality fresh produce forms the basis of all the dishes, and some of it comes from the hotel's own gardens.

Directions: A36/A30 from Salisbury, turn onto B3089. 5 miles W of Wilton, 9 miles W of Salisbury

WARMINSTER,
Bishopstrow House Hotel ❀❀

Imaginative cooking complemented by a good list of wines

An inspiring menu and sound standards of cooking are strengths of the kitchen at Bishopstrow House. Modern English food either chosen from the *carte* or fixed-price menu may include a salad of baked smoked haddock with plum tomato and mustard vinaigrette, or rillette of salt cod, crab and avocado with a light curry oil dressing, chargrilled breast of East Knoyle chicken basted in olive oil and lemon served in a light tarragon Chablis wine sauce, and grilled Scottish sirloin steak with herb dumplings and mashed potato. At an autumn inspection chicken liver parfait showed good flavour and breast of guinea fowl came with a rich shepherd's pie of the leg, and a simple feuilleté of red berries made an enjoyable end. Other desserts might be rhubarb crème brûlée, or iced pineapple and rum terrine with passion fruit sauce, or there are farmhouse cheeses. The wine list includes some sound New World selections.

Directions: From Warminster take B3414 (Salisbury). Hotel is signposted

Warminster BA12 9HH
Map no: 3 ST84
Tel: 01985 212312
Chef: Christopher Suter
Proprietors: The Blandy family.
Manager: David Dowden
Cost: Alc £33, fixed-price
L £12.50/D £33. H/wine £12.50
❗ Service exc
Credit cards: 🖭 🖭 🖭 🖭 OTHER
Times: Last L 2pm, last D
9.30pm
Menus: A la carte, fixed-price L
& D, bar menu
Seats: 60. No smoking in dining
room
Additional: Children welcome,
children's menu; ❶ menu,
vegan/other diets on request

Basil is an aromatic plant which originated in India. The name is derived from the Greek 'basilikos' meaning royal, for in ancient Greece basil was known as 'the royal herb', since only the sovereign 'basileus' was allowed to cut it (with a golden sickle). In most of the Mediterranean it was used chiefly as a perfume and insect repellent. The herb is strongly connected with Provence and Italy, especially Liguria, the region that invented pesto sauce.

CHANNEL ISLANDS
ALDERNEY

ALDERNEY, **Inchalla Hotel** ✿✿

☺ *Simple but sophisticated cooking in a relaxed, modern hotel set in its own gardens near the centre of St Anne*

The recent arrival of chef Richard Cranfield, from Bistro 33 and The Mansion House in mainland Dartmouth, offers an exciting prospect for both hotel and island. A small bar is now planned to attract more local trade to the smart, conservatory-style restaurant. An interesting selection of dishes is offered from a daily-changing, fixed-price menu, supported by an extensive *carte*. The cooking impresses with fresh flavours and commendably straightforward style. A hot fish terrine starter was light in texture and subtle in taste, and the accompanying béarnaise sauce smooth and correctly made. Ingredients are mostly of a high quality, although a main course cassoulet, packed with flageolet beans, sausage, bacon and herbs, would have benefited from stronger flavours in general, and a less bland sausage in particular. Vegetables are excellent, and the enjoyable desserts always freshly made. Home-baked bread is a plus, and the short wine list offers something to suit all palates. Service is notably friendly, helpful and efficient.

Le Val, St Anne G79
Map no: 16
Tel: 01481 823220
Chef: Richard Cranfield
Proprietor: Valerie Willis
Cost: *Alc* £20.50, fixed-price D £14 (4 course)/Sun L £8.75 (4 course). H/wine £7 Service exc
Credit cards: 🔲 ▭ ▭
Times: Last D 9pm/Sun L 2pm. Closed Sun D, Xmas
Menus: *A la carte*, fixed-price D & Sun L
Seats: 40. No smoking in restaurant
Additional: Children welcome (over 5 at D); children's menu, ❤ dishes, vegan/other diets on request

GUERNSEY

PERELLE, **L'Atlantique Hotel** ✿✿

☺ *An award-winning restaurant overlooking Perelle Bay from its setting on the west coast of the island*

Perelle Bay GY7 9NA
Map no: 16
Tel: 01481 64056
Chef: Gary Kenley
Managing Director: Michael Lindley
Cost: *Alc* £21, fixed-price D £14.50 (4 course)/Sun L £9.95 (4 course). H/wine £6.95 Service exc

Now winner of the Guernsey Restaurant of the Year Award for the second time, the smartly presented L'Atlantique remains popular with both locals and holidaymakers. In its quite formal surroundings, chef Gary Kindley continues to present an interesting, daily-changing set-price menu and a good range of vegetarian dishes in addition to the imaginative modern *carte*. One evening in early summer, an inspection meal began with a simple but enjoyable pressed ham terrine topped with spinach and mint; was followed by a rather over-complicated suprême of guinea fowl – the breast filled with a Stilton and walnut farce then served on a cream sauce with basil and grapes – and a commendable (though possibly excessive) selection of vegetables. The highlight of the meal was a marbled chocolate terrine set off by strawberries and an apricot coulis. Freshly made coffee was served with home-made fudge and petits fours. Thirteen vintage clarets, together with labels from Germany, Italy and Spain, are included in a predominantly French wine list.

Directions: Situated on the west coast road overlooking Perelle Bay

Credit cards: 🔳 🔳 🔳
Times: Last L 2pm, last D 9.30pm daily
Menus: *A la carte*, fixed-price D & Sun L, bar menu
Seats: 55. No-smoking area
Additional: Children welcome, children's portions; ♥ dishes, vegan/other diets on request

ST MARTIN, Hotel Bella Luce ❀

☺ *Excellent meals are served in the atmospheric, candlelit dining-room of this 12th-century manor house. Local produce, including first-class local seafood, is used to create dishes such as a delicately flavoured fish terrine, and braised saddle of English lamb with rosemary, glazed shallots and roasted garlic*

Menus: *A la carte*, fixed-price D, bar menu
Seats: 62. Air conditioned. No-smoking area
Additional: Children welcome, children's menu; ♥ menu, vegan/other diets on request
Directions: Along seafront, up Le Val de Terres, through lights follow lane, 1000yds on left

St Martin GY4 6YB
Map no: 16
Tel: 01481 38764
Chef: James Scowen
Proprietor: Richard Cann.
Manager: John Cockcroft
Cost: *Alc* £16, fixed-price D £14.90. H/wine £7 ♥ Service exc
Credit cards: 🔳 🔳 🔳 OTHER
Times: Last L 2pm, last D 9.45pm daily

ST MARTIN, Idlerocks Hotel ❀

☺ *Both Raffles lounge, and the more formal Admirals restaurant, provide outstanding sea views, and a sound degree of cooking skills. Combine home-made bread rolls, local seafood when available, and carefully prepared, interesting dishes made from fresh ingredients, and the result is enjoyable food*

Menus: *A la carte*, fixed-price L & D, bar menu **Seats:** 100. No-smoking area **Additional:** Children welcome, children's menu; ♥ dishes, vegan/other diets on request
Directions: On cliffs above Jerbourg Point about 10 minutes' drive from St Peter Port & airport

Jerbourg Point GY4 6BJ
Map no: 16
Tel: 01481 37711
Chef: Anthony Lawson
Managing Director: Paul Hamill
Cost: Fixed-price L £9.60/D £14.50 (both 5 course). H/wine £8.80 Service exc
Credit cards: 🔳 🔳 🔳 🔳
Times: Last L 2pm, last D 9.30pm daily

ST MARTIN, La Barbarie Hotel ❀

La Barbarie took second place this year in the Guernsey restaurant of the year competition. It offers an extensive, good-value carte, is noted for seafood, and soundly cooked dishes may include mille-feuille of salmon, crab rilette, or game pie

Menus: *A la carte*, fixed-price D, bar menu **Seats:** 70. No-smoking area **Additional:** Children welcome, children's menu; ♥ dishes, vegan/other diets on request
Directions: At the traffic lights in St Martin take the road to Saints Bay; hotel is on the right at the end of Saints Road

Saints Road,
Saints Bay GY4 6ES
Map no: 16
Chef: Michael Carney
Manager: Andrew Coleman
Cost: *Alc* £16.50, fixed-price D £12.50. ♥ Service exc
Credit cards: 🔳 🔳 OTHER
Times: Last L 2pm, last D 9.45pm

ST PETER PORT, The Absolute End ✿

☺ *Fabulous views from the picture window and fresh seafood are the mainstays of this popular, smart restaurant. Antonio Folmi's cooking style is straightforward, and his various menus offer an extensive selection. Expect turbot with hollandaise sauce, good chocolate mousse and decent espresso*

Longstore GY1 2BG
Map no: 16
Tel: 01481 723822
Chef: Antonio Folmi
Proprietor: Gastone Toffanello
Cost: *Alc* £22, fixed-price L £11. H/wine £6.50. Service inc
Credit cards: 🂠 ▨ ▨ ▨ OTHER
Times: Last L 2pm, last D 10pm. Closed Sun, Jan
Menus: *A la carte* D, fixed-price lunch

Seats: 60. No cigars or pipes in dining room
Additional: Children permitted, children's portions; ✿ menu, other diets on request
Directions: On seafront 1 mile N of town centre past QE2 marina

ST PETER PORT, Café du Moulin ✿✿

Robust country dishes are served here, in the appropriate setting of a converted granary

Rue du Quarteraine GY7 9PB
Map no: 16
Tel: 01481 65944
Chef: David Mann
Proprietors: David & Gina Mann
Cost: *Alc* £24, fixed-price L £10.95 (2 courses), £13.95/D £15.95 H/wine £7.50 ❗ Service exc
Credit cards: 🂠 ▨ OTHER
Times: Last L 1.30pm, last D 9.30pm. Closed Sun D, Mon
Menus: *A la carte,* fixed-price L & D, bar menu
Seats: 46. Air conditioned. No smoking while others are eating
Additional: Children permitted (over 7 at D), children's portions; ✿ menu, vegan/other diets on request

Nestling in a wooded valley, down a very narrow lane, Café du Moulin is housed in a granite-built former granary. Here, imaginative chef David Mann presents an interesting range of robust modern dishes that make good use of game and locally-caught fish; the evening *carte* displays his talents to their full advantage, although the simpler lunches do offer excellent value-for-money. An early summer lunch, for example, began with a country pâté, the well flavoured, crumbly blend of pork and calves' liver accompanied by home-made chutney and freshly toasted wholemeal bread. Mediterranean fish casserole, a selection of salmon, monkfish, plaice and skate served with an attractive tomato butter sauce and a selection of vegetables, proved a particularly successful main course, and a traditional trifle – sherry-soaked macaroons topped by fruit, superb egg custard, lemon syllabub, a swirl of cream and toasted almonds – provided a fitting climax to the meal. Freshly made coffee came with cream and petits fours. A descriptive, predominantly French, wine list features a separate Australian section.

Directions: Take the Forest road from St Peter Port, left in St Peters, signed 'Torteval', take 3rd right, Restaurant in 0.25 mile

ST PETER PORT, La Fregate ❀

☺ *A very popular and long established hotel which benefits from a good location overlooking the town and harbour. A major attraction is the Anglo-French cooking. Both the seafood specialities and recipes using fresh local produce, such as the chilled timbale of gravlax and Guernsey crab, are impressive*

Menus: A la carte, fixed-price L & D
Seats: 70. Air conditioned
Additional: Children permitted by arrangement Sun L only; ♥ menu, vegan/ on request, other diets prior notice
Directions: Town centre above St. Julian's Avenue

Les Cotils GY1 1UK
Map no: 16
Tel: 01481 724624
Chef: Gunter Botzenhardt
Proprietor: Oswald Steinsdorfer
Cost: Alc £20, fixed-price L £12.50/D £18 (4 course). H/wine £8.50 Service exc
Credit cards: ▨ ▨ ▨ ▨ OTHER
Times: Last L 1.30pm, last D 9.30pm daily

ST PETER PORT, Le Nautique ❀

☺ *Freshly caught seafood and shellfish are specialities at this old-established French restaurant overlooking the picturesque harbour. Flambé cooking is a further strength along with very attentive and convivial service*

Times: Last L 2pm, last D 10pm Closed Sun, Dec 24-Jan 10
Menus: A la carte, fixed-price L & D
Seats: 68.
Additional: Children over 5 welcome, children's portions; ♥ dishes, vegan/other diets on request
Directions: Sea front opposite Harbour and Victoria Marina

Quay Steps GY1 2LE
Map no: 16
Tel: 01481 721714
Chef: Vito Garau
Proprietor: Carlo Graziani. Manager: Luigi Tramentano
Cost: Alc £20, fixed-price L /D £17.50. H/wine £7.50 Service inc
Credit cards: ▨ ▨ ▨ ▨ OTHER

ST PETER PORT, La Piazza Ristorante ❀

☺ *Authentic Italian cooking can be enjoyed at this courtyard restaurant with some al fresco seating. Choices include fresh local fish such as Brittany-style scallops in a cream sauce, or breast of chicken with Dolcellate cheese, and escalope of veal with mushroom sauce*

Seats: 54.
Menus: A la carte L & D
Additional: Children over 6 welcome; ♥ dishes, vegan/other diets on request
Directions: Under the Arch, Trinity Square

Trinity Square GY1 1LX
Map no: 16
Tel: 01481 725085
Chef: Emilio Bianco
Proprietor: Gaetano Bianco
Cost: Alc £20. H/wine £6.20. Service exc
Credit cards: ▨ ▨ ▨ OTHER
Times: Last L 2pm D10pm. Closed Sun, Dec 24 – Jan 24

ST PETER PORT, St Pierre Park Hotel ❀❀

An excellent range of fresh seafood is featured in this stylish hotel's elegant French restaurant

Dating from the 1980s, but retaining much of the character and style of the early 19th century college it replaced, this hotel shares its site with a 9-hole golf course designed by Tony Jacklin. The richly furnished, air-conditioned Victor Hugo French Restaurant provides an elegant setting in which to appreciate John Hitchen's contemporary carte and set-price menus of dishes from around the world. The seafood section is particularly noteworthy – the success of its classical and original recipes based not only on the local catch but also on purchases made from all the major fishing ports of the UK. Starters range from smoked Scottish salmon to a crab bisque flavoured with brandy and Guernsey cream, main courses from anything on the catch-of-the-day list cooked 'freestyle' (grilled,

Rohais GY1 1FD
Map no: 16
Tel: 01481 728282
Chef: John Hitchen
Proprietor: St. Pierre Park. Manager: Jonathan Raggett
Cost: Alc from £20, fixed-price L £11.95, £9.95 (2 course)/D £17.95. H/wine £9.25 Service inc
Credit cards: ▨ ▨ ▨ ▨ OTHER
Times: Last L 2.30pm, last D 10.30pm daily
Menus: A la carte, fixed-price L & D, pre- theatre, bar menu
Seats: 70+120 in Café. Air conditioned. No-smoking area

St Pierre Park Hotel

Additional: Children welcome, children's menu; ❤ dishes, vegan/other diets on request

fried, roasted or steamed, with a choice of sauces) to braised local lobster and asparagus tips flavoured with vanilla, cardamom, lime and cream. Though mainly French, the wine list includes some examples from the New World; house wine is available by a half-litre carafe.

Directions: 1 mile from town centre on route to the west coast

VALE, **Pembroke Bay Hotel** ❀

☺ *A selection of English and international dishes are available on the carte of the Pembroke Conservatory restaurant. Our inspector recently enjoyed lobster with fresh pasta, and tenderloin of lamb with a house speciality of strawberries cooked in vodka and ground pepper, with cream and ice cream to finish. Ludwigs forms part of the Pembroke Bay Hotel, and serves traditional Bavarian food. Dishes include ravioli filled with bacon, herbs and spring onions, a tender pan-fried liver topped with red onions, and 'apfelstrudel'.*

Pembroke Bay GY3 5BY
Map no: 16
Tel: 01481 47573
Chef: Keith Windsor
Proprietor: Mr & Mrs Bruxby
Cost: *Alc* £18.90, fixed-price L £11.95/D £16.50
Credit cards: 🔳 🔤
Times: Last D 9.30pm
Closed 3 Jan-15 Feb

Directions: North tip of island. Next to Royal Guernsey Golf Club

Chillies were one of the earliest plants to be cultivated in the pre-Columbian New World. Archaeological evidence suggests that they were used at least 8,000 years ago to impart flavour and spiciness to food. The Mayans used 30 different varieties of chilli and recent evidence shows that the Aztecs used them in almost every dish. Today chillies are grown throughout the world. The characteristic for which chillies are best known is their heat. The fiery sensation is caused by capsaicin, a potent chemical that survives both cooking and freezing. As well as causing a burning sensation, this substance triggers the brain to produce endorphins, natural pain killers that promote a sense of well-being and stimulation. Also, capsaicin is a natural decongestant. The hottest chilli in the world is probably the Scotch bonnet chilli (so named because its shape resembles a Highlander's cap). A single Scotch bonnet has the fire power of 50 jalapeno chillies. Grown in the Caribbean it is an essential ingredient in Jamaican jerk dishes. When handling chillies you should wear rubber gloves. Wash your hands with soap afterwards and take care not to touch your face, or eyes. If your hands start to sting after handling chillies, rub them with a little toothpaste.

VAZON BAY,
Les Embruns House Hotel ❀

Fresh flavours and quality ingredients are particular strengths of the kitchen at this small, family-run hotel. An extensive choice, on both fixed-price menus and carte, includes uncomplicated but enjoyable dishes along the lines of breast of chicken with a creamy asparagus sauce, and puddings such as blackcurrant mousse

Directions: On west coast. At Richmond end of Vazon Bay

Route de la Margion GY5 7LG
Map no: 16
Tel: 01481 64834
Proprietor: Mr J F Kennedy
Cost: Alc £25, fixed-price
L £11/D £14
Credit cards: 🔲 🔲 🔲 OTHER
Times: Last D 9pm

HERM

HERM, **White House** ❀

☺ *Top-value dinners and Conservatory lunches in this, the only hotel on an idyllic island, include dishes using locally farmed Herm oysters, Guernsey plaice, English calves' liver plus interesting vegetarian options*

Menus: Fixed-price L & D, bar menu
Seats: 118. No smoking in dining room
Additional: Children over 6 permitted; ❶ dishes, vegan/ other diets on request
Directions: Only hotel on island; 20 mins by ferry from St Peter Port

Guernsey GY1 3HR
Map no: 16
Tel: 01481 722159
Chef: Chris Walder
Manager: Michael Hester
Cost: Fixed-price L £11/D
£16.95. H/wine £7.45 ❢
No service charge
Credit cards: 🔲 🔲
Times: Last L 1.30pm, last D
9.30pm Closed Oct-Mar

JERSEY

GOREY, **Jersey Pottery** ❀❀

☺ *All-year-round popularity is assured for a seafood restaurant with large white umbrellas and abundant greenery*

The Garden Restaurant, incorporated within the pottery complex, is one of the most popular on the island. Cooking is modern British with fresh local produce, especially fish, inspiring the menu. Mussels in Jersey cider, peppered lady crab, 'served hot with a bib, only for experienced crab pickers', endive farcie, carpaccio of smoked Rannoch venison, and hot or cold vichyssoise, for example. Under the conservatory glass on a hot day, the cold version might be a good idea. A long list of main courses begins with a range of seafood salads, and there are few native fish or shellfish which do not show up in one form or another; grilled lobster, Dover sole, brill, langoustine, bass, and salmon. Meat eaters can breathe a sigh of relief as they spot grilled fillet steak, breast of guinea fowl and fillet of lamb at the bottom of the menu. But the Pottery is first and foremost a fish restaurant and it makes an extremely good job of it. The patissière shows how desserts should be made. Among the mainly French wines there is a white from Jersey.

Directions: In Gorey village, well signposted from main coast road

Gorey Village JE3 9EP
Map no: 16
Tel: 01534 851119
Chef: Anthony Dorris
Proprietor: Colin Jones.
Manager: Robert Jones
Cost: Alc £22. H/wine £9.50 ❢
Service inc
Credit cards: 🔲 🔲 🔲 🔲 OTHER
Times: Last L 4.pm. Closed Sun,
10 days Xmas
Menu: A la carte L
Seats: 250. No-smoking area
Additional: Children welcome, children's menu; ❶ menu, vegan/other diets on request

GOREY, **The Village Bistro** ✹✹

☺ *A friendly, up-and-coming restaurant in the shadow of Gorey Castle,*
one of Jersey's most impressive tourist attractions

Regulars will have followed David Cameron around the island,
from his earlier days at Granite Corner and Jersey Pottery; when
in London they might even have tracked him down to The Royal
Garden Hotel. Along the way he not only acquired a fine
reputation, but equipped himself with the wherewithal to run his
own place back in the Channel Islands. Formerly a church, the
Bistro has been skilfully transformed by Sandra Dalziel in a way
that recalls its earlier use by means of hanging suns, moons and
stars. Menus change regularly with new and exciting recipes using
fresh produce brought in from the islands and from the mainland.
There are fixed-price dishes, winter warmers, blackboard specials
and a vegetarian menu. From the *carte* on inspection day came
'very tender' scallops with a purée of carrots and flavoured with
basil vinaigrette, then rack of lamb served with a well judged sauce
and individual dauphinoise potatoes. Desserts include rhubarb
Bakewell tart, and a light textured bread and butter pudding.
Wines are carefully chosen, with good value house wine.

Directions: Village centre

Gorey
Map no: 16
Tel: 01534 853429
Chef: David Cameron
Proprietors: Sandra Dalziel and
David Cameron
Cost: *Alc* £20, fixed-price L
£9.50/Sun £10.50 (4 course).
H/wine £ 5.50 Service exc
Credit cards: ▧ ▨ OTHER
Times: Last L 2pm, last D 10pm.
Closed Mon except BH
Menus: *A la carte,* fixed-price L
Seats: 40.
Additional: Children welcome,
children's portions; ❂ dishes,
vegan/other diets on request

GROUVILLE, **Hotel Kalamunda** ✹

The restaurant at this modern hotel, close to St Helier, serves a selection of
interesting dishes from a range of menus, including carte, fixed-price and
snack selection. A recent meal included chicken liver pâté and beautifully
cooked loin of lamb

Seats: *60/100. No-smoking area. No cigars or pipes*
Additional: *Children welcome, children's menu/portions;*
❂ *menu, vegan/other diets on request; live entertainment*
Directions: On the seaward side of Gorey village

Gorey Village JE3 9ER
Map no 16
Tel: 01534 856656
Chef: *Arwell Williams*
Proprietor: *John Rice*
Cost: *Alc £20, fixed-price L*
£9.50/D £10.90. H/wine £5
❢ *Service exc*
Credit cards: ▧ ▨
Times: *Midday-last L 2pm, last*
D 10pm

L'ETACQ,
Lobster Pot Hotel ✹

☺ *Anglo-French cooking with a seafood emphasis distinguishes this*
popular, but remote, coastal restaurant. Fresh lobster soup, 'coquilles
St Jacques Parisienne', and fresh Jersey plaice basted with butter and
lemon juice, could feature on an extensive menu which also includes
steaks, duck and game

Menus: Fixed-price L & D, bar menu
Seats: 95. Air conditioned
Additional: Children welcome, children's portions; ❂ menu, vegan/
other diets on request
Directions: Follow Victoria Ave to Beaumont then A12 to B64, to
B35; Rest at end

St Ouens JE3 2FB
Map no: 16
Tel: 01534 482888
Chef: Gilbert Heliou
Proprietor: Gerald A Howe
Cost: Fixed-price L £10.95/D
£15.50. H/wine £8.50. Service
exc
Credit cards: ▧ ▨ ▨ ▨ OTHER
Times: Last L 1.45pm/Sun 2pm,
last D 9.45pm daily

ROZEL BAY, Chateau La Chaire ❀❀

Fresh home-grown herbs are an important element in the imaginative dishes served here

St Martin JE3 6AJ
Map no: 16
Tel: 01534 863354
Chef: Ian Samson
Proprietor: Hatton Hotels.
Manager: Alan Winch
Cost: *Alc* £28.50, fixed-price L
£11.75/D £21.50. H/wine £8.90
☘ service exc
Credit cards: 🟦 📶 📶 💳 OTHER
Times: Last L 2pm, last D 10pm
daily
Menus: *A la carte,* fixed-price L
Seats: 65. No-smoking area
Additional: Children over 7
permitted, children's portions;
❶ dishes, vegan/other diets on
request

Popular not only for its secluded position above the village but also for the high standards of customer care provided throughout, this hotel serves meals to suit every taste. The majority of new chef Ian Samson's dishes are innovative in style, sometimes with surprising combinations, salmon cooked with rhubarb, for example, or chicken combined with a stuffing of haggis and smoked fish. Simpler alternatives, a few classic old favourites and some good vegetarian options are all available. Fixed-price menus are supplemented by a *carte,* and it was from this that an inspection meal was chosen earlier this year. Sauce Jacqueline (which turned out to be a sweet carrot sauce) provided a simple but appropriate contrast to a starter of crab and sorrel cakes. This preceded a fine carpaccio of salmon, then carefully cooked fillet of lamb with Sicilian vegetables (beetroot and ratatouille). Puddings range from ice-creams and sorbets to such well established favourites as tarte Tatin, and a selection of British and continental cheeses is offered. Both Old and New Worlds are well represented on a wine list which includes some good vintages.

Directions: From St Helier head N/E towards Five Oaks, Maufant, then St Martin's Church & Rozel; 1st left in village, hotel 100m

ST BRELADE, The Atlantic Hotel ❀❀

Located in attractive gardens on a headland overlooking the sea, the Atlantic offers a good selection of well-balanced dishes

The hotel is a modern establishment set in landscaped garden overlooking the bay. The kitchen takes care with ingredients which runs to good home-baked bread of walnut, soda, or sun-dried tomato, and offers a mix of traditional, innovative and vegetarian dishes on the fixed-price menu and *carte.* A fairly typical inspection meal yielded an elaborate crab ravioli – pasta filled with a crab mousse and served with grapefruit-flavoured coriander butter sauce with salmon eggs and tomato concasse and garnished with deep-fried shredded leeks. A main course of honey-roasted duck with a herb-flavoured demi-glace was marred by the slightly dry duck and

La Moye JE3 8HE
Map no: 16
Tel: 01534 44101
Chef: Tom Sleigh
Gen. Manager: Simon Dufty
(Small Luxury Hotels of the
World)
Cost: *Alc* £30, fixed-price L
£15/D £21.50 (4 courses).
H/wine £7.50
Credit cards: 🟦 📶 📶 💳 OTHER
Times: Last L 2.15pm, last D
9.30pm
Menus: *A la carte* dinner, fixed-price lunch, Sunday lunch

The Atlantic Hotel

Seats: 80. No cigars or pipes in restaurant
Additional: Children welcome, children's portions; ❻ dishes, other diets on request

corresponding lack of crispness; accompanying vegetables were fresh if unexciting. Baked poached pear on a sponge base with cinnamon ice-cream and brandy snaps was the highlight of the meal. The wine list includes a decent selection of both Old and New World wines, plus a range of half bottles.

Directions: From St Brelade take the road to Petit Port, turn into Rue de Sergente and right again, signed to hotel

ST BRELADE, Hotel L'Horizon ❀❀

An ideal seaside setting in which to enjoy the local catch prepared in an accomplished, unpretentious manner

Find a stone if you can on St Brelade Bay's sandy beach, throw it carefully, and prove how close L'Horizon is to the sea. There is a choice of three places to eat, the informal Brasserie, the more upmarket Crystal Room and the intimate Star Grill. Appetisers, such as warm tartlets filled with fresh mussels and soft cod's roe, are complimentary. Fish from local waters, as might be expected, are usually available on the *carte* and fixed-price menu, and their potential is fully exploited by chef Peter Marek. Meat lovers might prefer something enjoyably rich like tender medallions of beef served with a leek and wild mushroom-textured, red wine glace de viande reduction, garnished with lardons of bacon and all set on crisp rösti potato. Even those same meat lovers might easily be tempted by vegetarian options such as timbale of wild mushrooms placed on a bed of spinach with cheese and lentil sauce. The well stocked dessert trolley offers some old familiar offerings such as crème brûlée. Be prepared to drink a bottle of wine because there are no halves. The choice is wide, with some good wines of the month.

Directions: Overlooking St Brelade's Bay

St Brelade's Bay JE3 8EF
Map no: 16
Tel: 01534 43101
Chef: Peter Marek
Proprietors: Arcadian International
Cost: *Alc* £25, fixed-price L £13.50/D £23.75
Credit cards: 🅴 🔳 🔳 🔳 OTHER
Times: 12.30-last L 2.15pm, last D 10.15pm
Menus: *A la carte* dinner, fixed-price lunch, Sunday lunch
Seats: 50. No cigars or pipes in restaurant. Air conditioned
Additional: No children under 12; ❻ dishes, vegan/other diets on request

> Confit, a speciality of south-western France, is one of the oldest methods of preserving food. A piece of pork, duck, goose, rabbit or turkey is cooked in its own fat and stored in a pot, covered in the same fat to preserve it. It can be eaten hot or cold.

ST HELIER, **Bistro Central** ❁

An interesting list of lunchtime plats du jour as well as an extensive carte are offered at this Belle Epoche-style bistro. Outside, a large awning extending almost across the street allows for al fresco dining (weather permitting). Reliable cooking has an emphasis on local seafood such as pan-fried scallops, mussels, monkfish and cod in a garlicky white wine and brandy sauce

9-11 Don Street
Map no: 16
Tel: 01534 876933
Chef: Michael Gallichan
Proprietor: Mr M Thebault
Cost: Alc £22, fixed-price
L/D £14.50
Times: Last L 2.15pm,
last D 10.15pm

Seats: 80. No-smoking area
Additional: Children welcome; ❶ menu
Directions: Just off pedestrian precinct

ST HELIER, **Broome's** ❁❁❁

Vibrant, imaginative and witty food underpinned by considerable skill and precision

Young chef, Kevin Broome, has moved from Shai in St Helier, to open this new restaurant in St Aubin. The tall, terracotta villa stands just back from the quayside, overlooking the boats and distant skyline. There are colourful tables in a fenced and bosky patio at the front where lunch, afternoon tea and dinner are served when weather permits. Guests eating inside, however, will have no complaint; Kevin, dreadlocked and energetic, and his effervescent partner, Liz Storie – who runs front of house – have created a bright and elegant Romanesque dining-room and small bar area, with trompe l'oeil landscapes and statuary (don't miss the loos). The sense of imagination and personal commitment is echoed in both the cooking and the menu – the latter has moody, black and white, food-as-art photos on the cover. The wine list is very well chosen, and includes a good number of halves.

Kevin worked for three years with Marco Pierre White, and his dishes show a zestful abundance of flavour and colour, with much use of fresh, local produce. He prefers the Californain/Pacific rim garnish of salsa, rather than the French constructed sauce, but he judges the balance of tastes and textures with a fine hand. Fresh crab gâteau came interleaved with avocado and apple, paired with a lively lime and shallot salsa; langoustine tortellini given a shot in the arm by a piquant tomato and coriander vinaigrette. More salsa came with salmon, this time one of tomato and baby aubergines. A succulent and rich daube of beef had a deep, finely balanced chocolate and chilli sauce. Puddings include old British favourites reworked with a small twist; a wicked banana and toffee crumble in a first-rate pasty case was laced with mango coulis. Two-fingered irreverence is everywhere – salt-baked quail comes with shallot jus and ketchup, foie gras with fried egg, and arctic roll (yes, really) with lemon sabayon. For the cheek of it alone, he deserves success.

St Aubin JE3 8AD
Map no: 16
Tel: 01534 42760
Chef: Kevin Broome
Proprietors: Mr & Mrs Broome
Cost: Alc £27.50, fixed-price
L £12.50, £14.50
Credit cards: ▨ ▧ OTHER
Times: Last L 2pm, last D 10pm.
Closed Sat L, Sun, 23 Dec-1 Feb
Seats: 38. No cigars or pipes
Additional: Children welcome;
❶ dishes

Directions: On the harbour

> Balsamic vinegar is made from the cooked and concentrated must of the white grapes of the Trebbiano vine and aged in 12 kegs of different woods. By law it must be at least 10 years old. A deep, rich dark brown in colour, it is a full-bodied vinegar with an intense aromatic fragrance and a distinctive flavour which is at once both sweet and sour.

ST HELIER, **The Grand Hotel** ❀

Victorian-style decor and a fun atmosphere, helped along by a lively contintental brigade of staff, are the hallmarks of the hotel's Victoria's Restaurant. The menu reads elaborately in French, but yields decent seafood omelette on a bed of deep-fried spinach, salmon timbale, and good monkfish with a smoked salmon sauce

The Esplanade JE4 8WD
Map no: 16
Tel: 01534 22301
Chef: Adrian Doolan
Proprietors: De Vere.
Manager: Timothy Brooke
Cost: *Alc* £30, fixed-price
L £15.50, £11.50 (2 course)/D
£23.50 (4 course). H/wine £8.50
Service exc
Credit cards: 🆑 💳 💳 💷
Times: Last L 2.15pm, last
D10pm. Closed Sun D
Seats: 140. Air conditioned.
No-smoking area
Additional: Children welcome,
children's portions; ♥ menu,
other diets on request

Directions: On outskirts of town, overlooking Victoria Park

ST HELIER, **Pomme D'Or Hotel** ❀❀

☺ *The formal main restaurant of this town-centre hotel is an appropriate setting in which to enjoy French cooking*

Liberation Square JE2 3NF
Map no: 16
Tel: 01534 880110/66608
Chef: Steve Le Corre
Proprietors: Pomme
d'Or/Seymour Hotels.
Manager: Tony Aguilar
Cost: *Alc* £25, fixed-price
L £13.50 (4 course)/D £15.50
(4 course). H/wine £5.50 ❗
Service inc
Credit cards: 🆑 💳 💳 💷 OTHER
Times: Last L 2pm, last D 10pm
Closed Sat L, Sun
Menus: *A la carte,* fixed-price
L & D, bar menu
Seats: 45. Air conditioned.
No-smoking area
Additional: Children welcome,;
♥ dishes, vegan/other diets on
request

La Petite Pomme is one of three restaurants contained within this leading town-centre hotel opposite the harbour – the others being an informal coffee shop and a very popular carvery – and in its relatively sophisticated surroundings you can experience the skilful French cooking of talented Jersey-born chef, Stephen Le Corre. On the occasion of a spring visit, a ravioli of salmon, lemon sole and spinach, accompanied by rather firm fresh prawns and crème fraîche textured with a julienne of smoked salmon, preceded tender medallions of veal with a Stilton and port wine sauce, then a well made lemon tart and fairly rich espresso coffee. The descriptive wine selection that accompanies the menu includes some 83 bins, ranging from an interesting connoisseurs' list to startlingly inexpensive French house wines. Service is extremely attentive and particularly well supervised, though sometimes not as knowledgeable as it might be. Car parking is difficult, and you would be well advised to arrive by taxi.

Directions: Opposite Harbour and Marina

ST SAVIOUR, **Longueville Manor**

Consistently high standards of hospitality and cuisine are maintained at this handsome, wisteria-clad manor house

St Helier JE2 7SA
Map no: 16
Tel: 01534 25501
Chef: Andrew Baird
Proprietor: Malcolm Lewis
(Relais & Chateaux)
Cost: Alc £35.50, fixed-price
L £18/D £30 (4 course). H/wine
£12.50 ! Service inc
Credit cards: ◼ ▨ ▨ ▨ OTHER
Times: Last L 2pm, last D
9.30pm daily
Menus: A la carte, fixed-price
L & D, bar menu
Seats: 65. Air conditioned.
No-smoking area.
Additional: Children welcome,
children's portions; ❂ menu,
vegan/other diets on request

Stone built and handsome, this wisteria-clad manor house dating from the 13th century stands in 40 acres of manicured grounds. These days the place incorporates a tennis court, good sized swimming pool, furnished sun terrace, and ornamental lake with real ducks. More pertinently, there is a kitchen garden providing herbs and vegetables. The medieval wood-panelled dining-room is where a range of set-price menus are offered. These include a commendable vegetarian selection and a tasting menu which features eight courses of the kind of cooking that has put the manor on the culinary map. Griddled foie gras with woodland mushrooms, fillet of Jersey sea bass, and a quail consommé with leek and ginger are the sort of dishes with which chef, Andrew Baird, has impressed.

Dishes sampled in late May were singled out for special praise. Poached scallops with roast lobster on a nest of vegetable 'noodles' was deemed to be 'very exciting'. Pot au feu of maize-fed chicken was a meltingly tender suprême, plus an exquisitely flavoured ballotine of the leg stuffed with chicken mousse spiked with tarragon. An orange crêpe soufflé was a thick Normandy pancake, crispy at the edges and filled with a well-risen soufflé and served with a delightful warm butter sauce textured with segments of fresh orange and raspberries. It was well worth the wait. Standards of service in the restaurant, under the supervision of the redoubtable Pedro Beuto, are a credit to the Lewis family, who have been running this unique hotel for over 35 years. Stick to the sommelier's recommendations from a voluminous wine list.

Directions: From St Helier take A3 to Gorey, hotel 0.75 mile on left

SARK

SARK, La Sablonnerie ⊛⊛

☺ *Arrive by ferry, continue in pony and trap and reach this tranquil hotel ready for a gourmet feast of local fare*

The Perreé family have owned this restaurant in the south of the island for nearly 50 years and present patron, Elizabeth Perreé, is charming and extrovert. Much of the produce used in her kitchen is grown or reared on the island, other ingredients coming from Guernsey or France. Every meal, from light snack to gourmet feast, can be catered for at La Sablonnerie and its adjacent tea garden. Choosing from the fixed-price dinner menu, our inspector began an enjoyable meal with a warm salad of calves' liver progressing to a cream of celery and Stilton soup with a smooth, light texture and well-balanced flavours. The main course was best end of lamb; lobster, salmon, pheasant and home-grown pork are other typical dishes. Puddings come with double cream from the local farm, and there is a good cheeseboard, including Sark cheese which is similar to Boursin. The comprehensive wine list is reasonably priced.

Directions: On southern part of island

Sark GY9 0SD
Map no: 16
Tel: 01481 832061
Chef: Colin Day
Proprietor: Elizabeth Perreé
Cost: Alc £21, fixed-price L £17.80/D £19.80. H/wine £6.50
❗ Service exc
Credit cards: ▧ ▨ ▨
Times: Last L 2pm, last D 9.30pm. Closed Sat L
Menus: A la carte, fixed-price L & D, bar/garden menu
Seats: 39
Additional: Children welcome, children's menu; ✪ dishes, vegan/other diets on request

SARK, Stocks Island ⊛

☺ *Forget 20th century pressures in this elegant and secluded stone farmhouse hotel run by the Armorgie family. The Cider Press restaurant has an acclaimed reputation with carte and good value fixed-price menus, while the Courtyard bistro, open throughout the day, offers lighter meals*

Menus: A la carte, fixed-price L & D, bar/bistro menu
Seats: 70. No-smoking area
Additional: Children welcome (over 8 in Rest), children's portions/L menu; ✪ menu, other diets on request
Directions: Tractor-drawn bus from harbour, then 15-minute walk

Sark GY9 0SD
Map no: 16
Tel: 01481 832001
Chefs: Martin Smith and David Sharps
Proprietor: Paul Armorgie
Cost: Alc £19.50, fixed-price L £13/D £16/£18 (4/5 course). H/wine £ 6 ❗ No service charge
Credit cards: ▧ ▨ ▨ ▨ OTHER
Times: Last L 2pm, last D 9.30pm Closed Sat L

ISLE OF MAN

DOUGLAS, Mount Murray ⊛

A luxury hotel and leisure complex with a sound standard of cooking. In Murray's Restaurant, a seafood terrine would make a good starter, followed by ragout of venison with rösti, navarin of lamb, or darne of salmon from the set-price menu. The 'Menu Gastronimique' offers Dover sole or magret of duck. Charlotte's Bistro is more informal

Directions: Four miles southwest of Douglas

Santon IM4 2HT
Map no: 6 SC37
Tel: 01624 661111
Chef: Michael Wilkinson
Credit cards: ▧ ▨ ▨ ▨
Times: Last L 2.30pm, last D 9.45pm

NORTHERN IRELAND
ANTRIM

BALLYMENA, Galgorm Manor ❀

Set beside the River Maine, within 85 acres of peaceful grounds, this splendid 19th-century mansion features an elegantly appointed restaurant where chef Charles O'Neill offers imaginative carte and daily menus. Confit of duck might be followed by guinea fowl served on a bed of spinach and shallots, then a lemon soufflé

Ballymena BT42 1EA
Map no: 1 D5
Tel: 01266 881001
Chef: Charles O'Neill
Proprietors: Messrs N & P Hill
Credit cards:
Times: Last D 9.30pm

Directions: One mile outside Ballymena on A42 between Galgorm and Cullybackey

PORTRUSH, Ramore Restaurant ❀❀

Simpler menus and an emphasis on fresh quality produce, especially fish, make it necessary to book at this popular habourside restaurant

A change in direction, necessitated by the effects of the recession, has resulted in regularly packed tables at this popular harbourside restaurant. The longer opening hours and a more realistic approach to pricing, together with chef George McAlpin's reliable and uncomplicated cooking, has proved successful and brought his band of loyal followers back in droves. Menus may not be as adventurous as before, but quality ingredients remain the order of the day and the emphasis on seafood has not been lost. The excellent value *carte* changes about every three or four months, with a reasonable choice at each stage, and this is supported by a range of daily changing blackboard specials. A meal could start with the delicious baby scallops, lightly grilled in garlic and parsley butter, and served with mixed crisp salad leaves. This might be followed by the tender home-smoked brill, accompanied by a delicately flavoured cream and chive sauce. To finish, choux pastry mille-feuille with fresh cream and strawberries and an accomplished chocolate sauce comes highly recommended. The wine list is extensive, but the quality bins do seem a little too much for the modestly priced menu.

The Harbour BT56 8DF
Map no: 1 C6
Tel: 01265 824313
Chef: George McAlpin
Proprietors: George & Jane McAlpin
Cost: *Alc* £24. H/wine £7.75
❢ Service exc
Credit cards: ▨ ▨
Times: 6.30pm-last D10.30pm
Menus: A la carte D
Seats: 80.
Additional: Children welcome; ❤ dishes, other diets on request

Directions: On the harbour

ARMAGH

WARINGSTOWN, Grange Restaurant ❀

☺ *A converted 17th-century planter's house is the setting for this delightful rural restaurant. Straightforward cooking places emphasis on quality ingredients and the carte is good value. A loyal following enjoys the likes of seafood crêpe, followed perhaps by a salmon fillet. Booking is advised*

Main Street BT66 7AH
Map no: 1 D5
Tel: 01762 881989
Chef: Robert Lynn
Proprietors: The Lynn Brothers
Cost: *Alc* £22
Times: *Last L 1.45pm/Last D 9.30pm. Closed Sun eve, Mon, 2 weeks mid Jul*

Additional: *Children permitted; children's portions;* ❤ *dishes*
Directions: On the main road in the village

BELFAST

BELFAST, **Roscoff** ❀❀❀

Super food at high-profile, modern restaurant belonging to well known TV cooking couple

Television can sometimes makes stars out of the unworthy but, equally, it can bring genuine talent to wider public acclaim. With two popular TV series (and books) under their belt, Paul and Jeanne Rankin's contemporary city-centre restaurant is now inundated with a new following of admirers. They deserve their success; the food is vibrant and the place buzzes with vitality. Despite the pressure, the staff cope admirably, providing a smooth, friendly and attentive service. The menu format has changed, and now a good value, set menu offers a choice of approximately seven dishes through each course. At lunch, there is a smaller, cheaper, but equally appealing, business menu.

Paul unites modern French cooking with Californian originality, and given his natural flair and attention to detail, the union is a marriage made in heaven. Dishes to cross the Irish Sea for, include sautéed sweetbreads with orchiette pasta, artichokes and roast garlic, chicken paillard with chargrilled vegetables and a sun-dried tomato butter, and breast of duck with asparagus, shittake mushrooms, soy and ginger. One starter of crispy duck confit with lentils, balsamic vinegar and crispy fried onions is so popular there would be uproar if it was withdrawn from the menu. The explanation lies in the full flavoured, tender and crispy duck, and contrasting creamy texture of the lentils, offset by the vinegar. Only a chargrilled wild salmon main course, on our inspection, accompanied by a colourful saffron mashed potato, sweet red pepper and sharp salsa verde, was slightly mistimed and a touch dry. Jeanne has to take the credit for the very best crème brûlée our inspector had experienced in a long time – a smooth custard flecked with vanilla seeds, topped with a thin caramel crust. A side portion of tender rhubarb brought a fine balance of flavours and sweetness.

Directions: On entering the city, the restaurant is on the left side of Shaftesbury Square, just at the start of Great Victoria Street

7 Lesley House
Shaftesbury Square
BT2 7DB
Map no: 1 D5
Tel: 01232 331532
Chef: Paul Rankin
Proprietors: Paul & Jeanne Rankin
Cost: Fixed-price lunch £14.50, £21.50; fixed-price dinner £21.50. H/wine £11.25 ☕
Service exc
Credit cards: ▨ ▩ ▦ ▨
Times: 12.15pm-last L 2.15pm, 6.30pm-last D 10.15pm. Lunch not served Sat. Closed Sun, Xmas, Easter Mon & 12-13 Jul
Seats: 75. No-smoking area. Air conditioned
Menus: A la carte, fixed-price lunch & dinner
Additional: Children welcome; children's portions; ♥ dishes, vegan/other diets on request

DOWN

ANNALONG, **Glassdrumman Lodge** ❀❀

Home-grown produce features in menus that offers a choice of accomplished country house cooking-styles

Peacefully situated between the Mourne mountains and the Co Down coastline, Glassdrumman Lodge serves accomplished cooking featuring fresh produce (much of it home-grown) and good honest flavours. The four-course fixed-price menu offers a choice of 'country house' and 'town house' dishes – the former having a rustic feel, while the latter are lighter and more refined. A recent inspection meal included a flavoursome seafood soup of hake, brill, prawns and fish stock which, despite its thin consistency, contained

85 Mill Road BT34 4RH
Map no: 1 D5
Tel: 013967 68451
Chef: Stephen Webb
Proprietor: Joan Hall
Cost: Alc from £25; fixed–price dinner £25. H/wine £10 ☕
Service exc
Credit cards: ▨ ▩ ▦ ▨ OTHER
Times: Last D 8pm
Menus: A la carte, fixed-price dinner, pre-theatre
Seats: 50. No pipes or cigars

bite-size pieces of hake; this was followed by scampi Joanne – delicately flavoured fresh scampi with an unusual, and perhaps not too successful, oxtail and peppercorn sauce – then tender shank of Mourne lamb on a light sauce of aromatic herbs and butter-enriched vegetable juices. The list of desserts is both short and simple, but flambéed pineapple on a fine layer of black pepper proved very enjoyable. Prompt and attentive service was provided throughout.

Additional: *Children permitted; children's portions;* ❤ *dishes, vegan/other diets on request*

Directions: From Newcastle take A2 coastal road to Kilkeel. 1 mile after Glassdrumman House, take first right at the pub into Mill Road. The Lodge is 1 mile on the right

BANGOR, Clandeboye Lodge Hotel ❀

☺ *An attractive restaurant which is styled, like the hotel, on the listed church school building found within the landscaped grounds. The fixed-price menu features 'Taste of Ulster' dishes, but the carte is more internationally flavoured. Pâté en croûte, loin of lamb with a damson plum sauce, and tarte tatin, show the range*

Menus: A la carte D, fixed-price D **Seats:** 55. No-smoking area
Additional: Children welcome, children's portions; ❤ dishes, vegan/other diets on request
Directions: Leave A2 at Newtownards sign, 1st junction left, 300yds

Bangor BT19 1UR
Map no: 1 D5
Tel: 01247 852500
Chef: Colin McCreedy
Proprietors: Pim Dalm and Peter Woolnough
Cost: *Alc* £16-£22.25, fixed-price D £15. H/wine £9.25 ❢ Service inc
Credit cards: 🌑 🏧 💳 📟
Times: 6.30pm-last D 10pm
Closed Dec 25/26

BANGOR, O'Hara's Royal Hotel ❀

☺ *Popular light meals are served in the bar while serious modern French cooking is offered on carte and fixed-price menus in the front restaurant. Friday night is gourmet night, when you may expect, for example, prawns in filo pastry, mango sorbet and pan fried sirloin steak*

Menus: A la carte, fixed-price D, bar menu **Seats:** 40. No-smoking area **Additional:** Children welcome, children's menu; ❤ dishes, vegan/other diets on request **Directions:** A2 from Belfast, 12 miles turn right at Seafront, opposite Bangor Marina entrance

Seafront BT20 5ED
Map no: 1 D5
Tel: 01247 271866
Chef: Alexander Taylor
Proprietor: Stephen O'Hara
Cost: *Alc* £17.50, fixed-price D £14.50. H/wine £7.25 Service exc
Credit Cards: 🌑 🏧 💳 📟
Times: Last L 2.30pm, last D 9.15pm Closed Dec 25

BANGOR, Shanks ❀❀❀

A bold, contemporary and very welcome addition to the culinary scene of Northern Ireland

This thoroughly contemporary restaurant shares premises with The Blackwood golf club, prominently signposted from the A2 Bangor to Belfast road. The bright and airy dining-room has a stripped and polished wooden floor, perky yellow walls hung with Hockney prints and a big window looking into the kitchen where Robbie Millar strives to produce imaginative, modern dishes. His menus are heavily dependent on the availability of quality seasonal produce and, upon our visit, were marked by wanton use of wild mushrooms.

Our inspector relished his starter of fresh, succulent prawns served on an asparagus frittata, with a duxelle of wild mushrooms, charred tomato and a smooth butter sauce bursting with tarragon. Despite the riot of flavours, this combination was very satisfying and augured well for a main course of roast squab with grilled fennel, more wild mushrooms and balsamic vinegar mellowed with veal jus. The meat was pink and tender, its gamey flavour enhanced

The Blackwood
Crawfordsburn Road
BT19 1GB
Map no: 1 D5
Tel: 01247 853313
Chef: Robbie Millar
Proprietors: Blackwood Golf Centre.
Manager: Shirley Millar
Cost: Fixed-price L £14.95/D £24.95. H/wine £11.50 ❢ Service exc
Credit cards: 🌑 🏧 💳
Times: Last L 2.15pm, last D 10pm Closed Sat, Sun & Mon L, Sun & Mon D, Dec 25, 26, 1 Jan
Menus: Fixed-price L & D, Sun lunch, bar menu
Seats: 60

by the well-judged sauce, and was accompanied by a colourful and well-seasoned selection of vegetables that included flageolet beans and peas, turned carrots and potatoes. Other intriguing possibilities included crispy duck confit with wilted greens and Chinese five spice, or tempura of monkfish with essence of soya, sesame and ginger. Such is the eclecticism at work here, it should come as no surprise to find that the chef is a graduate of the kitchen at Roscoff in Belfast, which is leading the culinary revolution in Northern Ireland. A warm apple and nut tart set upon a swirl of caramel and crème anglaise proved to be a fitting finale to a meal which demonstrated accomplished cooking skills from start to finish. Service, from a young staff lead by the chef's wife, Shirley, is both relaxed and attentive and the wine list is as switched-on as the rest of the operation.

Additional: Children welcome, children's portions; ❤ menu, vegan/other diets on request

Directions: From A2 (Belfast-Bangor), right into Ballysallagh Road 1 mile before Bangor. 1st left (Crawfordburn Road) to Blackwood Golf Centre. Shanks is in grounds

HOLYWOOD, **Culloden Hotel** ❀

One of Northern Ireland's foremost hotels, the carefully extended baronial mansion enjoys fabulous views over Belfast Lough. Food in the Mitre Restaurant may include chicken and spinach roulade, warm duck salad, roast pigeon with beetroot and hazelnuts, or salmon en croûte

Co Down BT18 0EX
Map no: 1 D5
Tel: 01232 425225
Chef: Paul McKnight
Proprietors: Hastings.
Director: Philip Weston
Cost: *Alc* from £21, fixed-price D £18, £15 (2 course). H/wine £8.50 Service exc
Credit Cards: 🔳 🔳 🔳 🔳
Times: Last L 2.15pm, last D 9.30pm Closed Sat L, Dec 25
Menus: *A la carte,* fixed-price D
Seats: 150. No-smoking area
Additional: Children welcome, children's portions; ❤ dishes, vegan/other diets on request

Directions: On A2 (Belfast-Bangor), half-way, 6 miles from city centre

PORTAFERRY, **Portaferry Hotel** ❀

A charming waterside hotel offering honest cooking prepared from quality fresh ingredients. Interesting selections are offered on the fixed-price and carte. At a recent meal our inspector enjoyed slivers of salmon in a roulade of poached salmon, and rack of Mourne lamb

Menus: *A la carte,* fixed-price L & D, bar menu
Seats: 80. No smoking in dining room
Additional: Children welcome, children's portions; ❤ dishes, vegan/other diets on request
Directions: Opposite Strangford Lough ferry terminal

Co Down BT22 1P
Map no: 1 D5
Tel: 012477 28231
Chef: Anne Truesdale
Proprietors: John & Marie Herlihy
Cost: *Alc* £25, fixed-price L £13.50 (4 course)/D £18.50 (4 course). H/wine £9 Service exc
Credit Cards: 🔳 🔳 🔳 🔳 OTHER
Times: Last L 2.30pm, last D 9pm Closed Dec 24/25

SCOTLAND
BORDERS

KELSO, **Sunlaws House Hotel** ❀❀

Aristocratic surroundings in which to enjoy hearty helpings of good quality cooking

Heiton
Roxburghshire TD5 8JZ
Map no: 12 NT73
Tel: 01573 450331
Chef: David Bates
Proprietor: Duke of Roxburghe
(Pride of Britain).
Manager: David Webster
Cost: Fixed-price L £10 &
£12.50/D £23 & £27. H/wine
£13.50 Service exc
Credit cards: ▨ ▧ ▨ ▨ OTHER
Times: Last L 2pm, last D
9.30pm
Menus: Fixed-price L & D,
country lunch
Seats: 40. No smoking in dining
room
Additional: Children welcome,
children's menu; ❤ dishes/
vegan/other diets on request

Two hundred acres of riverside woodland and gardens surround this fine ducal mansion, owned by the Duke of Roxburghe. Despite its aristocratic associations, the atmosphere is by no means stiff: staff are friendly and attentive to the shooting parties, fishermen, tourists and business executives, and a warm ambience is created by blazing log fires in season and by hearty portions of food served in the dining-room. While not extensive, the fixed-price menus are carefully chosen and change daily, lunch representing particularly good value for money. First courses may include marinated red snapper, egg cocotte and smoked haddock and leek bavarois. On an inspection visit, a pan-fried fillet of Angus beef was impressive, cooked exactly to order, succulent and flavoursome. Lime and lemon posset, chocolate truffles and caramelized pear have been recent puddings. There is an extensive wine list, including some half bottles.

Directions: On the A698, 3 miles south of Kelso in Heiton village

MELROSE, **Burt's Hotel** ❀

☺ *A former coaching inn, this well-established, family-run hotel on the market square is a popular place. Interesting dishes are served in both bar and restaurant. At inspection warm monkfish salad, rack of lamb on stir-fried vegetables and bavarois were all enjoyed*

Menus: *A la carte,* fixed-price L & D, bar menu
Seats: 50. No smoking in dining room
Additional: Children permitted, children's portions; ❤ dishes,
vegan/other diets on request
Directions: Centre of Melrose

Roxburghshire TD6 9PN
Map no: 12 NT53
Tel: 01896 822285
Chef: Gary Moore
Proprietor: Graham Henderson.
Manager: Nick Henderson
Cost: Alc £25, fixed-price
L £13.95/D £21 H/wine £9.80
Service exc
Credit cards: ▨ ▧ ▨ ▨ OTHER
Times: Last L 1.45pm, last D
9pm/9.30 Fri & Sat Closed Dec
26

PEEBLES, **Cringletie House Hotel** ✿

A fine baronial-style hotel, family-run, where a great effort is made over the food. The menu changes daily, with the emphasis on traditional country house cooking, but the dishes are innovative. Pumpkin and coconut soup really catches the eye, and apricot cheesecake comes highly recommended

Peeblesshire EH45 8PL
Map no: 11 NT24
Tel: 01721 730233
Chefs: Sheila McKellar and Paul Maguire
Proprietor: S L Maguire
Cost: *Alc* L £13, fixed-price D £25.50/Sun L £15.50. H/wine £11.50 Service inc
Credit cards: ▨ ▩ ▧ OTHER
Times: Last L 1.45pm, last D 8.30pm
Menus: *A la carte,* fixed-price D & Sun L
Seats: 56. No smoking in dining room
Additional: Children welcome, children's portions; ✔ dishes, vegan/other diets on request. No smoking in dining room

Directions: 2.5 miles north of Peebles on A703

SWINTON, **Wheatsheaf Hotel** ✿

A welcoming country inn, where a loyal following eat in either the atmospheric pine and stone clad restaurant or the cosy cottage-style lounge. Both blackboard and carte reflect seasonal availability of high quality produce in well executed dishes such as braised oxtail and seafood stew

Berwickshire TD11 3JJ
Map no: 12 NT84
Tel: 01890 860257
Chef: Alan Reid
Proprietors: Alan & Julie Reid
Cost: *Alc* £12.50-£25, fixed-price D on request. H/wine £8.45 ▮ Service exc
Credit cards: ▨ ▩
Times: Last L 2.15pm, last D 9.30pm Closed Sun D, Mon, last 2 wks Feb, last wk Oct

Menus: *A la carte* L & D, fixed-price D on request, bar menu
Seats: 26+18+12. No pipes or cigars in dining rooms
Additional: Children welcome (over 8 at D), children's portions; ✔ dishes, vegan/other diets on request
Directions: On B6461 between Kelso & Berwick-on-Tweed

WALKERBURN,
Tweed Valley Hotel ✿

☺ *A long established family-run hotel. The attractive oak-panelled restaurant is at the heart of the hotel offering a carte of Scottish inspired dishes. Fish from the hotel's own smokery, freshly baked bread and puddings are specialities. The restaurant staff are young and enthusiastic*

Galashiels Road EH43 6AA
Map no: 11 NT53
Tel: 01896 870636
Chef: Keith Miller
Proprietors: Charles, Joyce & Keith Miller
Cost: *Alc* £19.75, fixed-price L £8.50-£10.50/D £19. H/wine £10.50 No service charge
Credit cards: ▨ ▩ ▧ OTHER
Times: Last L 2pm, last D 9.30pm Closed Dec 25/6

Menus: *A la carte,* fixed-price L & D, bar menu
Seats: 30-40. No smoking in dining room
Additional: Children welcome, children's menu; ✔ dishes, vegan/other diets on request
Directions: A72 between Galashiels & Peebles at E end of village

CENTRAL

ABERFOYLE, **Braeval** ❀❀❀

Popular chef Nick Nairn continues to woo guests to his converted mill with set dinners expertly created from quality produce

Nick Nairn is now established as one of Scotland's brightest chefs and is very much in demand for talks and cookery demonstrations. Nevertheless, he maintains what is effectively a one-man operation from the compact kitchen of this converted mill just outside Aberfoyle. He continues to offer a set fixed-price menu, its content being explained to guests as they relax over aperitifs and canapés; any dislikes they may have will have been established at the time of booking.

One spring evening our inspector began a meal with a fairly mild chilli and parsnip soup garnished with croûtons and shaved Parmesan cheese. Rich chicken liver pâté was accompanied by a thick, sweet Cumberland sauce and a mixed leaf salad containing avocado, then a fillet of halibut with mussels, tomatoes and spring greens, artistically presented with a crisply topped tower of dauphinoise potatoes. A crème brûlée was slightly marred by part of the caramelised topping being burnt, but the texture was smooth and firm and there was evidence of vanilla seeds. Good filter coffee came with the traditional home-made 'tablet'.

A reasonably representative wine list covers the popular growing areas and includes both some good house selections and a realistic choice of half bottles. Surroundings, like service, are pleasant, fine glassware and table linen further enhancing the appeal of the flagged, stone-walled dining-room with its wood-burning stove. All in all, dining here is a delightful, relaxing experience.

Directions: On A81 Callander road 1 mile from Aberfoyle

Stirlingshire FK8 3UY
Map no: 11 NN50
Tel: 01877 382711
Chef: Nick Nairn
Proprietors: Nick & Fiona Nairn
Cost: Fixed-price Sun L £18.95
(4 course)/D £28.50 (4 course).
H/wine £12 ❢ Service exc
Credit cards: ▨ ▧ OTHER
Times: Last Sun L 1.30pm, last D 9.30pm Closed Mon
Menus: Fixed-price D & Sun L
Seats: 34. No smoking until coffee
Additional: Children over 10 permitted; other diets prior notice

BALQUHIDDER, **Monachyle Mhor** ❀❀

☺ *Surprisingly accomplished cooking in isolated, charmingly rustic farmhouse*

The converted farmhouse stands miles from anywhere at the loch head of a beautiful Trossachs glen. Nonetheless, many are happy to make the trek here to enjoy Jean Lewis' exemplary cooking. Both the three-course menus offer excellent value, whether at £16 or £20. Orders are taken in the lively small bar and most meals served in the front-of-house extension, which makes the most of the splendid views. Dinner starts with crusty, home-baked brown bread, served with generous amounts of lightly salted butter. A starter of roast quail set on red cabbage was tender and strong in flavour and combined well with a tangy apple chutney. Accurately cooked scallops with spring onion and ginger, served on a bed of squid tagliatelle, was as good as to be found anywhere. Vegetables are fresh and abundant. Our inspector, though, was truly taken with his innovative pudding – 'one of the best this year', was the enthusiastic report. Described as bread and butter soufflé, it was melt-in-the-mouth light, with all the right flavours to round off a highly enjoyable meal.

Directions: A84 11 miles N of Callander turn right at Kingshouse Hotel

Perthshire FK19 8PQ
Map no: 11 NN52
Tel: 01877 384622
Chef: Jean Lewis
Proprietors: Robert & Jean Lewis
Cost: Fixed-price L £15/D £18 & £22 (4 course). H/wine £8.25 Service exc
Credit cards: ▨
Times: Last L 2pm, last D 9pm
Menus: Fixed-price L & D, bar menu
Seats: 30. No smoking in dining room
Additional: Children permitted at L; ♥ menu, other diets on request

BRIDGE OF ALLAN, **Royal Hotel** ✿

☺ *A business and conference hotel situated on the main street of the village. The menu roams the world with oriental samosas, Texas nachos and tagliatelle carbonara, but Scotland gets a look in. Try Loch Fyne mussels as a starter, followed by Highland venison and apricot casserole*

Menus: A la carte, fixed-price L & D, bar menu
Seats: 80
Additional: Children welcome, children's portions; ❤ menu, vegan/other diets on request
Directions: Village centre, 2 miles from Stirling, 1 mile from M9

Henderson Street
Stirlingshire FK9 4HG
Map no: 11 NS79
Tel: 01786 832284
Chef: Stewart Harrow
Proprietor: Aristo Hotels.
Manager: David A Kerr
Cost: Alc £18.95, fixed-price L £9.50/D £16.95 H/wine £9.10
❢ Service exc
Credit cards: 🔳 🔳 🔳 🔳 OTHER
Times: Last L 2.30pm, last D 9.30pm

CALLANDER, **Lubnaig Hotel** ✿

A charming small hotel with a kitchen offering carefully prepared dishes based on fresh ingredients. Unfortunately, only hotel guests can be catered for. Typical dishes include pancake stuffed with smoked trout pâté, celery and Stilton soup, and steak and pigeon pie with bacon, mushroom and red wine

Leny Feus
Perthshire FK17 8AS
Map no: 11 NN60
Tel: 01877 330376
Chef: Susan Low
Proprietors: Crawford & Sue Low
Cost: Fixed-price D £18 (4 course). H/wine £10. Service exc
Credit cards: 🔳 🔳
Times: Rest. open to residents only. Last D 8pm. Closed mid Nov-Mar
Menu: Fixed-price D
Seats: 20. No smoking in dining room
Additional: Children over 7 welcome, children's portions; ❤ /other diets prior notice

Directions: Through Callander to western outskirts, right to Leny Feus

CALLANDER, **Roman Camp Hotel** ✿✿

An historic house in a picturesque setting serving accomplished and imaginative food

The entrance to the drive of this 17th-century hunting lodge is located between two cottages on the main road through town. Set in 20 acres of wooded and lawned grounds, including an historic walled garden, the hotel looks out over the river Teith. Within, the candlelit restaurant disguises its relatively modern origins, the ceiling decorated with 16th-century Scottish designs and engraved with Robbie Burns' 'Selkirk Grace'. Chef Simon Burns uses the best of Scottish produce to create imaginative dishes that show a keen awareness of what is currently fashionable. At a recent meal, for example, chicken and wood pigeon terrine was followed by a clear burgundy beetroot consommé – the latest 'in' vegetable. Baked salmon came next, served on crisp asparagus spears. Extras

Perthshire FK17 8BG
Map no: 11 NN60
Tel: 01877 330003
Chef: Simon Burns
Proprietors: n/a.
Manager: Eric M Brown
Cost: Alc £40, fixed-price L £13.50 (2 courses) & £19/D £34 (4 course). H/wine £12 Service exc
Credit cards: 🔳 🔳 🔳 🔳 OTHER
Times: Last L 2pm, last D 9pm
Menus: A la carte, fixed-price L & D
Seats: 45. No smoking in the dining-room

such as sorbets and canapés do not leave much room for pudding, but our inspector managed to enjoy a caramelised pear and shortbread gâteau. The wine list has a pronounced French bias.

Directions: Turn left into driveway at east end of Callander main street

DUNBLANE, **Cromlix House Hotel** ✿✿

Stylish modern Scottish cooking in elegantly furnished period residence

Anyone who thinks that haggis eating is, at best, an acquired taste and, at worst, something that should be left to the natives, will be converted by the warm haggis beignets served along with the aperitifs. It's a clever touch, typical of chef Stephen Robertson's polished style. The five-course set menu is concise but, nonetheless, full of appeal and balance. Few could fail to appreciate an exceptionally fine ravioli of guinea fowl and wild mushrooms in a mustard sauce, or a smooth, deeply flavoured asparagus soup. Breast of Norfolk duck, offset by a prune gravy, was accurately cooked pink, although the quality of the meat could, perhaps, have been of a higher grade. No quibbles about the dessert – a dariole moulded bread and butter pudding, so light as to mimic a soufflé, served with a rich, real custard. The wine list offers a selection of considerable quality, and the smartly uniformed table staff are both alert and genuinely friendly. Highly polished surfaces and sparkling cut glass and silverware all add to the highly enjoyable experience of dining in this elegant Edwardian house.

Directions: 3 miles NE of Dunblane. From A9 take B8033 turning to Kinbuck, through village, 2nd left after small bridge

GRANGEMOUTH, **Grange Manor Hotel** ✿

☺ *A business hotel where Eric Avenier's effort in the kitchen is attracting wide local interest. The menu emphasises fresh produce and runs to game terrine served with pine nut and balsamic dressing, chicken stuffed with scallop and salmon mousse, and profiteroles with coffee cream*

Directions: M9 exit 6 200m on right, M9 exit 5/A905 2 miles

Additional: Children welcome (over 3 at D), children's menu; ☻ menu, vegan/other diets on request

Kinbuck
Nr Stirling
Perthshire FK15 9JT
Map no: 11 NN70
Tel: 01786 822125
Chef: Stephen Robertson
Proprietors: David & Ailsa Assenti (Pride of Britain)
Cost: Fixed-price lunch £17 (2 courses), £24; fixed-price dinner £35. H/wine £11. Service exc
Credit cards: 🔲 🔲 🔲 🔲
Times: 12.30pm-Last L 1.15pm, 7pm-Last D 8.30pm. Sat & Sun Lunch only served Oct-Mar. Closed mid Jan-mid Feb
Menus: Fixed-price L & D, Sunday lunch
Seats: 40, 22. No smoking in dining rooms
Additional: Children permitted (over 8 at dinner); children's portions; ☻ menu, vegan/other diets on request

Glensburgh Road FK3 8XJ
Map no: 11 NS98
Tel: 01324 474836
Chef: Christopher Lafferty
Proprietor: W M Wallace
Cost: Alc £16-£27, fixed-price L £10.50/D £17.50 H/wine £8.65 Service exc
Credit cards: 🔲 🔲 🔲 🔲 OTHER
Times: Noon-last L 2.30pm, 7pm-last D 9pm/10pm Fri & Sat Closed Dec 26, 1st wk Jan
Menus: A la carte, fixed-price L & D, bar menu
Seats: 70. No-smoking area
Additional: Children welcome, children's portions; ☻ dishes, vegan/other diets on request

PORT OF MENTEITH, **Lake Hotel** ❀❀

A unique location for traditional cuisine given an imaginative spin

Perthshire FK8 3RA
Map no: 11 NN50
Tel: 01877 385 258
Chef: Stuart Morrison
Proprietor: J L Leroy.
Manager: Douglas Little
Cost: *Alc* £22, fixed-price L £12
(Sun £15.95)/D £21.90 (4
- course). H/wine £8. Service exc
Credit cards: 🆒 🆒 OTHER
Times: Last L 2pm, last D 8.30pm
Menus: *A la carte,* fixed-price
L & D
Seats: 30
Additional: Children permitted
at L, children's portions; ❶
menu, other diets on request

The shore of Scotland's only lake is the setting for this attractive
art-deco hotel. Stunning views of Inchmahome Priory (where Mary,
Queen of Scots took refuge) radiate from the windows of the
conservatory restaurant. Here, chef Stuart Morrison's imaginatively
presented dishes, served by friendly and highly professional staff,
are based on fresh Scottish produce. The fixed-price menu includes
warm pigeon salad, game terrine and, as sampled at a recent meal,
chicken and herb terrine on a tomato and mint sauce. A soup or
sorbet is offered between first and second courses – on this occasion
a refreshing sweet apple sorbet. Main courses may feature fillet of
cod with citrus couscous, salmon with ratatouille and mashed
potato and beef fillet with horseradish sabayon accompanied by
roast shallots and bacon. This was complemented by a simple
selection of fresh vegetables. A light flaky pastry filled with creamy
custard and plums made an excellent finale, though the home-made
petits fours are worth leaving room for. The wine list shows a good
selection of vintages and countries of origin.

Directions: On the A873 in Port of Monteith

STIRLING,
Stirling Highland Hotel ❀❀

☺ *An historic setting for accomplished French/Scottish cooking*

Imaginatively converted from the old High School and retaining
much of that building's original features, this hotel is set high above
the town, close to the castle, yet just five minutes walk from the
centre. Its quadrangle design houses two dining areas: Rizzio's, a
cheery trattoria on two levels, and the more formal Scholars, the
main restaurant. Here chef Kieran Grant displays his skilful
French/Scottish cooking, offering starters such as warm salad of
wood pigeon and smoked salmon – smoked over whisky cask
chippings – from the Summer Isles. Main courses may include
breast of Grampian chicken, mille-feuille of filo pastry and ragout
of west coast shellfish. Sauces are particularly good; our inspector

Spittal Street
Stirlingshire FK8 1DU
Map no: 11 NS79
Tel: 01786 475444
Chef: Kieran Grant
Proprietor: Scottish Highland.
Manager: Chris Hansen
Cost: *Alc* £25-£30, fixed-price
L £10.95/D £21.50. H/wine
£10.45. Service exc
Credit cards: 🆒 🆒 🆒 🆒 OTHER
Times: Last L 2pm, last D
9.30pm. Closed Sun D
Menus: *A la carte,* fixed-price
L & D
Seats: 70. No smoking in dining
room

very much enjoyed a ravioli served with Noilly Prat sauce. Desserts are a feature of the *carte*. There is an extensive wine list from most major producing areas and a selection of halves.

Directions: In the road leading to Stirling Castle – follow Castle signs

STRATHYRE, **Creagan House** ❀

☺ *An attractive former farmhouse, with views across a river valley, is now a restaurant with rooms. It has an awe-inspring dining hall where patron/chef Gordon Gunn serves original dishes created with flair, imagination and skill*

Menus: A la carte, fixed-price D & Sun L
Seats: 15. No smoking in dining room
Additional: Children permitted (over 10 at D), children's portions; other diets prior notice
Directions: On A84, 0.25 miles north of the village

Additional: Children welcome, children's portions; ❶ dishes, vegan/other diets on request

Callander, Central FK18 8ND
Map no: 11 NN51
Tel: 01877 384638
Chef: Gordon A Gunn
Proprietors: Gordon & Cherry Gunn
Cost: Alc £21, fixed-price D £16.50/Sun L £14.50. H/wine £8.50 ❶ Service exc
Credit cards: 🔳 🔳 🔳
Times: Last L 1pm, last D 8.30pm. Closed Feb, 1 wk Oct

DUMFRIES & GALLOWAY

AUCHENCAIRN, **Collin House** ❀❀❀

A short menu, but accomplished cooking served with tender loving care at this pretty, pink Georgian house

Castle Douglas
Kirkcudbrightshire DG7 1QN
Map no: 11 NX75
Tel: 01556 640292
Chef: John Wood
Proprietors: Pam Hall and John Wood
Cost: Fixed-price (L £10.50 Residents only)/D £28 (4/5 course). H/wine £8 ❶ Service exc
Credit cards: 🔳 🔳
Times: D 7.30pm for 8pm Closed Jan 1-1st w/e in Mar
Menus: Fixed-price D (Non-residents must book)
Seats: 16. No smoking in dining room

Pam Hall and John Wood have firmly established themselves over the past five years at this little Georgian gem of an hotel. It can be recognised by its pink facade, sitting pretty on the hillside and enjoying magnificent views across Auchencairn Bay. The dining room seats only 16, so non-residents must be sure to book for what is bound to be a memorable dining experience. The co-proprietors operate with minimal staff – he in the kitchen, she front-of-house – and their good-natured hospitality makes for an eminently relaxing atmosphere. The set-price menu offers only two choices at each course, but the dishes are well-chosen and make full use of the local ingredients, demonstrating a creditable seriousness of culinary purpose.

An inspection meal in May started with perfectly cooked scallops on a julienne of vegetables, with beurre blanc; a simple dish that is easy to get wrong, but this was just right. Mussel and saffron soup is something of a trademark, but the spicy, slightly curried parsnip soup offered on this occasion was smooth, creamy and subtly flavoured. Fillet of sea bass with its own mousseline on a bed of fennel and wild basil scented juices is another signature dish which is beautifully presented and accurately cooked – the mousseline providing a textural contrast to the gently flaky fish. The crispy lattice of celeriac and potato served with it was especially appreciated. For pudding, Apple Brown Betty was the nursery favourite of apple baked with brown sugar, cinnamon and Calvados with a crusty breadcrumb topping. There is also a resolutely local selection of cheeses.

The concise wine list is presented in an adapted photo album, with tasting notes that come in handy when discussing the less familiar names, and includes ample choice for under £15.

Directions: Signposted right turn off A711 1 mile E of Auchencairn

Additional: Children over 11 permitted; other diets by arrangement

MOFFAT,
Beechwood Hotel ❀

☺ *The candlelit dining-room of this charming Victorian villa is the setting for some imaginative and good value cooking. Fixed-price menus roam the world for dishes such as lamb samosas, pork curry and Scottish fillet steak*

Menus: Fixed-price L & D **Seats:** 20. No smoking **Additional:** Children welcome, children's portions; ✪ dishes/other diets on request **Directions:** N end of High Street turn right into Harthorpe Place, hotel signed

Harthorpe Place
Dumfriesshire DG10 9RS
Map no: 11 NT00
Tel: 01683 220210
Chef: Carl S Shaw
Proprietor: J P Rogers
Cost: Fixed-price L £13.50
(4 course)/D £21 (6 course).
H/wine £8.75 ❢ Service exc
Credit cards: ▨ ▨ ▨
Times: Last L 2pm, last D 9pm.
Closed Jan 2-Feb 15

MOFFAT, Well View Hotel ❀❀

☺ *A small, homely hotel serving modern Scottish cooking with a strong French influence*

A delightful Victorian house overlooking the town and named after one of the sulphurous wells that made it famous for a while as a spa. It is owned and personally run by the Schuckardts – John, who looks after front-of-house, and Janet, who cooks. Dinner, preceded by canapés, is good value, consisting of five courses, including home-made sorbet and a selection of fine cheeses. There are four or five starters, such as brioche filled with lardons and mushrooms in a herb and garlic cheese sauce, or carrot and apricot soup. Then comes the sorbet followed by one of the three main courses, perhaps – to take one day's menu at random – medallions of venison with a wild cherry sauce, escalope of pork fillet with an apricot farce and a flambé sauce, or lemon sole with an orange and watercress sauce. Sauces are a key note. Meat is served pink and vegetables crisp, unless the kitchen is requested otherwise. The delicious sweets are home-made and coffee and sweetmeats are served in the lounge. The wine list has been carefully selected and offers a wide range from all major areas.

Directions: From Moffat take A708 (Selkirk) turn L after fire station, hotel is 300 yds

Ballplay Road
Dumfriesshire DG10 9JU
Map no: 11 NT00
Tel: 01683 20184
Chef: Janet Schuckardt
Proprietors: Janet & John
Schuckardt
Cost: Fixed-price L £13/D £24
(4 course). H/wine £8.75 ❢ No
service charge
Credit cards: ▨ ▨ ▨
Times: Last L 1.30pm/last D
8.30pm. Closed Sat L
Menus: Fixed-price L & D
Seats: 24. No smoking in dining
room
Additional: Children welcome
(over 5 at dinner); children's
portions & high tea, ✪ dishes/
other diets on request

NEWTON STEWART,
Kirroughtree Hotel ❀❀

Highly acclaimed modern cooking in a luxurious and elegant setting

Set in eight acres of landscaped gardens, Kirroughtree is a majestic 18th-century mansion, now converted into a luxurious country house hotel. It occupies a fine elevated position and commands superb views over the Galloway countryside. Flanking the elegant main lounge are two resplendent dining-rooms, one red, the other blue, suitable backdrops to the acclaimed dishes of chef Ian Bennett. Cooking is modern British in style, presented on a four-course daily-changing set menu, usually with a choice of three dishes. These may include andouille of smoked salmon and brill and ravioli of lobster and, among main courses, tournedos of venison and breast of Barbary duck. Typical of the home-made puddings offered are iced nougat glace and panaché of pistachio, caramel and vanilla ice-cream. A shorter menu is offered at lunchtime. Several outstanding wines appear on the list, as do more modest bottles at very affordable prices.

Directions: From A75, turn onto A712 (New Galloway), hotel entrance is 300 yds on left

Minnigaff
Wigtownshire DG8 6AN
Map no: 10 NX46
Tel: 01671 402141
Chef: Ian Bennett
Proprietor: McMillan Hotels.
Manager: James Stirling
Cost: Fixed-price L £12/D £27.50 (4 course). H/wine £10. Service inc
Credit cards:
Times: Last L 1.30pm, last D 9pm. Closed Jan 3-mid Feb
Menus: Fixed-price L & D,
Seats: 50. No smoking in dining room
Additional: Children permitted; ❷ dishes, other diets on request

PORTPATRICK,
Knockinaam Lodge ❀❀❀

Increasingly individual cooking in a remote, but idyllic location overlooking the Irish Sea

Wigtownshire DG9 9AD
Map no: 10 NW95
Tel: 01776 810471
Chef: Stuart Muir
Proprietors: Michael Bricker & Pauline Ashworth (Pride of Britain)
Cost: Fixed-price D £32. H/wine £11 Service exc
Credit cards: 🔲 🔲 🔲 🔲
Times: Last L 2pm, high tea 6pm, last D 9.30pm
Menus: Fixed-price D, bar menu, children's high tea
Seats: 35. No smoking in dining room

New owners have been very quick to inject their own enthusiasm in the running of this remote, but superbly situated hotel. It sits on its own beach, surrounded on three sides by cliffs and overlooks the Irish Sea. The French has been dropped from Stuart Muir's daily-changing menus, which are now in plain English and restrict choice to two dishes per course, allowing the chef to concentrate on displaying his considerable imagination and artistry.

Our inspector had some misgivings about the combination of scallops with a pineapple butter sauce, but all doubts were swept aside by what turned out to be a very effective liaison; the succulent scallops barely cooked, encased in light pastry and set upon a bed of spinach, with the fruity sauce lending a welcome touch of tartness to the dish. This was followed by a fillet of halibut steamed in Champagne and served with a potato purée seasoned with olive oil and garlic, a light and delicate combination with the perfectly-cooked fish being garnished with fine strips of leek and asparagus. Judicious portioning leaves ample room for desserts, which are uniformly splendid. A warm chocolate tartlet with a creamy cappuccino sauce was described as 'lovely'. Details such as warm and freshly-baked bread rolls, home made crisps served with aperitifs and petits fours with coffee, are commendable, as is the pleasant service from cheerful lasses with local accents.

The voluminous and profusely-annotated wine list is quite remarkable, but makes for such exhaustive reading that it's as well to ask for directions from the omnipresent host and head gardener, Michael Bricker. He is also happy to arrange post prandial tours through an ever-growing collection of malt whiskies.

Additional: Children welcome (over 12 after 6pm), children's portions; ❷ dishes, vegan/other diets on request

Directions: Turn left off A77 (Stranraer to Portpatrick) 3 miles south of Portpatrick on a well-signposted lane

FIFE

ANSTRUTHER, **Cellar Restaurant** ❀❀❀

An excellent range of fresh, locally caught seafood is, as one would expect, the strength of this unpretentious restaurant in a fishing village

Tucked away among narrow side streets, close to the harbour front of this picturesque fishing village, The Cellar continues – justifiably – to be one of the most popular restaurants in this part of Fife. Meals are served on tables converted from old Singer sewing machines, and a cosy atmosphere is created by the real fire which burns at one end of the room. Fresh local seafood is still Peter Jukes' speciality, on both the lunchtime *carte* and fixed-price three or four-course dinner menus. Starters alone might offer quiche of lobster and smoked sea-trout, a small omelette filled with creamy smoked haddock, crayfish and mussel bisque gratinée, locally dressed crab and a trio of cured Shetland salmon. Among the main courses, grilled suprême of prime East Neuk halibut, simply flavoured with citrus juices and served with hollandaise sauce vies for attention alongside collops of monkfish, peeled langoustine tails and Isle of Man scallops roasted with spiced herb and garlic butter, or – our inspector's choice – pan-fried tuna with caramelised onions, oyster mushrooms and Madeira pan juices. This was preceded by a rich, smooth liver parfait with red onion relish, with a layered chocolate mousse partnered by real vanilla sauce to finish. Though the quality of meat dishes is excellent, their range is limited to such staples as roast loin of Perthshire lamb with a Dijon mustard and herb crust, or medallions of beef fillet with green peppercorn sauce. No accusation of brevity could possible be levelled, however, at the vast and predominantly French wine list, now revised and even more impressive; allow yourself plenty of time to peruse it. Interesting labels include a Bekka Valley Chateau Musar, 1981 and 1985, from the Lebanon, and there is a good selection of ports.

24 East Green KY10 3AA
Map no: 12 NO50
Tel: 01333 310378
Chef: Peter Jukes
Proprietor: Peter Jukes
Cost: A/c L £13.50, fixed-price D £28.50-£32.50. H/wine £12.95 ❗ Service exc
Credit cards: ▨ ▩ ▨
Times: Last L 1.30pm, last D 9.30pm. Closed Sun, Mon, 1 wk Nov, Xmas
Menus: A la carte L, fixed-price D
Seats: 30. No smoking in dining room
Additional: Children permitted at L, children's portions; ❷ dishes, vegan/other diets on request

Directions: Behind the Scottish Fisheries Museum

FLETCHER RESTAURANT

CUPAR, Ostlers Close Restaurant ❀❀❀

Imaginative use is made of local produce by the enthusiastic proprietors of this unpretentious restaurant

Simple and unadorned, its distressed walls and candlelit wooden tables complemented by understated wild flower arrangements, this value-for-money restaurant has been run by Jimmy and Amanda Graham for more than ten years. Not only is their enthusiasm undiminished, but they have also built up a clientele so loyal that they often contribute to the produce which appears on the frequently changing short *carte* of modern British dishes; Jimmy himself remains an inveterate gatherer, still making dawn raids on secret woodland locations to collect mushrooms and other wild food.

One cold evening in March, our inspector very much appreciated a starter – a variation on Cullen Skink – of deliciously browned smoked haddock set on creamed potatoes and surrounded by a smooth sauce skilfully created from reduced fish stock. This was followed by a selection of game including pigeon, wild duck and venison, served with a tasty jus and a mound of puy lentils and wild mushrooms. The array of imaginatively presented (if slightly over-elaborate) seasonal vegetables that accompanied this was impressive, offering sliced peppered potatoes in pastry, a sandwich of turnip and mashed swede, red and spring cabbage with caraway seeds to flavour, broccoli and leeks topped with melted mozzarella and breadcrumbs, and carrots sweated in white wine. Perhaps by comparison with this, the meal ended rather disappointingly, the chocolate mousse being a little heavy and slightly stewed Cona coffee was unaccompanied by any kind of petits fours, but this may well have been a temporary lapse. The recently updated wine list provides a good selection. Service is friendly and informed, the owners obviously enjoying the opportunity to discuss their food.

Directions: In small lane off main street (A91) of Cupar

Bonneygate KY15 4BU
Map no: 11 NO31
Tel: 01334 655574
Chef: James Graham
Proprietors: James & Amanda Graham
Cost: *Alc* L £15/D £25. H/wine £8 ¶ Service exc
Credit cards: ▨ ▩ ▧ OTHER
Times: Last L 2pm, last D 9.30pm Closed Sun. Mon
Menus: *A la carte* L & D
Seats: 30. No smoking in dining room
Additional: Children welcome (over 6 at D), children's portions; ❤ dishes, vegan/ other diets on request

DUNFERMLINE, Keavil House Hotel ❀

Popular, rurally located hotel which dates in part from the 16th century. Adventurous cooking is to be had in the conservatory restaurant. Look out for courgette and Brie soup, fresh crab wrapped in smoked salmon with a dill and Arran mustard sauce and Tay salmon with nettle cream sauce

Directions: Two miles west of Dunfermline on A994

Crossford KY12 8QW
Map no: 11 NT19
Tel: 01383 736258
Chef: Volker Steinemann
Proprietor: Town and Country Hotels Ltd (Best Western)
Credit cards: ▨ ▩ ▧ ▣ OTHER
Time: Last D 9pm

ELIE, Bouquet Garni Restaurant ❀❀

Technical accuracy and inspired flavour combinations make innovative cooking successful in this popular restaurant

This cosy little restaurant goes from strength to strength. Not only does patron/chef Andrew Keracher use top quality ingredients, but his cooking is strong on accurate, distinctive flavours which he has the ability to combine imaginatively and successfully. Seafood figures prominently on the *carte*, and a first course of west coast scallops, sampled at a recent meal, was perfect. It was accompanied by an innovative orange and Noilly Pratt cream sauce, the zesty flavour of which complemented the scallops precisely. To follow,

51 High Street KY9 1BZ
Map no: 12 NO40
Tel: 01333 330374
Chef: Andrew Keracher
Proprietors: Norah & Andrew Keracher
Cost: *Alc* £23, fixed-price L £12.50 ¶ Service exc
Credit cards: ▨ ▩ ▧ OTHER
Times: Last L 2pm, last D 9.30pm. Closed Sun, 2nd & 3rd wks Jan

Bouquet Garni Restaurant

Menus: *A la carte,* fixed-price L
Seats: 50. No smoking in dining
room
Additional: Children permitted
(over 10 at D), children's
portions; other diets on request

saddle of venison had the edge over a loin of lamb in a duo of meats,
and finally an artistically presented degustation of puddings
consisted of a 'shortie' biscuit with butterscotch sauce, a brandy
basket and a white chocolate mousse. Like all the food here it was
light, delicate and despite the description, unfussy. Supper and lunch
menus are equally appealing and offer excellent value. The wine list
offers a good balance between French and New World bottles.

Directions: Village centre: from A915 (St Andrews) take the A917 to
Elie

GLENROTHES, **Rescobie Hotel** ✿

☺ *Enthusiastically run Edwardian country house hotel providing good*
food in a cosy atmosphere. Both the fixed-price menu and carte are
supplemented by steak and vegetarian dishes. At inspection a smooth
chicken liver parfait with a redcurrant and orange glaze was particularly
liked

Valley Drive
Leslie KY6 3BQ
Map no: 11 NO20
Tel: 01592 742143
Chef: Ian McEwen
Proprietor: Tony & Wendy
Hughes-Lewis
Cost: *Alc* £17.45-£24.65,
fixed-price D £16. H/wine £8.
Service exc
Credit cards: 🔲 🔲 🔲 🔲
Times: Last L 2pm/last D 9pm.
Closed Dec 24-26
Menus: *A la carte,* fixed-price D
Seats: 40. No-smoking area
Additional: Children welcome,
children's menu; ✆ menu,
other diets on request

Directions: At west end of Leslie village, turn S off A911

KINCARDINE-ON-FORTH,
The Unicorn Inn ●●

☺ *Mediterranean-style bistro no longer hiding its light under a bushel*

The 'on-Forth' suffix is not commonly applied, but it does distinguish this Kincardine from those in Grampian, Highland and Tayside. It might be a small, unassuming town, and the Unicorn might indeed be in a back street where an authentic Mediterranean atmosphere is unexpected, but chef/patron Douglas Mitch's split-level bistro works well. The daily-changing blackboard menu has a finger on the culinary pulse, making judicious use of chargrilling, herbs and spices. The kitchen's repertoire encompasses Catalan broth, steamed scallops and fresh ginger, or chargrilled haloumi cheese as starters, and some fine fish dishes, such as chargrilled red snapper, a medley of shellfish, and parcels of filleted sea-bass. Meats might include spiced fillet of beef with chillies, or open-roast sucking pig. Hearty Hungarian game broth can be recommended for its flavour and firm, tasty vegetable content, and Greek dorado, chargrilled and served with a powerful garlic mayonnaise. Accompanying vegetables are pan-fried with a touch of honey to give a sweet, almost caramelised touch. Desserts might include iced chocolate and brandy mousse, cranachan, or vanilla cheesecake with apricot and peach purée.

Directions: From S cross Kincardine Bridge 1st left, left again & 1st right

15 Excise Street FK10 4LN
Map no: 11 NS98
Tel: 01259 730704
Chefs: Douglas & Lesley Mitch
Proprietors: Douglas & Lesley Mitch
Cost: *Alc* £24.50, fixed-price L £6.50 (2 course). H/wine £9.95 Service exc.
Credit cards: 🔳 🔳 🔳
Times: Noon-last L 1.45pm, 6pm-last D 9.30pm Closed Sun L, Mon, 2 wks. July
Menus: *A la carte*, fixed-price L
Seats: 50. No-smoking area
Additional: Children welcome (over 5 after 7.30pm), children's portions; ❤ dishes, vegan/other diets on request

LUNDIN LINKS, Old Manor Hotel ●

Fine views over the golf-course and Fife coast line make a magnificent backdrop to a meal in the restaurant of this converted manor house. The kitchen prepares a mix of classically inspired dishes and makes good use of local produce such as asparagus spears in a puff pastry case, and baked fillet of salmon

Leven Road KY 8 6AL
Map no: 12 NO40
Tel: 01333 320368
Chef: Alun Brunt
Proprietor: Clark Family.
Manager: Alistair Clark
Cost: *Alc* from £25, fixed-price L £10.50 (2 course)/D £25 (4 course). H/wine £9.95 ! Service exc
Credit cards: 🔳 🔳 🔳 OTHER
Times: Noon-last L 2pm, 7pm-last D 9.30pm. Closed Dec 25 D, Jan 1
Menus: *A la carte*, fixed-price L & D, bar menu
Seats: 40. No smoking
Additional: Children welcome in Bistro only, children's menu; ❤ menu, other diets on request

Directions: On A915 Leven–St Andrews road in the village

MARKINCH, **Balbirnie House** ❀❀

A delightful setting made memorable by first-class Scottish cooking

Under the capable direction of Ian MacDonald, the kitchen brigade at Balbirnie House brings expertise to the preparation of every meal: guests enjoy carefully cooked breakfasts, old fashioned steak and kidney pudding for lunch and delicate pastries with afternoon tea. Dinner shows the kitchen working at its best, cooking food of a modern slant backed by fine local produce. Mixed seafood, for example, might be enlivened by the addition of spring onions and ginger, or a robust saddle of venison paired with pungent beetroot. Delicious appetisers – light but full of flavour – include tartlets of pheasant or prawn and avocado mousse, while such vegetables as hollandaise broccoli and battered courgettes avoid monotony without being over-fussy. Notable among the desserts is a light Drambuie mousse served in a crisp praline basket, drizzled with an intense raspberry coulis and topped with fine spun sugar. Cafetière coffee is served with attractive petits fours. The varied wine list that accompanies the meal has been carefully chosen, and an attentive staff provides professional service.

Directions: M90 exit 3/A92 (Glenrothes); turn right onto B9130 to Markinch and Balbirnie Park

Balbirnie Park KY7 6NE
Map no: 11 NO20
Tel: 01592 610066
Chef: Ian MacDonald
Proprietor: Alan Russell
Cost: *Alc* lunch £13.75, fixed-price D £25 (4 course)/Sun. L £13.75. H/wine £12.50 ❢
Service inc
Credit cards: 🔳 💳 💳 💳 OTHER
Times: Last L 2.30pm, last D 9.30pm
Menus: *A la carte* L, fixed-price D & Sun L, bar menu
Seats: 80+35. No-smoking in dining room
Additional: Children welcome, children's portions; ❷ menu, vegan/other diets on request

PEAT INN, **Peat Inn** ❀❀❀

Lovers of good food will drive a long way to sample the specialities of this village restaurant

Actually a restaurant with rooms, The Peat Inn bases its reputation firmly on the provision of excellent food. Two set menus supplemented by a *carte* provide a choice of attractively presented dishes – skilfully prepared in a blend of French and Scottish styles – that must surely contain something to tempt everyone. After a succulent cut of salmon topped with charred Thai spices and set on a smooth purée of celeriac, for example, you could enjoy full-flavoured saddle of venison, cooked pink and served with crunchy red cabbage, delicately turned new potatoes and a sauce of stock jus infused with bacon and wild mushrooms. Puddings include a platter of caramel desserts comprised of a miniature crème caramel, rich caramel ice-cream in a crisp almond basket and a mille-feuille of apples. Similarly, the tasting menu (which can only be ordered for a whole table) allows guests to sample slightly smaller portions of all the house specialities – perhaps lobster cake with scallops, smoked fish fillet with a chive sauce, julienne of pigeon breast on a confit of spiced pork, roast rack of lamb served with stewed shoulder in a thyme-flavoured sauce and, finally, a choice of cheese and/or dessert. Good espresso coffee is served with very acceptable petits fours, service is first-class. An outstanding wine list – richest in French labels, but also including prominent growers from Italy, Austria and California – was being updated as we went to press.

Directions: At junction of B940/B941 6 miles south-west of St Andrews

Cupar KY15 5LH
Map no: 12 NO40
Tel: 01334 84206
Chefs: David Wilson and Angus Blacklaws
Proprietors: David & Patricia Wilson
Cost: *Alc* £34, fixed-price L £18.50 (4 course)/D £28/£42 (4/6 course). H/wine £14 ❢
Service inc
Credit cards: 🔳 💳 💳 💳 OTHER
Times: Last L 1pm, last D 9.30pm Closed Sun, Mon, Dec 25, Jan 1
Menus: *A la carte*, fixed-price L & D
Seats: 48. No smoking in dining room
Additional: Children welcome, children's portions; ❷ dishes, vegan/other diets on request

ST ANDREWS,
Parkland Hotel ❀

Kinburn Castle
Double Dykes Road
Fife KY16 9DS
Map no: 12 NO51
Tel: 01334 73620
Chef: Brian J MacLennan
Proprietor: Brian J MacLennan
Cost: Alc £18.50, fixed-price L £10/D £18.50. H/wine £8.95
Service exc
Credit cards: 🔲 💳 OTHER
Times: Last L 2pm, last D 8.30pm Closed Sun D, Mon, Dec 25-27, Jan 1-3

☺ *At the heart of this well-maintained hotel on the west side of town is the restaurant which offers good value fixed- price and 'Menu en surprise' selections. Typical dishes have included seafood tartlette, Pittenweem dab soles and spicy chicken*

Menus: A la carte, fixed-price L & D
Seats: 50. No smoking in dining room
Additional: Children welcome, children's portions; other diets on request
Directions: West of town centre, opposite Kinburn Park

ST ANDREWS,
Rufflets Hotel ❀

Strathkinness Low Road
Fife KY 16 9TX
Map no: 12 NO51
Tel: 01334 472594
Chef: Robert Grindle
Proprietor: Ann Russell
Cost: Alc £15 min, fixed price L £15/D £25. H/wine £10 ▼
Service inc
Credit cards: 🔲 💳 💳 💳 OTHER
Times: Last L 2pm, last D 9pm
Menus: A la carte, fixed-price L & D, bar L menu
Seats: 80. No smoking in dining room
Additional: Children permitted, children's portions; ❤ dishes, other diets on request

In the Garden Restaurant, with views giving onto award-winning grounds, acclaimed modern Scottish cooking is presented in carte and set price menus. Poached roulade of sole, loin of venison and vegetarian ratatouille are sample dishes, supported by an international wine list

Directions: On B939 1.5 miles before St Andrews

ST ANDREWS,
St Andrews Golf Hotel ❀

40 The Scores KY16 9AS
Map no: 12 NO51
Tel: 01334 472611
Chef: Adam Harrow
Manager: Justin Hughes
Cost: Alc £28, fixed-price L £12/D £25 (4 course), H/wine £9.50 ▼ Service exc
Credit cards: 🔲 💳 💳 💳 OTHER
Times: Last L 2.30pm, last D 9.30pm

Wonderful views are to be had from this popular seafront golfing hotel. For many though, the main attraction is the proximity to the famous Old Course. The menu offers interesting choices, perhaps saddle of wild rabbit, or an 'enjoyable' salmon en-croûte with apple strudel for dessert

Menus: A la carte, fixed-price L & D, bar menu
Seats: 60 (Restaurant)+100 (Bistro). No smoking in dining room
Additional: Children welcome; children's menu; ❤ dishes, vegan/other diets on request
Directions: Entering St Andrews on A91 turn left at Golf Place & 1st right into The Scores, hotel 200 yards on right

ST ANDREWS,
St Andrews Old Course Hotel ❁❁

An interesting range of international dishes is served in 'the home of golf'

Golf enthusiasts the world over are attracted by this hotel's setting beside the famous 17th Road Hole of the championship golf course. The fourth-floor Road Hole Grill – whilst obviously capitalising on this proximity – is an attractive proposition in its own right. The imaginative dishes on the *carte*, 'Taste of Scotland' and gourmet menus, all show a kitchen that has not wavered in its ability to keep up with the times. Beetroot-flavoured pasta crackers filled with tender fried chicken livers, goats' cheese and olive oil cream, for example, made an original starter to a recent dinner. This was followed by grilled darne of Orkney salmon with braised salsify, pesto oil and crisp vegetables, then apple tart accompanied by cider ice-cream. For the health-conscious there are 'spa cuisine' dishes – nutritionally balanced and low in both cholesterol and sodium as well as calories – and during the summer season the conservatory offers an alternative, less formal eating option. Whatever you choose, a comprehensive, carefully selected list of fine wines from around the world will include a suitable accompaniment.

Directions: Situated close to the A91 on the outskirts of the city

Old Station Road KY16 9SP
Map no: 12 NO51
Tel: 01334 474371
Chef: Mark Barker
Proprietor: Old Course Hotel Ltd.
Manager: Patrick Elsmie
Cost: Fixed-price Sun L £16.50/D £32.50 (5 course) H/wine £14.50 ❗ Service exc
Credit cards: 🟦 ▦ ▦ 🟦
Times: Last D 10pm. Closed Christmas
Menus: Fixed-price D & Sun L, bar menu, gourmet menu
Seats: 80. Air conditioned
Additional: Children welcome, children's menu; ♥ menu, vegan/other diets on request

---

GRAMPIAN

ABERDEEN, **Ardoe House** ❁

A baronial mansion which is set in extensive parkland and reached by a tree-lined driveway. The menus provide a good and varied choice, and a typical meal could include chicken liver parfait, followed by a well presented chicken Wellington in a very alcoholic Burgundy sauce, with crème brulée for dessert

Seats: 65. No smoking in dining room **Menus:** *a la carte*, pre-theatre, bar menu **Additional:** Children welcome, children's menu; ♥ dishes, vegan/other diets on request
Directions: 3 miles from Aberdeen on B9007, on left hand side

Blairs, South Deeside Road Aberdeenshire AB1 5YP
Map no: 15 NJ90
Tel: 01224 867355
Chef: Ed Cooney
Proprietor: Macdonald.
Manager: Derek Walker
Cost: *Alc* £27.25, H/wine £11.95 Service exc
Credit cards: 🟦 ▦ ▦ 🟦 OTHER
Times: noon-last L 2.30pm, 6.30pm-last D 9.45pm

ARCHIESTOWN, **Archiestown Hotel** ❁❁

Country cooking full of robust flavours with an emphasis on fish

Judith and Michael Bulger and their small staff team take pains to ensure guests feel at home in their country hotel. With its relaxed atmosphere and informal bustle of fishermen (for the salmon on the River Spey), visitors would find it hard not to feel comfortable. The Victorian stone building has been sympathetically renovated to retain its character and increase its comfort; the dining-room is a delight. Here Judith presents good country cooking, with international influences, using the best seasonal and local produce available. Seafood is a speciality, with game also featuring on the menu. A short set price selection is offered in the dining-room; a more informal atmosphere can be found in the bistro where diners can

Morayshire AB38 7QX
Map no: 15 NJ24
Tel: 01340 810218
Chef: Judith Bulger
Proprietors: Judith & Michael Bulger
Cost: Fixed-price D £25. H/wine £10. Service exc
Credit cards: 🟦 ▦ ▦
Times: Last L 2pm, Last D 8.30pm. Closed mid Oct-mid Feb
Menus: Fixed-price D, Sun L, bar menu

enjoy the same dishes plus daily choices from a blackboard. Quality is assured and portions generous, as proved by an inspection meal of pigeon terrine followed by oxtail with port sauce, a dish full of honest, robust flavours. The wine list includes a section on clarets.

Directions: Turn off A95 at Craigellachie onto B9102

BALLATER,
Balgonie Hotel ❀❀

The best of Scotland's game, meat and seafood is used to good effect in the imaginative set-price menus of this country house hotel

Its preoccupation with every aspect of guests' well being makes this charming hotel really stand out from the rest. Chef David Hindmarch has played a key role in this achievement by creating a range of delicious French dishes which demonstrate both originality and flair. During the course of a typical dinner, lightly battered monkfish in a mustard-dressed salad might be followed by freshly made herb tagliatelle bound with a cream sauce and strips of salmon, then succulent fillet of lamb garnished with lambs' kidneys, oyster mushrooms and a rosemary jus. Just two choices – one hot, the other cold – are provided at the pudding stage, but a duo of white chocolate and dark chocolate mousse might provide a fitting conclusion. No detail is neglected: a selection of tempting canapés is offered with aperitifs, home-made bread rolls are served warm, and good cafétière coffee comes with petits fours. A well chosen, predominantly European wine list includes some which are sold by the glass as well as a selection of half bottles.

Directions: On outskirts of Ballater, off A93 (Braemar) near end of 30mph zone

Braemar Place AB35 5RQ
Aberdeenshire
Map no: 15 NO39
Tel: 013397 55482
Chef: David J Hindmarch
Proprietors: John & Priscilla Finnie
Cost: Fixed-price L £16.50 / D £27.50 (4 course). H/wine £13.50 ❢ Service exc
Credit cards: 🌑 💳 💳 OTHER
Times: Last L 1.45pm /D 9pm. Closed mid Jan-mid Feb
Seats: 25. No smoking in dining room
Additional: Children permitted, children's portions/other diets by arrangement

Seats: 25. No smoking in dining room
Additional: Children permitted, children's portions; ❤ dishes, other diets on request

BALLATER, Craigendarroch ❀❀

A well-equipped hotel, popular with families, offering a choice of restaurants and dining styles

A red sandstone mansion is at the heart of this hotel and country club complex. It nestles into the hillside, offering panoramic

Braemar Road
Aberdeenshire AB35 5XA
Map no: 15 NO39
Tel: 013397 55858
Chef: Eric Faussurier
Proprietor: Craigendarroch Ltd.
Manager: Eric Brown
Cost: *Alc* £27, fixed price L £17.50/D £27 (4 course) H/wine £11.75 ❢ No service charge
Credit cards: 🌑 💳 💳 💳 OTHER
Times: Last L 2.30pm, last D 9.45pm
Menus: *A la carte*, fixed-price L & D
Seats: 48. No smoking in dining room
Additional: Children over 8 welcome, children's menu; ❤ dishes, vegan/other diets on request

mountain and woodland views. Craigendarroch has extensive facilities for families, including a creche, adventure playground, indoor pool and gym. To cater for different tastes, there are three restaurants, each with its distinct style, from the informal Clubhouse next to the pool, to the Oaks situated in the main building. Here, chef Eric Faussurier's uses fresh ingredients imaginatively combined and well-presented. The fixed-price menu, with supplementary *carte*, features first courses such as roast duck and heather honey consommé, terrine of Deeside game and, enjoyed on a recent visit, roulade of lemon sole. This was followed by pink loin of lamb topped with morel mousseline and accompanied by carrot and broccoli timbale and crisp vegetables. The highlight of the meal was a creamy Drambuie parfait, well contrasted with a rich berry coulis. The extensive wine list offers a good choice of old and New World wines.

Directions: On A93 to Braemar, 0.5 mile from village centre

BALLATER, **Darroch Learg Hotel** ❀❀

Cooking of a particularly high quality in a country house hotel overlooking the River Dee and the mighty mountain of Lochnagar

If Lochnagar is the stuff of princes and fairy tales, then the cuisine at Darroch Learg is fit for kings and queens. Chefs Robert MacPherson and Philippe Wagenfuhrer have established an eclectic partnership which can sometimes produce quite outstanding cooking. On a quiet night, a special menu had been created, featuring an unusual starter of croûstillant of black pudding, rilette and apple. This was followed by a perfectly pan-fried piece of Shetland salmon, set on puy lentils in a light, carrot butter sauce. A very well crafted main course of a brace of boneless quail, stuffed with chicken, set on a slice of foie gras in an elderberry jelly juice, excelled in well-balanced ingredients, each retaining an individual flavour. After all this, a hot chocolate pudding may have seemed foolish, but not here; it was as light as a soufflé, and served with poached pears and real vanilla ice-cream. In our inspector's words, he 'scoffed the lot'. The wine list complements the menu well, offering good value for money, as well as all the popular wine growing areas.

Braemar Road
Aberdeenshire AB35 5UX
Map no: 15 NO39
Tel: 013397 55443
Chef: Robert MacPherson
Proprietors: Nigel Franks
Cost: Fixed-price Sun L
£12.75/D £23.75. H/wine £11
❗ Service inc
Credit cards: 🔷 ▨ ▨ 🔳 OTHER
Times: Last L 2pm, last
D8.30pm/9pm Fri & Sat Closed
Xmas
Menus: Fixed-price Sun L & D
Seats: 48. No smoking in dining room
Additional: Children welcome, children's portions; other diets on request

Directions: On A93 at the west end of village

BALLATER, **Green Inn** ❀❀

☺ *The combination of traditional recipes and superb fresh ingredients cannot fail to impress visitors to Scotland*

Service is outstandingly efficient at this restaurant with rooms which stands in the square of a Deeside village. Although there is an inviting lounge, most guests choose to have aperitifs served to their table. Chef/proprietor Jeff Purves brings out the best in Scottish meats, game and seafood, retaining their honest and distinctive flavours, and cheese buffs will appreciate an impressive range of regional varieties (served with oatcakes). For visitors to Scotland there will be something excitingly different about a starter of chicken and haggis sausage served on a bed of clapshot with mushroom and chive sauce, or spare rib of wild boar with a heather

9 Victoria Road
Aberdeenshire AB35 5QQ
Map no: 15 NO39
Tel: 013397 55701
Chef: J J Purves
Proprietors: Mr & Mrs Purves
Cost: *Alc* £22.75. H/wine £7.95
❗ Service exc
Credit cards: 🔷 ▨ ▨
Times: Last L 2pm, last D 9pm
Closed Sun from Nov-Mar, 2 wks. Dec
Seats: 32. Smoking restricted
Menus: *A la carte*

Green Inn

Additional: Children welcome, children's portions; 🕈 menu, vegan/other diets on request

honey and star-anise sauce. At the main course stage, too, one can sample the specialities of the area, perhaps baked sûpreme of salmon with creamed leeks and gravadlax sauce, or slightly underdone fillet of Aberdeen Angus set on creamed carrots and whole lentils and accompanied by a Sauternes and foie gras sauce. A predominantly straightforward wine list featuring a few interesting bottles will provide something to suit most tastes.

Directions: On A93 in centre of Ballater on the Green

BANCHORY, **Banchory Lodge Hotel** 🏵

Game, salmon and Aberdeen Angus feature regularly on the five-course menu offered at this popular riverside hotel. Traditional dishes could include fillet of beef Wellington, or honey roast duckling with orange sauce, with chicken liver pate and salmon mousse with spicy tomato coulis, to start

Menus: A la carte, fixed-price D & Sun L, bar L menu
Seats: 80-100. No cigars or pipes
Additional: Children welcome, children's menu; 🕈 dishes; vegan/other diets on request
Directions: 18 miles W of Aberdeen off A93 beside River Dee

Kincardineshire AB31 3HS
Map no: 15 NO69
Tel: 01330 822625
Chef: Miss E Cooper
Proprietors: Dugald & Margaret Jaffray
Cost: Alc £15, fixed-price D £25.50/Sun L £15.50 H/wine £8.50 ❢ Service inc
Credit cards: 🄰 📰 📰 💷 OTHER
Times: Last L 2pm, last D 9.30pm

BANCHORY, **Raemoir House Hotel** 🏵

A well-known and long established country mansion, dating from the 18th century, and lying in extensive grounds. Raemoir is as much a home as a hotel. In the restaurant friendly staff offer a choice of menus and at a recent visit the first class cream of pheasant soup was particularly enjoyed

Seats: 60+. No smoking in dining room
Menus: A la carte D, fixed-price D & Sun L, bar L menu
Additional: Children welcome until 7.30pm, children's L menu; 🕈 menu, vegan/other diets on request
Directions: A93 to Banchory then A980, hotel at crossroads in 2.5 miles

Kincardineshire AB31 4ED
Map no: 15 NO69
Tel: 01330 824884
Chef: Derek Ayton Smith
Proprietors: Mrs Kit Sabin and the Ollis Family.
Manager: Mike Ollis
Cost: alc £35-£50, fixed-price D £25 (4 course), Sun L £14.50. H/wine £11 ❢ Service exc
Credit cards: 🄰 📰 📰 💷
Times: Last L 2pm /D 9pm. Closed first 2 wks Jan

BRAEMAR, **Braemar Lodge Hotel** ✿

Cordon Bleu-style cooking, served in a dining-room decorated with oil lamps and fresh flowers, provides a good range of dishes using fresh ingredients. The four-course fixed-price menu offered at a test meal in May included chicken liver pate with orange and lemon sauce, and escalopes of salmon with herb butter

Times: Last D 9pm. Lunch by arrangement. Closed 31 Oct-23 Dec
Additional: Children over 12 permitted; ✿ dishes, vegan & other diets on request
Directions: On A9 near centre of village

Glenshee Road
Aberdeenshire AB35 5YQ
Map no: 15 NO19
Tel: 013397 41627
Chef: Caroline Hadley-Smith
Proprietors: Edna Coyne
Cost: Fixed-price D £21. H/wine £9.50 ✦ Service inc
Credit cards: 🅰 🆅
Seats: 20. No smoking in dining room

BRIDGE OF MARNOCH,
The Old Manse of Marnoch ✿✿

An attractively situated restaurant making skilful use of first-class local produce

Aberdeenshire AB54 5RS
Map no: 15 NJ55
Tel: 01466 780873
Chef: Keren Carter
Proprietors: Patrick & Keren Carter
Cost: Fixed-price D £25 (4 course). H/wine £9. Service exc
Credit cards: 🅰 🆅
Times: Last D 8.30pm Closed 2 wks Nov
Seats: 20. No smoking in dining room
Menus: Fixed-price D, (Residents L)
Additional: Children over 12 permitted, childrens portions; other diets prior notice

Beautiful grounds leading down to the River Devoran surround the interesting, early 19th-century house which is the setting for this restaurant. A bold colour scheme, nautical prints and a harmonious blend of antiques, with Far Eastern souvenirs, provide a striking backcloth to the service of an eclectic range of dishes in which chef/proprietor Keren Carter makes excellent use of quality Scottish produce. Gravlax – their own dill-cured salmon – or tagliatelli with smoked strips of Lorne beef might, for example, be followed by celery soup with Stilton, then medallions of venison with chocolate sauce, or turkey collops with rowan and rosemary jelly. Traditional shortbread will accompany your choice from a range of coffees or a wide variety of teas that includes herbal infusions as well as China, Ceylon and Indian. The more adventurous palate will be tempted by a number of unusual wines appearing alongside the clarets, Burgundies and Rhones, and a careful selection of single malts illustrates the characteristic qualities of Scottish whisky.

Directions: On B9117, just off the A97 (Huntly/Banff) road

CRAIGELLACHIE, **Craigellachie Hotel**

Banffshire AB38 9SR
Map no: 15 NJ24
Tel: 01340 881204
Chef: David Tilbury
Proprietor: Mermaid (Small Luxury Hotels).
Manager: Ian Fleming

Tempting regional dishes, fish casseroles using local salmon, and traditional roasts all feature in the hotel's Ben Aigan restaurant. A test lunch included an excellent chicken liver terrine, and some superlative guinea fowl. Dinner selections might be beef and haggis sausage, or braised halibut

Cost: Fixed-price L £14.50/D £28 (4 course). H/wine £14.50
Service exc
Credit cards: ◼ ▦ ▦ ▣
Times: 12.30-last L 2pm, 7pm-last D 9.30pm
Menus: Fixed-price L & D, bar L menu
Seats: 45. No smoking in dining room
Additional: Children welcome (D with Nanny in Games Room), children's menu; ◗ dishes, vegan/other diets on request

Directions: In the village centre, off A95

DRYBRIDGE,
The Old Monastery Restaurant ✿✿

Buckie
Banffshire AB56 2JB
Map no: 15 NJ46
Tel: 01542 832660
Chef: James Douglas Gray
Proprietors: J D & M G Gray
Cost: Alc £20-£30 H/wine £8.50. Service exc

Good use is made of fine, locally-caught seafood and quality Scottish meats in the kitchens of this charming restaurant

Credit cards: ◼ ▦ ▦ OTHER
Times: Last L 1.45pm / D 9.30pm. Closed Sun, Mon, 3 wks Jan, 2 wks Nov
Menus: A la carte L & D
Seats: 40. No smoking in dining room

Don't hope to wander into this delightful, original restaurant and get a meal on spec, for it has built up the sort of reputation that makes booking essential. Its setting is inevitably part of the attraction, the former monastery that houses it being surrounded by an attractive garden and enjoying superb views over the Moray Firth. In the kitchen, Douglas Gray and his team continue to treat the finest of Scottish ingredients with imagination and subtlety, creating honest, delicately flavoured dishes that continually delight visitors. The lunchtime menu is appropriately light, a good example being the delicious tomato and chive mousse, served with mixed peppers marinated in a sharp vinaigrette, which was enjoyed on a recent visit. The dinner *carte* offered in the Chapel Restaurant, on the other hand, assumes that your appetite will have been sharpened by a day out and about so includes more substantial main courses such as noisettes of Scotch lamb, medallions of Highland venison or pan-fried Aberdeen Angus sirloin steak. The accompanying wine list roams the world and offers some good choices.

Directions: Leave A98 at Buckie junction onto Drybridge Road for 2.5 miles; do not turn into Drybridge village

Additional: Children over 8 permitted; children's portions; ❤ menu, vegan/other diets on request

DUFFTOWN, **A Taste of Speyside** ❀

Set in the middle of the Whisky Trail, this unpretentious restaurant offers a short but good value menu based on prime raw materials. A wide range of malt whiskies is available for those unable to make it to the distilleries. The most popular dish is 'The Taste of Speyside' which includes smoked salmon, sweet-cured herring and smoked venison

10 Balvenie Street
Dufftown AB5 4AB
Map no: 15 NJ34
Tel: 01340 820860
Chef: Raymond McLean
Proprietors: Raymond McLean and Joe Thompson

Directions: Approaching Dufftown from Elgin, the restaurant is on the right just before the town square

ELGIN, **Mansefield House Hotel** ❀

☺ *Local seafood is a speciality with the extensive carte offering the likes of lobster prepared to request. Regional dishes feature too, as in chicken and haggis in puff pastry. A live pianist plays at weekends*

Seats: 80. Air conditioned. No smoking in dining room
Additional: Children welcome, children's menu; ❤ dishes, vegan/other diets on request
Directions: From A96 to town centre, right at 1st roundabout, right at mini roundabout, 1st left

Mayne Road
Morayshire IV10 1NY
Map no: 15 NJ26
Tel: 01343 540883
Chef: Robin Murray
Proprietors: Ross & Kathleen Murray
Cost: *Alc* £20-£25, fixed-price L £12 H/wine £9.95 ❢ Service exc
Credit cards: ▨ ▩ ▧ OTHER
Times: Noon-last L 2.30pm, 6.30pm-last D 9.30pm

ELGIN, **Mansion House Hotel** ❀

☺ *The turreted baronial mansion sits on the banks of the River Lossie but is close to the town centre. Modern cooking features in the elegant restaurant where typical dishes could be warm chicken and duck liver salad, game consommé, and deep-fried monkfish with a green peppercorn sauce*

Menus: *A la carte*, fixed-price L & D, bar menu
Seats: 40. No smoking
Additional: Children welcome, children's portions; ❤ dishes, vegan/other diets on request
Directions: In Elgin turn off the A96 into Haugh Road; hotel is at the end of the road by the river

The Haugh
Morayshire IV30 1AW
Map no: 15 NJ26
Tel: 01343 548811
Chef: John Alexander
Proprietors: Mr & Mrs Stirrat
Cost: *Alc* £23.50, fixed-price L £12.50/D £23.50 (4 course). H/wine £8 Service exc
Credit cards: ▨ ▩ ▧ ▨ OTHER
Times: Last L 2pm, last D 9pm daily

FORRES, **Knockomie Hotel** ✿

Knockomie Hotel is a fine country house which dates from 1821. In the tastefully decorated restaurant, the menus combine to provide carefully chosen dishes featuring the best of Scottish game, meat and seafood. The cooking is of a modern, yet unfussy style featuring, for example, first class feuilletté of seafood

Seats: 30. No smoking in dining room
Menus: A la carte, fixed-price L & D, bistro menu
Additional: Children welcome to 7.30pm, children's portions;
❂ dishes, vegan/other diets on request
Directions: On A940 one mile S of Forres

Gramtown Road
Morayshire IV36 0SG
Map no: 14 NJ05
Tel: 01309 673146
Chef: Ian White
Director: Gavin Ellis (Scotland's Commended)
Cost: Alc £20, fixed-price L £7.50/D £23.50. H/wine £10.95 Service inc
Credit cards: ▨ ▨ ▨ ▨ OTHER
Times: Last L 2pm, last D 9pm daily

FORRES, **Ramnee Hotel** ✿

☺ This attractive hotel, set in large pleasant gardens, offers Scottish and French cooking on fixed-price and carte menus. Black pudding with a béarnaise sauce, duckling with Cassis flavoured jus and peppered pineapple, and sweet pancake filled with apple and raspberries are typical sample dishes

Victoria Road
Morayshire IV36 0BN
Map no: 14 NJ05
Tel: 01309 672410
Chefs: James Murphy and Craig Wilson
Proprietors: Garry & Roy Dinnes
Cost: Alc £20-£27, fixed-price L £10.75/D £19.50 (4 course). H/wine £8.50 ❢ No service charge
Credit cards: ▨ ▨ ▨ ▨ OTHER
Times: Last L 2pm, last D 9pm. Closed Dec 25, Jan 1-3
Menus: A la carte D, fixed-price L daily
Seats: 34. No cigars or pipes
Additional: Children welcome, children's menu; ❂ menu, vegan/other diets on request

Directions: Turn off A96 into eastern side of Forres; hotel is 200yds on the right

INVERURIE,
Thainstone House Hotel ✿✿

Contemporary cooking features in the elegant Simpson's restaurant of this grand Palladian mansion

The tree-lined driveway sweeps up to the the grand portalled entrance of this recently renovated Palladian mansion. Within, the sophisticated Simpson's restaurant continues the stylish theme with swags and drapes and dramatic colour, and complements the elegant, contemporary cooking. The choice is from three and four-course fixed-price menus, which could commence with first-class canapés such as haggis wrapped in filo pastry. Reports suggest that an over-elaborate mixing of ingredients can, on occasion, miss the mark – some work, others do not. A terrine of wood pigeon and

Aberdeenshire AB51 5NT
Map no: 15 NJ72
Tel: 01467 621643
Chef: Gordon Dochard
Proprietor: Peter Medley. Managed by Macdonald Hotels.
Cost: Alc L £15/D £29.50, fixed-price L £9.50 (1 course)-£14.50; fixed-price D £23.50. H/wine £12.50. No service charge
Credit cards: ▨ ▨ ▨ ▨
Times: Last L 2pm, Last D 9pm
Menus: A la carte, fixed-price L & D, Sunday lunch, bar menu
Seats: 45. No smoking in dining room

venison in Cumberland sauce on continental leaves and fruit, for example, had some good flavours but the fruit was found to be superfluous and the dish slightly lacking in sauce. An excellent cream of autumn chanterelle soup with port wine was smooth and creamy with accurate flavours, though the tarragon cream topping was rather unnecessary, while Aylesbury duck on a bed of spinach was slightly dry and chewy but came with a superb blackberry and honey sauce. Orange crème brulée was good. The wine list has a strong French presence.

Directions: 2 miles from Inverurie on the A96 Aberdeen road

Additional: *Children welcome, children's portions/menu;* ● *menu; other diets on request*

KILDRUMMY,
Kildrummy Castle Hotel ✺

The ruins of the 13th-century castle stand dramatically beside the modern version – a grand, castellated country mansion built in 1900. Traditional cooking features 'Taste of Scotland' dishes such as roast saddle of wild hare, or there could be salmon en croûte and Aberdeen Angus steak

Aberdeenshire AB33 8RA
Map no: 15 NJ41
Tel: 019755 71288
Chef: Kenneth Whyte
Proprietor: Thomas Hanna
Cost: *Alc* £29, fixed-price L £14/D £27 (4 course). H/wine £9.50. No service charge
Credit cards: 🔳 🔳 🔳
Times: Last L 1.45pm, last D 9pm. Closed Jan 4-Feb 10
Seats: 42. No smoking in dining room
Additional: Children welcome, children's portions; ● dishes, vegan/other diets on request

Directions: Off A97 (Huntly–Ballater road) adjacent to Castle ruins

NEWBURGH, Udny Arms Hotel ✺

The pleasant Victorian dining-room of the Udny Arms provides a friendly and relaxed environment in which to enjoy interesting meals prepared from fresh quality produce. Fish features prominently. Look out for Shetland salmon fillet with a tomato and red onion salsa on a leek and potato pancake

Menus: *A la carte* L & D, bar menu
Seats: 75. No cigars or pipes in dining room
Additional: Children welcome, children's portions; ● dishes, other diets on request
Directions: Village centre – A92 Aberdeen/Peterhead turn right to Newburgh

Aberdeenshire AB41 0BL
Map no: 15 NJ92
Tel: 01358 789444
Chef: Cameron Kelly
Proprietors: Jennifer & Denis Craig
Cost: *Alc* from £20. H/wine £10.95 Service exc
Credit cards: 🔳 🔳 🔳 🔳 OTHER
Times: Last L 2pm, last D 9.30pm Closed Dec 25 D, Dec 26 D

TOMINTOUL,
The Gordon Hotel ✸

☺ *This old traditional fishing hotel has been completely renovated. The now stylish Cromdales Restaurant provides a short but carefully chosen menu with the emphasis on quality local produce cooked in the modern manner. Dishes offered include a tender cannon of lamb, cooked pink and topped with a mint mousse*

Seats: 45. No smoking in dining room
Menus: Fixed-price D, bar L menu
Additional: Children welcome, children's portions; ✪ dishes, vegan/other diets by arrangement
Directions: In centre of Tomintoul

The Square
Banffshire AB37 9ET
Map no: 15 NJ11
Tel: 01807 580206
Chef: Drew Heron
Proprietor: David Ian Adby
Cost: Fixed-price D £22.50
(4 courses). H/wine £14.50 ❢
Service inc
Credit cards: 🖸 💳 💳
Times: Last L 2.30pm, last D
9.30pm Closed Nov 1-Feb 1

HIGHLAND

ARISAIG, **Arisaig House** ✸✸

An impressively located country house hotel offering a consistently good standard of cooking from a short daily menu

Beasdale
Inverness-shire
Map no: 13 NM68
Tel: 01687 450622
Chef: David Wilkinson
Proprietors: Ruth, John &
Andrew Smither (Relais et
Chateaux)
Cost: *Alc* L £15, fixed-price D
£29.50. H/wine £14.50. No
service charge
Credit cards: 🖸 💳 💳 OTHER
Times: Last L 2pm, last D
8.30pm. Closed Nov 1-Easter
Menus: *A la carte* L, fixed-price
D, bar L menu
Seats: 36. No smoking dining
room
Additional: Children over 10
permitted; ✪ dishes, other diets
on request

A richly decorated 19th-century residence, Arisaig House is set amid breathtaking Highland scenery and sheltered by magnificent redwoods, beech and oak trees. The Smither family are the welcoming proprietors and son-in-law David Wilkinson the chef. A daily changing fixed-price menu is offered alongside a menu of 'alternatives' giving a choice of around four dishes at each stage. A meal might commence with warm melted goats' cheese in a salad with fine slices of pigeon, or Shetland salmon cured gravad lax-style. The next course is usually a soup (the subtly flavoured mushroom soup has been highly recommended), though alternatives include Cullen skink or tossed salad leaves. The more traditional main courses might offer fresh turbot drizzled with lemon oil, or Norfolk duckling sliced and served with a robust gravy of its juices. To finish there are French and local cheeses or a tempting range of desserts. The lunch menu provides a varied

choice: soup and sandwiches, light dishes available as a starter or main course, then more substantial items such as marinated Highland venison medallions with juniper sauce.

Directions: On A830 Fort William to Mallaig road, 3 miles east of Arisaig village

CANNICH, **Mullardoch House Hotel** ❀

☺ *Magnificent views across Loch Sealbanach to the Affric mountains can be enjoyed from the elegant dining room of this former hunting lodge. The short four-course, fixed-price menu offers a decent choice of well-prepared dishes, though service is not as sharp as it could be*

Directions: 8 miles West of Cannich (A831) on unclassified Glen Cannich road to Loch Mullardoch

Glen Cannich, Beauly
Inverness-shire IV4 7LX
Map no: 14 NH23
Tel: 01456 415460
Chef: John Kirk
Proprietors: A R Johnston
Cost: Fixed-price D £17-19
Credit cards: 🟦 💳 💳
Times: Last D 8.30pm

CONON BRIDGE, **Kinkell House** ❀

☺ *A good value, short carte is offered by chef/patron Marsha Fraser at her charming 19th-century farmhouse restaurant overlooking the Cromarty Firth. Increasing popularity has stimulated a more adventurous approach in the use of quality local ingredients, including seafoods and game. Puddings are recommended*

Menus: *A la carte* L & D
Seats: 30. No smoking in dining room
Additional: Children welcome, children's portions; ❷ dishes, vegan/other diets on request
Directions: On the B9169, 1 mile from the A9 & A835

Ross-shire IV7 8HY
Map no: 14 NH55
Tel: 01349 861270
Chef: Marsha Fraser
Proprietor: Marsha Fraser
Cost: *Alc* L £11/D £18.75.
H/wine £8.50. Service inc
Credit cards: 🟦 💳
Times: Last L 2pm, last D 9pm.
Closed Jan, Feb

CONTIN, **Coul House Hotel** ❀

A Victorian mansion, surrounded by lovely Highland scenery, is personally-run and radiates great charm. Its elegant dining-room is the ideal setting for carefully prepared 'Taste of Scotland' specialities: game and brandy terrine, quail and herbs, and Summer Isles scallops. The wine list contains some superb clarets

By Strathpeffer
Ross-shire IV 14 9EY
Map no: 14 NH45
Tel: 01997 421487
Chef: Chris Bentley
Proprietors: Martyn & Ann Hill (Scotland's Commended)
Cost: Alc £22-£30, fixed-price D £25.50 (5 course). H/wine £12 (ltr)
Credit cards: 🟦 💳 💳 💳 OTHER
Times: Last L 2pm, last D 9pm
Menus: *A la carte*, fixed-price D, bar menu
Seats: 40. No smoking in dining room
Additional: Children welcome (over 6 at D), children's menu; ❷ menu, vegan/other diets on request

Directions: A9 & A835 to Contin, private drive on right

DULNAIN BRIDGE,
Muckrach Lodge Hotel ❀

Robust modern cooking in the the attractive conservatory restaurant of this former Victorian hunting lodge. Now under new ownership, a new carte was being planned as we went to press. The present fixed-price menu offers traditional dishes such as salmon timbale, Cullen skink, and seafood medley

Menus: A la carte, fixed-price Sun L, bar menu
Seats: 90. No-smoking area
Additional: Children welcome, children's menu; ❂ menu, vegan/other diets on request
Directions: On A938, 0.5 mile from Dulnain Bridge

Morayshire PH26 3LY
Map no: 14 NH92
Tel: 01479 851257
Chef: Eric Mathew
Proprietors: Indah Hotel.
Manager: Mike Croarkin
Cost: Alc £22.50, fixed–price
Sun L £10.95. H/wine £8.50 ❢
Service inc
Credit cards: ▨ ▨ ▨ ▨ OTHER
Times: Last L 1.45pm, last D
9pm

DUNDONNELL, Dundonnell Hotel ❀

☺ *A daily-changing fixed-price menu features a number of 'Taste of Scotland' dishes, supported by seafood specials. An inspection meal featured a large cap mushroom filled with Stilton cream, an intensely-flavoured cauliflower soup, and tender grilled sole stuffed with crab meat*

Menus: A la carte, fixed-price D, bar L menu
Seats: 80. No smoking in dining room
Additional: Children welcome, children's menu, ❂ dishes by arrangement
Directions: A 832 (Ullapool/Gairloch) 14 miles from Braemore junction

Ross & Cromarty IV23 2QS
Map no: 14 NH08
Tel: 01854 633204
Chef: n/a
Proprietor: Selbie N Florence
Cost: Alc £19.50, fixed-price D
£22.75 (4 course) H/wine £7.25
❢ Service exc
Credit cards: ▨ ▨ ▨ OTHER
Times: Last L 2.15pm, last D
8.30pm

DUROR, Stewart Hotel ❀❀

A daily-changing set menu makes best use of regional produce at this personally run, attractive hotel

Running this lovely hotel set in beautiful gardens on the popular Oban to Fort William coast road is very much a family affair for Michael and Chrissie Lacy. He cooks, along with Callum O'Neill and Lorraine McFadden, in an assured, modern British style. Together they produce a daily-changing four-course menu of limited choice allowing for flexibility in the use of local produce (which can become available right up to the last minute). Quail, haggis and Loch Linnhe salmon are typical first courses, followed by a soup – tomato and vodka, or at a sample meal, carrot and orange. The main course consisted of medallions of pork with spinach and Gruyère, the meat tender and well presented. Alternative dishes may include venison Wellington and breast of mallard duck. On this occasion an enjoyable meal was rounded off by a steamed pudding with Glayva and honey sauce. A good value wine list ensures this accomplished cooking is well complemented.

Directions: On the A828 towards 4 miles south of Ballachulish Bridge

Appin
Argyll PA38 4BW
Map no: 14 NM95
Tel: 0163174 268
Chefs: Michael Lacy, Callum O'Neil and Lorraine McFadden
Proprietors: Michael & Chrissie Lacy (Best Western)
Cost: Fixed-price D £25 (4 course). H/wine £9.50 ❢
Service exc
Credit cards: ▨ ▨ ▨ ▨
Times: 7pm-last D 9.30pm.
Closed Oct 16-Mar 31
Menus: Fixed-price D & Sun L, bar menu
Seats: 38. No smoking in dining room
Additional: Children welcome (until 8pm under 6), children's portions; ❂ dishes, other diets on request

---

Factual details of establishments in this Guide are from questionnaires we send to all restaurants that feature in the book.

FORT WILLIAM, Crannog Restaurant ❀

The setting is spectacular – on a pier jutting out into Loch Linnhe with superb sea views. The restaurant's own fishing boat supplies the fish and the straightforward menu allows the quality to shine through. Langoustines are a speciality, and bouillabaisse and hake in a herb crust are highly recommended

Seats: 60. No-smoking area
Menus: Fixed-price L & D
Additional: Children welcome, children's portions; ❂ dishes, vegan/other diets on request
Directions: On town pier in Fort William; access from bypass

Inverness-shire PH33 7NG
Map no: 14 NN17
Tel: 01397 705589
Chef: Susan Trowbridge
Proprietor: Susan Trowbridge
Cost: *Alc* £20. H/wine £7.95
❢ Service exc
Credit cards: 🅰 🅱 🅲
Times: Noon-last L 2.30pm, last D10.30pm (9.30pm winter). Closed Dec 25 & Jan 1

FORT WILLIAM, Factor's House ❀

Kevin Kivingstone trained up the road at Inverlochy Castle and is producing good things on his short menu supported by daily changing blackboard specials. Look out for terrine of goose confit, brochette of lamb on cumin-flavoured couscous, and rich chocolate cappuccino mousse. Note that the restaurant is closed Sunday and Monday

Menus: A la carte D
Seats: 25. No smoking
Additional: Children welcome, children's menu; other diets on request
Directions: A82 4 miles N of Fort William just past golf course

Torlundy PH33 6SN
Map no: 14 NN17
Tel: 01397 705767
Chef: Kevin Kivingstone
Proprietor: Peter Hobbs
Cost: *Alc* £20 H/wine £8.30
❢ Service exc
Credit cards: 🅰 🅱 🅲 OTHER
Times: Last D 9.15pm Closed Sun, Mon

FORT WILLIAM,
Inverlochy Castle Hotel ❀❀❀

Aberdeen Angus beef, game in season, west coast fish and Isle of Skye crabs all feature prominently on the menus of this impressive Highland hotel

Inverness-shire PH33 6SN
Map no: 14 NN17
Tel: 01397 702177
Chef: Simon Haigh
Proprietor: Grete Hobbs (Relais & Chateau)
Cost: Fixed-price dinner £39-£45 (4 course). H/wine £10 ❢ No service charge
Credit cards: 🅰 🅱 🅲 OTHER
Times: Last L 2pm, last D 9.30pm. Closed Nov-Mar
Menus: Fixed-price L & D
Seats: 40. No smoking in dining room
Additional: Children welcome at L only, children's menu

Long recognised as one of the world's leading hotels, Inverlochy Castle continues to impress. Indeed, it would be difficult for it not to do so, set against a backdrop as dramatic as Ben Nevis and the grandeur of the Scottish Highlands. But the setting alone cannot account for its power to draw guests back time after time.

Exemplary standards of hospitality and service can, however, and two dining-rooms with polished tables, French silver, fresh flowers and candles certainly play their part.

From delicate canapés to equally fine petits fours, chef Simon Haigh continues to delight guests with his daily-changing four-course dinner menu; the choice offered is limited, but advance requests for any particular item will readily be met. Cuisine, though international in style, gains a distinctive character through the widespread use of quality regional produce. A meal taken in late spring, for example, began with an attractively presented, creamy avocado mousse topped with roasted Loch Linnhe prawns and garnished with quite strongly dressed leaves surrounded by chopped red pepper. Soup was a refined broth of vegetables and watercress, then loin of Scottish lamb stuffed with spinach and sweetbreads – its serving delayed because the chef felt that his first attempt was not pink as requested – proved an honest, enjoyable dish. The highlight of the meal, however, was a perfectly constructed hot apple tart crowned with silky-smooth cinnamon ice-cream. A wine list particularly strong on Burgundy and claret offered the perfect complement to the food, featuring not only a library of great vintages but also a good range of half bottles.

Directions: 3 miles N of Fort William on A82, just past the Golf Club.

FORT WILLIAM, **Moorings Hotel** ❀❀

One of the most popular restaurants in the area, making the very best use of fine local produce

Banavie
Inverness-shire PH33 7LY
Map no: 14 NN17
Tel: 01397 772797
Chef: Kevin Francksen
Proprietor: Norman J A Sinclair
Cost: *Alc* £22, fixed-price D £25. H/wine £12.25 ❢ Service exc
Credit cards: 🟦 🟫 🟪 🔳
Times: Noon-last L 2pm, 7pm-last D 9.30pm. Closed Dec 25/6
Seats: 60. No smoking in dining room
Menus: *A la carte*, fixed-price D, bar menu
Additional: Children welcome, children's portions; ❶ dishes, vegan/other diets on request

Under the caring direction of Norman Sinclair, this captivating business and tourist hotel lying alongside the Caledonian Canal beside Neptune's Staircase, continues to grow from strength to strength. New chef Kevin Francksen (ex Middlethorpe Hall in York), has settled in quickly and produces interesting dishes based on prime beef, fish and game. There is an imaginative fixed-price menu with two or four-course options. The renowned 'Taste of Scotland' menu emphasises its use of fresh local produce. Canapés, including delicious hot, small haggis dumplings, are presented in the bar. Look out for the smooth, honest flavoured chicken liver parfait with a sweet apple jelly and green salad as a starter, or perhaps a creamy tomato and basil soup, and then for main course, collops of fresh monkfish tails, garnished with small scoops of pea purée served with a light, cream sauce. Crème brulée to finish with a delicious, light filling on top of raspberries. The handpicked staff are exceedingly hospitable and attentive, yet still remain unobtrusive.

Directions: 3 miles from Fort William by Caledonian Canal: follow A82 then A830 Mallaig road for 1 mile

GRANTOWN-ON-SPEY, **Garth Hotel** ❀

☺ *Skilfully prepared dishes feature the best of Scottish meat, game and seafood, with a main course of salmon with prawn and dill sauce the highlight of one inspection meal. The country house hotel is popular with fishermen, and the staff are particularly welcoming and relaxed*

Times: Last L 2pm/D 9pm daily
Seats: 50. No smoking in dining room
Menus: A la carte, fixed-price L /D, bar menu
Additional: Children welcome, children's portions; ❷ dishes, vegan/other diets on request
Directions: Overlooking historic town square

Castle Road
Morayshire PH26 3HN
Map no: 14 NJ02
Tel: 01479 872836
Chef: Stewart Anderson
Proprietor: Gordon D McLaughlan (Scotland's Commended)
Cost: *Alc* £25, fixed-price L £10 /D £24 (4 course). H/wine £8 Service exc
Credit cards: 🄰 🄼 🄴 🄳

INVERNESS, **Bunchrew House Hotel** ❀

A 17th-century mansion house which is beautifully set in large landscaped gardens beside the shores of the Beauly Firth. The daily-changing menu is inspired by fresh local ingredients and prepared with a care that combines interesting blends of textures and flavours – 'delicious' baked wild salmon, or the chef's own bread and butter pudding, for example

Seats: 60. No smoking in dining room
Menus: A la carte, fixed-price D
Additional: Children welcome, children's portions; ❷ dishes, vegan/other diets on request
Directions: 2.5 miles from Inverness on A862 towards Beauly

Bunchrew
Inverness-shire IV10 6TA
Map no: 14 NH64
Tel: 01463 234917
Chef: Walter Walker
Proprietors: Stewart and Leslie Dykes
Cost: *Alc* £20, fixed-price D £25 (4 course) H/wine £11.50 Service exc
Credit cards: 🄰 🄼 🄴
Times: Noon-last L 2pm, 7pm-last D 9pm

Rhubarb originated in northern Asia. It is botanically not a fruit but a vegetable, but is classed as a fruit since that is how it is normally eaten. The Chinese valued rhubarb medicinally, and it was so regarded when it arrived in Britain in the 16th century. Indeed, the first recipe for rhubarb did not appear until the late 18th century. Recipes for sweet pies and tarts followed in the 19th century, but it was Mrs Beeton who really popularised it with her extensive repertoire of recipes for rhubarb jams, rhubarb pudding, rhubarb tart and rhubarb wine. Rhubarb can be forced to provide fruit out of season which probably helped to increase its popularity in Victorian times. The normal growing season lasts from May to July, but early forced rhubarb (January - April) is tender, pink and delicious. By comparison, the unforced summer rhubarb can be coarse and sour. Early forced rhubarb makes a good accompaniment to fish, especially wild salmon.

INVERNESS, **Dunain Park Hotel** ✿

Genuine hospitality together with competent, French influenced food mean visitors return time and again to this comfortable country house hotel. The daily changing menu features prime beef, game and seafood plus a range of speciality steaks. Edward Nicoll has a choice of 130 malt whiskies to offer

Inverness-shire IV3 6JN
Map no: 14 NH64
Tel: 01463 230512
Chef: Ann Nicoll
Proprietors: Edward Nicoll
Cost: Alc D £25.50, fixed-price
L £16.50. H/wine £12.50.
Service exc
Credit cards: 🔲 🔲 🔲 🔲 OTHER
Times: Last L 1.30pm, last D
9pm. Closed 3 weeks Jan/Feb
Seats: 36. No smoking
Additional: Children permitted,
children's portions; ❤ dishes,
vegan on request

Directions: One mile from town boundary on A82 to Fort William

KENTALLEN, **Ardsheal House Hotel** ✿✿

Lying at the end of a mile-long single track road, a grand Scottish mansion with a reputation for fine food

The Morven hills rising impressively on the other side of Loch Linnhe make for a spectacular view. The house, and its 900 acres of land, are now back in the hands of the Sutherland family. Eighteen years ago they sold out and are delighted to have regained possession. Nothing else has changed. For about 10 years the kitchen has been George Kelso's domain, with Michelle Kelso looking after the rest. In the attractive dining-room, with its conservatory extension, a daily-changing, fixed-price menu offers an alternative at three of the four main stages, and is complemented by an appropriately comprehensive, well-chosen wine list. Game, prime beef, fish and seafood feature strongly, the latter particularly so one January inspection day. Ramekin of seafood (salmon, scallop, monkfish and prawn) garnished with pink grapefruit and cucumber sauce was followed by a tomato, apple and celery soup. For the main course, a very good, lightly grilled fillet of salmon with a brioche and horseradish crust, accompanied by a delicate, creamy leek sauce came with an accompanying salad. Then, to finish, banana baked in rum and served with a hot butterscotch sauce. The wine list offers a decent spread and puts little strain on the pocket.

Appin
Argyllshire PA38 4BX
Map no: 14 NN05
Tel: 0163174 227
Chef: George Kelso
Proprietor: Mr & Mrs
Sutherland
Managers: George & Michelle
Kelso
Cost: Fixed-price L £17.50 (4
course) /D £32.50 (6 course).
H/wine £11. Service exc
Credit cards: 🔲 🔲 🔲
Times: Last L 1.45pm, last
D 8.30pm
Menus: Fixed-price L & D,
children's high tea, snack L
Seats: 45. No smoking in dining
room
Additional: Children welcome,
children's portions/high tea;
❤ dishes, other diets by
arrangement

Directions: In village, on the A828 between Glencoe and Appin

KINGUSSIE, **The Cross** ❀❀❀

The exposed stone walls and timbers of a former tweed mill provide an appropriate backcloth to the enjoyment of quality Scottish produce

Despite the hint of Japanese minimalism in the modern eating area, a full range of Scottish delicacies is offered by this popular restaurant with rooms. West coast prawns, venison, and Drambuie, all figure regularly on a set five-course dinner menu with choices at the starter, main course and pudding stage. Self-taught chef Ruth Hadley also makes use of a wide range of local fruit and vegetables, but her skill is to subtly enhance their flavours rather than overwhelm them in the name of innovation. This certainly does not mean that her meals lack interest. On a recent visit, after a starter of langoustines served with an avocado fan and seafood sauce, our inspector was pleasantly surprised by a delicious, fresh-tasting capsicum soup – a colourful blend of red peppers and tomatoes with a hint of orange. This was followed by a boudin of pike (the fine mousse studded with firm flesh and served with a well flavoured leek sauce scented with lemon grass) then breast of duck with a sharp shallot and Madeira sauce. There was technical expertise behind the apparently simple dessert, a pear poached in white wine and served with a tiny baked vanilla cream and passion fruit coulis – it was perfect. Infectiously enthusiastic wine buff Tony Hadley is only too willing to share his knowledge with any guest who needs help; faced with a wine list the size of a small book – though modestly described as 'one person's incursions into the world of wines' – many may indeed appreciate his advice.

Directions: Town centre, 300m uphill from lights along Ardroilach Road & turn left onto Tweed Mill Brae

Tweed Mill Brae
Arbroilach Road
Inverness-shire PH21 1TC
Map no: 14 NH70
Tel: 01540 661166
Chef: Ruth Hadley
Proprietors: Ruth & Tony Hadley
Cost: Fixed-price D £ 35 (5 course). H/wine £11 Service exc
Credit cards: 🔲 🔲 OTHER
Times: Last 9pm. Closed Tue, Dec 1-26, Jan 6-Feb 28
Menus: Fixed-price D
Seats: 28. No smoking in dining room
Additional: Children over 8 permitted; other diets with notice

KINGUSSIE, **Osprey Hotel** ❀

☺ *This charming and popular holiday hotel has a relaxed and informal atmosphere where visitors can sample some sound cooking. There is a short daily-changing menu offering such dishes as pan-fried langoustines with a hint of ginger, and a wonderful mango brûlée*

Menu: Fixed-price D
Seats: 20. No smoking in dining room
Additional: Children over-10 permitted, children's portions; ❶ dishes, other diets with prior notice
Directions: South end of High Street

Ruthven Road
Inverness-shire PH21 1EN
Map no: 14 NH70
Tel: 01540 661510
Chef: Aileen Burrow
Proprietors: Aileen & Robert Burrow
Cost: Fixed-price D £19.75. H/wine £7. Service exc
Credit cards: 🔲 🔲 🔲 🔲
Times: Last D 8.30pm. Closed 2 wks Nov

KINGUSSIE, **The Scot House Hotel** ❀

The McConachie and Gilbert families have come up with a winner in their latest venture. Good fresh, local bread, a trio of smoked meats with orange salad, tender, fresh scallops wrapped in bacon and coated with oatmeal with tomato sauce, and a sound crème brulée were all components of one enjoyable inspection meal

Menus: A la carte, fixed-price D, bar menu
Seats: 24. No smoking
Additional: Children welcome, children's menu; ❶ menu, other diets with notice
Directions: South end of main street in village

Newtonmore Road PH21 1HE
Map no: 14 NH70
Tel: 01540 661351
Chef: Lynda MacKay
Proprietors: Morag & Bill Gilbert and Val & Nigel McConachie
Cost: Alc £21, fixed-price D £17 (4 course) H/wine £8.75 ❢ Service exc
Credit cards: 🔲 🔲 OTHER
Times: Last L 2pm/D 9pm daily

KINLOCHBERVIE, **Kinlochbervie Hotel** ❀

Set in a secluded fishing village, Kinlochbervie House boasts fine sea views. The kitchen offers a daily-changing fixed-price menu which could include smoked salmon from the hotel's own smokehouse, cream of tomato soup, pan-fried beef sirloin and home-made puddings to finish

Menu: Fixed-price D
Seats: 40. No smoking in dining room
Additional: Children welcome, children's portions; ❂ dishes, vegan/other diets on request
Directions: Off B801 overlooking harbour

Sutherland IV27 4RP
Map no: 14 NC25
Tel: 01971 521275
Chef: Rex Neame
Proprietor: Kate Neame
Cost: Fixed-price D £27.50 (4 course). H/wine £8.25 ♥ Service exc
Credit cards: 🂠 🂠 🂠 🂠
Times: Last D 8.30pm. Closed Nov 1-Mar 31

LOCHINVER, **Lochinver Larder** ❀

By day it is a coffee shop and take away, in the evening the Riverside Bistro comes into being. The spectacular views of the Inver River are matched by the high-quality local produce, cooked simply and sympathetically. Popular dishes include Minch halibut steak with lime and ginger butter, and some fine steaks

Menus: A la carte D
Seats: 44. No smoking
Additional: Children welcome, children's menu; ❂ menu
Directions: On A837, 2nd property on right from Ullapool direction

Lochinver
Map no: 14 NC02
Tel: 01571 844356
Chefs: Mrs W Webster, Mr & Mrs I N & D A Stewart
Proprietors: I N & D A Stewart
Cost: Alc £14-£25, H/wine £7.25 Service exc
Credit cards: 🂠 🂠 OTHER
Times: 6.30 pm-last D 9pm Closed Nov-Mar

MUIR OF ORD, **The Dower House** ❀

A country house in every sense – Robin Aitchison is out feeding the hens and ducks when not behind the scene – offering a quiet and relaxing atmosphere. His set, four-course menu offers no choice except on pudding and cheese. Look out for lightly cooked scallops with cabbage tossed in creamed mustard sauce

Menus: Fixed-price L & D
Seats: 26. No smoking
Additional: Children welcome (over 5 at D), children's portions; ❂ dishes, vegan/other diets on request
Directions: From Muir of Ord take A862 (Dingwall) 1 mile, left at double-bend sign

Highfield IV6 7XN
Map no: 14 NH55
Tel: 01463 870090
Chef: Robin Aitchison
Proprietors: Mr & Mrs Aitchison
Cost: Fixed-price L £17.50/D £28 (4 course) H/wine £13 Service inc
Credit cards: 🂠 🂠
Times: Last L by arrangement, last D 9.30pm Closed 1 wk Mar, 1 wk Oct

ONICH, **Allt-Nan-Ros Hotel** ❀❀

☺ *An enthusiastically-run family hotel producing a sound repertoire of tempting French influenced dishes*

A welcoming atmosphere prevails at the MacLeod's comfortable hotel. It was formerly a Victorian shooting lodge, and sits in well tended gardens beside the shore of Loche Linnhe. The dining-room offers uninterrupted views of the loch and is a fine setting for Alan Clark's innovative, French-influenced modern cooking. His daily-changing, fixed-price menu is market led, and is supported by a six-course 'Menu Surprise'. Prime Scottish beef, lamb, game and seafood all feature strongly, and saucing is first-class. A June dinner produced a 'delicious' light white fish and scallop terrine wrapped in cabbage leaves and served with crisp leaves and lemon mayonnaise. Cream of asparagus soup had real depth of flavour

Inverness-shire PH33 6RY
Map no: 14 NN06
Tel: 018553 210/250
Chef: Alan Clark
Proprietor: James MacLeod (Minotel)
Cost: Alc L £10.50, fixed-price D £19.50 (5 course). H/wine £9.75. Service exc
Credit cards: 🂠 🂠 🂠 🂠 OTHER
Times: Last L 2pm, last D 8.30pm
Seats: 50. No smoking in dining room

Allt-Nan-Ros Hotel

Additional: Children welcome, children's menu; ❂ dishes, vegan/other diets on request

and was followed by moist and tender monkfish tails served with a delicate ginger and grape sauce topped with deep-fried spaghetti leeks. Accompanying vegetables – mange tout, cauliflower and baby corn – were 'crunchy' and full of taste. Sweet strawberry tart to finish. A well chosen wine list of about 100 bins includes some good clarets; developing countries get a good showing.

Directions: On A82, in the village, 11 miles S of Fort William

PLOCKTON, **Haven Hotel** ❁

Now under the care and direction of Annan and Jill Dryburgh, the Haven remains one of the best small hotels in the Highlands. The menu features some Scottish produce. Look out for whisky-cured smoked salmon, tender Orkney scallops, rack of Highland lamb, fresh Mallaig salmon, and for dessert, cranachan with raspberries

Menu: Fixed-price D
Seats: 38. No smoking in dining room
Additional: Children over 7 permitted; ❂ dishes
Directions: On the main road, on the left just before the Lochside

Ross & Cromarty IV52 8TW
Map no: 14 NG83
Tel: 01599 544223
Chef: Ian James
Proprietors: Mr & Mrs Annan Dryburgh
Cost: Fixed-price D £22 (4 course). H/wine £6.50. Service exc
Credit cards: ▨ ▨
Times: Last D 8.30pm. Closed Dec 20-Feb 1

SHIELDAIG, **Tigh an Eilean Hotel** ❁

Uncluttered and well-defined traditional cooking is produced from good quality ingredients at this waterfront hotel. The short fixed-price menu includes fresh local seafood such as crab Dijonaise and excellent smoked salmon, plus well-prepared dishes along the line of rare roast rib of beef with home-made horseradish

Seats: 26. No smoking in dining room
Additional: Children welcome, children's portions; ❂ dishes on request
Directions: In the centre of Shieldaig, at the water's edge

Strathcarron
Ross-shire IV54 8XN
Map no: 14 NG85
Tel: 01520 755251
Chef: Callum F Stewart
Proprietors: Mr & Mrs Stewart
Cost: Fixed-price D £19.50. H/wine £4.20 (half litre). Service exc
Credit cards: ▨ ▨
Times: Last D 8.30pm. Closed Nov-Mar

> Pink peppercorns are, in fact, not a peppercorn at all. They are the processed berry of a South American relative of the poison ivy. They are toxic if eaten in large quantities.

SKYE, ISLE OF – ARDVASAR,
Ardvasar Hotel ❀

☺ *Uncomplicated, honest food representing excellent value-for-money is served from the daily-changing carte at this 18th-century inn. Regional Scottish cooking is mostly prepared from fresh island produce and includes dill-pickled herrings, and baked salmon en croute with vermouth sauce*

Menus: *A la carte,* bar menu
Seats: 25. Smoking discouraged
Additional: Children welcome, children's portions; ❂ dishes, other diets on request
Directions: From Armadale ferry turn left and on through village

Inverness-shire IV45 8RS
Map no: 13 NG60
Tel: 014714 223
Chef: Bill Fowler
Proprietors: Bill & Gretta Fowler
Cost: *Alc* £18. H/wine £1.50 glass ❢ Service exc
Credit cards: ▨ ▦
Times: Last L 2pm, last D 8.15pm

SKYE, ISLE OF – COLBOST,
Three Chimneys Restaurant ❀

Even the bread is home-made at this picturesque former croft. Two adventurous menus are offered and seafood is a particular feature. Look out for monkfish roasted in rosemary scented olive oil with whole garlic cloves and roast red pepper sauce. Pressure can overstretch the kitchen, however

Additional: Children permitted (please phone to check for dinner); children's portions; ❂ menu, vegan/other diets on request
Directions: From Dunvegan take B884 to Glendale. Restaurant is at Colbost 4.5 miles from main road turn off

Dunvegan IV55 8ZT
Map no: 13 NG24
Tel: 01470 511258
Chef: Shirley Spear
Proprietors: Eddie & Shirley Spear
Cost: *Alc* L £15, fixed-price D £27.50 (4 courses) H/wine £9.95. Service exc
Credit cards: ▨ ▦
Times: Last L 2pm, last D 9pm. Closed Sun, Nov-Mar
Seats: 30. No smoking in dining room

SKYE, ISLE OF – HARLOSH,
Harlosh House ❀❀

A small hotel restaurant serving a modern set menu specialising in local seafood

In a beautiful, solitary position on the shores of Loch Caroy, this little hotel has much to recommend it, especially the magnificent views of the Cuillin Hills. It is run with enthusiasm by Peter and Lindsey Elford. One of the great attractions is Peter's cooking which has gained quite a reputation. His set four-course dinner menu is built around local seafood, but Scottish meats and game also feature. Indeed, carefully cooked venison in a superb port sauce was the outstanding dish of an inspection meal, which began with a filo parcel of fresh scallops, smoked bacon and mushrooms, served with a chive sauce, and concluded with an apricot and apple strudel. The second course is generally a soup, such as herb loveage, or pea, mint and lettuce, and at the fourth stage a choice is offered – a couple of puddings, a trio of home-made sorbets, or a selection of Scottish cheeses with oatcakes. The dining room is small and invites conversation with fellow diners, as do the cosy tables where Lindsey serves drinks and takes orders. Peter feeds four guests every half hour, an unusual arrangement which works very well.

Directions: 4 miles south of Dunvegan, turn right off A863, signed Harlosh

Dunvegan IV55 8ZG
Map no: 13 NG24
Tel: 01470 521 367
Chef: Peter John Elford
Proprietors: Peter & Lindsey Elford
Cost: Fixed-price D £24.50 (4 course). H/wine £8.50. Service inc
Credit cards: ▨ ▦ OTHER
Times: 7pm-last D 8.30pm. Closed mid Oct-Easter
Menu: Fixed-price D
Seats: 16. No smoking in dining room
Additional: Children welcome, children's portions; other diets on request

SKYE, ISLE OF – ISLE ORNSAY,

Hotel Eilean Iarmain ✿

A whitewashed, harbourside inn offering the warmest of welcomes. The attractive small, candlelit dining-room with a sea view features a daily-changing, set-price menu in Gaelic and English. Natural flavours are apparent in dishes like carrot and coriander soup, fillet of cod with roast peppers and oregano, and brûléed apple pie with cinnamon custard.

Directions: Overlooking harbour

Sleat
Isle of Skye IV43 8QR
Map no: 13 NG71
Tel: 01471 833332
Chef: Patrick Gudgeon
Proprietor: Sir Ian Andrew Noble

SKYE, ISLE OF – ISLE ORNSAY,

Kinloch Lodge ✿✿

A civilised ambience and friendly welcome together with skilful cooking make this rural retreat a rare treat

Isle of Skye IV43 8QY
Map no: 13 NG71
Tel: 01471 833214
Chefs: Lady MacDonald, Peter MacPherson and Claire Munro
Proprietors: Lord & Lady MacDonald
Cost: Fixed-price D £28 & £33(5 course). H/wine £10. Service exc
Credit cards: ▧ ▨
Times: Last D by arrangement. Closed Dec 7-Feb 28
Menu: Fixed-price D
Seats: 28. No smoking in dining room
Additional: Children permitted (under 8 not encouraged), children's portions; other diets on request

The secluded home of Lord and Lady MacDonald, Kinloch Lodge is at the end of a forest track, with a splendid outlook over Loch Na Dal. Dating from 1680, the lodge is now a comfortable country house hotel, though the atmosphere is still very much that of a private home. Open fires and antiques abound, while the elegant dining-room is filled with family portraits and silver. Here, the daily changing fixed-price menu features the best of fresh island produce. Dinner is served at 8 pm and an enjoyable inspection meal consisted of an intensely flavoured smoked mackerel and horseradish mousse, followed by an unusual pea, pear and mint soup which proved to be a happy combination of flavours. The main course of devilled seafood was accompanied by a lightly spiced sauce flavoured with tabasco and tomato. Other main courses may include haunch of venison and fillet of hake in oatmeal. To finish, our inspector chose a superb dark chocolate terrine with coffee cream sauce. The food is supported by a reasonable wine list.

Directions: 1 mile off main rd, 6 miles S of Broadford on A851, 10 miles N of Armadale

SKYE, ISLE OF – PORTREE,
Cuillin Hills Hotel ✿

Highland IV59 9W
Map no: 13 NG44
Tel: 01478 612003
Chef: Jeffrey Johnstone
Manager: Murray McPhee
Cost: Fixed-price D £22 (4 course) H/wine £9.50 Service exc
Credit cards: 🔳 🔳 🔳 OTHER
Times: Last D 9pm

☺ *The Cuillin Hills hotel boasts superb views, overlooking the bay to the mighty Cuillin Mountains beyond. The restaurant offers modern, French-influenced cooking based on quality Scottish ingredients. Look out for dishes such as noisettes of mountain lamb with artichoke hearts filled with Provençal sauce*

Menus: Fixed-price D & Sun L, bar menu **Seats:** 48. No smoking in dining room **Additional:** Children welcome, children's menu; ◑ dishes, vegan/other diets on request
Directions: Signed to right 0.25 mile from Portree on A855 north

---

SKYE, ISLE OF – PORTREE,
Rosedale Hotel ✿

Isle of Skye IV51 9DB
Map no: 13 NG44
Tel: 01478 613131
Chef: Linda Thomson
Proprietor: Hugh Andrew
Cost: Fixed-price D £23 (5 course). H/wine £7 Service exc
Credit cards: 🔳 🔳
Times: Last D 8.30pm Closed Oct-April

☺ *A cluster of fishermens' cottages on the quayside have been converted into a simple but comfortable hotel boasting fine sea views. In the restaurant some sound modern cooking yields the likes of poached egg tartlets with avocado salad and watercress sauce, and smoked salmon fillet with apple and rosemary butter*

Menu: Fixed-price D **Seats:** 36. No smoking in dining room
Additional: Children permitted, children's portions; ◑ dishes
Directions: Follow signs to Harbourside; hotel faces loch at end of Quay Brae

---

SPEAN BRIDGE,
Old Station Restaurant ✿

Station Road
Inverness-shire PH34 4EP
Map no: 14 NN28
Tel: 01397 712535
Chef: Richard Bunney
Proprietors: Richard & Helen Bunney
Cost: Alc D £15-£22, fixed-price Sat D £21.50. H/wine £8.50. Service exc
Credit cards: 🔳 🔳
Times: Last D 9pm. Closed Sun-Wed from Oct-Apr, Dec 25/6, Jan 1-31

☺ *Popular with both locals and visitors, this converted station ticket office serves good food at reasonable prices. The carte changes to reflect seasonal availability and dishes may include teriyaki salmon fillet garnished with ginger, rich game casserole with pickled walnuts, or grilled duck breast with apricot and lemon sauce*

Seats: 30. No smoking in dining room
Additional: Children permitted; ◑ dishes, vegan/other diets by arrangement
Directions: In centre of village, follow signs for BR station

---

STRONTIAN, **Kilcamb Lodge** ✿✿

Acharacle
Argyllshire PH36 4HY
Map no: 14 NM86
Tel: 01967 402257
Chef: Peter Blakeway
Proprietor: Peter Blakeway
Cost: Fixed-price D £26 (4 course). H/wine £10 No service charge
Credit cards: 🔳 🔳 OTHER
Times: Last D 7.30pm. Closed Nov-mid Mar

A short choice based on good local ingredients served in a friendly hotel setting

On the shores of Loch Sunart to the west of the village, this former hunting lodge enjoys the most tranquil of settings. It is now a small hotel with comfortable lounges and a bar with a crackling fire, but the elegant dining room is popular with both house guests and non-residents alike, attracted by the quality of chef/proprietor Peter Blakeway's cooking. The short fixed-price menu provides a good value four-course dinner. Starters could offer salmon fish cakes served as a ball with a smooth sweet pepper sauce, and boneless quail stuffed with wild rice and apricots on an orange caramel sauce, followed by a soup such as cream of parsnip. Appearing among the main courses are baked cod with a herb crust, served with a hollandaise sauce, and roast noisette of Scottish lamb with a mixed herb sauce, accompanied by simply cooked vegetables. Desserts range from Swiss meringue roulade with passion fruit and oranges to traditional apple pie and custard, though a fresh fruit platter and selection of Scottish cheeses are also available.

Directions: Over the Corran ferry off A82. Follow A861 to Strontian. First left over bridge in centre of village

Menu: Fixed–price D
Seats: 26. No smoking in dining room
Additional: Children permitted, children's portions; ♥ dishes, other diets on request

TONGUE, **Ben Loyal** ❀

☺ *There are indications of chef Maire O'Keefe's Irish background in the locally inspired menus offered in this restaurant with superb views over the Kyle of Tongue. Tain mussels with a garlic and herb stuffing might be followed by tender breast of wood pigeon with a filo parcel of local game*

Directions: Tongue lies at the intersection of the A838 and A386, hotel is in the centre of village

Sutherland IV27 4XE
Map no: 14 NG95
Tel: 01847 611216
Chef: Maire O'Keefe
Proprietors: M & P Cook
Cost: Fixed-price D £18.50
Credit cards: 🔲 🔲
Times: Last D 8.30pm

TORRIDON, **Loch Torridon** ❀❀

Wild, romantic scenery and country house Cordon Bleu cooking give this waterside hotel an impressive charm

Wester Ross IV2 2EY
Map no: 14 NG95
Tel: 01445 791 242
Chef: Geraldine Gregory
Proprietors: David & Geraldine Gregory (Scotland's Commended)
Cost: Fixed-price D £29.75. H/wine £11.95 ▮ Service inc
Credit cards: 🔲 🔲 🔲 OTHER
Times: Last L 2pm, last D 8.30pm
Menus: Fixed-price D, light lunch menu
Seats: 40. No smoking in dining room
Additional: Children welcome, (Over 12 at D); ♥ dishes, vegan/other diets on request

The romance of the glens is tangible at this most Scottish of hotels. Diners can gaze through the restaurant's windows at Highland cattle grazing against a backdrop of Torridonian granite. They belong to proprietors David and Geraldine Gregory, charming hosts, who quickly make guests feel at home. Mrs Gregory is actively involved in the cooking, a blend of British and Cordon Bleu, and offers a daily-changing set-price menu, which may include Scottish lamb, lemon sole and roast venison. A recently enjoyed meal began with a salmon and sole terrine of good quality, followed by saddle of hare. This was tender and correctly cooked and had a satisfying gamey flavour, as did the light, delicious game jus accompanying it. A good leek purée and crisp haricots vert completed a successful dish. Pastry work is also skilled, demonstrated by the pudding, a pithivier of hazelnut frangipan, which made a spectacular finish to the meal. The bar offers a wide range of malt whiskies, and there can be few better locations than this in which to enjoy them.

Directions: On A896; do not turn off to Torridon village

ULLAPOOL, **Altnaharrie Inn** 🏵🏵🏵🏵

First time visitors usually come for one night but most return and stay two or three days, drawn back by the stunning food and idyllic setting

It is not just the food, the whole of Altnaharrie is something special. Here is the form: drive to Ullapool, park the car at the Royal Hotel and telephone Altnaharrie. The boat picks you up. In just ten minutes you are transported to a cluster of converted former drovers' dwellings in a setting that is the closest thing to peace and tranquillity imaginable.

It is a complete experience and all the elements, location, accommodation, service and the food, are all inter-related. The stylish attention to detail throughout is worthy of the highest praise: log fires, fresh flowers, paintings; in the dining-room, bare floorboards strewn with rugs, plain white walls, candles, polished antique wood tables, more flowers, good silver cutlery, goblet-style glasses, lovely loch views. Fred Brown presides amiably over the front-of-house, and Gunn Erickson cooks with a considerable degree of flair and artistry. Results on the plate are stunning. Yet such excellence and consistency of standard is not obtained without a great deal of hard work; Gunn exacts the highest standards from her suppliers, and applies them to herself.

At a dinner in May, canapés included langoustine split in half and roasted with a herb butter, and the 'lightest of pastry' topped with caviar flavoured sour cream. Fillet of turbot was very lightly cooked, and placed on a bed of 'fantastically young spinach' and accompanied by an excellent butter sauce and garnished with morels – 'wonderful aroma' – and knotted baby leeks. Crab soup, 'the most exciting soup I have ever tasted', was light, with a pronounced flavour heightened by cayenne and herb pesto. Medallions of Sitka deer came set on top of a mixture of white and red onions and green juniper berries contained within a strand of leek ('even this strand had a wonderful flavour') served with two sauces – venison cooking juices enhanced by some cream in one, red Burgundy in the other – and garnished with ravioli of mushrooms and grapes. For pudding there is a choice of three. If you hesitate you get all three on separate plates. Hesitate! Perhaps there will be a wonderful hot chocolate cake, baked banana in filo with an exceptional orange and Cointreau sauce, vanilla and caramel ice-cream with meringue, and caramelised apple and intense pineapple sauce. A comprehensive wine list complements the food, there is a particularly good range of half bottles. Altnaharrie is totally non-smoking.

Directions: Follow A835 north to Ullapool. Telephone from Ullapool for directions to ferry. Advance booking at Altnaharrie essential

Ross & Cromarty
Map no: 14 NH19
Tel: 01854 633230
Cost: Check when booking. The meal cost – approximately £55 – is included in the overnight stay. H/wine £12 ❢ No service charge
Credit cards: ▨ ▧ ▨
Menus: None, guests are consulted prior to arrival
Times: Dinner 8pm. No lunches
Chef: Gunn Eriksen
Proprietors: Fred Brown and Gunn Eriksen
Seats: 16. No smoking throughout
Additional: No children under 8

LOTHIAN

DUNBAR,
The Courtyard Hotel ✤

Wood Bush Brae
East Lothian EH42 1HB
Map no: 12 NT67
Tel: 01368 864169
Chef: Peter Bramley
Proprietor: Peter Bramley
Cost: *Alc* L£10/D£18 H/wine
£8.50. Service inc
Credit cards: 🎴 📧 🎴 📇
Times: Last L 2pm/D 9.30pm.
Closed Xmas Day evening
Seats: 26. No cigars or pipes

☺ *Local produce married with international inspiration results in interesting and varied dishes at this delightful small hotel converted from fishermen's cottages. Peter Bramley's recent dishes have included lamb noisettes in a rosemary and hawthorn cream sauce. The selection of puddings should not be missed*

Additional: Children welcome, children's portions; ✔ dishes, other diets on request
Directions: Situated on the seafront close to the town centre

EDINBURGH, **Atrium** ✤✤✤

Cambridge Street
Lothian EH1 2ED
Map no: 11 NT27
Tel: 0131 228 8882
Chef: Andrew Radford
Proprietors: Andrew & Lisa
Radford
Cost: *Alc* L£15-£20/D
£25/Snack L £12. H/wine £8.95
❗ Service exc
Credit cards: 🎴 📧 🎴 OTHER
Times: Last L 2.30pm, last D
9.30pm (11pm during Festival)
Closed Sat L, Sun
Menus: *A la carte* L & D
(changes twice daily), snack
L menu
Seats: 70. Air conditioned
Additional: Children welcome,
children's portions; ✔ dishes,
vegan/other diets on request

State of the art Scottish cuisine served with a smile in a stylish environment

Located within the same building as the innovative Traverse Theatre, the Atrium is also quite radical in concept: feeding the design conscious denizens of Edinburgh with eclectic, contemporary cuisine. Tables are crafted from old railway sleepers, the conical oil lamps are from the unique North Glen Gallery and menus are contained in slabs of copper. The trendy decor is softened by admirably well-informed and very friendly waiting staff. Andrew Radford rewrites his short but well-balanced menu for each meal and also provides a 'snack' lunch at bargain prices. His style borrows enthusiastically from wherever and has a distinctly Mediterranean accent, but is thoroughly Scots in its use of prime local produce.

At a dinner in early Spring, tiny rounds of Parmesan shortbread served with aperitifs were crisp and cheesy, an indication of good things to come. Our inspector's party nominated the softly-textured, full-flavoured crab cakes – served on a bed of al dente courgettes with a well-made tomato butter – as the top starter in a close-run contest. Meaty roast monkfish, served with thin fresh asparagus spears and baked cherry tomatoes topped with melted Parmesan was also a strong contender. A main course of slightly rare, perfectly pink baked salmon with beurre blanc was accompanied by crunchy sliced leeks and new potatoes that might have been dug from the ground within an hour of their appearance on the plate. Fillet of beef was also on the rare side, sauced with a good meaty jus and wild mushrooms, and served with creamy mashed potatoes mixed with butter beans, giving a surprising but successful combination of textures. For pudding, a banana baked in its skin and served with a cocoa sorbet proved to be the perfect marriage. Commensurate with the rest of the operation, the wine list is modish but sure of itself.

Directions: From Princes Street turn into Lothian Road, 2nd left & 1st right, by the Traverse Theatre

EDINBURGH, **Balmoral Hotel** ❀❀

Accomplished Scottish cooking with a French influence, plus a taste of the Orient, in regal surroundings

Princes Street
Midlothian EH2 2EQ
Map no: 11 NT27
Tel: 0131 556 2414
Chef: Billy Campbell
Proprietor: Forte Grand.
Manager: Iain Archibald
Cost: Alc £40, fixed-price
L £17.50 (2 courses+wine)/D
£29.50 (4 course+aperitif).
H/wine £15 ❢ Service inc
Credit cards: ▧ ▨ ▨ ▨ OTHER
Times: Last L 2.30pm, last D
10.30pm. Closed Sat L, Sun L
Menus: A la carte, fixed-price L
& D
Seats: 50. Air conditioned
Additional: Children welcome,
children's portions; ♥ menu,
vegan/other diets on request

The magnificent clocktower of this hotel is a familiar Edinburgh landmark. The Edwardian building was totally refurbished in 1992 and, while retaining its grandeur, is now fully fitted with modern comforts. It houses a Palm Court, reputedly the capital's premier afternoon tea venue; the Brasserie, for light bites and the renowned Grill. Here, an Eastern influence is evident in the decor of deep red lacquered walls contrasting with modern cream armchairs. And more than a touch of the Orient is reflected in dishes such as fresh asparagus and forest mushrooms served with a ginger and chilli dressing, and breast of duck with chilli, coriander and soya dressing served with stir fry vegetables. Very successful on a test visit was a succulent darne of River Tay salmon with tangy rhubarb sauce, the salted, crisp skin adding to both texture and flavour. Scottish produce is favoured and 'Taste of Scotland' dishes, such as noisettes of Scottish lamb, are highlighted. As the restaurant's name suggest, grills also make up a major section of the menu. A comprehensive wine list is available.

Directions: Hotel at east end of Princes Street; Grill has own entrance

EDINBURGH, **Caledonian Hotel** ❀❀

Imaginative cooking based on sound use of the best Scottish produce at this famous venue

Princes Street
Midlothian EH1 2AB
Map no: 11 NT27
Tel: 0131 459 9988
Chef: Tony Binks
Proprietor: Queens Moat
Houses.
General Manager: Stephen Carter
Cost: Alc £42.50, fixed-price
L £22.50/D £40 (4 course).
H/wine £18.50 ❢ Service inc
Credit cards: ▧ ▨ ▨ ▨
Times: 12.30pm-last L 2pm,
7.30pm-last D 10.30pm. Closed
Sat L, Sun L
Menus: A la carte, fixed-price
L & D
Seats: 60. Air conditioned.
No-smoking area

Affectionately known as 'the Cally,' this former railway hotel dominates the west end of the city with its magnificently restored facade. Public rooms have a traditional elegance, with the first floor Pompadour restaurant regarded as one of the finest dining-rooms in the city. Manager Jordi Figuerola continues to run the room with charm and elegance, with chef Tony Binks offering visitors a choice of fixed-price and 'Classic' menus and a *carte*. The 'Classic' may feature asparagus with hollandaise, duck and beetroot consommé and chateaubriand, while the *carte* allows a more imaginative approach, one that makes the best use of Scottish produce. On a recent visit, a light and creamy smoked haddock cheesecake was presented on an oatmeal base and set off by a garnish of sevruga caviar and tangy horseradish dressing. As a main course, medallions of wild fallow deer were peppered then pan fried and served with curly kale and a cherry sauce. There are trolleys for everything including dessert, but they are used without fuss or pretension. Carriages restaurant serves more informal meals.

Directions: At western end of Princes Street

EDINBURGH, **Carlton Highland Hotel** ❀

☺ *Scottish and international cooking is the mainstay of one of Edinburgh's best located hotels. There are three eating places – Carlyle's Patisserie, the Carlton Court Carvery serving snacks and grills all day, and Quill's Restaurant which offers a wide choice including haggis, and the famous Atholl brose*

Menus: A la carte, fixed-price L & D
Seats: 30. No smoking in dining room **Additional:** Children welcome, children's menu; ◑ dishes, vegan/other diets on request
Directions: Turn right onto North Bridge at E/end of Princes Street

North Bridge
Midlothian EH1 1SD
Map no: 11 NT27
Tel: 0131 567 7277
Chef: Charles Price
Proprietor: Scottish Highland.
Manager: Franco Galgani
Cost: Alc £27, fixed-price
L £14/D £19.75.
H/wine £10.50 ❢ Service inc
Credit cards: 🃏 📇 📇 💳 OTHER
Times: Last L 2pm, last D 10pm
Closed Sat L, Sun

EDINBURGH, **Channings** ❀

Welcoming staff, friendly service and good food make this discreet club-like hotel – made up of five Edwardian townhouses – an ideal eating place. Imaginative use of fresh Scottish produce results in recommended dishes such as Cullen skink, and a deliciously sharp lemon tart

Menus: Fixed-price L & D, bar menu
Seats: 65. No smoking in dining room
Additional: Children welcome; children's portions, ◑ dishes, vegan/other diets on request
Directions: 10 mins from W/end of Princes Street, just off Queensferry Road

South Learmonth Gardens
Midlothian EH4 1EZ
Map no: 11 NT27
Tel: 0131 315 2226
Chef: Colin Drummond
Proprietor: Peter Taylor
Cost: Fixed-price L £9.95/D £19.50. H/wine £9.95 ❢ Service exc
Credit cards: 🃏 📇 📇 💳 OTHER
Times: Last L 2.45pm, last D 9.30pm (10pm Fri & Sat)

EDINBURGH,
Dalmahoy Hotel ❀❀

☺ *An imaginative menu of dishes skilfully prepared in modern eclectic style is served in the idyllic surroundings of this impressive Georgian mansion*

Kirknewton
Midlothian EH27 8EB
Map no: 11 NT27
Tel: 0131 333 1845
Chef: Gary Bates
Proprietor: Country Club.
Manager: Rafael Torrubia
Cost: Alc £23.50, fixed-price
L £14.50/D £20 (2 course).
H/wine £10.95 Service exc
Credit cards: 🃏 📇 📇 💳 OTHER
Times: Last L 2pm/D 9.45pm
Closed Sat L (Terrace bistro open all day)
Menus: A la carte, fixed-price L & D, bar menu
Seats: 120 (+70 Terrace) Air conditioned
Additional: Children welcome in Terrace, children's menu; ◑ dishes, vegan/other diets on request

Additional: No children; ◑ menu, vegan/other diets on request

A fine Adam house which retains much of its original character, bounded by two golf courses and enjoying views of the Pentland Hills, is the setting for this stylish restaurant. Here, Gary Bates has succeeded in lending imagination and eclectism to an enterprising two or three-course menu that takes in careful cooking and thoughtful presentation. Good use is made of fresh produce, and a trio of West Coast seafood – terrine of red mullet, gateau of salmon rillette and tartlet of creamed crab – might be followed by rump of Scotch lamb served with pesto rösti, button onions and rosemary essence, or fillet of Angus beef topped with sautéed wild mushrooms, glazed with herbs and garnished with cherry tomatoes. An interesting selection of farmhouse cheeses provides an alternative to a choice of desserts which sometimes includes an elaboration on a regional delicacy such as mille-feuille of honey wafers and cranachan. Service is competent but friendly. Some New World labels are included in a mainly European wine list which offers a few half bottles.

Directions: On A71, 3 miles from Calder roundabout, opposite Ratho turn off

EDINBURGH,
George Inter-Continental

An elegant hotel, given warmth, charm and character by the opulence of its public rooms. The Carvers Table Restaurant portrays a particular grandeur, but it is the more intimate Le Chambertin which serves the better food. Try tagliatelle mixed with salmon in a delicate cream and mushroom sauce

Seats: 50+. No-smoking area
Additional: Children welcome, children's menu; ◑ menu, vegan/other diets on request
Directions: At East end of George Street near St Andrew's Square

19-21 George Street
Midlothian EH2 2PB
Map no: 11 NT27
Tel: 0131 459 2506
Chef: Klaus Knust
Proprietor: Inter-Continental.
Manager: Barnaby Hawkes
Cost: Alc £30, fixed-price L
£19-£23 (inc wine)/D £19.95.
H/wine £11.75 ❢ Service exc
Credit cards: 🔲 🔲 🔲 🔲 OTHER
Times: 12.30pm-last L 2pm,
7pm-last D 10pm Closed Sat L,
Sun, some BHs

EDINBURGH, Iggs

The charismatic 'Igg' and his staff, make for a lively atmosphere at this popular restaurant. Tapas are available lunchtime and early evening, and there is a more elaborate carte in the evening offering a mix of Spanish and Scottish dishes. Air-cured Spanish meats are served with sweet peppers roasted in garlic and olive oil, or try pan-fried hare with rhubarb sauce

Directions: Around the corner from John Knox House on High Street

15 Jeffrey Street EH1DR
Midlothian EH1DR
Map no: 11 NT27
Tel: 0131 5578184
Proprietor: Ignacia Campos

Cassoulet is a dish which originated in Languedoc. It consists of haricot beans cooked in a stewpot with pork rinds and a variety of meats (which vary from region to region) but in general include pork loin, ham, leg and sausage, with perhaps a piece of preserved duck or goose, and a breadcrumb topping added in the final stages. The word comes from 'cassole', the name of the glazed earthenware cooking pot traditionally used.

EDINBURGH, **King James** ✸

Centrally situated and linked to the St James shopping centre, the King James is a busy, modern hotel. On the third floor an American themed bar, restaurant and cocktail bar are to be found. In the St Jacques Brasserie, chef David Veal offers fresh Scottish produce prepared in modern style

Directions: Adjacent to St James shopping mall

107 Leith Street
Midlothian EH1 3SW
Map no: 11 NT27
Tel: 0131 556 0111
Chef: David Veal
Proprietor: Thistle Hotels.
Cost: Alc £26; fixed-price D £18.50, £23.50. H/wine £11.30
❢ Service exc
Credit cards: 🌑 ▤ ▤ 🖃
Times: Last L 2.15pm/D 10pm
Seats: 90. Air conditioned
Additional: Children welcome, children's portions/menu;
❶ menu, vegan/other diets on request

EDINBURGH,
L'Auberge Restaurant ✸✸

☺ *A long-established, centrally-located French restaurant offering particularly good value lunch and pre-theatre dinners*

L'Auberge has a deceptively simple façade, which belies the stylish, busy interior. A French atmosphere is promoted through both menus and extensive wine list, which complement each other well. Patron Daniel Vencker, now joined by co-chef Michel Bouyer, offer good value lunch and pre-theatre dinner menus plus a chefs' choice selection, while more elaborate fixed-price menus and *carte* are available in the evenings. A sample meal consisted of an attractively presented vegetable and aspic terrine, followed by fillet of salmon filled with an aniseed-flavoured stuffing and surrounded by a sweet honey and herb cream sauce. Other main courses may include lamb in strudel pastry and Perigord-style duck. For pudding, a rich Belgian chocolate terrine was served with cinnamon cream, a successful combination of flavours. More flamboyant *carte* desserts include apple tart cooked to order and crêpes Suzettes prepared at your table. The sound wine list has a definite bias towards France. Knowledgeable and attentive service is provided by all the staff.

Directions: City centre, off Royal Mile near John Knox House

56 St Mary's Street
Midlothian EH1 1SX
Map no: 11 NT27
Tel: 0131 556 5888
Chefs: Daniel Vencker and Michael Bouyer
Proprietor: Daniel Vencker.
Manager: G Aubertel
Cost: Alc £28, fixed-price L £15.50/D £23.50. H/wine £10.50 Service exc
Credit cards: 🌑 ▤ ▤ 🖃
Times: Last L 2pm, last D 9.30pm
Menus: A la carte, fixed-price L & D, pre-theatre
Seats: 60. Air conditioned
Additional: Children welcome, ❶ dishes, children's portions/vegan/other diets on request

> We endeavour to be as accurate as possible but changes in personnel and data can occur in establishments after the Guide has gone to press.

EDINBURGH, **Le Marché Noir** ☻☻

☺ *Assured French cooking and a warm atmosphere at this cheery city venue*

This cheery little restaurant serves French dishes in contemporary style. While the management adopts a light-hearted approach to French on both menu and wine list, proprietor Malcolm Duck and his friendly staff willingly offer translations, which establishes a nice rapport with diners. There are two fixed-price dinner menus; although prices differ, the standard of cooking is consistent. At a sample meal, an exceptionally good chicken liver parfait of intense flavour made an excellent first course. It was followed by roast fillet of lamb with a minted redcurrant sauce, capably cooked, with the lightest covering of a herb en croûte crust. Vegetables get sympathetic treatment here, and are judiciously cooked. Alternative main courses could include roast fillet of salmon with a smoked salmon cream with Cognac. Desserts range from a terrine of white chocolate and orange, to a hot lemon sponge with raisins, traditional poached pear with red wine, or a creamy textured crème brûlée.

Directions: Follow the 'Mound' across Princes Street, George Street, Queen Street to bottom of Dundas Street

2/4 Eyre Place
Midlothian EH3 5EP
Map no: 11 NT27
Tel: 0131 558 1608
Chef: David Connell
Proprietor: Malcolm Duck
Cost: Fixed-price L £10 (2 courses), £12.50/D £19.50. H/wine £7.90 ▮ Service exc
Credit cards: 🔲 🔲 🔲
Times: Last L 2.30pm, last D 10pm (10.30pm Fri & Sat, 9.30pm Sun). Closed Dec 25/6
Menus: Fixed-price L & D
Seats: 40-45. No smoking while food served
Additional: Children permitted; ✆ dishes, vegan/other diets on request

EDINBURGH, **Malmaison Hotel** ☻

Converted from the Seaman's Mission building, this stylish hotel offers a French influenced brasserie, where traditional Mediterranean cuisine can be enjoyed until late. A sample meal could include seared plum tomatoes on focaccia toast, coq au vin, and a particularly smooth and creamy crème brûlée to finish

Directions: From city centre follow Leith Docklands. Through 3 sets of lights (Leith Walk/Constitution Street), left to Tower Street

1 Tower Place
Leith EH6 7DB
Map no: 11 NT 27
Tel: 0131 555 6868
Chef: Roy Brett
Proprietor: Malmaison Hotel
Cost: Alc L/D£23
Credit cards: 🔲 🔲 🔲 🔲 OTHER
Times: Last D 10.30pm

EDINBURGH, **Martins Restaurant** ☻☻

Lively cooking and a bustling atmosphere in a popular restaurant

Rose Street in Edinburgh is renowned for its lively atmosphere. Tucked away in a lane on the north side of this bustling street is Martins, a restaurant which continues to entice customers back time and again. This is due not only to the efficient service and friendly staff, but also to the high standards of the daily changing menu. Forbes Stott produces a limited menu with the emphasis on fresh flavours, combined to create simple but delicious dishes. At a recent inspection 'mouth-watering' canapés of piping hot cheese and chive scones set the tone for a meal that commenced with roast monkfish with a puréed salt cod crust set on a bed of roasted peppers, marred only by being a little cool in temperature. The main course of pan-fried breast of guinea fowl, served with a delicious creamy sauce and oyster mushrooms, left a long, memorable, lingering taste. To finish, the imaginative and well sourced selection of Scottish and Irish cheeses is to be recommended.

Directions: Hidden in the back lane of Rose Street between Frederick and Castle Streets

70 Rose Street
North Lane
Midlothian EH2 3DX
Map no: 11 NT27
Tel: 0131 225 3106
Chefs: Forbes Stott and Peter Banks
Proprietors: Martin & Gay Irons
Cost: Alc £27.50-£30, fixed-price L £15. H/wine £9.95. Service exc
Credit cards: 🔲 🔲 🔲 🔲 OTHER
Times: Noon-last L 2pm, 7pm-last D 10pm. Closed Sat L, Sun, Mon, Dec 24-Jan 24, 1st w/e May & Sept
Menus: A la carte L & D, fixed-price L
Seats: 28+8. No smoking in dining room
Additional: Children over 8 permitted; ✆ dishes, vegan/other diets on request

EDINBURGH, **Norton House** ❀❀

*A much-extended Victorian country house restaurant in extensive
parkland, popular with the business community*

Working one's way through the 'Taste of Scotland' menu to the
muted strumming of a classical guitarist would, for many, be a
perfect way to spend an evening. The running order is Loch Fyne
scallops, haggis with neeps and tatties, followed by pigeon, duck,
venison and guinea fowl cooked in the pot, and ending up with
whisky and oat flummery with Highland berries. Otherwise, in The
Conservatory Restaurant, it is modern international cooking that
features on new chef Trevor Ward's daily-changing, fixed-price menu
and seasonal *carte*. A dinner in May featured chicken boudin blanc
with sesame seed dressing and onion marmalade, followed by turbot
with creamy chive sauce. Collops of venison with a beetroot and
raspberry vinegar and juniper-scented jus, roast Lothian turkey with
a chestnut gravy and watercress, and grilled aubergine with polenta
and spicy tomato sauce are also typical of the style. For those after
less formality, the Tavern pub and restaurant in converted stables
close to the hotel is a good alternative.

Directions: M8, exit 2, off the A8, 0.5 mile past Edinburgh Airport

Ingliston
Midlothian EH28 8LX
Map no: 11 NT27
Tel: 0131 333 1275
Chef: Trevor Ward
Proprietor: Alan Campbell
(Virgin) **Manager:** J S Gibbs
Cost: *Alc* £33, fixed-price
L £15.50/D £22.50.
H/wine £11.95 ❗ Service exc
Credit cards: 🔲 ▧ ▩ 🔲 OTHER
Times: Last L 2pm, last D 10pm
Closed Sat L
Menus: *A la carte*, fixed-price L
& D
Seats: 80. No-smoking area
Additional: Children welcome,
children's portions; ❷ menu,
vegan/other diets on request

EDINBURGH,
The Sheraton Grand Hotel ❀❀

Intimate setting for imaginative cooking in city centre hotel

1 Festival Square
Midlothian EH3 9SR
Map no: 11 NT27
Tel: 0131 229 9131
Cost: *Alc* £34, fixed-price
L £19.50, fixed-price D £28.50
Times: Last D 11pm
Menus: *A la carte*, fixed-price
L & D

Munro means a high Scottish mountain, and is thus appropriate
menuspeak for a pyramid-shaped confection of three chocolate
mousses served with orange sauce and a tuile basket. You have
been warned. The cooking at the Grill Room owes much to the
Aulde Alliance. Typical is a classic starter of hare and wood pigeon
terrine on a light tomato and shallot chutney with confit of apples.
Well textured and served at the proper temperature, it was marred
only by a slight saltiness from the ham casing, and some minute
garnishing which contributed little to the overall effect. A main
course of tournedos of Inverurie beef with wild mushrooms in
claret and foie gras sauce with Anna potatoes, was a superior piece
of beef, excellently cooked. Nonetheless, the accompanying fungi

were a little gritty, and the sauce something of a misnomer, being two separate ones. Both were well reduced with good flavour, but risked mutual oblivion by running into each other. Details were generally good, especially the seasoned breads and the home-made petits fours. The wine list effectively balances the New World with some interesting French selections.

EDINBURGH, **The Vintners Room** ❀❀

Close to the redeveloped Leith dock area, an elegant, intimate and atmospheric restaurant popular with locals

Cherubs indulging in cherubic pleasures feature on the sooty, 350-year-old Venetian stucco plasterwork in the candle-lit Vintners Room. Dinner and lunch can also be enjoyed in the Long Room, flanked with wood and brick and adorned with gilt mirrors. Underneath are 12th-century vaults where Augustinian friars once stored wine from Holyrood Palace. Lunchtime menus offer two or three courses and are good value, but the *carte* offers more elaborate choices. The best Scottish game and seafood is selected daily to create a variety of well thought-out mainly French and Scottish dishes, such as guinea fowl with lime and white port sauce, or baked halibut fillet with sweet pepper and anise sauce. On a cold February night there was a colourful terrine of scallops, salmon and monkfish with an avocado sauce, followed by tender and gamey wild venison noisettes, served with a fragrant honey and lemon sauce and a pear poached in red wine. To finish, an iced white and dark chocolate parfait and delicate coffee bean sauce. The wines are thoughtfully selected from around the world.

87 Giles Street, Leith
Midlothian EH6 6BZ
Map no: 11 NT27
Tel: 0131 554 6767
Chef: A T Cumming
Proprietors: A T & S C Cumming
Cost: Alc £27, bar L from £6.
H/wine £ 10 Service exc
Credit cards: ▨ ▨ ▨
Times: Last L 2.30pm, last D 10.30pm Closed Sun, 2 wks at Xmas
Menus: A la carte L & D, bar L menu
Seats: 66. No smoking in dining room
Additional: Children welcome, children's portions; ♥ dishes, vegan/other diets on request

Directions: At end of Leith Walk: left & right into Henderson Street. Restaurant is in old warehouse on the right

EDINBURGH,
The Witchery by the Castle ❀❀

Enviable location at the top of the Royal Mile for formal restaurant with two separate dining-rooms

A touch of sorcery always adds spice to a meal, and the Witchery by the Castle is happy to play up its arcane connections as the reputed site of secret meetings of the nefarious Hell Fire Club. The two candlelit dining-rooms share the same menu. The Secret Garden is the more luxurious of the two, with tapestries, painted ceilings and a plant filled terrace. The food blends Scottish produce with classic French cuisine. A typical starter may be smoked bacon strips and oyster mushrooms in a white wine and cream sauce. Salmon fishcakes, on a bed of creamed leeks with parsley sauce, had a decent texture but arrived slightly over-browned on the plate. Vegetables failed to inspire. The out-of-season strawberry mousse was, nonetheless, a smooth and fruity finale. Allow time to study the extensive wine list with its useful descriptions and careful selections of vintages. Service is formal and attentive, with long opening hours enabling diners to enjoy meals at their own pace.

Castle Hill, Royal Mile
Midlothian 2 1NE
Map no: 11 NT27
Tel: 0131-225 5613
Chef: Andrew Main
Proprietor: James Thomson
Cost: Alc £25; fixed-price L £10.40 (2 courses), £12.95; fixed-price dinner £19.95.
H/wine £10.95 ❢ Service exc
Credit cards: ▨ ▨ ▨ ▨ OTHER
Times: Noon-Last L 4pm, Last D 11.30pm. Closed 25/26 Dec, 1 Jan
Menus: A la carte, fixed-price L & D, Sunday lunch, after theatre
Seats: 120
Additional: Children permitted (over 8 after 8pm); ♥ dishes, vegan/other diets on request

Directions: At the entrance to Edinburgh Castle at the very top of the Royal Mile

GULLANE, **Greywalls Hotel** ✿✿

Skilful cooking in Edwardian Lutyens house next to championship golf course

A bracing day on the links, particularly for those fortunate enough to play on the legendary Muirfield course, needs to be followed by a good supper. The dining-room at Greywalls directly overlooks the fairways and chef Paul Baron rewards both 18th and 19th holers with a short, well-structured, four-course dinner menu that changes daily. Locally grown asparagus with a chive butter sauce might be a good early summer starter, followed by an interesting sorbet or soup, such as rich broth of mussel, leek and saffron stew. Main courses might include steamed Scottish scallops with a lobster and basil jus, oven-cooked quail with a port wine sauce, or the slightly under par pan-fried fillet selected by our inspector. Desserts, however, scored the equivalent of a hole in one, with a warm, passion fruit soufflé, although the blackcurrant sauce was judged to be gilding the lily. The first-class wine list impresses, not only for its range of French classics, but also for its wider range and sensible pricing structure.

Directions: Signposted on A198 (North Berwick) in village of Gullane

Muirfield
East Lothian EH31 2EG
Map no: 12 NT48
Tel: 01620 842144
Chef: Paul Baron
Proprietor: Giles & Ros Weaver.
Manager: Sue Prime
Cost: *Alc* L £19, fixed-price D
£33 (4 course)/Sun L £20,
H/wine ☻ £11.50. Service exc
Credit cards: 🖪 📠 🖿 🖭 OTHER
Times: 12.30-last L 1.45pm,
7.30pm-last D 9.15pm. Closed
Nov-Mar
Menus: *A la carte* L, fixed-price
D & Sun L, bar menu
Seats: 50. No smoking in dining
room
Additional: Children permitted
at lunch; special diets on request

GULLANE, **La Potinière** ✿✿✿

A well-practised wife and husband team offer set menus of simple French(ish) food matched by excellent wines at their charming cottage

An unassuming little cottage, not far from Muirfield golf course, where David Brown performs a cunning juggling act in simultaneously serving a roomful of people with well judged and satisfying food. It is cooked by his wife Hilary in a style which she describes as 'French(ish)'. It is a double act that the pair have perfected over twenty years and can now carry off with apparently effortless, friendly flair. Mr Brown is also the keeper of one of the country's most extraordinary cellars and it is worth arriving early to peruse his list, especially if you are eager to discover some of the lesser-known wines from the South West of France.

The routine is this: Hilary decides on the set menu, drawing on the best available local produce and, having checked an index card reference system to ensure her guests aren't offered the same dishes twice, meals are served promptly at 1pm, lunch, and 8pm, dinner. This creates a rare conviviality among total strangers and a palpable atmosphere of expectation in the dining-room, which features dried flowers hanging from overhead beams and a framed collection of wine labels on the walls. Our last meal more than confirmed expectations of simple cooking full of uncluttered flavours. It consisted of a rich tomato and basil soup, followed by moist poached salmon with a salt crust served on a bed of lentils with some wine-soaked morels. Breast of Guinea fowl came with a sweet stuffing of dried apricots and dates spiked with mint. Then came a crisp salad of green vegetables, sunflower seeds and new potatoes in a light dressing. 'Citron Surprise' – a sort of flopped soufflé with custard at the bottom and whisked, browned egg white on top – rounded it all off wonderfully well.

Directions: Village centre

Main Street
East Lothian EH31 2AA
Map no: 12 NT48
Tel: 01620 843 214
Chef: Hilary Brown
Proprietors: David & Hilary
Brown
Cost: Fixed-price (4 course) L
£18.75/£19.75 Sun/D £29.50 (5
course). H/wine £9.75 ☻ Service
exc
Credit cards: None taken
Times: Last L 2pm, last D
9.30pm Closed Sat L
Menus: Fixed-price L & D
Seats: 30. No smoking in dining
room
Additional: Children permitted;
other diets prior arrangement

LINLITHGOW, Champany Inn ֎֎֎

Primarily a steakhouse of superb quality, this period restaurant appeals particularly to the business community and for special occasions

West Lothian EH49 7LU
Map no: 11 NS97
Tel: 0150683 4532/4388
Chef: Clive Davidson
Proprietors: Clive & Anne Davidson
Cost: Alc £38-£40, fixed-price L £13.75/D £27.50. H/wine £10.50 ♥ Service exc
Credit cards: ▨ ▨ ▨ ▨ OTHER
Times: Last L 2pm, last D 10pm Closed Sat L, Sun Dec 25/26, Jan 1/2
Menus: A la carte, fixed-price L & D, bar menu
Seats: 50.
Additional: Children over 8 permitted; ♥ dishes, other diets on request

The buildings that make up the Champany Inn date from the time of Mary, Queen of Scots, and it was apparently her fondness for picnicking 'a la campagne' in the area that gave rise to its name. Today's guests eat in more formal style, passing through a cocktail bar where lobster, crayfish and oysters are kept in sea water, then entering a hexagonal dining room with views over an attractive garden which is floodlit in the evenings. If you are a steak lover this is the place to go – Clive Davidson selects only the best Aberdeen Angus which is then hung for three weeks to ensure that it arrives on the plate in perfect condition.

Our inspector enjoyed a huge, tender piece of fillet steak accompanied by a light, tarragon-flavoured béarnaise sauce. Variations include 'carpet bagger', a thick fillet of beef stuffed with an oyster. Chargrilled salmon also provides a good alternative to beef, as does lamb, in season. Fresh vegetables are brought in a basket, your selection then being cooked to order, and you should try the traditional Champany chip – an excellent accompaniment to any cut of meat. This is not the place for people with small appetites, and few make it to dessert. Those who do, however, will be offered a selection of fruits and sorbets as well as more substantial sweets. A meal here is not cheap but you do get what you pay for, both in terms of quantity and quality. Staff provide professional service, and some one thousand bins make up a comprehensive wine list that fills a 300-page book.

Directions: 2 miles N/E of Linlithgow at junction of A904 & A803

LINLITHGOW, Earl O'Moray Inn ֎

A Grade II listed Georgian mansion east of the town, now an inn, which has both an elegant 'fine dining-room' (open only on Fridays and Saturdays at present) and an excellent value brasserie-style operation. The latter specialises in grills – its success soundly based on quality fresh ingredients innovatively prepared and carefully presented

West Lothian EH49 7NU
Map no: 11 NS97
Tel: 01506 842229
Chef: Joe Queen
Proprietor: Nicholas Holmes
Cost: Alc L £16/D£22
Credit cards: ▨ ▨ ▨ OTHER
Time: Last D 9.30pm

Directions: From M9 on A803, just before town

ORKNEY

ST MARGARET'S HOPE,
Creel Restaurant ✸

☺ *The emphasis is on seafood and fresh Orkney produce at this popular seafront restaurant. A typical meal might be dressed parton (crab) followed by local salmon in puff pastry stuffed with currants and flavoured with ginger. Orkney fudge comes with the coffee*

Menus: A la carte D
Seats: 34
Additional: Children welcome; ✌ dishes, special diets on request
Directions: Take A961 south from Kirkwall. Turn right at St Margaret's Hope. Parking on seafront

Front Road KW17 2SL
Map no: 16
Tel: 01856 831 311
Chef: Alan Craigie
Proprietors: Alan & Joyce Craigie
Cost: Alc £20, H/wine £7.50. Service exc
Credit cards: ▨ ▨
Times: Last D 9pm. Open daily Jun-Oct, Closed Sun-Thur Nov-May, 2 wks Oct, 1 wk Jan

STRATHCLYDE

ARDUAINE, Loch Melfort Hotel ✸

With a spectacular outlook over Asknish Bay you would expect the emphasis on fish and you find it here: Islay scallops, Luing lobster and langoustine, Isle of Seil oysters, Ardmaddy salmon. Philip Lewis's competent cooking has a light, modern touch which also takes in roasted or chargrilled meats with simple sauces

Arduaine
Argyllshire PA34 4XG
Map no: 10 NM71
Tel: 01852 200233
Chef: Philip Lewis
Proprietors: Philip & Rosalind Lewis
Cost: Fixed-price L £4-£20/D £25 (5 course). H/wine £11.95. Service exc
Credit cards: ▨ ▨ ▨ OTHER
Times: Last L 2.30pm/D 9pm Daily. Closed Jan 4-end Feb
Seats: 70. No smoking in dining room
Menus: Fixed-price L & D, bar menu
Additional: Children permitted, children's portions; ✌ dishes, vegan/other diets with notice

Directions: On A816 midway between Oban and Lochgilphead

ARRAN, ISLE OF, BRODICK,

Auchrannie Country House Hotel ✤

A renovated Victorian mansion stands in extensive landscaped grounds and has a warm atmosphere and sound cooking. The Garden restaurant showcases Scottish produce such as Highland venison with a port and redcurrant sauce, or baked fillet of salmon. The Bistro offers a more relaxed atmosphere

Seats: 60 + 60. No-smoking area **Menus:** *A la carte* L & D (Bistro), fixed-price D (Rest) **Additional:** Children welcome in Bistro, children's menu; ❤ dishes, other diets on request
Directions: Through village take second left past Brodick Golf Club

Strathclyde KA27 8BZ
Map no: 10 NS03
Tel: 01770 302234
Chef: George Ramage
Proprietors: Iain & Linda Johnston
Cost: *Alc* (Bistro) L £12.50, fixed-price D (Rest) £23 (4 course). H/wine £10.50 Service exc
Credit cards: ▨ ▩ OTHER
Times: 10am-last D 9.30pm (Bistro), 6.30pm-last D 9.30pm (Restaurant)

ARRAN, ISLE OF, BRODICK,

Kilmichael Country House Hotel ✤

Set in a small glen outside Brodick, Kilmichael has the atmosphere of a private country house. The restaurant is relaxed and guests are offered hearty portions of wholesome, competently cooked food. Flair is shown in the preparation of, for example, Arran scallops, or duck with kumquats. Puddings are highly recommended

Menus: Fixed-price D **Seats:** 18. No smoking **Additional:** Children over 12 permitted; ❤ menu, other diets on request
Directions: Golf course road, turn L inland on sharp bend past Church

Glen Coy
Isle of Arran KA27 8BY
Map no: 10 NS03
Tel: 01770 302219
Chefs: Antony Butterworth and Geoffrey Botterill
Proprietors: Antony Butterworth and Geoffrey Botterill
Cost: Fixed-price D £24.50 (5 course) H/wine £8.45 Service exc
Credit cards: ▨ ▩
Times: 7.30pm-last D 8.45pm Closed Mon, Christmas

AYR, # The Boathouse Restaurant ✤

An attractive, split-level, riverside restaurant, close to the fish quay and the town centre. Sound cooking is inspired by fresh regional produce and offered on either a bar-style menu or full carte. Typical dishes might be mille-feuille of salmon mousse and roast saddle of hare on a thyme and sherry jus

Menus: *A la carte,* fixed-price L, bar menu
Seats: 50. No cigars or pipes in dining room
Additional: Children welcome, ❤ dishes, other diets on request
Directions: By the riverside at bottom of Fort Street

4 South Harbour Street
Ayrshire KA7 1JA
Map no: 10 NS32
Tel: 01292 280212
Chef: Matt Thomson
Proprietors: Robert Jones and Heather Clark
Cost: *Alc* £25,fixed-price L £7.95. H/wine £9.90
No service charge
Credit cards: ▨ ▩ ▨ OTHER
Times: Last L 2.30pm/D 9.30pm Closed Tue

AYR, # Fairfield House ✤✤

A fine, restored and extended Victorian mansion in a quiet residential area, where meals may be taken in the dining room or a conservatory brasserie

From the house there are unrestricted views over the Firth of Clyde to the Isle of Arran. The building has an air of elegance throughout. The formal Fleur de Lys restaurant offers a set-price menu and a *carte* along with a reasonable wine list that is a bit short on half bottles. The separate list of specials is worth studying. For example, a starter available in the summer was poached pear wrapped in smoked salmon on a bed of endive lettuce with a raspberry and strawberry vinaigrette. Then there was a choice of medley of local

Fairfield Road
Ayrshire KA7 2AR
Map no: 10 N532
Tel: 01292 267461
Chef: Ian Mitchell
Manager: Geoffrey Dibble
Cost: *Alc* £22, fixed-price L £10.95/D £22
H/wine £11.75 ❢ Service inc
Credit cards: ▨ ▩ ▨ OTHER
Times: Last L 2.30pm, last D 10pm

seafood in champagne butter sauce and samphire grass, or pan-fried fillet of beef, on a red wine and thyme jus, with morels and fresh asparagus tips, or roast duck, filled with wild mushrooms, glazed with ginger and served on a bed of egg noodles. Ayrshire lamb, pan-fried suprême of pheasant and guinea fowl, or roulade of salmon and sole are other examples. Desserts include steamed sultana and syrup pudding with warm anglaise sauce. The conservatory brasserie serves simpler meals in a brighter, more spacious setting.

Menus: A la carte, fixed-price L & D, pre-theatre, bar menu
Seats: 40 (+30 Brasserie). No smoking in dining room
Additional: Children welcome, children's menu; ❶ dishes, vegan/other diets on request

Directions: From Ayr centre: down Miller Road, left at lights & immediately right

AYR, **Fouters** ❀❀

☺ *Fresh local produce cooked with the influence of the traditional French kitchen helps to account for a loyal local following*

The British Linen Bank opened its branch here in 1720. Long since absorbed by something bigger, its vaulted basement became a restaurant owned by Fran and Laurie Black. In the kitchen John Winton and Robert Brown rely on tried and tested favourites but they are still prepared to try new ideas. Blackboard specials support the separate lunch and dinner *cartes* in the three dining areas downstairs, each with a flagstone floor, white stucco walls and red clothed tables. On Saturday a set-price menu takes over. To some extent starters like tartlet of seafood in a smooth Thermidor sauce, or Loch Fyne mussels with garlic, parsley, wine and cream might happily be followed by Gressingham duck with cherry apples and ginger, accompanied by a stock-based wine, cream and herb sauce flavoured with apple jelly. Seafood is plentiful because Ayr fish market is so close. For those with a taste for real meat the char-grilled steaks are proving popular. Bread and butter pudding with brandy sherry can be recommended to finish. The wine list, with a decent selection of some 16 half bottles, is sensible in size and price.

2A Academy Street
Ayrshire KA7 1HS
Map no: 10 NS32
Tel: 01292 261391
Chef: John Winton and Robert Brown
Proprietors: Laurie & Fran Black
Cost: Alc £22, fixed-price L from £4.95 (1 course)/D £19.50 (2 course). H/wine £10.50 Service exc
Credit cards: 🅰 ▨ ▨ ▨ OTHER
Times: Last L 2pm, last D 10.30pm Closed Mon, 3 days Xmas & N/year
Menus: A la carte, fixed-price L & D, pre-theatre
Seats: 38. No-smoking area
Additional: Children welcome, children's menu; ❶ dishes, vegan/other diets on request

Directions: Town centre, cobbled lane opposite Town Hall

BALLOCH,
Cameron House Hotel ❀❀

A very civilised place for some serious eating, the kitchen successfully combining traditional skills with modern ideas

On the bonny banks of Loch Lomond is a sympathetically restored and enlarged, rather splendid, Georgian turreted mansion. It is beautifully set in well-tended grounds and successfully manages to combine the grace and charm of the 18th-century with up-to-date facilities and comforts. A sensible change has been the Brasserie's removal from the chlorine-laden atmosphere of the pool area to the new Grill Room, providing an informal alternative to the elegant Georgian Room Restaurant. At lunchtime, Jeff Bland's two/three-course menu is good value for money; in the evening, however, the price for the four-course set dinner rises steeply. There is, besides, an imaginative *carte* and a special six-course surprise 'Celebration' dinner menu. The highlight of an inspection lunch was a delicious timbale of salmon soufflé in a delicate hollandaise sauce. This was followed by a fresh, lightly steamed fillet of turbot on a bed of

Alexandria
Dunbartonshire G83 8QZ
Map no: 10 NS38
Tel: 01389 55565
Chef: Jeff Bland
Proprietor: Craigendarroch Group.
Manager: Rody Whiteford
Cost: Alc £40, fixed-price L £16.50/D £32.50 (4 course) H/wine £11.65 ❢ Gratuities not accepted
Credit cards: 🅰 ▨ ▨ ▨ OTHER
Times: Noon-last L 2pm, 7pm-last D 10pm. Closed Sat L, Sun L
Menus: A la carte, fixed-price L & D, bar menu
Seats: 45. No smoking in dining room.

Cameron House Hotel and Country Estate

Additional: Children permitted, children's menus;  menu, vegan/other diets on request

sautéed spinach, enhanced by a slightly spiced peanut and orange butter sauce. Home-made choux pastry amply filled with Drambuie flavoured cream, served with a sauce anglaise, and fresh berries was an ideal finish. There is no service charge and gratuities are not accepted.

Directions: M8/A82 to Dumbarton: take road to Luss, hotel signed 1 mile past Balloch on right

BIGGAR, **Shieldhill** ❀❀

800 years of traceable history and providing some of the best modern British cooking in the region

Shieldhill can date its history to three years before the Fourth Crusade began in 1202 AD. Presumably the gently rolling Lanarkshire countryside that surrounds it rolled just as gently then. There has been a change in the kitchen since last year's Guide, the new pairing being Paul Whitecross, who had his own AA two-rosette restaurant in Inverness, and Ashley Gallant. There is no *carte*, but set-price, two-course (three on Sundays) lunch, and three and four course dinner menus. These are changed daily to good effect. On our chosen night salmon tortellini on puréed broccoli with a light saffron cream sauce, and an oyster garnished with caviar, looked super, and mostly it was – only a slightly chewy pasta case let it down. Much better was the pavé of halibut perfectly accompanied by a well made Niçoise tatin and a sauce à l'antiboise. Vegetables were simply prepared to retain flavour. The sweet selection was not particularly impressive, but the 'theme of Banana' worked well – a small tartlet filled with sliced banana, a banana mousse, a small banana fritter and ice-cream to match.

Directions: Off B7016 (Carnwath), turn left 2 miles from centre of Biggar

Quothquan
Lanarkshire ML12 6NA
Map no: 11 NT03
Tel: 01899 20035
Chef: Paul Whitecross and Ashley Gallant
Proprietors: Joan & Neil Mackintosh (Scotland's Commended)
Cost: Fixed-price L £10 (2 course)/D £27. H/wine £9.50 Service exc
Credit cards: ◪ 🌐 🌐 ◪ OTHER
Times: Last L 1.30pm, last D 9pm
Menus: Fixed-price L & D, bar menu
Seats: 28. No smoking in dining room
Additional: Children over 8 permitted, children's portions;  dishes, vegan/other diets on request

---

Tapenade takes its name from the Provençal word for caper – 'tapeno', It is made with capers, desalted anchovies and stoned black olives, pounded in a mortar, and seasoned with olive oil, lemon juice, aromatic herbs, and perhaps a drop of marc (or brandy).

CLACHAN-SEIL, **Willowburn Hotel** ❀

Isle of Seil
Argyllshire PA34 4TJ
Map no: 10 NM71
Tel: 018523 276
Chef: Maureen Todd
Proprietors: Archie & Maureen Todd
Cost: *Alc* £20, fixed-price D £17.50 H/wine £6.95 Service inc
Credit cards: 🔲 🔲
Times: Last L 2pm/D 8pm.

☺ *A small, homely, holiday hotel beside the Seil Sound, with a garden leading down to the water. Local and regional produce appear on a menu that changes daily. Highly recommended are the roast Aberdeen Angus beef and the baked crab. A less formal bar menu is also available*

Menus: A la carte, fixed-price D, bar menu
Seats: 40. No smoking in dining room
Additional: Children welcome, children's menu; ❤ dishes, vegan/other diets on request
Directions: A816 S from Oban 8 miles, B844 (Easdale) 3 miles, cross Atlantic Bridge

COLONSAY, ISLE OF – SCALASAIG,
Colonsay Hotel ❀

Argyllshire PA61 7YP
Map no: 10 NR39
Tel: 01951 200 316
Chef: Christa Bryne
Proprietors: Kevin & Christa Bryne (Scotland's Commended)
Cost: Fixed-price D £21 (4 course). H/wine £8.50 Service inc
Credit cards: 🔲 🔲 🔲 🔲 OTHER
Times: Last D 7.30pm. Closed Nov 5-Feb 28

☺ *Remote, relaxing and friendly, the Colonsay hotel offers uncomplicated cooking based on island produce, especially seafood. Christa Byrne's popular Scottish/European set menus may feature hot blue cheese strudels, smoked haddock and mushroom, and bread and butter pudding*

Menus: Fixed-price D, bar menu
Seats: 28. No smoking in dining room
Additional: Children permitted, children's high tea; ❤ dishes, vegan/other diets on request
Directions: 400yds west of Scalasaig Pier

CUMBERNAULD,
Westerwood Hotel ❀❀

1 St Andrew's Drive,
Westerwood G68 0EW
Map no: 11 NS77
Tel: 01236 457171
Chef: Tom Robertson
Proprietors: Westerwood Hotels Ltd. Manager: Andrew Thrush
Credit cards: 🔲 🔲 🔲 🔲
Times: Last D 10pm

A smart, modern hotel restaurant especially popular with the business community

The smart, modern Westerwood is set high above the town overlooking an 18-hole golf course (designed by Seve Ballesteros) and the Campsie Fells to the north west. As well as a good range of leisure facilities, there is a contrasting choice of bars and restaurants. The Club Bar is quite lively while the Tipsy Laird Restaurant offers an informal alternative to the more refined, octagonal Old Masters Restaurant (not currently open every night, but this is under review). Chef Tom Robertson aims to produce memorable dishes and uses the best ingredients to achieve this. An inspection meal in the Old Masters Restaurant took in an appetiser of warm chicken and herb mousse, a deeply flavoured crayfish bisque garnished with Dublin Bay prawns, fresh tomato and chervil, and 'delicious' baked fillet of haddock with a herb and horseradish crust, served with an intense cream, kipper and chive sauce (which could have benefitted from being less intense in flavour). Sticky toffee pudding rounded it all off. The comprehensive wine list is strong on clarets and the New World and there's a good range of half bottles.

Directions: Take exit from A80 signposted Ward Park. At mini roundabout take first left, at 2nd roundabout turn right, leads into St Andrew's Drive

DALRY, **Braidwoods** ❀❀

☺ *A range of imaginatively devised and skilfully prepared dishes ensures the continued popularity of this small country restaurant*

This charming cottage-style restaurant – surrounded by fields and situated about a mile southwest of the village – has very quickly built up an enviable reputation. Be sure to book in advance (especially for dinner) as its honest dishes, relaxed environment and affordable prices mean that it is often full. The experience that Keith and Nicola Braidwood both have in several of Scotland's better country house hotels, together with their flair and imagination, stands them in good stead in their simple aim of providing the customer with the best of local produce. Lunch – predictably popular with the business fraternity – offers the choice of either two or three courses from a fixed-price menu with three options at each stage; dinner, whilst following a similar pattern, provides an intermediate course and slightly more choice. A delicious confit of Gressingham duck on a bed of lentils, for example, might be followed by fillet of Shetland salmon lightly baked in a fresh herb crust then crème brûlée flavoured with orange and Grand Marnier. Menus are accompanied by a reasonably priced wine list of moderate length.

Directions: From centre of Dalry take the A737 (Kilwinning). On outskirts turn right (unclassifed road signed Saltcoats). On right after 1 mile

Dalry KA24 4LN
Map no: 10 NS34
Tel: 01294 833544
Chefs: Keith & Nicola Braidwood
Proprietors: Mr & Mrs Braidwood
Cost: Alc £14.50, fixed-price £23
Credit cards: ▨ ▨ ▨ ▨
Times: L 12-2pm, D 7.9.30pm. Closed L Mon & Tue, Sun & Mon eve, 3 wks Jan

DUNOON, **Beverley's Restaurant** ❀

This charming Victorian hotel stands in wooded grounds overlooking the Firth of Clyde. The elegant Mackintosh-inspired dining room offers a variety of local seafood, game and prime beef. Cooking is modern in style, and the delicate saucing of dishes such as the scampi Prince Charlie attracts much praise

Seats: 40. No smoking in dining room
Additional: Children welcome, children's portions/menu; ❂ dishes, other diets on request
Directions: At the west end of Dunoon overlooking West Bay

Ardfillayne Hotel
West Bay, Dunoon
Argyllshire PA23 7QS
Map no: 10 NS17
Tel: 01369 702267
Chef: William McCaffrey
Proprietor: William McCaffrey
Cost: Alc £20, fixed-price D £25. H/wine £11 ❢ Service exc
Credit cards: ▨ ▨ ▨ ▨
Times: Last D 10pm. Closed Sun or Mon in winter

DUNOON, **Enmore Hotel** ❀

Overlooking the Firth of Clyde, the Enmore Hotel continues to earn praise for its daily changing five-course menu. Chef/Patron David Wilson uses quality raw ingredients to carefully prepare dishes such as pork forestière; pan fried strips of pork fillet with a mushroom, wine and cream sauce

Menus: A la carte, fixed-price L & D, bar menu **Seats:** 35. No smoking **Additional:** Children welcome (over 7 at D), children's menu; ❂ dishes, vegan on request
Directions: Between two ferries 1 mile N of Dunoon

Argyllshire PA23 8HH
Map no: 10 NS17
Tel: 01369 702230
Chef: David Wilson
Proprietors: Angela & David Wilson
Cost: Alc £18, fixed-price L £15 (4 course)/D £26 (6 course) H/wine £8.50 ❢ Service inc
Credit cards: ▨ ▨
Times: Last L 3pm/D 9.30pm Daily

Entries in this Guide are based on reports filed by our team of professionally trained, full-time inspectors.

ERISKA, Isle of Eriska 🏵🏵

The superb natural setting and charming public rooms of this hotel make a visit to its restaurant a trip to a different world

For over 21 years Robin and Sheena Buchanan-Smith have been welcoming guests to their unpretentious, comfortable Scottish baronial home situated on its own private island and surrounded by magnificent scenery. Now, however, they have passed over much of the running of the enterprise to their son, Beppo. Public rooms – which retain the timeless charm of fine wood-panelling, deeply cushioned sofas and real fires – include an attractively appointed dining-room where chef Craig Rodgers offers a daily-changing six-course dinner menu which each night features a particular roast (or, on Fridays, salmon) carved from the copper-domed trolley. A recent inspection meal commenced with a starter of chicken livers in a puff pastry case, was followed by thick, pleasantly flavoured carrot and coriander soup, and then scallops with beef fillet with wild mushroom sauce. There is a sensibly chosen wine list, attentive service and a pleasant environment. The breakfast buffet is in true country house style and includes kedgeree and pancakes.

Directions: From Connel take A828, signposted Fort William, for Benderloch village. Follow signs to Isle of Eriska

Ledaig by Oban
Argyllshire PA37 1SD
Map no: 10 NM94
Tel: 01631 720371
Chef: Craig Rodgers
Proprietors: The Buchanan-Smith family (Scotland's Heritage Hotels)
Cost: Fixed-price D £35. H/wine £8.50 ! No service charge
Credit cards: 🟦 🟫
Times: Last D 9pm. Closed Dec-Mar
Menus: Fixed-price dinner
Seats: 40. No cigars or pipes
Additional: Children over 10 permitted; ✪ dishes, vegan/other diets on request

GIRVAN, Wildings 🏵🏵

Good modern cooking, with an emphasis on fish, in a friendly village restaurant

Under the ownership of Brian and Dorothy Sage, a major transformation has taken place at this delightful, small restaurant. The lemon and blue interior is light and airy, and the ornamental fish adorning the walls and waistcoats of the staff clearly signal that seafood is the speciality. Meat-eaters, however, are well catered for. At lunch, the short, daily-changing set menu is excellent value for two courses at £7.95, and three at £10.50. In the evening, the format is similar, but with a slightly more adventurous choice of dishes. An enjoyable inspection meal began with a delicious smoked and fresh salmon roulade, liberally laced with pistachio nuts. This was followed by a selection of fish straight from the local harbour, which included salmon, turbot, monkfish, cod and trout. Lightly pan fried, they were served with a basil and tomato vinaigrette, and crunchy, market-fresh vegetables. To finish, a richly flavoured dark chocolate pot, with a hint of Grand Marnier, was topped with fresh orange and whipped cream. The wine list is sensible, both in size and price, and the staff made this the 'friendliest restaurant visited in some time'.

Directions: Just off A77 at the north end of village

Montgomerie Street KA26 9HE
Map no: 10 NX29
Tel: 01465 713481
Chef: B J Sage
Proprietors: B & D Sage
Cost: Fixed-price L £7.95-£10.50/£15.95-£18.50
Credit cards: none taken
Times: Last L 2pm. last D 9pm. Closed Mon, Tue L and Sun eve. Xmas & New Year
Seats: 40
Additional: ✪ dishes

> Pecorino is an Italian cheese produced in every region of central and southern Italy. It is made from sheep's milk and takes its name from 'pecora', the Italian for sheep. The pecorino we are most familiar with outside Italy is 'romano', a hard, pungent grating cheese from Rome.

GLASGOW, **Buttery Restaurant** ❀❀

In unlikely surroundings, judge it for content not appearance, it's one of Glasgow's institutions

Still holding out against a tide of redevelopment, and overshadowed by the Kingston Bridge, the Buttery with its splendid Victorian interior always makes first-timers exclaim. It continues to delight regulars too. Commitment and consistency have for years been the twin hallmarks of success, thanks to the combined efforts of front-of-house manager James Wilson and chef Stephen Johnson. The business community flock here for the good value three-course set-lunch but, if dinner it has to be, then the *carte* takes some beating. Try pan-fried strips of calves' liver in a light Cointreau sauce, home-made duck ravioli in a dark Madeira sauce or a pressed, layered fish and spinach terrine with a roast pepper and balsamic dressing. Recommended main courses might be lattice of salmon and sole with dill and keta sauce; roast suprême of pheasant on a green leaf and pine nut pancake with a foie gras butter sauce; or perhaps sliced loin of Highland venison on game haggis with a game and bayleaf-flavoured jus. Finish with bees' pollen ice-cream in a brandy snap basket with a thick, mixed berry sauce or the sugar-glazed raspberry crème brûlée. On the wine list France, especially the better regions, is well represented, and halves are in good supply.

Directions: City centre

652 Argyle Street
Lanarkshire G3 8UF
Map no: 11 NS56
Tel: 0141 221 8188
Chef: Stephen Johnson
Proprietor: Alloa.
Manager: James Wilson
Cost: *Alc* £25-£27, fixed-price L
£14.85. H/wine £10.95. Service
inc
Credit cards: 💳 💳 💳 💳 OTHER
Times: Last L
2.30pm/D10.30pm. Closed Sat
L, Sun, BHs
Menus: *A la carte*, fixed-price L,
bar L menu
Seats: 50. Air conditioned
Additional: Children permitted;
❤ menu, vegan/other diets on
request

GLASGOW, Crannog Seafood Restaurant ❀

A bistro-style restaurant in the heart of the city where West Coast seafood can be enjoyed. A two-course blackboard menu lists lunchtime choices and specials to supplement the evening carte. Recommended are Crannog bouillabaisse, fresh langoustines and salmon every which way

Menus: *A la carte*, fixed-price L, pre-theatre **Seats:** 52
Additional: Children welcome, children's portions; ❤ dishes,
vegan/other diets on request
Directions: 2 mins city centre – along Broomielaw, right into
Cheapside Street

28 Cheapside Street
Lanarkshire G3 8BH
Map no: 11 NS56
Tel: 0141 221 1727
Chef: Paul Laurie
Proprietor: Crannog Ltd.
Manager: Lisa Potter
Cost: *Alc* £22, fixed-price L
£10. H/wine £7.95 Service exc
Credit cards: 💳 💳 OTHER
Times: Last L 2.30pm/D
10.30pm. Closed Sun, Mon,
Xmas, New Year

GLASGOW, **Ewington Hotel** ❀

The arrival of a new chef has led to a more adventurous approach in the kitchen of the Ewington Hotel. Innovative dishes might include parcels of smoked salmon stuffed with horseradish mousseline, and duo of duck and pigeon with a raspberry and bitter chocolate sauce

Menus: Fixed-price L & D, pre-theatre
Seats: 60. Smoking area
Additional: Children permitted until 7pm, children's menu;
❤ dishes, vegan/other diets on request
Directions: From A77 pass through 8 sets of traffic lights then take
2nd left after Allison Street; overlooking Queen's Park

132 Queens Drive
Lanarkshire G42 8QW
Map no: 11 NS56
Tel: 0141 423 1152
Chef: Paul Moore
Proprietor: (Best Western).
Manager: Marie-Clare Watson
Cost: Fixed-price L £7.25/D
£14.95. H/wine £9 Service exc
Credit cards: 💳 💳 💳 💳
Times: 12.30pm-last L 2pm,
6pm-last D 9pm, pre-theatre
5.30pm-6pm

GLASGOW, **Hilton Hotel** ❀❀

The Hilton's Scottish/British cooking is proving a real winner in a city with an enviable gastronomic reputation

The Hilton is a striking modern building: twenty storeys of polished granite and mirrored glass. Within, it is equally impressive with a spacious and stylish lobby leading to a range of eating and drinking places, including the colonial-themed Raffles Bar, the Scotch Bar, specialising in West Coast whiskies, Minsky's New York Deli, and, for fine dining, Camerons. Here, Michael Mizzen works wonders with Scottish produce like Aberdeen Angus beef, Loch Fyne oysters, Arran smoked salmon and Highland game. He manages to be imaginative without getting too complicated and, the portions are generous. Rather heavy, over-firm tortellini of squat lobster mousse came with shelled langoustines and a full-flavoured tomato fondue; the pasta in a lasagna of wild salmon with Arran mustard sauce was much more refined. Foie gras encased in salmon, and served with crispy artichokes, created an interesting combination of tastes and flavours. Suprême of Barbary duck was served with its own ham and confit of leg meat, on a subtle cinnamon and juniper sauce. Patisserie is a strength with good, flavoured breads, well made desserts and fine petits fours. The wine list is adequate, although the half bottle selection is quite limited.

Directions: Charing Cross exit from M8, turn right at first traffic lights, right again & follow signs for hotel

1 Williams Street
Lanarkshire G3 8HT
Map no: 11 NS56
Tel: 0141 204 5555
Chef: Michael Mizzen
Proprietor: Hilton International.
Manager: Paul Cleary
Cost: Alc £30, fixed-price
L £17.50 (2 course), £20.50/D
£29.50. H/wine £12.50 Service
exc
Credit cards: 🔳 🔤 🔳 🔳 OTHER
Times: Last L 2.30pm, last D
10.30pm Closed Sun, Bhs
Menus: A la carte, fixed-price
L & D
Seats: 48. Air conditioned
Additional: Children welcome;
♥ dishes, vegan/other diets on
request

GLASGOW, **Moat House Hotel** ❀❀

A surprisingly good restaurant in one of the city's larger hotels

Being next to the Scottish Exhibition and Conference Centre makes the Moat House super-convenient for the business fraternity. Despite being in a city with some outstanding restaurants, many stay in the hotel to eat in the Mariner Restaurant. Starters include peppered tomato salad, Atlantic prawn and ricotta gâteau, or pimento crab parfait, poached oysters, chicken liver and wild mushroom pithiviers, or lobster and tomato ravioli. Soups are offered too. While seafood dominates the starters, it is the other way round with the main courses, so that there are three fish dishes – tranche of salmon, seared red snapper, and poached scallops – and seven meat options. Among them are roast veal fillet, tournedos of beef, saddle of venison, and rack of lamb. The nearest to a surprise on the desserts list is banana and raspberry tartlet, with a raspberry mousse. Lighter meals may be chosen from the Pointhouse Selection and Buffet menu. The wine list is mainly French.

Directions: Adjacent to Scottish Exhibition & Conference Centre, follow signs

Congress Road
Lanarkshire G3 8QT
Map no: 11 NS56
Tel: 0141 306 9988
Chef: Thomas Brown
Proprietor: Moat House.
Manager: Robert Campbell Aird
Cost: Alc £29.50, fixed-price
L £16.50/D £18.95(Buffet/5
course). H/wine £10.75 ❢
Service exc
Credit cards: 🔳 🔤 🔳 🔳
Times: Last L 2.30pm, last D
10.30pm
Menus: A la carte, fixed-price
L & D, pre-theatre, bar menu
Seats: 170. Air conditioned.
No-smoking area
Additional: Children welcome,
children's menu available;
♥ menu, vegan/other diets on
request

> Pesto is a sauce made with basil, olive oil, pecorino and Parmesan. Walnuts or pine nuts may be added. The Genoese claim to have invented it, and insist that true pesto cannot be made without their own small-leafed basil and a marble mortar.

GLASGOW, **Killermont Polo Club** ❀

☺ *The distinctive cooking of northern India is served in this unusual restaurant which combines the ambience of the days of the Raj with that of a polo club. Jaipuri and Nentara dishes of chicken, lamb and king prawns are particularly worth trying, as are the tikka and tandoori dishes*

Times: Last L 2pm/D 10.30pm. L not served Sun. Closed 1 Jan
Additional: Children permitted; ❷ dishes, vegan/other diets on request
Directions: From the city centre travel towards the West End, then Bearsden on the Maryhill Road. The driveway for the restaurant is before the Science parks

2002 Maryhill Road
Mary Hill Park
Lanarkshire G20 0AB
Map no: 11 NS56
Tel: 0141 946 5412
Chef: Bahadur Singh Dhaliwad
Proprietor: Killermont Polo Club
Cost: Alc £15, fixed-price L
£6.95 (2 courses), £7.95; fixed-price buffet D Sun & Mon £9.95.
H/wine £8.25. Service exc
Credit cards: 🂱 ▨ ▨ 🖳 OTHER
Seats: 96

GLASGOW, **La Parmigiana** ❀❀

Booking is essential at family-run, traditional Italian restaurant

The spaghetti carbonara here is the real thing – as authentic and delicious as any Momma ever made. As well as home-made pasta, this popular, unpretentious Glasgow-Italian restaurant features a number of European dishes, as well as the expected range of traditional Italian ones. Classic specialities include 'carpaccio, pollo all diavola' and scallops of veal with Parma ham and mozzarella. Our inspector was also impressed with 'zuppa di pesce', an exciting fish and shellfish stew flavoured with onions, celery, tomato and chillies. To finish there is a good choice of mouth-watering sweets, and crêpes al Grand Marnier can be safely recommended. At lunchtime, the excellent three-course menu is great value; in the evenings, the more adventurous *carte* comes into its own. Friendly and attentive staff are smartly turned out in black waistcoats, bow ties and long, white aprons, and Italian music adds to the atmosphere of the narrow interior.

Directions: Close to Kelvinbridge underground station

447 Great Western Road
Strathclyde
Map no: 11 NS56
Tel: 0141 334 0686
Chef: Sandro Giovanazzi
Proprietor: Angelo & Sandro Giovanazzi
Cost: Alc £18, fixed-price L £6.90. Service exc
Credit cards: 🂱 ▨ ▨ 🖳 OTHER
Times: Last L 2.30pm, last D 11pm Closed Sun, BHs, Dec 25, Jan 1
Menus: A la carte, fixed-price L
Seats: 45. Air conditioned
Additional: Children welcome, children's portions; ❷ dishes, vegan/other diets on request

GLASGOW, **Malmaison Hotel** ❀

In the heart of the city centre, this exciting new hotel offers style and simplicity, particularly in the chic brasserie. Traditional French cooking has been livened up with oriental spices and other influences to create light and tempting dishes which do not disappoint; try the sautéed mushrooms with garlic

Times: Last D 11pm

278 West George Street G2 4LL
Map no: 11 NS56
Tel: 0141 221 6400
Chef: Kenny Colthan
Proprietor: Arcadian International Plc
Cost: Alc L/D £20
Credit cards: 🂱 ▨ ▨ 🖳 OTHER

GLASGOW,
One Devonshire Gardens Hotel ❀❀

An opulent town house hotel serving a short choice of innovative dishes with a strong modern signature

A distinctive Victorian hotel in a tree-lined terrace, One Devonshire Gardens is unique. It comprises three adjoining, but not interconnecting, town houses with interiors that are dramatic, different, but completely in sympathy with the grandeur of the

1 Devonshire Gardens
Lanarkshire G12 0UX
Map no: 11 NS56
Tel: 0141 339 2001
Chef: Andrew Fairlie
Proprietor: One Devonshire Gardens.
Manager: Beverley Payne
Cost: Alc £37.50, fixed-price L £25. H/wine £16 ! Service exc
Credit cards: 🂱 ▨ ▨ 🖳 OTHER

whole property. Much interest is focused on the stunningly elegant restaurant, where Andrew Fairlie's innovative modern cooking is producing some imaginative juxtapositions of flavours and textures. There are influences from France, the Mediterranean and the Far East, and the end result reveals good taste. Successful dishes sampled this year have included seared scallops with beansprouts and spiced Thai sauce, a 'delicious' swede soup with a hint of rosemary, fillet of fresh halibut served on a basil cous cous with a tomato, olive and green bean dressing, and, to finish, a dessert of apple and Calvados gratin with a spicy fruit compote. The short daily menus offer three-courses at lunch and four-courses at dinner, along with a carefully chosen list of fine wines from around the world. Service is unobtrusively attentive.

Directions: On Great Western Road turn left at lights towards Hyndland, 200 yards turn right and right again

Times: Last L 2.30pm/D 10.15pm Daily
Menus: *A la carte,* fixed-price L, post-theatre
Seats: 30. Air conditioned
Additional: Children welcome, Ⓥ menu, vegan/other diets on request

GLASGOW, Rogano ❀❀

In a fashionable part of the city, one of Glasgow's popular eating places

A vibrant city atmosphere sets the lunch-time pace at one of Glasgow's long established restaurants, located in a pedestrianised area just off fashionable Buchanan Street. The stylish Art Deco interior has been carefully conserved. Seafood remains the house speciality, though other tastes, including vegetarian, are well catered for. Chef Derek Marshall has taken over in the kitchen, but has retained his predecessor's tried and tested favourites, at the same time stamping his own style. The no-choice, three-course, fixed-price menu is good value and immensely popular. Even cheaper are the Oyster Bar and Café menus but, when splashing out on dinner, the *carte* comes into its own. A successful inspection meal began with an old favourite, the Rogano fish soup with rouille and Parmesan croûtons, followed by lightly seared scallops with lime, ginger and spring onions in soya sauce, accompanied by a crisp green salad and fresh vegetables. The carefully chosen wine list is strong on Burgundies and Bordeaux, but the newer producing countries still get a pretty good look in. Staff in their black waistcoats and long white aprons look the business, and are attentive and eager to please.

Directions: City centre between Buchanan Street & Royal Exchange Square

11 Exchange Place
Lanarkshire G1 3AN
Map no: 11 NS56
Tel: 0141-248 4055
Chef: Derek Marshall
Proprietor: Alloa.
Manager: Gordon Yuill
Cost: *Alc* £31.50 (Rest), £18.50 (Cafe), fixed-price L £16.50 (£15 Sat-Sun). H/wine £9.50 Service exc
Credit cards: OTHER
Times: Last L 2.30pm (Cafe all day), last D 10.30pm (Cafe 11pm) Closed Dec 25-26, Jan 1-2
Menus: *A la carte,* fixed-price L, bar menu
Seats: 100. Air conditioned
Additional: Children welcome; Ⓥ dishes, vegan/other diets on request

GLASGOW, **The Town House Hotel**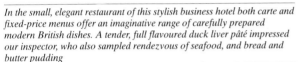

In the small, elegant restaurant of this stylish business hotel both carte and fixed-price menus offer an imaginative range of carefully prepared modern British dishes. A tender, full flavoured duck liver pâté impressed our inspector, who also sampled rendezvous of seafood, and bread and butter pudding

Menus: *A la carte,* fixed-price L & D, pre-theatre, bar menu
Seats: 40 **Additional:** Children welcome, children's portions; ❷ menu, vegan/other diets on request
Directions: On the corner of West George Street and Nelson Mandela Square

West George Street
Lanarkshire G2 1NG
Map no: 11 NS56
Tel: 0141 332 3320
Chef: John Shields
Proprietor: John P Campbell
(Select Hotel)
Cost: *Alc* £25, fixed-price L/D
£12.95 (2 course) & £15.95.
H/wine £9.75 Service exc
Credit cards: 🔳 🔳 🔳 🔳 OTHER
Times: Last L 2pm, last D 10pm.
Closed Sat L, Dec 25-Jan 2

KILCHRENAN, **Ardanaiseig Hotel** ❀❀

Good French wines find their match in a range of imaginative modern dishes based on excellent Scottish produce

The atmosphere of a very civilised private house prevails throughout this impressive 19th-century baronial mansion superbly set on the shore of Loch Awe. Beautiful wooded grounds where rhododendrons, azaleas and rare shrubs abound are an additional attraction. Talented young chef Simon Bailie continues his innovative modern treatment of quality Scottish ingredients and produces good results, with honest flavours shining through. An enjoyable warm salad, for example, features oven-roasted pigeon with a pink peppercorn sauce, while the intense flavour of plum tomato soup is sharpened by basil cream; cod baked in herb crust is complemented by a well made pimento dressing and served on a bed of flavoursome spinach and leeks, and desserts include a rich dark chocolate marquise garnished with a fresh strawberry and set on a coulis of the same fruit. Strong cafetière coffee comes with cream and petits fours. The short fixed-price menu is supported by a limited *carte* – normally produced on request. A thoughtfully compiled wine list is rich in examples from the better French regions.

Directions: From A85 take B845 south. At Kilchrenan village bear left. Hotel at end of this road

Taynuilt
Argyllshire PA35 1HE
Map no: 10 NN02
Tel: 01866 3 333
Chef: Simon Bailie
Proprietors: Mrs Julia Smith
(Small Luxury Hotels of the World)
Cost: *Alc* £30; fixed-price lunch £15, fixed-price dinner £33.50, *H/wine £9* ❢ Service exc
Credit cards: 🔳 🔳 🔳 🔳
Times: Last L 2pm, Last D 9pm. Closed Oct-Good Friday
Menus: *A la carte,* fixed-price lunch, Sunday lunch, bar menu
Seats: 30. No smoking in dining room
Additional: Children over 8 permitted; children's portions; ❷ dishes

KILCHRENAN, **Taychreggan Hotel** ❀❀

A captivating hotel in a stunning location, offering a set five-course dinner of modern Scottish cooking

The dining-room of this former drovers' inn enjoys fabulous views over Loch Awe, inviting a rather obvious pun. The decor is all polished wood, cut crystal and crisp linen, with some original works of art around the walls. Hugh Cocker is a talented chef whose dishes are inspired by fresh local produce, and by current trends. The menu is a set five-course affair, though a choice might be offered at the starter or soup stage. A spring inspection meal yielded a starter of tender confit of duck with a powerful mushroom risotto that would have 'graced a fashionable London brasserie', a judiciously seasoned curried cream of pear and parsnip soup, and a medley of fish with a delicate saffron sauce. The vegetables weren't quite as appealing: some roughly turned swede, oatmeal and butter

Taynuilt
Argyllshire PA35 1HQ
Map no: 10 NN02
Tel: 01866 833211/833366
Chefs: Hugh Cocker and Neil Mellis
Proprietor: Annie C Paul
Cost: Fixed-price D £28 (5 course). H/wine £9 Service exc
Credit cards: 🔳 🔳 🔳 OTHER
Times: Last L 2.15pm, Last D 8.45pm
Menus: Fixed-price D, bar L menu
Seats: 60. No smoking in dining room

Taychreggan Hotel

Additional: Children permitted L only; ✿ dishes, other diets prior notice

coated potatoes, and beans. The meal concluded happily with a yoghurt and honey ice-cream, cheeses, and petits fours. The wine list is very good, concentrating on the personal favourites of enthusiastic proprietor Annie Paul.

Directions: One mile before Taynuilt, turn left on to B845, follow signs to loch side

KILFINAN, **Kilfinan Hotel** ❀❀

A small hotel in a secluded spot serving the finest Scottish produce, classically prepared by a Swiss chef

Two elegant Victorian dining-rooms lit by candle light provide the appropriate setting for the classical cooking of this rather civilised establishment. The hotel, a former coaching inn, is owned by the Otter Estate and capably managed by Rolf and Lynne Mueller. He is a Swiss-trained chef, and offers a daily fixed-price four-course menu with a choice of two or three dishes at each stage, she is a natural host, and is responsible for the front-of-house. Good use is made of fresh local produce, prime beef and lamb, game from the estate, and fish from the sea and loch. A recent inspection meal began with delicious hot smoked salmon and a salad dressed with honey and fennel vinaigrette, followed by a deeply flavoured courgette and watercress soup. The main course, roast breast of duck, was carefully cooked and served with a well-judged sauce of cranberries and tarragon. A good pavé au chocolat to finish, with an equally accomplished Grand Marnier sauce anglaise. Wine is served from coolers, and coffee with petits fours at the table or in the bar.

Directions: On B8000 between Tighnabruaich and Otter ferry

Argyllshire PA21 2EP
Map no: 10 NR97
Tel: 01700 821 201
Chef: Rolf Mueller
Proprietors: Rolf & Lynne Mueller
Cost: Fixed-price L £12/D £25 (4 course). H/wine from £9.50 Service inc
Credit cards: 🂠 🂡 🂢
Times: Last L 2.30pm/D 9.30pm. Closed Feb
Menus: Fixed-price D, bar menu
Seats: 22. No smoking in dining room
Additional: Children welcome, children's portions; ✿ dishes, other diets on request

Balsamic vinegar is made from the cooked and concentrated must of the white grapes of the Trebbiano vine and aged in 12 kegs of different woods. By law it must be at least 10 years old. A deep, rich dark brown in colour, it is a full-bodied vinegar with an intense aromatic fragrance and a distinctive flavour which is at once both sweet and sour.

KILMARTIN, **Cairn Restaurant** ✿

Good honest food at affordable prices served in relaxing surroundings by friendly local staff sounds the answer to any diner's prayer. You will find it all at this refreshingly unpretentious bistro where the menu strengths are speciality steaks and seafood dishes

Times: Last L 3pm/D 10pm. Closed Mon, Tue, Wed during Oct-Mar
Seats: 40-80. No cigars or pipes. Air conditioned
Additional: Children permitted (over 10 at dinner); children's portions; ✿ dishes, vegan/other diets on request
Directions: On A816 Lochgilphead–Oban road

Lochgilphead
Argyllshire PA31 8RG
Map no: 10 NR89
Tel: 01546 5254
Chef: Marion Thomson
Proprietors: Ian & Marion Thomson
Cost: Alc from £13.35. H/wine £8.20 (litre). Service exc
Credit cards: None taken

KILNINVER,
Crannog Seafood Restaurant ✿

☺ *One of a small chain of fish restaurants that evolved from the fishing industry. This one is the place to go for bouillabaisse, langoustines, moules marinières, smoked salmon (they smoke their own), oysters and plenty more. Daily blackboard specials, including vegetarian, and a children's menu*

Directions: 10 miles south of Oban

Salmon Centre PA34 4QS
Proprietors: Crannog Ltd
Cost: Alc £15-£20
Times: Noon-last L 3pm, 6pm-last D 9.30pm
Closed Oct-April
Menu: A la carte
Seats: 60

KILWINNING, **Montgreenan Mansion House Hotel** ✿

☺ *A good selection of imaginative dishes is offered at this fine 19th-century mansion, set in 45 acres of wooded grounds. Choices from the carte and the fixed-price menu might include fresh local mussels and braised haunch of venison. There's a good comprehensive wine list*

Ayrshire KA13 7QZ
Map no: 10 NS34
Tel: 01294 557733
Chef: Alan McCall
Proprietor: Dobson Family.
Manager: Darren Dobson (Best Western)
Cost: Alc £23, fixed-price L £9.95/D £24.25 (6 course). H/wine £9.90. Service inc
Credit cards: ▨ ▦ ▦ ▣
Times: Last L 2.30pm, last D 9.30pm
Menus: A la carte, fixed-price L & D, bar menu
Seats: 60. No smoking in dining room
Additional: Children permitted, children's portions; ✿ dishes, vegan/other diets on request

Directions: 4 miles N of Irvine on A736, turn off at Torranyard

LANGBANK, **Gleddoch House Hotel** ❀

Panoramic views of the River Clyde are a striking feature of this sympathetically converted country house. David Dunn's imaginative fixed-price menus and carte reveal competent modern cooking which could include lobster and crayfish bisque, and timbale of scallops with a delicate brandy and cream sauce

Additional: Children welcome: children's portions/menu; ❂ dishes, vegan/other diets on request
Directions: From Glasgow take the M8 (Greenock) then the B789 Langbank exit. Follow signs to hotel

Renfrewshire
Map no: 10 NS37
Tel: 0147550 711
Chef: David Dunn
Proprietor: LW Conn (Scotland's Heritage Hotels)
Cost: *Alc* L £27/D £35, fixed-price L £15, £18.50/D £29.50. H/wine £9.95. Service inc
Credit cards: 🔳 🔳 🔳 🔳 OTHER
Times: Last L 2.30pm/D 9pm
Seats: 80/90. Air conditioned

LARGS, **Brisbane House** ❀

☺ *An attractive Georgian house on the Esplanade with lovely views over the Firth of Clyde, this hotel is a popular venue for local functions. Innovative modern cooking is featured on the fixed-price and carte menus, now supplemented by a speciality seafood selection*

Menus: *A la carte*, fixed-price D, bar menu
Seats: 150. Air conditioned
Additional: Children welcome, children's menu; ❂ dishes, vegan/other diets on request
Directions: On main road, 200 yds from the Pier

14 Greenock Road
Ayrshire KA30 8NF
Map no: 10 NS25
Tel: 01475 687200
Chef: Michael Hughes
Proprietors: Mr Maltby and Mr Bertschy
Cost: *Alc* from £15, fixed-price D £19.75. H/wine £8.75 ! No service charge
Credit cards: 🔳 🔳 🔳 🔳 OTHER
Times: Last L 2.30pm, last D 9pm

MAYBOLE, **Ladyburn** ❀

A civilised small country house, run by enthusiastic owner Jane Hepburn and her family. Thoroughly enjoyable home-cooking is served in an elegant dining-room complete with candles and lace table clothes; tranquillity and a warm welcome pervade the air. No wonder guests are tempted back year after year

Times: Last D 8.15pm. Closed 2 weeks Nov, 4 weeks Jan-Mar
Additional: No smoking in dining room. No children under 14.
❂ dishes by arrangement
Directions: A849 to Bunessan, pass village school on right, take unclassified road on left to hotel

Ayrshire KA19 7SG
Map no: 10 NS20
Tel: 01655 74585
Chef: Jane Hepburn
Proprietors: Mr & Mrs D J S Hepburn
Cost: Fixed-price L £12.50/D £25
Credit cards: 🔳 🔳 🔳

MULL, ISLE OF – BUNESSAN,
Assapol Hotel ❀

☺ *Peacefully set by Loch Assapol, this informal, civilised small hotel – now under new ownership – serves uncomplicated, robust home cooking, to residents only, in portions to satisfy the most hearty appetites. A short menu offers a choice of starters and puddings with set main courses*

Menus: Fixed-price D
Seats: 11. No smoking in dining room
Additional: Children over 10 permitted, children's portions; other diets prior arrangement
Directions: From Craignure on A849 signed on left after village school

Argyll PA67 6DW
Map no: 10 NM32
Tel: 01681 700258
Chef: O Robertson
Proprietors: O & T A Robertson
Cost: Fixed-price D £15 (4 course) H/wine £8 Service inc
Credit cards: 🔳 🔳 OTHER
Times: D served at 7.45 pm daily

MULL, ISLE OF – DERVAIG,

Druimard Hotel ❀

☺ *The Druimard makes the most of its proximity to the Mull Little Theatre by offering pre-theatre dinner. The short fixed-price menu features fresh local seafood and speciality cheeses. Look out for mushrooms and fresh prawns in a white wine and cream sauce and noisettes of lamb with fresh tomato and basil sauce*

Dervaig PA75 6QW
Map no: 13 NM45
Tel: 01688 400345
Chef: Wendy Hubbard
Proprietors: Mr & Mrs Hubbard
Cost: Alc D £16
Credit cards: ◩ ▨ OTHER
Times: Last D 8.45pm

Directions: From the Craignure ferry turn right to Tobermory. Go through Salen, turn left at Aros, signposted Dervaig on right-hand side

MULL, ISLE OF – KILLIECHRONAN,

Killiechronan House ❀

Dramatically situated at the head of Loch na Keal, Killiechronan House was once the lodge to this vast 6,000 acre estate. The elegant dining-room now serves a five-course, fixed-price menu with dishes such as tournedos of beef in a crushed peppercorn and cognac cream sauce

Directions: From ferry follow Salen. Through village, turn left to Ulva ferry. After 2 miles turn right at T-junction for hotel

Killiechronan Estate
Aros, Isle of Mull PA 72 6JU
Map no: 110 NM53
Tel: 01680 300403
Chef: Patrick Freytag
Proprietor: Killiechronan Estate, J L Leroy
Cost: Fixed-price D £21.90
Credit cards: ◩ ▨ ▨ OTHER
Times: Last D 8.30pm

MULL, ISLE OF – TOBERMORY,

Strongarbh ❀❀

A hillside restaurant overlooking the bay, with fish as a speciality on the Scottish/French-style menu

The elegantly appointed Victorian restaurant, owned by the McAdam family, really is worth seeking out. It is set high above the town, surrounded by lovely gardens and overlooking the bay; not surprisingly, considering the proximity of the sea, the emphasis is on seafood. Chefs Ian McAdam and Graham Horne keep the dishes simple and let flavours speak for themselves. Starters may include a platter of fresh local seafood, with oysters, prawns, scallops, mussels and salmon; a home-made soup and perhaps smoked Argyll ham, followed by a sorbet. Main course options, other than around three seafood dishes, perhaps cod with saffron butter sauce, or halibut steak with avocado and local cheese, might be chargrilled fillet of Scotch steak or traditional roast grouse. An inspection meal

Strathclyde PA75 6PR
Map no: 13 NM55
Tel: 01688 2328
Chefs: Graham Horne and Ian McAdam
Proprietor: Ian McAdam & Family
Cost: Fixed-price D £20 (4 course). H/wine £9.55 Service exc
Credit cards: ◩ ▨
Times: 7pm-last D 9pm Closed Dec 25
Menus: Fixed-price D, Sun L (Winter months only)
Seats: 32. No smoking in dining room

included lightly grilled Mull salmon with a well-constructed watercress and cream sauce, and was followed by a delicately flavoured pear poached in ginger scented wine. As an alternative to dessert there is a selection of cheeses with oatcakes and biscuits. The wine list offers a reasonable choice.

Directions: 500m uphill from main street; turn left at Western Isles Hotel

OBAN, **Dungallen House** ✤

Lovely Victorian mansion which occupies an elevated position overlooking the Firth of Lorn to the Isle of Mull. An inspection meal yielded competent cooking which included richly flavoured cream of spinach soup, grilled whole prawns in garlic butter

Directions: Close to entrance to MacBrayne ferries

Gallanach Road
Argyllshire PA34 4PD
Map no: 10 NM82
Tel: 01631 563799
Chef: Janice Stewart
Proprietors: Mr & Mrs Stewart

OBAN, **Manor House Hotel** ✤

Candle-lit tables and views over Oban Bay form the setting for Neil O'Brien's competent, modern cooking. The daily-changing fixed-price menu is supported by an interesting, varied carte with fresh seafood featuring strongly. The pan-fried scallops, accompanied by garlic butter are not to be missed

Times: Last L 2pm, last D 8.30pm. Closed Jan **Seats:** 24. No smoking in dining room **Menus:** A la carte, fixed-price D, bar menu **Additional:** Children permitted, children's portions; ✿ dishes, vegan/other diets on request **Directions:** 300m past entrance to MacBrayne ferries

Gallanach Road
Argyllshire PA34 4LS
Map no: 10 NM82
Tel: 01631 62087
Chef: Neil O'Brien
Proprietors: Patrick & Margaret Freytag.
Manager: Gabriel Wijker
Cost: Alc from £22, fixed-price D £21.90 (4 course) H/wine £7.50 ▼ Service exc
Credit cards: ▨ ▨ OTHER

PORT APPIN, **Airds** ✤✤✤

Some of the finest food in Scotland is to be found in a former ferry inn, set amid spectacular scenery

Argyllshire PA38 4DF
Map no: 14 NM94
Tel: 0163 1730 236
Chef: Graeme Allen
Proprietors: Mr & Mrs E Allen, Mr & Mrs G R Allen (Relais & Chateaux)
Cost: Fixed-price D £35 (4 course). H/wine £11-16 Service exc

The proven formula varies little at this comfortable country hotel on the shores of Loch Linnhe, where two generations of the Allen family have finely honed their inimitable brand of relaxed

Additional: Children welcome, children's portions; ✿ dishes, vegan/other diets on request

hospitality. It is no secret that Airds serves some of the finest food in Scotland, or that the dining-room is on the small side so non-residents must book well in advance and be prepared to order before 7pm for dinner at 8. The menu changes daily, features well-handled local produce and is matched by a wine list that is one of Scotland's chief attractions, featuring a splendid selection of well-known names from the most reputable shippers, balanced by the cream of the New World crop. Our inspector was initially disappointed to discover that Graeme was alone in the kitchen, without the support of Betty, his esteemed mother. His misgivings were somewhat borne out by a couple of clumsy sauces: one, supposedly a dill and mustard combination accompanying salmon mousse, tasted of honey; the other, a slightly curried sauce served with guinea fowl, was over-reduced and rather sticky. On the other hand, the mousse, wrapped in smoked salmon, had perfect texture and the bird's roasted leg and breast was accurately-cooked, tender and garnished with morel and plump shitake mushrooms. With the main course came a simple, but sound selection of vegetables: cabbage with juniper, courgettes with parsley. A hearty swede and leek soup was also appreciated. The meal was bracketed by well-made canapés and a prettily-presented shortcake of poached pears with a zesty lime-spiked caramel sauce that should be patented. If our man felt slightly let-down it is because Airds' reputation for excellence arouses such great expectations, but even the most gifted cooks have the occasional off night.

Directions: Leave the A828 at Appin, hotel is 2.5 miles between Ballachulish and Cannel

Credit cards: ▨ ▩ ▨
Times: Last L 2pm, last D 8pm (one sitting) daily
Menus: Fixed-price L & D
Seats: 36. No smoking in dining room
Additional: Children welcome, children's menu; ❂ dishes, other diets by arrangement

---

STEWARTON,
Chapeltoun House Hotel ❀

The McKenzie brothers extend a genuine welcome at their civilised, small country house hotel. In the kitchen, Tom O'Donnell continues to offer an imaginative menu based on the best of Scotland's rich larder: game terrine, fricassee of seafood, poached pear with a sweet honey and oatmeal mousse

Menus: Fixed-price L & D, bar menu
Seats: 50. No smoking in dining room
Additional: Children over 12 permitted; ❂ dishes, special diets on request
Directions: B778 at Stewarton Cross then B769 (Irvine) 2 miles

Ayrshire KA3 3ED
Map no: 10 NS44
Tel: 01560 482696
Chef: Tom O'Donnell
Proprietors: Colin McKenzie & Graeme McKenzie
Cost: Fixed-price L £15.90/D £23.90. H/wine £10.60. Service exc
Credit cards: ▨ ▩ ▨ OTHER
Times: Last L 2pm/D 9.15pm Daily Closed first wk Jan

TROON, Highgrove House ❀❀

☺ *A restaurant that's going places, serving well-prepared food set against a backdrop of stunning coastal views*

From a hillside position above the town, Highgrove House surveys the Ayrshire coast and the Firth of Clyde to the Isle of Arran 15 miles away. Under the joint care and direction of proprietor Bill Costley and manager Michael Poggi, this attractive, well-run hotel is going from strength to strength. The emphasis on competent and imaginative cooking doesn't change – Bill sees to that – and his enthusiastic kitchen team backs him fully. The split-level dining room has been opened up with a lobster tank as a new central

Old Loans Road
Ayrshire KA10 7HL
Map no: 10 NS33
Tel: 01292 312511
Chefs: William Costley and James Allison
Proprietor: Costley & Costley Hoteliers Ltd.
Manager: Michael Poggi
Cost: Alc L £12/D£20, fixed-price L £14.95/D £22.50 (4 course) H/wine £9.95 ❢
Service exc

feature (which is not to everyone's taste). At lunchtime the bar-style menu is excellent value, but the serious eating takes place at dinner. Here the *carte* takes centre stage although a good value, fixed-price menu is available on request, and a competitively priced brasserie menu is proving increasingly popular. An inspection meal started with an intensely flavoured goose and chicken liver terrine with Cumberland sauce, was followed by shallow pan-fried fillet of moist, tender wild salmon in a beurre blanc sauce and finished with an enjoyable bread and butter pudding with fresh oranges, ice-cream and spun sugar.

Directions: Situated on hill overlooking Troon

Credit cards: ▩ ▦ ▦ OTHER
Times: Last L 2.30pm, last D 9.30pm
Menus: *A la carte*, fixed-price L & D, bar menu
Seats: 100. Air conditioned. No cigars or pipes
Additional: Children welcome, children's portions; ❂ dishes, vegan/other diets on request

TROON, Lochgreen House ❀❀

A welcoming country house restaurant with a menu of considerable appeal

In the days when lawyers admitted to making money, one of them built Lochgreen as tangible proof of his success. Set in 16 acres with views across golf links to the sea, it is now a popular country house hotel with a welcoming atmosphere and a solid reputation for good Scottish food. Anyone wary of trying haggis should take advantage of the canapés which include the tiny breaded species. A three-course lunch may be chosen from the *carte* and a four-course dinner from a set-price menu. An inspection meal began with a warm salad of wild mushrooms and seared monkfish, flavoured with ginger and garlic, with a coriander butter sauce. Then came a 'surprisingly good' intermediate course of more haggis, this time with 'neeps 'n' tatties', before a main course of medallion of beef topped with a horseradish crust, glazed shallots and red wine jus. Crispy duckling was less crisp than it ought to have been, but its accompanying kumquat marmalade and green lentil and Madeira sauce worked well. The filling of a chilled lemon tart was better than the pastry; it came with Drambuie and oatmeal ice-cream and custard. Wines are well selected, with a strong showing of clarets.

Directions: Off A77 (Prestwick Airport) onto B749, S/E of Troon

Monktenhill Road
Southwood
Ayrshire KA10 7EN
Map no: 10 NS33
Tel: 01292 313343
Chef: Andrew Hamer
Proprietors: Mr & Mrs William Costley
Cost: Fixed-price L £16.95/D £25 (4 course). H/wine £12.50 Service exc
Credit cards: ▩ ▦ ▦ OTHER
Times: Last L 2pm, last D 9.15pm daily
Menus: Fixed-price L & D, bar menu
Seats: 100. No smoking in dining room
Additional: Children permitted; ❂ dishes, vegan/other diets on request

TROON, Marine Highland Hotel ❀

☺ *A long established, international hotel set next to the championship golf course. An attractive split level restaurant has spectacular views across the Firth of Clyde and offers a formal carte with a variety of local dishes. Try honest flavoured crayfish bisque, or tender pan-fried scallops with a mild garlic butter*

Menus: *A la carte*, fixed-price L & D, bar menu
Seats: 120. No-smoking area
Additional: Children welcome, children's menu; ❂ menu, vegan/other diets on request
Directions: Overlooking 18th fairway of Troon's championship golf course

Ayrshire KA10 6HE
Map no: 10 NS33
Tel: 01292 314444
Chef: Richard Sturgeon
Proprietor: Scottish Highland. Manager: Andrew M Overton
Cost: Alc £28, fixed-price L £10.75/D £22.95 (4 course). H/wine £10 ❢ Service inc
Credit cards: ▩ ▦ ▦ ▩ OTHER
Times: Last L 2pm/2.30pm Sun, last D 10pm

TROON, **Piersland House Hotel** ❀

☺ *A mock Tudor house set in its own grounds next to the championship golf course. The restaurant offers competent cooking based on Scottish regional produce. Look out for lobster bisque and trout and scallop timbale. The staff are smartly turned out*

Directions: Opposite Royal Troon Golf Club

Craigend Road
Ayrshire KA10 6HD
Map no: 10 NS33
Tel: 01292 314747
Chef: John Rae
Proprietor: Aristo.
Manager: Michael Lee
Cost: Alc £18, fixed-price
L £10.95/D £17.50.
H/wine £8.95 ! Service exc
Credit cards: 🟦 💳 💳 💳 OTHER
Times: Noon-last L 2.30pm,
7pm-last D 9.30pm
Menus: A la carte, fixed-price L
& D, brasserie menu
Seats: 60. No cigars or pipes
Additional: Children welcome,
children's menu; ❤ menu/other
diets on request

TURNBERRY, **Malin Court** ❀

☺ *Close to the championship golf course, overlooking the Firth of Clyde offering a successful blend of modern cooking mixed with traditional Scottish dishes in the Carrick Restaurant. The fixed-price menu changes daily and is ably supported by a tempting carte. Hospitality is a major strength*

Menus: A la carte, fixed-price L & D, high tea **Seats:** 60. Smoking not encouraged **Additional:** Children welcome, children's portions; ❤ dishes, vegan/other diets on request
Directions: On N side of the village on A719, 1 mile from A77

Strathclyde KA26 9PB
Map no: 10 NS20
Tel: 01655 331457
Chef: Andrea Beech
Proprietor: (Best Western)
Manager: W R Kerr
Cost: Fixed-price L £10.95/D
£18.95 (4 course). H/wine
£10.50 Service exc
Credit cards: 🟦 💳 💳 💳 OTHER
Times: Last L 2pm, last D 9pm
daily

TURNBERRY,
Turnberry Hotel ❀❀

A wide choice of dining in a legendary golfing hotel

The splendid Edwardian hotel stands on high ground overlooking the two world-famous golf courses and endlessly fascinating sea view. There are several restaurants, of various levels of formality, but the cooking throughout is of a consistently high standard, and aims to use local ingredients whenever possible. The Bay Room features light, modern cooking, along the lines of pasta strips, scampi, monkfish and salmon, bound with cream. More luxurious dishes, as befits a grand hotel, are available in the main restaurant. A classic turbot mousse, with a fish stock mousseline, might be followed by mushroom consommé with delicate thyme dumplings, and a succulent breast of guinea fowl. The latter came stuffed with foie gras mousse, and was served with an excellent Sauternes sauce. Desserts in both restaurants are worth saving room for. In the

Ayrshire KA26 9LT
Map no: 10 NS20
Tel: 01655 31000

Turnberry Hotel

Chefs: Stewart Cameron and Derek Abbot
Proprietor: Director & Manager: C J Rouse (Independent)
Cost: *Alc* £16.30 (Clubhouse)/£26.65 (Bay)/£45 (Turnberry), fixed-price Sun L (Turnberry) £20.50.
H/wine £18
Credit cards: 🃏 💳 💳 💳 OTHER
Times: Last L 2.30pm/last D 7pm (Clubhouse) 9.30pm (Bay) 10.30pm (Turnberry)
Menus: *A la carte* L & D, fixed-price L/D/Sun L (Turnberry)
Seats: 180 (Turnberry) 64 (Clubhouse) 54 (Bay).
Air conditioned
Additional: Children welcome, children's menu, 🟊 menu, vegan/other diets on request

restaurant, the famous Scottish sweet, cranachan, was light and not too sugary. A particularly felicitous combination of rosewater and lemon sorbet, honey macerated berries and crisp biscuits flecked with pistachio, proved a Bay Room winner. Although there is a fine wine list, these days a few more halves or wines by the glass would not go amiss.

Directions: On north side of the village on A719

TAYSIDE

ABERFELDY,

Guinach House Hotel ❀❀

☺ *A charming little hotel offering high standards of imaginative cooking*

By the 'Birks'
Urlar Road
Perthshire PH15 2ET
Map no: 14 NN84
Tel: 01887 820251
Chef: Albert Mackay
Proprietor: Albert Mackay
Cost: Fixed-price D £22.50
H/wine £8.95 Service inc
Credit cards: 🃏 💳
Times: Last D 9.30pm Closed Dec 25/6
Menus: Fixed-price D

A delightful place, a genuine home from home, is how regulars regard the Mackay's charming, small country house hotel, standing in its own grounds on the edge of the village. Guinach House has many virtues, not least of which is Bert Mackay's passion for innovative, modern British cooking. His daily-changing, fixed-price menu of competently cooked dishes is really good value for money and he makes excellent use of the best of Scotland's seasonal larder. Prime beef and lamb, game and seafood all feature strongly and he also grows many of his own vegetables. Real flavours shine through in dishes such as a lightly cooked rendezvous of fresh seafood in a delicate, creamy Chablis sauce with spaghetti vegetables, and the smoked salmon soup is something of a house speciality. Scented with rosemary and thyme, noisettes of lamb, though lacking the expected pinkness on one occasion, proved successful, served with an interesting mint and sherry sauce. Fresh, sliced pineapple flambéed in Kirsch can also be recommended. Discerning locals love the place and house-guests feel little need to eat out.

Directions: From Aberfeldy: A826 (Crieff) restaurant is on the right

Seats: 22. No smoking in dining room
Additional: Children welcome, children's portions; ❤ dishes, vegan/other diets on request

AUCHTERARDER,
Auchterarder House ❀❀

The Ochil Hills to the south and the Grampians to the north are grand backdrops to a delightful hotel serving quality Scottish cooking

Perthshire PH13 1DZ
Map no: 11 NN91
Tel: 01764 663646
Chef: Kiernan Darnell
Proprietor: Mr & Mrs Ian L Brown
Cost: Fixed-price L £15-£25/D £27.50-£45. H/wine £12.50 Service exc
Credit cards: 🆇 🆇 🆇 🆇 OTHER
Times: Last L 3pm, last D 9.30pm daily
Menus: Fixed-price L & D
Seats: 30. No smoking in dining room
Additional: Children by arrangement; other diets on request

Picture a typical Scottish baronial mansion and the likelihood is that something like Auchterarder House will come to mind. It was built some 165 years ago as a family home, set in seventeen and a half acres of lawns and woodland. The cooking is in the care of Kiernan Darnell, whose mainly Scottish food complements the splendid dining room. Dinner can run from three to five courses, according to the *carte*, which is sprinkled with Scottish references such as medallion of Aberdeen Angus fillet, saddle of Perthshire lamb, and Shetland Isles salmon fillet. Even without a geographical key one could still locate the menu's source, with clues like oak-smoked haddock soup with whisky and green lentils, terrine of local pigeon, served with spiced beetroot and sultana chutney, and medallions of red deer encrusted with oatmeal and thyme, presented with a cock-a-leekie sauce. Sweets include hot frangipane pastry with a moneybag of Amaretto sultanas and a vanilla roast hazelnut sauce, and spiced savarin flavoured with Earl Grey, lemon and cinnamon, with rum ice-cream and figs. The list of thoughtfully selected world wines contains sensible descriptions of the varieties.

Directions: On B8062 Crieff road for 1.5 miles N of Auchterarder

AUCHTERARDER,
Duchally House Hotel ❀

Perthshire PH3 1PN
Map no: 11 NN91
Tel: 01764 663071
Chefs: Derek & Liz Alcorn
Proprietors: Maureen Raeder
Cost: *Alc* £23.50, fixed-price
L £12.50/D £17.50.
H/wine £8.50 Service inc
Credit cards: 🌑 💳 💳 📖
Times: Last L 2.15pm, last D
9.30pm

☺ *Crisp linen and sparkling silverware in the dining-room complement the Victorian architecture of this comfortable manor house hotel. Expect soundly prepared dishes such as tagliatelle with chicken and café au lait sauce, Tay salmon with languoustine mousse, and Scottish cranachan with poached pears and Drambuie*

Menus: *A la carte*, fixed-price L & D, pre-theatre, bar menu
Seats: 36. No-smoking area **Additional:** Children welcome, children's menu; ❤ menu, vegan/other diets on request
Directions: From A9 take A823 (Crieff/Dunfermline), after 1 mile turn left at sign for Duchally. Hotel in 0.25 mile

AUCHTERARDER,
The Gleneagles Hotel ❀❀

Perthshire PH3 1NF
Map no: 11 NN91
Tel: 01764 662231
Chef: Alan Hill
Managing Director: Peter Lederer
Cost: *Alc* £40, fixed-price Sun L £26/D £41. H/wine £15.50 ❢
Credit cards: 🌑 💳 💳 📖 OTHER
Times: Noon-last L 2pm/2.30 Sun, 7.30pm-last D 10pm
Menus: *A la carte*, fixed price L & D
Seats: 240. No-smoking area
Additional: Children welcome, children's menu; ❤ dishes, vegan/other diets on request

An internationally renowned resort and sporting hotel with a staggering range of services, The Gleneagles offers a choice of food at a variety of venues, led by the Strathearn Restaurant

Live violin and harp music, traditional flambé cooking at the table and the carving of chateaubriands creates an extravagant and formal atmosphere in the Strathearn, which heads the range of the Gleneagles restaurants. The wine is all baskets and buckets and the sommeliers wear tasting ladles. There is no proper dress code, because of the international clientele, but everyone is perfectly smart. Chef Alan Hill caters for a wide range of guests' needs, with simple dishes such as smoked salmon and the daily roast, to more complex recipes including a well reported Crinan scallops with a soft gâteau of artichokes, and delicious venison with onion gravy and pears. The pudding, coulibac of winter fruits, was less successful on this occasion: rhubarb appeared to be the only fruit and the filo pastry was undercooked. Menus offer a baffling choice – with a top class wine list to match – and all the dishes are based on good local ingredients. Prices aren't cheap, as one would expect from a hotel of this calibre, but a visit to the grand Edwardian establishment is an exhilarating experience.

Directions: Just off the A9, well signposted

AUCHTERHOUSE,
Old Mansion House Hotel ❀

Forfarshire DD3 0QN
Map no: 11 N033
Tel: 01382 320366
Chef: Campbell Bruce
Proprietors: Nigel & Eva Bell
Cost: *Alc* £27, fixed-price L £15.
H/wine £9.95. Service exc
Credit cards: 🌑 💳 💳 📖
Times: Last L 1.45pm/D 9.15pm.
Closed Dec 24 Jan 4
Menus: *A la carte*, fixed-price L, bar menu
Seats: 50. No smoking in dining room

A 16th-century baronial mansion, magnificently converted into an atmospheric hotel. The kitchen relies on local produce. Poor Cullen skink, and slightly overcooked baked salmon in filo pastry, but top marks for a well made red pepper sauce, good vegetables, and an outstanding crème brûlée

Additional: Children welcome (over 7 at D); children's portions. ❤ menu, vegan/other diets on request
Directions: A923 from Dundee to Muirhead, take B954, hotel 2 miles on Alyth road

BLAIRGOWRIE,
Kinloch House Hotel ❀❀❀

Welcoming and friendly Scottish country house serving outstanding food that leaves a lasting impression

Perthshire PH10 6SG
Map no: 15 NO14
Tel: 01250 884237
Chef: Bill McNicoll
Proprietors: David & Sarah Shentall
Cost: Fixed-price L £15.95/ D£27.90 (4 courses). H/wine £11.50 ▯ Service inc
Credit cards: ▨ ▨ ▨ ▨ OTHER
Times: 12.30-Last L 2pm, 7pm-Last D 9.15pm closed Dec 15-30
Menus: Fixed-price L & D, bar L menu
Seats: 50. No smoking in dining room
Additional: Children permitted (over 7 at dinner), children's high tea; ❂ dishes, vegan/other diets on request

Sarah and David Shentall's delightful creeper-clad country house sits in 25 acres of parkland grazed by highland cattle, and offers fine views of nearby Marlee Loch. The house itself exudes a welcoming atmosphere which is difficult to resist. The spacious and elegant dining-room lends itself well to the stylish cooking of Chef Bill McNicholl, who prepares a daily four-course menu with a varied choice, as well as some supplementary dishes and a Scottish speciality menu. The food is prepared with loving care with the lightest of touches, and flavours and ingredients are honestly balanced.

Freshly-made canapés opened a recent inspection dinner. Smoked salmon mousse was so richly flavoured and densely textured that it was more a parfait than a mousse, served with a sharply contrasting sauce of avocado purée with horseradish and chive dressing. A perfect smoked haddock quennelle with a clean and distinctive taste followed, before the main course of loin of lamb topped with apple and herb breadcrumbs. Vegetables included lightly battered cauliflower, a mini-tower of courgette provençale, and a croquette of almond potato. Regulars may be mourning the demise of the dessert trolley, but should be pleased with the choice of puddings still on offer, and, as compensation, may have as many portions as they wish. Bread and butter pudding, a firm creation made from brioche, and served with a delicious caramel sauce, is highly recommended. Other inspectors have praised the pigeon and green lentil terrine which was 'moist and literally bursting with flavour', and quenelle of locally caught pike 'of an unimaginable lightness', perfectly supported by an airy shellfish butter sauce with diced tomato. There is a well-balanced wine list with some impressive French bins and a good selection of half bottles and wines by the glass.

Directions: Three miles west of Blairgowrie on A923

BRIDGE OF CALLY,
Bridge of Cally Hotel ❁

A great location with grounds stretching down to the river. Local produce is used to good effect. The full restaurant menu is only available during the hotel's busy periods, but the bar menu provides an enjoyable alternative. Look out for peppery chicken liver pâté and tender venison liver

Seats: 35
Additional: Children welcome, children's portions/menu; ❤ dishes, other diets on request
Directions: Six miles north of Blairgowrie, on A93 beside bridge of River Ardle

Near Blairgowrie
Perthshire PH10 7JJ
Map no: 15 NO15
Tel: 01250 886231
Chefs: Michael Wright and William McCosh
Proprietor: William McCosh
Cost: *Alc* L £12.50/D 16.50, fixed-price L £16/D £17.50. H/wine £7.50. Service exc
Credit cards: ▨ ▤
Times: Last D 9.30pm. Closed 25-26 Dec

CLEISH, **Nivingston House Hotel** ❁

☺ *Peace and comfort abound at this 18th-century former farmhouse which stands in extensive grounds. Well-produced menus are offered at both lunch and dinner, with dishes based on fresh local produce whenever possible. A typical meal could include spinach and apple soup, pan-fried chicken, and raspberry brûlée*

Menus: A la carte, fixed-price L & D, bar menu
Seats: 45. Smoking discouraged
Additional: Children welcome, children's portions; ❤ menu, vegan/other diets on request
Directions: M90 exit 5 + B9097 (Crook of Devon) 2 miles on left

Cleish Hills
Kinross KY13 7LS
Map no: 11 NT09
Tel: 01577 850216
Chef: Michael Thompson
Proprietor: Allan Deeson (Scotland's Commended)
Cost: *Alc* from £15.50, fixed-price L £15.50/D £25. H/wine £10.95
Credit cards: ▨ ▤ ▨ OTHER
Times: Last L 2pm, last D 9pm

DUNDEE, **Stakis Dundee Earl Grey** ❁

The quayside location means that the restaurant of this purpose-built hotel enjoys panoramic views over the Tay estuary. The cooking features stuffed goose breast, seafood ragoût and collops of venison, plus a grill selection. A well-displayed carvery buffet operates at lunchtimes

Menus: A la carte, fixed-price L & D, bar menu
Seats: 120. Air conditioned. No-smoking area
Additional: Children welcome, children's menu; ❤ dishes, vegan/other diets on request
Directions: City centre, from Station follow signs for Olympia Leisure Centre

Dundee DD1 4DE
Map no: 11 NO43
Tel: 01382 229271
Chef: Eddie Sharkey
Proprietor: Stakis plc.
Manager: Carlo Capaldi
Cost: *Alc* £30, fixed-price L £9.95/D £16.50 H/wine £9.75 Service exc
Credit cards: ▨ ▤ ▨ ▨ OTHER
Times: Last L 2pm, last D 10pm

DUNKELD, **Atholl Arms** ❁

Good honest cooking is the order of the day at this former coaching inn close to the Tay. Hearty portions of popular dishes such as steak pie, and huge meringues with apricot sauce, plus a good selection of vegetarian options are served in both the bar and the restaurant

Menus: A la carte, bar menu
Seats: 30. No smoking in dining room
Additional: Children permitted (over 8 after 6pm), children's portions; ❤ dishes, vegan/other diets on request
Directions: A9 & A923 (Blairgowrie) to Dunkeld, 1st building on right

Bridgehead
Perthshire PH8 0AQ
Map no: 11 NO04
Tel: 01350 727219
Chef: Annie Darbishire
Proprietor: Callum Darbishire
Cost: *Alc* £10.15. H/wine £7.50 Service inc Cover charge £1.50
Credit cards: ▨ ▤ ▨ OTHER
Times: Last L 1.45pm, last D 8.45pm

DUNKELD, **Kinnaird** ❀❀❀

A glorious, privately-owned country house hotel serving imaginative Modern British cooking

Kinnaird
Perthshire PH8 0LD
Map no: 11 NO04
Tel: 01796 482440
Chef: John Webber
Proprietor: Constance Ward
(Relais et Chateaux)
Cost: fixed-price L £24/D
£39.50 (4 course). H/wine £15
❢ Service exc
Credit cards: ▨ ▩ ▦ OTHER
Times: Last L 1.45pm/D 9.30pm.
Closed Mon/Tue/Wed from Jan-Mar
Menus: fixed-price L & D
Seats: 35. No smoking in dining room
Additional: Children permitted
(over 12); ❤ dishes, vegan/
other diets on request

Kinnaird is a magnificent secluded house, built in the late 18th century, with a 9000-acre estate which can offer guests some fine shooting, stalking, and salmon and trout fishing on the River Tay. A sumptuous cedar-panelled drawing room, discreet study and billiard room are all antique-filled and tastefully appointed. In one of the dining-rooms there are original Italianate frescoed walls, and in this stunning setting visitors can enjoy fine views to the Tay river. The cooking lives up to the decor, chef John Webber maintains not only a high standard in terms of produce and execution, but it is all elegantly presented.

Lunch and dinner are offered on short but well-balanced menus, and each evening a few extra dishes are added to the main four-course list. Typical of starters available at dinner could be ravioli of rabbit and morels with a Madeira sauce, and shellfish minestrone of squat lobster, scallops and mussels. Main courses might include braised boned oxtail cooked with red wine and stout, pot roast guinea fowl in sherry wine vinegar and braised vegetables, and poached fillet of wild salmon in a light herb and vegetable liquor. Inspection yielded a terrine of confit of duck with white beans, wrapped in dried ham and served with a scattering of green lentils and tiny beetroot cubes – an attractive-looking dish that lived up to expectations. Fillet of fresh cod with brown fried slices of fennel was packed with flavour, and was followed by a soft banana soufflé with a ring of caramelised slices and orange rind. The kitchen is very flexible, and can lighten or simplify dishes according to request. The wine list includes a short list of house recommendations, is strong on half bottles, and leans heavily towards France, although the rest of Europe and New World wines do get a look in.

Directions: Take B898 exit on A9 (Dalguise and Balnaguard) Kinnaird is 4.5 miles along

We endeavour to be as accurate as possible but changes in personnel and data can occur in establishments after the Guide has gone to press.

GLAMIS, **Castleton House Hotel** ❀

William and Maureen Little have built up a loyal following over the years at their civilised hotel. In the kitchen, a decent range of dishes reflects the best available raw ingredients. Foie gras of duck livers was the highlight of an inspection meal

Additional: Children permitted; children's portions/menu; ❶ dishes, vegan/other diets on request
Directions: 3 miles west of Glamis on A94, between Forfar and Coupar Angus

Forfar
Angus DD8 1SJ
Map no: 15 NO34
Tel: 01307 840340
Chef: William Little
Proprietor: Mr & Mrs Little
(Scotland's Heritage Hotels)
Cost: *fixed-price lunch £11.75/D £19.50. H/wine £9.50*
Credit cards: 🔳 🔳 🔳
Times: *Last L 2.30pm/D 9.30pm*

INVERKEILOR, **Gordon's Restaurant** ❀

A delightful country restaurant with a kitchen reliant on fresh local produce. A mainly French menu (with English translations) offers fish market soup, chicken liver pâté with Cumberland sauce, scampi poached in Noilly Prat and cream, noisettes of Scotch lamb with a plum sauce, and rich home-made ice-cream

Menus: A la carte, fixed-price L, high teas
Seats: 25. No smoking
Additional: Children welcome, children's menu; ❶ menu, other diets on request
Directions: Situated north end of main street

Main Street
Angus DD115RN
Map no: 15 NO64
Tel: 01241 830364
Chef: Gordon Watson
Proprietors: Gordon & Maria Watson
Cost: *Alc £18.95, fixed-price L £10.40 H/wine £8. Service exc*
Credit cards: 🔳 🔳
Times: 12.30-last L 2.30pm, 6pm-last D 9.30pm. Closed Mon & last 2 wks Jan

KILLIECRANKIE,
Killiecrankie Hotel ❀❀

A relaxing small country hotel with a sound reputation for its food

Killiecrankie means a wood of aspen trees and, just to the south, is the still heavily wooded Pass of Killiecrankie where the Jacobites defeated William lll in 1689. The hotel restaurant has built up a popular following, partly because of its impressive lunch and dinner menus, and partly because of Colin and Carole Anderson's hands-on approach. The enthusiastic attitude of their friendly young staff is a further plus. It is, however, chef John Ramsay and his team's four-course set dinner on which the hotel has built its reputation. Dishes are well presented without being over-fussy and good use is made of local meats, game and fish. Sauteed lambs' kidneys with Meaux mustard and Madeira sauce might be followed by breast of pheasant en croûte with Stilton and pineapple, served with wild mushrooms in a Dubonnet glaze. The only niggle from an inspector was that an otherwise 'super' lemon tart with crème anglaise was marred by a poorly textured lime custard. The cheeseboard is first-class. An interesting wine list covers most significant areas without specialising, and there is a good range of halves.

Directions: Turn off A9 at sign for Killiecrankie. Hotel in 3 miles

Pitlochry
Perthshire PH16 5LG
Map no: 14 NN96
Tel: 01796 473220
Chef: John Ramsay
Proprietors: Colin & Carole Anderson
Cost: Fixed-price D £26.50. H/wine £11.50 Service exc
Credit cards: 🔳 🔳 OTHER
Times: Last D 8.30pm. Closed Jan & Feb
Menu: fixed-price D, pre-theatre, bar menu
Seats: 34. No smoking in dining room
Additional: Children permitted (over 5), children's portions; ❶ dishes, other diets on request

Cassis is a liqueur with a rich, velvety fruit flavour that is made by macerating blackcurrants in spirit and sweetening the final result. It is a speciality of Dijon and the Côte d'Or and was first made commercially in 1841.

KINCLAVEN, **Ballathie House Hotel** ✿

For those seeking a place to relax and unwind this delightful mansion on the banks of the Tay is the ideal location. There is good food, too. The menu is rich in local produce offering the likes of terrine of seafood, Aberdeen Angus beef and Ballathie's home cured salmon served with Arran mustard cream

Ballathie
Perthshire PH1 4QN
Map no: 11 NO13
Tel: 01250 883268
Chef: Kevin McGillivray
Manager: Chris Longden
Cost: fixed-price L £13.50/D
£27.50 (4 course). H/wine £9.50
❢ Service exc
Credit cards: 🅰 ▒ ▒ 🔃 OTHER
Times: Last L 2pm, last D 9pm
Menus: Fixed-price L & D, bar menu
Seats: 70. No smoking in dining room
Additional: Children welcome, children's portions; ♥ menu, vegan/other diets on request

Directions: Off A93 at Beech Hedges, follow signs for Kinclaven, approx 2 miles

KINNESSWOOD, **Lomond Country Inn** ✿

Situated close to Loch Leven, the restaurant of this small inn boasts fine panoramic views. The main attraction here, however, has to be the honest cooking at good-value prices, with fresh local produce being used to create such delights as wild salmon en-croute and superb home-made desserts

Menus: A la carte, fixed-price L & D, bar menu
Seats: 80. No-smoking area
Additional: Children welcome, children's /menu; ♥ dishes, vegan/other diets on request
Directions: On the A911 10 mins from M90 exit 5 (Glenrothes) or exit 7 (Milnathort)

Kinross-shire KY9 7HN
Map no: 11 NO10
Tel: 01592 840253
Chef: Mark Cooper
Proprietor: David Adams (Logis of GB)
Cost: Alc £12.50, fixed-price L £5/D £9.50 H/wine £7.25 ❢ Service inc
Credit cards: 🅰 ▒ ▒ 🔃 OTHER
Times: Last L 2.30pm, last D 9pm

KINROSS, **Croft Bank** ✿✿

Well-executed and occasionally innovative cooking at fair prices is the main attraction at this small Victorian hotel

A Victorian villa where chef/proprietor Bill Kerr specialises in combinations that can sound tricksy on the page, but are brought off on the plate with panache and laudable use of seasonal produce. Our inspector was the solitary customer one Summer lunch time, but business is usually better for dinner and this enterprising and good value restaurant certainly deserves an appreciative audience. A filo pastry parcel filled not only with Brie, but also with chunks of celery and apple, was an interesting variation on a dish that has become something of a cliché and was served with a plum sauce that added a contrasting fruity flavour. Pieces of sautéed monkfish

30 Station Road
Kinross-shire
Map no: 11 NO10
Tel: 01577 863819
Chef: Bill Kerr
Proprietor: Bill & Diane Kerr
Cost: Alc £22.50, fixed-price L £13.50, £10.95 (2 course)/D £18.95. H/wine £9.95 Service exc
Credit cards: 🅰 ▒
Times: Last L 1.45pm, last D 9pm Closed Mon, Dec 25, Jan 1-2

Croft Bank

Menus: *A la carte,* fixed-price L
& D, bar L menu
Seats: 50. No smoking in dining
room
Additional: Children welcome,
children's portions; ❤ dishes,
vegan/other diets on request

served on a bed of lentils with a rich and garlicky sauce were
accompanied on the plate by a cylinder of dauphinoise potatoes and
crisp mange touts which rendered the selection of vegetables served
on the side somewhat superfluous. Dessert was a slightly over-iced
rhubarb parfait surrounded by a rather sharp coulis of this same
fruit, which refreshed the palate at the end of what was a
thoroughly enjoyable meal.

Directions: Just off M90 exit 6 towards Kinross

PERTH, **Huntingtower Hotel** ✿

*Innovative modern French/Scottish cooking makes good use of raw
materials. Diners can choose to eat in the new, informal conservatory
serving a brasserie-style menu, or in the more formal and elegant wood-
panelled restaurant. The selection of dishes could include a tasty crayfish
and crab bisque*

Crieff Road
Almondbank
Perthshire PH1 3JT
Map no: 11 NO12
Tel: 01738 583771
Chef: Kevin Graham
Proprietor: Gordon Sneddon
(Aristo Hotels)
Cost: *Alc* £20, fixed-price L
£9.95/D £19.95 (4 course).
H/wine £9.65 ▌ Service exc
Credit cards: ▨ ▧ ▧ ▨ OTHER
Times: Last L 2pm, last D
9.30pm
Menus: *A la carte,* fixed-price L
& D, pre-theatre, bar menu
Seats: 50. No cigars
Additional: Children welcome,
children's menu; ❤ dishes,
vegan/other diets on request

Directions: 1 mile west of Perth on A85 (Crieff), 2nd turning on right

PERTH,
Murrayshall Hotel ❀❀

☺ *The atmosphere of this hotel restaurant is now less formal, but the food is as good as ever, making excellent use of the best regional produce*

Magnificent though it is, this superb mansion – surrounded by 300 acres of parkland centred on a golf course – is not intimidating; even the delightful Old Masters Restaurant has shed the 'starchy' image of the early 90s and is now friendly and relaxed. Food, too, has become less flamboyant in an attempt to appeal to a wider market, but no concessions have been made on quality: Andrew Cambell (who trained under Bruce Sangster) continues to cook soundly. Short but interesting and well structured, his *carte* and fixed-price menus are in modern style with French and Scottish influences. A starter of breast of Perthshire pigeon, for example, set on a compote of red cabbage and accompanied by a light blackcurrant and thyme jus, might be followed by whole monkfish tail seasoned with fresh oregano and coriander spice, oven-roasted and served with a herb butter. Meat is presented pink and vegetables crisp, but no homage is paid to 'correctness' in this respect and guests should mention any preferences when placing their order. A wine list representing both Europe and the New World includes a selection of half bottles and bin ends.

Directions: From Perth A94 (Coupar Angus) turn right signed Murrayshall before New Scone

New Scone
Perthshire PH2 7PH
Map no: 11 NO12
Tel: 01738 551171
Chef: Andrew Cambell
Proprietor: Antony Bryan
Cost: *Alc* £18.24, fixed-price L £7.50 (2 course)/D £16.95. H/wine £12.50. Service inc
Credit cards: 🁢 💳 💳 💳 OTHER
Times: Last L 2.30pm, last D 9.30pm
Menus: *A la carte*, fixed-price L & D
Seats: 55. Air conditioned
Additional: Children over 5 welcome, children's portions; ❂ dishes, vegan/other diets on request

PERTH,
Newton House Hotel ❀

Situated in its own attractive gardens, this former dower house offers good food in a relaxing setting. Regional produce cooked with a French accent might include gourmet scampi and Scottish queen scallops with herbs, or grilled Perthshire lamb cutlets

Menus: *A la carte*, fixed-price L & D, pre-theatre, bar menu
Seats: 40. No smoking in dining room
Additional: Children welcome, children's menu; ❂ menu, vegan/other diets on request
Directions: On the A90 4 miles from Perth, 13 miles from Dundee

Glencarse
Perthshire PH2 7LX
Map no: 11 NO12
Tel: 01738 860250
Chef: Moira MacRae
Proprietors: Carole & Christopher Tallis
Cost: *Alc* £24, fixed-price L £15.75/D £19. H/wine £10.50
Credit cards: 🁢 💳 💳 💳 OTHER
Times: Last L 2pm, last D 9pm

PERTH, Number Thirty Three Seafood Restaurant ❀

A centrally located restaurant known for skilfully prepared fish dishes served with a selection of home-made bread. An inspection meal yielded smoked trout and apple mousse, baked salmon with spicy avocado salsa, and a brandy snap basket with vanilla ice-cream and ginger and apricot sauce

Seats: 24. No cigars or pipes
Additional: Children permitted (over 5); children's portions; ❂ dishes
Directions: In the city just off the High Street, near the river

33 George Street
Perthshire PH1 5LA
Map no: 11 NO12
Tel: 01738 633771
Chef: Mary Billingshurst
Proprietors: Mary & Gavin Billingshurst
Cost: H/wine £9.60
Credit cards: 🁢 💳
Times: Last L 2.30pm/D 9.30pm. Closed 10 days Xmas/New Year

PERTH, **Parklands Hotel** 🏵

Parklands was created by linking two houses together. It stands in mature gardens overlooking South Inch Park. The restaurant menu features regional dishes including grilled Scottish salmon served with a coarse grain mustard hollandaise, and lightly roasted pheasant with a blackcurrant vinegar and grape sauce

Menus: *A la carte*, fixed-price L /D, bar menu, pre-theatre
Seats: 30. No smoking in dining room
Additional: Children welcomed, children's portions; ❂ dishes, vegan/other diets on request
Directions: overlooking South Inch Park, round the corner from train & bus stations

St Leonards Bank
Perthshire PH2 8EB
Map no: 11 NO12
Tel: 01738 622451
Chef: Craig Wilson
Proprietor: Allan Deeson
(Scotland's Commended)
Cost: *Alc* from £20.90, fixed-price L £15.50 /D £24.95.
H/wine £10.95 Service exc
Credit cards: 🆑 🖃 🖾 💷 OTHER
Times: last L 2pm/D 9pm daily
Closed Dec 23-Jan 7

PITLOCHRY, **Knockendarroch House Hotel** 🏵

A substantial Victorian mansion with splendid views over the town and the Tummel valley. Enthusiastic owners create a welcoming atmosphere and a short menu offers home cooking at its best. Unfortunately the hotel does not accept non-resident diners

Seats: 24. No smoking
Additional: Children welcome, ❂ dishes, vegan/other diets on request
Directions: First right after the Atholl Palace Hotel, then second left, last hotel on left

Higher Oakfield
Perthshire PH16 5HT
Map no: 14 NN95
Tel: 01796 473473
Chefs: James McMenemie
Proprietor: The McMenemie family
Cost: Fixed price D £15, H/wine £5.90
Credit cards: 🆑 🖃 🖾 💷
Times: Last D 7.45pm

PITLOCHRY, **Pine Trees Hotel** 🏵

This magnificent country mansion built in 1892 is situated in 14 acres of secluded wooded gardens rising high above the town. Light modern cooking is a feature of the kitchen. Indeed, loin of lamb was the best our inspector had tasted all season, and the lemon tart was 'a treat'

Strathview Terrace
Perthshire PH16 5QR
Map no: 14 NN95
Tel: 01796 472121
Chef: Richard Axford
Proprietors: Mr & Mrs J T MacLellan
Cost: Fixed-price L £12.50/D £23 (4 course) H/wine £11 Service exc
Credit cards: 🆑 🖃 🖾
Times: Last L 1.30pm, last D 8.30pm
Menus: Fixed-price L & D, pre-theatre, bar menu
Seats: No smoking in dining room
Additional: Children welcome, children's portions; ❂ dishes, vegan/other diets on request

Directions: Turn right off main street and follow signs to Golf Course

ST FILLANS, Achray House ⊛

'Quite staggering' views over Loch Earn can be enjoyed from the bar and restaurant of this popular little hotel. The kitchen offers simple but effective dishes such as fetta cheese, asparagus and tomato tart or wild venison and red wine casserole, but the highlight of any meal is the delicious home baking and traditional desserts

Crieff Perthshire PH6 2NF
Map no: 11 NN62
Tel: 01764 685231
Chef: Bernard Steinka
Proprietors: Tony & Jane Ross
Cost: *Alc* £19, fixed-price D
£15. H/wine £6.50. Service exc
Credit cards: ▩ ▩ ▩ OTHER
Times: Noon-last L 2pm, 6pm-
last D 9pm. Closed Nov-Feb
Menus: *A la carte,* fixed-price D,
bar menu
Seats: 34. No smoking in dining
room
Additional: Children welcome,
children's portions; ♥ menu,
vegan/other diets on request

Directions: Off A85 five miles west of Comrie overlooking Loch Earn

ST FILLANS, Four Seasons ⊛⊛

Enterprising cooking with the accent on seasonal flavours inspires a loyal local following

This popular, family-run hotel, which stands at the eastern end of Loch Earn with panoramic views of the surrounding hills, is closed from Christmas Eve until the first of March, so perhaps it should be called the Three Seasons. Andrew Scott's hand-written, daily-changing, set price menus promise 'A Taste of Scotland' and feature the pick of local produce, which is handled with a delicate touch that allows natural flavours to shine. Hence Scotch beef is complemented by Arran mustard, smoked haddock combined with poached eggs and crispy bacon or made into a soup with leek and potato, mussels from Skye served with saffron cream to accompany steamed fillet of sole. The dessert trolley is well-stocked with all manner of home-made temptations and there's a fine selection of Scottish cheeses, served with oaties. Service is all smiles and there's a comprehensive wine list which offers few surprises, but is decent value.

Crieff Perthshire PH6 2NF
Map no: 11 NN62
Tel: 01764 685333
Chef: Andrew Scott
Proprietors: Mr & Mrs J A Scott
Cost: Fixed-price L £13.50/D
£22.50 (4 course). H/wine
£10.50 Service exc
Credit cards: ▩ ▩ ▩ ▩
Times: Last L 2.15pm, last D
9.45pm Closed Dec 24-Mar 1
Menus: Fixed-price L & D, bar
menu
Seats: 50. No smoking in dining
room
Additional: Children welcome,
children's portions; ♥ dishes,
vegan/other diets on request

Directions: On A85 at western edge of village overlooking Loch Earn

Sashimi is very fresh raw fish, shellfish and molluscs, trimmed, boned and cut with a long, thin knife. It is served with daikon (Japanese radish, thinly sliced and eaten raw), seaweed, slices of fresh ginger, soy sauce and horseradish paste. Sashimi should not be confused with sushi - Japanese vinegar rice and raw fish rolls.

STANLEY, **The Tayside Hotel** ✿

☺ *A popular Edwardian sporting hotel which has retained much of the original character. Liz Robertson's robust cooking, based on the best of fresh local ingredients, continues to satisfy the hearty appetites of the mostly sporting clientele. Try tomato soup, haggis (from the local butcher), neeps and tatties*

Mill Street
Perthshire PH1 4NL
Map no: 11 NO13
Tel: 01738 828249
Chefs: Peter Graham and Liz Robertson
Proprietor: Edgilton Hotels Ltd
Manager: Margaret Clark
Cost: *Alc* from £16.50, fixed-price D £16.50. H/wine £7.50. Service exc
Credit cards: 🟦 🟰 OTHER
Times: Last L 1.45pm/D 8.30pm, Sun high teas 4pm-6pm
Menus: *A la carte,* fixed-price D, bar L menu
Seats: 32. Smoking discouraged
Additional: Children welcome, children's portions; ❶ dishes, vegan/other diets on request

Directions: 5 miles N of Perth on B9099; turn right at village green, then left

Chillies were one of the earliest plants to be cultivated in the pre-Columbian New World. Archaeological evidence suggests that they were used at least 8,000 years ago to impart flavour and spiciness to food. The Mayans used 30 different varieties of chilli and recent evidence shows that the Aztecs used them in almost every dish. Today chillies are grown throughout the world. The characteristic for which chillies are best known is their heat. The fiery sensation is caused by capsaicin, a potent chemical that survives both cooking and freezing. As well as causing a burning sensation, this substance triggers the brain to produce endorphins, natural pain killers that promote a sense of well-being and stimulation. Also, capsaicin is a natural decongestant. The hottest chilli in the world is probably the Scotch bonnet chilli (so named because its shape resembles a Highlander's cap). A single Scotch bonnet has the fire power of 50 jalapeno chillies. Grown in the Caribbean it is an essential ingredient in Jamaican jerk dishes. When handling chillies you should wear rubber gloves. Wash your hands with soap afterwards and take care not to touch your face, or eyes. If your hands start to sting after handling chillies, rub them with a little toothpaste.

WALES
ANGLESEY, ISLE OF

BEAUMARIS,
Ye Olde Bulls Head Inn ❀❀

Historic inn, where both Charles Dickens and Samuel Johnson once stayed, with a good reputation for carefully prepared food

Anywhere called 'ye olde' something or another, runs the risk of terminal quaintness. Ye Olde Bulls Head Inn, however, wears its history well, offering a high standard of hospitality and up to date cooking. The well-furnished inn dates from 1472, and features enough timbers, beams and antique weaponry to sink the proverbial ship. The restaurant, under the guidance of Keith Rothwell, offers a large, fixed-price, no choice, daily menu augmented by a large *carte*. Table service is also available in the spacious lounge. Good local produce is a strong point, especially the Welsh lamb and the superb fish from the surrounding waters. The latter starred in a fine dish of smoked salmon and crab parcels, balanced with a tangy side salad, as well as a main course of roast sea bass with garlic. Vegetables were crisp and fresh and included new potatoes 'tasting as they really should'. A tulip-shaped chocolate mousse with a garnish of fresh, exotic fruit and a crème anglaise was sharp and refreshing.

Directions: Town centre, main street

Castle Street LL58 8AP
Map no: 6 SH67
Tel: 01248 810329
Chefs: Keith Rothwell and Soames Whittingham
Proprietor: David Robertson (Welsh Rarebits)
Cost: *Alc* £24, fixed-price Sun L £14.75/D £19.75. H/wine £12.50 Service exc
Credit cards: ▨ ▦ ▧ OTHER
Times: Last bar L 2.30pm, Sun L 1.30pm, last D 9.30pm
Menus: *A la carte*, fixed-price D & Sun L, bar L menu
Seats: 70. No smoking in dining room
Additional: Children welcome (over 7 at D), children's portions; ❷ dishes, vegan/other diets on request

LLANGEFNI, Tre-Ysgawen Hall ❀❀❀

Even the most jaded appetite should be stimulated by the fusion of quality produce and original ideas encountered here

As peaceful and quiet as its location in central Anglesey would suggest, this restaurant is a sympathetically designed modern addition to a fine country mansion. Chef Mark Colley demonstrates considerable style in fixed-price and *carte* menus of English/French dishes, his light touch with seafood immediately obvious in the pan-fried scallops with Chinese spices and a ginger and soya vinaigrette that began a recent inspection meal. A rack of Welsh lamb, though firm, had all the expected flavour and was accompanied by an excellent home-made black pudding sausage, a good Madeira sauce and al dente vegetables. The rum and banana soufflé which completed the meal betrayed little evidence of alcohol but was delicately textured and enjoyable, served with a pleasant fruit ice-cream and diced fruit in a soft tuille. Liqueur coffees provide an alternative to the standard cafetière, a different one being featured on each day's menu; Café Année 1993, for example, contains both peach schnapps and apricot brandy and is topped with lightly whisked Anglesey cream. A well structured wine list includes some unusual items and staff are friendly and attentive – the house policy being that guests need only request a service for it to be provided.

Directions: A5 to Llangefni, take B5111 to Llanerchmedd through Rhosmeirch. After 1 mile turn right for Capel Coch

Capel Coch LL77 7UR
Map no: 6 SH47
Tel: 01248 750750
Chef: Mark Colley
Proprietors: Ray & Pat Craighead
Cost: *Alc* £30, fixed-price L £14/D£19.95. H/wine £9.80. Service exc
Credit cards: ▨ ▦ ▧ ▨ OTHER
Times: Noon-Last L 2.30pm, 7pm-Last D 9.30pm
Menus: *A la carte*, fixed-price lunch & dinner, Sunday lunch, pre-theatre
Seats: 64. No-smoking area; no pipes or cigars in dining room
Additional: Children permitted (over 8 at dinner); children's portions; ❷ menu, vegan/other diets on request

CLWYD

ABERGELE, **Kinmel Arms** ✿

☺ *In addition to its good bar meals, this 17th-century coaching inn offers a restaurant carte featuring locally caught fish (notably sea bass and monkfish), game from a nearby park and, of course, Welsh lamb. Another speciality is local goats' cheese – sometimes interestingly served with a beetroot and roast garlic salad*

Seats: 38
Additional: Children welcome; ❶ dishes
Directions: Take A55 towards Conwy. Left turn signed 'St George'. Left at top of hill and restaurant on left

St George LL22 9BP
Map no: 6 SH98
Tel: 01745 832207
Chef: Gary Edwards
Proprietors: G Edwards and C Buckley
Cost: *Alc* £17, fixed-price Sun L £6.95-£8.95
Credit cards: 💳
Times: Last L 2pm, last D 9pm

COLWYN BAY, **Café Niçoise** ✿✿

☺ *An evocation of the Côte d'Azur is attempted at this relaxed, French restaurant*

124 Abergele Road LL29 7PS
Map no: 6 SH87
Tel: 01492 531555
Chef: Carl Swift
Proprietors: Lynne & Carl Swift
Cost: *Alc* £18.50, fixed-price L £12.95, £10.75 (2 course)/D £12.95. H/wine £6.95 ❢ Service exc
Credit cards: 💳 💳 💳 💳
Times: Last L 2pm, last D 9.30pm Closed Sat L
Menus: *A la carte*, fixed-price L & D
Seats: 32
Additional: Children permitted, children's portions; ❶ dishes, vegan/other diets on request

As its name implies, Café Niçoise is styled after a typical Nice café, romantically candlelit with a background of French music. Carl Swift combines traditional and modern provincial French cooking, with a touch of his own personality, to provide an interesting range of dishes. Lynne Swift takes care of front-of-house. There is a good value 'Menu Touristique' during the week plus a large blackboard selection – lunch is served on Thursday, Friday and Saturday only. Venison, wild boar and turbot make their appearance along with Welsh lamb and beef. A vegetarian option is always listed, perhaps baked vegetable charlotte with tomato fondue or asparagus and courgette tartlet. A test meal began with a smooth salmon and sole terrine textured with leek and served with an orange vinaigrette salad. Then 'delicious' pan-fried turbot came with poached asparagus and fresh dill. The dessert 'assiette du chef' is strongly recommended, although an alternative might be Anglesey honey and almond tart with lemon anglaise or a choice of Welsh and French cheeses from the cheeseboard.

Directions: From A55 take exit signed Old Colwyn, left at slip road, right at mini-roundabout, right towards Bay, Restaurant is on the left

ERBISTOCK, **Boat Inn** ❀❀

Lovely riverside location for this ancient inn and restaurant, now under new management

A waterfront setting always seems to favour romance, so anyone looking for a good place to pop the question could do worse than head for the Boat Inn on the banks of the river Dee. After a chequered history, the kitchen is back in business under the control of Duncan Laurie's sound, mainstream British menu. Prominence, quite correctly, is given to Dee salmon – as a tartare starter, perhaps, or more elaborately wrapped in puff pastry, served on a compote of red cabbage and sultanas. Simply roasted game – quail or Gressingham duck – also feature strongly. A good alternative main course would be the chicken suprême, stylishly parcelled in smoked bacon and spinach leaves. A spinach and wild mushroom tartlet with sorrel butter sauce also pleased for its fine array of flavours, an example of the broad selection of vegetarian dishes available. At lunchtime, the menu also includes tried and tested favourites such as steak and kidney pie, and Cumberland sausage with redcurrant sauce.

Directions: At Erbistock turn left off A528 just past Cross Foxes pub. Follow road to the River Dee

Wrexham LL13 0DL
Map no: 7 SJ34
Tel: 01978 780143
Chef: Duncan Laurie
Proprietor: Louise Marubbi
Credit cards: 🔳 🔳 🔳 🔳
Seats: 70
Additional: Children permitted:
❷ dishes

EWLOE, **St Davids Park Hotel** ❀

An extensive carte, a chef's gourmet menu and a carvery-style menu offer a wide range of dishes in this modern business hotel's Fountain Restaurant. Choices may include terrine of salmon and crab wrapped in smoked salmon, loin of pork filled with Swiss cheese, and Parma ham on home-made black pudding

Menus: A la carte, fixed-price L & D, pre-theatre, bar menu
Seats: 140. Air conditioned. No-smoking area **Additional:** Children welcome, children's menu; ❷ menu, vegan/other diets on request
Directions: At junction of A55 & A494,10 minutes from M56

St Davids Park CH5 3YB
Map no: 7 SJ36
Tel: 01244 520800
Chef: Graham Tinsley
Proprietor: St Davids Hotels.
Manager: Hamish Ferguson
Cost: Alc £30, fixed-price L
£11.95 (2 course), £17.50/D
£17.50. H/wine £ 10.50 ❗
Service inc
Credit cards: 🔳 🔳 🔳 🔳 OTHER
Times: Last L 2pm, last D 10pm
daily

HAWARDEN,
Swiss Restaurant Imfeld ❀❀

☺ *Genuine Swiss cooking in a quiet village restaurant with several intimate corners*

Swiss cooking is somewhat overshadowed by that of Switzerland's neighbours, France and Italy. But the country that gave us Gruyère and rösti has an interesting, varied style of cookery that draws extensively on its multinational origins. And here, Markus Imfeld proves it with a successful culinary microcosm of his motherland, competently assisted by Robert John. Starters might include tagliatelle Zurich, 'raclette Valaisienne' (melted cheese garnished with new potato, gherkins and silver skin onions), and 'grabboregglor knopfli' (pasta dumplings with mushrooms and onions gratinated with Alp cheese). There are more Swiss dishes among the main courses, together with more familiar dishes such as fillet of Barbary duck, mushroom Stroganoff, and catch of the day from the Fleetwood fish market chalked on the blackboard. This Lancashire town supplies most of the fish for Imfeld's seafood

68 The Highway CH5 3DH
Map no: 7 SJ36
Tel: 01244 534523
Chef: Markus Imfeld
Proprietor: Yvonne Imfield.
Manager: Pauline Lancaster
Cost: Alc £19, fixed-price D
£19/Sun L £10.95. H/wine £8.50
❗ Service exc
Credit cards: 🔳 🔳 OTHER
Times: Last D10pm, last Sun L
3pm Closed Sun D, Mon D, 2
wks Spring
Menus: A la carte, fixed-price D
& Sun L
Seats: 38. No-smoking area
Additional: Children welcome,
children's portions; ❷ dishes,
vegan/other diets on request

specialities menu – moules marinière, spicy jumbo prawns sautéed with garlic. The main *carte* and set-price menu change monthly and there are also special gourmet and fondue evenings. Some of the desserts are Swiss and, patriotic to the last, there are ten Swiss wines, including the house red and white.

Directions: Off A55 signed to Hawarden/Airport, through village centre & Restaurant is on left

HOLYWELL,
Kinsale Hall Hotel ❀

Holywell CH8 9DX
Map no: 7 SJ17
Tel: 01745 560001
Chef: Kevin Steel
Manager: Paul A W Roebuck
Cost: *Alc* from £16, fixed-price L £14/D £18. H/wine £10.25
Service exc
Credit cards: 🔳 🔳 🔳 🔳 OTHER
Times: Last L 2pm, last D 9pm/9.30pm Fri-Sat

A small restaurant offering modern English cooking. A typical meal might start with an avocado, brie and tomato salad, followed by a fillet of wild salmon baked in a herb crust with caper sauce, and home-made praline and nougat ice, and framboise sauce to finish

Menus: A la carte, fixed-price L & D, bar menu   **Seats:** 36. No smoking in dining room   **Additional:** Children welcome, children's portions (menu 6pm-7pm); ❤ dishes, vegan/other diets on request
Directions: A55 onto A548 (Prestatyn), at large white ship take side road for Maes Pennant, hotel in 1st driveway on left

LLANDEGLA, **Bod Idris Hall** ❀❀

Nr Wrexham LL11 3AL
Map no: 6 SJ25
Tel: 01978 790434
Chef: Philip Weale
Proprietor: T. Williams (Welsh Rarebits)
Cost: *Alc* D £18, fixed-price L £12.75/D £18
Credit cards: 🔳 🔳 🔳 🔳
Times: Last D 9.30

An historic house in a lovely setting serving fresh, imaginative cooking

More than five hundred years of history is embodied within the walls of this creeper-clad country house hotel. It is set in eleven acres of mature parkland which includes a lake complete with swans. The original manor house was rebuilt in Tudor times and visitors cannot fail to be influenced by its magical surroundings. Fine oak panelling and magnificent inglenooks remain. Phillip Weale leads the team in the kitchen, working from a 'Taste of Wales' menu in addition to daily changing choices. An inspection meal yielded parfait of chicken livers and ginger, fresh salad and rich apricots that had been preserved on the premises. Sweet rack of lamb was served with roast parsnips and a mild sauce of juniper and port; crisp vegetables included cauliflower, broccoli, new potatoes, asparagus and carrots. A lovely lemon tart, slightly caramelised and served with ginger ice-cream concluded the meal. Attention to the smallest detail is keen. All bread, preserves and ice-creams are made on the premises.

Directions: Llandegla is on A525 (Wrexham–Ruthin). In village (from Wrexham direction) turn right on to A5104. Hotel is signed in 1 mile on left

LLANDRILLO,
Tyddyn Llan Hotel ❀❀

Corwen LL21 0ST
Map no: 6 SJ03
Tel: 01490 440264
Chef: Dominic Gilbert
Proprietors: Peter & Bridget Kindred

Good Welsh produce is used imaginatively by this hotel in the lovely Vale of Edeyrnion

Comfortable, relaxing surroundings and service that combines friendliness with unobtrusive professionalism are the hallmarks of

Tyddyn Llan Hotel

Cost: Fixed-price L £10.75
(2 courses), £12.75/D £23, £25
(5 course). H/wine £10.25 ❗
Service exc
Credit cards: 🔳 🔳 🔳 🔳 OTHER
Times: Last L 2pm, last D 9.30.
Closed last 3wks Jan
Menus: Fixed-price L & D, bar
menu
Seats: 60. No pipes or cigars in
dining room
Additional: Children permitted
(D by arrangement); children's
portions; ❂ dishes, vegan/other
diets on request

this unpretentious hotel. The elegant, spacious dining-room –
efficiently designed in two sections – provides a pleasant setting in
which to enjoy reliable cooking. Inventive four-course fixed-price
menus, soundly based on local produce (including herbs from the
garden), reflect a style that comes over well. Marinated salmon with
capers and olive oil provided an effective starter to a recent meal,
and this was followed by good cream of broccoli soup. A main
course of boned quail stuffed with chicken then served with wild
mushrooms and a port sauce was less successful, the flavour of the
bacon wrapped around the bird predominating; vegetables – green
beans and a sliced baked potato – were disappointing too, both in
their simplicity and lack of range, but a delicious sticky toffee
pudding served with home-made ice cream left little to be desired.
A well chosen and annotated wine list should contain something to
suit most palates, with 100 bins spanning a wide variety.

Directions: Take B4401 from Corwen to Llandrillo. Restaurant on the
right leaving the village

LLANGOLLEN,
Bryn Howel Hotel ✿✿✿

*A lovely hotel in a magnificent setting serving an interesting choice of
modern British cooking*

From the Cedar Tree Restaurant, the eyes take in the magnificent
Vale of Llangollen, the beautiful lawns and the narrowboats on the
canal. It would be understandable if, occasionally, a diner, inspired
by such a view, were to get up and sing. For Llangollen is, of course,
the home of that great annual Bardic congress, the International
Eisteddfod.
    Cooking is based on the availability of the fresh local produce
which each day determines the fixed-price, three-course lunch
menu and dinner *carte*. An inspection lunch began with deep fried,
crisp, perfectly cooked cod fillets in breadcrumbs, followed by
excellently textured pan-fried lamb's liver, with shreds of bacon,
mushrooms and slices of mango. On another occasion dinner
commenced with beautifully cooked fillet of codling in light, black
bean batter with a strongish curry sauce. But it was the main course
– charred breast of Goosnargh duckling, served with a timbale of
stir-fry vegetables infused with leg rillettes – that was the star of the

Clwyd LL20 7UW
Map no: 7 SJ24
Tel: 01978 860331
Chef: Dai Davies
Proprietor: John E Lloyd (Best
Western/Welsh Rarebits)
Manager: Anne M Lloyd
Cost: *Alc* L £15-£17/D £18-£27,
fixed-price Sun L £13.50.
H/wine £12.90 ❗ Service exc
Credit cards: 🔳 🔳 🔳 🔳 OTHER
Times: Last L 2pm, last D 9pm
Closed Dec 25-27
Menus: *A la carte* L & D, fixed-
price Sun L, bar menu
Seats: N/A.
Additional: Children permitted,
children's portions; ❂ dishes,
other diets on request

show. Everything about it was right. Other possible starters are
Mediterranean ham salad, finished with pickled vegetables and
grilled prosciutto; nage of sea trout, infused with cockles in a black
olive cream sauce; and tian of avocado, layered with crab and slices
of mango, topped with yoghurt, and fried celeriac. Main courses:
roast loin of Usk Valley farmed venison, with a tartlet of leek and
goats' cheese crumble; pan-fried escalope of salmon, with a dill fish
cream; and steamed pudding of Welsh lamb's fillet and heart, with
onion gravy and glazed sweetbreads. Desserts include Welsh honey
wafers filled with raspberry cream and fresh berries, and prune and
Armagnac tart with vanilla sauce. The seventy or so wines are
mostly well under £20 a bottle. From a local vineyard come apple
and blackcurrant meads.

Directions: Two miles east of Llangollen on A539

ROSSETT, Llyndir Hall Hotel ❀

*This is a fine country-house hotel near Chester, where the chef and his
team prepare a choice of well liked food. Dishes sampled at inspection
included a 'delicious' ragout of mushrooms and bacon, a parcel of brill
with a mushroom mousse and a 'very rich' caramelised pear*

Menus: *A la carte,* fixed-price L & D, bar menu
Seats: 60. No-smoking area
Additional: Children permitted before 8pm, children's menu;
❂ dishes, vegan/other diets on request
Directions: South from Chester on A483 to Wrexham, follow signs
for Pulford/Rossett B5445. Llyndir Hall signed on the right

Wrexham LL12 0AY
Map no: 7 SJ35
Tel: 01244 571648
Chef: Jeremy Stone
Proprietor: Mr Tucker
(Celebrated Hotels)
Cost: *Alc* £24.95, fixed-price
L £14.50, £12.50 (2 course)/D
£18.50 (4 course). H/wine
£10.50 ❢ Service exc
Credit cards: ▨ ▨ ▨ ▨ OTHER
Times: Last L 2pm, last D
9.30pm Closed Sat L

ROSSETT, Rossett Hall Hotel ❀

☺ *Lying in extensive grounds, this splendid country house dates back to
1750. As well as the daily menu, a carte offers a wide choice of dishes.
An inspection meal, which included chicken with lobster stuffing, and
a syrup steamed pudding, was much enjoyed*

Directions: Turn off A483 (Chester & Wrexham) to Rossett. In centre
of village on B5445

Chester Road LL12 0DE
Map no: 7 SJ35
Tel: 01244 571000
Chef: Neil Baker
Proprietors: Mrs K A Craven
(Best Western)
Cost: Fixed-price L £11.50/D
£18.50
Credit cards: ▨ ▨ ▨ ▨ OTHER
Time: Last D 10pm

RUTHIN, Ye Olde Anchor Inn ❀❀

☺ *Visitors are attracted from a wide area by the carefully cooked food
served at this delightful 18th-century inn*

This atmospheric inn was once a stopping place for drovers on their
way from Holyhead to Shropshire. Many original features, such as
low oak-beamed ceilings, have been retained and the whole place
has been decorated with real character. There are two cosy bars and
a small restaurant which offers an extensive menu based on fresh
ingredients and simple preparation. An inspection meal
commenced with chicken liver pâté with added nutmeg, cracked
pepper and Grand Marnier and a good cranberry glaze. For main
course, a dish of tender pork with Indonesian spices and braised
rice was chosen. It was accompanied by a good selection of well
timed, simply presented vegetables, namely sweet braised leeks,
new potatoes and green cabbage. Other dishes could include

Rhos Street LL15 1DX
Map no: 6 SJ15
Tel: 01824 702813
Chef: Rod England
Proprietor: Rod England
Cost: *Alc* £15-£20, fixed-price L
£5.25/D £12.95. H/wine £7.95
Service exc
Credit cards: ▨ ▨ OTHER
Times: Last L 2pm, last D
9.30pm
Menus: *A la carte,* fixed-price L
& D, bar L menu
Seats: 60. No smoking in dining
room

Ye Olde Anchor Inn

Additional: Children welcome, children's meu; ♥ dishes, vegan/other diets on request

chateaubriand, breast of duck or fresh fish. To finish there is excellent home-made vanilla ice-cream or perhaps crêpe suzette or crème brûlée. Service is informal and friendly.

Directions: Situated in Ruthin at the junction of the A525 & A494

DYFED

ABERYSTWYTH, **Belle Vue Royal** ❀

A set-price carte in modern style now supplements the traditional menu of Royals Grill Room – the attractive restaurant of this seafront hotel. Shank of Ystwyth lamb, for example, is infused with rosemary and sweet garlic then served with fried couscous and a purée of creamed swede with nutmeg

Directions: On the seafront

Marine Terrace SY23 2BA
Map no: 6 SN58
Tel: 01970 617558
Chef: Michael Stagg
Proprietors: Mr Davies and Mr Jones
Cost: Fixed-price L £11.50/D £19
Credit cards: ▨ ▤ ▦ ▨ OTHER
Times: Last D 9.30pm

ABERYSTWYTH, **Conrah Hotel** ❀❀

Modern cooking with a sound classical base, in relaxed, well-run surroundings

Originally the mansion house to an old estate, Conrah is tucked away at the end of a long rhododendron-lined drive, magnificently set in 22 acres of rolling landscaped grounds. The twin hallmarks of this immaculately kept hotel are care and attention, nowhere more evident than in the dining-room. Stephen West's *carte* and set-price menus offer an imaginative choice, based on a marriage between classical and modern styles of cooking, and fresh produce. Laverbread and salmon sausage on a bed of steamed cucumber spaghetti with lemon sauce, or grilled brochette of vegetables with a peanut and herb sauce, could start the meal. Main courses include roast rack of Welsh lamb, with a honey and grain mustard glaze on a sauce of Cassis and pine nuts, chargrilled fillet of Welsh Black beef with roasted shallots, wild mushrooms and a rich claret sauce,

Ffosrhydygaled,
Chancery SY23 4DF
Map no: 6 SN58
Tel: 01970 617941
Chef: Stephen West
Proprietor: Frederick John Heading (Welsh Rarebits)
Cost: Alc £28.50, fixed-price L £15.75/D £23.50. H/wine £10. Service exc
Credit cards: ▨ ▤ ▦ ▨ OTHER
Times: Last L 2pm, last D 9pm daily Closed Christmas wk
Menus: A la carte, fixed-price L & D, bar menu
Seats: 50. No-smoking in dining room

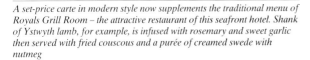

or ragout of mixed mushrooms in a port wine, garlic and cream sauce served in a puff pastry pillow. Warm treacle tart, almond and Amaretto syllabub and chocolate and meringue soufflé number among the sweets. The wine list draws deeply on France, is sensibly priced, and offers a decent selection of half bottles.

Additional: Children permitted (over 5), children's portions; ♥ dishes, vegan/other diets on request

Directions: On A487, 3 miles south of Aberystwyth

ABERYSTWYTH, Groves Hotel ❀

44-46 North Parade SY23 2NF
Map no: 6 SN58
Tel: 01970 617623
Chef: Steve Albert
Proprietors: The Albert family (Minotel)
Cost: Fixed-price D £15.50, Sun L £12.50. H/wine £7.95 ▮ Service inc
Credit cards: 🖾 ▆ ▆
Times: Last D 9pm
Closed Sun D

☺ *Pleasant, attractive restaurant of a small privately-run hotel. Good choice of soundly prepared food, includes speciality 'Taste of Wales' dishes. Recommended are crab salad and a delicious roast leg of Welsh lamb served with a savoury, light suet dumpling*

Menus: Fixed-price L & D, bar menu
Seats: 70. No smoking in dining room
Additional: Children welcome, children's menu; ♥ dishes, vegan/other diets on request
Directions: Town centre, take road opposite station & 2nd right

BRECHFA,
Ty Mawr Country Hotel ❀

Brecha SA32 7RA
Map no: 2 SN53
Tel: 01267 202332
Chef: Beryl Tudhope
Proprietors: Dick & Beryl Tudhope
Cost: Fixed-price D £ 19-£22. H/wine £8.95 Service inc
Credit cards: 🖾 ▆ ▆
Times: 7pm-last D 9.30pm
Closed Tue, end Nov-early Dec, Dec 25/26, last 2 wks Jan

☺ *Laden with accolades, this 'little jewel' of a hotel is popular with a wide range of people. It offers accomplished cooking, a lovely atmosphere and beautiful rustic surroundings. The food is delicious, too. Try prawn and mussel ravioli, and the wonderful dessert of chocolate and almond puff is fully recommended*

Menus: Fixed-price D & Sun L
Seats: 35. No smoking in dining room
Additional: Children welcome (over 8 at D), children's menu; ♥ menu, vegan/other diets on request
Directions: In the centre of the village 6.5 miles from the junction of A40/B4310

CARMARTHEN,
Old Cornmill Restaurant ❀

Cynwyl Elfed SA33 6UJ
Map no: 2 SN42
Tel: 01267 281610
Chef: Jack de Wreede
Proprietors: Sue & Jack de Wreede
Cost: Alc £16, fixed-price L £10. H/wine £6.90 No service charge
Credit cards: 🖾 ▆ OTHER
Times: Last L 2.30pm, last D 9pm Closed Sun D, Mon,Tue, Feb

☺ *Classical French and traditional English cooking share the bill at this intimate cottage-style restaurant. The carte changes three times a year but is supplemented by a specials board. Chicken livers and lentils, fried with sliced mushrooms and diced vegetables, are recommended*

Menus: A la carte, fixed-price L
Seats: 35. No cigars or pipes in dining room
Additional: Children welcome, children's menu; ♥ dishes, vegan/other diets with notice
Directions: 0.5 mile from village on A484 7 miles N/W of Carmarthen

LLANDEILO, **Cawdor Arms Hotel** ❁

A Georgian hotel with a large, period-style restaurant, which can be partitioned to accommodate private parties, offering straightforward, but perfectly pleasing cooking. Try the home-made mushroom soup, fresh fillet of cod, and the 'refreshing' trio of home-made lemon desserts

Menus: Fixed-price L & D, lounge menu
Seats: 56.
Additional: Children permitted, children's portions; ✆ dishes, vegan/other diets on request
Directions: Town centre, large Georgian building

Rhosmaen Street SA19 6EN
Map no: 3 SN62
Tel: 01558 823500
Chef: Gareth Passey
Proprietor: Sir Gar Gyf.
Managing Director: Philip Thomas
Cost: Fixed-price L £21, £16 (2 course)/D £21. H/wine £7.95 ❢ Service exc
Credit cards: 🂫 ▦ ▩ OTHER
Times: Last L 2pm, last D 9.45pm

MACHYNLLETH,
Ynyshir Hall ❁❁❁

A former shooting lodge maintaining the highest standards of food and service

Machynlleth SY20 8TA
Map no: 6 SN69
Tel: 01654 781209
Chef: Ian White and Chris Dawson
Proprietors: Rob & Joan Reen (Pride of Britain/Welsh Rarebit)
Cost: Fixed-price L £17.50/D £27.50. H/wine £12 ❢ Service inc
Credit cards: 🂫 ▦ ▩ 🂠 OTHER
Times: Last D 8.45pm
Menus: Fixed-price L & D, bar menu
Seats: 30. No smoking
Additional: Children permitted (over 9); ✆ menu, other dishes on request

Co-owner Rob Reen's calligraphic skills grace the wine list and the menus. Queen Victoria, adept no doubt at writing in the compulsory copper-plate hand of her day, would have admired the style. She rates this utterly gratuitous mention because she used to own the estate on which the attractive house was once a shooting lodge. Rob writes a fresh dinner menu every day; but only has to prepare one lunch menu a week – on Sundays.

The skilful cooking at Ynyshir Hall has merited an increase this year to three rosettes. As much produce as possible comes from west Wales, including seared Dyfi salmon with roasted vegetables and sauce vièrge, and noisettes of Welsh lamb with black pudding sausage and fondant potato. Local sea-fish goes into the bourride, with fettucini, ratatouille and a tomato coulis, and Welsh deer end up as fillet of venison on polenta, with a spiced cake of venison mousse. Lambs' sweetbreads may turn up as starters, perhaps with a thyme and beer coating on a bed of wild mushrooms. Desserts include timbales, délices, soufflés, crème brûlée and tartlets and are in the same creative vein. A selection of Welsh cheeses is offered with a glass of port.

Directions: On the A487, 6 miles from Machynlleth & 11 miles from Aberystwyth

PEMBROKE, Court Hotel ❀

Visitors can look forward to fine food in a lovely setting at this large, elegant country house. Dishes are based on English and Welsh recipes, and there is a separate vegetarian menu. An enjoyable recent main course was a tasty beef Cromwell. Staff are friendly and efficient

Directions: Hotel signed in Lamphey

Lamphey SA71 5NT
Map no: 2 SM90
Tel: 01646 672273
Chef: Kevin Shaw
Proprietor: A W Lain (Best Western)
Manager: R F Koomen
Cost: *Alc* from £20, fixed-price D £15.95 (4 course). H/wine £8.95. Service inc
Credit cards: ▨ ▧ ▧ ▨ OTHER
Times: Last L 1.45pm, last D 9.30pm
Menus: *A la carte,* fixed-price D, bar menu
Seats: 60. Air conditioned
Additional: Children welcome, children's menu; ❶ dishes, other diets on request

ST DAVID'S, Warpool Court Hotel ❀❀

Carefully presented food is offered at this superbly located hotel

A superb coastal location is a fitting setting for this impressive stone-built Victorian property. Warpool Court stands in lovely gardens on the outskirts of the city, overlooking St Brides Bay and the off-shore islands. John Daniels has taken over in the kitchen. His seasonally changing, fixed-price menus make good use of freshly available produce, cooked in a 'not over-elaborate style'. A high degree of care clearly goes into both preparation and presentation of food. A meal in winter sampled cream of mushroom soup – which could have used a little more seasoning but had plenty of flavour – followed by pan-fried sirloin steak, cooked to order and accompanied by a well executed garlic and red wine sauce. A wide selection of vegetables included broccoli, mashed swede, firm sliced carrots, cabbage with bacon, garlic potatoes and some very good new potatoes. Dessert was a light almond and raisin sponge on a hot creamy custard.

Directions: From Cross Square, left by Midland Bank into Goat Street, at fork follow hotel signs

Haverfordwest SA62 6BN
Map no: 2 SM72
Tel: 01437 720300
Chef: John Daniels
Manager: Rupert Duffin (Logis of GB)
Cost: Fixed-price L £16.95/D £28 (4 course). H/wine £8.40 No service charge
Credit cards: ▨ ▧ ▧ ▨ OTHER
Times: Last L 2pm, last D 9.15pm Closed Jan
Menus: Fixed-price L & D, pre-theatre, bar menu
Seats: 60. No cigars or pipes in dining room
Additional: Children welcome, children's menu; ❶ dishes, vegan/other diets on request

TENBY, Atlantic Hotel ❀

A personally-run hotel enjoying a lovely location above the South Beach with delightful views of the sea and Caldey Island. The menu changes every three days in order to take full advantage of the fresh produce available, especially the good choice of fish, seafood, and local meats

Menus: *A la carte* L & D, bar menu **Seats:** 90. Air conditioned
Additional: Children's menu; ❶ dishes, other diets on request
Directions: Town centre, half way along Esplanade, on right

Esplanade SA70 7DU
Map no: 2 SN10
Tel: 01834 842881
Chef: Julian Rees
Proprietor: Mr & Mrs W G U James
Cost: *Alc* £16 min. Service exc
Credit cards: ▨ ▧ OTHER
Times: Last L 1.30pm, last D 8.30pm Closed Christmas

TENBY,
Penally Abbey Country House 🏵🏵

An upgraded country house restaurant with a small but interesting menu making good use of local, quality produce

The Warren's charming 200-year-old country house, above Penally village, overlooks Carmarthen Bay and Caldey Island and its six acres of wooded grounds include the ruins of a 14th-century chapel. When winds from the Atlantic are blowing full blast outside, the tastefully decorated house with its comfortable period furnishings is best appreciated, especially the cosy bar, a particularly good place to browse through Ellen Warren's frequently changing fixed-price menu. The elegant, romantic dining-room is where to savour dishes drawing fully on good quality produce. Green lip mussels in cider, presented attractively with a crisp salad, and Dover sole, with a delicate lime and ginger butter sauce, formed the components of one inspection meal. Vegetables were firm, bar the broccoli which was rather flabby. There is a good selection of home-made desserts, including light and creamy bread and butter pudding. Staff are friendly and willing, mercifully free of any stuffiness.

Directions: 1.5 miles from Tenby, just off Penally village green

Penally SA70 7PY
Map no: 2 SN10
Tel: 01834 843033
Chef: Ellen Warren
Proprietors: Mr & Mrs S T Warren
Cost: *Alc* £23.50, fixed-price L £16.50/D £23.50. H/wine £9.95
❗ Service inc
Credit cards: 🔲 🔳 🔳 OTHER
Times: Last L 2pm (Sun L to order only), last D 9.30pm
Menus: *A la carte,* fixed-price L & D
Seats: 46. No smoking in dining room
Additional: Children over 7 welcome, children's menu; ❶ dishes, vegan/other diets on request

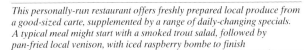

GWENT

ABERGAVENNY,
Llanwenarth Arms Hotel 🏵

This personally-run restaurant offers freshly prepared local produce from a good-sized carte, supplemented by a range of daily-changing specials. A typical meal might start with a smoked trout salad, followed by pan-fried local venison, with iced raspberry bombe to finish

Menus: *A la carte* L & D, bar menu   **Seats:** 60. No-smoking area
Additional: Children welcome, children's menu; ❶ dishes, other diets on request
Directions: On A40 midway between Abergavenny and Crickhowell

Brecon Road NP8 1EP
Map no: 3 SO21
Tel: 01873 810550
Chefs: D'Arcy McGregor, J O'Leary and R Gardener
Proprietors: Angela & D'Arcy McGregor
Cost: *Alc* £20. H/wine £7.50 Service inc
Credit cards: 🔲 🔳 🔳 🔳 OTHER
Times: Last L 1.45pm/1.15pm Sun, last D 9.30pm/8.15pm Sun

CHEPSTOW, **Beaufort Hotel** 🏵

A former 16th-century coaching inn with a pleasant, informal atmosphere and a decent standard of cooking. At a recent inspection meal an excellent moules marinière was followed by chicken breast stuffed with cabbage and bacon and an enjoyable fresh lemon tart

Menus: *A la carte,* fixed-price D, bar menu
Seats: 65. No-smoking area
Additional: Children welcome, children's portions; ❶ dishes, other diets on request
Directions: Town centre

St Mary Street NP6 5EP
Map no: 3 ST59
Tel: 01291 622497
Chef: Justin Sterry
Proprietor: Michael Collins. Manager: Chris Ashton
Cost: *Alc* £12.50, fixed-price D £10.95. H/wine £6.90 ❗ Service exc
Credit cards: 🔲 🔳 🔳 🔳
Times: Last L 2.30 pm, last D 10pm

CHEPSTOW, St Pierre Hotel ❀

Surrounded by its own golf course, St Pierre is a stunning complex. The more formal Orangery restaurant offers a range of carefully prepared, skilfully cooked dishes that make the most of quality ingredients. The brandy snap basket filled with cinnamon ice cream served with a caramel sauce is a dessert to note

St Pierre Park NP6 6YA
Map no: 3 ST59
Tel: 01291 625261
Chef: Mark Lindsey
Proprietor: Country Club.
Manager: Rene Brunet
Cost: *Alc* £21.45, fixed-price
Sun L £11.95. H/wine £10.95 ▌
Service exc
Credit cards: ▨ ▧ ▧ ▨
Times: Last Sun L 2pm, 7pm-
last D 10pm, daily
Menus: *A la carte,* fixed-price
Sun L, bar menu
Seats: 96. Air conditioned.
No smoking in dining room
Additional: Children welcome,
children's menu; ❂ dishes,
vegan/other diets on request

Directions: M4 exit 22, hotel 2.25 miles on A48 (Caerwent)

LLANDDEWI SKYRRID,
The Walnut Tree Inn ❀❀❀

Inspirational Italianate cooking with Oriental flourishes at a unique and influential country pub in the wilds of South Wales

Abergavenny NP7 8AW
Map no: 3 SO31
Tel: 01873 852797
Chef: Franco Taruschio
Proprietors: Franco & Anne
Taruschio
Cost: *Alc* £28 approx. H/wine
£10.50 (ltr) ▌ Cover charge
No service charge
Credit cards: None taken
Menu: *A la carte* L & D
Times: Noon-last L 3pm, 7pm-
last D 10.15pm. Closed Sun,
Mon, Xmas, 2 wks Feb
Seats: 46+60 (Bistro).
Air conditioned
Additional: Children welcome,
children's portions; ❂ dishes,
vegan/other diets on request

No ordinary Inn, but an institution which occupies a unique position in the culinary landscape. Franco and Ann Taruschio's whitewashed country pub has, over thirty years, become one of the most influential restaurants in Britain and the point of pilgrimage for a generation of indigenous chefs. Not that it looks terribly grand, but grandeur is not what people come here to find. They come for gutsy cooking in which the natural flavours of first rate ingredients are always the priority, served with natural charm and complete lack of pretension.

The hand-written menu changes in part twice a day, but offers as much choice for lunches eaten in the cosy bar and cramped bistro as it does for dinner, which is served in the more formal dining room. Signature dishes include home cured Bresaola and the definitive Llanover Salt Duck. Oriental influences crop up, sometimes unexpectedly, in starters such as the crispy crab pancake and goujonettes of cod with a Thai dip. At our last inspection, the wonderful aroma of freshly shaved white truffle permeated the bar and lifted both a white leek soup and a 'lasagna' composed of layered porcini, Parma ham and Parmesan to sublime heights. Game is handled with utmost care – pigeon was meltingly tender and a young roast partridge quite pink, but perfectly cooked. Vegetables can be unremarkably plain, but baked fennel and sliced potatoes with mozzarella and tomato were superb.

The plate of desserts, made for sharing, included praline ice-cream and a dense chocolate brandy loaf with coffee bean sauce.

Our inspector was disappointed by a rather dull pot of filter coffee, but the chocolate fudge 'kisses' that came with it more than compensated. Wines are carefully-chosen and well-described, but, like the rest of the operation, by no means cheap.

Directions: Three miles N/E of Abergavenny on B4521

LLANGYBI, Cwrt **Bleddyn Hotel** ❀❀

Relax in this tranquil setting and enjoy an excellent meal prepared by award-winning chefs

Usk NP5 1PG
Map no: 3 ST39
Tel: 01633 450521
Chef: Kevin Brookes
Managed by: Virgin Hotels.
Manager: Andrew Cole
Cost: Fixed-price D £24.95,
Gourmet menu £32.50 menu
Credit cards: 🃏 💳 💳 💳
Times: Last D 10pm (9.30 Sun)

A tranquil setting in which to slough off the stresses of modern urban life, this appealing property – parts of which date from the 14th century – stands in extensive parkland near the village of Llangybi, between Caerleon and Usk. A talented kitchen team is headed by Kevin Brookes, a winner of the Welsh Chef of the Year Award. Predictably, standards of both preparation and presentation are very high, and the two fixed-price menus offer a varied range of dishes which takes maximum advantage of fresh seasonal produce. Prime Welsh black beef figures prominently, and on the most recent visit our inspector enjoyed a fillet of sirloin served with a robust red wine and shallot glaze and a mille-feuille of veal kidneys and tarragon. The ravioli of sea scallops and king prawns that preceded this was complemented by a coriander-scented nage, and the meal ended with a beautifully light and creamy bread and butter pudding accompanied by an apricot sauce and vanilla crème anglaise. An already comprehensive wine list was to be changed as we went to press, to include more examples from the New World.

Directions: Near Llangybi village on A449 between Caerleon and Usk

NEWPORT, Celtic **Manor Hotel** ❀❀

Popular manor house with a range of modern amenities, serving a predominantly business clientele

Coldra Woods NP6 2YA
Map no: 3 ST38
Tel: 01633 413000
Chef: Trefor Jones
Proprietors: Mr & Mrs R Dawes
Cost: A/c £25.95 fixed-price
L £15.95/D £19.50. H/wine
£10.50. Service exc
Credit cards: 🃏 💳 💳 💳

Trefor Jones is a former Welsh Chef of the Year, and his cooking is characterised by well-executed dishes of depth and quality. An inspection meal at this busy manor house, perched in a high, commanding position above the M4, typifies his range. A terrine of rabbit came moist and full of flavour, with a hint of garlic, wrapped in Parma ham and accompanied by a bright, basil dressing. Pan-fried scallops with chanterelle mushrooms had a light, buttery sauce. A trio of fillets – tender beef with red wine and shallots, first-class lamb noisette with rosemary, and veal with good, home-made pasta – was a little ambitious but worked well. The main criticism was the veal, which could have been served in a far less meagre portion. Vegetables were straightforward or unexciting, depending on one's point of view. Puddings, however, such as assiette of chocolate, nougatine parfait and shortcake mille-feuille with fresh raspberries, soundly bring up the rear. More informal dining, also under Trevor's supervision, is available in the congenial brasserie.

Directions: On A48 just off junc 24 of M4 towards Newport

Times: Last L 2pm, last D 10.30pm. Closed Sat L, Sun, Bhs
Seats: 60. No-smoking area. No pipes
Additional: Children permitted; children's portions/menu; ❶ menu; special diets on request

TINTERN,
Parva Farmhouse Hotel ❁

☺ *A converted 17th-century farmhouse with a homely and relaxed atmosphere. Good use is made of fresh local produce with honest textures and flavours apparent in well-presented, soundly cooked dishes, such as moist tender rack of Welsh lamb. There is also a small selection of tempting puddings and good Welsh cheeses*

Additional: Children welcome, children's portions; ❶ dishes, vegan/other diets on request
Directions: Northern end of Tintern on A466 alongside the Wye, 0.75 mile from the Abbey

Chepstow NP6 6SQ
Map no: 3 SO50
Tel: 01291 689411
Chef: Dereck Stubbs
Proprietors: Dereck & Vickie Stubbs
Cost: Fixed-price D £16.50 (4 course). H/wine £8.50 Service inc
Credit cards: 🔳 🔳
Times: 7pm-last D 8.30pm
Menus: Fixed-price D
Seats: 24. Smoking discouraged

TINTERN, Royal George Hotel ❁

☺ *Good, sound cooking from quality local produce is the hallmark of this 17th-century inn close to the famous abbey. An inspection meal, chosen from the fixed-price menu, produced chicken terrine and medallions of local venison with gin and juniper sauce. Desserts are strongly recommended*

Menus: Fixed-price L & D, bar menu
Seats: 80. No smoking in dining room
Additional: Children welcome, children's menu; ❶ dishes, vegan/other diets on request
Directions: On A466 between Chepstow & Monmouth, 6 miles from M4 exit 22

Chepstow NP6 6SF
Map no: 3 SO50
Tel: 01291 689205
Chef: David Parkinson and Cliff Randal
Proprietor: Consort Hotels
Managers: Tony & Maureen Pearce
Cost: Fixed-price L £11.50/D £16.50. H/wine £6.90 Service exc
Credit cards: 🔳 🔳 🔳 💳 OTHER
Times: Last L 2pm, last D 9.30pm/10pm Fri-Sat daily

USK, Three Salmons ❁

Now vastly improved by renovation, this former coaching inn in the town centre is gaining a well deserved reputation for good food. Thick home-made soups are distinctively flavoured, and a simple dish of calves' liver is transformed by a good port wine sauce and a garnish of white grapes

Directions: In town centre, on A472

Bridge Street NP5 1BQ
Map no: 3 SO40
Tel: 1291 672133
Chef: Martyn Williams
Proprietors: K G & E L Burke
Cost: Alc L/D £12.95-£30, Fixed-price D £15
Credit cards: 🔳 🔳 🔳 OTHER
Times: Last D 9.30pm

WHITEBROOK,
Crown at Whitebrook ❀❀

Comfortable surroundings for a good choice of provincial French cooking

A restaurant with rooms renowned for the quality of its food as well as its comfort and hospitality, the Crown is a cosy retreat perched high in the lovely Wye Valley. It is owned and run by Sandra and Roger Bates; she cooks commendable French provincial dishes, he looks after front-of-house. Everything is home made from breads to sorbets, and good use is made of quality fresh local ingredients. Among the starters there might be 'boudin du poulet', a smooth sausage of chicken with caramelised apples and morels served on a bed of creamed leeks; and pan-fried scallops with bacon and a spaghetti of vegetables and shallot dressing. Robust main courses include 'canard au foie', a full flavoured duck breast and intense mousse of chicken livers presented with a delicate mushroom scented gravy. Chargrilled medallions of veal with wild mushrooms and Marsala flavoured sauce has been an equally impressive offering. 'Parfait de café' is recommended for dessert, which is followed by good high roast coffee and hand-made petits fours.

Directions: Turn W off A466 immediately S of Bigsweir Bridge (5 miles from Monmouth), 2 miles up this unclassified road

Monmouth NP5 4TX
Map no: 3 SO50
Tel: 01600 860254
Chef: Sandra Bates
Proprietors: Sandra & Roger Bates (Logis, Welsh Rarebits, Jouansons)
Cost: Fixed-price L £14.95/D £25.95. H/wine £8.50 ❢ Service exc
Credit cards: 🃏 💳 💳 💳 OTHER
Times: Last L 2pm, last D 9.30pm Closed Sun D, Mon L, 2 wks Jan & Aug
Menus: Fixed-price L & D, bar menu
Seats: 36. No-smoking area
Additional: Children welcome, children's portions; ❻ dishes, other diets on request

GWYNEDD

ABERDOVEY, **Maybank Hotel** ❀

This delightful small hotel, with a fine, attractive restaurant, is situated on the edge of the village. The menu changes regularly, and the kitchen produces enjoyable and imaginative food. Sea bass and sea trout are not to be missed, and local lamb is also superb

4 Penhelig Road
Penhelig LL35 0PT
Map no: 6 SN69
Tel: 01654 767500/767622
Chef: Elizabeth A Dinsdale
Proprietors: Elizabeth A Dinsdale and Paul C Massey
Cost: Fixed-price D £17.95. H/wine £ 10.95 ❢ Service inc
Credit cards: 🃏 💳
Times: 7pm-last D 8.30pm (10.30pm in busy times) Closed Nov 2-Dec 22, Jan 2-Feb 13
Menus: Fixed-price D
Seats: 26. No smoking in dining room
Additional: Children over 10 permitted; ❻ dishes, vegan/ other diets with notice

Directions: On A483 (Machynlleth–Aberdovey), 500yds from village

ABERDOVEY,

Penhelig Arms Hotel ✿

☺ *A relaxed, informal seafront hotel with lovely views over the Dovey estuary, noted for soundly prepared fresh fish and game. Inspection yielded an enjoyable roulade of spinach and cream cheese, and monkfish wrapped in bacon. Staff are particularly friendly and attentive*

Aberdovey LL35 0LT
Map no: 6 SN69
Tel: 01654 767215
Chef: Jane Howkins
Proprietors: Robert & Sally Hughes
Cost: Fixed-price D £19, Sun L £12.50. H/wine £8 ❗ Service exc
Credit cards: 🅰 💳 💳 OTHER
Times: 7pm-last D 9.30pm, last Sun L 2pm. Closed Dec 25/6
Menus: Fixed-price D & Sun L, bar L menu
Seats: 34. Smoking not encouraged
Additional: Children welcome, children's portions; ✪ dishes

Directions: On A493 coastal road to Aberdovey 10 miles from Machynlleth

ABERSOCH, **Tudor Court Hotel** ✿

Lovely sea views are to be had from this cosy family-run hotel. Locally caught fresh fish features on the menu, but there is a wide selection of dishes and a particularly good main course for meat eaters could be roast breast of duck in plum and orange sauce

Menus: A la carte, fixed-price L & D
Seats: 40. No smoking in dining room
Additional: Children welcome, children's menu; ✪ dishes, other diets on request
Directions: In the centre of the village on the main road

Lon Sarn Bach LL53 7EB
Map no: 6 SH32
Tel: 0175 871 3354
Chef: Jack Courtney
Proprietor: Jennifer Jones
Cost: Alc £22.50, fixed-price L £10.50/D £12.50. H/wine £8.50 ❗ Service exc
Credit cards: 🅰 💳 OTHER
Times: Last L 2pm, last D 9.30pm

BANGOR, **Menai Court Hotel** ✿

A former Victorian gentleman's residence, situated off the Menai Bridge road, has been converted into a small, relaxing hotel. A daily fixed-price menu and a good sized carte feature dishes such as mille-feuille of chicken livers, rack of Welsh lamb, and guinea fowl on a bed of leeks and wild mushrooms

Menus: A la carte, fixed-price L & D
Seats: 60. No smoking in dining room
Additional: Children permitted, children's portions; ✪ dishes, other diets on request
Directions: Turn left out of railway station, right at top of hill by Bank into College Road, first left into Craig y Don Road

Craig y Don Road LL57 2BG
Map no: 6 SH57
Tel: 01248 354200
Chef: Stephen Brown
Proprietors: Judy & Elwyn Hughes
Cost: Alc £14.50-£21.50, fixed-price L £11.50/D £15.95. H/wine £9.20 (ltr) Service exc
Credit cards: 🅰 💳 💳
Times: Last L 2pm, last D 9.30pm Closed Dec 26-Jan 8

BARMOUTH, Ty'r Graig Hotel ❀

With prominent features which still reflect the Victorian origin of the house, this popular hotel enjoys splendid views over Cardigan Bay. The restaurant offers a good choice of skilfully prepared food, featuring dishes such as 'cig oen Caerfille', a fillet of Welsh lamb, stuffed with minced lamb, leeks, herbs and cheese

Menus: A la carte, fixed-price L & D, bar menu
Seats: 30. No smoking in dining room
Additional: Children permitted, children's portions; ❷ dishes, other diets on request
Directions: On coast road 0.75 mile towards Harlech

Llanaber Road LL42 1YN
Map no: 6 SH61
Tel: 01341 280470
Chef: Jillian Wright
Proprietors: Mr & Mrs Wright
Cost: Alc £16-£20, fixed-price L £9.45/D £15.50 (4 course). H/wine £9 ❗ Service exc
Credit cards: 💳 💳
Times: Last L 2pm, last D 8.30pm Closed Nov-mid Mar

BARMOUTH, Wavecrest Hotel ❀

Simple dishes carefully prepared from fresh local produce are offered on the daily changing fixed-price menu. An inspection meal produced an excellent, well-made watercress and fennel soup, an enjoyable roast lamb with redcurrant, orange and mint sauce, and crêpe suzette

Times: Last D 7.30pm. Closed Dec-Easter
Directions: On the seafront, at the centre of the promenade

8 Marine Parade
LL42 1NA
Map no: 6 SH61
Tel: 01341 280330
Chef: Mrs S Jarman
Proprietors: Mr & Mrs Jarman
Credit cards: 💳 💳 💳

BONTDDU, Bontddu Hall Hotel ❀

Built as a country residence in the late nineteenth century, this is now a fine hotel featuring a conservatory style restaurant with excellent views over the Mawddach Estuary. A good selection of classic British and French dishes is offered and there is a good selection of Welsh farmhouse cheeses

Menus: A la carte, fixed-price L & D, bar menu
Seats: 60. No smoking in dining room
Additional: Children over 3 welcome, children's menu; ❷ dishes, vegan/other diets on request
Directions: Village centre, 3 miles from junction of A470 & A496

Dolgellau LL40 2SU
Map no: 6 SH61
Tel: 01341 430661
Chef: Didier Bienaime
Proprietor: Mike Ball (Virgin)
Cost: Alc £23.50 fixed-price L £12.75/D £23.50. H/wine £9.25 Service exc
Credit cards: 💳 💳 💳 💳 OTHER
Times: Last L 2pm, last D 9.30pm Closed Nov-Mar

CAERNARFON, Seiont Manor Hotel ❀

Stunningly situated a few miles from the foot of Snowdon in 150 acres of parkland, Seiont Manor offers fixed-price menus of British inspired dishes based on fresh local produce. Dishes might include chicken liver pâté and roast leg of lamb with sage and onion stuffing

Seats: 60. No smoking in dining room
Additional: Children welcome, children's portions/menu; ❷ menu, vegan/other diets on request
Directions: From Caernarfon follow A4086 toward Llanrug, hotel on left

Llanrug LL55 2AQ
Map no: 6 SH46
Tel: 01286 673366
Chef: Richard Treble
Proprietor: Virgin Hotels
Cost: Gourmet £29.95, fixed-price L £7.50/D £19.50. H/wine £8.95. Service exc
Credit cards: 💳 💳 💳 💳 OTHER
Times: Last L 2.15pm, last D 10pm. Closed Sat L

'Alla parmigiana' means the way it is made in Parma. As the name suggests it includes Parmesan and prosciutto although the latter is an optional ingredient.

CONWY, **Castle Bank Hotel** ❀

Good estuary views are to be had from this charming, family-run hotel situated near the town walls. The restaurant offers a daily changing fixed-price menu emphasising traditional British dishes such as steak, kidney and mushroom pie, and roast Welsh lamb with onion sauce, all based on fresh local produce

Mount Pleasant LL32 8NY
Map no: 6 SH77
Tel: 01492 593888
Chef: Marilyn Gilligan
Proprietors: Mr & Mrs Sean Gilligan
Cost: Fixed-price L £8.50/D £12.50. H/wine £7.90 Service exc
Credit cards: 🌅 📰 📰 OTHER
Times: Last L 1pm, last D 8pm Closed Jan-mid Feb
Menus: Fixed-price L & D
Seats: 40. No smoking
Additional: Children welcome, children's portions; ❤ dishes, vegan/other diets on request

Directions: Drive through Conwy to Bangor Archway. Turn left into Mount Pleasant, then right through public car park

CONWY, **The Old Rectory Country House** ❀❀❀

Fresh regional produce cooked with great skill in a stylish Georgian hotel with superb views

Llanrwst Road
Colwyn Bay LL28 5LF
Map no: 6 SH77
Tel: 01492 580611
Chef: Wendy Vaughan
Proprietors: Wendy & Michael Vaughan
Cost: Fixed-price D £27.50 (4 course). H/wine £12.90. Service inc
Credit cards: 🌅 📰 📰 💳 OTHER
Times: D 7.15pm for 8pm (Non-res by reservation only) Closed Dec 20-Feb 1
Menu: Fixed-price

A steep drive leads to the elegant Georgian house on the eastern side of the valley, with stunning views of Conwy Castle (floodlit at night), the Conwy estuary and the Snowdon range. The attractive and spacious dining room, in two sections, is a fitting location for Wendy Vaughan's set menus. Guests now have the option of dining with others at a communal table or at separate tables. Michael Vaughan serves drinks and canapés in the cosy pine-panelled lounge full of paintings, books and ornaments. A no-choice, four-course meal may start with a distinctly Mediterranean-style grey mullet with wild mushrooms and a tomato and chicory vinaigrette, then tender and nicely pink poached loin of Welsh lamb wrapped in leek with roast shallots and a tarragon jus with a 'tasty' stuffing of breadcrumbs, garlic and parsley. Good vegetables could be baby carrot and corn, courgette and broccoli, all centred around a puree of potato set in a baked potato jacket and topped with finely shredded deep-fried leek. Desserts include pine nut tartlet with apricot sauce or chocolate snowball and coffee parfait. The Welsh cheeses are always worth sampling. The wine list is informative and well prepared. Booking is essential for non-residents.

Directions: On A470 1/2 mile S of junction with A55

Seats: 16. No smoking in dining room
Additional: Children over 5 permitted; other diets prior notice

DOLGELLAU,
Clifton House Hotel ✿

The building was once the county gaol, but it has been transformed into a restaurant that has attracted a good local following. Fresh local produce is emphasised in the cooking, and the carte offers the likes of rack of Welsh lamb, or marinated breast of duck with pink peppercorn sauce

Smithfield Square LL40 1ES
Map no: 6 SH71
Tel: 01341 422554
Chef: Pauline Dix
Proprietors: Rob & Pauline Dix
Cost: *Alc* £17. H/wine £8 ❢
Service exc
Credit cards: 🔳 ▦
Times: 7pm-last D 9.30pm.
Closed Christmas
Menu: Fixed-price D
Seats: 22. No smoking in dining room
Additional: Children permitted, children's portions; ❤ dishes, vegan/other diets on request

Directions: Town centre, on left in one-way system ,100yds from main square

DOLGELLAU, **Dolmelynllyn Hall** ✿

A secluded country house situated in a magnificent woodland settings. The half-panelled restaurant boasts some beautiful stained glass windows. The daily-changing five-course menu offers the likes of devilled crab galettes on two pepper coulis, monkfish fried in light beer batter, and hot pear rarebit

Menus: Fixed-price D, bar menu
Seats: 20. No smoking in dining room
Additional: Children over 10 welcome; ❤ dishes, vegan/other diets on request
Directions: Village centre on the A470, 4 miles N of Dollgellau

Ganllwyd LL40 2HP
Map no: 6 SH71
Tel: 01341 440273
Chef: Joanna Reddicliffe
Proprietor: Jonathan Barkwith
Cost: Fixed-price D £22.50.
H/wine £8.75 ❢ No service charge
Credit cards: 🔳 ▦ ▦ 🔳
Times: Last D 8.30pm Closed Dec 1-Feb 28

DOLGELLAU, **Dolserau Hall Hotel** ❀

A converted Victorian mansion set in five acres of attractive grounds which stretch down to the river. The Winter Garden Restaurant has views over the Wnion valley and offers a daily-changing fixed-price menu of sound British cooking. Try poached mussels in white wine, and pan-fried venison steaks

Menu: Fixed-price D
Seats: 40. No smoking
Additional: Children over 5 welcome, children's portions; ❷ dishes, other diets on request
Directions: 1.5 miles N of Dolgellau on lane between A470 & A494, turn left (going S) at Esso station

Dolgellau LL40 2AG
Map no: 6 SH71
Tel: 01341 422522
Chef: Huw Roberts
Proprietors: Marion & Peter Kaye
Cost: Fixed-price D £18.50 (4 course). H/wine £6.95
Credit cards: ▨ ▧
Times: 7pm-last D 8.30pm

DOLGELLAU, **Penmaenuchaf Hall** ❀❀

An idyllic setting in which to enjoy food that has become more adventurous with the arrival of a new hand in the kitchen

An elegantly-appointed country house hotel that truly does nestle at the foot of Cader Idris, in an idyllic setting overlooking Mawddach Estuary, Penmaenuchaf has weathered a few recessionary years and is now well into the upswing. A new conservatory restaurant was under construction at the time of writing, but in the meantime the standard of cooking offered in the old panelled dining-room has undergone a marked improvement. The current chef, Lee Jones, is unafraid to introduce slightly exotic flavours to an adventurous menu which is changed monthly. His 'little stew of fish' is spiked with star anise, and pan-fried tuna served with a stir-fry of peppers and chillies. Medallions of beef with a carrot and parsnip purée was singled out for special praise by our inspector, who found the chicken livers in the salad he had as a starter a tad too rubbery. Earthy flavours are matched by a strong, annotated wine list that offers unexpected bargains. Those who enjoy the marriage of chocolate with fruit for dessert could be in for a treat.

Directions: From A470, take A493 (Tywyn/Fairbourne), entrance 1.5 miles on left by sign for Penmaenpool

Penmaenpool LL40 1YB
Map no: 6 SH71
Tel: 01341 422129
Chef: Lee Jones
Proprietors: Mark Watson (Welsh Rarebits/Taste of Wales)
Cost: Fixed-price L £11.95 (2 courses), £13.95/D £23 (4 course). H/wine £9.95. Service exc
Credit cards: ▨ ▧ ▧ ▨ OTHER
Times: Last L 2pm/2.30pm Sun, last D 9.30pm/9pm Sun
Menus: Fixed-price D, bar L menu
Seats: 35. No smoking in dining room
Additional: Children permitted, over 7 & until 8pm, children's portions; ❷ dishes, vegan/other diets on request

HARLECH, **Castle Cottage** ❀

A cosy, 16th-century beamed restaurant close to Harlech's ancient castle. Glyn Roberts offers a regularly changing two or three course fixed-price menu based on local produce. Inspection yielded 'juicy and sweet' noisettes of Welsh lamb with a parsnip purée. Anglesey steaks often feature, and there is a good choice of puddings

Menus: Fixed-price D & Sun L
Seats: 45. No smoking in dining room
Additional: Children welcome, children's menu; ❷ dishes, vegan/other diets on request
Directions: Just off High Street (B4573) 100yds from Harlech Castle

Pen Lech LL46 2YL
Map no: 6 SH53
Tel: 01766 780479
Chef: Glyn Roberts
Proprietors: Glyn & Jacqueline Roberts
Cost: Fixed-price D £16.50 (2 course), £18.50. H/wine £7.95 ❢ Service exc
Credit cards: ▨ ▧ ▧ OTHER
Times: 7pm-last D 9.30pm
Closed Feb 3 wks

LLANBERIS, **Y Bistro** ❀

Husband and wife team Danny and Nerys Roberts run this popular, attractive village restaurant entirely by themselves. Food is distinctly Welsh with French overtones with full use made of local lamb, fish and poultry. Highly recommended is tomatoes, garlic and basil roasted in olive oil, served with smoked lamb

Menu: Fixed-price D
Seats: 60. No smoking in dining room
Additional: Children welcome, children's portions; ❂ dishes, vegan/other diets on request
Directions: In middle of town, next to Tourist Office

Glandwr
43-45 Stryd Fawr LL55 4EU
Map no: 6 SH56
Tel: 01286 871278
Chef: Nerys Roberts
Proprietors: Danny & Nerys Roberts
Cost: Fixed-price D £22. H/wine £8.50. Service exc
Credit cards: ▨ ▨ OTHER
Times: Last D 9.45pm approx Closed Sun except Bhs

LLANDDEINIOLEN, **Ty'n Rhos Country House** ❀

A successful rural hotel serving quality British food inspired by fresh seasonal produce. The four-course set menu is now supplemented by an imaginative carte. At a recent visit our inspector enjoyed salmon bavarois, tender chicken suprême served with baked fennel, and rhubarb crumble for dessert

Caernarfon LL55 3AE
Map no: 6 SH56
Tel: 01248 670489
Chefs: Lynda Kettle and Bill Ashton
Proprietors: Nigel & Lynda Kettle
Cost: Alc £21 £23.50, fixed-price D £19 (4 course). H/wine £8.50 Service exc
Credit cards: ▨ ▨ ▨ OTHER
Times: 7pm-last D 9pm Closed Sun, Mon
Menus: A la carte, fixed-price D
Seats: 30. No smoking in dining room
Additional: Children over 6 welcome, children's portions; ❂ dishes, other diets on request

Directions: In the hamlet of Seion between B4366 & B4547

LLANDUDNO, **Bodysgallen Hall Hotel** ❀❀

A new chef strives for excellence in the imposing setting of this magnificent, rambling hall

A grand 17th-century country house set in 200 acres of verdant parkland with marvellous gardens – worth a visit in themselves either to work up an appetite or walk off a heavy lunch. Mike Penny, who has taken over in the kitchen this year, strives to produce mature cuisine that avoids unexpected juxtapositions in favour of classic combinations, such as poached salmon with minted potatoes, and honey-glazed Hereford duck with a red wine sauce. Our inspector enjoyed a warm crab mousse, creamy of texture and

Map no: 6 SH78
Tel: 01492 584466
Chef: Mike Penny
Proprietor: Historic House Hotels.
Manager: R Nigel Taylor
Cost: Alc £36, fixed-price L £15.90/D £27.50. H/wine £11.75 Service inc
Credit cards: ▨ ▨ ▨ OTHER
Times: Last L 2pm, last D 9.45pm daily
Menus: A la carte, fixed-price L & D, bar menu

Bodysgallen Hall Hotel

Seats: 50. No smoking in dining room
Additional: Children permitted if over 8; ❷ dishes, other diets on request

delicate of flavour, served with marinated scallops and a rather overpowering chilli dressing. Beef, accompanied by caramelised parsnips and sauced with a rich wine reduction, was first rate. Soufflés are something of a speciality. An extensive list even includes a couple of wines from Wales and offers exceptional value in its Cellarman's Choice and selections from the Petits Chateaux of Bordeaux. The menu carries an injunction against smoking between courses: guests are respectfully asked to save their cigarettes until after the coffee is served.

Directions: On A470 (Llandudno) 1 mile on right past A55 junction

LLANDUDNO, **Empire Hotel** ✤

☺ *The daily changing menu in the Watkins & Co restaurant offers a varied selection of reliably cooked dishes. The inspiration is traditional British, and could include the likes of a locally smoked salmon platter, or Empire game pies of duck, lamb, beef and venison. Compote of plums and apricots for dessert*

Church Walks LL30 2HE
Map no: 6 SH78
Tel: 01492 860555
Chef: Michael Waddy
Proprietors: Leonard & Elizabeth Maddocks, Elyse & Michael Waddy
Cost: Fixed-price Sat/Sun L £10.50/D £16.85. H/wine £10 Service inc
Credit cards: 🆇 🔳 🔳 🔳 OTHER
Times: Last L 2pm, last D 9.30pm daily Closed Dec 22-Dec 30
Menus: Fixed-price Sat/Sun L & D, bar menu
Seats: 100. No-smoking area
Additional: Children welcome, children's portions/menu; ❷ dishes, vegan/other diets on request

Directions: At end of Pier end of Promenade, turn left, 150 yds on left

LLANDUDNO, **Imperial Hotel** ✿

☺ *A seafront hotel noted for a good selection of dishes from the regularly changing fixed-price menu. An inspection meal produced parfait of ducks' liver, fillet of red mullet, roast Welsh lamb, and white chocolate mille-feuille*

Menus: Fixed-price L & D, bar menu
Seats: 150. No-smoking area
Additional: Children welcome, children's menu; ❤ dishes, vegan/other diets on request
Directions: On the Promenade

The Promenade LL30 1AP
Map no: 6 SH78
Tel: 01492 877466
Chef: Andrew Goode
Manager: Geoffrey Lofthouse
Cost: Fixed-price L £10.95/D £19.50. H/wine £8.95 Service inc
Credit cards: 🔳 💳 💳 💳 OTHER
Times: Last L 2pm, last D 9.30pm/9pm Sun daily

LLANDUDNO, **St Tudno Hotel** ✿✿✿

An inconspicuous but quietly excellent hotel that serves first rate modern British cuisine, with Welsh influences, in the delightful Garden Room

The Promenade LL30 2LP
Map no: 6 SH78
Tel: 01492 874411
Chefs: David Harding and Ian Watson
Proprietors: Janette & Martin Bland
Cost: Fixed-price L £15.50/D £27.50. H/wine £9.50 Service inc
Credit cards: 🔳 💳 💳 💳 OTHER
Times: Last L 2pm, last D 9.30pm/9pm Sun
Menus: Fixed-price L & D, bar menu
Seats: 55. No smoking in dining room
Additional: Children welcome (except very young at D), children's menu; ❤ dishes, vegan/other diets on request

At the west end of the promenade, opposite the pier, this charming hotel does not immediately stand out from its neighbours. As soon as you cross the threshold, however, the owners' expertise and attention to detail becomes apparent. Martin and Janette Bland have a friendly, caring approach which evidently rubs off on their courteous and smartly turned-out staff. Meals in the Garden Room are delightful, with chefs David Harding and Ian Watson providing a set-price five-course dinner that is well balanced, deftly prepared, and uses local produce as much as possible. A £3 supplement may be charged for locally-smoked salmon, but it's worth it. Otherwise, Welsh lamb is a permanent feature, Herefordshire duckling is a regular visitor and Conwy fish – mussels with laverbread and a saffron sauce, seabass with a Llanboidy cheese sauce and fried leeks – is a speciality.

Our inspector particularly relished a pasta dish with beautifully seared chicken livers in Madeira sauce and thought the salmon, baked with spinach in pastry, as good as any he'd ever had. The selection of Welsh cheeses is exemplary and the wine list comprehensive, with many different and unusual bottles offered at bargain prices. Service, led by the hospitable Mrs Bland, was attentive and very friendly. The one cavil was with the burnt Trinity College cream for dessert, which turned out to be a form of crème brûlée with grapes lurking beneath an uneven caramelised topping. This was probably a bad choice, since the kitchen has something of a reputation for its pastry. Cafetière coffee is freshly ground and the petits fours home-made, showing admirable attention to detail. Smokers are required to repair to the lounge bar to indulge their vice.

Directions: Town centre, on Promenade opposite the pier entrance

PORTMEIRION,
The Hotel Portmeirion ❀

A distinctive hotel, in a stunning, secluded estuary setting, part of Sir Clough Williams-Ellis's unique Italianate village. Modern British cooking, based on prime local produce, could include carrot and garlic soup with herb cream, baked salmon with truffle butter sauce and hazelnut flan with coffee bean sauce

Portmeirion LL48 6ET
Map no: 6 SH53
Tel: 01766 770228
Chef: Craig Hindley
Manager: Menai Williams
Cost: Fixed-price L £13.50, £10.50 (2 course)/D £25. H/wine £9.50. Service exc
Credit cards: 🌑 🔲 🔲 🔲 OTHER
Times: Last L 2pm, last D 9.30pm. Closed Mon L, Jan 10-Feb 4
Menus: Fixed-price L & D
Seats: 100. No smoking in dining room
Additional: Children welcome, children's portions; ✆ dishes, other diets on request

Directions: Signposted off A487 at Minffordd

TAL-Y-LLYN, **Minffordd Hotel** ❀

The dining room is the real heart of Mark Warner and Mary McQuillan's old hotel. The short, daily changing menu might include mushroom and apple soup, salmon and prawn roulade, or duck breast with kumquat and brandy sauce. The location, at the foot of Cader Idris with Talylln lake a short walk away, is spectacular

Menu: Fixed-price D **Seats:** 22. No smoking in dining room
Additional: Children over 5 permitted, children's portions; other diets on request
Directions: At base of Cader Idris mountain, A487/B4405 junction

Minffordd LL36 9AJ
Map no: 6 SH70
Tel: 01654 761665
Chef: Mark Warner
Proprietors: Mary McQuillan and Mark Warner
Cost: Fixed-price D £18 (4 course). H/wine £7.65 Service inc
Credit cards: 🌑 🔲
Times: 7pm-last D 8.30pm Closed Jan & Feb

TALSARNAU, **Maes y Neuadd** ❀❀❀

Standards continue to rise at this marvellous country house hotel, set in the heart of Snowdonia, which is renowned as a bastion of modern Welsh cuisine

Hidden up a narrow lane and set in eight acres of landscaped hillside which affords spectacular views of Tremadoc Bay and the

Harlech LL47 6YA
Map no: 6 SH63
Tel: 01766 780200
Chef: Peter Jackson
Proprietors: June & Michael Slatter, Olive & Malcolm Horsfall (Pride of Britain/Welsh Rarebits)

Lleyn Peninsula, tranquillity is surely the keynote at this superb country house. Since it was acquired in 1981 by the Horsfall and Slatter families, the manor has been extensively and tactfully renovated to quite luxurious standards. The chef, Peter Jackson, is a leading exponent of modern Welsh cuisine and dinner here can be a serious gastronomic affair, if one opts for the full five courses from a set-price menu that changes daily. Many of the vegetables and herbs are gathered straight from the garden, meat and fish are locally-produced and the wide range of home-baked bread all testify to an industrious kitchen that strives to be self-sufficient. Welsh lamb and Welsh cheeses are always on the menu, which otherwise flourishes laverbread, Trelough duck and locally-caught fish among its indigenous delights.

Our inspector went the fish route and enjoyed a superbly grilled piece of monkfish on a bed of garlicky vegetables, drizzled with olive oil, followed by wild salmon which may have been poached a minute too long but was accompanied by perfect, fresh vegetables including baby broccoli and steamed spinach. Dessert, billed as the 'Grand Finale', offers a choice of three sweets, or a confusion solution, consisting of small helpings of each. Our inspector managed three rhubarb dishes, comfrey fritters and three varieties of home-made ice-cream. Michael Slatter takes justifiable pride in his extensive wine list, which has a strong French accent but includes a judicious selection from the New World at prices that are not cheap, but eminently reasonable.

Directions: 0.75 mile off B4573 between Talsarnau & Harlech (sign on corner of unclassified road)

Cost: Fixed-price L £9.75 (2 course), £11.75, (Sun £14.25)/D £22, £25 (5 course). H/wine £8 Service exc
Credit cards: 🅰 🔤 🔤 💳 OTHER
Times: Last L 2pm, last D 9.15pm daily
Menus: Fixed-price L & D
Seats: 50. No smoking in dining room
Additional: Children welcome (over 7 at D), children's portions; ❶ dishes, vegan/other diets on request

---

TREARDDUR BAY,

Trearddur Bay Hotel ✿

This fine, modern hotel offers a wide range of dishes cooked with style and intelligence. An inspection meal yielded well prepared field mushrooms with red peppers, roast rack of lamb, and orange and champagne sponge to finish

Holyhead LL65 2UN
Map no: 6 SH27
Tel: 01407 860301
Chef: Ian Biddlecombe
Proprietor: N/A (Welsh Rarebits)
Manager: Ian Murdoch
Cost: Alc £25, fixed-price L £11/D £20. H/wine £9.95
Service exc
Credit cards: 🅰 🔤 🔤 💳 OTHER
Times: Last L 2pm, last D 9.20pm Closed Sat L
Menus: A la carte, fixed-price L & D, bar menu
Seats: 80. No smoking in dining room
Additional: Children welcome, children's menu; ❶ dishes, vegan/other diets on request

Directions: A5 from Bangor to Valley crossroads onto B4545, left after 3 miles

TREFRIW, Hafod House Hotel ❀

A converted farmhouse enjoying a lovely setting in the Conwy Valley and some superb views. The food is good too. Game sausage has been highly recommended, and other dishes on the fixed-price menu might include Conwy salmon, or pan-fried turbot

Menu: Fixed-price L & D
Seats: 30. No smoking in dining room
Additional: Children over 11 welcome; ❷ dishes, other diets on request
Directions: At the south end of village on B5106 (Conwy/Betws-y-Coed)

Trefriw LL27 0RQ
Map no: 6 SH76
Tel: 01492 640029
Chef: Norman Barker
Proprietor: Norman Barker
Cost: Fixed-price L £9.95/D £17.95, £21.95 (4 course).
H/wine £6.95 Service exc
Credit cards: ▨ ▨ ▨ ▨ OTHER
Times: Last L 2.15pm, last D 8.45pm Closed Mon, Tue

MID GLAMORGAN

BRIDGEND, Coed-y-Mwstwr Hotel ❀

Set high on the hillside in the heavily wooded Vale of Glamorgan, and overlooking the village of Coychurch, this is the place for seekers of tranquillity. The restaurant offers fixed-price menus and a carte. A new chef had just started as we went to press

Menus: *A la carte,* fixed-price L & D, bar menu
Seats: 45.
Additional: Children welcome, children's menu; ❷ dishes, vegan/other diets on request
Directions: M4 exit 35, A473 (Bridgend) into Coychurch, right at petrol station, up the hill for 1 mile

Coychurch CF35 6AF
Map no: 3 SS97
Tel: 01656 860621
Chef: Scott Morgan
Proprietor: Philip Warren (Virgin)
Cost: *Alc* £28, fixed-price L £10.95/D £24. H/wine £9.95 Service inc
Credit cards: ▨ ▨ ▨ ▨ OTHER
Times: Last L 2pm, last D 9.30pm Closed Sat L

MISKIN, Miskin Manor Hotel ❀

Enjoyable cooking is offered at this large and elegant stone-built manor house set in extensive wooded grounds and gardens. A great deal of care and imagination goes into the preparation of dishes. A highly recommended dessert is steamed orange pudding with home-made marmalade ice-cream

Menus: *A la carte,* fixed-price L & D, bar menu
Seats: 60
Additional: Children welcome, children's menu; ❷ dishes, other diets on request
Directions: M4 exit 34, follow hotel signs

Pontyclun CF7 8ND
Map no: 3 ST08
Tel: 01443 224204
Chef: Ian Presgrave
Proprietor: John Millard
Cost: *Alc* £26.40, fixed-price L/D £19.50. H/wine £ 9.75 Service exc
Credit cards: ▨ ▨ ▨ ▨
Times: Last L 2pm, last D 9.45pm

PONTYPRIDD, **Llechwen Hall Hotel** ✿

Overlooking four surrounding valleys, this one-time farmhouse stands in six acres of grounds, yet is conveniently close to the A470. Well executed dishes are prepared from quality fresh produce and include excellent desserts such as a light coconut parfait on a passion fruit coulis surrounded with chocolate

Llanfabon CF37 4HP
Map no: 3 ST08
Tel: 01443 742050/740305
Chef: Louis Huber
Proprietors: Louis Huber, Helen Huber and John Mackie
Cost: *Alc* £20-£30, fixed-price L £8.95/D £17.95. H/wine £7.75 Service inc
Credit cards: 🔳 🔳 🔳 💳 OTHER
Times: Last L 2.30pm, last D 9.30pm daily
Menus: *A la carte*, fixed-price L & D, bar menu
Seats: 32 x 2
Additional: Children welcome, children's menu; ✿ menu, vegan/other diets on request

Directions: 1 mile off the A4054 (Cilfynydd) N/E of Pontypridd

PORTHCAWL, **Heritage** ✿✿

Diminutive restaurant offering fresh, well-sourced dishes in a variety of cooking styles

'Surprising to find such a little gem tucked away amidst all the other small hotels and guest houses close to Porthcawl's seafront', comments one inspector's report. The restaurant is small and offers enthusiastic cooking inspired by fresh seasonal produce, especially fish. Due to the size, booking is essential. Free-range chicken breast with mushrooms and asparagus, marinated Llandello lamb steak, Oriental stir-fried vegetables, and spinach and mushroom crêpes are just some of the dishes to expect from three wildly different menus. One is based on Welsh produce and recipes, the other is vegetarian, and the third Chinese. Vegetables are well timed and plentiful and desserts range from the old fashioned to the positively wicked.

24 Mary Street CH36 3YA
Map no: 3 SS87
Tel: 01656 771881
Chef: Jimi Miller
Proprietor: Jimi Miller
Cost: *Alc* £18, fixed-price D £13.95. H/wine £7.95. Service exc
Credit cards: 🔳 🔳
Times: 6.30pm-last D 9.30pm/10pm Fri-Sat
Menus: *A la carte*, fixed-price D, seasonal L as required
Seats: 36. No-smoking area
Additional: Children welcome, children's portions; ✿ dishes, vegan/other diets on request

Directions: Town centre; from seafront St Mary St runs r/h side of the Pavillion, Restaurant is just past car park

'A la parisienne' describes classic styles of presentation that are typical of the repertoire of Parisian restaurants. Fish or shellfish 'à la parisienne' is a cold dish made with mayonnaise and accompanied by artichoke hearts garnished with a mix of small diced vegetables in mayonnaise, stuffed hard boiled eggs and/or cubes of aspic. Soup 'à la parisienne' is made with leeks and potatoes, finished with milk, and garnished with chervil leaves.

POWYS

CRICKHOWELL, **Bear Hotel** 🏵🏵

Imaginative modern cooking can be enjoyed in an ancient inn

Crickhowell NP8 1BW
Map no: 3 SO21
Tel: 01873 810408
Chef: Graham Mallia
Proprietor: Stephen Sims-Hindmarsh
Cost: Alc £20-£25. H/wine £7.90 Service exc
Credit cards: 🔲 🔲 🔲
Times: Last L 2pm, last D 9.30pm daily
Menus: A la carte L & D, bar menu
Seats: 60
Additional: Children permitted; 🕐 menu, other diets on request

Conveniently situated in the town centre and resplendent with exposed beams, stone-flagged floors and an attractive garden, this 15th-century coaching inn offers warm and friendly hospitality. An imaginative choice is provided on the *carte*, with typical dishes including baby haggis with a wild sage sauce, or home-made pigeon and chestnut sausage, with perhaps game hot-pot with juniper berries as a main course. On an inspection visit in April some very enjoyable dishes were sampled. The meal began with a good portion of fresh mussels in a sauce of smoked bacon, cream and garlic (unfortunately lacking the bacon due to shortage of stock). A main course of prawn and fresh coconut curry was cooked with sesame seeds, spices and oyster sauce and served with nicely-cooked rice; the wide range of fresh vegetables included whole baby corn, new potatoes in their jackets and sliced carrots. A creamy lemon crunch pie for dessert was served with a strong-flavoured lemon sorbet.

Directions: Town centre off the A40

CRICKHOWELL,

Gliffaes Hotel 🏵

A long-established country house hotel surrounded by acres of park land and set in the beautiful Usk valley. It has been run by the same family for more than forty years. The menu changes daily and offers a good variety. Puddings are recommended; try sticky toffee pudding, or orange timbale with passion fruit

Menus: Fixed-price D & Sun L, bar L menu
Seats: 70. No smoking in dining room
Additional: Children welcome, children's portions; 🕐 dishes, other diets on request
Directions: 1 mile off A40, 2.5 miles W of Crickhowell

Crickhowell NP8 1RH
Map no: 3 SO21
Tel: 01874 730371
Chef: Peter Hulsmann
Proprietor: Nick Brabner
Cost: Bar L £2.50-£12.50, fixed-price Sun L £18.50 (4 course)/ D £19.90 (4 course). H/wine £8.50 ‼ Service inc
Credit cards: 🔲 🔲 🔲 🔲 OTHER
Times: Last L 2.30pm/2.15 Sun, last D 9.15pm Closed Jan 5-Feb 23

HAY-ON-WYE, **Old Black Lion** ✿✿

A characterful hotel serving solid, praiseworthy food in its popular restaurant and bar

Oliver Cromwell stayed here and this predominantly 17th-century coaching inn has bags of old world charm, but also some first rate cooking served in the traditionally furnished Cromwell Restaurant and in the King Richard bar. Chef John Morgan's training at The Walnut Tree is evident in dishes described on the specials board: Thai mussels, Glamorgan sausages, a rustic ragout of wild boar and a straightforward, but impeccable grilled lobster with garlic and prawns. The printed menu makes less interesting reading, although the description of a 12 oz T-bone on a section headed 'Simply Steaks' as being 'for the ladies and those of a smaller appetite,' might upset some notions of political correctness. Our inspector liked the bouillabaisse, but felt that it could have been better with just a little more care and some of the skin and bones removed. The canon of lamb that followed was stuffed with spinach and garlic, which threatened to overwhelm the delicate flavour of the meat. Rhubarb crumble for pudding was plain good. The wine list is perfunctory, but serviceable.

Directions: Town centre, 30 yards from junction of Lion Street & Oxford Road

26 Lion Street HR3 5AD
Map no: 3 SO24
Tel: 01497 820841
Chef: John Morgan
Proprietor: J Collins
Cost: *Alc* D £15-£17, L £7-£10, fixed-price Sun L £9.25. H/wine £7.60 Service inc
Credit cards: 🂠 🂠 🂠
Times: Last L 2.30pm, last D 9.15pm
Menus: *A la carte*, fixed-price Sun L, bar menu
Seats: 50. No smoking in dining room
Additional: Children over 5 welcome, children's portions; ✪ dishes, vegan/other diets on request

HAY-ON-WYE, **The Swan Hotel** ✿

Modern British cooking is the order of the day at this comfortable hotel with a relaxed atmosphere. Visitors choose from a short carte. At inspection the main course of medallions of fillet beef was excellent, followed by a superior Banoffi pie

Menus: *A la carte*, fixed-price D & Sun L, bar menu
Seats: 46 x 2. No smoking in dining room
Additional: Children welcome; ✪ menu, children's portions/menu, vegan/other diets on request
Directions: On S/W edge of town centre

Church Street HR3 5DQ
Map no: 3 SO21
Tel: 01497 821188
Chef: Nathan Millikin
Proprietors: Colin & Rosemary Vaughan (Best Western)
Cost: *Alc* from £17.50 , fixed-price D £17.50/Sun L £10.95. H/wine £7.95 No service charge
Credit cards: 🂠 🂠 🂠 🂠 OTHER
Times: Last L 2pm, last D 9.30pm

KNIGHTON, **Milebrook House Hotel** ✿

A pleasant, small hotel set in countryside near the River Teme with a kitchen garden providing many of the vegetables and herbs used in the kitchen. Local produce is featured on the fixed-price menus which, at inspection, yielded a warm salad of scallops with lardons of bacon, followed by fillet of beef

Menus: Fixed-price L & D, bar menu
Seats: 30. No smoking in dining room
Additional: Children welcome, children's menu; ✪ dishes, vegan/other diets on request
Directions: 2 miles east of Knighton on A4113, Ludlow road

Milebrook LD7 1LT
Map no: 7 SO27
Tel: 01547 528632
Chef: Beryl Marsden
Proprietor: Rodney Marsden
Cost: Fixed-price L £10.75/ D £16.50 & £19.50. H/wine £8.40 Service exc
Credit cards: 🂠 🂠 🂠 🂠 OTHER
Times: Last L 1.45pm, last D 8.30pm Closed Mon L

Prices quoted in the Guide are based on information supplied by the establishments themselves.

LLANFYLLIN, Seeds ✿

A pleasant little market town restaurant run by Felicity and Mark Seager. Cooking is quite simple. Expect fillet of red sea bream with lime and dill butter, roast rack of Welsh lamb with redcurrant crust and pistachio ice-cream and coconut water. There is a selection of Welsh cheeses

Times: Last L 2.30pm, last D 9pm/9.30pm Sat/8.30pm Sun
Closed Mon (Oct-Mar), 2 wks Nov & Jan
Menus: *A la carte* L, fixed-price D
Seats: 22. Totally no smoking
Additional: Children welcome (no babies); ❶ dishes, vegan/other diets on request
Directions: Village centre, on A490 13 miles from Welshpool

High Street SY22 5AP
Map no: 7 SJ11
Tel: 01691 648604
Chef: Mark Seager
Proprietors: Mark & Felicity Seager
Cost: *Alc* £13.55, fixed-price D £15.75. H/wine £7.25 Service exc
Credit cards: 🆇 🆇

LLANGAMMARCH WELLS,

Lake Hotel ✿✿

Although popular with birdwatchers and fishermen, they really come for the expertly prepared food, just as everyone else does

Powys LD4 4BS
Map no: 3 SN94
Tel: 01591 620202
Chef: Richard Arnold
Proprietor: Jean-Pierre Mifsud (Welsh Rarebits)
Cost: Fixed-price L £15.50 (4 course)/D £24.50 (5 course). H/wine £9.75 Service inc
Credit cards: 🆇 🆇 🆇 🆇 OTHER
Times: Last L 2pm, last D 9pm daily
Menus: Fixed-price L & D, bar menu
Seats: 50. No smoking in dining room
Additional: Children welcome (over 7 at D), children's portions; ❶ dishes, other diets on request

More than a hundred different species of birds have been recorded in the 50 acres of mature woodland, riverside walks and large trout lake. The country house itself retains much of the character and charm of a Victorian spa hotel, but notions of complete time warps are part-dispelled by modern comforts and amenities. A meal taken late in August, before the wood-burning fires were lit, began with a light, clear tomato and basil consomme with a parcel of Provençal vegetables bound by thin film pastry. Expertly boned roast quail came with a sauté of spinach with chanterelle mushrooms, puy lentils and thyme flower juice, and rack of delicately flavoured lamb, topped with pistachio nuts, shallots and rosemary, served with a potato basket of honey-glazed vegetables; the accompanying boiled and turned château potatoes, carrot batons, parsnips rolled in Parmesan and cabbage with bacon, all contributed their individual tastes. Dark and white chocolate cups filled with chocolate mousse and served with a raspberry coulis with summer fruits was artistically presented.

Directions: A483 from Garth, turn left for Llangammarch Wells & follow signs to hotel

LLANWDDYN, **Lake Vyrnwy Hotel** ❀❀

Good huntin', shootin', fishin' and some fine cookin' is to be had at this grand country retreat

Lake Vyrnwy SY10 0LY
Map no: 6 SJ01
Tel: 01691 870 692
Chef: Andrew Wood
Proprietor: J P Talbot
Cost: Fixed-price L £13.75/D £22.50. H/wine £9.20 Service exc
Credit cards: 🔳 🔳 🔳 🔳 OTHER
Times: Last L 1.45pm, last D 9.15pm daily
Menus: Fixed-price L & D, bar menu
Seats: 80. No smoking in dining room
Additional: Children welcome, children's menu; ❤ dishes, vegan/other diets on request

Billed as a sporting country house offering rooms with a view, this much improved and expanded hotel sits in 24 acres of mature woodland, promising great potential for hunting and fishing. It stands in an elevated position over the lake, affording some glorious vistas of the Berwyn mountains. The kitchen, under chef Andrew Wood, has also come on in leaps and bounds over recent years and can be relied upon not only for better than competent cooking, but also for delicious canapés and wholesome, home-baked bread. A fairly long wine list complements a daily set-price, four-course menu upon which the signature dish of Welsh lamb and apple pudding with leek and onion bread and fruity Cumberland sauce is a staple. A variation on traditional black pudding, it's indicative of an inventive style that makes great play of local ingredients. Our inspector was full of praise for a meal that commenced with smoked salmon wrapped around a fillet of bream, with a smooth basil sauce, followed by spicy loin of pork with caramelised apple and leek that was 'quite delicious.'

Directions: Follow Tourist signs on A495/B4393, 200 yards past dam at Lake Vyrnwy

Antoine Augustin Parmentier (1737 - 1813). A military pharmacist and French agronomist who was an enthusiastic propagator of the potato. Although the potato had been cultivated in France since the 16th century, the French regarded the potato as unwholesome and indigestible, food for cattle and the poor. But, as a prisoner-of-war in Westphalia, Parmentier discovered the nutritional value of the vegetable, for it was highly prized by the local population. He encouraged the spread of the potato throughout France through booklets describing its cultivation and uses. For a time the potato was known as the 'parmentier' in his honour and he gave his name to various dishes based on potatoes, including a potato garnish for lamb and veal, a cream of potato soup, scrambled eggs mixed with sautéed cubes of potato, eggs cooked in nests of potato purée and omelettes filled with diced fried potatoes.

LLANWRTYD WELLS,
Carlton House Hotel ❀❀

Fine cooking of depth and imagination in an intimate small town restaurant in deepest Wales

Reputedly the smallest town in Britain, Llanwrtyd was given a promotional boost in the 19th-century by the addition of Wells, in recognition of the local spa waters. Although not quite the country's smallest restaurant dining-room, it only holds 12 people, so booking is essential. Proprietor Alan Gilchrist is responsible for the general feeling of informality and relaxation front-of-house and his wife, Mary Ann, takes credit for the cooking. She prepares everything herself, including the bread rolls which are 'something special'. There is a daily fixed-price, four-course menu, two, three or four-course Epicurean menus, as well as a *carte*, and a vegetarian selection. All throw up a choice of modern dishes helped along by inventive flourishes – fresh peeled prawns with Thai spiced dressing, pan-fried Haloumi cheese with a lime and caper vinaigrette and roasted vegetables with cous cous, for example. Meat is first-class, and well-handled. An inspection meal kicked off with good canapés, followed by slices of duck served on a bed of herbs and red lentils, then fillet steak with crushed black peppercorns in a brandy and cream sauce. A sharp lemon posset, cafetière coffee and fudge finished the meal nicely.

Directions: In the town centre

Dolycoed Road LD5 4SN
Map no: 3 SN84
Tel: 01591 610248
Chef: Mary Ann Gilchrist
Proprietors: Dr & Mrs A J Gilchrist
Cost: *Alc* £23, fixed-price D £17.50. H/wine £9. Service exc
Credit cards: 🆇 🆇
Times: 7pm-last D 8.30pm. Closed Sun, Xmas, New Year
Menus: *A la carte* D, fixed-price D
Seats: 12. No smoking in dining room
Additional: Children permitted, children's portions; ❂ dishes, other diets on request

LLYSWEN, **Griffin Inn** ❀

An established, homely, fishing and sporting inn, set in the Wye valley. A relaxed atmosphere, enhanced by log fires and sound country cooking, ensures popularity with visitors and local fishermen alike. Much of the produce is local, such as hare, venison, and salmon. Try the traditional bread and butter pudding

Menus: *A la carte* L & D, bar menu
Seats: 40. No smoking in dining room
Additional: Children welcome, children's portions; ❂ dishes, vegan/other diets on request
Directions: On A470

Brecon LD3 0UR
Map no: 3 SO13
Tel: 01874 754 241
Chefs: Eileen Harvard and Sharon Williams
Proprietors: Richard & Di Stockton
Cost: *Alc* £18-£20. H/wine £8 ❢ Service exc
Credit cards: 🆇 🆇 🆇 🆇 OTHER
Times: Last L 2pm, last D 9pm daily Closed Dec 25/26

LLYSWEN, **Llangoed Hall** ❀❀

Part of an idyllic country house hotel, this restaurant presents imaginative menus of expertly prepared dishes in modern English style

Sir Bernard Ashley's dream of creating the perfect hotel have come together in this luxurious house. Set in grounds stretching down to the River Wye, it features spacious public areas where the many fine pieces of furniture and art are complemented by Persian rugs casually scattered across polished wooden floors. In the elegant dining-room, talented chef Ben Davies (ex Calcot Manor) brings an innovative touch to the daily-changing fixed-price five-course menu and *carte*. An autumn dinner was preceded by delicate canapés and firm-crusted brown and white rolls were offered hot with Ecriré butter. Chicken and sweetbread terrine with warm potato salad was

Brecon LD3 0YP
Map no: 3 SO13
Tel: 01874 754525
Chef: Ben Davies
Proprietor: Sir Bernard Ashley. Managers: Gareth & Helen Pugh
Cost: Fixed-price L £17, £14 (2 course)/D £29.50 (4 course). H/wine £ 14.50 ❢ Service exc
Credit cards: 🆇 🆇 🆇 🆇 OTHER
Times: Last L 2pm, last D 9.30pm Closed Sat L
Menus: *A la carte*, fixed-price L & D

Llangoed Hall

Seats: 40. No smoking in dining room
Additional: Children over 8 permitted; ❤ dishes, other diets on request

followed by excellent, generously filled ravioli of crab with ginger and spring onions. An intensely flavoured grapefruit sorbet came before the main course – tender sliced loin of local lamb with spinach and girolles, set on a well made potato galette and served with an intense jus. An assiette of desserts provided a taste of the house specialities. A fine wine list includes many vintage and château-bottled wines as well as examples from the New World.

Directions: On A470, 2 mile from Llyswen heading towards Builth Wells

THREE COCKS, **Three Cocks Hotel** ❀❀

Sound, country-style cooking served in atmospheric, tranquil surroundings

Brecon LD3 0SL
Map no: 3 SO13
Tel: 01497 847215
Chef: Michael Winstone
Proprietors: Michael & Marie-Jeanne Winstone
Cost: *Alc* £28, fixed-price D £25 (5 courses) H/wine £8. Service inc
Credit cards: 🆇 ▦
Times: Noon-Last L 1.30pm, last D 9pm. L not served Sun. Closed Tues, Dec-10 Feb,
Menus: *A la carte*, fixed-price L & D, bar menu
Seats: 30. No cigars or pipes in dining room
Additional: Children welcome, children's portions; special diets on request

Wrapped in ivy, the Three Cocks Hotel offers a tranquil 15th-century setting for an enjoyable meal. The age-old charm of the building is continued inside with worn steps, uneven floors and original beams. Marie-Jeanne Winstone and her team of local staff provide a friendly and attentive service and Michael Winstone's kitchen skills account for the restaurants reputation for food. He prides himself on the freshness and quality of the ingredients, whilst his Belgian origins greatly influence the dishes on offer. At a recent meal a thick carrot and celery soup was made all the better by the hunks of freshly baked bread which came with it. Wild mushrooms covered with puff pastry and a sour cream sauce were followed by a superb John Dory served with a white butter sauce and accompanied by courgettes, new potatoes and a parcel of chopped cabbage. The meal was finished with a light, fluffy apple soufflé with cinnamon sauce, and plenty of good coffee. Welsh lamb and lobster feature regularly.

Directions: In the village of Three Cocks, 4 miles from Hay-on-Wye, 11 miles from Brecon

WELSHPOOL, Golfa Hall Hotel ❀❀

An hotel restaurant which impresses with its sound cooking

Llanfair Road SY21 9AF
Map no: 7 SJ20
Tel: 01938 553399
Chef: David Ostle
Proprietor: David Ostle
Cost: Fixed-price D £16.95. H/wine £6.95 ❢ Service exc
Credit cards: ▧ ▦ ▦ ▨ OTHER
Times: Last L 2pm, last D 9pm daily
Menus: Fixed-price D, bar menu
Seats: 60. No smoking in dining room
Additional: Children welcome, children's portions; ♥ dishes, other diets on request

A delightful hotel, in eight acres of grounds adjoining 13th-century Powis Castle, is the setting for David Ostle's honest cooking. He is meticulous in his efforts to obtain the best ingredients, and the resulting clear flavours reflect his flair and dedication. Select two or three courses from a regularly changing menu, which also includes a vegetarian dish – the choice is yours. One inspector dined with a party and their meal yielded an 'excellent' vegetable soup with chives, wild mushrooms and baby onions in a puff pastry case with a delicious cream and Madeira sauce, monkfish terrine, from which the flavour of the fish 'shone out', clear-flavoured, pan-fried venison medallions with a rich gravy, as well as various chicken, salmon and steak dishes. An apple and Calvados crumble was 'not really a crumble in the traditional sense', but it was rich and was enjoyed, crème brûlée 'seemed just right' and cheesecake had just the right degree of sharpness. In addition, the option of well chosen British cheeses is worth following up. Wines are reasonably priced.

Directions: On A458 (Dollgelau), 1.5 miles W of Welshpool on right

SOUTH GLAMORGAN

BARRY, **Egerton Grey Hotel** ❀❀

A welcoming hotel, handy for Cardiff Airport, serving imaginative seasonal food

Egerton Grey is an elegant 19th-century former rectory. Although Cardiff Airport is not far away, the place is secluded in seven acres of gardens at the head of a steep wooded valley, which ends in a golf course and a shingle beach. Period decor and a mahogany-panelled restaurant make the perfect setting for dining. Craig Brookes arrived a short time ago to head the kitchen, with promising results. His more imaginative seasonal menus comprise well-made dishes, often vigorously textured and flavoured. Recent inspection meals have yielded delicate steamed crab and salmon with tomato and leek butter sauce, sturdy venison medallions with peppercorn crust and juniper-scented jus, set off with compote of sliced apple, fillet of pork served on a confit of shallots and chives, accompanied by chestnut sausage and a mustard sauce. Dark chocolate and rum truffle with elderflower sauce is highly commended. Sunday lunch offers a mix of traditional and modern, perhaps duck liver parfait with a salad of sun-dried tomatoes, followed by roast leg of Welsh lamb with a casserole of lentils on a port wine jus.

Directions: M4 exit 33, follow signs for Airport then Portkerry, & left at hotel sign by thatched cottage

Porthkerry CF62 3BZ
Map no: 3 ST16
Tel: 01446 711666
Chefs: Craig Brookes
Proprietor: Tony Pitkin
Cost: Fixed-price L/D £21/Sun L £12.50. H/wine £10.50 Service inc
Credit cards: 🔲 🔲 🔲 🔲 OTHER
Times: Last L 2pm, last D 9.30pm Closed Jan 1
Menus: Fixed-price L & D, pre-theatre
Seats: 40. No smoking in dining room
Additional: Children permitted, children's portions; ❂ dishes, other diets on request

CARDIFF,
Chikako's Japanese Restaurant ❀

Popular restaurant offering Japanese food in an attractive and unfussy setting. Choose sashimi, chicken or beef teriyaki, pork tonkatsu, various noodle dishes, or have meat or seafood teppanyaki, sukiyaki or shabu shabu (Japanese-style fondue) cooked at your table

Menus: Fixed-price D **Seats:** 70. Air conditioned
Additional: Children welcome; ❂ dishes, children's portions/vegan/other diets on request
Directions: City centre opposite Marriott Hotel, left at top of main street

10-11 Mill Lane CF1 1FL
Map no: 3 ST17
Tel: 01222 665279
Chef: Chikako Cameron
Proprietor: Chikako Cameron
Cost: Fixed-price D £11.80-£19.50. H/wine £7.50 ❢ Service exc
Credit cards: 🔲 🔲 🔲
Times: 6.30pm-last D 11.30pm daily. Closed Dec 25

CARDIFF, **The Copthorne** ❀

Raglans, the Copthorne's stylish restaurant, enjoys a lakeside setting, and offers simple but effectively presented food. A recent meal included smoked salmon mousse with tangy mustard and dill sauce, and nicely cooked calves' liver with mango and Madeira

Directions: From M4 (jnct 33) take A4232 for 2.5 miles towards Cardiff West and then A48

Copthorne Way,
Culverhouse Cross CF5 6XJ
Map no: 3 ST17
Tel: 01222 599100
Chef: Mark Jameson
Proprietor: Copthorne.
Manager: P Taylor
Credit cards: 🔳 🔳 🔳 🔳

CARDIFF, **Le Cassoulet** ❀❀

A charming bistro where earthy cooking is served with an authentically Gallic air

A corner of provincial South West France transplanted to South Wales by a couple called Viader, who maintain the authentic ambience with amiable, Gallic good humour. The current chef, Mark Freeman, keeps up the culinary standard with reliable interpretations of French provincial classics, like carré d'agneau and magret de canard. The speciality, naturally, is cassoulet Toulousain: a stew of white haricot beans which is then baked in an earthenware bowl with coarse pork sausage, confit of duck and neck end of pork. Our inspector's meal was marred by vegetables that were somewhat over seasoned and slightly over-cooked, but sound enough in all other departments. His asparagus mousse, wrapped in leek, had good texture, tasted fine and was complemented by a simple butter sauce. A main course of stuffed guinea fowl and braised oxtail proved to be a busy plate with an intriguing variety of flavours. Lemon tart was accompanied with an unnecessary, but enjoyable passion fruit sorbet. The chauvinistic wine list tours the more familiar appellations, is well-selected and not over priced.

Directions: From M4 follow B4267 Canton, Restaurant is next to Post Office

5 Romilly Crescent,
Canton CF1 9NP
Map no: 3 ST17
Tel: 01222 221905
Chef: Mark Freeman
Proprietors: Mr & Mrs G Viader
Cost: Fixed-price L £19, £16 (2 course)/D £26. H/wine £9.50 Service exc
Credit cards: 🔳 🔳 🔳 🔳 OTHER
Times: Last L 2pm, last D 10pm Closed Sat L, Sun, Mon, 2wks Xmas, Aug
Menus: Fixed-price L & D
Seats: 40
Additional: Children welcome, children's portions; ❂ dishes, vegan/other diets on request

CARDIFF,
Manor Parc Hotel ❀

Set in rural surroundings, yet only ten minutes from the city centre, Manor Parc boasts an attractive conservatory-style restaurant complete with stylish Italian furnishings. Italian dishes also feature amongst the international-based cooking, and seafood is a strong point, perhaps squid, or sea bass

Seats: 65. No smoking in dining room **Additional:** Children welcome, children's portions; ❂ dishes, vegan/other diets on request
Directions: Outskirts of Cardiff; M4 exit 32 & A470, left onto A469 Cardiff/Caerphilly, hotel signed

Thornhill Road CF4 5UA
Map no: 3 ST17
Tel: 01222 693723
Chef: Russell Palfrey
Proprietors: S Salimeni and E Cinus
Cost: Alc £28, fixed-price L £13.95/D £24.50. H/wine £8.95 Service exc
Credit cards: 🔳 🔳 🔳 OTHER
Times: Last L 2pm, last D 9.30pm Closed Sat L
Menus: A la carte, fixed-price L & D, bar menu

Anchoïade is an anchovy paste from Provence. It consists of a purée of anchovies mixed with crushed garlic and olive oil. It is usually served with raw vegetables, or spread thickly on slices of fresh bread, drizzled with olive oil, and browned in the oven.

CARDIFF, **New House** ❀❀

A Georgian country house hotel with panoramic views of Cardiff and ambitious food served in generous portions

A lovely old place in a delightful setting, New House was acquired by Julian Hitchcock at the tail end of 1994 and the new proprietor has set about making improvements with great brio. Ian Black is the enthusiastic and talented chef, who is given to demonstrating his expertise in culinary competitions. Both his monthly changing *carte* and the set price menu, which is changed weekly, are written in terse English that does not quite prepare one for what appears on the plate – carefully prepared and artfully presented dishes served in heaping portions with one eye firmly on metropolitan fashion. Hence the choice might include smoked halibut with guacamole, baked cod with pesto, or venison braised in stout and served with pickled walnuts. Our inspector found a ham shank served on black eye peas a touch salty but otherwise fine and appreciated the selection of crisp vegetables served with it. This was bracketed by fresh, plump mussels cooked simply in white wine and herbs and by an unusual, home-made Advocaat and cherry ice-cream. A good selection of Welsh cheeses would have been an alternative, served with home-made bread.

Directions: Take the A469 to the north of city. Entrance on the left shortly after crossing the M4 flyover

Thornhill
Map no: 3 ST17
Tel: 01222 520280
Chef: Ian Black
Proprietor: Julian Hitchcock
Cost: *Alc* £22, fixed-price L £11.95/D £14.95. H/wine £8.50
❢ Service exc
Credit cards: 🔳 🔳 🔳 OTHER
Times: Last L 2pm, last D 9.45pm daily
Menus: *A la carte,* fixed-price L & D
Seats: 40. No-smoking area
Additional: Children welcome until 8pm, children's portions; ❂ dishes, vegan/other diets on request

WEST GLAMORGAN

LANGLAND BAY, **Langland Court** ❀

A Tudor-style house situated in a peaceful residential area close to Langland Bay. The Oak Room offers fricassée of seafood Gwyr, medallions of pork fillet finished with country cider, apple and cream and desserts from the trolley. More informal meals are served in Polly's Bistro

Directions: A4067 (Swansea/Mumbles) then left B4593 (Caswell), left at St Peter's Church, hotel signed

Langland Court Road
SA3 4TD
Map no: 2 SS68
Tel: 01792 361545
Chef: Kevin Strangward
Proprietors: Colin R Birt (Best Western)
Cost: *Alc* £23.70, fixed-price L £8.65/D £18. H/wine £8.25
Service exc
Credit cards: 🔳 🔳 🔳 OTHER
Times: Last L 2pm, last D 9.30pm daily
Menus: *A la carte,* fixed-price L & D, pre-theatre, bar menu
Seats: 50. Air conditioned. No-smoking area
Additional: Children welcome, children's menu; ❂ dishes, vegan/other diets on request

REYNOLDSTON, **Fairyhill Hotel** ❀❀

A comfortable, congenial country house hotel that serves confident modern Welsh cuisine in elegant surroundings

A steadily improving establishment with a choice of rooms in which to dine and where food is taken seriously. Paul Davies has taken over in the kitchen this year, with no apparent diminution in standards at the table. His menu changes daily and makes great play of local produce in signature dishes such as free range Gower eggs scrambled with Penclawdd cockles and roasted peppers, or a rare breast and crispy leg of Pembrokeshire duckling served with a white onion sauce and sherried jus. Otherwise there are confident interpretations of contemporary classics, like sea bass with ginger and spring onion, smoked salmon with a chive cream, and roast rack of lamb with sautéed liver and kidneys. The wine list has a depth that is commensurate with such an ambitious operation. It has a page devoted exclusively to Château Latour, but also includes two pages of wines priced at under £15, a useful selection of house wines and daily recommendations at eminently reasonable prices.

Directions: Just outside Reynoldstown, off the A4118 from Swansea

Swansea SA3 1BS
Map no: 2 SS48
Tel: 01792 390139
Chef: Paul Davies
Proprietors: Jane & Peter Camm, Paul Davies and Andrew Hetherington
Cost: Fixed-price L £13.95, £10.95 (2 course)/D £24.50. H/wine £9.50 ❗ Service inc
Credit cards: ▨ ▬ ▭ OTHER
Times: Last L 2.15pm, last D 9.15pm Closed Su D in Winter
Menus: Fixed-price L & D
Seats: 70. No cigars or pipes in dining room
Additional: Children over 8 permitted at L, children's L portions; ❂ dishes, vegan/other diets on request

SWANSEA, **Beaumont Hotel** ❀❀

Not in the grand style but a charming hotel, just off the city centre, where food is good and staff are friendly

A real find. Situated between the city centre and the Uplands area, this is a well-run commercial and family hotel, its homely feel accentuated by soft furnishings and lots of fresh flowers. Wynne Jones and John Colensos pay attention to the smallest details, as can be seen clearly in the intimate conservatory dining room, with fine silver and cut glass complementing the assured style of cooking. Fixed-price menu and *carte* dishes, although tried and trusted, still reveal a desire to avoid sameness. The deep flavours and bright presentation which are his hallmarks were evident in a recent smooth, well-balanced chicken liver and asparagus terrine, salmon tartare with crème fraîche and dill vinaigrette, followed by fillet of venison with expertly reduced juniper and port sauce. Portions of vegetables are generous as are the home-made puddings and petits fours. Vegetarians are well looked after with dishes such as mushroom and leek mille-feuille with garlic cream; vegan requirements can also be met. The sizeable wine list has a good sprinkling of half bottles and house wines.

Directions: N/W of town centre on A4118, opposite St James' Church in an area called Uplands

72 Walter Road SA1 4QA
Map no: 3 SS69
Tel: 01792 643956
Chef:
Proprietors: J Wynne Jones and J K Colenso
Cost: Alc £25, fixed-price L £14.50/D £21.75. H/wine £9.50 Service exc
Credit cards: ▨ ▬ ▭ ▨ OTHER
Times: Last L 2pm, last D 9.30pm Closed Sat L
Menus: *A la carte*, fixed-price L & D, pre-theatre
Seats: 40. No cigars or pipes dining room
Additional: Children over 8 welcome, children's portions; ❂ dishes, vegan to order, other diets on request

---

Cotechino is a traditional northern Italian sausage made with pork rind mixed with coarsely chopped, lean pork meat and back fat. Seasoned with salt and pepper, spiced with cinnamon and cloves and pushed into pig casing, it is ready to eat in two to three weeks. It is usually served with lentils, polenta, or Savoy cabbage, and is part of a 'bollito misto' (a mixture of boiled meats not dissimilar to the French pot au feu).

SWANSEA, **Windsor Lodge Hotel** ❀

Anglo/Welsh cooking at this delightful Georgian house with a strong local following. Good use is made of quality, fresh produce, and honest textures and flavours predominate in dishes such as cassolet of mussels and cockles with spinach, and new season Welsh lamb with ham and walnut stuffing

Mount Pleasant SA1 6EG
Map no: 3 SS69
Tel: 01792 642158
Chefs: Hervé Chataignere and Ron Rumble
Proprietors: Ron & Pam Rumble (Logis)
Cost: Fixed-price L £11.99, £8.99 (2 course)/D £14 & £19.50. H/wine £5.95 ❢ Service exc
Credit cards: 🔲 🔲 🔲 🔲 OTHER
Times: Last L 2pm, last D 9.30pm Closed Sun, Dec 25/26
Menus: Fixed-price L & D, bar menu
Seats: 60. No-smoking area
Additional: Children welcome, children's portions; ❤ dishes, vegan/other diets on request

Directions: M4 /A483 town centre, left by station, through next lights & right at next pedestrian lights

Index

Greater London

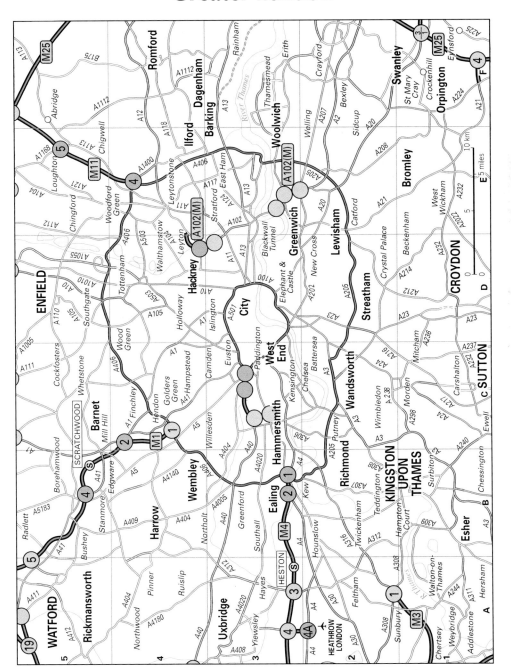

Central London

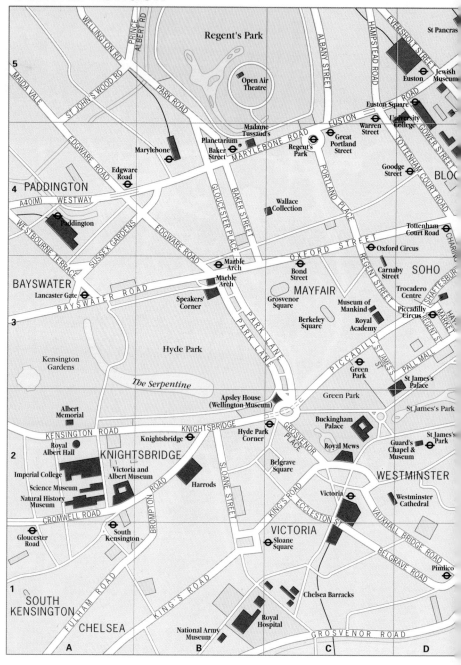

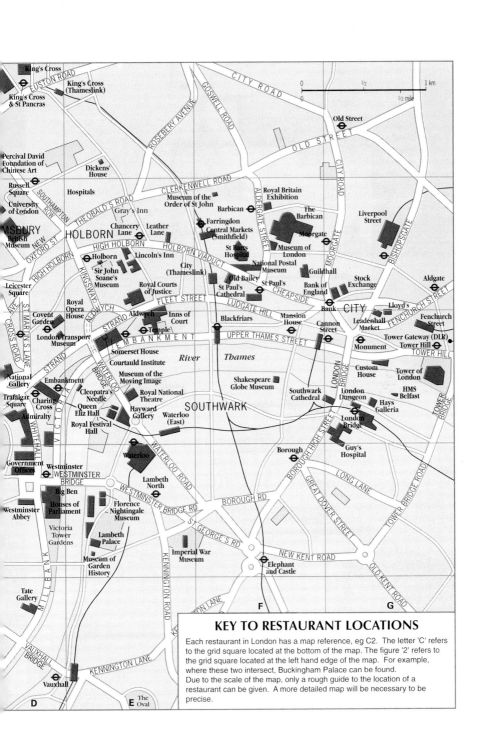

KEY TO RESTAURANT LOCATIONS

Each restaurant in London has a map reference, eg C2. The letter 'C' refers
to the grid square located at the bottom of the map. The figure '2' refers to
the grid square located at the left hand edge of the map. For example,
where these two intersect, Buckingham Palace can be found.
Due to the scale of the map, only a rough guide to the location of a
restaurant can be given. A more detailed map will be necessary to be
precise.

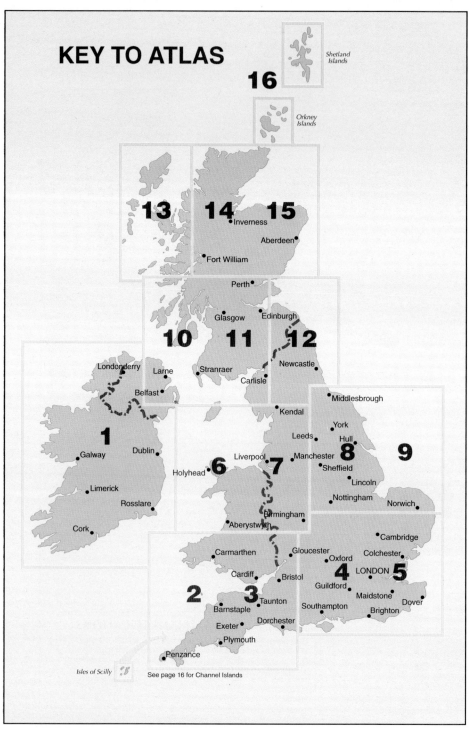

KEY TO ATLAS

Shetland Islands

16

Orkney Islands

13 **14** **15**
•Inverness
Aberdeen•
•Fort William

Perth•

10 **11** **12**
Glasgow• •Edinburgh
Newcastle•

Londonderry• Larne• •Stranraer
Belfast• Carlisle•
Kendal•

•Middlesbrough
1 York•
Galway• Leeds• Hull
Dublin• Manchester• **8** **9**
Liverpool• Sheffield•
Holyhead• **6** **7** Lincoln•
Limerick• Nottingham• Norwich•
Rosslare• Birmingham•
Cork• Aberystwyth•

Carmarthen• Gloucester• Cambridge•
Cardiff• Oxford• Colchester•
2 **3** Bristol• **4** LONDON **5**
Taunton• Guildford• Maidstone•
Barnstaple• Southampton• Dover•
Exeter• Dorchester• Brighton•
Plymouth•
Penzance•

Isles of Scilly See page 16 for Channel Islands

© The Automobile Association 1995

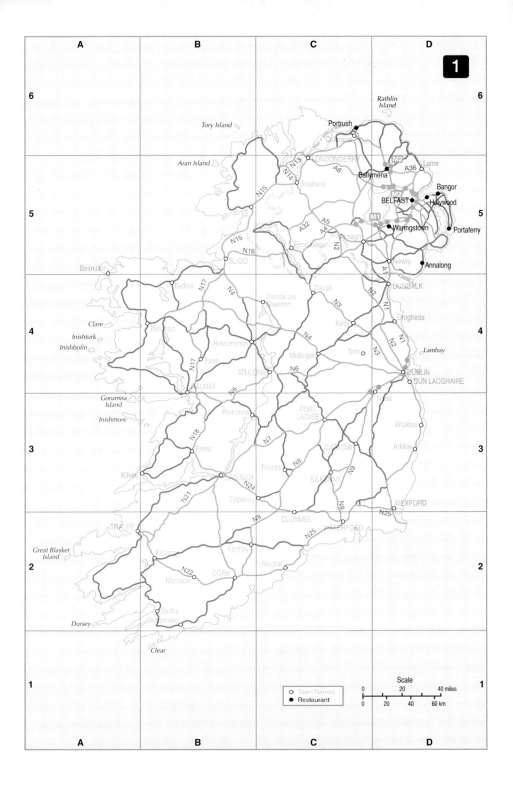

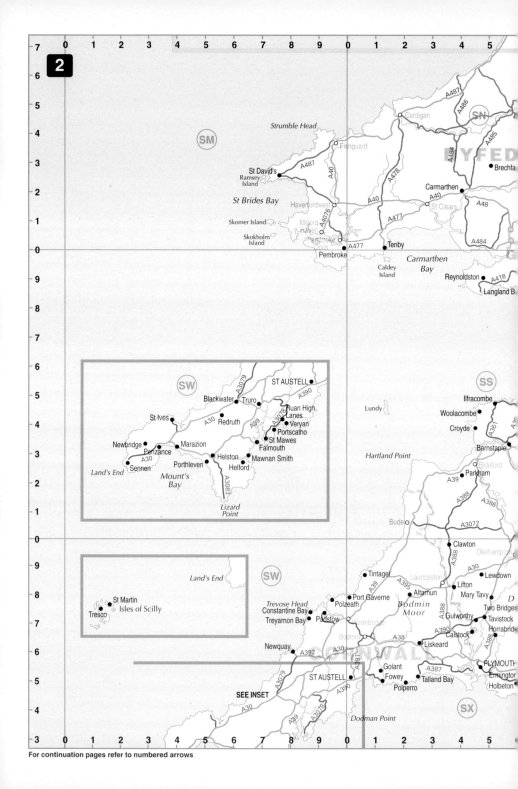

For continuation pages refer to numbered arrows

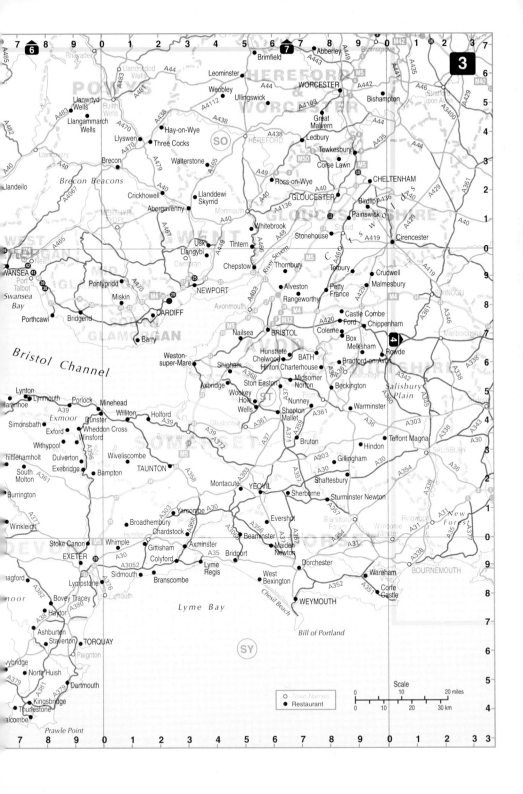

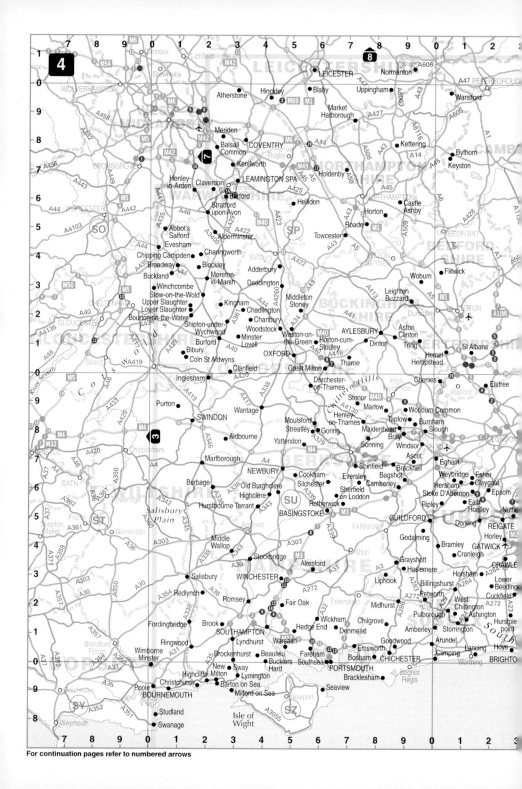

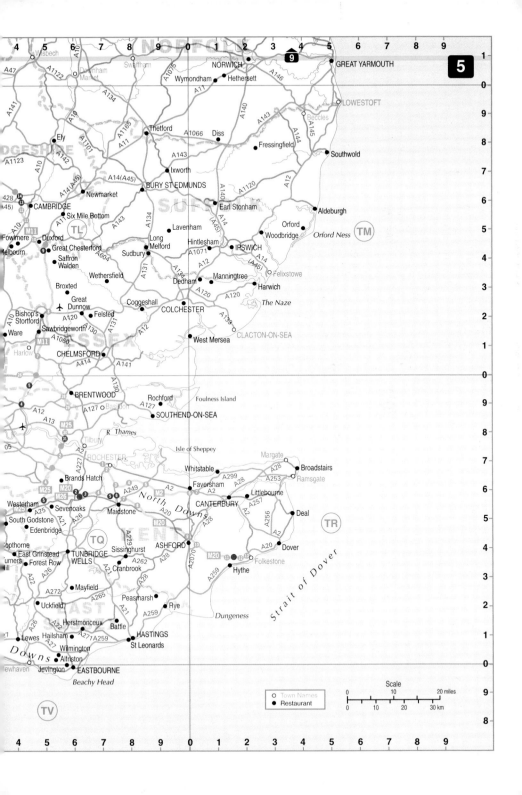

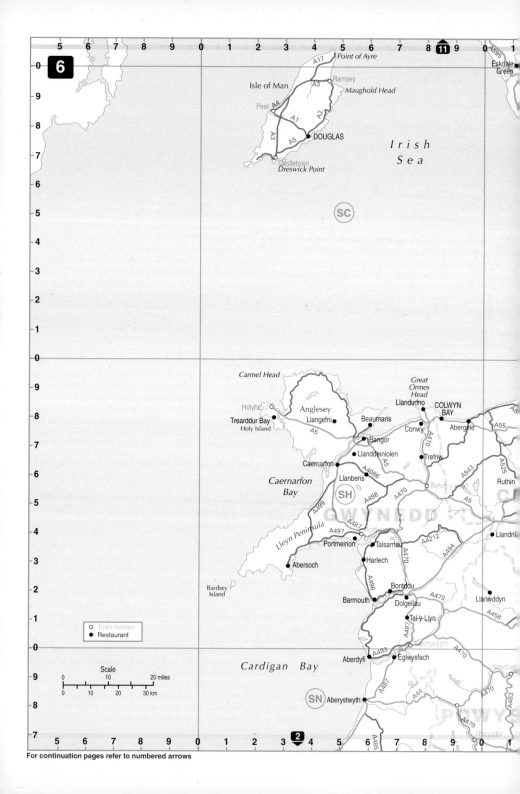

0

9

8

7

6

5

4

3

2

1

0

9

8

7

6

5

4

3

2

1

0

9

8

7

A17 Point of Ayre
Eskdale Green

Isle of Man
A3 Ramsey
Maughold Head

Peel A4
A1 A2

A3
A5 DOUGLAS

Castletown
Dreswick Point

Irish Sea

SC

Carmel Head

Great Ormes Head
Holyhead
Anglesey
Llandudno
COLWYN BAY

Treaddur Bay
Holy Island
Llangefni
Beaumaris
Conwy
Abergele
A55
A5

Bangor
A470
Trefriw

Caernarfon
Llanddeiniolen
Betws-y-coed
Ruthin

Caernarfon Bay
Llanberis
A4086
A5
A543
A525

SH
A498
A470
A5

A499
A487
Llandril

Lleyn Peninsula
A497
Portmadog
A212
A494

Portmeirion
Talsarnau
A470

Bardsey Island
Harlech

Abersoch
A496
Bontddu
Llanwddyn

Barmouth
Dolgellau
A470

Tal-y-Llyn
A487
A458

Machynlleth
A493
A470

Cardigan Bay
Aberdyfi
Eglwysfach
Newtown

SN
A487
A44
A483

Aberystwyth
A458
A470

Rhayader

○ Town Names
● Restaurant

Scale
0   10   20 miles
0   10   20   30 km

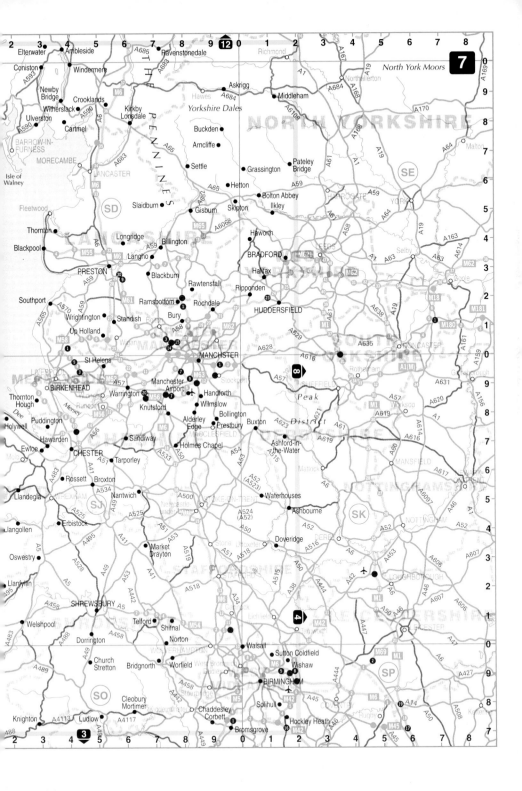

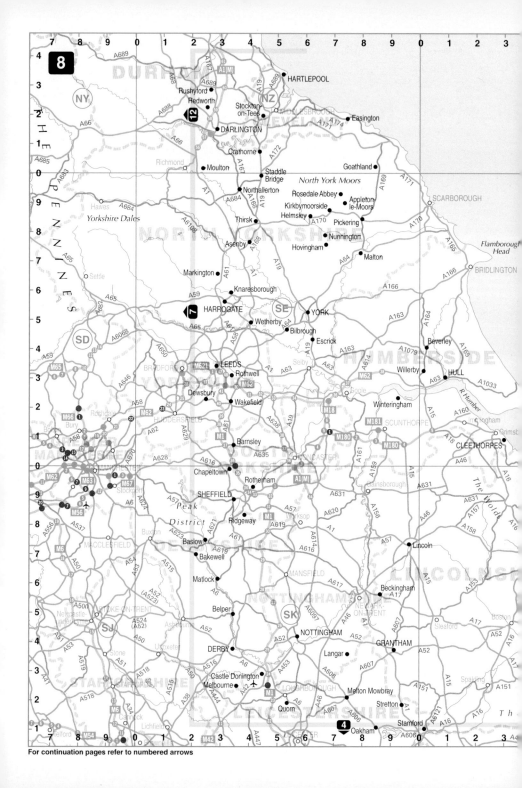

9

| 4 | 5 | 6 | 7 | 8 | 9 | 0 | 1 | 2 | 3 | 4 | 5 | 6 | 7 | 8 | 9 | 0 |

Spurn Head

Sutton-on-Sea

A1031

A52

A158

Skegness

A52

TA

TF

TG

The

Wash

Scale

| 0 | | 10 | | 20 miles |
| 0 | 10 | 20 | 30 km |

○ Town Names
● Restaurant

Wells-next-
the-Sea

Titchwell

Burnham
Market

A149

Blakeney

A148

Holt

Cromer

Erpingham

King's
Lynn

A148

Grimston

A1065

A10

A149

A1067

A149

A1151

A149

A17

A47

NORFOLK

The
Broads

Fen

Wisbech

A10

Downham
Market

Swaffham

A47

NORWICH

A47

Great Yarmouth

5

| 4 | 5 | 6 | 7 | 8 | 9 | 0 | 1 | 2 | 3 | 4 | 5 | 6 | 7 | 8 | 9 | 0 |

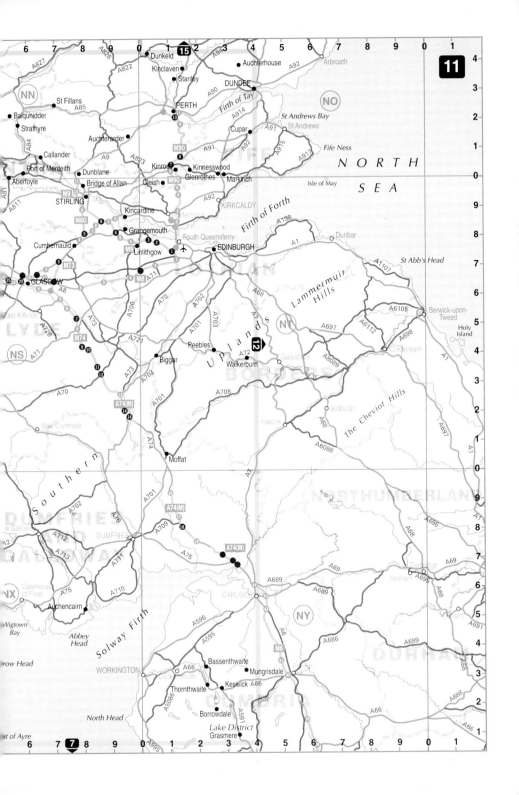

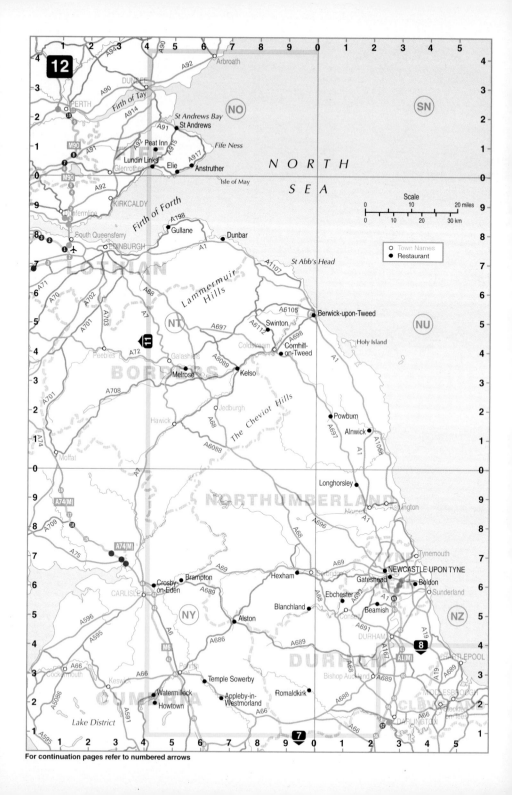

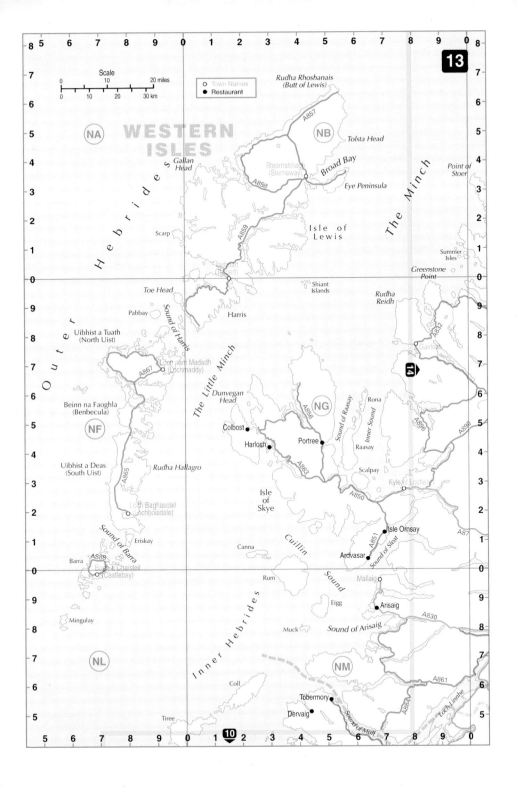

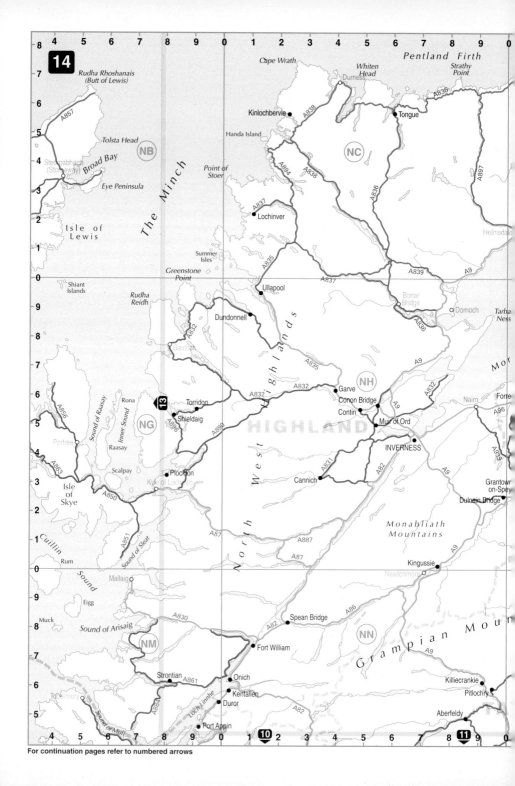

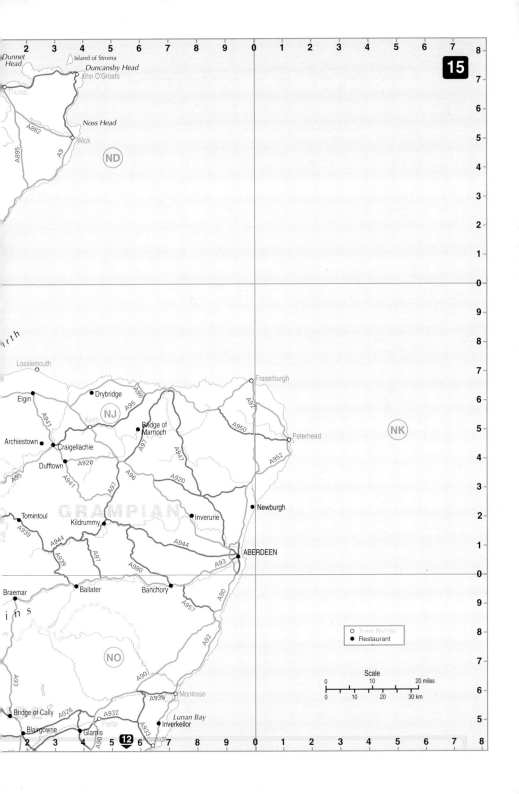

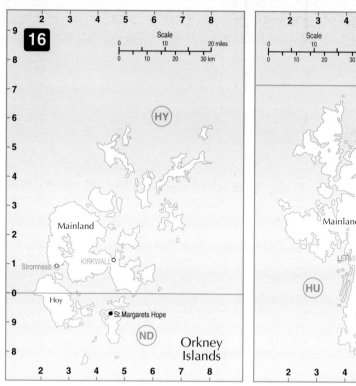

10

Orkney Islands

16

Scale
0   10   20 miles
0   10   20   30 km

HY

Mainland

Stromness ○   KIRKWALL ○

Hoy

● St Margarets Hope

ND

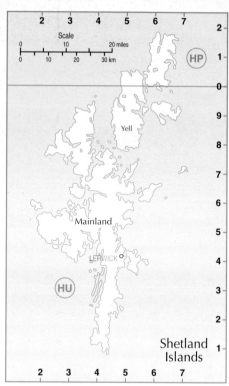

Shetland Islands

Scale
0   10   20 miles
0   10   20   30 km

HP

Yell

Mainland

LERWICK ○

HU

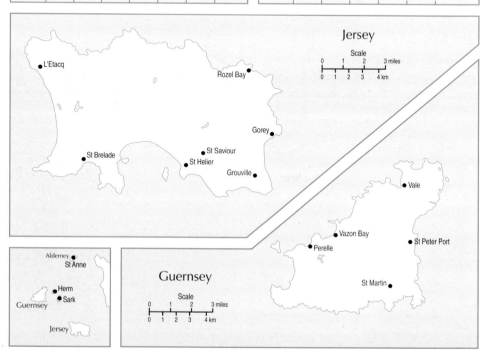

Jersey

Scale
0   1   2   3 miles
0   1   2   3   4 km

● L'Etacq

Rozel Bay ●

Gorey ●

● St Brelade

● St Saviour
● St Helier

Grouville ●

Guernsey

Scale
0   1   2   3 miles
0   1   2   3   4 km

Vale ●

Vazon Bay ●

● Perelle   St Peter Port ●

St Martin ●

Alderney ●
St Anne

● Herm
● Sark

Guernsey

Jersey

Special AA Membership Offer

Join today and you gain all the benefits of membership of the AA - the 4th Emergency Service - as well as being able to use the AA Hotel Guide Discount Card.

You're the Member, Not the Car

AA membership is personal - that means whatever car you are in, even if you are travelling simply as a passenger, you can use your AA cover to get you out of trouble.

Priority for Motorists at Risk

The AA has the world's largest patrol force and helps someone out of trouble every 8 seconds. Almost 90 per cent of breakdowns are fixed at the roadside, and priority is given to lone women and members in vulnerable situations.

Option 100 - Roadside Assistance
Option 200 - Roadside Assistance and Relay
Option 300 - Roadside Assistance, Relay and Home Start
Option 400 - Roadside Assistance, Relay, Relay Plus and Home Start

The affordable options are designed to make membership easy. Available as Single, Joint or Family membership, you simply select the option that's right for you.

AA Membership Benefits

extend beyond motoring emergencies and include:
• AA Handbook
• AA Magazine
• AA Member Benefits booklet
• Route planning services
• Legal and technical information services

To join or for further details, call today free on 0800 919 595, quoting ref RGPC

When you join* you may receive a free copy of the AA's celebrated THE HOTEL GUIDE 1996

• Over 4000 inspected hotels with AA Star Rating
• Many Special Award winners
• Up-to-date details and colour location maps
• Free Prize Draw to Win a Luxury Weekend for Two
• Published November 1995
• Price £13.99

*This offer is not available in conjunction with any other promotional offer and is only available for new members joining by bank direct debit or credit card continuous authority. Offer closes 31st December 1996.

The photograph above is the Lythe Hill Hotel at Haslemere, Surrey.

Reader's Recommendations

If you have recently eaten well at a restaurant that is not included in this guide, we should be interested to hear about it. Please send this form to Head of Guidebooks, Editorial Department, AA Publishing, Fanum House, Basingstoke RG21 4EA.

Recommendations, and/or any adverse comments will be carefully considered and passed on to our Hotel and Restaurant Inspectors, but the AA cannot guarantee to act on them nor to enter into correspondence about them. Complaints are best brought to the attention to the management of the restaurant at the time, so that they can be dealt with promptly and, it is hoped, to the satisfaction of both parties.

Your name and address

Name and address of the restaurant

Was the meal lunch or dinner?

Approximate cost for two £

Type of cuisine English/French/Itaila/Italian/Indian/Chinese/Other

Comments